# THE OXFORD ENCYCLOPEDIA OF
# AMERICAN LITERATURE

# THE OXFORD ENCYCLOPEDIA OF
# AMERICAN
# LITERATURE

*Jay Parini*

*Editor in Chief*

Volume 1

ACADEMIC NOVELS–THE ESSAY IN AMERICA

OXFORD

UNIVERSITY PRESS

2004

# OXFORD

## UNIVERSITY PRESS

Oxford   New York

Auckland   Bangkok   Buenos Aires   Cape Town   Chennai
Dar es Salaam   Delhi   Hong Kong   Istanbul   Karachi   Kolkata
Kuala Lumpur   Madrid   Melbourne   Mexico City   Mumbai   Nairobi
São Paulo   Shanghai   Taipei   Tokyo   Toronto

Copyright © 2004 by Oxford University Press, Inc.

Published by Oxford University Press, Inc.

198 Madison Avenue, New York, New York 10016

http://www.oup.com

**Library of Congress Cataloging-in-Publication Data**

The Oxford Encyclopedia of American Literature / Jay Parini, editor-in-chief.
p. cm.
Includes bibliographical references and index.
ISBN 0-19-515653-6 (set: alk. paper)
ISBN 0-19-516724-4 (v. 1: alk. paper)
ISBN 0-19-516725-2 (v. 2: alk. paper)
ISBN 0-19-516726-0 (v. 3: alk. paper)
ISBN 0-19-516727-9 (v. 4: alk. paper)
1. American literature—Encyclopedias. I. Parini, Jay.
PS21 .E537 2003
810'.3—dc21
2002156325

Printing number:   9   8   7   6   5   4   3   2   1

Permission credits are on p. 517 of vol. 4, which constitutes
a continuation of the copyright page.

Printed in the United States of America
on acid-free paper

# EDITORIAL AND PRODUCTION STAFF

*Acquiring Editor*
Ralph Carlson

*Development Editor*
Beth Ammerman

*Project Editor and Photo Researcher*
Mark Gallagher

*Copyediting*
Louise B. Ketz Agency

*Proofreaders*
Fred Dahl   Sue Gilad   Carol Holmes   Matthew Miller   Kaari Ward

*Index prepared by*
Cynthia Crippen, AEIOU, Inc.

*Compositor*
Laserwords Private Limited

*Manufacturing Controller*
Chris Critelli

*Designer*
Joan Greenfield

*Cover Design*
Eve Siegel

*EDP Director*
John Sollami

*Editorial Development Director*
Timothy J. DeWerff

*Publisher*
Karen Day

# CONTENTS

THE OXFORD ENCYCLOPEDIA OF

# AMERICAN LITERATURE

# LIST OF ARTICLES

## VOLUME 1

## VOLUME 3

## VOLUME 4

# PREFACE

*by Jay Parini*

The *Oxford Encyclopedia of American Literature* represents an attempt, necessarily limited by space, to provide a comprehensive discussion of literary practices within the United States from colonial times to the present. It includes discussions of individual authors, notable texts, and literary movements, institutions, and—for lack of a better term—aggregations (such as the academic novel or the production of "little magazines"). The term "encyclopedia" itself, while old-fashioned in its resonances, has some meaning here, in the most literal sense: this project might be considered an attempt to "walk around" the subject, encircling authors and texts, literary developments, ideas, programs, and themes. This walk has been taken by an array of critics, many of them well-known scholars, without much in the way of restraining orders. My only charge, as editor, was that each critic write for the so-called general reader, a term that includes high school and university students, as well as the sort of person who might visit a public library in the evening after work to find out about someone or something connected to American literature.

Anyone looking for a consistent theoretical approach to the subjects at hand will be disappointed, since no effort was made to enforce a particular theoretical method, critical approach, or ideological strain, apart from a general openness to multicultural dimensions and feminist theory. (The sheer number of articles devoted to, say, African-American or feminist topics will be obvious at a glance.) Jargon, as such, has been discouraged, and the writers of these articles—some very lengthy, some relatively short—have been steered away from excessive theorizing, although theory itself is the subject of one detailed essay, and many aspects or branches of literary theory and criticism are treated separately. It would be fair to say that many, if not most, of the articles in these pages reflect a serious attempt on the part of the writers to grapple with the subject before them in the context of recent theory and literary practice. In this sense, the articles included meet a high professional standard while remaining accessible to general readers.

Attempts to encircle, or represent, the subject of American literature on a broad scale have been relatively few and far between. Several historians of literature in the nineteenth century approached the subject with distinction, such as Moses Coit Tyler, who published the two-volume *A History of American Literature during the Colonial Time, 1607–1765* (1878), which regarded American literature as a "noble and distinctive branch" of English literature. Another excellent critic was Charles F. Richardson, who in *American Literature: 1607–1885* (1896) wrote: "No critical task is more difficult and delicate than that of estimating the rank and analyzing the achievements of American authors." With palpable displeasure he noted that Victor Hugo had declared Poe "the prince of American writers" while saying he had never even heard of Emerson. Richardson also viewed American literature as a local branch of English literature and described his project as an effort to comprehend and describe "the Saxon mind in America." His two-volume study remains valuable and fascinating. Perhaps the most visible project of the era was *Appleton's Cyclopedia of American Biography*, edited by James Grant Wilson and John Fiske in six volumes between 1887 and 1889. For decades, this remained the standard history of American literature, taking a strongly biographical and belletristic approach.

In the twentieth century, a number of historical surveys of American literature were published by individual scholars or groups of scholars. Among the major publications of this type were Walter C. Bronson's lucid and meticulous *Short History of American Literature* (1900) and Isaac Woodbridge Riley's *American Thought: From Puritanism to Pragmatism and Beyond* (1915). The latter was an especially useful study that weighed the influence of European—as opposed to English—thought on American writers and thinkers. Riley was especially interested in American authors who had managed to digest the great German authors, such as Goethe and Schiller, remaking an American tradition from these influences as well as the more obvious British sources.

The first modern, cooperative study of American literature was the *Cambridge History of American Literature* (1917–1921), which remains readable to this day. One might well trace the beginnings of the multicultural approach currently secure within the academy to this impressive effort to include many voices, American and Canadian, and to attempt to avoid what the editors called "the temptation of national pride." There was a chapter on Native American writing and other chapters on American literary work written in languages other than English, such as Yiddish. The Continental origins of American movements such as transcendentalism were traced with considerable energy and vision to European sources. This work was comprehensive and remarkably lucid and in many ways provided a model of sorts for this enterprise, although we have stepped away from a strict historical approach in presenting this material in a nonchronological fashion, allowing the alphabet, with its arbitrary sequencing, to govern the shape of the whole.

A few well-known and ambitious surveys of American thought and literature were published during the middle decades of the twentieth century, ranging from Vernon Louis Parrington's *Main Currents in American Thought* (1927) to Robert Spiller's *Literary History of the United States* (1948). Each of these attempted to "place" American literature within the context of British and European culture, showing how American authors had transmogrified their sources, made something new from something old, giving a national inflection to their writing and thus helping to shape American national identities. There was also a fresh sense that American literature was not simply a passive receptor of Old World energies but that American writers and writing had begun to influence European writing, as the widespread impact of Emerson, Poe, and Cooper on European literature exemplifies.

More recent attempts to assemble comprehensive histories of American literature include Emory Elliott's excellent one-volume *Columbia History of American Literature* (1988) and Sacvan Bercovitch's *Cambridge History of American Literature* (1994–). These volumes, written by many hands, reflected earnest attempts to encompass the pluralist nature of American writing, exploring literary texts as a reflection of the tensions and disruptions that are part of any living culture, but especially one as complex and heterogeneous as that which has arisen within the geographical and spiritual boundaries of the United States. Both Elliott and Bercovitch tended to bring forward and emphasize the immense cultural diversity of American literature, giving weight to multicultural and feminist texts in particular. If anything, I have taken my cue from these first-rate studies, although my aim is more directly focused on the general reader than were these "histories," which made no attempt to provide the sort of basic information and "coverage"—a dreadful but useful term—that one will find in these pages.

Critics of these recent historical surveys have been suspicious of attempts merely to gather discordant, even dissenting, voices into an imaginary tent of some kind—the liberal nation-state itself—that totalizes and somehow undermines the bite and fierce independence of voices coming from the margins. This tendency inevitably will exist in anything resembling an encyclopedia, with its heavily Enlightenment accent, its aspirations to comprehensiveness. I'm hoping that, by the variety of critical voices present here, representing a considerable range of approaches to literary studies and textual interpretations, something fresh will be made available. These volumes do contain a lot of old-fashioned "close readings," and no apologies need be offered for this. These articles, on works ranging from *Adventures of Huckleberry Finn* and *The Great Gatsby* to *A Raisin in the Sun* and *Beloved*, should prove useful to students in particular. But interested readers will also find speculative essays here in which critics explore the multicultural dynamics of African American, Native American, Hispanic, Asian American (including Filipino), Italian American, and Jewish American as well as gay and lesbian writing.

In keeping with the encyclopedic tradition, we have included a lot of facts in these articles. Readers will find reliable surveys of the lives and works of most well-known American authors from Anne Bradstreet through the usual suspects, such as Longfellow, Emerson, Thoreau, Whitman, Dickinson, Hawthorne, and Melville: the great procession, which still continues. To a degree, the canonical authors—Whitman, Dickinson, and so forth—have been given more space in this project than lesser-known authors. It goes without saying that many readers will (quite rightly) question whether So-and-So was given too much or too little space. Certainly the "major" authors have all been thoroughly examined in essays by leading scholars. Their writing lives are presented, with bibliographies of primary works and selected secondary works that include brief commentaries on those critical and biographical texts.

The most difficult part of this project involved deciding on which lesser-known or contemporary authors to include and which to exclude. In any work of this kind, exclusion is necessary. This is true of any text not randomly produced. I would hope that the *Oxford Encyclopedia* offers many pleasant surprises for readers, treating authors and texts and subjects not often discussed in projects such as this one. As for the contemporary authors included, I will only say that every effort was made to include subjects who might interest high school and college students as well as the general reader. Certain texts receive separate analytical essays simply because they have proven popular in the classroom in recent years. We make no apologies for the fact that this encyclopedia can (and will) be historicized, and that it reflects current tastes and prejudices. All literary histories suffer from this limitation. (There will be supplements in due course, taking up authors and texts and literary movements that have been excluded in the original four volumes for one reason or another.)

Many of the "topic" essays, such as those on Puritanism or naturalism or nature writing, include references to authors who are treated elsewhere in greater detail. Readers should consult the index entry on a given author or work to see where these are discussed and in what context. There is also a good deal of cross-referencing, designed to help readers find out where they can find out more about a given subject. Readers will also discover that many authors and texts are discussed in various articles in different ways, and this is intentional. In the case of masterworks, such as *Moby-Dick* or *The Great Gatsby*, readers may wish first to consult the longer essay on the authors, Melville or Fitzgerald, where brief discussions of the major text are offered; the longer essays on individual works are supplementary, allowing the critic room to explore a text in a closer way.

Readers will find articles on ethnic literature (Jewish, Italian-American, and so forth), on movements (transcendentalism, the Black Arts Movement, the Beats, or the Black Mountain school), on city-specific movements (the Harlem Renaissance, the Chicago school), on broad themes (the literature of war or the academic novel), or on specific genres (the slave narrative or the long poem). Major literary figures in all these periods, movements, or genres are given a separate article, so that while Henry David Thoreau is discussed as part of the transcendental movement, there is also a longer article on his life and work and, indeed, a separate essay on *Walden* itself. In this way, a reader interested in the movement as it relates to Thoreau will have both a broad context for understanding his work and an opportunity to look closely at a given text.

Embracing four centuries of writing, mostly in English, *The Oxford Encyclopedia of American Literature* should prove valuable to researchers at many levels of inquiry and stimulating for readers who simply want to find out about a particular author or text, movement or period. If anything, this project testifies to the astonishing diversity and range of writing—poems, novels, plays, journals, letters, memoirs, criticism, history—subsumed under the heading of "literature" within these national borders. What the term "American" means is open to interpretation, a term that specifies a geographical space, to be sure, but something much less definable as well: a patchwork of individual and group desires, a vision, a power play, a palimpsest of constructions, represented by a wild and vivid assortment of texts produced in time, and thus governed by limits which have, in many instances, proved affirming.

# CHRONOLOGY

| DATE | LITERARY WORKS AND AUTHORS | HISTORICAL CONTEXT |
|---|---|---|
| 1607 | — | Colony of Jamestown established in Virginia |
| 1619 | — | First slaves arrive in America |
| 1620 | — | The *Mayflower*, carrying Pilgrims from Plymouth, England, lands at New Plymouth, Mass. |
| 1638 | — | Anne Hutchinson banished from Massachusetts Bay Colony after Puritan clergy find her guilty of heresy |
| 1649 | | Charles I deposed and executed |
| 1650 | Bradstreet, *The Tenth Muse Lately Sprung Up in America* | Oliver Cromwell comes to power |
| 1657 | ca. William Bradford | — |
| 1672 | d. Anne Bradstreet | — |
| 1675 | — | Wampanoag Indians destroyed after attacking English colonists in King Philip's War, 1675–1676 |
| ca. 1680 | Taylor, *God's Determinations Touching His Elect* | — |
| 1682 | Mary Rowlandson, *The Captivity Narrative* Taylor, *Preparatory Meditations* begun (1682–1725) | — |
| 1692 | — | Witch trials in Salem, Mass., result in 20 executions |
| 1693 | Mather, *Wonders of the Invisible World* | — |
| 1711 | — | — |
| 1724 | — | Jewish settlers exiled from Louisiana colony |
| 1728 | d. Cotton Mather | — |
| 1729 | d. Edward Taylor | — |
| 1734 | — | — |
| 1735 | — | John Peter Zenger, editor of *New York Weekly*, acquitted of sedition and libel, establishing doctrine of freedom of the press |
| 1739 | — | War of Jenkins's Ear, between England and Spain over control of seaways, 1739–1748 The "Great Awakening," a religious revival movement spawned by Jonathan Edwards and others, spreads across American colonies |
| 1741 | Edwards, *Sinners in the Hands of an Angry God* | — |
| 1745 | — | King George's War, between England and France for control over North America, 1745–1748 |

| DATE | LITERARY WORKS AND AUTHORS | HISTORICAL CONTEXT |
| --- | --- | --- |
| 1754 | — | French and Indian War, continued territorial struggle pitting France, its Canadian colonies, and its American Indian allies against Britain and its American colonies, 1754–1763 |
| 1758 | d. Jonathan Edwards | — |
| 1761 | — | Slavery abolished in mainland Portugal |
| 1765 | — | Stamp Act, a tax imposed by Britain on American colonies, provokes movement against "taxation without representation" |
| 1766 | — | Daniel Boone explores Kentucky Territory |
| 1768 | Sampson Occom, *A Short Narrative of My Life* | — |
| 1770 | Freneau, *Father Bombo's Pilgrimage to Mecca* | British soldiers fire into a crowd, killing five persons in the Boston Massacre |
| 1772 | Freneau, "A Poem on the Rising Glory of America" | — |
| 1773 | Wheatley, *Poems on Various Subjects, Religious and Moral* | Colonists destroy British tea at Boston Tea Party, signaling American opposition to the Tea Act of 1773 |
| 1775 | — | Clashes between American troops and British army at Lexington and Concord, Mass. Begin Revolutionary War<br>Second Continental Congress meets in Philadelphia<br>British defeat Americans at Bunker Hill, near Boston |
| 1776 | — | Thomas Paine publishes *Common Sense*<br>Second Continental Congress adopts the Declaration of Independence<br>George Washington's army defeats British at Trenton, New Jersey<br>First state constitutions written |
| 1777 | — | Articles of Confederation adopted |
| 1780–1781 | | Americans defeat British in Battle of Cowpens, in South Carolina<br>Articles of Confederation ratified |
| 1782 | Crèvecoeur, *Letters from an American Farmer* | — |
| 1783 | — | Treaty of Paris with Great Britain recognizes American independence |
| 1784 | d. Phillis Wheatley | — |
| 1786 | — | — |
| 1787 | — | Daniel Shays leads armed rebellion of debtor farmers against courts in western Mass., spurring drive for stronger national government<br>Constitutional Convention, meeting in Philadelphia, adopts Constitution<br>The *Federalist Papers*, a collection of essays supporting the United States Constitution and the idea of a strong federal government, written by Alexander Hamilton, James Madison, and John Jay under the pseudonym "Publius," published in New York City newspapers, 1787–1788<br>States ratify Constitution, 1787–1788 |

| DATE | LITERARY WORKS AND AUTHORS | HISTORICAL CONTEXT |
| --- | --- | --- |
| 1789 | | First elections held under Constitution<br>George Washington becomes first president<br>Bill of Rights adopted by Congress<br>French Revolution, abolishing the monarchy and establishing a republican form of government, 1789–1799 |
| 1790 | d. Benjamin Franklin | First American cotton mill established in Pawtucket, R.I. |
| 1791 | Franklin, *The Autobiography of Benjamin Franklin* | — |
| 1794 | — | Whiskey Rebellion, an uprising against the federal excise tax on corn liquor in western Pennsylvania, put down by federal troops |
| 1796 | — | Washington leaves presidency |
| 1798 | — | Alien and Sedition Acts, imposing far-reaching restrictions on freedom of speech and of the press, passed by Congress |
| 1801 | — | Thomas Jefferson becomes president |
| 1802 | | The Library of Congress established |
| 1803 | — | Supreme Court rules in *Marbury* v. *Madison* that the court has the power to invalidate acts of Congress when they are determined to be unconstitutional<br>Louisiana Purchase, the acquisition by the United States of more than 800,000 square miles of territory from France, extends U.S. holdings from Mississippi River to the Rocky Mountains<br>Lewis and Clark begin expedition to investigate the territory added by the Louisiana Purchase (1803–1806) |
| 1806 | First edition of *Webster's Dictionary* | — |
| 1807 | — | Embargo Act bans all foreign trade |
| 1812 | — | U.S. declares war on Britain, beginning War of 1812 |
| 1813 | d. J. Hector St. John de Crèvecoeur | British erect naval blockade |
| 1814 | | British troops capture and burn Washington<br>Treaty of Ghent ends war between U.S. and Britain |
| 1819 | Irving, *The Sketch Book of Geoffrey Crayon, Gent.* (1819–1820) | — |
| 1821 | — | Cherokee language transcribed |
| 1823 | — | James Monroe issues Monroe Doctrine, declaring that any military incursions by European nations into the Americas would be considered a threat to U.S. sovereignty. |
| 1825 | — | Erie Canal opens, linking the Great Lakes to the Hudson River |
| 1826 | Cooper, *The Last of the Mohicans* | — |
| 1827 | Poe, *Tamerlane and Other Poems* | First railroad tracks laid on American soil |

| DATE | LITERARY WORKS AND AUTHORS | HISTORICAL CONTEXT |
|---|---|---|
| 1830 | — | Indian Removal Act, giving the president power to negotiate the removal of Indian tribes from areas east of the Mississippi River, passed by Congress and signed by President Andrew Jackson |
| 1831 | Prince, *The History of Mary Prince, A West Indian Slave* | William Lloyd Garrison begins publishing abolitionist newspaper *The Liberator* |
| 1832 | d. Philip Freneau | — |
| 1834 | — | Slavery abolished in British Colonies |
| 1835 | Simms, *The Yemasee* | — |
| 1836 | Emerson, *Nature* | Transcendentalist movement (ca. 1836–1882), promoting intuitive idealism, the divinity of humankind, and the importance of the individual's own moral insight as opposed to the rule of the many, becomes major influence in American literature, theology, and social thought |
| 1838 | — | Cherokee Nation forced to move from Georgia to Indian Territory (Oklahoma) in Trail of Tears, 1838–1839 |
| 1839 | Very, *Essays and Poems* | — |
| 1840 | Dana, *Two Years before the Mast* <br> Poe, *Tales of the Grotesque and Arabesque* <br> Tocqueville, Alexis de, *Democracy in America (1835–1840)* | — |
| 1841 | Cooper, *The Deerslayer* <br> Emerson, *Essays* | — |
| 1843 | Poe, "The Tell-Tale Heart" | — |
| 1844 | | — |
| 1845 | Douglass, *The Narrative of the Life of Frederick Douglass* <br> Poe, *The Raven* <br> Poe, *Tales* | — |
| 1847 | Longfellow, *Evangeline* | — |
| 1848 | — | Women's rights convention at Seneca Falls, New York demands equal rights for women, including the right to vote <br> John Humphrey Noyes founds Oneida Perfectionist colony, a Christian socialist society that becomes a leading example of the American Utopian movement, 1848–1900 |
| 1849 | Thoreau, *Civil Disobedience* <br> d. Edgar Allan Poe | Gold rush in California, 1849–1850 |
| 1850 | Hawthorne, *The Scarlet Letter* | Fugitive Slave Act, part of the Compromise of 1850, denies right of escaped slaves to a trial by jury and authorizes government authorities to return escaped slaves to former owners |
| 1851 | Hawthorne, *The House of the Seven Gables* <br> Melville, *Moby-Dick* <br> d. James Fenimore Cooper | — |

| DATE | LITERARY WORKS AND AUTHORS | HISTORICAL CONTEXT |
|---|---|---|
| 1852 | Hawthorne, *The Blithedale Romance*<br>Stowe, *Uncle Tom's Cabin* | — |
| 1853 | Melville, "Bartleby the Scrivener" | — |
| 1854 | Thoreau, *Walden; or, Life in the Woods* | Republican Party formed |
| 1855 | Douglass, *My Bondage and My Freedom*<br>Irving, *Life of George Washington* (five vols., 1855–1859)<br>Longfellow, *The Song of Hiawatha*<br>Whitman, *Leaves of Grass* | — |
| 1856 | Melville, *The Piazza Tales* | — |
| 1857 | — | Supreme Court issues decision in *Dred Scott* v. *Sandford* case, declaring that a black slave cannot become a citizen under the U.S. Constitution |
| 1858 | Longfellow, *The Courtship of Miles Standish* | — |
| 1859 | d. Washington Irving<br>d. Alexis de Tocqueville | John Brown leads raid on U.S. arsenal at Harper's Ferry, Virginia, hoping to inspire slave uprising |
| 1860 | — | Abraham Lincoln elected president |
| 1861 | | Confederate States of America formed<br>Fort Sumter, S.C., falls to Confederate forces, beginning Civil War<br>In first major armed conflict of Civil War, Confederates defeat Union army in (First) Battle of Bull Run in Virginia |
| 1862 | d. Henry David Thoreau | Both armies sustain enormous casualties in battles of Shiloh, (Second) Bull Run, Antietam, and Fredericksburg |
| 1863 | Thoreau, *The Maine Woods* | Lincoln issues Emancipation Proclamation, freeing the slaves |
| 1864 | d. Nathaniel Hawthorne | Antidraft riots break out in New York City; homes of wealthy looted and scores of African Americans lynched<br>Union armies victorious at crucial battles of Vicksburg and Gettysburg<br>General Sherman captures Atlanta, begins "March to the Sea" to destroy Confederacy<br>Lincoln re-elected president |
| 1865 | Whitman, *Drum Taps* | General Lee of the Confederacy surrenders to General Grant of the Union Army at Appomattox Courthouse, Virginia, ending the Civil War<br>President Lincoln assassinated; Andrew Johnson becomes president. Thirteenth Amendment outlaws slavery<br>Freedmen's Bureau established to aid and assimilate freed slaves |
| 1866 | — | Congress approves Fourteenth Amendment, granting citizenship to "all persons born or naturalized in the United States" and prohibiting states from reducing the "privileges and immunities of citizens"<br>Ku Klux Klan formed in South |

| DATE | LITERARY WORKS AND AUTHORS | HISTORICAL CONTEXT |
| --- | --- | --- |
| 1868 | Alcott, *Little Women*<br>Alger, *Ragged Dick* | Military Reconstruction Act outlines plan of Reconstruction, placing the South under temporary military occupation, enfranchising African Americans and disenfranchising former Confederate leaders<br>Andrew Johnson impeached but not convicted<br>Fourteenth Amendment ratified<br>Ulysses S. Grant elected president |
| 1869 | Twain, *The Innocents Abroad* | Congress passes Fifteenth Amendment<br>Transcontinental railroad completed |
| 1870 | Harte, *The Luck of Roaring Camp and Other Sketches*<br>d. William Gilmore Simms | John D. Rockefeller founds Standard Oil |
| 1871 | — | Great Chicago Fire destroys large portion of city's central district |
| 1872 | Twain, *Roughing It* | First national park, Yellowstone, established |
| 1873 | — | Andrew Carnegie founds Carnegie Steel |
| 1874 | | Financial panic disrupts national economy |
| 1876 | Twain, *The Adventures of Tom Sawyer* | General George Custer dies in battle with Sioux at Little Big Horn (Montana)<br>Alexander Graham Bell invents the telephone<br>Baseball's National League founded |
| 1877 | | Last federal troops withdrawn from South after "Compromise of 1877," an agreement between Southern Democrats and Republicans to end federal intervention in South |
| 1878 | James, *Daisy Miller* | |
| 1879 | — | Edison invents the light bulb |
| 1880 | Harris, *Uncle Remus*<br>d. Jones Very | — |
| 1881 | Alger, *From Canal Boy to President*<br>James, *The Portrait of a Lady* | President Garfield assassinated |
| 1882 | Howells, *A Modern Instance*<br>Lazarus, *Songs of a Semite*<br>d. Richard Henry Dana<br>d. Ralph Waldo Emerson<br>d. Henry Wadsworth Longfellow | Congress passes Chinese Exclusion Act, outlawing immigration from China |
| 1883 | Twain, *Life on the Mississippi* | Brooklyn Bridge opens |
| 1884 | Twain, *Adventures of Huckleberry Finn* | First steel girder "skyscraper" built in Chicago |
| 1885 | Howells, *The Rise of Silas Lapham* | — |
| 1886 | d. Emily Dickinson | — |
| 1887 | d. Emma Lazarus | — |
| 1888 | Bellamy, *Looking Backward*<br>d. Louisa May Alcott | — |
| 1889 | — | Jane Addams opens Hull House in Chicago to help assimilate immigrants |

| DATE | LITERARY WORKS AND AUTHORS | HISTORICAL CONTEXT |
|---|---|---|
| 1890 | Dickinson, *Poems of Emily Dickinson* | Battle of Wounded Knee (S. Dakota), the last major clash between federal troops and American Indians, results in massacre of hundreds of Sioux<br>Sherman Antitrust Act outlaws contracts, combinations, and conspiracies "in restraint of trade"<br>"Jim Crow" laws establishing strict segregation passed throughout South (ca. 1890s) |
| 1891 | d. Herman Melville | — |
| 1892 | Gilman, *The Yellow Wallpaper*<br>d. Walt Whitman | People's Party formed in Omaha on behalf of debtor farmers, launching "Populist" movement |
| 1893 | — | Depression begins<br>Chicago World's Fair<br>Anti-Saloon League founded |
| 1894 | Garland, *Crumbling Idols*<br>Twain, *The Tragedy of Puddn'head Wilson* | — |
| 1895 | Crane, *The Red Badge of Courage*<br>d. Frederick Douglass | First Coney Island amusement park opens<br>Insurrection against Spanish begins in Cuba |
| 1896 | Dunbar, *Lyrics of Lowly Life*<br>Jewett, *The Country of the Pointed Firs*<br>d. Harriet Beecher Stowe | William Jennings Bryan wins Democratic nomination after "Cross of Gold" speech denouncing gold standard<br>William McKinley elected president<br>Yukon Gold Rush<br>*Plessy* v. *Ferguson* upholds racially segregated railroad cars; further discriminatory (Jim Crow) laws follow |
| 1897 | — | The advent of sensationalistic newspaper reporting known as "Yellow Journalism" |
| 1898 | Crane, *The Open Boat and Other Tales of Adventure*<br>James, *The Turn of the Screw* | Spanish-American War, 1898–1899; Treaty of Paris cedes Puerto Rico, Philippines, and other Spanish possessions to U.S. and recognizes Cuban independence<br>U.S. battleship *Maine* explodes in Havana harbor<br>Revolt against American rule begins in Philippines (1898–1902) |
| 1899 | Chesnutt, *The Conjure Woman*<br>Chopin, *The Awakening*<br>Norris, *McTeague*<br>d. Horatio Alger | — |
| 1900 | Baum, *The Wizard of Oz*<br>Chesnutt, *The House behind the Cedars*<br>Dreiser, *Sister Carrie*<br>d. Stephen Crane | Eugene Debs runs for president as candidate of Socialist Party<br>Hawaii becomes U.S. territory |
| 1901 | — | President McKinley assassinated; Theodore Roosevelt becomes president<br>J. P. Morgan creates United States Steel Corporation<br>Baseball's American League founded |

| DATE | LITERARY WORKS AND AUTHORS | HISTORICAL CONTEXT |
| --- | --- | --- |
| 1902 | Hapgood, *The Spirit of the Ghetto*<br>James, *The Wings of the Dove*<br>Wister, *The Virginian*<br>d. Bret Harte<br>d. Frank Norris | — |
| 1903 | Du Bois, W. E. B., *The Souls of Black Folk*<br>James, *The Ambassadors*<br>London, *The Call of the Wild* | Ford Motor Company founded<br>Wright brothers launch first airplane flight at Kitty<br>  Hawk, North Carolina<br>First motion picture debuts in America |
| 1904 | Henry, *Cabbages and Kings*<br>James, *The Golden Bowl*<br>d. Kate Chopin | Construction of Panama Canal begins |
| 1905 | Wharton, *The House of Mirth* | Roosevelt elected president |
| 1906 | London, *White Fang*<br>Sinclair, *The Jungle*<br>d. Paul Laurence Dunbar | San Francisco earthquake and fire destroy much of the<br>  city<br>Meat Inspection Act, requiring government inspection<br>  of slaughterhouses, passed by Congress<br>Pure Food and Drug Act, restricting sale of dangerous<br>  or ineffective medicines, passed by Congress<br>Henry Ford produces his first automobiles |
| 1907 | Adams, *The Education of Henry Adams* | Sinn Fein, an Irish nationalist movement, founded |
| 1909 | d. Sarah Orne Jewett | National Association for the Advancement of Colored<br>  People (NAACP) founded<br>Admiral Peary reaches North Pole |
| 1910 | d. O. Henry<br>d. Mark Twain | Boy Scouts of America founded |
| 1911 | Bierce, *The Devil's Dictionary*<br>Wharton, *Ethan Frome* | Standard Oil Company declared a monopoly and<br>  broken up |
| 1912 | Lindsay, *Rhymes to Be Traded for Bread* | *Titanic* sinks<br>Girl Guides (later Girl Scouts of America) founded<br>Woodrow Wilson elected president |
| 1913 | Cather, *O Pioneers!*<br>Frost, *A Boy's Will* | — |
| 1914 | Pound, *Des Imagistes*<br>Stein, *Tender Buttons*<br>Tarkington, *Penrod*<br>d. Ambrose Bierce | Panama Canal opens<br>Austria invades Serbia, beginning World War I<br>First federal income tax established by Congress |
| 1915 | Lindsay, *The Art of the Moving Picture*<br>Masters, *Spoon River Anthology* | D. W. Griffith's film *The Birth of a Nation* features<br>  stereotypical images of African Americans and<br>  negative portrayal of Reconstruction<br>Great Migration of African Americans from the South<br>  to Northern cities begins |
| 1916 | Lardner, *You Know Me, Al*<br>d. Henry James<br>d. Jack London | The Easter Rebellion in Dublin, Ireland; Irish<br>  Republican Army is established<br>Margaret Sanger opens first birth control clinic in<br>  Brooklyn<br>Wilson re-elected |

| DATE | LITERARY WORKS AND AUTHORS | HISTORICAL CONTEXT |
|------|---------------------------|--------------------|
| 1917 | Eliot, *Prufrock and Other Observations*<br>Lowell, *Tendencies in Modern American Poetry*<br>Millay, *Renascence and Other Poems*<br>Sinclair, *King Coal* | Russian Revolution, 1917–1921<br>Soviet Union established<br>U.S. enters World War I<br>Puerto Ricans granted U.S. citizenship |
| 1918 | Cather, *My Ántonia*<br>Tarkington, *The Magnificent Ambersons*<br>d. Henry Adams | Spanish flu epidemic kills millions (1918–1919)<br>Armistice ends war |
| 1919 | Algonquin Round Table begins meeting, 1919–1932<br>Anderson, *Winesburg, Ohio*<br>Mencken, *The American Language* | Paris Peace Conference convenes<br>Treaty of Versailles signed by Germany, Britain, France,<br>    Italy, and Japan, but not ratified by U.S. Senate<br>Eighteenth Amendment (Prohibition) ratified<br>Race riots break out in Chicago and other cities |
| 1920 | Lewis, *Main Street*<br>Wharton, *The Age of Innocence*<br>d. William Dean Howells | In "Red Scare" federal government reacts to radicalism<br>    and raids leftist organizations<br>Prohibition goes into effect<br>Women given the right to vote (Nineteenth<br>    Amendment)<br>Partition of Ireland |
| 1921 | Dos Passos, *Three Soldiers*<br>Robinson, *Collected Poems* | *Reader's Digest* founded |
| 1922 | Cummings, *The Enormous Room*<br>Eliot, *The Waste Land*<br>*The Fugitive* magazine founded, 1922–1925<br>Garland, *A Daughter of the Middle Border*<br>Lewis, *Babbitt* | Harlem Renaissance, 1922–1929<br>Motion Picture Association, under Will Hays, founded<br>    to regulate film industry |
| 1923 | Cummings, *Tulips and Chimneys*<br>Frost, *New Hampshire*<br>Loy, *Lunar Baedeker*<br>Millay, *The Harp-Weaver and Other Poems*<br>Stevens, *Harmonium* | Warren G. Harding dies; Calvin Coolidge becomes<br>    president<br>*Time* magazine founded |
| 1924 | Lardner, *How to Write Short Stories [with Samples]*<br>Melville, *Billy Budd, Foretopman*<br>H. L. Mencken cofounds *American Mercury*<br>Robinson, *The Man Who Died Twice* | Stalin takes power in the Soviet Union after Lenin's<br>    death<br>National Origins Act severely restricts immigration<br>    from Asia and southern and eastern Europe<br>The Ku Klux Klan reaches peak membership |
| 1925 | Dreiser, *An American Tragedy*<br>Fitzgerald, *The Great Gatsby*<br>Lowell, *What's O'Clock?*<br>d. Amy Lowell | Scopes trial in Dayton, Tennessee, highlights attempts<br>    by religious fundamentalists to forbid the teaching of<br>    evolution<br>*The New Yorker* begins publication |
| 1926 | Hemingway, *The Sun Also Rises*<br>Hughes, *Weary Blues*<br>Parker, *Enough Rope*<br>Tate, *Ode to the Confederate Dead* | National Broadcasting Company (NBC) formed |
| 1927 | Wilder, *The Bridge of San Luis Rey*<br>Lewis, *Elmer Gantry*<br>Cather, *Death Comes for the Archbishop* | Sacco and Vanzetti, Italian immigrants and admitted<br>    anarchists, executed<br>Charles Lindbergh's solo flight across the Atlantic<br>Columbia Broadcasting System (CBS) formed |

| DATE | LITERARY WORKS AND AUTHORS | HISTORICAL CONTEXT |
|------|----------------------------|--------------------|
| 1928 | Benét, *John Brown's Body*<br>Jackson, *Anarchism Is Not Enough*<br>Sandburg, *Good Morning, America* | Herbert Hoover elected president<br>Alexander Fleming discovers penicillin |
| 1929 | Aiken, *Selected Poems*<br>Faulkner, *The Sound and the Fury*<br>Hemingway, *A Farewell to Arms*<br>Wolfe, *Look Homeward, Angel* | Stock market crash<br>Great Depression begins, 1929–1939 |
| 1930 | Auden, *Poems*<br>Crane, *The Bridge*<br>Eliot, *Ash Wednesday*<br>Faulkner, *As I Lay Dying*<br>The Fugitives publish *I'll Take My Stand: The South and the Agrarian Tradition* | The Dust Bowl, a decade of severe drought and dust storms in U.S. Plains, begins |
| 1931 | Buck, *The Good Earth*<br>Wilson, *Axel's Castle*<br>Louis Zukofsky edits objectivist issue of *Poetry* magazine<br>d. Vachel Lindsay | Scottsboro case attracts national attention when a group of black teenagers is convicted and sentenced to death for the rape of two white women on a train near Scottsboro, Alabama |
| 1932 | Faulkner, *Light in August*<br>Caldwell, *Tobacco Road*<br>d. Charles W. Chesnutt<br>d. Hart Crane | Franklin Delano Roosevelt elected president<br>Tuskegee syphilis project begins |
| 1933 | Stein, *The Autobiography of Alice B. Toklas*<br>West, *Miss Lonelyhearts*<br>d. Ring Lardner | New Deal begins<br>Adolf Hitler becomes chancellor of Germany<br>Twenty-first Amendment ends prohibition<br>U.S. recognizes USSR<br>Tennessee Valley Authority (TVA) created to revitalize the region |
| 1934 | Fitzgerald, *Tender Is the Night*<br>Miller, *Tropic of Cancer*<br>Pound, *Make It New*<br>Roth, *Call It Sleep* | Revised Production Code mandates self-censorship among Hollywood studios |
| 1935 | Moore, *Selected Poems*<br>O'Hara, *Butterfield 8*<br>Wolfe, *Of Time and the River*<br>d. Charlotte Perkins Gilman<br>d. Edwin Arlington Robinson | Works Progress Administration and other relief agencies, including Federal Writers' Project and Federal Arts Project, created to keep millions of people employed<br>Social Security Act creates pension system for working Americans and provides government assistance to the poor and elderly<br>National Labor Relations Act (Wagner Act) encourages collective bargaining between employers and employees, fostering union growth |
| 1936 | Barnes, *Nightwood*<br>Mitchell, *Gone with the Wind*<br>Sandburg, *The People, Yes!* | Roosevelt re-elected president<br>Spanish civil war, 1936–1939<br>Jesse Owens wins four gold medals in Berlin Olympics<br>*Life* begins publication |
| 1937 | Hurston, *Their Eyes Were Watching God*<br>Steinbeck, *Of Mice and Men*<br>d. Edith Wharton | The *Hindenburg* hydrogen airship explodes in Lakehurst, New Jersey |

| DATE | LITERARY WORKS AND AUTHORS | HISTORICAL CONTEXT |
|---|---|---|
| 1938 | Dos Passos, *U.S.A.* trilogy (collected)<br>Wilder, *Our Town*<br>Wright, *Uncle Tom's Children*<br>d. Thomas Wolfe | Germany annexes Austria and Czech Sudetenland<br>Munich Conference |
| 1939 | Hellman, *The Little Foxes*<br>Miller, *Tropic of Capricorn*<br>Steinbeck, *The Grapes of Wrath*<br>Thurber, "The Secret Life of Walter Mitty"<br>West, Nathanael, *The Day of the Locust* | Germany invades Poland<br>World War II begins, 1939–1945<br>New York World's Fair |
| 1940 | Hemingway, *For Whom the Bell Tolls*<br>McCullers, *The Heart Is a Lonely Hunter*<br>O'Hara, *Pal Joey*<br>O'Neill, *The Iceman Cometh*<br>Wright, *Native Son*<br>d. Hamlin Garland<br>d. F. Scott Fitzgerald<br>d. Nathanael West | Roosevelt re-elected president |
| 1941 | Agee, *Let Us Now Praise Famous Men*<br>Glasgow, *In This Our Life*<br>Ransom, *The New Criticism*<br>d. Sherwood Anderson | Japan attacks Pearl Harbor<br>U.S. enters World War II |
| 1942 | Frost, *A Witness Tree*<br>Kazin, *On Native Grounds*<br>Stevens, *Notes toward a Supreme Fiction*<br>White, *One Man's Meat* | News of the Holocaust reaches U.S.<br>Japanese Americans interned<br>Manhattan Project, government-sponsored research<br>that produced atomic bomb, begins |
| 1943 | Eliot, *Four Quartets*<br>d. Stephen Vincent Benét | Zoot-suit riots break out in Los Angeles when white<br>sailors attack Mexican-American youth |
| 1944 | Williams, *The Glass Menagerie*<br>d. Hutchins Hapgood | Roosevelt re-elected president<br>Allied forces storm the beaches at Normandy (D day)<br>GI Bill of Rights provides financial and educational<br>support to U.S. WWII veterans |
| 1945 | White, *Stuart Little*<br>Wright, *Black Boy*<br>d. Theodore Dreiser<br>d. Ellen Glasgow | Franklin D. Roosevelt dies; Harry S. Truman becomes<br>president<br>Mussolini killed by rioters<br>Hitler commits suicide<br>Germany surrenders, ending WWII<br>America drops atomic bombs on Hiroshima and<br>Nagasaki, Japan<br>Japan surrenders<br>United Nations founded |
| 1946 | Lowell, *Lord Weary's Castle*<br>Warren, *All the King's Men*<br>Welty, *Delta Wedding*<br>d. Gertrude Stein<br>d. Booth Tarkington | Literary figures develop New Criticism, which focuses<br>on text and language in literary analysis<br>Benjamin Spock, pediatrician and pacifist, publishes<br>*Baby and Child Care* |

| DATE | LITERARY WORKS AND AUTHORS | HISTORICAL CONTEXT |
|---|---|---|
| 1947 | Kees, *The Fall of Magicians*<br>Stafford, *The Mountain Lion*<br>Williams, *A Streetcar Named Desire*<br>d. Willa Cather | Jackie Robinson plays with Brooklyn Dodgers, breaking baseball's color line<br>House Un-American Activities Committee (HUAC) begins its investigation of communists in the Hollywood Motion Picture Industry<br>Construction begins on Levittown, New York, symbolizing suburban growth |
| 1948 | Jackson, "The Lottery"<br>Jarrell, *Losses*<br>Mailer, *The Naked and the Dead*<br>Pound, *The Pisan Cantos*<br>Roethke, *The Lost Son and Other Poems*<br>Vidal, *The City and the Pillar* | Truman signs Economic Cooperation Act (the Marshall Plan), sending financial aid to European countries suffering the effects of WWII<br>State of Israel established |
| 1949 | Algren, *The Man with the Golden Arm*<br>Brooks, *Annie Allen*<br>Miller, *Death of a Salesman*<br>d. Margaret Mitchell | North Atlantic Treaty Organization (NATO) established<br>Mao Zedong declares People's Republic of China a communist state |
| 1950 | Sandburg, *Complete Poems*<br>Trilling, *The Liberal Imagination*<br>d. Edgar Lee Masters<br>d. Edna St. Vincent Millay | North Korea invades South Korea, beginning Korean War (1950–1953)<br>UN troops, led by U.S. General Douglas MacArthur, launch counterattack against North Korea<br>China enters Korean War<br>Senator Joseph McCarthy alleges that certain State Department members hold communist loyalties |
| 1951 | Hughes, *Montage of a Dream Deferred*<br>McCullers, *The Ballad of the Sad Café*<br>Salinger, *The Catcher in the Rye*<br>Styron, *Lie Down in Darkness*<br>d. Sinclair Lewis | Julius and Ethel Rosenberg convicted as Soviet spies (executed 1953) |
| 1952 | Ellison, *Invisible Man*<br>Hemingway, *The Old Man and the Sea*<br>Malamud, *The Natural*<br>O'Connor, *Wise Blood*<br>Steinbeck, *East of Eden*<br>White, *Charlotte's Web* | U.S. tests hydrogen bomb<br>Dwight D. Eisenhower elected president |
| 1953 | Baldwin, *Go Tell It on the Mountain*<br>Bellow, *The Adventures of Augie March*<br>Jarrell, *Poetry and the Age*<br>Miller, *The Crucible*<br>Roethke, *The Waking: Poems, 1933–1953*<br>d. Eugene O'Neill | Watson and Crick document DNA<br>Korean war ends in stalemate |
| 1954 | Stevens, *Collected Poems*<br>Swenson, *Another Animal*<br>Robert Creeley founds *The Black Mountain Review* | Supreme Court decides *Brown* v. *Board of Education* case, ruling against racial segregation in public schools and declaring separate education facilities unequal<br>North and South Vietnam divided after communists under Ho Chi Minh defeat French colonials<br>Southeast Asia Treaty Organization (SEATO) established |

| DATE | LITERARY WORKS AND AUTHORS | HISTORICAL CONTEXT |
|---|---|---|
| 1955 | Baldwin, *Notes of a Native Son*<br>Bishop, *Poems: North and South—A Cold Spring*<br>Miller, *A View from the Bridge*<br>Nabokov, *Lolita*<br>O'Connor, *A Good Man Is Hard to Find*<br>O'Neill, *Long Day's Journey into Night*<br>Williams, *Cat on a Hot Tin Roof*<br>d. James Agee<br>d. Weldon Kees<br>d. Wallace Stevens | Montgomery, Alabama, bus boycott sparked by Rosa Parks refusing to give up her seat<br>American Federation of Labor and Congress of Industrial Organizations merge to become the AFL-CIO |
| 1956 | Barth, *The Floating Opera*<br>Ginsberg, *Howl*<br>Wilbur, *Things of This World*<br>d. H. L. Mencken | Eisenhower re-elected president |
| 1957 | Agee, *A Death in the Family*<br>Cheever, *The Wapshot Chronicle*<br>Kerouac, *On the Road*<br>McCarthy, *Memories of a Catholic Girlhood*<br>Singer, *Gimpel the Fool and Other Stories* | Soviet Union launches satellite *Sputnik*<br>European Economic Community (Common Market) established<br>Federal courts order desegregation of Central High School in Little Rock, Ark.<br>Martin Luther King Jr. establishes the Southern Christian Leadership Conference (SCLC) in Atlanta |
| 1958 | Capote, *Breakfast at Tiffany's*<br>Kerouac, *Dharma Bums*<br>Kunitz, *Selected Poems: 1928–1958*<br>Williams, *Paterson* (five volumes, 1946–1958) | National Aeronautics and Space Administration (NASA) established |
| 1959 | Albee, *The Zoo Story*<br>Burroughs, *Naked Lunch*<br>Hansberry, *A Raisin in the Sun*<br>Lowell, *Life Studies*<br>Paley, *The Little Disturbances of Man*<br>Roth, *Goodbye, Columbus*<br>Schwartz, *Summer Knowledge*<br>Thurber, *The Years with Ross*<br>White, *The Elements of Style* | Revolutionaries led by Fidel Castro overthrow Fulgencio Batista in Cuba<br>Alaska and Hawaii become states |
| 1960 | Barth, *The Sot-Weed Factor*<br>Kinnell, *What a Kingdom It Was*<br>Knowles, *A Separate Peace*<br>Lee, *To Kill a Mockingbird*<br>Plath, *The Colossus and Other Poems*<br>Sexton, *To Bedlam and Part Way Back*<br>Updike, *Rabbit, Run*<br>d. Zora Neale Hurston<br>d. Richard Wright | John F. Kennedy elected president<br>U.S. Food and Drug Administration approves the birth control pill |

| DATE | LITERARY WORKS AND AUTHORS | HISTORICAL CONTEXT |
|---|---|---|
| 1961 | Ginsberg, *Kaddish and Other Poems*<br>Gunn, *My Sad Captains*<br>Heller, *Catch-22*<br>Salinger, *Franny and Zooey*<br>d. H.D.<br>d. Ernest Hemingway<br>d. James Thurber | Attempted invasion of Cuba at the Bay of Pigs ends in defeat of U.S.-led forces<br>Construction of Berlin Wall begins<br>Peace Corps established |
| 1962 | Albee, *Who's Afraid of Virginia Woolf?*<br>Ashbery, *The Tennis Court Oath*<br>Auden, *The Dyer's Hand*<br>Baldwin, *Another Country*<br>Nabokov, *Pale Fire*<br>Stafford, *Traveling through the Dark*<br>d. E. E. Cummings<br>d. William Faulkner<br>d. Robinson Jeffers | Soviet Union removes missile sites from Cuba after U.S. threatens military attack<br>Socialist writer Michael Harrington publishes *The Other America*, documenting poverty in America |
| 1963 | McCarthy, *The Group*<br>Plath, *The Bell Jar*<br>d. W. E. B. Du Bois<br>d. Robert Frost<br>d. Sylvia Plath<br>d. Theodore Roethke<br>d. William Carlos Williams | Martin Luther King Jr. delivers "I Have a Dream" speech at March on Washington<br>President Kennedy assassinated; Lyndon B. Johnson becomes president<br>Betty Friedan publishes *The Feminine Mystique*, helping launch "second-wave" feminism |
| 1964 | Berryman, *77 Dream Songs*<br>Lowell, *For the Union Dead*<br>d. Flannery O'Connor | Civil Rights Act legislates against discrimination<br>The Beatles come to the U.S.<br>Free Speech Movement begins at University of California at Berkeley<br>Gulf of Tonkin resolution gives president power to "take all necessary measures" against communist insurgents in Vietnam<br>Johnson elected president |
| 1965 | Haley, *The Autobiography of Malcolm X*<br>Matthiessen, *At Play in the Fields of the Lord*<br>Plath, *Ariel*<br>d. T. S. Eliot<br>d. Lorraine Hansberry<br>d. Randall Jarrell<br>d. Shirley Jackson | U.S. sends combat troops to Vietnam, beginning Vietnam War (1965–1973)<br>Malcolm X assassinated<br>National Endowment for the Arts established<br>Race riot breaks out in Watts, Los Angeles<br>Voting Rights Act (Civil Rights Act of 1965) passed, providing federal protection to African Americans exercising their right to vote |
| 1966 | Capote, *In Cold Blood*<br>Hayden, *A Ballad of Remembrance*<br>Malamud, *The Fixer*<br>Pynchon, *The Crying of Lot 49*<br>Sexton, *Live or Die*<br>d. Mina Loy<br>d. Delmore Schwartz | National Organization for Women established |

| DATE | LITERARY WORKS AND AUTHORS | HISTORICAL CONTEXT |
|---|---|---|
| 1967 | Hecht, *The Hard Hours*<br>Levertov, *The Sorrow Dance*<br>McPhee, *Oranges*<br>Reed, *The Free-lance Pallbearers*<br>Stone, *A Hall of Mirrors*<br>Styron, *The Confessions of Nat Turner*<br>Tate, *The Lost Pilot*<br>d. Langston Hughes<br>d. Carson McCullers<br>d. Dorothy Parker<br>d. Carl Sandburg | Israel and Arabs clash over territory in Six-Day War<br>Thurgood Marshall becomes first African-American<br>   Supreme Court Justice<br>Race riots break out in Detroit and Newark |
| 1968 | Didion, *Slouching towards Bethlehem*<br>Momaday, *House Made of Dawn*<br>d. Upton Sinclair<br>d. John Steinbeck | Martin Luther King Jr. assassinated<br>Robert Kennedy assassinated<br>Viet Cong launch Tet offensive, intensifying war with<br>   U.S.<br>Richard Nixon elected president |
| 1969 | Bukowski, *Notes of a Dirty Old Man*<br>Howard, *Untitled Subjects*<br>Oates, *them*<br>Roth, *Portnoy's Complaint*<br>Stafford, *Collected Stories*<br>Vonnegut, *Slaughterhouse-Five*<br>d. Jack Kerouac | Stonewall Riot in New York City launches gay rights<br>   movement<br>Americans land on the moon<br>Woodstock music festival |
| 1970 | Angelou, *I Know Why the Caged Bird Sings*<br>Dickey, *Deliverance*<br>Didion, *Play It As It Lays*<br>Merwin, *The Carrier of Ladders*<br>Morrison, *The Bluest Eye*<br>d. John Dos Passos<br>d. John O'Hara | National Guard soldiers shoot antiwar protesters at<br>   Kent State University in Ohio, killing four |
| 1971 | Bukowski, *Post Office*<br>Gardner, *Grendel*<br>Stegner, *Angle of Repose*<br>Wright, *Collected Poems* | — |
| 1972 | Welty, *Optimist's Daughter*<br>d. John Berryman<br>d. Marianne Moore<br>d. Ezra Pound<br>d. Edmund Wilson | Nixon re-elected president<br>Watergate break-in<br>Israeli athletes killed at Munich Olympics<br>Congress approves Equal Rights Amendment,<br>   supporting the women's movement<br>Antiballistic Missile (ABM) Treaty (SALT I agreement)<br>   between U.S. and Soviet Union<br>Bloody Sunday sets off civil unrest in Ireland |
| 1973 | Jong, *Fear of Flying*<br>Pynchon, *Gravity's Rainbow*<br>Rich, *Diving into the Wreck*<br>Vidal, *Burr*<br>Vonnegut, *Breakfast of Champions*<br>d. Conrad Aiken<br>d. W. H. Auden<br>d. Pearl S. Buck | *Roe* v. *Wade* case invalidates anti-abortion laws<br>Paris Peace Accords produce cease-fire in Vietnam<br>U.S. withdraws from Vietnam<br>Members of the American Indian Movement (AIM)<br>   occupy town of Wounded Knee<br>Arab oil embargo and OPEC price increase creates<br>   spurring energy crisis |

| DATE | LITERARY WORKS AND AUTHORS | HISTORICAL CONTEXT |
| --- | --- | --- |
| 1974 | Ammons, *Sphere: The Form of a Motion*<br>Dillard, *Pilgrim at Tinker Creek*<br>Snyder, *Turtle Island*<br>d. John Crowe Ransom<br>d. Anne Sexton | Impeachment proceedings begin against Nixon<br>Nixon resigns; Gerald Ford becomes president<br>OPEC raises oil prices<br>"Stagflation" (recession and inflation together) begins |
| 1975 | Ashbery, *Self-Portrait in a Convex Mirror*<br>Bellow, *Humboldt's Gift*<br>Doctorow, *Ragtime*<br>Levertov, *The Freeing of the Dust*<br>Mamet, *American Buffalo*<br>Pinsky, *Sadness and Happiness*<br>d. Lionel Trilling<br>d. Thornton Wilder | South Vietnam falls to Communists |
| 1976 | Beattie, *Distortions*<br>Carver, *Will You Please Be Quiet, Please?*<br>Kingston, *The Woman Warrior*<br>Stegner, *The Spectator Bird* | Jimmy Carter elected president<br>Viking II space probe lands on Mars |
| 1977 | Hugo, *31 Letters and 13 Dreams*<br>Jordan, *Things That I Do in the Dark*<br>King, *The Shining*<br>Shepard, *Curse of the Starving Class*<br>d. Vladimir Nabokov<br>d. Robert Lowell | — |
| 1978 | Angelou, *And Still I Rise*<br>Gardner, *On Moral Fiction*<br>Hayden, *American Journal*<br>Irving, *The World According to Garp*<br>Lopez, *Of Wolves and Men*<br>Matthiessen, *The Snow Leopard*<br>Rich, *The Dream of a Common Language* | First test-tube baby born |
| 1979 | Justice, *Selected Poems*<br>Levine, *Ashes*<br>Mailer, *The Executioner's Song*<br>Styron, *Sophie's Choice*<br>d. Elizabeth Bishop<br>d. Jean Stafford<br>d. Allen Tate | Ayatollah Khomeini leads revolution in Iran against<br>    Shah Reza Pahlavi<br>American diplomats taken hostage in Iran<br>SALT II agreement between U.S. and Soviet Union<br>    further attempts to control nuclear armaments<br>Soviet troops invade Afghanistan; U.S. backs Muslim<br>    guerrilla fighters<br>Partial meltdown at Three Mile Island nuclear plant |
| 1980 | Kingston, *China Men*<br>Shepard, *True West*<br>d. Robert Hayden<br>d. Henry Miller<br>d. Katherine Anne Porter<br>d. Muriel Rukeyser<br>d. James Wright | Ronald Reagan elected president<br>U.S. boycotts Moscow Olympics |
| 1981 | Prose, *Household Saints*<br>Silko, *Storyteller*<br>d. Nelson Algren | Sandra Day O'Connor becomes first female Supreme<br>    Court justice<br>John Hinckley Jr. shoots President Reagan |

| DATE | LITERARY WORKS AND AUTHORS | HISTORICAL CONTEXT |
| --- | --- | --- |
| 1982 | Kinnell, *Selected Poems*<br>Merrill, *The Changing Light at Sandover*<br>Naylor, *The Women of Brewster Place*<br>Walker, *The Color Purple*<br>White, *A Boy's Own Story*<br>d. Djuna Barnes<br>d. John Cheever<br>d. John Gardner<br>d. Richard Hugo | First case of AIDS confirmed in America<br>Equal Rights Amendment fails to obtain necessary 38 state ratifications by deadline<br>U.S. invades Grenada |
| 1983 | Barthelme, *Overnight to Many Distant Cities*<br>Carver, *Cathedral*<br>Sandra Cisneros, *The House on Mango Street*<br>Kennedy, *Ironweed*<br>d. Tennessee Williams | — |
| 1984 | Erdrich, *Love Medicine*<br>Mamet, *Glengarry Glen Ross*<br>Olds, *The Dead and the Living*<br>Wolff, *The Barracks Thief*<br>d. Truman Capote<br>d. Lillian Hellman | Reagan re-elected president<br>Apple Computer introduces the Macintosh, the first personal computer with graphic user interface |
| 1985 | Banks, *Continental Drift*<br>DeLillo, *White Noise*<br>Irving, *The Cider House Rules*<br>Kincaid, *Annie John*<br>Wilson, *Fences*<br>d. E. B. White | Mikhail Gorbachev becomes leader of Soviet Union |
| 1986 | Erdrich, *The Beet Queen*<br>Lopez, *Arctic Dreams*<br>Ostriker, *The Imaginary Lover*<br>Taylor, *Summons to Memphis*<br>d. Bernard Malamud | Space shuttle *Challenger* explodes<br>Iran-Contra affair exposed; U.S. concedes selling weapons to Iran and illegally funding "contra" rebels in Nicaragua<br>Chernobyl nuclear power accident |
| 1987 | Morrison, *Beloved*<br>McNally, *Frankie and Johnny at the Claire de Lune*<br>Stevenson, *Selected Poems*<br>d. James Baldwin | U.S. stock market crashes |
| 1988 | White, *The Beautiful Room Is Empty*<br>d. Raymond Carver | George H. Bush elected president<br>Soviet troops withdraw from Afghanistan |
| 1989 | Banks, *Affliction*<br>Irving, *A Prayer for Owen Meany*<br>Kingston, *Tripmaster Monkey: His Fake Book*<br>Ozick, *The Shawl*<br>Wolff, *This Boy's Life*<br>d. Donald Barthelme<br>d. Mary McCarthy<br>d. May Swenson<br>d. Robert Penn Warren | Berlin Wall falls; end of the Cold War<br>Exxon *Valdez* runs aground in Alaska<br>Chinese military massacres pro-democracy demonstrators in Tiananmen Square, Beijing<br>U.S. invades Panama |

| DATE | LITERARY WORKS AND AUTHORS | HISTORICAL CONTEXT |
|---|---|---|
| 1990 | O'Brien, *The Things They Carried*<br>Simic, *The World Doesn't End*<br>Styron, *Darkness Visible*<br>Walcott, *Omeros*<br>Wideman, *Philadelphia Fire*<br>Wilson, *The Piano Lesson* | Nelson Mandela released after 27 years in South African prison |
| 1991 | Alvarez, *How the Garcia Girls Lost Their Accents*<br>Berry, *Standing on Earth*<br>Elkin, *The MacGuffin*<br>McNally, *Lips Together, Teeth Apart*<br>d. Laura Riding Jackson<br>d. Isaac Bashevis Singer | U.S. and allies force Iraq out of Kuwait in (first) Persian Gulf War<br>START I agreement between U.S. and Soviet Union calls for reduction and eventual dismantling of each country's nuclear weapons<br>Soviet Union collapses<br>Launch of the World Wide Web<br>Official end of Apartheid in South Africa |
| 1992 | Gioia, *Can Poetry Matter?*<br>Glück, *The Wild Iris*<br>Kushner, *Angels in America (1992–1995)*<br>McCarthy, *All the Pretty Horses* | Los Angeles race riot sparked by acquittal of police officers accused in the Rodney King beating<br>War breaks out in Yugoslavia as a result of ethnic tensions<br>Bill Clinton elected president |
| 1993 | Ammons, *Garbage*<br>Proulx, *The Shipping News*<br>d. Wallace Stegner<br>d. William Stafford | First bombing of New York's World Trade Center by Islamic terrorists<br>START II agreement between U.S. and Russia<br>Federal agents besiege and later burn Waco, Texas, compound of the Branch Davidians religious cult after a 51-day standoff |
| 1994 | Hacker, *Winter Numbers*<br>Levine, *Simple Truth*<br>d. Charles Bukowski<br>d. Ralph Ellison<br>d. Peter Taylor | Proposition 187 denies social services to illegal immigrants in California<br>Russian military begins suppression of Chechnyan secessionists<br>Genocide in Rwanda leaves 800,000 dead<br>North American Free Trade Agreement (NAFTA) eliminates trade barriers between U.S., Canada, and Mexico |
| 1995 | Carruth, *Scrambled Eggs and Whiskey: 1991–1995*<br>Ford, *Independence Day*<br>Kunitz, *Passing Through: The Later Poems*<br>Soto, *New and Selected Poems*<br>d. Stanley Elkin<br>d. James Merrill<br>d. Henry Roth | Oklahoma City bombing kills 169<br>O. J. Simpson criminal trial ends in acquittal<br>Bosnia, Serbia, and Croatia sign peace treaty<br>Israeli prime minister Yitzhak Rabin assassinated<br>Partial shutdown of U.S. government over budget disputes |
| 1996 | Brodkey, *This Wild Darkness*<br>Kincaid, *Autobiography of My Mother*<br>Matthews, *Time & Money*<br>Ostriker, *The Crack in Everything*<br>Pinsky, *The Figured Wheel*<br>Snyder, *Mountains and Rivers without End*<br>d. Harold Brodkey | Montana militia members (freemen) surrender to FBI after 81-day standoff<br>U.S. missile strike against Iraq<br>Bill Clinton re-elected |

| DATE | LITERARY WORKS AND AUTHORS | HISTORICAL CONTEXT |
|------|---------------------------|-------------------|
| 1997 | Beattie, *My Life, Starring Dara Falcon*<br>DeLillo, *Underworld*<br>Wright, *Black Zodiac*<br>d. William S. Burroughs<br>d. James Dickey<br>d. Allen Ginsberg<br>d. Denise Levertov<br>d. William Matthews | Diana, Princess of Wales, dies in car accident<br>Kyoto conference addresses global warming |
| 1998 | McPhee, *Annals of the Former World*<br>Ponsot, *The Bird Catcher*<br>Stern, *This Time: New and Selected Poems*<br>Strand, *Blizzard of One*<br>d. Alfred Kazin | Lewinsky scandal and the Starr Report lead to<br>    impeachment of Bill Clinton<br>India and Pakistan begin nuclear testing |
| 1999 | Ellison, *Juneteenth*<br>d. Joseph Heller | Columbine High School shootings<br>The Euro is officially launched in 11 countries |
| 2000 | Oates, *Blonde*<br>Williams, *Leap*<br>d. Gwendolyn Brooks | 2000 Census indicates Hispanic Americans become<br>    largest minority group in the U.S.<br>Controversy over U.S. presidential election ends in<br>    victory for George W. Bush<br>Class-action suit against tobacco industry<br>Microsoft charged in violation of antitrust laws<br>Dot-com crash |
| 2001 | Collins, *Sailing Alone around the Room*<br>d. A. R. Ammons<br>d. Eudora Welty | Enron scandal disclosed<br>Islamic terrorists destroy twin towers of New York's<br>    World Trade Center, damage Pentagon, and kill<br>    thousands in September 11 attacks<br>Anthrax powder mailed to media and political targets<br>China joins World Trade Organization |
| 2002 | McClatchy, *Hazmat*<br>d. June Jordan | Sniper attacks in Maryland, Virginia, and Washington,<br>    D.C. |
| 2003 | | U.S.-led troops invade Iraq; Saddam Hussein regime<br>    falls<br>SARS epidemic strikes Asia and other regions<br>Space shuttle *Columbia* breaks apart<br>North Korea reactivates nuclear program |

# TOPICAL OUTLINE OF ARTICLES

The entries in *The Oxford Encyclopedia of American Literature* are conceived according to the general conceptual categories listed in this topical outline. Some entries are listed more than once because the conceptual categories are not mutually exclusive. Entries in the encyclopedia proper are organized alphabetically.

## AUTHORS

Adams, Henry
Agee, James
Aiken, Conrad
Albee, Edward
Alcott, Louisa May
Alger, Horatio
Algren, Nelson
Alvarez, Julia
Ammons, A. R.
Anderson, Sherwood
Angelou, Maya
Ashbery, John
Auden, W. H.

Baldwin, James
Banks, Russell
Barnes, Djuna
Barth, John
Barthelme, Donald
Beattie, Ann
Bellow, Saul
Benét, Stephen Vincent
Berry, Wendell
Berryman, John
Bierce, Ambrose
Bishop, Elizabeth
Bradstreet, Anne
Brodkey, Harold
Brooks, Gwendolyn
Buck, Pearl S.
Bukowski, Charles
Burroughs, William S.

Capote, Truman
Carruth, Hayden

Carver, Raymond
Cather, Willa
Cheever, John
Chesnutt, Charles W.
Chopin, Kate
Collins, Billy
Cooper, James Fenimore
Crane, Hart
Crane, Stephen
Creeley, Robert
Crèvecoeur, J. Hector St. John de
Cummings, E. E.

Dana, Richard Henry
DeLillo, Don
Dickey, James
Dickinson, Emily
Didion, Joan
Dillard, Annie
Doctorow, E. L.
Dos Passos, John
Douglass, Frederick
Dreiser, Theodore
Du Bois, W. E. B.
Dunbar, Paul Laurence

Edwards, Jonathan
Eliot, T. S.
Elkin, Stanley
Ellison, Ralph
Emerson, Ralph Waldo
Erdrich, Louise

Faulkner, William
Fitzgerald, F. Scott
Ford, Richard
Franklin, Benjamin
Freneau, Philip
Frost, Robert

Gardner, John
Garland, Hamlin
Ginsberg, Allen
Gioia, Dana
Glasgow, Ellen
Glück, Louise
Gunn, Thom

Hacker, Marilyn
Hapgood, Hutchins
Harte, Bret
Hawthorne, Nathaniel
Hayden, Robert
H.D. (Hilda Doolittle)
Hecht, Anthony
Heller, Joseph
Hellman, Lillian
Hemingway, Ernest
Henry, O.
Hoagland, Edward
Howard, Richard
Howells, William Dean
Hughes, Langston
Hugo, Richard
Hurston, Zora Neale

Irving, John
Irving, Washington

Jackson, Laura Riding
James, Henry
Jarrell, Randall
Jeffers, Robinson
Jewett, Sarah Orne
Jong, Erica
Jordan, June
Justice, Donald

Kazin, Alfred
Kees, Weldon
Kennedy, William
Kerouac, Jack
Kincaid, Jamaica
King, Stephen
Kingston, Maxine Hong
Kinnell, Galway
Kunitz, Stanley
Kushner, Tony

Lardner, Ring
Lazarus, Emma
Levertov, Denise
Levine, Philip
Lewis, Sinclair
Lindsay, Vachel
London, Jack
Longfellow, Henry Wadsworth
Lopez, Barry
Lowell, Amy

Lowell, Robert
Loy, Mina

Mailer, Norman
Malamud, Bernard
Mamet, David
Masters, Edgar Lee
Mather, Cotton
Matthews, William
Matthiessen, Peter
McCarthy, Cormac
McCarthy, Mary
McClatchy, J. D.
McCullers, Carson
McNally, Terrence
McPhee, John
Melville, Herman
Mencken, H. L.
Merrill, James
Merwin, W. S.
Millay, Edna St. Vincent
Miller, Arthur
Miller, Henry
Momaday, N. Scott
Moore, Marianne
Morrison, Toni

Nabokov, Vladimir
Naylor, Gloria
Norris, Frank

Oates, Joyce Carol
O'Brien, Tim
O'Connor, Flannery

O'Hara, John
Olds, Sharon
O'Neill, Eugene
Ostriker, Alicia
Ozick, Cynthia

Paley, Grace
Parker, Dorothy
Pinsky, Robert
Plath, Sylvia
Poe, Edgar Allan
Ponsot, Marie
Porter, Katherine Anne
Pound, Ezra
Prose, Francine
Proulx, Annie
Pynchon, Thomas

Ransom, John Crowe
Reed, Ishmael
Rich, Adrienne
Robinson, Edwin Arlington
Roethke, Theodore
Roth, Henry
Roth, Philip
Rukeyser, Muriel

Salinger, J. D.
Sandburg, Carl
Schwartz, Delmore
Sexton, Anne
Shepard, Sam
Silko, Leslie Marmon
Simic, Charles

Simms, William Gilmore,
   and Antebellum
   Southern Literature
Sinclair, Upton, and
   the Muckrakers
Singer, Isaac Bashevis
Smith, Dave
Snyder, Gary
Soto, Gary
Stafford, Jean
Stafford, William
Stegner, Wallace
Stein, Gertrude
Steinbeck, John
Stern, Gerald
Stevens, Wallace
Stevenson, Anne
Stone, Robert
Stowe, Harriet Beecher
Strand, Mark
Styron, William
Swenson, May

Tarkington, Booth
Tate, Allen
Tate, James
Taylor, Edward
Taylor, Peter
Thoreau, Henry David
Thurber, James
Tocqueville, Alexis de
Trilling, Lionel
Twain, Mark

Updike, John

Very, Jones
Vidal, Gore
Vonnegut, Kurt

Walcott, Derek
Walker, Alice
Warren, Robert Penn
Welty, Eudora
West, Nathanael
Wharton, Edith
Wheatley, Phillis
White, E. B.
White, Edmund
Whitman, Walt
Wideman, John Edgar
Wilbur, Richard
Wilder, Thornton
Williams, Tennessee
Williams, Terry Tempest
Williams, William Carlos
Wilson, August
Wilson, Edmund
Wolfe, Thomas
Wolff, Tobias
Wright, Charles
Wright, James
Wright, Richard

## WORKS

*Adventures of*
   *Huckleberry Finn*
*Age of Innocence, The*
*All the King's Men*
*Ambassadors, The*
*American Buffalo*
*As I Lay Dying*
*Autobiography of Malcolm X,*
   *The*
*Ballad of the Sad Café, The*
"Bartleby the Scrivener"

*Bell Jar, The*
*Beloved*
*Catcher in the Rye, The*
*Death of a Salesman*
*Four Quartets*
*Glass Menagerie, The*
*Gone with the Wind*
*Grapes of Wrath, The*
*Great Gatsby, The*
*Lolita*

*Long Day's Journey*
   *into Night*
"Lottery, The"
*Moby-Dick*
*Native Son*
*Notes toward a*
   *Supreme Fiction*
*On the Road*
*Our Town*
*Paterson*
*Pisan Cantos, The*

*Portrait of a Lady, The*
*Raisin in the Sun, A*
*Red Badge of Courage, The*
*Scarlet Letter, The*
*Slaughterhouse-Five*
*Song of Myself*
*Sound and the Fury, The*
*Streetcar Named Desire, A*
*Sun Also Rises, The*
*Tender Is the Night*

*Their Eyes Were
Watching God*

*Things They Carried, The
To Kill a Mockingbird*

*Walden
Waste Land, The*

*Winesburg, Ohio
"Yellow Wallpaper, The"*

## THEMES

Academic Novels
Algonquin Round Table
Asian American Literature
Autobiography:
    General Essay
Autobiography:
    Slave Narratives
Autobiography: White
    Women during the
    Civil War
Beat Movement, The
Black Arts Movement
Black Mountain Poetry
Chicago Renaissance
Children's Literature
Colonial Writing in America
Confessional Poetry
Detective Fiction

Essay in America, The
Fireside Poets, The
Fugitives and Southern
    Agrarianism, The
Gay Literature: Poetry and
    Prose
Harlem Renaissance
Imagism and American
    Poets
Italian-American
    Literature
Jewish-American Fiction
Latino/Latina Fiction
    in America
Literary Theory in America
Little Magazines
Long Poem, The
Metafiction

Native American
    Literature
Naturalism and Realism
Nature Writing: Poetry
Nature Writing: Prose
New Critics, The
New Formalism, The
New Journalism, The
New York School
    of Poets
Objectivism (Reznikoff,
    Zukofsky, Oppen)
Poetess in
    American Literature, The
Popular Fiction
Proletarian Literature
Puritanism: The Sense of an
    Unending

Romanticism in America:
    The Emersonian
    Tradition
Science Fiction
Sentimental Literature
Short Story in America,
    The
Theater in America
Transcendentalism
Vietnam in Poetry and
    Prose
War Literature
West Coast School
Western Fiction: Grey,
    Stegner, McMurtry,
    McCarthy
Writing as a Woman in the
    Twentieth Century

# THE OXFORD ENCYCLOPEDIA OF
# AMERICAN LITERATURE

# ACADEMIC NOVELS

*by Rob Morris*

The academic novel answers two questions: What happens on a college campus? and What is college for? To answer the first question, the academic novel takes the form of high-spirited realism or mean-spirited satire. Its source material is the actual condition of living and working on a college campus at a certain time in a certain era. It wears the fashions of the day and is easily dated. The answer to the second question follows the answer to the first. The purpose of a college education varies from era to era, sometimes from year to year. In the academic novel, the college—the institution and the *idea* of college—is always in crisis. The purpose of college is shown to be warped, compromised, or ill-defined.

Novels that belong to this genre may answer other questions as well, but they take as their primary concern the workings of higher education. They describe the social lives of students—the parties, the pranks, the late-night conversations. They describe contentious faculty meetings and weighty encounters between administrators and teachers. They describe romantic liaisons, on campus and off. Infrequently, they describe students and teachers engaged in the work of formal education; taken as a whole, academic novels offer remarkably few scenes in which a teacher teaches and a student learns.

No one novel describes all of these things, but any description in an academic novel—any character or scene or setting—is limited as much by its source material as by the requirements of the genre. The favorite tropes of the academic novel are easily listed. The college is located in New York or Pennsylvania or is nestled in a forest in New England. When a university appears in the novel, it is massive, impersonal, and midwestern. Administrators, especially the president, know how to shake hands, make small talk, and raise funds. Professors come in one of three guises: the daft, otherworldly scholar; the irresponsible (and often lecherous) failure; and the venal, back-stabbing careerist. Students are clean-cut upper-class men, working-class "grinds," or unclassifiable outcasts.

The academic novel's most familiar narrative trope is that of high expectations brought low. Over and over, the genre tells us that American higher education promises much but delivers little. In this way, the academic novel constitutes a shadow history of the American university. It represents the academy's most hopeful vision of itself, and its ghostly sense of failing that vision.

## THE GENTEEL IDYLL

Two centuries after the founding of the first American college (Harvard, in 1636), the first college appeared in American literature. Nathaniel Hawthorne set his novel *Fanshawe* (1828) at the fictional Harley College, clearly modeled after Bowdoin College in Maine, from which he had recently graduated. Harley, a homely seminary tucked away in the New England woods, serves as a convenient backdrop for Hawthorne's melodramatic plot. The story has little to do with college life, but Hawthorne's sketch of Harley anticipates later portraits. The school is secluded; the students, with a few exceptions, have little interest in or aptitude for theoretical study; and they attend Harley to become slightly more polished men. Harley is a rustic version of the early idea of the American college: a genteel idyll, time away from the working world where boys grow into fine Christian men.

*Fanshawe's* main characters became stock types in later academic novels. Dr. Melmoth, the head of Harley, is a genial, dotty figure, a composite of the absentminded professor and the smiling, vapid dean. Fanshawe is a young scholar—a grind—whose devotion to his studies withers him and sends him to an early grave. Edward Walcott is the prototype of the college man: hale and hearty, glancingly interested in scholarship, a mild prankster, a gentleman. Ellen Langton represents the world outside the college. Walcott and Fanshawe battle for Ellen's heart. Walcott's victory suggests that he is ready to join the real world; Fanshawe's fatal loss is the consequence of single-minded intellectual pursuit.

*Fanshawe* was ignored by the public, and Hawthorne later disowned it. Thereafter, the American college was all but absent from American fiction until the nineteenth century drew to a close. In England, however, the British

1

author Thomas Hughes published *Tom Brown at Oxford* (1861), which offered an expanded and clearly defined template for American academic novels. Still green from public school, Tom Brown—a name as common as dirt—falls in with Drysdale, the ringleader of Oxford University's fast crowd—the rich, pranking, indolent boys. Soon, however, under the guidance of Hardy, a wise and patient tutor, Brown devotes himself to the practical business of living a decent, manly life. He rows hard for the Oxford crew and falls in love with a girl. He joins a feisty liberal crowd for a rowdy talk about the need to democratize the campus. Oxford is not perfect, but Tom is grateful to it and feels a preemptive nostalgia for the university. The story—wildly popular on both sides of the Atlantic—is a chronicle of innocence and experience, the story of a boy's emergence into manhood.

Owen Wister. (© *Corbis*)

As the American academic novel began to develop, it relied for support, by accident or design, on the tropes established in *Tom Brown*. In Helen Dawes Brown's *Two College Girls* (1886), a pair of Vassar roommates temper each other's rough edges and come to maturity. Edna, from rural New England, is a prim version of Tom Brown, and Rosamund, from Chicago, is a lightened version of Drysdale; together they overcome their prejudices and prepare themselves for healthy, fulsome womanhood outside Vassar's gates. In Charles Macomb Flandrau's *Harvard Episodes* (1897), a series of sketches offers the genre's signal characters and themes: the shy public school student intimidated by rich cosmopolitans and their pose of casual indifference, the frank discussion of the aims of the college experience and the conclusion that the college has fallen short, and the clear social hierarchy and the effort to subvert it. In Owen Wister's *Philosophy Four* (1903), two indolent Harvard sophomores, Bertie and Billy, exploit their hard-working tutor, Oscar Maironi, as they prepare for an exam. Bertie and Billy are Drysdale's cousins; Maironi is an ethnic Hardy. After Harvard the two boys find success in the business world, while Maironi lives a dull, grinding life at the fringes of the literary world.

The most successful academic novel, popularly if not critically, is Owen Johnson's *Stover at Yale* (1912). With the exception of a few particulars, Johnson's novel turns out to be a fully realized plagiarism of *Tom Brown*. Dink

Stover, a bluff, clean-cut fellow, arrives at Yale with more clout than Brown; he was a football star at his prep school, Lawrenceville. But Dink's years at Yale run parallel to Brown's at Oxford. Dink falls in with the society crowd but later rejects it; joins a feisty liberal crowd for a debate on the need to democratize Yale's campus; is transfixed by an older student's tales of the nobility of hard work; devotes himself to the practice of living a decent, manly life; excels at football; and falls in love with his friend's sister. Yale does not fully realize its democratic promise, but, as is Tom Brown, Stover is filled with gratitude and a kind of preemptive nostalgia for the college. The keynotes of *Stover at Yale* sound throughout the academic novel's history. The notes are plaintive (is this all there is?), hopeful (we can make it better), bitter (good-bye to all that), and sweet (wasn't it grand?).

The Yale described in *Stover at Yale* is more than a genteel idyll. In Johnson's novel, the college undertakes a social experiment in which all the standard student types—college men, grinds, and outcasts—meet on equal footing before they assume their roles in the real world. To Stover, this is a great American experiment. When he finds that it has gone awry—the mix hasn't taken and the social hierarchy is still intact—he uses his considerable power to set it right. Although the novel glamorizes the genteel tradition, it hopes for something new, something that is chaotic and democratic and fine.

## AWAKENINGS

*Stover at Yale* became a guidebook for aspiring college students—an audience that grew after the turn of the century. American higher education had by this time entered the age of the university; it had arranged itself into formal disciplines, each with a trained faculty; and some colleges had grown into universities, offering specialized study in specific fields leading to a doctorate. *Stover*, published in 1912, stood nearly at the midpoint of the American college's maturation process. In 1870, America counted roughly 500 institutions of higher education; by 1930 the number had nearly trebled, to 1,400. During the same period, the number of students in college exploded, from 52,000 to more than 1,100,000. This was the chaotic democratic mass that *Stover* saw on the horizon in 1912.

By the time *Stover*'s influence faded, the university was an institution, and college life—the fashions, athletic contests, slang, rituals, pranks, and romances of college students—was a fixture in the American imagination.

Amory Blaine, the hero of F. Scott Fitzgerald's first novel, *This Side of Paradise* (1920), studies *Stover* like a textbook before he heads to Princeton University. But Blaine himself is a desiccated version of Stover: cynical, ironic, narcissistic. He chooses Princeton because he has heard that it is run like a country club. He fancies himself the hero of a vaguely drawn philosophical drama; he adopts and discards poses and styles, mocking them and himself as he does so. He smokes, he lounges, he writes bad poetry. He is indifferent to the world war that interrupts his college years. Stover wouldn't have understood him in the least.

Yet Stover and Blaine share a kinship. Blaine, like Stover, is frustrated by his college's social system, which is roughly divided between "Philistines" and grinds. Blaine, like Stover, feels that his college has failed him, and comes to maturity despite his formal education rather than because of it. What splits the two, in the end, is the war. Fitzgerald wrote the first draft of his novel partly at Princeton, where he had quit his studies, and partly at an army training camp, where he waited for the war to come. Blaine—like Fitzgerald himself—is the fevered creation of this hopeless moment. His indifference to the war is another ironic pose; he is disillusioned not simply with higher education but with humankind. His specific protest against the genteel notion of higher education gains force as the war spends itself. What good are ideals—what good is character, or manhood, or morality—in the face of such savagery? Even so, Blaine feels the familiar pang of nostalgia for his college years, though he is certain that Princeton itself did not provide an education. He is nostalgic for the freedom, the leisure, the irresponsibility of his time at college.

*This Side of Paradise* shows a certain stylistic daring that is unusual in the genre—though some of that daring is better described as incoherence. Fitzgerald rushed to finish the novel and was seemingly indiscriminate in choosing and arranging its material; the novel feels at once slapdash and innovative. In general, the academic novel of the 1920s and 1930s showed little awareness of the experimentation with form and style that was being applied to literature at the time. George Anthony Weller's *Not to Eat, Not for Love* (1933) makes a modest attempt to toy with experimental techniques, but the genre is implacably realistic. The pretense of the academic novel is that it offers access to the actual college experience; its primary interest is documentation, not stylistic innovation.

*This Side of Paradise* is notable for two other reasons. First, it signaled a greater permissiveness in describing the younger generation's behavior. In Fitzgerald's novel, the drinking is more reckless (one character dies in a drunken car crash), the petting more serious (the novel's world-weary lovemaking scenes scandalized older readers), and the disillusionment deep and thoroughgoing (Stover and his ilk are essentially optimists). Second, though Blaine is as uninterested in his formal studies as Stover, he does gain enlightenment from extracurricular reading—novels and poems recommended to him by a fellow poet. If *Stover at Yale* describes the main character's moral and social awakening, *This Side of Paradise* describes the main character's intellectual and artistic awakening.

A handful of academic novels were published every year in the 1920s, 1930s, and 1940s, most taking their cues from *Stover* or *This Side of Paradise*. Percy Marks's *The Plastic Age* (1924) mimics Fitzgerald's often savage cynicism. Several of Thomas Wolfe's novels, including *Look Homeward, Angel* (1929), *Of Time and the River* (1935), and *The Web and the Rock* (1939), deal glancingly with college life and offer scenes that are by turns stylishly colored, intellectually rich, and deeply bitter—a concerted attempt to do what Fitzgerald had done halfheartedly. William Maxwell's *The Folded Leaf* (1945) is a sensitive recasting of *Stover*; timid Lymie Peters comes to maturity by stepping out of the shadow of his Stover-like hero, Spud Latham.

Willa Cather's *The Professor's House* (1925) occupies its own quiet corner. Cather is concerned more with the house than with the professor; nevertheless, there are glimpses of a midwestern state university that suffers from a flood of new students and the development of a practical curriculum. The genteel idyll has ended. College is a business; it develops practical skills, not moral character. In Cather's novel, and the majority of academic novels to follow, the nostalgia of former students for their glowing college years is replaced by the sour protest of teachers who find themselves trapped in a dysfunctional bureaucracy.

## A TERMINAL IRONY

American higher education continued to expand after World War II; by 1960, three and a half million students were enrolled in the country's colleges and universities. The American academic novel grew as well. The decades from the 1950s through the 1980s saw a steady increase of titles in the genre—an increase that does not imply increased respect. In these novels the academy is portrayed as a farce. This is not the farce of student pranks and drunken larks; it is the farce of administrative hypocrisy and petty squabbles among faculty over teaching methods or ideologies. The authors of these novels are not former students—they are professional writers who have made their livings as teachers in the academy. Their novels are as plainly autobiographical as the genre's earliest novels, but their approach toward their subject is markedly different.

Two of the genre's defining texts, published within two years of each other, establish the tenor of many of the works to follow. Mary McCarthy's *The Groves of Academe* (1952) and Randall Jarrell's *Pictures from an Institution* (1954) are pitiless satires of academic life. McCarthy had taught recently at Bard, Jarrell at Kenyon, and both at Sarah Lawrence. If the colleges described in their novels are not exact replicas of these campuses, they are close enough to suggest that the authors were writing from experience. In both novels the colleges themselves take starring roles; individual characters are rendered as caricatures, and, in Jarrell's novel especially, the plot is immaterial. The point of the novels is to expose the flaws of American higher education—to mock its pretensions and lay bare its hypocrisies.

The novels are set at progressive colleges. We learn that progressive education is an oxymoron, that what passes for education at these schools is a kind of high-minded recess. Both are arranged around writers who teach or teachers who write; and we learn that the study of literature is subject to personal whim and political fancy, such that no literature is actually studied. We also learn that college presidents are at once vacuous and scheming; that professors are doddering eccentrics or small-minded guardians of meager intellectual turf; that the sciences are at odds with the humanities; and that no one in his or her right mind—no one, that is, outside the academy—would care about any of this.

Some of this criticism is frivolous, some vicious, and some, very rarely, sympathetic—but all of it goes to suggest that college achieves the opposite of its aims. This simple irony—people who are supposed to be thoughtful and broad-minded are in fact petty and parochial—echoes the plaintive and bitter tones found in *Stover*. Is this all there is? If so, good-bye to all that. Here, though, there is no hope, no sweetness, no nostalgia. The irony is terminal.

A flood of academic novels followed, many of them taking McCarthy's and Jarrell's works as models, some fashioning a slightly different model. May Sarton's *Faithful*

*Are the Wounds* (1955) and several of Alison Lurie's novels, beginning with *Love and Friendship* (1962), take a special interest in the personal relationships of faculty and their lovers and friends. In Sarton's novel, a brilliant and politically engaged Harvard English professor named Edward Cavan commits suicide. In chapters that adopt the point of view of his friends and colleagues, we learn that Cavan was unable to reconcile his professional and political lives. Sarton suggests that academia is walled off from the real world, and the attempt to break through the wall can be fatal. *Love and Friendship* chronicles an affair between a faculty wife and a music teacher at a small college in rural New England. The novel offers several comic scenes and is fashioned in part as a comedy of manners, but its characters are treated with some seriousness.

Vladimir Nabokov, who, like Lurie, taught for a time at Cornell University, produced two novels that could be classified as academic novels if they were not, like most of Nabokov's work, unclassifiable. *Pnin* (1957) stays closest to the form. Timofey Pnin arrives from overseas to teach Russian at a small college that seems much like Cornell. His American colleagues mock his eccentric habits and his arcane scholarship; their niggling callousness forces the reader to feel sympathy for Pnin and disdain for academia. We are relieved when, at the end of the year, Pnin leaves the college. *Pale Fire* (1962) is a burlesque of literary scholarship. It purports to be the critical edition of an epic poem by John Francis Shade, with a foreword and commentary by Shade's neighbor and colleague Charles Kinbote. Kinbote's gloss on the text is smothering; the critic has superceded the author.

Novels by Joseph Heller—*Something Happened* (1974) and *Good as Gold* (1979)—and John Barth, such as *The End of the Road* (1958) and *Giles Goat-Boy* (1966), subject the academy to withering scrutiny. Barth's work employs considerable formal experimentation—a rarity in the genre. Novels by Philip Roth, including *The Breast* (1972), *My Life as a Man* (1974), and *The Professor of Desire* (1977), and Saul Bellow, including *Herzog* (1964) and *The Dean's December* (1982), use the university as a backdrop but are not primarily concerned with academic life. Roth and Bellow are creatures of the academy, and it is an enduring presence in their work. Joyce Carol Oates, too, has spent her professional life in academia and makes frequent use of the university in her fiction, for example, *Unholy Loves* (1979), *Solstice* (1985), and *Marya, a Life* (1986). In her work, the ironies of the academy are deep and cruel.

## FOOLS AND FAILURES

Academic novels since the beginning of the 1990s are direct descendants of *The Groves of Academe* and *Pictures from an Institution*. They are, with few exceptions, written by men and women who teach English (especially creative writing) in colleges or universities. Their main characters are typically members of the department of English, which is riven by political gamesmanship and skirmishing over arcane theories. They tend to be self-consciously literary; they allude to works of literature and draw much of their humor from punning or wordplay. Their characters tend toward stereotype, and their plots toward slapstick. Their academy is a collection of fools, failures, and freaks.

There is, for example, Jane Smiley's *Moo* (1995), an episodic tale in which one of the primary characters is a hog named Earl Butz. In a former slaughterhouse at the center of Moo U., a large midwestern university (Smiley taught at Iowa State), Butz gorges himself at his trough—a symbol of the university's appetite for funds. In Richard Russo's *Straight Man* (1997), set at a failing branch of a state university in Pennsylvania, the cast includes an overweight, overperfumed poet who has not fulfilled the promise of her youth; a loutish, irresolute fiction writer who also has not fulfilled the promise of his youth; and the English department's most recent hire, a professor of literature who claims that literature is bogus and requires his students to turn in their assignments on video. Francine Prose's *Blue Angel* (2000) tells the story of a drifting, washed-up professor of creative writing (who has not fulfilled the promise of his youth) in a small New England college. The professor becomes involved with the only student in his fiction workshop who shows a genuine interest in literature. She happens to be the campus freak—pierced and tattooed and sullen.

A similar list might include Michael Chabon's *Wonder Boys* (1995), whose main character is yet another aimless teacher of creative writing. Grady Tripp is a fat marijuana addict who wrote an acclaimed novel when he was younger, but has not fulfilled the promise of his youth. Another could be James Hynes's *The Lecturer's Tale* (2001), which chronicles the freakish, even supernatural, activities of an English department at a midwestern university that includes professors who write about the lesbian phallus, show pornographic films to their students, and nurture a costume fetish.

These novels tell us that college faculties comprise people who cannot function in the real world. A sense of failure hangs over them; their ambitions, their ideas, their lives seem meager and mean. The college itself appears in one of two familiar guises: the massive university, overseen by a soulless bureaucracy and run like a corporation, or the secluded rural idyll, hapless and inconsequential. Students, when they appear, are dull-witted and earnest; for the most part, they are invisible. In the contemporary academic novel, the professors take center stage.

There are a few exceptions. Tom Perrotta's *Joe College* (2000) and Elwood Reid's *If I Don't Six* (1998) are cast in the mold of *Stover at Yale*; they describe the awakening and maturing of the young soul. In *Joe College*, a Yale junior named Danny tries to reconcile his college life (parties, a job at the dining hall, a modest interest in classwork, a potential romance with a brainy classmate) with his life at home (friends from high school who have lost their way, a job driving his father's food truck, a suddenly serious romance with a former high school classmate who is now a secretary). *If I Don't Six* chronicles Elwood Riley's first year as a football recruit at the University of Michigan. Riley is an intellectual—he carries around a copy of Marcus Aurelius's *Meditations*—and his term culminates in Stover-like disillusionment when he realizes that the football team is not a pure meritocracy.

There are, as well, novels by esteemed writers who return to the academy as a setting. Saul Bellow's *Ravelstein* (2000) and Philip Roth's *The Human Stain* (2000) do not strictly conform to the genre. *Ravelstein* functions as a character sketch and a protest novel, in which the character is an academic and the protest is, in part, against academia—but its heart is elsewhere. *The Human Stain* hinges on a professor's remark that is wrongly interpreted as politically incorrect—but again, the scope of the novel is panoramic, not bound by genre.

## A SHADOW HISTORY

As an object of critical attention, the academic novel is seen as a diversion; it lies outside the province of serious literature. This vision is strikingly similar to the popular image of the academy itself. The Puritans prized education and founded Harvard; and though a Puritan faith in the value of education hovers over American culture like a guilty conscience, the country's id and ego are obsessed with material wealth, physical labor, and obvious utility. From its inception the American academy has had to justify its existence in terms of practical value: What can a college education *do*? The lamentation of the parent of the twenty-first century undergraduate ("My tuition bills are paying for *this*?") is an echo of thousands of such complaints leveled at American higher education over the past three and a half centuries. The country wrings its hands over the fate of its education system, and every upstanding middle-class parent will affirm the necessity of attending college. But in the popular imagination the college experience is a diversion from the hard labor of making money. The real world begins after college.

The genre is treated as the poor cousin of a handful of more distinguished genres: the comic novel, the social novel, the bildungsroman (novel of spiritual awakening), and the *Kunstlerroman* (novel of artistic awakening). Although the academic novel is distinguished by certain repeated themes and characters and episodes, it is most clearly marked by its setting: An academic novel takes place primarily on a college campus. This limited scope might play to an author's strengths, yet the academic novel inevitably suffers from its confinement. The academic novels most likely to last are those that escape the campus or take up concerns beyond the academy—works that cannot, in other words, properly be considered academic novels.

The three novels that serve as the genre's standard-bearers are minor works. Randall Jarrell's *Pictures from an Institution* and Mary McCarthy's *The Groves of Academe* are neither actively read nor much loved outside a cultish circle of current and former professors. Owen Johnson's *Stover at Yale* is familiar only to students of the genre and old-time Yale alumni. The critical attention paid to these works, and to the genre itself, is slight. There is only one comprehensive survey of the genre—*The College Novel in America* (1962) by John O. Lyons. It is out of print, outdated, and so dyspeptic as to discourage future critics from attempting a fresh survey.

We can point to a list of great writers who have worked within the genre: Hawthorne, Fitzgerald, Cather, Nabokov, Oates, Bellow, and Roth. But our list must be heavily qualified. Hawthorne's *Fanshawe* is academic only in its setting; it is, in any case, a clumsy first novel. Fitzgerald's *This Side of Paradise* is more fully an academic novel, but it is many other things as well and reads less as a coherent academic novel than a pastiche of several different novels, plays, and poems. *The Professor's House* is one of Cather's minor works, and its central concerns lie far beyond the walls of the academy. Nabokov's *Pnin* is minor as well; his *Pale Fire* is sui generis. Oates's academic novels are mostly forgotten, as are some of Roth's and Bellow's. *Herzog* and *The Human Stain* may last, but they escape the genre.

What of the handful of most recent writers who have achieved critical success and embraced the genre?

Jane Smiley, Michael Chabon, and Richard Russo won the Pulitzer Prize for fiction (in 1992, 2001, and 2002, respectively) for works that were not academic novels. Russo and Chabon wrote their academic novels before writing the novel that won the Pulitzer, and Smiley's novel followed her prize-winner. Their academic novels appear to us as warm-ups or cool-downs—exercises before or after the main event. The writers are cutting loose, larking about; the result is (sometimes) an entertainment, but not a lasting work of literature.

We might say that real literature begins after genre. Yet some genres—the detective novel comes to mind—have produced works of lasting importance. Not so the academic novel. But if the genre's literary value is insignificant, its sociological and historical value is substantial.

## WHAT WENT WRONG?

The history of the academic novel, broadly drawn, is the history of the American university. The academic novel begins as a series of sketches, becomes a full-blown genre, then hardens into an institution. The American academy begins as a series of sketches (Harvard, Yale, and a handful of others, scattered and remote), becomes a full-blown part of American culture (the development of the university, the formation of disciplines and professional degrees), and hardens into an institution. Attending an institution of higher education is now the rule, not the exception, in American life. The academic novel, like its subject, has grown from a novelty into a profession.

The history we find in the academic novel is, perhaps not surprisingly, incomplete. It is largely the history of the Ivy League and the big state schools—and within those schools, it is the history of relatively privileged Caucasian boys and men, most of whom, as the novel reaches its maturity, are shown to be fools or failures. It is, in other words, the history of the decline of an American aristocracy—the class of white, Anglo-Saxon, Protestant men. The genre tells us little about the fortunes of other classes and other populations. Since the 1950s, for example, the number of Americans attending junior or community colleges has shot from a few hundred thousand to more than ten million. Yet this college experience—this radically different idea of college—is invisible in American fiction.

Beneath every fictional college lurks a single ideal college—the college of *Stover*, even of *Fanshawe*: a cloistered verdant quad where boys grow into men. When the academic novel is realistic, it describes colleges that want to embody this image. (Their tragedy is that they cannot.) When the novel is satirical, it mocks colleges (or, frequently, universities) for pretending to want that vision at all. Most academic novels present their colleges and universities as proof of their failure. They are lost; they cannot reclaim that ideal vision. What went wrong? The academic novel does not know. It offers a critique, not a remedy.

[*See also* Barth, John; Bellow, Saul; Cather, Willa; Fitzgerald, F. Scott; Hawthorne, Nathaniel; Heller, Joseph; Jarrell, Randall; McCarthy, Mary; Nabokov, Vladimir; Oates, Joyce Carol; Roth, Philip; *and* Wolfe, Thomas.]

## FURTHER READING

Hofstadter, Richard. *Anti-intellectualism in American Life*. New York, 1963. Indispensable survey of America's tormented relationship to intellectual work.

Horowitz, Helen Lefkowitz. *Campus Life: Undergraduate Cultures from the End of the Eighteenth Century to the Present*. Chicago, 1987. Persuasive historical analysis of student culture in American higher education.

Lyons, John O. *The College Novel in America*. Carbondale, Ill., 1962. The only comprehensive (but now outdated) study of the genre.

Marchalonis, Shirley. *College Girls: A Century in Fiction*. New Brunswick, N.J., 1995. A helpful corrective to Lyons's male-focused work.

Proctor, Mortimer R. *The English University Novel*. Berkeley, Calif. 1957 (reprint New York, 1977). A brisk treatment of the subject that neatly foreshadows the American academic novel.

Veysey, Laurence. *The Emergence of the American University*. Chicago, 1965. An authoritative history and the real-life guide to the settings of academic novels.

# HENRY ADAMS

*by Edward Halsey Foster*

Henry Adams's paternal great-grandfather and grandfather were, respectively, the second and sixth presidents of the United States. His father, Charles Francis Adams, was among the distinguished diplomats of his time, serving as American ambassador to Great Britain during the Civil War. Henry Adams himself, however, did little public service. He published several books, was a distinguished editor and college professor, and spent most of his life at the center of Washington's social world, living in an elegant mansion almost as close to the White House as he could get without actually living in it. To the general public, however, he was far better known for his name than for who he was.

In *The Education of Henry Adams* (1907), the book for which Adams is best known, he wrote that "probably no child" born the same year as he "held better cards," but he "was born

Henry Adams.
(*Courtesy of the Library of Congress*)

an eighteenth-century child," scrupulous about morals in a world where successful people were more likely to be scrupulous about investments. He watched his country abandon its ethical constraints in a frenzied scramble for material success. In the process, the Adams name, he felt, become a nostalgic memento of the past.

## A CHILD OF PRIVILEGE

Had Adams's family been almost any but the one it was, he would have had difficulty presenting himself as a failure; but he did, after all, spend his childhood certain that he would someday be president. Born in Boston, Massachusetts, on 16 February 1838, he graduated from Harvard University near the top of his class in 1858, followed by travel in Europe and legal studies

in Germany. His maternal grandfather, among Boston's wealthiest men, left his grandson a substantial fortune that eliminated the need for gainful work.

In 1861, Adams's father became the United States minister to the Court of Saint James, a post he held for seven years, during which the son served as his private secretary. Henry Adams's position left him time to travel and to begin a career in journalism. While friends and classmates fought on Civil War battlefields and then began the task of reconstructing the Union, he toured Scotland, Italy, and other scenic places and wrote articles on British economics, Pocahontas, and Darwin. Returning to the United States in 1868, when he was thirty, he wrote and published well-regarded articles on American finance and politics. Two years later, he became an assistant professor of history at Harvard, a position he held until 1877.

In 1871, he and his brother, Charles Francis Adams Jr., published *Chapters of Erie*, dealing with financial scandals in the management of American railroads. In 1877, Adams began to work on a biography of Albert Gallatin, secretary of the treasury under Thomas Jefferson and James Madison, and on an edition of Gallatin's writings; both appeared in 1879.

In 1872, Adams married Marian Hooper, the daughter of a distinguished Boston physician. After Adams resigned from Harvard, they lived in Washington at the center of social and political life. Marian became the model for the title figure in Adams's novel *Esther*, which he published in 1884 under the pseudonym Frances Snow Compton. The book sympathetically portrays the independent or "new woman," in late-nineteenth-century America, but it also rejects conventional religious and spiritual beliefs. In both social and theological matters,

Adams would have appeared deeply controversial to his contemporaries.

In 1884, Henry and Marian Adams engaged Henry Hobson Richardson, a celebrated architect who had been among his classmates at Harvard, to design a townhouse across Lafayette Square from the White House. The house was receiving its final touches on 6 December 1885, when Marian, depressed over the recent death of her father, killed herself by drinking chemicals she used in her work as a photographer. Some have speculated that Adams's distant, ironic nature contributed to his wife's suicide, but there is no direct evidence of this. In fact, all accounts indicate that it had been a strong marriage and that Adams was devastated by her death. He rarely spoke of her during the rest of his life, and *The Education* does not mention her, skipping from 1871 to 1893, including the years of their marriage.

Adams's other writings during the 1880s are often somber or deeply serious, mingling desire for freedom with a bleak historical and spiritual vision. His major work in these years was the nine-volume *History of the United States during the Administrations of Thomas Jefferson and James Madison* (1889–1891), considered one of the monuments of historical writing. The principal issue with which he dealt is the degree to which individual freedom is possible or permissible. "The Federalist leaders [in Massachusetts]," wrote Adams, "had more difficulty to restrain than to excite the people, and felt themselves strong enough to assume the air of cautious and conservative men." The freedoms desired for the new nation by the author of the Declaration of Independence were not universally celebrated, and, wrote Adams, "the great mass of Federalists wished at heart no more harm to the country than to overthrow and humiliate Jefferson, and to cripple Madison from the start."

Men like Jefferson and Gallatin had looked forward to a time when the "vast creative power" of the American people "might rise to the level of that democratic genius which found expression in the Parthenon"; but Adams lived in an era in which he saw all around him a very different kind of democratic genius—one that had, with a greed unparalleled in the history of the Republic, funneled wealth and power into the hands of a few. Adams's *History* was an obituary for American ideals.

## CORRUPTION IN THE REPUBLIC

Earlier, Adams had published anonymously a novel, *Democracy* (1880), which taught the same lessons but had a much larger readership than the *History*. In part, the novel's popularity can be attributed to the fact that it is a roman à clef, revealing intimate details of life in the capital that only an insider could know. The novel concerns a wealthy and well-connected widow, Mrs. Lightfoot Lee, who moves to Washington "bent upon getting to the heart of the great American mystery of democracy and government." She is not merely a student of politics, however; she wants a place in it: "What she wanted," says Adams, "was POWER."

Mrs. Lee gets more than she bargains for as she watches the corruption of men in public life unfold before her. One diplomat tells her at the beginning of her quest:

> I declare to you that in all my experience I have found no society which has had elements of corruption like the United States. The children in the street are corrupt, and know how to cheat me. The cities are all corrupt, and also the towns and the counties and the States' legislatures and the judges. Everywhere men betray trusts both public and private, steal money, run away with public funds.

As the coauthor of *Chapters of Erie* who had seen one less-than-sterling president follow another, Adams knew that the diplomat had good reason to speak as he did. In the course of the novel, Mrs. Lightfoot Lee learns how accurate he is, realizing ultimately what power had become in her own day:

> Had she not penetrated the deepest recesses of politics, and learned how easily the mere possession of power could convert the shadow of a hobbyhorse existing only in the brain of a foolish country farmer, into a lurid nightmare that convulsed the sleep of nations? . . . She had got to the bottom of this business of democratic government, and found out that it was nothing more than government of any other kind.

Her conclusion, which Adams shared, was deeply shocking to many readers in the 1880s and undoubtedly would have been even more so had the author's identity been known. Adams had no taste for notoriety, however; he not only published his novels pseudonymously but also printed the books for which he is best known, *Mont-Saint-Michel and Chartres* (1904) and *The Education*, at his own expense and circulated copies only among friends. Adams was preeminently an aristocrat in temperament, with little apparent wish or need for public acclaim. As a young man living in London, he had acquired a British accent that he never lost, and his reserve and irony made him seem formidable even among friends. His public persona was perhaps his response to a democracy that had despaired of its ideals.

This man of immense reserve and intelligence, living across from the White House and studying its occupants with little confidence in their abilities, was the close friend of some of the most powerful figures of the day, notably John Hay, Lincoln's private secretary and the secretary of state from 1898 until 1905. Adams informally advised Hay on foreign policy, a fact unknown to the public, but in general he had little political influence. *The Education* in effect is an attempt to explain why.

## A VICTIM OF HISTORY?

Adams's life, as recounted in *The Education of Henry Adams*, was a weave of failures and false starts that served him mainly to show how ill prepared he had been for the world in which he lived. He presented himself in *The Education* as profoundly self-aware and well-intentioned, but defeated by a historical moment ruled by values he did not share. His relationship to his era was, therefore, ironic: he knew many who achieved great power while he himself, burdened with principles, was unable either to enter into the struggle for power or to relish the rewards that accompanied the little power that came his way.

As Adams admitted in *The Education*, he changed almost nothing in the world of public affairs, yet his significance elsewhere was considerable. Out of his conflict with his age, he developed penetrating, if at times bitter, insights into the motivations behind successful contemporaries. Adams imagined a historical process that ran counter to the notions of laissez-faire capitalism proposed by the economist Adam Smith, who had written that self-interest drove the ambitious to create a dynamic economy through which everyone benefited. As Adams understood it, however, the laissez-faire capitalist benefited primarily himself.

Emerson argued in his essay "History" (1841): "There is one mind common to all individual men. Every man is an inlet to the same and to all of the same . . . . Who hath access to this universal mind is a party to all that is or can be done, for this is the only and sovereign agent." The "universal mind" found its expression in the individual, and therefore, "All history becomes subjective; in other words, there is properly no history; only biography." Adams's historical works follow that conclusion, focusing strongly on individuals. In *The Education*, the life of a failed man—as Adams felt himself to be—is shown to exemplify historical process as fully as the lives of those who succeed.

Adams was not an Emersonian (the Adams family, he wrote, "had little or no affinity with the pulpit, and still less with its eccentric offshoots, like . . . the philosophy of Concord"), but Emerson's view of history, centering on the individual while recognizing history as a transcendent force, is remarkably close to Adams's. Emerson was the most respected American intellectual during Adams's youth, and even if the Adams family kept its distance from "eccentric offshoots," they could hardly avoid Emerson's ideas: these were discussed everywhere, and it is not surprising to see them reflected in Adams's work.

*The Education* is not an autobiography, but it uses elements of the author's life to explain a historical moment from which he was largely excluded. History is seen through the example of the author himself; he is not a player in a laissez-faire struggle of self-interested individuals but the representative victim of historical developments through which older, morally guided politics lost their control over public life. Failure though he was in his own eyes, Adams can present himself as what Emerson called a "representative man," illustrating in his life the history of his times as amply as those who created it.

More important to Adams than Emersonian notions of history was Charles Darwin. Adams read *On the Origin of Species by Means of Natural Selection* (1859) soon after its publication and claimed to be "a Darwinist before the letter." Although he had not the scientific training to defend or refute Darwinism and felt its conclusions had to be accepted on trust, he followed the general trends in science in the late nineteenth century, which argued that the human will was not a prime mover in the universe. He viewed the dynamo, which he first saw at Chicago's World Columbian Exposition in 1893, as the "moral force" at the core of the modern world. Significantly, that force was not human; its power was abstract and absolute. It was also indifferent to human moral principles.

Adams's grandfather and father, leaders in the antislavery movement, believed in an immutable moral law at work in the universe that ensured that in the end things would work out for the best, but this moral law was inadequate for a generation permeated by corrupt politics and business. Adams retained the notion of history driven by moral force, but he reconceived that force to be something that could as easily serve an individual's greed as lead to human betterment. No government, including a democracy, was likely to change that. Adams labeled himself a "conservative Christian anarchist"—"conservative" reflecting his temperament, "Christian" identifying his values, and "anarchist" freeing him from full commitment to any one political or system, including the one that had passed him by.

An heir to Calvinist doctrines that viewed the world as essentially predetermined, Adams constructed a secular determinism in which history as a force could, with frightening ease, annul the ambitions of individuals. In this way, Adams escaped from responsibility, from his dilemma as one who should have done much but who, according to his own standards, had achieved little. Born two years after the publication of Emerson's *Nature*—the consummate expression of American individualism—Adams remade Calvinism for a secular world. God, in his cosmology, was essentially historical force.

### ADAMS AND THE "NEW WOMAN"

Adams wrote in *The Education* that "American art, like the American language and American education, was as far as possible sexless." He noted that few American artists had "insisted on the power of sex" and singled out Walt Whitman as one of the few exceptions. Obviously Adams was overlooking many writers—his friend Henry James is a case in point—but certainly among American historians, none before him had "insisted on the power of sex." His own life was apparently for the most part celibate. Adams's biographers discuss his late friendship with Elizabeth Sherman Cameron as if that intimacy, together with his marriage to Marian Hooper, were enough to explain his sexual nature. Yet Adams did not marry until he was thirty-four, and after his wife's suicide fourteen years later, he never again lived with a woman except for his nieces and the other young women who cared for him in his old age. Whatever his sexual nature, for most of his life he had no intimate companion.

Adams, however, viewed the Virgin Mary as a transcendent force that motivated society and gave it purpose during the late Middle Ages. She is the subject of his *Mont-Saint-Michel and Chartres*, in which he argued that in the twelfth century, she became a figure more powerful and sweeping in her authority than the Trinity:

Not only was the Son absorbed in the Mother, or represented as under her guardianship, but the Father fared no better, and the Holy Ghost followed. The poets regarded the Virgin as the "Templum Trinitatis"; "totius Trinitatis nobile Triclinium." . . . The Trinity was absorbed in her.

The great Gothic cathedrals of medieval France became her royal seat: "Man came to render homage or to ask favors. The Queen received him in her palace, where she alone was at home, and alone gave commands." The petitioner, Adams showed, survives at the will of the monarch, but the monarch survives at the will of no one

but herself. She is the supreme deity, but her power is maternal and sexless.

In the United States, neither the Virgin nor any other woman had such power:

Why was [the woman] . . . unknown in America? For evidently America was ashamed of her, and she was ashamed of herself, otherwise they would not have strewn fig-leaves so profusely all over her. When she was a true force, she was ignorant of fig-leaves, but the monthly-magazine-made American female had not a feature that would have been recognized by Adam. The trait was notorious, and often humorous, but anyone brought up among Puritans knew that sex was sin. In any previous age, sex was strength.

Adams himself was among those "brought up among Puritans," and it should not surprise one to find in him the same reserve toward, or fear of, women that Adams found in his compatriots. Edward Chalfant states in his biography of Adams's final years, *Improvement of the World* (2001), that Adams was a "normal male" who "differed sexually from other males only in having strong wishes and more than usual energy." Chalfant may be right if by "normal" he means that Adams was not homosexual, but Adams's essentially solitary sexual life remains an enigma, especially in light of his reverence toward women in his writings. Chalfant argues that Adams thought Marian Hooper was "irreplaceable," but that does not explain away the solitude, broken only by brief encounters with Elizabeth Sherman Cameron, that Adams chose for the last thirty-two years of his life.

Observations like this would be idle were it not that Adams's theories of historical process are tightly interwoven with his notions of sexuality. His Virgin offers release only to those who allow their identities to be subsumed in hers. She requires submission and in this way destroys her penitents, or at least their independence, at the same moment that she protects them. Why, then, did Adams consider the Virgin's power to be desirable, as he clearly did, in his understanding of the Middle Ages? Something in his deepest nature seems to have hungered for the kind of submission he felt the Virgin required.

Chalfant begins his three-volume biography of Adams by saying, "Henry Adams was set apart from other human beings mainly by having always known he mattered," but in reality, he seldom mattered much at all. American history would not be much different if he had never lived. He was not, as he saw it, in control of his fate, and one may speculate that both his submissive sexuality and his deterministic view of history were entwined with his failure to become what, as a child, he had imagined, or had been led to believe, he should become. At the same time, he needed to explain that failure if he were not to leave the world as a mere descendant of famous men.

Although *Mont-Saint-Michel and Chartres* and *The Education* see history, or its embodiment in the Virgin and the dynamo, as a power to which one can only submit, the books themselves required a master of language, and in this Adams achieved a freedom from the yielding, deferential, compliant role that he wished to believe history had set out for him. In his writings, he could become the subject of his own rhetoric rather than merely the subject of events.

Art gave Adams a way to deal with the apparently inflexible power of history. *The Education* transforms history into a personal style and is less a record of what happened than a record of his impressions and how they were formed. The facts of history become material for language: thus, he writes: "[Theodore] Roosevelt, more than any other man living within the range of notoriety, showed the singular primitive quality that belongs to ultimate matter—the quality that medieval theology assigned to God—he was pure act." Whatever Roosevelt actually did and was, he had become material for Adams's stylistic brilliance.

Adams distanced himself from his readers in *The Education* by never referring to himself in the first person. His subject is a character named "Adams," who is born into a world to which he does not belong and who is rarely in control of his circumstances, but Adams the writer was in full control, shaping his sentences with a mastery of nuance that made him one of the great stylists in the language. The biological Henry Adams gave place to a literary construction named Adams. The world thereby shifted, becoming no longer a sequence of events as such but a literary narrative in which the author could both explain away his failures and reveal his mind and insights to be far more brilliant than those of people who had taken a place in the world that, in another age, might have been his. Roosevelt might reveal "the singular primitive quality that belongs to ultimate matter," but it was Adams who had the sophistication and wit to say it.

In *The Education*, and to some degree all of his writings, Adams was concerned with history, politics, and economics as essentially aesthetic problems. The Virgin and her nineteenth-century parallel as historic force, the dynamo, gave a culture order, and it was this essentially aesthetic quality that intrigued Adams. He did not study history in order to change it—he was too much a determinist for that; rather, he took pleasure in its

design, and that design in turn found its expression in the perfectly modulated sentences of his prose.

## HISTORY AS ART

Adams commissioned the leading American sculptor of the day, Augustus Saint-Gaudens, to create a statue to mark Marian's grave at Rock Creek Cemetery in Washington, D.C. The statue, which is widely considered St. Gaudens's masterwork, was immediately famous, and many people visited it every day. In *The Education*, Adams noted that "Like all great artists, St. Gaudens held up the mirror and no more"; people saw in the statue what was already in themselves. Thus, "[t]he interest of the figure was not in its meaning, but in the response of the observer," and since observers felt they saw in it "the expression . . . of despair, of atheism, of denial," Adams concluded: "The American layman had lost sight of ideals; the American priest had lost sight of faith."

Adams suggested here much about his own perceptions, for that layman who "had lost sight of ideals" was one with those who had most succeeded. Further, Adams aligned himself here with the discourse of fin-de-siècle aesthetes such as Walter Pater and Oscar Wilde, who believed that works of art were not themselves moral and that their "meaning" would be whatever the observer found in them. Pater argued in *Studies in the Renaissance* (1873) that art is understood and interpreted through "one's own impressions," and one person's impressions are not another's. Aesthetics, in this view, allows one to make of the work of art what one wills. This is the antithesis of the determinist's vision.

History, as Adams understood it, decisively shaped an individual's destiny but, at the same time, remained open to aesthetic perception and presentation. History may have removed Adams from even the possibility of achieving power and position, but he had his revenge, transforming history into art. In turn—this is the lesson St. Gaudens's statue illustrated—as art, history was whatever an individual might make of it, and Adams quite likely made more of it than any other American of his time.

## WORKS

*Chapters of Erie and Other Essays* (1871)
*Title Documents Relating to New-England Federalism* (1877)
*The Life of Albert Gallatin* (1879)
*The Writings of Albert Gallatin* (1879)
*Democracy: An American Novel* (1880)

*John Randolph* (1882)

*Esther: A Novel* (1884)

*History of the United States of America during the Administrations of Thomas Jefferson and James Madison* (1889–1891)

*Historical Essays* (1891)

*Memoirs of Arii Taimai e Marama of Eimeo, Teriirere of Tooarai, Teriinui of Tahiti, Tauraatua i Amo* (1901)

*Mont-Saint-Michel and Chartres* (1904)

*The Education of Henry Adams* (1907)

*A Letter to American Teachers of History* (1910)

*The Life of George Cabot Lodge* (1911)

*Letters to a Niece and Prayer to the Virgin of Chartres* (1920)

*Letters of Henry Adams* (1930–1938)

*Henry Adams and His Friends; A Collection of His Unpublished Letters* (1947)

*The Making of a History: Letters of Henry Adams to Henry Vignaud and Charles Scribner, 1879–1913* (1959)

*The Letters of Henry Adams* (1982–1988)

*The Correspondence of Henry James and Henry Adams, 1877–1914* (1992)

## FURTHER READING

Adams, Henry. *A Henry Adams Reader.* Edited by Elizabeth Stevenson. Garden City, N.Y., 1958. This anthology of selections by one of Adams's earliest biographers provides an excellent introduction for those encountering his work for the first time.

Blackmur, R. P. *Henry Adams.* Edited by Veronica A. Makowsky. New York, 1980. Blackmur spent forty years on this sympathetic study of Adams's imaginative thought in *Mont-Saint-Michel and Chartres* and *The Education.*

Chalfant, Edward. *Both Sides of the Ocean: A Biography of Henry Adams, His First Life, 1838–1862.* Hamden, Conn., 1982. This and the following two volumes now constitute the standard resource.

Chalfant, Edward. *Better in Darkness: A Biography of Henry Adams: His Second Life, 1862–1891.* Hamden, Conn., 1994.

Chalfant, Edward. *Improvement of the World: His Last Life, 1891–1918.* Hamden, Conn., 2001.

Contosta, David R., and Robert Muccigrosso, eds. *Henry Adams and His World.* Philadelphia, 1993.

Decker, William M. *The Literary Vocation of Henry Adams.* Chapel Hill, N.C., 1990. Examines Adams's attempts to find literary means to convince his readers of his social and political acuity.

Dusinberre, William. *Henry Adams: The Myth of Failure.* Charlottesville, Va., 1980. Adams's invention of the persona and legend through which he presents himself and his culture.

Levenson, J. C. *The Mind and Art of Henry Adams.* Stanford, Calif., 1957. Levenson, editor of Adams's letters, wrote the initial version of this book as his dissertation, but it stands with Blackmur as one of the best critical introductions to Adams.

Samuels, Ernest. *The Young Henry Adams.* Cambridge, Mass., 1948. Samuels's three-volume biography has been superseded by Chalfant's but remains one of the great interpretative studies.

Samuels, Ernest. *Henry Adams: The Middle Years.* Cambridge, Mass., 1958.

Samuels, Ernest. *Henry Adams: The Major Phase.* Cambridge, Mass., 1964.

# JAMES AGEE

*by Donna Seaman*

James Agee. (*Photograph by Walker Evans. Courtesy of the Library of Congress*)

For James Agee, night was the most enchanting and blessed part of the day, and he often wrote about its hushed, starry beauty and the wonder of being awake when nearly everyone else was under the strange and necessary spell of sleep. Agee also loved movies, another form of magic that takes place in the dark, and both of these passions are manifest in the opening pages of his best-known work, the posthumously published, Pulitzer Prize–winning novel, *A Death in the Family* (1957). Although Agee completed few books over the course of his somewhat frenetic, all-too-brief writing life—one volume of poetry, two works of fiction, and the provocative prose lyric *Let Us Now Praise Famous Men* (1941)—he wrote scores of ardent, impeccable, and far-reaching movie reviews and ultimately left behind a highly concentrated yet remarkably innovative and profoundly influential oeuvre.

## EARLY CAREER: CHANNELING OF PASSIONS

A native of Knoxville, Tennessee, James Rufus Agee, born on 27 November 1909, was seven years old when his father died in an automobile accident. Two years later, Agee entered St. Andrew's, an Episcopalian boarding school, and befriended Father James Harold Flye, thus establishing a nourishing and enduring relationship, the foundation for the compelling volume, *The Letters of James Agee to Father Flye* (1962). It was obvious at an early age that Agee was a natural-born writer driven by irrepressible curiosity, free-flowing compassion, an acute moral sensibility, a distrust of institutions and authority, and a deep attunement to the sonorous music of language. His imaginative and relentlessly critical turn of mind animates his frank and ruminating letters to Father Flye, which primarily cover his years at Phillips Exeter

Academy and Harvard, and the launching of a brilliant and unique writing career. His frequently prescient correspondence with his supportive and understanding confidant provides a fascinating and moving record of the evolution of a multitalented, original, conflicted, and often self-destructive artist.

Agee's vision of a free and creative life clashed, as artists' dreams almost always do, with everyday reality and the need to earn a steady living. Agee married three times in rapid succession and had four children, and thus felt that he had to toe the line and work as a full-time journalist. However, his frustration over having to defer his dreams of writing creatively, of being free of assignments, and of writing and directing his own movies goaded him into indulging his gargantuan appetite for socializing (Agee was a captivating, even legendary conversationalist), womanizing, and nightlife, all fueled by large quantities of nicotine and alcohol. Yet despite his own venomous self-condemnation for failing to achieve his desired goals, and the commentary of critics who feel that he should have accomplished more, Agee remains a vital and important figure in American literature. He was able to pour the radiance of his fiery moral and artistic convictions into everything that he wrote, from the confines of magazine articles and movie reviews to the finer chalice of fiction.

In a letter to Father Flye written from Cambridge, Massachusetts, in November 1930, Agee describes his ambition to write symphonically, and reports that he "thought of inventing a sort of amphibious style" that would combine prose and poetry. He put this vision to work during the late 1930s when, as a staff writer for *Fortune*, he turned what—for someone else—would have been a straightforward assignment to report on the lives of poor tenant farmers into a masterpiece of empathic observation, excruciatingly candid self-portraiture, and searing social commentary. This resounding testimony to the redoubtable human spirit was the still not fully appreciated or easy to categorize *Let Us Now Praise Famous Men*.

In tandem with Walker Evans, a master photographer, Agee lived for eight weeks with three different Alabama tenant farm families in the summer of 1936 during the terrible Dust Bowl drought and the Great Depression. While Evans coolly used the camera to document the materially impoverished yet nonetheless dignified lives of the Ricketts, Woods, and Gudger households, Agee wrote about his and Evans's transformative experiences with these strangers abruptly turned intimates in a fever of awe, respect, despair, and guilt. Preternaturally aware and tortuously self-conscious, Agee asks, in effect, Who am I to invade and exploit such private terrain, only to retreat back to the safety and security of my privileged world? Was he, he quizzes himself, in any measure capable of conveying the nobility of these good and suffering people, the unexpected beauty of their dirt-poor lives?

Agee perceives a "sorrowful holiness" in this alien world, and his lush prose acquires a biblical tone as he catalogs in exhaustive yet glorious detail every physical aspect of their spare homes and threadbare clothes, their plain food and "simple and terrible work." This generates a veritable river of observations that infuses everything he describes with emotion and meaning. Focusing on the families themselves, he records the subtlest of body language and the most delicate nuances of temperament and interaction among family members. And he decries the lack of mental stimulus in their work-weary, uneducated lives even more sharply than their physical deprivations. Here are people cruelly isolated and denied education, literature, art, and hope; people entrenched in the Deep South, a place, Agee perceives, of deep prejudice, institutionalized cruelty and ignorance, fear, and violence. This is a land of virulent racism, and Agee does not hesitate to say so or to lament such hate.

Always poetic, sometimes grandiose, overwrought, or self-serving, *Let Us Now Praise Famous Men* recounts a young artist's spiritual quest, one that demands an unflinching inquiry into the interloper's responsibilities. Valuing both the reportorial eye and the fruits of the imagination, Agee struggles to balance actuality and interpretation, and wonders if the camera is not a more reliable tool than the pen. His sojourn inspired intense self-scrutiny, an attempt at absolute honesty, and myriad philosophical musings. By making analysis of his own experiences, thoughts, and feelings integral to his reportage, Agee helped lay the groundwork for what became known, after his death, as New Journalism and creative nonfiction, literary arts performed with verve by the likes of Joan Didion, Tom Wolfe, and John McPhee.

## AGEE ON FILM

It was not easy to find a publisher for this symphonic contemplation of poverty and sacredness, nor did it improve Agee's financial situation, so immediately after *Let Us Now Praise Famous Men* was published, Agee became a film critic, writing for both *Time* and *The Nation*. Ultimately, he assembled a solid body of critical writing that seeded the high-impact film reviewing of Pauline Kael, and established serious criticism of popular media as a crucial element in magazine and newspaper publishing and in American letters. Film was still a relatively new, albeit already much-loved, medium when Agee began critiquing it in 1941, and no critic could have written about a burgeoning art form in a more explosive and significant time. Agee wrote about movies regularly, faithfully, and with undiminished enthusiasm from 1941 to 1948, a span of all-but-apocalyptic years that began with the creeping horrors of Hitler and Stalin and ended with the deployment of the atomic bomb in Japan. Because television had not yet emerged as the dominant force in communication and entertainment, movies—both newsreels and features—were the most immediate and visceral medium available. Agee wrote about them with corresponding intensity, placing each film within the context not only of the times but also of the entire pageant of human history.

Each perfectly composed review is a model of concise, hard-hitting, fresh, witty, and astute prose, as well as clarion and morally oriented interpretation. Agee was a gallant and fair-minded reviewer, bringing the same attention and open-mindedness to B movies as to cinema's most artistic achievements, to comedies as well as dramas. Concerned with the questions of authenticity versus artifice, romanticism versus accuracy, Agee's judicious dissection of how the war was presented in both documentaries and features is more relevant now than ever before in this age of sensationalized television coverage of violent, tragic, and scandalous events.

So powerful and far-reaching are Agee's film reviews, the poet W. H. Auden was inspired to write a now-famous letter in praise of Agee's film column to the editors of *The Nation*. So highly regarded was Agee in Hollywood, he ended up writing screenplays, including those for *The*

*African Queen* and *The Night of the Hunter* (1955). After his death, his cinematic writings were collected in *Agee on Film*, an outstanding and enduring two-volume set.

## AGEE WRITES FICTION

Although given to excess both in life and on the page (insiders claim that Agee's original screenplay for *The Night of the Hunter* was as thick as a big-city phone book), Agee was so skilled and versatile a writer and so cued to the realm of archetypes and symbols that he could—when motivated—hone the torrents of ideas and feelings that assailed him down to the tightest of compositions. This creative discipline is evident in his to-the-point film reviews, his poetry, and the succinct but mighty novella *The Morning Watch* (1951).

Young Richard, a boarding school student, is a serious boy obsessed with fantasies of martyrdom and sainthood. As the tale begins, he is struggling to satisfy his boarding school's religious demands, including participation on Good Friday in the morning watch, the symbolic reenactment of the hour during which Christ was betrayed. Even as he strives to be good, Richard, smart and terribly sensitive, is painfully aware of the vanity inherent in his ambitious piety, of his smug pleasure in self-generated wretchedness, and of how this self-gratification negates the very purity of spirit he seeks. Filled with self-disgust as he finally leaves the church, as well as a boy's irrepressible energy and rebelliousness, Richard instigates a forbidden escapade in the woods with two other boys.

Agee's tracking of his intrepid young hero's revelations is at once spellbinding and cleverly humorous, but what he is really after, and what he creates, is an unveiling of the dichotomies that shape our confounding lives. Agee's precise chronicling of the predawn church service perfectly conjures both the holiness and repressiveness of the tradition, while his vivid depiction of nature discloses an earthy sacredness in which every plant and animal, every spear of light and shadow, reflects the endless cycle of birth, death, and rebirth, the essence, after all, of the story of Christ. Richard is fascinated by two biblical creatures—a ghostly locust shell and the unnerving grace and gleam of a snake—and undergoes a spontaneous form of self-baptism when he dives naked into deep, cold water. Whether kneeling in church or romping in nature, Agee's scrupulous young hero bravely confronts his failure to live up to religious teachings and his own spiritual intimations. Thus, Agee's poetic and piercing tale of one boy's moral awakening becomes emblematic of every human being's seemingly impossible struggle to consistently do right.

An intrinsically autobiographical writer compelled by temperament to examine morality's gray scale, the many facets of guilt, sin (especially pride), and the repercussions of loss, Agee once again unveils the inner reality of a boy's life much like his own in his tour de force, *A Death in the Family*. This psychologically exacting, dramatically taut, and iridescently textured novel illuminates the minds of a Tennessee family in shock after the sudden death in a freak car accident of Jay Follet, a thirty-six-year-old husband and father. This parallels Agee's own father's death, and, in an odd way, anticipates Agee's death in a taxicab in May 1955, where he was felled by a heart attack at age forty-five.

The Follet boy is named Rufus, which is Agee's middle name and the name he went by as a boy, and the exquisitely detailed renderings of Knoxville and the geography of one family's grief are as much the product of memory as of the imagination. Agee's magnificent second novel is a far grander work than *The Morning Watch*, as electric with dialogue as with description, and richly evocative in structure and pacing.

The novel's time frame is compact. Jay and Mary Follet are pulled from sleep by the ringing of the telephone. Jay listens skeptically as his drunken brother, Ralph, insists that their father is near death, but decides to make the trip anyway, just in case. He is reluctant to leave his warm bed, loving wife, and sweetly sleeping children, and he and Mary are very affectionate toward each other as he prepares for the long drive. Death is indeed imminent, but its aim is off: Follet Sr. lives to bury his favorite son. And obedient Mary and inquisitive Rufus are forced to test the resiliency of religious beliefs and family bonds.

Agee's articulation of his characters' stunned psyches is striking in its fluency and authority; the characters are authentic and alive both in terms of their streaming consciousness and their physical particularity and voice. Their tragedy and their awkward attempts to find solace in conventional rituals—and to quickly reestablish normalcy—are universal and timeless. Anguish is deftly counterbalanced with wit, and every paragraph glows with tender regard for humanity in all its absurdity and courage, vanity and love. This is a powerful novel, an abiding work of literature, and Agee will long be treasured for his empathy, passion, exactitude, moral imperative, and splendidly lyrical writing.

## WORKS

### NONFICTION

*Let Us Now Praise Famous Men* (1941)
*Agee on Film* (1958, 1960)

*Letters of James Agee to Father Flye* (1962)
*The Collected Short Prose of James Agee* (1969)

### POETRY

*Permit Me Voyage* (1934)
*The Collected Poems of James Agee* (1968)

### FICTION

*The Morning Watch* (1951)
*A Death in the Family* (1957)

### FURTHER READING

Bergreen, Laurence. *James Agee: A Life*. New York, 1984. A comprehensive and unsurpassed biography.

Kramer, Victor A. *Agee and Actuality: Artistic Vision in His Work*. Troy, N.Y., 1991.

Lofaro, Michael A., ed. *James Agee: Reconsiderations*. Knoxville, Tenn., 1992.

Madden, David, and Jeffrey J. Folks, eds. *Remembering James Agee*. 2d ed. Athens, Ga., 1997. A forum of wonderfully personal discussions about various facets of Agee's life and work featuring family members, friends (including Father Flye), and fellow writers.

Moreau, Genevieve. *The Restless Journey of James Agee*. Translated by Miriam Kleiger and Morty Schiff. New York, 1977. A European perspective on the American writer.

Spiegel, Alan. *James Agee and the Legend of Himself: A Critical Study*. Columbia, Mo., 1998.

# CONRAD AIKEN

*by Arnold E. Sabatelli*

Conrad Potter Aiken (1889–1973) epitomized the well-educated intellectual, scholar, and writer. Like his contemporary, friend, and fellow Harvard University graduate T. S. Eliot, he was one of the most admired and respected writers of his time. Given that he was so prolific in several genres (poetry, essays, critical analysis, fiction) and so popular during his life, it is surprising that he is not as well known today as he was in his time.

## LIFE AND CAREER

Aiken was born in Savannah, Georgia, on 5 August 1889. When he was very young, his father shot his mother and then himself while Aiken was in the house. Aiken found the bodies, and this event shaped his intellectual and artistic outlook for the rest of his life. In his experimental autobiography *Ushant* (1952), he discusses the link between this event and his artistic viewpoint. He was raised by a great-great-aunt in Massachusetts from the age of eleven. Even as a child, Aiken was intent on becoming a writer. His years at Harvard coincided with those of Eliot, E. E. Cummings, and Ezra Pound. He graduated from Harvard in 1912. He later worked with Pound on the journal *Dial*, and they became close friends. He published his first volume of poetry, *Earth Triumphant*, in 1914, and soon established his place as an important poet. Stating that poetry was an "essential industry," he never served in World War I. Like Eliot, he spent a considerable amount of time in England, and during much of the 1920s and 1930s he traveled extensively, moving back and forth between New England and England and marrying three times before settling in the United States at the outbreak of World War II. (His daughter from his first marriage with Jessie McDonald is the writer Joan Aiken.)

Aiken edited Emily Dickinson's *Selected Poems* (1924), almost single-handedly establishing her posthumous reputation as a great poet. In 1930, Aiken was awarded the Pulitzer Prize for his *Selected Poems* (1929). From 1934 to 1936, while in Rye, Sussex, Aiken wrote "London Letters" to *The New Yorker*. He was poetry consultant to the Library of Congress (now the U.S. poet laureate) from 1950 to 1952. His other honors included the Bollingen Prize, the Gold Medal in Poetry from the American Academy of Arts and Letters, and a National Medal for Literature. He died in Savannah on 17 August 1973.

## INTELLECTUAL AND ARTISTIC SOURCES

Aiken worked for a short time as a reporter but soon decided to live off a modest inheritance in order to devote his time entirely to writing and academic pursuits. He made specific reference to the works of Sigmund Freud as a major influence and was one of the first writers to openly acknowledge and self-consciously attempt to integrate Freud's theories into his body of work. Freud himself admired Aiken's work, especially the overtly psychological novel *Great Circle* (1933). Aiken also drew on the writings of literary figures and philosophers including Henry James, the philosopher William James, Edgar Allan Poe, and the French symbolists. Much of his poetry has been seen in a kind of dialogue with Eliot, who concurrently based a number of his more famous images and poetic structures on Aiken's work. The phrase "handful of dust," from *The Waste Land* (1922), is often considered a reference to Aiken's *The House of Dust* (1920). He also clearly learned much from his extensive close reading and reviews of fellow poets such as Ezra Pound, Wallace Stevens, and William Carlos Williams.

## POETRY

From the outset, Aiken's poetry was formal and direct, seizing hold of a theme and pursuing it at length through highly stylized forms frequently grounded in the structures of classical music. Often romantic, stemming from the works of Keats and Poe, his work is also self-consciously in step with the innovative, modern poets of his own time. While his work evolved in content and approach, he never really abandoned more traditional forms, instead trying to state the modern consciousness through the traditional. In *Ushant*, Aiken puts special emphasis on the term "consciousness," suggesting that the poet's act of creation emerges hand in hand with the acquisition of knowledge. That is to say, the poet steps forth actively into the unknown hoping to shape it or to find shape in it—ordering and embedding or extracting meaning where once there was chaos. The act of poetry, for Aiken, springs both from incessant, sharp observation of the physical world and a welcome acceptance of subconsciously derived imagery and event.

Later in life, Aiken dismissed much of his early poetry as derivative or juvenile, with little intellectual substance. In his works that became known as the "symphonies"—*The Jig of Forslin* (1916), *The Charnel Rose* (1918), *Senlin* (1918), *The House of Dust, The Pilgrimage of Festus* (1923), and *Changing Mind* (1925)—he began a much more self-conscious attempt to merge form and content and instill his work with the depth of intellect he so admired and frequently reviewed or commented on in Eliot and Pound. Written largely between 1915 and 1920, these works were later revised and reordered in *The Divine Pilgrim* (1949), with some undergoing extensive changes. Although overly lavish and at times pretentious, these lengthy poems are also brilliant, ambitious, and intellectually forceful and marked a critical move toward his maturity as a poet.

In the years between publication of the "symphonies" and what would become his other most ambitious and accomplished works, known as the "preludes," Aiken produced *Punch: The Immortal Liar* (1921)—one of his most popular works, written in the voice of a puppet who tells of his life and loves—and *John Deth, a Metaphysical Legend* (1930), light dramatic sketches that demonstrate Aiken's willingness to pursue many and varied artistic genres. He was always writing, willing to follow any and all ideas that came to him, and because of this his writing shows a remarkable range of type, quality, and seriousness.

With *Preludes for Memnon* (1931) and *Time in the Rock: Preludes to Definition* (1936), Aiken reached poetic maturity and established himself as a major poet in his time. These poems, especially *Time in the Rock*, bring together all of his earlier concerns—emphasis on the reflective, speculative, and philosophic; a deep desire to lay bare the dark mysteries of human consciousness and the ways in which the self both views these mysteries and is an integral part of them—but without the self-consciousness and excess of his earlier work. Although the seven volumes of poetry he produced after the "symphonies" are more understated and the poems completed after the "preludes" are competent, none are on a par with these two formidable works. Overall, then, Aiken was a prolific poet who authored two substantial

masterpieces and a large number of successful but not nearly as important collections, ranging from humorous dramatic monologues to more unwieldy experiments.

## FICTION

Aiken published five novels and numerous short stories. A number of his contemporaries thought that he would ultimately become more known for his fiction (and criticism) than for his poetry—and this may one day prove to be true. In all his fiction there is a clarity of description, an awareness of the mundane details of ordinary life, and a wonderful ear for natural yet highly charged dialogue. Ultimately, his fiction seeks to demonstrate the theme of how the human consciousness functions. His novels and short stories are notable for their intense emotional and dramatic struggles, voyages both real and emotional, and vivid descriptions of real places, especially New England landscapes.

In his first novel, *Blue Voyage* (1927), the story of a man who sails from New York to England in search of a lost love, the primary dramatic quest becomes lost in the character's day-to-day life onboard. Aiken painstakingly explores the collision of the man's past with his looming future meeting and a barrage of subtle, largely internal dramas. The novel is often criticized for its lack of event, but it establishes Aiken as a master of dialogue and convincingly demonstrates the complexities of the human psyche, a theme he would pursue much more extensively, and in a more surreal and jarring manner, in *Great Circle*.

In *A Heart for the Gods of Mexico* (1939), a dying man's need to get to Mexico to be both divorced and married is almost overshadowed by the cataloging of characters and details during his long cross-country train ride. Here and elsewhere, there is a sense in Aiken's fiction that the central dramatic and emotional event is nearly subsumed by descriptions and dialogue—in other words, by the complex interplay between the human psyche and the outside world. Yet the endless descriptions and seemingly disassociated dialogue actually provide a complex and more purely metaphoric response to the central dramatic tension. In this novel, for instance, we find the narrator in the opening pages begging a friend for money to make the trip to Mexico, but the descriptions of the various eateries and bars and neighborhoods of Boston are dwelled on more than the matter at hand. Thus the trip to Mexico is in large part shown to be a more spiritual and metaphoric journey away from intense familiarity, comfort, and constancy, and the plot itself takes a back seat to Aiken's sketching out of the intricate workings of human perception and consciousness. While Aiken's fiction is sometimes overwhelmingly intense in its portrayal of the human mind—which is often engaged in the most mundane of events—there is an ease of tone in these novels that is not as apparent in his poetry.

## ESSAYS, CRITICISM, LETTERS

Aiken produced a large body of academic and nonfiction prose. First as coeditor with Eliot of Harvard's literary journal, later as a reviewer for the *Dial* and a correspondent for *The New Yorker*, and finally as an author of his own critical texts, *Scepticisms* (1919) and *A Reviewer's ABC* (1958), Aiken frequently examined his deep commitment to the literary text as a doorway to deeper self-understanding. The experimental autobiography *Ushant* frequently blurs together elements of autobiography, essay, fiction, and poetry and is one of his most successful works. In it he depicts his friendships with Malcolm Lowry, Eliot, and other major figures and friends, juxtaposing visions of the literary world between the wars with ad lib psychoanalytic and autobiographical wanderings. Its freedom from the constraints of both poetry and fiction allowed Aiken to give voice in complex and free-flowing fashion to many of the concepts and concerns in the whole body of his work. Here he arguably may have found the perfect form to synthesize the many and disparate forces at work in his creative consciousness. The *Selected Letters of Conrad Aiken* (1978) provides further understanding of Aiken's complex and varied approach to literature and life, with many letters to the major literary figures of his time.

## ABUNDANCE OF WORK

Aiken was the consummate self-consciously forged intellect, writer, and scholar. At his best, his work transforms that intellect into art—transcending his own notions of what the work is trying to say and remaining elusive, natural, challenging, and rewarding. At its worst, his work is uneven, too overtly intellectualized and overdone. Many critics conclude that Aiken published too much. But amid all of his many volumes of poetry, short stories, novels, essays, and criticism stands a substantial body of rich and powerful work for which he is perhaps deserving of more prominence in the literary canon.

## WORKS

*Earth Triumphant and Other Tales in Verse* (1914)
*Turns and Moves and Other Tales in Verse* (1916)

*The Jig of Forslin: A Symphony* (1916)
*Nocturnes of Remembered Spring and Other Poems* (1917)
*The Charnel Rose, Senlin: A Biography, and Other Poems* (1918)
*Scepticisms: Notes on Contemporary Poetry* (1919)
*The House of Dust: A Symphony* (1920)
*Punch: The Immortal Liar, Documents in His History* (1921)
*Priapus and the Pool* (1922)
*The Pilgrimage of Festus* (1923)
*Priapus and the Pool and Other Poems* (1925)
*Changing Mind* (1925)
*Bring! Bring! and Other Stories* (1925)
*Blue Voyage* (1927)
*Selected Poems* (1929)
*John Deth, a Metaphysical Legend and Other Poems* (1930)
*The Coming Forth by Day of Osiris Jones* (1931)
*Preludes for Memnon* (1931)
*And in the Hanging Garden* (1933)
*Great Circle* (1933)
*Landscape West of Eden* (1935)
*King Coffin* (1935)
*Time in the Rock: Preludes to Definition* (1936)
*A Heart for the Gods of Mexico* (1939)
*And in the Human Heart* (1940)
*Conversation; or, a Pilgrim's Progress* (1940)
*Brownstone Eclogues and Other Poems* (1942)
*The Soldier: A Poem* (1944)
*The Kid* (1947)
*Skylight One: Fifteen Poems* (1949)
*The Divine Pilgrim* (1949)
*Ushant: An Essay* (1952)
*Collected Poems* (1953)
*Mr. Arcularis* (1953)
*A Letter from Li Po and Other Poems* (1955)
*A Reviewer's ABC* (1958)
*Sheepfold Hill: Fifteen Poems* (1958)
*The Collected Short Stories of Conrad Aiken* (1960)
*Selected Poems* (1961)
*The Morning Song of Lord Zero* (1963)
*The Collected Novels of Conrad Aiken* (1964)
*Cats and Bats and Things with Wings* (1965)
*Collected Poems* (1968)
*Collected Criticism* (1968)
*Collected Poems* (1970)
*A Little Who's Zoo of Mild Animals* (1977)
*Selected Letters of Conrad Aiken* (1978)
*Selected Poems* (1980)

## FURTHER READING

Hoffman, Frederick J. *Conrad Aiken.* New York, 1962. A comprehensive work on Aiken's writing up to the late

1950s. It does an excellent job of critiquing Aiken's poetry, but the chapter on his fiction is quite thin and incomplete.

Marten, Harry. *The Art of Knowing: The Poetry and Prose of Conrad Aiken*. Columbia, Mo., 1988. Chapter 6, "Absolute Fiction and Beyond," offers a very good explication of Aiken's fiction.

Seigel, Catharine F. *The Fictive World of Conrad Aiken*. DeKalb, Ill., 1993.

Spivey, Ted R., and Arthur Waterman, eds. *Conrad Aiken: A Priest of Consciousness*. New York, 1989. A collection of essays offering incredible breadth—from comparisons with Melville to the metafictional aspects of *Ushant*.

# EDWARD ALBEE

*by Victoria D. Sullivan*

When Edward Albee broke upon the American theater scene in 1960 with *The Zoo Story*, he was immediately recognized as a brilliant and exciting young voice. Critics, magazine editors, and the public all welcomed this handsome, somewhat morose young man into the world of serious art. In fact he was the first recognized American absurdist, tapping into the post–World War II European tradition of Samuel Beckett, Eugène Ionesco, and Jean Genet. A loud chorus of critical praise met his early works, including *The Sandbox* (1960) and *The American Dream* (1961), in addition to *The Zoo Story* (1959). When *Who's Afraid of Virginia Woolf?* opened on Broadway in 1962, his fame was sealed. But that was also, in some rather American sense, the beginning of the end. It was, certainly, the end of the uncritical adulation.

Over the next forty years he wrote a number of serious plays and had numerous productions, on Broadway and off. Although since the Pulitzer Prize–winning production of *Three Tall Women* in 1994, Albee's reputation has been on the rise, never again has he risen to those early heights of critical esteem. In the last decades of the twentieth century, his work did not attract the ongoing theater attention received by the plays of Sam Shepard or David Mamet. In college drama courses and anthologies, the same few early Albee plays have been represented again and again. Since the early 1960s, of course, when absurdism defined the cutting edge, it has never engaged the theatergoing public much in America—as opposed to Europe, where audiences have been much more comfortable with it and with experimentalism in general.

Certainly, Albee has left a definitive mark on contemporary theater. He is a boldly experimental playwright with an ongoing avant-garde orientation, sometimes absurdist, sometimes symbolist, sometimes surrealist. With his fresh theatrical voice, he influenced other young playwrights of the 1960s like Rochelle Owens, Maria Irene Fornes, Jean-Claude Van Itallie, Israel Horovitz, Adrienne Kennedy, John Guare, Megan Terry, David Rabe, Sam Shepard, Lanford Wilson, and others. As an absurdist, Albee is

Edward Albee. (*Photo by Jerry Speier*)

committed to playing games with the audience, mocking communication, breaking the rules of realism, introducing imaginary or surreal but nonetheless potent threats onto the stage, and generally refusing to create easy, answer-providing work. His most famous play, *Who's Afraid of Virginia Woolf?*, is more naturalistic than most of his work, and as such it continues to attract respect and attention.

Despite stylistic variations, in his subject matter Albee has remained intrigued with certain characteristic themes: attacks on the dysfunctional American family, particularly the sadistic, self-serving mother and her powerless mate; American manhood under siege; infants and children at risk of loss or dismemberment; and the terror of wasted lives. Real and pseudo-families dominate his plays, which convey a constant sense that the ties that bind people also destroy them. A recurring issue is the crippling effects of familial transactions, along with the ways in which people refuse to grow. His is a nightmare vision, but usually treated with acidic humor so that the mood is more satiric than tragic, often falling into the category of black humor. Albee has one core story that he tells repeatedly: a baby arrives in a home and by hook or by crook is destroyed. Of course, since that happened to Oedipus in ancient Greece (although he survived the attempt at infanticide), it is a story with a strong classical resonance.

Looking at Albee's career, one impressive aspect is his refusal to shape his plays to commercial expectations or even to the desires of serious critics. Although play after play in the 1970s and early 1980s provoked strong critical, often vituperative attack, Albee continued to walk his own path. He has obviously made a strong personal commitment to writing exactly what he needs to write in whatever challenging style he chooses. He has brought reptiles on stage as characters, persisted in his obsession with the very rich, and not moved in any overtly political direction. His plays contain stripped-down story lines, often of a fantastic nature, and highly stylized language. They possess a musical quality: self-doomed creatures singing arias of pain and betrayal in an ever-less-recognizable world. His approach may prove right in the long run, since such plays may last longer than those more closely tied to contemporary American society and its issues.

## ALBEE'S LIFE

Born on 12 March 1928, in Washington, D.C., Edward Albee was adopted as an infant by a very well-to-do couple, Reed Albee and Frances Cotter. They created an economically privileged existence for him, with sumptuous homes in Larchmont, New York; on Park Avenue in Manhattan; and in Palm Beach, Florida, during the winter. But as a child and afterward, Albee felt unloved and unappreciated by this couple, remote from his mostly silent father (who had inherited his wealth from the family's very profitable family vaudeville theaters) and alienated by his cold, manipulative mother. During his childhood, young Edward attended a number of private schools, settling at last at the prestigious Choate prep school in Wallingford, Connecticut, from 1944 to 1946. Choate proved to be his first intellectual home.

After only a year and a half at Trinity College in Hartford, Connecticut, Albee was asked to leave for failing to attend certain required courses and compulsory chapel. He then lived at home for some months, drinking, partying, commuting to New York City for a job as an office boy, and generally annoying his controlling mother. Following a particularly bitter family quarrel, he moved out at the age of twenty and did not return to see or speak with his mother again for seventeen years. He later said that he had felt "an enormous release" upon leaving; "That part of my life had absolutely ended" (Gussow, p. 71).

Albee headed immediately for Greenwich Village in New York City, an exciting place to be in the late 1940s and early 1950s. The art world was alive with abstract expressionism (including such artists as Jackson Pollock, Willem de Kooning, and Franz Kline), and the literary world was getting ready to burst forth in new directions with Norman Mailer, Philip Roth, Delmore Schwartz, and Allen Ginsberg. But at the time Albee hung out mostly with a crowd of serious music composers (William Flanagan, Ned Rorem, and Aaron Copland), going to their favorite haunts to drink and talk after hours spent at various insignificant and generally briefly held day jobs, like record store clerk or hotel desk clerk. His longest job was as a Western Union messenger; it gave him the most freedom and he liked walking around the city. Albee acknowledges that the character Jerry in *The Zoo Story* emerged from his experience delivering telegrams to the denizens of the decayed rooming houses on the Upper West Side of Manhattan.

Until he was around twenty, Albee occasionally dated women and even became briefly engaged to the sister of a good friend, but once he had severed his ties with home, he embraced his homosexual identity, a predilection he had been aware of since puberty. As he said looking back, "For God's sake, what did I think I was doing? I was going to bed with boys from age thirteen on and enjoyed it greatly" (Gussow, p. 70). An early and significant relationship—both close and volatile—was with the composer William Flanagan, five years his elder, but more than that, his teacher in the ways of sophistication and the artistic subculture. The gay world in Manhattan at the time (in the early 1950s) was cliquish, a tight-knit family in which heavy drinking and sexual freedom defined a kind of witty, noir, clandestine existence.

Once Albee entered the public world with his 1959 production of *The Zoo Story* in Berlin, Germany, his life changed significantly. The next several years were filled with productions of new plays, culminating in the extremely successful Broadway production of *Who's Afraid of Virginia Woolf?*; the drama jury awarded it a Pulitzer Prize that was then withdrawn by the advisory board, which—shocked by the play's language—decided to give no Pulitzer in drama that year. *Virginia Woolf* did win both the New York Drama Critics Circle best drama award that year and the Tony Awards for best play, best production, best director (Alan Schneider), best actress (Uta Hagen), and best actor (Arthur Hill). Nonetheless, the early Pulitzer Prize controversy set the tone for later battles fought over Albee's work so that in 1981, when he was writing the introduction to a collection of his early plays, he noted: "I have learned . . . that experimental plays, dense, unfamiliar and lacking proper road signs meet with considerable critical and audience hostility" (Gussow, p. 322).

It was a circumstance he would encounter repeatedly throughout the 1970s and 1980s. Yet Albee refused simply to leave the theater or quit writing plays. Instead, he turned some of his attention to nurturing other writers, to teaching playwriting, and to lecturing widely around the country on the subject of theater. His support of other artists and writers had been generous from the start; in 1969 he founded the William Flanagan Memorial Creative Persons Center in Montauk, Long Island, a place for artists to retreat and do their work.

In terms of his reputation, Albee's career could be divided into three phases. The first, early fame, ran from 1959 to 1966, its highlight being *Who's Afraid of Virginia Woolf?*, which played on Broadway for 664 performances and then was directed most effectively on film in 1966 by Mike Nichols, starring Elizabeth Taylor and Richard Burton. The second phase would be one of growing disaffection between Albee and theater critics; a number of plays opened and closed very quickly, culminating in *The Man Who Had Three Arms* (1982), which Frank Rich labeled in his *New York Times* review, "a temper tantrum

in two acts." It lasted on Broadway for only sixteen performances in 1983, and after that Albee did not open another major production in New York City until 1994, with *Three Tall Women*. That successful production, for which he received his third Pulitzer Prize for drama, would be the commencement of the third phase: the welcoming of Albee back into critical esteem, at least in terms of the New York theater reviewers. In Europe throughout his whole career there has been an ongoing interest in his work, with regular productions throughout eastern and western Europe. In 2002 Albee won the Tony Award for best play of the season for *The Goat; or, Who Is Sylvia?*. This marked his definitive return to the commercial limelight.

## EARLY PLAYS

Albee's first serious play, written as a thirtieth birthday present to himself, was *The Zoo Story*, which received its premier production in Berlin, Germany, in 1959. It is a brilliant theater piece, the perfect balance of two characters, Peter and Jerry, strangers who meet in Central Park in Manhattan and discover between them an attraction and repulsion that leads to violence and death. Jerry is the active, agitated, dangerous one of the pair, who tells his life story to the conventional Peter, while prodding him to face the stifling restrictions of his bourgeois life. Jerry's language is marvelously alive, filled with a brutal poetry and a searing vision of his existence. He tells the story of himself and his landlady's dog, a tragicomic monologue that almost alone assured Albee's continuing theatrical significance.

He followed up this play with *The Sandbox* (1960) and *The Death of Bessie Smith* (1960), both talented works, but of the two *The Sandbox* has had the longer stage life. It is a very short, darkly humorous, absurdist one-act play about fourteen minutes in production, in which Mommy and Daddy take Grandma to the beach to die. They place her in a large child's sandbox to wait for the end. On stage also are a musician and a handsome young man doing calisthenics, who is both the object of sexual desire and the angel of death. Mommy's callous disregard for her own mother is the classic Albee vision of motherhood—all false sentiment and concern with doing things by the book. Her husband, Daddy, is just a weak, foolish, yesman. Albee removed the characters for this play from his longer work, *The American Dream*, then in draft. The feisty grandmother is based on his own maternal grandmother, who lived with his family while he was growing up. The theme of facing death, and accepting it, is one that would persist in his work through the next four decades.

*The American Dream*, his most fully developed absurdist play, is a cutting attack on both the American dream of wealth and success and the American family as horribly dominated by the sick, self-centered matriarch, Mommy. The fatuousness of the characters—Mommy, Daddy, and the adoption lady, Mrs. Barker—produces high comic art. The story involves the escape of Grandma and the replacement of a defective baby adopted many years earlier by Mommy and Daddy.

The baby had not been up to Mommy and Daddy's standards, and so when it "put its hands under the covers, *looking* for it's you-know-what," of course they "*had* to cut off its hands at the wrists." This comes after they blind the baby because "it only had eyes for its Daddy" (p. 101). And for the last straw in aggravating behavior, the baby simply dies. The handsome stranger who shows up about twenty years later turns out to be the probable twin of the flawed baby, and he fits right into the household, now determined to get restitution for the prior loss. Grandma closes the play, deciding to leave things "while everybody's happy," Mommy most of all, with the exceedingly desirable young man in his role as baby replacement and cocktail maker.

Albee's next play, *Who's Afraid of Virginia Woolf?*, is his almost universally acknowledged masterpiece: a stunning examination of a long-married academic couple's fiercely destructive psychological games filled with delusion, denial, and rage as well as love. Their struggle takes place during one long night of drinking and entertaining, where—for their delectation—George and Martha play a committed game of "get the guests," along with an attempt at "hump the hostess," with a younger couple that is new to their college community. All the bitter bile of their long marriage, with its crushed hopes and mutual fantasies, gets spilled onto the rug in front of their embarrassed guests, who play both audience and victim, until finally the story of their "son" is dragged out to be exorcised.

As George tells it, this boy spends his summers away from home "because there isn't room for him in a house full of empty bottles, lies, strange men, and a harridan" for a mother (p. 226). But Martha sees herself stung by a "vile, crushing marriage" and sees her son as "the one light in all this hopeless . . . *dark*ness" (p. 227). On this night, George decides to kill off the imaginary son they have created. This seemingly sadistic act leads at the very end to some moments of truth, which for Albee are essential to leading a life worth living: "I think once they've brought their marriage down to level ground again and gotten rid of the illusion, they might be able to build a sensible

relationship" (Kolin, ed., *Conversations*, p. 187). Whether such hopefulness exists at the end of the play, there has been a strange, almost redemptive quality in the ceremony that rids them of illusion, with George murmuring in Latin the Mass of the dead.

## CRITICAL CONTROVERSY

With *Tiny Alice* (1964), Albee entered a new phase for critics and audiences, producing a stylized fable that confused many and annoyed others. For Albee it was a story of the sacrifice of innocence and the intriguing relationship of martyrdom to sexual hysteria. Its style is beyond naturalism, a kind of high allegory, with characters named the lawyer, the butler, and the Cardinal, along with Miss Alice and Brother Julian, the sacrificial lamb of the group. The play revolves around the dealings of the Catholic Church with a mysterious woman, Miss Alice, who plans to contribute $100 million a year to the church, exciting the interest of the worldly Cardinal. But certain of her conditions must be met. Furthermore, it is never made clear exactly why she is giving the money or what she hopes to achieve. It may be as simple as that her enormous wealth is enormously corrupting, and institutions like the Catholic Church are rarely as pure in their actions as they claim to be.

The absurdist elements in this play possess a frustrating quality: the dialogue seems loaded with subtext and even menace, but its mystery leads to no clear human insight. In Harold Pinter's plays the menace implicates the world in which we live, whereas in Albee the menace seems more abstract, even decorative, and at times simply didactic. The entire issue of the nature of reality plays out on stage in a somewhat surreal metaphor—the gigantic house model, which dominates the stage, exists in another dimension—and the audience is left afloat in a world of theological abstraction.

In his simple robes Brother Julian excites the perverse mansion dwellers, who engage in constant games of dominance and sexual power. As in both his earlier and later plays, Albee's fascination with games and game playing implies a certain worldview: the core nature of human interaction is the game. Such a view is in line with absurdist thinking, which denies standard morality and traditional religious values for a more existential vision.

With *A Delicate Balance* (1966), Albee returns to a more naturalistic scene: the family home of the comfortably upper-middle-class Agnes and Tobias. Other characters include their adult daughter Julia, Agnes's alcoholic sister Claire, and their best friends Edna and Harry. The play takes place over a single weekend, during which Edna and Harry show up uninvited to stay because alone at night in their own house, they have become frightened.

This fear is the thread tying the three acts together. Never precisely named, the fear appears existential in nature, as if to be alive and growing old in a wealthy Connecticut suburb is to be prey to nameless fears, terrors even—something akin to the dread of the dark that small children regularly experience. The home they enter for succor is filled with dysfunctional tensions of its own; Julia is there for a visit (or perhaps to stay) upon the breakup of her fourth marriage in her mid-thirties. No one seems particularly pleased to have her back. And the ever-tippling Claire is a thorn in Agnes's side. Tobias, the "man" of the house, keeps making mostly impotent gestures in the direction of taking some control over the family's endless, bitter squabbles. His manhood is regularly mocked by the three women with whom he lives. Their existence in close, familial conjunction is maintained only with a "delicate balance." Alcohol consumption plays a large and significant role in most of their lives (as it did in Albee's for at least twenty years before he gave up drinking altogether in the early 1980s).

Albee said in an interview that *A Delicate Balance* "is about the death of passion . . . about people realizing that they no longer have freedom of choice any more" (Kolin, ed., *Conversations*, p. 92). But what has their passion ever been? They talk of nothing of significance. They are wealthy, unhappy, bored, but nonetheless apparently healthy people in their late fifties or early sixties (except for Julia, who is thirty-six). These people remind one of characters in a late Woody Allen film. Yet the play has its fierce defenders, and it won Albee his first undisputed Pulitzer Prize for drama. Given that the year of this play is 1966, Albee is investigating the survival strategies of a certain small subset of Americans caught in a 1950s value system: money and comfort and a well-stocked bar. The big revolutions of the late 1960s have barely begun. This wealthy suburb is like Rome just before the arrival of the Vandals. Besides writing a number of theatrical adaptations from the 1960s to the beginning of the 1980s (*The Ballad of the Sad Café*, from Carson McCullers's novella; *Malcolm*, from James Purdy's novel; *Everything in the Garden*, from a play by Giles Cooper; and *Lolita*, from Vladimir Nabokov's novel), Albee also wrote more plays: *Box* (1968), *Quotations from Chairman Mao Tse-tung* (1968), *All Over* (1971), *Seascape* (1975), *Counting the Ways* (1976), and *Listening* (1977). There is no one theme that links these works. *Box* and *Quotations* are derivative of later Beckett, exercises in language as a kind of nonlinear stage music, whereas *All Over* is quite a realistic depiction of the deathwatch for a famous man, whose exact fame and eminence are never tied down (although critics in the 1970s saw him as a lawyer or a writer, while those reviewing the 2002 revival imagined him as a vastly wealthy, business mogul—which reveals more about critics than the play). *Seascape* involves an upper-middle-class couple who are apparently happily married (that rare thing in Albee, at least before *The Goat; or, Who Is Sylvia?*) and are on a seaside vacation when two lizard-like creatures emerge from the ocean to confront them, raising such issues as how one continues actually to live life—or evolve—as opposed to settling merely for a peaceful but unadventurous existence.

## FROM CAREER LOW TO RETURNING PROMINENCE

Albee produced five plays during the 1980s: *The Lady from Dubuque* (1980), his version of *Lolita* (1981), *The Man Who Had Three Arms* (1982), *Finding the Sun* (1983), and *Marriage Play* (1987). They all fell into the category of critical failures at the time, but no doubt will be revived under different circumstances in the future. *The Lady from Dubuque* involves a dying young woman, her glib crowd of friends, her confused and angry husband, and the mysterious lady—clearly not from Dubuque, although that is her claim—who arrives at the end of act one with a black man who eventually appears to be Mr. Death. Albee had been reading the work of psychologist Elisabeth Kubler-Ross and was interested in the issues surrounding death and dying: who gets to set the tone, who deserves comforting, and what the dying person actually needs on an emotional level. The play possesses a Strindberg-like poetry as the husband and the mystery lady struggle over who shall comfort the terminally ill woman.

Critics immediately became angry with *The Man Who Had Three Arms* because they saw in it an attack on themselves that expressed a bitter resentment on Albee's part for his loss of both talent and fame. Albee denied that the play was autobiographical since his protagonist—who had grown the strange third arm and therefore entered the world of celebrity (only to lose his luster when his third arm disappeared)—had originally been a very ordinary advertising man whereas he had been the fair-haired boy of the theater. In the form of an after-dinner speech by a former celebrity, the play reminds one in places of a Chekhov vignette. It is funny, cruel, and way too long.

Finally, in the early 1990s Albee brought to the stage a play with some of his old power. Critics and audiences alike were delighted with *Three Tall Women* (1991), a two-act play whose characters are three women, A, B, and C, and a young man of twenty-three, the approximate age of Albee when he skipped off to New York City, not to see his mother again for many years. As he explains in his introduction, this is the play in which he comes to terms with his mother—who she was and how she affected him (it is not forgiving but neither is it, according to him, coming from anger: "I felt no need for revenge," p. ii). A play about old age and dying, it illuminates the sense of different and yet linked selves possessed by one person throughout a lifetime: how shocked we might be at twenty-five to see our fifty-two-year-old self, how unprepared we are to glimpse our future history, and how mocking we might be of our younger selves from a later vantage point.

Albee plays here with time, self-perception, and the way we continually rewrite our lives and our memories. As C says in the second act: "They say you can't remember pain. Well, maybe you can't remember pleasure, either—in the same way, I mean, in the way you can't remember pain. Maybe all you can remember is the memory of it . . . remembering, remembering it" (p. 107). Like Beckett, Albee is concerned with the strangeness of time's passage and the way in which memory is a construct like fiction; so what is the truth is no longer the issue.

During the 1990s he also wrote *The Lorca Play* (1992), *Fragments* (1993), and *The Play about the Baby* (1998), this final work of the decade proving the most entertaining. The title reveals the level of self-consciousness: it is a "play"; it is playful; it plays with the audience. The four characters are Girl, Boy, Man, and Woman, and the action is quite simple: a girl delivers a baby that she and the boy love just as they love each other with a great youthful joy and innocence. The older couple intervene, mocking their youth, stealing their baby, and ultimately, in a kind exorcism reminiscent of the end of *Who's Afraid of Virginia Woolf?*, they make the baby disappear, not only from the stage but from the consciousness of the young couple—so that, like the audience, the young couple must recognize a world of illusions and delusions. Both witty and sad, the play presents life as theater or game, what *New York Newsday* described as a "devastating piece of emotional terrorism." As in *The Lady from Dubuque*, where characters turn and talk overtly to the audience, so the man and woman address us from the stage, gathering

us into their cynical conspiracy, summed up: "Without wounds, what are you?" (p. 50).

Then, in 2002, Albee again won a Tony Award, this time for *The Goat; or, Who Is Sylvia?*, a play that asks the audience to believe that a highly successful, award-winning, fifty-year-old, happily married architect might fall in love with a goat. As his teenage son says to him: "You're fucking a fucking goat and you tell me not to *swear*?!" The play is certainly humorous in places, but it is hardly profound; nor does it achieve the kind of shock value that Albee may have expected. He claims he wrote it to get "everybody to be able to think about what they can't imagine and what they have buried deep as being intolerable and insufferable" (*Charlie Rose* television program, Public Broadcasting System, transcript, 31 May 2002). The problem is that the premise is simply not believable as he wrote it; a dwarf would be more shocking. We do not believe that this nice, clean, upper-middle-class white man is having sex with a goat, and not just sex but intense romantic feelings.

## ALBEE'S ART AND LEGACY

Albee has said, "You see, I write plays about how people waste their lives" (Kolin, *Conversations*, p. 105). Certainly in interviews he emphasizes his desire to wake up the audience, to make them uncomfortable, to force them to let go of their illusions in order to move toward more troubling realities and insights. He claimed in 1963, "People would rather sleep their way through life than stay awake for it" (p. 25). One of the reasons he often professes a disdain for Broadway is that its audience is too comfortable: "Broadway audiences are such placid cows" (p. 22). For Albee, it is the role of the artist to shake up his audience. The one thing he never wants to be is safe.

The theatergoer both laughs and is horrified at a typical Albee play but ultimately is left with a sense that the world is a cruel and claustrophobic place, dominated by mothers who consume their young and infantilize their mates. It can have an almost comic-book aspect. Middle-class America and its materialistic values were under attack for most of the twentieth century, so Albee's subject matter is not unique. Basically what makes Albee significant is his style, although the cut-to-the-chase rigor in his early short plays dissipated in his later, longer works. Still, the dark, bleak, bitter, humorous, witty Albee does possess a powerful voice, and this voice is his gift to late-twentieth-century theater. As the character called Man says about our lives in *The Play about the Baby*:

What do we *want*. Well, I would imagine we want what almost everyone wants—eternal life, in great health, no older than we are when we want it; easy money with enough self-deception to make us feel we've earned it, are worthy people; a government that lets us do whatever we want . . . a bigger dick, a more muscular vagina; a baby, perhaps? (p. 27)

The playfulness, self-knowledge, and casual cruelty mark this character as quintessentially Albee-esque.

So, too, the elegant and surprising street speech of Jerry in *The Zoo Story*, the articulate upper-class musing of Agnes in *A Delicate Balance*, or the brilliantly urbane chatter of the Man in *The Play about the Baby*—all reveal Albee's ear for language. The audience is seduced and riveted. Right from the start of his career, he possessed a keen sense of theater as theater, that it is an imitation of reality, as Aristotle pointed out, and that since it is such a construct, it is not limited by reality. What this means in terms of the play's relationship to the audience is that they cannot sit back passively and wait to be entertained, as with television, but that they too must play a role in the event, not be mere witnesses, but guests at the feast.

In terms of his theatrical failures, Albee may have gotten frozen in the world in which he grew up: the world of the privileged Wasp. It is a group that was significant on the American scene in the 1940s and 1950s but ceased to have much impact in subsequent decades. The world of John O'Hara and John Cheever seems rather dated at the start of the twenty-first century. Inherited wealth tends to be a bore, and Albee's work supports such a view, since his very wealthy characters are usually both vicious and vacuous; they overdrink, they loathe their families, and they enjoy the mean remark and the selfish gesture disproportionately. They are, of course, witty. Albee has recognized this pattern in his art over time, remarking of the negative critical reaction to his play *All Over*: "Maybe they became impatient with these wealthy, self-indulgent people who seem to be most interested in the precision of their language. Maybe the play seemed too distant, too elegant. Of course it does have the problem that so many of my plays have of being about an almost extinct society" (Gussow, p. 285).

Albee's cerebral inclinations place him more in the post–World War II European tradition than the American, which tends toward realism in drama and senti-mentality in taste. Avant-garde and experimental theater has a long and significant European tradition: from Alfred Jarry's *Ubu roi* (1896) and Jean Cocteau's theater of cruelty through Luigi Pirandello and the theater of the absurd. By choosing to work in this other tradition, Albee has both

distanced himself from commercial success and intro-duced useful innovations of style and perception into the American scene, enormously enriching its theater in the process. It is rare in the United States for playwrights over age fifty to produce exciting new work. (O'Neill is the model here, with his late masterpiece *Long Day's Journey into Night* in 1957). Edward Albee has awakened Amer-ican theater to the world of the absurd, the illogical, the painful, the dreaded, and the blackly humorous, insisting in play after play that we confront our own darker selves.

[*See also* McCullers, Carson, and her *Ballad of the Sad Café*; Shepard, Sam; *and* Theater in America.]

## SELECTED WORKS (CHRONOLOGICALLY BY FIRST PRODUCTION)

*The Zoo Story* (Berlin, 1959)
*The Death of Bessie Smith* (New York City, 1960)
*The Sandbox* (Berlin, 1960)
*The American Dream* (New York City, 1961)
*Bartleby* (New York City, 1961)
*Who's Afraid of Virginia Woolf?* (New York City, 1962)
*The Ballad of the Sad Café* (New York City, 1962)
*Tiny Alice* (New York City, 1964)
*Malcolm* (New York City, 1966)
*A Delicate Balance* (New York City, 1966)
*Everything in the Garden* (New York City, 1967)
*Box* (Buffalo, N.Y., 1968)
*Quotations from Chairman Mao Tse-tung* (Buffalo, N.Y., 1968)
*All Over* (New York City, 1971)
*Seascape* (New York City, 1975)
*Counting the Ways* (London, 1976)
*Listening* (Hartford, Conn., 1977)
*The Lady from Dubuque* (New York City, 1980)
*Lolita* (New York City, 1981)
*The Man Who Had Three Arms* (Chicago, 1982)
*Finding the Sun* (Greeley, Colo., 1983)
*Marriage Play* (Vienna, 1987)
*Three Tall Women* (Vienna, 1991)
*The Lorca Play* (Houston, Texas, 1992)
*Fragments* (Cincinnati, Ohio, 1993)
*The Play about the Baby* (London, 1998)
*The Goat; or, Who Is Sylvia?* (New York City, 2002)

## FURTHER READING

Amacher, Richard E. *Edward Albee*. Rev. ed. Boston, 1982. Useful critical commentary on the plays up to *A Delicate Balance*, combining explication of the text with Aristotelian analysis.
Bigsby, C. W. E. *Albee*. Edinburgh, Scotland, 1969. A literary and psychological analysis of Albee's plays.

Bigsby, C. W. E., ed. *Edward Albee: A Collection of Critical Essays*. Englewood Cliffs, N.J., 1975.

Bloom, Harold, ed. *Edward Albee*. New York, 1987. Useful, full bibliography.

Bottoms, Stephen J. *Albee:* Who's Afraid of Virginia Woolf? Cambridge, 2000.

Cohn, Ruby. *Edward Albee*. Minneapolis, 1969.

Gussow, Mel. *Edward Albee: A Singular Journey*. New York, 1999. An excellent biography by a theater critic that deals with both Albee's life and art and provides detailed information about various productions of his plays.

Hayman, Ronald. *Edward Albee*. London, 1971. Covers both Albee's early plays and his adaptations through *All Over*.

Hirsh, Foster. *Who's Afraid of Edward Albee?* Berkeley, Calif., 1978. Sees Albee as a self-absorbed stylist and regards his work as growing increasingly arid.

Kolin, Philip C., ed. *Conversations with Edward Albee*. Jackson, Miss., 1988. Extremely useful collection of many in-depth interviews with Albee conducted by a variety of people.

Kolin, Philip C., and J. Madison Davis, eds. *Critical Essays on Edward Albee*. Boston, 1986. A large compilation of writers, ranging from Robert Brustein to Ruby Cohn to John Kenneth Galbraith, and including an annotated bibliography of Albee interviews.

Paolucci, Anne. *From Tension to Tonic: The Plays of Edward Albee*. Carbondale, Ill., 1972. Places Albee in a national context as an American and also in the tradition of the French absurdist writers.

Rose, Charlie. ''Charlie Rose Transcript'' #3216 (31 May 2002). Public Broadcasting System.

Roudané, Matthew C. *Understanding Edward Albee*. Columbia, S.C., 1987.

Roudané, Matthew C. Who's Afraid of Virginia Woolf?: *Necessary Fictions, Terrifying Realities*. Boston, 1990.

Rutenberg, Michael E. *Edward Albee: Playwright in Protest*. New York, 1969. Sees Albee as a social protester committed to the cause of human dignity.

Stenz, Anita Maria. *Edward Albee: The Poet of Loss*. New York, 1978.

Wasserman, Julian N., ed. *Edward Albee: An Interview and Essays*. Houston, Tex., 1983.

# LOUISA MAY ALCOTT

*by Angela M. Garcia*

Long recognized only for her children's books, Louisa May Alcott also wrote adult novels, Civil War hospital sketches, and at least fifty pieces of much-publicized "sensation" fiction, but her most popular legacy remains that curiously modern portrait of family life, *Little Women* (1868). Although the author mocked herself as providing mere "moral pap for the young," her audience in America, and later worldwide, responded enthusiastically to its edifying and entertaining truths. Readers have remained absorbed by and even enamored with Alcott's story; by the end of the twentieth century, several million copies had been sold in dozens of translations, and film and television adaptations continue to be produced.

Louisa May Alcott.
(*Hulton Archive/Getty Images*)

Beloved for her contributions to juvenile fiction, although not considered a serious writer by critical standards, Alcott was christened the "Children's Friend," and her work was relegated for about a century to the low position given to sentimental or domestic subjects. In the late twentieth century, however, with the reissuing of her sensation fiction or "blood-and-thunder tales" in numerous collections, Alcott's reputation as a writer has grown. Feminist critics in particular, addressing the dichotomy between the seemingly polar genres in which she engaged—from domestic to lurid or Gothic fiction—a have examined Alcott's writing and life more closely and have found a complex figure whose stories are not so simple or conventional as once believed.

Alcott, born in Germantown, Pennsylvania, lived a life that often contradicted the sweet and wholesome quality some critics have identified as central to her most popular book. Her parentage itself combined the illustrious and radical, the philosophical and eccentric. Her mother, Abba May Alcott, was born to one of the most respectable families in Boston. She married Amos Bronson Alcott, who aligned himself firmly with the transcendentalists through deep lifelong friendships with Ralph Waldo Emerson and Henry David Thoreau and their families, friendships which Louisa, their second daughter, also enjoyed. In fact, she claimed Emerson as one of her major influences, and her first novel, *Moods* (1864, reworked for publication in 1882), features characters based on Emerson and Thoreau. Nathaniel Hawthorne was also a family friend.

Her family's financial insecurity shadowed Alcott's youth and would shape her life and career. In one instance, Bronson Alcott had the family embark on an experiment in rural communal living that lasted six months. In Fruitlands, with restricted vegan diets and cold-water baths, his disciple-like devotion left the family traumatized. This experience, combined with her father's other noble but financially unproductive endeavors—he taught in the progressive but ultimately failed Temple School and once returned from a western lecture tour with one dollar in his pocket—drove Louisa to seek financial independence for herself and financial security for the family, and she soon became her household's sole supporter.

Louisa May Alcott often referred to her fiction as her bread and butter, duly noting in her journals the money each article earned, what it bought (for example, a new carpet), and the bills it paid. This practical side kept Alcott conscientious about her writing's marketability, keenly aware not only of her sales figures but also of her audience. Furthermore, the necessary mercenary quality of Alcott's writing, and her consequent catering to popular demand in her moral children's literature, undercut her own sense of a serious critical quality, or greatness, to her work. At the same time as she maintained the persona of the "Children's Friend," she disparaged domestic fiction and despaired over the lack of reception for her serious adult novels; she had worked on some of these for several years, yet they failed to garner positive reviews or comparable sales in her lifetime.

Before 1868 and the windfall that was *Little Women*, Alcott ventured into several genres, including short fiction, fairy tales and fantasies, and drama. With *Hospital Sketches* (1863), based on her short stint as a nurse for Civil War soldiers in Washington, D.C., she found her first book-length success. Her experience also left her chronically ill: the calomel (a mercury compound) prescribed for the typhoid she contracted there would slowly erode the author's health until her death, and nightmares from her battle with the illness ended up as material for the sensation stories Alcott produced for the next five years.

## THE THRILLERS

The extensive quantity of Alcott's sensation fiction was first identified by Leona Rostenberg in 1943, and it was reprinted, mainly by Madeleine B. Stern, beginning in the 1970s. Since then, the Alcott oeuvre has undergone a process of radical re-vision.

The melodramatic stories Jo March writes and publishes to her pride and delight in *Little Women*, and then gives up in deference to her husband's wishes, were stories Alcott actually wrote by the dozens. Unknown to her popular audience, these brought in regular and substantial sums for the Alcott family, and certainly some self-respect for Alcott as a professional writer. Critics also indicate the cathartic possibilities of this type of writing as a psychic outlet, even finding in its melodrama and obsessions an expression of suppressed rage.

Mostly published anonymously or under the pseudonym A. M. Barnard, the magnetic tales appeared in various ladies' or popular magazines. They tend to feature seduction, insanity, drug addiction, murder, power struggles, and illicit sexual encounters against exotic backgrounds. Their subjects reflect Alcott's deep-rooted theatrical interest, also documented in *Little Women*—the dark streak that drew her, stagestruck, toward the lurid. Her page-turners also exhibit high-flown language and incorporate nearly impossible coincidences.

The genre's virtual catalogue of deviance, which includes adultery, bigamy, transvestism, androgyny, and incest themes, has led scholars, especially since the 1970s, to reexamine this pulp fiction mainly in a feminist light, noting in these wild stories women's subversion of the power structure. Several of Alcott's heroines, seen by critics as a feminine challenge to gender stereotypes

or expectations, manipulate as well as they are being manipulated. How Alcott's sensation fiction differs from other such work of the period, however, seems a topic left largely uninvestigated.

Critics' attention to this experimentation with the reverse side of domestic tranquility has both heightened Alcott's stature within the American canon and drawn attention to her politics—for instance, her dedicated work for social reform. Feminist scholars have emphasized her involvement in a sphere beyond the cozy home depicted in *Little Women* through Alcott's work for the abolitionist, suffrage, and temperance movements her parents also espoused, and they have highlighted her Civil War experience. Her Gothic stories, in addition to representing often sexualized feminine power, are seen as evidence for Alcott's forward-thinking views on themes based in race and gender issues, such as her beliefs in racial integration and egalitarian marriage. Finally, *Work* (1873), another adult novel, echoes Alcott's own experience in tracing Christie Devon's work history as servant, actress, companion, and seamstress; her thoughts of suicide; and finally her advocacy of women's rights.

Scholarship has moved full circle to the immense success of *Little Women*, drawn to reconcile the didacticism in it and her other "children's" novels with her often immoral adult fiction. Alcott added seven books to the successful series, including *Little Men* (1871) and *Jo's Boys* (1886), the latter completed a few years before her death.

Critics have also worked to analyze the secrets behind the persistent appeal of her classic. Recent articles and essays that apply feminist and postmodern criticism to Alcott's "sentimental" writing reread the novel as subversive and intertextual. Through its numerous allusions and ambiguity, the novel is said to allow for multiple readings, including social critique; thus, the text has been shown essentially to question conventional gender roles, particularly girls' and women's domesticity, even while it appears to further the principles of feminine duty and self-sacrifice.

## RE-SEEING *LITTLE WOMEN*

Alcott's moody tomboy heroine, Jo March, embodies a mass of contradictions, not the least of which is her girl/boy identity. Sharp-witted and self-castigating, she is most "herself" when at play with the adolescent boy next door, Laurie, and both refer to her as a boy. She longs for a boy's freedoms; cuts her hair, said to be her one beauty; and sells it to support the family. While Jo eschews all fashion and bewails her sister Meg's marriage as a betrayal of the much-adored circle of mother-and-sisterhood (a loss even comparable to her sister Beth's death), the father is notably and conveniently absent through much of the story; this chaplain/hero character has abandoned the family for the greater good of serving in the Civil War.

The authoritarian mother, Marmee, with her loving, cautionary words and gestures, is thus the central, idealized figure in the all-feminine circle and is responsible for much of the joy and all of the moral guidance for her four daughters in their happy home. When she leaves to nurse the father, there is a palpable void. In both Marmee's and Jo's cases, one might read the combination, interchangeability or fluidity of gender roles as an ideal for the creation of a truly whole individual in society, rather than as an advocation of androgyny, as some critics have suggested.

Despite the conspicuous absence of churchgoing, Christian virtues (seen in *Little Women* as practical) such as charity and good works predominate. The novel begins with the shabby-genteel Marches giving their Christmas breakfast to a poor family. The father has gone to help the soldiers. Their mother, Marmee, also advocates self-improvement. Her drive to help Jo gain self-control over her anger leaves its mark as—with Beth as her conscience and role model and *Pilgrim's Progress* as her Christian guide—Jo manages largely to overcome her temper, though not without a charming and very human series of pitfalls and consequent passionate repentance. In fact, all four sisters have weaknesses they must work to overcome, including vanity, timidity, and selfishness.

Although Marmee emphasizes their happiness and struggle toward goodness in spite of their financial problems, the family's poverty is realistically deplored, especially by the oldest and youngest daughters, Meg and Amy, ever drawn toward the fashionable. Meg and Jo must work as governess and companion, and they dislike it immensely, yet they find their wealthy employers no happier than they. In choosing to write and publish to earn money, Jo succeeds in a traditionally male role rather than in an acceptable female position, again subverting expectations for her gender.

Yet love and marriage seem to undo artistic ambition in the novel, as if the two cannot coexist. Romance and marriage, though a goal in the daughters' theatrics and soon a reality for Meg, are not at first an ostensible goal for Jo. She forthrightly refuses the marriage proposal of her best friend and neighbor, Laurie Laurence, the male insurgent into the feminine circle, but Jo is moved after her gentle sister Beth's death to accept that of German professor Friedrich "Fritz" Bhaer. (Alcott's refusal to marry her off to Laurie works as a sabotage in itself.) However, the professor keeps Jo from publishing any more of her sensational tales; the protagonist's submission is a problematic one for feminist critics. Alcott herself stopped writing sensation fiction for almost a decade after her runaway hit with *Little Women* and its sequels.

Balancing on this girl/woman edge or verge—the threshold that for Jo signifies a loss in individuality and independence along with the initiation into womanhood—became Alcott's special territory, and she, by public acclaim, its expert. Adolescence's threshold carries much fear and confusion in *Little Women*, as well as humor, but the daughters, at their mother's advice and at Jo's inclination, remain on the girlhood side as long as possible. Only Beth escapes growing up through her premature death, and even as the most domestic and angelic sister, she features in an unsentimentalized death scene and a turning point for the March family.

In frankness and innocence the sisters are most comfortable, but the title's word "women," with all the changes it invokes, is writ large in their psyches. Though working always against her boyish nature to stifle her exuberance and temper, Jo nevertheless remains recognizable throughout the series. Even in *Jo's Boys*, as a matriarch at a college, having given up writing for storytelling and living through her boys' (foster as well as natural sons) travels and adventures, she retains a bit of her rumpled self, perhaps less wild but never completely chastened.

## CRITICAL CONNECTIONS

The challenge for many Alcott scholars lies in finding common themes within two seemingly divergent strands of fiction. Actually, the Faust-inspired *A Modern Mephistopheles* (1877) marks Alcott's only known return to the shocker genre. It was written for the No Name Series, in which well-known authors each contributed an anonymous piece. The tale follows a love triangle and breeds speculation on the question of authorship and the hidden literary identity, topics central to Alcott's professional life.

Although no seductress, madhouse inmate, or opium eater, Alcott's assertive Jo wields feminine power and dodges society's narrow gender constraints as capably as any of Alcott's shocker heroines; as one critic contrasted the two, Jo plays daylight to the heroine's midnight. Yet complicated questions are raised in *Little Women*.

Indeed, whether the goals of egalitarian marriage and creating art—two themes delineated in her novels—need be mutually exclusive for a woman is a question not easily answered either in Alcott's work or in her life. However, that these are suggested as viable ambitions for a young woman of the 1860s is in itself an achievement.

Life never exactly imitated art for Alcott. Even in a generous matriarchal role, Jo's character conveys the unease of having gained marriage and lost writing through the last of the series, *Jo's Boys*. Having allowed the vibrant, contentious tomboy to make an unconventional, even rebellious match for herself, and to sacrifice her art, the author herself chose to forgo marriage and children for the liberty to write. But her mother's death in late 1877 and the news of her younger sister May's death in Europe two years later dealt Alcott severe blows, as she battled slowly deteriorating health from mercury poisoning. May had designated her famous author sister to adopt her child, and so "Lulu" Nieriker spent ten years in Alcott's New England home until Alcott's death in 1888, at fifty-five.

## THE WORK'S ENDURANCE

Behind the renewed interest in Alcott the woman writer, or Alcott the masked writer, lies the quiet avowal of Alcott as a professional at her craft. In her art, Alcott at her best brought her characters and scenes remarkably to life. Her work singularly animates nineteenth-century New England family life in a relevant, modern fashion, even as it introduces the necessarily contingent questions of woman's role and feminine power that remain pivotal in American society today. With the right to vote and the right and often the economic necessity to labor, more women enjoy the freedoms Alcott sought, yet they continue to identify with her frankly role-subverting, convention-defying Jo.

For Alcott and all her heroines, passivity, at least, is not a virtue. While they might also dream, they work toward their goals, professional and otherwise. After all, it is when Jo initiates, whether by writing and selling a story to the newspaper or by marching into the next-door mansion of the shy neighbor boy and his uncle, that she reaps the rewards. Where there is poverty, Jo and her family bring a family their breakfast. When Amy is hit at school as punishment, Marmee immediately withdraws her from the school. Alcott merged with Jo in that as a child she loved movement, loved to run; likewise, as an adult she found satisfaction in action, whether working toward abolition, suffrage, temperance, and women's rights, or in her work-deliriums, scribbling her forty books.

What lives and breathes most in *Little Women* is the unmistakable truth of Jo, who for all her conventionality and unconventionality bounds off the pages. Jo March in her vitality, hope, and despair has been compared to Huckleberry Finn in American literature; this quality of immediacy in all her fiction, wholesome or not, has become recognized as an Alcott trademark.

[*See also* Emerson, Ralph Waldo; Hawthorne, Nathaniel; *and* Thoreau, Henry David.]

## SELECTED WORKS

*Hospital Sketches* (1863)
*Moods* (1864)
*Little Women, or Meg, Jo, Beth and Amy*, 2 vols. (1868–1869)
*An Old-Fashioned Girl* (1870)
*Little Men: Life at Plumfield with Jo's Boys* (1871)
*Work: A Story of Experience* (1873)
*Eight Cousins; or, The Aunt-Hill* (1875)
*Rose in Bloom: A Sequel to "Eight Cousins"* (1876)
*A Modern Mephistopheles* (1877)
*Jack and Jill: A Village Story* (1880)
*Jo's Boys, and How They Turned Out: A Sequel to "Little Men"* (1886)
*The Selected Letters of Louisa May Alcott* (1987)
*The Journals of Louisa May Alcott* (1989)
*Louisa May Alcott Unmasked: Collected Thrillers* (1995)

## FURTHER READING

Anderson, William. *The World of Louisa May Alcott: A First-Time Glimpse into the Life and Times of Louisa May Alcott, Author of* Little Women. New York, 1995. Offers intriguing photographs of Alcott's homes, furnishings, and the Boston area; a visual gloss of her life and times.

Auerbach, Nina. *Communities of Women: An Idea in Fiction*. Cambridge, Mass., 1975. Includes a fascinating study comparing *Little Women* with *Pride and Prejudice*, and discusses Jo March's relationship to (male) history.

Bedell, Madelon. *The Alcotts: Biography of a Family*. New York, 1980. Provides extensive information on Alcott's parents, their radical thought, and their marriage.

Delamar, Gloria T. *Louisa May Alcott and* Little Women: *Biography, Critique, Publications, Poems, Songs, and Contemporary Relevance*. Jefferson, N.C., 1990. This collection is of particular interest for its song lyrics by Alcott and contemporary comments on the relevance of her classic.

Doyle, Christine. *Louisa May Alcott and Charlotte Brontë: Transatlantic Translations.* Knoxville, Tenn., 2000. Establishes valuable biographical and thematic connections between two woman artists of the same period.

Eiselein, Gregory, and Anne K. Phillips, eds. *The Louisa May Alcott Encyclopedia.* Westport, Conn., 2001. Alphabetizes and synopsizes the people and places, books and themes for easy access.

Elbert, Sarah. *A Hunger for Home: Louisa May Alcott and Little Women.* Philadelphia, 1984. A detailed biography that analyzes Alcott's life in connection with her lesser-known works as well as the most popular.

Keyser, Elizabeth Lennox. *Whispers in the Dark: The Fiction of Louisa May Alcott.* Knoxville, Tenn., 1993. This contemporary textual analysis focuses on the wide variety of Alcott's work as subversive writing.

Saxton, Martha. *Louisa May: A Modern Biography of Louisa May Alcott.* Boston, 1977. An example of the psychoanalytical slant that some criticism took in the 1970s in liberally interpreting the life from the thrillers.

Stern, Madeleine, B., ed. *Critical Essays on Louisa May Alcott.* Boston, 1984. Wide range of early book reviews and modern reappraisals of Alcott's work.

Stern, Madeleine B. *Louisa May Alcott.* New York, 1996. In a traditional biography originally published in 1950, the best-known Alcott critic traces the author's life through the places she inhabited.

Strickland, Charles. *Victorian Domesticity: Families in the Life and Art of Louisa May Alcott.* University, Ala., 1985. Addresses the Civil War context in which Alcott wrote and the contradictions inherent in the sentimental familial ideal versus the reality of the time.

# HORATIO ALGER

*by Glenn Hendler*

Horatio Alger wrote approximately one hundred novels, as well as biographies of public figures, short stories, and poetry. Alger emerged from the same New England cultural milieu that produced major authors and intellectuals from Jonathan Edwards to Nathaniel Hawthorne, Ralph Waldo Emerson, and William and Henry James, but he came to exemplify the mass-produced popular fiction that such writers generally abhorred. In a related irony, Alger's stories of a virtuous boy or young man ascending into the middle class were widely accepted early in his career as appropriate for children, but by the end of his career many critics lumped them together with more sensationalistic and ambiguously moral books. Alger's reputation—along with the dominant interpretation of his fiction—took yet more turns after his death, as his books went through at least two different twentieth-century revivals. Any understanding of Alger should encompass not only his actual life and works but also the various meanings that "the Horatio Alger story" has accrued.

Horatio Alger. (© *Bettmann/Corbis*)

## CAREER CHANGES

Alger was expected to follow his father into the Unitarian ministry, and so at age sixteen left Chelsea, Massachusetts, where he was born on 13 January 1832, to matriculate at Harvard. There he began writing and publishing poems and essays, mostly in the popular sentimental vein of the period. Some of these were later collected in his first book, *Bertha's Christmas Vision: An Autumn Sheaf* (1856). He received an advanced degree from the Divinity School in 1860 and then left to travel in Europe. Deemed unqualified for service in the Union army, in 1864 Alger wrote a book about the home front. *Frank's Campaign* (1864), the story of a boy who keeps up the family farm while his father fights in the war, sold well and met with positive reviews.

At first it seemed Alger might maintain both careers. He accepted an offer to preach at the First Unitarian Church in Brewster, Massachusetts, and while there he published another boys' novel and started work on a book for girls. However, in another personal and moral twist difficult to reconcile with his reputation as a moral exemplar of the virtues of acquisitiveness, his Brewster parishioners charged him with pederasty. Alger may not have denied that he had committed "a crime of no less magnitude than the abominable and revolting crime of unnatural familiarity with boys, which is too revolting to think of in the most brutal of our race," for he voluntarily left Brewster for New York City. The charges did not come up again publicly during his lifetime. Henry James Sr. remarked in 1870 that "Alger talks freely about his own late insanity—which he in fact appears to enjoy as a subject of conversation" (Scharnhorst and Bales, 1985, pp. 67, 70).

The Brewster charges ended Alger's ministerial career. However, his move to New York gave him the elements out of which he would construct his most famous character, Ragged Dick. Alger became friendly with Charles Loring Brace, founder of the Children's Aid Society and the Newsboys' Lodging House, and through Brace met the street children and bootblacks who would so often be the protagonists of his stories. Drawing on this material, in January of 1867 the serialization of "Ragged Dick; or, Street Life in New York" began in the magazine *Student and Schoolmate*. In 1868 the story appeared in book form, rapidly becoming a best-seller.

## *RAGGED DICK* AND THE HORATIO ALGER MYTH

Later promoters of the Alger myth would describe his tales as "rags to riches" stories, and the first part of this description certainly applies to the title character of *Ragged Dick*. As the novel opens, Dick is living on the street, selling newspapers and shining shoes. Dick is no paragon of virtue; his faults—theatergoing, smoking, and gambling—are made evident early on. Like all of Alger's protagonists, though, Dick is honest by nature, "frank and straightforward, manly and self-reliant." Perhaps most important, his virtues are evident to anyone willing to look for them. In the novel's opening chapters, a wealthy businessman hires the boy to give his son a tour of New York, and Dick proves a good choice. He demonstrates his knowledge of the city, and along the way outwits a swindler and returns the money to its owner, is accused and proven innocent of theft himself, and displays a clever, punning wit. Dick's encounter with the wealthier boy and the generosity of the boy's father inspire him to renounce his vices, save enough money to find lodging, and generally improve himself both morally and financially.

As in other nineteenth-century American tales of self-making such as slave narratives, *Ragged Dick* dramatizes its hero's acquisition of literacy. Dick learns to read and write in an exchange both emotional and economic, as he offers to share his bed with his friend Fosdick if the younger boy will teach him. In another prototypical scene, Dick selflessly rescues a rich man's daughter from drowning. The girl's father thanks Dick by sending him new clothes and hiring him as a clerk. This almost accidental intervention into the boy's life is more typical of Alger's formula than is the "rags to riches" version of the story, in which hard work and thrift are what propel the boy to great wealth. Most often the story hinges on a wealthy patron recognizing the boy's virtue despite his visible poverty; as one such patron describes the hero of *Silas Snobden's Office Boy* (1899): "He is a very good-looking boy, and he looks *good*, which is still better." And the boy's "rise" usually culminates in a position no more exalted than a job in middle management. Only in a few fairly atypical stories do the boys acquire great wealth, and in some of these cases this is the result of unexpected inheritance rather than hard work.

Thus, Alger's writings themselves did not purvey quite the same fantasy that twentieth-century politicians and businessmen meant to evoke when they referred to a "Horatio Alger tale." That is not to say that Alger was an urban realist or social critic. But he and his supporters distinguished his stories from those of his predecessors by claiming that they possessed qualities of realism and material specificity that had been lacking in earlier boys' fiction. Some of his novels took readers on geographically and sociologically plausible tours of New York City, from lodging houses for the poor to luxury suites in the Astor Place Hotel. They taught readers that there were children sleeping in boxes on city streets, and somewhat undercut the potentially excessive sentimentality of such scenes by depicting his boys as witty and lively personalities, many of whom had the wherewithal to cope with their poverty. Even the novels that took him beyond New York City had aspirations to verisimilitude; Alger took a trip to the West in 1876–1877 to gather material and experiences for a series to be set there. Although they may seem didactic to us today, Alger's morals were conveyed somewhat more subtly than those in most antebellum children's fiction. Mark Twain's parodies of children's fiction targeted writers like Jacob Abbott's *Rollo* books, but Twain may have incorporated elements of Alger's formula into, for instance, the half-serious possibility he holds out that Tom Sawyer would grow up to be a respectable and virtuous young man.

Alger's writings veer farthest into fantasy in their understanding of the virtuous benevolence of the Gilded Age. For Alger, a boy who prominently displays his virtue will be noticed by a wealthy patron who is ready to reward him for rescuing a girl from drowning, for foiling a confidence man, for aiding a younger boy in distress. In turn, the boy aspires to become this sort of benevolent man himself, a moral aspiration that to some extent displaces the economic aspirations that might have looked to contemporary readers like naked greed. This aspiration, with which most of his stories conclude, also sets up the promise of a sequel. In the next novel in the series, the previous book's protagonist is generally a minor character who provides the recognition a younger boy needs to set him on his own path to respectability. Thus, *Ragged Dick* was followed by *Fame and Fortune* (1868), *Mark, the Match Boy* (1869), and three more in the Ragged Dick series, which in turn were followed by *Luck and Pluck; or, John Oakley's Inheritance* (1869), which initiated the eight-book *Luck and Pluck* series.

Alger struck gold with *Ragged Dick*, and a few of his other novels sold well enough that he was able to make a decent living from his writing. But most of his books were not massive best-sellers, which was perhaps a reason he wrote so many. Only rarely did he deviate from his blueprint, making at least two attempts to write novels for women: *The Disagreeable Woman* (1895) and *A Fancy of Hers* (serialized in 1877). One interesting variation came in the *Tattered Tom* series, beginning in 1871 with *Tattered Tom; or, The Story of a Street Arab*, which largely stuck to the formula except that the eponymous protagonist turns out to be a girl named Jane. Alger's biography of James Garfield might seem to represent a more expansive ambition, but the title alone—*From Canal Boy to President* (1881)—indicates that he was not straying far from familiar narrative ground.

## REPRINTS, REINTERPRETATIONS, AND REEVALUATIONS

While the texts do not vary much, readers' interpretations of Alger's works shifted significantly during his lifetime and after. As early as 1879, the Library Associations of America drew unusually large crowds to their Boston convention treating the topic of "Fiction in Libraries and the Reading of Children," and sparked a lively debate in which Alger's works figured prominently. The librarians categorized Alger's works as comparable to, for instance, those of his former mentor William T. Adams, who published under the name "Oliver Optic," but also to those of more sensational writers such as Mrs. E. D. E. N. Southworth, author of *The Hidden Hand* (written about 1867) and *Ishmael; or, In the Depths* (1876). Some speakers acknowledged that Alger and such other writers "mean[t] well," and many defended children's reading such works as a phase that could lead to better literature. But critics castigated these authors for writing "insipid or sensational fiction" that threatened to "emasculate" the minds of their readers, and advocated removing their books from public libraries. There is no record of Alger's response to such claims, but they certainly represent an interpretation of his fiction at variance with both his intentions and the ways in which he would be read in the twentieth century.

Alger reached unprecedented levels of posthumous popularity. Beginning in 1900, Edward Stratemeyer published eleven novels of his own under Alger's name, and soon began reprinting the older ones, some of which had annual sales of a million or more. Sales dropped again in the 1920s, but references to "the Horatio Alger story" did not. A 1943 issue of *Atlantic Monthly*, for instance, described Alger's novels as evincing a "faith in *laissez-faire*, in the best of all possible worlds, in the inevitability of rags to riches" (Scharnhorst and Bales, p. 154). Repeatedly in the twentieth century, new and mostly inaccurate readings of the Horatio Alger myth were cited for particular ideological reasons, perhaps most notably by President Ronald Reagan, who—like Dwight Eisenhower, Conrad Hilton, Norman Vincent Peale, and Alfred Fuller, founder of the Fuller Brush Company—was a recipient of the Horatio Alger Award granted annually by the Horatio Alger Association of Distinguished Americans.

Perhaps the most egregiously inaccurate Horatio Alger story came in the first published biography of the author, *Alger: A Biography without a Hero*, written in 1928 by Herbert R. Mayes, a journalist. Mayes admitted fifty years later that he had simply made up the supposed facts in his biography, and that the sources he cited—including a diary and personal letters—did not exist. In the interim, other biographers used this hoax as a source, and so perpetuated Mayes's tales of, for instance, Alger's affairs with women on his trip to Europe. The rediscovery of the Brewster incident added sensational detail to the author's story, but no reliable and sober account of his life was published before Gary Scharnhorst and Jack Bales's 1985 *The Lost Life of Horatio Alger Jr.*

## WORKS

*Bertha's Christmas Vision: An Autumn Sheaf* (1856)

*Frank's Campaign; or, What Boys Can Do on the Farm for the Camp* (1864)

*Ragged Dick; or, Street Life in New York with the Boot-Blacks* (1868)

*Fame and Fortune; or, The Progress of Richard Hunter* (1868)

*Mark, the Match Boy; or, Richard Hunter's Ward* (1869)

*Luck and Pluck; or, John Oakley's Inheritance* (1869)

*Rough and Ready; or, Life among the New York Newsboys* (1869)

*Tattered Tom; or, The Story of a Street Arab* (1871)

*Paul, the Peddler; or, The Adventures of a Young Street Merchant* (1871)

*Phil, the Fiddler; or, The Story of a Young Street Musician* (1872)

*Strive and Succeed; or, The Progress of Walter Conrad* (1872)

*Bound to Rise; or, Harry Walton's Motto* (1873)

*Julius; or, The Street Boy Out West* (1874)

*Risen from the Ranks; or, Harry Walton's Success* (1874)

*Brave and Bold; or, The Fortunes of a Factory Boy* (1874)

*The Young Outlaw; or, Adrift in the Streets* (1875)

*The Western Boy; or, The Road to Success* (1878)

*From Canal Boy to President; or, The Boyhood and Manhood of James A. Garfield* (1881)

*From Farm Boy to Senator; Being the History of the Boyhood and Manhood of Daniel Webster* (1882)

*Abraham Lincoln, the Backwoods Boy; or, How a Young Rail-Splitter Became President* (1883)

*The Train Boy* (1883)

*The Store Boy; or, The Fortunes of Ben Barclay* (1887)

"Are My Boys Real?," *Ladies' Home Journal* 7 (November 1890): 29

*$500; or, Jacob Marlowe's Secret* (1890)

*Struggling Upward; or, Luke Larkin's Luck* (1890)

*Only an Irish Boy; or, Andy Burke's Fortunes and Misfortunes* (1894)

*The Disagreeable Woman. A Social Mystery* (1895)

"Writing Stories for Boys," *Writer* 9 (March 1896): 36–37

*Silas Snobden's Office Boy* (1899)

*A Debt of Honor. The Story of Gerald Lane's Success in the Far West* (1900)

## FURTHER READING

Cawelti, John G. *Apostles of the Self-Made Man.* Chicago, 1965.

Hendler, Glenn. "Pandering in the Public Sphere: Masculinity and the Market in Horatio Alger." *American Quarterly* 48:3 (September 1996): 414–438.

Mayes, Herbert R. *Alger: A Biography without a Hero.* New York, 1928.

Moon, Michael. " 'The Gentle Boy from the Dangerous Classes': Pederasty, Domesticity, and Capitalism in Horatio Alger." *Representations* 19 (Summer 1987): 95–97.

Nackenoff, Carol. *The Fictional Republic: Horatio Alger and American Political Discourse.* New York, 1994.

Scharnhorst, Gary, and Jack Bales. *Horatio Alger Jr.: An Annotated Bibliography of Comment and Criticism.* Metuchen, N.J., 1981.

Scharnhorst, Gary, and Jack Bales. *The Lost Life of Horatio Alger Jr.* Bloomington, Ind., 1985.

# ALGONQUIN ROUND TABLE

*by Rob Morris*

The Algonquin Round Table refers to a place, a group, a sensibility, and an era. The place was indeed a round table, near the center and toward the back of the Rose Room in the Algonquin Hotel, on West 44th Street in Manhattan, in New York City. The group was a rotating cast of writers, critics, actors, and hangers-on, most in their twenties and thirties, who for a decade or more met at the table for lunch, sometimes every day. The group's sensibility was witty, urbane, and sophisticated, but also depressive and parochial. The era was the twenties, the decade when America became the center of the world and New York City became the center of America.

## A SEAT AT THE TABLE

The origins of the Round Table, like much of its history, are shrouded in legend. This much is known: on a summer day in 1919, a press agent named John Peter Toohey invited Alexander Woollcott, the drama critic of *The New York Times*, to lunch at the Algonquin. They were or were not joined by Murdock Pemberton, another, more established press agent. Toohey tempted Woollcott with a confection made by the Algonquin's pastry chef—either angel cake or deep-dish apple pie. Toohey's aim was either to encourage Woollcott's interest in a new playwright, Eugene O'Neill, or to satisfy his friend's sweet tooth.

The lunch quickly became a performance, as any gathering with Woollcott eventually did. Woollcott regaled his friends with tales of his time as a war reporter in Paris. Woollcott's blustery, oft-repeated stories, at this or another lunch, led Pemberton and Toohey (or Pemberton and another friend, Bill Murray) to plan a joking luncheon in honor of Woollcott's return from the war. They invited the city's drama critics and editors, a group that numbered in the several dozens and included most of the men and women who would become members of the Round Table.

The luncheon was held in the Algonquin's Pergola Room, at a long table bedecked with a banner mocking Woollcott's service. Guests received a typed agenda that listed twelve speeches, all to be given by Woollcott,

each Woollcott spelled a different way. The tone of the event is hazily recalled by the attendees (affectionate teasing? worshipful tolerance?), but the upshot is clear: the establishment of a daily lunch at the Algonquin. How it was established—who suggested it, who agreed to it—this, too, has been forgotten.

What seems clear is that the principals had no clear sense that they were establishing anything. They simply began to meet every day at one o'clock for lunch—because they worked nearby, because they worked in the same fields (media, public relations, performing arts), because they were young and vaguely ambitious and satisfied with each other's company. They met at first at the long table in the Pergola Room. Soon the hotel's manager, Frank Case, moved them to a round table in the Rose Room, not only because they needed the space, but because their presence drew a crowd. Eventually, Case blocked off the room with a velvet rope to hold back gaping lunch-hour star watchers; by 1928, when the members' achievements had made them famous, Case moved them back to the more private Pergola Room.

Who were they? Even this essential fact has softened with time. Certainly they included Woollcott, Dorothy Parker, Robert Benchley, Robert Sherwood, Marc Connelly, George S. Kaufman, Franklin P. Adams, Heywood Broun, and Harold Ross. Other, less familiar names associated with the group include Deems Taylor, Art Samuels, Toohey, Pemberton and his brother Brock, Murray, Jane Grant, and Ruth Hale. Harpo Marx became a standing member in 1924; Edna Ferber (who won the Pulitzer Prize in 1925 for her novel *So Big*) maintained a tenuous relationship with the group; and Ring Lardner, whom many of the regular members admired greatly, was often linked to the group but spent little time at the table.

## WIT FOR WIT'S SAKE

What did they do? As a group, of course, they ate lunch—a meager lunch at first, when they were relatively poor and unknown. Within a year or two of their first meeting, some of the men formed a poker group that claimed a second-floor room of the hotel on Saturdays and Sundays. The Thanatopsis Poker and Inside Straight Club (called by many other names; *thanatopsis* is Greek for "contemplation of death") drew yet more members, who played with considerable venom for increasingly high stakes. Also, within a year or two of their first meeting, the Round Table began to spend weekday afternoons at the studio of Neysa McMein, a painter who became a favorite of Woollcott's. In the evenings they would find each other at speakeasies like Tony Soma's. In time they would spend weekends together at Woollcott's Vermont retreat or the country estates of friends. They played croquet, charades, and word games. They drank, many of them to excess. They tried and failed to maintain marriages, sometimes to one another.

They also nurtured their careers. When the Round Table began, Franklin P. Adams (known as F.P.A.) was the group's elder statesman at thirty-eight; his column, "The Conning Tower," a miscellany of droll observation, light verse, and mild opinion, had established itself in the *New York Tribune*. "The Conning Tower" would last for three decades, moving first to the *New York World*, then to the *New York Post*. Adams's Saturday column, "The Diary of Our Own Samuel Pepys," became a running tally of the Round Table's activities. For a time F.P.A., Woollcott, and Broun were all writing for the *World* and served as tastemakers for their sizable readership. Woollcott achieved significant fame not only as a literature and drama critic but also as a spokesperson and a radio personality. Broun became increasingly political, and in 1928 he split with the *World* over his columns defending Sacco and Vanzetti, two immigrants accused, on questionable grounds, of murder. In 1933 Broun helped found the American Newspaper Guild.

In 1919 Parker, Benchley, and Sherwood worked for *Vanity Fair*; in 1920 Parker was fired (for writing an unflattering review of a play produced by one of the magazine's advertisers), and Benchley and Sherwood quit in protest. Sherwood became an editor at *Life* (then a humor magazine) and wrote roughly a play per year; Benchley joined him as the magazine's drama critic, and gained renown as a performer, first of comic monologues, then in short comic films. Parker wrote poems, stories, and reviews for *Esquire*, *The New Yorker*, and other magazines; her first collection of poems, *Enough Rope* (1926), became a best-seller.

Kaufman and Connelly collaborated on several successful plays; Kaufman worked with the Marx Brothers on

*The Cocoanuts* (1925) and *Animal Crackers* (1928), wrote *The Royal Family* (1927) with Edna Ferber, and in 1932 won the Pulitzer Prize for *Of Thee I Sing*. Connelly won the Pulitzer in 1930 for *The Green Pastures*. Ross founded *The New Yorker* in 1925, with an editorial board hastily assembled from his Round Table friends. Woollcott and Parker became closely associated with the magazine, Woollcott for his "Shouts and Murmurs" column and Parker for her stories and reviews, but the board made its influence felt mostly in the form of an attitude, an ethos. The promotion of that attitude is the Round Table's real achievement.

What defined the Round Table's ethos? First, a respect for the hard, cold facticity of life and language. The Round Table prized precision and scorned vagueness. They came together in the aftermath of World War I, a time when exalted feeling and soft sentiment seemed a betrayal of what the war had shown. Their conversation was a sport in which the winner showed the sharpest tongue. Their word games were fiercely contested; language mattered to them, not because it transcended the real but because it deflated it. *The New Yorker*'s prospectus promised that the magazine would "hate bunk"; this is a neat crystallization of the Algonquins' pose.

Paired with precision was wit. Although they were given to pranks and puns and verbal nonsense, and though they behaved at times like vaudeville hams, the Round Table's humor was more profound than slapstick. This is not to say that their humor was political or philosophical. The humor of the Round Table stood against many things—dullness, conformity, carelessness with language—but all it stood for, in the end, was itself. It was wit for wit's sake. Its positive function was anesthetic: it allowed the members of the group to think of nothing more than the next punchline.

Precision and wit implied sophistication—the ability to discriminate between fine and false. The Round Table served as a barometer of taste in a time when the cultural atmosphere was chaotic. The decade saw the expansion of radio, the beginning of the Book-of-the-Month Club and the Literary Guild, and the birth of the talking motion picture. New York City saw a surge of theatrical productions on Broadway, a booming newspaper business, and an explosion in advertising. The Round Table sat, quite literally, at the center of this. In their columns and criticism, in their plays and performances, in their stories and humorous essays, they satirized the burgeoning American popular culture—its conformity, its routine, its bloodless love of business.

## DRIFTING AWAY

Such was the public face of the Round Table. Yet each char-acteristic—the razor wit, the cultivated taste—demands closer scrutiny. Much of the Round Table's humor was self-directed. The name they gave themselves soon after they met—the Vicious Circle—was apt: their humor was whip-smart and easily turned against them. Much of their gossip, published or passed along, was about each other. When they reviewed plays or books, they were often reviewing their friends. Often they were kind (they were frequently subject to charges of logrolling); sometimes they were not. Two of the most prominent members, Parker and Benchley, were notorious for their masochistic humor. Parker's poems and stories are colored by self-loathing; the premise of her reviews is typically that her presence is an accident and her qualifications are nil. In his humorous essays and short films, Benchley plays the role of the bewildered duffer, the pale, bumbling modern-day male who would just as soon wake up the next morning in the nineteenth century, when life was so much simpler.

Their taste, too, suffered from parochialism. F.P.A., Broun, and Woollcott—whose reach was enormous, whose columns were read by millions, who were, for at least two decades, as popular and respected as any cultural commentators—cast no shadow on American letters through their opinions. Woollcott and Broun championed F. Scott Fitzgerald and Ernest Hemingway, but as a whole their criticism offered no vision and made no lasting impression. Parker developed an abject admiration for Hemingway, but her most famous review is a one-sentence put-down of A. A. Milne, the author of the Winnie the Pooh stories. As critics, the Algonquins are best known for puncturing middling work for the entertainment of middle-class readers—or for writing about themselves.

As artists, the Algonquins left a meager legacy. Parker and Benchley are the only writers whose work is still in active circulation. Both were acutely conscious of having failed in their artistic ambitions. A selected volume of Benchley's work confirms the narrow scope of his talent; he played one note exceptionally well. Parker's selected work is at once bracing and depressing—we feel the sting of her wit, and then we sense the hollowness of its purpose. Several of Kaufman's plays are routinely revived. Ross's New Yorker is perhaps the Round Table's most enduring contribution to American letters—the magazine itself, but especially the aura around it: the obsessive concern for factual accuracy, the habitual tone of detached wit, the bemused evaluation of literature and the arts.

The Round Table ended in 1932. The members drifted away, as they had drifted together. The Great Depression had taken hold and the Roaring Twenties had come to a crashing end—but some members had drifted long before that. Ross became consumed with his magazine soon after it began. Connelly moved to Hollywood in 1926; around the same time, Sherwood abstained from the table at Ferber's urging. (He was more productive as a result.) Few of the members talked about the group in later years; when they did, their comments tended toward bitterness.

## SOMETHING TO WRITE ABOUT

Today the Algonquin Round Table is used as a romantic term by anyone with literary ambitions and a desire to be surrounded by smart, funny, cultured people. There is something heroic about the Round Table's attempt to survive only on wit in the face of a swarming mass culture. That they were part of this culture—that their work was widely circulated, that their readers were as often middle-class folks aspiring to sophistication as actual sophisticates—dims only slightly the glow of their legend.

The Algonquins were, for a time, as visible as any clutch of Hollywood stars today. One of their legacies is the public memory of an active literary culture—even of writers as celebrities. They were known, talked about, admired, feared. They *mattered*. We know them now because they came of age in a time when the art of fashioning a public self—public relations, advertising, self-promotion—was coming of age. Woollcott, F.P.A., and Benchley, to name three, were genuine literary personalities. As a group, the Round Table wielded tremendous power.

One of their ironies is that they seemed not to know what do with that power. Woollcott often lamented that he could be a great writer if only he had something to write about—a remark that captures perfectly the Round Table's depressive, inward-looking worldview. There was everything to write about in the twenties—sweeping political and social change, radical artistic experimen-tation—but again and again, when they searched for something to write about, the Algonquins simply looked across the lunch table.

The Round Table constitutes not so much a literary movement as a social exemplar. Like the New England transcendentalists of the mid-1800s and the New York Intellectuals of the mid-1900s, they mark a time in American culture when writers and thinkers occupied the public stage. The Round Table would have rolled their eyes at the transcendentalists' fuzzy exaltations, and they would have scoffed at the pretensions of the New York Intellectuals. They rightly belong between these groups. They belong, that is to say, in the middle. They flourished during the birth of the American middle class, which they mocked and served. They wrote in the shadow of the first war fought on a world scale, which signaled the death of one civilization, and during the rise of the world's first mass culture, which signaled the growth of another. They pledged allegiance to neither civilization. They stood in the valley between the two and pledged allegiance to themselves.

[*See also* Parker, Dorothy.]

## FURTHER READING

Benchley, Robert. *The Benchley Roundup*. Chicago, 1983. Slim volume of selected works. Useful introduction to the Round Table's sensibility.

Douglas, Ann. *Terrible Honesty: Mongrel Manhattan in the 1920s*. New York, 1995. Magisterial portrait of "the capital of the twentieth century." Many of the Algonquins play supporting roles.

Drennan, Robert E., ed. *The Algonquin Wits*. New York, 1968. A sampler of humor from around the Table.

Gaines, James R. *Wit's End: Days and Nights of the Algonquin Round Table*. New York, 1977. A critical group biography that attempts to counter the legend. Lavishly illustrated.

Harriman, Margaret Case. *The Vicious Circle: The Story of the Algonquin Round Table*. New York, 1951. A rambling, sunny reminiscence by the daughter of the Algonquin's manager and owner.

Parker, Dorothy. *The Portable Dorothy Parker*. Rev. and enl. ed. New York, 1976. Perennially popular collection of Parker's poems, reviews, and stories. Introduction by Brendan Gill is especially helpful.

# NELSON ALGREN

*by Bill Savage*

Nelson Algren was born Nelson Ahlgren Abraham on 28 March 1909 in Detroit, Michigan, but was raised in Chicago. He died days after his election to the American Academy of Arts and Letters, his fiction out of print and largely forgotten, in Sag Harbor, New York, on 9 May 1981. Profound shifts in American political and literary culture shaped the trajectory of Algren's life and literary career. He was radicalized by the Great Depression and set out, like Mark Twain, Theodore Dreiser, and Walt Whitman before him, to depict America from the point of view of the outsider. His subjects were the disinherited of Texas jail cells; the wanderers of the New Orleans waterfront; and the petty thieves, strong-arm boys, hookers, and cops of Chicago's Polish-American ghetto. Like the modernist writers he admired, Algren wrote and rewrote and rewrote again, trying to create truth and beauty out of the language of shuttered barrooms and backroom card games, police lineups, and Chicago Avenue streetcars. Uniquely among American novelists, Algren melds the political eye of naturalism with the written craft of modernism and the vernacular voice of realism.

Algren was the grandson and namesake of a Swedish convert to Judaism; Algren's father was a machinist, his mother a housewife. He earned a degree in journalism from the University of Illinois in 1931, and as he traveled the country seeking work, his experiences convinced him of the fundamental injustice of capitalism. He returned home and joined Chicago's left-wing intellectual scene along with writers such as James T. Farrell and Richard Wright. Like many struggling artists of the day, he worked various jobs, including one at the Works Progress Administration's Federal Writers' Project. At the start of his career, he dropped the "Abraham" and became Nelson Algren.

## FINDING HIS PLACE
## AND VOICE

His first published short story, "So Help Me," appeared in *Story* magazine in August 1933 and led to a contract for a novel with the Vanguard Press. *Somebody in Boots* depicted the human consequences of the Depression; it was edited in part by Farrell and appeared in 1935. Like most novels, it disappeared without making any impression on critics or readers, much less transforming the American political and economic system. In 1942 his second novel, *Never Come Morning*, had greater success. This work was set in the place that would be most associated with Algren: Chicago's near Northwest Side, centered around the Polish Triangle, the intersection of Division Street and Milwaukee and Ashland Avenues. While Algren found his literary voice here—a heightened and poeticized street talk, the slang of skid row bars, the in-the-know chatter of police stations and poolhalls, the inflection of first- and second-generation immigrants—he also earned the enmity of Chicago's Polish-American powers that be. They thought his depiction of the dehumanizing influences of corruption and the city on Polish immigrants and their children served as Nazi propaganda, and Algren was never highly regarded on his own turf.

After military service in World War II, Algren published his most successful books in quick succession: in 1947 *The Neon Wilderness*, a collection of short stories, and in 1949 his masterpiece, *The Man with the Golden Arm*. This novel—the story of Division Street and the doomed card dealer and morphine addict Frankie Machine, his wife Sophie, and his sidekick Sparrow—won the first National Book Award in 1950 and propelled Algren to the top rank of up-and-coming young writers. (In a letter to Algren, Hemingway said he was better than Faulkner.) In 1951 Algren published *Chicago: City on the Make*, a prose poem which is half love song and half history lesson about the hustlers who built Chicago and run it yet. Algren was relatively prosperous, at the height of his powers, and was involved in a romance with the French existentialist philosopher, novelist, and feminist Simone de Beauvoir, whom he had met in 1947.

## NEW RULES OF THE LITERARY GAME

But American literary culture had already begun to change, as the Red Scare of the postwar years festered and

Nelson Algren. (*Courtesy of the Library of Congress*)

the McCarthyism of the 1950s bloomed. The political climate and the expansion of the university system created a new class of literary tastemakers, academics heavily influenced by various types of formalism. These canon makers did not merely emphasize formal qualities over content; they rejected any work that—as far as they were concerned—focused on a particular political situation rather than timeless or universal human nature. They defined work with political concerns, however well written, as not really Literature with a capital "L." Form had, it seemed, triumphed over content.

It would be more productive, however, to understand this conflict by focusing on what critics and writers considered proper literary subject matter. Those novelists canonized by the same critics who downgraded Algren wrote about themselves. Their protagonists were academics, writers, or intellectuals struggling to live well in contemporary American culture. Algren's continued insistence that people who did not read—much less write—were worthy subjects of novels and stories and poems reached back beyond naturalism to the roots of realism, to the essential democratic notion that everyone, regardless of social position, is worthy of art. Algren never wrote fiction about himself. With clear-eyed compassion, humor, and humanity, he wrote of people limited—if not destroyed—by the American class structure and the material reality of their urban situation. In a prosperous

postwar America, such an emphasis on the alienated and dehumanized had few fans.

In 1956, *A Walk on the Wild Side*, the last Algren novel published in his lifetime, appeared. In reviews published in prominent journals, famous critics dismissed Algren as someone living in the past, a purveyor of voyeuristic pulp fiction obsessed with the Depression, out of touch with his times, and so beneath the attention of the serious reader. The bitter irony of this attack is that *Wild Side* was a revision of *Somebody in Boots*, a revision crafted especially for Eisenhower's America. When contracted to do a quick revision of his long-forgotten first novel for the paperback trade, Algren reread it and saw that his tone of humorless leftist outrage would no longer work—not because the politics were wrong, but because Algren believed that an audience for such political art had disappeared. Like writers such as Joseph Heller and Kurt Vonnegut, Algren saw satire as the only way to address this new America, and so while keeping some of the characters and settings, he transformed his first book into a comic fable about the American Dream of upward class mobility, set largely in the bars and brothels of New Orleans. There Dove Linkhorn strives for success—by trying to learn how to read.

## ON THE SKIDS

The process by which a writer like Algren goes from next-big-thing to would-be-has-been extends beyond the opinions of literary critics to wider aspects of literary culture and the writer's own actions. The historical moment of Algren's exile from the realm of serious literature coincided with the rise of the paperback. Such commercial and material aspects of the world of books often go overlooked, but in Algren's case it is clear that the way his works were packaged and sold to readers unfamiliar with him reinforced the critics' negative judgment. Just as the critics were dismissing him as a pop writer, his fiction was reissued in paperbacks, which confirmed this impression. Lurid cover art and sensationalistic blurbs cast Algren's work as though it were urban exposé or juvenile delinquent fiction. Film versions of his novels had the same lowbrow labeling.

Algren also contributed to some degree to his own critical fate by seeming to accept it. His critics dismissed him as a clown, and he wrote hilarious satirical essays in which he gave them comic nicknames and mocked their pretensions. His own feeling that his audience no longer existed led him to surrender rather than to soldier on, and without the steady publication of new work that marks the career of most successful novelists, he faded into the past to which his critics had relegated him.

Algren's personal life and career would never recover. The State Department, considering him a security risk, would not issue him a passport to visit de Beauvoir in Paris, and their relationship eventually ended badly. A habitual gambler, his financial situation was never stable, and he could not get an advance on a book contract to write another big novel. So he made a living with journalism and book reviewing. He published several collections of miscellaneous prose, poetry, and travel writing in the 1960s and 1970s. But his final attempt at a novel, one that told the story of Rubin "Hurricane" Carter, remained unpublished at his death. It first appeared posthumously in German translation as *Calhoun* in 1981 and only in 1983 did it appear in English as *The Devil's Stocking*.

## REVIVAL

Developments since Algren's death suggest that he had an audience all along, as accomplished novelists such as Russell Banks credit Algren with showing them that they could write novels about people who do not attend universities. Publishers have gotten his work back in print. Other artists have produced work dramatizing his life or adapting his prose for the stage and television. American literary culture has shifted again, returning to the concerns of class, race, ethnicity, and gender which Algren grappled with throughout his career. New generations of scholars and critics have begun the process of having conferences and writing articles and books about Algren, the things that surround the creative work of any great writer. Yet the contradictions and irony that marked Algren's career continue. When the city of Chicago changed the name of West Evergreen Street, where he lived for many years, to Nelson Algren Avenue, the neighbors complained about the trouble involved. The city changed the name back and put up honorary street signs—which keep getting stolen. Then in 1999, the city dedicated the Nelson Algren Fountain at the intersection of Milwaukee, Division, and Ashland, so that now the successors to the jackrollers and neighborhood toughs whom Algren depicted with such accuracy, humanity, and humor sit on the edge of the fountain, cooling off on hot summer nights.

[*See also* Naturalism and Realism *and* Proletarian Literature.]

### SELECTED WORKS

*Somebody in Boots* (1935)
*Never Come Morning* (1942)
*The Neon Wilderness* (1947)
*The Man with the Golden Arm* (1949)
*Chicago: City on the Make* (1951)
*A Walk on the Wild Side* (1956)
*Nelson Algren's Book of Lonesome Monsters* (1962)
*Who Lost an American?* (1963)
*Conversations with Nelson Algren* (1964)
*Notes from a Sea Voyage: Hemingway All the Way* (1965)
*The Last Carousel* (1973)
*The Devil's Stocking* (1983)
*The Texas Stories of Nelson Algren* (1995)
*Nonconformity: Writing on Writing* (1996)

### FURTHER READING

Cappetti, Carla. *Writing Chicago: Modernism, Ethnography, and the Novel.* New York, 1993. Examines the relationship between the Chicago school of sociology and the sociological methods of Algren and other Chicago novelists.

Drew, Bettina. *Nelson Algren: A Life on the Wild Side.* New York, 1989. The definitive biography.

Giles, James R. *Confronting the Horror: The Novels of Nelson Algren.* Kent, Ohio, 1989. First full-length book on Algren's fiction. Giles argues that Algren melds existentialism with naturalism.

Rotella, Carlo. *October Cities: The Redevelopment of Urban Literature.* Berkeley, Calif., 1996. Examines Algren and other writers in Chicago, Philadelphia, and New York City as they grapple with the transformation from industrial to postindustrial America.

# JULIA ALVAREZ

*by Kathrine Varnes*

---

Julia Alvarez, born in New York City on 27 March 1950, lived in the Dominican Republic until 1960, when her family sought political refuge in the United States. The shock of being transplanted from a tropical paradise amidst an extended and well-respected family to Queens, New York, where she and her family—mother, father, and three sisters—were viewed as outsiders, informs much of her writing. Often her work is autobiographical, but even when not, her characters are caught between worlds: cultural, lingual, economic, national, political, and familial. Equally essential to her work is the experience of what it means to be a writer. The author of eleven books, Alvarez has proved herself a

Julia Alvarez.
*(Photograph by Bill Eichner)*

talented and flexible writer and has won many prizes and awards, including a fellowship from the National Endowment for the Arts and a Josephine Miles/PEN award. She was also a finalist for the National Book Award. Alvarez lives in Vermont and the Dominican Republic, where she visits relatives and tends the shade-grown coffee farm she started with her husband, Bill Eichner, a cookbook author and ophthalmologist.

## EARLY WRITINGS

Most readers know Alvarez mainly as a novelist, but her first publications were poems that garnered a dedicated group of readers. Her first widely available book, *Homecoming*, was published in 1984, when Alvarez was thirty-four years old, after many years of writing and itinerant teaching. *Homecoming*'s title poem, the first in the collection, describes a trip to the Dominican Republic for a cousin's wedding. While an uncle exclaims "*all this is yours!*," the poem's narrator realizes how this opulent wedding and lifestyle are built on the backs

of the many servants, a moral and social price she is unwilling to pay. Like an inoculation against nostalgia, this poem sets up for difficult balancing in the rest of the poems as they explore both the good and bad of life's choices. The first section, the housekeeping poems, depicts a strict mother and precocious child negotiating their relationship through household chores such as sewing, cleaning, cooking, and folding clothes. "Dusting," for instance, describes the mother erasing the daughter's fingerprints with her polishing flannel, but the daughter "refus[ing] with every mark/to be like her, anonymous." Other poems, such as the intricate villanelle "Women's Work" (added to the 1996 revision), assert that housework can be an art not unlike writing, which she describes as "housekeeping paper." The most dramatic achievement of *Homecoming* is "33," a series of forty-six sonnets turning around the speaker's thirty-third birthday. The poems explore her worries about lasting romantic love, growing old, achievement in writing, and political corruption while they employ fun technical experiments: a primer; a sonnet that uses all *w*-words for rhymes; mini narratives about her parents or the UPS man; a sonnet in He/She dialogue; and several lists and phrases reminiscent of the celebrated nineteenth-century American poet Walt Whitman.

Seven years after *Homecoming*, having landed a tenure-track position at Middlebury College in Vermont and having met her husband, Alvarez published her first celebrated novel, *How the García Girls Lost Their Accents* (1991). While mirroring some of her family's difficult experience fleeing with four daughters from the Dominican Republic to the United States, the novel reveals Alvarez's enduring penchant for narrative experimentation by moving backward in time, from the

United States in 1972 to the Dominican Republic in 1956. The effect is of falling deeper into memory, especially since each chapter takes the point of view of a different character. For the Garcia girls, the past contains not only the usual generational conflicts but also the clash between the expectations of a traditional Dominican culture and the allure of 1960s liberation in the United States.

Alvarez's second novel, *In the Time of the Butterflies* (1994), is based on the true story of the Mirabal sisters, also called *las Mariposas*, the butterflies. While traveling to visit their husbands imprisoned for resisting Rafael Trujillo (the same dictator against whom Alvarez's own father struggled), three of the four sisters were murdered—just months after Alvarez's family moved to New York. Alvarez was able to interview the eldest and survivor, Dedé, in 1992 in the Dominican Republic. As Alvarez explains in her postscript, her novel attempts to find a middle ground between facts and legends, so that her readers can celebrate the courage of the sisters as fully imagined, real people. Perhaps because these sisters' stories represent what might have happened in her own life, Alvarez portrays the emotional states of these national heroines with remarkable clarity, showing, among other things, how personal decisions about whom to love have political ramifications. Particularly poignant are the journal entries of María Terésa, which move from a childlike drawing of new shoes and a list of birthday gifts, to diagrams of how to build a bomb, then a drawing of her sister Minerva's meager home and a detached narrative of her brutal interrogation with names blacked out. Each sister has chapters in her own voice, and the novel is framed by Dedé's shuttling between 1994 and her haunting past.

*The Other Side/El Otro Lado* (1995), Alvarez's second collection of poems, is even more concerned with feeling suspended between two cultures, two nations, two languages, and the two selves of the past and the present. Rather than fight it, however, this collection embraces both positions, as its self-translated title suggests. While she revisits the style of domestic poems so successful in *Homecoming*, the innovations of *The Other Side* lie in the long title poem narrating her return to the Dominican Republic. Unsure of the direction her life had taken, and with the racist taunts of the Queens playground still echoing in her adult ears, the speaker "mounted a silver Pegasus and headed south to the island." Illustrating her continued sense of suspension is her accompanying North American boyfriend-masquerading-as-husband, Mike, who serves to dramatize the cliché "you can never go home again." Despite frustrations and difficulties, the trip confirms the importance of words and writing to her happiness.

## OTHER PUBLICATIONS

Alvarez reaches a new level of experimentation in her third novel, *Yo!* (1997). It is cast in voices of characters from *How the García Girls Lost Their Accents* except for Yo, a novelist whose "real life" family is not particularly pleased with the way their stories have been told. (Yo is short for Yolanda but is also Spanish for "I".) Although we might understand *Yo!* as the author's attempt to appease her disgruntled family, the novel achieves a much wider scope. Instead of reading the narrative from the first-person point of view (often erroneously) assumed to be the novelist's position, we learn of the novelist (the character) through others and their not always sympathetic perspectives: angry sisters (one of whom claims her husband changed after reading his depiction), a cousin and maid's daughter (both hurt by Yo's childhood writing—a journal and a school report), a professor, two illiterate workers who ask for her help, and Yolanda's third husband, who initially does not understand her rituals with, for instance, spirit water. As do her poetry collections, the novel ends with an affirmation of writing as a vocation—for Yo, this comes in her father's voice.

Her fourth novel, *In the Name of Salomé* (2000), picks up Alvarez's persistent themes: the importance of individual choices in the making of history, family strife and reconciliation, the crucial values of language, literacy, and storytelling, and, of course, the perennial searches for meaning and romantic love. Like her second novel, *In the Name of Salomé* is based on historical people, particularly the poet Salomé Ureña (1850–1897)—a woman whose early patriotic poems made her the Dominican Republic's national heroine—and her daughter, Camila, depicted by Alvarez as a shy and intelligent woman devoted to her family, to her work as a language professor, and to her privacy. The novel begins with Camila's third-person point of view, in 1960, as she retires and leaves Poughkeepsie, New York, after years of teaching; then comes Salomé's first-person voice describing her birth into a country fraught with revolutions, "eleven changes of government" during her first six years. As Camila's story travels backward in time, her mother's moves forward, alternating chapters until they meet in Salomé dying in childbirth. Finally, the epilogue brings Camila back to Santo Domingo in 1973, after thirteen years of revolutionary work in Cuba.

Alvarez puts her writing where her heart is. One sees this in her recent publications for younger readers—*The*

Secret Footprints (2000) for ages four to eight, *How
Tía Lola Came to Stay* (2001) for ages nine to twelve,
and *Before We Were Free* (2002) for ages thirteen and
up—and in *A Cafecito Story* (2001), a short narrative
about growing ecologically and socially responsible coffee.
In *Something to Declare* (1998), a book of autobiographical
essays, Alvarez describes herself as a "synthesizing
consciousness." Nervous about labels like "Latina writer"
that might limit her audience, she is committed to bringing
cultures together and eschewing old stories that no longer
work for contemporary life. For Alvarez, this synthesis
and revolution come through the transformational power
of the written and spoken word.

[*See also* Latino/Latina Fiction in America.]

## WORKS

*The Housekeeping Book* (1984)
*Homecoming* (1984, revised 1996)
*How the García Girls Lost Their Accents* (1991)
*In the Time of the Butterflies* (1994)
*The Other Side/El Otro Lado* (1995)
*Yo!* (1997)
*Something to Declare* (1998)
*The Secret Footprints* (2000)
*In the Name of Salomé* (2000)
*How Tía Lola Came to Stay* (2001)
*A Cafecito Story* (2001)
*Before We Were Free* (2002)

## FURTHER READING

Bing, Jonathan. "Julia Alvarez: Books That Cross
Borders." *Publishers Weekly* 241:51 (December 1996):
38–39. This brief interview offers a good picture of the
author in her early years and her sense of the writing
world.

García-Tabor, María, and Silvio Sirias. "The Truth
According to Your Characters: An Interview with
Julia Alvarez." *Prairie Schooner* 74:2 (Summer 2000):
151–156. A conversation with college students from
a Latino literature course covers some of Alvarez's
thoughts about her works and writing in general.

Sirias, Silvio. *Julia Alvarez: A Critical Companion.*
Westport, Conn., 2001. The only book-length study of
Julia Alvarez, this resource includes a helpful overview
of the author's life and the Latino novel and a chapter
devoted to each novel.

# A. R. AMMONS

*by Aaron K. DiFranco*

One of the most prolific poets of the late twentieth century, A. R. Ammons generated a poetic style versatile enough to handle hard, controlled lyrics as well as more expansive, contemplative meditations in his long poems. Although most often placed in an American tradition from Emily Dickinson, Walt Whitman, and Ralph Waldo Emerson through Wallace Stevens, his innovative voice perhaps best supports his proposition that he had been influenced by "everyone." In one of his few poetic statements, "A Poem Is a Walk," he indicates a debt to Samuel Coleridge's "secondary imagination," Lao-tzu's Taoist configurations, as well as his own frequent walks, each of which served as a model for encountering the contradictions of the world's shifting details. Often associated with the poet John Ashbery for the way his reflexive verse presents the motions of mind, Ammons's attention to the details of nature encountered on his excursions also invites comparison to poets Robert Frost and Gary Snyder. Restless and circumspect, believing more in process than pattern, Ammons produced more than twenty volumes of poetry over his celebrated career.

### EARLY YEARS AND *OMMATEUM*

Born Archibald Randolph Ammons on 18 February 1926, in a farmhouse outside Whiteville, North Carolina, Ammons spent his early years in a South burdened by the Great Depression. Although the Ammons family farm provided enough to live and barter with, the family struggled continually against debt as well as the contingencies of land, weather, and daily survival. This rural backdrop against which Ammons and two older sisters lived—another sister and two younger brothers died as infants—directs many of his lyrics toward the pastoral, but the bleaker years of struggle also give his poems a sometimes stark, unsentimental edge that does away with simple idyllic notions.

After graduating from high school, Ammons worked in a shipyard before joining the U.S. Navy in 1944. He spent nineteen months in the service, most of them working as a sonar operator with a destroyer escort in the South Pacific. Upon his release from the navy, he used the GI Bill to attend Wake Forest University and earn a general science degree. There he also met Phyllis Plumbo, his Spanish instructor, whom he married in 1949. For a year he worked as principal of a small elementary school in Cape Hatteras, North Carolina, before enrolling at the University of California, Berkeley. He stayed only three semesters, enough time to complete an English degree and some graduate work before moving to New Jersey in 1952. He lived there for the next twelve years, working mostly in sales for the biological glass-manufacturing firm owned by his father-in-law.

Ammons began writing in the South Pacific when he found a poetry anthology aboard his ship and attempted his own experiments. Already becoming removed from the content, if not the spiritual passion, of his southern Pentecostal and Baptist roots, he turned to poetry to provide him a way to engage with and articulate a world ungoverned by a god yet no less astonishing in its dynamic processes. Like his contemporaries, he had to contend with the modern crisis of faith that led to T. S. Eliot's *The Waste Land*, and his early work confronted the isolation of the individual in the universe, turning frequently to the natural world as a source of support. Often the poems—especially those with his "Ezra" persona—were dramatic monologues that attempted to protect the poet from the disorientations of existence but contained a somber recognition of the temporary and often destructive aspects of these attempts. The publication of these early poems has developed its own legend: appearing in 1955 as *Ommateum: With Doxology* through the vanity press Dorrance, the book sold only sixteen of the one hundred volumes bound. His father-in-law later bought forty copies, sending them to acquaintances in South America; Ammons bought thirty of the remaindered copies himself. Nine years of struggle without an audience followed before Ammons's next book appeared.

### ITHACA AND A POETRY OF SHIFTING GROUNDS

With the favorable critical reception of *Expressions of Sea Level* (1964), Ammons's fortunes slowly turned. Invited to give a reading at Cornell University in Ithaca, New York, he was asked to join their English department and help run their poetry program. Although suspicious of the institutional arrangement between poets and university writing programs, and as always deprecating of his own ability as a teacher, Ammons nevertheless joined the faculty in 1964 and championed poetry for its own sake, with all the passionate and desperate connotations that involves. Expressing humble bewilderment at times that the university would support his need to write, Ammons, known to everyone as Archie, became a conspicuous campus fixture, always meeting mornings with friends, colleagues, and students in the Temple of Zeus coffeehouse and eventually becoming the Goldwin Smith Professor of Poetry. Two years after he and Phyllis moved to Ithaca, their son, John, was born. And it was here, too, that Ammons would meet the critic Harold Bloom, an early supporter of Ammons's work as well as a good friend.

Over the next decade, Ammons's poetry grew in strength and complexity as he brought out another eight volumes, including *Corsons Inlet* (1965), *Uplands* (1970), and *Briefings* (1971). Bloom's influential praise cast this early poetry into a transcendental tradition, as the poems seek a provisional balance with the natural and contingent details of the speaker's local surroundings. Recalling memories of North Carolina and Ammons's walks along the New Jersey coast, the poems of *Expressions at Sea Level* and *Corsons Inlet*, in particular, reflect a more fluid engagement with the shifting coastal environment. Ammons, like other poets of his generation, concerned himself with establishing a poetic self receptive to the fluctuations of his surrounding world; however, he was also more sensitive than most to the violent mental changes this self often had to accommodate in its perceptions. As unwelcoming as many as these poems were in their dismissal of easy lyric closure and abstract absolutes, they nevertheless provided a conditional firmness for the poet's existential anxiety. Extremely personal, the poems' solitary voice helps avoid the dramatic exposures of the confessional poets and the rant of the Beats, tending toward more reticent, discursive expressions.

The poems of this era also demonstrated a growing control and comfort within the poetic "field" conceptualized by Charles Olson. Responding with ever-greater openness to the world's motions, Ammons refined a signature style marked by enjambment and the use of the colon. Punctuating with the colon not only allowed a more fluid pacing of the poems but also marked the equivalence of the propositions on both sides, an egalitarianism between the parts that make up the whole. In the poems *Uplands* and *Briefings*, he used this technique to concentrate on how the concrete particulars of the world reveal their own small "radiances." Maturing into small praises, the poems still hold their resistance to absolute radiance and gesture back to the passing world, for the comfort of an ideal beauty nevertheless brings limits and the fear of annihilation. Spare before, the verse now turned with clearer precision into complexity, showing a mind actively engaged in encountering and structuring the universe. These early lyrics, gathered with others in *Collected Poems: 1951–1971* (1972), helped establish Ammons as a major American poet.

## LONG POEMS AND LYRIC NATURE

Even as he was cultivating his lyric, Ammons was experimenting with longer forms. *Tape for the Turn of the Year* (1965) inaugurated his use of adding machine tape to type his poems (Ammons wrote using an Underwood standard upright, manual typewriter). The tape provided new formal possibilities for the poet: its length encouraged a downward motion for the poem, while its narrow margins structured how the lines would break for emphasis. Strewn with the details of dailiness from 6 December 1963 through 10 January 1964—his labor at the typewriter, job worries, Christmas gifts from Phyllis—*Tape* tested the poet's ability to improvise extended meditations and explore the limits of freedom within an arbitrary, imposed form. The follow-up to this test was the tour de force *Sphere: The Form of a Motion* (1974), a single, flamboyant sentence of 155 sections each made up of four three-line stanzas typed, again, on adding machine tape. Deftly employing his trademark colons to find rhythm for his lines between the tape's margins, Ammons took the image of the whole earth—like that just recently seen from space—as an image of the times that could uphold movement and multiplicity. With its publication, Ammons received the Bollingen Prize in 1975.

Never satisfied with his own products, Ammons continued his explorations, probing the limits of language's ability to establish congruence with the world. Nothing was beneath consideration, though the backyard ecology out his window was a primary source. Often noted for his work's inclusion of contemporary scientific ideas, Ammons would perhaps consider this inclusion more a matter of finding an adequate diction. Poems like those in *Diversifications* (1975) confronted language's inability to represent reality completely, yet they were nevertheless able to use language's ambiguities to assert the poem's real ability to turn us both toward *and* away from the world. This was followed with *The Snow Poems* (1977), a long poem sequence, which asserted with self-conscious irritability that everything could be turned into poetry, including store receipts, weather reports, and word games. Strenuous in its critical resistance to lyric modes, Ammons's accumulations here attempted to express the inexhaustible variety of the inexpressible.

Although still prone to occasional explosive lyrics, Ammons's next volumes became more attuned to slower, simpler motions and experiences. Poems touched with Taoist diction are collected within *A Coast of Trees* (1981), *Worldly Hopes* (1982), and *Lake Effect Country* (1983), as the poet now turned more calmly to particulars and how they unwind their own small, unexpected becomings. Resisting romantic impulses by looking for the way plain thought and feeling were configured by a nonverbal world, his naturalistic observations take on metaphysical implication: a miscellany of birds, bushes, brooks, as well as an illustrative "Shit List," become material evidence for the immaterial and spiritual. Consideration of nature and ecological systems remains a continuous element of his work, especially as he attempted to set his concrete, individual experiences in the context of an expansive universe. Often listening for the hum of the world's constant motion, he is never indolent, feeling his way between the general and the specific in his praises.

Ammons will probably be best remembered, however, for his continued mastery of the long poem, including two volumes brought out in the last decade of his career. The audaciously titled *Garbage* (1993) focused on the processes of the world that—as the poet does with language—break down material and prepare its energies for further transmissions. Inspired by a mound of garbage he saw in Florida off Interstate 95, the poem's couplets irreverently trace the resemblances between the high and the low, the sacred and the profane. Acknowledging how the ideal and the material mix in our experiences of life, the poem nevertheless drives toward a contact with the real world that is both reasonable and palpable. *Glare* (1997) balances this with a sharp meditation on the airy and transient, trying to catch the least things in its dispersing grasp. Bawdy and reverent, laconic yet garrulous, "Glare" follows the other long poems in presenting the absurd pathos of existence while demonstrating how Ammons used poetry to make for himself a way to live life.

With his wife, Ammons maintained his hermitage in Ithaca throughout his career, writing, teaching, and painting expressionist watercolors. Even after he retired from active service at Cornell in 1998, he still continued his ritual morning coffee at the Temple of Zeus. Although he had suffered from various ailments through his life, he remained inexhaustibly active. Unapologetically dedicated to the poem, Ammons produced only one slim but significant collection of prose. *Set in Motion: Essays, Interviews, and Dialogues* (1996) reveals how the tension between the one and the many, the center and the periphery, unity and diversity—as well as the problem of how to engage this tension without limiting possibility—remained a lifelong theme of his work. Ammons's poems glide between these extremes with sophistication, wit, and sensitivity to the world beyond statement, clinging to something sufficient for a life always headed toward death. Numerous honors have been awarded him for his work, including two National Book Awards, the Robert Frost Medal from the Academy of American Poets, and a MacArthur Prize. He died in his home on 25 February 2001.

[*See also* Long Poem, The, *and* Nature Writing: Poetry.]

## WORKS

*Ommateum: With Doxology* (1955)
*Expressions of Sea Level* (1964)
*Corsons Inlet* (1965)
*Tape for the Turn of the Year* (1965)
*Northfield Poems* (1966)
*Selected Poems* (1968)
*Uplands* (1970)
*Briefings* (1971)
*Collected Poems: 1951–1971* (1972)
*Sphere: The Form of a Motion* (1974)
*Diversifications* (1975)
*The Snow Poems* (1977)
*Highgate Road* (1977)
*The Selected Poems: 1951–1977* (1977)
*Selected Longer Poems* (1980)
*A Coast of Trees* (1981)
*Worldly Hopes* (1982)
*Lake Effect Country* (1983)
*The Selected Poems: Expanded Edition* (1983)
*Sumerian Vistas* (1987)
*The Really Short Poems* (1990)
*Garbage* (1993)
*Brink Road* (1996)
*Set in Motion: Essays, Interviews, and Dialogues* (1996)
*Glare* (1997)

## FURTHER READING

"A. R. Ammons." Special issue of *Diacritics: A Review of Contemporary Criticism* III, no. 4 (1973). Edited by David I. Grossvogel. Contains poetry and excellent essays dealing with Ammons's early lyrics.

Bloom, Harold, ed. *A. R. Ammons.* New York, 1986. A strong collection of critical essays.

Bloom, Harold. *Ringers in the Tower: Studies in the Romantic Tradition.* Chicago, 1971. Although it deals with numerous contemporary poets, this text provides an extensive reading of Ammons's work and argues for his place in a transcendental tradition.

Gilbert, Roger. *Walks in the World: Representation and Experience in Modern American Poetry.* Princeton, N.J., 1991. Although this work deals with numerous twentieth-century poets, Ammons provides a critical frame for Gilbert's analysis of poetic "walks."

Holder, Alan. *A. R. Ammons.* Boston, 1979. Offers solid analysis, especially for the poetry through the 1970s.

Kirschten, Robert, ed. *Critical Essays on A. R. Ammons.* New York, 1997. Offers new critical perspectives and engages the more recent developments in his poetry.

Schneider, Steven P. *A. R. Ammons and the Poetics of Widening Scope.* Rutherford, N.J., 1994.

Schneider, Steven P., ed. *Complexities of Motion: New Essays on A. R. Ammons's Long Poems.* Madison, N.J., 1999. A comprehensive selection of essays addressing Ammons's engagement with the long-poem form.

Scigaj, Leonard M. *Sustainable Poetry: Four American Ecopoets.* Lexington, Ky., 1999. An academic study, this text analyzes Ammons's poetry from an "ecocritical" perspective.

"The Work of A. R. Ammons." Special issue of *Pembroke Magazine.* No. 18 (1986). Edited by Shelby Stephenson. Essays on, personal accounts of, and poems by and for Ammons. Containing an extensive range of submissions, the issue is a good source of criticism for Ammons's middle career.

# SHERWOOD ANDERSON

*by Nancy Bunge*

On 13 September 1876 in Camden, Ohio, Sherwood Anderson, the third of seven children, was born to Irwin McLain Anderson and Emma Smith Anderson. Irwin Anderson struggled to support his large family by making harnesses as industrialization rendered his craft increasingly obsolete. His search for employment eventually took the Andersons to Clyde, Ohio, where Sherwood worked hard at a variety of jobs to compensate for his father's tendency to simply disappear, sometimes for weeks. Sherwood brought great energy to his entrepreneurial efforts, whether as a stable hand, a bicycle factory worker, or a newsboy. For instance, when a train stopped at Clyde, he hopped on, sold papers to passengers, and jumped off just before it continued its journey. The admiring townspeople nicknamed Sherwood "Jobby." At age nineteen, after his mother's death, Anderson's ambition led him to Chicago, but he found only menial work there. So when the Spanish-American War broke out in 1898, he enlisted in the Ohio National Guard and discovered that he relished the camaraderie of army life.

Sherwood Anderson. (*Photograph by Carl Van Vechten. Courtesy of the Library of Congress*)

After leaving the service, he briefly attended Wittenburg Academy (1899–1900) in Springfield, Ohio, his only successful school experience. Still, his hunger for money and status drew him back to Chicago. There, he began a successful career in advertising at the Long-Critchfield Agency, married Cornelia Lane, and started a family. The Andersons settled in Elyria, Ohio, where he founded and became president of the American Merchants Company. In a room set aside for him at home, Anderson began writing because he believed it allowed him to discover and articulate the truth. Since he drafted fiction that used events from his life, he apparently hoped that through his imagination he could understand and reevaluate his choices. First, he wrote *Windy McPherson's Son* (1916), a book centering on a young man named Sam McPherson who leaves his hometown for Chicago, where he makes money and marries but fails to find happiness. After going out on the road to explore his options, Sam returns to his wife, Sue, so they can rebuild their marriage. Next, Anderson drafted *Marching Men* (1917), a book celebrating the unity with others he had enjoyed in the service. Sitting in his room writing, Anderson apparently discovered the limits of the conventional achievement he had so passionately sought.

Meanwhile, Anderson still tried to meet his obligations until, on 28 November 1912, he said something to his secretary about wet feet and the river outside his window, left his office, and disappeared for four days. He reappeared in Cleveland, filthy and uncertain of his identity. Eventually, he remembered who he was, but his scattered recollections of what happened during his disappearance and the baffling notes he wrote and mailed to his wife while he was gone supply only tantalizing hints of how he spent his time. Still, the significance of his amnesia seems clear: Anderson had to change his life so that it coordinated more completely with his values. So his Ohio business was sold, and in February 1913 he returned to the renamed Taylor-Critchfield advertising agency in Chicago, where his family joined him. Through his brother Karl, a painter, he met other artists and, for one of the few times in his life, he felt accepted by a group of like-minded people. After retreating to an Ozark hunting lodge in late 1913, he and his wife concluded after a few months that their marriage should end, and Anderson was left on his own in Chicago with the new knowledge that writing had to play a central role in his life.

## WINESBURG, OHIO AND OTHER SHORT STORIES

Karl Anderson introduced Sherwood to Gertrude Stein's *Tender Buttons* (1915), a work that expanded his sense of writing's possibilities. One night in 1915 he used what he had learned from Stein to write a story called "Hands," about a schoolteacher named Wing Biddlebaum who is forced into isolation by false charges of child abuse. When Anderson finished this tale, his elation drove him out to walk the Chicago streets. His rereading of the story after he returned home confirmed his sense that he had written something fine. Most readers and critics who have encountered "Hands" in the decades since would agree. It stands at the beginning in *Winesburg, Ohio* (1919), a collection of short stories subtitled *The Book of the Grotesque: A Group of Tales of Ohio Small Town Life*, held together by its narrator, its characters' shared isolation, and the empathy of the book's main character, a young man named George Willard learning about life in a small town. Anderson saw a similarity between the book's structure and that of Ivan Turgenev's *Sportsman's Sketches* (1852), but finally considered it his own invention.

In *Winesburg, Ohio*, George's tolerance for and curiosity about people who seem to have failed—"twisted apples"—encourage many of them to share their stories with him. Talking with George, they briefly transcend their isolation. Anderson's book displays the hidden depths of ordinary lives, showing how a mother's reprimands cloak her intense love and hope for her child, how a businessman's religious fervor can drive him to ruthlessness, and how the young man who flits from one job to the next enjoys a rich fantasy life.

Anderson claimed that his affection for his mother explained his lifelong empathy with "thwarted lives." This sympathy achieves its most compelling realization in *Winesburg, Ohio* and in short stories such as "I Want to Know Why," "The Man Who Became a Woman," "The Triumph of the Egg," and "Death in the Woods," where Anderson attends to people theretofore ignored in literature, especially children and women, and using simple language, offers lyrical renditions of their lives. Anderson greatly admired the American poet, Walt Whitman, but when he tried to articulate his sympathy with others, as Whitman did, in poetry (*Mid-American Chants*, 1918), he failed utterly. In his stories, particularly those collected in *Winesburg, Ohio*, Anderson gets it right, producing work rich in imagery, complexity, and most important to Anderson, emotional resonance.

Anderson declared it essential for writers to face and describe the commonplace. He argued that the rocky ground in New England encouraged its authors to flee both natural and human reality and urged midwestern writers to continue the tradition Mark Twain started with *The Adventures of Huckleberry Finn* (1884) of making compelling literature from ordinary speech, people, and dilemmas. So when Hart Crane claimed that *Winesburg, Ohio* offered crucial insight into America's psyche, Anderson did not dispute this characterization. Nor did he apologize when critics complained that his characters had sex lives. Instead, he repeatedly allied himself with Theodore Dreiser, another midwestern writer whose book *Sister Carrie* (1900) had also provoked outrage by acknowledging sexuality's power.

## ANDERSON'S MARRIAGES AND MARRIAGE NOVELS

Anderson married Tennessee Mitchell, an artistic woman who enjoyed spicing up his dress, four days after his divorce to Cornelia was final in July 1916. He believed that Tennessee's independence would allow the marriage to nourish rather than impede his work, but to protect himself from intrusion, he and Tennessee had separate residences. Still, even his limited interactions with Tennessee made him uncomfortable, he complained in letters to Marietta Finley, a woman to whom he wrote from 1916 until 1933 after informing her that she would serve as his muse but should expect no more from him. Appropriately, Anderson began a series of novels about men struggling to establish good relationships with women, titled *Poor White* (1920), *Many Marriages* (1923), and *Dark Laughter* (1925).

In *Poor White*, Hugh McVey—a loner urged to resist his imaginative tendencies by Sarah Shepherd, the flinty New Englander who raised him—finds himself irresistibly drawn to fantasy. As a result, he imagines that a corn-planting machine could release the farm workers from the task that forces them into grotesque shapes. Hugh wins financial backing, makes the device, and becomes wealthy as mechanization spreads. Hugh's integrity and reliability attract Clara Butterworth, the daughter of the wealthiest man in town. But unable to forget Sarah Shepard's admonition that he is "white trash," Hugh struggles to find the courage to consummate their marriage. Although Clara helps him discover the naturalness of making love, after three years she still does not know him. As the novel ends they go into the house together, leaving the reader hopeful but uncertain that they will establish a genuine bond.

After drafting this book, Anderson felt that both his marriage and his writing were flagging. In 1920 he fled to Mobile, Alabama, where he lived alone, revised *Poor White*, wrote stories, painted, and sculpted, all in an attempt to fully explore himself. He also began his next novel, *Many Marriages*, the story of John Webster, who feels trapped in his marriage but cannot find the courage to leave. Although Anderson allowed Tennessee to join him near the end of this Mobile retreat, his new book did not bode well for their union.

In the fall of 1920, Anderson returned to Chicago and the Taylor-Critchfield advertising agency. In January 1921 he began visiting a group of lively young people at a house called the Domicile. Here, Anderson met the novelist Ernest Hemingway, whose talent he recognized immediately; Anderson urged him to turn away from the nineteenth-century literary models Hemingway favored and write about what he knew. Hemingway listened even though Anderson's openness and vulnerability offended him. On 14 May 1921 Anderson and Tennessee sailed to Europe with Paul Rosenfeld, an editor at an influential magazine called *The Seven Arts*. Anderson wept at the sight of the Louvre, marveled at Chartres, and met James Joyce, Ezra Pound, and Gertrude Stein, whom he told of her enormous influence on him. When he returned to Chicago, Anderson urged Hemingway to go to Paris, giving him letters of introduction to Joyce and Stein.

In January 1922 Anderson again fled to the South, this time to New Orleans; there he frantically resumed writing *Many Marriages*, having John Webster resolve his frustrations with his marriage by leaving his wife and running off with his secretary to an uncertain future. This weak novel seems a virtual confession that Anderson's marriage to Tennessee had failed. In the fall of 1922, he met Elizabeth Prall in New York City and thought that marriage to her might work out well since she combined Cornelia's conventionality with Tennessee's interest in art. Prall and Anderson married after his divorce from Tennessee came through in 1924 and settled in New Orleans, where in November 1924 they welcomed a young writer named William Faulkner. Anderson urged him to stop writing poetry and produce prose about the Mississippi town that nurtured him. In the fall of 1924, Anderson rapidly wrote *Dark Laughter*, another bad, inconclusive novel about marital difficulties. In this book a man named Bruce Dudley leaves his conventional life and marriage to return to the town where he lived as a child. There he falls in love and runs off with a married woman named Aline Grey, who spends her evenings assuming poses in her garden because that gives her an illusion of unity with nature. Hemingway parodied this book in *Torrents of Spring* (1926).

## FINAL NOVELS

In July 1925 the Andersons retreated to the Virginia countryside, where they built a house called Ripshin, but happiness eluded them. Anderson thought that getting out among other people would help, so in 1927 he bought two country newspapers, the *Smyth County News* and the *Marion Democrat*. Anderson wrote whatever his papers required, sometimes in the voice of a folksy character named Buck Fever. In December 1928 Anderson urged Elizabeth to go visit family in California; then, he wrote begging her to stay there. In 1929 he began a understandably pessimistic novel about relationships between men and women called *Beyond Desire* (1932). A smart, lively, socially aware woman named Louise, whom the narrator suspected would make a fine wife if she met a courageous man, sounded the book's only hopeful note. Anderson modeled Louise on Eleanor Copenhaver, his next wife. His prediction proved accurate: not only did his relationship with Eleanor bring him the intimacy he had sought all his life, but—because of her social activism—she also taught him much about the lives of working people. This new knowledge informs *Beyond Desire*, making it a richer book than the marriage novels preceding it.

Anderson's contentment apparently freed his imagination. His final novel, *Kit Brandon* (1936), has a female protagonist and reviews the difficulties of marriage and modern life from her perspective. Perhaps Anderson's detachment from her issues explains why this novel has a sharper plot and livelier characters than his other marriage novels.

Anderson's tendency to put his emotional problems at the center of his books undoubtedly helps explain their vagueness and confusion, but he had too much integrity to pursue any other course, no matter what the aesthetic consequences. From the start, he valued writing principally because it allowed him to face the truth.

## ANDERSON AS SOCIAL COMMENTATOR

Anderson realized early in his career that one cannot separate any individual from his or her culture, so starting with *Poor White*, Anderson interrupts the narrative flow of his novels with lectures about American society. Anderson argues repeatedly that industrialism has separated men and women from themselves and each other and urges his contemporaries to cure themselves by ceasing their frantic, futile attempts to find happiness by dominating their environments and other people. Instead, Anderson recommends a return to nature, community, and intimacy. Although these sociological analyses persist in his novels until the end of his career, he apparently felt he had more to say than these asides would allow, so Anderson wrote nonfiction. He began with *A Story Teller's Story* (1924), a fictionalized version of his evolution as a writer, and continued with *The Modern Writer* (1925), an essay on the writer's obligation to resist corruption by the same forces destroying society at large. Eventually, Anderson wrote social criticism without bothering to link it to his craft, as in his book *Perhaps Women* (1931), where he argues that cooperating with machines has rendered modern men impotent, leaving all hope of salvation with women, whose ability to give birth has kept them tied to nature. Although these books add little to Anderson's literary achievement, they show how strong was his compulsion to speak the truth as he saw it, especially when he thought it could help others through the difficulties that clogged his own life and work.

In *No Swank* (1934), when Anderson talks of storytellers he admires, including Ring Lardner, Theodore Dreiser, D. H. Lawrence, and two unnamed Irishmen, he praises not their artistry but their kindness and passion. One could argue that, despite several excellent short stories that appeared later, Anderson's literary career peaked when he published *Winesburg, Ohio*. But this seems too harsh a judgment for someone who valued writing primarily as a way of helping himself and others live more fully. No matter what its aesthetic value, his later work—fictional and otherwise—reflects intelligently on the emptiness of modern life, the difficulties men and women have working out good relationships, and the role art can play in helping people resolve these problems. Moreover, the same integrity and decency that equipped him to produce moving accounts of overlooked lives also allowed Anderson to make significant contributions to American literature even after his death on 8 March 1941, in the town of Colon in the Panama Canal Zone. For example, Ernest Hemingway and William Faulkner both followed Anderson's advice and example, wrote out of their own experience, and as a result, won the Nobel Prize for literature.

[*See also* Short Story in America, The.]

## SELECTED WORKS

*Windy McPherson's Son* (1916)
*Marching Men* (1917)
*Mid-American Chants* (1918)
*Winesburg, Ohio* (1919)
*Poor White* (1920)
*The Triumph of the Egg* (1921)
*Many Marriages* (1923)
*Horses and Men* (1923)
*A Story Teller's Story* (1924)
*Dark Laughter* (1925)
*The Modern Writer* (1925)
*Sherwood Anderson's Notebook* (1926)
*Tar: A Midwest Childhood* (1926)
*A New Testament* (1927)
*Hello Towns!* (1929)
*Nearer the Grass Roots and Elizabethton* (1929)
*Perhaps Women* (1931)
*Beyond Desire* (1932)
*Death in the Woods and Other Stories* (1933)
*No Swank* (1934)
*Puzzled America* (1935)
*Kit Brandon* (1936)
*Plays: Winesburg and Others* (1937)
*Home Town* (1940)
*Sherwood Anderson's Memoirs* (1942)
*Letters of Sherwood Anderson* (1953)
*Return to Winesburg: Selections from Four Years of Writing for a Country Newspaper* (1967)
*The Buck Fever Papers* (1971)
*Sherwood Anderson/Gertrude Stein* (1972)
*The "Writer's Book" by Sherwood Anderson* (1975)
*France and Sherwood Anderson: Paris Notebook, 1921* (1976)
*Sherwood Anderson: Selected Letters* (1984)
*Letters to Bab: Sherwood Anderson to Marietta Finley, 1916–33* (1985)
*The Sherwood Anderson Diaries 1936–1941* (1987)
*Sherwood Anderson's Love Letters to Eleanor Copenhaver Anderson* (1990)
*Sherwood Anderson's Secret Love Letters: For Eleanor, a Letter a Day* (1991)

## FURTHER READING

Anderson, David. *Sherwood Anderson: An Introduction and Interpretation*. New York, 1967. An insightful and sound introduction to Sherwood Anderson.

Howe, Irving. *Sherwood Anderson*. New York, 1951. The standard literary biography.

Townsend, Kim. *Sherwood Anderson*. Boston, 1987. A critical biography and a fine study.

See also the article on *Winesburg, Ohio*, immediately following.

# SHERWOOD ANDERSON'S
# *WINESBURG, OHIO*

*by Tanya Jarvik*

Legend has it that Sherwood Anderson began writing *Winesburg, Ohio* (1919) in a state of ecstasy; one rainy night in the autumn of 1915, feeling suddenly inspired, he sprang naked from his bed and dashed off the first story, never afterwards changing a word of it. Indeed, Anderson maintained that each of the twenty-two stories in *Winesburg* had been composed quickly, effortlessly, and almost without subsequent revision. Though there are reasons to doubt the accuracy of such a claim, it is true that Anderson had finally found his niche. When he began the tales that would eventually become *Winesburg*, Anderson had already laboriously produced drafts of several novels, but those, he felt, were derivative. This time he would draw his characters from people he observed in a Chicago tenement and construct a new setting for them based on his memories of the small Ohio town where he had grown up. This time he would write out of what he called the "repressed, muddled life" around him. The result would be the greatest achievement of Anderson's career.

Although *Winesburg, Ohio* first appeared in 1919, many of the stories had previously been published piecemeal in literary magazines. The book is neither a novel nor a collection of short stories; perhaps its original subtitle, *A Group of Tales of Ohio Small Town Life*, describes it best. Anderson, however, had wished to call it "The Book of the Grotesque," the title of the first tale in the group. In this story, an old writer dreams that a "young indescribable thing within himself" is "driving a long procession of figures before his eyes." These figures, all "grotesques," eventually make their way into a book, which the story's narrator claims to have seen although it was never published. We are thus implicitly invited to read "The Book of the Grotesque" as a framing device for the remaining *Winesburg* stories, each of which functions much like a character sketch.

## THEMES

Another way to read the book is as a bildungsroman. *Winesburg* charts the growth of one character, George Willard, in particular detail. While many of the characters in *Winesburg* appear in more than one story, George figures in almost all of them. Even when the narrative focus is clearly upon someone else, he often plays the role of listener; as a reporter for the town newspaper, George Willard becomes privy to the secrets and stories of others. The final tale in the book, "Departure," concludes with this young man "going out of his town to meet the adventure of life." We are told that when the train pulls out of the station, Winesburg will become "but a background on which to paint the dreams of his manhood." Anderson himself held that the "central theme" of *Winesburg* "is the making of a man out of the actual stuff of life," but there are other themes that help to make an organic whole out of the many disparate stories.

The most obvious of these recurring themes is encapsulated by a single word: adventure. In fact, this word appears so often that the sight of it can begin to grate upon the reader's nerves. A sentence like, "One evening in July . . . Elizabeth Willard had an adventure" will later be reincarnated several times: "One day in August Doctor Parcival had an adventure," for example, or, "One night when it rained Alice had an adventure." *Winesburg* also accords mantra status to another, related, sentence: "And then something happened." The tales echo one another to such a degree that what began as a theme becomes in the end a veritable obsession, as if the text were compelled to repeat itself. But the sort of thing that qualifies as an event in *Winesburg* might not have registered at all if the narrator of these stories had not seized every opportunity to remind us that any character who thinks a new thought or goes on a walk or feels some vague desire "present in the spirit of the night" is having an adventure. By dint of repetition, then, *Winesburg* suggests that its characters' lives are so prescribed by custom that anything offering even the slightest respite from dull everyday existence will pass as a major event. At the same time, the stories seem to insist that small epiphanies experienced by ordinary people are more worthy of our attention than the most trumped-up adventures could ever be.

## EXPLORING THOUGHT

With *Winesburg*, Anderson was consciously working against a tradition that had been established by writers such as O. Henry (William Sydney Porter), whose short stories were much admired for their ingenious plots. The twists and surprises characteristic of O. Henry's fiction failed to interest Anderson. Convinced that these "poison-plot" tales were nothing but cheap entertainment, he set out to explore the richness of the human psyche instead. Although Anderson had not yet read Sigmund Freud's work, Freudian theories were often discussed in the circles he frequented, and there is some evidence of this influence in the *Winesburg* stories. "Surrender," for example, introduces us to Louise Bentley, a character who "was from childhood a neurotic, one of the race of over-sensitive women that in later days industrialism was to bring in such great numbers into the world." Whether or not Anderson's book owes a debt to Freud's new psychoanalytic method, its focus on the inner lives of its characters makes *Winesburg* an early example of the modern psychological novel.

Kate Swift, the Winesburg schoolteacher, describes Anderson's own philosophy of writing when she tells George Willard, "You must not become a mere peddler of words. The thing to learn is to know what people are thinking about, not what they say." Above all, *Winesburg* is an attempt to get at what people in a small American town might be thinking about. Since in Anderson's estimation the people there typically keep their own counsel, the task is a difficult one. The reader is enlisted as a kind of analyst, asked to pay attention as the stories "express something" for characters who cannot put into words the "vague and intangible hunger" they feel. These people desperately want a real connection, someone who will listen and understand, but they are denied the meaningful interaction they crave. Even though many of the stories explore relationships between characters, each character seems to come to the conclusion that he or she is ultimately alone—that this is the essential human condition. Another theme, then, is loneliness.

## COMMUNICATIONS FAILURE

Nearly everyone in *Winesburg* suffers from the same malady. They may try to communicate their thoughts and feelings to some other character, but no one really listens. Female characters, especially, have trouble making themselves understood. After trying—and failing—to bridge the gap between themselves and others, they retreat back into an isolation made even more desolate by their sense of defeat. Louise Bentley's husband responds to her efforts to communicate by kissing her lips, stopping her speech. She ends by not wanting to be kissed. Elizabeth Willard was once a tall and beautiful girl "forever putting out her hand into the darkness and trying to get hold of some other hand," but not one of her half dozen lovers was the "real lover" she wanted. Because her search for human intimacy has been fruitless, her desires continually thwarted, the middle-aged Elizabeth is now a "drab meaningless figure" incapable of any "expression of joy." Kate Swift pins her hopes on George Willard, an aspiring writer who, she believes, "might possess a talent for the understanding of life." One night she seeks him out and begins talking to him with "passionate earnestness" about life, urging him to "interpret it truly and honestly." Ironically, he mistakes her interest in him for a sexual invitation. Their conversation ends when George takes her into his arms and she, betrayed, begins to "beat on his face" with her fists.

A woman's complex desire for intimacy is misinterpreted as a simple statement of sexual availability, a tragedy that is replayed over and over in *Winesburg*. But the best example of such a mix-up occurs in "Hands," which is not about a woman at all. It is about Wing Biddlebaum, "one of those rare, little-understood men" who are rather like "the finer sort of women in their love of men." It is also about what happens when a young schoolmaster's love for his pupils is perverted by rumor into something indecently sexual. As a young man, Biddlebaum had been a teacher with a habit of talking with his hands, "caressing the shoulders of the boys [and] playing about the tousled heads." Then one of his pupils became "enamoured" of him, imagined "unspeakable" things, and "went forth to tell his dreams as facts." Biddlebaum narrowly escaped being lynched. Chased out of the Pennsylvania town where he taught, he eventually settled in Winesburg. Wing does not understand what happened to him all those years ago, but he holds his hands responsible. Though they are "the piston rods of his machinery of expression," he struggles to keep his "slender, expressive fingers" concealed. Afraid of himself and everyone else, Wing has lived alone for twenty years, a recluse on the edge of town.

## REACTION TO *WINESBURG*

The frankness with which *Winesburg* addresses sex and sexuality shocked some of its first readers. One reviewer went so far as to call the book "plain dirt." Anderson resented this criticism, and he took pains to defend crudity as "an inevitable quality in the production of a really significant present-day American literature." Anderson was well aware that *Winesburg* flew in the face of the kind of decorous fiction preferred by some of his contemporaries. Critics such as William Dean Howells had argued that American writers should set themselves apart from their European counterparts by concentrating on the purer and more polite aspects of American life; Anderson disagreed. He believed that a "true" novelist was "a man gone a little mad with the life of his times." The *Winesburg* stories were his attempt to share with his fellow Americans "the crude expression of their lives."

Anderson recalled every hard word that was ever said about *Winesburg*, claiming in his *Memoirs* that he had been widely condemned as a pervert for writing it. The truth, however, is that the book was favorably reviewed by all but a very few critics. H. L. Mencken praised it, declaring, "Nothing quite like it has ever been done in America." His opinion was seconded by many others. Gertrude Stein was particularly impressed, and well she might be, for her influence on *Winesburg* was considerable. Although Anderson cultivated the myth that *Winesburg* was a personal revelation, something that just occurred to him one night, the book borrows from other traditions and texts. Writing the *Winesburg* stories, Anderson put into practice techniques he had learned by reading Stein: simple diction and the application of what he referred to as "word color." Like Stein, Anderson admired the impressionist painters and sought to develop an impressionistic prose style. Anderson was not gracious about acknowledging other models for *Winesburg*, but he probably conceived of the book after reading Edgar Lee Masters's *Spoon River Anthology*, which also dealt with life in small town America.

## WINESBURG'S SIGNIFICANCE

*Winesburg* did not just spring from Anderson's head fully formed, but its arrival did mark the beginning of a new direction for American literature. The book was a crucial precursor to some of the best work to come out of the modernist period. Compared with these later works, *Winesburg* seems neither bold nor especially innovative, but for many years after its publication it served as a kind of handbook for aspiring and adventurous writers. Anderson himself also had considerable clout in the literary world of the 1920s, and writers who later eclipsed him in fame acknowledged his influence on their early work. Without Sherwood Anderson's *Winesburg, Ohio*, there might never have been Jean Toomer's *Cane* (1923), Ernest Hemingway's *In Our Time* (1925), or William Faulkner's *Go Down, Moses and Other Stories* (1942). *Winesburg* established Anderson as a major writer, and he continues to be considered an important figure in American literary history. However, his reputation rests on that one slim volume. None of his later books quite matched up to the promise of *Winesburg*, to the wide-eyed simplicity of its prose or the frank tenderness with which it treats its crudely drawn characters.

[*See also* Henry, O.; Howells, William Dean; Masters, Edgar Lee; Mencken, H. L.; Short Story in America, The; *and* Stein, Gertrude.]

### FURTHER READING

Crowley, John W., ed. *New Essays on Winesburg, Ohio.* Cambridge and New York, 1990. Crowley's introduction is especially helpful.

White, Ray Lewis. *Winesburg, Ohio: An Exploration.* Boston, 1990.

---

See also the article on Sherwood Anderson, immediately preceding.

# MAYA ANGELOU

*by Stefanie K. Dunning*

Maya Angelou was born Marguerite Johnson in St. Louis, Missouri, in 1928. Because her brother Bailey could not say her whole name as a child, Marguerite became Maya. Angelou's life is synonymous with her work; she has published a series of five autobiographies, her most famous being *I Know Why the Caged Bird Sings* (1970). In each of these five works, Angelou writes about particular and important parts of her life. Yet not only does each book elucidate periods in Angelou's own life, but these books also paint a picture of the time she is writing about within the black community. Angelou's work demonstrates that the personal is political and that the events that shape and inform an individual life are often related to large political movements and events that affect an entire community.

Long before the publication of *I Know Why the Caged Bird Sings*, Maya Angelou had been a poet, a dancer, a singer, and an actor. After a party one evening where Angelou had regaled her guests with humorous stories of her childhood, she was approached by a publisher and asked to write an autobiography. At first Angelou refused, but she eventually accepted the offer and wrote her now-famous autobiographical account of her childhood. In *I Know Why the Caged Bird Sings*, Angelou details her childhood, which she and her brother Bailey spent being shuttled from her paternal grandparents, her mother and her father.

In this her first work, Angelou's writing is resplendent and taut; it is perhaps Angelou's most lyrically successful autobiographical account. Angelou draws a quaint portrait of her life in Stamps, Arkansas, with her paternal grandmother and her partially disabled uncle. In Stamps, Maya and Bailey's lives are steady, healthy, and regulated by school, the commerce of her grandmother's thriving store, and their church schedule. In Stamps, young Maya is protected from the brutalities of her mother and father's worlds, which she would come to know too soon. After a few years in Stamps, their mother reclaims Maya and Bailey and they move to St. Louis to live with her. There, Maya is molested by one of her mother's boyfriends and suffers not only bodily trauma but also psychological trauma as she attempts to grapple with what has happened to her. This experience will make the young Maya feel "tainted" as she proceeds through the difficulties of adolescence. She is eventually returned to her grandmother, only to move once again in her life to California, where she lives with both her mother and her father alternately. Angelou's narrative ends when she becomes pregnant at sixteen and gives birth to a boy, whom she named Guy Johnson.

Angelou's first autobiography received rave reviews, but it has lately come under fire, along with a host of other books that have been considered American classics. Banned along with some works by Mark Twain in several states, among them Georgia and Texas, *I Know Why the Caged Bird Sings* was thought to be so sexually explicit that it was pornographic; some parents felt Angelou's descriptions of her sexual molestation were too graphic for children to read. Despite this controversy, *I Know Why the Caged Bird Sings* remains one of the most widely read and best-selling autobiographical accounts in American literature.

## ANGELOU'S LIFE AS HER WORK

In 1971, Angelou published a book of poetry, *Just Give Me a Cool Drink of Water 'fore I Diiie*. Like her autobiography, her poetry in this volume deals with the difficult themes of sexuality, race, and gender. Her poem "The Mothering Blackness," in the section entitled "Where Love is a Scream of Anguish," perfectly illustrates this conjunction of issues in Angelou's poetry. "She came home running / back to the mothering blackness / deep in the smothering blackness / white tears icicle gold plains of her face / she came home running." This poem also reminds us of Angelou's own homeward journey from St. Louis after her horrific sexual abuse at the hands of her mother's boyfriend. Angelou's poetry has yet to receive the critical praise some of her autobiographical work has garnered. Despite the lack of critical acclaim or interest in Angelou's poetry, her volumes continue to sell well with popular readers.

Angelou followed this volume of poetry with another autobiographical work, *Gather Together in My Name* (1974). In this book, Angelou writes about her and her brother's relationship with their grandmother and the widening rift between them. She also chronicles her experience in a variety of professions—most notable is her work as a prostitute and madam. At the end of *Gather Together in My Name*, Angelou realizes she was "tricked" into prostituting herself by a lover. The novel ends as a repentant Angelou beseeches her readers to forgive her for the insights, some of which are tawdry, she reveals in this book. Yet Angelou's colorful past exposes far more than simply the salacious nature of some of her jobs; her frank portrayal of her life demonstrates her showmanship, highlighting that Angelou is a consummate performer and she brings to her work the kind of difficult honesty that makes art meaningful, worthwhile, and beautiful.

The forthright nature of Angelou's work and art has meant that she was never without work; during the period between the publication of her autobiographies, Angelou toured with the State Department's production of *Porgy and Bess* on a twenty-two-nation tour, wrote songs for Hollywood movies, and perhaps most notably, wrote the script for the film *Georgia, Georgia* and became the first black woman to write a Hollywood film.

Between the publication of her second and third book of autobiography, Angelou published a book of poetry titled *Oh Pray My Wings Are Gonna Fit Me Well* (1975). In *Oh Pray My Wings Are Gonna Fit Me Well*, Angelou continues to confront issues of race and racism. This volume, however, reflects her experiences abroad and in Africa, as the poem simply titled "Africa" demonstrates. Of Africa, she notes, "Now she is rising / remember her pain / remember the losses / her screams loud and in vain / remember her riches / her history slain / now she is striding / although she had lain." This volume of poetry reflects a more mature Angelou, who is contemplating aging as well as celebrating those who have died, as evidenced in titles from the volume such as "Turning Forty" and "Elegy."

Angelou's next autobiographical publication is the enigmatic *Singin' and Swingin' and Gettin' Merry Like Christmas* (1976). In this work, Angelou chronicles her failed marriage to a Greek sailor, Tosh Angelos. The two were married for five years but eventually separated; Angelou devotes the second half of the book to describing her experiences as a dancer in the State Department's world tour of *Porgy and Bess*. While touring with *Porgy and Bess*, Angelou had to leave her son, Guy Johnson, behind, and this guilt at not being with her son was almost more than she could bear. Battling severe depression and at times considering suicide, Angelou spent a year bouncing between astounding emotional highs and lows. After one year the tour ended, and she moved to a houseboat in Sausalito and lived in a commune with her son.

## THE IMPACT OF MAYA ANGELOU'S WORK

Angelou then published the book of poetry *And Still I Rise* (1978). This volume of poetry produced Angelou's best-known poem among African-American women, "Phenomenal Woman." Reproduced on T-shirts, posters, and greeting cards, Angelou's poem celebrated African-American beauty, and though published in 1978, fifteen years later a new generation of racially conscious readers would rediscover this poem as an enduring ode to the beauty and strength of African-American women. Her mainstream popularity among a younger generation of African Americans undoubtedly is linked in part to the success of her poem "On the Pulse of Morning," which she delivered at the inauguration of President William Jefferson Clinton in 1992. Her poem, which rhymes and seems to move with a beat akin to rap music, begins "Pretty women wonder where my secret lies. / I'm not cute or built to suit a fashion model's size." Angelou goes on to write, "It's in the reach of my arms, / The span of my hips, / The stride in my step, / The curl of my lips. / I'm a woman / Phenomenally. / Phenomenal woman, / That's me." Though Angelou never explicitly posits two economies of racial beauty (white versus black) in this poem, it has been interpreted and claimed as a validation of the physical features of black women that have long been labeled as unacceptable by mainstream American society. This poem represented a rallying cry for African-American women everywhere to embrace themselves as they were, rather than subscribe to white standards of beauty.

Angelou's fourth and fifth autobiographies, *The Heart of a Woman* (1981) and *All God's Children Need Traveling Shoes* (1986), continued to explore the themes of race and racism in her work as well as questions of gender and sexuality. In *The Heart of A Woman*, Angelou recaptures some of her former linguistic acuity as she finds herself committed to the cause of civil rights. Quite notably, Angelou served as the Northern Coordinator of the Southern Christian Leadership Conference. The book has been hailed as an important contribution to African-American history, as it covers the pivotal civil rights moment. Her fifth autobiography, *All God's Children Need Traveling Shoes*, explores the four years Angelou spent in Africa and the devastating car accident that endangered the life of her son. In Africa, Angelou becomes deeply depressed as she waits for Guy to recover from a broken neck; yet she also finds herself in Africa and reconnects her African-American self to the home of her ancestors. Angelou falls in love with Kwame Nkrumah's Ghana and portrays an extremely important moment in African history—the opening years of Africa's first postcolonial republic.

Though all of Angelou's work (as well as her many professions, which include teaching, journalism and performing) is too numerous to name here, it is worth noting that she also published a volume of poetry in 1983 titled *Shaker, Why Don't You Sing!* Another autobiographical novel, *A Song Flung Up to Heaven* (2002), deviates from her previous autobiographies in that she takes a longer look over her entire life rather than focusing on one specific period. Angelou recounts her return from Africa, her depression over the deaths of Martin Luther King Jr. and Malcolm X, and her growing disappointment with the emotional distance growing between her and her son, Guy. She also provides vivid accounts of her friendship with James Baldwin.

Despite Angelou's previous success, African-American poet Wanda Coleman reviewed *A Song Flung Up to Heaven* negatively. Of Angelou's latest work, she wrote in the 14 April 2002 issue of the *Los Angeles Times* that the book was full of "empty phrases and sweeping generalities . . . dead metaphors ('sobbing embrace,' 'my heart fell in my chest') and clumsy similes ('like the sound of buffaloes running into each other at rutting times')." Coleman's criticism of Angelou sparked an enormous controversy in the African-American literary community; Coleman was subsequently uninvited by Eso Won Books, the premiere African-American bookstore in southern California, to a book signing. Coleman, however, was not alone in her criticism of the book; the reviews for the book were generally mixed, with quite a few strongly negative reviews of it.

Though Coleman's negative review of Angelou's latest autobiography generated a great deal of press (Coleman was even featured in the *Village Voice* after the fallout from her review), Angelou's work has often received mixed reviews. Critics have long discounted her poetry as simplistic. It is, perhaps, for this reason that her poetry is less known than her other works. And of all

her works, Angelou is still most critically lauded for her autobiographical novel *I Know Why the Caged Bird Sings*. Despite some critical disapproval, Angelou's work continues to inspire and sustain readers all over the world. Maya Angelou is currently serving as Reynolds Professor of American Studies at Wake Forest University in Winston-Salem, North Carolina.

## SELECTED WORKS

*I Know Why the Caged Bird Sings* (1970)
*Just Give Me a Cool Drink of Water 'fore I Diiie: The Poetry of Maya Angelou* (1971)
*Gather Together in My Name* (1974)
*Oh Pray My Wings Are Gonna Fit Me Well* (1975)
*Singin' and Swingin' and Gettin' Merry Like Christmas* (1976)
*And Still I Rise* (1978)
*The Heart of a Woman* (1981)
*Shaker, Why Don't You Sing!* (1983)
*All God's Children Need Traveling Shoes* (1986)
*I Shall Not Be Moved* (1990)
*Wouldn't Take Nothing for My Journey Now* (1993)
*Phenomenal Woman: Four Poems Celebrating Women* (1994)
*Even the Stars Look Lonesome* (1997)
*A Song Flung Up to Heaven* (2002)

## FURTHER READING

Bloom, Harold, ed. *Maya Angelou's* I Know Why the Caged Bird Sings. Philadelphia, Pa., 1998. A thorough and authoritative collection of important essays about Angelou by leading literary critics.
Courtney-Clarke, Margaret. *Maya Angelou: The Poetry of Living.* New York, 1999. An interesting book of photographs and quotations about Angelou.
Elliot, Jeffrey M., ed. *Conversations with Maya Angelou.* Jackson, Miss., 1989. A great set of interviews with Angelou from the 1970s and 1980s.
Lupton, Mary. "Singing the Black Mother: Maya Angelou and Autobiographical Continuity." *Black American Literature Forum* 24, no. 2 (Summer 1990): 257–275. An interesting discussion of Angelou and the tradition of autobiography.
McPherson, Dolly. *Order out of Chaos: The Autobiographical Works of Maya Angelou.* New York, 1990. A critical review of Angelou's autobiographies through 1986.

# JOHN ASHBERY

*by Susan M. Schultz*

Insofar as John Ashbery has a group affiliation as a poet, it is with the New York School of Poets, populated by Frank O'Hara, Kenneth Koch, James Schuyler, Barbara Guest, and Bernadette Mayer, among others. These are witty, erudite, urbane, and profoundly urban poets whose work is at once about the place, New York City, and written according to its pace. It is ironic, then, that Ashbery, born on 28 July 1927 in Rochester, New York, grew up in a white wood house on an apple farm outside the small town of Sodus, located in the western part of the state. More than seven decades later, Sodus's population hovers below ten thousand, and its Chamber of Commerce advertises such special events as bowling at Papa Joe's restaurant; the town's Web site features a mere three photos of its scenic areas, mostly water scenes, including one of a Boy Scout sailboat near Sodus Point.

Ashbery has said that he was lonely and unhappy on the farm and with his father, so he lived for a time with his grandparents in Rochester, a city most famous for being the home of Kodak. Ashbery's father was a carpenter

and his mother a science teacher; he had a brother who died at nine. As Ashbery writes in *The History of My Life* (from *Your Name Here*, 2000): "Once upon a time there were two brothers. / Then there was only one: myself." He was educated at Deerfield Academy, in rural western Massachusetts, then at Harvard University (B.A. degree, 1949) and Columbia University (M.A. degree, 1951). Less formally, his education took him from country to city and then back again, from Sodus to Cambridge to New York City to ten years as a freelance art writer in Paris, from 1955 to 1965, and back to New York City. He lives there and in the small town of Hudson, New York.

## YALE YOUNGER POET: POEMS OF THE 1950s

While Ashbery's first published poems were printed in *Poetry Magazine*, they were not published under his name but under that of a roommate at Deerfield who later became a realtor. Fearful that he would be considered a plagiarist, Ashbery did not for many years submit more work to the magazine, one of the few poetry publishers in the country at that time. At Harvard, which he attended in the late 1940s along with Frank O'Hara, Robert Creeley, Adrienne Rich, Donald Hall, and other later-famous poets, Ashbery worked on the *Advocate*, a literary journal that provided a place for his and his friends' work. He and O'Hara formed a friendship that would remain close until O'Hara's premature death in 1966, and the latter's casual use of colloquial American English was to have an influence on Ashbery's own rendering of the demotic. Also, O'Hara and Ashbery were rivals for the attention of W. H. Auden, who selected Ashbery's volume, *Some Trees* (1956), for the Yale Younger Poets Prize in 1956 over O'Hara's work after threatening not to give the prize to anyone.

*Some Trees* is a highly self-conscious book whose author was obviously immersed in visual and poetic art. Many of the poem titles refer to kinds of writing: "Popular Songs," "Eclogue," "Pantoum," "Sonnet," "Canzone," "A Long Novel," "Sonnet," and "A Pastoral." While the tone of the work is at times stern—the first line of the

John Ashbery. (*Margaretta K. Mitchell Photography*)

first poem, *Two Scenes*, for example, echoes Marianne Moore's most moralizing tendencies with "We see us as we truly behave"—the book itself does not altogether behave well. Consider the poems called "Sonnet." These poems are wrought of fourteen lines, as they should be (John Hollander's *Rhyme's Reason* [1981] gives the reasoning behind this form), but they otherwise disobey rules kept even by Robert Frost, William Butler Yeats, Hart Crane, and other twentieth-century poets. The first "Sonnet" discards rhyme, beginning:

> Each servant stamps the reader with a look.
> After many years he has been brought nothing.
> The servant's frown is the reader's patience.

Not only does Ashbery's form diverge from that of the traditional sonnet, but the content of this poem surely astonishes an American reader accustomed to the American line of democratic poets from Whitman through Frost. For one thing, there is the servant, and then there is the rapid tumble into obscurity as the poem ends—not with a Shakespearian final judgment, but with something more tenuous: "Dear, be the tree your sleep awaits; / Worms be your words, you not safe from ours." Typical of most Ashbery poems, this one concludes by saying at once too little (if the reader likes clarity) and too much (by following standard English syntax without rewarding its usual cause-and-effect logic). Death and poetry are allied here, as one might expect, but it is not clear who the "dear" is, or where servant or tree fit into a larger narrative structure.

The second sonnet in *Some Trees* follows some idiosyncratic rules, even as it pokes fun at the regularity they foist upon the poet. Note the incessant rhymes of the opening:

> The barber at his chair
> Clips me. He does as he goes.
> He clips the hairs outside the nose.
> Too many preparations, nose!

The poem concludes by shifting focus from the expected barber to the razor, from rhyme to what one might call clipped-off rhyme:

> To be the razor—how would you like to be
> The razor, blue with ire,
> That presses me? This is the wrong way.
> The canoe speeds toward a waterfall.
> Something, prince, in our backward manners—
> You guessed the reason for the storm.

There had been a "raincoat" in the first octave of the sonnet, which explains "the storm" at the end of the sestet. Otherwise, again, one has the feeling of plenty amid the playful diminishment of this traditional form, a plenty that is more postmodern than modern, unanchored as it is from the very traditions it mocks.

Better-known poems from this first unself-published collection (Ashbery had himself published *Turandot* in 1953) include "The Instruction Manual," an imagined tour of Mexico, and the somewhat autobiographical "The Picture of Little J. A. in a Prospect of Flowers," based as it is on Andrew Marvell's "The Picture of Little T. C. in a Prospect of Flowers." While this last poem includes such lines as "In a far recess of summer / Monks are playing soccer," clearly unassociated with a biographical Ashbery, except perhaps very tangentially, it ends with a self-reference (to the photograph), which is also a statement of poetic principle. It bears lingering on this statement, since it marks an early instance of what might be called Ashbery's poetic criticism. (He writes it almost exclusively within poems, not without them.) It also offers an example of Ashbery's version of autobiography, more like Gertrude Stein's *Everybody's Autobiography* (1937) than like Robert Lowell's *Life Studies* (1959). He asserts that he "cannot escape the picture / Of my small self in that bank of flowers," a picture that is, through time's "emulsion" (as he will call it later on), less serious than comical:

> so I am not wrong
> In calling this comic version of myself
> The true one. For as change is horror,
> Virtue is really stubbornness
>
> And only in the light of lost words
> Can we imagine our rewards.

The shift from "comic" self to "horror" is swift, perhaps unexpected, but typical of Ashbery, for whom nostalgia is at once sustenance and terror, marking as it does the constantly inconstant passage of time. Like Yeats, Ashbery has always been a poet of old age, even as he has explored his (and our) progress toward it, stage by stage. Here, in his twenties, he can only imagine "reward" as "loss."

## THE SIXTIES: *THE TENNIS COURT OATH TO RIVERS AND MOUNTAINS*

Ashbery's second volume, *The Tennis Court Oath* (1962), written in France, is either his greatest work (judging by enthusiastic responses by members of the school of Language poets, including Charles Bernstein, who proclaimed the book a "critique of clarity and transparency") or a "fearful disaster" (if one listens to Harold Bloom, otherwise Ashbery's most prominent supporter). While the techniques and experiments employed by the poet in creating many of the poems in this book were avant-garde (cut-ups and collages, for example), his intentions consisted of what is called the "New Realism" in the book. Of *Leaving the Atocha Station* he has commented: "The dirt, the noises, the sliding away seem to be a movement in the poem. The poem was probably trying to express that, not for itself but as an epitome of something experienced; I think that is what my poems are about." His emphasis on the "not for itself" of language, of experiment, explains why Ashbery has not retained his following among Language writers; his work post-*Tennis Court Oath* has been more engaged with meaning than with arbitrary form, with experience more than with the disruption of it.

Yet in this book, as Andrew Ross argues, "we are shown how and why language has nothing at all to do with unmediated expression, except when it chooses to voice parodically the fallacy of such an idea." "Thoughts of a Young Girl," like many Ashbery poems, appears to promise a story, then fails to deliver it. This fairy tale–like setup begins with a quotation attributed to "The Dwarf" and ends with a first-person call to "My sweetheart, daughter of my late employer, princess," without offering a context in which these two voices speak the same sense. "They Dream Only of America" tells what seems to be a detective story, but then lapses not into anticipated answers but into questions:

Now he cared only about signs.
Was the cigar a sign?
And what about the key?
He went slowly into the bedroom.

Of course the signs alluded to have more to do with psychoanalysis than with a crime scene marked by "the murderer's ash tray." *The Tennis Court Oath* was published by Wesleyan University Press but was otherwise hardly noticed on Ashbery's home turf. He has said that he never anticipated having an audience for his poems, and this book would seem to validate that fear. As he writes in *The History of My Life*, published in *Your Name Here* (2000): "I thought of developing interests / Someone might take an interest in. No soap." Soap, cigar, the signs were not visible to the poetry audience of the early 1960s, but Ashbery toiled on, even as he wrote art criticism for the *Herald Tribune* in Paris, work that is included in *Reported Sightings: Art Chronicle, 1957–1987*, published by Knopf in 1989.

Ashbery mediated between his own extremes—that of spare formal aestheticism and avant-garde experiment—in his next book, *Rivers and Mountains* (1966).

When reading a later book of Ashbery's, one encounters a style that had its origins in *Rivers and Mountains* and is characterized by spells of meditation, by a very American vocabulary and rolling syntax, and by a roving "I" who may also appear on the poetic stage as "he" or "you" or "one." This volume also features two of Ashbery's long poems ("Clepsydra" and "The Skaters"), a form to which he has been drawn over and again through the years. Throughout the book, his use of form is more playful than pedantic; in the title poem he plugs in one river per line, beginning "Far from the Rappahannock, the silent / Danube moves along toward the sea," ignoring conventional geography as he goes. "The Skaters" includes cutout work, along with Ashbery's contemplative interventions, including interludes about "system," a concern that reappears at greater length in his *Three Poems* (1972).

Inventing systems,
We are a part of some system, thinks he, just as the sun is part of
The solar system.

This from a poet perhaps the most consistently antisystematic of American poets of the twentieth century. And from one of the most romantic, this swat at Shelley, at Keats:

The west wind grazes my cheek, the droplets come
Pattering down;
What matter now whether I wake or sleep?

## ASHBERY AND THE ROMANTIC INHERITANCE: THE 1970s

Ashbery's complicated relationship with the romantic tradition lies at the center of his next book, *Double Dream of Spring* (1970), a book featured on Harold Bloom's contemporary poetry reading list at Yale around 1980. Bloom is among the most positive and powerful of Ashbery's promoters; he is also the self-appointed guardian of romantic traditions (both European and American) in American poetry. Hence, a poem like "Evening in the Country" can be read as a remake of Wordsworth's "Tintern Abbey," a poem in which the past is recollected quite happily (Ashbery's poem launches with the line, "I am still completely happy"). Perhaps he protests too much in this opening, but the poem does celebrate "the new sign of being," describing the poet "refreshed and somehow younger," despite "the incredible violence and yielding / Turmoil that is to be our route." The book is full of such paradoxes as "violence and yielding": in "Soonest Mended," Ashbery writes of "action, this not being sure, this careless / preparing," and "Spring Day" begins not simply with "immense hope" but also "forbearance." But, if Ashbery employs stereotypical romantic tropes, like "casements" and rural settings, in these poems, he also employs an undecidedly unromantic American vernacular. "Decoy" begins,

> We hold these truths to be self-evident:
> That ostracism, both political and moral, has
> Its place in the twentieth-century scheme of things

and "Definition of Blue" starts with "The rise of capitalism parallels the advance of romanticism / And the individual is dominant until the close of the nineteenth century." Here, a romantic veneer collapses into the patriotic, the political, the bureaucratic, the banal. This is perhaps appropriate in a postromantic work that directly addresses John Clare, not his more renowned contemporaries. In *For John Clare*, written in prose, in the voice of that marginal romantic poet, Ashbery calls into question the traditional landscape of romanticism, one where the poet finds himself, above all else, inscribed. Instead, "There ought to be room for more things, for a spreading out, like. Being immersed in the details of rock and field and slope—letting them come to you for once, and then meeting them halfway would be so much easier. . . . Alas, we perceive them if at all as those things that were meant to be put aside."

In his Norton Lectures on poetry, delivered in the early 1990s and published in 2000, Ashbery writes about how "Clare's modernity is a kind of nakedness of vision that we are accustomed to, at least in America, from the time of Walt Whitman and Emily Dickinson. . . ." When he notes, further on, that "Clare's poems are dispatches from the front" rather than emotions recollected in tranquillity or in Keats's music, we see Ashbery carving out a place for himself somewhere between high romanticism and William Carlos Williams's "no ideas but in things" objectivism. As ever, Ashbery does not choose between polarities, he synthesizes them. Or, as he puts it in "Soonest Mended," his is "a kind of fence sitting / raised to the level of an esthetic ideal."

In 1969 Ashbery and his fellow New York poet (one also rural in his inclinations) James Schuyler published *A Nest of Ninnies*, a novel written collaboratively. This venture into prose traveled the camp world of the suburbs; as the jacket reads, "[it] masterfully dissects the discreet charm of an eccentric cross section of America's bourgeoisie." This novel has never been considered central to the Ashbery canon, but his next venture into prose is one of the most

significant works of his long career. It is *Three Poems*, a sequence of three prose meditations influenced by the mystical investigations of Renaissance writer Thomas Traherne. *Three Poems* was written during a crisis in Ashbery's psychic life, after his therapist recommended he read the mystics. In *Three Poems*, Ashbery's long, discursive poetic lines, developed in *Rivers and Mountains* and *The Double Dream of Spring*, jump loose into even longer prose sentences. It is as if his lyric poems had, quite literally, exploded; as he writes in "The System," "one can almost hear the beginning of the lyric crash in which everything will be lost and pulverized, changed back into atoms ready to resume new combinations and shapes again." Characteristically, the poet ventures into philosophical speculations that are quickly undercut. He writes of a world where ideas are evanescent, as are the systems we live by (whatever remains of them after world wars, after *The Waste Land*). Thus, at the beginning of the second meditation, "The System," Ashbery writes, suggesting a city self that has broken into its constituent, more suburban and rural parts:

> The system was breaking down. The one who had wandered alone past so many happenings and events began to feel, backing up along the primal vein that led to his center, the beginning of a hiccup that would, if left to gather, explode the center to the extremities of life, the suburbs through which one makes one's way to where the country is.

If the system is to break down, then the poet is confronted with a choice: whether, as he puts it on the first page of the book, in *The New Spirit*, to "put it all down" or to "leave all out," which "would be another, and truer, way." Ashbery opts slyly for the less true way, that of (seemingly) putting it all down. Where Eliot took the fragments he shored against his ruin and propped them up, leaving them fragmentary, Ashbery's prose suggests a lack of fragment (despite coming on the heels of "Fragment," the last poem in *The Double Dream of Spring*), except in the excess that results from the explosion that inspired it. It is perhaps the very fullness of this book that makes it both Ashbery's own favorite and the most influential of all his books, as John Shoptaw points out in *On the Outside Looking Out: John Ashbery's Poetry* (1994). While prose was not a widely used poetic form in the early 1970s, the 1980s and 1990s saw Language poets "filling their pages with prose they published as poetry," Shoptaw observes. In 1975 Ashbery was nearly fifty years old and still labored in poetic obscurity ("poetic" and "obscurity" being synonyms in some parts). *Self-Portrait in a Convex*

*Mirror* (1975) changed that, garnering for Ashbery the Pulitzer Prize, the National Book Award, and the National Book Critics Circle Award. This volume hardly marks Ashbery's venture into clarity, or the kind of lucidity that often earns the attention of the mainstream press. Instead, the prizes indicate that Ashbery had educated the poetry public, readers both traditional and experimental in their tastes, to his modes of writing. In a way typical of Ashbery's syntheses of his own tendencies, *Self-Portrait*'s version of Ashberyese mediates between the prose of *Three Poems* and the lyricism of *The Double Dream of Spring* (and vice versa). The title poem of this collection, written in response to a painting by Parmigianino, argues that what is most important about works of art is not the finished product so much as the elusive activity occurring around its creation. "Is there anything," the poet asks,

> To be serious about beyond this otherness
> That gets included in the most ordinary
> Forms of daily activity, changing everything
> Slightly and profoundly, and tearing the matter
> Out of our hands

*Self-Portrait* is nothing if not a serious portrait of the ordinary world, and its language is plainer than that in any Ashbery book to this point, aside perhaps from the little-known collaboration with Joe Brainard, *The Vermont Notebook* (1975), published at nearly the same time by Black Sparrow Press in California.

While *Self-Portrait* opens with the romantic, nearly vatic, tones of "As One Put Drunk into the Packet-Boat," which alludes to Andrew Marvell's poem about bad poets, it quickly loses that sheen. More typical than the opening line of this poem ("I tried each thing, only some were immortal and free") are the following phrases, culled almost at random: "Puaagh. Vomit. Puaaaaaagh. More vomit"; " 'Once I let a guy blow me' "; "A pleasant smell of frying sausages"; and "I have not told you / About the riffraff at the boat show." While Ashbery places the statement about the blow job in quotations, thus distancing himself from it, the homosexual (or "homotextual," as John Shoptaw calls it) content of the poem from which it comes ("Poem in three parts: 1. Love") is more direct than what has preceded it in Ashbery's oeuvre. As a young man, Ashbery had to inform the draft board of his homosexuality to get out of the Korean War; he did so at the beginning of the McCarthy years. The indirections in Ashbery's poetry, while not entirely because of the danger, for a gay man, of confession (which came into vogue among some heterosexual poets

in the 1950s and 1960s), were doubtless rendered more desirable by it.

At this point in his career, Ashbery begins to respond to Harold Bloom's notions about poetry, as if to play with ideas that were, almost accidentally, making him famous. In *Grand Galop*, for example, he writes, seemingly cribbing his notes from a Bloom lecture:

> And one is left sitting in the yard
> To try to write poetry
> Using what Wyatt and Surrey left around,
> Took up and put down again
> Like so much gorgeous raw material.

Very little in this book seems related to the work of Sir Thomas Wyatt or the Earl of Surrey, including the American vernacular Ashbery trucks in. So Ashbery's engagement with Bloom's "anxiety of influence," whereby later poets "misread" earlier ones and write a thereby diminished version of the poems that were once possible, is an ambivalent one. He would engage Bloom agonistically again, and at much greater length, in his 1991 volume, *Flow Chart*. But for now, the attention he pays to what might otherwise be considered unpoetic material is itself an intervention in criticism as well as poetry. It is one that contravenes Bloom's vaunting of the romantic, of Ashbery as a follower of Wallace Stevens rather than, say, Gertrude Stein.

Two years after *Self-Portrait*, Ashbery published *Houseboat Days* (1977), a kind of separated Siamese twin of the previous volume. Here again, Ashbery ventures into commentaries about poetry; he was, by now, a professor of poetry at Brooklyn College, eager to give his students the definitions they demanded of poetry. So, in "And *Ut Pictura Poesis* Is Her Name," he writes: "You can't say it that way any more," and asserts that

> Something
> Ought to be written about how this affects
> You when you write poetry:
> The extreme austerity of an almost empty mind
> Colliding with the lush, Rousseau-like foliage of its desire to
>   communicate.

*Houseboat Days* continues Ashbery's pendulum sweep between romantic "casements" and Daffy Duck, between "Street Musicians" and "The Nut Brown Maid." His style has settled into a poetic-prosaic mode, with poems "spoken" by a poet-translator adept in more than one poetic language, one level of diction, just as interested in Disney's America as he is in European art.

*As We Know* (1979) and *Shadow Train* (1981) rounded out Ashbery's poetic production of the 1970s. The 1979 volume featured a long poem, "Litany," written in two columns, influenced by Elliott Carter's music for violin and piano. Again, Ashbery playfully engages the issues of literary criticism at the time, proclaiming in this, his seventh volume of the decade, that, "Alone with our madness and favorite flower / We see that there really is nothing left to write about." Or rather, he continues in *Late Echo*, "it is necessary to write about the same old things / In the same way." And again, as he had done throughout this prolific, marvelous decade, he writes poetry that is intellectually rigorous, meditative, intimately informal, and often funny, as in the punch last lines of "The Other Cindy": "The contest ends at midnight tonight / But you can submit again, and again." *Shadow Train* is a slighter work, in all senses of the term, but Ashbery can be seen experimenting with a sonnetlike, sixteen-line form in each of these poems.

## ASHBERY AS INDUSTRY: THE 1980s

In 1980 *Beyond Amazement: New Essays on John Ashbery*, edited by David Lehman, became the first full-length book of criticism of Ashbery's work. It included essays by the Douglas Crase, Marjorie Perloff, John Koethe, Lehman, and other noted critics. Topics ranged from prophecy (Crase) to metaphysics (Koethe) to "Ashbery's Dismantling of Bourgeois Discourse" (Keith Cohen). Strangely, not until the mid-1990s, with the publication of John Shoptaw's *On the Outside Looking Out* and *The Tribe of John: Ashbery and Contemporary Poetry* (1995), edited by Susan M. Schultz, was so much published on his work.

Or perhaps it was not so strange. Ashbery is a prolific poet, one with whom it is difficult to keep pace. As soon as the critic sits down to write about his work, Ashbery has published another volume—or two. The relative lack of criticism stems not only from the difficulty of his work, the way in which the poems unravel the critic's claims even as they are being made, but also from the sense that one simply cannot stand still amid the constantly evolving work. A book like David Herd's *John Ashbery and American Poetry*, published in 2000, hardly addresses Ashbery's work after 1984's *A Wave*; while Herd suggests that Ashbery's work after the mid-1980s is not up to snuff, an arguably just statement, one also sympathizes with the difficulty of following Ashbery's work through to what is only today "the end." Marjorie Perloff has written of the normalization of John Ashbery by mainstream critics and argued vociferously that Ashbery remains an experimental poet, hardly normal at all.

Indeed, Ashbery's work of the 1980s, *A Wave* (and the long title poem, which again argues Ashbery's relationship to romanticism) and *April Galleons* (1987) (with its constant allusions to fairy tales), does not so much transform Ashbery's oeuvre as elaborate it, or spin off from the strengths of his earlier work. There is an autobiographical force to the work in these years that remains abstract and understated, and yet that meditates more directly on "life" (see Fred Moramarco's chart of Ashbery's references to this concept in Schultz's *Tribe of John*) than any poems since *Three Poems*. *A Wave* foreshadows 1991's *Flow Chart* in its contemplations of life's (and a career's) possible shapes:

> One idea is enough to organize a life and project it
> Into unusual by viable forms, but many ideas merely
> Lead one thither into a morass of their own good intentions,

he writes in the title poem. The use of a wave, more untenable than the somewhat more stable construction of a houseboat, suggests that Ashbery thinks such organizations cannot be maintained for long, that after "pass[ing] through pain," one emerges always "on an invisible terrain," as new as any encountered by the hapless Buster Keaton. Poems are like lives, Ashbery asserts,

> And the new wondering, the poem, growing up through
> the floor,
> Standing tall in tubers, invading and smashing the ritual
> Parlor, demands to be met on its own terms now

The poem ends by promising only more questions, and compares walls to veils, which "are never the same." Its last sentence, "But all was strange," suggests a world of dream, yet one actively inhabited by the poet. Marianne Moore's real toads in imaginary gardens never had a better poet laureate than John Ashbery.

In *April Galleons* this anxiety, marked in the poem *A Wave* by the walls that are also veils, inspires, if only at one instant, directly autobiographical writing, or seems to. In *Sighs and Inhibitions*, Ashbery begins by rehearsing issues he had taken up in *A Wave*:

> On the way life manages itself, though its beginning
> And end seem clear enough as givens, as does
> The quasi-permanent siesta of noon that our long day
> Is fabricated of.

But life management has not always been so easy, has on occasion been desperate:

> I remember in the schoolyard throwing a small rock
> At some kid I hated, and then, when the blood began
> To ooze definitively, trying to hug the teacher,

The boy, the world, into ignoring what I'd done,
To lie and thus escape through a simple
Canceling, not a confession, to wipe the slate clean
So as to inhabit another world in which
I bore no responsibility for my acts: life
As a clear, living dream.

What had been "a lie," a "canceling," has become, for the least confessional of contemporary poets, just that—a confession. This banal confession of ordinary childhood misbehavior is nearly shocking in the context of a life's work devoted to life, but not to the way in which it is tethered to the poet's ego. The work has been "as a clear, living dream," but here we see it turned on end, so that the limpid poems we know are shown to come out of ordinary drama or trauma. Ashbery has defended escapism as a function of art, but here we see how escape comes out of an urgent need to escape from something. It makes sense, then, that this passage comes in a book full of fairy-tale motifs, and in which "The castle was infested with rats" (*Savage Menace*) and where "Even ghost stories are fairly prevalent, and about to be believed" (*Dreams of Adulthood*).

Perhaps the greatest reshaping of Ashbery's career in the 1980s occurred with the mid-decade publication of his *Selected Poems* (1985), which contained work from *Some Trees* to *A Wave*—and contained precious little work from *The Tennis Court Oath*. The more radical poems from that collection are missing, whereas *A Last World* and "The New Realism" suggest continuity, rather than discontinuity, in Ashbery's overall career. By contrast, *Shadow Train* is probably overrepresented.

### ASHBERY NORMALIZED?: THE 1990s AND BEYOND

Ashbery's work of the 1990s, aside from the book-length meditation, *Flow Chart*, which eulogizes his mother even as it explores the shape (and shaping) of his poetic career, is largely written in one mode, which is thoughtful but often less persistently philosophical or meditative than Ashbery's work of the 1960s and 1970s. Where Ashbery had published only three books in the 1980s, along with his *Selected Poems*, in the 1990s he began publishing a book almost every year. Yet while there is a sameness to a lot of this work, there are still surprises, experiments, grand ideas. *And the Stars Were Shining* (1994) can be read as a colonial allegory:

I read Ashbery's latest volume, *And the Stars Were Shining* (at least in certain moods) as a colonial allegory, manipulated by Ashbery to his own ends. This allegory reads as follows:

a famous American poet, wishing to write about his own inevitable decline and fall, uses his own position as an intellectual well-versed in European art, music and literature, to tell his story. The decline of the West is embodied (or disembodied) in the poet's decadence (or belatedness). In so doing, he reveals the extent to which Americans are still colonized by Europe, even as Europe ingests large quantities of American culture. And so Ashbery appropriates his own appropriation: "What! Our culture in its dotage! / Yet this very poem refutes it," he proclaims. He becomes an odd colonist of the colonial.

(Schultz, 1994)

*Can You Hear, Bird* (1995), dedicated in part to Harry Mathews, features a table of contents done in alphabetical order, perhaps acknowledging Ashbery's Oulipo-ian friend's interest in rule-based poetry. *Girls on the Run* (1999) is based on the works of Henry Darger, who painted and wrote about little girls for much of his (secret) artistic life. Ashbery's *Chinese Whispers* (2002), much of it published in *As Umbrellas Follow Rain* (2001), continues Ashbery's ongoing meditation on old age, as in the poem "In the Time of Pussy Willows":

My goodness, I thought I'd seen a whole lot of generations,
but they are endless, one keeps following another,
treading on its train, hissing.

History is not yet done with Ashbery. He has grown into a reputation larger than that of any other American poet of the late-twentieth- and early-twenty-first centuries. His influence is pervasive, if not to be heard in every poet's cadence. As Marjorie Perloff argues, John Ashbery's work cannot, finally, be normalized, even if it so often dwells inside confined domestic spaces. He has shown contemporary poets that there are yet poems to be written out of the "scraps" left by earlier writers. We may not know what will happen to his reputation in fifty or one hundred years' time. But to have had the experience of reading Ashbery, for the first, second, or third time is one of the great privileges of being alive at this moment, in and not out of time.

[*See also* Long Poem, The; New York School of Poets; *and* Transcendentalism.]

### SELECTED WORKS

*Some Trees* (1956)
*The Tennis Court Oath* (1962)
*Rivers and Mountains* (1966)
*A Nest of Ninnies* (1969)
*The Double Dream of Spring* (1970)
*Three Poems* (1972)
*The Vermont Notebook* (1975)

*Self-Portrait in a Convex Mirror* (1975)
*Houseboat Days* (1977)
*As We Know* (1979)
*Shadow Train* (1981)
*A Wave* (1984)
*Selected Poems* (1985)
*April Galleons* (1987)
*Reported Sightings: Art Chronicles, 1957–1987* (1989)
*Flow Chart* (1991)
*Hotel Lautréamont* (1993)
*And the Stars Were Shining* (1994)
*Can You Hear, Bird* (1995)
*Wakefulness* (1998)
*Girls on the Run* (1999)
*Your Name Here* (2000)
*Other Traditions* (2000)
*As Umbrellas Follow Rain* (2001)
*Chinese Whispers* (2002)

## FURTHER READING

Herd, David. *John Ashbery and American Poetry*. Manchester, U.K., 2000. Herd is an English critic, writing for what is usually considered to be a skeptical audience. His book covers Ashbery's career from the beginning through 1984, more or less dismissing everything that comes after. Less a book on Ashbery and American poetry than on Ashbery and writers who influenced him, including Boris Pasternak, it is most valuable, perhaps, as a portrait of the artist as conversationalist (in interviews and in dialogue with other poets and poems).

Lehman, David, ed. *Beyond Amazement: New Essays on John Ashbery*. Ithaca, N.Y., 1980. Lehman's collection was the first major grouping of essays about Ashbery's work and includes contributions by many of the finest critics and poet-critics of the time, including Marjorie Perloff, Douglas Crase, John Koethe, and Lehman himself. The subjects covered include everything from prophecy to irony to an early revaluation of *The Tennis Court Oath* by Fred Moramarco. Diffuse, but appropriately so, in the case of Ashbery.

Perloff, Marjorie. "Normalizing John Ashbery." Available from *http://wings.buffalo.edu/epc/authors/perloff/ashbery.html*. 1998. Marjorie Perloff has long been the primary advocate of avant-garde writing in the United States. In this essay she takes on more conservative critics, including James Longenbach and Vernon Shetley, who normalize Ashbery's work by fitting it neatly into a twentieth-century tradition beginning with T. S. Eliot and Wallace Stevens. Perloff sees Ashbery's work even his poetry of the 1990s, as more radical than that.

Schultz, Susan M. "Decline of the West: Review of Lois-Ann Yamanaka's *Saturday Night at the Pahala Theatre* and John Ashbery's *And the Stars Were Shining*." *RIF/T: An Electronic Space for Poetry, Prose, and Poetics* 3.1 (Summer 1994).

Schultz, Susan M., ed. *The Tribe of John: Ashbery and Contemporary Poetry*. Tuscaloosa, Ala., 1995. Schultz's collection includes essays on Ashbery's poetry (including his use of landscapes, his love poetry, and his use of typical language) as well as essays on Ashbery's influence on such writers as Ann Lauterbach, Jorie Graham, and Charles Bernstein and his noninfluence on William Bronk. The book's preface and conclusion are poem-essays, suggesting that one of Ashbery's influences can be found in the use of mixed genres.

Shoptaw, John. *On the Outside Looking Out: John Ashbery's Poetry*. Cambridge, Mass., 1994. Shoptaw's book provides an intense close reading of Ashbery's oeuvre up to the early 1990s, with information from the poet on the origins of the poems. Shoptaw argues that Ashbery's texts are "homotextual," if not exactly "homosexual." A fascinating appendix, with drafts of *A Wave*.

# ASIAN AMERICAN LITERATURE

*by Kella Svetich*

Any discussion of "Asian American literature" must address the inadequacy of the term to describe the array of writings that spring from a multiplicity of cultures and experiences. Ultimately, the phrase has come to encompass writers of Asian heritage living in, writing about, born in, or having sojourned to America. This set of definitions is not limited to written literatures or those originally created in the English language; it can also be extended to transcribed Chinese oral narratives, narratives written in Vietnamese and translated into English, or Chinese characters carved into walls. The term Asian American literature also prompts questions regarding national boundaries. "America" need not be limited to the United States; the fluid concept of nation can spill over geographical boundaries to reach neocolonies where complex constructions of "America"—economic and cultural—significantly affect other countries.

Asian American literature, therefore, reflects contexts of immigration, discrimination, and international relations—including war. Historically, reception of immigrants from Asian countries by Euroamericans has been fraught with racism. The Exclusion Laws of 1882, 1888, and 1892 refused entry to Chinese laborers. Employment opportunities largely available only to men and laws prohibiting the immigration of Asian women created unequal sex ratios that initially attenuated the development of many Asian American communities. Antimiscegenation legislation in states including California exacerbated this situation, and Asian immigrants were furthermore prohibited from becoming U.S. citizens or owning property. Although antimiscegenation laws were eventually declared unconstitutional and the Immigration and Nationality Act of 1965 finally allowed quotas of Asian immigrants equal to European immigrants, racism continues to surface as a theme in contemporary Asian American literature. Circumstances of war have also inflected these writings: the Philippine-American War (1899–1902), World War II and the Japanese occupation of Asian countries, the internment of Japanese Americans, wars in Korea and Vietnam—these conflicts are recorded throughout Asian American literature.

The conditions under which Asian American writers labor are connected to a number of recurring issues running throughout this enormous body of work: loss of homeland, alienation in a new country, cultural conflicts, issues of identity, family, gender relations, class differences, hope in America, anger against America, memory, longing, history. The recent proliferation of Asian American literature has been accompanied by an ever-broadening range of scholarly studies on these texts. Literary approaches to these works include analyses of class, gender, and sexuality; postcolonialism and neocolonialism; transnationalism; and cultural studies. Controversies have arisen in the field, most notably in the prioritization of racism over sexism and the question of who may write about and therefore represent "the Asian American experience." Rather than rely on the concept of the "native informant" of impossibly pure origins, scholarly studies have shifted toward recognizing hybrid identities and multiple representations that defy homogenizing descriptions of human experience.

This increasing emphasis on multiple identities includes a resistance to categories that limit people to one tidy but narrow ethnicity. Writers like the poet Cathy Song, whose background is Chinese and Korean and whose bioregion is Hawaii, or Alison Kim, a Chinese Korean lesbian writer and activist raised in California and also born in Hawaii, suggest a particular complex of cultural identities unique to Asian Hawaiian literature. Further demonstrating a need for flexible boundaries are Sui Sin Far and Diana Chang, both of Chinese and white parentage, and Brenda Wong Aoki, a playwright who describes herself as Chinese, Japanese, Spanish, and Scots and draws on Western and Japanese traditions in her drama (*The Queen's Garden*, 1992). Sigrid Nunez's novel *A Feather on the Breath of God* (1995) reflects Nunez's experiences as a child born in New York City to a Chinese Panamanian father and a German American mother. The short-story writer Marie Murphy Hara (*Bananaheart*,

1994), who comes from Asian and white parentage, edited the anthology *Intersecting Circles* (2000), a collection of writings by women of mixed ethnicities. This embrace of multiplicity and its concomitant resistance to homogeneity does not, however, preclude the possibility for individuals within ethnic groups to share historical experiences that allow for groupings helpful in organizing essays such as this one. Nonetheless, the following categorizations must be viewed as nonrigid and always open to intersections between ethnic identities.

## CHINESE AMERICAN LITERATURE

Large-scale immigration from China to America began in the nineteenth century with the importation of Hawaiian plantation workers, the 1848 discovery of gold in California, and the construction of the transcontinental railroad from 1863 to 1869. A rich oral tradition arrived with these early immigrants, traces of which were recorded in the publication of folk verse known as *muk yu* (wooden fish) in the 1860s San Francisco Chinese newspapers. Lee Yan Phou's *When I Was a Boy in China* was published in 1887, and in the late 1880s short pieces by Sui Sin Far (a.k.a. Edith Eaton) began appearing in American periodicals. Some of Sui Sin Far's writings were collected in *Mrs. Spring Fragrance* (1912), which was noted for its nonstereotypical Asian and American characters; her autobiographical sketch "Leaves from the Mental Portfolio of an Eurasian" (1909) details her years growing up in Canada and the United States. Other early works documenting the lives of Chinese immigrants include *Songs of Gold Mountain: Cantonese Rhymes from San Francisco Chinatown* (edited by Marlon K. Hom, 1987), which were originally published in 1911 and 1915.

Among the injustices suffered by Chinese immigrants was their detention in holding centers like Angel Island, where they were forced to wait off the coast of California—sometimes for years—while officials perused their paperwork and subjected them to interrogation. The barracks walls at Angel Island (the center operated from 1910 to 1940) bear Chinese characters registering that experience; these poems have been translated and collected in *Island* (edited by Mark Him Lai et al., 1980). The period immediately preceding World War II saw the publication of Huie Kin's *Reminiscences* (1932), which describes his experiences as a Christian minister in America, and H. T. Tsiang produced a wealth of writings throughout the 1930s, including the novel *And China Has Hands* (1937).

With the onset of World War II, anti-Asian discrimination shifted toward Japanese Americans, and China

became an ally of the United States. The resulting change in atmosphere contextualizes works by Chinese American writers like Helena Kuo, whose autobiography *I've Come a Long Way* (1942) details her career as a journalist. U.S.-born writers Pardee Lowe (*Father and Glorious Descendant*, 1943) and Jade Snow Wong (*Fifth Chinese Daughter*, 1945) depict San Francisco's Chinatown, while on the opposite coast, Louis Chu's *Eat a Bowl of Tea* (1961) confronts the emasculation of Chinese men in America. The 1950s saw the appearance of Su-ling Wong's *Daughter of Confucius* (1952) as well as Diana Chang's autobiographical novel *The Frontiers of Love* (1956), which describes the life of a young Eurasian girl growing up in China.

As the civil rights movement exploded in the 1960s and students on American campuses demanded the inclusion of ethnic studies in university curricula, Chinese American texts found new venues for expression. In 1974 the playwright Frank Chin, together with Jeffery Paul Chan, Lawson Fusao Inada, and Shawn Hsu Wong (*Homebase*, 1979; *American Knees*, 1995), published the seminal anthology of Asian American literature *Aiiieeeee!* (1974). In 1976 Maxine Hong Kingston's debut novel, *The Woman Warrior: Memoirs of a Girlhood among Ghosts*, created a sensation with its genre-subverting style and its representation of a Chinese American girl's coming of age. *The Woman Warrior* and Kingston's later works, *China Men* (1980) and *Tripmaster Monkey: His Fake Book* (1989), echo with a unique Chinese American cultural history drawn from Chinese and American myths and sensibilities. The novels of Amy Tan share with Kingston's work an attention to mother-daughter relationships; Tan's most famous book, *The Joy Luck Club* (1989), enjoyed particular success as an established best-seller and a Hollywood film.

More women's perspectives are offered by Louise Leung Larson, whose autobiographical *Sweet Bamboo* (1989) recalls the life of her immigrant family in Los Angeles at the turn of the century; Gish Jen, whose multiethnic experiences growing up in New York are reflected in *A Typical American* (1991) and *Mona in the Promised Land* (1996); and Fae Myenne Ng, whose novel *Bone* (1993) depicts a family with three daughters growing up in San Francisco's Chinatown. Chinese American writers who create representations of strong women are Ruthanne Lum McCunn (*Thousand Pieces of Gold*, 1981; *The Moon Pearl*, 2000), Alice Murong Pu Lin (*Grandmother Had No Name*, 1988), and Katherine Wei (*Second Daughter*, 1984). Fiona Cheong's novels re-create her native Singapore: *Scent of the*

*Gods* (1991) reconstructs the political upheaval following the country's independence in 1965, and *Shadow Theatre* (2002) channels a little girl's ghost who follows around a young unwed mother.

In 1972, *Aiiieeeee!* editor Frank Chin, whose works also include the novels *Donald Duk* (1991) and *Gunga Din Highway* (1994), saw his *Chickencoop Chinaman* become the first Asian American play to be performed on the New York stage, signaling the beginnings of a flourishing Chinese American drama scene. The celebrated David Henry Hwang wrote his first play, *FOB*, in 1978, and a decade later his *M. Butterfly* (1988), based on the true story of a twenty-year affair between a French diplomat and a Chinese transvestite opera singer, garnered a Tony award for best play of the year. Laurence Yep's *Pay the Chinaman* (1990) reveals a group of Chinese immigrants' struggles with identity in Northern California at the end of the nineteenth century; the journalist and playwright Elizabeth Wong comments on the boycott of Korean stores by African Americans in *Kimchee and Chitlins* (1990); and *Paper Angels* (1991), by the poet, performance artist, and playwright Genny Lim, portrays Chinese immigrants in Angel Island's detention center. The Chinese Filipino playwright Paul Stephen Lim's *Figures in Clay* (1989) subverts heterosexism with his portrayal of an Asian American writer and his two homosexual lovers, and Ping Chong's multimedia performances such as *Nuit Blanche* (1981) explode genre boundaries.

Among a wealth of Chinese American poets is Mei-mei Berssenbrugge, whose early verse has been characterized as imagistic (*Summits Move with the Tide*, 1974) and whose later work weds poetry and medical terminology in images of the body (*Four-Year-Old Girl*, 1998). Marilyn Chin's collections of poetry, such as *Dwarf Bamboo* (1987) and *The Phoenix Gone, the Terrace Empty* (1994), reveal the melding of Eastern and Western poetic forms, and New York–born Arthur Sze (*Dazzled*, 1982; *The Redshifting Web*, 1998) is celebrated for his striking poetic evocations of nature. The prolific Chinese Malaysian writer and literary scholar Shirley Geok-lin Lim has won a number of literary honors including the Commonwealth Poetry Prize for *Crossing the Peninsula and Other Poems* (1980) and the American Book Award for her memoir *Among the White Moon Faces* (1996); Lim's first novel, *Joss and Gold* (2001), challenges stereotypes of Asian American women and gender relationships. Also noteworthy for its attention to women's issues is Nellie Wong's *The Death of Long Steam Lady* (1986), and the writers Kitty Tsui (*The Words of a Woman Who Breathes Fire*, 1983) and Merle

Woo (*Yellow Woman Speaks*, 1986) espouse a specifically lesbian sensibility. Gay sexuality and politics provide the focus for Timothy Liu's poetry collections *Vox Angelica* (1992) and *Say Goodnight* (1998).

A contingent of Chinese American writers dedicate their texts to representations of Hawaii. Darrell H. Y. Lum's work (*Sun: Short Stories and Drama*, 1980 and *Pass On, No Pass Back!*, 1990) deploys pidgin English to assert preservation of Hawaiian linguistic culture, and Norman Wong's prose collection *Cultural Revolution* (1994) explores the experiences of a gay Chinese American man whose family moves from China to Hawaii. The Chinese Korean poet Cathy Song, influenced by visual artists like Kitagawa Utamaro and Georgia O'Keeffe, paints poetic collages of Oahu rains, quotidian details of domestic life, and the mysteries of her ancestors, from her picture-bride grandmother to her aging parents; her collections include *Picture Bride* (1983), *Frameless Windows, Squares of Light* (1988), and *The Land of Bliss* (2001). Eric Chock's poetry collections *Ten Thousand Wishes* (1978) and *Last Days Here* (1990) speak of the poet's lifelong experiences of Hawaii; other poets who evoke the islands are Wing Tek Lum (*Expounding the Doubtful Points*, 1987) and John Yau (*Radiant Silhouettes*, 1989).

Among numerous other voices in Chinese American literature are the poets Fay Chiang (*In the City of Contradictions*, 1979), Alexander Kuo (*Changing the River*, 1986), Alan Chong Lau (*Songs for Jadina*, 1980), Li-Young Lee (*The City in Which I Love You*, 1990), George Leong (*A Lone Bamboo Doesn't Come from Jackson Street*, 1977), Russell Leong (*The Country of Dreams and Dust*, 1993), Amy Ling (*Chinamerican Reflections*, 1984), Stephen Liu (*Dream Journeys to China*, 1982), the Chinese Malaysian poet Chin Woon Ping (*The Naturalization of Camellia Song*, 1993), and John Yau (*Radiant Silhouette*, 1989). Fiction writers include Adet Lin and Lin Taiyi, who published in the 1940s (their father, Lin Yutang, published *Chinatown Family* in 1947); Virginia Lee (*The House That Tai Ming Built*, 1963); Betty Lee Sung (*Mountain of Gold*, 1967); and sojourner Yung Wing (*My Life in China and America*, 1909).

## FILIPINO AMERICAN LITERATURE

The circumstances of American colonization of the Philippines from 1899 to 1946 and the continued use of English in government, schools, and other settings inflect the concept of Filipino American literature, so a strict differentiation between Filipino literature in English and Filipino American literature becomes problematic.

Among early examples of Filipino writing in English is Paz Marquez Benitez's short story "Dead Stars" (1927) and the works of José García Villa, who is often described as a modernist writer; his short stories (*Footnote to Youth*, 1933) and poetry (*Have Come, Am Here*, 1941) drew praise from such notables as W. H. Auden and Edith Sitwell. Angela Manalang Gloria's poetry, written in the 1930s and 1940s, conveys daring exposures of women's oppression so controversial that the Commonwealth Literary Award committee for 1940 rejected Gloria's work, including the poem "Revolt from Hymen." Also among important writers of Filipino literature in English is F. Sionil José, who began writing short stories and novels while working as a journalist in Manila. The Rosales saga, including *The Pretenders* (1962) and *Po-on* (1984), is considered José's masterpiece, a five-volume work spanning four generations and more than a hundred years of Philippine history. The novelist, poet, playwright, and essayist Nick Joaquin references Spanish colonization as well as Filipino heritage; his works include the novel *The Woman Who Had Two Navels* (1961) and *The Aquinos of Tarlac* (1983), a biography of the assassinated presidential candidate Benigno Aquino.

After the Spanish-American (1898) and Philippine-American (1899–1902) wars, the Philippines became a "protectorate" of the United States, rendering the Filipino people U.S. "nationals." Thus began a major wave of immigration from the Philippines to the United States; these immigrants included mostly laborers who moved along the West Coast between the Alaskan canneries and California's agricultural fields. Carlos Bulosan is the most prominent writer from this cohort of immigrants, which also includes Manuel Buaken (*I Have Lived with the American People*, 1948) and Benny Feria (*Filipino Son*, 1954). Bulosan, who came to the United States in 1931, produced an outpouring of prose and poetry, including the autobiographical novel *America Is in the Heart* (1946). Although the book refuses to elide the racism encountered by Filipino immigrants in the United States, Bulosan's most famous work was considered an example of optimism and faith in "America." A contemporary of Bulosan, Bienvenido Santos (*Scent of Apples*, 1979) came to the United States under different circumstances. As a *pensionado*, or government-sponsored scholar, Santos traveled the American Midwest and East Coast, but his academic adventure was overshadowed by the distant Japanese invasion of the Philippines. In 1949 N. V. M. Gonzalez arrived in America on a writing fellowship. He embraced the conviction that Filipino languages shape

Filipino writing in English, an aesthetic evident in his novels *The Bamboo Dancers* (1959) and *A Season of Grace* (1956).

Linda Ty-Casper began her prolific writing career in 1963 with the appearance of *The Transparent Sun and Other Stories*; however, political censorship prevented the publication of her novel *Awaiting Trespass* (1985) in the Philippines, and the book became her first American publication. Political circumstances also inform the work of Ninotchka Rosca (*State of War*, 1988), who came to the United States as an exile after martial law was declared under Ferdinand Marcos in the 1970s. Jessica Tarahata Hagedorn has pursued a multifaceted career that includes singing, performance art, and writing fiction, plays, and poetry. *Danger and Beauty* (1993), a collection of poetry and prose published between 1968 and 1992, offers a sampling of her work; her 1990 novel *Dogeaters* garnered a nomination for the National Book Award.

Writers who also present Filipina perspectives include Sabina Murray, whose 1990 novel *Slow Burn* portrays the downward slide of a Manila party girl, and Marianne Villanueva, who explores family and gender relationships in her collection *Ginseng and Other Tales from Manila* (1991). The impacts of American cultural and military presence upon women in the Philippines are inscribed in Michelle Cruz Skinner's stories (*Balikbayan*, 1988; *Mango Seasons*, 1996), while M. Evelina Galang's *Her Wild American Self* (1996) features women's perspectives deriving mainly from the experiences of a U.S.-born generation of Filipino Americans living in the Midwest. Filipino American narratives published at this time also include Peter Bacho's novel *Cebu* (1991), which recounts the story of a Filipino American priest and issues of identity, religion, and morality, and Cecilia Manguerra Brainard's *Song of Yvonne* (1991), which evokes Filipino myth while simultaneously revealing the horrors of Japanese occupation. Brian Ascalon Roley's novel *American Son* (2001) portrays the cultural conflicts of a U.S.-born generation, specifically of two brothers living in Southern California with their Filipino mother. Other Filipino American voices in fiction include Gina Apostol (*Bibliolepsy*, 1997), Tess Uriza Holthe (*When the Elephants Dance*, 2002), Lia Relova (*Sacred Places*, 1997), Sophia G. Romero (*Always Hiding*, 1998), Lara Stapleton (*The Lowest Blue Flame before Nothing*, 1998), and Sam Tagatac (*The New Anak*, 1974).

The "Flip" writers of the San Francisco Bay Area presented selections from their poetry in the anthology *Without Names* (1985), edited by Al Robles, whose volume *Rappin with Ten Thousand Caribou in the Dark* appeared in 1996. Among the poets in *Without Names* are Virginia Cerenio (*Trespassing Innocence*, 1989), Jeff Tagami (*October Light*, 1987), Shirley Ancheta, Oscar Peñaranda, and Jaime Jacinto. The ingenuity and vision of Filipino American poetry is also evident in work from Nick Carbó (*El Grupo MacDonald's*, 1995; *Secret Asian Man*, 2000); Eileen Tabios, whose *Beyond Life Sentences* (1998) won the Philippines' National Book Award for poetry; Myrna Peña-Reyes (*The River Singing Stone*, 1983); Maria Luisa B. Aguilar Cariño (*In the Garden of the Three Islands*, 1994); Gémino H. Abad and his daughter Cyan Abad (*Father and Daughter: The Figures of Our Speech*, 1996); Fatima Lim-Wilson (*Crossing the Snow Bridge*, 1995); Nerissa S. Balce; Jean Vengua Gier; Karina Africa-Bolasco; Mila D. Aguilar; Carlos A. Angeles; and Catalina Cariaga. Many of these poets are published in the anthology *Returning a Borrowed Tongue* (1995), edited by Nick Carbó.

Filipino American dramatists have drawn upon tales of immigration, family histories, and regional connections in their theater pieces. The playwright Jeannie Barroga has written dozens of plays, including *Talk-Story* (1990), which portrays the relationship between an immigrant father and his U.S.-born daughter, and *The Bubble-Gum Killers* (1999), based on the true story of a Filipino immigrant gang leader. Han Ong has authored over thirty plays including *Bachelor Rat* (1992) and *Middle Finger* (2001); Ong's first novel, *Fixer Chao*, was published in 2001 to critical acclaim, and in 1997 he became the first Filipino American to be awarded the prestigious MacArthur Fellowship. *Balangiga* (2002), by Ralph B. Peña and the Korean American playwright Sung Rno, exposes the horrors of the Philippine-American War, and other Filipino American artists bringing Filipino cultural scenes to the stage are Louella Dizon (*Till Voices Wake Us*, 1992) and Linda Faigao-Hall (*Americans*, 1987).

An extensive body of Filipino American writing is dedicated to exploring gay and lesbian sexualities. R. Zamora Linmark's *Rolling the R's* (1995) deploys pidgin English and 1970s popular cultural references to portray a group of teenagers coming of age in Hawaii; in his novel *The Umbrella Country* (1999), Bino A. Realuyo depicts a family tormented by domestic violence and poverty in the Philippines; and Chea Villanueva's lesbian erotica is collected in *Jessie's Song* (1995). Anthologies include *Ladlad: An Anthology of Philippine Gay Writing* (1994) and *Ladlad 2* (1996), both edited by J. Neil C. Garcia and

Danton Remoto, as well as *Tibok: Heartbeat of the Filipino Lesbian* (1998), edited by Anna Leah Sarabia.

Although Filipino American literature suggests writing in English, works in native dialects cannot be excluded from this designation. Since 1971 the writers group Gunglo Dagiti Mannurat Nga Ilokano Iti Hawaii has published Ilokano-language texts by Filipino American writers in Hawaii; the group works to preserve their native tongue as well as the literary forms particular to Filipino and Ilokano cultures. Poetry written in English and translated to Cebuano, or written in Kinaray-a or Ilokano and translated into English, appears in the anthology *Babaylan: An Anthology of Filipina and Filipina American Writers* (2000), edited by Nick Carbó and Eileen Tabios, demonstrating the possibilities for subverting the restrictions of an English-only Filipino American literary canon.

## JAPANESE AMERICAN LITERATURE

Although literature regarding Japanese American internment receives much attention, the years before World War II also produced writing that reflects the experiences of first-generation immigrants. This generation of Japanese Americans, known as Issei, arrived toward the end of the nineteenth century, when the Chinese Exclusion Acts and the easing of Japanese emigration laws spurred male Japanese immigrants to Hawaii and the mainland. *Miss Numé of Japan* (1899) by Onoto Watanna is considered by some the first Asian American novel to be published in the United States; other early Issei literary figures include Carl Sadakichi Hartmann, a critic, writer, and artist working at the turn of the century, known particularly for composing haiku in English. Etsu Sugimoto, raised and educated in Japan, sought to describe her culture for American audiences through four novels and an autobiographical narrative, *A Daughter of the Samurai* (1925); poet Bunichi Kagawa's *Hidden Flame* was published in 1930.

The internment during World War II of more than 110,000 Japanese Americans raised questions of national loyalty and identity, particularly for the Nisei (second-generation Japanese Americans); consequently, internment literature often reflects Japanese Americans' ambivalence toward the United States. John Okada's *No-No Boy* (1957) directly confronts the loyalty oath that Japanese Americans were forced to sign; Monica Sone's autobiographical account of internment in Minidoka, Idaho, *Nisei Daughter* (1953), is also among works that portray life in the camps; and Jeanne Wakatsuki Houston's narrative of conditions at Manzanar, California, *Farewell to Manzanar* (1973, cowritten with James Houston), was made into a television film in 1976. In 1949 Toshio Mori published his collection of short stories, *Yokohama, California*. Although Mori was incarcerated at Topaz, Utah, his work leans away from internment themes to envision a community of first- and second-generation Japanese Americans living in the San Francisco Bay Area of the 1930s. Hisaye Yamamoto, who was interned at Poston, Arizona, wrote a number of short stories collected in *Seventeen Syllables* (1988). Her fiction reflects camp life but delves into other experiences, such as jobs as a reporter and as a cook in Massachusetts. Mitsuye Yamada's poetry and fiction (*Camp Notes*, 1976; *Desert Run*, 1988) confront crises of racism and sexism during World War II and within the camps; her work also reaches back to ancestral forms, as in her translations of her father's senryu poems. In 1982 Yoshiko Uchida published her war and internment memoirs, *Desert Exile* (1982), but such literature is not limited to the United States; Joy Kogawa's novel *Obasan* (1981) weaves recollections of the camps in Canada.

Japanese American writers drawing upon their parents' lives as immigrants include Akemi Kikumura (*Promises Kept*, 1991) and R. A. Sasaki (*The Loom and Other Stories*, 1991). Cynthia Kadohata's *The Floating World* (1989) portrays a Japanese American migrant-worker family driving through the United States in the 1950s and 1960s, and David Mas Masumoto's short-story collection *Silent Strength* (1984) focuses on California farming communities in the 1930s. In 1988 the journalist and fiction writer Gene Oishi expanded Asian American investigations of racism to reference discrimination by whites against African Americans and Native Americans in his book *In Search of Hiroshi*, and in 1989 Tooru J. Kanazawa's *Sushi and Sourdough* appeared, an account of Japanese Americans living in Alaska from the late 1890s through the early 1920s. Lydia Minatoya's memoir *Talking to High Monks in the Snow: An Asian American Odyssey* was published in 1992; her first novel, *The Strangeness of Beauty* (2001), depicts three generations of Japanese and Japanese American women as they reunite in pre–World War II Japan. The filmmaker, poet, playwright, and performance artist David Mura has produced the book *Turning Japanese: Memoirs of a Sansei* (1991); a multimedia performance titled *Relocations: Images from a Sansei* (1990); and a poetry collection, *The Colors of Desire* (1995).

Early Japanese Americans rendering literary visions of Hawaiian culture include Shelley Ota (*Upon Their Shoulders*, 1951), Margaret Harada (*The Sun Shines on the Immigrant*, 1960), and Kazuo Miyamoto (*Hawaii: End of the Rainbow*, 1964). Edward Sakamoto's plays (*In the Alley*, 1961; *Aloha Las Vegas*, 1998) create characters whose use of pidgin English helps them carve out identities from their positions among several cultures. Milton Murayama's novels *All I Asking for Is My Body* (1975) and *Plantation Boy* (1998) also experiment with pidgin to present stories of Japanese Americans working and living on Hawaiian plantations. Sylvia Watanabe's short-story collection *Talking to the Dead* (1992) evokes the islands' natural and cultural phenomena, and Juliet S. Kono's volume of poems *Hilo Rains* (1988), haunted by Pearl Harbor and internment, sketches family dynamics with special awe for the maternal. The award-winning poet Garrett Hongo (*Yellow Light*, 1982; *The River of Heaven*, 1988) draws landscapes of Hawaii and the American West Coast, asking questions regarding identity and place and connecting with ancestors and their cultural mythos.

The injuries of racism, war, and internment also emerge through Japanese American poets such as Lawson Fusao Inada, whose jazz-influenced verse reflects the political sensibilities of the 1960s and 1970s; his collections include *Before the War* (1971) and *Legends from Camp* (1992). Janice Mirikitani's poetry is gathered in *Awake in the River* (1978), *We, the Dangerous* (1995), and her ferocious volume *Shedding Silence* (1987), which calls up racism and internment in association with scenes of sexual violence. The National Book Award–winning poet Ai, born in Arizona of Native American, African American, and Japanese heritage, presents visions that intertwine the personal and the political, particularly in terms of racist historical atrocities (*Cruelty*, 1973; *Fate*, 1991). Notable Japanese American poets also include Kimiko Hahn (*Mosquito & Ant*, 1999), Geraldine Kudaka (*Numerous Avalanches at the Point of Intersection*, 1979), James Mitsui (*Crossing the Phantom River*, 1978), Yasuo Sasaki (*Village Scene/Village Herd*, 1986), and Ronald Tanaka (*Shino Suite*, 1981).

Japanese American playwrights include Wakako Yamauchi, who was interned at Poston with Hisaye Yamamoto and whose drama often centers around her childhood observations of Issei women, as in *And the Soul Shall Dance* (1973) and *The Music Lessons* (1977). Philip Kan Gotanda's plays (*Yankee Dawg You Die*, 1988; *Floating Weeds*, 2001) have been produced internationally, and Dwight Okita's *The Rainy Season* (1996) portrays the relationship between a mother and her gay son. Velina Hasu Houston's *Asa Ga Kimashita* (1981) reflects her experiences as the daughter of an African American serviceman and a Japanese mother, and the critically acclaimed play *Tea* (1987) depicts Japanese American women in Kansas in the 1960s. Other dramatists offering performances of culture and identity are Amy Hill (*Tokyo Bound*, 1990), Momoko Ito (*Gold Watch*, 1970), Denise Uyehara (*Hiro*, 1994), and Karen Tei Yamashita (*Godzilla Comes to Little Tokyo*, 1990).

## KOREAN AMERICAN LITERATURE

Korean American literature shares with other Asian American literatures the historical contexts of immigration and discriminatory legislation as well as experiences of racism and alienation in the United States. The circumstances of Japanese occupation (1910–1945), World War II, and the Korean War (1950–1953) and its aftermath are also present in the works of immigrant and U.S.-born Korean American writers. New Il-han's *When I Was a Boy in Korea* (1928) exemplifies an early text that proffers an immigrant's description of Korean culture for an American audience, but perhaps the most prominent writer from this time period is Younghill Kang, who came to America in 1921. Kang's novel *The Grass Roof* (1931) offers a glimpse of Kang's life in Korea; his second book, *East Goes West* (1937) focuses upon life in America and a bachelor society of intellectuals whose dreams of success are destroyed. Other early Korean American autobiographical works include Induk Pahk's *September Monkey* (1954), which describes American missionaries and Japanese colonization in Korea, and Taiwon Koh's *The Bitter Fruit of Kom-pawi* (1959).

Richard E. Kim's novel *The Martyred* (1964), set in the North Korean city of Pyongyang during the Korean War, remains the only Asian American book to be nominated for a Nobel Prize. Kim's next novel, *The Innocent* (1968), renders a sympathetic portrayal of South Korean military officers during a coup, and his *Lost Names* (1970) recounts his boyhood in Korea under Japanese occupation. Other immigrant Korean American writers include Ty Pak, author of two volumes of short stories (*Guilt Payment*, 1983; *Moonbay*, 1999) and a novel (*Cry Korea Cry*, 1999). Sook Nyul Choi, who emigrated to the United States in 1968, has crafted a number of works for young readers, including *Year of Impossible Goodbyes* (1991), which portrays Japanese occupation and Soviet invasion from the perspective of a ten-year-old girl, and *Gathering of Pearls* (1994). Ahn Jung-Hyo originally wrote his novel *White Badge* (1989) in Korean and then translated the text into English to present his experiences in the Korean army during the Vietnam War to an American audience.

Writers who base their art on their immigrant families' experiences include Margaret K. Pai, whose *The Dreams of Two Yi-Min* (1989) is an autobiographical account of her parents' immigration from Korea and their attempts to settle in America. Like Pai's work, Mary Paik Lee's *Quiet Odyssey: A Pioneer Korean Woman in America* (1990) describes the struggles of Lee's family upon arriving in the United States. *Clay Walls* (1986), a novel by Ronyoung Kim (a.k.a. Gloria Hahn), shows how U.S.-born children are influenced by their immigrant parents' culture. Other depictions of young people navigating their parents' cultures are Marie G. Lee's *Finding My Voice* (1992) and *If It Hadn't Been for Yoon Jun* (1993); Heinz Insu Fenkl's *Memories of My Ghost Brother* (1996), which fictionalizes the author's experiences as the child of a white American soldier and a Korean mother in a military camptown in South Korea; and Nora Okja Keller's *Comfort Woman* (1997), which intertwines the narratives of a mother, previously a comfort woman, and her mixed-ethnicity daughter.

Gary Pak's fiction (*The Watcher of Waipuna*, 1992; *A Ricepaper Airplane*, 1998) explores a multiplicity of ethnicities and sexualities and draws upon Hawaiian plantation history and narrative traditions such as talk-story and pidgin English. *Native Speaker* (1995), by Chang-rae Lee, deals with a Korean American protagonist who feels caught between cultures; the novel garnered great critical praise, which led to Lee's inclusion in *The New Yorker* magazine's list of the twenty best writers under the age of forty. Other Korean American writers include Leonard Chang (*Over the Shoulder*, 2000), Susan Choi (*The Foreign Student*, 1998), Sun-Won Hwang (*The Descendants of Cain*, 1997), Peter Hyun (*Man Sei!*, 1986), Nancy Kim (*Chinhominey's Secret*, 1999), Frances Park and Ginger Park (*To Swim across the World*, 2001), Therese Park (*A Gift of the Emperor*, 1997), Mira Stout (*One Thousand Chestnut Trees*, 1998), and Mia Yun (*House of the Winds*, 1998).

The poet Willyce Kim, whose work espouses lesbian Asian American sensibilities replete with humor and play, has published two volumes of verse, *Eating Artichokes* (1972) and *Under the Rolling Sky* (1976), as well as two novels, *Dancer Dawkins and the California Kid* (1985) and *Dead Heat* (1988). Myung Mi Kim's poetry takes on more somber tones: *Under Flag* (1991) portrays immigration, national identity, and the legacy of war; *The Bounty* (1996) invokes the maternal; and *Dura* (1998) wields fragments of haunting natural imagery. Other writers representing Korean American experiences in verse are Debra Kang Dean (*News of Home*, 1998), Chungmi Kim (*Selected Poems*, 1982), Won Ko (*The Turn of Zero*, 1974), Priscilla

Lee (*Wishbone*, 2000), Yearn Hong Choi, and Moon Hee Kim.

Performance and playwriting are represented by a group of versatile Korean American artists. Writer, filmmaker, and performance artist Theresa Hak Kyung Cha created a multigenre masterpiece with her book *DICTEE* (1982), which portrays Korean women's suffering under Japanese occupation while simultaneously demonstrating cultural displacement through the use of Korean, French, and English languages. Diana Son, a fiction writer and dramatist, saw the premier of her production *R.A.W. Plays: Short Plays for Raunchy Asian Women—R.A.W. ('Cause I'm a Woman)* in 1993. Performing the relationship between a Korean American brother and sister in the Midwest, Sung Rno's play *Cleveland Raining* was produced in several U.S. cities in 1995, and his 1999 play *wAve* boasts a pastiche of images from Asian and American cultures. Rob Shin's *The Art of Waiting* (1991) explores the uneasy relationship between Korean Americans and African Americans, and Susan Kim, besides writing a number of plays, adapted Amy Tan's novel *The Joy Luck Club* for the theater; the play premiered in 1997.

## SOUTH ASIAN AMERICAN LITERATURE

The term "South Asian American," like the term "Asian American," inevitably homogenizes a group of people who derive from India, Pakistan, Sri Lanka, Bangladesh, Nepal, and the Maldive Islands, or who have sometimes arrived in the United States or Canada by way of East Africa and South America. Early South Asian immigrant laborers arrived on the American West Coast between 1904 and 1924; their narratives represent some of the earliest records of South Asian American lives. This literature today often reflects influences of Western literary traditions as well as South Asian classic and folk literatures; many South Asian American writers have lived or live now in Canada or England, demonstrating the vestiges of British colonization also apparent in the proliferation of English-language South Asian literature.

Prolific among South Asian American writers is Ved (Parkash) Mehta, who came from India to the United States to attend the School for the Blind in Arkansas. A writer for *The New Yorker*, his numerous works include the autobiographical narrative *Face to Face* (1957), a novel (*Delinquent Chacha*, 1966), and a book of short stories (*Three Stories of the Raj*, 1986). Raja Rao, whose writing is deeply rooted in Brahmanism and Hinduism, has published a number of works, including *The Serpent and the Rope* (1960), a narrative of the search for spiritual

truth, and *Cat and Shakespeare* (1965), in which a cat symbolizes karma. Bharati Mukherjee, a fiction writer who immigrated from Calcutta to Canada and then to the United States, claims identity as an American writer while acknowledging her roots in Indian culture. Her books *The Wife* (1975), *The Tiger's Daughter* (1972), and *Jasmine* (1989) allude to the experiences of upper-class women moving from Calcutta to the United States, their displacement and alienation, and their disillusionment with the "American Dream." Bapsi Sidhwa, a Pakistani diasporic novelist, reveals attention to women's issues and her own childhood exposure to storytelling: *The Crow Eaters* (1979), *Cracking India* (1991), and *An American Brat* (1993).

Other South Asian American writers have found voice through verse. G. S. Sharat Chandra began a career as a lawyer and turned instead to poetry; he has published numerous collections, including *Family of Mirrors* (1993), which was nominated for the Pulitzer Prize, and *Immigrants of Loss* (1994), which won nominations for the Commonwealth Poetry Prize and the T. S. Eliot Prize. Agha Shahid Ali has composed five volumes of poetry, including *In Memory of Begum Akhtar* (1979) and *A Nostalgist's Map of America* (1991). Ali's work is particularly inscribed by the loss of and longing for home; his own wanderings from Kashmir, India, to New Delhi and then to the United States are revealed in his work's vision of regional history and geography. Zulfikar Ghose, from prepartition India and Pakistan, moved in 1969 to the United States. His work demonstrates attention to identity issues such as religious affiliation; his oeuvre includes *The Triple Mirror of the Self* (1992) and *Veronica and the Góngora Passion* (1998).

South Asian American women have also forged writing careers throughout the 1980s and 1990s. Chitra Banerjee Divakaruni's *Vine of Desire* (2002), the sequel to her novel *Sister of My Heart* (1999), continues the narrative of two women's friendship in India and the United States; her collections of poetry include *Black Candle* (1991). The poet, fiction writer, and essayist Meena Alexander has published several volumes of poetry, a novel (*Nampally Road*, 1991), and a memoir (*Fault Lines*, 1993); her work details the nuances of women's perspectives of family, migration, and memory. The Pakistani American literary critic and writer Sara Suleri depicts her relocations between Pakistan, England, and the United States in the narrative *Meatless Days* (1989), and Indira Ganesan created a bildungsroman of a young Indian girl who has an affair with an older American man in *Inheritance*

(1998). Tanuja Desai Hidier's novel *Born Confused* (2002) presents the story of an aspiring woman photographer encountering questions of cultural authenticity against the backdrop of the New York nightclub scene.

Santha Rama Rau's prolific writing career has yielded cookbooks, travel books, fiction, and poetry, including the novel *The Adventuress* (1971) and a theatrical adaptation of E. M. Forster's *A Passage to India*. Anita Desai's works are infused with the cultural divisions that she witnessed and experienced with an Indian father and a German mother, including *In Custody* (1984), which was made into a motion picture, and *Fasting, Feasting* (1999), which also focuses on women's experiences within Pakistani culture. Vikram Seth's books of poetry include *Mappings* (1982) and *Three Chinese Poets* (1992), and his critically acclaimed *A Suitable Boy* (1993), at 1,349 pages, is the longest single-volume novel published in English. Shashi Tharoor has written several novels, including *Riot* (2001), *India: From Midnight to the Millennium* (1997), and *Show Business* (1992), a rollicking look at the Indian filmmaking industry that was made into the film *Bollywood*. *The Glass Palace*, Amitav Ghosh's novel about a young man seeking a childhood love against the backdrop of a politically unstable Burma, appeared in 2000.

Not limited to English-language texts, South Asian American literature also encompasses poets writing in other languages. Panna Naik, whose work has been described as Indian feminist, has written several volumes of poetry in Gujarati; Usha Nilsson (Priyamvada) composes poetry in Hindi; and A. K. Ramanujan composes in English and Kannada (*Speaking of Siva*, 1973). South Asian American literature is further highlighted by the works of the poet Indran Amirthanayagam (*The Elephants of Reckoning*, 1993); the novelist Boman Desai (*The Memory of Elephants*, 1988); the memoirist and writer Kartar Dhillon, whose granddaughter Erika Surat Andersen adapted Dhillon's work for the short film "Turbans" (1999); the Pakistani American short-story writer and translator Tahira Naqvi (*Attar of Roses* 1995); the novelist Kirin Narayan (*Love, Stars, and All That*, 1994); and the playwright Bina Sharif (*My Ancestor's House*, 1992). South Asian Canadian writers include Michael Ondaatje (*The English Patient*, 1992), the poet Rienzi

Santha Rama Rau. (© *Corbis*)

Crusz (*The Rain Does Not Know Me Anymore*, 1992), and Uma Parameswaran (*The Door I Shut Behind Me*, 1990).

## VIETNAMESE AMERICAN LITERATURE

Over the course of just a few days in April 1975, more than 86,000 Vietnamese refugees came to the United States, fleeing the aftermath of the fall of Saigon. Although a number of immigrants came from Vietnam before this influx, the beginnings of Vietnamese American literature are often pinpointed on or about 1975. Soon after, a number of Vietnamese American narratives began to appear, albeit in the form of translated, transcribed, and/or edited interviews like Al Santoli's *To Bear Any Burden: The Vietnam War and Its Aftermath in the Words of Americans and Southeast Asians* (1985) and James M. Freeman's *Hearts of Sorrow: Vietnamese-American Lives* (1989). Other writings appearing in the late 1980s also took the form of collaborations, such as the poetry and prose collection by Wendy Wilder Larsen and Tran Thi Nga, *Shallow Graves: Two Women in Vietnam* (1986). *When Heaven and Earth Changed Places* (1989) and *Child of War, Woman of Peace* (1993), two volumes representing Le Ly Hayslip's autobiographical writing, were coauthored by Jay Wurts and James Hayslip, respectively; the two works were made into a film directed by Oliver Stone (*Heaven and Earth*, 1993).

A number of autobiographical narratives not reliant upon collaboration have emerged since the mid 1990s; among these is Nguyen Qui Duc's *Where the Ashes Are: The Odyssey of a Vietnamese Family* (1994), which focuses on his family members' inability to escape Vietnam during the war, and Jade Ngoc Huynh's *South Wind Changing* (1994), which describes the horrific conditions of war and the author's imprisonment in a forced labor camp. *Catfish and Mandala* (1999), Andrew X. Pham's travel memoir of a Vietnamese American man traveling through Mexico, Japan, and Vietnam, won the Kiriyama Pacific Rim Book Prize for nonfiction, and Kien Nguyen's *The Unwanted* (2001), a memoir of his experiences as a half-white American, half-Vietnamese boy growing up in Vietnam after the fall of Saigon, is being planned as a Hollywood film.

More writing that draws upon experiences of war includes Lan Cao's novel *Monkey Bridge* (1997), which portrays the strain within a mother-daughter relationship as the pair flee Vietnam for Virginia in 1975, and Mong-Lan's *Song of the Cicadas* (2001), a collection of poems and drawings that garnered the Juniper Prize. Truong Tran's collection *Placing the Accents* (1999) intertwines food and family dynamics with Vietnamese and French phrases, layers of language that reveal multiple national influences. Linh Dinh, who also writes as a poet (*Drunkard Boxing*, 1998) and translator, returned in 1999 to Vietnam after spending twenty-four years as a refugee in the United States. Half of the short stories in his collection *Fake House* (2000) take place in America; the other half are set in Vietnam. In *The Book of Salt* (2003), the literary critic and writer Monique T. D. Truong evokes Paris between the world wars, as seen from the viewpoint of Gertrude Stein and Alice B. Toklas's male Vietnamese cook.

The performance artist and writer le thi diem thuy transforms her memories of Vietnam into theater in *Mua He Do Lua* (*Red Fiery Summer*, 1994), and Vietnamese American histories and narratives are further traced in the works of Jackie Bong-Wright (*Autumn Cloud*, 2001), Nancy Tran Cantrell (*Seeds of Hope*, 1999), Duong Van Mai Elliott (*The Sacred Willow*, 1999), and Mai Nguyen (*Little Daisy*, 1993). Other Vietnamese American literary figures include Bao-Long Chu, Maura Donohue, Lan Duong, Elizabeth Gordon, Lai Thanhha, Andrew Lam, Trinh T. Minh-ha (also an important critic and theorist), Bich Minh Ngyuen, Minh Duc Nguyen, Dao Strom, and Barbara Tran.

## MORE ASIAN AMERICAN LITERATURES

Works by writers who have arrived in America from Laos include *Where the Torches Are Burning* (2002), a poetry chapbook by the Hmong American Pos Moua that recounts his family history in Southeast Asia, his flight from Laos, and his adaptation to life in the United States. The novelist T. C. Huo was born in Laos of Canadian descent and came to the United States in 1979; his first book, *A Thousand Wings* (1998), takes place in present-day San Francisco and in Laos during the Vietnam War. Huo's second novel, *Land of Smiles* (2000), which depicts a family living in a Thai refugee camp in the late 1980s, won the Asian Pacific American Award for Literature in adult fiction.

The Burmese American writer Wendy Law-Yone, born in Mandalay and raised in Rangoon, published her first novel, *The Coffin Tree*, in 1983 and a second book,

*Irrawaddy Tango*, in 1993. *The Coffin Tree* reflects the painful experiences of the narrator and her half-brother as they flee the volatile situation in Burma after a violent political coup in the 1960s. In America they suffer such discrimination and poverty that the narrator is driven to a suicide attempt and her brother to death. The Cambodian American writer Loung Ung's autobiographical account of her childhood, *First They Killed My Father* (2000), describes the tyranny of the Khmer Rouge regime under which Ung and her family were sent to forced labor camps. The book garnered the 2001 Asian Pacific American Award for Literature in adult nonfiction, and Ung currently continues her vocation as an activist working to increase awareness of the global consequences of landmines.

[*See also* Kingston, Maxine Hong, *and* Vietnam in Poetry and Prose.]

## FURTHER READING

Asian Women United of California, eds. *Making Waves: An Anthology of Writing by and about Asian American Women.* Boston, 1989. A collection of prose and poetry from Asian American women; includes historical and sociological essays.

Chan, Jeffery Paul, Frank Chin, Lawson Fusao Inada, and Shawn Wong, eds. *The Big Aiiieeeee!: An Anthology of Chinese American and Japanese American Literature.* New York, 1991. The follow-up volume to the first; focuses exclusively on Chinese American and Japanese American writers.

Chan, Sucheng. *Asian Americans: An Interpretive History.* Boston, 1991. An often-referenced work describing Asian immigrants in America and the legal and socio-economic obstacles they have historically encountered.

Cheung, King-Kok, ed. *An Interethnic Companion to Asian American Literature.* Cambridge, 1997. A collection of overviews on different Asian American literatures, accompanied by a selection of essays dealing with specific topics such as gender, journalistic representations, and Hawaiian literature.

Cheung, King-Kok, and Stan Yogi, eds. *Asian American Literature: An Annotated Bibliography.* New York, 1988. References to numerous primary and secondary sources for literary research.

Chin, Frank, Jeffery Paul Chan, Lawson Fusao Inada, and Shawn Hsu Wong, eds. *Aiiieeeee!: An Anthology of Asian-American Literature.* Washington, D.C., 1974. A collection of novel excerpts and short stories by Asian Americans; includes introductory essays on various literary histories.

Chock, Eric, and Darrell H. Y. Lum, eds. *Pake: Writings by Chinese in Hawaii.* Honolulu, 1989. A broad selection of writers conveying their various perspectives on Hawaiian culture.

Fenkl, Heinz Insu, and Walter K. Lew, eds. *Kori: The Beacon Anthology of Korean American Fiction.* Boston, 2001. Comprising book extracts and short fiction from sixteen noteworthy Korean American writers.

Francia, Luis H. *Brown River, White Ocean: An Anthology of Twentieth-Century Philippine Literature in English.* New Brunswick, N.J., 1993. Short stories and poetry written in English by Filipinos and Filipino Americans; accompanied by an introduction and brief biographies.

Francia, Luis H., and Eric Gamalinda, eds. *Flippin': Filipinos on America.* New York, 1996. Literature from Filipino American artists; includes English-language writers and poets in the Philippines.

Hagedorn, Jessica, ed. *Charlie Chan Is Dead: An Anthology of Contemporary Asian American Fiction.* New York, 1993. A range of Asian American literature including poetry, novel excerpts, and short stories.

Hara, Marie Murphy, and Nora Okja Keller, eds. *Intersecting Circles: The Voices of Hapa Women in Poetry and Prose.* Honolulu, 2000. A collection of writing by women of mixed Asian and white backgrounds and their representations of their experiences living between ethnic categories.

Hongo, Garrett, ed. *The Open Boat: Poems from Asian America.* New York, 1993. Thirty poets are collected in this anthology, which features contemplations of identity and culture.

Houston, Velina Hasu, and Roberta Uno, eds. *But Still, Like Air, I'll Rise: New Asian American Plays.* Philadelphia, 1997. A selection of recent plays by Asian American dramatists; includes a foreword by Uno.

Kim, Elaine H. *Asian American Literature: An Introduction to the Writings and Their Social Context.* Philadelphia, 1982. A seminal literary study of a range of Asian American writers from Younghill Kang to Carlos Bulosan; historically contextualizes authors and works.

Lew, Walter, ed. *Premonitions: The Kaya Anthology of New Asian North American Poetry.* New York, 1995. Anthologizes seventy-three poets, descended from a multitude of Asian regions, writing in traditional and experimental forms.

Lim, Shirley Geok-lin, and Mayumi Tsutakawa, eds. *The Forbidden Stitch: An Asian American Woman's Anthology.* Corvallis, Oreg., 1989. This American Book Award–winning anthology encompasses poetry, prose, and visual art (including photographs of art pieces) by Asian American women.

Lim, Shirley Geok-lin, and Amy Ling, eds. *Reading the Literatures of Asian America.* Philadelphia, 1992. A collection of essays discussing issues portrayed in Asian American literature, such as gender and nationality.

Lim-Hing, Sharon, ed. *The Very Inside: An Anthology of Writing by Asian and Pacific Islander Lesbian and Bisexual Women.* Toronto, 1994. A collection of Asian American and Asian Canadian lesbian and bisexual women's writing.

Rustomji-Kerns, Roshni. *Living in America: Poetry and Fiction by South Asian American Writers.* Boulder, Colo., 1995. A gathering of verse and prose with introductory material from the editor and Rashmi Sharma.

Srikanth, Rajini, and Esther Y. Iwanaga, eds. *Bold Words: A Century of Asian American Writing.* New Brunswick, N.J., 2001. Memoirs, poetry, and fiction from an impressive range of Asian American writers; includes a general introduction.

Tran, Barbara, Monique T. D. Truong, and Luu Truong Khoi, eds. *Watermark: Vietnamese-American Poetry and Prose.* New York, 1998. Represents a group of Vietnamese American artists writing on themes of war and beyond.

Wong, Sau-ling Cynthia. *Reading Asian American Literature: From Necessity to Extravagance.* Princeton, N.J., 1993. A literary study that analyzes themes, including food and landscape, in a range of literature by Asian American writers.

# W. H. AUDEN

*by Philip Hobsbaum*

Wystan Hugh Auden was born on 21 February 1907 in the cathedral city of York. He was the youngest of three sons of a physician, George Auden, and his wife, Constance, née Bicknell. His unusual name was a result of his father's archaeological interests, which included the editorship of the *Historical and Scientific Survey of York and District* (1906). St. Wystan was a Mercian prince whose martyrdom led to the foundation of the church of that name in Derbyshire. In 1908 his father left a lucrative practice to serve as the first-ever school medical officer in Birmingham. The family lived outside that industrial city in the then village of Solihull, which today is a Birmingham

W. H. Auden. (*Courtesy of the New York Public Library*)

suburb. When Auden was eight years old, he went as a boarder to a preparatory school called St. Edmund's in Surrey, where he met Christopher Isherwood, who was to become a close friend and also, in due course, a distinguished writer. In 1920 Auden went to the public school, Gresham's, where his parents had to pay high fees. It had developed under the headmastership of G. W. S. Howson from being a local school to a leading establishment with an interest in science. Although brought up by his mother to be a High Anglican, Auden began to lose his religious beliefs. This may have been coincidental with his recognition that he had homosexual proclivities. Robert Medley, a schoolfellow and later a noted theatrical designer, interested him in writing poetry.

In 1925 Auden went up to Christ Church, Oxford, in order to study natural sciences, with especial emphasis on biology. Toward the end of his first year, however, he sought to change his subject to English literature. At first he approached the eighteenth-century scholar David Nichol Smith of Merton College to be his tutor, as there was nobody professing that subject at Christ Church. Nichol Smith, unimpressed by Auden's manner

and appearance, refused to teach him. Auden was taken on by a young medievalist at Exeter called Nevill Coghill. They agreed well, but Coghill was unable to protect his pupil from the examiners, who in the final examinations awarded Auden only a third-class degree. It is hard not to feel that there was prejudice involved in this result, because Auden was already phenomenally well read and was the best-known poet in Oxford at a time when John Betjeman and Louis MacNeice were among his contemporaries. He had obtained an intellectual ascendancy over these and others of his fellow students—C. Day Lewis, for example, Stephen Spender, Rex Warner, Richard Crossman, all of whom were to make a considerable mark in the world.

On the whole, Auden was not himself influenced by his contemporaries. One exception to this was the future politician Tom Driberg. Auden reacted not to Driberg's own work but to a back number of a magazine called the *Criterion* that Driberg showed him. The number in question contained a poem by the editor, T. S. Eliot, called *The Waste Land*. Immediately Auden bought Eliot's *Poems, 1909–1925*. Shortly after, he went in to his tutor, Coghill, to say that he had torn up all his poems because they were no good.

Before reading Eliot, Auden wrote in the tradition of Thomas Hardy and Edward Thomas. His poems were normally about country matters and were couched in formal stanzas with full rhymes, as in "The Carter's Funeral" (1925):

> Sixty odd years of poaching and drink
> And rain-sodden wagons with scarcely a friend;
> Chained to this life—Rust fractures a link,
> So—the end.
>
> Sexton at last has stamped down the loam
> He blows on his fingers and prays for the sun;

Parson unvests, and turns to his home,
Duty done.

Little enough stays musing upon
The passing of One of the Masters of things;
Only a bird looks peak-faced thereon
Looks and sings.

This shows a promising grasp of basic form, the reconciliation of meaning with structure—which is usually a problem for an aspiring poet. There are no forced syntactical constructions, nor is there any undue disarrangement of the stanza once established. One might quibble at the omitted article "the," which might have been expected in front of the words "sexton" and "parson," and at the archaic "thereon." However, the poem is competent enough, though without any sign of originality or personal sensibility.

Within eighteen months we have, untitled, this:

Taller to-day, we remember similar evenings,
Walking together in the windless orchard
Where the brook runs over the gravel, far from the glacier.

Again in the room with the sofa hiding the grate,
Look down to the river when the rain is over,
See him turn in the window, hearing our last
Of Captain Ferguson.

It is seen how excellent hands have turned to commonness.
One staring too long, went blind in a tower,
One sold all his manors to fight, broke through, and faltered.

Nights come bringing the snow; and the dead howl
Under the headlands in their windy dwelling
Because the Adversary put too easy questions
On lonely roads.

But happy now, though no nearer each other,
We see the farms lighted all along the valley;
Down at the mill-shed the hammering stops
And men go home.

Noises at dawn will bring
Freedom for some, but not this peace
No bird can contradict; passing, but is sufficient now
For something fulfilled this hour, loved or endured.

We are in a different world. There is a degree of displacement in vocabulary and syntax from what previously might have been expected in poetry. Notice the emphasis on the definite article—"the windless orchard," "the brook," "the glacier," "the room," "the grate," "the river," "the window." Notice, also, the tendency toward obscure allusion: "hearing our last / Of Captain Ferguson," "One staring too long, went blind in a

tower"—often, incidentally, with a sinister overtone. There is trickery in the utterance. Why, for example, is it necessary to specify that an orchard is "windless"? Why do the dead howl "Because the Adversary put too easy questions?" We would expect them to howl if the questions were difficult. This early poem was thought good enough to be placed in Auden's first trade collection, *Poems* (1930).

### POEMS (1930)

The jewel of the collection was a miniature play, "Paid on Both Sides." This originated as a charade performed at the family home in Somerset of a Christ Church contemporary, Bill McElwee. It was an ad hoc production dressed with ordinary household furniture, but that does not alter the fact that Auden tapped emotional roots in this work. The plot concerns the unending war between two rival families, and that mirrors the conflict we see to this day of tribe against tribe. It suggests that contention between tribes is part of human nature. What is most appealing in the work, however, is not its political implications but the rhythm and character of its lyrical passages. It is punctuated by choruses. An example, early in the text, follows the shooting of a spy found hiding in an outhouse:

The Spring unsettles sleeping partnerships,
Foundries improve their casting process, shops
Open a further wing on credit till
The winter. In summer boys grow tall
With running races on the froth-wet sand,
War is declared there, here a treaty signed;
Here a scum breaks up like a bomb, there troops
Deploy like birds. But proudest into traps
Have fallen. These gears which ran in oil for week
By week, needing no look, now will not work;
Those manors mortgaged twice to pay for love
Go to another . . .

The word "scum" above is a misprint for "scrum," that is to say a pack formed in playing the game of rugby football. But it is safe to say that the early readers would not have noticed. The form is the half-rhyme in five-stress lines adopted by Wilfred Owen for his poem "Strange Meeting," but the idiom is something distinct from Owen and, in fact, from that of English poetry hitherto. That compressed diction—"But proudest into traps / Have fallen"—derives from an American form of modernism, as does, indeed, the insistence on the definite article in the previously quoted poem. The first line here—"The Spring unsettles sleeping partnerships"—would not have achieved that particular pattern had the author not already read T. S. Eliot. One must remember that "The Waste Land" begins "April is the cruellest month, breeding / Lilacs out of the dead land. . . . "

Of the poems in the rest of the book, all untitled, the most interesting today seem to be number IV ("Watch any day his nonchalant pauses, see / His dextrous handling of a wrap"); XVI ("It was Easter as I walked in the public gardens"); XXIV ("From scars where kestrels hover"); XXIX ("Consider this and in our time / As the hawk sees it or the helmeted airman"); and XXX ("Sir, no man's enemy, forgiving all / But will his negative inversion, be prodigal"). There are opacities among the brilliances but also a magical lyricism that delighted a generation.

That little book in blue paper wrappers, *Poems* (1930), set the literary world alight. Like the young Byron, Auden, then no more than twenty-three years of age, woke up one day to find himself—at least in the world of contemporary letters—famous. Of "Paid on Both Sides," William Empson, a contemporary of Auden, wrote, "it has the sort of completeness that makes a work seem to define the attitude of a generation" (*Experiment* 7, spring 1931). Michael Roberts, soon to be the most influential anthologist of the period, declared of *Poems* as a whole, "Mr. Auden approaches that integration, that acceptance of the dynamic nature of life, which we are all seeking" (*Adelphi*, December 1930). The American critic Morton D. Zabel suggested that "The progressive consonance in rhymes and phrases, the dove-tailing of images . . . combine to evoke a music wholly beyond the reason, extraordinarily penetrating and creative in its search of the significance behind fact" (*Poetry*, May 1931). A less enthusiastic critic, F. R. Leavis, was to remark that Auden's admirers spoke of him as having superseded T. S. Eliot (*New Bearings in English Poetry*, rev. ed., 1950).

All this time, after a break spent with Christopher Isherwood in Germany, Auden had been working as a schoolteacher, first at Larchfield Academy in Helensburgh, Scotland, then at the Downs school at Colwell on the Malvern Hills looking westward toward Wales. He seems to have been unpredictable in his methods: rather than producing set essays, he encouraged his pupils to perform impromptu plays, and to restore order, he played the piano with his feet. He was writing poems that superficially seem politically leftward but which really celebrate a sense of sexual release associated with D. H. Lawrence, whose work he greatly admired. During this period he was homosexually promiscuous, with laborers and with undergraduates at Oxford.

It was not until June 1935 that Auden freed himself from the schoolmastering that he claimed to have enjoyed. Briefly he worked as a scriptwriter with the General Post Office Film Unit, his best-known production being *Night Mail* (1935), with music by Benjamin Britten, also a homosexual. He further collaborated with Britten on a work for the Norwich and Norfolk Triennial Festival, contributing to it the lyric that gave the composition in question its title, "Our Hunting Fathers." F. R. Leavis used to put this forward in his lectures at Cambridge as an example of obscurity in modern verse, but in fact it is one of Auden's less obscure poems:

Our hunting fathers told the story
Of the sadness of the creatures,
Pitied the limits and the lack
Set in their finished features;
Saw in the lion's intolerant look,
Behind the quarry's dying glare,
Love raging for the personal glory
That reason's gift would add,
The liberal appetite and power,
The rightness of a god.

Who nurtured in that fine tradition
Predicted the result,
Guessed love by nature suited to
The intricate ways of guilt?
That human ligaments could so
His southern gestures modify,
And make it his mature ambition
To think no thought but ours,
To hunger, work illegally,
And be anonymous?

The last lines might make the reader think the poem is about serving as a secret agent, but beyond that it refers to the secrecy imposed upon homosexual behavior by a legal system that rendered this a criminal offense. The poem is really about self-consciousness. The animals are limited, but their limitation confers this advantage, that they do not feel guilt concerning their actions. The human being, however, with his developed superego, is well aware of what he is doing and frets at the hiatus between what is performed and what is enjoined. That plot in itself would not render the poem distinctive, although it is worth considering that Auden's daily life could, if brought to the attention of the appropriate authorities, have ensured him a term in prison. But the songlike nature of the text and magic of its phraseology make one see why Britten, the supreme master in his time at setting words to music, should have been enthusiastic enough to render it the climax of his composition.

## THE ORATORS (1932)

Auden resigned from the Film Unit in February 1936, eight months after he joined it. He needed more time for writing and felt confident enough now to depend for his income on what he could earn by his pen. After *Poems*, Faber and Faber published *The Orators: An English Study* (1932). It is often said that a poet's second book is a disappointment, and this is no exception. The work is a mixture of prose and verse, each genre in a jumble of styles, drawing upon memories of childhood, school, and college and replete with private reference. *Poems* sought to avoid clichés, but *The Orators* is full of them. They are not redeemed by a species of defensive irony that implies the writer is parodying that which he asserts: "That one always in hot water with the prefects"; "No use saying 'The mater wouldn't like it' "; "I had outbursts, wept even, at what seemed to me then your insane jealousy"—

The cousins you cheated shall recover their nerve
And give you the thrashing you richly deserve.

The author as narrator goes on to say, "Now I see that all that sort of thing is juvenile and silly," but it does not prevent what has gone on before from seeming precisely that, juvenile and silly. Nor can one say that the clichés are protected by their context. There is no context, at least not any context that helps.

There is indeed a semblance of external form. The work is couched in component parts: "Address for a Prize-Day," "Argument," "Statement," "Letter to a Wound," "Journal of an Airman," "Six Odes." But this arrangement is arbitrary, and the impression is that this heap of undigested matter would require some narrative structure in order to arrive at a degree of comprehensibility. As an unsigned review in *The Listener* (22 June 1932) said, "It is evident that he has not taken enough trouble to make his private counters effective currency." Nobody will deny there are individual brilliances in *The Orators*, found especially in "Address for a Prize-Day" and in the fine epilogue with its balladlike swing—" 'O where are you going?' said reader to rider." But as a whole, the work seems in need of further recension.

## GROUP THEATER

A degree of popular recognition came with Auden's involvement in the theater. He was lucky in knowing the designer Robert Medley, who introduced him to his friend the director Rupert Doone. After one or two abandoned projects, Auden presented the Group Theatre, as the Doone enterprise was called, with *The Dance of Death*. Doone and Medley had asked for a play on the theme of Orpheus. What they got was a piece of political propaganda, couched in doggerel, centering on the figure of death symbolized by a dancer. This work was performed on two successive Sunday nights, 25 February and 4 March 1934, in tandem with the Noah's Flood play from the medieval Chester cycle of dramas based on aspects of the Bible, and again in tandem in 1935 with T. S. Eliot's *Sweeney Agonistes*. *The Dance of Death* had been poorly received in 1933 as a printed text published by Faber and Faber. But it was a success with audiences when presented on the stage, and reviewers hailed it as a welcome contrast to the etiolated commercial theater of the time. Michael Sayers wrote, "Here is theatre springing from the rhythms and idiom of your own life, the only life you know, with its slang and jazz heightened into poetry" (*New English Weekly*, 10 October 1935).

A further dramatic venture developed as "The Chase," a work that incorporated earlier incomplete ventures and finally emerged as a collaboration with Christopher Isherwood called *The Dog beneath the Skin*. Published as an insufficiently revised text in 1935, this received chilly reviews but, as with its predecessor, did far better on the stage. It opened on the night of 30 January 1936, with a strong cast and music by Herbert Murrill. The basic plot involves a village boy, together with an intelligent dog, searching through various decadent monarchies and republics for the missing lord of the manor. In the end they return to their village, Pressan Ambo, and it turns out that the lord himself is the dog. He delivers a sermon explaining to the villagers that he left because he was disgusted with them as representatives of humanity but now finds they are much the same as the people anywhere else. For this he is stabbed to death by a lady with a hatpin. The village explodes: "O Day of Joy in happiness abounding / Streams through the hills with laughter are resounding." The play was taken by some as social satire and by others as a revue. The truth is that it was produced as an eccentric musical comedy. In this guise it ran for six weeks, which was not bad for an unconventional play in an unconventional theater.

This relative success induced Doone and Medley to commission from Auden and Isherwood another script for the Group Theatre. This started off as *The Summit* but finally became *The Ascent of F6*. F6 is a mountain in a country somewhat like Nepal, its name being analogous with the already existing mountain K2. The central figure, Michael Ransom, is driven to climb it, not through mystic revelation as the abbot of the monastery thinks, nor through patriotism, as the statesmen of his country think, but through compulsion stemming from his mother. So the apparent strong man in fact turns out to be a weak man, and the career of the adventurer T. E. Lawrence—subject of Auden's contemporary sonnet ("A shilling life will give you all the facts")—had a good deal to do with its conception. The play is wordier than its predecessors, with some detachable lyrics such as "Stop all the clocks." It was produced with mixed reviews at the Mercury Theatre, opening on 26 February 1937, then transferring after two months to the West End, where it ran for a further five weeks. It appears to have been improved greatly on revival in 1939 at the Old Vic.

Auden and Isherwood now craved commercial success, and they wrote a further play for Doone and Medley. This was *On the Frontier*, the frontier being a concern in several of Auden's earlier poems. The struggle between two fictitious countries, Westland and Ostnia, had featured in the two previous plays, but the form was an attempt at something that could thrive in the West End. Its theme seems to be that the political leaders of both countries have little power compared with that of a cartel, whose chairman in this play is called Valerian. But Valerian is shot by one of Leader Westland's bodyguards as the result of a personal grudge, so the drama fizzles out. It opened at the Arts Theatre, Cambridge, on 14 November 1938 with music by Benjamin Britten; was staged for one night only at the Globe Theatre, London; failed to interest any West End management; and, as Isherwood said, "passed away painlessly."

## ON THIS ISLAND (1937) AND ANOTHER TIME (1940)

One must not imagine Auden anchored in England all this time. There were several trips to Germany to pick up boys and a visit to Iceland with Louis MacNeice. This resulted in another joint venture, a book called *Letters from Iceland* (1937) with comic poems such as Auden's *Letter to Lord Byron* and some rather jokey prose. All this time, however, the lyrics steadily progressed. A revised version of *Poems* appeared in 1933. Some poems were dropped and new ones included: "Doom is dark and deeper than any sea-dingle," "Between attention and attention," and several pieces that look like cabaret songs—"It's no use raising a shout" and "What's in your mind, my dove, my coney?"

*Look, Stranger* (1936), published in the United States as *On This Island* (1937), contained the elegiac "O Love, the interest itself in thoughtless heaven," which may have been intended as the prologue to a play, as well

as lyrics such as "O what is that sound?," "Fish in the unruffled lakes," "Our hunting fathers"—this last rescued from the composition Britten had produced for the Norfolk Festival—and "Stop all the clocks," rescued from *The Ascent of F6* (1936) and later to find fame when recited in the film *Four Weddings and a Funeral* (1994). There were also meditative poems such as "Hearing of harvests rotting in the valleys," later known as "Paysage Moralisé"; "The earth turns over; our side feels the cold," later known as "Through the Looking Glass"; and terse sonnets containing a degree of biographical content, such as one already mentioned, "A shilling life will give you all the facts"—which may refer to T. E. Lawrence. What makes the poems of this book memorable, what renders Auden remarkable as a whole, is the gift of charismatic phrase—that slight derangement of language that heightens the sense: "the enormous comics," "the policed unlucky city," "the long aunts," "August for the people," "your map of desolation." Several of these phrases have served other writers as titles. The book itself is dedicated to the daughter of the novelist Thomas Mann—Erika, outspokenly anti-Nazi, with whom Auden had gone through a form of marriage on 15 June 1935 in order to rescue her from Germany.

*Another Time* (1940) continues the approach of its predecessor. Here are some of Auden's best-known lyrics ("Lay your sleeping head, my love, / Human on my faithless arm") and ballads, such as "Miss Gee," "Victor," and "James Honeyman." The biographical poems, mostly but not entirely sonnets, have increased in quantity and sharpened in quality: "The Sphinx," "Rimbaud," "The Novelist" (who may be Isherwood), "The Composer" (who may be Britten), "Edward Lear," and "Matthew Arnold," who "thrust his gift in prison till it died." Further, there are larger and more affirmative poems: "Voltaire at Ferney," the nonchalantly authoritative "Musée des Beaux Arts"—deriving from a visit to the Royal Museum at Brussels—and "In Memory of W. B. Yeats," where Auden achieves a flawless pastiche and makes it work for him:

> Earth, receive an honoured guest;
> William Yeats is laid to rest:
> Let the Irish vessel lie
> Emptied of its poetry.

Perhaps the most famous of all is a work, Yeatsian in title and to some extent in form, "September 1, 1939." This broods over the coming war and utters a line that echoes through history: "We must love one another or die."

## JOURNEY TO A WAR (1939)

Auden had already experienced more than a taste of conflict. He had visited Spain in January 1937, during the civil war, and had been shocked at the vandalized churches of Barcelona. He had planned to enlist with an ambulance unit in Valencia, but the extent of disorganization on the part of a Republican Medical Aid committee rendered this impossible. He seems to have done some propagandistic broadcasting. By March he was back in England and wrote a rhetorical poem, "Spain," which he later disowned.

However, there was to be a further excursion. War had broken out between China and Japan, and Auden's American publisher, Bennett Cerf, jointly with Faber and Faber, commissioned Auden and Isherwood to write a book about the Far East. They went to China as observers, Auden remarking "We'll have a war all of our very own."

They reached Canton (Guangzhou), sailing via Marseilles, Port Said, and Hong Kong. They visited Hankow (Wuhan) and reached the battlefront at Süchow (Xuzhou) by April 1938. They managed by using diplomatic connections to get into Shanghai, even though it was under Japanese occupation. During their stay they interviewed mainly middle-class politicians and intellectuals and made little contact with the troops. The resulting book, *Journey to a War* (1939), contains many photographs of provincial governors and city mayors, and these are authentically portrayed in the downbeat prose of Isherwood's travel diary. The main value of the book, however, is Auden's concluding sequence, "In Time of War," which contains some of his best sonnets—dry, terse, ironic. These include number VIII ("He turned his field into a meeting-place"), XI ("He looked in all His wisdom from the throne"), and XVI:

Here war is simple like a monument:
A telephone is speaking to a man;
Flags on a map assert that troops were sent;
A boy brings milk in bowls. There is a plan
For living men in terror of their lives,
Who thirst at nine who were to thirst at noon,
And can be lost and are, and miss their wives,
And, unlike an idea, can die too soon.

To this sequence is appended a verse commentary.

The chums sailed from Shanghai on 12 June, with little more than a tourist's acquaintance with China. The decision had been taken to return to England via the United States. They landed at Vancouver and went by train to New York. There they spent two triumphantly happy weeks. Back home they were faced with the increasingly grim situation in Europe and decided to go back to the United States, this time to settle. Some of the best poems in *Another Time* were written during this period of decision.

## SETTLING IN AMERICA

On 18 January 1939 Auden and Isherwood sailed for New York. Auden was well known in America; Random House had published several of his books. With Isherwood he rented an apartment in the Yorkville district of Manhattan. He gave many lectures and poetry readings at universities and other institutions. At one of the latter, he made the acquaintance of a young poet, Chester Kallman, who called on his home a couple of days later. Kallman was to prove to be the decisive influence on Auden's later life. He was fourteen years younger than Auden, blond and Jewish, and Auden fell in love with him. Much has been written of this relationship, but in one way it was beneficial to the world: Kallman got Auden interested in opera.

He did not move into Auden's apartment but continued to live with his parents while he studied at Brooklyn College. His father was a dentist with artistic tastes, but Kallman did not get on with his stepmother. It is not too much to say that Auden supplied a maternal need for affection in his life. Though both Auden and Kallman were homosexual, their preferences were different, and physical passion played little part in their relationship. It may have been Kallman's dependence on Auden—financial as well as emotional—that helped to shape the connection. In one way or another, it persisted until the end of Auden's life. Kallman's promiscuity pained Auden, who would have at this stage preferred a settled partnership. Auden's consolation was a series of brief relationships with other young men.

Auden regularized his presence in the United States by leaving the country for Canada and returning as part of the regular quota of British immigrants. He had already visited New Mexico and California with Kallman but remained basically in New York. He began regularly to attend an Episcopalian church and moved into a house in Brooklyn Heights purchased by the literary editor George Davis. It quickly filled with artistic friends. Though merely a paying guest himself, Auden dominated the ménage, insisting that meals be served punctually and himself sitting at the head of the table. He initiated several rules, including one that parties should cease by 1 A.M. Although he was ingesting greater and greater quantities of alcohol, Auden was playing the role of mother. The role intensified after he learned, in August 1941, that his own mother had died. Her death also bound him closer to the church.

## LONGER POEMS

The work of this period, 1940, consisted of a long poem, *The Double Man* (*New Year Letter* in the U.K.), a meditation upon art and life. This poem was published together with a further sequence of sonnets, *The Quest*, in 1941. It is often said that there was a falling off in Auden's work after he went to the United States. This may be so as regards intensity, but there are fine passages in *The Double Man*, including an invocation addressed to past poets:

> Great masters who have shown mankind
> An order it has yet to find,
> What if all pedants say of you
> As personalities be true?
> All the more honour to you then
> If, weaker than some other men,
> You had the courage that survives
> Soiled, shabby, egotistic lives,
> If poverty or ugliness
> Ill-heath or social unsuccess
> Hunted you out of life to play
> At living in another way;
> Yet the live quarry all the same
> Were changed to huntsmen in the game,
> And the wild furies of the past,
> Tracked to their origins at last.

A good deal of the pressure here may come from the fact that Auden is justifying his own failures: as an unloved homosexual, as a person assailed as a traitor for leaving Britain in the teeth of an impending war, as one living a shiftless life with no settled occupation, as—in short—someone who never satisfied his mother's standards. His justification would seem to be his quality as a poet. That was an early ambition, and by now he seemed to have fulfilled it. In this instance he is allying himself with the past masters, but such a standing could never be certain:

>                         Who
> That ever has the rashness to
> Believe that he is one of those
> The greatest of vocations chose,
> Is not perpetually afraid
> That he's unworthy of his trade
> · · ·
>
> For I relapse into my crimes:
> Time and again have slubbered through
> With slip and slapdash what I do,
> Adopted what I would disown,
> The preacher's loose immodest tone
> · · ·

> Yet still the weak offender must
> Beg still for leniency and trust
> His power to avoid the sin
> Peculiar to his discipline . . .

These lucid four-beat lines, so unlike those early verses accused of obscurity, must stand as Auden's justification. So should *The Quest*, whose sonnets may be seen as an appendage to those of *In Time of War*. Like those, they are terse and witty, but only one or two have the charisma of the earlier efforts: "One should not give a poisoner medicine, / A conjurer fine apparatus, nor / A rifle to a melancholic bore" (No. 2).

Auden was in demand as a lecturer and became associate professor of English at the University of Michigan. At this time he was writing a further long poem, *For the Time Being* (1944), a kind of oratorio without music, dedicated to his late mother. It bears something of the same relation to the story of Jesus' birth as does a real oratorio, Handel's *Messiah*. That is to say, it is a meditation on the event rather than a retelling of the biblical story. Auden's oratorio may be found uneven, owing to his wavering conception of Christianity. However, it contains some attractive writing, chiefly of a humorous kind. His "Herod" is a genuine creation—an inflated sensualist who has never grown up: "How dare He allow me to decide? I've tried to be good. I brush my teeth every night. I haven't had sex for a month. I object. I'm a liberal. I want everyone to be happy. I wish I had never been born."

Published with this work is "The Sea and the Mirror," presented as a commentary on Shakespeare's play *The Tempest*. This was written in 1943 at Swarthmore College, Pennsylvania, where Auden transferred himself when his contract at Ann Arbor finished. His methods of teaching at the college level were as ingenious as those he had used when he was a schoolteacher. For example, he circulated scripts of a poem with blanks instead of certain key words and asked the students to supply the deficiencies. This he used as a way of teaching the students respect for the precision with which a poet deploys the language.

The Swarthmore lectureship was a part-time appointment and so afforded opportunity for Auden to compose "The Sea and the Mirror." It is an uneven work, a result of uncertainty as to form, but the enormous speech by Caliban about the nature of illusion bears scrutiny. Caliban represents the raw material of art, yet speaks in the accents of that most dedicated of artists, Henry James. Here is how he describes the creative process, with Ariel acting as muse:

Lying awake at night in your single bed you are conscious of a power by which you will survive the wallpaper of your boardinghouse or the expensive bourgeois horrors of your home. Yes, Ariel is grateful; He does come when you call, He does tell you all the gossip He overhears on the stairs.... So it goes on from exasperated bad to desperate worst until you realize in despair that there is nothing for it but you two to part.... [T]o your dismay He whose obedience through all the enchanted years has never been less than perfect, now refuses to budge. Striding up to Him in fury, you glare into His unblinking eyes and stop dead, transfixed with horror at seeing reflected there, not what you had always expected to see, a conqueror smiling at a conqueror, both promising mountains and marvels, but a gibbering fist-clenched creature with which you are all too unfamiliar.... [A]t last you have come face to face with me, and are appalled to learn how far I am from being, in any sense, your dish.

This has reverberations not only concerning the nature of art but about the nature of Man and, indeed, the nature of God.

Notice, however, that the high points of both *For the Time Being* and "The Sea and the Mirror" are prose. In a letter to the radio producer Frederick Bradnum seventeen years later, Auden declared "Caliban to the Audience" to be the poem of which he was most proud. All this shows an indecision as to genre, so it is not surprising to find him, once back in New York, embarking upon *The Age of Anxiety* (1947), which he termed "A Baroque Eclogue." There is a good deal of prose by way of connective tissue in this work that, however, is superficially a play in which the characters think and speak in verse. They coincide in a New York bar on All Souls' Night. An epigraph could be Marlowe's "Nature, that framed us of four elements"(*Tamburlane the Great*, part 1, act 2).

Quant is a widower who works as a clerk and represents Intuition. Malin is an intelligence officer in the Canadian air force and represents Thinking. Emble has dropped out of college to enlist in the U.S. Navy; he represents Sensation. Rosetta is a young Jewish woman, buyer for a New York department store, and she represents Feeling. They do not at first address one another but brood separately, each in an interior monologue. At Rosetta's suggestion they move from their separate bar stools into a booth, where they proceed to discuss the nature of man.

This is a work that may have been more enjoyable to write than to read. Auden has no special insight into these particular characters, even though Rosetta is based upon his one serious heterosexual partner, Rhoda Jaffe.

Their thoughts are couched in the manner of medieval alliterative verse, and this manner becomes more marked when they break into speech: "On picnic days / My dearest doll was deaf and spoke in / Grunts like grandfather." It might have worked as a special effect over a short period, but *The Age of Anxiety* is a poem 126 pages long, and probably the best thing about it is its title. That, for Auden, suggested the human need for the unifying factor, God.

Auden left Swarthmore in 1945 in order to take part in a overseas mission to Germany, the purpose of which was to ascertain the effects on the civilian population of Allied bombing. His main qualification for this task was the German he had picked up in numerous visits of a recreational nature to Austria and Germany in the 1930s. He returned to New York in mid-August but not to any teaching post, though he gave talks and poetry recitals and from time to time coached young poets. He rented a succession of apartments, ending up in an upper floor on St. Mark's Place in New York's East Village, apparently in the hope that Kallman would live there with him permanently.

*The Collected Poetry* came out in 1945. It incorporated lyrics such as "Law Like Love," "Say this city has ten million souls," and "Lady Weeping at the Crossroads" as well as biographical poems such as "Herman Melville," "In Memory of Sigmund Freud," and "At the Grave of Henry James." John Van Druten wrote in the *Kenyon Review* (Summer 1945): "he is the only poet to have bridged the Atlantic, to have absorbed completely the essence of both England and America, and to have made himself bilingual and bisensual as artist and as human being." An abridged version of this *Collected Poetry* came out in Britain, influentially for the rising generation of that time, as *The Collected Shorter Poems* (1950). Auden selected poets to be published by the Yale University Press, edited anthologies, wrote introductions to books by other authors, and published a good deal of occasional prose. He became a citizen of the United States on 20 May 1946.

## OPERA

In September 1947 Auden was asked through an intermediary by the expatriate Russian composer Igor Stravinsky to write a libretto for an opera based on *The Rake's Progress*, a sequence of engravings by the eighteenth-century English artist William Hogarth. Auden met Stravinsky in Hollywood, where the latter was living, and the two built up a plot from that only sketchily suggested by Hogarth's engravings. Returning to New York, he found that Chester Kallman—who knew a good deal about opera—was keen to involve himself in the project and indeed came up with the invention of Nick Shadow and the songs accorded to Anne Truelove. This collaboration resulted in probably the best libretto ever to have been originally written in English. The opera opened on 11 September 1951 at the Teatro La Fenice in Venice, and Auden and Kallman took their bows alongside Stravinsky to excited applause that was followed by enthusiastic notices.

The climate of New York was getting too much for Auden, and he leased a house on the island of Ischia in the Bay of Naples, usually spending the late spring and summer there and the autumn and winter in New York. *Nones*, nostalgic and topographical, came out in 1951, and *The Shield of Achilles*, with its much-applauded title poem, in 1955.

In 1956 Auden was elected professor of poetry at Oxford, an honor that his father, who died in May 1957, lived long enough to appreciate. That was the year in which Auden moved from Ischia to Kirchstetten, in Austria. There was a constant stream of visitors, but over the years he and Kallman managed to complete some opera librettos: *Elegy for Young Lovers* (1961), *The Bassarids* (1966), *Love's Labour's Lost* (1972), and a translation of *The Magic Flute*.

## LITERARY CRITICISM

More important, Auden put together a notable collection of essays called *The Dyer's Hand* (1962), based in part on his Oxford lectures and in part on occasional journalism. He said in his introduction that he had never written criticism except in response to demand. We must be grateful to the importunities of such organs as *The New York Times* and *The New Yorker*. These resulted in some of the finest criticism of the age. Auden's work in this mode is impressionistic, akin to such poetry of his as was biographically based. His aperçus can be searching:

[of Iago] He manipulates others but, when he finally reveals his identity, his victims learn nothing about his nature, only something about their own.

("The Joker in the Pack")

In our minds Mr. Pickwick is born in middle age with independent means; his mental and physical powers are those of a middle-aged man, his experience of the world that of a newborn child.

("Dingley Dell & The Fleet")

Even when Lawrence talks nonsense, as when he asserts the moon is made of phosphorous or radium, one is convinced that it is nonsense in which he sincerely believed.

("D. H. Lawrence")

His most sustained work of criticism previously had been *The Enchaféd Flood* (1950), which originated as the Page-Barbour Lectures at the University of Virginia and which is largely a thought-provoking analysis of *Moby-Dick*, about whose author he had already written a brilliant poem. A late collection of reviews is called *Forewords and Afterwords* (1973)—too modest a title and hence undervalued. It contains pieces that will be found remarkable for their insight into, for example, the sonnets of Shakespeare as well as the works of Alexander Pope, Richard Wagner, Rudyard Kipling, A. E. Housman, and Walter de la Mare—"It is only with the help of wonder...that we can develop a virtue which we are certainly not born with, compassion, not to be confused with its conceit-created counterfeit, pity" (Walter de la Mare).

## DECLINE AND FALL

There were further books of verse. The bookish *Homage to Clio* came out in 1960, taking leave of the Mediterranean—"Go I must, but I go grateful (even / To a certain Monte) and invoking / My sacred meridian names." In 1965 appeared *About the House*, based on his Austrian cottage and containing a moving apologia for poetry, "The Cave of Making." This is a successful pastiche of Louis MacNeice, in mourning for whose untimely death the poem is written:

After all, it's rather a privilege
amid the affluent traffic
to serve this unpopular art which cannot be turned into
background noise for study
or hung as a status trophy by rising executives,
cannot be "done" like Venice
or abridged like Tolstoy, but stubbornly still insists upon
being read or ignored.

There were signs in this later work that Auden's ear for verse was beginning to deteriorate, and when a new *Collected Shorter Poems* came out in 1966 it incorporated some unacceptable revisions. The last three books—*City without Walls* (1969), *Epistle to a Godson* (1972), and *Thank You, Fog* (1974)—added little to his reputation. Mere grumbling in verse, one might call these, though the verse is certainly that of a past master. That reputation, however, revived decisively with the publication in 1977 of Edward Mendelson's brilliant compilation *The English Auden*, where the early work was republished in the original versions without the omissions and revisions of an increasingly tiresome old age.

For some years now Kallman had refused to return to New York. Auden gave up the St. Mark's

Place apartment—which, like its district, had become squalid—in favor of returning to Christ Church where, in 1972, the college offered him a small house on its grounds. However, he felt he was not welcome at High Table and found it a relief to return to Kirchstetten. On 28 September 1973 he gave a poetry recital for the Austrian Society of Literature in Vienna. He declined dinner and returned to his hotel. The next morning Kallman found him dead. Years of alcoholism and self-neglect had worn him out at the age of sixty-six. He was buried in Kirchstetten to the recorded music of Siegfried's funeral march from the *Ring* cycle by Wagner.

There is little doubt that, had we only the poetry from Auden's American period, he would rank as a major poet. So far as the earlier English period is concerned, Auden's distinction was to have brought about a change of idiom. There was a reliance on free association and a loosening of verse form learned from such Americans as T. S. Eliot and Ezra Pound. What never quite left him was his lyrical instinct, heard in its pristine quality in "From scars where kestrels hover," "Consider this," "Sir, no man's enemy," and the choruses from "Paid on Both Sides." He is also the poet of meditation and biography: "Musée des Beaux Arts," "In Memory of W. B. Yeats," "Voltaire at Ferney," "In Memory of Sigmund Freud," and the speeches of Herod in *For the Time Being* and of Caliban in "The Sea and the Mirror." These contain perceptions so remarkable that they shade over into the illuminating literary criticism contained in *The Enchaféd Flood*, *The Dyer's Hand*, and *Forewords and Afterwords*.

## WORKS

*Poems* (1930)
*The Orators: An English Study* (1932)
*The Dance of Death* (1933)
*The Dog Beneath the Skin* (1935)
*The Ascent of F6* (1936)
*Look, Stranger* (1936; published in the United States as *On This Island*, 1937)
*Letters from Iceland* (1937)
*On the Frontier* (1938)
*Journey to a War* (1939)
*Another Time* (1940)
*The Double Man* (1941; published in the United Kingdom as New Year Letter, 1940)
*For the Time Being* (1944)
*The Collected Poetry* (1945)
*The Age of Anxiety* (1947)
*The Collected Shorter Poems, 1930–1944* (1950)
*The Enchaféd Flood* (1950)
*Nones* (1951)

*The Rake's Progress* (1951)
*The Shield of Achilles* (1955)
*The Magic Flute* (1956)
*Homage to Clio* (1960)
*Elegy for Young Lovers* (1961)
*The Dyer's Hand* (1962)
*About the House* (1965)
*The Bassarids* (1966)
*City without Walls* (1969)
*Epistle to a Godson* (1972)
*Love's Labour's Lost* (1972)
*Forewords and Afterwords* (1973)
*Thank You, Fog* (1974)
*Collected Poems* (1977)
*The English Auden* (1977)
*Juvenilia: Poems, 1922–28* (1994; published posthumously)

## FURTHER READING

Bahlke, George W. *The Later Auden*. New Brunswick, N.J., 1970. Pays special attention to the four major poems of Auden's earlier American period, including *For the Time Being* and "The Sea and the Mirror."

Callan, Edward. *Auden: A Carnival of Intellect*. New York and Oxford, 1983. Good on Auden's ideas and development.

Carpenter, Humphrey. *W. H. Auden: A Biography*. London and Boston, 1981. Reliable biography, with some cogent contextualization of poems.

Davenport-Hines, Richard. *W. H. Auden*. London and New York, 1995. Biographical approach; the most recent study.

Farnan, Dorothy J. *Auden in Love*. New York, 1984; London, 1985. Amusingly written and shows the place in Auden's life of Chester Kallman.

Fuller, John. *A Reader's Guide to W. H. Auden*. New York and London, 1970.

Fuller, John. *W. H. Auden: A Commentary*. London and Princeton, N.J., 1988. Poem-by-poem commentaries by an English poet.

Haffenden, John, ed. *W. H. Auden: The Critical Heritage*. London, 1983. Collects and reprints contemporary reviews of all Auden's books.

Hecht, Anthony. *The Hidden Law: The Poetry of W. H. Auden*. Cambridge, Mass., 1993. Major study by a major American poet.

Smith, Stan. *W. H. Auden*. Oxford, 1985. Helpful and illuminating study by British critic.

Spears, Monroe K. *The Poetry of W. H. Auden: The Disenchanted Island*. New York and Oxford, 1963. Pioneer American study with cogent criticism not yet outmoded.

# AUTOBIOGRAPHY: GENERAL ESSAY

*by Susan Balée*

We are living in an autobiographical era, as readers all over America can readily attest. Jay Parini, in his introduction to the *Norton Book of American Autobiography* (1999), deduces that "the immense interest in this form of writing owes something to a moment when our culture as a whole has turned introspective, interested in (some might say obsessed by) self-definition" (p. 19). According to Paul Gray, writing in an April 1997 issue of *Time*, memoirs have now replaced novels as the major American publishing product, with hundreds published every year, many by first-time writers. These recent memoirs deal with topics once reserved for fiction—child abuse, alcoholism, mental illness, incest—and some critics wish that fiction is where such "taboo" subjects would stay. Those who deplore the upsurge in self-writing note its emphasis on narcissism and self-pity: one such critic even titled his review of the new memoirs "Read about Why I Love Me and How Much I've Suffered."

These critics, however, may be missing the point of the self-absorbed narrative—narcissists dwell on themselves not because they have a strong self-identity but because their sense of self is so very fragile. Autobiography stems from the need to construct a unique self, an identity that is clear and clearly differentiated from all others. Indeed, for the first three hundred years of American self-writing, autobiographers had the task of both constructing themselves and building a national identity; the well-known phrase "American individualism" suggests the double goal. The invention of America began as it does in every other nation: with words.

## AUTOBIOGRAPHIES "INVENT" AMERICA

National identity emerges and coalesces in the literature of a nation. Nations are built from sentences and paragraphs as much as from nails and lumber and labor. Settlers tell themselves who they are and why they are here, and then export their identity with all the other products of a new country. In the early nineteenth century, America's cultural identity resonated in the words of Nathaniel Hawthorne's Puritans and Augustus Baldwin Longstreet's southern frontiersmen as clearly as it must have emanated from the country's tangible goods, the cotton, whale blubber, cranberries, maple sugar, beaver pelts, freshly sawed hardwoods, molasses, tobacco, indigo, and maize that emerged from the holds of sailing ships recently returned to Europe from the New World.

Europeans stepped onto the shores of North America and cast off their Old World selves like salt-stained garments. Very quickly, the new land defined Americans. New settlers carved a fresh identity out of the wilderness; they differentiated themselves from the English and other Europeans as well as from the Native Americans; they rebelled against the mother country and its patriarchal demands, even as they modified its old customs and laws to suit the new community. By breaking away from England, America gained a sense of national identity far more quickly than, say, Canada, the sibling colony to the north.

As Puritans and Protestants and Christians concerned with spiritual salvation, Americans quickly contrasted themselves with the heathens, the Indian peoples, living in their midst. Outside forces—wars and winters and pestilence—helped Americans define themselves. So did the experience of religious oppression, slavery, immigration. For three hundred years, the majority of American autobiographies reflected individual identities constructed in response to external pressures.

But in the space of a scant five decades, all of that has changed. Americans have ceased to see themselves as primarily shaped by external events. Instead, American autobiography has moved from outer environments to inner landscapes. In this century, the external forces that forged individual identities up through the 1940s—the Depression, the First and Second World Wars, the rise of industry and technology, the assimilation of immigrants—took a step inward in the 1950s. In fact, the last generation of American writers who felt themselves largely at the mercy of historical forces came of age in the 1920s and 1930s—they were the writers and artists who formed part of America's Lost Generation after World War I.

Alienated from mainstream American values, they rebelled against the established culture. In addition to a great deal of thinly disguised autobiographical fiction, anguished coming-of-age autobiographies were penned by Eugene O'Neill, Gertrude Stein, F. Scott Fitzgerald, and Ernest Hemingway. These were the works of giant writers, and they cast long shadows. That may be why the generation of autobiographers who came after them—including Norman Mailer, Malcolm X, Jack Kerouac, and Mary McCarthy—had to be particularly audacious in order to be original.

## AUTOBIOGRAPHERS OF THE 1950s: LOOKING INSIDE FOR ANSWERS

The Cold War generation's writers, then, began to look inward to find the sources of self-identity. Several of these autobiographers discovered that their identities derived not from the pressure of external, historical forces but quite literally from forces within the family. Mary McCarthy's *Memories of a Catholic Girlhood*, published serially in *The New Yorker* between 1946 and 1957, presents a self shaped by family dynamics. McCarthy's parents died during the Spanish influenza epidemic in 1918, when she was six years old, and she and her brothers were sent to live with a great-aunt and her husband in Minneapolis. The impetus for McCarthy's autobiography is the unfair treatment she endured at the hands of these guardians. Further, she recognizes that if her parents had not died, she would probably not have become a writer nor her brother Kevin McCarthy an actor.

> If [my parents] had both lived, we would have been a united Catholic family, rather middle class and wholesome. I would probably be a Child of Mary. I can see myself married to an Irish lawyer and playing golf and bridge, making occasional retreats and subscribing to a Catholic Book Club. (p. 16).

Her parents were beautiful people, though her father, she later discovers, was also a spendthrift and a binge drinker. But all of this she forgives, because they enter the realm of the Ideal Parents before she ever has a chance to see them as equals and also because "I could not accept the idea that anyone beautiful could be bad." When she arrives at the home of the great-aunt delegated by her father's parents to raise the orphans, her life as Cinderella begins. But McCarthy, far from coming off as a pathetic victim, mints a new version of the underdog: Cinderella with an attitude. She observes acidly, "Even if my guardians had been nice, I should probably not have liked them because they were so unpleasing to look at and their grammar and

accents were so lacking in correctness. I had been rudely set down in a place where beauty was not a value at all" (p. 17).

Although it is not her own parents McCarthy blames for her wretched childhood, the fact that her oppressors are within the family rather than outside of it marks this autobiography as a trailblazer. In *Memories of a Catholic Girlhood*, McCarthy opens the closet door on her family's secrets and inaugurates the "tell-all" genre of American autobiography. She publicly indicts her grandparents for permitting their son's children to suffer in front of them. Her wealthy, rosy-cheeked and white-haired grandfather originally appears to Mary and her brothers as beneficent, in keeping with "the family myth."

> We were too poor, spiritually speaking, to question his generosity, to ask why he allowed us to live in oppressed chill and deprivation at a long arm's length from himself and hooded his genial blue eye with a bluff, millionairish grey eyebrow whenever the evidence of our suffering presented itself at his knee. (p. 31)

Perhaps because of McCarthy's belief that no one beautiful can be truly bad, her handsome old grandfather escapes serious criticism. Alas, his wife, her Grandmother McCarthy, doesn't get off the hook as easily. In fact, Mary McCarthy positively gigs her on the spear point of her prose as "an ugly, severe old woman, with a monstrous bosom of a balcony," a cruelly ungenerous old lady who "was a great adherent of the give-them-an-inch-and-they'll-take-a-mile theory of hospitality, [who] never, so far as I can remember, offered any caller the slightest refreshment, regarding her own conversation as sufficiently wholesome and sustaining."

Despite the fact that "all of the paraphernalia of motherliness were hers," this grandmother's identity remained that of "a cold, grudging, disputatious old woman" in the eyes of her granddaughter. The autobiography form itself allows McCarthy to unmask the cruelty of her grandmother without forcing her to explain it. As she notes, "luckily, I am writing a memoir and not a work of fiction, and therefore I do not have to account for my grandmother's unpleasing character" (p. 33).

An unpleasing character, however, is not necessarily an abusive one. In the lexicon of social workers, Grandmother McCarthy may have "neglected" her orphaned grandchildren, but she did not actively abuse them. Their new guardians, Myers and Margaret, become the real villains of this autobiography because Myers does actively abuse the children, both emotionally and physically. Curiously, he nevertheless remains beyond the pale of the family, even as he rules the roost. The first two sentences of "The Tin Butterfly," the chapter detailing some of his more iniquitous deeds, announces, "The man we had to call Uncle Myers was no relation to us. This was a point on which we four orphan children were very firm." Although McCarthy is breaking new ground with an autobiography that details child abuse, she is careful to assert that the abuse was not at the hands of a biological parent. Revelations of that sort of abuse appear much later, in popular autobiographies such as Christina Crawford's *Mommy, Dearest*, and literary ones such as Mary Karr's *The Liars' Club* (1995).

Still, at the hands of Myers, the McCarthy children "were beaten all the time, as a matter of course." Their mouths were taped shut at night to prevent "mouth breathing," their poor diet of root vegetables was supplemented with daily doses of castor oil, and, on weekends year round, even at twenty below zero, the children were forced outside to "play" for six hours a day. They were not allowed to have friends or toys because "our lives, in order to be open, had to be empty." Naturally this regimen failed to achieve its goal; instead, Mary and her brothers managed to contrive rich inner lives, telling each other stories in lieu of playing with toys and living in their imaginations in lieu of external stimulation.

At last the sad story ends, as all Cinderella memoirs do, when Mary is rescued by her Grandfather Preston, her mother's father, who suspects and then uncovers the abuses endured by his only daughter's children. Alas, Cinderella's brothers don't fare as well; they are packed off to a midwestern boarding school, where they remain even during holidays—only Mary escapes entirely and is restored to a life of wealth and privilege in Seattle. Still, the memory of her mistreatment no doubt instilled in her what Richard Rhodes, recalling his own abusive childhood (described in *A Hole in the World: An American Boyhood*, 1990), terms "a rage to speak" (and its accompanying goal, to be heard and validated). In McCarthy's words, "The injustices my brothers and I had suffered in our childhood had made me a rebel against authority, but they had also prepared me to fall in love with justice, the first time I encountered it."

Nevertheless, McCarthy must question how just her own motives are in telling a story that indicts—or at least reveals—the inner life of her family. An Irish presentiment of doom darkens her prose when she observes, "starting to tell that story now, to publish it, so to speak, abroad, I feel a distinct uneasiness.... If I believed in the afterlife, I would hold my peace" (p. 198). Fortunately for

literature, she published her piece and provided a bridge for many important autobiographers who followed her. After *Memories of a Catholic Girlhood*, the family lost its sacred, private status; it ceased to be exempt from the scrutiny of memoirists.

## AMERICAN AUTOBIOGRAPHIES IN THE 1960s: "TELL ALL ... "

By the 1960s, the tell-all-about-how-my-family-shaped-me autobiographies had produced some very powerful testaments of self-identity. One of the best of these is Loren C. Eiseley's *The Unexpected Universe*, a collection of autobiographical essays first published in 1969 and republished posthumously in 1978 with other of his favorite essays in *The Star Thrower*. Eiseley slowly recognizes that his way of perceiving the world comes—both genetically and socially—from his mother, who spent much of her life on the edge of mental chaos.

> It began ... with the skull and the eye. I was the skull. I was the inhumanly stripped skeleton without voice, without hope, wandering alone upon the shores of the world.... There was, in this desiccated skull, only an eye ... a search beam revolving endlessly in sunless noonday or black night.

Eiseley, an anthropologist, writes of wind and weather and tribes, of tricksters and dualism. He notes that humans have almost always believed their lives were caught between the dual forces of good and evil. But it is clearly his own identity that Eiseley is trying to find as he looks back to the origins of humans. "We gaze backwards into a contracting cone of life until words leave us and all we know is dissolved into the simple circuits of a reptilian brain." Our lives as humans are merely constructs, Eiseley argues, "Our identity is a dream."

The image of the searching eye continues to haunt Eiseley; he struggles to identify the eye that is so mingled with his "I." His mind's eye casts him back on childhood images.

> There was the beaten, bloodshot eye of an animal from somewhere within my childhood experience. Finally there was an eye that seemed torn from a photograph, but that looked through me as though it had already raced in vision up to the steep edge of nothingness and absorbed whatever terror lay in the abyss.... I knew the eye and the circumstance and the question. It was my mother. She was long dead, and the way backward was lost.

Eiseley shifts away from the eye whose gaze he cannot bear for long; he cloaks himself again in the protective garb of the anthropologist, the man of science. He diverts his personal narrative to speak of Darwin and Einstein and Freud, but in the end the persistent memory of the skull and eye brings him home—home to his childhood house, to a satchel he discovers after his parents are dead. In it, he finds a lock of his mother's hair and a note—"This satchel belongs to my son, Loren Eiseley"—written in his mother's hand.

In the satchel he finds a photo of his mother and her sister, taken when his mother was six years old in Dyersville, Iowa (the "dire place," he realizes suddenly, reflecting on the word).

> Six years old, I thought, turning momentarily away from the younger child's face. Here it began, her pain and mine. The eyes in the photograph were already remote and shadowed by some inner turmoil. The poise of the body was already that of one miserably departing the peripheries of the human estate. The gaze was mutely clairvoyant and lonely. It was the gaze of a child who knew unbearable difference and impending isolation. . . . All her life she had walked the precipice of mental breakdown. Here on this faded porch it had begun—the long crucifixion of life.

At this point, Eiseley realizes how absolutely he is his mother's son. His view of humanity grows likewise dark; he sees the history of the species as "a tale of desolations." Walking along the beach at Sanibel Island, Florida, the beach (called "costabel" in his narrative) he identifies as a coast "set apart for shipwreck," he feels this desolation fully.

Eiseley, an emotionally drowning "I" at this point in his memoir, finds unexpected salvation in the act of "a star thrower": literally a man throwing living starfish back into the sea. This man, whom Eiseley had at first deemed a madman, suddenly looks more like a brother, a fellow human. The star thrower is actually saving the starfish before they suffocate on the shore, and Eiseley stoops to help him. "I picked up a star whose tube feet ventured timidly among my fingers while, like a true star, it cried soundlessly for life." Eiseley imagines God flinging real stars, somewhere else in the universe. "Perhaps he, too, was lonely, and the end toward which he labored remained hidden—even as with ourselves."

Eiseley, in the act of throwing stars, transcends his mother's legacy; it doesn't crush him as her life did her. "Somewhere, my thought persisted, there is a hurler of stars, and he walks, because he chooses, always in desolation, but not in defeat."

Vivian Gornick, perhaps the best-known autobiographer of the my-mother-made-me-who-I-am variety, is likewise a walker—she and her mother walk the streets of Manhattan, talking, fighting, connecting. Her memoir, *Fierce Attachments* (1987), describes a daughter bound, for better or worse, to her deeply demanding mother. Gornick and her mother have a relationship that contemporary psychologists would doubtless term "co-dependent," but "co-combative" might be a better description. They fight to live, they live to fight, and in argument they find intimacy.

> "So, I'm reading the biography you gave me," [my mother] says. I look at her, puzzled, and then I remember. "Oh!" I smile in wide delight. "Are you enjoying it?"
>
> "Listen," she begins. The smile drops off my face and my stomach contracts. That "listen" means she is about to trash the book I gave her to read. She is going to say, "What. What's here? What's here that I don't already know? I *lived* through it. I know it all. What can this writer tell me that I don't already know? Nothing. To *you* it's interesting, but to me? How can this be interesting to me?"
>
> . . . Invariably, when she speaks so, my head fills with blood and before the sentences have stopped pouring from her mouth I am lashing out at her. . . . However, in the past year an odd circumstance has begun to obtain. On occasion, my head fails to fill with blood. I become irritated but remain calm. Not falling into a rage, I do not make a holocaust of the afternoon.

They fail to fight because of Gornick's forbearance, and then the daughter learns something important about her mother. They walk silently for blocks, and then her mother again mentions the book her daughter gave her.

> "That Josephine Herbst," my mother says. "She certainly carried on, didn't she?"
>
> Relieved and happy, I hug her. "She didn't know what she was doing either, Ma, but yes, she carried on."
>
> "I'm jealous," my mother blurts at me. "I'm jealous she lived her life, I didn't live mine."

Gornick writes this memoir of herself and her mother when she is herself middle age and her mother is old. Old, but not dead—still alive and able to witness her daughter's revelations about the two of them. *Fierce Attachments*, however, is not the *Mommy, Dearest* revenge memoir it might at first seem. Instead, it is a far more complex, more subtle autobiography of a mother/daughter dyad. Their bond occurs at the point where separate worlds intersect—the immigrant world of the Russian-born mother, the urbane world of the Manhattan-born daughter—and the city itself serves as the place where, for generations, different worlds have coexisted.

Vivian Gornick has written elsewhere that the current boom in memoir writing is simply the response to a postmodern "need to testify," to share truths with others. Interestingly, however, these truths follow the path of a late-twentieth-century course of psychotherapy: autobiographers move from recognition of abuse and consequent anger (McCarthy), to depression about their roles as victims (Eiseley), to ultimate acceptance of the relationship with the offending parent (Gornick). The difference between the revelations of such truths lies not in the experiences but in the audience for them—revelations that were once reserved only for the ears of the therapist are now trumpeted to the world for all to hear and judge.

In an attempt to catch the attention of readers no longer shocked by what memoirists are willing to confess about themselves, writers have had to become increasingly outrageous to gather an audience. Kathryn Harrison, for example, has dynamited her own private gold shaft out of the mountain of autobiographies dealing with familial sexual abuse. Her memoir, *The Kiss* (1997), turns the concept of child-sexually-victimized-by-adult on its head. Instead, Harrison writes the daughter-does-daddy memoir of a gleeful victim. *The Kiss*, which has garnered a fair amount of outrage from critics, details Harrison's sexual relationship with her own father—a relationship not forced upon her as a helpless child but *chosen* by the adult Harrison.

It is difficult to imagine what, if anything, American autobiographers can do with the parent/child memoir after *The Kiss*.

### ALSO IN THE 1960s: THE DRUG-DRENCHED MEMOIR

Drug experimentation in the 1960s induced another series of reflections on inner states—altered ones. Tom Wolfe's *The Electric Kool-Aid Acid Test* (1968) is perhaps the best-known literary work about the drug-induced musings of the era, but the most popular ones were surely the "Don Juan" books of Carlos Casteneda, nine of which have been published since *The Teachings of Don Juan: A Yaqui Way of Knowledge* appeared in 1968. In these books, Casteneda, a graduate student in anthropology at UCLA, mingled his knowledge of medicinal plants used by southwestern Indians with the received wisdom of his Yaqui mentor, Don Juan.

Tom Wolfe. (© *Bettman/Corbis*)

Mood-altering drugs such as peyote put Casteneda in an insightful mood, and he wrote spiritual advice worthy to brush covers with Khalil Gibran on the counterculture bookshelf. Indeed, Casteneda's higher purpose in getting stoned stands out when compared with the self-reports of more mundane trippers of the time. Joan Didion, who covered a covey of LSD tab poppers in 1967 San Francisco ("Life Styles in the Golden Land," collected in *Slouching Towards Bethlehem*, 1968), sat with them through an afternoon trip. She records the detailed description of the altered mental state related to her by one of the participants: "Wow."

As the drug-induced memoirs of the 1960s and 1970s attest, the primary impetus for autobiography had moved even further inward: the effects of inner experiences shaped the psychedelic self. The era's slogan was "Tune in, turn on, drop out." Although Timothy Leary probably meant that young Americans should tune in to something larger than themselves—peace and love instead of war, for example—his mantra became far more self-referential for most of its practitioners, who instead tuned in to music, turned on to drugs, and dropped out of the establishment culture.

### AUTOBIOGRAPHIES OF ILLNESS

In another two decades, the autobiography of ill health—in particular, memoirs by writers with cancer or AIDS—became a primary vehicle through which Americans achieved identity, the self shaped because of, or in spite of, the body. In a similar vein, a spate of autobiographies about discovering one's (homo)sexuality appeared in the 1980s—again, the autobiographer revealed an identity formed in response to inner impulses rather than outer pressures. The best memoir of the period combines both: Paul Monette's *Borrowed Time: An AIDS Memoir* (1988). (Monette's 1992 *Becoming A Man: Half a Life Story* focuses more exclusively on his coming of age as a gay man.) If the autobiographies of drug users had focused on the body as the site of pleasurable experiences, the autobiographies of AIDS sufferers focused on it as the site of a protracted war—a battleground with no known survivors.

Monette himself uses the imagery of war to describe the way AIDS descended on the gay men of his generation:

Then someone you know goes into the hospital, and suddenly you are at high noon in full battle gear. They have neglected to tell you that you will be issued no weapons of any sort. So you cobble together a weapon out of anything that lies at hand, like a prisoner honing a spoon handle into a stiletto. You fight tough, you fight dirty, but you cannot fight dirtier than it.

All you can do is watch the landscape of your body for signs that the enemy has invaded: night sweats, tongue sores, diarrhea, fevers, bruises that didn't heal, weight loss. Monette soon found himself examining his body on a daily basis, "inch by inch as cowering people must have done in medieval plague cities, when X's were chalked on afflicted houses."

AIDS memoirs like Monette's differ from memoirs about other types of illness both because the virus was linked to homosexuality initially and also because it was transmissible.

Has anything ever been quite like this? Bad enough to be stricken in the middle of life, but then to fear that your best and dearest will suffer exactly the same. Cancer and the heart don't sicken a man two ways like that.

The disease itself bred alienation and isolation in its sufferers—in those early days, jobs and careers were lost; victims were often abandoned by their lovers and families. As Monette details his beloved companion's deepening struggle with AIDS and his own reactions to Roger's decline, he observes, "Within three months, this sense of separateness [became] so acute that I didn't want to talk to anyone anymore who wasn't touched by AIDS, body or soul." Finally, the book reaches the point it has always been moving toward: Roger's death. But before he dies, Paul Monette has a chance to both cherish and memorialize their love. As he observed, "Loss teaches you very fast what cannot go without saying." Monette himself is now dead of AIDS, but this memoir will endure as a testament to the early years of the epidemic. In fact, Monette's reputation is likely to rest on this memoir and on *Becoming a Man*. His response to the assault on the body of his lover, and then his own, produced his best writing. Had he lived in another era, Monette would probably only have rated a footnote (as a minor poet and novelist) in the annals of literature; instead, he is likely to be remembered as one of the important recorders of gay life in the plague years of fin-de-millennium America.

## THE NEXT WAVE OF AMERICAN AUTOBIOGRAPHY: MADNESS MEMOIRS

If AIDS memoirs—like the illness itself—are on the wane in the new millennium, memoirs of madness are waxing. The book that inaugurated this genre of memoirs remains its classic: *Darkness Visible: A Memoir of Madness*, by William Styron (1990). The great novelist's account of his own descent into depression landed the book on best-seller lists for years. Styron gave readers a writerly account of his own personal tour of hell, realizing that depression is "so mysteriously painful and elusive in the way it becomes known to the self—the mediating intellect—as to verge close to being beyond description."

As Monette does with the symptoms of AIDS, Styron lists "some of [depression's] most sinister hallmarks: confusion, failure of mental focus and lapse of memory. At a later stage *my entire mind would be dominated by anarchic disconnections*" [italics added]. Styron's depression, which causes his mind to revolt, to be "dominated by anarchic disconnections," threatens his very sense of identity. American autobiography has come full circle when the memoir no longer serves to construct the self but questions even the possibility of identity. Autobiographies of insanity (temporary or otherwise) such as Styron's show that the inward movement of self-definition has reached not a core of identity but a lacuna where that identity should be.

In fact, as his mental health worsens, Styron's consuming desire becomes oblivion; much of the book discusses the attractiveness of suicide for people enduring the despair that comes with major depression. Unable to hang on to a sense of self-preservation, Styron recognizes that he is losing his mind. "I had now reached that phase of the disorder where all sense of hope had vanished, along with the idea of a futurity; my brain, in thrall to its outlaw hormones, had become less an organ of thought than an instrument registering, minute by minute, varying degrees of its own suffering" (p. 58).

At last, Styron's personality is so assailed by inner pain that it actually splits. The depressed autobiographer records the phenomenon of a second self, "a wraithlike observer who, not sharing the dementia of his double, is able to watch with dispassionate curiosity as his companion struggles against the oncoming disaster, or decides to embrace it" (p. 64).

Styron's memoir is a slender book, but it has been succeeded by thicker, more comprehensive accounts. One of the initial twenty-first-century best-sellers about depression that follows in the track initially set down by

Styron is Andrew Solomon's *The Noonday Demon: An Atlas of Depression* (2001). Like Styron, Solomon stresses the loss of self that accompanies major depression: "What is so unattractive is the idea that in addition to all other lines being blurred, the boundaries of what makes us ourselves are blurry. There is no essential self that lies pure as a vein of gold under the chaos of experience and chemistry" (p. 21).

Other memoirs of mental illness—depression, schizophrenia, multiple personality, and bipolar disorder—now abound. Some of the best of these are Susanna Kaysen's *Girl, Interrupted* (1993); Donna Williams's "extraordinary autobiography of an autistic," *Nobody Nowhere* (1992); *The Magic Daughter* (1995), by a college professor with multiple-personality disorder who writes under the pseudonym Jane Phillips; and several new books by psychotherapists writing about their own mental illnesses: Kate Redfield Jamison's *Unquiet Mind* (1995) and Lauren Slater's *Welcome to My Country* (1996) and *Prozac Diary* (1998). Slater, like her cohort Elizabeth Wurtzel in *Prozac Nation* (1994), tackles the subject of the new serotonin-enhancing drugs and their effects on mental illness and, by extension, identity.

Still, one of Slater's best short pieces, "Black Swans," which first appeared in *Best American Essays 1997*, insists on the presence of a bedrock of identity that cannot be dislodged by either external or internal pressures. "Black Swans" describes Slater's struggle with obsessive-compulsive disorder, another mental illness that robs an individual of selfhood by robbing her of self-will. Slater is at the mercy of counting rituals to get through a doorway, a page, a room, a day. Nevertheless, as Gornick found an island of independence in the ocean of her mother's presence, Slater finds one despite the tempest in her brain. "Part of me was still free, a private space not absolutely permeated by pain. A space I could learn to cultivate."

Elizabeth Wurtzel. (© *Corbis*)

## THE INVERSION OF AMERICAN AUTOBIOGRAPHY: FROM THE OUTSIDE IN

The question to cultivate here is this: How did American autobiography travel so far from its origins? How did autobiographies progress from firmly delineating individual identities to questioning the very possibility of a unified self? Perhaps what has been termed, in another context, "America's isolationist tendencies," has brought this nation to the brink of unthinking itself. Left to elaborate their paranoid fantasies—and paranoia has ever been a hallmark of American thought—contemporary autobiographers are busy dismantling the idea of a clear and transcendent identity one text at a time. The big picture seems to be dissolving into so many pixels; American identity, once so clearly demarcated from European identity, or Native American identity, has fragmented at the core—the corpus callosum. Contemporary American autobiography has turned back to the original questions: Who am I? Why am I here?

In the beginning, if you read the words of the early colonizers, Americans *knew* the answers to those questions. William Bradford's memoir *Of Plymouth Plantation* (1620–1647) describes the Pilgrims wrestling with the wilderness, becoming who they are in the act of subduing their new landscape. Captain John Smith's accounts of the colonization of Virginia (1608–1630) likewise detail the transformation of the new settlers from denizens of the Old World to crafters of the New. His accounts also initiated the American tradition of seeing the Indians as characters in the European drama of colonization rather than as the original authors of America.

The Puritan journalists—of whom there were scores—kept records of their lives in the same way they kept records of their household accounts; they accounted for their lives in a book of deeds and thoughts reminiscent of God's account book, the one the Bible says will be brought forth on Judgment Day. Everything in its place and a place for everything (America seemed to be the place for every thing). Although these Puritan writers were ostensibly concerned with their inner states, hence the term "spiritual autobiographies," invariably external factors such as the wilderness bordering the New England colonies or invasions of the settlements by hostile Indian tribes influenced their conversion narratives. Faith was achieved in adversity, grace through a spiritual progress paralleling the pilgrim's progress in nature. The early settlers saw themselves as pilgrims in both senses.

## EARLY FEMALE AUTOBIOGRAPHERS: A FEW VOICES THAT CARRIED

As the voices of women and minorities are largely missing from early American history, autobiographies marking the seventeenth-century colonial experience issued mainly from male pens; in addition to the memoirs of William Bradford and John Smith, other self-reflective writings of the period come from Thomas Shepard, Samuel Sewall, William Byrd, and Cotton and Increase Mather. Spiritual self-examinations by seventeenth-century women appeared in other genres: Anne Bradstreet's poetry, for example, or Anne Hutchinson's testimony at the trial that precipitated her banishment from Massachusetts—she believed God had spoken directly to her soul to tell her she was saved. The forefathers of Massachusetts had little patience for women who claimed access to the minds of supernatural beings—witches and antinomians alike could expect harsh treatment from the Puritans.

But what could a woman expect who had been captured by Indians and returned to tell the tale? Fame, apparently. *Narrative of the Captivity and Restoration of Mrs. Mary Rowlandson* (1682) was among the most popular prose works of its time. Rowlandson describes the day in early February 1676 when the frontier village of Lancaster, Massachusetts, was attacked by Indians. Rowlandson watched her own house go up in flames around her.

> Now is the dreadful hour come, that I have often heard of (in time of war as it was the case of others), but now mine eyes see it. Some in our house were fighting for their lives, others wallowing in their blood, the house on fire over our heads, and the bloody heathen ready to knock us on the head if we stirred out. Now might we hear mothers and children crying out for themselves and one another, "Lord, What shall we do?"

The blazing fire made the choice inevitable; Mary took her children and left the house. The Indians shot her in the side, the bullet first going through the intestines of her young daughter Sarah whom Mary held in her arms. In the same melee, her brother-in-law and nephew were murdered by the Indians. Mary Rowlandson's depiction of the horror had to have been riveting reading for her fellow Americans.

> There were twelve killed, some shot, some stabbed with their spears, some knocked down with their hatchets. When we are in prosperity, oh! the little that we think of such dreadful sights, and to see our dear friends and relations lie bleeding out their heartblood upon the ground. There was one who was chopped into the head with a hatchet, and stripped naked, and yet was crawling up and down. It is a solemn sight to see so many Christians lying in their blood, some here, and some there, like a company of sheep torn by wolves, all of them stripped naked by a company

of hellhounds, roaring, singing, ranting, and insulting, as if they would have torn our very hearts out; yet the Lord by His almighty power preserved a number of us from death, for there were twenty-four of us taken alive and carried captive.

Rowlandson's narrative sharply distinguishes between the Christians and the "heathen" Indians, between the wolves and the sheep, the predators and the victims. Although forced to live for eleven weeks with the Indians, her own identity builds in resistance to that of her captors. An autobiography like this one had to have encouraged early Americans to differentiate themselves from the natives whose land they were settling. Indeed, an account like this would have helped justify the Indian removal bills that later became an accepted part of American domestic policy.

What is worth remembering here, although it does not show up in the autobiographies of the times, is that the Christian settlers were equally barbaric in their treatment of the Indians. Mary Rowlandson's narrative takes place during King Philip's War, and she ultimately encounters "King Philip" himself, the Wampanoag chief so named by the colonists for his proud manner. What Rowlandson does not mention is that when King Philip was killed in August 1676, the colonial militia ripped him limb from limb and hung his dismembered parts—and decapitated head—on trees. Another incident from the same period involved a group of Massachusetts women who, upon leaving church, encountered two Indian prisoners from Maine: these good Christian women tore them to pieces with their bare hands. Further, a darker version of Rowlandson's narrative is the story of Hannah Duston, another woman captured by Indians in Haverhill, Massachusetts, in 1697. Duston retaliated for the death of her newborn by killing and scalping ten of her captors. Although she looks like a murderer in our enlightened days, she was revered in her own: Duston was the first woman in the United States to have a monument erected in her honor.

## CONVERSION NARRATIVES TO RAGS-TO-RICHES AUTOBIOGRAPHIES

Jonathan Edwards, a rhetorically violent Puritan, wrote what is probably the most important spiritual autobiography of the eighteenth century. But the "Great Awakening" of religious fervor that Edwards helped foment among his fellow Puritans did not outlive him, nor did his memoir of religious conversion seem to strongly influence the personal narratives that followed his. Instead, the most important memoir of the eighteenth century is scarcely spiritual but, rather, deeply pragmatic: *The Autobiography of Benjamin Franklin* (1770–1791).

Franklin's autobiography not only outlived him by hundreds of years, it provided the template of the American dream as it would continue to be imagined until midway through the twentieth century. Indeed, Jay Parini believes "American literature begins with Benjamin Franklin. Before that, there was colonial literature" (p. 13). It is certainly true that the rags-to-riches tale of the self-made man Franklin originated in his autobiography has become a staple of American literature, both in fiction and nonfiction. In fact, revealing the secret of his material success is the reason Franklin gives for writing this book at all.

> From the poverty and obscurity in which I was born and in which I passed my earliest years, I have raised myself to a state of affluence and some degree of celebrity in the world. As constant good fortune has accompanied me even to an advanced period of life, my posterity will perhaps be desirous of learning the means which I employed, and which, thanks to Providence, so well succeeded with me.

After giving his purpose for writing the autobiography, Franklin quickly presents his credentials as an American to the potential consumers of his text: he informs readers that he is "the youngest son of the youngest son for five generations back." A truism of America's founding fathers is that they were frequently the offspring of "younger" sons. The English laws of primogeniture were such that eldest sons inherited the family property in England, younger sons being thus induced to try their fortunes in the colonies. Franklin's father, a nonconformist in the Church of England, came to America in 1685 to escape religious persecution—another common credential for early Americans. Ben Franklin was therefore born in Boston, the fifteenth of Josiah Franklin's seventeen children and the youngest boy.

It's a wise father who knows his own child: Josiah Franklin soon perceived that his youngest son hated the family chandlery and, to prevent the spirited Ben from running off to sea (a serious temptation for Boston-bred boys with a taste for adventure), Josiah indentured him as an apprentice printer to James Franklin, Ben's much older brother. Again, Ben's "younger son" mentality brought his rebellious tendencies to the fore in his new relationship with his elder brother.

> Though a brother, [James] considered himself as my master and me as his apprentice, and accordingly expected the same services from me as he would from another, while I thought he degraded me too much in some he required from me,

who from a brother expected more indulgence. . . . Perhaps this harsh and tyrannical treatment of me might be a means of impressing me with the aversion to arbitrary power that has stuck to me through my whole life.

In addition to the depredations of his big brother, young Franklin had the English Assembly to deal with—he and James had been publishing anti-English editorials in their paper, the *New England Courant*. Between his brother's abuse and the ire of the English governors, Franklin soon decided to leave Boston and become a printer elsewhere in the colonies.

In October 1723, Franklin settled as a printer's assistant in Philadelphia. After a few years, he quarreled with his employer and set up his own shop. Again, in his recounting of these events, Franklin's narrative underscores the rebelliousness and urge for independence that would become the trademarks of American character.

After opening his own print shop and soon becoming a wizard of industry and efficiency, Franklin did not neglect his own spiritual education. He read constantly and set himself daily tasks to improve both his mind and his character. The wisdom he attained he gives to his readers in the *Autobiography*: "I grew convinced that *truth, sincerity*, and *integrity*, in dealings between man and man, were of the utmost importance to the felicity of life." This sounds like the motto of the Rotary Club of America. He goes further: "In order to secure my credit and character as a tradesman, I took care not only to be in *reality* industrious and frugal, but to avoid the appearances of the contrary. I dressed plain and was seen at no places of idle diversion." Scientist, inventor, linguist, lover, father, and ambassador, Franklin minted the archetype of a successful American. His autobiography even prescribes a list of thirteen moral virtues for self-betterment: temperance, silence, order, resolution, frugality, industry, sincerity, justice, moderation, cleanliness, tranquillity, chastity, and humility.

In his autobiography, Franklin reveals himself as a man shaped by his times—the oppression of the English governors of the American colonies—and by his circumstances: born poor but bright, oppressed by his elder brother and his less-talented employers. These two major external influences inculcated in him a desire for independence from tyranny. Franklin is the model of the self-made man—born in poverty, he achieved both riches and respect. He is the exemplar of what Thomas Jefferson claimed for American society (as opposed to European): a meritocracy based on talent and ability rather than birth and wealth.

## TOCQUEVILLE'S ASSESSMENT OF AMERICAN LITERATURE IN THE 1830s

Franklin had been dead for nearly half a century when Alexis de Tocqueville visited America in 1831–1832; many of nineteenth-century America's greatest writers—Walt Whitman, Henry David Thoreau, Herman Melville—were mere boys, while three others, Henry Wadsworth Longfellow, Ralph Waldo Emerson, and Nathaniel Hawthorne, were still very young men, the majority of their accomplishments yet to come. The country's greatest achievements were still political rather than literary when de Tocqueville took his measure of the nation. Thomas Jefferson had only died a few years before, and his and Franklin's eighteenth-century ideas about democracy had taken root and grown lushly into the nineteenth. Thus, Alexis de Tocqueville, who had come to America to study the prison system, instead left with a consuming passion to write about democracy in America. His book of the same title appeared in America in 1840, four years after Ralph Waldo Emerson published *Nature* and five before Henry Thoreau would give up teaching to move to a cabin at Walden Pond and write his autobiography.

Tocqueville's description of an American bookseller's shop in 1831, however, would still have been recognizable to readers a decade later:

> [A traveler] will first find a multitude of elementary treatises, destined to teach the rudiments of human knowledge. Most of these books were written in Europe; the Americans reprint them, adapting them to their own use. Next comes an enormous quantity of religious works, Bibles, sermons, edifying anecdotes, controversial divinity, and reports of charitable societies; lastly appears the long catalogue of political pamphlets. In America, parties do not write books to combat each other's opinions, but pamphlets, which are circulated for a day with incredible rapidity, and then expire.

Unsurprisingly, Tocqueville found little to admire in American letters, which he deemed largely derivative ("the Americans constantly draw upon the treasures of English literature"). In fact, other than journalism, Tocqueville concluded, "the inhabitants of the United States have then, at present, properly speaking, no literature." Without naming Franklin and Jefferson, he accurately notes that those who dabble in belles lettres in democratic nations "are either engaged in politics or in a profession which only allows them to taste occasionally and by stealth the pleasures of the mind." "The pleasures of the *book*" would be more precise in the case of Jefferson and Franklin; certainly they tasted aplenty the pleasures of the mind.

Nevertheless, these two founding fathers might have been mainly men of letters had they been born in Europe rather than in eighteenth-century America. Instead, they became leaders of their new republic, and when they picked up the pen to write for an audience it was primarily to instruct and persuade rather than to entertain. Their aims were practical rather than aesthetic.

Tocqueville, like every other commentator on the new republic before him (and many after him), believed that the necessity of conquering the wilderness had drained the poetic impulse out of Americans. He seems to have utterly missed the transcendentalist movement budding around him when he observes:

> I readily admit that the Americans have no poets; I cannot allow that they have no poetic ideas. In Europe, people talk a great deal about the wilds of America, but the Americans themselves never think about them: they are insensible to the wonders of inanimate nature, and they may be said not to perceive the mighty forests which surround them till they fall beneath the hatchet. Their eyes are fixed upon another sight: the American people views its own march across these wilds,—drying swamps, turning the course of rivers, peopling solitudes, and subduing nature.

From his perspective in the early 1830s, Tocqueville could not foresee the way the destruction of the American wilderness would profoundly alter the landscape of the nation's literature. He could not, properly speaking, have envisioned Thoreau.

## THOREAU AND THE TRANSCENDENTAL AUTOBIOGRAPHY

Henry David Thoreau, however, was a prominent feature of the New England landscape and not a destructive one. He moved to Walden Pond in 1845, built his own house, grew his own food, and lived quietly and contentedly as a sojourner in nature. He had no intention whatever of subduing nature, preferring to live in harmony with it. Frankly, he has little good to say at all about industry, either in England or America, but much to praise in the Native American way of life. He is particularly drawn to a purification ritual practiced annually by the Mucclasse Indians: on one particular day of the year, they cleaned their houses, consigning all of their old goods to a bonfire, and then fasted for three days. At the end of this time, they would feast and rejoice in their newly purified homes and bodies. Thoreau notes, "I have scarcely heard of a truer sacrament, that is, as the dictionary defines it, 'outward and visible sign of an inward and spiritual grace,' than this...."

Still, like other autobiographers of the nineteenth century, Thoreau remains more at the mercy of outside forces than inner desires. *Walden* could be subtitled "A Train Runs through It," because the not-so-distant rumbling of train wheels on the newly laid tracks does run through his narrative. Although he longs to turn inward, Thoreau is ever influenced by the world outside him: the woods, the pond, his bean field *and* his neighbors, his community (he was jailed for failing to pay his taxes), and the industrial culture burgeoning all around him.

In addition, Thoreau, like Franklin, wants to advise his readers. Much of *Walden*, though written in an "I" voice ("it is, after all, always the first person that is speaking") is directed to a "you" audience. For all his seeming iconoclasm, Thoreau doesn't want to simply smash established practices; he wants to prescribe new ones. His advice to readers is vintage American: "I desire that there may be as many different persons in the world as possible; but I would have each one be very careful to find out and pursue *his own* way, and not his father's or his mother's or his neighbor's instead."

The main reason Thoreau stands out among nineteenth-century American autobiographers is that he opposed the destruction of the American wilderness and did his best to preserve the small part with which he came in contact: "I let it lie, fallow perchance, for a man is rich in proportion to the number of things he can afford to let alone." Alexis de Tocqueville, for all his perspicacity in describing America, could not imagine that the destruction of the wilderness would engender a spiritual and literary backlash and that the "progress narrative" of America would be challenged by the spiritual ideology of the transcendentalists.

## ARCHETYPAL AMERICAN AUTOBIOGRAPHIES: SLAVE NARRATIVES

Any discussion of nineteenth-century American autobiography must include those that are the most archetypally American: slave narratives. Scores of these memoirs have been republished since the 1960s, but the best remain *Narrative of the Life of Frederick Douglass* (1845), written by himself, and *Incidents in the Life of a Slave Girl* (1861) by Harriet Jacobs. Slave narratives invariably show the construction of a self in opposition to a suffocating external force: the oppression of the white culture around them. Jacobs writes:

> I had not lived fourteen years in slavery for nothing. I had felt, seen, and heard enough, to read the characters, and question the motives of those around me. The war of my life had

begun; and though one of God's most powerless creatures, I resolved never to be conquered.

Far from being conquered by what she endured, Harriet Jacobs's identity was clearly forged in the furnace of that oppression.

This theme of the self, created in spite of the attempts of the majority white culture to crush it, runs through virtually every autobiography by an African American. It represents the self-defining experience for American blacks, and some description of it appears in nineteenth-century autobiographies by Douglass and Jacobs up through late-twentieth-century memoirs by Henry Louis Gates and Brent Staples. This passage from James Baldwin's *Notes of a Native Son* (1955) is representative:

> I . . . contracted some dread, chronic disease, the unfailing symptom of which is a kind of blind fever, a pounding in the skull and fire in the bowels. . . . There is not a Negro alive who does not have this rage in his blood—one has the choice, merely, of living with it consciously or surrendering to it.

The autobiographies of Americans who identify themselves as minorities continue to follow this pattern, whether written a century ago or now.

Excepting those autobiographies then, a more general movement in this genre of literature—the impetus for self-construction shifting from external forces to inner—distinguishes the historical trajectory of American autobiography. This general trend becomes strikingly obvious in the autobiographies of the last half of the twentieth century. However, its seeds may have been initially sown in the most important American autobiography of the early part of the twentieth century: Henry Adams's *The Education of Henry Adams* (1905).

## HENRY ADAMS'S "EDUCATIONAL" AUTOBIOGRAPHY

In this book, Henry Adams discovers that the more he learns, the less he understands. Education has failed to clarify the workings of the world for this intellectual; instead, the more knowledge he acquires, the more baffling and complex the modern world appears. Tellingly, Adams subtitled his autobiography "Studies in Twentieth-Century Multiplicity." The passage below suggests the crux of his third-person narrative of himself.

> All one's life, one had struggled for unity, and unity had always won. The national government and the national unity had overcome every resistance, and the Darwinian evolutionists were triumphant over all the curates; yet the

greater the unity and the momentum, the worse became the complexity and the friction. . . . the multiplicity of unity had steadily increased, was increasing, and threatened to increase beyond reason.

As this excerpt from Adams suggests, the path traced in this essay through American autobiography may stem from the increasing complexity of American society. When settlers first arrived here, they had a clear purpose—hack a living space out of the forest, build houses and churches, erect a community. Their lives were brutal but simple. Their identity derived more from who they were not—not European (any longer), not Indians, not animals—than who they were. They pitched their lives on the edge of the wilderness and spent their days clearing land, chopping wood, finding or planting food, having and raising children. They were too busy surviving to reflect long on the meaning of their existence, but if they were tempted to do so, they were Christians and could look in the Bible.

Well into the nineteenth century, Americans who had the intellect to reflect on the meaning of their lives were too pragmatic to linger long over the task. Jefferson and Franklin gave themselves to their communities; what they discovered about themselves they applied to others. Both of these men were products of the Enlightenment, and they firmly believed in the power of knowledge. Of course, they also lived in a time when knowledge itself was not yet so vast that it could daunt the intelligent generalist. It was still possible to "know the world," and Franklin and Jefferson were philosophers—they believed any intelligent individual could know it if he simply applied himself to the task. From their perspective in history, they could not have envisioned the objections to education—to knowledge itself—that Henry Adams would raise at the outset of the twentieth century.

## WHERE (WHO) WE ARE NOW

Inevitably, certain types of knowledge led to the development of the technology that would revolutionize American life. In this country, as in the rest of the Western world, the single-family farm that conjoined both work and family and represented the occupation of most of the population has steadily fragmented into a myriad of employments outside the home and away from the family. Most people nowadays work in "service industries" and have no tangible products to show for their labors. Many people find it difficult even to describe to their children what they spend their workday doing.

Generalization has given way to specialization, knowledge has both exploded and fragmented. External events—such as the world wars of the twentieth century, the Holocaust, the invention of the nuclear bomb, the destruction of the World Trade Center—have grown increasingly difficult to comprehend in both their magnitude and their implications. Knowledge has ceased to enlighten but rather to darken our brows; knowledge now seems malevolent, as it was in the Garden of Eden. Progress no longer looks as good as it did in the earlier centuries of this country—it no longer even looks like progress.

The fragmentation evident everywhere in the larger society is echoed in the fragmentation of individual identity. A passage in Sonia G. Austrian's *Mental Disorders, Medications, and Clinical Social Work* (2000) attempts to explain the upsurge in depression among Americans:

> Depression appears to have been on the increase since World War II, and this may be due to the mobility of the population, which removes people from familial support systems and hinders them from establishing long-term close friendships. The increase may also be caused by the demands of the workplace or the greater complexity of the postwar world. In the past decade, increasing unemployment, the continued breakdown of the nuclear family, and the faltering economy have likely been contributing factors.

For Americans, individual identity has never been more fragile than it is now. The narcissism so prevalent in America has logically found its niche in the autobiography, but such memoirs do not wallow in self-identity so much as question it. The narcissist stares at himself because he fears his image will disappear if he doesn't constantly monitor it. He isn't reveling in himself so much as hoping to catch a glimpse of who he might really be.

American autobiography in the twenty-first century, then, records the rupture of both national and self-identity. Certainty about the world has given way to confusion—even one's senses can no longer be trusted to provide accurate information. We can be fooled, and we are fooled all the time—we live in the era of virtual reality and this lends our lives a surreal quality. Contemporary American memoirists are simply encoding these doubts about the nature of the reality and the instability of identity.

No one can predict what direction American autobiography will take after this point; we can only see where we are now. To misquote Henry Adams, "All one's life, one had struggled for unity, and unity had finally been lost."

[*See also* Adams, Henry; Autobiography: Slave Narratives; Autobiography: White Women during the Civil War; Baldwin, James; Bradstreet, Anne; Confessional Poetry; Didion, Joan; Douglass, Frederick; Edwards, Jonathan; Franklin, Benjamin; Haley's *Autobiography of Malcolm X*; McCarthy, Mary; Styron, William; Thoreau, Henry David, and his *Walden*; Tocqueville, Alexis de; Transcendentalism; *and* Wolfe, Thomas.]

## FURTHER READING

Benstock, Shari, ed. *The Private Self*. Chapel Hill, N.C., 1988.

Dillard, Annie and Cort Conley, eds. *Modern American Memoirs*. New York, 1995.

Eakin, John Paul. *Fiction in Autobiography: Studies in the Art of Self-Invention*. Princeton, N.J., 1985.

Eakin, John Paul. *Touching the World: Reference in Autobiography*. Princeton, N.J., 1992.

Heilbrun, Carolyn G. *Writing a Woman's Life*. New York, 1988.

Parini, Jay, ed. *The Norton Book of American Autobiography*. New York, 1999.

Smith, Sidonie. *A Poetics of Women's Autobiography: Marginality and the Fictions of Self-Representation*. Bloomington, Ind., 1987.

Stone, Albert E. *Autobiographical Occasions and Original Acts*. Philadelphia, 1982.

# AUTOBIOGRAPHY: SLAVE NARRATIVES

*by Lynn Orilla Scott*

Slave narratives are autobiographical accounts of the physical and spiritual journey from slavery to freedom. In researching her groundbreaking 1946 dissertation, Marion Wilson Starling located 6,006 slave narratives written between 1703 and 1944. This number includes brief testimonies found in judicial records, broadsides, journals, and newsletters as well as separately published books. It also includes approximately 2,500 oral histories of former slaves gathered by the Federal Writers' Project in the 1930s. The number of separately published slave narratives, however, is much smaller. Although exact numbers are not available, nearly one hundred slave narratives were published as books or pamphlets between 1760 and 1865, and approximately another one hundred following the Civil War. The slave narrative reached the height of its influence and formal development during the antebellum period, from 1836 to 1861. During this time it became a distinct genre of American literature, and achieved immense popularity and influence among a primarily white, northern readership. A few, in particular *The Narrative of the Life of Frederick Douglass, An American Slave. Written by Himself* (1845), displayed a high level of rhetorical sophistication. With the end of slavery, however, interest in the narratives declined sharply. Furthermore, one consequence of the social and political repression of the black population following Reconstruction was the "loss" of the slave narratives for sixty years. During the last few decades of the twentieth century, scholars recovered, republished, and analyzed slave narratives. Both historians and literary critics came to value their importance to the historiography of American slavery and to the development of African-American autobiography and fiction.

## THE EARLY NARRATIVES

The form and content of the slave narratives evolved over the course of the eighteenth, nineteenth, and twentieth centuries. Several eighteenth-century narrators were African-born freemen of high status who contrasted their lives before captivity with their enslavement. Their narratives assailed slavery, especially the Atlantic slave trade, on moral and religious grounds. The narrator's journey through the trials of slavery to freedom was represented in conjunction with his conversion to Christianity and his westernization. Similar to the questing hero of *Pilgrim's Progress* (1678), the subjects of eighteenth- and early-nineteenth-century black autobiography reflected Puritan religious values and the popular modes of writing of the time, which included conversion narratives, spiritual autobiography, Indian captivity narratives, and criminal confessions. Most early black autobiographical accounts were dictated to a white amanuensis or editor who selected and arranged the former slave's oral report, "improved" the style and wording, and provided an interpretive context in the preface and in the choice of metaphors that gave shape and meaning to the former slave's story. Consequently, as William L. Andrews has pointed out, in much early African-American autobiography it is often impossible to separate the voice of the black autobiographical subject from that of the white writer recording and interpreting the story.

An important exception to this literary ventriloquism is *The Interesting Narrative of the Life of Olaudah Equiano, or Gustavus Vassa, the African, Written by Himself*, first published in London in 1789. The most famous and influential of the eighteenth-century slave narratives, Equiano's *Life* went through eight British editions and one American edition in his lifetime and numerous editions after his death. Equiano's narrative includes descriptions of his early life among the Igbo people of Africa, his kidnapping and enslavement at eleven years of age, and the terror of the middle passage. Eventually sold to a British Royal Navy captain, Equiano was spared the crueler existence of life on a Caribbean or American plantation, and in 1766 he purchased his freedom. One of the most well-traveled men of the eighteenth century, Equiano served in the Seven Years' War in Canada and in the Mediterranean, accompanied the expedition of Constantine John Phipps to the Arctic in 1772 and 1773, and spent six months among the Miskito Indians in

Central America. A strong indictment of the Atlantic slave trade and the evils of human bondage, Equiano's narrative was presented to members of the British Parliament and played an important part in the eventual abolition of the British slave trade. It also served as a prototype for many of the later fugitive slave narratives.

## THE ANTEBELLUM SLAVE NARRATIVES

By the 1830s slave narratives had undergone a transformation. The African, freeborn narrator had disappeared and was replaced by the American-born fugitive slave narrator who escapes southern bondage to northern freedom. American slavery had not declined following the abolition of the African slave trade in 1807, as some had believed it would. On the contrary, the growth and profitability of cotton agriculture resulted in increasingly harsh conditions for many enslaved people. In contrast to the earlier narratives, antebellum narratives explicitly indicted slavery as an institution, emphasizing its dehumanizing and hellish aspects. Sold at antislavery meetings and advertised in the abolitionist press, the fugitive slave narratives were an activist literature that developed in the context of a growing and increasingly militant antislavery movement. As a reviewer of Henry Bibb's narrative wrote in 1849:

> This fugitive slave literature is destined to be a powerful lever. We have the most profound conviction of its potency. We see in it the easy and infallible means of abolitionizing the free states. Argument provides argument, reason is met by sophistry. But narratives of slaves go right to the heart of men.

A number of antebellum narratives went through multiple editions and sold in the tens of thousands, far exceeding sales of contemporary works by Herman Melville, Henry David Thoreau, or Nathaniel Hawthorne. Among the best-selling were *A Narrative of the Adventures and Escape of Moses Roper from American Slavery* (1837); *Narrative of the Life of Frederick Douglass, An American Slave. Written by Himself* (1845); *Narrative of William Wells Brown, a Fugitive Slave, Written by Himself* (1847); Solomon Northrup's *Twelve Years a Slave* (1853); and Josiah Henson's second autobiography, *Truth Stranger than Fiction: Father Henson's Story of His Own Life* (1858). Frederick

The Reverend Josiah Henson.
(© *Bettmann/Corbis*)

Douglass's narrative sold more than 30,000 copies in the first five years and became an international best-seller. Douglass would go on to write two later versions of his autobiography: *My Bondage and My Freedom* (1855) and *The Life and Times of Frederick Douglass* (1881; expanded edition, 1892). Josiah Henson, who became identified with Harriet Beecher Stowe's character Uncle Tom, of *Uncle Tom's Cabin* (1852), also published multiple versions of his autobiography.

The authors of the antebellum narratives wrote within an established literary tradition. Often written after the fugitive slave's story had been told at antislavery gatherings, the material was honed by repeated oral performance and influenced by the narratives of other slaves. The result is a highly formulaic body of literature with a number of features in common, beginning with the title page, which asserts that the narrative was written by the slave himself or dictated to a friend. Before the narrative proper, and sometimes after it as well, are authenticating documents written by prominent white citizens and editors who describe their relationship to the fugitive slave and testify to his good character and to the veracity of the story. In addition, the introduction often claims that the narrative understates rather than overstates the brutality of slavery.

Following the prefatory material, the narratives almost always begin with the phrase, "I was born." Then, in contrast with the conventions of white autobiography, the slave narrator emphasizes how slavery has denied him specific knowledge of his birth and parentage. The slave narrator goes on to describe the precarious and dehumanizing aspects of slavery, including scenes where slaves are brutally beaten, sold at auction, and separated from family members. A critical turning point in most narratives describes the slave's desperate awakening in which he determines to be a slave no longer. Following this determination, he plans and eventually executes his escape. Often the details of the narrator's escape are suppressed so as not to compromise those individuals who helped him or to limit the possibilities for other slaves to use similar means of escape. However some slave narratives focus on an adventurous escape such as the *Narrative of Henry Box Brown, Who Escaped from Slavery in a Box Three Feet*

*Long, Two Wide, and Two and a Half High* (1849). An example is *Running a Thousand Miles for Freedom; or, the Escape of William and Ellen Craft from Slavery* (1860). The antebellum slave narrative moves from south to north, from rural to urban, and from slavery to freedom. The typical narrative ends with the narrator's arrival in either the northern states or Canada and with the former slave's adoption of a new name.

## THEMES AND STYLE

Drawing from techniques used in popular historical novels and sentimental fiction, the antebellum slave narratives are episodic in structure, melodramatic in tone, and didactic in their appeal to commonly held moral values. Slave narrators appealed to the religious and secular values of their white audiences, arguing that slavery dehumanized the masters as well as degraded the slaves. They often noted that the most fervently religious masters were the most brutal. Thus, the narratives sought to expose slaveholding ideology as religious hypocrisy and to distinguish the slave as the true spiritual pilgrim. Similarly, the slave narrative appealed to the national values of liberty and equality as stated in the Declaration of Independence. It is the American romance with freedom, in particular, that the nineteenth-century Unitarian minister Theodore Parker had in mind when he stated that

> there is one portion of our permanent literature, if literature it may be called, which is wholly indigenous and original. . . . I mean the Lives of Fugitive Slaves. But as these are not the work of the men of superior culture they hardly help to pay the scholar's debt. Yet all the original romance of Americans is in them, not in the white man's novel.

In addition to arguing against slavery by appealing to the religious and political values of the white readers, the slave narratives are arguments for literacy as evidence of black humanity. European intellectuals had long equated being human—or at least being mentally and culturally superior humans—to having a written language. The value Europeans gave to writing is reflected in a key metaphor of early African-American autobiography, which Henry Louis Gates Jr. (1985, p. xxvii) has identified as "the figure of the talking book." Gates has argued that early black autobiography is a self-conscious refutation of the European charge that blacks could not write. The direct link between literacy and freedom is a thematic matrix that occurs in all of the major antebellum narratives as well. By the nineteenth century, it was generally illegal and believed dangerous to teach a slave to read and write. A number of fugitive narrators vividly recount their struggle to gain an education despite the prohibitions and denounce slavery's attempt to limit the slave's awareness of his condition and his capacity to learn. In the classic slave narrative, the acquisition of literacy is the precondition for the slave's decision to revolt against his enslavement, and literacy becomes the first step toward mental as well as physical freedom. This process is expressed most eloquently in the *Narrative of the Life of Frederick Douglass, An American Slave. Written by Himself* (1845). Douglass recounts the moment when he first understands the importance of literacy. He hears his master, Hugh Auld, tell his wife, "if you teach that nigger . . . to read, there would be no keeping him. It would forever unfit him to be a slave." Douglass's response is often cited as evidence of the rhetorical art, which makes his narrative the finest example of the genre.

> These words sank deep into my heart, stirred up sentiments within that lay slumbering, and called into existence an entirely new train of thought. . . . I now understood what had been to me a most perplexing difficulty—to wit, the white man's power to enslave the black man. It was a grand achievement, and I prized it highly. From that moment, I understood the pathway from slavery to freedom. . . . Though conscious of the difficulty of learning without a teacher, I set out with high hope, and a fixed purpose, at whatever cost of trouble, to learn how to read. The very decided manner with which he spoke, and strove to impress his wife with the evil consequences of giving me instructions, served to convince me that he was deeply sensible of the truths he was uttering. It gave me the best assurance that I might rely with the utmost confidence on the results that, he said, would flow from teaching me to read. What he most dreaded, that I most desired. What he most loved, that I most hated. That which to him was a great evil, to be carefully shunned, was to me a great good, to be diligently sought; and the argument which he so warmly urged, against my learning to read, only served to inspire me with a desire and determination to learn. In learning to read, I owe almost as much to the bitter opposition of my master, as to the kindly aid of my mistress. I acknowledge the benefit of both.

While the slave narratives provided a voice for black experience, they also circumscribed that voice. The antebellum slave narrator portrayed himself as an objective and representative witness of southern slavery in order to persuade white northern audiences to join the antislavery cause. This narrative stance required that the slave's subjective experience be repressed or in some cases excised from the text. The pressure to speak in representative terms of the slave's experience left little room for the individual voice or for a discussion of the narrator's interior life except as it specifically related to slavery. In her *Witnessing Slavery: The Development of Antebellum Slave Narratives* (1994), Frances Smith Foster has argued that "the desire to recognize oneself and to be recognized as a unique individual had to counter the desire to be a symbol, and it created the tension that is a basic quality of slave narratives." In addition, slave narrators had to be careful not to offend their white audiences, and thus the narratives did not directly challenge the ideology of white supremacy or sharply criticize the northern racism that negatively affected the lives of the fugitive and newly freed blacks.

## WOMEN'S NARRATIVES

Male narrators and male experience dominate the slave narrative genre. Nineteenth-century cultural prohibitions against women's involvement in the public sphere carried over to the antislavery movement, in which women's "proper" role was of considerable controversy. Of the known slave narratives, women wrote only 12 percent. The first known woman's slave narrative is *The History of Mary Prince, a West Indian Slave, Related by Herself*, published in London in 1831. Prince asserts herself as an authentic voice of the slave experience when she says,

> All slaves want to be free—to be free is very sweet. . . . I have been a slave myself—I know what slaves feel—I can tell by myself what other slaves feel, and by what they have told me. The man that says slaves be quite happy in slavery—that they don't want to be free—that man is either ignorant or a lying person.

The finest of the antebellum narratives written by a woman is *Linda: Incidents in the Life of a Slave Girl. Written by Herself*. Originally published under the pseudonym Linda Brent in 1861, the narrative was long thought to be a fiction written by Lydia Maria Child. In 1981, Jean Fagan Yellin demonstrated that it is, in fact, the autobiography of Harriet Jacobs, who did, indeed, write it herself. Employing techniques from sentimental fiction, Jacobs describes her struggle to avoid the predatory sexual advances of her master and to gain freedom for herself and her children. While enslaved women are portrayed as passive victims of sexual exploitation in narratives written by men, women narrators portray themselves as active and heroic agents in the struggle for freedom. Women-authored narratives also tend to place a greater emphasis on the role of family relationships.

## POSTBELLUM NARRATIVES AND BEYOND

Following the Civil War, newly freed blacks wrote autobiographies that clearly borrowed from the conventions of the antebellum narratives; however, the emphasis and purposes of these autobiographies were different. After 1865 slave narratives argued for full participation of black Americans in the new postwar society and therefore downplayed the past horrors of slavery. As William L. Andrews has stated in *To Tell a Free Story: The First Century of Afro-American Autobiography, 1760–1865* (1986), narratives written during this period depicted slavery "as a kind of crucible in which the resilience, industry, and ingenuity of the slave was tested and ultimately validated." An early example of a Reconstruction-era slave narrative is Elizabeth Keckley's *Behind the Scenes; Thirty Years a Slave and Four Years in the White House* (1868). The most famous slave narrative of this post-Reconstruction period, Booker T. Washington's *Up From Slavery* (1901), is a classic success story that testifies to black economic progress and promotes interracial cooperation.

The influence of slave narratives on American literature should not be underestimated. Harriet Beecher Stowe's enormously popular novel, *Uncle Tom's Cabin* (1852), was directly influenced by a number of slave narratives that Stowe had read before writing her novel. White authors were not only influenced by slave narratives; a few composed fraudulent ones and attempted to pass them off as genuine. Richard Hildreth's *The Slave; or, Memoirs of Archy Moore* (1836) and Mattie Griffiths's *Autobiography of a Female Slave* (1857) are such imitations. However, scholars have been most interested in the influence of the slave narrative on the African-American literary tradition. Vernon Loggins, Arna Bontemps, Henry Louis Gates Jr., Robert B. Stepto, Joanne M. Braxton, and several other scholars have long argued that the antebellum slave narrative is the foundation of African-American autobiography and fiction.

A number of twentieth-century classics of African-American literature, including Richard Wright's *Black Boy* (1945), Ralph Ellison's *Invisible Man* (1952), Alex Haley's *The Autobiography of Malcolm X* (1965), Maya Angelou's *I Know Why the Caged Bird Sings* (1969), and Alice Walker's *The Color Purple* (1982) contain many of the formal patterns and thematic concerns of the slave narrative. These patterns include the movement from south to north, from slavery or neoslavery to freedom, and from perceptual blindness to enlightenment or illiteracy to literacy. Like the slave narratives, these twentieth-century works provide a sharp critique of the effects of racial injustice and challenge America to live up to its stated values of freedom and equality. A number of twentieth-century African-American writers are interested in reimagining slavery in ways that give voice to the kinds of subjective and psychological experience repressed in the slave narrative. Examples of these neo-slave narratives include Ernest Gaines's novel *The Autobiography of Miss Jane Pittman* (1971), Ishmael Reed's parody of the slave narrative *Flight to Canada* (1976), Octavia E. Butler's science-fiction novel *Kindred* (1979), Sherley Anne Williams's novel *Dessa Rose* (1986), Toni Morrison's novel *Beloved* (1987), and Charles Johnson's novel *Middle Passage* (1990). As a form that embodies the collective experience of an oppressed people and the individual struggle to control one's own destiny, the slave narrative genre continues to offer a rich vein of exploration for contemporary African-American writers.

[*See also* Autobiography: General Essay; Haley's *Autobiography of Malcolm X*; Douglass, Frederick; *and* Stowe, Harriet Beecher.]

## FURTHER READING

Andrews, William L. *To Tell a Free Story: The First Century of Afro-American Autobiography, 1760–1865*. Urbana, Ill., 1986. Analyzes the history of African-American autobiography as "one of increasingly free story telling." The slave narrators not only write about freedom as a goal in life, but through a variety of rhetorical means show that they regard the writing of autobiography as self-liberating. A comprehensive study, one of the best in the field.

Braxton, Joanne M. *Black Women Writing Autobiography: A Tradition within a Tradition*. Philadelphia, 1989. Argues for a redefinition of the genre of black American autobiography to include women's writing. Demonstrates that slave narratives and spiritual autobiographies written by black women developed common themes and archetypal figures that established a tradition evident in contemporary black women's autobiography. Since most earlier writing only treated male slave narratives, Braxton's book is key in expanding the field.

Davis, Charles T., and Henry Louis Gates Jr., eds. *The Slave's Narrative*. New York, 1985. A collection of essays and reviews about slave narratives, including a selection of those written at the time of the original publication of various narratives. Modern essays on the slave narrative include historical analysis and literary criticism and focus on a range of specific texts. The volume includes

an excellent introduction and a selected bibliography of black narratives from 1760 to 1865. An important resource for the student of slave narratives.

Foster, Frances Smith. *Witnessing Slavery: The Development of Antebellum Slave Narratives*. 2d ed. Madison, Wisc., 1994. First published in 1979. Examines slave narratives in their cultural matrix by looking at the social and literary influences, the development of plot, the role of racial mythology, and the influence of the slave narrative on postbellum black writing. The focus is on separately published, male-authored narratives, but the second edition includes an essay on the differences in the portrayal of women by male and female slave narrators. A very readable work and a fine introduction to the genre.

Gates, Henry Louis, Jr. "Introduction: The Language of Slavery." In Davis and Gates, ed. pp. xi–xxxiv.

Jackson, Blyden. *A History of Afro-American Literature*. Vol. 1, *The Long Beginning, 1746–1895*. Baton Rouge, La., 1989. A comprehensive history of early African-American poetry, autobiography, prose, and fiction that includes but is not limited to a discussion of the slave narratives. Helpful for seeing the slave narrative in the larger context of African-American literature.

McDowell, Deborah E., and Arnold Rampersad, eds. *Slavery and the Literary Imagination*. Baltimore, 1989. A selection of papers from the English Institute that examines the evolution of the relationship between slavery and the American literary imagination from the antebellum slave narratives through nineteenth- and twentieth-century autobiography and fiction. An important source for understanding the influence of slave narratives.

Sekora, John, and Darwin T. Turner, eds. *The Art of the Slave Narrative: Original Essays in Criticism and Theory*. Macomb, Ill., 1982. Twelve essays that focus on the rhetorical art of the slave narrative, including studies of form, metaphor, and point of view, especially the challenge of creating a controlling self to serve as protagonist and author. The collection includes an essay on the practical use of the slave narrative in literature courses and a checklist of criticism of slave narratives. A good resource for the student of slave narratives.

Starling, Marion Wilson. *The Slave Narrative: Its Place in American History*. 2d ed. Washington, D.C., 1988. Originally presented as a Ph.D. thesis in 1946, Starling's was the first extensive study of the slave narrative. It inspired historians and literary scholars to study early

African-American writing. Starling located 6,006 slave narratives. Her work includes a list of primary sources in which slave narrative sketches were found and a list of separately published narratives. An excellent source of information on testimony in its historical and social context.

Stepto, Robert B. *From Behind the Veil: A Study of Afro-American Narrative*. Chicago, 1979. Identifies the quest for literacy and freedom as a "pre-generic myth" manifest in the historical consciousness of African-American written narrative. Categorizes the slave narratives into four types and examines how modern African-American narratives revoice and "answer the call" of the slave narratives. An important argument for the slave narrative as the foundation for later African-American literature.

# AUTOBIOGRAPHY: WHITE WOMEN DURING THE CIVIL WAR

*by Lynn Domina*

In the decades immediately following the Civil War, and even to some extent throughout the years of actual battle, hundreds of Americans published memoirs describing their experiences during this cataclysmic event. Such an outpouring of autobiographical material following the war is not surprising, since otherwise ordinary individuals are often prompted to write their life stories after extraordinary experiences. Because the American Civil War was arguably the most extraordinary event in this nation's history, as attested to by the debate that raged (occasionally even to this day) over its proper title—the Civil War, the War between the States, the War for Southern Independence, the War of Northern Aggression—the personal experiences of Americans who lived through it retain substantial contemporary interest. Many of these autobiographers were men, soldiers who had fought with Grant or Lee or Sherman and who often identified themselves with these heroes in their titles. Yet women also wrote of the war, in diaries and memoirs, describing their experiences as the mothers and sisters who stayed home or became refugees, as nurses in military hospitals, as spies, even as soldiers. This essay discusses several diaries composed during the war itself as well as memoirs published soon after the war's end. While such memoirs continued to be published for decades, the writers' goals shifted—and their memories became less reliable—as Reconstruction ended. (By 1900, for example, very few writers claimed to have supported slavery.) These writers consistently return to similar questions: What exactly is an appropriate role for a patriotic woman during a war? What is the enemy like, and how does one respond when he quite literally steps onto one's front porch? What will or should happen to the thousands of slaves whose very existence is so peculiarly entangled with the war itself?

## WOMEN'S CONVENTIONAL ROLES DURING THE CIVIL WAR

In their diaries and journals many women, especially those supporting the Confederacy, express frustration at their apparent inability to contribute actively to the war effort. This frustration became especially acute after Union victories. Sarah Morgan, a nineteen-year-old woman living in Baton Rouge, Louisiana, when the war began, expresses outrage when her city is surrendered in May of 1862 without significant resistance. She argues that if women had been defending the city, they would never have capitulated so easily, and she speculates that women soldiers would show the men how to fight if only women could fight. This longing to participate in the action is most pronounced among younger women, those who are envious of their brothers rather than worried over their sons; as the war dragged on, however, and as the exuberance of the young men faded, the envy of the young women would also convert to concern. In contrast, Kate Stone, twenty years old and also living in Louisiana, simply resigns herself to a woman's lot: suffering in silence. While she may wish that her options were less limited, she doesn't fantasize over the possibility of change.

By the final years of the war, after it had become clear that the substantial population advantage of the Northern states would become a contributory factor in any Union victory, Confederate women began to express overt disdain for any men who weren't off fighting. Kate Stone suggests that men who permit their compatriots to die while they themselves lounge about at home must lack any developed conscience. Even Sarah Emma Edmonds, a Canadian woman who disguised herself as a man and fought with a Michigan regiment, quotes a former Confederate soldier who insists that Southern women refuse to tolerate the presence of men who do not enlist.

Nevertheless, women created ways to contribute to the war effort within the sphere of appropriate feminine behavior. They raised money through various fairs and raffles and joined together in sewing circles to manufacture uniforms and other necessities for the soldiers. Kate Stone cites her own inadequacy in this regard compared with some of her neighbors. She can knit woolen mufflers but lacks sufficient skill for gloves or even socks. Eventually her lack of effort pricks her conscience, but her mother

Sarah Edmonds leaving hospital tents for battlefield. (© *Bettmann/Corbis*)

dismisses her desire to sew uniform jackets, stating that the family has enough work just to ensure its own survival—and implicitly the survival of its slaves—a response that was likely realistic if not patriotic.

Early on, however, other women looked to the example of Florence Nightingale, who had become famous for her nursing during the Crimean War (1853–1856). If refined English ladies could nurse soldiers far from home, the argument went, American ladies need not be ashamed to follow that example—indeed, they should be ashamed not to. Kate Cumming, who was twenty-six years old and living in Mobile, Alabama, when the war began, is particularly forceful on this point. The decision to permit women to serve in military hospitals rather than assign male soldiers the duty of nursing evoked significant controversy. Doctors as well as officers resisted the change. Socially, the idea of women changing the bandages on or bathing or even so boldly witnessing the bodies of male strangers was scandalous. Until the Civil War and the subsequent westward movement, women who affiliated themselves with military regiments were generally referred to as "camp followers" and implicitly understood to be prostitutes. Yet women like Cumming eventually demonstrated their value, particularly as Confederate soldiers were more and more desperately needed on the battlefront. While engaging in this struggle to shift

nursing from an exclusively male activity to one that included women, however, writers sought less to redefine women than to redefine nursing; the rhetoric employed often describes the ideal nurse in stereotypically feminine terms: compassionate, gentle, maternal, soothing.

Life in military hospitals during the mid-nineteenth century was far from appealing. Antibiotics were nonexistent and anesthetics much less precise or effective than they are today. Sanitary conditions appall the modern imagination, as writers frequently comment on the piles of amputated limbs outside the surgery. Clearly such a hospital filled to capacity with dirty, bloody, groaning, and dying men was "no place for a lady," at least by the conventional standards of the day. Cumming in particular, however, asserts that a woman's virtue would not be endangered by such an experience; she implies that any woman who could lose her respectability by performing her duty could not have been respectable to begin with. Throughout her journal, Cumming insists that working in the hospitals is the duty of every available Confederate woman, analogous to a man's duty to fight. By the end of the war she essentially blames the Confederacy's defeat on Confederate women who did not volunteer as nurses. She is particularly critical of young women who had no other family obligations, women who felt the frustration or ennui expressed by Morgan or Stone.

## FEMALE SPIES AND SOLDIERS

Despite these controversies, many women chose to participate directly with the military, often as spies and occasionally as soldiers. Since women who enlisted in either army did so under male names and masculine disguise, exact figures are impossible to establish, but contemporary scholarship suggests that as many as one thousand women fought for the Confederacy or Union (Edmonds, p. xiv). Others exploited their female identity and became successful spies because male officers simply didn't take their conversations with women seriously. Women, in other words, used gendered stereotypes as a military tactic. The most famous of these spies was Belle Boyd, who describes several of her ruses in her memoir *Belle Boyd in Camp and Prison*, published immediately as the war ended. Boyd, a strong Confederate sympathizer, infiltrated Union camps and Union-held towns. Through these actions, she attained notoriety not only among Union supporters but also within the Confederacy. Although the information she gathered was undeniably helpful to the Confederacy—even if she has exaggerated her role—the fact that a woman had become such a public figure in itself led to questions of her respectability. In her own diary, Lucy Rebecca Buck, who lived in Front Royal, Virginia, one of Boyd's residences, critiques Boyd for her coarse behavior, linking this critique to Boyd's renown. Buck implies that a woman who refuses her proper place, regardless of her effectiveness in other arenas, likely would lack the refinement preferred in middle-class women.

Boyd appears to be aware of critiques of this sort, for she concludes her section of her memoir (the book continues with a narrative by her husband) with a description of her marriage. At this point, Boyd presents herself as suddenly romantic, as if to demonstrate that she has been a true woman all along. Descriptions of Boyd's wedding were printed in newspapers throughout North America and Europe, and Boyd reproduces two of them. Nevertheless, the event that should most appease her critics instead earned her even more notoriety.

Other women defied gender constraints even more dramatically, though few left detailed accounts of their experiences. Sarah Emma Edmonds, however, published her memoir in 1864 under the title *Unsexed; or, The Female Soldier*. That title was apparently too direct, as the book was reissued in 1865 with a new one: *Memoirs of a Soldier, Nurse, and Spy*. Perhaps to deflect any criticism of her decision, Edmonds opens her memoir with an assertion that God directed her to do as she did. In her description of her enlistment, however, she simply describes her first assignment as a field nurse, neglecting any discussion of exactly how she managed her subterfuge. Throughout the memoir, Edmonds freely confesses her willingness to act violently—to respond, that is, appropriately as a soldier if not as a woman. In one memorable incident, Edmonds shoots a Confederate woman in the hand, but only after that woman has twice shot at Edmonds. When the woman falls to the ground, however, Edmonds binds her wound and bathes her face, playing the chivalrous soldier even if her foe hasn't played the proper lady. The woman eventually reveals that four of her family members, sharpshooters in the Confederate army, had recently been killed; Edmonds implies that such a strain led to the woman's psychological inability to behave appropriately. Given Edmonds's own identity, the implication that only an unbalanced woman could commit violence is highly ironic.

Edmonds also functions as a spy on several occasions. She disguises herself as a male slave and as an Irish peddler woman. Her impersonations range through gender, race, ethnicity, and class; like many spies, she discards each false identity after it has served its purpose to reduce her risk of discovery. Unlike her fundamental impersonation of a man, none of these disguises is considered potentially scandalous, in part because her deception functions only against the enemy. Additionally, however, these disguises generally place her at a lower level on the social hierarchy, so she is clearly not attempting personal gain by "passing." As a spy, she is understood to be a man temporarily acting *like* a slave or Irish peddler; she is not attempting to *be* of another race, gender, or ethnicity. In her role as a soldier, however, she has, according to any public perceptions, become a man, and though she will eventually again don women's clothing, her original deceit is so much more profound and long-lived than any spy's disguise that it threatens to disrupt the foundations of her society. If soldiers can't trust the manliness of their peers, a manliness they witness with their own eyes, every other bit of empirical knowledge must also be suspect. Hence the potential for scandal that surrounds Edmonds's choice.

Edmonds herself provides evidence that soldiers such as herself were not as rare as we might assume. After the battle of Antietam in September 1862, Edmonds reaches a severely wounded soldier. This soldier reveals her own identity as female as Edmonds provides what little palliative care she can; the soldier is most concerned that her identity remain secret and begs Edmonds to bury her personally, a request to which Edmonds readily agrees. Like Edmonds, this soldier presents herself as a believing

Christian who has made her peace with God and who chose to fight because of her belief in the righteousness of the cause.

## CHARACTERIZING THE ENEMY

Although women may have seldom encountered their opponents in actual battle, Southern women especially interacted with Union soldiers as the Union army gained control of Confederate territory. These writers describe officers arriving at their homes to demand dinner and enlisted men pillaging their barns and fields. Not unexpectedly, the enemy is demonized almost by default, "Yankee devil" being a common phrase in several diaries and memoirs. Belle Boyd describes an officer in the Illinois cavalry as both physically and culturally primitive and then extrapolates criminal tendencies from her description of his appearance. She describes another Union officer as the devil himself and suggests that he would feel at home in the work of Edgar Allan Poe. Kate Cumming suggests that it is not only individual Yankees who are devils incarnate, but the Union temperament itself.

By far the most notorious of Union officers is General Benjamin Butler, frequently referred to as "Beast" Butler because of an order he issued while in command of New Orleans. This order, General Order No. 28, known as the "woman order," essentially stated that any woman who spoke or otherwise behaved disrespectfully to Union soldiers, who behaved, in other words, unlike a lady, should be treated as a prostitute. The order shocked residents of the city and became notorious throughout the Confederacy. Butler himself therefore appears as an object of disgust and a representative of Yankee degradation in many Southern women's diaries and memoirs, including those of Morgan, Boyd, Cumming, Stone, and Mary Chesnut.

## THE PLACE OF POLITICS IN WOMEN'S LIVES

Although agitation for women's suffrage had begun before the Civil War, women's political influence in the mid-nineteenth century was still generally perceived to be most appropriately exercised in their maternal influence over their sons. Because of their family connections and geographic location, some women acquired more direct and more reliable knowledge of events as the war progressed than did others, who were forced to rely almost exclusively on unconfirmed rumors. Mary Chesnut, for example, was married to James Chesnut Jr., who was a U.S. senator from South Carolina until he was recalled when the state seceded. She is the most well known of

Civil War diarists, in part because her husband served as an aide to Jefferson Davis and she was personally acquainted with many other members of the Confederate government, individuals who are occasionally mentioned in her diary. Chesnut's situation—and the knowledge it permitted—was clearly unusual. Yet even she refers to women's legal status as a form of slavery, not entirely distinct from what she terms "African slavery." Married women are enslaved to their husbands, she states, and single women are enslaved to their fathers.

More typical was Kate Stone, who spent the war's opening years in Louisiana under Union occupation and the last years of the war as a refugee in Texas. Mail from the North, including magazines and newspapers, was embargoed. Even letters from her brothers in the Confederate army were scarce, since the Union army often occupied territory between them. This lack of news exacerbated the anxieties of women like Stone, who longed not only for news of Confederate victory but also for reliable accounts of the safety of relatives. In December 1863, for example, Stone received word of her brother Coleman's death in Mississippi on 22 September. Yet before this, an acquaintance had assured her of Coleman's safety as of 10 October. Only the worst news, it seems, could be trusted.

Yet lack of direct access to political structures hardly dampened women's patriotism. In diary after diary and memoir after memoir, by Northerners as well as Southerners, the nation and its symbols earn consistent, sometimes even obsessive attention. Writers discuss their flags—stars and stripes or stars and bars—with reverential awe. With anger bordering on rage, they describe scenes during which the enemy replaces their flag with his. Military regulations often specified that as soon as one army gained control of a particular town, all signs and symbols of loyalty to the opponent be repressed. Such regulations could often be outwitted, but these small victories were generally more symbolic than substantive. Belle Boyd, for example, relates how she was, day after day, able to attain small Confederate flags, despite being held in prison. In another scene, she describes raising a contraband Confederate flag while being escorted with a group of prisoners into a Baltimore jail. This incident is treated more as a prank than as outright mutiny, however; Boyd remains a prisoner, and Baltimore remains within the Union.

Such scenes occurred more frequently in Southern women's writing because most of the battles were fought in Confederate territory, but Northern women also relied on the power of their flag's symbolic value. Born in

Southbridge, Massachusetts, in 1827, Caroline Seabury moved to Mississippi in 1854 in order to teach at the Columbus Female Institute, a position she held until 1862, when the school's principal determined that only Southerners should be employed. In 1863, Seabury determined to return to the North. She initially attempted to secure passage on Mississippi riverboats by waving a white flag, but the crews ignored her. So in order to secure the trust of Union soldiers occupying the region, Seabury constructed a makeshift flag from appropriately colored silk and cut-out paper stars. The strategy worked.

## SLAVES AND SLAVERY IN WHITE WOMEN'S AUTOBIOGRAPHIES

To contemporary readers who identify slavery as the primary cause of the war, the issue of slavery appears in these texts surprisingly infrequently. While this could indicate that the writers themselves did not perceive slavery to be of central importance, it more likely indicates how deeply ingrained slavery was in Southern culture. Kate Stone, as much as she expresses hatred toward Yankees, is one of the only Southerners who implies that owning slaves might in itself be sinful, even if one treats one's slaves comparatively humanely. When the moral aspects of slavery are addressed, the writers are more likely to express concern over miscegenation between masters and slaves than they are over the question of slavery itself. Mary Chesnut sarcastically suggests that slave children include the biological children of slave masters on virtually every plantation and that mistresses agree that some slave children remarkably resemble the master's acknowledged children—on all the neighboring plantations, that is, but not on their own. Northern women are more likely to remark on the pale complexions of some slaves, implicitly indicting white slave owners. Sarah Emma Edmonds notes the surprise she felt when she initially encountered a "Negro" slave with pale skin and blue eyes. Caroline Seabury describes the auction of a slave woman whose complexion was only slightly darker than her own. Esther Hill Hawks, a physician from New Hampshire who served as a teacher for the Freedmen's Aid Society during the war, critiques Union troops as well, asserting that no African-American woman is safe from their advances. In a comment unique to these texts, Hawks even argues that interracial marriage should be legally acceptable, though her tone indicates that she would be unlikely to consider such a relationship herself. In addition, white women frequently express misgivings about their lack of protection from male slaves once the white men leave their plantations to fulfill their military duties.

Additional racial stereotypes abound in these texts, even among the writers who could be considered most progressive. Most of these comments involve African Americans, but members of other ethnic groups, especially the Irish, also receive derisive comments. Most commonly, black speech is conveyed in dialect, while white speech is conveyed in standard English. Sarah Morgan suggests that her family's slaves enjoy her appearance as much as she does their service. She fails to consider the possibility that slaves who refer to her as a "queen" or in other flattering terms might be mocking her. Even Sarah Emma Edmonds classifies African Americans according to type, and each type is a stereotype: the cheerful, the lazy, the bestial.

If Mary Chesnut could, with apparent equanimity, define wives as slaves, other Southerners used the terms of slavery to clarify the psychological severity of a Confederate defeat. White Southerners would not be made slaves, writer after writer asserts, to white Northerners. The outcome of the war is continually expressed in terms of subjection, as if in so frequently declining to speak of the profound role slavery played in this war, the writers are experiencing a return of the repressed. Because so few of these journals or memoirs continue into the period of Reconstruction, however, we cannot accurately assess how these women felt after the nation was reunited, after they were, to use their own term, enslaved.

[*See also* Autobiography: General Essay; Autobiography: Slave Narratives; *and* War Literature.]

## FURTHER READING

Andrews, Eliza Frances. *The War-time Journal of a Georgia Girl, 1864–1865.* Lincoln, Neb., 1997. First published in 1908.

Boyd, Belle. *Belle Boyd in Camp and Prison.* Baton Rouge, La., 1998. First published in 1865. Memoir of a confederate woman who became notorious for her role as spy.

Buck, Lucy Rebecca. *Shadows on My Heart: The Civil War Diary of Lucy Rebecca Buck of Virginia.* Edited by Elizabeth R. Baer. Athens, Ga., 1997.

Chesnut, Mary. *Mary Chesnut's Civil War.* Edited by C. Vann Woodward. New Haven, Conn., 1981. First published in 1904.

Culley, Margo, ed. *A Day at a Time: The Diary Literature of American Women from 1764 to the Present.* New York,

1985. Foundational text for the study of diaries, particularly useful in situating diaries as autobiographical texts. Useful beginning to theoretical work that remains to be done in analyzing the narrative and retrospective structure of diaries.

Cumming, Kate. *Kate: The Journal of a Confederate Nurse.* Edited by Richard Barksdale Harwell. Baton Rouge, La., 1987. First published in 1866.

Daly, Maria Lydig. *Diary of a Union Lady, 1861–1865.* Edited by Harold Earl Hammond. New York, 1962. Northern Democrat and wife of New York City judge, Daly spent the war years in Washington, D.C., and New York.

Edmonds, Sarah Emma. *Memoirs of a Soldier, Nurse, and Spy: A Woman's Adventures in the Union Army.* Introduction by Elizabeth D. Leonard. DeKalb, Ill., 1999. First published in 1865.

Faust, Drew Gilpin. *Mothers of Invention: Women of the Slaveholding South in the American Civil War.* New York, 1997. Thorough and engagingly written analysis of women's contributions to the war effort and of the shifts in gender roles resulting from the war. Much evidence for Gilpin's conclusions is gleaned from diaries and memoirs of the period.

Hawks, Esther Hill. *A Woman Doctor's Civil War: Esther Hill Hawk's Diary.* Edited by Gerald Schwartz. Columbia, S.C., 1989. First published in 1984.

Kemble, Frances A., and Frances A. Butler Leigh. *Principles & Privilege: Two Women's Lives on a Georgia Plantation.* Ann Arbor, Mich., 1995. Abolitionist journal of the British actress while she resided in the United States and a pro-Confederacy memoir of her daughter.

McDonald, Cornelia Peake. *A Woman's Civil War: A Diary, with Reminiscences of the War from March 1862.* Edited by Minrose C. Gwin. Madison, Wis., 1992. First published in 1935.

McGuire, Judith W. *Diary of a Southern Refugee during the War, by a Lady of Virginia.* Lincoln, Neb., 1995. First published in 1867.

Morgan, Sarah. *The Civil War Diary of a Southern Woman.* Edited by Charles East. New York, 1991. First published in 1913.

Rable, George C. *Civil Wars: Women and the Crisis of Southern Nationalism.* Urbana, Ill., 1991. Analysis of changes wrought in women's lives as a result of the war. Relies substantially on women's "private writings" to reinterpret women's notions of patriotism and duty during the war.

Seabury, Caroline. *The Diary of Caroline Seabury, 1854–1863.* Edited by Suzanne L. Bunkers. Madison, Wis., 1991. Northerner opposed to slavery who spent much of the war in the Confederacy.

Stone, Kate. *Brokenburn: The Journal of Kate Stone, 1861–1868.* Edited by John Q. Anderson. Baton Rouge, La., 1995. First published in 1955. Diary of a young Louisiana woman who spent the end of the war as a refugee in Texas.

Wink, Amy L. *She Left Nothing in Particular: The Autobiographical Legacy of Nineteenth-Century Women's Diaries.* Knoxville, Tenn., 2001. Chapter 3 considers Civil War diaries. Suggests that the keeping of diaries and writing of memoirs helps experience become comprehensible, especially when a given experience is otherwise so incomprehensible.

# JAMES BALDWIN

*by Greg Miller*

As a teenager James Baldwin abandoned the pulpit after a year and a half, but it would be fair to say that he always remained a preacher. For Baldwin, the life of an artist was a higher vocation, and he plunged into that life with inexhaustible, at times desperate, fervor. While he insisted that the writer's primary responsibility is to his or her craft, he was equally adamant that the writer has an obligation to serve as witness for society; in doing so, the writer plays an essential role in the construction of a better future. Baldwin certainly demanded of himself this double purpose, and when the two are in accord—often in his essays, occasionally in his fiction—it is easy to see his work as among the most important in twentieth-century American literature. For many, though, Baldwin's early promise as a novelist was never fully realized; according to this not entirely unsound perspective, the tumult of the 1960s took a heavy toll on the writer and rendered his fiction didactic and disheveled. His reputation sagged, not least among black radicals who considered Baldwin to have been co-opted by the (white) literary establishment. Years after his death, opinion is still divided over the merits of Baldwin's fiction and even his later essays. What Baldwin wrote in his essay, "Alas, Poor Richard" (1961), published after the death of Richard Wright, could be said of himself: "The fact that [Wright] worked during a bewildering and demoralizing era in Western history makes a proper assessment of his work more difficult."

In a 1959 review of a Langston Hughes collection, Baldwin concluded that Hughes was "not the first American Negro to find the war between his social and artistic responsibilities all but irreconcilable," and here, too, Baldwin could have been speaking of his own struggle. The key words here are "all but," a phrase that allows for a

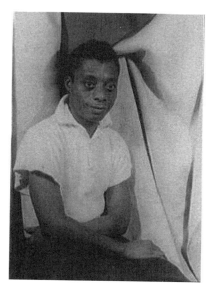

James Baldwin. (*Photograph by Carl Van Vechten. Courtesy of the Library of Congress*)

narrow passageway, an elusive but not wholly inaccessible path that may be likened to a spiritual journey. Baldwin's way forward, his own literary project of reconciling the social with the artistic, was indeed arduous. If Baldwin was only fitfully successful, this does not detract from the quality of his best work; one might even argue that Baldwin's so-called failures are equally instructive and, given his refusal to sanitize or streamline the unpleasant realities of American society, equally exemplary.

From the beginning of his writing career, American literature's most famous former preacher would speak in terms of "vision" and "revelation." In his first great essay, "Everybody's Protest Novel" (1949), Baldwin is already insisting that it is the "power of revelation which is the business of the novelist, this journey toward a more vast reality which must take precedence over all other claims." The artist must provide vision, he states in "The Black Boy Looks at the White Boy" (1961), because "where there is no vision the people perish." And in his essay "The Creative Process" (1962), he writes: "Societies never know it, but the war of an artist with his society is a lover's war, and he does, at his best, what lovers do, which is to reveal the beloved to himself, and with that revelation, make freedom real." Baldwin's primary theme as novelist, playwright, and essayist is the redemptive power of love. His invocation of "a lover's war" in the above quote is by no means metaphorical: the romantic entanglements of his fictional protagonists, their restless relationships and trysts and obsessions, should be seen as simultaneously personal and social, intimate and political, as complex movements toward a more meaningful reality. Such is Baldwin's literary territory. At times he approaches melodrama and at times he seems to lose control of form, but he writes beautifully and his vision has lost none of its urgent power.

## EARLY YEARS

Baldwin was born in Harlem on 2 August 1924. He never knew the identity of his biological father; the man whom he always called his father, David Baldwin, married his mother, Emma Berdis Jones, in 1927. David Baldwin was a severe man, an introverted and increasingly bitter minister. In his autobiographical essay, "Notes of a Native Son" (1955), Baldwin starkly declares of his father: "I do not remember, in all those years, that one of his children was ever glad to see him come home." It was a tense, poverty-stricken household. From an early age Baldwin was torn between his love of reading and his father's expectation that his sensitivity and intelligence would serve ministerial ends. Although Baldwin's childhood hardly seemed favorable for a budding artist, his precociousness attracted fortuitous attention, beginning with Countee Cullen, who oversaw the literary club at Baldwin's junior high school. Another crucial influence was Orilla ("Bill") Miller, a young white female teacher who took the boy under her wing, exposing him to theater and film—and, crucially, provided a lasting counterexample to his father's demonization of all white people. He soon developed an enthusiasm for writing, and while his father distrusted this side of his son, Baldwin's instructors were encouraging (and one of his poems even brought a congratulatory letter from Mayor Fiorello La Guardia). In 1938 Baldwin began to preach at the Fireside Pentecostal Assembly in Harlem. That same year, he began attending DeWitt Clinton High School in the Bronx. He showed flair as a preacher; indeed, his impassioned, poetic sermons drew away many from his father's congregation. But he was also a gifted student, and in his sophomore year Baldwin stopped preaching to concentrate on extracurricular activities, foremost among them his work as coeditor (with classmate Richard Avedon) of the school literary magazine. Upon graduating from high school, Baldwin made the difficult, yet inevitable decision to renounce the ministry altogether. He knew he wanted—in fact, *needed*—to become a writer; in the meantime, he began working at a railroad in New Jersey. David Baldwin died in 1943 after struggling with mental and physical illness. The next year, James Baldwin moved to Greenwich Village.

He instantly took to the Village; indeed, where else in the United States could a black, openly homosexual artist thrive? He was introduced to Richard Wright, who discerned the young writer's potential and was instrumental in setting Baldwin on track. Baldwin began work on a first novel, "In My Father's House" (which would become *Go Tell It on the Mountain*, 1953). Largely on Wright's recommendation, Baldwin was awarded a literary fellowship in 1945. His first published work was a book review on Maxim Gorky in 1947 for *The Nation*. His work began to appear in various magazines: reviews and essays in *The Nation* and *The New Leader*, along with essays and a first short story ("Previous Condition," 1948) in *Commentary*. Baldwin was awarded another fellowship in 1948, and later that year he moved to Paris. Although never a permanent exile, Baldwin experienced more freedom abroad. He was on the verge of becoming both a major writer and a public figure and stateside pressures (racism, of course, not least among them) made him happy to spend the majority of his time abroad for the rest of his life.

His time in Paris gave him a more nuanced perspective of his country's particular racial problems, and no doubt the distance was also helpful psychologically. Baldwin began to find his literary voice. He published essays that would be collected in *Notes of a Native Son* (1955). In "Everybody's Protest Novel," Baldwin argues that American protest novels are in fact only radical on the surface; for Baldwin, the protest novel makes the mistake of favoring theoretical frameworks rather than "the man of the flesh," and in doing so, it ultimately becomes "an accepted and comfortable aspect of the American scene." That Baldwin uses Wright's *Native Son* (1940) as his contemporary case is perhaps a pure example of anxiety of influence. In any event, Baldwin found himself alienated from Wright when the essay was published, and the rift was never effectively repaired. His next significant essay, "Many Thousands Gone," was published in 1951 in the *Partisan Review*. Here Baldwin extends his discussion of Wright in more positive terms. More important, the essay serves as Baldwin's first sustained meditation upon race in America. "Negroes are Americans," writes Baldwin, "and their destiny is the country's destiny. They have no other experience besides their experience on this continent and it is an experience which cannot be rejected, which yet remains to be embraced." Baldwin would always insist upon the entwined destinies of black and white Americans; this was an arranged marriage, with no possibility of divorce.

## THE NOVELIST EMERGES

Together, "Everybody's Protest Novel" and "Many Thousands Gone" sketched out an aesthetic of a black American fiction that might broaden the prescribed territory and so render black experience without succumbing to the self-defeating reactivism that, to Baldwin's mind, had marred even the best work of its kind (such as *Native Son*). If Baldwin's essays to date had helped him think through his own approach to fiction, they had also set the stakes imposingly high. Baldwin sensed the quality of the novel on which he was currently working, but was finding it difficult to finish, and so he jumped at an opportunity to leave behind the distractions of Paris for an extended stay in a Swiss village. In Switzerland, with his beloved Bessie Smith records playing in the background, he finished *Go Tell It on the Mountain*. It was received with enthusiasm and earned a National Book Award nomination in 1953, the year of its publication.

Many find Baldwin's first novel to be his best. Certainly it is an impressive debut. Baldwin skillfully presents the semiautobiographical narrative from several points of view and demonstrates a firm structural command that he would not equal in subsequent novels. On the other hand, Baldwin's astonishing, insightful lyricism depends on a somewhat ramshackle foundation—or, at least, moments of excess—and on the whole *Go Tell It* is too polite, too self-consciously literary to achieve such heights. The book's correspondence to Baldwin's own life should not be overemphasized, and yet connections clearly exist. John Grimes, the novel's protagonist, is born into the poverty of Harlem, as was Baldwin; like Baldwin, his father is an intimidating preacher, and John is expected to follow suit. The senior Grimes considers all whites to be wicked, and he makes fun of his son's physicality (he calls John "frog eyes," for example, as did Baldwin's stepfather). John Grimes inherits his father's hatred, and the thrust of the plot involves John's overcoming of this inheritance, achieved by a mixture of the flesh and the spirit. James Joyce's *Portrait of the Artist as a Young Man* (1916), which Baldwin had read a few years back, is an obvious influence. The other main influences would remain so throughout his career: the language and imagery of Christianity (especially the King James Version of the Bible); music (spirituals, blues, and jazz), and Henry James. The influence of James would grow stronger and more varied in future works; in *Go Tell It*, the characterization bears a Jamesian mark.

The success of *Go Tell It on the Mountain* made Baldwin's publishers eager for a follow-up novel, but the last thing Baldwin wanted to do was to become pigeonholed. He was especially eager to make it as a playwright (another similarity with Henry James, and Baldwin was only marginally more successful in this regard), and he completed his first play, *The Amen Corner*, in 1954. When Baldwin's publishers passed on it, the novelist-playwright (as he considered himself) oversaw its performance by the Howard University drama troupe; it had a fairly successful run in Europe, but the play was not published for more than a decade. Meanwhile, some of Baldwin's essays were collected and published in 1955 as *Notes of a Native Son*. The book attracted enormous attention, most of it positive. Besides "Everybody's Protest Novel" and "Many Thousands Gone," the book's high points are the title essay and "Stranger in the Village." The latter, drawn from Baldwin's time spent in Switzerland, begins strikingly: "From all available evidence no black man had ever set foot in this tiny Swiss village before I came" (p. 159). Baldwin goes on to provide a shrewdly elegant examination of the "Negro problem" from a European vantage point. It was in Europe that Baldwin learned to accept his inevitable identity as American. While the black American has "arrived at his identity by virtue of the absoluteness of his estrangement from his past," American whites, claims Baldwin, long for a recovery of their European innocence, a time "in which black men do not exist" (p. 174). Baldwin concludes by cautioning against the desire for racial separation, and he eloquently links this desire with larger concerns of identity and the desire to take refuge in an apolitical netherworld:

> It is only now beginning to be borne in on us—very faintly, it must be admitted, very slowly, and very much against our will—that this vision of the world is dangerously inaccurate, and perfectly useless. For it protects our moral high-mindedness at the terrible expense of weakening our grasp of reality. People who shut their eyes to reality simply invite their own destruction, and anyone who insists on remaining in a state of innocence long after that innocence is dead turns himself into a monster. (p. 175)

Baldwin insists that America's racial drama has led to the creation of a new kind of black person and also a new kind of white. The last sentence of the essay—and the last sentence of the book—asserts that the "world is white no longer, and it will never be white again" (p. 175).

"Notes of a Native Son," surely one of Baldwin's finest pieces of writing, brilliantly moves between intimate memoir and polemic. In large part, the essay is a portrait of his stepfather, and of the writer's difficulty with the late man's legacy of hatred. Baldwin realizes that hatred, however justifiable, inevitably results in self-destruction, and the essay accordingly becomes a testament to Baldwin's survival as both man and artist. The concluding paragraph dialectically outlines the problem of how to live one's life in troubled times, and it is a passage that is essential for comprehending Baldwin's literary project:

> It began to seem that one would have to hold in the mind forever two ideas which seemed to be in opposition. The first idea was acceptance, the acceptance, totally without rancor, of life as it is, and men as they are: in the light of this idea, it goes without saying that injustice is a commonplace. But this did not mean that one could be complacent, for the second idea was of equal power: that one must never, in one's own life, accept these injustices as commonplace but must fight them with all one's strength. This fight begins, however, in the heart and it now had been laid to my charge to keep my own heart free of hatred and despair.

## THE ROLE OF THE WRITER

Baldwin was now firmly established as one of the most promising American writers, and *Notes of a Native Son* in particular made him almost overnight the representative black voice of his generation. Baldwin had no intention of playing this role, but it was one that he ultimately could not escape. With *Giovanni's Room* (1956), Baldwin sought not to repeat himself, but his American publishers were hardly enthusiastic about the result. (Indeed, since they initially passed on publication, the novel first appeared in England.) Although tame by later standards, *Giovanni's Room* was a landmark book in its frank depiction of homosexuality. For the first and only time, not a single black character makes an appearance. The novel concerns David, a young midwestern man who is in Paris while his fiancée, Hella, travels in Spain. David meets and falls in love with Giovanni, a handsome Italian who is primarily homosexual. David, who until now has mainly repressed his homosexual inclinations, cannot come to terms with his happiness, and he ends up shunning Giovanni when Hella returns from Spain. Giovanni becomes desperate; he prostitutes himself, commits murder, and is sentenced to be executed. David, meanwhile, is overcome with remorse. He is unhappy with Hella, and takes to picking up sailors in gay bars. His fiancée eventually catches David and leaves him. The narrative is related by David on the night before Giovanni's execution, as he prepares to return to America. Despite some overwritten passages, this may be Baldwin's finest novel. The theme is typical—a young American loses his innocence in Europe—but Baldwin imbues the story with a genuinely tragic, almost unbearably painful account of man's failure to pursue his nature.

It is a moral failure; David lacks the strength to honestly confront and accept love when it comes into his life. The influence of Henry James upon Baldwin—always evident in Baldwin's comma-heavy, multiclause sentences—can be seen in Baldwin's complex rendering of Old and New World societies.

By now, Baldwin rarely stayed in the same place for more than a few months. He returned to the United States after the publication of *Giovanni's Room*, and in 1957 he visited the South for the first time. His personal life was becoming cluttered and chaotic. Ceaseless socializing (and important friendships with, among others, Norman Mailer, James Jones, William Styron, and Marlon Brando) and painful romantic relationships took up much of his time. It would be another six years before he would finish his next novel.

In the meantime, Baldwin remained prolific as essayist and short story writer. A fellowship from the *Partisan Review* gave him time to write "Sonny's Blues" (1957), a lengthy short story in which, once again, Baldwin powerfully examines the question of how one should live one's life. The story concerns two brothers (perhaps the central relationship in Baldwin's fiction from this point on) whose outlooks on life could hardly be more different. The unnamed narrator is Sonny's older brother.

As the story opens Sonny, a jazz musician, has just been arrested (again) for drug possession. The narrator has escaped the projects, and now works as a high school math teacher and lives with his wife. Although he had promised his mother that he would take care of his younger brother, he finds Sonny's world so mystifying and threatening that he has, guiltily, generally kept clear. When the narrator's little daughter dies, the narrator finds himself ready to reach out, as best he can, to Sonny. The story chronicles their relationship and ends as the brother watches Sonny perform for the first time, a scene that becomes an extended meditation upon the artist's invaluable yet sacrificial contribution to society: "Sonny moved, deep within, exactly like someone in torment. I had never before thought of how awful the relationship must be between the musician and his instrument. He has to fill it, this instrument, with the breath of life, his own" (*Going to Meet the Man*, p. 138). Narratively complex yet never strained, "Sonny's Blues" also benefits from Baldwin's treatment of his protagonists' complicated, confused, and not entirely understood responses to a world that will not stay fixed. Their inner lives come through with a force and precision that for once makes comparisons with Henry James apt not only in manner but in quality.

Baldwin is not normally convincing as a short story writer; he needs a broader canvas than short fiction usually allows, so it makes sense that his best stories—"Sonny's Blues" and "This Morning, This Evening, So Soon" (1960)—are nearly of novella length. In the years following "Sonny's Blues," Baldwin increasingly applied himself to the national struggle for civil rights. Even though he lived mostly in Paris, Baldwin was the movement's most important spokesperson from the artistic ranks. His visit to the South resulted in numerous essays, and his views were continually sought on a wide range of topics. The 1961 collection, *Nobody Knows My Name: More Notes of a Native Son*, finds Baldwin in top form once again, addressing civil rights issues as well as (and sometimes simultaneously) Faulkner, Mailer, and Ingmar Bergman ("What he saw when he looked at the world did not seem very different from what *I* saw."). In "Notes for a Hypothetical Novel: An Address," Baldwin reasserts his view of the writer's social work in terms that reflect the escalating sense of urgency that the civil rights movement was developing:

> Now, this country is going to be transformed. It will not be transformed by an act of God, but by all of us, by you and me. I don't believe any longer that we can afford to say that it is entirely out of our hands. We made the world we're living in and we have to make it over. (p. 154)

Such expectations, for himself and for others, reveal Baldwin's inheritance of the romantic tradition. Like Shelley, Baldwin saw the artist as legislator of the world. But the decade ahead would bring bitter disappointment, and a wavering reputation.

### TUMULT

The same year that *Nobody Knows My Name* was published (and became a best-seller), Baldwin wrote an essay on Martin Luther King Jr. for *Harper's*. He began to speak frequently with King and with Malcolm X, and traveled to Africa in 1962. Just before he left for Africa, Baldwin's next novel, *Another Country* (1962), appeared to mixed reviews, although it would be his most popular success. *Another Country* is primarily concerned with the redemptive possibility of love. The plot is perhaps insignificant; Baldwin instead explores the interrelationships of seven characters, most of them musicians or writers from New York City and Paris. They are black and white, heterosexual, homosexual, and bisexual, and it seems that by novel's end virtually everyone has slept with everyone else. Baldwin himself felt he was losing the thread of the plot, and some of the sexual encounters seem to emit an image of the novelist throwing up his hands. Despite accusations of obscenity, however, Baldwin's perspective remains primarily ethical; the healing, enabling aspect of the sexual encounter was always stressed ahead of the physical release. While the writing is occasionally clumsy, Baldwin's evocation of New York City in the 1950s cannot be faulted. What comes through, finally, is the failure of the black and white characters to transcend their racial identity and connect as equals. Still, the title's metaphorical reference to the possibility of change conveys a strain of hope, and the overall effect of the book is powerful. For all its shortcomings, *Another Country* remains the clearest embodiment of Baldwin's contribution to the twentieth-century American novel. It is easy to see why it attracted the largest audience that Baldwin would ever have. Unfortunately, among *Another Country*'s less impressed readers was J. Edgar Hoover; the FBI would keep an extensive file on Baldwin for the rest of his life, a file that swelled to nearly eighteen hundred pages.

The year 1962 also saw the publication of two essays in *The New Yorker* that would be published in book form the following year as *The Fire Next Time*. The book once again mixes personal memoir with overtly political passages, including Baldwin's negative impressions of the Black Muslim movement. It is the cautionary sermon of a brilliant man, and it signaled the sweeping, multilayered style of his later book-length essays. *The Fire Next Time* also reveals Baldwin hardening toward Christianity. In this striking passage, for instance, the author sounds almost Nietzschean:

> Whoever wishes to become a truly moral human being must first divorce himself from all the prohibitions, crimes, and hypocrisies of the Christian church. If the concept of God has any validity or any use, it can only be to make us larger, freer, and more loving. If God cannot do this, then it is time we got rid of him.

His tone had become increasingly prophetic; as an essayist he was in complete control. Baldwin did not know it, but he would never command such influence or widespread acclaim.

A long essay, *Nothing Personal* (1964), was released in book form accompanied by the photographs of former high school friend Richard Avedon. It is a trenchant essay that reveals Baldwin's increasing pessimism about race relations in the United States. In a society that "permits one portion of its citizenry to be menaced or destroyed," Baldwin warns, "then, very soon, no one in that society is safe." His ambitions as a playwright were realized when *Blues for Mister Charlie* was staged in 1964 under the direction of Burgess Meredith. The play itself is a rather tedious treatment of the Emmett Till murder, and its primary interest today resides in the manner in which Baldwin seems to be staging his own vacillation between the nonviolent philosophy of Martin Luther King Jr. and the less conciliatory approach of Malcolm X. The Foreign Drama Critics named it the best play of the year; stateside reaction was less enthusiastic, and Baldwin's increasingly confrontational political tone, however justified, was beginning to bother his white liberal readers.

Times were changing. Baldwin's aesthetic debt to the white literary canon was not unnoticed by his black readership. Baldwin's own increasing radicalism affected his aesthetic sensibility as well. His always shaky relationship with religion had become almost hostile during the tumultuous 1960s, especially after the assassinations of King and Malcolm X, and he was less likely to dwell upon the Bible's literary influence on his writing. As for James and other important canonical influences (Dickens, Dostoyevsky, Hemingway, and Fitzgerald), Baldwin's willingness to discuss them depended on the audience. He was now more interested in stressing the African-American tradition; to this end, Baldwin wanted his fiction to sound like Miles Davis, Billie Holiday, Bessie Smith. No other writer of his time could make such a claim, but Baldwin's prose justifies such comparisons. Still, one suspects other reasons for Baldwin's shift in emphasis: a new generation of black artists and activists was beginning to find Baldwin irrelevant, and they certainly were not interested in hearing about the novelist's reverence for *The Portrait of a Lady* (1881). More cynically, one might relate his public identification with musicians rather than other writers to the opening passage of Baldwin's early essay, "Many Thousands Gone": "It is only in his music, which Americans are able to admire because a protective sentimentality limits their understanding of it, that the Negro in America has been able to tell his story" (*Notes of a Native Son*, p. 24). Baldwin deeply cared about the opinion of others, so much so that his work sometimes suffered as a result. He was particularly wounded by criticism from black leftists—some of the militants began referring to him as Martin Luther Queen—since his influence among that segment had once been so great.

His next novel, *Tell Me How Long the Train's Been Gone* (1968), was written at the lowest point in Baldwin's life. Its narrator, Leo Proudhammer, is an obvious stand-in for Baldwin, and the book may reasonably be read as Baldwin's attempt to make sense of his own fractured existence. Proudhammer is a famous actor who is recovering from a massive heart attack. The narrative drifts from flashbacks that take place throughout his life to ruminations on his present state. The novel's most successful, most moving passages involve Leo's boyhood relationship with his brother Caleb. Stylistically, the novel can be read as a parable despite its length and its autobiographical bent. Leo is representative of the "successful" black American artist, but his heart attack signals the profound sickness of American society. The latter, somewhat bewildering section of the novel chronicles Leo's complicated relationship with a black activist. Baldwin was clearly not interested in shaping *Tell Me How Long the Train's Been Gone*, and there are passages that, to quote Baldwin reviewing a collection by Langston Hughes, "a more disciplined poet would have thrown into the waste-basket." Oddly, though, the novel's formal sloppiness manages to convey the narrator's confusion—which is not to say that the result is a great novel, but simply that the emotional experience of reading the book is somehow intensified as a result. The reviews, though, were the worst of Baldwin's career.

The reviews of his next publication, the long essay *No Name in the Street* (1972), were scarcely better. This was particularly unfortunate, since *No Name in the Street* is one of Baldwin's finest books. Formally, it bears resemblance to *The Fire Next Time*: an admixture of the personal and the polemic, and a roving survey of subtopics. The main difference is that, whereas the earlier book was sad yet hopeful, in *No Name in the Street* grief often becomes fury. It is Baldwin's survey of the 1960s and early 1970s, and it offers this stinging summation of its author's disillusionment regarding American democracy:

> The necessity for a form of socialism is based on the observation that the world's present economic arrangements doom most of the world to misery; that the way of life dictated by these arrangements is both sterile and immoral; and, finally, that there is no hope for peace in the world so long as these arrangements obtain.

The intellectual reach in *No Name in the Street*, the clarity of prose and the inspiring vision, are quintessential Baldwin; it is the ideas themselves that gave reviewers trouble, but then leftist thought has never gone down easily in the United States. In the years since his death, however, Baldwin's views have become increasingly relevant. In many ways, he is America's Orwell.

Baldwin seems to have listened to critics of *Tell Me How Long the Train's Been Gone*; his next novel, *If Beale Street Could Talk* (1974), is a model of brevity. For the first time, Baldwin tells his story exclusively through a female narrator. The twenty-one-year-old Tish lives with her family in Harlem; she is pregnant with the child of her lover, a Puerto Rican man who is in prison on false charges of rape. Critics have often found fault with the tendency for Baldwin's narrators to echo Baldwin the essayist. But these narrators usually resemble their creator enough so that the asides and conjectures actually enrich Baldwin's fiction. Tish, however, could hardly be more dissimilar than her creator, so in this case the effect is wholly jarring. Many passages are moving but, as with most of Baldwin's short stories, the brevity renders the narrative too schematic. Baldwin returned to form with *The Devil Finds Work* (1976), an extended reflection on American cinema (focusing on representations of African Americans) and an absorbing work of cultural film criticism. The book was briefly prefigured at least twice, in an essay for *Commentary*, "On Catfish Row: *Porgy and Bess* in the Movies" (1959), and in a delightful scene in *Tell Me How Long the Train's Been Gone*, in which Leo and Caleb go to the movies and are subjected to *King's Row* (1942). *The Devil Finds Work* is not on the same level as Baldwin's best essays (he too often resorts to generalities), but his insights into such films as *The Birth of a Nation* (1915), *Guess Who's Coming to Dinner* (1967), *Lady Sings the Blues* (1972), and *The Exorcist* (1973) are of much interest.

Baldwin had high hopes for his last novel, the ambitious *Just above My Head* (1979). In this book Baldwin's prose is leaner (to the unfortunate extent that a sense of place, always a strong aspect of Baldwin's fiction, is nearly absent), and for the first time his characters converse in black English. The novelist seems to be consciously providing a summation of his philosophy and themes, and the result is paradoxically both bloated and threadbare, although the novel has its admirers.

James Baldwin died at age sixty-three on 1 December 1987, in St. Paul de Vence in southern France. He was buried a week later in Ferncliff Cemetery, Hartsdale, New York. On the bottom of the memorial program was this passage from "Sonny's Blues":

> For, while the tale of how we suffer, and how we are delighted, and how we may triumph is never new, it always must be heard. There isn't any other tale to tell, it's the only light we've got in all this darkness.

And this tale, according to that face, that body, those strong hands on those strings, has another aspect in every country and a new depth in every generation.

(*Going to Meet the Man*, p. 139)

[*See also* James, Henry *and* Wright, Richard.]

## SELECTED WORKS

*Go Tell It on the Mountain* (1953)
*Notes of a Native Son* (1955)
*Giovanni's Room* (1956)
*Nobody Knows My Name: More Notes of a Native Son* (1961)
*Another Country* (1962)
*The Fire Next Time* (1963)
*Blues for Mister Charlie* (1964)
*Nothing Personal* (1964)
*Going to Meet the Man* (1965)
*The Amen Corner* (1968)
*Tell Me How Long the Train's Been Gone* (1968)
*No Name in the Street* (1972)
*One Day, When I Was Lost: A Scenario Based on "The Autobiography of Malcolm X"* (1972)
*If Beale Street Could Talk* (1974)
*The Devil Finds Work* (1976)
*Just above My Head* (1979)
*The Evidence of Things Not Seen* (1985)
*The Price of the Ticket: Collected Non-fiction, 1948–1985* (1985)

## FURTHER READING

Balfour, Lawrie. *The Evidence of Things Not Said: James Baldwin and the Promise of American Democracy*. Ithaca, N.Y., 2001. A valuable consideration of Baldwin's continued relevance within the context of political theory.

Bloom, Harold, ed. *James Baldwin*. New York, 1986. Baldwin's fiction and nonfiction are examined in eleven essays.

Campbell, James. *Talking at the Gates: A Life of James Baldwin*. London, 1991. The best critical—though surely *too* critical—biography of Baldwin.

Harris, Trudier, ed. *New Essays on* Go Tell It on the Mountain. Cambridge, 1996.

Johnson-Roullier, Cyraina E. *Reading on the Edge: Exiles, Modernities, and Cultural Transformation in Proust, Joyce, and Baldwin*. New York, 2000. The author looks at *Notes of a Native Son* and *Giovanni's Room*.

Köllhofer, Jakob, ed. *James Baldwin: His Place in American Literary History and His Reception in Europe*. Frankfurt, Germany, 1991.

Leeming, David. *James Baldwin: A Biography*. New York, 1994. Leeming was Baldwin's secretary and friend, and this is probably the most sensitive and complete treatment of Baldwin's life and thought. Baldwin's work, however, is dealt with too uncritically.

McBride, Dwight A., ed. *James Baldwin Now*. New York, 1999. A wide-ranging collection of essays intended to reassess the writer along the interconnected lines of race, class, and gender. Particularly valuable regarding Baldwin's later works.

Standley, Fred L., and Nancy V. Burt, eds. *Critical Essays on James Baldwin*. Boston, 1988. Includes scholarly essays alongside popular book reviews. Baldwin's fiction, nonfiction, and plays are covered.

Standley, Fred L., and Louis H. Pratt, eds. *Conversations with James Baldwin*. Jackson, Miss., 1989. An excellent collection of interviews from 1961 to 1987.

Washington, Bryan R. *The Politics of Exile: Ideology in Henry James, F. Scott Fitzgerald, and James Baldwin*. Boston, 1995.

# RUSSELL BANKS

*by Lani Wolf*

Russell Banks's short stories and novels portray working-class people trapped in mundane lives filled with violence and trauma. His themes include the cycle of violence from father to son and the exploration of the difference between the psyches of women and men and between those of people of varying races and economic classes. In Banks's world, these dichotomies lead to conflict, the outcome of which is most often tragic, and to a crushing sense of personal guilt. Redemption, however, is always hard-bought. In addition, Banks's work offers one of the most severe indictments of the American dream ideology in contemporary literature. His characters reach

Russell Banks. (*Photograph © Jill Krementz*)

after what they think will make them happy, striving for self-transformation and "successful" lives. All but a few, however, find themselves thwarted.

## THE LIFE OF RUSSELL BANKS

The first of four children, Russell Banks was born in New Hampshire in 1940 into a working-class family headed by an alcoholic and physically and emotionally abusive father, a recurrent character type in Banks's fiction. His parents fought constantly, both verbally and physically, his father asserting dominance over all other members of the family. In search of a "better life," Earl Banks moved the family often, from one economically depressed northeastern town to another, but could not escape the chaos and poverty from which they had fled. When Russell was twelve, his father abandoned the family to live with a girlfriend, and his parents divorced. Banks strove throughout his adult life to improve his relationship with his father.

Precocious in school, Banks was offered a scholarship to the prestigious preparatory school, Andover Academy; it was withdrawn when he and a friend ran away from home, embarking on a cross-country trip in a stolen car. These acts of self-sabotage and flight became a pattern in Banks's early life. For example, he won an academic scholarship to Colgate University in 1958 (he was the first in his family to attend college) but dropped out in the first semester. As Banks later explained, success through academic and intellectual achievement, and with it the possibility of crossing social and economic boundaries, was considered by his father a betrayal of the family, and this in part accounted for his subconscious undermining of his future.

Inspired by Jack Kerouac's *On the Road*, Banks headed south with the intention of joining Fidel Castro's guerrilla fighters in Cuba. He never made it out of Florida, however, where he lived a bohemian lifestyle and began thinking of himself as an artist. By his early twenties, he had married Darlene Bennett, a salesgirl in a local department store where he worked as a window dresser, and soon thereafter they had a daughter. Faced with living out his life in small-town central Florida, working hard at menial jobs to support his family, he grew bored, frustrated, and lonely and began echoing his father's pattern of violence, familial abuse, and heavy drinking. In an effort to escape, he moved with his wife and daughter to Boston, but the marriage crumbled completely, and Darlene and the child returned to Florida.

In Boston he befriended aspiring beatnik artists, writers, and musicians and became disciplined about his writing. He also met his second wife, Mary Gunst, a theater major at Emerson College. Reeling from the emotional strain of this relationship, Banks returned to Florida, this time to the Keys, and then spent the early 1960s in a series of hitchhiking adventures across the United States. In severe debt, he returned to New Hampshire, where his father helped him get jobs as a pipe fitter and plumber, and Russell managed a tolerable, though still strained, relationship with his father. Still pursuing his vision of himself as an artist, he attended the 1963 Breadloaf Writers' Conference in Vermont, where he met Nelson Algren, who would become his mentor and encourage Banks to see himself as a "real" writer.

Another turning point in his life came when his wealthy in-laws sent him to the University of North Carolina at Chapel Hill, where he studied English literature, graduating with honors in 1967. During his years there, he became politically active, helping to found a chapter of Students for a Democratic Society. His friendships with several African Americans led him to see African Americans as real people with a set of problems much like his own, and to understand race relations as an integral part of American history. These experiences planted the seed for his critically acclaimed 1998 novel *Cloudsplitter*, about the radical abolitionist John Brown. At the University of North Carolina he also helped found a small press, Lillabulero, which published his first two books of poetry, along with the work of such emerging writers as Gary Snyder and Malcolm Cowley. As Banks himself has admitted, he was not a natural poet, but his poetry gave him a place to explore themes that would later emerge in his fiction, for example, the intersection of alien worlds and the passage of the compulsion toward violence from father to son, "like a secret blood disease" (*Snow*).

In 1968, Banks, his wife, and their daughters moved to New Hampshire, where Banks taught at Emerson College and the University of New Hampshire. During this time, he also published stories in respectable journals, receiving several short story awards. From 1975 to 1984 he wrote four novels, *Hamilton Stark* (1978), *The Book of Jamaica* (1980), *The Relation of My Imprisonment* (1983), and *Family Life* (1988), very innovative works that many critics call "experimental," a term that Banks himself would disagree with, feeling that "all fiction is experimental" (Niemi, p. 68). Although about widely divergent subjects, these apprentice works all employ the rococo style, freely shifting points of view, highly unconventional narration, and rejection of realist illusion typical of 1970s metafiction.

Interspersed with his metafictional novels were more conventional works employing the social realism, naturalistic language, and Dreiserian style for which Banks has become known. Set in New Hampshire and the tropics, these melancholy stories, collected in *Searching for Survivors* (1975), *The New World* (1978), *Trailerpark* (1981), and *Success Stories* (1986), explore class conflict and social issues in America, focusing on the pain and loneliness of the poor and on the illusion of the American dream ideology.

In 1976, Banks received a Guggenheim Fellowship, which he used to spend eighteen months in Jamaica. He grew to love and respect the Jamaican people, ideology, and culture, and would integrate his Jamaican experiences into many of his future novels. His increasingly unstable marriage to Mary Gunst failed at this time, however, and his family returned to the United States without him.

Banks spent the 1980s and 1990s living in the Northeast, a professor at several universities, including Sarah Lawrence, Columbia, and most recently, Princeton. In 1982 he married his third wife, Kathy Wilson, an editor at Harper and Row. In 1988, he married a fourth time, to Chase Twitchell, a poet at Princeton. He has continued to write prolifically, in 1985 publishing *Continental Drift*, widely regarded, with *Cloudsplitter*, as his best work, and bringing him from a respected but little-known writer to a commercial and critical success. Four critically acclaimed novels followed: *Affliction* (1989), about adult male rage and violence instilled by childhood abuse at the hands of an alcoholic father; *The Sweet Hereafter* (1991), about the guilt, grief, and fragmentation of a small town that has lost its children to a bus accident; *Rule of the Bone* (1995), about the alienation and flight of a young man from a broken, abusive home; and *Cloudsplitter* (1998), a historical novel about the troubled father–son relationship between the radical abolitionists John and Owen Brown. Banks also contributed numerous poems, short stories, and essays to such esteemed publications as *Harper's*, *Esquire*, *Vanity Fair*, and *The New York Times Book Review*. In addition, *Affliction* and *The Sweet Hereafter* were made into feature films in the 1990s.

## AWARDS

Banks has been the recipient of numerous literary awards throughout his career: a grant from the National Endowment for the Arts; a Guggenheim Fellowship; the Ingram Merrill Award; the Saint Lawrence Award for Short Fiction; the O. Henry and Best American Series short-story awards; the Jon Dos Passos Award; the American Academy of Arts and Letters Award; and a nomination for the 1986 Pulitzer Prize, the last three for *Continental Drift*. Additionally, he was short-listed for both the PEN-Faulkner Fiction Prize and the Irish International Prize for *Affliction* and was elected president of the International Parliament of Writers in 2001.

## EARLY WORKS

Banks's first novel *Family Life* (1975) is about the sexually and emotionally dysfunctional relationship between a king and queen and their three sons, a combination of tall tale, fable, and social satire that explores the theme of paternal violence transmitted to the next generation. Despite poor critical reviews, Banks continued writing, publishing *Hamilton Stark* (1978), an epistemological detective novel about the death of Hamilton Stark, a Paul Bunyanesque, larger-than-life, fearless man, whom the narrative reveals to be a thief, liar, drunkard, bigot, and deserting father—analogous, like the king in *Family Life*, to Earl Banks. The novel is told in shifting points of view, that of Stark's daughter and the sensitive, intelligent and articulate narrator, a friend of Stark's. Out of Banks's Jamaican experiences came *The Book of Jamaica* (1980), told by a New England college professor interested in the Maroons, the mountain-dwelling descendants of escaped slaves, and their guerilla war against the British. Like the narrators of *Hamilton Stark*, the professor seeks to define himself by obsessive exploration of something outside the self, which he sees as heroic and larger-than-life. The general critical success of *The Book of Jamaica* comes in part from its more straightforward narrative style, the only innovation being a shift from first- to second- to third-person voice by the book's end. *The Relation of My Imprisonment*, published in 1984 and written in Jamaica, is an odd, puzzling work, perhaps Banks's most difficult. The protagonist, a death-obsessed coffinmaker, leads a cult whose members lie in coffins during prayer and meditation. He is incarcerated when the state makes coffins illegal and, while imprisoned, writes his "Relation," a type of first-person narrative first introduced by jailed seventeenth-century Puritan divines to relate the tests of their faith while in prison and read aloud to a congregation for inspiration, instruction, and spiritual regeneration. Banks later explained that he needed the distancing effect and artifice of these highly allegorical tales to be able to approach the disarray and pain of his past as figured in these works, particularly regarding his father (Lee, p. 212).

Banks's first collection of short stories, *Searching for Survivors* (1975), ranges from fantastic tales of Che Guevara, one of his early heroes, in America to a largely autobiographical account of his younger brother's sudden death in a train accident. *The New World* (1978), his second collection, contains two sets of stories, the first in "Renunciation," set in New England, concerned with domestic themes, and generally realistic, the second in "Transformation," based on a variety of historical events and personages and employing unusual modes of narration, for example, the second person. *The New World* is a good example of what Banks refers to as his "bipolarity," his swinging back and forth between New England and the tropics, a characteristic of much of his later work. The stories also contain his persistent theme of self-fashioning and discovery of the "new world" of the self. *Trailerpark* (1981), thirteen interwoven stories about the lives of the residents of Granite State Trailerpark in New Hampshire, completed his transformation into a writer of working-class fiction in the naturalist mode. Similar to Sherwood Anderson's *Winesburg, Ohio* in their exposure of personal and communal anguish and neurosis, these interrelated stories examine the popular stereotypes of urban poverty, seeking to illuminate the humanity of the poor, the fact that they too possess complex and rich personal histories worthy of exploration. The ironically titled *Success Stories* (1986), a striking demystification of the American dream ideology, portrays characters who achieve what appears to be success, only to find that it leads to crushing defeat. One group of stories, the semiautobiographical, "Earl Painter" stories, relate episodes from Banks's past, for example, his dropping out of Colgate and his marriage to Darlene Bennett. The second group are sociopolitical fables, the most powerful of which is "Sarah Coles: A Type of Love Story," in which the handsome, upper-class narrator, Ron, falls in love with a conventionally unattractive, lower-class woman, Sarah. The story ends with Ron's symbolic destruction of Sarah and the reader's realization of the illusory nature of Ron's "success" in a world that privileges physical beauty, material wealth, and social status above all else.

## MAJOR WORKS: *CONTINENTAL DRIFT*

In his early writing career, Banks favored realism for his shorter works and metafiction for his novels. He resolved both dichotomies in his fourth novel, *Continental Drift* (1985). Written in a neo-Dreiserian realist idiom, it brings together working-class New England and the Caribbean by alternating between two narrative threads, the stories of Bob DuBois, a middle-class, white American male and Vanise Dorinsville, a young, poor, unmarried Haitian mother. The story charts the symbolic migrations of DuBois, a thirty-year-old oil burner repairman who moves from a depressed town in New Hampshire to central Florida in search of a better life for himself and his family, and Vanise, who is forced to flee the political repression, poverty, and violence of Haiti with her infant son and nephew. The two migrations converge off the coast of Florida with heartbreakingly tragic results.

*Continental Drift*, nominated for the 1986 Pulitzer Prize, was highly praised for its vivid, readable prose, the intense forward drive of the narrative, and Banks's convincing evocation of the desperate reality of the lives of contemporary Americans. Some critics, however, found fault with Banks's attempt to capture the story of Vanise, a poor Haitian unwed mother, and also for his handling of the voodoo elements in the book, for example, the invocation of the *loa*, the voudon spirit of the dead that speaks through the mouth of the living, to call DuBois back to life and tell his tale. Banks's nonconventional narrative method of indirect discourse received mixed reviews. This device allows an omniscient narrator to step in and comment on his often inarticulate characters' unspoken inner lives. This technique exposes the central theme that, as Niemi puts it, "a man's feelings and perceptions, no matter how sketchy or deluded, often have more of an effect on shaping his destiny than do actual circumstances" (Niemi, p. 107) in a way that DuBois himself cannot. Instead, he manifests the pain of his life through drinking, philandering, and sporadic bouts of violence—yet another reflection of Earl Banks—blaming himself, rather than the exploitative class system, for the failure of the American dream in his life. With the guidance of the narrator, we see that it is more a psychological than economic imperative that compels his migration to Florida to join his brother Eddie in the liquor retail business.

Vanise is forced to flee Haiti when she, her infant son, her nephew Claude, and the entire village community face brutal retaliation for partaking of a ham Claude had stolen from an overturned delivery van because they were starving. Her chapters detail the brutal sexual enslavement and violence she, her son, and Claude are subjected to during her passage by boat to Florida. She begins her journey "on the further side of resignation, where people, especially women, laugh and cry too much and too often, where nothing matters and a second later everything matters," but slips into derangement as a result of her profound physical, emotional, and sexual victimization.

DuBois's life in Florida with Eddie, a vicious, exploitative man and a racist, is by far worse than what he left. Not only does his marriage fail, but, unhappy with his sales job at the liquor counter, he is pulled into the criminal underworld. Finally, he becomes involved in smuggling drugs and illegal aliens into the country from the Caribbean. Thus, the two story lines converge when DuBois pilots a boat on which Vanise and other illegal aliens have bought passage to Florida. Tragedy

ensues when the boat is spotted by the Coast Guard, and DuBois naively takes the first mate's advice to throw the immigrants overboard. All drown in the rough seas, except Vanise, who washes ashore on the coast of Florida, near-dead and now demented.

Plagued with guilt, DuBois learns of Vanise's survival. Desperate for her forgiveness, seeing her as his only hope for redemption, he finds her and pleads with her to take the money that the immigrants gave him to smuggle them into the United States. She refuses the money—whether for reasons of mental instability or higher morality is left unclear—and he is stabbed to death by a group of teenagers. As Niemi points out, his death *does* achieve the moral redemption he so desperately sought. Instead of indulging in another selfish act of greed and self-advancement, he dies in an act of renewed integrity, of trying to do the right thing at the highest personal cost, and thus achieves moral regeneration (Niemi, p. 119).

## OTHER MAJOR WORKS

Banks's next three novels, *Affliction*, *The Sweet Hereafter*, and *Rule of the Bone*, are alike in their treatment of working-class life in the Northeast, the blunt neorealist idiom in which they are written, and the straightforward manner of their narration, largely devoid of metafictional tropes that detract from the immediacy of the story. Likewise, they share the common theme of personal and familial disruption by an evolving trauma.

*Affliction* (1989), considered Banks's most autobiographical novel, portrays the patterns of rage and violence passed from father to son. Wade Whitehouse, the protagonist, lives in Lawton, New Hampshire, the kind of economically and morally depressed northeastern mill town typical of Banks's work. After the inevitable breakup of his marriage, he lives alone in a trailer and works as a part-time policeman, well driller, and snowplow driver. His father's physical and mental abuse of him as a child has scarred him emotionally, and, unable to better his situation and thus his self-concept, he mimics his father, a sadistic, self-pitying, narcissistic man consumed with fear and loathing. His young daughter's rejection of him deepens his pain, and by the end of novel he self-destructs, murdering his father and another man, and finally fades into oblivion, doomed to continue his life of anonymity, loneliness, and self-hatred.

The story is told through the empathetic perspective of his younger brother, Rolfe, who tries to piece together the events surrounding Wade's disappearance and represents another of Banks's sensitive, articulate, and intelligent narrators seeking self-definition through exploration of something outside the self. A high-school history teacher living near Boston, Rolfe attained a college education and, with it, escaped from his working-class origins, the dead-end town of Lawton, and, most important, the violence and rage that consumed Wade and his father and led to the demise of his family. As Banks has observed, Wade and Rolfe are the "before and after" versions of himself (Brown, p. 70).

In *The Sweet Hereafter* (1991) four consecutive first-person narrators tell the story of a school bus accident on a snowy road that claims the lives of fourteen children. Each version advances the plot, rather than simply reiterating what happened, and each narrator embodies a different and crucial perspective on the events. The bus driver, Dolores Driscoll, a matronly, sincere, caring, meticulous, very sympathetic woman, becomes the town scapegoat. Billy Ansel, the Vietnam veteran and cancer widower who loses his twin children in the crash, represents all the bereaved parents. Mitchell Stevens, the New York attorney specializing in negligence cases, stands for corporate society; his job is to legally assign blame and deny the existence of accident. Nichole Burnell, the eighth-grade cheerleader and beauty queen crippled in the accident, is both victim and survivor.

What drives the plot is an exploration of the varied ways survivors cope with issues of acceptance and blame, the difficulty of the mystery of life and death, and the eventual fragmentation of the community of Sam Dent. The novel ends with the Sam Dent County Fair, the first occasion of the town's coming together since the accident. The ostracized Dolores Driscoll, recognizing the physical and emotional rifts throughout the community, observes that this is now "a town of solitaries living in the sweet hereafter."

*Rule of the Bone* (1995), narrated by fourteen-year-old Chapman Dorset, an upstate New York "mall rat" with a nose ring, Mohawk hairdo, and marijuana habit, once again engages the theme of the father-son relationship. Chappie, a lost, lonely and isolated teenager, bears a striking resemblance to both Huck Finn and Holden Caulfield in his high intelligence, advanced state of awareness, often sardonic view of the world, and likability as a narrator. Reacting against his parents' divorce and the abuse and perversion of his stepfather, Chappie runs away from home with a friend, renames himself "Bone," and enters the underworld of bikers, drugs, child pornography, and homelessness. True to the form of the bildungsroman, the formation or upbringing novel, Bone achieves moral redemption through the guidance of a Rastafarian mentor figure, a father substitute named I-Man, and begins to takes moral responsibility for the people around him. For example, he returns Sister Rose, a nine-year-old girl caught in child pornography, to her mother, a well-meant though ultimately disastrous decision. Later he travels to Jamaica with I-Man and becomes a Rasta: "Even though I was a white kid I could still become a true heavy Rasta myself as long as I didn't ever forget I was a white kid, just like black people could never forget they were black people." Like Huck Finn's friend Jim, I-Man is a black surrogate father who teaches the importance of acceptance, love and loyalty over prejudice, convention and fear (Niemi, p. 170).

*Cloudsplitter* (1998), a novel that many critics consider Banks's finest, addresses his classic father–son story in a historical context. The radical abolitionist John Brown, leader of the failed 1859 raid on Harpers Ferry, Virginia, is the overpowering, larger-than-life father, but this time a father whose son Owen passionately admires and wishes to emulate. A tyrant in private rather than in public, John Brown both neglects his family and then demands their devoted participation in his holy war to end slavery. At first, Owen resists his father's dominance, rebelling against him. In addition, he is struggling with probable homosexuality but lacks the societal or personal means to understand his feelings and thus form a healthy self-concept. Ultimately, Owen cannot get out from under his father's shadow; he feels tied to him "like a slave" and can find no meaning in his life other than as a diminished form of his father. His feelings of unworthiness lead him to join his father's cause and later to commit terrifying acts of violence that sometimes surpass even his father's. The narrative traces their joint movement from idealism to extreme activism to guerrilla warfare to terrorism to martyrdom—the classic Banksian father–son mimicry.

The novel is structured as a manuscript written in period language by Owen to Miss Mayo, a researcher engaged in writing a biography of the Brown family fifty years after Harpers Ferry. Owen, having lived the majority of life after the Civil War as a hermit, is now a guilt-ridden old man consumed with a desire to justify the extremity of his behavior, at times gratuitously murderous and bloodthirsty, and so come to peace with himself. Owen's neurotic temperament, arising from both his thwarted sexuality and his fixation with his father, complicates this process, and therefore, as a narrator, he is most unreliable, his story a "snarl of truths, lies, memories, [and] fantasies." Like so many of Banks's narrators, Owen Brown is engaged in the process of personal redemption, striving for lucidity out of chaos, and, ultimately, the sense of a life well-lived.

## WORKS

### NOVELS AND SHORT STORIES

*Family Life* (1975)
*Searching for Survivors* (1975)
*Hamilton Stark* (1978)
*The New World: Tales* (1978)
*The Book of Jamaica* (1980)
*Trailerpark* (1981)
*The Relation of My Imprisonment* (1983)
*Continental Drift* (1985)
*Success Stories* (1986)
*Affliction* (1989)
*The Sweet Hereafter* (1991)
*Rule of the Bone* (1995)
*Cloudsplitter* (1998)

### UNCOLLECTED SHORT STORIES

"Crossing the Line." *New York Times Magazine* (20 December 1992)
"Just Don't Touch Anything." *GQ* (May 1993)
"Plains of Abraham." *Esquire* (July 1999)
"That." In *Statements: New Fiction from the Fiction Collective*. Compiled by John Baumbach. New York, 1975
"The Visitor." In *Disorderly Conduct: The VLS Fiction Reader*. Edited by M. Mark. New York, 1991
"Xmas." *Antaeus* 64/65 (Spring-Autumn 1990): 176–180

### POETRY

*15 Poems*. With William Matthews and Newton Smith (1967)
*30/6*. With Peter Wild, Charles Simic, Robert Morgan, William Matthews, and Doug Collins. Supplement to *The Quest* 3, 2 (Winter-Spring 1969)
*Waiting to Freeze: Poems* (1969)
*Snow: Meditations of a Cautious Man in Winter* (1974)

### OTHER WORKS

*Brushes with Greatness: An Anthology of Close Encounters with Greatness*. Coedited with Michael Ondaatje and David Young (1989)
*The Invisible Stranger: The Patten, Maine, Photographs of Arturo Patten* (1999)

## FURTHER READING

Brown, Wesley. "Who to Blame, Who to Forgive." *The New York Times Magazine* (10 September 1989).

Hennessy, Denis M. "Russell Banks." *Dictionary of Literary Biography*, vol. 130: *American Short-Story Writers Since World War II*. Edited by Patrick Meanor. Oneonta, N.Y., 1993. pp. 22–27.

Lee, Don. "About Russell Banks." *Ploughshares* 19, no. 4 (Winter 1993). Excellent and thorough biographical sketch.

Niemi, Robert. *Russell Banks*. New York, 1997. Excellent discussion of Banks's life and writing career and on *Continental Drift*.

Niemi, Robert. "Russell Banks." *American Writers*. Supplement 5. Edited by Jay Parini. New York, 2000.

Pfiel, Fred. "Beating the Odds: The Brechtian Aesthetic of Russell Banks." In *Another Tale to Tell: Politics and Narrative in Postmodern Culture*. New York, 1990.

# DJUNA BARNES

*by Joy Arbor*

Djuna Barnes was a poet, journalist, playwright, theatrical columnist, and novelist. She was also an accomplished graphic designer and artist, often illustrating her own work. But Barnes is mostly known for writing the modernist classic *Nightwood* (1936).

Djuna Barnes was born 12 June 1892 near Cornwall-on-Hudson, New York, to Wald Barnes, an American, and Elizabeth Chappell Barnes, a British subject. Barnes was raised in Cornwall-on-Hudson until her father bought a 105-acre farm on then-undeveloped Long Island because he desired a life free from society and its conventional morality. In fact, he built a mostly self-sufficient (some say polygamous) family

Djuna Barnes. (© *Oscar White/Corbis*)

unit and also wrote a credo, a statement of the beliefs by which he shaped his life. Young Djuna Barnes was educated at home by her paternal grandmother, Zadel Barnes, an early feminist and journalist who lived with the family.

As a young adult, Barnes studied at the Pratt Institute and the Art Students League. Her first job was as a journalist and illustrator for the *Brooklyn Eagle*. When she joined the Provincetown Players in 1919, her imagist poems and stories were already appearing in a number of periodicals. She had also published a book of poems and drawings called *The Book of Repulsive Women* (1915). Her play, *Three from the Earth*, appeared on the same bill as the premiere performance of Eugene O'Neill's *The Dreamy Kid*, bringing both Barnes and O'Neill to public attention. Two more of Barnes's one-act plays also opened that 1919–1920 season: *Kurzy of the Sea* and *Irish Triangle*.

At the end of the season, Barnes left for Europe to write and to interview famous personalities, such as D. W. Griffith, for *McCall's* magazine. In Europe, Barnes became friends with James Joyce, the Irish novelist; T. S. Eliot, the American-turned-British poet; Ezra Pound, the

poet and proponent of the imagist movement; and the poet William Carlos Williams. Becoming a part of the modernist movement's expatriate set, she also became part of another important expatriate group: the circle of lesbians who frequented the salons of the heiress Natalie Barney and the writer Gertrude Stein. An unconventional woman who was not seeking conventional romances, Barnes had a number of affairs in Europe. The most important and turbulent one was with sculptor Thelma Wood, who many say was the inspiration for Robin Vote in *Nightwood*.

In Europe, Barnes proved herself a witty, unconventional reporter. Her work becoming sought after when in 1923 a collection of her plays, poems, and short fiction, titled *A Book*, was published. This work was revised and published in 1929 under the title *A Night among the Horses*. Barnes's short fiction centers mostly on European immigrants estranged from American life, each other, and themselves. In 1928 Barnes wrote, illustrated, and privately published *Ladies Almanack*, a satire of Natalie Barney and her salon. Written in Elizabethan prose and often said to be parodying the eighteenth-century novel of manners, the book depicts a lesbian society in which one woman is sainted. Also appearing in 1928, *Ryder* is a family chronicle revolving around a man who wants to father the world. The parodying of countless literary styles and the use of Elizabethan diction evident in *Ryder* moved Barnes into the ranks of important modernist innovators like Joyce and Eliot, who yoked literary models of the past with boldly experimental techniques and content.

In 1929 Barnes famously refused to answer any questions about herself or her work in response to a survey by *The Little Review*, haughtily stating that she did not have much respect for the public. This act reflected Barnes's attitude that the writer's only obligation is to her art. She felt that art is not part of consumer culture, a mass-produced product for everyone. An artist cannot sell herself to the world and be true to her art. For this reason, Barnes rarely rushed into print.

Barnes went back and forth between Europe and America, working on *Nightwood*. It was published in 1936 with an introduction by T. S. Eliot. In 1940 she moved to Greenwich Village in New York City, where she lived at 5 Patchin Place for the rest of her life, rejecting most publicity and leading a reclusive life. Returning to the Elizabethan and Jacobean literary influences absent in *Nightwood*, *The Antiphon* (1958; produced in 1961) is a blank-verse tragedy about a family reunited through the efforts of one son, who by the end of the play causes both his mother and sister to die. Djuna Barnes died on 18 June 1982 in New York City.

## NIGHTWOOD

*Nightwood* charts the destructive love affairs of a young woman, Robin Vote, in 1920s Paris. She first marries Baron Felix Volkbein, leaves him for American journalist Nora Flood, and then leaves Nora for widow Jenny Petherbridge. Yet the novel is not a soap opera or an indulgent display of sexual antics. Nor is it a character study, though the characters do seem realistic. Instead, this experimental novel focuses on those who are affected by Nora's unthinking actions, those who are left in her wake to make sense out of her actions and of their own lives in her absence. The novel takes to task a number of cultural myths, not least of which is the fairy-tale romance plot. It does not focus on the intimate moments and actions of a romance but, for the most part, centers on conversations and narrations that interpret the experiences of, for the most part, those who have been left behind. The most important interpretative lens in the novel is Dr. Matthew O'Connor, to whom both Felix and Nora speak about the most crucial shaping forces in their lives.

Matthew is the most intriguing character in the novel. A great deal of *Nightwood* is taken up by his speeches and discussions. In brief, he frames the novel by providing the characters and us, the readers, with interpretations of the events. For example, he points out to Nora that the fairy tale cultural myth that she is imposing on her relationship with Robin is actually narcissistic. What she has really been looking for is not another person to save or to save her (the way the prince on the white horse saves the heroine) but, rather, herself.

Matthew also discusses issues of sexuality and identity. He describes himself as a man who should have been

a woman. One day, Nora finds him dressed up in women's clothes in his apartment. This opens their discussion to the idea that Robin is a woman who should have been a man. Here the discussion reveals ideas of gender and sexuality contemporaneous with the novel. While homosexuality has since the 1930s often been theorized to be a fixed and single aspect of one's identity, Matthew points out in the novel that sexuality determines one's comfort or discomfort with one's gender in a world where heterosexuality is the rule. Since the novel turns almost entirely on those for whom ideas of masculine and feminine are not simply affixed to physical gender, *Nightwood* anticipates theories of gender that posit masculine and feminine as poles on a continuum.

Although Matthew is clearly the most knowledgeable person in the book, the one to whom everyone comes for wisdom, one cannot believe his stories about himself. There are those within the book that actively question the validity of his truth telling. But it is the very role he plays as a storyteller and provider of wisdom that, he says, makes him a liar. No one is more uncomfortable with Matthew's role as interpretative lens and truth sayer than he is as he questions notions of unassailable truths while describing the human longing for them.

Matthew's words, his interpretative lens, and his insistent presence throughout the novel is juxtaposed against Robin's empty, voiceless center. Robin is the hub around which the story turns, yet it is her absence that affects people more than her presence. Although Robin is described by her lovers as speaking, we, the readers, only infrequently hear her voice. In fact, Robin's most pivotal interactions with people, the interactions that change other people's lives, are generally silent. For example, Robin and Felix get married because "Robin's life held no volition for refusal." The important moment that precipitates Robin and Nora's love affair is Nora removing a crying Robin from the circus, saving Robin from recognition of her animal nature as she looks at the lions. Jenny steals Robin away from Nora by appealing to her animal instincts; Jenny attacks and claws at Robin. That this is the appropriate and effective way to communicate with Robin is shown by the conclusion, when Robin has traveled from Jenny's to Nora's. Robin has lit candles in Nora's chapel. When Nora's dog faces off with Robin, Robin fights back; after barking and tussling, both Robin and the dog give up in a heap.

Robin is continually described as bestial, an animal arrested in an incomplete transformation into the human. When we are first introduced to her, she is unconscious on a bed. Described as surrounded by plants, she can be seen as an animal in her lair; she gives off natural and fungal odors rather than perfume. And since she lacks the self-reflection that distinguishes the human in the animal kingdom, she can truly be understood to be an animal. She is interested only in her physical desires for alcohol, sex, and walking. She wanders like a somnambulist; half asleep to her own life, she does not think about where she is going or those whom she might hurt in pursuit of her own physical desires. She gets drunk and stays out all night, worrying her partners. She arrives back home to the lairs her lovers maintain, but only to sleep. Incomplete as a human or an animal, she belongs nowhere.

Felix also belongs nowhere. The novel begins with his concerns as a Jew with no family and a manufactured past: he pretends to be a baron and a Christian. An ardent appreciator of wealth and titled privilege, he admires yet is afraid of the past, since it is the past that can undo him. He feels displaced everywhere, since Jews have been evicted at one time from every European country, but he travels through Europe as easily as Robin travels through her life. Because he knows that he is a fraud, however, it seems unsurprising that he chooses the company of the theatrical and bohemian set, who name themselves as they please and who are always on the periphery. Felix decides that he wants a son who will admire the past as much as he does. He has a mentally retarded son (the mental deficiency possibly a result of Robin's drinking during pregnancy) through his marriage to Robin. His son, regardless of his deficiency, shapes the rest of Felix's life as they return to live in Vienna. Not only does Felix embody the Wandering Jew, but he resembles the characters in Joyce's and Eliot's writings; like them, and arguably like Joyce and Eliot themselves, Felix is a simultaneously nostalgic and alienated other.

Nora, who many claim is actually Barnes herself, is obsessed with her suffering over the loss of Robin. Yet because she is so insistent on suffering and taking on the role of victim, empathy for her, on the part of both Matthew and the reader, is difficult. After Matthew explains to Nora that she is participating in a narcissistic obsession that grows out of the fairy-tale myth that our culture perpetuates, it is easier to feel a degree of sympathy for the suffering and now more self-reflective Nora.

## BARNES'S LEGACY

Djuna Barnes remains a fascinating and critical enigma of the Lost Generation. Since she eschewed fame and

success in her lifetime, it would seem only too easy to forget her. Yet she is the author of the masterwork *Nightwood*, a novel that begs to be remembered. In addition to T. S. Eliot's stamp of approval as the author of its introduction, Dylan Thomas called *Nightwood* "one of the three great prose books ever written by a woman." In addition, even in a day when the literary canon is being reformed, *Nightwood* continues to be one of the only novels by a woman, if not the only one, regularly taught in courses on American modernist literature. Indeed, *Nightwood* has often been cited as a very influential novel for subsequent writers.

While *Nightwood* was never forgotten by literary critics and historians (it has also never been out of print since its publication), Barnes's other works, including her newspaper pieces, have only recently been unearthed and reprinted by those interested in experimental writing, women's writing, feminism, and modernism. Now that Barnes can no longer prohibit the reprinting of her early work, her reputation as a feminist modernist, and perhaps the most important female modernist, has begun to flourish.

[*See also* Writing as a Woman in the Twentieth Century.]

### SELECTED WORKS

*The Book of Repulsive Women: 8 Rhythms and 5 Drawings* (1915)
*A Book* (1923)
*Ladies Almanack* (1928)
*Ryder* (1928)
*A Night among the Horses* (1929)
*Nightwood* (1936)
*The Antiphon* (1958)
*Selected Works: Spillway, The Antiphon, Nightwood* (1962)
*Vagaries Malicieux: Two Stories* (1974)
*Greenwich Village As It Is* (1978)
*Creatures in an Alphabet* (1983)
*Smoke and Other Early Stories* (1983)
*Interviews* (1985)
*I Could Never Be Lonely without a Husband* (1987)
*New York* (1989)
*At the Roots of the Stars: The Short Plays* (1995)
*Poe's Mother: Selected Drawings of Djuna Barnes* (1995)
*Collected Stories* (1996)

### FURTHER READING

Broe, Mary Lynn, ed. *Silence and Power: A Reevaluation of Djuna Barnes.* Carbondale, Ill., 1991. An excellent collection of essays that both summarizes previous scholarship and extends it with personal reflections from scholars and friends.

Field, Andrew. *Djuna: The Life and Times of Djuna Barnes.* New York, 1983. The most often-quoted biography of Barnes.

Herring, Phillip. *Djuna: The Life and Work of Djuna Barnes.* New York, 1995. A good critical biography, discussing her often-ignored childhood.

Herring, Phillip. "The Stories of Djuna Barnes." In *Collected Stories by Djuna Barnes.* Los Angeles, 1996. Good introduction to Barnes's short fiction.

O'Neal, Hank. *"Life is painful, nasty and short . . . in my case it has only been painful and nasty." Djuna Barnes 1978–1981: An Informal Memoir.* New York, 1990. A portrait of Barnes's later and reclusive life.

Scott, James B. *Djuna Barnes.* Boston, 1976. An admirable introduction to Djuna Barnes that nevertheless simplifies *Nightwood* and effaces some of her early biography.

# JOHN BARTH

*by Ian Bickford*

John Barth is counted among the first generation of American postmodernist writers. Of this group, which includes Thomas Pynchon, William Gass, John Hawkes, and Donald Barthelme, Barth has been identified by turns as the most nihilistic and the most hopeful; indeed, his fiction explores just this sort of irreconcilable dualism.

Barth and his twin sister were born on 27 May 1930 in Cambridge, Maryland, and named, at the suggestion of their older brother, Jack and Jill. They were inseparable through early childhood, and Barth often puts forth his twinship as both literal source and metaphorical illustration of his approach to writing—his preoccupation with opposites and his tendency

John Barth. (© Alex Gotfryd/Corbis)

to endow characters with variant and often contradictory personae. Most recognizably at the beginning of his career, though also later, Barth has written books in pairs. *The Floating Opera* (1956) and *The End of the Road* (1958) are his first, completed in one year. Both are novels of a comically nihilistic attitude; both showcase first-person antiheroes suffering from a sense of purposelessness; both maintain a surface realism, though they hint at an aesthetic of the bizarre that will later fill Barth's writing. *The Sot-Weed Factor* (1960) and *Giles Goat-Boy* (1966), Barth's third and fourth books, explore traditional and mythical ideas of the questing hero in fast-paced, alliterative, lengthy prose. Bawdy and brash, they pit the dangers of experience against the irresponsibility of innocence. Next, *Lost in the Funhouse* (1968) and *Chimera* (1972) are collections of shorter prose in which Barth fleshes out his signature techniques of metafiction—fiction concerned with fiction itself. He won the National Book Award for *Chimera*. Later major works include *LETTERS* (1979), *The Tidewater Tales: A Novel* (1987), *The Last Voyage of Somebody the Sailor*

(1991), and *Once upon a Time: A Floating Opera* (1994). His first six books are his most important.

A drummer, Barth attended the Juilliard School of Music in New York City for a short time. He decided, however, that his musical talent was not of a professional level and returned to his childhood Chesapeake Bay environs to study writing at Johns Hopkins University. There, to help fund his studies, Barth worked shelving books in the university library. In the stacks he encountered the multivolume ancient story cycles that would later so thoroughly inform his sensibilities as a writer: *The Thousand and One Nights*, *Ocean of Story*, *Decameron*, and others. The "arabesque" frame structure of these texts, embedding stories within stories, fed a direct line to Barth's boundary-testing methods. Barth completed an M.A. degree in 1952. During the years of his graduate study he married Harriet Anne Strickland; their first two children, Christine and John, were born in 1951 and 1952. Barth began work on a Ph.D. at Johns Hopkins, but instead of completing the degree he began his teaching career in 1953 as an instructor of English composition at Pennsylvania State University. His third child, Daniel, was born in 1954.

A little more than a decade later, having written and published three controversial but well-regarded novels, Barth moved with his family to Buffalo, New York, to teach at the state university. He describes his time there as rich with artistic experimentation. Working on *Lost in the Funhouse*, Barth attempted to push the possibilities of literature beyond print, composing stories to be recorded on tape and played to an audience in litany with a live performer. This way he made room for multiple voices and combinations of voices to come through in a narrative.

Barth and his first wife divorced in 1969. In the winter of that year he encountered a former student, Shelly Rosenberg, at a reading in Boston, and they married in 1970. In 1973, Barth returned to Johns Hopkins to teach in the writing seminars, where in 2002 he was professor emeritus. Since the 1970s his life on the Chesapeake as a professional teacher and an amateur sailor provided the setting for much of his writing.

## LITERATURE OF EXHAUSTION

From the publication of *The Floating Opera* in 1956 through the early 1960s, Barth was dubbed variously an existentialist, a black humorist, and a fabulist. His early writing, heavily philosophical yet verging on a nihilism of ideas in its continual discarding of any one standpoint, flirted with but did not settle into contemporary categories. Then, in 1967, Barth published an essay entitled "The Literature of Exhaustion," in which he discusses the feeling held by many critics and writers that narrative fiction has been used beyond usefulness and has become an anachronistic form. Many read and dismissed this essay as an overly simple proclamation of the death of the novel. It was pointed out that the novel's demise had been predicted countless times before but had not yet happened; in his essay Barth himself likens this phenomenon to a cry-wolf doomsday impulse, discounted because it is so often repeated. But he also suggests that whether the novel does or does not fade from relevance, the perception of its fading is vital to literature. In fact, this endgame sensibility begins to propel artistic imagination.

We can see Barth struggling in this essay toward a definition of postmodernism, a movement he helped create and into which his writing would settle. He offers as an example of his argument the case of Jorge Luis Borges (1899–1986), the Argentinean poet, essayist, and short story writer who became greatly influential to Barth's work in the 1960s. Borges's stories are often accounts of fictional texts or sets of texts (in one, an encyclopedia of an invented world; in another, an infinite library which itself is a world); these phantom texts are always much larger and more encompassing than the stories that tell of them. Borges evokes an image of literature birthing literature. A single short story contains the possibility of an entire genealogy of new stories, new textual tracks. An endlessness seems possible and, far from being exhaustible, literature for Barth is propelled in the same moment that it is spent.

In his attempt at a "replenishment" of literature, as he terms the issue in another essay, Barth joins his instincts as a musician to his habits as a writer through the idea of arrangement: as a jazz composition will refashion established themes and melodies, constantly evaluating and renovating the old to form the new, Barth's work almost always emerges from preexisting stories, riffing on the foundations of culture. For Barth, who in explaining his own project as a writer has often proposed an investigation of all that "goes without saying," this is a key element of postmodernism. In response to the worry that everything has already been said, standard among most of the early postmodernist cohort, he wants to acknowledge overindulged cultural tropes—not to discard them but to build a new literature from them.

"Arranging" literature, Barth has recycled stories from the Bible to *The Thousand and One Nights* to ancient Greek heroic myths. His choices of texts from which to work show a fascination with cultural relevance and perseverance. Although on occasion he will rescue a historical tale from obscurity in order to retell it (the most obvious instance being the story of Ebenezer Cooke, "Poet Laureate of Maryland," on which *The Sot-Weed Factor* is based), for the most part Barth draws from a mainstream narrative heritage. The first "story" in *Lost in the Funhouse* is a Mobius strip: on each side of the page is a fragment of text; when cut out, twisted, and fastened end to end, the text yields a story that repeats itself forever, an invocation of continual beginning. This idea of continuity in literature informs all of Barth's work. He is devoted to history and future, to stories resurrected over and over, exhausting and replenishing themselves in the concurrent celebration of source and search for new form. While this is Barth's link to modernism via James Joyce and T. S. Eliot, whose ideas of literary heritage were similar, it is also his departure into postmodernism. In recycling material, Barth joins the Italian writer Italo Calvino in declaring that one cannot simply restate an idea; one must at the same time acknowledge the chain of precedent for that idea and inform the reader that he or she is being fed a leftover concoction. The result is a self-aware fiction often steeped in irony and humor. When sincere, it mocks its own sincerity; when joking, its jokes are severe.

## FRAMING AND METAFICTION

Barth's relationship to Borges's texts within texts is an extension of his long-standing obsession with frame structures in ancient story cycles. The main protagonist of *The Thousand and One Nights*, Sheherazade, must keep the king, her lover, entertained night after night with her prolific storytelling ability; to keep the narrative going, she often has a character in a story begin to tell a second story. The first story becomes a frame for the second, the second might frame a third, and so forth, while the story of Sheherazade and the king acts as an initial frame for the entire structure. Barth's first significant experiment with framing in his own writing appears in *Giles Goat-Boy*, in which a series of fictional secondary texts—"Publisher's Disclaimer," "Cover-Letter to the Editors and Publisher," and others—serve to contain and complicate the book's primary narrative. The short stories in *Lost in the Funhouse*, produced largely in response to Barth's reading of Borges, further explore such many-layered structures. Characters become narrators, narrators reenter stories as characters, and in the process of dipping into and emerging from the various digressive plots we forget the line between the story and the teller. Stories, in essence, become the occasion for other stories. It often seems like a daredevil game for Barth to test how deep he can dive into the structure of his narrative frames without losing control, without having to come back up for air.

One of Barth's essential tenets is that, in the layering of narratives, reality itself acts as a frame. As Sheherazade's stories are contained within the story of Sheherazade, the story of Sheherazade is contained within the story of the actual reader, the person holding a volume of *The Thousand and One Nights*. In the short piece "Tlön, Uqbar, Orbis Tertius," Borges proposes that, given a realistic enough and complete enough text, fiction could invade and ultimately replace reality. Barth steps into a similarly disorienting set of ideas when, in *Giles Goat-Boy*, a girl at a library information desk reiterates a couple of words of a preceding narrative passage, breaking the surface of the text by violating rules of omniscience: this character appears to read the mind of the author instead of the normal opposite, and we are jolted out of the illusion that text is separate from reality. Although in this instance Barth quickly reapplies the varnish of narrative distance, it is impossible afterward to read without a suspicion that we are partners in a textual hoax, that the border between fiction and fact is unstable, that one side could easily infiltrate and occupy the other. It furthermore becomes impossible for Barth to write without this suspicion.

Almost all of Barth's writing in and after this breakthrough involves the irrigation of a system of metafiction, a self-referential mode of writing in which fiction itself is under scrutiny. In the title story of *Lost in the Funhouse*, for instance, Barth continually interrupts himself to painstakingly document his writerly anxieties.

Lecturing on proper storytelling form while complaining that his own story-in-progress is all wrong, he asserts that narrative depends on the act of writing and that therefore an understanding of the writer's presence is vital. Dissatisfied with the discrete roles of reader, author, and text, he opts out of the system. He steps into the story. Barth's instinct is always to demonstrate the synthetic nature of the walls between the inside and the outside of a narrative. As in his funhouse, the partitions are mazelike but thin. Barth's project is to find where light shows through the cracks.

## WORKS

*The Floating Opera* (1956)
*The End of the Road* (1958)
*The Sot-Weed Factor* (1960)
*Giles Goat-Boy; or, The Revised New Syllabus* (1966)
*Lost in the Funhouse: Fiction for Print, Tape, Live Voice* (1968)
*Chimera* (1972)
*LETTERS: An Old Time Epistolary Novel by Seven Fictitious Drolls & Dreamers, Each of Whom Imagines Himself Actual* (1979)
*Sabbatical: A Romance* (1982)
*The Friday Book: Essays and Other Nonfiction* (1984)
*The Tidewater Tales: A Novel* (1987)
*The Last Voyage of Somebody the Sailor* (1991)
*Once upon a Time: A Floating Opera* (1994)
*Further Fridays: Essays, Lectures, and Other Nonfiction, 1984–1994* (1995)
*On with the Story: Stories* (1996)
*Coming Soon!!!: A Narrative* (2001)

## FURTHER READING

Bowen, Zack R. *A Reader's Guide to John Barth*. Westport, Conn., 1994.

Harris, Charles. *Passionate Virtuosity: The Fiction of John Barth*. Urbana, Ill., 1983.

Lindsay, Alan. *Death in the Funhouse: John Barth and Poststructural Aesthetics*. New York, 1995. The second volume of the series Studies in Literary Criticism and Theory.

Schultz, Max F. *The Muses of John Barth*. Baltimore, 1990.

Tobin, Patricia. *John Barth and the Anxiety of Continuance*. Philadelphia, 1992. From the series Penn Studies in Contemporary American Fiction.

Waldmeir, Joseph J., ed. *Critical Essays on John Barth*. Boston, 1980. Essays by various authors on Barth's early work.

# DONALD BARTHELME

*by Ian Bickford*

Donald Barthelme was born in Philadelphia on 7 April 1931. He was the oldest of five children, all of them talented writers—including the prominent minimalist Frederick Barthelme (b. 1943). From the late 1960s until his death in 1989, Donald Barthelme produced a body of experimental fiction regarded as central to the postmodernist movement. Along with Thomas Pynchon, John Barth, and others, Barthelme tested boundaries of perception and assumptions about fiction in the development of a new style. Although he shared with other postmodernists an ironic tone and a keen imagination for literary structure, Barthelme was in many ways ideologically separate from his peers. Through his father, a renowned architect, he internalized the principles of the Bauhaus—a school of artists, designers, and architects that originated in Germany early in the twentieth century whose proponents firmly believed that excellence of form and design could substantively improve the quality of human existence. Whereas many postmodernists were busy breaking down overused literary structures in order to demonstrate the fundamental flimsiness of them, Barthelme wanted to hatch new forms that could hold up under scrutiny. His short stories, which make up most of his work, almost always engage a distinctive innovation of form. Each of his four novels, too—*Snow White* (1967), *The Dead Father* (1975), *Paradise* (1986), and *The King* (1990)—playfully redirect novelistic conventions.

Shortly after Barthelme's birth, his family moved to Houston. Their home, designed by the elder Barthelme, was an odd but lovely building reminiscent of Bauhaus architect Ludwig Mies van der Rohe; it became something of a tourist curiosity, and the Barthelme brood had fun performing antic dances on the front lawn for ogling passersby. Barthelme attended the University of Houston, majoring in journalism. His first job was as an arts reporter for the *Houston Post*. In 1953 Barthelme was drafted and sent to Korea, where he was stationed in the public information office of the Second Infantry. Upon his homecoming to Houston the following year, he returned to the university to work in the public relations department. This proved to be a vital time in Barthelme's literary growth. He studied philosophy, gathering the disperse strings of Western thought that became essential to his fiction. He also founded the literary journal *Forum*, which was minimally funded by the university. The idea behind *Forum* was to mesh seemingly discrete scholars and writers into an elaborate but cohesive presentation. Always concerned with design, Barthelme managed on his small budget to produce an attractive and professional journal, and though he could not pay his contributors, he attracted an impressive array of emerging and established intellectual figures such as William H. Gass and Henri Cartier-Bresson.

Barthelme served on the board of trustees for Houston's Contemporary Arts Museum, and in 1961 he became the museum's director. Through this job he met Harold Rosenberg (1906–1978), a major arts critic, and before long Rosenberg invited him to edit a new literary magazine out of New York City entitled *Location*. Although only two issues of *Location* were ultimately produced, this editorship delivered Barthelme into the situation for which he had been aiming. Between the management of *Forum* and the directorship of the Contemporary Arts Museum, Barthelme had formed contacts with a broad range of the country's intellectual elite. Now he was in the midst of the New York publishing world with which he had interacted from afar. He had also been widely publishing his own short fiction, notably in *The New Yorker* magazine, and his place as a key literary figure was secure.

## SHORT STORIES

Barthelme likened his short stories to collages. Indeed, they often seem to be a collection of images and ideas taken piecemeal from the world and assembled anew. As an arts writer for the *Houston Post*, Barthelme would frequently comb through philosophical and critical texts in search of an intellectual buttress for his reporting. He usually did not read these texts closely, but would glean from them whatever major ideas might be useful to him. The same sort of grazing intellectualism appears in his short stories. For instance, in "A Shower of Gold," from Barthelme's first book of short fiction, *Come Back, Dr. Caligari* (1964), a minor character blithely quotes Pascal's idea of mortality as an abject and irreparable state, bringing to the forefront of the story its philosophical underpinnings. For Barthelme, ideas are part of the geography of human life, and he points to them in his stories as easily as he might point to a physical object. Ideas are props, vital to the narrative setting.

Popular culture and politics also weigh heavily into Barthelme's writing. One of his favorite devices is to bring an untouchably famous or important figure into his stories as a character. The president of the United States recurrently fills this role—markedly in the story "The President," from the volume *Unspeakable Practices, Unnatural Acts* (1968). In this piece the president is tiny (he fits in a box), mysterious, and may be the cause of an epidemic of fainting. In turning a recognizable and commonplace figure into this bizarre image, Barthelme creates a vertiginous template for viewing cultural preoccupations. Similarly, in "A Shower of Gold," a very different but equally strange president enters the apartment of the protagonist and begins smashing pieces of art. Finally, in "Robert Kennedy Saved from Drowning," also from *Unspeakable Practices, Unnatural Acts*, Barthelme uses short vignettes to construct a portrait of a real-life figure associated with the presidency. Although the portrait of Kennedy is, for the most part, of a much more realistic public figure than the two weird presidents, this story nevertheless ends in the same vein as the others: the narrator, who has until this point remained unseen, saves a sword-wielding, cape-clad Kennedy from drowning. Barthelme cannot help but deliver his characters into an immediate and touchable, yet peculiar, context. His view of the world is one in which all figures and facets are equal; all are strange and behave strangely; and everything and everyone, from president to Pascal, can potentially fit into a single room, a single vision.

## NOVELS

Barthelme's four book-length works are regarded as "novels," but their relationship to the novelistic form constitutes a wholesale departure from convention. His first novel, *Snow White*, equates an ultimate futility of language with the impossible demands that men and women make on each other. Barthelme allows himself freer formal range here than in most of his earlier short stories; whereas his short fiction seems bottled and carefully structured, *Snow White* at times lets its chapters

spiral and digress in its demonstration of language as a frustrating and self-defeating endeavor. Encasing this experimental prose in the most static and recognizable of fairy tales, Barthelme enacts a simultaneous destruction and renewal: tradition yields to invention, and yet the traditional story survives in a new body.

Barthelme admired French poet Stéphane Mallarmé, and in the formal liberty of his longer fiction he often invokes Mellarme's distinctive connectivity of ideas, launching surprising meanings in a continual, elastic wordplay. This is especially evident in his second novel, *The Dead Father*, a sort of shaggy-dog story whose thin plot (an alternately omniscient and bumbling "dead" father, in some ways very much alive, is literally dragged by a crew of men toward a vague redemption) serves as a foil for an exploration of associative logic and linguistic humor that at times reads more as a long prose poem than as a proper novel. Here, in contrast to the mythic recycling of *Snow White*, Barthelme creates his own myth, describing a world populated by confused heroes and dominated by a godlike creator (the "dead father") whose fussy temperament leads him storming off repeatedly into the woods to slay whomever or whatever he finds there. *The Dead Father* has often been censured for maintaining a cold, distant attitude; indeed, its situation is bleak and its dialogue tersely unforgiving. But its connective progression always steers toward humor, and Barthelme's mindfulness of the bizarre and complex properties of language reveals a warmth and sensitivity generally overlooked by critics.

Barthelme's final novel, *The King*, was published posthumously. Employing a conceit similar to the fairy-tale reinvention of *Snow White*, Barthelme casts the story of King Arthur against the backdrop of World War II. This final piece in Barthelme's experimental resumé can be seen as a summing-up of his overall project: an attempt to use the debris of popular and mythic consciousness in explaining the circumstances of an aesthetically and morally embattled century. As Snow White must evaluate the ideal of romantic destiny in the contemporary atmosphere of infidelity and communicative failure, so must King Arthur, the symbol of chivalry and fairness, confront the nuclear bomb.

Barthelme married four times and had one daughter with his third wife. He won a Guggenheim Fellowship in 1966 and a National Book Award in 1972 for his children's book, *The Slightly Irregular Fire Engine; or, The Hithering Thithering Djinn*. On 23 July 1989, in Houston, Barthelme died of cancer.

[*See also* Short Story in America, The.]

## WORKS

*Come Back, Dr. Caligari* (1964)
*Snow White* (1967)
*Unspeakable Practices, Unnatural Acts*
  (1968)
*City Life* (1970)
*The Slightly Irregular Fire Engine; or, The Hithering Thithering Djinn* (1971)
*Sadness* (1972)
*Guilty Pleasure*s (1974)
*The Dead Father* (1975)
*Amateurs* (1976)
*Great Days* (1979)
*Sixty Stories* (1981)
*Overnight to Many Distant Cities* (1983)
*Paradise* (1986)
*Sam's Bar* (1987)
*Forty Stories* (1987)

*The King* (1990)
*The Teachings of Don B.* (1992)
*Not Knowing: The Essays and Interviews of Donald Barthelme* (1997)

## FURTHER READING

Barthelme, Helen Moore. *Donald Barthelme: The Genesis of a Cool Sound*. College Station, Tex., 2001. This biography by Barthelme's first wife is both a personal memoir and a comprehensive account of Barthelme's life and work.

Patteson, Richard F., ed. *Critical Essays on Donald Barthelme*. New York, 1992. A range of essays regarding Barthelme's writing and career.

Trachtenberg, Stanley. *Understanding Donald Barthelme*. Columbia, S.C., 1990. A good overview of Barthelme's career and place in the American critical landscape.

# THE BEAT MOVEMENT

*by Chuck Carlise*

The Beat movement was America's first major Cold War literary movement. Originally a small circle of unpublished friends, it later became one of the most significant sources of contemporary counterculture, and the most successful free speech movement in American literature. It is at once a reclamation of poetry from the modernist pedestal of the New Critics and an attempt to infiltrate the academy itself; as closely associated with the proliferation of Eastern spirituality in America as it is with the drug culture and jazz rhythms of the street.

The Beat movement is often identified by its three highest-profile writers: Jack Kerouac, Allen Ginsberg, and William Burroughs—three friends who met in New York City in the mid-1940s. However, the nucleus always included numerous influences and fellow writers, whose lives form the plot through which the Beat movement travels.

## "A NEW VISION": NEW YORK

A good starting point for understanding the significance of the Beat scene is to consider the context within which its members found their collective voice. The early 1940s was a relatively prosperous time for the United States. Having recovered from the Great Depression and high on World War II patriotic zeal, the country was in the early stages of learning the power of commodity capitalism while also developing the most destructive weapon in the history of the world. The seeds of communist paranoia were planted but still developing, and craftless, mechanized assembly line monotony would soon become the preferred method of production for everything from cars to homes.

It was beneath this shadow that, in 1943, Allen Ginsberg and Lucien Carr, students at Columbia University, became friends. Ginsberg was a seventeen-year-old prelaw student who switched to English after studying with Mark Van Doren and Lionel Trilling. His father was a published lyric poet, and his mother, a radical communist and Russian émigré, had spent much of Allen's childhood slowly deteriorating into paranoid schizophrenia—a fact that compounded his own shaky sense of sanity in the years

before he became open about his homosexuality. Carr was a charming transfer student from St. Louis, Missouri, who had been followed east by David Kammerer, a thirty-one-year-old friend who was romantically obsessed with him. The group came to include twenty-nine-year-old William Burroughs, a Harvard graduate with a sardonic wit and an infatuation with criminal life, all of which contributed to his status as an elder statesman in the circle. Soon they met Jack Kerouac, a twenty-one-year-old former football star and Columbia dropout who aspired to become a writer. Kerouac was a devout Catholic, the son of working class, French-Canadian parents. Sensitive, idealistic, and both shy and bursting with energy, he was already a mild alcoholic, and he would never completely dry out. Kerouac's girlfriend, Edie Parker, and her roommate, Joan Vollmer, also entered the picture, and a veritable salon was formed that conducted frenzied discussions on literature and politics and enjoyed an open sexual climate. Ginsberg and Carr declared their intention to create a "New Vision" for literature, and this "libertine" circle began collaborating on projects—reading their work to each other and generally supporting each other's literary aspirations—a practice they would continue long after their respective publications and fame. Marijuana and Benzedrine were commonly used by the circle, and before long, Burroughs had started using morphine and heroin. In his drug expeditions, Burroughs met Herbert Hunke, a Times Square hustler, who introduced them all to the real criminal life, as well as to the language of hip culture, including the term "beat" as a way of expressing the exhaustion of being down-and-out.

This group thrived until, in 1944, after a night of drinking, Kammerer made a frighteningly desperate sexual advance, and Carr stabbed him to death with a Boy Scout knife. Kerouac and Burroughs were both arrested as accessories, for aiding Carr after the incident, and the group temporarily disintegrated: Carr was in a reformatory, Burroughs was at home in St. Louis, and Kerouac bargained a quick marriage for Edie Parker's family to bail him out of prison.

The group reassembled before long, however, and by 1946, Neal Cassady, a friend of Hal Chase (Vollmer's roommate) had come from Colorado to visit. The appearance of Cassady, a twenty-year-old Denver con man and car thief with an endless supply of energy and irresistible sex appeal, altered the lives of Kerouac and Ginsberg forever. While in New York, Cassady had a short affair with Ginsberg and quickly became the first and great unrequited love of the poet's life, as well as a paradigm for sexuality (Burroughs and Hunke were also homosexual but were not nearly as attractive to Ginsberg as Cassady, who was bisexual). To Kerouac, Cassady embodied the explosive, spiritual energy he felt was so lacking in the age. Cassady asked Kerouac to teach him how to write before returning to the West. The two exchanged letters often, and Kerouac was deeply affected by the spontaneous energy of Cassady's prose. A fan of the improvisational bop jazz of Charlie Parker and Miles Davis, Kerouac saw Cassady's huge monologues as verbal bop, and began developing a writing method based on this that he later outlined in "The Essentials of Spontaneous Prose" (1957), including the notion of "first-thought best-thought," which would greatly influence Ginsberg.

Neal Cassady.
(© *Ted Streshinsky/Corbis*)

## ROAD YEARS: BEYOND COLUMBIA

Much of this nucleus was dispersing by the late 1940s. Kerouac, who had been in and out of the merchant marine during the war, spent 1946 to 1948 traveling the country with and without Cassady. He spent time in Denver, Los Angeles, San Francisco, New Orleans, Mexico City, and other places, and occasionally stopped at his mother's house to work on what would become his first book, the autobiographical, Thomas Wolfe–inspired novel, *The Town and the City*, which was published in 1950. These trips were eventually immortalized in his greatest work, *On the Road*.

Ginsberg, after having a hallucinated vision of William Blake and having gone through several failed romantic advances with Cassady, was arrested in 1949 for possession of Hunke's stolen property, stored at Ginsberg's apartment. Hunke went to prison, and Ginsberg was sent to the Columbia Presbyterian Psychiatric Institute.

While there, he met Carl Solomon, a fellow intellectual and publisher, who connected to Ginsberg profoundly at a pivotal moment in the young poet's life, and was ultimately the muse to whom Ginsberg dedicated his masterwork, "Howl." In 1950, out of the hospital, working a steady job, and even occasionally dating women in an attempt to "cure" his homosexuality, Ginsberg met twenty-year-old Gregory Corso, an idealistic "jail-kid" who was obsessed with the romantic poetry of Shelley and Rimbaud.

Meanwhile, Burroughs and Vollmer married and settled in Mexico City to cultivate their respective drug habits. One night in 1951, while waiting in an apartment to sell a gun, someone suggested that Burroughs (an excellent marksman) demonstrate his "William Tell act." Vollmer put a glass on her head, but Burroughs shot low. She was struck in the forehead and died quickly. Burroughs ultimately faced very few legal consequences but was haunted by the act for the rest of his life. He later, and famously, cited this as the beginning of his writing career, because it put him in touch with "the Ugly Spirit" that he believed possessed him at the time and thrust him into a lifelong struggle, from which he had to write his way out. Two years later, *Junky* was published under the pseudonym William Lee. Influenced by the hard-boiled detective stories of Dashiell Hammett and Raymond Chandler, it is essentially a true confession of Burroughs's heroin addiction. Ace Paperbacks (owned by Solomon's uncle) published it as part of a two-volume set—the other volume being an antidrug tract by a former narcotics officer.

Kerouac, experiencing the most prolific writing time of his career, eventually moved to San Jose, California, with Cassady and his wife, Carolyn (a three-way affair later documented in Carolyn's memoir *Off the Road*). Among the numerous projects he had completed by this time was *On the Road*, which was written in a twenty-day Benzedrine-induced frenzy on a single spool of typing paper. The book would remain unpublished for several years, rejected even by Ace. In 1954, Ginsberg traveled to San Jose to join them. Spurned by Cassady, and not wanted around by Carolyn, he quickly found himself in the bustling cultural scene just to the north, in San Francisco.

## CONFLUENCE: THE SAN FRANCISCO RENAISSANCE

During these same years, another scene was emerging in the San Francisco area. Often considered an entirely different (if overlapping) movement by critics, as well as by some of the writers within each scene, the San Francisco Renaissance ultimately found its roots in the crossing of many spiritual, political, and literary influences.

Through the 1940s, small literary magazines like *Circle* and *Ark* had been publishing experimental and radical poetry and prose, producing manifesto-like mission statements and attracting the disillusioned youth of the West Coast. Then, in 1946, Robert Duncan, a twenty-seven-year-old Oakland native, returned to Berkeley from New York, where he had known and helped publish Henry Miller, Anais Nin, and Kenneth Patchen. Bringing a surrealist sensibility with him, Duncan soon met twenty-one-year-old Jack Spicer, a fan of Federico Garcia Lorca, who believed in the inherent magic of poetry and relentlessly pushed spoken word readings around town. The two also became regulars at the lively anarchist literary meetings of Kenneth Rexroth. Rexroth was an established poet, slightly older (forty-five years old in 1950), a founder of the radical radio station KPFA, and a tireless anarchist who contributed greatly to the sense of San Francisco as a legitimate cultural center.

Also flourishing in this scene by the early 1950s were three friends who had moved down from Reed College in Portland, Oregon: Gary Snyder, Philip Whalen, and Lew Welch. Snyder, a serious outdoorsman and Zen Buddhist with an interest in Native American mythology, had studied linguistics and Asian culture—interests Rexroth shared. Whalen, too, studied Buddhism—he later was ordained a Buddhist monk—and occasionally worked as a fire lookout in the Cascade Mountains. Welch was a scholar of Gertrude Stein; he had greatly impressed William Carlos Williams with his dissertation on her. Welch suffered occasional nervous breakdowns and committed suicide in 1971, but wrote with and influenced many of the San Francisco writers in this period.

It was into this scene that Allen Ginsberg stepped in 1954, bearing a letter of introduction to Rexroth from Williams, a fellow native of Paterson, New Jersey, to whom Ginsberg often wrote for literary mentoring. (Some of Ginsberg's early letters were later published in Williams's postmodern masterpiece *Paterson*). Intrigued by the scene and moved by many of the personalities within it, particularly Snyder, Ginsberg was soon joined by Kerouac. Not long after Kerouac's arrival, Ginsberg met Peter Orlovsky, a model for the painter Robert La Vigne, who would become Ginsberg's lover and life partner.

Poetry readings were popular in San Francisco around this time, thanks to people like Spicer and Bob Kaufman, a jazz poet who had known Kerouac briefly while they were both in the merchant marine. Kaufman was known not to write his poems down; rather, he would enter a café or meeting hall and begin reciting from memory, or simply make them up as he went. (There is also some dispute as to whether "beatnik" was an improvised bop term of Kaufman's or whether the *San Francisco Chronicle*'s Herb Caen originated it as the degrading slang it became.) Along with presenting readings and selling radical magazines, City Lights bookstore, in North Beach, raised the literary consciousness of the city. Founded, and still owned by the poet Lawrence Ferlinghetti, a Sorbonne-educated veteran of World War II who saw Nagasaki just weeks after the atomic bomb was dropped on it, City Lights was modeled after the great paperback bookshops of Paris, and catered to a decidedly pacifist revolutionary sensibility. Ferlinghetti also ran a small publishing house, City Lights Press, whose Pocket Poets series was intended to make poetry more accessible to the general public.

As literature became a more prominent part of the public consciousness in San Francisco, Rexroth decided to help showcase some of his younger poet friends. He asked Ginsberg to organize a reading, which Rexroth would host, at a converted garage on Fillmore Street, called the Six Gallery. On 7 October 1955, Ginsberg, Snyder, and Whalen were joined by Phillip Lamantia and Michael McClure. Lamantia, a surrealist who had known Ginsberg in New York, read poems by his late friend John Hoffman. McClure, the youngest reader at only twenty-three, had never met Snyder or Whalen until the reading. A Kansas native with a keen interest in animism and natural science, he had entered the poetry scene after taking a workshop with Duncan. Kerouac had been asked to read, but declined, and instead took a collection for wine and sat on the edge of the low stage in the packed gallery. Ginsberg, the penultimate speaker, had been working frantically for two months on a visionary poem unlike any others he had written. He read the first completed section of the poem, "Howl," in an incantatory and climactic rhythm, with Kerouac pounding on a wine jug, hollering "Go!" at each long-breath line. The reading left the astonished crowd of hipsters stunned, Rexroth in tears, and Ferlinghetti echoing Ralph Waldo Emerson's famous declaration on seeing Walt Whitman's first edition of *Leaves of Grass*: "I greet you at the beginning of a great career. When do I get the manuscript?"

## PUBLICATION AND FAME

The reading made them all instant local celebrities, particularly Ginsberg, who quickly set to work finishing the poem and gathering a collection for Ferlinghetti's Pocket Poets series—in which *Howl and Other Poems* would be number four. After this, things began to happen very quickly. A degree of notoriety had come to the San Francisco Renaissance, and the movement thrived for a short time, then dispersed. Gary Snyder was first to go, leaving for Japan, where he would spend most of the next ten years in a Zen monastery. Before leaving, he took Kerouac on a climb up Matterhorn Mountain in Yosemite,

Lawrence Ferlinghetti.
(© *Ed Kashi/Corbis*)

an adventure that resulted in a spiritual breakthrough for Kerouac, which he would document in *The Dharma Bums*, along with the reading itself. There was a going-away party for Snyder in 1956, followed later in the year by the publication of *Howl and Other Poems*, which was seized by customs officials as obscene. Ferlinghetti was arrested for selling the book, and went to work amassing an army of intellectuals and critics to testify to its literary worth. Ginsberg, who had recently received news of his mother's death in a mental hospital, wanted little to do with the legal battle. He and Orlovsky left on an extended overseas vacation while the trial progressed. Ferlinghetti's defense overwhelmed the censors; the book was declared to have literary merit, and thus could not be considered obscene. The ramifications of this decision were tremendous; publishing houses such as Grove Press began dusting off works by such banned authors as Henry Miller and D. H. Lawrence.

Another impact of the success of "Howl" was the sudden interest in Beat work. Beginning in 1955, numerous novels and poetry collections by this circle of writers found their way into print, most notably Kerouac's *On the Road* in 1957. It became a sensation among the disaffected youth, but was harshly reviewed by most critics, including Truman Capote's famous declaration that the book was not writing but typing. The public was fascinated, though, and *On the Road* and *Howl and Other Poems* sold extremely well. By 1958, Kerouac had added, among other titles, *The Dharma Bums*, which features Snyder as the main character. Snyder later published *Riprap and the Cold Mountain*

*Poems* (1965). Also published in 1958 were Corso's nuclear ode, *Bomb*, and Ferlinghetti's *A Coney Island of the Mind*, which, with *Howl and Other Poems*, is still one of the best-selling poetry books of all time.

Through all this, Burroughs had been living and writing in the Moroccan city of Tangier. He had a steady correspondence with Ginsberg and Kerouac, who visited him after the Six Gallery reading. What they found Burroughs developing was a writing style he called "routines." Burroughs would start with an image—often something from a dream or begun while extremely high—and begin typing, improvising on it for as long as he could, not unlike the jazzy spontaneous prose Kerouac preached. The difference was that when he came to a block, Burroughs simply stopped and began later on a different image. When Ginsberg, Kerouac, and Corso visited Burroughs, in Tangier and later at the famous "Beat Hotel" in Paris, they found uncountable routines scattered around his dingy apartment, and each attempted to help Burroughs gather, retype, and structure them into a text that Kerouac had dubbed "Naked Lunch." Burroughs's work was raw and often even more graphic than Ginsberg's, making it virtually unprintable in most countries. Ginsberg was a relentless promoter of his friend's work, however, and gathered some of the less outrageous routines to send to publishers back home.

In March 1958, Robert Creeley published several poems by Beat writers, including routines by Burroughs, in the *Black Mountain Review*, and soon after, Irving Rosenthal printed more in the *Chicago Review*. A conservative outcry followed, and when Rosenthal was instructed not to print Burroughs's work in the next issue, he resigned to found *Big Table* magazine. By the middle of 1959, *Big Table* I had been seized by U.S. postal authorities. Apparently influenced by the decision at the "Howl" trial, a judge ruled that the Burroughs routines were not obscene. The scandal surrounding the book prompted a French publisher to ask Burroughs for a full manuscript, and by August, *Naked Lunch* was in print.

## RIPPLES AND REPERCUSSIONS

While many of the early Beat texts received harsh reviews by academic publications, such as the *Partisan Review*, there were those who recognized their significance. In 1960, Donald Allen's *The New American Poetry* appeared. Allen divided the era's poets into several categories, splitting many of these friends into separate subgroups. Kerouac and Ginsberg were listed as "Beats," and Ferlinghetti and Welch as "San Francisco Renaissance," while Snyder and Whalen were in a third, unclassified section.

Besides gathering these writers into one literary anthology (the Black Mountain poets and New York school were also represented), this volume continued to widen the conception of what "Beat" meant to the rest of the actual generation. Many talented writers across the country, living in unconnected bohemian pockets, were gradually becoming aware that they were not alone. Writing in New York, Diane DiPrima and LeRoi Jones were two of the most talented and tenacious of these writers—founding the literary magazine *Floating Bear* and publishing it on a mimeograph machine through the early 1960s. Jones and his wife, Hettie, also ran *Yugen*, an experimental magazine, for several years, but it was *Floating Bear*'s cheaper and more immediate format that allowed for a crossing of styles and, as another publisher pointed out, gave the writers freedom to fail. *Floating Bear* 9 was eventually seized on obscenity charges, but Jones and DiPrima were never indicted. Many small literary magazines operated at this time, publishing experimental work for eager audiences, notably including Ed Sanders's *Fuck You: A Magazine of the Arts*.

Jones, DiPrima, and Sanders were among the more talented young Beat writers to emerge in the wake of "Howl" and *On the Road*, along with Ted Joans, John Wieners, Ray Bremser, and Brenda Frazer. Jones (who later changed his name to Amiri Baraka) published the excellent *Preface to a Twenty-Volume Suicide Note* in 1961, and was included in Allen's *New American Poetry*. His poetry references Kerouac, Snyder, and Ginsberg at times, and draws connections between the early 1960s black American experience and the Beat Generation, in that both represent a generally unwanted, but still distinctly present, sector of American life. DiPrima, a strong female voice in a movement often considered exclusively male, ultimately made her mark through her intensely honest and often uncensored poetry and prose. Her meditation on an early abortion, "Brass Furnace Going Out," and other poems, such as "Poetics," prefigure a feminist voice in American poetics by several years, and her love poems, such as "Three Laments" and "Song for Baby-O, Unborn," are among the stronger jazz poetry of the era. Sanders helped begin a transition to political activism. He wrote his first

published poem, "Poem from Jail," while he was in jail following his arrest at an early protest for peace.

The original wave of writers continued to disperse, however. Snyder and the poet JoAnne Kyger were married in Tokyo in 1960, and both continued writing while abroad. Michael McClure received much attention for his play *The Beard*, which was both critically acclaimed and challenged as obscene in 1965. Kerouac moved to a cabin in Big Sur, California, owned by Ferlinghetti, in an attempt to cure his alcoholism. The result was disastrous: the solitude and sublimity of the seaside cabin tested his resolve daily, and ultimately sent him into a mental and emotional downward spiral from which he never recovered. His book *Big Sur* (1962) documents the experience and is, in many ways, his last truly honest writing. Meanwhile, Ginsberg, Burroughs, and Corso spent the summer of 1961 in Tangier, taking part in Timothy Leary's early LSD experiments, later dubbed "Psychedelic Summer." Ginsberg also published his tribute to his mother, "Kaddish," in 1961—a poem many critics, and Ginsberg himself, believed to be his finest work. He would later travel in Asia with Snyder and Kyger, experiencing a spiritual awakening along the way. Kyger would document this trip in *Strange Big Moon: Japan and India Journals, 1960–1964*. In Paris, Burroughs had connected with the painter Brion Gysin, and the two had begun collaborating on a method of writing that included cutting previously written texts and rearranging them at random. Burroughs would devote the next decade to perfecting this "cut-up" method.

### WHOSE GENERATION?: CULTURAL SIGNIFICANCE

The Beat movement was unique in that it directly affected the popular culture of the time—a fact even more significant when one considers how ostracized these writers were by the contemporary literati. Given that odd balance, the question remains of what pulse the Beats were able to tap into that had been so neglected before.

In 1948, Kerouac and an aspiring writer, John Clellon Holmes, sat in Holmes's New York apartment discussing their generation. Kerouac characterized the postwar youth as a generation of furtives, not simply knowing, but having grown accustomed to living with, the nuclear threat. In the face of such constant, dull fear, the only sense of meaning they were given for their lives was in the form of Cold War propaganda, and the meaninglessness of their soon-to-be-inherited corporate-cog futures. Holmes noted Kerouac's comment, that the entire generation was beat, as the first use of the term "Beat Generation." In 1952, Holmes published a famous article in *The New York Times*, "This Is the Beat Generation." In it, he expands on these ideas, differentiating between the Lost Generation of the 1920s and his own, calling attention not simply to the current youths' sense of being used, but also to an objectless sense of loss that manifested itself in a desperate search for something to believe in. The Beat Generation, then, as Kerouac often noted, was as much about spirituality as it was about restlessness and rebellion. Kerouac would later insist that "beat" referred to street authenticity, exhaustion of the down-and-out, the rhythms of both the heart and the speaker, and ultimately to the beatitudes, which speak directly to the powerless masses.

When *On the Road* became a sensation five years later, it was due in part to Kerouac's mad exuberance and unorthodox improvisational writing style, but also to his ability to embody the frenetic desperation Holmes had written about. Sal Paradise (Kerouac's alter ego in the book) was the soul of the generation, constantly searching and celebrating, declaring that "the only ones for me are the mad ones," and seeing holiness in nearly everyone he met. Dean Moriarty (Cassady) was the ideal—the urban cowboy living by his own rules, never stopping long enough to acknowledge that anything could go wrong. Snyder noted years later that the nerve Cassady touched in the New York Beats was in some way connected to the spirit of the old West, the American dream that had been pushed westward a century before. The expansiveness, possibility, and constant, unself-conscious motion Cassady embodied were irresistible in that they were utterly opposed to the deliberate Old World paranoia of the time. In that sense, the Beat tie to San Francisco is much more of an organic expansion than an arbitrary lumping of separate literary movements. To take the search for meaning and belief to its ultimate ends by continuing westward across the Pacific, the introduction of Buddhism, particularly Snyder's celebratory Zen practice, touched that same nerve. Kerouac's blending of Buddhism with his Catholic traditions is also truly a Beat phenomenon—the search for new meaning without erasing one's existing sense of individual self. In addition, the common study and discussion of these things among friends truly dictates the other half of the Beat aesthetic—the search for connection to another person. It is ultimately the same impulse that compelled Kerouac to write his strongest work about his friends (Cassady and Snyder), and the resolution that Ginsberg provides at the end of "Howl," whose

redemptive closing image is a dream of Carl Solomon tearfully arriving at Ginsberg's door in Berkeley.

These same pressures that brought the original Columbia scene together in the mid-1940s affected and catalyzed many of the other arts being produced at this time. The influence of bop jazz on the Beat writers is well documented, particularly in Kerouac's vignette "Jazz of the Beat Generation." The intensely emotional and unscripted solos of Charlie Parker, Thelonius Monk, Dizzy Gillespie, and Lester Young, and later Miles Davis and John Coltrane, surely were pivotal in Kerouac and Ginsberg's literary development; but more important, these musicians were ultimately after the same things as their literary progeny. The intense jams were diametrically opposed to the acceptable sense of 1940s and 1950s decorum and uniformity, and therefore much closer to *real*. This same sense of abandon drove Jackson Pollock's chaotically revolutionary 1940s work; his large canvases splattered with paint seem to have an organic motion to them. Pollock, a raging alcoholic like Kerouac, did not believe that he was getting closer to nature, but rather that he *was* nature, when painting that way. In Hollywood—arguably the most potentially bourgeois, moneymaking sector of the arts—Marlon Brando's stunning Method acting, in films such as *A Streetcar Named Desire*, *On the Waterfront*, and *The Wild One*, also speak to this search. Brando's ability to give himself over to the role and improvise action and emotion were essentially the silver screen version of this same spontaneous abandon. This would come to a head in James Dean's 1955 classic *Rebel without a Cause*—almost the entire film is ad-libbed, with very little direction and no script. Even in stand-up comedy, exuberance and energy found their way to the fringes with new performers like Lord Buckley and Lenny Bruce. Buckley's performances were extremely energetic and utterly unique, while Bruce specialized in pushing the envelope, to the point of often being harassed for obscenity.

The one major missing link in the Beat literary movement is in the lack of attention given to women writers of the period. When asked about this, Gregory Corso asserted that there were many brilliant women rebelling within this scene, but that this led to family-imposed institutionalization for many of them. Nonetheless, there are several striking female writers, poets, and publishers who emerged from this movement. Diane DiPrima is usually the first to be mentioned, and perhaps the strongest voice, but poets such as Kyger, Elise Cowen, and Lenore Kandel are more recently receiving deserved critical attention. Kandel's erotic love poems, as well as her manifesto "Poetry Is

Never Compromise," are as powerful and indicative of the Beat aesthetic as any writing of this period, and the uncollected poetry of Cowen, who committed suicide in 1962, is striking and original. Hettie Jones and Joyce Johnson (née Glassman) have both enjoyed successful careers as writers and editors. Jones's memoir *How I Became Hettie Jones* (1990) and Johnson's *Minor Characters* (1983) operate as both strong autobiographies and statements on women in the Beat Generation.

### LATTER-DAY BEATS AND LATER WORK

Beat influence was enormous on the next generation's counterculture, whose dominant issues centered on the Vietnam War, civil rights, and legalization of drugs such as the new LSD. Ken Kesey, the author of *One Flew over the Cuckoo's Nest,* had begun a traveling bohemian circle around his own LSD experiments, and recruited the ageless Cassady to drive their bus. Ginsberg would later become involved with this scene as well. Highly influenced by their own conceptions of *On the Road* and *The Dharma Bums,* this circle, dubbed "the Merry Pranksters," would later define the bohemian, hippie aesthetic. The New Left also reflected the protest sensibility of writers like Rexroth, Ferlinghetti, and Ginsberg—who also involved himself in this scene, supporting or actively participating in nearly every major counterculture event of the 1960s, including the 1968 Democratic Convention in Chicago, where he helped organize protests with Black Panther and Yippie leaders. Burroughs covered the convention for *Esquire,* teamed with the French avant-garde playwright Jean Genet and the coauthor of *Easy Rider,* Terry Southern. The previous year, Ginsberg, Snyder, and McClure had been leaders at the San Francisco Be-In; Snyder blew the conch shell to inaugurate the event.

The strongest young voice of this new protest generation, Bob Dylan, was profoundly influenced by the Beats, and became a close friend of Ginsberg during the 1970s. Meanwhile, Burroughs's cut-ups, strange sci-fi scenarios, and heroin awareness were hugely influential in the new proto-punk scene emerging in New York under the wing of Andy Warhol, and on musicians like Lou Reed and David Bowie. The energy of Kerouac's writing can also be seen in the New Journalism of Tom Wolfe and Hunter Thompson, and in the later jazzy readings of Tom Waits.

By the end of the 1960s, Cassady and Kerouac had died, after too many years of hard living. Already hugely important in pop culture by this time, Kerouac died without seeing real critical support for his writing. Other Beats were more fortunate. The 1970s saw Ginsberg

receiving the National Book Award for *The Fall of America* in 1974, and Snyder the Pulitzer Prize for his *Turtle Island* collection in 1975. In 1976, Ginsberg and the poet Anne Waldman were asked to found a writing school at the Naropa Institute in Boulder, Colorado—the first accredited Buddhist college in the western hemisphere. They named the program the Jack Kerouac School of Disembodied Poetics, and it quickly became a stopping point for most remaining bohemian writers to lecture and read.

In the early 1990s, a resurgence of interest in Beat literature began at universities, along with conferences and academic journals on or influenced by their work. In addition, outside the academy, Beat-influenced poetry slams and readings increased in number across the country. Many retrospectives and long-term projects by Beat writers were produced, including collected works and recordings of many Beat writers, among them Kerouac and Ginsberg, Snyder's book-length, forty-year project *Mountains and Rivers without End* (1996), and a marathon reading of *On the Road* on the fortieth anniversary of its publication. By the time of Ginsberg's and Burroughs's deaths in 1997, university courses on the Beats were becoming common, and in 1998, Ferlinghetti was named poet laureate of San Francisco. Later that year, the Modern Library placed *On the Road* at number 55 on its "Top 100 English Language Novels of the 20th Century."

[*See also* Burroughs, William S.; Ginsberg, Allen; Kerouac, Jack, and his *On the Road*; *and* Snyder, Gary.]

### FURTHER READING

Allen, Donald M., ed. *The New American Poetry, 1945–1960.* New York, 1960. Among the first texts to acknowledge Beat as a significant literary movement. Also draws distinctions between Beat, San Francisco Renaissance, Black Mountain, New York school, and other movements.

Ball, Gordon, ed. *Allen Verbatim: Lectures on Poetry, Politics, Consciousness.* New York, 1974. Ginsberg essays on other Beat writers, happenings.

Bartlett, Lee, ed. *The Beats: Essays in Criticism.* Jefferson, N. C., 1981. Critical work on all the major Beat writers.

Breslin, James E. B. *From Modern to Contemporary: American Poetry, 1945–1965.* Chicago, 1984. Some discussion of Beat texts, including a long essay on "Howl."

Charters, Ann, ed. *The Beats: Literary Bohemians in Postwar America.* Detroit, 1983. Many excellent essays on almost every figure in this movement, by their biographers, fans, and sometimes by one another. A very good biographical perspective.

Charters, Ann. *The Portable Beat Reader*. New York, 1992. Selections by many key figures in the Beat movement, along with Charters's editorial and biographical commentary. An excellent starting point in the study of the Beat movement.

Davidson, Michael. *The San Francisco Renaissance: Poetics and Community at Mid-century*. New York, 1989. Analysis of historical context, as well as the writings that came out of this literary scene.

George-Warren, Holly, ed. *The Rolling Stone Book of the Beats*. New York, 1999. Cultural and biographical essays and retrospectives.

Gifford, Barry, and Lawrence Lee. *Jack's Book*. New York, 1979. Oral history of Kerouac's life.

Ginsberg, Allen. *Howl: Original Draft Facsimile, Transcript and Variant Versions*. Edited by Barry Miles. New York, 1986. Interesting background and compositional history of the poem.

Goodman, Michael Barry. *Contemporary Literary Censorship: The Case History of Burroughs'* Naked Lunch. Metuchen, N.J., 1981. Complete background of the seminal obscenity trial.

Hickey, Morgen. *The Bohemian Register: An Annotated Bibliography of the Beat Literary Movement*. Metuchen, N.J., 1990. Good listing of primary and secondary sources.

Holmes, John Clellon. *Passionate Opinions*. Fayetteville, Ark., 1988. Many of Holmes's definitive essays on the Beat Generation, with his later commentary as well.

Johnson, Joyce. *Minor Characters*. Boston, 1983. Memoir by Kerouac's former girlfriend. First definitive statement on women in the Beat Generation.

Knight, Brenda, ed. *Women of the Beat Generation*. Berkeley, Calif., 1996. Very good collection of writings on and by Beat women.

McClure, Michael. *Scratching the Beat Surface*. San Francisco, 1982. Firsthand account of Six Gallery reading, among other things.

Morgan, Ted. *Literary Outlaw: The Life and Times of William S. Burroughs*. New York, 1988. Very good biography, including much information on Burroughs's Tangier and Paris years not often noted in other sources on the Beats.

Rexroth, Kenneth. *American Poetry in the Twentieth Century*. New York, 1971. Evaluation of how Beat writers affected development of American poetics.

Tonkinson, Carole, ed. *Big Sky Mind: Buddhism and the Beat Generation*. New York, 1995. Excerpts from many Beat writers on or inspired by Buddhist thought, along with biographical and critical commentary on the subject.

Waldman, Anne, ed. *The Beat Book: Poems and Fiction of the Beat Generation*. Boston, 1996. Selections from many Beat writers, including previously excluded women, such as Kyger and Kandel.

# ANN BEATTIE

*by Donna Seaman*

Enthralled by literature but disenchanted with graduate school, Ann Beattie began writing short stories and resolutely submitting her unsolicited manuscripts to *The New Yorker*. She racked up nearly two dozen rejections, but her determination finally bore fruit when the preeminent weekly magazine accepted "A Platonic Relationship" in 1974, thus launching a controversial and significant writing career.

Born Charlotte Ann Beattie on 18 September 1947, the now-renowned short-story writer and novelist, a camera's darling with her high cheekbones, large eyes, long, blond hair, and charmingly offbeat style, had no blazing desire to become a writer while an only child growing up in a middle-class household in the staid suburbs of Washington, D.C. She was, however, an imaginative girl who learned early on how to amuse herself by painting pictures and composing stories.

An indifferent public school student, Beattie nonetheless excelled at American University, where her interest in literature earned her a guest editorship at *Mademoiselle* in 1968 and carried her on to graduate school in English at the University of Connecticut. Beattie earned her M.A. degree there, but as she began working toward a Ph.D. degree, she became impatient with academia's stale approach to literature and in protest started writing her own distinctive short stories, ultimately withdrawing from the program altogether.

## ESTABLISHING A VOICE, FINDING AN AUDIENCE

Published with exhilarating frequency in *The New Yorker*, Beattie's early stories startled all and riled many with their spare style, piercing realism, quirky wit, and frank intimacy with the morose and ironic so-called Woodstock generation. As Beattie so shrewdly observed, the heady exuberance of the counterculture faded rapidly, leaving many participants in the grip of an emotional hangover and a philosophical backlash. Beattie's fiction of the mid-1970s and 1980s perfectly reflects this disillusioned and cynical time, and she took her place in the literary pantheon with a big bang in 1976 when her first short-story collection, *Distortions*, and her debut novel, *Chilly Scenes of Winter*, were published at the same time. Both books feature anxious, intelligent, funny, skeptical, disenfranchised, unreliable, and lonely men and women in their twenties burdened with family responsibilities, weary of the cryptic subtexts of unstable relationships, and longing for escape from the crassly mercantile and hypocritical mainstream world. Beattie's people—the clever but aimless, pot-smoking, music-loving, and fantasy-ridden descendants of the characters of J. D. Salinger, John Cheever, and John Updike—depend on the indulgence of friends and siblings as they attempt the tightrope walks of career, marriage, and parenthood, or try their damnedest to avoid them.

In stories like the seminal "Vermont," wistful vacuity and paralyzing irony pervade as couples abruptly break up and the tenuous security of their fledgling adult lives drains away. Beattie's besieged narrator, one of her many smart, amusing, modestly valiant, winsome, yet depressed women characters, struggles both to decipher and to suppress her feelings after her husband walks out, leaving her to care for their young daughter and cope with the dogged courtship of a neighbor whose adulterous wife has also decamped. All of Beattie's signature qualities are present in this involving tale: barbed, ping-pong-quick dialogue that reveals the confounding and fitful complexities of relationships; adroitly sketched, acutely telling physical details; and the plight of a young child whose divorced parents are more preoccupied with their own angst than with the profound emotional needs of their vulnerable offspring.

Atmosphere and place are key elements in Beattie's moody fiction, whether it is in brooding, overcast New England, the exhausting in-your-faceness of New York City, or the profusion and funkiness of Key West. But if one ambiance dominates her work, it is the isolating cold and darkness established in *Chilly Scenes of Winter*. The novel's eloquent but dispirited protagonist, Charles, is already worried about growing old at age twenty-seven. He feels burdened by his mother's aggressive craziness, his protective concern for his younger sister and his feckless roommate, and his obsessive love for a married woman and devoted stepmother. A lucid dissection of the paralysis of depression and the unconscious use of romanticism as a form of escape, Beattie's first novel introduces her preoccupation with the idea of dysfunctional inheritance and presents the first of many carefully parsed sibling relationships.

Beattie's insightful portraits of brothers and sisters provide a stereo perspective on a troubled marriage (that of their parents); explore two variations on one genetic and domestic legacy; ponder the dimensions and complications of familial love and loyalty; and address questions of identity, independence, and duty. The sisters she portrays enable her to generate an almost cubist perspective on the female self, while symbiotic brother and sister relationships neatly contrast closely aligned yet essentially divergent male and female points of view. Part of the power of Beattie's family-focused fiction is her ability to write convincingly from the perspectives of men and women, boys and girls. And children loom large in Beattie's unnerving universe. In fact, they are the soul of her fiction, particularly the neglected children of self-absorbed parents or struggling single and divorced mothers, not to mention children who become orphaned—thanks to spectacular car crashes and other bizarre accidents—and subsequently relegated to the care of distant relatives, neighbors, or even a parent's former lover.

## THE CRITICS DISAGREE: MINIMALISM VERSUS SUBTLETY

Critics and reviewers responded with unusual vehemence to newcomer Beattie's work, initiating a sustained, often didactic debate. Avid dissection of her fiction pitted those who believe that literature has a straightforward moral imperative against those who believe that works of the imagination stand on their own aesthetic terms and values. Beattie's gestural prose, with its allusions to rock and roll, art, and the flotsam and jetsam of pop culture, her comfort with ambiguity and chance, her adroit use of silence (what is not said being as significant as what is), and, finally, her refusal to use fiction as a forum for passing overt moral judgments struck certain critics as facile, glibly reductive, and morally bankrupt. Her work was grouped dismissively with that of Raymond Carver (a comparison that Beattie, as would so many writers, considered a great compliment) and saddled with the inaccurate and perjorative label of minimalism.

The most vociferously negative critic was Joshua Gilder, who wrote specifically about Beattie in 1982 in a *New Criterion* article titled, "Down and Out: The Stories of Ann Beattie," and a year later in the same publication, about minimalist literature in general in "Less is Less." In an all-out attack on Beattie's characters, he writes, "They're not socially or economically blocked but psychologically burnt out; they drag themselves around her stories like worn sneakers sucking up the mud of despair, making little squishy, sighing noises as they go." Gilder's untempered objections ignore Beattie's technical mastery, sophisticated wit, acuity, and compassion, and stand exposed not only as overwrought reactions against her strongly conveyed, flawed, hence quintessentially human characters, but also as a denigration of psychological inquiry, literature's raison d'être.

Larry Husten, one of the many critics who have perceived the deeper levels and meaningful subtleties of Beattie's thoughtful and elegant fiction, describes her as "a sharp cultural observer" who "focuses on the interaction between her characters and their culture." Beattie's alignment with F. Scott Fitzgerald has been recognized by astute readers, and she has been praised for her fluent insights into the lost generation she portrays. Beattie corroborated this interpretation of her work in a 1978 interview with G. E. Murray in which she says, "The spirit of what Fitzgerald was getting at was something I wanted to restate. I do see some similarities between the 1920s and 1960s—that whole idea of being in a frantic state and still seeing real-life possibilities. That was deliberate."

Heated critical discussion only swelled the ranks of Beattie's enthusiastic readers. As the 1970s sped by, *The New Yorker* published one story after another, a film version of *Chilly Scenes of Winter* was released, and Beattie served as the Briggs-Copeland lecturer in English at Harvard and visiting writer and lecturer at the University of Virginia, where she has continued to teach. In 1978 she received a Guggenheim Fellowship, and her second short-story collection, *Secrets and Surprises*, was published. A more accomplished volume than the first, it contains some wonderfully memorable stories, including "A Vintage Thunderbird," which exemplifies Beattie's profound sensitivity to the volatile chemistry of relationships, their arbitrariness and fragility, their confusion and peril.

In her second novel, *Falling in Place* (1980), which unfolds during the summer of 1979 when Skylab was falling to Earth, Beattie ventures into the most harshly scrutinized of modern literary terrains, East Coast suburbia. Here Beattie revitalizes the world of Cheever and Updike, delving thoroughly and slyly into domestic strife and sorrow in her alternately funny and harrowing portrait of the fractured Knapp family. Gutsy and hard-hitting, *Falling in Place* is a scathing indictment of the neglect of children by affluent and selfish parents and society at large.

*The Burning House* (1982), Beattie's third story collection, extends her inquiry into the tenuousness of relationships and the precariousness of existence. As critics have noted, story titles such as "Learning to Fall," "Gravity," "Waiting," "Afloat," and "Like Glass" attest to a brittle, imploding, and doomed universe, an insubstantial realm in which people float and drift in limbo passively, at the mercy of forces greater than themselves. These stories embody the terrible instability of life and the chilling truth that you cannot count on anything, neither love nor sex nor money, not even the fundamentals of the physical universe. But even though Beattie is a lyricist of bleakness, she does unveil the path to transcendence, offering this Zen-like close to "Learning to Fall": "What will happen can't be stopped. Aim for grace."

## IRONY & PITY, INC.

In response to criticism of her allegedly arch and distancing irony, Beattie, drolly riffing on Ernest Hemingway (the writers she alludes to most often form quite a coterie: Fitzgerald, Hemingway, Yeats, Joyce, Flannery O'Connor, Chekhov, and Beckett), began copyrighting her work under the rubric Irony & Pity, Inc., a perfect example of her agile wit and lack of pretension. Stung yet undaunted, perhaps even inspired by adversity, Beattie went for broke, irony-wise, in her third novel, *Love Always* (1985).

Hilarious and melancholy at the same time, this loopy, metaphysical comedy of manners skewers the mores of three capitals of 1980s trendiness: Manhattan, Vermont, and Los Angeles. Lucy Spenser writes as Cindi Coeur in a parody of a lonely hearts column in "Country Daze," an ultra hip, highly cynical magazine, and her fearless fourteen-year-old niece plays an abused teenage alcoholic on a soap opera called, in one of Beattie's more mordant witticisms, "Passionate Intensity." (The phrase is Yeats's.) Both magazine and soap opera provide Beattie's central characters with alternate identities and mirror their unhappy predicaments as Beattie charts the morphing of hippies into yuppies, the dreamy haze

of marijuana into the harsh buzz of cocaine, and the vague, romantic notion of going back to the land and living the simple life into full-blown, me-first capitalism. People behave very badly here, as they do in all of Beattie's fiction, and love does not always triumph, although self-indulgence does give way to the demands of sheer survival.

Beattie is profoundly intrigued with the American preoccupation with crime and violence, especially the weird and unforeseen. Freakish accidents and outlandish attacks repeatedly punctuate and shift the action in her fiction, derailing and forever changing lives. Beattie's proclivity for plotting unexpected and wrenching occurrences points to her keen awareness of the most disturbing aspect of life, its unpredictability and vulnerability, but the violent acts and accidents she concocts all take place offstage and are recounted tersely, without emotion, objection, or even curiosity. This stoicism, born in shock and evolved from the survivor's instinct to try to maintain the status quo under even the most traumatic circumstances, interests Beattie no end and plays a crucial role in her much analyzed fourth novel, *Picturing Will* (1989).

Jody, a single mother, struggles to earn a living as a wedding photographer, although her dream is to concentrate solely on her own work. She all but sells her soul to make it as a fine art photographer, carelessly neglecting her five-year-old son, Will, in the process, prompting her thoughtful lover to muse, "There can hardly be a more serious test of a person's sanity than surviving childhood." Beattie, married to a painter, Lincoln Perry, often writes about photographs and paintings as emblematic of specific states of mind and ways of seeing. In *Picturing Will*, this motif allows her to consider what is revealed and concealed in photographs, and, more importantly, in one's picturing, or understanding, of one's self and others.

## HIDDEN LIVES, MULTIPLE SELVES: BEATTIE'S FICTIONAL UNIVERSE EXPANDS

In "Where You'll Find Me," the title story in Beattie's fourth short-story collection (published in 1986), a character listens to "the very quiet kind of Miles Davis." This seemingly casual detail is a clue to the nuanced, restrained, yet potent music of Beattie's meticulously detailed and socially grounded, yet genuinely poetic and mysterious fiction. Miles Davis was a master at purposeful improvisation; Beattie believes that "people are living improvisations," and she herself improvises when she writes. What brings her to the page, Beattie says, is a

> physiological feeling that I should write something. . . . Something in me has built up . . . it's not totally amorphous, there is something in the back of my mind: it's a name, it's a sentence, it's a sense of remembering what it is like to be in the dead of winter and wanting to go to the beach in the summer, some vague notion like that. It's never more than that. I've never in my life sat down and said to myself, "Now I will write something about somebody to whom such-and-such will happen."

However instinctively she has worked, Beattie's stories have become far more lustrous, intricately assembled, and discerning and her novels more substantial in terms of both narrative structure and psychological depth. *Another You* (1995) and *My Life, Starring Dara Falcon* (1997) are each concerned with the forging of the self and the acquisition of self-knowledge and with questions of identity, verity, reliability, and growth. In *Another You*, Beattie portrays an English professor at a small New Hampshire college who becomes entangled with a pretty student, who tells him a shocking story about a colleague of his who allegedly sexually abused her roommate. Meanwhile, his stepmother, who has secrets of her own, is dying, and his wife is having an affair with her boss. This setup has all the trappings of predictability, but instead Beattie works magic, deftly exploding clichéd situations to examine our diabolical capacity for living double lives, sustaining emotional denial, and failing to understand those closest to us. There is much suspense in this superbly executed novel, as well as some of Beattie's most brilliant comedy.

*My Life, Starring Dara Falcon* portrays yet another character who loses her parents at a young age and who consequently grows up uncertain of the validity of her existence. Cautious Jean Warner drops out of college to marry the first man she has sex with and then diligently seeks to subsume herself within his large New Hampshire family. But then she meets and becomes nearly bewitched by Dara Falcon (real name Darcy Fisher), a mercurial, commanding, and conniving self-invented and self-serving creature, whose cold-hearted machinations ultimately force Jean out of her exile from her true self into a more fulfilling life. Here Beattie keenly analyzes the masks people don to protect themselves and considers how very hard it is to "see things as they really are" because "we are so much in our own worlds."

## ACHIEVING GRAVITAS

Beattie is an award-winning member of the American Academy of Arts and Letters, and her short stories are included in three O. Henry Award collections and in the prestigious *The Best American Short Stories of the Century* (1999), edited by John Updike. In 2000 Beattie received the PEN/Malamud Award for lifetime achievement in the short-story form, a fitting recognition that ushered in her seventh story collection, the universally acclaimed *Perfect Recall* (2001) and her masterful seventh novel, *The Doctor's House* (2002), in which Beattie once again considers the pathos of families and the anguish of dysfunctional inheritance by positing her most complicated and most erotically charged brother-sister relationship to date. She also employs a favorite form, a triptych of narratives (the third voice is their widowed mother's) designed to disclose slowly the confounding fact that each family member possesses a unique and inevitably skewed perspective on their shared lives. In her most exacting dramatization of the elusiveness of truth, the dangers of delusion, the debilitating nature of isolation and fear, and the failure of love, Beattie achieves an aura of almost sacred mystery.

At this stage in Beattie's writing life, she evinces an exquisite authority. Her undiminished candor regarding the flaws of human nature makes her an uncompromising chronicler of the yin and yang of relationships and the sorrowful consequences of the precipitous loss of innocence. Beattie's artistic oeuvre has grown and evolved in sync with the writer herself, and her books grant readers a gracefully imaginative, insightful, and indelible record not only of an era and a generation, but of the human heart.

[*See also* Cheever, John; Fitzgerald, F. Scott; O'Connor, Flannery; Short Story in America, The; *and* Updike, John.]

## SELECTED WORKS

*Chilly Scenes of Winter* (1976)
*Distortions* (1976)
*Secrets and Surprises* (1978)
*Falling in Place* (1980)
*The Burning House* (1982)
*Love Always* (1985)
*Where You'll Find Me* (1986)
*Picturing Will* (1989)
*What Was Mine* (1991)
*Another You* (1995)
*My Life, Starring Dara Falcon* (1997)
*Park City: New and Selected Stories* (1998)

*Perfect Recall* (2001)
*Unholy Ghost: Writers on Depression* (2001)
*The Doctor's House* (2002)

## FURTHER READING

Montresor, Jaye Berman, ed. *The Critical Response to Ann Beattie*. Westport, Conn., and London, 1993. This generous and enlightening collection of essays, interviews, and reviews presents diverse perspectives on Beattie and her work up to 1991 and *What Was Mine*, her fifth short-story collection.

Murphy, Christina. *Ann Beattie*. Boston, 1986. The first biographical-critical monograph on Beattie presents a vivid portrait of the still young and successful writer along with an invaluable analysis of the critical reception of her early work.

# SAUL BELLOW

*by Sanford Pinsker*

In much the same way that William Faulkner created the necessary conditions for serious literature about the modern South and, in the process, inspired generations of literary followers, Saul Bellow made serious literature about modern urban Jewish Americans possible. His fiction brought the immigrant Jewish sensibility, in all its restless striving and ethnic vividness, to national attention. With novel after impressive novel he slowly emerged as the only contemporary fictionist who could be mentioned in the same breath with Faulkner and Henry James. "As the external social fact grows larger, more powerful and tyrannical," Bellow wrote in a 1951 application to the Rockefeller Foundation, "man appears in the novel reduced in will, strength, freedom and scope." The Foundation turned down his request for badly needed funding, but he continued to explore ways in which fiction might celebrate humanity's essential spirit. Humor is an essential ingredient in Bellow's formula because wit (in his case, the Yiddish quip) is a traditional way that oppressed people counter the fists and guns of a majority culture. Moreover, humor is, in Bellow's words, "more manly" than complaint. Thus, Bellow explores the human comedy, as did Shakespeare, Dante, and Joyce before him, but he does so with a distinctively Yiddish flavoring.

Saul Bellow was born in Lachine, Quebec, a suburb of Montreal, on 10 June 1910, as Solomon Bellows. His father, Abraham, had emigrated from St. Petersburg, Russia, just two years before Solomon's (later changed to Saul) birth. Abraham was a daring but largely unsuccessful businessman (Bellow remembers him as a "sharpie circa 1905"), but he cast a large, often oppressive shadow over Saul, the youngest of his children, because he did not believe that anyone could make a living as a writer.

Saul Bellow. (© *Bettmann/Corbis*)

The Bellows family moved to Chicago when Saul was nine years old, and it was in Chicago that Bellow spent much of his life trying to prove his father wrong and to earn his blessing. The task was a daunting one, not only because he received little encouragement at home (his mother hoped he would become a Talmudic scholar), but also because white Anglo-Saxon Protestants controlled the avenues of high culture. Nonetheless, Bellow made his way through the public library stacks not, as he puts it, "to read the Talmud, but the novels and poems of Sherwood Anderson, Theodore Dreiser, Edgar Lee Masters, and Vachel Lindsay." To this muscular, thoroughly realistic and American prose, Bellow added the Yiddish, Hebrew, and French of his childhood.

As an undergraduate at Northwestern University, Bellow majored in anthropology because he was told that anti-Semitism would thwart his literary ambitions. Taken together, everything that militated against Bellow becoming a writer was met by his stiff resistance. Later, when intellectuals made much of alienation, Bellow said kind words about accommodation; when Marxism was fashionable, Bellow quickly outgrew the fashion, just as he would move beyond the appeal of Reichian psychology, the drumbeats for a 1960s-style radicalism, or the later fascination with multiculturalism. Bellow has always been his own man, even if this meant earning the disapproval of critics who mounted a number of angry charges against him: elitist, misogynist, racist. As a serious artist he regarded elitism as a badge of honor rather than one of shame; as for the other accusations, his best defense has always been a careful reading of his fiction.

Although Bellow has been showered with every important literary prize—three National Book Awards, the Pulitzer Prize, and in 1976 the Nobel Prize in literature—he has not generated the wide public adulation that we associate with the careers of American modernists such as William Faulkner, F. Scott Fitzgerald, and most especially, Ernest Hemingway. Of his books, only *Herzog* (1964) spent a stretch of time on the best-seller list (*Ravelstein* [2000] made a brief appearance), but Bellow's works have obtained considerable attention from reviewers, critics, and scholars. There are literally hundreds of articles exploring his themes, dozens of book-length studies of his novels, and a healthy number of Ph.D. dissertations The Bellow industry gives no sign of slowing down, even if Saul Bellow himself is not the household word that Ernest Hemingway once was, and in many ways still is.

## EARLY FICTIONS

Bellow began his career in the mid-1940s, at a time when Ernest Hemingway dominated the literary landscape and his sparse style was being imitated by many aspiring young authors. A man was defined, Hemingway argued, by the manner in which he faced his death, usually on a battlefield or in the bull ring. At such existential moments, action spoke louder than words, and a character's inner life was often sacrificed to more pressing external facts. *Dangling Man* (1944) was Bellow's strenuously inward-looking account of a man who finds himself uneasily "dangling" between a civilian life that no longer matters and a military call-up that keeps being postponed. The novel announced a new direction in American literature, not only because it was a study in alienation, isolation, and claustrophobia or because it was a "proof" book—one that showed Bellow's intimate acquaintance with the masterpieces of world literature—but also because *Dangling Man* made its differences from the Hemingway aesthetic of manly stoicism abundantly clear: "Most serious matters are closed to the hard-boiled [that is, Hemingway and his disciples]. They are unpracticed in introspection, and therefore badly equipped to deal with opponents whom they cannot shoot like big game or outdo in daring." By contrast, Bellow's testy protagonist is a character study in introspection: he writes up his thoughts in the form of a journal. His ruminations, set against the backdrop of a gloomy Chicago landscape, are restricted to four months—from mid-December 1942 until April 1943—during which Joseph simultaneously "dangles" and gives an accounting of his inner life. While his wife works, Joseph wanders about the neighborhood or holes himself up in their tiny apartment; he lunches in restaurants (invariably alone), listens to the radio, and reads the newspaper. With the exception of the daily record he obsessively keeps (for example, "the day the waitress refused to take back the burned toast"), Joseph lives what can only be called an appallingly uneventful life.

The poet-critic Delmore Schwartz praised the novel for its catalog of "the typical objects of a generation's sensibility" while Bellow's biographer, James Atlas, felt that *Dangling Man* was about "the struggle to sustain a sense of identity and worth amid the patriotic clamor of wartime." Casting his eye over the buildings outside his window, Joseph wonders about what, in all this, "speaks for man?" That basic question, perhaps more existential than anything Hemingway encountered on the battlefield, has remained a primary concern throughout Bellow's career.

*Dangling Man* ends as Joseph seemingly embraces the regimentation that will await him in the army, but as Bellow himself assured David Bazelon, this was an "ironic statement": "I don't encourage surrender. I'm speaking of wretchedness and saying that no man by his own effort finds his way out of it. To some extent the artist does. But the moral man, the citizen, doesn't. He cannot." In the case of *Dangling Man*, echoes of Dostoyevsky's *Notes from the Underground* (1864) suggest a bitter irony that represents Joseph inwardly resisting even as he outwardly stumbles toward accommodation.

Bellow's next published novel, *The Victim* (1947), was yet another work out to establish his intellectual credentials and to further his exploration of urban claustrophobia. This time modeled on Dostoyevsky's *The Eternal Husband* (1870), the novel follows an insecure Jewish protagonist (Asa Leventhal) as he deals with Kirby Allbee, an anti-Semitic antagonist who, on a steamy summer's night, comes out of the psychological shadows to accuse Leventhal of causing his ruin. Allbee argues that he is the "victim" of the novel's title, just as Leventhal would insist that he is the one who has been singled out for the blame of Allbee's lost job, smashed marriage, and chronic alcoholism.

The two men are psychological doubles, each bonded to the other in rhythms of attraction and repulsion, and each trying to convert the other to his version of the "real." Coming so close to the raw memories of the Holocaust, some critics objected to the psychic affinities Bellow suggested between anti-Semite and Jew. (Were they really just opposite sides of the same coin?) But for Bellow, Leventhal was simply an up-against-it human being, neither more nor less. As he grapples with the outlandish accusations leveled against him, Leventhal shows us just how dispiriting urban life can be: its subways hot and crowded, its streets oppressive, its sheer mass of competing bodies (for jobs, for space, even for air) utterly relentless.

After writing *The Victim*, Bellow needed what he called "a fantasy holiday," and this would come when he temporarily set aside yet another claustrophobic city novel (*Seize the Day*, 1956) for the high energy, picaresque expansiveness of *The Adventures of Augie March* (1953), just as he would engineer another such holiday when sending the protagonist of *Henderson the Rain King* (1959) off to an Africa of the imagination. As Bellow scholars have amply demonstrated, the publication dates of Bellow's works are not necessarily a reliable index of when they were written. Bellow tended to have several projects bubbling along simultaneously. That is why *Seize the Day*, possibly Bellow's most tightly constructed work, belongs in the category of early fiction, while *The Adventures of Augie March*, published three years earlier, deserves a separate heading.

*Seize the Day*, which was initially printed in the pages of *Partisan Review*, the premier journal of the New York intellectuals, revolves around a single day in the life of a middle-aged flop. A series of bad decisions have forced Tommy Wilhelm, a former salesman for a line of kiddy furniture, to move to the Hotel Gloriana on Manhattan's Upper West Side, where his father, the icy Dr. Adler, can pay his bills and otherwise offer him fatherly aid and comfort. Dr. Adler, however, refuses—partly because Tommy changed his name from Wilhelm Adler when he dropped out of college to pursue an ill-fated career as a Hollywood actor and partly because Dr. Adler can scarcely bear to look at his untidy, altogether unpromising son.

In a work fairly bursting with water imagery, Tommy is always on the verge of drowning. His estranged wife makes increasingly shrill demands for money. His father refuses to carry Tommy, or anyone else for that matter, on his back. Finally, when a con man bilks Tommy out of his last dollars on an ill-advised plunge in the commodities market, he effectively hits rock bottom.

Bellow renders Tommy's efforts to "seize the day"—as Dr. Tamkin, half wise man, half crackpot, keeps recommending—with near-Olympian detachment. Dr. Adler's hard heart is set against Tommy's sloppy sentimentality; the steaming hydrotherapy pool in the bowels of the Hotel Gloriana is at odds with the city in springtime that only Tommy seems to notice; and "the inexhaustible current of millions of every age, of every genius, possessors of every secret" contrasts with

the funeral home Tommy stumbles into as he chases after a specter he thinks is Tamkin. What follows is among the most resonant and moving of any passage in Bellow's canon. Tommy finds himself standing before an unknown corpse (who may symbolically represent his father, himself, or some combination) and unleashing his blocked heart at last: "The source of all tears had suddenly sprung open within him." As the flowers, lights, and music fuse within him, Tommy "sank deeper than sorrow, through torn sobs and cries toward the consummation of his heart's ultimate need." He has, at long last, managed to "seize the day"—not as a victory in the world of Tamkin's getting and spending, but rather in a deeply elegiac moment to which the novella had been pointing from its opening page.

### THE ADVENTURES OF AUGIE MARCH AND HENDERSON THE RAIN KING

As a minor character observes about Augie March, "There's opposition in him." Unlike the brooding protagonists of his early fiction, Augie is "larky" (Bellow's word), ever on the move and unfailingly optimistic. If the precursors of Joseph and Asa Leventhal were the brooding figures found in German or Russian novels, Augie's closest antecedent is Mark Twain's *Adventures of Huckleberry Finn* (1884). Just as well-meaning adults wanted to adopt, and then to "sivilize," the eminently resourceful thirteen-year-old Huck, so too do a wide variety of people want to press Augie to their bosoms—that is, if he will simply agree. But he is unadoptable. His opening line, "I am an American, Chicago-born . . . and I go at things as I have taught myself, free-style" not only announces the utter "Americanness" of *The Adventures of Augie March* (this as opposed to having a protagonist defined by his immigrant status), but it also suggests just how much of an independent agent he will become as the novel unfolds.

Augie fares best in the first third of the novel (Bellow himself has remarked on how wearying his character's unalloyed spunkiness became), because his childhood years are dominated by the altogether wonderful con person, Grandma Lausch, and later by William Einhorn, possibly the most vividly etched "cripple" in all of American literature. Grandma Lausch teaches Augie the lessons necessary for the immigrant survivor, while Einhorn introduces him to the world of the streets. Each of these early mentors is cast larger-than-life, with the allusions clinging to Grandma Lausch suggesting that she is a member in good standing of the czar's court, while Einhorn is the king of his West Side neighborhoods of pool rooms and shady characters.

It is only when Augie is old enough to be thought a gigolo to the North Shore matron, Mrs. Renling, or when his ambitious brother Simon marries into a wealthy family, that Augie musters up the necessary resistance to avoid being ensnared by a harsh, destructive world. Ultimately, Grandma Lausch's Machievellian cynicism ends with children who treat her cynically and Einhorn's smartness finally outsmarts himself.

Only Augie seems able to bound effortlessly past the nets set in place to snare us, but even Augie is not as wound free as his status as a picaresque hero might suggest. If the mythic details that surround the denizens of his Chicago neighborhood elevate them, the same magnifications also reduce and ultimately darken them. By the midsections of Bellow's freewheeling novel, moments of doubt begin to creep in. Most reviewers, however, had nothing but praise for Bellow's stylistic achievement. Square inch by square inch, his verbal portraiture had texture, density, and not least of all, wit. If Augie's buoyant spirit smacked of Huck Finn, Bellow's meticulously rendered catalogues reminded one of Whitman. In addition, Bellow's vigorously American anthem came during the Cold War, a time when such exercises were decidedly welcome. If our nation was pitted against the Soviet Union in a propaganda war out to decide if democratic values could speak to the common man more eloquently than could communist rhetoric, a novel such as *The Adventures of Augie March* was just what those times, those places, required.

The critic-essayist Norman Podhoretz cast one of the few dissenting votes about Bellow's breakthrough. He much preferred *Dangling Man*, a novel that captured his own sense of "dangling" as he put aside a promising literary career and waited to hear from his draft board. As for *Augie*, Podhoretz dared to say in print what (he later claimed) many of New York intellectual crowd were thinking silently—namely, that "*Augie* was largely the product not of a state of being already achieved, but rather of an effort on Bellow's part to act as though he had already achieved it. As a test case of the buoyant attitudes of the [post-war] period . . . *Augie* fails—and it fails mainly because its buoyancy is embodied in a character who is curiously untouched by his experience, who never changes or develops, who goes through everything yet undergoes nothing." For Podhoretz there was a "quality of willed and empty affirmation" in Bellow's novel. The book may have wanted to trumpet American virtue, but its author did not fully believe in the message.

Podhoretz's cavils aside, what *The Adventures of Augie March* demonstrates brilliantly is Bellow's liberation from the closed-upness of his first books and the effervescent style that warmly attached itself to his protagonist. In his pursuit of a "worthwhile fate," Augie will travel anywhere, try everything. That he does not find what he so optimistically seeks is no proof that the journey was a failure. "Columbus too," Augie points out, " thought he was a flop, probably when they sent him back in chains. Which didn't prove there was no America"—and by extension, Augie's own disappointments do not alter the fact that *The Adventures of Augie March* is a distinctly American book.

If Bellow has expressed some misgivings about *The Adventures of Augie March* (he went "too far" and thus violated formal unity), *Henderson the Rain King* remains the favorite of his novels. Eugene Henderson is a six-foot-four, two-hundred-thirty-pound gentile—hardly the sort of character one expects to meet in a Bellow novel. At age fifty-five, Henderson's life thus far can be summarized this way: He has an M.A. from a prestigious university, a second wife, seven children, a $3-million-dollar estate, and most important of all, an inner voice that incessantly cries, "I want . . . I want . . . I want . . ." Henderson's quest is to fill in the direct object, to assuage both his unhappiness and his aspiration.

*Henderson the Rain King* is a comic novel, one not only out to parody Joseph Conrad's "Heart of Darkness" (1902), but also to ruminate about spiritual journeys rendered as farce. What Henderson wants to do is no less than "burst the spirit's sleep," to move beyond his chaotic life as a pig farmer given to bouts of gratuitous violence. In Africa, he means to find his soul, and to follow its directives.

Bellow himself has noted his similarities with Henderson—not in such surface details as ethnicity or overblown physical size, but in their secret sharer sense of being quixotic seekers of a higher truth. But the world in which author and character do their questing remains dark and mysterious, just as it was in Bellow's earlier fiction. "Truth comes in blows," we learn from Henderson's experience, and it is in great error and pain, albeit comically rendered, that he steps into a dreamlike Africa and fastens himself to Dahfu (daffy?), the Wariri king. Dahfu is everything that Henderson is not: relaxed; confident; a man formed by his study of Ralph Waldo Emerson, William James, and Wilhelm Reich. Bellow, who once dabbled in Reich's regimen of orgone boxes and other sexual therapies, frees himself of such foolishness by making Dahfu appear as (dangerously) foolish at the same time that the novel's tone suggests there is a nub of truth hiding inside Dahfu's speeches.

Taken in by all that is impressive about Dahfu, Henderson enters the lion den, as he must in a mythic tale that mingles fire, water, and tests of courage involving wild animals. Had this been a Hemingway novel (some critics have noted the similarity between the names Henderson and Hemingway, as well as their gun-toting, swashbuckling tendencies), the existential moment of killing the lion, and thus appropriating its soul, would have been rendered with a straight face and an eager enthusiasm. By contrast, Bellow gives this scenario a comic twist, preferring to see his antihero celebrating life as he joyously dances with a lion cub and a Persian orphan at his side. The dance takes place in Newfoundland, a heavy-handed piece of symbolism perhaps, but one that makes it clear that Henderson is headed toward community and life: "God does not shoot dice with our souls," he exclaims, echoing a belief first expressed by Albert Einstein, "and therefore . . . I believe there is justice, and that much is promised." Many of Bellow's critics were not convinced that he had earned the sentiments expressed in the novel's concluding paragraphs, but given its overall comic vision, what other ending is possible? Like Augie, Henderson may not know precisely what his "worthwhile fate" is, much less which direct object to place after the words "I want," but he is a less troubled, probably wiser man for his dreamy, largely internal trip through Africa.

### HERZOG

In an age that pays both lip service and hard cash to the special importance of intellect, Bellow's protagonists grow to expect the gingerly treatment due an endangered species. Thus, Moses Herzog easily earns his way from grant to grant as a bona fide egghead, the author of a highly regarded work of intellectual history entitled (significantly enough) *Romanticism and Christianity. Herzog* (1964) is Bellow's most vivid portrait of a New York intellectual losing his grip not only on his "work" as a scholar but also his life. That Bellow's protagonist has more than a few similarities to the tumultuous life of its author (both found themselves going through messy divorces) is true enough, but once again it was Bellow's uncanny ability to put his finger squarely on the pulse of his cultural times that made the novel remarkable.

"If I am out of my mind," Herzog declares in the opening sentence, "it's all right with me" The statement, however, is problematic because nothing means more

to Herzog—and nothing is more self-defining—than his intellectual prowess. Since his wife Madeleine walked out on him for another man, Herzog has been suffering through a bad patch by writing "mental letters" to a wide range of the living and the dead. Overcome by "a need to explain, to have it out, to justify, to put in perspective, to clarify, to make amends," Herzog spends the novel in the grip, often a comic one, of his hyperconsciousness.

By contrast, others respond to Herzog's high-mindedness with nearly equal doses of admiration and thinly veiled condescension: "Though Simkin was a clever lawyer, very rich, he respected Herzog. He had a weakness for confused, high-minded people with moral impulses like Herzog—Hopeless! Very likely he looked at Moses and saw a grieving childless man trying to keep his dignity." In Herzog's case, the populist wisdom that figures "if you're so smart, why ain't you rich?" becomes the unspoken: "And if you were *really* so smart, how come you got cuckolded?" That is bad enough, but those who would instruct poor Herzog in the nature of the *real* are even worse. They elbow their way into his life with teeth bared and a stomach for the brutalities of quotidian life.

Herzog is peculiarly unequipped to deal with the hard edges of a reality cut off from Time and wrenched from continuity. What we need, he half-playfully insists, is a "good five-cent synthesis," one that would provide "a new angle on the modern condition, showing how life could be lived by renewing universal connections: overturning the last of the Romantic errors about the uniqueness of the social meaning of Nothingness." It is a grand, wonderfully nutty dream, the stuff that make later protagonists such as Artur Sammler and Charlie Citrine tick. These historians are more likely to be men of moral vision than accountants of hard fact. In Herzog's case everything militates against him making good on his early promise as a scholar: the sleazy cultural moment; assorted "operators" (Mermelstein, Shapiro, and other competing academics); Reality Instructors; Potato Lovers; virtually any woman; and of course, himself.

*Herzog* is built upon a foundation of painful memories and *trepverter*, a Yiddish word defined in the novel as "retorts that came too late, when you were already on your way down the stairs." He has been systemically betrayed—by his second wife, his (former) best friend, assorted lawyers, psychiatrists, and priests. All of them know what Herzog only found out as Madeleine delivered a carefully composed speech beginning with the words, "We can't live together anymore." Valentine Gersbach, an intellectual wannabe, has stolen Madeleine away from him. Each member of the newly formed couple is an actor in a novel filled with "actors": Valentine plays the role of culture maven, even though his shameless bid for popularity is a sad joke, while Madeleine's conversion to the Catholic Church tells us more about "theater" than religious feeling. In addition, Madeleine's father is the egomaniacal director who announced his productions in posters that put his own name, Poinsetter, in large capital letters above names such as Eugene O'Neill and Anton Chekhov.

Although the novel's actual events are severely restricted, flashbacks present an international cast of Herzog's former lovers, intellectual friends (and enemies) from his past, and perhaps most of all, warm memories of his Montreal boyhood. Throughout it all, Herzog worries if his children will somehow inherit his "Herzog heart." He fantasizes about striking Madeleine and even of murdering her, but such violence runs counter to everything he both was, and is.

At one point Herzog writes himself down as a "*suffering joker*," and his letters, real or imaginary, suggest both terms. At times he fires off playful quips (writing to Herr Nietzsche, he feels obliged to point out that many of his phrasings have "a very Germanic ring"); but on other occasions his sermonizing is in deadly earnest: "*We must get it out of our heads that this is a doomed time,*" he upbraids one all-too-trendy scholar, "*that we are waiting for the end, and the rest of it, mere junk from fashionable magazines. Things are grim enough without these shivery games.*" He will often put himself up short, realizing, in a burst of sanity, that he is conducting a Great Books course to people who couldn't give a fig about high culture. But if Herzog is hard on others, he is hardest on himself: "*Lord, I ran to fight in Thy holy cause but kept tripping, never reached the scene of the struggle.*"

Herzog's struggle reminds us of how much the spirit continues to matter, and if his battle to recover his sanity ultimately exhausts Herzog himself, the very fact that he no longer feels the compunction to write "mental letters" is a sign of health, or at least of its future possibility. He can, at long last, let go, without, as the novel's last lines put it, any "messages for anyone. Nothing. Not a single word."

## SHORT FICTION AND OTHER ASSORTED WRITING

Bellow may be better known as a novelist, but his short fiction is every bit as distinctive. *Collected Stories* (2001) puts most, but not all, of Bellow's short fiction between hard covers and justifies the words that the critic

James Wood uses in his Introduction to the volume. Wood argues that what distinguishes Bellow from other contemporary writers is that he is "greatly abundant, greatly precise, greatly vast."

Bellow has published five collections of short fiction. They include *Seize the Day, with Three Short Stories and a One-Act Play* ("A Father-to-Be," "The Gonzaga Manuscripts," and "Looking for Mr. Green" and the play *The Wrecker*) (1956); *Mosby's Memoirs, and Other Stories* ("Leaving the Yellow House," "The Old System," "Looking for Mr. Green," "The Gonzaga Manuscripts," "A Father-to-Be," and "Mosby's Memoirs") (1968); and *Him with His Foot in His Mouth, and Other Stories* ("Cousins," "A Silver Dish," "What Kind of Day Did You Have?," "Zetland: By a Character Witness," and "Him with His Foot in His Mouth") (1984). The stories cover a wide range of situations and characters, from Bellow's fictionalized memories of the writer Isaac Rosenfeld ("Zetland: By a Character Witness") or the art critic Harold Rosenberg ("Him with His Foot in His Mouth") to evocations of how an older generation of immigrant Jews differs from their more Americanized children ("A Silver Dish" and "The Old System"). *Something to Remember Me By: Three Tales* consists of three novellas (*Something to Remember Me By, A Theft*, and *The Bellarosa Connection*) (1991).

In most instances spiritual yearning is coupled with the heart's pang as Bellow investigates what it is to live amid the world's messiness even as the soul is eager to abide in higher regions. *Collected Stories*—something of a misnomer because it is really a selection of the shorter works Bellow most values—also includes the novellas he published as paperback originals: *The Bellarosa Connection* and *A Theft*. *The Actual* (1997) can be added to this last grouping of novellas that were too long for magazines but too short to warrant hardback publication.

Like Henry James, Bellow is a stylist who tried to turn his accomplishments on the page to success in the theater; like James, he could not pull it off. In addition to *The Wrecker*, he wrote three one-act comedies under the general heading *Under the Weather* (*Orange Soufflé*, 1965; *A Wen*, 1965; and *Out from Under*, 1966) and *The Last Analysis* (1965). Each had a short run. From time to time Bellow turned his hand to nonfiction. *To Jerusalem and Back: A Personal Account* (1976) details his trip to Israel and the desperate confusions he found there. Bellow's egghead protagonists often convey the sense that they could solve the world's problems if only they were not so distracted by personal grief; but in this memoir Bellow reveals that he is no savvier about the Middle East than the wide range of experts he reads and interviews.

*It All Adds Up: From the Dim Past to the Uncertain Future* (1994) is a collection of Bellow's essays that no serious Bellow reader can ignore. It is not that he changes his mind about the artist's role in assessing his culture and the continuing need to preserve humane values from attack, but that he unloads his message with increasing conviction and eloquence.

## MR. SAMMLER'S PLANET

*Mr. Sammler's Planet* (1970) has become a politically controversial novel because its elderly protagonist, Artur Sammler, attacks the moral excess of the mid-1960s youth culture and because of a highly charged scene in which an elegant black pickpocket exposes himself as a means of intimidation. If *Herzog* is a tapestry of "explanations," an older, possibly wiser Sammler knows that they alone can never be entirely sufficient. What begins with his cranky hectoring about "intellectual man" as "explaining creature"—complete with a cultural list that includes "fathers to children, wives to husbands, lectures to listeners, experts to layman, colleagues to colleagues, doctors to patients"—ends with the terms of our human "contract," which "in his inmost heart each man knows": "as I know mine. As all know. For that is the truth of it—that we all know, God that we know, that we know, we know, we know."

Between such airy metaphysics falls the shadow of the City and that shoddiness that prompts Sammler into becoming an "explainer" extraordinaire. If the subways were hot and crowded in *The Victim*—thus causing an already testy Asa Leventhal to grow even more irritated—things have steadily worsened. Sammler walks through "invariably dog-fouled" streets, no longer surprised that the counterculture's young look "autochthonous" or that one must search like Diogenes for a working telephone booth.

Sammler is a variation on the themes central to William Butler Yeats's "Sailing to Byzantium." Caught in a city that has added genital bullying to our century's "mackerel-crowded" landscape, Sammler, rather like Yeats's speaker, concludes that "that is no country for old men." This is not to suggest, however, that Sammler opts either for an artsy Byzantium or the moony craters of scientist-philosopher Dr. Govinda Lal. Rather, he wonders if "perhaps the best is to have some order within oneself. Better than what many call love. Perhaps it *is* love."

In *Mr. Sammler's Planet* the rage for a "charmed and *interesting* life" turns minor characters into menagerie grotesques and the City itself into a Theater of Decadence. Not since the days of T. S. Eliot has there been such an eloquent appeal on behalf of reestablishing that necessary relationship between tradition and the individual talent. As Sammler puts it, "Antiquity accepted models, the Middle Ages—I don't want to turn into a history book before your eyes—but modern man, perhaps because of collectivization, has a fever of originality." Because Sammler is an explainer, despite his reservations about the value of explanations, and because he is such a crank, the novel struck many as a neoconservative polemic against the times that Bob Dylan assured us, were "a-changin'." But from an artist committed to telling the cultural truth (as he saw it), the novel is not only a marvelously rendered portrait of a man in old age but also a rumination on the soul stuck in the midst of an ongoing, mind-blowing revel.

## HUMBOLDT'S GIFT

In Bellow's early fiction the lot of praising the City fell to the likes of Augie March, a breathlessly picaresque Hero with a sharp eye for possibilities. In *Humboldt's Gift* (1975) Charlie Citrine may be more dupe than con man, but his civic cheers take on the force of an aesthetic credo: "I was trained in Chicago to make something out of such a scant setting. In Chicago you become a connoisseur of the near nothing. With a clear eye I looked at a clear scene." As Bellow likes to put it, one must develop a taste for Chicago—and he clearly has. His apprentice years as a writer were spent in New York City and in his later years he moved to Boston, but it is Chicago that remains his most congenial psychic turf.

As with other Bellow protagonists before him, Citrine fumbles his way between elevated thought and rude circumstance, and it is this collision between ongoing mediations and a genuine affection for the street savvy that makes *Humboldt's Gift* so resilient, its comedy of Ideas so affecting. At least part of the blame for the downward spiral of Von Humboldt Fleisher's tragic career (one modeled on that of the poet Delmore Schwartz) rests in the nature of lyric poetry itself, in the restless urge to exert power via song, to rekindle the shaman's healing magic in a land of technology and ever-bigger conglomerates. But New York City is not entirely blameless, for its appetite for dazzling talk helped to turn poor Humboldt into a "Mozart of conversation," a man dying from unwritten poems.

By contrast, Citrine is neither an Anglophile hot to crack into the Bloomsbury group (as was Sammler), nor is he bent upon becoming the *Partisan Review* crowd's darling by out-Humboldting Humboldt himself with dazzling intellectual performances that linked Bela Kun with Babe Ruth, Tocqueville with Ruggles of Red Gap. Rather, Citrine is a man who suspects that real ideas do not generate either in committee or over delicatessen counters. But when he is not musing about his projected study on the nature of boredom or trying to make sense out of Rudolf Steiner's anthroposophy, it is Chicago that keeps Citrine busy.

Like Bellow himself, Citrine often finds himself bowing to "low-life expertise," to people with their hands firmly gripped on solid, no-nonsense ropes. The attraction is one that much appeals to a side of Bellow's consciousness and it surely helps to generate the comic side of his fiction, but Citrine's needs speak louder than his reflective asides. To be a Historian of Ideas in a novel like *Herzog* or *Humboldt's Gift* is to wonder, as a child might wonder, about the quotidian world and to ask again and again: "With everyone sold on the good how does all the evil get done?"

### THE DEAN'S DECEMBER

*The Dean's December* (1982) is as much the tale of two cities—Chicago and Bucharest, Romania—as it is a study in the dark ruminations of its protagonist, Dean Albert Corde. Corde is a journalist turned academic and he brings his critical eye to the two cities, one capitalist, the other communist, that he regards as emblematic of a general decline in Western civilization. In his *The Modern American Novel* (1992), Malcolm Bradbury argues that the novel "confirms the late Bellow as the novelist of a world which has lost cultural bearing, moved into an age of boredom and terror, violence and indifference, private wealth and public squalor."

Chicago and Bucharest are very different cities, but when Corde makes an extended visit to the latter (the mother of his Romanian-born wife is dying and in need of support), he comes to realize that—in the contemporary world—disorder, violence, and death know no politics. "I imagine, sometimes, " Corde muses, "that if a film could be made of one's life, every other frame would be death." The Death Question is one of Bellow's major obsessions, but his work usually leavens this preoccupation with generous dashes of humor. Not so in *The Dean's December*; Corde becomes a "moralist of seeing" as his mind moves from a spectacular rape case and the rapid deterioration of Chicago's Cabrini Green housing project to his mother-in-law's death amid the grimness of Bucharest.

As Bellow told Matthew C. Roudané in an interview for *Contemporary Literature* (1984), "there is a correspondence between the outer and inner, between the brutalized city land and the psyche of its citizens. Given their human resources I don't see how people today can experience life at all." The distance between protagonist and author is nearly nonexistent in *The Dean's December*; generous slabs of Corde's journalism rise to the condition of art at the same time that Bellow's novel becomes what Roudané calls "a nonfiction novelistic style." Much of Bellow's later fiction has a preachy side, as did many of his later essays, but in *The Dean's December* his conviction that we are living through the death pangs of civilization itself was expressed in self-righteous, often sour notes.

### MORE DIE OF HEARTBREAK

What is at stake in *More Die of Heartbreak* (1987) is not merely the saga of a man who was a "visionary with plants" and a "dub with the women." It is also the difficult, painful business of fashioning a soul when one adds the complicating factors of love, marriage, and domesticity to the mix.

Kenneth Trachtenberg, the protagonist-narrator of *More Die of Heartbreak*, explains the phenomenon this way: "If you venture to think in America, you also feel an obligation to provide a historical sketch to go with it, to authenticate or legitimize your thoughts. So it's one moment of flashing insight and then a quarter of an hour of pedantry and tiresome elaboration—academic gabble. Locke to Freud with stops at local stations like Bentham and Kierkegaard. One has to feel sorry for people in such an explanatory bind. Or else (a better alternative), one can develop an eye for the comical side of this." Bellow's richest fictions explore this "better alternative"—namely, the "comical side" of dreamy intellectuals with lives in great disorder. Urban comedians like Moses Herzog and Charlie Citrine are better architects of moral vision than accountants of hard fact. Bellow leaves it to others, drawn from the growing mélange of wacky but memorable minor characters, to set these eggheads straight.

Trachtenberg is presumably on a mission of mercy. His Uncle Benn Crader, a world-renowned botanist, needs massive doses of hand-holding as the disastrous consequences of a recent marriage become increasingly clear, but uncle and nephew are so nearly identical that it often becomes difficult to keep the two players straight. Moreover, both of them sound suspiciously like dead ringers of their author. The result is a novel longer on self-indulgence than discipline; and at the same time a novel that fails to elicit our sympathies in the ways that earlier journeys into the heart of grief once did.

As Trachtenberg, an assistant professor of Russian, freely admits: "I had to be vigilant with myself, too, for I have a similar weakness for setting things straight and I know how futile it is to work at it continually.... We were doubly, multiply, interlinked. Neither of us by now had other real friends, and I couldn't afford to lose him." This is Kenneth and Benn as psychic doubles, doppelgängers of the first water. Not since *The Victim* has Bellow given himself over to such an extended exercise in secret sharing. Trachtenberg can and does match his uncle in the give-and-take of erudite conversation and, more important, in the high stakes, "pain schedule" game of pitting heartbreak against heartbreak, kinky affair against kinky affair. Both men subscribe to the dream of living peacefully—"two human beings bound together in love and kindness"—and not surprisingly, both are shocked, and then plunged into confusion, when their respective women give them such drubbings.

To the rest of the family, Benn is a schlemiel, pure and simple. As his sister puts it in one of the novel's more memorable quips: "In love, my brother is the kind of hemophiliac who would shave in the dark with a straight razor." And although Trachtenberg might demur, he too is cut from the same self-delusional cloth. Thus, one leaner leans on the other.

## *RAVELSTEIN*

The magisterial Abe Ravelstein, modeled on Allan Bloom, Bellow's friend and long-time colleague at the University of Chicago's Committee on Social Thought, is a world-class intellectual with a wide network of former students and a man who never stopped thinking about the condition of his soul. Bellow has always been fatally attracted to the type, especially if (as is the case with Ravelstein) he also has enough hard cash to indulge his outrageously expensive tastes and to stay (often for extended periods) in the finest hotels Paris can offer.

Bellow tries hard to separate the lines between Ravelstein, his fictional character, and the real Allan Bloom, but those who have read Bellow's remarks at Bloom's funeral know better. There, he said this: "What I was seeing, as I well knew, was the avidity for life particularly keen in him.... On a lesser level this avidity was apparent also in the delight he took in acquiring Persian carpets, Chinese chests, Hermès porcelain, Ultimo cashmere coats, and Mercedes-Benzes. In general, his attitude toward money was that it was something to be thrown away, scattered from the rear platform of luxury trains."

Many of the same examples of wealth and turns of phrase find their way into *Ravelstein*. No doubt some will take Bellow to task for writing a book that lets Ravelstein-Bloom off the hook too easily, but such people have been dogging Bellow's heels ever since he wrote the introduction to *The Closing of the American Mind* (1987), a surprising best-seller given the book's difficult, no-holds-barred arguments about higher education and American culture. To say a few kind words about Bloom—even if they are balanced by a realistic assessment of his foibles and eccentric folly—is to risk the censure of those who are quite willing to write both Bellow and Bloom off as pinch-faced conservatives.

But Ravelstein (or Bloom, if you prefer) is not reducible to a simple, formulated phrase—and that is where the continuing strength of Bellow's style comes in. In old age he can still write rings around most of the younger competition. Which contemporary American novelist, one wonders, could write lines as tightly packed with ideas and their consequences as these: "[Ravelstein was going to give his students] a higher life, full of variety and diversity, governed by rationality—anything but the arid kind. If they were lucky, if they were bright and willing, Ravelstein would give them the greatest gift they could hope to receive and lead them through Plato, introduce them to the esoteric secrets of Maimonides, teach them the correct interpretation of Machiavelli, acquaint them with the higher humanity of Shakespeare—up to and beyond Nietzsche. It wasn't an academic program that he offered—it was more freewheeling than that." Chick's narrative crackles with sharp observations and memorably turned sentences. Bellow is nearly at the top of his game—this, surprisingly, wonderfully, as death and the Death Question press ever more urgently. *Ravelstein* gives him the opportunity to reflect not only about Allan Bloom's death and about the true nature of male friendship but also about the life-threatening *cigua* toxin he got from eating poisoned fish during a Caribbean vacation. Like "Papa" Hemingway after his two plane crashes in Africa, Bellow was written off, prematurely, as a goner.

The extraordinary thing about Saul Bellow is that cultures high and low have always managed to coexist in his fictional worlds (Ravelstein, the deep thinker, loves vaudeville patter, Michael Jordan, and Mel Brooks movies) and that he remains possibly the only contemporary American novelist not ashamed to use the word "soul." All this and much, much more is compressed into the biographical portrait of Ravelstein that Chick had, ostensibly with reluctance, agreed to write. *Ravelstein* is that biographical sketch. In outlining how the chain-smoking Ravelstein looked in his sleek Japanese kimono or what he thought about Athens and Jerusalem—for him, the twin towers of our civilization—Chick (and Bellow) tell us what life means, or can mean, in our new century.

Taken as a whole, Saul Bellow's long career at the writing desk speaks to his imperfect, vulnerable characters seeking, as best they can, to fuse head, heart, and soul amid the corruptions of contemporary American life. Their struggles are a reflection of our time, and of us.

[*See also* Jewish-American Fiction.]

## SELECTED WORKS

*Dangling Man* (1944)
*The Victim* (1947)
*The Adventures of Augie March* (1953)
*Seize the Day, with Three Short Stories and a One-Act Play* (1956)
*Henderson the Rain King* (1959)
*Herzog* (1964)
*Mosby's Memoirs, and Other Stories* (1968)
*Mr. Sammler's Planet* (1970)
*Humboldt's Gift* (1975)
*To Jerusalem and Back: A Personal Account* (1976)
*The Dean's December* (1982)
*Him with His Foot in His Mouth, and Other Stories* (1984)
*More Die of Heartbreak* (1987)
*The Bellarosa Connection* (1989)
*A Theft* (1989)
*Something to Remember Me By: Three Stories* (1991)
*It All Adds Up: From the Dim Past to the Uncertain Future* (1994)
*The Actual* (1997)
*Ravelstein* (2000)
*Collected Stories* (2001)

## FURTHER READING

Atlas, James. *Bellow: A Biography*. New York, 2000.

Bloom, Harold, ed. *Saul Bellow*. New York, 1986.

Bradbury, Malcolm. *Saul Bellow*. New York, 1982.

Braham, Jeanne. *A Sort of Columbus: The American Voyages of Saul Bellow's Fiction*. Athens, Ga., 1984.

Clayton, John Jacob. *Saul Bellow: In Defense of Man*. 2d ed. Bloomington, Ind., 1979.

Cohen, Sarah B. *Saul Bellow's Enigmatic Laughter*. Urbana, Ill., 1974.

Cronin, Gloria L., and Ben Siegel, eds. *Conversations with Saul Bellow*. Jackson, Miss., 1994.

Dutton, Robert R. *Saul Bellow*. Rev. ed. Boston, 1982.

Goldman, L. H. *Saul Bellow's Moral Vision: A Critical Study of the Jewish Experience*. New York, 1983.

Tanner, Tony. *Saul Bellow*. London, 1965.

Trachtenberg, Stanley, ed. *Critical Essays on Saul Bellow*. Boston, 1979.

# STEPHEN VINCENT BENÉT

*by Paul Johnston*

Stephen Vincent Benét is remembered primarily for two works: the long narrative poem *John Brown's Body* and the short story "The Devil and Daniel Webster." These two works are characterized by qualities that can be found in varying degrees in Benét's less familiar work: formal craftsmanship combined seamlessly with an easy, informal diction; a love of America that is not blind to America's shortcomings; a liberal view of both political and domestic relationships; and a commitment to the progress of humanity.

Stephen Vincent was born in Bethlehem, Pennsylvania, on 22 July 1898, the third child of Frances Neill (Rose) and James Walker Benét. Both his older brother, William Rose, and their older sister, Laura, also became writers. Benét attributed the family's strong interest in poetry to his father, an amateur poet much interested in craft. James Walker Benét was a military officer by profession, as was James's father, and Benét's sense of service to his country can be attributed to his father's influence. He completed his first book of poetry when he was just seventeen. By the time he died at the age of forty-five, he had published the Pulitzer Prize–winning *John Brown's Body*, seven volumes of shorter verse, five novels, two short story collections, and a popular history of the United States, as well as radio scripts and pamphlets written to rally Americans and the world to the American cause in World War II. After his death, portions of a second long narrative poem on American themes, *Western Star*, were published from his extant manuscripts, and brought him a second Pulitzer Prize.

## POETRY

In 1926 Benét was awarded a Guggenheim Fellowship, which allowed him to live with his young family in Paris for two years and write *John Brown's Body*. At the time

Stephen Vincent Benét.
(© *Bettmann/Corbis*)

he had already published four volumes of poetry and four novels, supporting himself in part by writing short stories for popular magazines. Little that he had written up to that point indicated the phenomenal success that was to come with *John Brown's Body* (1928). Benét was not particularly gifted as a novelist, and though his chief aspiration was to be remembered as a poet, much of his poetry had been more earnest than successful. His greatest success had come with a handful of narrative ballads primarily on popular American themes, most notably "The Mountain Whippoorwill." The story of the boy who gives his all and emerges triumphant in a contest with the great fiddlers of the Georgia hills, climaxing with the exclamation "Hell's broke loose in Georgia!" quickly became a part of American folklore.

*John Brown's Body*, a narrative of the American Civil War, develops this American voice, embracing North and South, wealthy and poor, farmer and dandy, black and white, general and private. Its story interweaves fictional characters with historical figures of the Civil War. The moral evil of slavery is presented in the prelude, a vignette aboard a Yankee slave ship, but the poem that follows, in eight books and over eleven thousand lines, is not a melodrama of good and evil but a complex study of courage and weakness, characterized more often by failure than by triumph. If human progress prevails in the end, symbolized by the two marriages that follow the death and destruction of the war, it comes at a cost in individual aspirations and lives that evokes the reader's sympathies.

The struggle to maintain human values in the face of the forces of destruction informs the best of Benét's lesser-known poetry. As the United States moved through financial depression toward World War II, Benét wrote a series of nightmare poems that came to focus on the title image of his last collection of poems, *Burning City* (1936), evoked in "Litany for Dictatorships," which opens with the lines: "For all those beaten, for the broken heads, / For the fosterless, the simple, the oppressed, / The ghosts in the burning city of our time...." Yet Benét retained his belief in the ultimate triumph of progress embodied in American liberal populism, called forth in his poem on the reelection of Franklin Roosevelt, "Tuesday, November 5th, 1940" (1941), which concludes: "A country squire from Hyde Park with a Harvard accent, / Who never once failed the people / And whom the people won't fail."

## FICTION

Although Benét desired to be remembered as a poet, he wrote short stories from the time he completed his master's degree at Yale for the income they provided. The market for magazine fiction in the 1920s and even the 1930s was lucrative for someone who could write the expected formulas—which Benét could do with ease, though he considered the stories he produced vapid. "The Devil and Daniel Webster" was as much a revelation for Benét himself as for the reading public when it appeared in 1936, as it established that Benét could make money writing stories reflecting his true ability. The three dozen stories he wrote between 1936 and the coming of World War II, together with half a dozen of the best of his earlier stories, constitute a diverse body of work more successful than his poetry, *John Brown's Body* excepted.

"The Devil and Daniel Webster," like "The Mountain Whippoorwill," is a local color story, capturing the essence of a region, in this case New Hampshire, through a well-crafted story told in colloquial language. But Benét is thinking as well of the United States—what Daniel Webster in the story calls "the Union"—as a whole. In Daniel Webster, Benét finds a character representative of his own complex American feeling. Webster is shrewd, strong, generous, eloquent, good-humored, and down-to-earth. Yet he is also flawed; his career ends not in triumph but in compromise, as he makes his last important speech as a senator defending the Missouri Compromise, which would allow the extension of slavery into new states of the Union. Jabez Stone, who has sold his soul to the devil, is a smaller man and not really admirable—though not really evil either—yet a man and an American nevertheless. The jury that gathers to try him are likewise Americans, though traitors and criminals. Even the devil declares himself to be as American as any, pointing to the injustices done in the name of America to the Indians and the enslaved. In all this motley crew, however, there is something

worth defending and preserving. Benét's own ironic good humor, intelligence, and generosity prevail in the end, as Stone is rescued and the devil acknowledges that, in spite of all that threatens it, including its own worst tendencies, the Union will be preserved.

Benét's short stories vary widely in time, place, and kind, from historical fictions such as "The Devil and Daniel Webster" to contemporary stories of Manhattan socialites to fantasies of the future. They differ widely in tone as well, from the whimsical to the serious. "Into Egypt," published in 1939, shows Benét's awareness of what was happening to the Jews of Europe, while "The Blood of the Martyrs" anticipates the fate of intellectuals in dictatorial regimes around the world in the latter half of the twentieth century. "All around the Town" celebrates the working men and women who built Manhattan, while "The King of the Cats" celebrates the yielding of white American culture to the global multiracial culture that was already transforming Manhattan in the 1920s. In keeping with his nightmare poems is "By the Waters of Babylon," written in 1937, perhaps the first story to imagine a postapocalyptic Manhattan. On a more personal level, "A Death in the Country" focuses on the difficulties of marriage. "The Die-hard" explores both the social and the personal, combining a story of the dangers of political obsession with a story of the need for fathers in the imaginative lives of children.

## DEMOCRATIC PROPAGANDA

For Benét, as for Thomas Paine, the cause of America was the cause of all mankind. With the coming of World War II, Benét set aside all other work to devote himself to the American cause. *America* (1944), a history of the United States written at the suggestion of the War Department, was distributed around the world. Broadcasts of his radio plays—"Dear Adolf," "Listen to the People," "We Stand United," "The Watchers by the Stone"—were listened to by Americans across the country. Pamphlets and public statements written on behalf of various patriotic organizations declared Benét's belief in liberal democracy, "unalterably opposed to class hatred, race hatred, religious hatred, however manifested, by whomever instilled." Not just the United States, but its best ideals, must prevail.

Benét accepted no payment for this work, though he gave it his all. He suffered a heart attack while writing *America*, and though he seemed to recover, he suffered a second attack while working on yet another radio script. He died 13 March 1943. His second Pulitzer Prize, for the unfinished "Western Star," was a recognition not of the merits of that work so much as of his work on behalf of his country and his fellow man.

## WORKS

### POEMS

*Five Men and Pompey: A Series of Dramatic Portraits* (1915)
*Young Adventure* (1918)
*Heavens and Earth* (1920)
*Tiger Joy* (1925)
*John Brown's Body* (1928)
*Ballads and Poems 1915–1930* (1931)
*A Book of Americans* (1933)
*Burning City* (1936)
"Western Star" (1943)

### NOVELS

*The Beginning of Wisdom* (1921)
*Young People's Pride* (1922)
*Jean Huguenot* (1923)
*Spanish Bayonet* (1926)
*James Shore's Daughter* (1934)

### SHORT STORIES

"The Devil and Daniel Webster" (1937)
"Thirteen O'Clock" (1937)
"Tales before Midnight" (1939)
*Twenty-five Short Stories* (1943)
"The Last Circle" (1946)
*Selected Letters of Stephen Vincent Benét* (1960)

### MISCELLANEOUS

"The Magic of Poetry and the Poet's Art." In *Compton's Pictured Encyclopedia*, vol. 11 (1936)
*The Headless Horseman* (libretto, 1937)
*The Devil and Daniel Webster* (libretto, 1939)
"My Most Unforgettable Character." *Reader's Digest* 37 (October 1940): 113–116.
*A Summons to the Free* (1941)
"Daniel Webster." In *There Were Giants in the Land* (1942)
*Selected Works of Stephen Vincent Benét* (1942)
"A Creed for Americans." In *The Democratic Tradition in America* (1943)
*America* (1944)
*We Stand United and Other Radio Scripts* (1945)
*Stephen Vincent Benét on Writing* (1964)

## FURTHER READING

Bacon, Leonard, et al. "As We Remember Him." *Saturday Review of Literature* (27 March 1943): 5–7, 14. Reminiscences by fourteen contemporaries, including Archibald MacLeish, Muriel Rukeyser, and Thornton Wilder.

Benét, Laura. *When William Rose, Stephen Vincent and I Were Young.* New York, 1976.

Benét, William Rose, and John Farrar. *Stephen Vincent Benét.* New York, 1943. Includes a bibliography.

Fenton, Charles A. *Stephen Vincent Benét: The Life and Times of an American Man of Letters, 1898–1943.* New Haven, Conn., 1958.

Moffet, Judith. "Stephen Vincent Benét: An Appreciation on the Centenary of His Birth." *American Poet* (Fall 1998): 30–33.

Stroud, Parry. *Stephen Vincent Benét.* New York, 1962.

# WENDELL BERRY

*by Aaron K. DiFranco*

One of the most versatile contemporary authors, Wendell Berry is renowned for his prolific output of poetry, fiction, and essays. The quality of his craft is even more impressive considering his lifelong dedication to the land-based values and practices learned in the rural valleys of Kentucky. Grounded in the realities of running a small farm increasingly under threat from America's urban-centered industrial society, his work recalls that of the southern Agrarians for the way it promotes the traditional values of agricultural communities. Although all his work is infused with a sense of historical continuation, it also shuns the

Wendell Berry. (*Photograph courtesy of Wendell Berry*)

sentimentally nostalgic as well as the unthinkingly "innovative," preferring instead tested methods of stewardship that help promote an ethical relationship to the land, the community, the family, and the self. His vocal advocacy for the environment from an agricultural standpoint has paralleled Gary Snyder's more wilderness-oriented position. Frequently compared to Henry David Thoreau for his retreat to and promotion of a life lived in effective balance with the land, Berry's firm dedication to *place* has enabled him to refine his skills as farmer, husband, and writer.

## AGRARIAN ETHICS AND REINHABITATION

Wendell Erdman Berry was born on 5 August 1934 in the town of Newcastle, Henry County, Kentucky. His ancestors had settled in Henry County over a century earlier, and Berry grew up on his family's farm. He attended the University of Kentucky, receiving a B.A. in English in 1956 and his M.A. the following year. In 1957 he also married Tanya Amyx, beginning a lifelong commitment to family and home, and the couple remained briefly in Kentucky while Berry taught for a year at Georgetown College. They then moved to California in 1958, when Berry received a Wallace Stegner Fellowship

from the writing program at Stanford University. Stegner himself would become a good friend to Berry, and much of Berry's clear, powerful writing shows the influence of his mentor. But Berry surely established his own voice, rooted in the rhythms and diction of his home region. His first book, *Nathan Coulter* (1960), a coming-of-age story set against the struggles of a Kentucky farming town, was finished while Berry taught for a year in Stanford's Department of English.

In 1961, Berry traveled to Europe for a year on a Guggenheim fellowship. Afterward, he joined the faculty at New York University's English Department. His first two books of poetry appeared in 1964: *November Twenty Six, Nineteen Hundred Sixty Three* and *The Broken Ground*. The first—a slender edition of a single poem first published in *The Nation* (21 December 1963)—is a stirring elegy for President John F. Kennedy and brought Berry immediate public attention. The second volume introduces what have become recognizable themes throughout his oeuvre. An attention to the cycles of nature, family, and community displayed in his crafted verse is intensified by sharp knowledge of the politics and science of agriculture, a strong personal reverence for the created world, and a sense of social history. Like other poetry of the era, his poems probe emotional and psychological dimensions of a persona caught within an astonishing but unstable world, but Berry also demonstrated a formal clarity more reminiscent of Robert Frost than of his more radical contemporaries.

Berry left New York in 1964 and returned to Kentucky after being invited to join the English Department at the University of Kentucky in Lexington. The following year, Tanya and he made the homecoming complete by purchasing a twelve-acre farm in Henry County. Located in the town of Port Royal along the Kentucky River,

Lanes Landing Farm was intended as a second home; it became not only the family's primary residence but also their vocation. Here the couple raised their two children, Mary Dee and Pryor (Den) Clifford, while working to build a place for themselves. Dedicated to the traditional agrarian culture that evolved in that region, Berry has championed small-scale, local farming while critiquing damaging agribusiness practices and America's commercial industrialism.

The next decade marked a period of increasingly abundant publication while Berry continued to work on his farm and teach at the university. A succession of poetry volumes not only demonstrated his continued mastery of line and concern with artistic representation but also became more concretely grounded in his efforts to build a home. *Openings* (1968) and *Findings* (1969) both trace the concerns and desires that drove Berry to return to his rural Kentucky values. Many of his plainspoken accounts embrace the dark and bright mysteries of his native region, but the poems also demonstrate sophisticated attention to language. His "Window Poems" especially are meditative yet playful, implicating the poetic seer in the vision of the world beyond his window. The workings of the larger world are present as well: criticism of the war in Vietnam, and the economic and industrial drives behind it, resonates with the era's countercultural tendencies. With *Farming: A Handbook* (1970), Berry introduces the persona of the Mad Farmer, whose cunning madness grounds him in the knowledge of the workings of nature and satirizes institutional conformity. *The Country of Marriage* (1973) emphasizes Berry's valuation of marriage as a model of commitment to the land, the community, and the universe, although the relationship can be just as bawdy and difficult as it is sacramental.

The earlier essays of this period tend toward personal reminiscences, but they are always attuned to larger social and political issues. Where *The Hidden Wound* (1970) explores how the history of slavery and racism mix with his heritage, *The Long-Legged House* (1969) addresses more public, timely concerns, such as Vietnam and transformations to the environment via strip mining. The essays of *A Continuous Harmony* (1972) take up his poetry's marriage and agricultural themes in their observations of American cultural transformation. Despite his call for revolutionary change to American systems, his continued emphasis on a holistic society, his promotion of marriage, and his Christian disposition have led some to criticize his acceptance of "traditional" Western conventions. Conscious and self-critical, Berry explores how his practices implicate him in the world while he works toward an ideal of atonement.

Appointed a professor of English in 1973, Berry remained at the University of Kentucky only until 1977. Wary of institutional obligations and determined to dedicate more time to writing about agriculture, he became a contributing editor for Rodale Press, providing practical pieces for *New Farm Magazine* and *Organic Gardening and Farming* over the next four years while improving his homestead. With Wes Jackson, founder of the Land Institute of Salina, and Bruce Colman, he helped edit a collection of essays on farming called *Meeting the Expectations of the Land* (1984).

## WRITING, COMMUNITY, AND BELIEF

The same year he resigned from the university, Berry's next volume of nonfiction was published by Sierra Club Books. *The Unsettling of America* (1977) continues his analysis of the country's culture and agriculture begun in *A Continuous Harmony*. Here he recounts Thomas Jefferson's agrarian ideals as a lens for considering contemporary society's ecological mistreatment of the land. One of the harshest critiques of Western culture's deterioration due to its reliance on industrial agriculture, the text argues that such a reliance has lead to parallel disunities within the self, the family, the community, and the earth. Erudite, challenging, and historically grounded, he nonetheless scrutinizes his own positions, knowing the real difficulties of trying to live a life of principle. *The Gift of Good Land* (1981) intensifies his call for individual and communal stewardship of the land. During this period, two well-received volumes of new poetry also appeared: *Clearing* (1977) and *The Wheel* (1982). Several volumes that explore the problems and possibilities of cultural change followed. *Standing by Words* (1983) not only provides a framework for Berry's own poetic practice, but also critiques academics and society as a whole for not paying more attention to the way language allows individuals to participate fully with other people and the world. The impact of this participation on the physical and social environment is taken up in *Home Economics: Fourteen Essays* (1987) and *What Are People For?* (1990). Although committed to the processes of nature, Berry recognizes that human communities develop their own manners in response to local conditions. His charge, therefore, is not just for modes of living that are closely integrated into these processes. In stressing the interdependence of humanity with the rest of nature, Berry also demonstrates the responsibility citizens have for taking care of both nature and culture, thereby extending the notion of a land ethic as posed by Aldo Leopold.

Berry's commitment to his home region shows through even in his fiction. Often compared to William Faulkner's Yoknapatawpha County, Berry's Port William is a fictional town that serves as a grounding locale throughout his novels and stories. Reminiscent of his own home of Port Royal, Port William is less a setting for the characters to perform in than a character in itself. His second novel, *A Place on Earth* (1967), develops this idea by exploring how the members of the town participate in the seasons of loss and renewal affecting the town. Set against the backdrop of World War II, the book demonstrates how individual action determines one's location, and how that location changes in response to the characters' perceptions as well as to the motions of natural and human history. History is also a particular concern in *The Memory of Old Jack* (1974), which traces the extensive memory of its protagonist through a century of social transformations affecting the region. But Berry's fiction remains full of sensitive, rounded personalities who must confront essential human desires and basic needs. *Remembering* (1988), more formally experimental, follows the crisis of Andy Catlett as he tries to deal with the loss of his hand from a farming accident as well as with the discontinuities between the expectations of modern agribusiness and Port William's rural heritage. Several story collections, including *The Wild Birds* (1986) and *Fidelity* (1992), increase the populace of the town as well as expand Berry's narrative range. Bawdy, tender, tragic, and considered, the stories play out the idiosyncrasies and beliefs of a town working through their place in the present and redefining how to belong together in that place.

Berry returned to teaching at the University of Kentucky in 1987. This time, however, he shunned institutional course offerings, designing classes that emphasized the fundamental skills of reading and writing in academically unconventional contexts. A new book of poetry, *Sabbaths*, appeared that same year to wide acclaim. Comprising poems written by Berry after taking meditative walks each Sunday morning, the volume is rich with close observation of the world and patient rumination. Religious in tone but never dogmatic, these small sermons console and brace as they connect spiritual needs with the natural environment. This and a second volume were collected into *A Timbered Choir: The Sabbath Poems 1979–1997* (1998), a moving sequence demonstrating Berry's dedication to his poetic craft as well as to a hallowed earth.

Berry has added to the saga of Port William with several books, including *A World Lost* (1996), *Two More Stories of the Port William Membership* (1997), and Jayber Crow (2000), all of which chronicle the manners and mores of a slowly disappearing Kentucky lifestyle. Numerous essay collections have also appeared, with Berry's attention turning increasingly toward national and global concerns. While *Sex, Economy, Freedom, and Community* (1992) broadly announces its topics, broader ecological concerns direct his attention in *Another Turn of the Crank* (1995). Besides promoting the preservation of resources, the book addresses the effect of increasing globalization on the economic and environmental health of the country. In *Life Is a Miracle: An Essay against Modern Superstition* (2000), Berry cogently defends the functions of art and religion, especially their ability to express the mysteries of nature and experience that rational science still cannot address.

Berry's visionary social criticism complements his visionary literary imagination, both of which contain moments of prophecy and of moralizing. These are directed by a sense of responsibility to the community he lives in and a need to preserve its collective memory for the future. Numerous other works of every genre have been published, many of which are slender editions that Berry produced in support of smaller presses. Berry continues to write and work the farm he shares with Tanya. Their organic farm has grown to more than 100 acres, and they continue to cultivate food and raise livestock to sustain their family.

[*See also* Nature Writing: Poetry *and* Nature Writing: Prose.]

## SELECTED WORKS

*Nathan Coulter* (1960)
*November Twenty Six, Nineteen Hundred Sixty Three* (1964)
*The Broken Ground* (1964)
*A Place on Earth* (1967)
*Openings: Poems* (1968)
*The Rise* (1968)
*Findings* (1969)
*The Long-Legged House* (1969)
*Farming: A Handbook* (1970)
*The Hidden Wound* (1970)
*The Unforeseen Wilderness: An Essay on Kentucky's Red River Gorge* (1971)
*A Continuous Harmony: Essays Cultural and Agricultural* (1972)
*The Country of Marriage* (1973)
*An Eastward Look* (1974)
*The Memory of Old Jack* (1974)
*Horses* (1975)
*Sayings and Doings* (1975)

*To What Listens* (1975)

*The Kentucky River: Two Poems* (1976)

*There Is Singing around Me* (1976)

*Clearing* (1977)

*Three Memorial Poems* (1977)

*The Unsettling of America: Culture and Agriculture* (1977)

*The Gift of Gravity* (1979)

*A Part* (1980)

*The Gift of Good Land: Further Essays Cultural and Agricultural* (1981)

*Recollected Essays, 1965–1980* (1981)

*The Wheel* (1982)

*Standing by Words* (1983)

*Meeting the Expectations of the Land: Essays in Sustainable Agriculture and Stewardship* (1984)

*Collected Poems: 1957–1982* (1985)

*The Wild Birds: Six Stories of the Port William Membership* (1986)

*Home Economics: Fourteen Essays* (1987)

*The Landscape of Harmony: Two Essays on Wildness and Community* (1987)

*Sabbaths* (1987)

*Remembering* (1988)

*Traveling at Home* (1988)

*The Work of Local Culture* (1988)

*What Are People For?* (1990)

*Harlan Hubbard: Life and Work* (1990)

*The Discovery of Kentucky* (1991)

*Standing on Earth: Selected Essays* (1991)

*Fidelity: Five Stories* (1992)

*Sex, Economy, Freedom, and Community* (1992)

*Entries: Poems 1994* (1994)

*Watch with Me and Six Other Stories of the Yet-Remembered Ptolemy Proudfoot and His Wife, Miss Minnie, Née Quinch* (1994)

*Another Turn of the Crank* (1995)

*A World Lost* (1996)

*A Timbered Choir: The Sabbath Poems 1979–1997* (1998)

*The Selected Poems of Wendell Berry* (1998)

*Jayber Crow* (2000)

*Life Is a Miracle: An Essay against Modern Superstition* (2000)

*Three Short Novels: Nathan Coulter, Remembering, A World Lost* (2002)

## FURTHER READING

Angyal, Andrew J. *Wendell Berry*. New York, 1995. A lucid introduction to the author.

Goodrich, Janet. *The Unseen Self in the Work of Wendell Berry*. Columbia, Mo., 2001. Examines Berry's oeuvre as a mode of autobiography.

Merchant, Paul, ed. *Wendell Berry. Confluence American Author Series*. Lewiston, Idaho, 1991. A substantial collection of criticism and testimony, it also includes an extensive selected bibliography of journal articles.

Quetchenbach, Bernard W. *Back from the Far Field: American Nature Poetry and the Late Twentieth Century*. Charlottesville, N.C., 2000. Traces the way a number of nature poets—including Berry—pursue a social advocacy role for nature through their poems.

Scigaj, Leonard. *Sustainable Poetry: Four American Ecopoets*. Lexington, Ky., 1999. An academic text, this study attempts to theoretically place Berry "ecocritically" with close readings of his poetry.

Slovic, Scott. *Seeking Awareness in American Nature Writing: Henry Thoreau, Annie Dillard, Edward Abbey, Wendell Berry, Barry Lopez*. Salt Lake City, Utah, 1992. Places Berry in a tradition of nonfiction nature writers.

Weiland, Steven. "Wendell Berry Resettles America: Fidelity, Education, and Culture." In *Earthly Words: Essays on Contemporary American Nature and Environmental Writers*, edited by John Cooley. Ann Arbor, Mich., 1997. A good introduction to several of Berry's main themes.

Wirzba, Norman, ed. *The Art of the Commonplace: The Agrarian Essays of Wendell Berry*. Washington, D.C., 2002.

# JOHN BERRYMAN

*by Philip Hobsbaum*

John Berryman was born John Allyn Smith Jr. on 25 October 1914 in McAlester, Oklahoma. He was named after his father, a bank clerk. His mother was Martha Little Smith, and both parents were Roman Catholics. His father, dismissed from his bank for nonattendance, became a game warden, then bought a restaurant in Tampa, Florida. The family lived in a tenement owned by John Angus Berryman. There is little doubt that Martha Smith began an affair with their landlord. Early on the morning of 26 June 1926, her husband was found shot dead at the rear of the tenement. It is generally held that he committed suicide.

John Berryman, from *Collected Poems: 1937–1971*. (*Photograph by Tom Berthiaume. Courtesy of Farrar, Straus and Giroux*)

### SEED TIME

Within nine weeks of Smith's death, his widow married John Angus Berryman, and the young John and his brother, Robert, five years his junior, took their stepfather's name. The family moved to New York and in 1928 John entered South Kent School, Connecticut, where he was bullied, and he attempted suicide in 1931. Nevertheless, he made academic progress, and in 1932 he entered Columbia University. Here, Berryman came alive to the possibilities of writing poetry, inspired by Mark Van Doren's teaching of Shakespeare, by the literary criticism of R. P. Blackmur, and by his own reading of W. H. Auden. Several of his poems were accepted by the *Columbia Review* and by *The Nation*, and he was encouraged further by winning the Mariana Griswold van Rensselaer Prize. Berryman went on to win the Euretta J. Kellett scholarship, by means of which he was enabled to study at Clare College, Cambridge, where his supervisor was George Rylands, celebrated as a director of plays at the Marlowe Society.

It was Cambridge—where he met and conversed with Auden—that provided the key stimulus to his early work.

The Audenesque "Meditation" (1937) dates from this period. Berryman always retained the happiest memories of Cambridge, where he won the highly competitive Charles Oldham Shakespeare Scholarship and met his fiancée, the actress Rosalie Crutchley, whom he called "Beatrice."

### FIRST MARRIAGE AND *THE DISPOSSESSED*

Berryman returned to the United States, where he was appointed as an instructor, first at Wayne State University in Detroit, then, on a temporary contract, at Harvard. After his tempestuous engagement to "Beatrice" was broken off, in 1942 he married Eileen Mulligan, a clerk whom he had encountered the year before at a party. Berryman became part-time poetry editor of *The Nation*, met Delmore Schwartz—who was to become a lifelong friend—through the *Partisan Review*, and was included in a project organized by James Laughlin. This came out as *Five Young American Poets* (1940), comprising Randall Jarrell, W. R. Moses, George Marion O'Donnell, and Mary Barnard, as well as Berryman. Twenty of Berryman's poems were published, including "Meditation" and "Night and the City."

A volume of his work appeared as *Poems* (1942), another of James Laughlin's projects. This contained "The Statue," which became something of an anthology piece. The formality of its verse leads one to expect even more by way of a rhyme scheme than is provided, suggesting that Berryman's style had not developed yet. Nevertheless, that poem went on to appear in *The Dispossessed* (1948), a troubled collection for which Berryman wrote three pieces at the last minute: "Fare Well," "Narcissus Moving," and "The Dispossessed." This last seems to be a parallel between a play and the poet's life. It gave the volume, hitherto called "Traditional Poems," its title.

That volume was published by William Sloane Associates. While suffering anxiety about its reception—which was to include adverse reviews by Yvor Winters and Randall Jarrell—Berryman safeguarded his self-confidence by penning the first stanza of "Homage to Mistress Bradstreet," a long poem that was to occupy him for the next five years.

## BERRYMAN'S SONNETS

In 1946, Berryman had secured a position at Princeton University through R. P. Blackmur to teach creative writing. During 1947 he fell in love with the wife of a neighbor. He called her "Lise" but her real name seems to have been "Chris"—surname unknown. This period saw the composition of a sequence eventually published as *Berryman's Sonnets* (1967). These are all in the difficult Petrarchan form that demands a plenitude of rhymes. They are allusive—to the Bible, Petrarch, Sidney, Balzac, among others—and keep up a peculiar tone throughout. It is not so much that of a man in love, as of one intensely scrutinizing some ever-fascinating entity that he seems almost to have invented: "Once in the car (cave of our radical love) / Your darker hair I saw than golden hair / Above your thighs whiter than white-gold hair." This, and sonnets 10, 11, 13, 14, 19, 23, 77, and 103 are probably the best, together with the last, which finishes the affair: "my lady came not / in blue jeans and sweater."

*Homage to Mistress Bradstreet* (1956) may be seen as a successor to the "Lise" poems. Berryman was distracted by his teaching at Princeton, by a commission he had undertaken to write a book about Stephen Crane, which eventually appeared (in 1950), and an edition of *King Lear*, which did not. The emphasis on Freudian psychology that characterizes the former effort arises from the fact that, since the end of the affair with "Lise," Berryman had been drinking heavily and undergoing treatment at the hands of a series of psychiatrists. His appointment at Princeton had terminated, and he taught first at the University of Washington in Seattle, and then in 1952 as Elliston Professor of Poetry at the University of Cincinnati. In 1953 he split up with Eileen after a trip to Europe in which she had become incapacitated owing to an injury to her back. Once back in the United States, he accepted a job in Iowa from which he was dismissed in 1954 following a drunken altercation with his landlord that resulted in his arrest by the local police. Through Allen Tate, he became a lecturer at the University of Minnesota in 1955, and Minneapolis became his base for the sixteen years that remained of his life. However, it was in Cincinnati that most of *Mistress Bradstreet* was written.

## HOMAGE TO MISTRESS BRADSTREET

This work is in essence a reverie of Berryman's, interrupted by the voice of Anne Bradstreet, the first woman poet in America. She tells of her life and difficulties, but she is also opening out before the wooing of the poet. Anne Bradstreet was taken in 1630, when she was eighteen, to the then-primitive colony of Massachusetts with her father and her husband—whom she had married two years previously. Stanzas 1–4 of the poem are a kind of love elegy, spoken by Berryman in *propria persona*. Stanza 5 begins Part One of the poem, in which Anne describes her daily life in the colony. Berryman intervenes at stanza 12, line 5 to express surprise that Anne wrote her rhymes to please her father. In stanza 13, line 2 she replies, detailing the carnal lusts that still took hold of her and the smallpox that had ruined her looks, but she also states that this did not diminish the love her husband, Simon, bore her. In stanza 17 she fears that she is barren, but by stanza 21 she glories in childbirth. Her child, Samuel, grows to question her about death—"Then he takes us one by one"—all this, in the course of a religious revival in the community.

Part Two of the poem begins at stanza 25, line 4, with a dialogue between the poet and Anne. It is a love-duet over the centuries—the quotation here is altered in styling, to elucidate interpretation of this interchange:

| Berryman: | I miss you, Anne, |
| | day or night weak as a child, |
| | tender & empty, doomed, quick to no tryst. |
| Anne: | I hear you. Be kind, you who leaguer |
| | my image in the mist. |
| Berryman: | Be kind you, to one unchained eager far & wild |
| | and if, O my love, my heart is breaking, please |
| | neglect my cries and I will spare you. Deep in Time's grave, Love's, you lie still. |
| | Lie still. |
| Anne: | Now? That happy shape |
| | my forehead had under my most long, rare, ravendark, hidden, soft bodiless hair |
| | you award me still. |
| | You must not love me, but I do not bid you cease. |

There is tenderness in this passion for a woman long dead, and her delighted yet cautious response. There is Berryman's pleasure also in cuckolding, if only in imagination, the rigorous Simon, protégé and son-in-law of the wintry governor of Massachusetts. Berryman is, so to speak, showing this long-dead Puritan woman a glimpse of another world. He is also showing his mastery, as poet, over time and space.

Even so, the poet's voice fades out at the end of stanza 35, though the dialogue continues, with only Anne's voice speaking and Berryman silently listening—until stanza 39, line 4. At that point, Part Three begins, and the verse reverts to Anne's chronicling of the domestic life of the colony: converse with her daughter, Dorothy; death of her father; converse with her daughter Mercy; death of Dorothy; and in stanza 53, her own sickness and death. Then there is a coda, spoken by the poet in the vein of elegy, where he bids farewell to this phantom whom his art has summoned up—"whom my lost candle like the firefly loves."

## SECOND AND THIRD MARRIAGES

*Homage to Mistress Bradstreet* was published in 1956 to considerable applause. The *Partisan Review* awarded Berryman a Rockefeller Fellowship in Poetry and he was also awarded the Harriet Monroe poetry prize. Berryman met a Jewish girl, Ann Levine, a Bennington graduate much younger than himself. They married in the same year that *Mistress Bradstreet* was published and had a son, Paul, in 1957. However, Berryman depended more and more on his students for company, reciting his poems to all who would listen. He also drank a great deal. Thus, tensions arose between him and Ann, and they split up in 1959.

One of the many students with whom Berryman had affairs introduced him to a friend, Kate Donahue, and Kate and Berryman were married in 1961. She was only twenty-two and he was by then forty-seven. A series of minor breakdowns both preceded and followed the birth of their daughter Martha, in December 1962. Money problems pursued him. He had always done a certain amount of reviewing, and he worked hard on a set of essays including "Conrad's Journey" and "The Freedom of the Poet." These, together with penetrating studies of Elizabethan drama, were published posthumously in 1976 in volume form under the title *The Freedom of the Poet.*

## THE DREAM SONGS

From as far back as June 1955, Berryman had been writing short poems, the generic name of which came to him while he was teaching T. S. Eliot's *The Waste Land,* James Joyce's *Ulysses,* and Sigmund Freud's *Interpretation of Dreams.* He called these strangely biographical pieces *Dream Songs.* Berryman experienced trouble in sorting them out to form a coherent entity. He decided to publish an interim

volume, *77 Dream Songs* (1964), and was awarded the Russell Loines Award from the National Institute of Arts and Letters and the Pulitzer Prize in poetry. He was also given a Guggenheim Fellowship for the academic year 1966–1967, which he decided to spend with his wife and daughter in Dublin. There, he wrote more Dream Songs, and organized a selection that formed the volume *His Toy, His Dream, His Rest* (1968)—collected, together with the earlier pieces, in 1969. He won the National Book Award and shared the award of the Bollingen prize for Poetry with Karl Shapiro.

Berryman's Dream Songs thrust the actualities of a tortured life into our sensibilities. This is done by means of a persona, "Henry," who is patently the poet himself. The persona in question masquerades as a Negro minstrel; that is to say, a white man who has painted his face black for the purpose of entertaining the public. He is catechized throughout the Dream Songs—as used to happen in the singing troupe called the Kentucky Minstrels—by an interlocutor, who represents death. This interlocutor addresses Henry as "Mr. Bones."

A good many dead people are invoked, and there is a central block of Dream Songs concerned with the alcoholic poet Delmore Schwartz. Berryman, by now himself an alcoholic, is additionally obsessed with his father, who committed suicide:

> in a modesty of death I join my father
> who dared so long agone leave me.
> A bullet on a concrete stoop
> close by a smothering southern sea
> spreadeagled on an island, by my knee.
> —You is from hunger, Mr. Bones

(Dream Song 76)

The Dream Songs are a kind of modern equivalent to Shakespeare's sonnets. Each is in three parts, rather than the two of a sonnet, and is loosely related to the conceptual shape of the syllogism in logic. For example, in the Dream Song just cited, the first section states "Nothin' very bad happen to me lately," the second section—the one quoted—states "in a modesty of death I join my father," and the third, "I saw nobody coming, so I went instead." The whole amounts to an exposition of stasis.

With some exceptions, each section of these poems consists of six lines. The third and sixth lines tend to be shorter than the others. Quite often the first line of a Dream Song has a feminine ending; that is, the line ends on a heavy syllable followed by a light syllable, as in the word "lately."

As the Dream Songs proceed, Berryman engages in some astonishing feats of syntax. In an elegy for the much-feared critic, Randall Jarrell, he writes:

> Let Randall rest, whom your self-torturing
> cannot restore one instant's good to, rest:
> he's left us now.
> The panic died and in the panic's dying
> so did my old friend. I am headed west
> also, also, somehow
>
> (Dream Song 90)

The apparent contortion of that initial sentence may be straightened out if we omit the second "rest," which is there by way of emphasis, and alter the word-order to something like "Your self-torturing cannot restore one instant's good to Randall." However, in revising thus we are losing the intricate speech-rhythm and indeed what may be styled as the characteristic tone of Berryman, which is something like a confidential signaling for attention.

## DETERIORATION AND SUICIDE

The remainder of his work appears fragmented. *Love and Fame* (1970), largely in unrhymed quatrains, is a crude autobiography; it is interesting mostly in its quotations from other texts. *Delusions, Etc.* (1972) looks like poems that failed to get into the preceding volume. The novel *Recovery* (1973) is a clinical account of struggle from and lapse back into alcoholism. *Henry's Fate and Other Poems* (1977) looks like poems that failed to get into the *The Dream Songs*.

Berryman's ten years of marriage to Kate represent a decline, despite her ministrations, into an abyss. Their second daughter, Sara Rebecca, was born in June 1971. But he had deteriorated in inverse proportion to his growth in reputation. Here was a damaged personality somehow retrieving distinguished verse from its gradual disintegration. Berryman committed suicide on 7 January 1972 by jumping off the Washington Avenue Bridge in Minneapolis. He had already abandoned his novel, which somehow presaged, as its title suggests, recovery.

[*See also* Auden, W. H.; Confessional Poetry; Jarrell, Randall; Lowell, Robert, *and* Schwartz, Delmore.]

## SELECTED WORKS

*Poems* (1942)
*The Dispossessed* (1948)
*Stephen Crane* (1950)
*Homage to Mistress Bradstreet* (1956)
*77 Dream Songs* (1964)
*Berryman's Sonnets* (1967)
*His Toy, His Dream, His Rest: 308 Dream Songs* (1968)
*The Dream Songs* (1969)
*Love and Fame* (1970)
*Delusions, Etc.* (1972)
*Recovery* (1973)
*The Freedom of the Poet* (1976)
*Henry's Fate and Other Poems, 1967–1972* (1977)
*We Dream of Honour: John Berryman's Letters to His Mother* (1988)
*Collected Poems, 1937–1971* (1989)

## FURTHER READING

Alvarez, A. *The Savage God: A Study of Suicide*. New York, 1990. A readable account of suicide and literature (as distinct from suicide in literature).

Dodsworth, Martin, ed. *The Survival of Poetry: A Contemporary Survey*. London, 1970. Contains essays on John Berryman by Martin Dodsworth and on other contingent figures such as Robert Lowell (by Gabriel Pearson) and Sylvia Plath (by Barbara Hardy).

Haffenden, John. *John Berryman: A Critical Commentary*. New York, 1980. A thorough and searching discussion, especially useful concerning the Dream Songs.

Haffenden, John. *The Life of John Berryman*. Boston, 1982. A sympathetic and detailed biography.

Mariani, Paul L. *Dream Song: The Life of John Berryman*. 2d ed. New York, 1996. Contains more recent information than above.

Phillips, Robert S. *The Confessional Poets*. Carbondale, Ill., 1973. Puts Berryman, along with contingent writers, in context.

Simpson, Eileen B. *Poets in Their Youth: A Memoir*. New York, 1982. John Berryman's first wife writes evocatively about her former husband, about Delmore Schwartz, Randall Jarrell, Robert Lowell, and others.

# AMBROSE BIERCE

*by Molly McQuade*

Ambrose Bierce, an ironist whose choice of genre roved from predatorially sardonic verse to artfully detached war writing, was born Ambrose Gwinett Bierce on 24 June 1842, in the Ohio village of Horse Cave Creek. He was the tenth of thirteen children of Marcus Aurelius Bierce, a struggling Congregationalist farmer; Protestant evangelism helped to dictate the community's calendar. Bierce left his family's faith and their rural penury behind him as soon as he could, beginning work at age fifteen as a printer's devil for the antislavery *Northern Indianan* newspaper. And yet the barnyard did not forever leave the writer; in it Bierce may have found his origins as a literary mocker. For example, the biliously independent title character in Bierce's short story "Curried Cow" could be readily understood as the writer's alter ego.

Phoebe the cow is well known to kick at anything that moves, and at many things that don't. Not only that; the quality of her kicking is judged superb. Like the author, Phoebe is a high-minded herd rebel, unwilling to compromise and impossible to subdue on a permanent basis—a lone troublemaking purist whose original motives remain mysterious. She won't give milk, and is no longer expected to. But the cow is habitually curried with a comb by a farmhand, her owner's only regular effort to break Phoebe's spirit. To be curried as if she were a horse is thus a delicately debasing punishment. Dedicated readers of Bierce may recognize the currying as a subtly disguised metaphor for editing, that barbarism routinely inflicted on the indignant writer when he was a *San Francisco Examiner* columnist from 1887 to 1909, in the hire of William Randolph Hearst. Bierce, who would tender his resignation without delay or remorse whenever his copy was too much altered by another, became infamous for his editorial scruples. Yet

Ambrose Bierce.
(*Courtesy of the Library of Congress*)

the editors usually wanted him back, and on his return to the office, Bierce would take his revenge by submitting ever more incendiary columns. Similarly, Phoebe the bovine endures her momentary humiliation only to resume her treachery twofold.

As one hired hand after another is kicked by Phoebe while currying her and then quits, her owner, the widowed Aunt Patience, resolves to marry someone new who can put Phoebe in her place. She exchanges vows with the Reverend Berosus Huggins—spindly, drab, and grim of face. The Reverend, bidden to busy himself with routing farm weeds, also contrives a scheme for besting the cow: he dresses an iron pump in his own black Methodist garb, hoping the cow will believe the pump is himself, kick it, and suffer or die. After delivering the inevitable wallop to the steadfast iron instrument, Phoebe blacks out, visibly injured. Yet when approached weeks later by the guilt-stricken, peacemaking Aunt Patience, Phoebe kicks her harder than ever before, leaving Aunt Patience both upended and dumbfounded: her husband, "Huggy," has failed.

Composed, as Bierce's fiction often was, in a spare, compressed, and deceptively understated style, the story nonetheless strikes blows to a long-standing authorial foe, men of the cloth. The Reverend, "conspicuously unnatural and inhuman" (*The Stories and Fables of Ambrose Bierce*, 1977, p. 78), believes he is clever enough to overcome cattle with cheap tricks, but lives to rue that assumption. All too preoccupied by "my strife with Satan" (p. 79), he cannot pay the proper attention to Phoebe's "sinful traits" (p. 80), and so the battling cow's will and skill have their way. The art of kicking by beast (or writer) is proposed in "Curried Cow" as a lifetime's livelihood.

## BATTLING BIERCE

To that peculiar livelihood Bierce devoted himself only after enlisting in 1861 as a private in the Ninth Indiana Infantry Regiment and seeing battle, during four years of service, at Shiloh, Murfreesboro, Chickamauga, and Chattanooga, among other sites. In 1864 a bullet hit him in the head. While recovering, he went on furlough; sadly, his hometown sweetheart, Bernie Wright of Warsaw, Indiana, lost interest in Bierce once she saw he had been wounded. He returned to fighting, and was discharged in 1865 as a first lieutenant.

The Civil War gave Bierce a ferocious education that far surpassed his routine high-school learning in the Midwest and his brief experience studying, in 1859, at the Kentucky Military Institute. Some of his best fiction and essays later emerged from his memories of the four years he spent at war before even suspecting that he would become a writer. The war itself may have helped to refine in Bierce an accurate passion for offensive strategy, eventually aiding him not only as a satirist but also as an investigative journalist. Perhaps more important, his wartime encounters may have excised whatever potential he had as a sentimentalist. Bierce's essays about war are lucid, and then some: he describes with a scrupling fairness the moral surprises of warfare, while evoking the battleground landscape with an ironic serenity.

As a narrator of war, Bierce was never tendentious or melodramatic. His brief essay "On a Mountain," for example, recalls with a guilefully selfless voice the failure of Bierce's regiment to manage a successful reconnaissance mission against the Confederate army in the region of Cheat Mountain. As their regiment retreats, Bierce and his fellow soldiers come across some of their own fallen men, now being eaten by wild pigs. The soldiers kill the predators, but can do nothing for the prey, already dead from combat with the human enemy.

The achievement of the writing is tonal: rarely resorting to the first-person pronoun, and deliberately avoiding portrayal of his fellow soldiers as individuals, Bierce elegantly eschews any sentimentality and ironizes the bungling of the mission without stating directly that it was bungled. Likewise, he writes with unremitting realism to undermine any hope the patriotic soldiers may have held for their own military prowess. According to Bierce, who fought with them and does not exempt himself, they were more interested in savoring the beauty of pine cones and the unfamiliarly idyllic mountain woodland than they were in military action—"a mountain region was a perpetual miracle" (*A Sole Survivor*, 1998, p. 7).

For this reason and others, they failed in their effort at reconnaissance to overpower the enemy; instead, the enemy overpowered them, "so we parted from him in anger and returned to our own place, leaving our dead—not many" (p. 8). The regiment then proceeded to guard a mountain pass and enjoy themselves while "tracking bruin" (p. 9) (they fail, though, to bag any). Afterward, they embark on a "movement in force" (p. 9) on the enemy, but are rebuffed. Finally, in the essay's closing, they come upon their own dead being eaten by "a herd of galloping swine" (p. 10), and the soldiers begin to shoot the pigs. The anticlimax on which the essay ends receives no conspicuous commentary from Bierce. Rather, he implicitly asks the reader to consider the typically strange luck of soldiers: those in his regiment could neither conquer nor defend meaningfully.

Although Bierce's cool head allowed him to write with soaring self-effacement about wartime, Bierce the man and the moralist was anything but chilly by temperament. His celebrated short story "Chickamauga," for instance, follows a child of the South, "son of a poor planter" (*The Stories and Fables of Ambrose Bierce*, p. 8), as the six-year-old boy wanders uncomprehending through the outskirts of that famously grueling battle. When he glimpses a rabbit, the unnamed child is frightened, but when he discovers a corps of wounded soldiers, struggling to retreat, he misunderstands their suffering as comic circus antics: "To him it was a merry spectacle" (p. 11). Prankishly the small boy mounts and tries to ride a soldier who is crawling along on hands and knees, his jaw blown away. Finally realizing the man's misery, the child feels misery in turn. But as flashes of a distant conflagration illuminate the scene, he regains his composure and gallantly pretends to lead the ghoulish army as it desperately seeks a source of water. The army falls open-mouthed upon a creek; many are too weak to rise again, and drown there. Innocent, baffled, and amused at the sight, the child "danced with glee" (p. 15) until recognizing a nearby house, ruined by war, as his own. He sees the body of his mother, her brain "overflowing the temple" (p. 17) through a wound. And the child begins to shriek—he "was a deaf mute" (p. 17).

Paradoxically, Bierce's compassion allowed him to assume the distant narrative position necessary in "Chickamauga" for exposing with decisive clarity the improbable, incongruous carnage of the war. The unhearing and unspeaking child cannot fathom it; neither should we, if we are fortunately ignorant. Following the child as he learns, we learn from Bierce's immaculately discerning prose that emotion can be summoned by a stealthily neutral voice. The same voice can be heard in other stories based on the author's Civil War experiences, notably "A Horseman in the Sky" and "An Occurrence at Owl Creek Bridge."

## LEARNING TO WRITE

After Bierce was discharged, he worked as an agent for the U.S. Treasury Department, based in Selma, Alabama, locating and confiscating "enemy" Confederate cotton as federal property before it could be smuggled out by boat for illegal export. Bierce's role in Reconstruction led him to canvass deserted plantations for booty and also to befriend ex-Confederates: seemingly as incorruptible as he was unprejudiced, Bierce came to disapprove of American postbellum punishment of the South. In 1866, at the orders of the War Department, he left his work as an agent to help General William Hazen map and survey the West from Nebraska to California. When the Hazen party arrived in San Francisco, Bierce declined an army commission as second lieutenant, resigned from the surveying assignment, and took up a post as night watchman at the U.S. subtreasury in San Francisco. While guarding the U.S. Mint and getting to know a very lively new city, Bierce taught himself to write by reading the classics: Voltaire, Burke, Swift, Bacon, Plato, Mill, Coleridge, and others. By 1867 he was publishing poetry in local venues such as *The Californian*, and then essays, articles, and humor pieces in the *San Francisco News Letter and California Advertiser*, edited by two Englishmen, and in the *Overland Monthly*, edited by Bret Harte. In late 1868 he joined the *News Letter* staff as editor and began writing a satirical column, "The Town Crier," which became known and admired as far away as England. Bierce's first published short story, "The Haunted Valley," appeared in *Overland*'s July 1871 issue. On Christmas Day, 1871, he married a San Francisco heiress, Mary Ellen "Mollie" Day. Funded by his new father-in-law, he and his wife went to live in London in 1872.

As his first years in San Francisco suggest, Bierce's versatility as a writer and a journalist was established early in his career. Poetry, essays, articles, epigrams, and satire: throughout his life he chose them all. Yet Bierce regarded his poetry with misgivings, although he venerated the calling. As the scholar and critic Mary Elizabeth Grenander has observed in *Poems of Ambrose Bierce*, Bierce the versifier went to poetry to express emotion and awaken it in a reader without abandoning the effort to keep on thinking. His demanding expectations

may have fatigued his own writing of poems. Nevertheless, his abiding interest in diction as a literary issue may have originated in his reading and writing of poetry; even in his prose, Bierce's unusually fastidious choosiness about words, whether vernacular or literary in their register, helps to give paragraphs the unlikely polish of stanzas. Whether or not he failed to meet the high standards set historically by the best verse, poetry—and other poets—thus influenced all of Bierce's writing. Byron and Pope were among his favorites, and the swaggering precision of their rhyming satire left an impression on his poetry and his prose. Known to write occasionally "after" the slyly sneering Alexander Pope, he penned the following four-liner about Leland Stanford, the notoriously greedy and arrogant California railroad and mining magnate:

Here Leland Stanford lies, who thought it odd
That he should go to meet his God.
He looked, until his eyes grew dim,
For God to hasten to meet him.

(*Poems of Ambrose Bierce*, 1995, p. 113)

Such calculated concision and exacting wit would also come to serve the cause of Bierce's sardonic high kicks in prose works, such as his satirical *The Devil's Dictionary* (1906), where the word "once" was defined by the lone word "enough."

His three-year stay in England confirmed Bierce's sense of literary style and his zest for fearless mockery. Received well by his British colleagues, he contributed regularly to English magazines such as *Fun* and *Figaro*. He also published his first three books in England: *Nuggets and Dust* (1872), *The Fiend's Delight* (1873), and *Cobwebs from an Empty Skull* (1874). All were collections of essays; the first two gathered his old "Town Crier" columns, among other pieces. In addition, while in England, Bierce was contracted to write in their entirety the first two (and only) issues of a new magazine, *The Lantern*, sponsored by the exiled Empress Eugenie of France. *The Lantern* was devised by her as a means to defend herself from the threat of a Communard, Henri Rochefort, to publish in England a version of his periodical *La Lanterne*, which in France had regularly and humorously impugned the royal family. For this short-lived journal Bierce invented a new column for himself, dubbed "Prattle," and later transferred with great success to San Francisco. Of the *Lantern* experiment he would write in 1882, "I still think it a sufficient distinction to be probably the only American journalist who was ever employed by an Empress in so congenial a pursuit as the pursuit of another journalist" (*A Sole Survivor*, p. 128).

## BACK TO SAN FRANCISCO

When Bierce returned to San Francisco in 1875, he was the father of two sons and was expecting a third child. His wife preferred to see the third born on home ground, and Bierce's recurrent asthma had in any case bedeviled him in England, so the move back, though disappointing to him, was only practical. Regardless, San Francisco was to give Bierce his base for many years to come. At first he worked at the U.S. Mint; his older brother Albert was then employed there. From 1877 to 1879 he joined the staff of a new magazine, *The Argonaut*, where the old "Prattle" column resurfaced, and Bierce's yen for sizzling satirical attack, offered to any number of subjects, found fulfillment. Scolding San Francisco's poets, for example, Bierce wrote in an *Argonaut* column of 26 May 1877:

> We have a letter from a gentleman who writes verses, complaining that, not content with breaking the bones of the local poets once or twice each, we persist with tiresome assiduity in breaking them over and over again. Perseverance is, indeed, reckoned amongst our virtues, but then it is also one of the vices of the local poets. Have they stopped writing?
>
> (*A Sole Survivor*, p. 139)

In other columns Bierce took a stand against San Franciscans' anti-Chinese bigotry, wrote about issues of government and the press, and on anything else that struck his fancy or provoked his contempt. "Prattle" was again revived from 1881 to 1886 when Bierce became editor of *The Wasp*, a San Francisco weekly.

But before he did, in 1880 Bierce unexpectedly entered the world of commercial mining in the Black Hills, where he was hired as an overseer by the Black Hills Placer Mining Company to finish the work on a dam and flume in Rockerville, Dakota Territory. The badly managed New York City–based company had been defrauded by a previous Rockerville employee, and in taking over from him, Bierce inherited numerous financial problems and staff frictions. Although he built the flume, he left the company after a few months. Perhaps it was inevitable that Bierce would return for good to writing. He became editor of *The Wasp* in 1881, staying with it for five years. Less inevitable was that William Randolph Hearst would hire him. Hearst, a twenty-three-year-old Harvard dropout, appeared on the writer's Oakland, California, doorstep only a few weeks after assuming the editorship of the *Examiner* on 4 March 1887. (His father, the miner George Hearst, had bought the paper in 1880.) As Bierce recalled his first disarming meeting with Hearst, "One day as I was lounging in my lodging there was a gentle, hesitating rap at the door and, opening it, I found a young man, the youngest young man, it seemed to me, that I had ever confronted" (*A Sole Survivor*, p. 201). Hearst wanted Bierce's by now locally legendary invective, especially the "Prattler" column, to bedizen his newspaper. Bierce said yes to the offer, insisting that his column occupy a regular spot on the paper's editorial page, a far more prominent placement for a much larger readership than any of the column's previous homes had provided.

Despite the boss's recklessly crass business instincts, the uncannily upright Bierce was to remain in his hire until 1909, though bolting whenever his words were defaced by staff copy editors. Wrote Bierce of the unlikely professional alliance with Hearst, "If ever two men were born to be enemies he and I are they. Each stands for everything that is most disagreeable to the other, yet we never clashed" (*A Sole Survivor*, p. 202). The reason was simple: "He did not once direct nor request me to write an opinion that I did not hold, and only two or three times suggested that I refrain for a season from expressing opinions that I did hold.... As to Mr. Hearst's own public writings, I fancy there are none: he could not write an advertisement for a lost dog" (p. 202), chided the cheeky hireling. Still, "this amusing demagogue is nobody's dunce," Bierce conceded (p. 202).

What Hearst might well have recognized as valuable invective sparkles in one of Bierce's *Wasp* columns about the 1882 San Francisco visit of the English writer and wag Oscar Wilde. Observed the columnist on 31 March of that year:

> That sovereign of insufferables, Oscar Wilde, has ensued with his opulence of twaddle and his penury of sense. He has mounted his hind legs and blown crass vapidities through the bowel of his neck, to the capital edification of circumjacent fools and foolesses, fooling with their foolers....
>
> The ineffable dunce has nothing to say and says it—says it with a liberal embellishment of bad delivery, embroidering it with reasonless vulgarities of attitude, gesture, and attire. There was never an imposter so hateful, a blockhead so stupid, a crank so variously and offensively daft. Therefore is the fool enamored of the feel of his tongue in her ear to tickle her understanding. (p. 192)

For Hearst, Bierce was to write attacks on Charles Dickens, Thomas Edison, sundry senators, policemen, vintners, almost anyone—he referred in print to the publisher of the *San Francisco Chronicle* as "Sir Simian" (O'Connor, p. 159). However, while working for Hearst's *Examiner*, his *New York Journal*, and his magazine

*Cosmopolitan*, Bierce also extended his range, with Hearst's approval and sometimes at his urging. He was sent to Washington, D.C., by Hearst to investigate and expose shenanigans associated with the funding bill supported by the unscrupulous railroad mogul Collis P. Huntington; by writing about it, Bierce played a significant role in the 1896 congressional defeat of the bill. Two years later, he produced a series of articles vitriolically opposing the Spanish-American War. As a result of these two journalistic efforts alone, Bierce would have achieved national stature. But meanwhile, he was also writing fiction, fables, epigrams, and poems. *Tales of Soldiers and Civilians*, a collection of his short stories, appeared in 1891. His satirical poetry was published in *Black Beetles in Amber* (1892). *Fantastic Fables* came out in 1899. In 1906 *The Devil's Dictionary* was released under a more cautious title: *The Cynic's Word Book*.

## THE DEVIL AND HIS DICTIONARY

Into his mock dictionary Bierce swept bits and pieces of his past columns that had seized as their pretext the practice and conventions of lexicography. The writer borrowed the conventions only to overturn them. *The Devil's Dictionary* redefined words in Bierce's own words with a stinging critical celerity, a longing to expose ugly truths of the world, and an eye open to observe human inanity. Each definition is a sort of essay. Some definitions are tersely epigrammatic: Bierce defined a hearse, for example, merely and memorably as "Death's baby carriage." A fork is summed up as "An instrument used chiefly for the purpose of putting dead animals into the mouth." And the saturnine writer, as though taking stock of his disreputable colleagues, the ink-stained wretches of newspaperdom, described ink as "A villainous compound of tannogallate of iron, gum-arabic and water, chiefly used to facilitate the infection of idiocy and promote intellectual crime."

Other definitions in his renegade dictionary go on for paragraph after paragraph in finely reckless burlesque of human failings. At times Bierce includes poetry in the definitions, written by himself but typically attributed to fictitious authors with silly Dickensian names; the poetry allows Bierce to exemplify and expatiate on a word's customary usage (or to send it up) while crucifying the habits and the language of fusty Victorian crackpot poetasters. Writing jubilantly as an American extremist in the lexicographical tradition of such enthusiastic self-appointed dictionary makers as Samuel Johnson and Gustave Flaubert (*The Dictionary of Received Ideas*), Bierce in his own work may also have been hearkening back to

his days as a fledgling writer in San Francisco, when he read not only the classics but also the dictionary in an effort to educate himself. Although composed on the fly and over the years, his dictionary entries together offer a fairly comprehensive sidelong portrait of the writer as a timeless, scathing ironist.

*The Devil's Dictionary* may also have served to flog or exorcise the various devils importuning the author's life, such as his career-long hatred of editors and hack journalists; his disdain for doctors, dogs, and lawyers, among others; his worsening asthma; the early deaths of his sons Day (1889) and Leigh (1901); and the deterioration of Bierce's marriage in 1889. An often absent father and husband, he demanded unconditional loyalty during his long intermissions from family life. During one of these, Mollie Bierce had been receiving the attentions—and then the courtly letters—of a Danish admirer, leading Bierce to assume her breach of faith in marriage, true or not. She filed for divorce in 1904 and died in 1905.

Bierce spent extended portions of his later solo life in Washington, D.C., where a circle of acolytes gathered around him, including various women: for although the handsome Bierce, blue-eyed and mustachioed, seemed to be a stickler for moral probity, he attracted more than a few admirers of his own. Among his major efforts of this time was the preparation of his twelve-volume *Collected Works* for publication; the volumes were released between 1909 and 1912.

Bierce's last days may be best left to the imagination, since no reliable record exists. After revisiting familiar U.S. Civil War sites in 1913, late that year Bierce apparently entered Mexico to observe, as a journalist, the corps of Pancho Villa, then fighting the government of General Victoriano Huerta in the Mexican civil war. The circumstances of Bierce's death are unknown; his body was not recovered.

The disappearance of the writer was appropriate to the thematic burden of his writing. As an author and a war veteran, Bierce was for years preoccupied with death, as is revealed in an *Examiner* column of 24 July 1887, when he recalled the three main recurrent dreams of his life. During the first dream, he wanders in a wood, "the only living thing in it" (*A Sole Survivor*, p. 309) and discovers a brook of blood leading to a white marble "tank" containing more blood and surrounded by naked dead men. In the second dream, a burned nocturnal "plain" (p. 310) receives him as he travels it alone, with humanity "long ages dead" (p. 310) and where "God lies dead" (p. 310) as well. In the third dream, he journeys through a more habitable yet still unpeopled "glade" (p. 311), where a horse "speaks my own tongue, but I never know what it says. I suppose I vanish from the land of dreams before [the horse] finishes expressing what it has in mind" (p. 311).

Three seeming battlefields, death everywhere, and no one in sight save the writer, who vanishes before the tongue he best knows how to speak can tell him what he most needs to hear—and before he can reply to it. In this brief survey of his dominant dreams, Bierce could have been foretelling his own silent exit from the field.

## WORKS

*Nuggets and Dust* (1872)
*The Fiend's Delight* (1873)
*Cobwebs from an Empty Skull* (1874)
*Tales of Soldiers and Civilians* (1891)
*Black Beetles in Amber* (1892)
*In the Midst of Life—Tales of Soldiers and Civilians*
    (1892, 1898)
*The Monk and the Hangman's Daughter* (1892)
*Can Such Things Be?* (1893)
*Fantastic Fables* (1899)
*Shapes of Clay* (1903)
*The Cynic's Word Book* (1906); retitled *The Devil's*
    *Dictionary* (1911)
*A Son of the Gods and A Horseman in the Sky* (1907)
*Write It Right* (1909)

*The Shadow on the Dial and Other Essays* (1909)
*The Collected Works of Ambrose Bierce* (1909–1912)
*Selections from Prattle* (1936)
*The Collected Writings of Ambrose Bierce* (1946)
*The Enlarged Devil's Dictionary of Ambrose Bierce*
    (1967)
*The Ambrose Bierce Satanic Reader: Selections from the*
    *Invective Journalism of a Great Satirist* (1968)
*The Stories and Fables of Ambrose Bierce* (1977)
*Poems of Ambrose Bierce* (1995)
*A Sole Survivor: Bits of Autobiography* (1998)

## FURTHER READING

Fatout, Paul. *Ambrose Bierce, The Devil's Lexicographer.* Norman, Okla., 1951. Solidly informative treatment of the man and his work.

Grenander, M. E. *Poems of Ambrose Bierce.* New York, 1971. A careful and concise biographical summary combined with a substantial critical overview of Bierce's writings.

McWilliams, Carey. *Ambrose Bierce: A Biography.* New York, 1929; 2d ed., Hamden, Conn., 1967. An early study, still useful.

O'Connor, Richard. *Ambrose Bierce: A Biography.* Boston, 1967. A very readable full-length biography of Bierce.

Saunders, Richard. *Ambrose Bierce: The Making of a Misanthrope.* San Francisco, 1985. The most compact biographical account.

# ELIZABETH BISHOP

*by Tyler Hoffman*

Elizabeth Bishop is one of the most original lyric voices of the twentieth century, standing with such other American poets as Robert Frost, Wallace Stevens, and Marianne Moore, who was Bishop's mentor and shared Bishop's thirst for accuracy. Like these poets, Bishop was not part of any school and so did not align herself with any program or spend time framing manifestos. Instead, she forged her own aesthetic based on close observation of the thing itself, and in the process generated new idioms and rhythms that convey with wit and a keen moral sense her beliefs about the power of the human imagination to build upon and alter our world.

Born on 8 February 1911, in Worcester, Massachusetts, to William Thomas Bishop and Gertrude Bulmer, Elizabeth Bishop had a troubled childhood: her father died just eight months after she was born, and her mother, who suffered from mental illness, was institutionalized in 1915. After being essentially orphaned at such a young age, Elizabeth went to live with her mother's family in Great Village, Nova Scotia, and she saw her mother for the last time in 1916. In 1917, at the age of six, she was taken back to Worcester to live with her paternal grandparents, spending summers in Nova Scotia until she was seventeen. In her posthumously published short story "The Country Mouse," Bishop remarks on her early sense of estrangement from her "home" in Nova Scotia and her vexed nationalism, as she clung to the patriotic songs and emblems of Canada while being forced to give those up for "the Star-Spangled Banner" and all things American. "I didn't want to be an American," Bishop recalls feeling, and her condition of rootlessness brought on by her expatriation would last a lifetime.

Setting up residences in New York, Key West, Brazil, and, finally, Cambridge, Massachusetts (where she died on

Elizabeth Bishop.
*(Courtesy of the Library of Congress)*

6 October 1979), among other places, she led a peripatetic existence that is reflected in her poetry, which documents the people, customs, and cultures that she encountered along the way. Although she spent the longest time (fifteen years) in Brazil living with her partner, Lota de Macedo Soares, and later referred to Brazil as having become her home, Bishop insisted that her poetry was grounded in North America: "I am influenced by Brazil certainly, but I am a completely American poet, nevertheless." At the same time, though, she felt an overwhelming sense of being countryless, of never particularly feeling at home anywhere. Indeed, what is most striking about Bishop is not so much her Americanism as it is her cosmopolitanism. Her ability to portray at least three nations (Canada, the United States, and Brazil) in such subtlety and depth—her multinational imagination—is unmatched in American poetry.

## NORTH & SOUTH

Bishop's first book of poems, *North & South* (1946), represents the varied experiences of her years living in the northeastern and southeastern United States. In the book she moves from one region to the other, and in doing so moves from poems that are largely allegorical to ones that are more particular and detailed; it is these latter poems that point in the direction of her future work. This shift in representational strategy bespeaks her own deeper penetration into the interior life of the country and her increasingly urgent effort to locate herself in her world. "The Map" is the lead poem in the book, and it first appeared in print in *Trial Balances*, an anthology published in 1935 that included three of Bishop's poems along with an introduction to her work by Marianne Moore. In the poem a speaker stares at a map, considering the tension between its aesthetic features—"delicate" colorings and formal markings—and its representational function. Invariably, that tension relates to poetic representation, to the question of the relationship between her art and the world it seeks to portray. The map is, she says, a "shadowed" world, but it is unclear whether the shadows are produced by art or nature (the poem opens with the line, "Shadows, or are they shallows, at its edges"). Her effort to place herself is made difficult by the uncertainty of representation, and the imaginary travel allowed by the map competes with the actual travel for which the map might be used. In her effort to make sense of the cartographic field, she ends by claiming to prefer formalism to historical reality: "More delicate than the historians' are the map-makers' colors"; however, in her emotional response to the map, she suggests also her deep interest in historical fact and its relationship to abstract topographical display. Indeed, the prosodic form of "The Map" bears on this theme: The poem is divided into three eleven-line stanzas each ending in a rhymed couplet, but, within that form, the metrical pattern fluctuates, with iambic pentameter lines occasionally yielding to longer and shorter ones. This unevenness emblematizes the hold of the actual world on the lines of pure art.

In the next poem, "The Imaginary Iceberg," which was published in the same year as "The Map" (when Bishop was twenty-four), she again explores the pressures of the world of art and the responses of the imagination to it. The title figure represents both the "self-made," self-enclosed art object and the benighted soul, the mind's interior. The poem begins, "We'd rather have the iceberg than the ship, / although it meant the end of travel," and in that formulation we feel the pull of the pure crystalline of the "rhetorical" on the speaker. As an emblem of art, the iceberg represents the dangerous lure of the artificial ("imaginary") and hermetic that must be steered away from if one is to create poetry out of the reality of travel and the engagements that travel affords. The poem ends with a vision of the isolation that comes from a rejection of reality, "The iceberg cuts its facets from within. / Like jewelry from a grave / it saves itself perpetually and adorns / only itself," and it is this fate that Bishop is warning herself against as a creative artist.

Other poems in the first half of the book also examine the plight of the modern artist, who is seen as caught up in the seemingly impossible effort to negotiate between the self and the world outside the self. "The Gentleman of Shalott" is about an artist's effort to make the best of a rather precarious situation. Playing on Alfred Lord Tennyson's "The Lady of Shalott," where we find a female artist living exclusively in a world of shadows, Bishop depicts a man who is off balance, a split personality who believes that because he is perfectly symmetrical: one side of his body is a mirror image of the other. He is therefore unable to determine which side of him is real and which is illusion ("mirrored reflection"), and his "uncertainty" about his identity is a product of the solipsistic world he has constructed and to which he is "resigned." In love with "that sense of constant re-adjustment" that he must undergo, the artist keeps trying to figure out the connection between his imagination and the facts of existence. In "The Man Moth," one of Bishop's New York poems (though there is no attempt to ground it in the particulars of that city), she makes a similar point. The poem's symbolist cityscape depicts both the alienated artist and the alienation and dislocation of modern urban man. The allegorical title figure, which is based on a typographic error for "mammoth" that Bishop saw in a newspaper, is both sad and funny: He is heroic in his struggle to succeed in his climb up skyscrapers to the moon, though doomed to failure. The Man Moth chooses not to expose himself, concealing the tear he sheds in the final stanza, and Bishop's ironic suggestion is that the creative artist must choose otherwise, remaining open to the world in order to nourish the imagination.

In her poem "Large Bad Picture" Bishop continues her inquiry into our relations to art, responding to a banal picture painted by her great-uncle. The speaker begins in close observation of the items represented on the canvas, pointing out as she does the conventional and not very masterful brushstrokes ("perfect waves"; "hundreds of fine black birds / hanging in *n*'s in banks"). However, in the sixth quatrain her perception shifts, as she imagines about these birds, "One can hear their crying, crying." She invests herself emotionally in the painting, and finds value in the calming influence of the lines and colors: "the small red sun goes rolling, rolling, / round and round and round at the same height / in perpetual sunset, comprehensive, consoling." Ascribing therapeutic effects to the work of art, the speaker overlooks its poor quality to find in this ordinary—and not very aesthetically exalted—object a beauty, a "consoling" illusion of the world that she inhabits. The form of the poem suggests the commonplace nature of the picture, its ballad stanzas linking to the idea of folk art and its rhythmic and sonic irregularities resisting perfection, as she does not want to translate the picture into something superior but instead honor it on its own terms.

Although Bishop does not take political issues of the day head-on in this book, she does include in it her sestina "A Miracle for Breakfast," a Depression-era poem that Bishop wrote in New York when breadlines were common and which she described to Moore as her " 'social conscious' poem, a poem about hunger." The speaker is one of a number of poor people isolated on their separate balconies, waiting for food. When a man brings to each only a drop of coffee and "rather hard crumb," it becomes apparent that no religious miracle will occur; however, through careful observation, her "eye close to the crumb," the speaker brings to mind an earthly paradise: "My crumb, / my mansion, made for me by a miracle, / through ages, by insects, birds, and the river / working the stone." This secular vision is fleeting, though, and the envoi of the sestina brings us back to the poverty of the present: "We licked up the crumb and swallowed the coffee. / A window across the river caught the sun / as if the miracle were working, on the wrong balcony." Bishop shows through her manipulation of traditional Christian symbols that any miracle or alteration of consciousness, even if momentary, will be a product of the imagination.

Bishop took her first trip abroad in the summer of 1935, traveling to Paris and then on to London, Morocco, and Spain, before returning to New York the following year. While in France, Bishop became interested in literary and visual surrealism, and the four Paris-inspired poems that she wrote show the extent of her debt to surrealist poetics. Rather than getting a detailed description of the city of Paris, we get an impressionistic view of interior space, a sort of dreamscape. "Sleeping on the Ceiling" opens with the line, "It is so peaceful on the ceiling." This topsy-turvydom continues in "Sleeping Standing Up": "As we lie down to sleep the world turns half away / through ninety dark degrees; the bureau lies on the wall." In "Paris, 7 A.M." the speaker tries to determine what is actual and what is not, as the conception of time and space is wholly distorted. These poems, standing at the pivot between north and south in the book, figure the displacement of the narrator, her altered psychic state and instability; here, as in other poems from throughout her career, Bishop depicts what she called the "surrealism of everyday life."

The second half of *North & South* arises out of the landscape and people she encountered in Key West, Florida, where she lived off and on for nine years, beginning in 1938. In the poem "Florida" she hails "The state with the prettiest name" and documents in stunning detail the flora and fauna of that ecosystem, taking in the tropical mangrove roots, pelicans, tanagers, and fireflies. The accumulation of sensuous natural images represents a turning point in Bishop's aesthetic, as she moves away from the intense interiority of her earlier poems and toward a fuller attention to the external contours of her world. At night, however, Bishop sees that the state of Florida radiates a "corrupt" image, turning into "the poorest / post-card of itself"; as she bears witness, even in this vital landscape there lurks the presence of death, but there is no sermonizing here or adoption of abstract philosophical turns of phrase; natural facts speak for themselves.

"The Fish" is another remarkable poem in Bishop's body of work, and in it she charts the fluctuating emotions of a speaker who has caught a fish and who comes to know it in relation to herself. The poem begins with objective description: "I caught a tremendous fish / and held him beside the boat / half out of water, with my hook / fast in a corner of his mouth." However, the scene is soon infused with the observer's subjectivity, as she begins to see something both like and unlike herself in her catch. The careful depiction of the fish on the hook is based on an actual experience that Bishop had in Key West, and she brims with emotion as she looks on the fish who bears scars from previous battles ("five big hooks / grown firmly in his mouth" are seen "Like medals with their ribbons / frayed and wavering"). This decorated soldier reminds her of her kinship to it, and in the shock of recognition—in her flush of excitement—she exclaims, "I stared and stared / and victory filled up / the little rented boat"; with oil spilling about her and creating a rainbow, she ends the poem in the epiphanic "everything / was rainbow, rainbow, rainbow! / And I let the fish go." Ultimately, Bishop is able to see the beauty of the ordinary, and her moral decision at the end of the poem to "let the fish go" recognizes its uniqueness and integrity.

"Roosters," first published in *New Republic* in April 1941, is another Key West–inspired poem and one of the few in which she moves firmly into the realm of politics. Although Marianne Moore and her mother objected to some of the language of the poem (including what they believed to be the crude word "water-closet") and largely rewrote it, Bishop stood behind her choices, and in her defense revealed that the poem related to the aggression and brutality of World War II: "I cherish my 'water-closet' and the other sordidities because I want to emphasize the essential baseness of militarism." One of those "other sordidities" was the triple rhyme scheme, whose "grating" quality imitated the harsh cry of the rooster, which "grates like a wet match / from the broccoli patch, / flares, and all over town begins to catch." As Bishop remarked to Moore: "I can't seem to bring myself to give up the set form, which I'm afraid you think fills the poem with redundancies, etc. I feel that the rather rattle-trap rhythm is appropriate." In the poem Bishop meditates on the violence of war and the responsibilities it thrusts on us, with the pugilistic roosters "At four o'clock / in the gun-metal blue dark" standing as a symbol of an intimidating fascism ("Deep from protruding breasts / in green-gold medals dressed, / planned to command and terrorize the rest"). Ironically, the rooster is also a reassuring symbol, representing the capacity to forgive, a biblical reference to the apostle Peter's betrayal of Christ and his repentance. The poem points up this redemptive potential ("those cock-a-doodles yet might bless, / his dreadful rooster come to mean forgiveness"), and attests to Bishop's increasing interest in our heroic endurance as historical subjects.

Alert to the politics of class, Bishop also wrote poems about poor black and Cuban residents of south Florida. In the dramatic monologue "Jerónimo's House" the figure of Jerónimo joyfully describes the homemade domestic space that he inhabits, a space made up of fragile materials but woven together with great imagination. In the poem "Cootchie," Bishop writes about the relationship between Miss Lula, who ran a boardinghouse in Naples, Florida, where Bishop stayed on her first trip there, and her servant, Cootchie. The poem is an elegy for Cootchie, whose worth Miss Lula cannot see even after she is gone. The speaker of the poem asks, "but who will shout and make her understand?" but no amount of shouting will make Miss Lula understand, as racism has performed its work too well. Through these portraits, Bishop as poet-ethnographer reveals her concern for both the geographical and cultural coordinates of her world.

### A COLD SPRING

When Bishop's next book, *Poems: North and South—Cold Spring*, appeared in 1955, it took the form of a reprint of *North & South* together with a collection of eighteen new poems under the heading *A Cold Spring* and won for her the Pulitzer Prize. Much had changed in Bishop's life between 1946 and 1955, and those changes are reflected in her new work. She served as Consultant in Poetry for the Library of Congress from 1949 to 1950 (her poem "View of the Capitol from the Library of Congress" reflects on that experience), and, in 1951 she went on a trip to Brazil and ended up staying, living there for fifteen years with Lota Soares. Her life in Brazil was the happiest

period of Bishop's life, and it is here that she attained her international reputation. Although the majority of her Brazil poems appear in the later *Questions of Travel*, *A Cold Spring* records some of her experiences in that country and also includes some of her earliest meditations on her childhood territory of Nova Scotia, as she continued to explore the meaning of travel and the work of the mind in the shaping of human experience.

The trajectory of Bishop's "At the Fishhouses" is typical of her best poetry, moving as it does from a precise description of the physical (a Nova Scotia seascape with its five old fishhouses) to a meditation on the metaphysical (knowledge and being in the world). Drawn into the visceral details of this scene on a cold evening, the speaker is attracted to the silver color that coats everything, in particular the "iridescent" herring scales that line the fish tubs and wheelbarrows, as well as the vest and thumb of the old fisherman with whom she talks. She finds beauty in all of this, but she is also aware of the sense of decline and decay that hovers over it. Turning to the water, she communes with a seal, and sings it hymns, joking that like the seal she is "a believer in total immersion," and she is fully immersed as an observer of the details of this place. In the final passage of the poem, Bishop's precise painting gives way to more abstract considerations, as she is baptized into a new and deeper understanding of her world. The sea, which she earlier had described as "opaque," now is legible, and she sees that it is not subject to decay, as is the land, but instead is a source of life and death; in that body of water she finds a metaphor for human knowledge, "It is like what we imagine knowledge to be: / dark, salt, clear, moving, utterly free," and she ends in the epistemological insight, "our knowledge is historical, flowing and flown," a formulation that acknowledges the interpenetration of the past and the present. The hypnotic lexical repetitions of the finale ("Cold dark deep and absolutely clear" appears twice as does "the same") symbolize the mysterious qualities of the sea, its immortal allure, positioned as it is "above the stones and then the world."

In "Over 2,000 Illustrations and a Complete Concordance," Bishop continues her investigation into the significance of travel and registers her awareness of the ways in which travel does not measure up to our desires and expectations, our rage for order. After examining a set of Bible engravings, she finds: "Thus should have been our travels: / serious, engravable." At first it appears that the pictures in the Bible are at odds with her fragmented memories of actual travel. As in "The Map," she is confronted by the difference between the representation of the world and her personal experience of it, and she finds appealing the order and permanence of the Bible's engravings, especially in light of her own random memories. However, as she goes on to inspect the book, she finds that the images are in fact "tired / and a touch familiar," that they are impoverished for not being real. When she recounts her own travels, there similarly is no sense of order or purpose, with "Everything only connected by 'and' and 'and.' " (The idea of our memory as merely a "litter" of "correspondences" is the submerged subject of another poem in the book, "The Bight.") To the final question, "Why couldn't we have seen / this old Nativity while we were at it? / . . . and looked and looked our infant sight away," the implied answer is that our efforts for a unified and exalted vision based on travel are doomed to failure, and yet, she seems to insist, it remains important to try to refresh our sense of the world by seeing again through the wondering eyes of a child.

Finally, her incantatory lyric "An Invitation to Miss Marianne Moore" is based upon a poem by Pablo Neruda entitled "Alberto Rojas Jimenez Viene Volando" ("Comes Flying"), and in it Bishop uses the refrain, "you come flying," that underpins Neruda's poem to invoke the spirit of Moore, one of her closest friends and most important mentors. In her poem the speaker begins by asking Moore, "From Brooklyn, over the Brooklyn Bridge, on this fine morning, pleases come flying"; later in the poem, Moore is seen "Bearing a musical inaudible abacus," a reference to her work in syllabic verse. Her encouragement of Moore includes the following line as well, "Manhattan / is all awash with morals this fine morning, / so please come flying," as Bishop appeals to Moore's highly refined moral sensibility, a sensibility reflected in her poems and one that she hails in her prose tribute to Moore entitled "Efforts of Affection." In that piece, Bishop pays homage to Moore's spontaneity, her close observation of the objects of this world, and at the same time establishes her independence from Moore and her particular poetic vision.

### QUESTIONS OF TRAVEL

*Questions of Travel* is divided into two parts, "Brazil" and "Elsewhere," and takes up matters of both public and private history. In the early part of "Brazil" Bishop begins to question the essential value of travel and records her first tentative steps as a tourist in what amounts to a sort of initiation into the South American country. In the first poem, "Arrival at Santos," which is dated January, 1952 and was originally part of *A Cold Spring*, the expectations of the tourist are unfulfilled by what she finds

in the Brazilian port: "is this how this country is going to answer you // and your immodest demands for a different world, / and a better life, and complete comprehension / of both at last, and immediately, / after eighteen days of suspension?" She had not thought of there being a national flag and monetary system; she was not ready for the realities of travel. The strange but rather "feeble" and "unassertive" features of Santos are disappointing, and she comes to the realization that "Ports are necessities, like postage stamps, or soap, / but they seldom seem to care what impression they make."

The ballad rhyme scheme of the poem suggests the commonness of the experience the tourist undergoes. One prosodic trick in the poem owes a debt to Lewis Carroll's *Alice's Adventures in Wonderland*, and, indeed, Alice's experience of seeing a world in a different scale is very much in keeping with the disorientation of the tourist in Bishop's poem. In wonderland Alice listens as the Mock Turtle "sighed deeply, and began, in a voice sometimes choked with sobs, to sing" a song called "Turtle Soup," a song that includes the lines, "Who would not give all else for two p / ennyworth only of Beautiful Soup?" Here Carroll is parodying a popular sentimental song of his day, "Star of the Evening," which is marked by an overblown sentimentality. Bishop, too, splits a word across a line break for the sake of rhyme in describing a fellow passenger, Miss Breen: "Her home when she is at home, is in Glens Fall // s, New York." This effect is meant to highlight the "wonderland" feeling of Brazil for the speaker and to mock the sentimental notions that tourists carry with them on their journeys. At the end of the poem the tourist declares "We leave Santos at once; / we are driving to the interior," and those lines of departure point us toward the education of the tourist, toward the transformation of the "tourist" into a "traveler."

In "Brazil, January 1, 1502" Bishop delves into the colonial history of the country, and evokes the fabulous nature of the flora and fauna that proliferates there. However, as Bishop describes, the densely textured landscape that these Portuguese explorers encounter is "not unfamiliar," "corresponding" as it did to the embroidered art of tapestries they left at home, that is, "to an old dream of wealth and luxury / already out of style when they left home— / wealth, plus a brand-new luxury." Here she shows how our response to the alien is conditioned, how our understanding is impacted by our expectations and our sense of the already known. Representing the violence of conquest, she writes that these men "ripped away into the hanging fabric, / each out to catch an Indian for himself," the women in swift retreat. The hypocrisy of these "Christians" "Directly after Mass" pursuing the natives is not lost on Bishop, and she is careful, without sermonizing, to point up the horror of the nationalist enterprise of conquest.

In the title poem we are back in the present, with the traveler overwhelmed by the plenitude of the environment of Brazil: "There are too many waterfalls here; the crowded streams / hurry too rapidly down to the sea." Indeed, there is an overabundance and overactivity to everything, and that feeling leads her to question her desire to drive to the interior of this country, to experience for herself what she could have read in a book: "Should we have stayed at home and thought of here? / Where should we be today? / Is it right to be watching strangers in a play / in this strangest of theatres?" She is self-conscious about her foreignness and the voyeurism that it entails and wonders further if it is simply some "childishness" that makes us want "to rush / to see the sun the other way around": "*Is it lack of imagination that makes us come / to imagined places, not just stay at home?*" Yet the answer to these questions is finally a firm "No," as she finds virtue in travel as an aid to the imagination: "surely it would have been a pity not to have seen" the fantastic sights and sounds of this clime. Her ironic and final "*Should we have stayed at home, / wherever that may be?*" suggests that for Bishop there really is no alternative to travel and the pleasures it affords, that there really is for her no stable "home" from which she is leaving or to which she can easily go back.

As "Brazil" progresses, the female traveler-poet is quickly assimilated into the indigenous culture, interacting with people on a personal level as she draws on Brazilian folklore and mythology to come even closer to the lived history of the native scene. She becomes more patient and less desirous of immediate and rushed sensation as time goes on, and, as she is initiated into a new order of things, her privileged native position creates a sense of rootedness even though culturally she is only a resident alien. In her poem "Squatter's Children," Bishop paints a picture of poverty with a girl and a boy on a hillside and ponders what their "rights" are. The dramatic monologue "Manuelzhino," which is told from the perspective of Lota (the poem states that "*A friend of the writer is speaking*"), is about the gulf that separates the rich from the poor in Brazil. Manuelzhino is a worker on Lota's estate, and the paternalism of the rich is pointed up here, and with it the condescension that marks their treatment of those beneath them on the social scale. The speaker says toward the end of the poem, "You helpless,

foolish man, / I love you all I can, / I think. Or do I?" and she puzzles ("perhaps...") throughout the poem over the life he lives, admitting that she called him names to visitors, for which she "apologize[s] here and now." The speaker calls attention to her many generosities, including providing money for medicine and other items for his family, and her ironic tone calls on us to make judgments about her attitude toward Manuelzhino, even as she is making her own judgments about him.

"The Armadillo," a poem dedicated to the poet Robert Lowell, whom Bishop met in 1947 and with whom she remained friends throughout her life, taps into local history, as it records her impression of the traditional celebration of St. John's Day, a holy day celebrated with the release of fire balloons into the air. Lowell's high praise for Bishop's handling of idioms, rhythms, and images in this poem led him to write "Skunk Hour," a poem he said was deeply indebted to Bishop's, though Bishop's is not confessional in the way Lowell's is. "The Armadillo" begins in casual observation, with the speaker watching the "frail, illegal" balloons ascend in flight, attracted to their desire to transcend the earthly plane. However, she also recognizes in them a danger and sees one fall and burst into flame; in the aftermath, "a glistening armadillo left the scene, / rose-flecked, head down, tail down, // and then a baby rabbit jumped out, / *short*-eared to our surprise. / So soft!—a handful of intangible ash / with fixed, ignited eyes." These lines suggest the exuberance of the narrator, who is happy to see the survival of these animals, but who is also very aware of their fragility. The poem ends in the following italicized ballad quatrain: "*Too pretty, dreamlike mimicry! / O falling fire and piercing cry / and panic, and a weak mailed fist / clenched ignorant against the sky!*" Here the speaker notes the weakness of the armadillo in the face of the man-made balloons, which imitate the stars, and registers the hopelessness of the animal's protest against the forces that cause his suffering. The poem ends, then, not in transcendence but rather in a painful reminder of the agonies of the body that we all must endure.

The ballad "The Burglar of Babylon" pivots on yet another native legend, the folk hero and criminal Micuçú. In the poem Micuçú, "a burglar and killer" and hero of the poor, escapes from the penitentiary and is pursued by the police, who finally kill him. Bishop said that she watched the pursuit of Micuçú through binoculars from her apartment in Rio and modeled her poem on stories about the incident she read in the newspaper. As Bishop makes clear in a twice repeated quatrain, he is a product of his environment: "On the fair green hills of Rio /

There grows a fearful stain: / The poor who come to Rio / And can't go home again." However, we also learn from Micuçú's grieving aunt that Micuçú "was always mean," that not everyone chose the life he did: " 'I raised him to be honest, / Even here, in Babylon slum.' " Bishop's attention in the poem to the gap between rich and poor, though, suggests that class plays a large role here, as "Rich people in apartments / Watched through binoculars" while the fugitive hid on the hill of Babylon. In the end, in the wake of Micuçú's death, the police are "after another two" criminals, the cycle of violence, poverty, and despair spiraling on.

In the section of the book entitled "Elsewhere" Bishop ranges more widely, taking up multiple locations and points of view in her exploration of her personal past, a past that revolves around images of pain and loss. In its original form, it begins with the autobiographical story "In the Village," which is about the loss of Bishop's mother to insanity when she was five years old. The little girl's mother's refusal to give up mourning for her dead husband produces a scream that haunts the narrative and the girl's memory: "A scream, the echo of a scream, hangs over that Nova Scotia village." The story shifts perspective (moving from first-person to third-person accounts) and migrates back and forth in time, conflating "the past, the present, and those years in between." Bishop's confusion of events in her representation of the ruptured world of the child symbolizes the grave indeterminacy of identity with which she struggles.

In the poems that follow this story, Bishop charts her losses further. "First Death in Nova Scotia" is about the death of her young cousin Arthur and her attempts to make sense of that loss. In "Manners" she addresses the death of a social order from a child's perspective. "Sestina" also returns us to her Nova Scotia childhood and proves, as Helen Vendler (Schwartz and Estess, 1983) has noted, that "the strange can occur even in the bosom of the familiar, even, most unnervingly, at the domestic hearth" in Bishop's work. In the poem a grandmother tries to "hide her tears" from a child, who draws a "rigid" and an "inscrutable" house in recognition of the buried emotions that engulf her. The title highlights the verse form that the poet chooses—one that runs on lexical repetition at the ends of lines—and ironically comments on the losses and absences (the lack of repetition) that she feels. In these poems Bishop drifts backwards and forwards in history to offer up a concordance of unprivileged perspectives, insisting that home is variable, not some deeply rooted constant. Even though certain events take place in Nova Scotia, this location is often not explicit, and the ambiguity of time and place relates to the ambiguity of selfhood that these poems map.

In "Visits to St. Elizabeths" Bishop treats yet another figure in decline, giving her impression of her visits (while at the Library of Congress) to the poet Ezra Pound, who was confined to a mental hospital and under indictment for treason for his radio broadcasts from Italy during World War II. Written to the tune of the nursery rhyme "This is the House that Jack Built," the poem paints a picture of disturbing dislocation, of a world that is out of balance and in danger of collapse. The fact that the poem is based on a familiar one from childhood indicates that condition is not one of comfort for Bishop. Pound, "the man / that lies in the house of Bedlam," is seen in various takes as "tragic," "honored," "cranky," "cruel," and "wretched," but the portrait that emerges through the repetitions of the poem is not only of Pound but of the post-war world that makes the crisis of establishing a solid identity particularly acute. In this poem Bishop's engagements of private and public history in *Questions of Travel* collide.

## GEOGRAPHY III

Bishop's final book of poetry begins with a series of questions and answers from an 1884 textbook entitled *First Lessons in Geography*. To the questions of Lesson VI, which include "What is Geography?" and "What is the Earth?," we are provided with simply stated answers ("A description of the earth's surface" and "The planet or body on which we live"). In Lesson X, though, the answers are not always forthcoming. About the map, questions proliferate: *"In what direction is the Volcano? The Cape? The Bay? The Lake? The Strait? The Mountains? The Isthmus?"* These sorts of locational questions are those Bishop sought answers to throughout her life, and it is appropriate that she rounds back to them here, still in search of a positive identity in a shifting world.

Her poem "In the Waiting Room" is the first that Bishop wrote in which she calls herself by name, and in it she pursues the questions of personal identity that shape *Questions of Travel*, especially the Nova Scotia poems of "Elsewhere," even as she resists the confessional strain of Lowell and other contemporary poets. Drawing on her personal history, Bishop represents a scene in which as a child of six she went to the dentist's office with her Aunt Consuelo. Leafing through a *National Geographic* in the waiting room, she is confronted by the "horrifying" naked breasts of "black, naked women with necks / wound round and round with wire / like the necks of light bulbs." Her surprise midway through the poem at her identification with them by virtue of her gender creates confusion. What she believes to be a scream from her aunt in the doctor's chair turns out to be her own scream: "Without thinking at all / I was my foolish aunt, / our eyes glued to the cover / of the *National Geographic*, / February, 1918." In her existential crisis she remembers feeling, "you are an *I*, / you are an *Elizabeth*, / you are one of *them*. / *Why* should you be one, too?" Indeed, she goes on to ask, "Why should I be my aunt, / or me, or anyone?" Her movement back into the flow of history at the end of the poem, where we are told "The War was on," suggests the continuing imbrication of public and private, as Bishop struggles to make sense of herself in the world.

Picking up another thematic strand from an earlier book, "Poem," which is about a painting by her great-uncle George Hutchinson that Bishop inherits, is, like the earlier "Large Bad Picture," a meditation on the nature of art and the work of the imagination that makes art meaningful to us. Unlike the large picture, though, there is no pretension to grandeur here; this picture is little ("About the size of an old-style dollar bill, / American or Canadian"), and the detailed brushstrokes make vivid impressions, even though they are conventional. In the second stanza the narrator points out what she recognizes in the painting, the human touch. After a rather unengaged observation, she suddenly discovers something ("Heavens, I recognize the place, I know it!"), feeling her connection to the artist through the familiar scene, which she actively reconstructs through memory: "We both knew this place, / apparently, this literal small backwater, / looked at it long enough to memorize it, / our years apart. How strange." The painting mirrors the world so accurately that she is unsure which is actual and which imagined: "art 'copying from life' and life itself, / life and the memory of it so compressed / they've turned into each other. Which is which?" In the end the speaker's emotional response to the "touching detail" of the work of art creates its value, and she finds that the world the picture memorializes—one that stands beyond the ravages of time—has the power to console. The title ("Poem") calls attention to Bishop's own art, which is itself a re-description (of the painting) and which likewise attempts to make meaning out of the commonplace, to represent the blurring of the boundaries between art and life.

The meaningfulness of the quotidian is also the subject of Bishop's dramatic monologue "Crusoe in England," where the figure of the castaway Robinson Crusoe back in England reminds us of other displaced and solitary figures from Bishop's early poetry; on a metaphorical (and autobiographical) level it also suggests Bishop's isolation and deep sense of loss after her return to America and Lota's suicide. Crusoe claims of his life story that "None of the books has ever got it right," and here he works to set the record straight. Once off the island, Crusoe says he missed the charged nature of every object that was his: "The knife there on the shelf—/ it reeked of meaning, like a crucifix. / It lived . . . / Now it won't look at me at all. / The living soul has dribbled away"; as he discovers, the items of his life in misery on the island were in fact dear to him, even though at the time he often "gave way to self-pity." An anachronistic passage from Wordsworth's poem "I wandered lonely as a cloud" (" 'They flash upon that inward eye, which is the bliss . . . ' ") that Crusoe could not fully recall while on his island allows Bishop to critique romantic solipsism in her insistence on the need for companionship in the world. When we learn that his friend Friday is no longer with him, having died of the measles, we feel the full weight of Crusoe's sense of dispossession.

Another of the most celebrated lyrics from *Geography III*, "The Moose," Bishop's longest poem, returns us once again to the landscape of Nova Scotia and to the theme of travel, as the speaker journeys on a bus from Nova Scotia to Boston, away from home. As the familiar and domestic recedes, the traveler enters into a dreamy moonlit world, with fog enveloping the bus and an air of mystery infusing the scene. The traveler dozes off, and overhears conversations within the bus, talk that seems to be going on "in Eternity": she listens to the losses that families have endured ("deaths, deaths and sicknesses") and begins to see that these losses must be accepted as part of life. Suddenly, the bus comes to a stop when a moose comes out of "the impenetrable wood" to stand in the middle of the road. The moose is curious, sniffing around the bus, and so are the passengers, whose excitement is keen; the animal's "otherworldly" presence prompts the speaker to ask, "Why, why do we feel / (we all feel) this sweet / sensation of joy?" This joy they experience brings the passengers together and is in counterpoint to the human experience of deprivation and loss that is articulated in earlier stanzas. When the bus finally moves on, the passengers descend again to the mundane facts of existence, symbolized by the smell of gasoline emanating from the bus, but the moose, "Towering, antlerless, / high as a church, / homely as a house," will not be forgotten; instead, she will continue to inhabit the imagination of the people who witnessed her, her magical presence carried with them into the future.

Finally, Bishop's villanelle "One Art" takes up in a personal way the losses that the poet has suffered in her life, and her opening lines ironically suggest the depth of her despair: "The art of losing isn't hard to master; / so many things seem filled with the intent / to be lost that their loss seems no disaster." The speaker goes on to catalogue the precise nature of these losses, including "three loved houses" (one in Key West and two in Brazil) and "two cities, lovely ones. / And, vaster, some realms I owned, two rivers, a continent. / I miss them but it wasn't a disaster." Bishop's choice of the villanelle, which is built on the repetition of words at the ends of lines, adds to the irony, since it is a verse form that requires the artist to remember words and the order of those words; however, her looseness in the villanelle form is typical of her easy way with most of the fixed forms that she wields. The ending of the poem illustrates how the compulsions of form enable her to articulate the deep emotional losses that she has suffered and that she is often reluctant to reveal: "—Even losing you (the joking voice, a gesture / I love) I shan't have lied. It's evident / the art of losing's not too hard to master / though it may look like (*Write it!*) like disaster."

Bishop said that she prized clarity and simplicity, and her poetry of travel, which treats on a small scale the largest questions of human experience, shows this to be true. Her keen visual sense and ability to map (often with irony) the geographical and cultural boundaries of our world allow us to see anew that world and our place in it. As Bishop once remarked: "I've never felt particularly homeless, but, then, I've never felt particularly at home. I guess that's a pretty good description of a poet's sense of home. He carries it within him." For her, identity and geography are inextricably linked, and her awareness of her cultural in-betweenness yields a powerful ethnographic poetry, one that takes the measure both of life's losses and of its joys.

[*See also* Moore, Marianne; Pound, Ezra; *and* Poetess in American Literature, The.]

## WORKS

*North & South* (1946)
*Poems: North & South—A Cold Spring* (1955)
*Questions of Travel* (1965)
*The Complete Poems* (1969)
*Geography III* (1976)
*The Complete Poems, 1927–1979* (1983)
*The Collected Prose* (1984)

## FURTHER READING

Bloom, Harold, ed. *Elizabeth Bishop*. New York, 1985.

Costello, Bonnie. *Elizabeth Bishop: Questions of Mastery.* Cambridge, Mass., 1991. An excellent treatment of Bishop that is attuned to the relation of her work to visual art.

Diehl, Joanne Feit. *Elizabeth Bishop and Marianne Moore: The Psychodynamics of Creativity.* Princeton, N.J., 1993. An engaging intertextual reading of the two writers' works through the lens of object-relations theory.

Doreski, C. K. *Elizabeth Bishop: The Restraints of Language.* New York, 1993. An examination of Elizabeth Bishop's rhetorical strategies and the way they shape the formal and thematic movements of her poetry and stories.

Goldensohn, Lorrie. *Elizabeth Bishop: The Biography of a Poetry.* New York, 1992.

Harrison, Victoria. *Elizabeth Bishop's Poetics of Intimacy.* Cambridge, 1993. An evaluation of the various phases of Bishop's career, with particular attention to biographical events that influenced Bishop's poetic style.

Kalstone, David. *Becoming a Poet: Elizabeth Bishop with Marianne Moore and Robert Lowell.* Ann Arbor, Mich., 2001.

Lombardi, Marilyn May, ed. *Elizabeth Bishop: The Geography of Gender.* Charlottesville, Va., 1993.

McCabe, Susan. *Elizabeth Bishop: Her Poetics of Loss.* University Park, Pa., 1994. A study of Bishop in a postmodern and feminist light.

Merrin, Jeredith. *An Enabling Humility: Marianne Moore, Elizabeth Bishop, and the Uses of Tradition.* New Brunswick, N.J., 1990.

Millier, Brett C. *Elizabeth Bishop: Life and the Memory of It.* Berkeley, Calif., 1993. A thorough account of Bishop's life and work, with discussion of her homosexuality, alcoholism, and depression as they relate to her art.

Parker, Robert Dale. *The Unbeliever: The Poetry of Elizabeth Bishop.* Urbana, Ill., 1988.

Schwartz, Lloyd, and Sybil P. Estess, eds. *Elizabeth Bishop and Her Art.* Ann Arbor, Mich., 1983. This edited collection includes major essays by leading American critics and also contains previously uncollected material by Bishop herself.

Travisano, Thomas J. *Elizabeth Bishop: Her Artistic Development.* Charlottesville, Va., 1988. A superb overview of the development of Bishop's career and poetry.

# BLACK ARTS MOVEMENT

*by William R. Nash*

The term "Black Arts Movement" describes a set of attitudes, influential from 1965 to 1976, about African-American cultural production, which assumed that political activism was a primary responsibility of black artists. It also decreed that the only valid political end of black artists' efforts was liberation from white political and artistic power structures. Just as white people were to be stripped of their right to proscribe or define black identity, white aesthetic standards were to be overthrown and replaced with creative values arising from the black community.

Larry Neal, one of the movement's founders, noted in his essay "The Black Arts Movement" (1968) that this agenda made the Black Arts Movement "the aesthetic and spiritual sister of the Black Power concept." Like Black Power, the Black Arts ideology had roots in earlier African-American historical moments; also like Black Power, the specifics of the movement arose in response to the integrationist ethos of the late 1950s. As such, it marked an important era in the evolution of African-American artistry, a moment when black writers, visual artists, and musicians forged their own declarations of independence from white America. Because of the proscriptive nature of its tenets, it also created much controversy. Through its evocation of such resistance, the Black Arts Movement also prepared the way for subsequent black artists, who have moved away from essentialist racial characterizations to articulate a more sweeping, multifaceted understanding of racial identity.

## THE BLACK ARTS MOVEMENT AND THE EVOLUTION OF AFRICAN-AMERICAN LITERATURE

In many ways the Black Arts Movement was a lineal descendant of the Harlem Renaissance, or at least of the wing that privileged the art and experiences of "the folk" over the high art of white culture. The link is so strong, in fact, that some scholars refer to the Black Arts Movement era as the Second Renaissance. One sees this connection clearly in a reading of Neal's essay alongside Langston Hughes's "The Negro Artist and the Racial Mountain" (1926). Indeed, "The Negro Artist" was deemed sufficiently important to the architects of the Black Aesthetic for Addison Gayle to include it among the selections in his definitive 1971 anthology of the theory of the movement, *The Black Aesthetic*. The Black Arts Movement overlapped with the articulation of the principles referred to as the Black Aesthetic. One might say the former is practice, the latter theory. Hughes's seminal essay advocates that black writers resist external attempts to control their art, arguing instead that the "truly great" black artist will be the one who can fully embrace and freely express his blackness. The hallmark of this, in Hughes's vision, is an artist's ability to reject bourgeois posturing and to privilege instead the more elemental experience of the black masses, those whom he refers to as "low-down folks." This call resonates strongly with Neal's call for "a cultural revolution in art and ideas [that] speaks to the spiritual and cultural needs of Black people, regardless of whether or not whites approve." Neal and his peers went a step farther than their predecessors, however, arguing that it was not enough to reject white aesthetic standards; instead, they claimed, white artistic standards must be destroyed.

Such extreme terminology created, or at least exacerbated, rifts within the African-American literary community. Perhaps no single break is more illustrative or more troublesome than the Black Aestheticians' rejection of Ralph Ellison. Ellison's *Invisible Man* (1952) set a standard for African-American fiction and established its author as a preeminent man of American letters. Although the novel challenges simplistic, white-defined portrayals of black identity, its fundamental ethos is undeniably integrationist. Furthermore, with its evocation of classic white texts like Herman Melville's *Moby-Dick* (1851), Mark Twain's *Adventures of Huckleberry Finn* (1884), and Fyodor Dostoyevsky's *Notes from the Underground* (1864), *Invisible Man* supported the values of a traditional Western (read "white") literary aesthetic, even though Ellison extended those standards through his concomitant celebration of black folk culture. For this, Ellison earned a number of "establishment" accolades, including the National Book Award. Also, in 1965 a group of American scholars and authors named *Invisible Man* the most accomplished American novel published since 1945. The 1965 designation came at the time when African-American writers were mounting the struggle to find a black literary voice that would shortly arise in the form of the Black Arts Movement; the honor only confirmed these young writers' opinions of Ellison as an assimilationist. This, by extension, also made him irrelevant to the movement and an Uncle Tom in their eyes.

Ellison was far from the only figure whose work was deemed politically inadequate by the Black Aestheticians; rather, one might best view their reaction to him as illustrative of a tendency in the movement to make restrictive pronouncements about what art by African Americans qualified as "black enough" for the movement's purposes. The profound irony of this particular case is that Ellison, like the Black Aestheticians, sought to reimagine black identity and to break it out of the strictures imposed on notions of blackness by a white majority. Recognizing this link between Ellison and his detractors proves useful, as it allows one to contextualize the Black Arts Movement in the continuum of efforts to redefine black being. Without the Black Aestheticians' call for a strict separation of black and white creative identity, African-American literature likely could not have evolved as it did. At the same time, however, the commonalties between Black Arts artists and those predecessors like Ellison, whom they so pointedly rejected, illustrate why the movement was necessarily a step in a process. Only with the expansion of notions of black identity can true creative freedom come, and real expansion by definition demands movement beyond any group's rigid definition of identity, be it externally or internally imposed.

## IMMEDIATE ANTECEDENTS AND THE BLACK ARTS LABEL

As the 1960s began, African Americans' struggle for civil rights gradually began to shift from accommodationism to militancy. This was true for literary groups just as it was for other kinds of political organizations. In 1962

Amiri Baraka (aka LeRoi Jones of the Black Arts Repertory Theatre/School [BART/S] in Harlem). (*Courtesy of the Library of Congress*)

the Umbra poets' workshop was founded on Manhattan's Lower East Side; this group of young black poets, which published two issues of the journal *Umbra* before it self-destructed, sought to define a position for itself outside the boundaries of the white aesthetic. Group members included several writers who subsequently became well-known: Ishmael Reed, Calvin Hernton, Askia Touré, Lorenzo Thomas, Tom Dent, David Henderson, Joe Johnson, and Norman Pritchard. For the first two years, Umbra was a dynamic, active organization. Eventually, however, political differences caused important rifts within it, which eventually led to its dissolution. One result of this balkanization of the group was the articulation of newer, more strictly nationalist standards for evaluating black art. Another key development that came in the wake of Umbra's collapse in 1965 was the founding by LeRoi Jones of the Black Arts Repertory Theatre/School (BART/S) in Harlem. With the founding of this group, Jones gave the nascent movement a name; he also became one of its most prominent promoters and theoreticians.

Jones began publishing poetry in the style of the Beat poets of the late 1950s and early 1960s; his first volume of poetry, *Preface to a Twenty-Volume Suicide Note* (1961), shows the poet seeking a new means of expressing black experience but operates within the conventions of white English usage. As Jones moved toward his Black Arts phase, he changed his name to Amiri Baraka ("blessed prince" in Bantu). He also changed the form and content of his poetry, adopting a more violent stance and adopting the vernacular of the urban community. One sees these elements in play quite clearly in Baraka's poem, "Black Art" (1969):

Poems are bullshit unless they are
teeth or trees or lemons piled
on a step. . . . Fuck poems
and they are useful, wd they shoot
come at you, love what you are,
breathe like wrestlers, or shudder
strangely after pissing. We want live
words of the hip world live flesh &
coursing blood.

(Randall, ed., *The Black Poets*, p. 223)

The aim of this black art is clear, as the poem explicitly equates activism and artistry; the only valid art, in Baraka's view, is art that strikes a blow against white hegemony.

For the artist, words can best be weapons when he or she uses them to create a unique black speech. In addition to using street language, Baraka also occasionally adopts nontraditional orthography, in this instance substituting "wd" for "would." This practice of adopting alternate spellings would become a standard of the movement, especially in the work of Black Arts Movement poets like Sonia Sanchez and Haki Madhubuti. Irregular orthography has a dual purpose for the poet. First, it jolts the reader out of complacency, forcing him or her to acknowledge inherent biases about how language "should" look and work. It follows logically from this that the reader who overcomes a narrow interpretation of linguistic form will likely be receptive to similar challenges to linguistic meaning. Second, and following from that, the artist who successfully asserts his or her control of language explicitly rejects white domination. Given that language had traditionally been a tool that whites had used to define and confine black identity, black artists' seizing of the power of linguistic construction and definition is a significant blow for creative and communal freedom.

This is not to suggest that all of the poetry of the Black Arts Movement saw this differentiation from white culture in terms of violent rebellion. The poet's ability to celebrate black lives and experiences without concern for interracial inclusiveness in audience appeal is another means of differentiation that many artists of the period used. One sees this clearly in Angela Jackson's poem "Second Meeting" (1975), which frames an interaction between a black man and woman exclusively in terms of their common African heritage; the poet does not attempt to make the poem relevant or appealing to anyone with a European-American background.

The poem opens with an evocation of an African past, as the speaker talks to her male auditor:

memba the time . . .
we met at home
that slow age ago.
(Parks, 1987, p. 122)

In that place, she encounters a hunter "hone / n a spear" as she moves "with a water jar balanced on my head / to fetch from the river." They share a beautiful day, eating together and performing a "fertility dance." Clearly, for her the first meeting was a powerful experience, an event that figures into the speaker's sense of self. Equally clearly, the event is not actual memory, but rather the dream of a former life.

The Africa she sees in her mind is an idealized homeland, a place free of the corrupting Western value systems that poison interaction between black men and women.

Nevertheless, real or imagined, this is what sustains her. It also guides her thought and action in this second meeting in the subway. Teasing her male auditor for his "hey sista wuts happen / n" opening, she says "i guess / u forgot" that common past. In the moment, though, the speaker gave not rejection but a smile that prompted another line:

don't i know u
from
sum
where??"

And again, her dream of the past controls her response:

I nod
ed softly: yes.
afraid I'd tip
ova
the water jar
I always think
is
balanced on my head (Parks, 1987, p. 122)

In this moment, the speaker's defense against white America embraces her male companion. The message is one of possibility, an image of who these individuals can be and what kind of community they can build in a harsh urban environment.

One sees a similar range of attitudes in Black Arts drama. Baraka was as crucial to the movement for his plays as for his poems, and he worked to make the black theater a powerful political weapon. His most anthologized play, *Dutchman* (1964), presents a murderous confrontation between a white woman, Lula, and a young black intellectual named Clay. As Lula tries to seduce Clay (in preparation for murdering him), she pushes him into a violent rage in which he equates black art with murder. As he puts it, "If Bessie Smith had killed some white people she wouldn't have needed that music" (p. 97). In *Great Goodness of Life: A Coon Show* (1967), Baraka takes that violence into the black community; the play describes the trial of Court Royal, a middle-aged black man who is hauled before a white judge known only as "the Voice" and accused of harboring a murderer. In order to be free he must kill the murderer, who turns out to be his own son. As the curtain closes, Royal has apparently forgotten his actions and is heading out to go bowling, happy and secure in the knowledge that white society accepts and affirms him.

The message of these plays is clear: white America actively seeks to exterminate any blacks it sees as potentially dangerous. The goal is very much to arouse black empathy and to mobilize African Americans to resist white oppression. One finds a sharp contrast in the plays of Ed Bullins, another prominent Black Arts dramatist. In works such as *Goin' A Buffalo* (1968) and *In the Wine Time* (1968), he portrays interactions among blacks that have no real connection to white society. Rather than reacting violently against whites, the characters in Bullins's plays operate with no real sense of white presence. One might think of Baraka's and Bullins's plays as something of a continuum that, taken together, raise two crucial questions. First, Baraka asks, what can be done to destroy the white man's world; then, when that is done, Bullins wonders, what sort of world can the black community make for itself in place of the old order?

## PROLIFERATION OF THE MOVEMENT AND *THE BLACK AESTHETIC*

Although Baraka and Bullins occupied such significantly different intellectual space, they both worked primarily in the metropolitan New York area. Given the high concentration of venues available in New York City, it is perhaps no surprise that many Black Arts events occurred there. Unlike the Harlem Renaissance, however, this Second Renaissance was not so localized as to be given a geographic name. Indeed, one found major Black Arts Movement workshops spread across the nation. The Bay area of San Francisco was home to Black Arts West and a prominent site for Black Aestheticians; Black Arts Midwest and Concept East were both located in Detroit. Los Angeles had at least three groups operating in the city: the Ebony Showcase, the Inner City Repertory, and the Performing Arts Society of Los Angeles. New Orleans housed BLKARTSOUTH. All were dynamic groups that promoted the values and aesthetic standards of the movement.

Perhaps the most interesting, though, was Chicago's Organization of Black American Culture. Founded in 1967, this group (whose name contains the Yoruba word for leader, "Oba") sought to create a "leader culture" that would help it counteract the social and economic forces of racism that they saw threatening their community. As Abdul Alkalimat notes in his "OBAC Position Paper" of 1967, participants have "the job of building OBAC into an organization deeply grounded in the Black community ... which far transcends individual differences ... so people will have faith in themselves and

the strength of self confidence" (Parks, ed., *Nommo: A Literary Legacy of Black Chicago (1967–1987)*, p. 12). At the heart of the group's program was a belief that art could have significant social impact; one sees this clearly in the title of its journal, *Nommo*, which derives from the Bantu and means "the power of the word to make material change."

This impulse toward change is part of what cofounder Hoyt Fuller called the workshop's "generative idea." Fuller was an important figure in this era. When Addison Gayle compiled *The Black Aesthetic*, he selected Fuller to write the introduction; in that brief essay, Fuller explained how OBAC was founded and how it embodied and advanced the values of the Black Arts Movement. In the same statement, Fuller also noted that OBAC participants strove "to invest their work with the distinctive styles and rhythms and colors of the ghetto" and to "set in motion the long overdue assault against the restrictive assumptions of the white critics" (p. 10).

Like BART/S, OBAC was essential to the evolution of the Black Arts ethos; unlike Baraka's group, however, OBAC existed for almost twenty-five years, ceasing to function only in the 1990s. Its longevity made it unique among Black Arts era organizations. This demonstrated something crucial about both the group and the Black Arts Movement itself. OBAC survived because it evolved, moving away from the essentialist values of its early years to a broader, more inclusive understanding of blackness and the black community that was sensitive to changes in national attitudes about race and racial identity. Black Arts Movement groups that adhered strictly to the separatist ethos of BART/S and its peer institutions eventually found themselves obsolete.

## BACKLASH AGAINST THE BLACK AESTHETIC

In the mid-1970s artists began a serious effort to replace the essentialism of the Black Arts Movement with something more expansive. As a result, the movement foundered around 1976, leaving space for other attempts at defining black identity to come to the fore. One such effort came from a small but active group of African-American writers dissatisfied with the principles of the Black Aesthetic. Often referred to as the New Breed, these writers—including Ishmael Reed, Al Young, Cecil Brown, and Quincy Troupe Jr.—"found the Black Aesthetic too prescriptive and narrowly political" and "felt the battleground was not the street but the mind. They wanted to dethrone the Western mind from the seat of intellectual power and prestige" (Andrews,

Smith Foster, and Harris, "Black Aesthetic" *The Oxford Companion to African-American Literature*, p. 69). In their work, white standards were usually not ignored; if anything, they were brought to the forefront and mocked, as in Reed's early parodies of genre fiction. In some ways, the work of this group resembled that of Black Arts Movement writers; however, as a general rule one finds less of an emphasis on violence and more of a willingness to engage creatively with the Western tradition. These variations allowed for writers and critics to expand their definitions of black arts and artistry.

In the wake of the New Breed writers, black artists and critics advanced an even broader range of aesthetic positions. Trey Ellis's suggestion that a New Black Aesthetic had grown from within the African-American artistic community was one important innovation; bell hooks's call for an "aesthetic of blackness" represented another. Challenging the values of the Black Aesthetic, hooks promoted a more diverse understanding of African-American artistry, characterized in part by a breadth of vision she said was lacking in most works identified with the Black Arts Movement. She recognized that discussions of aesthetic issues must not be cast in binary terms, pitting black against white and eliminating other sources of inspiration. Instead, hooks argued, blacks and whites alike must recognize "the need to see darkness differently" (Hooks, 1990, p. 113) and to celebrate the beauty of darkness that runs counter to conventional Western aesthetics. In some ways a modified version of "black is beautiful," the rallying cry of the Black Arts and Black Power movements, her choice had important implications. Awareness of white art was, in her view, an entry point into the interrogation of a dominant culture; this process would lead ultimately to black empowerment.

Trey Ellis, the representative man of the New Black Aesthetic, offered another response to the Black Arts Movement. Chief among the traits of the New Black Aestheticians was an awareness and acceptance of their "cultural mulatto" status, a term recognizing their immersion in and indebtedness to "a multi-racial mix of cultures" (Ellis, 1989, p. 235). Like the New Breed artists, Ellis saw the New Black Aesthetic as a means to black empowerment, a goal he deemed attainable because "today's popular culture is guided by blacks almost across the board" (p. 237). For all of the breadth of his artistic vision, then, the goal was still the political aspiration that the Black Aestheticians and the New Breed writers shared.

## LEGACY OF THE BLACK ARTS MOVEMENT

Ellis's and hooks's efforts to balance political activism for the community with more expansive visions of black identity mark the legacy of the Black Arts Movement. Were it not for the efforts of Baraka, Fuller, Neal, and the host of writers, visual artists, and musicians who adhered to their principles, African-American literature could not have evolved as it has. Some critics argue that the African-American tradition has always been political; one can certainly trace a tradition of political writing by African Americans back to the beginning of the tradition. What characterizes much of the early writing, however, is a tension between the desire to adhere to traditional literary forms and to present a radical message. The result is often an uneasy marriage of content and style that leads many to say that black literature was not really concerned with artistic questions until the twentieth century. With the Black Arts Movement, much of this tension was resolved, as form and content melded in the service of the common cause of black liberation. It is this ability to fuse structure and subject that gives the literature of this era significance beyond its specific historical moment and makes the Black Arts era a crucial chapter in the evolution of African-American writing.

## FURTHER READING

Andrews, William L., Francis Smith Foster, and Trudier Harris, eds. *The Oxford Companion to African-American Literature*. New York, 1997.

Elam, Harry J., and David Krasner, eds. *African-American Performance and Theater History: A Critical Reader*. New York, 2001.

Ellis, Trey. "The New Black Aesthetic." *Callaloo: A Journal of African-American Arts and Letters* 12 (1989): 233–251.

Hay, Samuel A. *African-American Theatre: An Historical and Critical Analysis*. New York, 1994.

Henderson, Stephen. *Understanding the New Black Poetry: Black Speech and Black Music as Poetic References*. New York, 1973. A standard work on the poetry of the period, it gives excellent insights into the theory and practice of Black Arts Movement authors.

Hooks, Bell. *Yearning: Race, Gender, and Cultural Politics*. Cambridge, Mass., 1990.

Johnson, Abby Arthur, and Ronald Maberry Johnson. *Propaganda and Aesthetics: The Literary Politics of African-American Magazines in the Twentieth Century*.

Amherst, Mass., 1991. Paperback ed. Originally published in 1979. This volume has an excellent chapter on the literary magazines of the 1960s.

Lacey, Henry C. *To Raise, Destroy, and Create: The Poetry, Drama, and Fiction of Amiri Baraka (LeRoi Jones)*. Troy, N.Y., 1981.

Parks, Carole A., ed. *Nommo: A Literary Legacy of Black Chicago (1967–1987)*. Chicago, 1987. The definitive OBAC anthology.

Randall, Dudley, ed. *The Black Poets*. New York, 1971. An excellent collection of poems from the era.

Redmond, Eugene B. *Drumvoices: The Mission of Afro-American Poetry*. New York, 1976. Insightful analysis of the period and of specific writers; an excellent complement to the Henderson volume.

Sanders, Lesile G. *The Development of Black Theater in America: From Shadows to Selves*. Baton Rouge, La.,1989.

# BLACK MOUNTAIN POETRY

*by Lacy Schutz*

In 1960 the poet Donald M. Allen published an anthology titled *The New American Poetry*. Just three years earlier, the poets Donald Hall, Robert Pack, and Louis Simpson had edited *New Poets of England and America*. Although each purported to be a definitive survey of contemporary poetry, these books could not boast a single poet in common. *New Poets of England and America* contained academic poets working largely within traditional form, poets influenced by predecessors such as Robert Frost and T. S. Eliot. Mainstream poets like Adrienne Rich, John Hollander, and Richard Wilbur were included. Allen's collection, however, provided a forum for the many experimental poets working in the United States. He viewed these poets as inheritors of the innovations set in motion by Ezra Pound and William Carlos Williams. The work of this new generation had heretofore reached its growing audience only through publication in small magazines and by independent presses or through readings. The Beats, including Allen Ginsberg and Jack Kerouac, were represented, as well as poets of the New York school and the San Francisco Renaissance. Allen also created a new designation for a group of writers otherwise difficult to categorize: the Black Mountain School. To this school he assigned Charles Olson, Robert Creeley, Denise Levertov, Edward Dorn, Joel Oppenheimer, Paul Blackburn, Jonathan Williams, Paul Carroll, Robert Duncan, and Larry Eigner. They were named for the short-lived but much storied Black Mountain College, of which Olson was the rector from 1951 until it dissolved in 1956.

## BLACK MOUNTAIN COLLEGE

Black Mountain College was founded in North Carolina in 1933 by the educator John Andrew Rice as an experimental school along the lines of Evergreen College in Washington and Bennington College in Vermont. He envisioned the school as an experiment in democratic and liberal education. Because Rice believed practical responsibilities, along with study in the creative arts, are essential to the development of the intellect, students participated in running the school: constructing buildings, serving meals, and working on the college's farm. Administrative decisions were made by consensus among a faculty board, with input from an elected student representative. Students created their own courses of study. There were no set requirements for graduation, and each student was evaluated individually by the faculty and an outside scholar to determine fitness to graduate.

Rice brought with him a cadre of professors who had recently either been fired or resigned from Rollins College in Florida. He also engaged the artist Josef Albers, who had lately come to the United States after leaving his teaching position at the Bauhaus in Germany. Immensely influential in the community, Albers brought to Black Mountain College many of the pedagogies of the Bauhaus, including an emphasis on practical skills and the view of students as apprentices to their artisan teachers. With Albers came his wife, Anni Albers, a prominent textile artist who had run the weaving studio at the Bauhaus. Together with their Bauhaus legacy, the Alberses lent Black Mountain College added credibility and brought the school to the attention of members of the artistic community, including many fellow refugee artists who also had fled the growing turmoil in Europe.

By the time Olson became involved with Black Mountain College in 1948, Albers had succeeded Rice as the college's rector. Olson was invited to fill a position vacated by his friend and mentor, the poet and novelist Edward Dahlberg. Albers left Black Mountain College for Yale in 1949. The departure of many of the staff and students around this time, over philosophical and administrative disagreements, caused the college to become even less structured academically, and Black Mountain College began its transformation into something that, in its final years, came to resemble a community of working artists more than a college.

The school's constantly precarious financial situation reached epic proportions after Olson became rector in 1951. During these final years, many of the biggest names in the American avant-garde were associated with the college. The composer John Cage, the choreographer

Merce Cunningham, the architect Buckminster Fuller, and the painters Franz Kline and Robert Motherwell taught and worked there. The painters Robert Rauschenberg and Cy Twombly, and the sculptor John Chamberlain were students and went on to be some of the most successful and influential artists of their generation. Olson brought in Creeley and Duncan as teachers, and asked Creeley to edit the newly founded and instrumental *Black Mountain Review*, which, along with the poet Cid Corman's magazine, *Origin*, published early work of many of the Black Mountain poets, the Beats, and other innovative writers.

Of Allen's original Black Mountain poets, Olson, Creeley, and Duncan were instructors at the college. Dorn and Oppenheimer were students. Others, like Levertov, never set foot on the campus. Michael Rumaker and Russell Edson were two poets who attended Black Mountain College but were not included in Allen's anthology; John Wieners, another student at the school, appeared in the anthology, but under the Miscellaneous category. Though Olson invented many schemes to try to save Black Mountain College from dissolution, the financial situation finally became entirely infeasible and the school began to self-destruct. There was no money to buy coal to heat the facilities, the land was about to be foreclosed on, enrollment had sunk to barely more than a dozen students. The school closed but its legacy lived on, its reputation as an important and formative institution growing as the poets and artists associated with Black Mountain College became better known.

## PROJECTIVE VERSE

Olson was the undisputed leader of the Black Mountain poets not only because of his position as rector at the college but also through his seminal statement on poetics, "Projective Verse." Born in 1910 in Worcester, Massachusetts, Olson was the son of a postman. He was raised in a working-class family and distinguished himself as a scholar during his high school years. He attended Wesleyan College (B.A., 1932; M.A., 1933), returning to Worcester during the summer to help his father deliver mail. Olson was one of the first people to enter Harvard's American Studies graduate program, an interdisciplinary course of study designed to facilitate the kind of broad-minded curiosity that later informed Olson's work. Though he had finished his course work, Olson left Harvard without receiving his doctorate when he was awarded a Guggenheim Fellowship in 1939. Later, during World War II, Olson worked as the assistant chief in the Foreign Language Division of the Office of War Information (later the U.S. Information Agency) during President Franklin Delano Roosevelt's administration. He quit in 1945, however, over disputes regarding censorship of his news releases. He straggled through various jobs with the Democratic Party before quitting the political life to devote himself to poetry. Olson's first mark on the literary map was the publication in 1947 of *Call Me Ishmael*, a study of Herman Melville's *Moby-Dick* that remains one of the outstanding contributions to American belles lettres. His essay "Projective Verse" was published in pamphlet form in 1950 and enthusiastically quoted in William Carlos Williams's *Autobiography* the following year.

In his manifesto, Olson laid out the necessities of forging a new kind of form, something that took the work of Pound and Williams and their modernist experimentation to a new level. Olson was, in fact, the first to use the term "postmodern" in its present meaning. He picked up a number of different threads to weave into his new poetic: Williams's interest in vernacular speech and his dictum "No ideas but in things"; the idea of the French symbolist poet, Paul Valéry, that the lyric can be defined as content and form realized simultaneously; Milton's attention to syllabic prosody; Melville's expansiveness. This particular intersection in American history was one in which jazz was changing the musical terrain and abstract expressionism held the art world in its thrall. Both of these movements were responding to the social and political changes set in motion during World War II and amplified by America's use of the atom bomb on Japan in 1945. They represented, in part, artists' and musicians' attempts to understand and depict America's new understanding of irreversibility and mortality. Jazz broke down and restructured traditional elements of melody, while abstract expressionism rendered moot standard expectations that paintings be pictorial and figurative. Traditional forms clearly were no longer adequate in any genre. Olson felt it was necessary for poetry to adapt to these changes.

"Projective Verse" proposes a kind of instantism in poetry and something Olson called "composition by field." Academe was in the grips of New Criticism, a method of critique in which readers were forbidden to consider any factors outside the work. The New Critics insisted all interpretation must be generated from the text itself, without reference to history, culture, biography, or theory. Mainstream poets were working almost entirely within the strictures of traditional English prosody and poetics. Olson believed that the poet, the process of writing a poem, the form of the piece, and the final product are inextricably linked. Just as contemporary musicians and painters were engaged as much in their process of creation as in its product, so Olson posited that the poet must preserve and convey in the poem elements of the original energy that propels him or her to begin the poem.

Olson rejected inherited notions of the line, stanza, and other elements of closed form. If poets surrender themselves wholly to the poem, they will be led into its individual field, and both the poet and the poem will be projected forward on a series of perceptions that lead instantly to other perceptions, the way each breath leads to the next. The field represents not only the whole page that the poet may put to use but also the realm of content available to the writer. Olson urged poets to use their ears to hear the poem's individual syllables, which he felt were the fundamental building blocks, and far more important than meter or rhyme. Olson was suggesting, in some ways, a return to poetry, like that of Milton, which relied heavily on syllabic verse. Paying attention to the syllables of a poem was a way to engage with the piece on a minute and intimate level as well as a kind of pre-sense way of communicating directly from the poet's ear to the reader's. Once syllables are mastered, the poet can move on to the line. The line, Olson believed, necessarily varies from person to person and is determined by breath. Olson was a huge man, well over six feet tall, who could smoke a cigarette in one inhalation. Consequently his lines tend to be very long and more than an average person could pronounce in one breath. He wrote that syllables come to the poem from the head by way of the ear, while lines come from the heart by way of the breath.

Once Olson established the form projective verse should take, he moved on to content and the rhetorical devices necessary to convey it. He dismissed the simile as too easy and cautioned against excessive description as a potential drain on the energy of the piece. Instead, Olson positioned objects as the most important part of the content and suggested they must be encountered in the poem as objects would be encountered in a field. Olson believed that grammar should be toyed with and should serve the line rather than traditional rules. He hailed the typewriter as the tool that frees the poet to record thoughts and speech exactly as he or she hears or conceives of them, as a composer scores music on the staff and bar. Olson cited the typographical experimentation of the poet E. E. Cummings as an example of the way a poet can convey pauses, breath, and speed to readers.

Olson wound up the essay with a discussion of the content a projective poem should take up. Subjects, he argued, should expand beyond tradition, should spring from the dramatic center of the poet. The poet will be able to achieve this paragon of content only if he or she can simultaneously dwell deep within, connect with the larger forces of nature and history, and assert primacy over these forces. The individual poet, therefore, is more important than any tradition or doctrine. In short, the poet transmits a message of experience or emotion to the reader through a neutral and natural language.

Although all the poets in *The New American Poetry* were experimenters, and most revered Pound and Williams, the various schools focused on different influences and subjects. The New York school produced poems that were more overtly playful and looked to the French avant-garde of the early twentieth century for sources and philosophy. The Beats were more inclined to take up timely political issues as subject matter, and they were interested in exploring Eastern religion in both their lives and their poetry. The work of all these poets provides a substantial part of the foundation upon which contemporary poetry is built, and Allen's categories have become largely obsolete. "Projective Verse," however, was the most influential manifesto for Olson's generation and the generation immediately following, and is one of the few statements of poetics produced during the midcentury that remains alive and relevant to today's poets.

## THE POETS

Robert Creeley (b. 1926) and Charles Olson (1910–1970) were close friends who became acquainted when Cid Corman published their work in *Origin*. They maintained a correspondence for several years before meeting when Olson invited Creeley to teach at Black Mountain College in 1954. Like Olson, Creeley came from a working-class, New England family and had attended Harvard (though not when Olson was there), leaving before completing a degree. Creeley joined the American Field Service, married shortly after returning from India and Burma, raised chickens in New Hampshire, then moved to Aix-en-Provence in France, where his neighbors were a friend from college and that friend's wife, Denise Levertov.

Levertov (1923–1997) came to be an influential and highly respected poet, but her connection to the Black Mountain poets is tenuous at best. She neither taught at nor attended Black Mountain College, and she rejected any attempts to categorize her work. It's notable that she is the only woman Allen included among the Black

Mountain poets. Olson treated women in a patriarchal and dismissive way, alienating many of the female students and faculty at Black Mountain College. Born in England, Levertov immigrated to her husband's native United States shortly after publishing her first book, and is considered an American poet rather than a British one. Her poetic style is informed by William Carlos Williams's vernacular more than by projective verse, and she was, in fact, very close to the older poet.

She was also close to Robert Duncan (1919–1988), who had written a letter to her that praised her first book. Levertov and Duncan remained astute readers of one another's work and dedicated correspondents until they had a falling out over the overtly political bent Levertov's work took in the 1960s. The first issue of *The Black Mountain Review* contained an attack on Duncan by Olson. Later, however, when Duncan read "Projective Verse" and was invited to teach at Black Mountain College in 1955, he revised his opinion of Olson. While teaching at the college, Duncan worked on the poems for *The Opening of the Field*, published in 1960, which clearly show Olson's influence.

Olson, Creeley, Levertov, and Duncan are the most recognized and influential of the Black Mountain poets. Even the most cursory examination of their poetry, however, reveals vast differences in style and content. All four retain utterly individual voices. Olson's sprawling work discloses his interest in mythology, cultural studies, postmodern theory, anthropology, and language. Creeley's work couldn't look more different from Olson's on the page. His tight, spare poems dwell primarily in the realms of the abstract and emotional. Duncan's poems physically resemble Olson's, but his interest in the mystical and in writers like Gertrude Stein and the poet H.D. (Hilda Doolittle) set him apart. Hailing from the West Coast, he also provides a connection to the poets of the San Francisco Renaissance. He and his long-term partner, the collage artist Jess (Collins), were close friends of such San Francisco poets as Jack Spicer and Robin Blaser. Levertov had a much greater interest in subverting rather than in rejecting traditional prosody and pursued her own agenda of spiritual mysticism and political conscience.

Edward Dorn.
(© *Christopher Felver/Corbis*)

The remaining six poets never achieved the same recognition as the primary four, and their work in *The New American Poetry* is, stylistically, largely interchangeable. At the time of Allen's anthology they were, however, still very much under Olson's spell, and many went on to develop somewhat more distinct voices.

Edward Dorn (1929–1999), born in rural Illinois, attended the University of Illinois before becoming a student at Black Mountain College. He holds the distinction of being one of the few students to graduate from that institution. He is immortalized in Olson's 1964 work *A Bibliography on America for Ed Dorn*. In 1968 Dorn published the first volume of his three-part *Gunslinger* series, an epic poem of the American West, hallucinogenic drugs, the 1960s, and the creation of a self mythology. *Gunslinger* bears the unmistakable mark of Olson's *Maximus* poems. Dorn also gained from Olson an interest in Central and South American languages and became a noted translator of contemporary and historical literature from indigenous Mayan, Toltec, and Nahuatl cultures. By the time of Dorn's death in 1999, he had been teaching at the University of Colorado in Boulder for almost two decades and had produced more than forty books and chapbooks of poetry, prose, and translations.

Originally from North Carolina, Jonathan Williams (b. 1929) has distinguished himself as a publisher and has consistently brought to light the poetry of young and/or experimental poets. He founded Jargon Books (later the Jargon Society) in 1951 to publish neglected poets, particularly those associated with Black Mountain College. He was a student at Black Mountain College from 1951 until 1956. In addition to being an influential force in the world of independent publishing, Williams is a noted photographer and essayist. He and Robert Creeley are the only original Black Mountain poets still living.

Joel Oppenheimer (1930–1988) was born in Yonkers, New York, and went to Black Mountain College in 1950 to learn to paint, but changed his path after studying with Olson. After a number of jobs, including journalist and typographer, he became the first director of New York City's St. Mark's Poetry Project in 1966, and he wrote a regular column for the *Village Voice* from 1969 to 1984. In

1982 Oppenheimer moved to New Hampshire to teach at New England College, and he died there from lung cancer six years later.

Paul Blackburn (1926–1971) is connected to the Black Mountain poets through his acquaintance with Robert Creeley. The two men started a correspondence after Ezra Pound encouraged Blackburn to write to Creeley. Creeley's Divers Press published Blackburn's first book, *The Dissolving Fabric*, in 1955, and the men were briefly neighbors on Mallorca. Blackburn became known as much for his controversial but adept translations of Provençal troubadour poetry as for his own poetry. He helped found St. Mark's Poetry Project before dying of esophageal cancer in 1971 in Cortland, New York, leaving behind eighteen books of poetry.

Larry Eigner's (1927–1996) first book, *From the Sustaining Air* (1953), was published by Divers Press. Eigner was born in Massachusetts. Disabled by cerebral palsy from birth, he spent his life in a wheelchair and had difficulty speaking clearly. His poetry, though he was limited to what he could see from his window, contains vivid and astute observations on nature and human interaction. After living for fifty-one years in his parents' house in Swampscott, Massachusetts, Eigner moved to Berkeley, California, where he joined a community of writers eager to integrate this man whose work they'd long admired. Eigner was tremendously valued by younger poets, to whom he was a generous mentor, and many writers took inspiration from the commitment he showed, despite his physical difficulties, to poetry. He published more than forty books before his death from pneumonia and attendant complications in 1996.

Paul Carroll (1927–1996) did not make it into Donald M. Allen's revised edition of *The New American Poetry*. This follow-up volume, *The Postmoderns: The New American Poetry Revised* (1982), dropped five of the poets from the original, including Carroll. Like Eigner, Carroll was immensely important to the younger generation of avant-garde poets, and he encouraged them with his contagious enthusiasm. In the 1970s, he founded the Poetry Center of Chicago and the Program for Writers at the University of Illinois-Chicago.

Though none of these poets gained the kind of renown Duncan, Olson, Creeley, and Levertov enjoyed, all of them left their marks on the generations of poets who followed. Besides serving as dedicated teachers and mentors, many of them proved to be generous editors, facilitating the publication of younger poets' work by small presses and in literary journals. They are remembered more in these roles as promoters of poetry than for the work they published, and in this way have made important contributions to the state of American poetics.

[*See also* Creeley, Robert; Levertov, Denise; *and* New Critics, The.]

## FURTHER READING

Allen, Donald M. *The New American Poetry*. New York, 1960.

Colclough Little, Anne, and Paul, Susie, eds. *Denise Levertov: New Perspectives*. West Cornwall, Conn., 2000. Essays on Denise Levertov by various authors, including the poets Anne Waldman and Lucille Clifton.

Elmborg, James K. *"A Pageant of Its Time": Edward Dorn's "Slinger" and the Sixties*. New York, 1998. A critical discussion of Dorn's *Gunslinger* and its relation to the counterculture of the 1960s.

Foster, Edward Halsey. *Understanding the Black Mountain Poets*. Columbia, S.C., 1995. A short, basic study addressing Olson, Creeley, and Duncan.

Fox, Willard. *Robert Creeley, Edward Dorn, and Robert Duncan: A Reference Guide*. Boston, 1989.

Fredman, Stephen. *The Grounding of American Poetry: Charles Olson and the Emersonian Tradition*. Cambridge, 1993. A study of Olson, Creeley, and Duncan and their relationship to influence and experimentation in American poetry.

Gilmore, Lyman. *Don't Touch the Poet: The Life and Times of Joel Oppenheimer*. Jersey City, N.J., 1998.

O'Leary, Peter. *Gnostic Contagion: Robert Duncan and the Poetry of Illness*. Middletown, Conn., 2002. An interdisciplinary study of Duncan's life and work, including psychological analysis and discussion of religious history.

Paul, Sherman. *Olson's Push: Origin, Black Mountain and Recent American Poetry*. Baton Rouge, La., 1978.

# ANNE BRADSTREET

*by Daniel G. Brayton*

Anne Bradstreet has long been the best-known English-language woman poet of the seventeenth century and one of the most famous early American literary figures. While numerous women writers of her era have, in the past two decades, gained a wider readership than ever before, largely because of the recuperative efforts of feminist literary scholars, Bradstreet has needed no such resurrection. She has been widely admired since her poems were first published in 1650. Her fame is often attributed to her status as one of the first English poets, male or female, writing in the Americas. Indeed, the title of the first published volume, *The Tenth Muse Lately Sprung Up in America*, suggests that the novelty of a poet writing in New England was a significant part of her appeal. Yet there can be no doubt that Bradstreet's work stands on its own. Readers appreciate her poetry for its passionate treatment of familial and theological themes and for its simple elegance.

Like Emily Dickinson two centuries later, Bradstreet has become as famous for her remarkable life as for her poetic achievement. Both poets wrote personal, meditative verses; the major theme of both poets was the relationship of the natural world to a distant and domineering creator-god whose ways were ultimately incomprehensible to mortals; and they both created literary microcosms based on local topics when momentous historical events were transpiring around them. Perhaps because both poets were women writing in the adverse circumstances of isolated, provincial, male-dominated surroundings, poets whose works might never have been published or known to readers without the intervention of benevolent admirers, both have become the heroines of romantic cultural narratives. Students are at least as likely to be exposed to the cultural narratives, or myths, as they are to read the poems. In the case of Anne Bradstreet, the poetic achievement has everything to do with the life of the poet.

## LIFE AND EDUCATION

Anne Bradstreet was born Anne Dudley, the second child of Thomas Dudley and Dorothy Yorke, in Northampton, England, in 1612 or 1613. More is known of her father than of her mother, although the latter was of "gentle" status and was described by Cotton Mather as "a gentlewoman whose extract and estate were considerable." Thomas Dudley came from a rather illustrious family; in fact, the great sixteenth-century poet Sir Philip Sidney once wrote, "my chiefest honor is to be a Dudley." While the religious reformers somewhat misleadingly known as Puritans often came from the emergent middle class of cities, the Dudleys were of high social status, a noble family with a heraldic shield and connections to some of the most powerful families in England. Yet notwithstanding their noble lineage, the Dudleys were Puritans through and through. Thomas Dudley was a follower of the Puritan preacher John Dod, and later of the renowned John Cotton.

Dudley was a capable man whose active and successful career followed from his talents as an administrator and his nonconformist religious sympathies. He was orphaned at the age of ten, served as a page in a household of distinction, and was a soldier under Queen Elizabeth. In 1619 he became the steward of the earl of Lincoln, a noted nonconformist, and this position made him a relatively prominent and well-connected figure among Lincolnshire Puritans. A steward's job was to manage the estate of a wealthy lord or lady; to be the steward of an earl entailed a great deal of trust and responsibility. The job meant that the Dudley family lived in close proximity with its wealthy and aristocratic patron, with access to lovely grounds and a well-stocked library. The young Anne Dudley, thus, spent the first part of her life in far different circumstances than the relative wilderness of New England where she would spend the better part of her life.

Being a Puritan did not mean living a monastic life, but it did entail certain forms of discipline that non-Puritans often found amusing or even ridiculous. This discipline had the benefit of instilling literacy, however, for reading Scripture (the Bible) was an important feature of Puritan religious practice. Radical Protestants such as the Dudleys were suspicious of all religious paraphernalia—gaudy clothes, symbols, the church hierarchy—that mediated their relationship to the deity. They believed in immediate access to the word of God, which for them meant the reading and interpretation of the Bible. The Bible was a best-seller in the sixteenth and seventeenth centuries, and numerous editions were available. The English Protestant William Tyndale translated much of the Bible in the 1520s, and in 1535 Miles Coverdale published the first complete English Bible. Other English editions included the Great Bible of 1540, the Geneva Bible of 1560, the Bishops' Bible of 1568, and the official King James Version of 1611. Many of these translations contained significant differences as they were the work of different religious groups. Bradstreet, like many Puritans, read the Geneva Bible.

Reading Scripture was, inevitably, a major part of Anne's upbringing, something that, according to her own memoir, she began at a young age. Her knowledge of biblical lore and of the rhythms and vocabulary of its more Protestant translations (the Tyndale and Geneva versions) resonate in her verse. But it was not just the language of the Bible that influenced her writing; it was also the thematic content. The Bible contains passages critical of kings, a fact that religious dissenters tended to emphasize. The eminent historian Christopher Hill has argued that the English Bible was one of the major causes of the seventeenth-century revolution in England. The biblical culture that developed in England in the sixteenth and seventeenth centuries promoted literacy as well as widespread criticism of the prelates, the powerful church leaders who opposed religious nonconformists. In the decades before the English Revolution, the tension between the king and his powerful prelates on the one hand, and the various groups of nonconformists on the other, became unbearable for a large number of the latter category. For those Puritans considering whether or not to settle in New England, a new land where they could build the kingdom of God, or at least a society safe for Puritans, the Bible was an agent of motivation.

Committed as they were to a culture of literacy, Puritans did not limit their reading to Scripture. Anne Dudley's reading was thoroughly up-to-date and included the works of Edmund Spenser, Philip Sidney (to whom she wrote an elegy in 1638), Walter Raleigh's *History of the World* (1614), William Camden's *Annals of Queen Elizabeth* (1615), and the writings of the French Calvinist Guillaume du Bartas (to whom she wrote a tribute in 1641). The last two of these were no doubt the most influential. *La Sepmaine; ou, du Creation du Monde*

(1578) of Du Bartas had recently been translated into English by Joshua Sylvester as *The Divine Weeks and Works* (1608), a popular text among English Puritans and others. Bradstreet shared with du Bartas an interest in reading "the book of nature," or understanding the natural world as a cornucopia of signs attesting to the presence of a divine creator. As Bradstreet herself wrote of du Bartas in the Prologue to *The Four Elements*,

> But when my wond'ring eyes and envious heart
> Great Bartas' sugared lines do but read o'er,
> Fool I do grudge the Muses did not part
> 'Twixt him and me that overfluent store;
> A Bartas can do what a Bartas will,
> But simple I according to my skill.

While du Bartas undoubtedly influenced Bradstreet's interest in the natural world as a book of divine signs, she did not slavishly imitate his style, and the relationship of the two poets is hardly that of master and apprentice. Nevertheless, du Bartas was a formative influence on the young Anne Bradstreet.

Puritanism was a culture of hard work and self-discipline, and Anne's education was clearly a rigorous one. Her connection with Emmanuel College, Cambridge, which her brother and her father's employer both attended, undoubtedly contributed to her learning. So, too, did the rhetorical performances of the Puritan preachers who played a large part in her family life. The radical Protestantism of the day was, to some extent, a rhetorical culture, defined as much by its habits of expression as by the content of its doctrines. Indeed, the poetic works of devoutly Protestant poets such as Philip Sidney and George Herbert vividly attest to the expressive power of the more extreme forms of Protestantism that flourished in England in the Elizabethan and Jacobean eras. Religious writing and preaching was often stylistically innovative and compelling, and the young poet could not help but be influenced by the fiery and often quite powerful sermons of her family's circle. Her interest in worldly matters—love, devotion, suffering, desire—reflects a religious practice that was hardly ascetic.

In 1622 Simon Bradstreet, a graduate of Emmanuel College and a fellow Puritan, became Thomas Dudley's assistant at the earl of Lincoln's estate at Sempringham. Although a younger man, Bradstreet resembled Dudley in many ways, having been orphaned, espousing the Puritan cause, and developing into a capable administrator after years of service. Both men would later become prominent leaders in the Massachusetts Bay Colony, and both would eventually hold the position of governor there. Dudley put great trust in Bradstreet, and when he moved with his family to the nearby town of Boston, also in Lincolnshire, where the Puritan cause was strong, Bradstreet took over his duties as steward at Sempringham. Soon Bradstreet, too, moved away, becoming for a time the steward of the countess of Warwick, a fellow Puritan. But this job was relatively short-lived; soon Bradstreet and the Dudleys would move on to an altogether new situation.

In the 1620s the growing religious and political turmoil in England began to put increasing pressure on nonconformist groups. These were hard times for Puritans. Eventually, during the revolution of the 1640s and 1650s, conditions would improve dramatically for Puritans and religious dissenters of many stripes. But in the period of simmering before the religious antagonisms exploded into war, there were many reasons for religious reformers and dissenters to leave England.

The monarch, Charles I (who would later be decapitated during the English Revolution), was never sympathetic to the Puritan cause and became increasingly difficult to bear as he asserted his power against the Puritan-dominated Parliament and attempted to consolidate his own absolutism. The Stuart kings were never particularly fond of hard-line Protestants, but James I, Charles's father, had been reasonably cautious in treading on their toes. Less cautious than his father, however, Charles sympathized with Catholics and stridently insisted on his own absolute authority to rule the nation—and the national church. Supported by his loyal nobles and churchmen, such as the brutal Archbishop William Laud, who saw Puritans as upstart commoners, he came down hard on the Puritan cause and fought continually with those elements of English society with which the Dudleys and Simon Bradstreet were associated.

The early years of Charles's reign were particularly dire for the likes of the Dudleys, and many Puritans actively made plans to leave the country to build God's kingdom in the New World. In 1627 Lord Lincoln was arrested for his opposition to the king's efforts to raise money by forced loan; soon, others of the Sempringham household were jailed, too. Thomas Dudley was in jeopardy. To make matters worse, his daughter, Anne, came down with smallpox and experienced a temporary loss of faith. In 1628, very soon after recovering her health and faith, Anne Dudley married Simon Bradstreet at the age of fifteen or sixteen. He was twenty-five.

The commonplace stereotype of Puritans portrays them as harsh, ascetic people completely opposed to all sensuality. This is an immense misconception. Not only were there many kinds of religious nonconformity in Renaissance England, but varieties of doctrine and attitude concerning earthly matters—desire, sex, gender roles—were many as well. The religious nonconformists of the seventeenth century, including many so-called Puritans, were often quite radical in their sexual mores. Women were particularly prominent in New England, although the Bay Colony elders often did their best to suppress them. One of the refreshing and, perhaps, surprising aspects of Bradstreet's poetry is its unabashed celebration of earthly love between a man and a woman. The following poem, addressed to her husband, does not refer to the pleasures of the flesh, but it bespeaks a pleasure in earthly union that those unfamiliar with the worldliness of the Puritans might find surprising.

> If ever two were one, then surely we.
> If ever man were loved by wife, then thee.
> If ever wife was happy in a man,
> Compare with me, ye women, if you can.
> I prize thy love more than whole mines of gold
> Or all the riches that the East doth hold.
> My love is such that rivers cannot quench,
> Nor ought but love from thee, give recompense,
> Thy love is such, I can no way repay,
> The heavens reward thee manifold, I pray.
> Then while we live, let's so persevere
> That when we live no more, we may live ever.

What is surprising about these lines is that they sound so modern. Bradstreet strikes a theological note in this poem of marital love, but the relationship described seems thoroughly mortal. The fact that she would bear eight children, not all of whom survived, was not unusual. But it was unusual that she would write about her love for her husband in powerful, compelling poetry that puts the two partners on a remarkably equal level.

Anne wrote a number of passionate poems and letters to Simon that express a powerful physical and spiritual sympathy between them. While it is potentially misleading to read such lines as a straightforward description of the poet's relationship with her husband, this and other poems strongly suggest that the relationship was a robust and loving one. Beginning as it did many years before those lines were penned, we can at least be certain that the relationship began at a time when Anne was returning to the fold after a temporary loss of faith, a fact that suggests a spiritual dimension to the marriage from the start. Yet time and again in her poetry, Bradstreet affirms the significance of worldly attachment.

The young Anne Bradstreet and her new husband were not destined to remain in England for long. In 1629 Simon Bradstreet and Thomas Dudley signed for the charter of the Great Seal of the Massachusetts Bay Company. Early in 1630 both the Dudleys and the Bradstreets sailed for America aboard the *Arbella*, landing at Salem on 12 June of that year after a difficult voyage. Soon after the Bay Colony expanded, as a large number of Puritans settled in and around Salem and Boston. Conditions were harsh, however, and a large number of settlers died in the first winter. Others later returned to England, preferring to brave political and religious persecution over the fierce New England winters and inhospitable landscape. But the Dudleys and Bradstreets remained. Once in Massachusetts they moved around a great deal, living for a time in Salem, Boston, Newtown (later Cambridge), Agawam (later Ipswich), and, finally, in 1644, North Andover, where Anne would spend her last years. She died there on 16 September 1672.

While her father and husband embarked on successful political careers in the Bay Colony, relatively little is known about the specifics of Anne Bradstreet's life in New England, although her life has been the subject of much speculation and myth. It is clear, however, that she spent a great deal of time bearing and raising children, as well as writing and revising her poems—poems that circulated among family members in manuscript form before making their way across the Atlantic and into print.

## POETIC CAREER

Bradstreet's enduring reputation as a poet owes much to the timely publication of her poems in England while she lived three thousand miles and a long sea voyage away in New England. She also had the distinct good fortune to have her works offered to the public by others, admirers who took upon themselves the task of seeing her poems to the press. The introductory letter that accompanied her first book, *The Tenth Muse*, claims that the author herself would not have approved the publication of her own poems: "I feare the displeasure of no person in the publishing of these Poems but the Authors, without whose knowledge and contrary to her expectation, I have presumed to bring to publick view what she resolved should never in such a manner see the Sun; but I have sent forth broken pieces to the Authors prejudice, which I sought to prevent, as well as to pleasure those that earnestly desired the view of the whole." The sentiments of the letter writer, I.W., most likely Bradstreet's brother-in-law, John Woodbridge, seem genuine, but such letters as this were quite frequently appended to published literature.

We must understand such expressions of reticence to publish in the context of the early modern "stigma of print." The publication of poetry, plays, and other sorts of literary fiction in seventeenth-century England was widely viewed as a vulgar form of self-display that, like the profession of acting, could render a person "common." The safest way to publish was to have someone else do it for you, and then protest against the display of one's private sentiments. These disavowals were generally penned by the author, but oftentimes they were written by someone else who invariably claimed a desire to rescue good poetry from oblivion. Frequent as were such statements of a poet's unwillingness to publish, literate amateurs, then as now, wrote poems for themselves, their friends, and family. It seems quite possible that Bradstreet wrote her poems with a small—even minute—readership in mind.

It is, indeed, possible that Bradstreet never intended to publish. The intimate nature of many of her poems supports this possibility. Bradstreet's lack of involvement in the initial publication of poems collected in *The Tenth Muse* is further indicated by her subsequent efforts to revise and amend the collection. *The Tenth Muse* does not represent Bradstreet's best work. With age she continued to grow and improve as a poet. Compared to *Several Poems*, the 1678 edition of her work, *The Tenth Muse* appears the work of an immature poet. Whether or not she wanted to publish, the fact remains that Anne Bradstreet took poetry quite seriously and had recourse to it to express powerful sentiments about her life, her novel circumstances, and her spirituality.

We should not think of Bradstreet as an accidental poet. She produced verses over many years, editing, revising, and improving them. If the young Anne Bradstreet was a talented if somewhat unpolished versifier, the mature Anne Bradstreet was a formidably skilled wordsmith. Moreover, publication established her identity as a poet in an era when many women writers struggled, quite often without success, to find their way into print. She not only wrote poems, which other English women did in the seventeenth century; one way or another, she found a wide readership for them, which most women did not. Of primary interest, then, is how a woman who led such an unusual and difficult life should become such an accomplished poet—and be recognized as such.

It should come as no surprise that a child born into an accomplished family, whose early life was spent in very comfortable circumstances in an era of spectacular religious and literary productivity, should write verses of a high quality. What is surprising, however, is that this poet should be female. In seventeenth-century England, not only were girls regularly given less formal education than boys, but the role of poet was only available to men. While women did write verse, it was a pursuit that only a few aristocratic women could safely indulge. It was not a recognized or generally available avocation for women, and numerous obstacles lay in the way of publishing. To be a woman and a published poet could have disastrous social consequences, a fact to which Bradstreet refers in several of her poems.

Difficult though conditions were for doing so, women did write poetry in the seventeenth century, and occasionally they took up arms against the prevalent sexism of the times that labeled them lesser poets than men. So, too, with Bradstreet. In a stanza of the Prologue she writes,

> I am obnoxious to each carping tongue
> Who says my hand a needle better fit,
> A poet's pen all scorn I should thus wrong,
> For such despite they cast on female wits:
> If what I do prove well, it won't advance,
> They'll say it's stol'n, or else it was by chance.

Here she undermines the potential tactics of sexist detractors, of whom there were many in the mid-seventeenth century, by disallowing the claim of theft or accident when a woman wrote good verses.

These lines rather forcefully assert the status of their author as a poet, a fact that not only speaks to Bradstreet's intellectual independence but also to the relative—and only relative—independence of nonconformist women in the seventeenth century. Nonconformist religious practice frequently gave women the opportunity to have a voice in spiritual matters. Prophetic writers such as Anna Trapnell, thus, claimed special access to spiritual truth. Others, such as the other famous Anne of the Massachusetts Bay Colony, Anne Hutchinson, became actively involved in matters of spiritual doctrine and worldly governance. Bradstreet's boldness in proclaiming her sex and her authorship, thus, was in part made possible by the unusual power of women in the particular spiritual subculture to which she belonged.

Part of the reason for the unusual prominence of women's voices in charismatic religion was the fact that, in Renaissance England, the forms of literary expression available to women—when they were available at all—were few. One of them was "child-loss" poetry, in which the poetic speaker is invariably a mother or grandmother lamenting the death of a child. It flourished in Elizabethan and Jacobean times. One of the strengths of

Bradstreet's poetry is the presence of a powerful speaking voice with which to express sentiments generally associated with conventional female verse forms. The combination of this direct voice and the forceful sentiments it expresses gives her poems a freshness that conventional women's verse forms often lacked. When Bradstreet writes about the death of a child, the conventional nature of verses written in epitaph shows through, but the emotions can also seem raw and immediate, in part due to the simplicity of the verse.

Such simplicity often hides a carefully chosen and tightly woven metaphoric structure. A case in point is her poem *In Memory of My Dear Grandchild Anne Bradstreet Who Deceased June 20, 1669, Being Three Years and Seven Months Old*.

> With troubled heart and trembling hand I write,
> The heavens have changed to sorrow my delight.
> How oft with disappointment have I met,
> When I on fading things my hopes have set.
> Experience might 'fore this have made me wise,
> To value things according to their price.
> Was ever stable joy yet found below?
> Or perfect bliss without mixture of woe?
> I knew she was but as a withering flower,
> That's here today, perhaps gone in an hour;
> Like as a bubble, or the brittle glass,
> Or like a shadow turning as it was.
> More fool than I to look on that was lent
> As if mine own, when thus impermanent.
> Farewell dear child, thou ne'er shall come to me,
> But yet a while, and I shall go to thee;
> Mean time my throbbing heart's cheered up with this:
> Thou with thy Saviour art in endless bliss.

As she does elsewhere, Bradstreet here meditates on the passing of love, happiness, and life itself, embodied in the deceased child. The child's death forces a meditative introspection that leads to a statement of faith. Typical of Bradstreet is the religious statement of faith—all will be well in the afterlife—as a means of tempering the sorrow of the preceding lines. The deity, here and elsewhere in her poems, is both the owner of all beings and the great account keeper who only lends mortal beings any joy they have "found below."

Women in the seventeenth century generally led difficult lives; the constraints of marriage, childbirth, and patriarchal subordination determined much of what they could and could not do. Like many other women of her time, Bradstreet bore numerous children; unlike many, she wrote about it, and she did so with an emotional directness that continues to captivate readers.

The following, very famous poem, *Before the Birth of One of Her Children*, exemplifies her characteristic focus on familial themes and the uncertainty of a world haunted by death and instability. Addressed to her husband, the poem gives voice to the fears of a woman for her children if she should die.

All things within this fading world hath end,
Adversity doth still our joyes attend
No tyes so strong no friends so clear and sweet,
But with deaths parting blow is sure to meet.
A common thing, yet oh inevitable;
How soon, my Dear death may my steps attend,
How soon't may be thy Lot to lose thy friend,
We both are ignorant, yet love bids me
These farewell lines to recommend to thee,
That when that knots untyd that made us one,
I may seem thine, who in effect am none.
And if I see not half my dayes that's due,
What nature would, God grant to yours and you;
The many faults that well you know I have,
Let be interr'd in my oblivious grave;
If any worth or virtue were in me,
Let that live freshly in thy memory
And when thou feel'st no grief, as I no harms,
Yet love thy dead, who long lay in thine arms:
And when thy loss shall be repaid with gains
Look to my little babes my dear remains.
And if thou love thyself, or loved'st me
These I protect from step Dames injury.
And if chance to thine eyes shall bring this verse,
With some sad sighs honour my absent Herse;
And kiss this paper for thy loves dear sake,
Who with salt tears this last Farewell did take.

These lines attest to Bradstreet's directness and vigor as a poet; they also tell a poignant story that appeals to the reader's desire for a stable narrative within which to cast the future.

In her striking development of the metaphoric connection between the writing of poetry and motherhood, Bradstreet consistently and quite self-consciously combats the notion of poetry as an exclusively masculine vocation. In *The Author to Her Book*, which accompanied the 1678 edition of her works, published six years after her death, Bradstreet develops the metaphor of her verse as a child to excellent effect.

Thou ill-formed offspring of my feeble brain,
Who after birth didst by my side remain,
Till snatched from thence by friends, less wise than true,
Who thee abroad, exposed to public view,
Made thee in rags, halting to th' press to trudge,

Where errors were not lessened (all may judge).
At thy return my blushing was not small,
My rambling brat (in print) should mother call
I cast thee by as one unfit for light,
Thy visage was so irksome in my sight;
Yet being mine own, at length affection would
Thy blemishes amend, if so I could:
I washed thy face, but more defects I saw,
And rubbing off a spot still made a flaw.
I stretched thy joints to make thee even feet,
Yet still thou run'st more hobbling than is meet;
In better dress to trim thee was my mind,
But nought save homespun cloth i' th' house I find.
In this array 'mongst vulgars may'st thou roam.
In critics hands beware thou dost not come,
And take thy way where yet thou art not known;
If for thy father asked, say thou hadst none;
And for thy mother, she alas is poor,
Which caused her thus to send thee out of door.

These lines typify Bradstreet's strengths and appeal as a poet. They connect the act of writing with child rearing, and the metaphor works beautifully.

The conceit here relies upon the double meaning of "feet" as those of a child and the meter of poetry. By figuring her poetry as a kidnapped child ("snatched . . . by friends") whose handicaps are partially the fault of its mother, Bradstreet both claims a certain amount of responsibility for the publication history of her works and insists on the right to edit and revise work that she never properly finished. She also excludes the possibility of a male hand having intruded in the writing of her verses by insisting that her "child" had no "father." This gendering of the act of writing, and of publication, was nothing new in her lifetime, but Bradstreet was particularly effective at insisting on her own double status as a woman and a poet. That she succeeded in this balancing act is attested by the introduction to *The Tenth Muse*, in which I. W. calls Bradstreet's writings "the work of a woman, honored, and esteemed where she lives, for her gracious demeanor, her eminent parts, her pious conversation, her courteous dispositions, her exact diligence in her place, and discreet managing of her family occasions."

## THE CRITICAL AFTERLIFE

Readers have admired Bradstreet's poetry since her own lifetime, but the critical consensus about the quality of her poetry and the importance of her work has waxed and waned a good deal. She received rapturous reviews from some of her contemporaries, including one N. H., who compared the brightness of her work to that of celestial bodies. In the nineteenth century, by contrast, a series of literary figures gave her far more tepid reviews. One noted editor, Charles Eliot Norton, claimed that the poetry "hardly stands the test of time," and another, John Harvard Ellis, agreed. In the middle of the twentieth century, the American historian Samuel Eliot Morison damned her with faint praise. Primarily biographical, not critical, John Berryman's lengthy poem of 1953, *Homage to Mistress Bradstreet*, contributes to the cultural mythology of Bradstreet's early New England life.

Since World War II, scholars have engaged in various debates about Bradstreet, but the general trend seems to be toward taking her seriously as a poet. In recent decades the poet's gender and her Puritanism are the two topics that have exercised scholars the most. While there is no space to summarize the scholarly discussion here, it is worth noting that her palpable comfort with the body and with love and desire, as well as her success in a professional arena where so many seventeenth-century women failed, make her a peculiar figure in the otherwise rather grim history of English literature by women during that century. There can be little doubt that the fact of her being a settler in New England at a time when the Massachusetts Bay Colony was scarcely well established and incredibly difficult to inhabit contributed to her fame, both in her own lifetime and afterwards. The general interest in Bradstreet's life has turned toward a more sophisticated critical assessment of her work. The recent increase in historicist literary scholarship will no doubt aid our understanding of Anne Bradstreet as a poet and as the heroine of an American cultural narrative of early New England.

[*See also* Colonial Writing in America; Poetess in American Literature, The; *and* Puritanism: The Sense of an Unending.]

## SELECTED WORKS

*The Tenth Muse Lately Sprung Up in America* (1650)
*Several Poems Compiled with Great Variety of Wit and Learning, Full of Delight.* 2d ed. (1678)
*Several Poems Compiled with Great Variety of Wit and Learning, Full of Delight* (Reprint, 1758)
*The Works of Anne Bradstreet, in Prose and Verse* (1867)
*The Poems of Mrs. Anne Bradstreet (1612–1672). Together with Her Prose Remains with An Introduction by Charles Eliot Norton.* Edited by F. E. Hopkins. 1897.
*The Works of Anne Bradstreet* (1967)

## FURTHER READING

Cowell, Pattie, and Ann Stanford. *Critical Essays on Anne Bradstreet.* Boston, 1983.

Daly, Robert. *God's Altar: The World and the Flesh in Puritan Poetry.* Berkeley, Calif., 1978. An excellent study of Puritan poetics that is particularly useful on the theological context, this book contains chapters on a variety of early American writers.

Greer, Germaine, et al., eds. *Kissing the Rod: An Anthology of Seventeenth-Century Women's Verse.* New York, 1988. A collection of primarily recuperative scholarship that contains annotated poems and biographies of a large number of women poets of the seventeenth century.

Hill, Christopher. *The English Bible and the Seventeenth-Century Revolution.* London, 1993. A brilliant account, by an eminent historian, of English biblical culture in the seventeenth century and its role in causing and sustaining the English Revolution.

Lauter, Paul et al., eds. *The Heath Anthology of American Literature.* Vol. 1. Lexington, Mass., and Toronto, 1990. An excellent anthology of American literature, with "American" taken in the broadest sense.

Marotti, Arthur. *Manuscript, Print, and the English Renaissance Lyric.* Ithaca, N.Y., and London, 1995. A thorough study of the social, economic, and technological conditions within which English poets of the sixteenth and seventeenth centuries produced and circulated their work.

Morison, Samuel Eliot. "Mistress Anne Bradstreet." In his *Builders of the Bay Colony.* 2d ed. Boston, 1958. An example of the tendency to focus on the sensational aspects of the poet's life at the expense of a fully engaged treatment of her works.

Piercy, Josephine K. *Anne Bradstreet.* New York, 1965.

Rosenmaier, Rosamond. *Anne Bradstreet Revisited.* Boston, 1991.

Wall, Wendy. *The Imprint of Gender: Authorship and Publication in the English Renaissance.* Ithaca, N.Y., and London, 1993. An intelligent and thorough study of the role of gender in sixteenth- and seventeenth-century English print culture.

While, Elizabeth Wade. *Anne Bradstreet: "The Tenth Muse."* New York, 1971.

# HAROLD BRODKEY

*by Philip Bufithis*

Harold Brodkey. (*Photograph © Jill Krementz*)

If we accept the well-known distinction that literary fiction is character driven and commercial fiction is plot driven, then the work of Harold Brodkey is the most literary American fiction of the twentieth century. Indeed, it is a critical commonplace to compare Brodkey's work with that of Marcel Proust (1871–1922), the French master of memory and psychological nuance. Born Aaron Roy Weintraub in Staunton (some sources say Alton), Illinois, on 31 October 1930, Harold Brodkey was adopted after the death of his mother by his father's cousins, Joseph and Doris Brodkey (the S.L. and Leila or Lila in his fiction), who lived in University City, Missouri, a suburb of St. Louis. Brodkey graduated from Harvard (*cum laude*) in 1952, the same year he married Joanna Brown (they were divorced in 1962), with whom he had a daughter, Emily Ann. In his early twenties he began to publish stories in *The New Yorker* magazine, which were collected to form his first book, *First Love and Other Sorrows* (1957). The title sardonically recalls the melancholic longing of the European romantic movement. The difference is that Brodkey's protagonists—boys, college students, young marrieds—are unheroic, suburban, and American. They reach for levels of passion and sublimity beyond their capacity, Brodkey all the while maintaining a tone of tender pathos. The first story, "The State of Grace," recounts the failure of an unnamed thirteen-year-old boy to make a connection of redemptive love with Edward, a beautiful seven-year-old. In the last five of the nine stories, Brodkey portrays Laura—sensitive, intelligent, a representative white middle-class female of the 1950s—from adolescence to marriage and young motherhood. Two of these five stories are parodically titled: "Piping down the Valleys Wild" (a William Blake poem of paradisiacal vision) and "The Dark Lady of the Sonnets"

(a reference to the powerfully sensual woman in William Shakespeare's sonnets). Laura and her world, Brodkey wants us to know, are poignantly distant from what Blake and Shakespeare evoked. In its depiction of innocence and loss, *First Love and Other Sorrows* resembles the stories of two other *New Yorker* writers of the 1950s—J. D. Salinger and John Updike.

With *Stories in an Almost Classical Mode* (1988), Brodkey comes into his own and establishes a narrative voice that typifies his fiction to the end of his career. He now portrays his characters more freely and more deeply. His style is ponderous, convoluted, inventively metaphoric. And the characters themselves have changed; they are charged beings of uncorrelated impulses, complex forces compelled to reckon with one another. Love and hate, nurture and deprivation, pride and degradation—all emotional contraries obtain in the relations between Brodkey's characters, though one emotion prevails: guilt. Half of these stories concern what Sigmund Freud called the "Family Romance." We are in the mind of Wiley Silenowicz as he recollects his childhood and boyhood with his adoptive parents, S.L. and Leila (or Lila); the three of them form an emotionally unhealthy love triangle. Each parent is a congeries of moods that destabilize Wiley. Each woos him as if he is a lover—he is a beautiful child—then rejects him, then woos him again. Despite their exhibitionistic complacencies, they also turn bitter toward themselves, each other, and Wiley, who, in his turn, tries to accommodate their turbulent needs or effect manipulations of his own. Intensifying this oppressive atmosphere is Wiley's malicious stepsister, Nonie. The voluble voices of Wiley's parents are a distinctive achievement of these familial stories. Mr. and Mrs. Silenowicz speak in clichés and idioms that revive for us the social tonalities of a gone era—America in the 1930s.

The adult protagonists in *Stories in an Almost Classical Mode* amplify a character type that has appeared in American fiction since the 1930s. Jewish, intellectual, artistic, somberly self-analytic, they gravitate toward attractive WASPs with whom they have difficult relations. In "The Abundant Dreamer," Marcus Weill, a director who is making a movie in Rome, remembers in intermittent flashbacks the experiences that shaped his life: a generous, dominant grandmother, young love and its attendant disillusion. Marcus realizes finally that for him permanence can only be found in the transformation of his dreams into film. Certainly, Brodkey's best-known story is the sensational yet honest "Innocence," his attempt at a kind of definitive presentation of sex. Wiley, now an undergraduate at Harvard, tries to bring his girlfriend Orra to climax and, after nearly ten thousand words of description, succeeds. Balanced against the sensual tour de force of "Innocence" is the last story in this collection, "Angel," a spiritual tour de force. We are again with Wiley at Harvard, but Brodkey's content is atypical: myth and mystery. An angel has been sighted in Harvard Yard. Neither religious, ideological, nor moral, it embodies an ontology whose meaning exists outside the operations of the educated mind and remains for the reader a haunting enigma.

Brodkey's long-awaited novel, *The Runaway Soul* (1991), appeared to the same kind of divided reviews as *Stories in an Almost Classical Mode*. Some critics called the novel shapeless, protracted, tortuous, egocentric. Other critics, acknowledging these aspects, explained that Brodkey had reached depths of psychological exploration no American fiction of the time equaled. *The Runaway Soul* is of a piece with the Wiley stories of *Stories in an Almost Classical Mode*; again we have a first-person narrator who analyzes himself, his memories, and the world with strangely imaginative scrupulosity. Characters selfishly tug at and threaten to capsize one another, as if they must to stay afloat. And always, Wiley's parents swamp him with goading advice. *The Runaway Soul* is hardly a novel in any traditional sense. Rather, it is an outsized fictional disquisition born of the insistences and complexities of desire—desire for sex and love, yes, but primarily desire to delineate, with the sharp interiority of an X-ray, the geography of consciousness from childhood to young manhood.

Set in Venice, Italy, Brodkey's novel *Profane Friendship* (1994), compared with *The Runaway Soul*, is well structured and unified. The narrator, Niles O'Hara, the son of an expatriate American novelist, tells the story of his boyhood love in the 1930s for Onni, an Italian boy. After World War II, Niles returns to Venice and has an adolescent affair with Onni. In the novel's last chapter, Niles humorously portrays himself and Onni as accomplished middle-aged men, fractious with one another, yet enduring friends. *Profane Friendship* is at once a rapturous homage to Venice and an intense sexual history that transmutes into a story of fraternal love.

Part memoir, part diary, part essay, *This Wild Darkness: The Story of My Death* (1996) is Brodkey's valedictory, an account of his two-and-a-half-year struggle with AIDS—its effects on him, his wife, his doctor, and friends. Writing with uncharacteristic clarity and directness, Brodkey monitors his deterioration unflinchingly. Yet he is so dedicated to the reportorial truth of his death that its emotional dimension remains undeveloped. Nonetheless, *This Wild Darkness* is a unique book and a brave gift to his readers. Harold Brodkey died on 26 January 1996, in New York City. He was survived by his daughter, a stepdaughter, two stepsons, and his second wife, the novelist Ellen Schwamm.

In addition to *This Wild Darkness*, three other of Brodkey's books were published posthumously. *The World Is the Home of Love and Death* (1997) is a collection of stories, most of them involving the Silenowicz family, that do not appreciably enhance Brodkey's themes in *Stories in an Almost Classical Mode*. *My Venice* (1998) is a ruminative adoration (with photographs) of the great city—boat rides, churches, statuary, shifting light. *Sea Battles on Dry Land* (1999) is a collection of essays on contemporary American culture and on literature, half of which first appeared in *The New Yorker*. Brodkey's literary honors include two first-place O. Henry Awards, a Prix de Rome, and fellowships from the National Endowment for the Arts, the American Academy in Rome, and the John Henry Guggenheim Memorial Foundation.

## WORKS

*First Love and Other Sorrows* (1957)
*Women and Angels* (1985)
*A Poem about Testimony and Argument* (1986)
*Stories in an Almost Classical Mode* (1988)
*The Runaway Soul* (1991)
*Profane Friendship* (1994)
*This Wild Darkness* (1996)
*The World Is the Home of Love and Death* (1997)
*My Venice* (1998)
*Sea Battles on Dry Land* (1999)

## FURTHER READING

Bawer, Bruce. "A Genius for Publicity." *New Criterion* (December 1988): 58–69. A mainly negative assessment of the author's first two story collections.

Bromwich, D. "The Art of Narcissism." *New Republic* (27 January 1992): 30+. An accurate comprehension of *The Runaway Soul*.

Kermode, Frank. " 'I Am Only Equivocally Harold Brodkey.' " *The New York Times* (18 September 1988): section 7, p. 3. A balanced assessment of *Stories in an Almost Classical Mode*.

Linville, James. "Harold Brodkey: The Art of Fiction." *Paris Review* (Winter 1991): 51–91. An interview with the author.

Moynihan, Robert. "Harold Brodkey." In *American Short Story Writers Since World War II*, edited by Patrick Meanor. Detroit, 1993, pp. 49–55. A mainly positive assessment of the author's first two story collections.

# GWENDOLYN BROOKS

*by William R. Nash*

Gwendolyn Brooks, American poet, novelist, activist, and teacher, stands out for her social engagement, her professional generosity, and her literary accomplishment. In a career that spanned six decades, Brooks concerned herself with portraying the lives of American blacks, especially people hampered by social and economic circumstances. Throughout her corpus, Brooks demonstrates sensitivity to the particulars of black life in America; when tracking the work chronologically, one sees evolving her sense of the black poet's most appropriate response to a racially charged society.

Brooks was born on 17 June 1917 in Topeka, Kansas, to David and Keziah Wims Brooks; her parents were residents of Chicago's South Side, who had returned home for the birth of their first child. They subsequently moved back to Chicago, where Brooks lived for most of her life. Despite her family's poverty, which necessitated both of her parents' foregoing career aspirations, Brooks grew up in a nurturing home environment. Unfortunately, her community experience was not similarly positive. In the face of intraracial prejudice aimed at her because of her appearance, Brooks found solace and self-confidence in her writing. Her mother was especially sensitive to her daughter's plight and encouraged Brooks to develop her creative talents. She also took Brooks to readings by authors such as James Weldon Johnson and Langston Hughes. Hughes strongly encouraged her in her attempts to establish a poetic career.

## YOUTH AND EARLY CAREER

By the age of thirteen, Brooks had already published a poem, "Eventide," in *American Childhood* magazine. At the age of seventeen, she became a regular contributor to the Chicago *Defender*, where eventually she published

Gwendolyn Brooks.
*(Courtesy of the Library of Congress)*

seventy-five poems. Heartened by her early success, Brooks continued to hone her craft, enrolling in a poetry workshop at the South Side Community Art Center that yielded her many of the pieces for her first book of poetry, *A Street in Bronzeville* (1945). In a series of polished, graceful poems, Brooks takes readers inside the world of the black poor, portraying the harsh realities of economic injustice without ever losing sight of the basic human dignity of her subjects.

The second poem of *Bronzeville*, "kitchenette building," establishes the volume's tone. The speaker is, as Brooks was, a resident of a tenement on Chicago's South Side; furthermore, like Brooks, the speaker experiences creative urges—the reader sees her wondering whether or not a dream could "sing an aria" in the confines of rooms marked with the stench of food smells and garbage. For all of her wondering, however, the speaker ultimately recognizes the futility of her speculation. First of all, there are practical needs to be met, such as a bath in the shared bathroom. Second, the speaker understands herself and her fellow residents as "things," a notion that the reference to a fellow resident as "Number Five" strongly reinforces. As long as she accepts this vision of herself, the speaker cannot really afford to dream, especially not of a world that values aesthetic sensitivity. This was not so for Brooks. As this and the other poems of *A Street in Bronzeville* demonstrate, Brooks sees making art as a viable, even a crucial, response to this environment. In short, making beauty in this world where it is so scarce becomes for the poet one means of surviving it.

Unfortunately, many of Bronzeville's residents are not as lucky as the poet. From the aborted babies of "the mother," to De Witt Williams, whose funeral procession the reader observes, to "poor Percy," the victim of his brother's violence in "the murder," the number of characters who die in the volume is sobering. Of the ones who do survive, most are scarred by their experiences. One sees, for instance, Matthew Cole, a reclusive bachelor who "Is everlasting sad" or the subject of "obituary for a living lady," who, like Cole, is among the dead living. These are adults so broken by events in their lives that they do not live, but only exist. As poignant as these portraits are, the children of Bronzeville are even more heart-wrenching. Percy perishes in flames of his brother Brucie's creation. The fires of poverty and intraracial oppression burn others. Of these, none is better known or more moving than Mabbie, the subject of "the ballad of chocolate Mabbie."

A shy seven-year-old whose dark skin suggested to others that she "was cut from a chocolate bar," Mabbie develops a crush on classmate Willie Boone. Innocently, Mabbie believes that declaring her feelings will win her young Boone's devotion. What she does not realize is that he is prone to the intraracial prejudice about skin color that makes light-skinned blacks reject those with darker complexions. Waiting outside the schoolhouse, she encounters Boone and the new object of his affections, a light-skinned girl with straight hair. The poem ends with an image of Mabbie's isolation, her belief that she is most fit for "chocolate companions" like herself. Although not directly autobiographical, the poem does reflect a crucial part of Brooks's experience: her own feelings of rejection and isolation associated with her darkness. Here, as in "kitchenette building," the experiencing consciousness in the poem can ill afford beauty as solace: chocolate Mabbie faces a life of isolation because of her color, a reality that simple beauty cannot ameliorate. For the poet, however, the opportunity to make art out of this painful experience is much more effective, perhaps even the best response that she has to injustice.

These motifs from *A Street in Bronzeville* resonate through her Pulitzer Prize–winning collection of poems, *Annie Allen* (1949), and through her only novel, *Maud Martha* (1953). Like chocolate Mabbie, Maud Martha knows the pain of color-based rejection; like the speaker of "kitchenette building," she struggles to keep her aesthetic dreams alive in the oppressive environment of a South Side tenement. The great strength of the novel (which has unfortunately been largely overlooked by critics), is its sustained examination of the impact of the Bronzeville environment on a single individual. With this shift from the street to the individual self, the poet trades breadth for depth and thereby mutually enriches both portraits.

And with these complementary approaches, Brooks fully illustrates the artist's power as chronicler of this segment of black life.

## AN INCREASING INTEREST IN POLITICS

In 1960, Brooks published another volume of poetry, *The Bean Eaters*. Here, as in the earlier work, one finds finely crafted portraits of African-American life; furthermore, as in *Bronzeville*, Brooks shows her readers many members of a community. What changes here, however, is the tone of the work. She balances her desire for making beauty with a clearer, more obvious call for political engagement. This takes the form of commentary on specific events in poems like "A Bronzeville Mother Loiters in Mississippi. Meanwhile a Mississippi Mother Burns Bacon" and "The Last Quatrain of the Ballad of Emmett Till," both of which deal with the 1955 lynching of Emmett Till, a Chicago teenager who ran afoul of a white mob in Money, Mississippi, by daring to speak familiarly to a white woman. For his boldness, he was tortured, shot, and drowned. Brooks uses the particular experiences of two women closely connected to Till's death to comment on the larger social disorder.

"A Bronzeville Woman . . ." shows the mental turmoil of a white Mississippi woman whose husband was among Till's lynchers. As she prepares breakfast, she feels the blood on her husband's hands staining her, her children, and her home. In response to his violence, she feels "hatred" for him, a sign of her new awareness of all that is wrong with the social order she has always known and, implicitly, valued. Brooks ends the description of her enlightenment with the following lines: "The last bleak news of the ballad. / The rest of the rugged music. / The last quatrain." Immediately following this is the poem entitled "The Last Quatrain of the Ballad of Emmett Till." In this poem, Brooks shows the reader Till's mother, Mamie Bradley, "after the murder, after the burial." Sitting quietly alone, she regrets what has happened to her son. The last lines of the poem "Chaos in windy grays / through a red prairie" suggest that the scene takes place back home in Chicago. With these two poems, Brooks reminds her reader that Till's death is more than an outrage against blacks, more than a southern crime. Through the ruminations of these two women, who share an outrage over the white man's action that comes at least partially from the shared experience of maternity, Brooks suggests that change can come only through mutual recognition of the cost of racial injustice. If blacks and whites can learn this lesson and work together in response, there is perhaps hope for some sort of racial reconciliation.

The same is true of "The Chicago Defender Sends a Man to Little Rock," which chronicles responses to the 1957 integration of Central High School in Little Rock, Arkansas. Here, as in the Till poems, Brooks strikes a balance between her accurate portrayal of historical events and her hope for some transcendent sympathy that will overcome injustice. What one needs to achieve such sympathy, in her view, is action; the poet's role in that is to raise her readers' awareness by pointing out to them instances where such action should be taken. Subsequent to the period of *The Bean Eaters*, she remained true to that ideal of action but restricted her focus almost exclusively to the black community.

## THE BLACK ARTS ERA AND BEYOND

In the mid-1960s, Brooks underwent what she called a transformation after attending the second Black Writers' Conference at Fisk University; there she met, among others, Don L. Lee (Haki Madhubuti). She subsequently became involved in Chicago's Black Arts Movement, running a workshop that included many future founders of the Organization of Black American Culture (OBAC). The younger poets Brooks met through her contact with OBAC also taught her much of the theory and practice of the Black Aesthetic. It was Brooks's immersion in this set of values and principles that moved her toward a new vision of the poet's role as activist.

Brooks acknowledges her indebtedness to the OBAC poets by offering tribute to thirteen workshop members at the beginning of *In the Mecca* (1968), her volume that maps the terrible, wonderful landscape of the Chicago ghetto. The title poem, which presents a mother's frantic search for her missing (and, the reader ultimately learns, murdered) daughter, reflects Brooks's conviction that the most significant art is relevant to the community that inspires it. In this case, part of the relevance of the poem comes in Brooks's effort to balance affirmation of and challenge to her community. That translates into a critique of individuals and institutions that harm the community; but even as she presents that commentary, she tries to locate whatever redeeming features her subject might have.

"In the Mecca" demonstrates that attempt. As Mrs. Sallie Smith roams the filthy halls of the decrepit, overcrowded building, searching for her abducted daughter, Pepita, she encounters a range of characters that inspire admiration and fear, often for similar reasons. For instance, she pairs St. Julia Jones, a devout Christian, with Prophet Williams, a charlatan whose transgressions

include killing his wife in a domestic abuse incident. In the process, she also creates conflicting emotional responses to this landscape. She describes one of Pepita's siblings, Thomas Earl, who "loves Johnny Appleseed" and notes "It is hard to be Johnny Appleseed." And yet, despite these challenges, Thomas Earl's love remains. Even in the face of this horrible environment, Thomas Earl does not surrender his hope. Brooks's representation of this tension suggests the conflict between hope and economic reality that one sees in "kitchenette building." Furthermore, in both instances, Brooks rejects a deterministic viewpoint. To be sure, the Mecca can kill people, as the Smith family soon learns, but dreams survive there.

Perhaps the most significant of these dreams belongs to Don Lee, the young Mecca resident who seeks a revolutionary art. One has the sense that his experiences living in the Mecca fuel his desire for a new world where blacks like the Mecca's residents have and exercise power. In making a character named for one of Chicago's most significant young poets a resident of this complex and awful world, Brooks aligns herself with Lee (and, by extension, his OBAC peers) and announces the role that the group can play in the community. Black artists may not be able to actually tear these buildings down, but they can change their meaning by going among the residents and spreading the message of their new art, their new vision. In a sense, Don Lee is the true Johnny Appleseed of the Mecca, and although it may be hard to be him, the fruit of his work makes the effort worthwhile.

Even as Brooks shows one of her younger peers in this role in the poem, she is adopting it herself. From *In the Mecca* forward, her work reflects a strong commitment to political action, a recognition that the poet's responsibility is to use words as weapons in the fight against injustice. She coupled that commitment with economic action in 1969, when she shifted from Harper, her publisher for twenty-five years, to a series of small black presses: Broadside in Detroit, Third World in Chicago, and, starting in 1982, her own companies, Brooks Press and the David Company. The result was increased business for these companies and no diminishment of Brooks's prominence or relevance. She continued her work, garnering awards that include a National Book Award nomination for *In the Mecca*, an appointment as poetry consultant to the Library of Congress in 1985, induction into the National Women's Hall of Fame in 1988, a Lifetime Achievement Award from the National Endowment for the Arts in 1989, the Frost Medal from the Poetry Society of America in 1989, the Jefferson lecturer award in 1994, and more than fifty honorary degrees from universities and colleges. As she continued, her vision of the boundaries of black community expanded; in the 1980s and 1990s, she connected herself to blacks all over the world, challenging the implications of the term "African American" as too narrow. Instead, she called for blacks from America to South Africa to unite in celebration of their common black humanity. At her death on 3 December 2000, she was hailed as a poetic and a political force in black life; such a designation reflects her own sense of how those roles can and should intertwine. In acting out those beliefs through her writing, Brooks helped change the face and the orientation of American literature.

[*See also* Black Arts Movement *and* Poetess in American Literature, The.]

## WORKS

*A Street in Bronzeville* (1945)
*Annie Allen* (1949)
*Maud Martha* (1953)
*Bronzeville Boys and Girls* (1956)
*The Bean Eaters* (1960)
*A Catch of Shy Fish* (1963)
*In the Time of Detachment, in the Time of Cold*
    (1965)
*In the Mecca* (1968)
*For Illinois 1968: A Sesquicentennial Poem* (1968)
*Riot* (1969)
*Family Pictures* (1970)
*Aloneness* (1971)
*Aurora* (1972)
*Report from Part One* (1972)

*The Tiger Who Wore White Gloves; or, What You Are, You*
    *Are* (1974)
*Beckonings* (1975)
*Primer for Blacks* (1980)
*To Disembark* (1981)
*Black Love* (1982)
*Mayor Harold Washington; and, Chicago, The I Will*
    *City* (1983)
*The Near-Johannesburg Boy, and Other Poems* (1986)
*Gottschalk and the Grand Tarantelle* (1988)
*Winnie* (1988)
*Children Coming Home* (1991)
*Report from Part Two* (1996)

## FURTHER READING

Evans, Mari, ed. *Black Women Writers (1950–1980): A Critical Evaluation*. Garden City, N.Y., 1984. Contains a useful profile of Brooks in the context of a women's tradition.

Kent, George. *Gwendolyn Brooks: A Life*. Lexington, Ky., 1990. The first full-length biography by a scholar of the Black Arts era.

Madhubuti, Haki R. *Say That the River Turns: The Impact of Gwendolyn Brooks*. Chicago, 1987. An analysis of Brooks's work by one of the principal Black Aestheticians in Chicago.

Mootry, Maria K. and Gary Smith, eds. *A Life Distilled: Gwendolyn Brooks, Her Poetry and Fiction*. Urbana, Ill., 1987. A comprehensive collection of essays that touches all periods of Brooks's career.

Wright, Stephen Caldwell, ed. *On Gwendolyn Brooks: Reliant Contemplation*. Ann Arbor, Mich., 2001.

# PEARL S. BUCK

*by Amanda Fields*

A best-selling writer who was the first American woman to win the Nobel Prize in literature (1938) and the Pulitzer Prize (1935), Pearl Comfort Sydenstricker Buck published more than seventy books, including novels, short-story collections, nonfiction, poetry, drama, children's literature, and English translations from the Chinese. In addition to enlightening Westerners about various Asian countries and traditions, Buck was active in the political sphere, advocating civil and women's rights, children's rights, and peace.

Pearl S. Buck was born on 26 June 1892 in Hillsboro, West Virginia, the fourth of seven children and one of three children to live to adulthood. Absalom and Caroline Sydenstricker, her parents, were southern Presbyterian missionaries in China. Buck grew up in Chinkiang (Zhenjiang), and she was fluent in both Chinese and English from childhood.

In 1910 Buck began to attend Randolph-Macon Woman's College in Lynchburg, Virginia. She graduated in 1914 and moved back to China. In 1915 she met John Lossing Buck, an agricultural economist. They married in 1917 and moved to Nanhsuchou (Nanxuzhou), a rural, poverty-stricken area. They divorced eighteen years later. Buck taught English at Nanking (Nanjing) University from 1920 to 1933, and her husband taught there during the same period. When her mother died in 1921, her father moved in with them. In 1921 Buck gave birth to a daughter, Carol, who had phenylketonuria (PKU). She eventually placed Carol in a New Jersey institution. Buck had a hysterectomy after the birth because a uterine tumor was discovered. In 1925 she adopted her second daughter, Janice, a decision that would affect Buck's later focus on the adoption process in the United States.

During the 1920s Buck had stories and essays published in prominent magazines like the *Atlantic Monthly* and *The*

Pearl S. Buck.
*(Courtesy of the Library of Congress)*

*Nation*. Her first novel, *East Wind, West Wind* (1930), was published in 1930. In 1935 she married Richard J. Walsh, the man at John Day who published her first novel. Her second novel, *The Good Earth* (1931), was the best-seller of 1931 and 1932. She received both the Pulitzer Prize and the Howells Medal for *The Good Earth* in 1935, and it was made into an MGM film in 1937.

While much of her work focuses on Chinese culture, she also wrote about other Asian countries and cultures. For instance, *The New Year* (1968) is a novel about a Korean American war orphan, while *Come, My Beloved* (1953) depicts American missionaries in India. In addition, Buck wrote critiques of the American government and explored American culture through both fiction and nonfiction. For example, *The Angry Wife* (1947), written under the pseudonym John Sedges (five of her books used this pseudonym), examines racism and southern white women in the United States, while *All under Heaven* (written in the 1950s but published in 1973) protests the Cold War.

## BUCK THE MULTICULTURALIST

In America, Buck's depiction of Chinese culture was often considered a definitive statement since this was the first time that a widespread American audience was reading about the lives of the Chinese people. It is telling that many Chinese critics today claim her portrayals to be fair and accurate.

Buck wrote about significant transitions in Chinese history, especially within the class system and subservience toward it. The progressive novels are evidence of the broad spectrum of her work with its continued interest in Chinese culture and history. For instance, *The Good Earth* follows the life of a Chinese farmer who marries a servant from a Great House. With a persistent focus on pragmatic farming and the eventual ownership of more land, Wang Lung and O-lan build up their own Great House, and Wang Lung is just as susceptible to corruption as those who were previously wealthy. Yet keeping the land remains the most significant act for Wang Lung, and the reader can witness a foreboding transition in the concluding passage as two of Wang Lung's sons secretively indicate that they will sell the land, never having known the importance of working, buying, and keeping land themselves. Thus, a new era in Chinese history is introduced, and Buck follows with other novels.

One of the strengths of Buck's fiction is its ability to present views of tolerance and intolerance without didacticism. Readers also become attuned to the concept that those who are oppressed are not immune to becoming oppressors themselves. For example, in *Peony* (1948), Buck concentrates on the pocket of Jewish people who have come to China to escape oppression and live safely. Through multiple narrative viewpoints, Buck reveals the perspective of the Chinese people, the Jewish people, and people with both Chinese and Jewish heritage. The main conflict in the story is a clash of cultures and class, once again pointing to the enduring relevance of Buck's writing. David, the dashing son of the Jewish house of Ezra, is torn. He believes that the rhetoric of Jehovah is at times hateful, while his Confucian tutor teaches him wise words of peace. The "heathen" people who serve and accept the Jewish people into China are closer to David than he is brought up to believe. He wants to learn about "his people," and he feels a connection to their suffering. At the same time, David is not fully Jewish since his father had a Chinese mother. David's mother, Madame Ezra, refuses to speak of this, and her staunch insistence upon keeping the traditions of her "chosen people" gives pause to her family. She arranges for David to marry Leah, the devout daughter of the rabbi. In a desperate, passionate moment, Leah severs her throat with the very sword through which she felt a connection with David. David eventually realizes his desire to accept more than one culture into his life. By the end of the novel, it is apparent that remnants of the Jewish culture will always remain; however, one of the most telling descriptions of the demise of the tradition is that no one could recite a prayer at Madame Ezra's funeral.

Buck was committed to a growing understanding between different peoples, and her dedication is evident not only in her novels but in her social work. With her second husband, Richard J. Walsh, she founded and led the East and West Association from 1940 to 1950 in order to improve relationships and encourage the accumulation of knowledge about different cultures. In addition, she was a member of the Citizen's Committee to Repeal Chinese Exclusion, the American Civil Liberties Union's Committee against Racial Discrimination, and the India League of America. She had an NAACP certificate of life membership and was published in *Crisis*, as well as the NAACP journal *Opportunity*. She was a trustee at Howard University for twenty years.

## A CALL FOR PEACE

Buck's views were not set in stone, which, ironically, was a source of criticism in later years since she delivered differing viewpoints as she saw fit. For example, she didn't view the cold war as "democracy" versus "communism"; she considered the issue to be much more complex and disagreed with this simplification of a conflict that seemed to promise violence. Buck worked to change the way violence is accepted in American culture. She opposed the aggressive use of U.S. power and military action. *American Argument* (1949), a book she cowrote with Eslanda Goode Robeson, articulates a few of her beliefs about the U.S. military. She spoke before the Senate in opposition of Truman's UMT (Universal Military Training) proposal, one of the many voices that helped defeat the concept. As is the case with many writers, the FBI assembled a dossier on Buck.

Buck also showed a great concern for the effects of militaristic cultures on women, believing that these cultures are inherently sexist. World War II and the subsequent nuclear arms race prompted her to voice her views through both writing and speaking. In *The Hidden Flower* (1952) Buck depicts American soldiers occupying Japan after World War II in relation to the sexual corruption that can occur with any sort of military conquest. Similarly, *Command the Morning* (1959), a novel about the creation of atomic bombs, called for recognition of the masculine nature of these weapons, as well as the necessity for women to protest the nuclear arms race. The dramatic version of *Command the Morning, A Desert Incident* (1959) was an unsuccessful Broadway play; however, judging by the initial women's peace movements of the 1960s and the global network of such movements and protests today, the play may have been ahead of its time.

## A FEMINIST OF HER OWN

Buck's cultural concerns played out in her dedication to women's rights and activism. She showed support for many women by including them in interviews and articles. For instance, she published a series of "talk books" in which she interviewed people of different backgrounds. The aim of the series was to introduce Americans to a plethora of cultures and values, and a majority of the people featured in these books are women.

Buck's concepts of womanhood, while not stagnant, were not always in compliance with the ideas of many of her American feminist contemporaries. For instance, she argued that Chinese women were stronger than American women, giving them a more significant role in their society, and that the restrictions of the Chinese culture had made them stronger through strife. Indeed, female protagonists in Buck's novels often seem stronger than male characters. In *The Good Earth*, Wang Lung is a protagonist whose weaknesses are offset by his wife, O-lan. Peony (*Peony*) is a Chinese bondmaid who has grown up with David's Jewish family, and she loves him throughout the novel, though class distinctions keep them apart. Even though her endurance and strength are motivated by her dedication to a man, Peony becomes a woman of high respect in the community, eventually becoming abbess of the Buddhist convent. By contrast, Madame Ezra and Leah, who are not Chinese, cannot endure even with privileged lives.

Another novel, *Pavilion of Women* (1946), centers on one woman's struggle to find a space to enrich herself amidst a Great House, as she directs everyone's life within the house. Madame Wu knows that she is more intelligent than her husband, and long before she turns forty, she is planning a way to pursue her own knowledge and goals while still providing her family and her husband with the things she believes they need. She buys a concubine for her husband and takes up residency by herself in another court. Even children do not move her yearning for independence. She thinks of the birth of her children as a freeing act; the children are never a part of herself.

Yet her freedom comes from being an unconscious oppressor. She does not realize this until she meets a foreign monk, Brother Andre, who informs her that her independence has come at the cost of causing pain to another woman, hurting her husband, and considering herself superior to the needs of all the women around her. Madame Wu does no favor to the concubine she purchases in order to satisfy her husband's sex life, nor does she consider that the woman who has served her since she was married continues to do so. The class distinctions remain. Eventually, though, Madame Wu envisions a more freeing goal.

Madame Wu is a feminist of her own, one who is concerned with her own personal freedom and pursuits. Brother Andre moves her to go beyond this concept and to consider the global implications of all she does. This shift reflects a conflict and introduces more than one type of feminism, which is an intriguing strength of Buck's writing. Buck's argument that the very restrictions of the Chinese culture upon women made them stronger and more capable than American women helped pave the way for attempts to understand and acknowledge different feminisms beyond the white middle-class viewpoint.

These feminisms can be intriguingly compared with the views presented by Buck's male characters. For example, in *Peony*, David is shaped by his mother, Peony, and Leah. Male characters often rely on the advice and knowledge of female characters, and the men are often depicted as rather clumsy without the women. After O-lan's death in *The Good Earth*, for example, Wang Lung's household is in disarray; for the first time he clearly sees that O-lan has quietly kept things in order. The class system determines beauty—O-lan is never beautiful to Wang Lung, but the accumulation of money and land (much of it due to her wise advice and hard work) introduces him to the aspect of leisurely time, and the wealthy men in his town spend their leisure time where the beautiful young women are. Beauty is tiny, painfully bound feet and soft hands, which implies a lack of knowledge about putting one's last ounce of breath into the land and the sustenance of life. O-lan has this knowledge, along with large feet and a frame fit for hard work. Yet even when she is on her deathbed, Wang Lung cannot bring himself to find physical beauty in her. O-lan presents a kind of womanhood that Wang Lung cannot accept in the state of his wealth. Thus, in a world where humans can trap themselves into restrictive definitions, Buck's presentations of feminism on many levels may be useful and fascinating.

## WELCOMING BUCK

Pearl S. Buck spent nearly forty years in China, where she finished her most popular books. When Buck and Walsh moved to the United States in 1934, they adopted six more children. With seven total adopted children, Buck was eager to help children from all over the world have the opportunity to be adopted into a family. Disturbed that many children were being turned away from adoption agencies because of their race and nationality, Buck established the first international, interracial adoption agency in 1949, Welcome House. In addition, she was outspoken about the plight of Asian children left behind by American soldiers who were the fathers. In 1964 she established the Pearl S. Buck Foundation to support such children who were ineligible for adoption. Both Welcome House and the Pearl S. Buck Foundation continue to thrive. Peter Conn, a prominent biographer of Buck, and his wife adopted a child through Welcome House.

Available criticism on Pearl S. Buck is limited, perhaps in part due to the undervaluing of this writer by the literary community. Many critics consider her later writing to be rather romanticized and filled with the rhetoric of the cold war, and the largely sexist attitude toward politically active women writers also influenced her lack of acceptance within academic culture. However, works such as Peter Conn's 1996 biography have motivated the academic community to examine more closely the values and agendas of this writer.

Buck's life and work continue to be influential. Green Hills Farm in Bucks County, Pennsylvania, where she lived with Walsh and was buried upon her death in March 1973 at the age of eighty-one, is a popular historic landmark. In May 2000 Buck's residence in east China's Jiangsu Province was opened to visitors at Nanjing University. Her humanitarian and literary contributions are expansive and noteworthy, making Pearl S. Buck a classic and enduring writer of American literature.

## WORKS

*East Wind, West Wind* (1930)
*The Good Earth* (1931)
*Sons* (1932)
*The Young Revolutionist* (1932)
*East and West and the Novel* (1932)
*Is There a Case for Foreign Missions?* (1932)
*The First Wife and Other Stories* (1933)
*The Mother* (1934)
*A House Divided* (1935)
*The Exile* (1936)
*Fighting Angel: Portrait of a Soul* (1936)
*This Proud Heart* (1938)
*The Patriot* (1939)
*Flight into China* (1939)
*Other Gods* (1940)
*Stories for Little Children* (1940)
*Of Men and Women* (1941)
*Today and Forever* (1941)
*Dragon Seed* (1942)
*American Unity and Asia* (1942)
*The Promise* (1943)
*Twenty-Seven Stories* (1943)
*The Dragon Fish* (1944)
*The Story of Dragon Seed* (1944)

*Portrait of a Marriage* (1945)
*Will This Earth Hold?* (1945)
*Pavilion of Women* (1946)
*Far and Near* (1947)
*The Angry Wife* (1947)
*Peony* (1948)
*The Big Wave* (1948)
*American Argument* (1949)
*The Long Love* (1949)
*The Child Who Never Grew* (1950)
*One Bright Day* (1950)
*God's Men* (1951)
*The Hidden Flower* (1952)
*Bright Procession* (1952)
*Come, My Beloved* (1953)
*Voices in the House* (1953)
*My Several Worlds* (1954)
*The Beech Tree* (1954)
*Imperial Woman* (1956)
*Friend to Friend* (1958)
*American Triptych: Three "John Sedges" Novels* (1958)
*Command the Morning* (1959)
*A Desert Incident* (1959)
*The Christmas Ghost* (1960)
*Fourteen Stories* (1961)
*Satan Never Sleeps* (1962)
*The Living Reed* (1963)
*Stories of China* (1964)
*The Gifts They Bring* (1965)
*The People of Japan* (1966)
*Matthew, Mark, Luke, and John* (1967)
*The New Year* (1968)
*The Three Daughters of Madame Liang* (1969)
*China As I See It* (1970)
*Mandala: A Novel of India* (1971)
*China Past and Present* (1972)
*All under Heaven* (1973)
*Mrs. Starling's Problem* (1973)
*The Rainbow* (1974)
*East and West* (1975)
*Secrets of the Heart* (1976)
*The Lovers and Other Stories* (1977)
*Mrs. Stoner and the Sea* (1978)
*The Woman Who Was Changed* (1979)

## FURTHER READING

Conn, Peter. *Pearl S. Buck: A Cultural Biography*. New York, 1996. An extensive, detailed treatment of Buck's life and work, including a bibliography, index, and several photographs.

Gao, Xiongya. *Pearl S. Buck's Chinese Women Characters*. Selinsgrove, Penn., 2000. Covering five novels in which she studies Buck's depictions of Chinese women, Gao makes a case for the characters' unique humanity and realism. Includes a bibliography and index.

Liao, Kang. *Pearl S. Buck: A Cultural Bridge across the Pacific*. Westport, Conn., 1997. Discusses Buck's depictions of Chinese culture through five sections, each with a label of her identity (for example, "A Neglected Laureate"). Includes an extensive bibliography and index.

Lipscomb, Elizabeth J., Frances E. Webb, and Peter Conn, eds. *The Several Worlds of Pearl S. Buck: Essays Presented at a Centennial Symposium, Randolph-Macon Women's College, March 26–28, 1992*. Westport, Conn., 1994. Essays collected at a symposium conducted at Buck's alma mater and divided into three themes: historical, humanitarian, and literary. Includes Peter Conn's keynote address, a bibliography, and an index.

Stirling, Nora. *Pearl Buck: A Woman in Conflict*. Piscataway, N.J., 1983. A biography that is personalized by interviews with Buck's friends and acquaintances.

# CHARLES BUKOWSKI

*by Mark Conway*

Charles Bukowski. (© *Fabian Cevallos/CORBIS SYGMA*)

Charles Bukowski fought, drank, and tirelessly wrote his way to international renown by defining a new American outsider poetry. A self-mythologizing and ingenious promoter, Bukowski was also an extremely prolific novelist, columnist, short-story writer, and poet best known for his hard-bitten, minimalist portrayals of Los Angeles's underbelly. Bukowski provokes extreme reactions to his work. On the one hand he is a cult hero, a writer who sees through the pretensions of life and literature to depict the world in all its brutality and beauty. On the other hand he is dismissed as a primitive writer who spewed out a facile mixture of juvenile bile, self-absorbed rant, and clever posturing designed to get a rise from his audience and raise sales of his books. Bukowski published over sixty volumes of poetry and prose, and his works have been translated into more than a dozen languages. Though he lived hard and drank determinedly for most of his life, he died on 9 March 1994 from leukemia. At the time of his death, he had become wealthy from his many writings and lived in the comfortable suburb of San Pedro.

Bukowski began his story like this: "I was born August 16, 1920, Andernach, Germany . . . something to do with the war. Old man American soldier. Brought his German wife and me over here in 1922 and the land was gifted with a hardmouth poet. Meaning me." Named for his father, Henry Charles Bukowski, he used Charles as his pen name and was later known as Hank or Buk to his friends and fans. Bukowski's father was a stern authoritarian who beat the young Charles regularly. His parents' desire for middle-class respectability drove them to force their son to wear his dress clothes at all times. In his teens, Bukowski was further alienated by disfiguring acne so severe he had to miss a half a year of school. The acne resulted in

scarring, physical and psychological. It was a long time before Bukowski had any contact with women his own age. Though he characterized himself as a troublemaker, most people from this time remember a quiet, polite, even bookish young man.

Bukowski barely considered college as an option because money was tight, and he attended Los Angeles City College mainly to forestall the future. After hostilities escalated with his father, Bukowski moved out and began his wanderings, writing relentlessly and submitting his stories to magazines. Already rejecting his parents' middle-class values, Bukowski was content to be deferred from the draft during World War II. He later said he had only the vaguest awareness about the war as he drank and drifted on the fringes of society. He wrote a short story a day, and his first story, "Aftermath of Lengthy Rejection Slip," was published in 1944, when he was twenty-four years old.

The next ten years are difficult to trace because details are hazy and Bukowski has placed an overlay of fable over that time. There is no doubt, however, that Bukowski grew discouraged with his literary prospects, all but abandoned writing, and spent much of the next decade seated at a bar. His ten-year binge ended in 1955 when he came close to dying from a bleeding ulcer. Soon after getting out of the hospital, Bukowski began writing poems rather than stories. He started to place this work in underground journals almost immediately.

Though Bukowski published often in small magazines, it still took some time for his first book to appear. *Flower, Fist, and Bestial Wail*, a chapbook of fourteen poems, came out in 1959, when Bukowski was forty. The switch from prose elicited an astonishing outpouring of poems. He would get a supply of beer, sit at the "typer" and write half a dozen poems a night. From 1962 to 1970, Bukowski published twenty-two titles of poetry, many of these chapbooks and collections of previously published poems.

Bukowski's verse style owed a great deal to his prose. Narrative and anecdotal, the poems are usually first person and largely autobiographical. The poems are narrated by Bukowski's invariable persona, the drunken, womanizing tough guy, and they cover familiar territory: gambling, drinking, whoring, and fighting.

While Bukowski sometimes proclaimed he was creating new modes of writing outside of any tradition, at other times he acknowledged his literary precursors. He read widely—Ernest Hemingway was a major influence. Throughout his career, Bukowski appropriated many of Hemingway's stylistic devices, such as a quick, staccato directness of narration. He also borrowed some of Hemingway's personality traits, including his famous pugnacity and machismo. He even adopted Hemingway's sentence structure for his poems. Bukowski's unit of composition for verse was the sentence rather than the line. The short lines are heavily, even arbitrarily, enjambed in a fluid style that to Bukowski's ear mimicked "bar-talk."

If Hemingway was the stylistic master, Dostoyevsky was the inspiration for Bukowski's natural subject: the defiant, underground hero who resisted God and all convention to create a new form of sanity and sanctity through his struggles with society. Bukowski, though often apolitical, felt a social responsibility to write for the common person. He valued clarity and consciously confined himself to a limited vocabulary. He did not use complicated or extended metaphors. He wished to bring about a confrontation through art, convinced that most people need to be jolted into seeing the world as it is. He strove for urgency and, above all, "blood"—colorful, rollicking writing that would surprise, offend, and ultimately seduce the reader. "Blood" also implied wildness, the irrational. Bukowski accessed surrealism through the actual by making an aesthetic of alcohol. In his view, hallucinations brought on by drinking have the otherworldly power to pierce the veil of reality, and so could "the morning after." In Bukowski's theology, there is a sacred quality to the hangover, a hushed and gentle resurrection where one's senses have been scrubbed clean. For the initiated, this can be an opportunity for vision.

What really made a name for Bukowski was a column he wrote starting in 1966 for the alternative newspaper, *Open City*. The completely uninhibited *Notes of a Dirty Old Man* (1969), a mixture of opinion, fiction, and autobiography, created Bukowski the cult hero, the raunchy and poetic postal worker, both drunkard and prophet. The column was raw, irreverent, like nothing ever seen before, obscene and hilarious. Always a party of one, Bukowski ridiculed everything, including the emerging hippie culture, and had no more use for antiwar protests than he had for World War II. He was always more of a hobo than a bohemian.

Bukowski forged another important relationship in 1966, with John Martin and Black Sparrow Press. Martin not only became a lifelong friend, he advanced Bukowski enough money to quit the post office. Bukowski went on to publish most of his later work with the press and, again with Martin's encouragement, branched out into novels that solidified his reputation at home and abroad. *Post Office*, published in 1971, told the story of Henry Chinaski, the alter ego who appeared in most novels and poems of this period. Chinaski is a disgruntled postal worker, a drinker and gambler who has numerous run-ins with his incompetent, sadistic supervisors. Bukowski soon became an international phenomenon. He was extremely popular in his birthplace, Germany, and praised in France as a working-class hero by Jean-Paul Sartre and Jean Genet.

Even after achieving these successes, Bukowski kept writing and publishing at the same frenetic pace. Never an innovative stylist, he continued to mine the same autobiographical material for both poems and prose and got them on the page with spontaneous verve. The novel *Factotum* (1975) later became the basis for a screenplay produced into a Hollywood movie, *Barfly*, in 1987. *Ham on Rye: A Novel* (1982) returned to Bukowski's childhood and recounted much of his parents' mistreatment of him. During this time, Bukowski built an ever-expanding following, though he received scant critical attention.

In the last decade of his life, Bukowski was as cantankerous and prolific as ever. Happily married to Linda Beighle, he gave in and finally started to look after his health. He settled down into a much more suburban existence and, though he still wrote often about the racetrack, he also wrote about driving around San Pedro in his BMW. This was no contradiction to Bukowski; he never rejected material wealth, just chaining oneself to a regular job. While some of the work from this period can be seen as seeking rapprochement with death, Bukowski was also writing some of his most biting, sarcastic work, and the most violent as well.

Since Bukowski died in 1994, Black Sparrow has continued to publish a posthumous volume nearly every year, including several editions of letters. Bukowski's irreverence, candor, and humor ensure his ongoing popularity, particularly among younger readers. The Internet has spawned a new cult following for Bukowski, with a number of Web sites devoted to his work. In 2002 Black Sparrow Press sold to Ecco/HarperCollins the rights to its three top authors, including Bukowski, for over one million dollars. Not only will Charles Bukowski stay in print, he will continue to rankle, the perennial outlaw and outsider, because the deal also includes the rights to five unpublished books.

[*See also* Hemingway, Ernest.]

## SELECTED WORKS

*Flower, Fist, and Bestial Wail* (1959)
*Longshot Poems for Broke Players* (1963)
*Poems and Drawings* (1962)
*Run with the Hunted* (1962)
*It Catches My Heart in Its Hands: New and Selected Poems, 1955–1963* (1963)
*Grip the Walls* (1964)
*Cold Dogs in the Courtyard* (1965)
*Crucifix in a Deathhand: New Poems, 1963–1965* (1965)
*All the Assholes in the World and Mine* (1966)
*Confessions of a Man Insane Enough to Live with Beasts* (1966)
*The Flower Lover* (1966)
*The Genius of the Crowd* (1966)
*The Girls* (1966)
*Night's Work* (1966)
*On Going Out to Get the Mail* (1966)
*To Kiss the Worms Goodnight* (1966)
*True Story* (1966)
*The Curtains Are Waving* (1967)
*2 by Bukowski* (1967)
*At Terror Street and Agony Way* (1968)
*Poems Written before Jumping out of an 8-Story Window* (1968)
*A Bukowski Sampler* (1969)
*The Days Run Away Like Wild Horses over the Hills* (1969)
*If We Take . . .* (1969)
*Notes of a Dirty Old Man* (1969)
*Another Academy* (1970)
*Fire Station* (1970)
*Post Office* (1971)
*Anthology of L.A. Poets* (1972)
*Erections, Ejaculations, Exhibitions, and General Tales of Ordinary Madness* (1972)
*Me and Your Sometimes Love Poems* (1972)
*Mockingbird, Wish Me Luck* (1972)
*Love Poems to Marina* (1973)
*South of No North: Stories of the Buried Life* (1973)
*While the Music Played* (1973)

*Burning in Water, Drowning in Flame: Selected Poems, 1955–1973* (1974)
*Africa, Paris, Greece* (1975)
*Chilled Green* (1975)
*Factotum* (1975)
*Tough Company* (1975)
*Weather Report* (1975)
*Winter* (1975)
*Scarlet* (1976)
*Art* (1977)
*Love Is a Dog from Hell: Poems, 1974–1977* (1977)
*Maybe Tomorrow* (1977)
*What They Want* (1977)
*We'll Take Them* (1978)
*Women* (1978)
*You Kissed Lilly* (1978)
*Legs, Hips, and Behind* (1979)
*A Love Poem* (1979)
*Play the Piano Drunk Like a Percussion Instrument Until the Fingers Begin to Bleed a Bit* (1979)
*Shakespeare Never Did This* (1979)
*Dangling in the Tournefortia* (1981)
*Ham on Rye* (1982)
*Horsemeat* (1982)
*The Last Generation* (1982)
*Bring Me Your Love* (1983)
*Hot Water Music* (1983)
*Sparks* (1983)
*There's No Business* (1984)
*War All the Time: Poems 1981–1984* (1984)
*You Get So Alone at Times That It Just Makes Sense* (1986)
*The Movie "Barfly": An Original Screenplay by Charles Bukowski for a Film by Barbet Schroeder* (1987)
*A Visitor Complains of My Disenfranchise* (1987)
*Beauti-Ful and Other Long Poems* (1988)
*The Roominghouse Madrigals: Early Selected Poems, 1946–1966* (1988)
*Hollywood* (1989)
*Septuagenarian Stew: Stories and Poems* (1990)
*People Poems: 1982–1991* (1991)
*The Last Night of the Earth Poems* (1992)
*Run with the Hunted: A Charles Bukowski Reader* (1993)
*Screams from the Balcony: Selected Letters, 1960–1970* (1993)
*Pulp* (1994)
*Confession of a Coward* (1995)
*Heat Wave* (1995)
*Living on Luck: Selected Letters, 1960s–1970s* (1995)
*Betting on the Muse: Poems and Stories* (1996)
*Bone Palace Ballet: New Poems* (1997)
*The Captain Is Out to Lunch and the Sailors Have Taken Over the Ship* (1998)

*What Matters Most Is How Well You Walk through the Fire* (1999)
*Open All Night: New Poems* (2000)

## FURTHER READING

Cherkovski, Neeli. *Hank: The Life of Charles Bukowski.* New York, 1991. A sympathetic biography completed before Bukowski's death.

Harrison, Russell. *Against the American Dream: Essays on Charles Bukowski.* Santa Rosa, Calif., 1994. A partisan attempt to bring scholarly attention to Bukowski's work.

Richmond, Steve. *Spinning Off Bukowski.* Northville, Mich., 1996. A remembrance written by a young bookstore owner befriended by Bukowski.

Weizman, Daniel, ed. *Drinking with Bukowski: Recollections of the Poet Laureate of Skid Row.* New York, 2000. An intimate look at Bukowski, with selections from former lovers, friends, fans, colleagues, and a movie star (Sean Penn).

# WILLIAM S. BURROUGHS

*by Chuck Carlise*

eat pioneer, heroin addict, expatriate, anarchist, gay rights advocate, gentleman, punk icon, free speech trailblazer, and member of the Academy of Arts and Letters, William Seward Burroughs was not only one of the most important American authors of the twentieth century but also one of the most fascinating.

Born in St. Louis, Missouri, on 5 February 1914, Burroughs was the grandson and namesake of the inventor of the Burroughs adding machine. He graduated from Harvard in 1936 and later moved to New York City, where he met Jack Kerouac and Allen Ginsberg and was introduced to heroin, an addiction he fought for four decades.

In 1946, Burroughs and Joan Vollmer were married and moved to Mexico City. There he began *Junky*—a stark account of his addiction. Written like a hardboiled detective story, the book was published under the narrator's alias, William Lee. *Junky* was issued by Ace Paperbacks as part of a two-volume set—the other an antidrug tract by a former narcotics agent.

On 6 September 1951, Vollmer and Burroughs (an excellent marksman) decided to put on a "William Tell act." Vollmer put a glass on her head, but Burroughs fired low, hitting her in the forehead and killing her. He famously described this event as putting him in touch with "the Ugly Spirit" that possessed him at the time and thrust him into a lifelong struggle, leaving him no choice but to write his way out.

In the next few years, he produced *Queer* (published in 1985) and *The Yage Letters* (published in 1963), dramatizing, respectively, a failed homosexual romance and a correspondence with Ginsberg while on a South American drug expedition. The latter is significant because it introduces what Burroughs referred to as "routines" (strange vignettes, sometimes including references to

William S. Burroughs.
*(© Alen MacWeeney/Corbis)*

dreams, and often hardly constituting any type of narrative structure).

He soon relocated to the North African city of Tangier, which was jointly ruled by four countries—that is, an international zone. The bizarre control structure in Tangier later crystallized for Burroughs as "Interzone." In 1958, he traveled to Paris and took a room in the unofficially named "Beat Hotel," where he befriended the painter Brion Gysin. By this time, routines from *Naked Lunch* began appearing in literary journals. American postal authorities seized one, *Big Table*, but the *Naked Lunch* excerpts in it were ruled not obscene. This scandal led the French publisher Maurice Girodias to ask Burroughs for a full manuscript. Burroughs and Gysin typed and sent out routines as they found them, a process that ultimately determined the order and structure of the book. *Naked Lunch* was finished and available in Paris by August 1959.

## "THE ALGEBRA OF NEED": *NAKED LUNCH*

In *Naked Lunch*, Burroughs posits that all of humanity is victimized by some form of addiction. One of the ways he accomplishes this is through the setting: "Interzone." Burroughs's description of Interzone's social structure is the "Algebra of Need"—which defines the power structure in terms of the average man's total need for drugs, sex, or power (the three most basic addictions). Burroughs describes the physical body's addictive nature as "the Human Virus," presenting need itself as a parasite rather than a condition. When infected, the addict regresses into a lower life-form, becoming one with the virus. As Burroughs says in the preface: "The face of 'evil' is always the face of total need. . . . In the words of total need: 'Wouldn't you?' Yes you would" (p. vii). The idea of physically regressing into a lesser being is dramatized throughout *Naked Lunch*, most notably in the famous "Talking Asshole" routine, as told by Dr. Benway, where the subject is literally taken over by one of his bodily functions.

The fourth political party of Interzone (along with the left, right, and centrist) is the Factualists, who are the only force challenging these parasites. The Factualists fight simply by revealing the plots of the more evil factions—and in fact the narrator, Lee, is a Factualist. Ultimately, the Factualists represent the underlying hope in *Naked Lunch*: the potential for intellectual freedom through the simple and subversive act of seeing clearly.

Structurally speaking, *Naked Lunch* itself defines this clarity by undermining standard ideas of what a story ought to look like. It is told, for one thing, in routines rather than a straight narrative style, with very little forward momentum. Moreover, the strange juxtaposition of many of the image montages forces the reader to make some kind of sense or connection between two otherwise unrelated elements. This new vision pulls the reader out of the predictable comfort of stories with beginning, middle, and ending. In doing so, the reader is forced to have an individual, almost anarchic, experience of the story, thus opening up new potentials to see past whatever smokescreens are in place.

## "RUB OUT THE WORD": THE CUT-UPS

Soon after *Life* magazine's famous 1959 Beat Generation article, Gysin fell upon the idea of cutting text and rearranging it at random. Calling it "the cut-up method," Burroughs soon began applying it to unused routines from *Naked Lunch*, introducing a new focal point: the idea that humanity is controlled fundamentally by "word/image locks" (language-based concepts that human beings are "locked into," processing all experiences through). The cut-ups feature not only Burroughs's own texts, but cut-up work by other authors as well, including Shakespeare, T. S. Eliot, and Kafka. (Critics of the technique cite this as a lack of craft. However, as was true for many conceptual and pop artists of this time, Burroughs's theoretical intent outweighed his need for critical endorsement, and the cut-ups continued.)

*The Soft Machine* (1961), the first of the cut-up trilogy, explores an imagined human history. In one routine, Burroughs explains humanity's evolution from apes as the result of a parasitic virus—making control the basis of human nature. Language and sexuality are introduced as solely human conventions, since both allow humans to be controlled in fundamental ways (intellectually and bodily). Even the title of the book reflects this, as the "soft machine" is a manipulative reference to the human body.

Revolt depends on the autonomous individual who can transcend the power structure. The most direct way to do this is to separate the elements of word/image lock and present the system's own materials in such a way that they are unable to evoke the desired effect. Therefore, the writer becomes (again) a revolutionary.

*The Ticket That Exploded* (1962) continues, positing that the bodily addictions Burroughs previously identified (sex, drugs, power) are secondary manifestations of the control of language. This book begins a sustained metaphor—the Nova mythology—featuring the Nova Mob, who seek control, and the Nova Police, who break down that force. The Mob invades Earth like a virus, forcing humanity to take part in "the reality film," which consists of endless repetition of the same scenes, scripts, and movements. This is indicative of the way words control mankind's concept of reality, shaping it so fundamentally that any conceptual change is nearly impossible to imagine. The Mob then complicates this through "Operation Other Half"—a scheme to control mankind by forging a feeling of separation that humanity obsessively yearns to close with another's body (an "Other Half").

The Nova Police fight in two ways: by exposing the plot and by silencing the word (taking away its power by cut-up). Burroughs, who had already positioned himself as a leader of the revolt in astonishingly real-life ways, closes this volume by disintegrating his text into the meaningless form-calligraphy of Brion Gysin. The introduction of Nova mythology suggests a wider metaphor as well. Since the Nova myth revolves around concepts such as Word and Reality, it is an open construct, and easily interprets any structure or story into its language.

*Nova Express* (1964), the final volume, has a more linear sequence of routines, and focuses again on the writer as resister. In one routine, the viruses' powers are suspended in a biological court. An appeal is made to "The Man at the Typewriter," but he upholds the suspension, and the viruses disintegrate. In the final episode, a character called "the Subliminal Kid" destroys reality by exposing the world to cut-ups of all past and present events. Now knowing that reality is a construct, the city dissolves, leaving a silent, bodiless world of sensory perception. It is important to note that while Burroughs is formulating social commentary, he does not suggest any program of change. Rather, he postulates that change can come only through new vision. Thus, the cut-up trilogy is a translating tool through which he helps each reader create his or her own concept of reality.

Burroughs spent much of the mid-1960s explaining the cut-up process to disbelieving audiences, and receiving praise from such unlikely sources as Norman Mailer. Also at this time, there was a highly publicized obscenity trial regarding *Naked Lunch*. The end of the decade brought Jack Kerouac's death, which profoundly saddened Burroughs.

In 1971, Burroughs completed *The Wild Boys*, a return to narrative style. *The Wild Boys* is a sci-fi fantasy about a tribal community of homosexual boys. They live naked, without family, religion, or country. They also have discovered the secret to immortality, which soon became a major theme in Burroughs's work.

In 1974, while lecturing at the City College of New York, Burroughs met James Grauerholz, who would be his secretary, manager, and caretaker for the next twenty-three years. Soon, Burroughs began a successful career of performance readings, thereby raising his already folkloric status in counterculture circles, including the underground punk music scene. The following year, while splitting time between lecturing at Ginsberg's Naropa Institute and a windowless New York loft (nicknamed "The Bunker"), Burroughs began *Cities of the Red Night*, which was published in 1981. In the early 1980s, he temporarily relocated to Lawrence, Kansas, where he would eventually spend the last years of his life.

## IMMORTALITY: THE *RED NIGHT* TRILOGY AND LATER WORKS

*Cities of the Red Night* is a threefold fantasy about an eighteenth-century homosexual pirate colony; the dystopian cities of the red night, and a contemporary detective story in which a private investigator discovers the biological trap of the cities and must rewrite history to prevent disaster. Burroughs invents the B-23 virus—the biological trap of sex and death—and the question arises of whether the writer can free humanity from this simply by erasing its acknowledgment. *Cities of the Red Night* is a creation instead of a destruction (as the cut-ups were), but explores similar territory. Rather than obliterating systems to achieve clarity, now Burroughs is concerned with manipulating these systems to defy other systems, namely space-time.

The sequels, *Place of Dead Roads* and *The Western Lands*, appeared in 1983 and 1987, respectively, featuring the writer-character William Seward Hall and bringing up questions about writing and immortality in new, complex ways. As *Place of Dead Roads* opens, Mike Chase kills Hall in a shoot-out. Hall's character and alter ego, Kim

Carsons, appears then—a Wild West literary outlaw. Carsons attempts to break the "lock" of time and reality. He reenacts the shoot-out, but wins this time, killing Chase (and thus, death itself). Since Carsons is tied to Hall, Hall survives, writing his way out of death with Carsons's life. After wild adventures and much blurring of character between Carsons and Hall, the shoot-out once again occurs; this time Carsons loses, shot in the back, ultimately affirming that he exists only within the writer's prose.

*The Western Lands* features both Hall and Carsons again. The title of the book refers to an ancient Egyptian term for the afterlife, and the novel itself deals directly with the subject of immortality. In this, Burroughs's last complete novel, one can feel the writer anticipating death. Carsons and Hall are very representative of this; for example, it is said that Carsons's only links to the living earth are his cats—that he is barely present even when he is present. Near the book's conclusion, Burroughs writes that "The Old Writer" has come to the end of what can be done with words.

In 1986, Brion Gysin died, another in a long succession of Burroughs's friends whom he outlived. Burroughs, deeply saddened, published a late collaboration titled *The Cat Inside*.

In the next decade, Burroughs worked sporadically, appearing in films such as *Drugstore Cowboy*, collaborating with Tom Waits and Kurt Cobain, and overseeing a 1991 film version of *Naked Lunch*, directed by David Cronenberg. He began publishing old journals and uncollected essays, continued writing (primarily about his cats), sold his splatter paintings, and received friends and fans at his house. On 2 August 1997, four months after the death of Allen Ginsberg, eighty-three-year-old William Burroughs passed away in Lawrence, Kansas, following a heart attack.

[*See also* Beat Movement, The; Ginsberg, Allen; *and* Kerouac, Jack.]

## SELECTED WORKS

*Junky: Confessions of an Unredeemed Drug Addict* (as William Lee) (1953)
*Naked Lunch* (1959)
*Exterminator* (with Brion Gysin) (1960)
*Minutes to Go* (with Brion Gysin, Sinclair Beiles, and Gregory Corso) (1960)
*The Soft Machine* (1961)
*The Ticket That Exploded* (1962)
*Dead Fingers Talk* (1963)
*The Yage Letters* (with Allen Ginsberg) (1963)

*Nova Express* (1964)

*APO-33: Bulletin Metabolic Regulator* (1965)

*Call Me Burroughs* (1965)

Darazt (with Lee Harwood) (1965)

*Roosevelt After Inauguration and Other Atrocities* (as Willy Lee) (1965)

*Time* (1965)

*Valentines Day Reading* (1965)

*White Subway* (1965)

*So Who Owns Death TV?* (with Claude Pelieu and Carl Wiessner) (1967)

*They Do Not Always Remember* (1968)

*Ali's Smile* (1969)

*The Dead Star* (1969)

*The Braille Film* (with Carl Weissner) (1970)

*The Job* (1970)

*The Last Words of Dutch Schultz* (1970)

*The Third Mind* (with Brion Gysin) (1970)

*Electronic Revolution* (1971)

*Jack Kerouac* (with Claude Pelieu) (1971)

*The Wild Boys: A Book of the Dead* (1971)

*Brion Gysin Let the Mice In* (with Ian Somerville) (1973)

*Exterminator!* (1973)

*Mayfair Academy Series More or Less* (1973)

*Port of Saints* (1973)

*The Book of Breething* (1974)

*Sidetripping* (with Charles Gatewood) (1975)

*Snack* (1975)

*Cobble Stone Gardens* (1976)

*Le Colloque de Tanger* (with Brion Gysin) (1976)

*Letters to Allen Ginsberg, 1953–1957* (1976)

*The Retreat Diaries* (1976)

*Naked Scientology* (1978)

*23 Skidoo* (1978)

*Ah Pook Is Here* (1979)

*Blade Runner: A Movie* (1979)

*Le Colloque de Tanger*, vol. 2 (with Brion Gysin and Gerard-Georges Lemaire) (1979)

*Dr. Benway* (1979)

*Cities of the Red Night* (1981)

*Early Routines* (1981)

*Nothing Here Now but the Recordings* (1981)

*Streets of Chance* (1981)

*With William Burroughs: A Report from the Bunker* (edited by Victor Bockris) (1981)

*You're the Guy I Want to Share My Money with* (1981)

*Sinki's Sauna* (1982)

*A William Burroughs Reader* (edited by John Calder) (1982)

*The Place of Dead Roads* (1983)

*The Burroughs File* (1984)

*The Four Horsemen of the Apocalypse* (1984)

*Ruski* (1984)

*The Adding Machine: Collected Essays* (1985)

*Queer* (1985)

*The Cat Inside* (with Brion Gysin) (1986)

*Interzone* (edited by James Grauerholz) (1987)

*The Western Lands* (1987)

*Apocalypse* (with Keith Haring) (1988)

*The Whole Tamale* (1988)

*My Education: A Book of Dreams* (1989)

*Tornado Valley* (1989)

*Uncommon Quotes* (edited by Kathelin Hoffman) (1989)

*Dead City Radio* (1990)

*Ghost of a Chance* (1991)

*Paper Cloud; Thick Pages* (1992)

*The "Priest" They Called Him* (with Kurt Cobain) (1992)

*Seven Deadly Sins* (1992)

*The Black Rider* (with Tom Waits) (1993)

*Collected Interviews of William S. Burroughs* (1993)

*Spare Ass Annie* (1993)

*Speed / Kentucky Ham: Two Novels* (1993)

*William S. Burroughs: Selected Letters* (1993)

*The Letters of William S. Burroughs: 1945–1959* (1994)

*Conversations with William Burroughs* (edited by Allen Hibbard) (1995)

*Last Words: The Final Journals of William S. Burroughs, November 1996–July 1997* (edited by James Grauerholz) (2000)

## FURTHER READING

Grauerholz, James, and Ira Silverberg, eds. *Word Virus: The William S. Burroughs Reader.* New York, 1998. Excerpts of Burroughs's work, with commentary provided by Grauerholz, Burroughs's longtime secretary. Compiled posthumously, it also includes later biological information excluded from earlier biographies.

Lydenberg, Robin. *Word Cultures: Radical Theory and Practice in William S. Burroughs' Fiction.* Urbana, Ill., 1987.

Miles, Barry. *William Burroughs: El Hombre Invisible.* London, 1992. A good biography with an annotated bibliography.

Morgan, Ted. *Literary Outlaw: The Life and Times of William S. Burroughs.* New York, 1988. Critical biography through the late 1980s. Extremely intricate in biographical information, with some consideration of Burroughs's texts as well.

Skerl, Jennie, and Robin Lydenberg, eds. *William S. Burroughs at the Front: Critical Reception, 1959–1989.* Carbondale, Ill., 1991.

# TRUMAN CAPOTE

*by Charles Robert Baker*

The author known as Truman Capote was born Truman Streckfus Persons on 30 September 1924 in New Orleans, Louisiana. His father, Archulus Persons, was a charming dreamer who believed that his big break was just around the corner; that his next get-rich-quick scheme would be the one that would establish him as a financially independent southern gentleman. One of the many people who fell for his charm and his dreams was a seventeen-year-old former Miss Alabama, Lillie Mae Faulk. Lillie Mae had dreams of her own and saw the twenty-five-year-old entrepreneur as her ticket to a better life. The two were married in Lillie Mae's hometown of Monroeville, Alabama, on 23 August 1923. Their honeymoon along the Gulf Coast was cut short when Persons ran out of money and Lillie Mae was sent home to the relatives who had raised her since her mother's death. Persons stayed in New Orleans, trying to raise some funds, and four weeks later returned to Monroeville with the expectation that the Faulks would take him in and care for him as a member of the family. He was mistaken.

Persons returned to New Orleans and was hired as a salesman for the Streckfus Company. Captain Vern Streckfus owned a fleet of excursion boats, and it was Person's job to book groups for tours along the Mississippi, from New Orleans to St. Louis. Although he proved to be remarkably successful at this, Lillie Mae continued to have misgivings about his ability to take care of her, and enrolled in a business school in Selma, Alabama. In the winter of 1924, she discovered she was pregnant and went to Persons in New Orleans, demanding that he pay for an abortion. It took all the charm Persons possessed to convince Lillie Mae to have the child. When the boy was born in the Touro Infirmary in New Orleans, Persons took it upon himself to choose his name: Truman, after

Truman Capote.
*(Photograph by Carl Van Vechten.
Courtesy of the Library of Congress)*

a boyhood friend, and Streckfus, to ingratiate himself with his employer.

The arrival of the child did nothing to unite the mismatched couple in a common bond of parenting. Persons continued to focus solely on his pursuit of riches, and Lillie Mae began a pursuit of other men and alcohol; Truman was an inconvenience, often left with friends or family, or, on occasion, alone.

In 1930, Truman was sent to live on a more or less permanent basis with Lillie Mae's relatives in Monroeville. The household consisted of three elderly sisters and their brother. Two of the sisters, Jennie and Callie Faulk, owned a hat store in town and were away from the house most of the day, and their bachelor brother, Bud, spent most of his time alone in his bedroom. Truman was left in the care of the painfully shy and simple older sister, Sook. Sook called Truman "Buddy" because he reminded her of a young boy she had once loved and lost. The time they spent together and their intense love for each other, the only unconditional love he was to ever know, were immortalized in Capote's *A Christmas Memory* (1966) and *The Thanksgiving Visitor* (1967). Truman's only other friend in Monroeville was a little girl almost two years younger than he, Harper Lee. Lee was later to capture Truman's precociousness in the character Charles Baker Harris, "Dill," in her classic novel *To Kill a Mockingbird*.

Lillie Mae, after many tries, finally found the man she was looking for: a well-to-do Cuban named Joseph Garcia Capote. Her petition for divorce was granted in 1931, and she married Joe Capote the following year. On St. Valentine's Day 1935 adoption papers were finalized, and Truman's name was legally changed to Truman Garcia Capote. Lillie Mae decided to choose a name for herself that better reflected her new, affluent lifestyle.

Henceforth, everyone other than her Alabama relatives knew her as Nina.

Capote knew from the age of nine or ten that he was destined to be a writer. He received encouragement from his high school English teacher, Catherine Wood, to whom *A Christmas Memory* is dedicated, to submit his stories to *Scholastic* magazine. Although he was a voracious reader and regularly won writing contests, Capote was a poor student. In interviews, he gave conflicting stories about whether or not he completed high school, but it is certain he never attended college. At the age of eighteen, Capote was hired as a copyboy by *The New Yorker* magazine. His hopes that this might lead to recognition by the literati of New York were dashed when he was fired for supposedly insulting Robert Frost at the Bread Loaf Writers' Conference in 1944. Joe Capote recalled Truman coming home in tears with the news of his firing. The generous and understanding stepfather comforted Capote with the assurance that he would support him while he worked on his writing. Soon thereafter, *Mademoiselle* magazine bought Capote's short story "Miriam." The gothic story of a little girl, who may or may not exist, and the lonely woman to whom she attaches herself, caught the attention of Robert Linscott, an editor at Random House. On 22 October 1945, Linscott signed Capote to a contract. Bennett Cerf, founder of Random House, remembered that day; "He looked about eighteen. He was bright and happy and absolutely self-assured. Everybody knew that somebody important had arrived upon the scene—particularly Truman!"

## EARLY FICTION

Capote wrote that his first novel, *Other Voices, Other Rooms* (1948), was an attempt to exorcise demons. Indeed, the novel can be read as a psychological autobiography filled with lush, dreamlike symbolism. Capote's protagonist, thirteen-year-old Joel Harrison Knox, is sent to live with his father after his mother's death. He travels from New Orleans to a mysterious, isolated, and run-down plantation that is the home of his spiteful stepmother, her exotic cousin Randolph, and the father he has never seen. In this eerie environment, Joel, desperately seeking love and understanding, makes the tortuous journey of self-discovery. When it becomes clear to Joel that he is homosexual, he is neither ashamed nor guilt-ridden. Instead, he takes one last look at the confused boy he used to be and joyfully accepts the young man he truly is. The novel created an immediate international sensation when it arrived in bookstores in January 1948. Although

most critics disliked it, the subject matter as well as the provocative photograph of the author that graced the back of the book jacket intrigued the reading public. The book stayed on *The New York Times* best-seller list for nine weeks, and Capote was propelled into the celebrity and notoriety that would follow him the rest of his life.

Random House kept its successful and mysterious young author in the public eye by publishing in rapid succession *A Tree of Night and Other Stories* (1949), a collection of eight of Capote's short stories, two of which, "Miriam" and "Shut a Final Door," had won the O. Henry Award; *Local Color* (1950), a book of travel vignettes; and another autobiographical novel, *The Grass Harp* (1951).

## STAGE, SCREEN, AND HOLLY GOLIGHTLY

Always anxious to try something new, Capote wrote a version of *The Grass Harp* for the New York stage. He likened the experience to making a statue out of a painting. The play opened at the Martin Beck Theater on 27 March 1952 to great expectations, but it failed to capture the critics or audience, and closed on 26 April. Capote quickly recovered from his disappointment and traveled to Ravello, Italy, with director John Huston and leading man Humphrey Bogart to film his comic screenplay *Beat the Devil*. While in Europe, Capote received news that his mother, after several earlier attempts, had successfully committed suicide.

Capote returned to the United States and created a Broadway musical based on his short story "House of Flowers." Although he gathered the best choreographers, songwriters, and actors in the business, critics and the public were again disappointed. A few devoted fans, however, managed to keep the show running at the Alvin Theatre from 30 December 1954 through 22 May 1955.

In December 1955, the first of what was hoped to be many Soviet–American cultural exchanges occurred. An all-American company was booked to perform Gershwin's *Porgy and Bess* in Leningrad and Moscow. Capote traveled with the troupe, and *The New Yorker* published the chronicle of his observations in two parts in October 1956. Random House published the pieces in a slim volume titled *The Muses Are Heard* later the same year. Capote's other contributions to stage and screen include *The Innocents* (1961), a screenplay based on Henry James's *The Turn of the Screw*; *Trilogy* (1969); a screenplay of three of his short stories, "Miriam," "Among the Paths to Eden," and "A Christmas Memory"; and acting the role of Lionel Twain in the Neil Simon movie *Murder by Death* (1976).

It had been seven years since Capote published any fiction when Random House released his novella *Breakfast at Tiffany's* in 1958. Critics and readers adored this story of a fascinating and beautiful young woman who has discarded her harsh life as Lulamae Barnes in Tulip, Texas, to reinvent herself in Manhattan as "Miss Holiday Golightly of the Boston Golightlys." A writer who had lived in the same brownstone apartment building as Holly in the early years of World War II tells her story in retrospect. He has returned to the old neighborhood after several years, drawn by a friend who has some news of Holly's possible whereabouts. The story of the ebullient, childlike woman who lived by her wits, loved freedom above all things, and disdained middle-class values and morality continues to startle and enchant readers decades later.

### IN COLD BLOOD

A small news item in the 16 November 1959 issue of *The New York Times* captured Capote's imagination. A wealthy farmer, Herbert W. Clutter, his wife, and two teenage children had been killed by shotgun blasts after being bound and gagged. Capote convinced *The New Yorker* to send him and his childhood friend, Harper Lee, to the scene of the crime in Holcomb, Kansas, where they would interview the townspeople about the murdered family and write a short piece about the effect the gruesome killings had on this small mid-American community. After weeks of work, Capote and Lee were close to wrapping up their story when news came that two men had been arrested and charged with the crime. Capote decided to expand upon his original idea, and spent the next five years interviewing the murderers and revising his manuscript. He gained the confidence of the two men, Perry Smith and Richard Hickock, and became quite close to them; so close, in fact, that he stood beside them at their request when they were hanged on 14 April 1965. Something of Truman Capote died on the scaffold that day as well.

### THE FALL FROM THE TOP

*Esquire* magazine prepublished *In Cold Blood* in four parts from 25 September through 16 October 1965. It was a major literary event that has been compared to the excitement felt when Dickens published his novels in anxiously awaited installments. Capote was hailed as the creator of a new genre: the nonfiction novel. To celebrate its completion and to honor his friend Katharine Graham, he invited more than five hundred of the world's most famous and glamorous people to a party at the Plaza Hotel in New York City: the legendary Black and White Ball. The book, published in January 1966, brought him fame and wealth, but the experience in Kansas exacted a terrible price. Never the shy, retiring type, Capote became self-destructively reckless in his public and private life. The 1960s and 1970s were decades of recreational drug use and recreational, faceless sex. Capote took his fill of both, along with ever-increasing amounts of alcohol. He was omnipresent, appearing in magazines and at trendy discotheques and as a guest on late-night talk shows. He regularly appeared on the *Tonight Show*, trading sharp-tongued insults with other authors and presenting himself as the final arbiter of everything from high fashion to high crime.

When *In Cold Blood* failed to win either the Pulitzer Prize or the National Book Award, Capote sank further into depression and depravity. He wrote little of importance in his final years; *The Thanksgiving Visitor* (1967), a companion piece to *A Christmas Memory*, showed a glimpse of Capote's storytelling genius, but his growing bitterness is evident in the fact that he makes the sweet-natured Buddy of the Christmas story commit a mean-spirited and hateful act of betrayal during a Thanksgiving dinner. Random House published a collection of previously printed magazine pieces, *The Dogs Bark: Public People and Private Places* (1973), but the public was hungry for something new. Capote had hinted for years that he was hard at work on a "tell all" nonfiction novel that he called *Answered Prayers*, taking the title from St. Teresa of Ávila, who is reputed to have said that more tears are shed over answered prayers than unanswered ones. Capote was hit with the full force of the truth of this aphorism when *Esquire* magazine published four chapters from the work in progress—"Mojave" (June 1975), "La Cote Basque, 1965" (November 1975), "Unspoiled Monsters" (May 1976), and "Kate McCloud" (December 1976)—and he found himself abandoned by the high society personalities who had been his mainstay. Friends and lovers, who were easily identifiable in the roman à clef "La Cote Basque, 1965," were enraged to find themselves lampooned and ridiculed. Capote was crushed; the feeling of being abandoned by his substitute family was as painful as the one he had often felt as a child when his mother would dispose of him when he became inconvenient.

Random House published a collection of Capote's magazine stories and sketches, *Music for Chameleons*, in 1980, and a slim Christmas story, *One Christmas*, in 1983. Although he claimed in the preface to *Music for Chameleons* that his personal and creative crises were over, his rapid descent continued. After a long series of overdoses and hospital stays, Capote retreated to the care of one of his few remaining friends, Joanne Carson, wife of the *Tonight Show* host, Johnny Carson. He arrived at her Los Angeles home on 23 August 1984, looking ill and much older than his fifty-nine years. Early on the morning of 25 August, Mrs. Carson knew that he required medical attention but Capote refused, telling her that he had enough of doctors and hospitals. The two sat in his bedroom at the Carson home and talked until he could talk no more; by noon, Truman Capote was dead. Mrs. Carson has said that as he grew weaker, she heard him say to someone only he could see, "It's me, it's Buddy."

Capote's influence on journalism and the writing of creative nonfiction can be seen in the works of writers like Norman Mailer, Carl Bernstein, and Bob Woodward. But he will perhaps be best remembered for his creation of characters who, like himself, felt lost, unwanted, unknown to themselves and others; characters who struggled to find a safe place for themselves, a "Tiffany's" where nothing bad could happen to them.

## WORKS

*Other Voices, Other Rooms* (1948)
*Tree of Night and Other Stories* (1949)
*Local Color* (1950)
*The Grass Harp* (1951)
*The Muses Are Heard* (1956)
*Breakfast at Tiffany's, A Short Novel and Three Stories* ("House of Flowers," "A Diamond Guitar," "A Christmas Memory") (1958)

*Observations* (with Richard Avedon) (1959)
*Selected Writings of Truman Capote* (1963)
*A Christmas Memory* (1966)
*In Cold Blood* (1966)
*The Thanksgiving Visitor* (1967)
*The Dogs Bark: Public People and Private Places* (1973)
*Music for Chameleons* (1980)
*One Christmas* (1983)
*Three by Truman Capote* (1985)
*Answered Prayers: The Unfinished Novel* (1987)
*A Capote Reader* (1987)
*A House on the Heights* (2002)

## FURTHER READING

Clarke, Gerald. *Capote: A Biography*. New York, 1988. The best biography available, it reads like a nonfiction novel.

Dunphy, Jack. *"Dear Genius": A Memoir of My Life with Truman Capote*. New York, 1987. Capote described Dunphy as the love of his life. The two had a long, often volatile relationship.

Garson, Helen S. *Truman Capote*. New York, 1980.

Garson, Helen S. *Truman Capote: A Study of the Short Fiction*. New York, 1992.

Grobel, Lawrence. *Conversations with Capote*. New York, 1985.

Plimpton, George. *Truman Capote: In Which Various Friends, Enemies, Acquaintances, and Detractors Recall His Turbulent Career*. New York, 1997.

Reed, Kenneth T. *Truman Capote*. Boston, 1981.

# HAYDEN CARRUTH

*by Mark Conway*

One of the most enduring figures in the literary world during the second half of the twentieth century, Hayden Carruth (b. 3 August 1921) has been publishing poems and reviews in prolific fashion since World War II. Carruth initially became known as an editor and critic. He was editor-in-chief of *Poetry* magazine from 1949 to 1950 and an associate editor at the University of Chicago Press from 1951 to 1952. His essays on the modernist masters William Carlos Williams, Wallace Stevens, and Ezra Pound appeared in such prominent venues as *The Nation* as early as 1950. His first book of poems, *The Crow and the Heart, 1946–1959* followed in 1959.

Carruth's early preeminence as a critic is partially due to the force and originality of his essays and reviews. He leapt to the defense of Pound, who was widely attacked for his politics when awarded the Bollingen Prize for poetry in 1948. Carruth, a U.S. war veteran who had served in Italy, defended Pound with characteristic courage, directness, and a touch of orneriness.

A seminal event occurred in 1953 when Carruth spent fifteen months in a psychiatric hospital. He described the reasons for his hospitalization in *The Bloomingdale Papers*, a sequence of poems named for the clinic: "The fact is I am here, / Having collapsed, because / I can't be anywhere else— / The case with most of us. / And because the terrors / Which clutch and shake me, / The drink which wards them off, / Equally reduced me / To inaction, paralysis, / And extreme pain." The hospital stay had a significant impact on Carruth's work. Part of his prescribed therapy consisted of exploring the causes of his psychological problems through writing, but more importantly, the experience became the demarcation line between the possibility of a meaningful life and an overwhelming sense of futility. Carruth wrote, "My poems, I think, exist in a state of tension between the love

Hayden Carruth.
*(Courtesy of Copper Canyon Press)*

of natural beauty and the fear of natural meaninglessness or absurdity." Poetry offered both a way to discern order in the face of chaos and to join the resistance, a means to contribute to the intellectual and cultural reserves that oppose chaos.

Carruth wrote often and openly about his hospitalization. For him, it is a symptom and symbol of human frailty rather than a personal failing. A disturbing number of his contemporaries and fellow poets fought with mental disabilities—Sylvia Plath, Robert Lowell, Anne Sexton, John Berryman, Delmore Schwartz, and Randall Jarrell. Unlike most of these poets, Carruth never explored "confessional" poetry, but instead turned outward, toward form and history, as a way to investigate the meaning of the experience. Much of Carruth's early work can be seen as a persistent testing of form against disorder, an attempt to find a home in an unfriendly and cold universe, a desire to find something, anything—an idea, a person, a work of art—one can trust.

The hospitalization also inspired the long poem *The Asylum*. This is Carruth's first sustained work and the most striking of the poems that appear in *The Crow and the Heart, 1946–1959*. *The Asylum* is written in thirteen stanzas of fifteen lines each, a form of Carruth's invention that he calls the "paragraph" and that he returned to episodically over his career. The paragraph sets for itself a complicated structure of required elements, repeated precisely, including an intricate scheme of metrics and rhyme. Despite its painful autobiographical subject, the poem typifies Carruth's initial reaction toward the personal—though inspired by his own individual experience, the primary focus is on collective history. The tone of the poem is cerebral, chilly, and ironic. The title plays on the dual meaning of the word "asylum" as refuge and as sanitarium and suggests that the natural state for mankind in the 1950s is exile: "And we shall search the air, / Turning drained eyes along the wind, as blind / Men do, but never find asylum here."

After leaving the hospital, Carruth lived with his parents in his childhood home in Pleasantville, New York, for five years. He recalls this time in *Reluctantly: Autobiographical Essays* (1998), referring to himself in the third person:

> He was loaded with Thorazine during this period, five hundred milligrams a day and sometimes more, but it didn't help him. He lived at night as much as he could . . . —guests were a serious problem for him. . . . Each night at about two o'clock he went out and walked down the sidewalk. Sometimes he walked a hundred feet, sometimes a hundred yards. He had been told that he should walk around the block, but in five years he never made it that far.

Even though he spent most of the time in solitude, he characterized this period as a positive move from "reclusion to seclusion."

James Laughlin, the poet and publisher, gave him a place to stay in Connecticut for two years starting in 1960. Carruth then cobbled together enough money to look for a place of his own. He and his new wife and son settled in northern Vermont, not as an early "back to the land" return to agrarian values, but because they could not afford anything closer to Connecticut. They bought a house and eleven acres of land for $5,725. Carruth put down $3,000 and took out a mortgage with a monthly payment of $27.54. Though they came to Vermont not by choice, Carruth eventually became an eloquent and ardent advocate of his new rural homeland, for his neighbors and the local ecology. Carruth later said of these years that his life was almost entirely unconnected with poetry, that "much of it was outdoors in the company of people who considered me a laborer or mechanic, never a writer."

## THE 1960s AND 1970s

Despite these protests, Carruth produced an amazing amount of work during this time. From 1959 to 1979, he published twenty-one books, including his only novel (*Appendix A*), a book of philosophical inquiry (*After "The Stranger": Imaginary Dialogues with Camus*), and several anthologies, as editor. He also began to win a steady stream of prizes; the monetary award often paid the monthly mortgage.

He kept in touch with such poet friends as Galway Kinnell, Adrienne Rich, and Denise Levertov, but for the most part he was on his own, writing voluminously and working in a broad variety of styles. Carruth constantly experimented with form and tinkered with every variation of meter and rhyme. He adapted forms from other traditions, such as the haiku, and tried out many different stanzaic structures. He wrote a number of narrative poems, often dramatic monologues, that relate stories of his Yankee neighbors in a conscious modernization of Robert Frost. At the same time, Carruth was attracted to the possibilities of free verse and organic forms. He explored these modes of expression often using his passion for jazz as an aesthetic model.

Carruth's books received little or no attention from the critics. Living in isolation in northern Vermont, Carruth mostly published with small presses. Furthermore, he was not part of any school of poetry, he was not connected to any academic circle, and he never gave readings. However, he did write, by his own reckoning, thousands of magazine and newspaper articles, and continued to publish striking, independent-minded pieces in *The Nation*, *Sewanee Review* and elsewhere. He also began a long relationship with the *Hudson Review* as an advisory editor and frequent contributor. In 1970 he edited a very influential anthology of twentieth-century American poetry, *The Voice That Is Great within Us*.

Carruth knew that other poets were doing well in what was essentially a new milieu for literature, one much more friendly for writers, "provided that they teach, recite, perform, expound, exhibit—in short that they tickle the institutional vanity of the age." Carruth was neither capable nor interested in returning to society; any temptation to "perform" was out of the question.

A turning point came in 1978 when *Brothers, I Loved You All: Poems, 1969–1977* won the Lenore Marshall Poetry Prize. In many ways, this collection is a compendium of Carruth's restless experimentation. It includes examples of most of the forms discussed above: "paragraphs," dramatic monologues on rural neighbors, short haiku-like meditations, and another invention, the poetic "essay." *Brothers* was generally regarded as a major achievement. It may simply be that Carruth's work finally found its moment because he published two other books of poetry around this time. Those books, largely neglected by the public, were written during the same period as *Brothers*, and the poems are virtually interchangeable with one another.

## A PUBLIC LIFE

Several developments occurred in the wake of *Brothers*. Carruth began two important professional relationships, one with *Harper's* magazine as poetry editor. He also relocated to New York in 1979 to teach at Syracuse University, significant because he felt capable of moving out of isolation. To his surprise, he found that he liked teaching and had something to offer creative-writing students. He taught there until his retirement in 1991.

Many critics consider *The Sleeping Beauty*, published in 1982, to be Carruth's masterpiece. The book-length poem composed over the course of the 1970s sustains the paragraph form for 125 stanzas. Even though he relaxed certain of the most stringent formal requirements of the paragraph, the result is a stunningly ambitious, virtuoso performance. The poem encapsulates all of history through the fairy tale story, creating a mythological context for Carruth's life. Carruth disperses himself throughout the poem in various guises, but always as an aspect of the prince, the masculine principle to Sleeping Beauty.

Following the move to Syracuse, *Asphalt Georgics* and *The Oldest Killed Lake in North America: Poems, 1979–1981*, both appeared in 1985. These books show the effects of Carruth's relocation, with the poems now taking place at the boundaries of civilization, where it fades into a borderland of fast-food joints, where the forests and lakes are turned into jobs and money. The Vermont dramatic monologues have been transposed to this blighted suburb; the dialect of the poems change into rough, street-smart harangues of bitterness.

On 24 February 1988, Carruth wrote, "I intentionally and massively overdosed myself with every pill I possessed." He survived and wrote about the experience in an essay entitled "Suicide." Part of the reason to write about the event was pragmatic. The essay states, "To be frank...no topic in fifty years of writing has blocked me as thoroughly and persistently as this one, my own suicide." The effort unlocked one of the most luminous of Carruth's essays, filled with a radiant sense of exhilaration that came from surviving, in some ways a telescoped version of his life.

In the early 1990s, Carruth's reputation as a critic still overshadowed his many achievements as a poet. When he won the National Book Critics Circle Award in 1993 for *Collected Shorter Poems, 1946–1991*, and followed this signal achievement with the National Book Award in 1996 for *Scrambled Eggs and Whiskey: 1991–1995*, his reputation as a poet was secured. A major retrospective of his work appeared in *Parnassus: Poetry in Review* in 1997 that took into account *Collected Shorter Poems, Scrambled Eggs and Whiskey, Collected Longer Poems* (1993), *Sitting In: Selected Writings on Jazz, Blues, and Related Topics*

(1986), and *Selected Essays and Reviews* (1996). His most recent poetry volume is *Doctor Jazz* (2001).

Carruth's unflinching honesty as a critic and ceaseless experimentation as a poet resulted in an astonishing diversity of writings. While some of the writing in this huge output is uneven, on the whole the work exhibits a rare boldness and passionate honesty. Carruth's project is different from many poets in the latter half of the twentieth century. One of his searches is for language with the exactitude of philosophical terms, to translate philosophy into a new kind of poetics. He tries to find a form that could convey the lyricism of an intellectual notion. Carruth is as enterprising as any poet of his time in fusing jazz riffs, common speech, and vast learning into a flexible idiom that could bear the weight of any idea or emotion.

[*See also* Long Poem, The; Pound, Ezra; Vietnam in Poetry and Prose; *and* Williams, William Carlos.]

## WORKS

### POETRY

*The Crow and the Heart, 1946–1959* (1959)
*In Memoriam: G. V. C.* (1960)
*Journey to a Known Place* (1961)
*The Norfolk Poems: 1 June to 1 September 1961* (1962)
*North Winter* (1964)
*Nothing for Tigers; Poems, 1959–1964* (1965)
*Contra Mortem* (1967)
*For You: Poems* (1970)
*The Clay Hill Anthology* (1970)
*From Snow and Rock, From Chaos: Poems, 1965–1972* (1973)
*Dark World* (1974)
*The Bloomingdale Papers* (1975)
*Loneliness: An Outburst of Hexasyllables* (1976)
*Aura: A Poem* (1977)
*Brothers, I Loved You All* (1978)
*Almanach du Printemps Vivarois* (1979)
*The Mythology of Dark and Light* (1982)
*The Sleeping Beauty* (1982, 1990)
*If You Call This Cry a Song* (1983)
*Asphalt Georgics* (1985)
*Lighter Than Air Craft* (1985)
*The Oldest Killed Lake in North America* (1985)
*Mother* (1985)
*The Selected Poetry of Hayden Carruth* (1985)
*Sonnets* (1989)
*Tell Me Again How the White Heron Rises and Flies across the Nacreous River at Twilight toward the Distant Islands* (1989)
*Collected Shorter Poems, 1946–1991* (1992)
*Collected Longer Poems* (1993)

*Selected Essays and Reviews* (1996)
*Scrambled Eggs and Whiskey: Poems, 1991–1995* (1996)
*Doctor Jazz* (2001)

### AS EDITOR

*A New Directions Reader* (1964)
*The Voice That Is Great within Us: American Poetry of the Twentieth Century* (1970)
*The Bird/Poem Book: Poems on the Wild Birds of North America* (1970)
*The Collected Poems of James Laughlin* (1994)

### OTHER WORKS

*Appendix A* (1963)
*After "The Stranger": Imaginary Dialogues with Camus* (1965)
*Effluences from the Sacred Caves: More Selected Essays and Reviews* (1983)
*Sitting In: Selected Writings on Jazz, Blues, and Related Topics* (1986, 1993)
*Suicides and Jazzers* (1992)
*Reluctantly: Autobiographical Essays* (1998)
*Beside the Shadblow Tree: A Memoir of James Laughlin* (1999)

*Listener's Guide: Reading from Collected Shorter Poems and Scrambled Eggs and Whiskey* (1999)
*Faxes to William* (2000)

### FURTHER READING

Dickey, James. *Babel to Byzantium: Poets and Poetry Now*. New York, 1968. See pages 127–131.

Miller, Mathew. "A Love Supreme: Jazz and the Poetry of Hayden Carruth." *Midwest Quarterly* 39, no. 3 (Spring 1998): 294.

Selinger, Eric Murphy. "Collected Shorter Poems, Collected Longer Poems, Scrambled Eggs and Whiskey, Sitting In: Selected Writing on Jazz, Blues, and Related Topics, Selected Essays and Reviews." *Parnassus: Poetry in Review* 22, no. 1–2 (Spring-Summer 1997): 250.

Solotaroff, Ted. "Hayden Carruth: Collected Shorter Poems, 1946–1991." *The Nation* 255, no. 16 (16 November 1992): 600.

Weiss, David, ed. "In the Act: Essays on the Poetry of Hayden Carruth." *Seneca Review*, Twentieth Anniversary Issue, 1990. Includes fourteen essays on Carruth.

# RAYMOND CARVER

*by James P. Austin*

Few writers have succeeded over hardship to become an indelible literary figure of their era quite like Raymond Carver. Born in 1938 in Clatskanie, Oregon, Carver was the son of a sawmill worker and he spent his formative years, and even much of his own adulthood, as a member of the working class. It is the men and women of the working class who populate the world of Carver's award-winning short stories. But the road from Clatskanie to the distinguished awards and respect Carver had earned by the end of his life was a long and winding one.

So much of Carver's life, including his choice to write short stories and poetry, was decided by the finite imperatives of time and money, both of which were in short supply from a young age. His father, C. R., moved the family several times throughout the 1940s and 1950s in search of better-paying work, first to Yakima, Washington, and on to several places after that. But the pay was no better, and with C. R.'s increasing dependence on alcohol, the Carver family scrambled for financial stability. These twin themes of alcoholism and financial difficulty would later play a significant role in Carver's adulthood and writing career, beginning in 1957 when, at nineteen years old, he married his sixteen-year-old girlfriend Maryann Burk. Several months later, their first child Christine was born. The following year, at age twenty, Carver and his wife welcomed a son, Vance. The pressure of being responsible for a family at such a young age shaped both Carver's worldview and writing, as he states in his essay "Fires": "[M]y children are . . . the main influence. They were the prime movers and shapers of my life and my writing" (*Fires: Essays, Poems, Stories*, p. 30).

## EARLY ADULTHOOD AND STORIES

Those "ferocious years of parenting" (*Fires*, p. 25) were so influential because, unlike so many other writers, the facts of Carver's family life dictated how much time and energy that he had left for writing. "I had to sit down and write something now," Carver writes, "tonight, or at least tomorrow night, no later, after I got in from work and before I lost interest" (*Fires*, p. 25). Thus was born Carver's decision to concentrate on short story and poetry writing.

Both Carver and his wife, however, desperately sought education as a means of escaping the endless series of menial jobs they held throughout their early years. They had also adopted the nomadic existence that Carver had lived as a child and that brought them to Paradise, California, in 1958, where they were able to rent a house for twenty dollars a month. Carver began attending Chico State University, and there met his first mentor, a then-little-known writer named John Gardner. It was Gardner who took Carver "seriously enough to sit down and go over a manuscript. . . . I knew something crucial was happening to me, something that mattered" (*Fires*, p. 29). Gardner also granted Carver access to his office to write on the weekends, which was important for a man with a wife and two small children at home. Carver was finally able to devote significant time to writing, and to concentrate in privacy.

But the financial imperative directing Carver's life would assert itself again, forcing the Carvers to move from Paradise to Eureka, California, in search of work. While there, Carver finally finished his college degree at Humboldt State College, and after a brief stay in Berkeley, he was admitted to the University of Iowa's prestigious Writer's Workshop. Carver was only able to stay for one of the two years, however, because the financial straits caused by being a graduate student were too much for his family to bear. They moved to Sacramento, close to Carver's parents, but life there also proved difficult and he was forced again to take menial positions in order to help support his family.

It was during this time that the second major theme of Carver's adulthood, alcoholism, began taking hold of his life. At the time, Carver worked as a custodian at Mercy Hospital in Sacramento, and instead of coming home after work, he began stopping for a drink. His drinking gradually escalated over the next several years, forcing the Carvers to declare bankruptcy at one point.

During this otherwise bleak period, Carver began having the first glimmerings of what would later become fabulous success as a writer. While studying at Humboldt, his teacher, Richard Day, lauded Carver's story "The Father," which would later appear in his 1976 collection *Will You Please Be Quiet, Please?* He had some more modest publishing successes, including a story in the *Western Humanities Review*. And in 1968, Carver's story "Will You Please Be Quiet, Please?" was selected for the *Best American Short Stories* annual. As his alcoholism worsened, Carver nevertheless continued to write stories that would later appear in his major collections.

Other successes followed, as readers and editors seemed drawn to Carver's subtle, pared style of writing and the often grim subject matter of his stories. Of further note is that Carver inadvertently helped shepherd a renaissance in the short story, which had for years been less marketable than the novel. Interest in his stories likely increased because his style and subject matter, too, were unique for the times. Carver wrote nearly all his stories in a severely pared style, sometimes so close to the bone that no light at all shone through. He also wrote of characters who, like Carver himself, "wanted their actions to count for something. But at the same time they've reached the point—as so many people do—that they know it isn't so. It doesn't add up any longer. . . . It's their lives they've become uncomfortable with, lives they see breaking down" (*Fires*, p. 201). These characters are rarely successful men and women; on the contrary, like Carver for so much of his life, the characters lead out-of-control lives, holding down jobs that they can barely stand and that hardly pay enough to cover the bills. Their stories correspond with the moments where, while things may be bad, they are about to somehow get worse.

## SUCCESS OVER DRINKING AND WITH WRITING

It was not until after Carver had finally taken his final drink of alcohol that his career took the shape we recognize today. Like his characters, Carver, too, had reached a point where he "felt spiritually obliterated" (*Fires*, p. 195) by the years of hard work that had led only to frustration, poverty, and debt, and with little time for writing. The early successes aside, Carver reached a point where he "threw in the towel" and "took to full-time drinking as a serious pursuit" (*Fires*, p. 195) as a method for coping with the dawning realization that his life was not what he had hoped it would be.

In 1971, however, Carver's story "Neighbors" appeared in *Esquire*, where Gordon Lish was the fiction editor, and whom Carver had known during their days in California. This renewed relationship lasted over a decade and had a dramatic impact on Carver's writing style. Lish encouraged Carver to pare down his style even further, using fewer words for greater impact. As this style eventually grew more successful in the 1970s, the concepts "minimalism" and "dirty realism" were used to characterize the style and mood of Carver's work.

Before Carver could realize these successes, however, he first had to triumph over his alcoholism, which had a dramatic impact on every aspect of his life. After "Neighbors" appeared in *Esquire*, Carver's problems with alcohol only increased. His wife Maryann, in fact, noted that the increasing problems with alcohol corresponded with Carver's new career as a university teacher. This new position was something Carver would eventually grow into, but his inherent shyness caused him to depend heavily upon alcohol in the meantime.

Teaching, too, led to the nomadic lifestyle that had characterized Carver's childhood. From 1971 to 1975, Carver taught at the University of California, Santa Cruz; the University of California, Berkeley; the University of Iowa Writer's Workshop; and finally at the University of California, Santa Barbara. It was at UC-Santa Barbara that Carver's escalating alcohol abuse finally overtook him. He rarely had class and was unable to fulfill his one-year teaching position for 1974–1975. In December of 1974, he was asked for his resignation, and he provided it.

For the next few years, until 1977, Carver did little writing and devoted himself to drinking. It was not until he had finally reached "a very grave place" (*Fires*, p. 197) that involved frequent blackouts and several trips to rehabilitation centers that Carver was finally able to stop drinking before it killed him: "I was dying of it, plain and simple, and I'm not exaggerating" (*Fires*, p. 197). His first short story collection, *Will You Please Be Quiet, Please?*, was published by McGraw-Hill Press in 1976, a success that did not curtail his drinking problem.

In 1977, Capra Press published his second collection of stories, *Furious Seasons*, that included nearly all his short fiction not appearing in *Will You Please Be Quiet, Please?* This was also the year that saw Carver achieve permanent sobriety, which he has called his greatest success. By early 1978, Carver was encouraged enough by his sobriety to teach a short course at Goddard College in Vermont, where he struck up friendships with two other emerging writers, Tobias Wolff and Richard Ford. Carver began writing more frequently during this period, too, particularly after he was awarded a John Simon

Guggenheim Fellowship, leading to his first new fiction since his drinking days: "Why Don't You Dance?" and "Viewfinder." He also spent time again in Iowa City, Iowa, with his wife, after which they separated, and then began a teaching position at the University of Texas, El Paso.

While there, he saw the poet Tess Gallagher again, whom he had first met the previous year at a writer's conference. Gallagher was herself in town for a conference being held at the university, and the two developed an instant rapport. She left town after the conference ended, but following an intense correspondence, she returned to El Paso. On New Year's Day 1979, she and Carver began living together, which they would continue doing until Carver's death in 1988. The two moved together to take temporary teaching positions in Tucson, Arizona, and again in 1980 to Syracuse, New York, where Carver was hired to the permanent faculty at Syracuse University.

The years of sobriety in Syracuse proved to be some of the most fruitful and illustrious of Carver's career. He wrote short stories more frequently than ever before, publishing, among others, "Gazebo," "A Serious Talk," and "One More Thing" in 1980 and 1981. These works would later comprise much of Carver's next collection of stories, *What We Talk about When We Talk about Love*, which was a critical success and secured Carver's place as a master of the genre. This collection was edited by Carver's old friend Gordon Lish, and he edited the stories severely, pushing Carver toward the pared-down style many consider his calling card. The extent of this editing was not known until years after Carver's death, when it became clear that Lish's editing hand was indeed a heavy one. Copies of Carver's stories show Lish editing extensively, pushing Carver to use fewer words. Several stories from *Furious Seasons*, for example, reappeared in this next collection in much more concise form. Strangely, it is Carver's work from this period that led to him being labeled a "minimalist," a term with which Carver himself never entirely agreed.

Nevertheless, *What We Talk about When We Talk about Love* was received warmly and with several glowing reviews. His story "The Bath" received *Columbia* magazine's Carlos Fuentes Fiction Award, "What We Talk about When We Talk about Love" appeared in the *Pushcart Prize*, and a new story, "Chef's House," appeared within the pages of *The New Yorker*.

## ASCENT TO THE TOP OF AMERICAN LETTERS

Following this string of successes, Carver soon wrote another story that would become one of his most famous, and the titular story of his third collection. "Cathedral" was a marked change for Carver; while the writing style was still efficient, it was no longer pared down to only its essentials. The story has a more expansive feel to it, and while its conclusion is hardly a "happy ending," it does offer a glimmer of light and hope not previously seen in Carver's work. Surely the end of his drinking, and the continuing success of his relationship with Tess Gallagher, brought Carver away from the darkness that had characterized so much of his life. It is natural to assume that all this success altered his worldview and affected his fiction. But "Cathedral" was also the first story that Carver wrote after he had ended his relationship with Lish, who had pushed him toward a minimalist, pared-down style. Without Lish and the old frustrations of life, Carver produced his most acclaimed work, the short story collection *Cathedral*.

In 1983, Carver was also awarded a Mildred and Harold Strauss Living Fellowship by the American Academy and Institute of Arts and Letters. It paid him a living stipend of $35,000 a year, with the only condition that he not hold any other job. To that end, Carver resigned from Syracuse and went to work completing the stories that would eventually comprise *Cathedral*. The collection was nominated for both the National Book Critics Circle Award and the Pulitzer Prize, and it assured Carver his place at the forefront of American literature and provided a certain degree of celebrity, as well.

The years following *Cathedral*'s success saw Carver write two collections of poetry, *Where Water Comes Together with Other Water* and *Ultramarine*; the former was awarded *Poetry* magazine's Levinson Prize. He also published several book reviews, collaborated with Gallagher on two screenplays that were never produced, and became guest editor for literary journals such as *Ploughshares* and annuals like the *Best American Short Stories*, 1986. Two years after the success of *Cathedral*, Carver began to write new fiction, and much of it appeared within the pages of prestigious literary magazines like *The New Yorker* and *Granta*.

In conjunction with his final birthday, Carver's fiftieth, he was awarded a Creative Arts Award Citation for Fiction from Brandeis University, a Doctor of Letters degree from the University of Hartford, and induction into the American Academy and Institute of Arts and Letters. His ascent to the top of the American literary scene, however, also came at a time of grave illness. Carver had been a heavy smoker nearly all his life, and in late 1987 he was diagnosed with lung cancer. Doctors at Syracuse University removed two-thirds of his left lung in an attempt to also remove the cancer from his body, but Carver was granted only a temporary reprieve from his illness. In early 1988, cancer appeared in his brain, and a few months later it recurred in his lungs.

Nevertheless, Carver published two final and significant works. In 1988, Atlantic Monthly Press published his short story collection *Where I'm Calling From*, a collection of his best fiction. And even as the seriousness of his cancer became clear and his health deteriorated, Carver completed a collection of poetry that would be published after his death, *A New Path to the Waterfall*.

In June 1988, Carver and Gallagher were married in Nevada and made a brief trip to Alaska. On 2 August 1988, Raymond Carver died at home in Port Angeles, Washington, at the age of fifty.

[*See also* Short Story in America, The *and* Gardner, John.]

## WORKS

### POETRY

*Near Klamath* (1968)
*Winter Insomnia* (1970)
*At Night the Salmon Move* (1976)
*Where Water Comes Together with Other Water* (1985)
*Ultramarine* (1986)
*A New Path to the Waterfall* (1989)

### FICTION

*Will You Please Be Quiet, Please?* (1976)
*Furious Seasons and Other Stories* (1977)

*What We Talk about When We Talk about Love* (1981)
*Cathedral* (1983)
*Where I'm Calling From: New and Selected Stories* (1988)

### OTHER WORKS

*Fires: Essays, Poems, Stories* (1983)
*Dostoevsky: A Screenplay* (1985)
*No Heroics, Please: Uncollected Writings* (1992)

### FURTHER READING

Campbell, Ewing. *Raymond Carver: A Study of the Short Fiction*. New York, 1992. Provides career overview and analysis of twenty-seven stories.

Meyer, Adam. *Raymond Carver*. New York, 1994. Summarizes Carver's life and writing career; provides analysis of his most famous fiction and poetry.

Nesset, Kirk. *The Stories of Raymond Carver: A Critical Study*. Athens, Ohio, 1995. A book-length version of a dissertation; provides useful introduction to Carver and his work.

Runyon, Randolph Paul. *Reading Raymond Carver*. Syracuse, N.Y., 1992. Asserts Carver's stories should be read in their sequence in each collection.

Saltzman, Arthur M. *Understanding Raymond Carver*. Columbia, S.C., 1988. First full-length study of Carver's work. Occasionally brief.

# WILLA CATHER

*by Susan J. Rosowski*

Willa Cather is remarkable for the excellence, productivity, longevity, consistency, and experimentation of her writing, and also for the absence in her life of the angst familiar in other authors' biographies: alienation, madness, scandal, alcoholism. Instead, she was faithful to her home, her family, and her friends. Her experience encompassed rural Virginia, frontier Red Cloud and Lincoln, Nebraska, Pittsburgh, Pennsylvania, and Park Avenue in New York City, with side trips to Europe, the American Southwest, and Canada; she was a Nebraska cosmopolite. Unlike writers such as Walt Whitman, Mark Twain, and F. Scott Fitzgerald, who lived their lives as extensions of the stories they told, Cather was known for the privacy of her life as well as for the openness of her writing. She once said, in a letter to *The Commonweal* describing her own methods, that a novelist should present "the experiences and emotions of a group of people by the light of his own . . . whether his method is 'objective' or 'subjective' " (*On Writing*, p. 13). Cather was a writer whose works were exceptionally infused with her own experiences, but at the same time she had the rare capacity for detachment and could make those experiences and emotions part of her characters' stories, not just her own.

Cather is strongly identified with place. Nebraska is the setting of six of her novels (though one is nominally located in Colorado), as well as of the majority of her short stories, but she also wrote of the Southwest and Quebec City. The common link is that these are all sites of exchanges, of the interplay of cultures and beliefs: in Virginia, of the North and the South; in Nebraska and Quebec, of the New World and the Old; in the Southwest, of Native Americans and Mexicans and Anglos. Cather

Willa Cather. (*Courtesy of the Library of Congress*)

sought within these changing worlds continuities broad enough to include our own.

## A VIRGINIA–NEBRASKA CHILDHOOD

Willa Cather was born in Back Creek Valley, Frederick County, Virginia, on 7 December 1873; though christened Wilella, she was called Willa even in the earliest family letters. She was born into a family of close ties and strong, independent, capable women. (Sidney Gore, her great-aunt, was a postmistress, teacher, and letter writer, and the namesake of Gore, Virginia.) The Shenandoah Valley, site of the Cather home, was split apart by feelings about slavery and states' rights; as a strategic crossroads between the North and the South, it was hotly contested in the Civil War. These divisions were mirrored in Cather's own extended family, some of whom fought for the Confederacy while others adhered to the Union.

In 1873, the same year Willa was born, the extended Cather family began to emigrate to Nebraska. Willa's uncle George and aunt Frances (Smith) Cather, newly wed, were the first settlers in a part of Webster County that came to be known officially as Catherton. Theirs was the classic pioneer experience: living first in dugouts, planting an orchard and digging a well, fighting grasshoppers, starting a school and church, establishing a post office. Friends and neighbors from Virginia, including Cather's grandparents, William and Caroline Cather, soon followed, giving the area the name of New Virginia. In 1883, Willa's parents, Charles and Virginia (Boak) Cather, emigrated with their four children (three others would be born in Nebraska), bringing with them the hired girl Margie Anderson and her brother, Willa's maternal grandmother, Rachel Boak, and two of her other grandchildren. Their neighbors included settlers from Germany, Scandinavia, Bohemia, and French Canada. This mixture of the familiar and the unknown helped to spark young Willa's imagination; the scenes and people she knew in these years would form the fabric of many of her works. As she said, "most of the basic material a writer works with is acquired before the age of fifteen" (Bohlke, p. 20).

The Charles Cather family lived in the country for nearly two years. In 1885, they moved into the frontier town of Red Cloud, which would appear in Cather's fiction as Hanover in *O Pioneers!*, Moonstone in *The Song of the Lark*, Black Hawk in *My Ántonia*, Sweet Water in *A Lost Lady*, Skyline in "Old Mrs. Harris," and Haverford in *Lucy Gayheart*. There, for the next five years, Cather experienced the stability and diversity of small-town life, as well as the interconnectedness of farms, villages, and cities. Country people came to town to buy finished goods and sell their produce; the expanding railroads connected villages to cities. Eight passenger trains a day stopped in Red Cloud on the run between Chicago and Denver, bringing traveling theater and opera companies that opened up new imaginative worlds for young Willa.

There was a diversity of cultures and characters in the growing town. Willa's mother was a Southern belle; the Cather's neighbors included an educated European Jewish couple (later appearing as the Rosens in "Old Mrs. Harris") who opened their fine library to her. The Miners (who appear as the Harlings in *My Ántonia*) were musical: Mrs. Miner's Norwegian father had played in Ole Bull's orchestra; and the Miners' hired girl, Anna Sadilek, the eldest daughter of Bohemian immigrants, inspired Ántonia herself.

Cather's journeys outward from Red Cloud began in 1890, when she enrolled in the second year of the preparatory school of the University of Nebraska. The rapidly growing university had opened its doors in 1871; when she was a freshman, there were three hundred to four hundred students, and three times that many when she graduated in 1895. The university was the site of interaction between American beginnings and Europe's rich past, between raw energy and cultural restraint. The dynamic chancellor, James Canfield, led a faculty that included the botanist Charles Bessey, Lieutenant (later General) John J. Pershing, and the linguist A. H. Edgren. The students included Dorothy Canfield, a best-selling novelist who also introduced the Montessori method into America; Alvin Johnson, founder of the New School for Social Research; Roscoe Pound, legal theorist and dean

of Harvard Law School; Louise Pound, folklorist and philologist, and the first woman president of the Modern Language Association; and Frederick Clements and Edith Schwartz Clements, founders of modern ecology. Cather intended to study medicine; at the university she awakened to ideas, an experience she would give to Jim Burden in *My Ántonia*. One day she saw an essay she had written on Carlyle in both the *Hesperian* (the student literary magazine) and the *Nebraska State Journal*, sent in, unknown to her, by her rhetoric teacher. She later said she became a writer because of this prep-school essay.

Becoming a writer meant learning all she could of literature: its history and its production, as well as its relations to other arts. That meant reading voraciously, writing, reviewing, editing, publishing, and marketing, and Cather did them all. She contributed to or edited five periodicals, ranging from student publications to two city papers, including the *Nebraska State Journal*, Lincoln's largest newspaper. In her junior year, she became the regular drama critic for the *Journal*, publishing 170 articles, reviews, and essays, 94 in her senior year alone. Her weekly columns provided a forum for her wide-ranging mind, interested in local events, classic and popular literature, painting, theater, music, and the artists who created them. They gave her practice in creating a scene, selecting the telling detail, and assessing what created art and what fell short—all (in the words of pioneer Cather scholar Bernice Slote) "Improvisations toward a Credo."

## PITTSBURGH: MAKING HER WAY IN THE WORLD

By the time she graduated in 1895, Cather had a reputation for talent, intellect, ambition, and opinion (she was known as the "meat-axe" critic). "[S]he is unquestionably destined to be among the foremost of American literary women," wrote the popular poet Walt Mason in 1896 (Slote, p. 27). She was ready to leave the parish and go into the world to experience places and cultures she had only read about. Getting out wasn't easy, however, in a decade of hard times. The dark side of the settlement experience came in the midst of the severe drought and the national depression of the 1890s, and Cather felt the desperation of being trapped in the cornfields, as she later said. She returned briefly to Red Cloud ("Siberia," she wrote), applied unsuccessfully for a teaching position at the university, and continued writing. Her break came in 1896, when she moved to Pittsburgh as editor of a new magazine, the *Home Monthly*, modeled on the successful *Ladies Home Journal*.

Cather's Pittsburgh years (1896–1906) were marked by the eclecticism of someone getting on in the world. She was responsible for editing, and often writing, "home and hearth" pap for the *Home Monthly*; within two months, she was also writing music and drama reviews for the *Pittsburgh Daily Leader,* Pennsylvania's biggest evening paper. Later she worked for the *Leader* as assistant "telegraph editor" and book and drama critic. She was briefly on the staff of the weekly *Library*; she spent some months in Washington, D.C., working as a translator in a government office and writing as a Washington correspondent for the *Nebraska State Journal* and the *Index of Pittsburgh Life.* Starting in 1901, her day job was teaching high school in Pittsburgh, while at night she kept involved in the city's vibrant social and cultural life, continuing as a columnist and music and drama critic for Lincoln and Pittsburgh papers.

It was through her theatergoing that Cather met Isabelle McClung in 1899. Cather and McClung had a mutual interest in the arts and complementary differences in background. McClung was the daughter of a prominent Presbyterian Pittsburgh family; her mother was from the wealthy Mellon family, and her father was a judge. She was interested in the arts and the Bohemian life (the counterculture of the day). Cather had artistic genius; Isabelle proved the guide into culture. Cather made her first trip abroad with Isabelle in 1902. She moved into the McClungs' large, gracious home, where she had an attic study for writing. Friendship with Isabelle McClung became an emotional center for Cather, as Nebraska became her creative center. She wrote all her books for Isabelle, she once said.

The year following their meeting yielded a burst of creative activity. Cather had published only a single, forgettable story in each of the preceding years, but in 1900 she published six, including "Eric Hermannson's Soul," her first in a magazine of national circulation (*Cosmopolitan*). In it, an awakened yearning for art releases the soul of the immigrant Eric Hermannson from the austere strictures of fundamentalism, when beautiful, talented, world-weary Margaret Elliot arrives "in the wilds of Nebraska" with her brother, Wyllis, from the East.

Other stories of merit followed during Cather's Pittsburgh years, including "A Wagner Matinee," "The Sculptor's Funeral," and "Paul's Case." Her themes include culture, class, and yearning for access to the world of art. Her first book, however, was a volume of poetry, *April Twilights*, published by a vanity press in 1903: bookishly imitative elegies, laments, and pastorals.

Cather later said she should have bought all the copies and thrown them "in a tarn" (Woodress, p. 165). Her poetic impulse was authentic, however: she introduced her true first novel with the poem "Prairie Spring."

Other events in 1903 were more important to Cather. While visiting in Lincoln, she met Edith Lewis, daughter of a banking family there. When Cather moved to New York to work for *McClure's Magazine,* she took a studio apartment in the house where Lewis was living, a "very sedate Bohemia," as Lewis recalled it, populated by poor, hard-working writers and artists—the studio Cather recalled in "Coming, Aphrodite!" Lewis was an editorial proofreader at *McClure's.* In 1908, Cather and Lewis took an apartment at 82 Washington Place, and they lived together for thirty-nine years, until Cather's death. Lewis, a published poet, remained at *McClure's* as assistant managing editor after Cather left, then worked as an advertising writer for J. Walter Thompson. This relationship sustained Cather both personally—they traveled together and shared a summer cottage on Grand Manan Island—and professionally: they read proof together, and some of Cather's typescripts reveal Lewis's hand.

In 1903, through the recommendation of Will Owen Jones, managing editor of the *Nebraska State Journal,* Cather also met S. S. McClure, a magazine publisher legendary for discovering talent and notorious for creating chaos. *McClure's Magazine* excelled in first-rate fiction as well as in muckraking journalism that exposed corruption in politics and business. In writing to thank Jones, Cather described meeting with McClure in New York: she had returned to Pittsburgh feeling elated, as if her life were now more valuable than it had been. McClure promised to publish her stories in his magazine, then as a book; he would place anything he didn't use.

McClure published Cather's first volume of fiction, *The Troll Garden*, in March 1905. The seven stories deal with the yearning to enter the seductive and dangerous world of art. Three stories are in a sense exorcisms of issues Cather was confronting in her own life. The body of a great sculptor is returned to his home town on the plains, where the uncomprehending townspeople ridicule him ("The Sculptor's Funeral"). A woman who had left the East to homestead in Nebraska returns to Boston, where her nephew takes her to a concert that reawakens her passion for art, a passion that must be frustrated again: "For her, just outside the door of the concert hall, lay the black pond with the cattle-tracked bluffs . . . the gaunt, moulting turkeys picking up refuse about the kitchen door" ("A Wagner Matinee"). In "Paul's Case: A Study in Temperament," a Pittsburgh high school boy seeks to escape working-class life by stealing money to go to New York, briefly entering the glamorous world he had imagined; he commits suicide rather than return to his old life.

## NEW YORK CITY AND *MCCLURE'S MAGAZINE*

When Cather joined McClure's staff in 1906, she moved to New York City, her home for the rest of her life. She entered the charged world of what her biographer James Woodress calls "a supernova in the journalistic firmament"; Ida Tarbell, Lincoln Steffens, and Ray Stannard Baker, all working for McClure at the same time, gave the magazine "a brilliance perhaps unsurpassed in American magazine history" (Woodress, pp. 185, 184). Cather's first big assignment was a controversial series on Mary Baker Eddy, founder of the Christian Science Church, to check the facts and rewrite a flawed manuscript by Georgine Milmine. She went to Boston, where she worked under imminent deadlines for much of 1907 and 1908; *Mary Baker G. Eddy: The Story of Her Life and the History of Christian Science* appeared in fourteen installments from January 1907 to June 1908. Increasingly, Cather took over administrative responsibilities at the magazine, serving from 1908 to 1911 as managing editor. McClure valued Cather as an editor (she ghost-wrote his *Autobiography*, published in 1914), but the political and reformist aspect of the magazine was not particularly congenial to her, and though her position gave her access to the literary and artistic life of New York and London, she had little time for her own work. She published only seven stories between 1904 and 1911.

However, while in Boston, Cather met Annie Fields, widow of the publisher James T. Fields, and through her, Sarah Orne Jewett, whose book of stories, *The Country of the Pointed Firs* (1896), Cather admired. In a critically important exchange of letters in December 1908, Jewett assessed Cather's equipment as a writer: "Your Nebraska life,—a child's Virginia, and now an intimate knowledge of what we are pleased to call 'the Bohemia' of newspaper and magazine office life." She advised her on how to find her self and her subject: "To work in silence and with all one's heart, that is the writer's lot; he is the only artist who must be a solitary and yet needs the widest outlook on the world." "You must find your own quiet centre of life, and write from that to the world... in short, you must write to the human heart, the great consciousness that all humanity goes to make up." "You can write about life, but never write life itself. And to write and work on this level, we must live on it." In her response, Cather described

her fears and her ambitions; this is one of the most revealing and important letters of Cather's life. Cather felt dispossessed of herself, like a trapeze performer putting all her energy into catching the bar lest she fall into the net, or like a rabbit being chased. She had been rereading Jewett's story "Martha's Lady," which made her feel humble and desolate—and made her want to begin again.

Cather left *McClure's* for a six-month vacation in late September of 1911, never to return to full-time staff work. In rapid succession, she wrote her first novels ("there were two," she later said). *Alexander's Bridge*, serialized as *Alexander's Masquerade* in *McClure's* (February–April 1912), was published by Houghton Mifflin later in 1912. This story of a bridge-building engineer is an updated approach to the tragic hero. The pattern was conventional, Cather later remarked, but the impressions she tried to communicate were genuine. Like Cather, Alexander's inner feelings are at odds with his public success. The narrative follows his restless movement between Boston and London, and between Winifred, his cultivated wife, and Hilda Burgoyne, the actress whom he had loved in his youth. In the end, when Alexander is called to inspect his cantilevered bridge, pushed beyond its limits, he realizes that "the whole structure has to come down." Before he can rebuild, the bridge collapses, and going down with it, he drowns.

Cather was returning to her Nebraska roots even before she wrote *O Pioneers!*, the second of her two "first novels." The short stories "The Joy of Nelly Deane" (1911) and "The Bohemian Girl" (August 1912) show both the beauty and the narrowness of life in the small plains towns she had excoriated in earlier stories. Two other stories, "The White Mulberry Tree" and "Alexandra," suddenly came together in what Cather described to her friend Elizabeth Sergeant as "a sudden inner explosion and enlightenment. She had experienced it before only in the conception of a poem. Now she would hope always for similar experience in creating a novel, for the explosion seemed to bring with it the inevitable shape that is not plotted but designs itself" (Sergeant, p. 116).

### O PIONEERS!

The country would be the hero, or heroine, of Cather's new book, and she had taken her themes from the long grass, as Anton Dvorák had in the *New World Symphony* (Sergeant, p. 92). Introduced with the poem "Prairie Spring," *O Pioneers!* (1913), Cather's first Nebraska novel, begins: "One January day, thirty years ago, the little town of Hanover, anchored on a windy Nebraska tableland, was trying not to be blown away." The opening scene introduces her country—the Divide, a strip of high land between the Republican and the Little Blue rivers. On this landscape appear the characters whose lives will play out in two intertwined stories of youth. Alexandra Bergson, the far-seeing eldest child of an immigrant Swedish family, who after her father's death assumes responsibility for the family, learns to love the wild land into which they have come; she transforms it into one of the most prosperous farms on the Divide, but with prosperity comes loneliness. Alexandra's youngest brother, Emil, falls in love with Marie, the young wife of a Bohemian neighbor; their passion ends unhappily when Marie's husband, Frank, kills them as they lie under the mulberry tree. In the end, the country gives rise to new life: "Fortunate country . . . to receive hearts like Alexandra's into its bosom, to give them out again in the yellow wheat, in the rustling corn, in the shining eyes of youth" (p. 274). These are the human stories repeated endlessly.

*O Pioneers!* marked something new not just in Cather's work but in American literature. "This was the first time I walked off on my own feet—everything before was half real and half an imitation of writers whom I admired. In this one I hit the home pasture and found that I was Yance Sorgeson and not Henry James," wrote Cather (Woodress, p. 240). She was referring not to her Nebraska material (she had written much Nebraska fiction before this time) but to her principle of design, the interrelatedness. The book's themes—yearning desire, attachment to place, ecstatic fulfillment in connection to something big, the loneliness and loss inevitable in human lives, and solace in the ongoing life of nature—as well as an interest in how individual lives unfold in a particular time and place and a belief in great truths underlying existence permeate all Cather's best works.

Despite the occasional review faulting *O Pioneers!* for its "slow-moving" plot (Frederick Taber Cooper) or misplacing its setting (a London reviewer praised its vivid pictures of "wild, lonely Canadian life"), critics who understood it celebrated its genius and described qualities that would remain consistent in Cather's writing. *O Pioneers!* "is touched with genius. It is worthy of being recognized as the most vital, subtle and artistic piece of the year's fiction." "One feels thru this narrative the spirit of the author, and comes to trust oneself completely in her hands. It is a spirit, an attitude toward life, that in its large and simple honesty has a kind of nobleness. Life, the course of events, as traced by such a mind, loses the taint of commonplace and becomes invested with

dignity" (O'Connor, pp. 49, 47). "This book provides an opportunity for the American Academy of Arts and Letters to justify its existence . . . one of the functions of an academy . . . is the discovery and recognition of genius," Floyd Dell wrote (p. 47).

Meanwhile, Cather was securing the conditions she needed to write. Long the editor of others' writing, she now had in Ferris Greenslet at Houghton Mifflin an interested and refined editor of her own. When in 1912 she and Lewis moved to number 5 Bank Street in Greenwich Village, she felt they had the ideal apartment, spacious and quiet, with their maid of four years to keep order in their lives. Freed of her full-time responsibilities at *McClure's Magazine*, Cather continued freelance work for the magazine, editing and writing to supplement her royalties. She settled into a working routine of writing two to three hours in the morning; she always wrote a first draft by hand and typed a second and sometimes additional drafts, revising each time. Equally important for her, Cather was living at the heart of the cultural as well as the publishing world. As her days combined writing and concerts and friends, her years combined "home" in New York with yearly visits "home" to Nebraska, and travels in the United States and abroad.

## THE SONG OF THE LARK

Cather had "hit the home pasture" with *O Pioneers!*, for the first time writing in her own voice as an artist, spontaneously, without arranging or inventing. It is characteristic that she next explored what it meant to find one's voice and come into one's own as an artist. She would write "Of Artist's Youth" (her original title), about a talented young girl's fight to escape commonness and succeed in the true sense of delivering herself completely to her art. *The Song of the Lark* (1915) is a *Künstlerroman*, a novel of an artist's development that reverses the genre's typical gender roles. For the details of her character's career, Cather drew loosely upon the opera singer Olive Fremstad, whose friendship she had enjoyed. For the emotional life of her heroine, however, Cather drew upon her own life. Thea Kronborg passes her childhood in Moonstone, Colorado, so precisely based on Red Cloud that a visitor today can follow a character's movements through the actual town; she moves into the world—for lessons in Chicago, for an awakening to herself as an artist in Panther Canyon, Arizona, and to New York City, where she comes into full possession of her powers. Thea Kronborg fights her way to the top, thereby (as Cather wrote in her 1932 preface) succeeding in delivering herself completely to her art; yet as she does so, her personal life pales.

This was a period of exceptional public ferment and change. In 1913, the Armory Show introduced Postimpressionism and Cubism to New York; in 1914, World War I began in Europe, with the United States entering the war in 1917. There were personal changes, too. In 1915, Judge McClung died and Isabelle and her brother sold the house that Cather had visited frequently even after moving to New York; and, most devastatingly for Cather, in 1916 Isabelle married the musician Jan Hambourg. She saw, however, that Isabelle was happy.

## MY ÁNTONIA

For her most beloved novel, Cather again drew upon her memories of growing up in Nebraska, this time by remembering an actual woman—Anna Sadilek, the oldest daughter of an immigrant Bohemian family. She created a narrator, Jim Burden, to whom she gave her own experiences of arriving from Virginia by train, living in the country and then moving to town, going to the university and from there to New York, and returning to visit Ántonia, now married and mother of ten children. Some of the scenes are among the most famous in American literature: the West, symbolized by a plow, magnified briefly against the setting sun, or children emerging from a fruit cave in an explosion of life. The book, like its title character, is one to "leave images in the mind that did not fade" (p. 342). Yet there is no flinching from the hardships and the dark possibilities of pioneering: the threat of starvation in first hard winter the Shimerdas live in a dugout; Ántonia's vulnerability to rape by her employer, Wick Cutter; her disgrace after following the railroad man she loved to Denver, then returning unwed and pregnant; the darker pasts of settlers such as Peter and Pavel, exiles from Russia, who in their homeland were groomsmen who threw a bride and groom to wolves in order to save themselves; the tramp who commits suicide by throwing himself into a threshing machine.

Cather included lessons on reading her novel in the novel itself. She addressed how to draw upon lived experiences and actual people through a conversation between friends in the introduction. Throughout the novel, characters tell their stories in conversations with others, who may comprehend the stories only as their own experiences grow. Cather had found in conversation a way to write about the people and places she loved without causing them pain.

Ferris Greenslet recalled reading *My Ántonia* as "the most thrilling shock of recognition of the real thing of any manuscript" he ever read (Woodress, p. 300). H. L. Mencken had noted Cather's steady advance and wrote that *My Ántonia* was "a sudden leap—a novel, indeed, that is not only the best done by Miss Cather herself, but also one of the best that any American has ever done, East or West, early or late" (O'Connor, pp. 88–89). Reviewers recognized that she belonged among the moderns. Randolph Bourne said of *My Ántonia* that Cather "has taken herself out of the rank of provincial writers and given us something we can fairly class with the modern literary art the world over that is earnestly and richly interpreting the spirit of youth" (Woodress, p. 301). "The most extraordinary thing about *My Ántonia* is the author's surrender of the usual methods of fiction in telling her story." She was giving aesthetic reality to America's remote, even exotic heartland: Mencken said, "I know of no novel that makes the remote folks of the western prairies more real than *My Ántonia* makes them, and I know of none that makes them seem better worth knowing. . . . There is no other American author . . . whose future promises so much" (O'Connor, pp. 88–89).

## CHANGING PUBLISHERS: ALFRED A. KNOPF

Although her relationship with her editor, Ferris Greenslet, remained cordial, Cather was increasingly unhappy with Houghton Mifflin as her publisher. With almost three decades of experience in the literary marketplace, she now had definite ideas about books as embodiments of visual as well as literary art, about design as creating a reading field, and about promotion as introducing a book to its readers. In *My Ántonia*, she had wanted square type, wide margins, rough cream-colored paper stock, and line drawings integrated into the text—features that would evoke a childlike play of imagination, a warmth of memory, a sense of sunlight and open space. But she had to fight every step of the way. As for promotion, "The firm didn't believe it could make much money on her; so they were careful not to lose very much either" (Woodress, p. 306).

At this point, Alfred Knopf entered Cather's life. After graduating from Columbia in 1912, at age twenty-three he founded his publishing house as a daring experiment in 1915. In Knopf, Cather found a publisher whose attention to design and manufacturing style gave all his Borzoi Press's titles a distinctive look; he was a passionate advocate of American literature, provided an international reach for his list with a program of literature in translation, and recognized Cather's genius.

Knopf offered to reprint *The Troll Garden*, and Cather took a break in 1920 from writing the book she was calling "Claude" to write "Coming, Aphrodite!," which became the lead story for her new collection. With its mix of old and new stories, a new, inspired title, beautiful design, and astute marketing (including a limited issue signed by Cather), Knopf's *Youth and the Bright Medusa* (1920) made as much for Cather in six months as *My Ántonia* had made for her in its entire first year at Houghton Mifflin. She wrote Greenslet, saying she was giving "Claude" to Knopf. He would remain her publisher for the rest of her life and would safeguard her legacy throughout his own. Edith Lewis has written:

> Next to writing her novels, Willa Cather's choice of Alfred Knopf as a publisher influenced her career, I think, more than any action she ever took . . . he gave her great encouragement and absolute liberty to write exactly as she chose—protected her in every way he could from outside pressures and interruptions—and made evident, not only to her but to the world in general, his great admiration and belief in her. Life was simply no longer a battle—she no longer had to feel apologetic or on the defensive. (pp. 115–116)

### CHANGING WORLDS, 1922–1923

The world broke in two about 1922, Cather was to write in a preface to a volume of essays provocatively titled *Not Under Forty* (1936). T. S. Eliot's *The Waste Land* and James Joyce's *Ulysses* were published that year, announcing a modernist sensibility of historical discontinuity, alienation, loss, and despair. The modern was saying that we create the world in perceiving it; meanwhile, in the real world Benito Mussolini was forming a fascist government in Italy and the Ku Klux Klan was gaining power in the United States. Cather responded with two books, *One of Ours* and *A Lost Lady*.

*One of Ours* appeared in 1922, Cather's first novel with Knopf, and her first major commercial success. For her plot Cather drew upon the life of her cousin G. P. Cather, who seemed destined for failure—unhappy in business, farming, school, and marriage—and then joined the American Expeditionary Forces and died in France. Cather's character Claude Wheeler yearns for something splendid, struggles to escape the commonplace, in France he embraces an Old World culture and finds himself before his death.

*One of Ours* was announced by a thoughtful review in *The New York Times* by Cather's friend from her university years, Dorothy Canfield Fisher. It became a best-seller, and Cather received royalties of nineteen thousand dollars in a year. "And for the rest of her life [she] had no money problems. The book stimulated sales of her other titles, and it brought her the Pulitzer Prize in 1923. In many ways it was a turning point in her career" (Woodress, p. 334). Critics were not as kind as the public, however. Though Cather maintained that she had not written a war novel, reviewers attacked her for presuming to do just that. Mencken wrote that her war scenes occurred "on a Hollywood movie-lot," and Ernest Hemingway described its last battle scene as coming from D. W. Griffith's film *The Birth of a Nation*: "I identified episode after episode, Catherized. Poor woman, she had to get her war experience somewhere" (Woodress, p. 333).

Perhaps in reaction, in late 1922 Cather went to Red Cloud for six weeks to be home for her parents' fiftieth wedding anniversary and Christmas. While there, she joined the Episcopal Church with her parents (her family were Baptists in her childhood), and she wrote to friends of her intense pleasure in being home "to watch the human stories go on and on among her farm friends, to see how the lives she knew so well were turning out" (Woodress, p. 337). Back in New York, she and Knopf mounted a counteroffensive by appealing to her readers directly, circumventing reviewers.

In April 1923, *The New Republic* published Cather's essay "The Novel Démeublé" (meaning "stripped of furnishings"), which would become a touchstone for understanding Cather's writing. It is, in effect, her tutorial, describing her principles and methods and claiming "her" readers, the ones who care about what endures. Realism does not consist in cataloguing objects, explaining processes, and describing physical sensations; instead, realism is a writer's attitude toward his or her material, the "candour with which he accepts, rather than chooses, his theme" (*On Writing*, p. 37). Cather called for simplification in presentation and style; the writer should suggest, for "Whatever is felt upon the page without being specifically named there—that, one might say, is created. It is the inexplicable presence of the thing not named, of the overtone divined by the ear but not heard by it . . . that gives high quality to the novel or the drama, as well as to poetry itself" (pp. 41–42).

Before its book publication, *A Lost Lady* (1923) was serialized in *Century*, with the first of three installments appearing in April. Following the third serial installment in June, Knopf advertised that the first edition of its first printing was "the largest edition I have ever printed of any book, and I have already ordered a second printing of

6000 copies," and on 1 September an advertisement stated that 32,000 copies were printed before first publication.

*A Lost Lady* was an enormous success upon publication and since, meeting critical and popular acclaim. Whereas *One of Ours* follows Claude Wheeler's struggle to escape the insularity, self-importance, and ignorance of an America that had broken with the Old World, *A Lost Lady*'s very design is that of a world broken in two. It is the story of the Old West told through the life of Marian Forrester, married to Captain Forrester, a railroad pioneer twenty-five years older than she. She is seen through the eyes of Niel Herbert, a boy who at first idealizes her, then turns from her in bitter disappointment. The two parts are perfectly balanced: the first set long ago when great things were expected, and the second after the financial panic when "a generation of shrewd young men, trained to petty economies by hard times" (p. 102) takes over. Captain Forrester loses his fortune, falls ill, and dies; without the protection of her husband and the railroad aristocracy, Mrs. Forrester becomes the "lost lady" of the title. With the power to live strong in her, unwilling to immolate herself with her husband, she betrays the ideals of Niel Herbert, and he turns away bitterly. In the coda, he comes to be glad that she had a hand in breaking him in to life, achieving a hard-won maturity of understanding and compassion.

Cather had arrived. The commercial success of *One of Ours* was followed in 1923 by its receiving the Pulitzer Prize and by critical acclaim for *A Lost Lady*. Celebrity status was conferred on her by interviewers, students, friends, and institutions, all making demands on her time. The one thing everyone seemed bent on was preventing her from working, Cather wrote; then she did what Fitzgerald wished he had done: she set about ensuring conditions that enabled her to continue to write. She hired a secretary who would remain with her the rest of Cather's life to turn away intrusions on her time and attention. She and Lewis began plans to build a cottage on Grand Manan Island in the Bay of Fundy, New Brunswick, where they had first summered in 1922; they found congenial both its setting and its people's respect for privacy.

Cather also began taking steps to protect her writing from exploitation, insofar as possible. Warner Brothers had bought the film rights to *A Lost Lady*. The results were dismal. The 1924 silent version, featuring Irene Rich and George Fawcett, was followed in 1934 by a freely adapted sound production conceived and promoted as a vehicle for its stars, Barbara Stanwyck, Frank Morgan, and Ricardo Cortez. The film's setting is a fashionable suburb of Chicago, Marian Forrester's lover Frank Ellinger is a World War I pilot, and Marian returns to her elderly husband after his heart attack. Having rejected the standard romantic plot, Cather saw her novel converted into melodrama, predictable and, worse, boring. Outraged, she drew up legal strictures in her will against any future adaptations of her work in any form then known or to be developed.

Cather explored questions of art's place in culture and feeling's relation to form in a series of essays, interviews, and talks in the early 1920s. She returned to her early mentor by preparing an edition of Sarah Orne Jewett's stories, selecting those that especially appealed to her and that she thought would endure. Cather's introduction explained the qualities of literary art that she valued in Jewett's work and her own: design "so happy, so right, that it seems inevitable"; "a cadence, a quality of voice that is exclusively the writer's own, individual, unique"; the "gift of sympathy," which is a writer's great gift, "the fine thing in him that alone can make his work fine. He fades away into the land and people of his heart, he dies of love only to be born again." Like Cather, "Miss Jewett wrote of the people who grew out of the soil and the life of the country near her heart, not about exceptional individuals at war with their environment." Her introductions to other writers' works give similar insight into Cather's ideas about art. Writing of *The Fortunate Mistress*, Cather faulted Daniel Defoe for not creating atmosphere and for his lack of imagination; she praised Gertrude Hall's *The Wagnerian Romances* for creating an emotional effect, translating the spirit of the music into words. In *Wounds in the Rain*, Stephen Crane, she said, showed how to handle detail for its emotional effect. Cather's essay on Katherine Mansfield praises the way "She communicates vastly more than she actually writes. . . . It is this overtone, which is too fine for the printing press and comes through without it, that makes one know that this writer had something of the gift which is one of the rarest things in writing, and quite the most precious" (*On Writing*, pp. 110–111).

In addition to writing, Cather was on the lecture circuit, speaking on the modern novel and taking on issues of commercialism and art. A 21 December 1924 interview with Rose Feld of *The New York Times* on book reading and book publication is revealing. Publishers (who are business men), she said, recognize a demand among a prosperous middle class who buy books to take the edge off boredom. These are the books published for a cinema public—quite a different thing from the fine books written for fine readers, those with mentality, spirituality, and character "that can bring an ardor and an honesty to a masterpiece and make it over until it becomes a personal possession" (Bohlke, p. 69). America has fostered industrial progress but lacks the discrimination of the French. "It's our prosperity, our judging success in terms of dollars," that produces comfort but not art. Unlike Americans, French minds "have been formed by rubbing up cruelly with the inescapable realities of life. . . . The Frenchman doesn't talk nonsense about art, about self-expression; he is too greatly occupied with building the things that make his home" (pp. 70–71).

### THE PROFESSOR'S HOUSE; MY MORTAL ENEMY; DEATH COMES FOR THE ARCHBISHOP

The questions of culture that sustains, of art that lasts, and of the modern novel as literary art became the subjects of Cather's next novels. Having established her reputation with five Nebraska novels, she moved on to other settings and materials. In three years—the most sustained and productive period of her life—Cather wrote three books, each radically different in style, exploring the modern novel's narrative form: different versions of the house of fiction.

"The moving was over and done," begins *The Professor's House* (1925). Professor Godfrey St. Peter, a writer-historian, has realized international success with his seven-volume *Spanish Adventurers in North America*. Recognition and prize money have enabled the St. Peters to build a new house, but he retains a study in the dismantled rented house where they had brought up their daughters. Book I, "The Family," re-creates the cluttered style of the modern commercial novel. Focusing on jealousies among members of a family consumed with buying, building, and decorating houses, it builds a claustrophobic atmosphere until, stifled, St. Peter responds by recalling his former student, Tom Outland. Book II, "Tom Outland's Story," is the narrative equivalent of an open window; its spare, uncluttered style recalls Tom's account of discovering ancient cliff dwellings in the American Southwest and learning about the society that had inhabited them, and then living alone on the mesa one summer, in possession. Finally, Book III, "The Professor," shows St. Peter alone in his attic study, losing consciousness when the flame of his gas stove burns out, and awakening to a meditation on the earth itself—the home—to which each living form returns.

*The Professor's House* is the most personal of Cather's novels, Lewis (p. 137) wrote, referring not to autobiographical details but to the feeling of having realized youthful dreams and, in midlife, contemplating a future without delight. Like her protagonist, Cather was in her fifties; beginning with *Alexander's Bridge*, she too had seven volumes published; her fourth, *My Ántonia,* evoked intense interest in her "experiment," and her latest books had brought her "a certain international reputation and what were called rewards," among them the Pulitzer Prize.

Cather next took her readers inside the sentimental love plot in *My Mortal Enemy* (1926), her sparest example of the unfurnished novel. The novel opens with the story of Myra Driscoll and Oswald Henshawe, who staked all on love by eloping in spite of certain disinheritance by her wealthy uncle. "But they've been happy?" the young narrator, Nellie Birdseye asks. "Oh, as happy as most people, I suppose," she is told (pp. 24–25). Thus launched, *My Mortal Enemy* pushes the narrative of romantic love beyond its usual ending to tell of Myra and Oswald as they grow older and fall on hard times; then Myra, dying, asks the fundamental questions about what sustains and what destroys.

*My Mortal Enemy,* Cather's most radical example of the novel démeublé, was followed immediately by *Death Comes for the Archbishop* (1927), not a novel at all but a narrative, written in the manner of a legend, without accent, as she said: "a kind of discipline in these days, when the 'situation' is made to count for so much in writing" (*On Writing,* p. 9). Inspired by her own travels in the American Southwest, the book is, John J. Murphy writes,

> more than any other Cather narrative a product of research, the fusion of an astounding array of sources that would be disparate if not combined within its text. Included are sources in U.S. military and political history; Roman Catholic Church history, tradition, and liturgy; Mexican and Indian myth, legend, and history; biblical scriptures; Southwestern flora and geography; accounts of Spanish conquest and exploration of the Americas; philosophy and theology; French history and geography; architecture; and others. (p. 381)

Cather traces the journeys of Father Jean Latour from France to the Southwest, eventually to become archbishop of Santa Fe, and those of Father Joseph Vaillant, his vicar. She had felt "something fearless and fine and very, very well-bred" in Archbishop Lamy, Latour's prototype: "What I felt curious about was the daily life of such a man in a crude frontier society" (*On Writing,* p. 7). The episodic narrative consists of their encounters with the people—Mexican, European-American, and Native

American—and the cultures and faiths embodied in their stories. The daily life of an individual provided a means for Cather to write once again of a place and time as a site of exchange, and to tell the age-old story of a search for continuities in a changing world.

Cather extended her range in history and geography with *Shadows on the Rock* (1931), which won the Prix Femina Américain in 1933. The rock—here, the rock on which Quebec City was built—is a recurring image in Cather's writing, beginning with "The Enchanted Bluff" in 1909. As Cather explained in a letter published in the *Saturday Review of Literature*, "To me the rock of Quebec is not only a stronghold on which many strange figures have for a little time cast a shadow in the sun; it is the curious endurance of a kind of culture, narrow but definite" (*On Writing*, p. 15). It is a coming-of-age story about Cécile Auclair and her apothecary-father, Euclide, as they try to re-create their old life in France out in the Canadian wilderness, and come to realize that they have made a new life in the New World. It is the quietest of Cather's novels, and arguably her most direct response to a modernist confrontation with isolation, the threat of annihilation. The colony of Quebec, cut off from the Old World by annihilating ocean, and from the rest of Canada by endless suffocating forest, maintains the continuities of its life, sustained by its faith in a well-ordered universe, the teachings of the Catholic Church, and the domestic rituals brought from France. Its sketches are subdued and seem slight: impressions of ships appearing and disappearing, weather changing, characters coming and going, visiting Auclair's shop and gathering around firesides. The whole evokes questions of what makes art, and faith, and life itself.

## COMING HOME: THE FINAL YEARS

"I had the sense of coming home to myself," Jim Burden reflects at the conclusion of *My Ántonia*. Like her narrator, Cather returned to early memories for her three final books: memories of Nebraska, and delving deeper still, of Virginia.

*Obscure Destinies* (1932) comprises three stories, reiterations of Cather's earlier Nebraska stories. For the first, "Neighbour Rosicky," Cather turned once again to Anna Sadelik and John Pavelka, her real-life models for *My Ántonia*, now a generation older and renamed Anton and Mary Rosicky. When, in the story's opening sentence, Dr. Burleigh tells neighbor Rosicky he has a bad heart, Rosicky protests, "So? No, I guess my heart was always pretty good" (p. 7). Thus launched, the story unfolds in a

series of scenes and inset stories demonstrating the power of such a heart as it meets with poverty, a succession of other cultures, and at last, marriage and family and kinship with the land. It concludes with Dr. Burleigh's pausing by the graveyard where Anton Rosicky is buried, reflecting upon the beauty of that place and that life.

For "Old Mrs. Harris," Cather again used her own family as models, as she had in *The Song of the Lark*. Now, rather than focusing on a girl's trajectory toward success, Cather encompassed three generations of women within the Templeton family, transplanted from the South to the western community of Skyline. Each feels the isolation that exists within family and community: the girl, Vicky, seeks to escape by going away to college; the mother, Victoria, feels herself trapped by yet another pregnancy; and the grandmother, Mrs. Harris, who alone understands the others, knows that she is dying. Only when the others are old will they begin to understand and say, "But now I know" (p. 157).

If Rosicky understands life, and the Templeton women come to understand it better, the friends of the last story, "Two Friends," never do. Their friendship with each other, which meant so much to the young narrator, is broken over a political disagreement. Each dies alone, unreconciled, and the narrator confronts the randomness of life: "the feeling of something broken that could so easily have been mended . . . of a truth that was accidentally distorted—one of the truths we want to keep" (p. 191).

In *Lucy Gayheart* (1935), set in 1901–1902, Lucy, an embodiment of life and beauty, leaves the Nebraska town of Haverford on the Platte River to study music in Chicago. Lacking Thea Kronborg's focus, Lucy falls in love with the baritone Clement Sebastian, an aging singer who breathes in her youth. When Sebastian drowns, she breaks down and flees back to Haverford, where she discovers that life, not Sebastian, was her lover. But before she can return to her life in Chicago, she accidentally drowns in the Platte. The third section shows the effect the memory of Lucy has on Harry Gordon, the Haverford banker who had not loved her more than his own pride. His memory of her remains, but only so long as those who knew Lucy live. Then there will be nothing left but her impression in a concrete sidewalk, "three light footprints, running away" (p. 231).

*Sapphira and the Slave Girl* (1940), Cather's last book, deepens this return with its Virginia setting, harking back not only to her own past but also to that of her grandparents. Based on family history and set in pre–Civil War Virginia, the story explores the intricate webs of race relations, the complications of characters, and the corrupting nature of slave ownership in the person of Sapphira, who plots to ruin a young slave girl of whom her husband is fond. Sapphira's daughter, Mrs. Blake (based, like Mrs. Harris, on Cather's maternal grandmother, Rachel Boak), helps the girl, Nancy, escape to the North. An epilogue, set twenty-five years later, retells Cather's own memory of the return of Nancy to visit her mother, Sapphira's devoted maid, and the ends of the stories set in motion so long ago.

Cather planned one more collection of short stories, which did not appear until after her death in 1947; it was published as *The Old Beauty and Others* (1948). The title character of "The Old Beauty" clings to the old, prewar order of things, looking disdainfully at the 1920s, the time in which the story is set; her companion, Cherry Beamish, a former music-hall star, is more amused and tolerant of the ways of youth. Lady Longstreet's death follows an apparently minor run-in with a car driven by two modern, trouser-wearing young women, and it seems to mark the end of an era, with both its grandeur and its faults. Cather's narrator holds the flaws and virtues of both times in a sympathetic balance. "The Best Years" returns to the Nebraska setting in a story of a young teacher and the woman who is her mentor; the focus is less on the death of young Leslie than on her close family life and the memories she leaves to them and Miss Knightley. "Before Breakfast," Cather's only story set on a fictionalized Grand Manan Island, follows the meditations of disillusioned Henry Grenfell on aging and the isolation of families; he feels withdrawn from his family—indeed, from his own life—until he accidentally witnesses a young girl plunging into the chill of the ocean for a morning swim. The courage he sees, even in so small a thing, helps to reconnect him to life.

Willa Cather's reputation, always solid among readers and other writers, in the last quarter of the twentieth century underwent a sea change among academics, who have gone from dismissing her as a minor regionalist to granting her canonical status. She has been interpreted in the light of various literary traditions (romantic, realist, naturalist, modern, elegiac, or pastoral), and appropriated by "isms" concerned with her feminism, gender, aestheticism, and colonialism. Unlike Fitzgerald, identified solely with the Jazz Age, Cather provides an opportunity for exploring issues as they have emerged: women and gender in the 1970s and 1980s, or the environment in the 1990s and into the twenty-first century. She wrote with an ecological sensibility of interconnectedness, a sense of the integrity,

complexity, and unity of the whole, whether in the natural or human community. Thus, because communities are never static, her premise is of change: emigration, aging, progress and degradation, modernity and tradition. She wrote about stories that keep repeating themselves, deeply rooted in a specificity of place; she understood that everlasting stories are reenacted in individual lives. Critics trying to "get at" her secret, as Niel Herbert attempted with Mrs. Forrester, have been frustrated by her contradictions. She evades classification and unsettles facile, reductive interpretations. The effect of reading her work is an opening of mind, a sense of expansiveness, and an engagement with life, grappling with its complexities.

## WORKS

*The Troll Garden* (1905)
*O Pioneers!* (1913; reprinted 1992)
*The Song of the Lark* (1915)
*My Ántonia* (1918; reprinted 1994)
*One of Ours* (1922)
*A Lost Lady* (1923; reprinted 1997)
*The Professor's House* (1925; reprinted 2002)
*My Mortal Enemy* (1926)
*Death Comes for the Archbishop* (1927)
*Shadows on the Rock* (1931)
*Obscure Destinies* (1932; reprinted 1998)
*Lucy Gayheart* (1935)
*Sapphira and the Slave Girl* (1940)
*The Old Beauty and Others* (1948)
*On Writing: Critical Studies on Writing as an Art* (1988)

## FURTHER READING

Bohlke, L. Brent, ed. *Willa Cather in Person: Interviews, Speeches, and Letters.* Lincoln, Nebr., 1986. The most authentic source for Cather's own voice about her writing.

Crane, Joan. *Willa Cather: A Bibliography.* Lincoln, Nebr., 1982. A reliable guide through Cather rare editions, as well as for readers tracing changes through Cather's texts.

Jewett, Sarah Orne. "Letters to Willa Cather." Ms., Houghton Library, Harvard University. A firsthand glimpse into Cather's world, especially important for providing insight into the mentor who changed her life.

Lewis, Edith. *Willa Cather Living: A Personal Record.* New York, 1953. A thoroughly respectful, and yet deeply intimate, account of Cather's life written by her companion of thirty-eight years.

Murphy, John J., ed. Explanatory Notes. In *Death Comes for the Archbishop*, by Willa Cather. Lincoln, Nebr., 1999. An example of the historical, explanatory, and textual materials supplied with the Willa Cather Scholarly Edition, published by the University of Nebraska-Lincoln.

O'Connor, Margaret Anne, ed. *Willa Cather: The Contemporary Reviews*. Cambridge, Mass., 2001. A reliable guide to Cather's contemporary reception. Insightful for criticism as well as reception.

Sergeant, Elizabeth. *Willa Cather: A Memoir*. Philadelphia, 1953. Valuable as a writer's remembrance of Cather as she came into her own.

Slote, Bernice, ed. *The Kingdom of Art: Willa Cather's First Principles and Critical Statements, 1893–1896*. Lincoln, Nebr., 1966. A ground-breaking study of Cather's early journalism, documenting the period in which Cather worked out principles of her art.

Woodress, James. *Willa Cather: A Literary Life*. Lincoln, Nebr., 1987. The standard biography.

# JOHN CHEEVER

*by Scott Donaldson*

In his memoir *Writing Was Everything* (1995), Alfred Kazin describes meeting John Cheever for the first time. The occasion was a 1937 party hosted by the *New Republic* magazine for contributors under the age of twenty-five. Kazin was impressed by the ease with which Cheever maneuvered around the room. They were both struggling young writers but very different in personality. As Kazin stammered around the periphery, the short and slight Cheever took over the party, as lithe in movement as Fred Astaire and bubbling with pleasure as he charmed everyone with his wit and cleverness. He seemed to possess an inborn social confidence.

In later years, the pattern remained the same. John Hersey, who saw a good deal of Cheever once he had become an established writer, found him a man of remarkable mental speed who at parties exhibited a sunny disposition and enjoyed himself almost beyond belief. Cheever might have been having trouble with his drinking and his career and his marriage and his sexuality, but the jocularity warded off discussion of such difficulties. "What was extraordinary" about his father, Benjamin Cheever wrote in his introduction to *The Letters of John Cheever* (1988), "was his joy and the talent he had for passing that joy on to the people around him" (p. 17). The joy was accompanied by, and may have derived from, a terrible darkness of spirit. Cheever could be deliriously happy, or unbearably despairing, or both at the same time, undergoing what John Updike called "a constant tussle between the bubbling *joie de vivre* of the healthy sensitive man and the deep melancholy peculiar to American Protestant males" (Weaver, ed., p. 20).

In his fiction as in his life, Cheever is blessed and/or oppressed with double vision, at once aware of the beauty and the degradation of the world around him. As he said

John Cheever.
(© *Bettmann/Corbis*)

in 1964, his underlying impulse was "to bring glad tidings to someone. My sense of literature is a sense of giving, not a diminishment." But he is not a facile celebrant, and much of his work exhibits a dichotomy between the tragic and the transcendent. The tension between these polar outlooks, and his struggle to resolve them, gives his fiction its distinctive tone and its power.

## THE BROTHER THEME

The duality between joy and despair is vividly embodied in "Goodbye, My Brother," the 1951 story that Cheever chose to lead off the Pulitzer Prize–winning *The Stories of John Cheever* (1978). He began writing "Goodbye, My Brother" during a summer vacation on Martha's Vineyard. In first draft, the story described a family in a summer house who spent their evenings playing backgammon. It was to be called "The Backgammon Game," and Cheever planned to use the apparatus of the game to symbolize tensions within the family. But the story wouldn't coalesce, and upon returning to New York he went over his journal notes from Martha's Vineyard. There he found only bad news: comments on an old friend lamenting his lost youth, on a promiscuous young woman, on a newly built island house that had been scored and stained to antique it. These morose observations, he understood, derived from his own heritage as a child of the Puritans. He was the descendant of those "who feel that there is some inexpungible nastiness at the heart of life and that love, friendship, Bourbon whisky, lights of all kinds—are merely the crudest deceptions." The one cheerful note he made all summer described the pleasure it gave him to watch his wife and another young woman walk out of the sea without any clothes on (O'Hara, pp. 106–108).

With the aid of these reflections, Cheever transformed "The Backgammon Game" into "Goodbye, My Brother," a subtle yet forceful evocation of the division in his spirit. There is still a family on a summer retreat, and they continue to play backgammon. But in revision Cheever invents two brothers who encompass the conflict between dark and light in himself. The somewhat "fatuous" son of the family who serves as narrator imagines that he sees only the bright side of things. He attributes his own dark thoughts to his dour brother Lawrence, who upsets everyone with his criticisms. Eventually the narrator, driven to distraction, strikes out at Lawrence, who promptly leaves the family gathering.

In the final paragraph, the narrator begins with a diatribe against Lawrence. "Oh, what can you do with a man like that? What can you do? How can you dissuade his eye in a crowd from seeking out the cheek with acne, the infirm hand; how can you teach him to respond to the inestimable greatness of the race, the harsh surface beauty of life; how can you put his finger for him on the obdurate truths before which fear and horror are powerless?" The answer, of course, is that you can do little or nothing to exorcise such a man, who resides within. What you can do, in Cheever's vision, is to glory in the wonder of the creation. As the story ends, the narrator watches his wife and sister swimming, their uncovered heads "black and gold in the dark water." When they walk out of the sea, he sees that they are "naked, unshy, beautiful, and full of grace" (*Stories*, p. 21).

The brother motif in "Goodbye, My Brother" derives in part from Cheever's own family background. In fact he had one sibling, his brother Fred, who was seven years older and who was also—as he told his daughter Susan—the strongest love of his life (Meanor, p. 4). "Some people have parents or children," he said to this essay's author in 1977, only a year after Fred died. "I had a brother." Fritz and Joey, as they called each other, lived together in Boston during the early 1930s and tramped through Germany's Black Forest one summer. In an uncollected early story called "The Brothers," Cheever depicted them as more closely bound to each other than any woman could be to either one of them. The bond between them was confining, Cheever decided. To escape, he moved down to New York and struck out on his own.

In stories and especially in his four novels, Cheever explored the brother theme. The two Wapshot novels—*The Wapshot Chronicle* (1957) and *The Wapshot Scandal* (1964)—follow the fortunes of brothers Moses and Coverly Wapshot. Moses, like Fred, is the older brother, hearty and outgoing, confident in his masculinity. Younger brother Coverly is shy, somewhat withdrawn, not at all sure of himself or his sexuality. In *Bullet Park* (1969), competition escalates into attempted murder—in a recurrent dream, Cheever imagined striking his brother with an oar and dumping him overboard—as Hammer conspires to destroy Nailles, or more literally, the son Nailles loves. The two men, not blood relations, are securely linked by nomenclature. Finally, Ezekiel Farragut in *Falconer* (1977) does in fact kill his brother and is sent to jail for the crime of "fratricide, zip to ten."

## A LIFE IN BRIEF

"Fiction is not crypto-autobiography," Cheever declared a hundred times. He proved the point almost every time he recounted an adventure or revisited a relationship from his own experience. The mere facts of the case didn't matter to him, and this was true whether he was actually putting the words down on paper or telling the story in conversation. When the stories had to do with his family background, he sometimes invested them with "the shine of decorum" (*Wapshot Scandal*, p. 5). In that spirit, he converted his father from shoe salesman to shoe manufacturer. More often, though, he simply aimed to attract the attention of his audience. In one legend, he pictured himself as an unwanted child who would never have been born had not his mother drunk two manhattans one afternoon. Even then, he liked to say, his father invited the abortionist to dinner.

As Father George W. Hunt put it, Cheever possessed a mega-faculty, or "interanimation of memory and imagination," which enabled him to transform "any personal incident into a magically altered story" (*Thirteen Uncollected Stories*, p. viii). It was a talent he practiced from early boyhood. In grammar school he would occasionally be called on to tell a story. Usually he did not know, as he walked to the front of the room, what the story would be about. He would start talking and the story would come. It was, Cheever said, rather like having been given a pleasant baritone voice. And it was a gift he never stopped enjoying. He would eavesdrop at dinner and invent an entire narrative from an overheard scrap of talk. He would single out a stranger on the street and imagine the details of his existence. One could not be with him for more than five minutes without seeing stories taking shape. As they did so, Cheever gave his inventive faculties full rein and overleaped the boundary between recollection and fiction.

John Cheever was born 27 May 1912 in Quincy, Massachusetts, the second and last child of Frederick and Mary

Liley Cheever. His father, forty-nine years old when John was born, largely ignored him, reserving his attentions for his elder son, Fred. The family was reasonably prosperous during Cheever's early years but suffered financial reversals when he was in high school. The Cheevers were forced to give up their home, and his mother opened a gift shop to make ends meet. An inattentive student, John was expelled from Thayer Academy for poor grades. He wrote a fictionalized account about the dismissal that the *New Republic* published when he was only eighteen.

With his parents separated, John moved in with his brother Fred in Boston. He never attended college, instead working in a department store and in a newspaper job. He continued to write stories and managed to publish a few of them—with anticapitalist overtones—in little magazines. In 1934 he relocated to New York City to pursue his writing career in earnest. In the next year, he followed the advice of his mentor Malcolm Cowley and began to churn out very short stories. *The New Yorker* took two of them, beginning an affiliation that was to last for most of Cheever's career. During the Depression he worked on the *New York City Guide* for the Federal Writers' Project. In 1939 he met and fell in love with Mary Winternitz. They were married in March 1941. Cheever enlisted in the army the next year, following Pearl Harbor. He trained as an infantryman in Georgia, but after his first book of stories—*The Way Some People Live*—was published in 1943, he was recruited to join the Signal Corps propaganda unit in Astoria, just across the Queensboro Bridge from Manhattan.

Though Cheever later chose not to republish any of the stories in *The Way Some People Live*, the book received favorable notices. Struthers Burt in the *Saturday Review* predicted a brilliant future for him as a writer of stories, novels, and plays. When the war was over, Cheever settled into an apartment on East Fifty-ninth Street and worked in all three mediums. The novel refused to jell. *Town House*, a play by Gertrude Tonkonogy based on a series of Cheever stories in *The New Yorker*, closed after only twelve performances. But he achieved an artistic breakthrough in his short fiction with such stories as "The Enormous Radio" and "Torch Song," both published in 1947 and collected in *The Enormous Radio and Other Stories* (1953).

In 1951 Cheever and his family—Susan had been born in 1943 and Benjamin in 1948, with second son Federico due to arrive in 1957—moved to Westchester County, which served as the locale of many of his best-known stories, including most of those in the four short story collections that appeared between 1958 and 1973. Although his writing career did not make him as prosperous as most of his suburban neighbors, Cheever received considerable recognition. He was awarded Guggenheims in 1951 and 1960. Individual stories won the Benjamin Franklin and O. Henry awards. He was elected to the National Institute of Arts and Letters in 1957, the same year that he published *The Wapshot Chronicle*, his first novel. That novel was given the National Book Award, and a second, *The Wapshot Scandal* (1964), was awarded the Howells Medal of the American Academy of Arts and Letters as the best work of fiction to be published during the period 1960–1965. *Bullet Park*, a dark and controversial novel, was published in 1969. The American Academy elected him a member in 1973.

Excessive drinking took a toll on Cheever's marriage and on his physical and mental health. Following disastrous extended absences from home to teach in the writing programs at the University of Iowa and at Boston University, in 1975 he underwent a successful rehabilitation at the Smithers Alcohol Rehabilitation Center in New York. There ensued a period of increasing public and critical recognition, fueled in part by *Falconer* (1977), a novel that took place in a jail where homosexuality and drug abuse were rampant. He won the Pulitzer Prize and the National Book Critics Circle award for *The Stories of John Cheever* (1978), a selection of sixty-one of his best stories. The book was welcomed with enthusiastic reviews and reached a wider audience than anything Cheever had written. In his last years he was widely interviewed by the media. Harvard and Skidmore awarded him honorary degrees. He won the MacDowell Award in 1979 and the National Medal for Literature in 1982, two months before his death from cancer on 18 June. A novella, *Oh What a Paradise It Seems*, was also published that year.

## REALISM AND ITS DISCONTENTS

Cheever has sometimes been pigeonholed as an observer and reporter of upper-middle-class life. Yet to dismiss him as a social realist is to ignore his emphasis on the magical and the fantastic and to undervalue how much he changed during the course of his career. The contest between joy and despair is waged throughout his fiction, but which of these attitudes emerges as dominant, and on what terms, is subject to considerable alteration. There are many excellent writers, Saul Bellow has observed, who do not develop and expand. "John Cheever was a writer of a different sort, altogether," he decided, one who went through a dramatic series of metamorphoses.

Roughly, Cheever's career as a writer can be divided into three stages. His writing through *The Wapshot Chronicle* and *The Housebreaker of Shady Hill and Other Stories* (1958) exhibits a contrast between an idealized past and a less hospitable present, in a tone ranging from genial to mildly satirical. In the second stage, the dark period of the 1960s that encompassed stories like "The Swimmer" as well as *The Wapshot Scandal* and *Bullet Park*, Cheever often adopted the stance of a visiting anthropologist— "at the time of which I'm writing," the narrator would intrude—who despite apparent objectivity regards the ills of modern life with an attitude of disillusionment. Finally, in *Falconer* and *Oh What a Paradise It Seems*, the dismayed observer manages to find affirmation in a deeply flawed universe. Miracles can, and do, happen. Cheever's narrative voice changes too from the flat, controlled style of his earliest stories to the distinctive voice he is most remembered by: a plangent eloquence balanced delicately between lamentation and celebration, tilting in one direction or another as the spirit requires.

In his earliest uncollected stories, Cheever depicted families down on their luck, struggling to achieve a viable economic existence. As his own fortunes improved, he shifted his focus to characters who were financially better off, although by no means secure. In two brilliant stories of 1947, he began mining the vein of the fantastic. "The Enormous Radio" in the story of that name broadcasts everything that happens to the occupants of a New York apartment building—their pleasures and sorrows, indecencies and cruelties, and above all their grasping materialism. Listening to these disclosures brings the principal characters to a bitter awareness of their own moral failings. "Torch Song" describes a young woman with a seemingly nurturing nature who takes in weak and unhappy men and sees them to their grave. At the end of the story, the narrator falls ill and goes into hiding from this young woman he now regards as the "lewd and searching shape of death." The misogynistic overtones of "Torch Song" are reflected in other stories and novels, notably "An Educated American Woman" and *Falconer*.

In creating his incredible radio and sinister handmaiden of death, Cheever combined his customary skillful evocation of surface details with plots that demanded a suspension of disbelief. William Maxwell, for decades Cheever's editor at *The New Yorker*, was initially taken aback by these stories that collided with the magazine's naturalistic approach to fiction. In mixing the quotidian with the magical, Cheever was trying "things that we felt just weren't possible. It turned out that anything was possible" (Cheever, 1984, p. 138).

Following the move to Westchester County in 1951, the setting of much of Cheever's fiction shifted from New York City to suburbia. Most of his characters, however, remained in the same social stratum: not members of the "power elite" as classified by C. Wright Mills but instead a vulnerable class seeking almost desperately to establish its credentials. As he observed their travails, Cheever looked to the past for a moral reference point. *The Wapshot Chronicle*, the novel he finally completed after several false starts, presents the New England village of St. Botolphs in a rosy glow of nostalgia. The patriarch, Leander Wapshot, now dwindled into ineffectuality, attempts to convey to his progeny the customs and standards of a better time. But mere observance of inherited ceremonies cannot keep his sons Moses and Coverly from seeking their fortunes elsewhere. The times have passed St. Botolphs by. Still, Cheever nostalgically laments, "Why do the young want to go away?" And at the end, he gives Leander the last word. He drowns himself in the sea, leaving behind a wonderful letter to his sons. "Fear tastes like a rusty knife," it concludes, "and do not let her into your house. Courage tastes of blood. Stand up straight. Admire the world. Relish the love of a good woman. Trust in the Lord" (*Chronicle*, p. 307). Leander's advice comes closer than anything Cheever wrote to providing the moral program of his work.

*The Wapshot Chronicle* was admired for its lyricism and, like all Cheever novels, criticized for its episodic nature. The book unravels various threads as Moses and Coverly and Leander and Cousin Honora Wapshot pursue their destinies, and the threads are not invariably tied together. Yet *Chronicle* remains engagingly readable, Cheever's finest achievement in the novel form. Cheever had a particular affinity for the short story, yet his career required that he write novels, which stood a far better chance of attracting money and attention. *The Wapshot Chronicle* and *The Housebreaker of Shady Hill*, his book of stories set in the suburban enclave of Shady Hill, proved the point. In effect he wrote both books simultaneously, between 1953 and 1957. *Chronicle* won the National Book Award and stayed in print for decades. *Housebreaker*, despite containing several excellent stories, generated some of the worst reviews of his life and soon disappeared from bookstores.

The Shady Hill stories were criticized for appealing too directly to the comfortable upper-middle-class readers of *The New Yorker* (where seven of the eight stories originally appeared) and for their suburban milieu. Cheever was denigrated as the "Dante of the cocktail hour" and "the poet of the exurbs." The consensus held that he would be well served to "say goodbye to Shady Hill." Suburbia and its inhabitants were unworthy of his talent. Cheever's attitude toward suburban life was complicated and ambivalent, but he refused to join in the general cultural attack on the suburbs. "It goes without saying," he commented in 1958 (the year *Housebreaker* was published), "that the people in my stories and the things that happen to them could take place anywhere." He wrote about suburbanites because he lived among them and discovered them to be as interesting as the wildest denizens of the East Village. The inhabitants of Cheever's Shady Hill are troubled by money woes, by loss of youth, by excessive drinking, by adultery. At the same time they share a common pretense that nothing bad can happen in a setting where the lawns are mowed, the hedges trimmed, and the silverware polished.

Vladimir Nabokov called "The Country Husband," the longest story in *Housebreaker*, "really a miniature novel beautifully traced," with the many things that happen nicely linked through "thematic interlacings." The principal unifying theme has to do with Shady Hill's refusal to acknowledge that anything can go wrong. Coming home from a business trip, Francis Weed's plane crashes in a cornfield. He survives and makes his way home, where no one wants to hear about his close call. Cheever studs the story with war imagery. The plane crash was "just like the Marne," a fellow passenger says. The Weeds' house, tranquil on the surface, is described as a battlefield where the children exchange blows and accusations. At a party, Francis recognizes the maid as a Frenchwoman he had seen stripped naked for consorting with the enemy during World War II. He decides it would be "unseemly and impolite" to tell his companions about it, for they "seemed united in their tacit claim that there had been no past, no war—that there was no danger or trouble in the world." Rebelling against convention, Francis becomes infatuated with the babysitter. But such things are not permitted in Shady Hill, which admits to no turpitude, no divorce, no scandal, nothing improper. So when a psychologist advises him to take up woodworking instead of pursuing the babysitter, he meekly complies. The only heroes in the story are those who break the rules—the child Gertrude Flannery who persistently intrudes on other peoples' privacy, and the dog Jupiter who, at the end, "prances through the tomato vines, holding in his generous mouth the remains of an evening slipper."

Cheever celebrates the moment with a blue sky coda. "Then it is dark; it is a night where kings in golden suits ride elephants over the mountains" (*Stories*, p. 345).

## THE DARK PERIOD

In "The Death of Justina" (1960), the suburb of Proxmire Manor goes one step farther than Shady Hill by legislating against death. The narrator's wife's cousin Justina dies during a visit, an unfortunate occurrence since she passes on in Zone B, where dying is against the law. The body must be moved to Zone C before it can be collected by the undertaker and prepared for burial. Other ills beset the narrator: his depressing job as an advertising man, his defeated attempts to stop drinking, the unhappiness he encounters on every hand. He cannot understand "why, in this most prosperous, equitable, and accomplished world. . . . everyone should seem to be disappointed" (*Stories*, p. 432).

Cheever was among those who felt the deepest disappointment. The 1950s began with great promise, he thought, but halfway through the decade something went terribly wrong. The most useful image of that downfall he could conjure up was that "of a man in a quagmire, looking into a tear in the sky." It seemed to him that contemporary vices had supplanted the virtues of the past. In the first chapter of *The Wapshot Scandal*, a much darker book than the *Chronicle*, he presents the vignette of a young girl runaway calling home on Christmas Eve from a drugstore in St. Botolphs. The carolers are singing "Good King Wenceslas" on the green as the girl, crying, assures her parents that she is not drunk, that she just wants to wish them a Merry Christmas. Cheever then comments that the voice of this girl, "with its prophecy of gas stations and motels, freeways and all-night supermarkets, had more to do with the world to come than the singing on the green" (*Scandal*, pp. 10–11).

As the wandering girl suggests, rootlessness lies at the heart of the evils Cheever associates with modern life. Later in the novel, Coverly Wapshot takes an international flight that is commandeered by skyjackers (one of the first fictional instances of such an event). The passengers are "helpless," the skyjackers announce. To ward off the fear of death, a woman begins to sing "Nearer, my God, to thee" and the others join in. Such courageous gestures do little to lighten the atmosphere of degradation in *Scandal*, however. Overcome by lust, Moses's wife, Melissa, runs off to Rome with the grocery boy. Moses dwindles into alcoholism. Coverly works at a missile base presided over by the terrifying Dr. Cameron, a scientist perceptive enough to realize that a "highly advanced civilization might well destroy itself with luxury, alcoholism, sexual license, sloth, greed and corruption" (a catalog of the ills that Cheever observed beneath the torn sky) but who is untroubled by the threat of nuclear holocaust.

The characters in Cheever's novels and stories of the 1960s seek to belong somewhere but are condemned to remain transients, forever in movement from suburb to city, one continent to another. "The Angel of the Bridge" (1961) presents three phobias occasioned by modes of travel. The narrator's seventy-four-year-old mother panics at the prospect of boarding an airplane. The narrator's older brother is terrified of elevators. The narrator cannot drive across the George Washington Bridge because he is afraid that it will collapse. Finally, he realizes that his fear of bridges, like the other phobic reactions, is an expression of his horror at what was becoming of the world—including freeways and Buffalo Burgers, expatriated palm trees and monotonous housing developments, canned music on trains and the destruction of familiar landmarks. He yearns for a "more vivid, simple, and peaceable world" (*Stories*, p. 495).

The concept of the arduous journey, a common motif in literature, is brilliantly evoked in "The Swimmer" (1964), perhaps Cheever's best-known story. On a hungover Sunday, Neddy Merrill sets out to traverse the county by swimming pool. As he makes his increasingly difficult way, time speeds up and passes him by. When he arrives home exhausted, he finds that his wife and children have gone and the house is boarded up. The story carries unmistakable mythic baggage and has been subject to Homerian, Ovidian, and Dantean interpretations—as well as to one motion picture that drastically alters the plot and simplifies the characters. Writing the story took a great deal out of Cheever. He spent two months on it, making 150 pages of notes for ten pages of text. As he narrowed the work down, Cheever observed, something mysterious began to happen. For him as for Neddy, "it was growing cold and quiet. It was turning into winter" (Meanor, pp. 114–121).

The drugging of America provides the central theme of *Bullet Park* (1969), Cheever's most controversial novel. The book was condemned by some critics for clumsiness of structure and for overindulgence in coincidence and admired by others for its exploration of a universe dominated by chance. Very much at issue is the question of how to value *Bullet Park*'s ending. In an improbable climax, Eliot Nailles rescues his son Tony from immolation on a church altar by his alter ego, Paul

Hammer. But this hardly amounts to a reawakening. Nailles must as usual meet his pusher for the fix that will enable him to endure the ride on the commuter train to New York. "Tony went back to school on Monday [the last words of the novel] and Nailles—drugged—went off to work and everything was as wonderful, wonderful, wonderful, wonderful as it had been" (*Bullet Park*, p. 245). The third "wonderful" might have been enough; the fourth one makes the satirical point clear.

## TRANSCENDENCE AND REPUTATION

In his later fiction Cheever reached for transcendence. He continued to believe that modern life presented virtually unsolvable problems yet unblushingly embraced miraculous resolutions in his last two works of fiction. He had summoned up miracles before, both in "A Vision of the World" (1964) and in *Bullet Park*. In "A Vision" the unhappy protagonist awakes from a dream of invigorating rain (for Cheever, the smell of rain is particularly beguiling) to proclaim aloud, "Valor! Love! Virtue! Compassion! Splendor! Kindness! Wisdom! Beauty!" As he recites these words, which seem to "have the colors of the earth," he feels his hopefulness mount (*Stories*, p. 517). In *Bullet Park*, Tony is similarly restored by chanting "cheers of place" that the Swami Rutuola coaches him to recite: "I'm in a house by the sea at four in the afternoon and it's raining and I'm sitting in a ladderback chair with a book in my lap and I'm waiting for a girl I love who has gone on an errand but who will return" (*Bullet Park*, p. 140). But these cures by chanting are notably secular, while in *Falconer*, Cheever specifically locates the source of wonder in religion.

Throughout his life Cheever attended Sunday services regularly and took comfort in his Anglican faith. "There has to be *someone* you thank for the party," he would say. Often he associated religious feelings with his admiration for the natural world: "Which came first? Christ the Saviour or the smell of new wood?" (Weaver, ed., pp. 8–9). But not until *Falconer* (1977) did he write a long work that is constructed around a full-scale acceptance of Christian doctrine. He was inspired to do so because of his deliverance in 1975 from a debilitating dependence on alcohol. "I wonder if this book is not simply a testament of conversion," he wrote in his notes. "Conceal this" (Meanor, p. 188).

An optimistic imagination defines Cheever's final two books. Like all of his longer works of fiction, *Falconer* was faulted for its loose and disjointed structure. In making such accusations, Glen M. Johnson argued in a seminal essay, critics failed to perceive that the form of the book followed the Christian pattern of redemption. Ezekiel Farragut, a heroin addict who has murdered his brother, must redeem himself by accepting his guilt, actively turning away from wrongdoing and receiving grace through love for others. Only after he has done so can he be freed by the angels Cheever sends to his assistance. The miracle derives from the transfiguring power of human relationships. At the end, Farragut has escaped from prison as from all his phobias. He walks toward freedom, his head held high. "Rejoice, he thought, rejoice" (p. 211).

*Oh What a Paradise It Seems* echoes the affirmation expressed in *Falconer*. The old man Lemuel Sears comes up from New York to skate on Beasley's Pond and feels reinvigorated. Outraged that commercial interests are contriving to turn the pond into a dump, Sears sets out to stop this act of defamation, finds an ally in Betsy Logan, and in spite of murderous profiteers and an apathetic public, manages to stop the polluting of Beasley's Pond. This victory, which challenges credibility, is only achieved on the grounds of an ethically dubious quid pro quo that Betsy devises. Stop poisoning the pond, she says, and she'll stop poisoning the food in the supermarket.

The pessimism that marked Cheever's work up to the mid-1970s vanished in the last half dozen years of his life. Now he looked to the future for relief, rather than to an unrecoverable past. In the contest between joy and despair, joy achieved the upper hand. He wasn't necessarily getting better as a writer, Cheever said in 1979, but there had been a change. It was "as if one were discovering more light, if light is what one is after." Light was what he was always after.

*Falconer* brought John Cheever to the attention of a wider public. For decades he had been identified with stories and novels about exurbia. "Ovid in Ossining," *Time* called him in its 1964 cover story. The Cheevers lived in a handsome home on Cedar Lane in Ossining, a place that was also the site of Sing prison, and for a time Cheever taught writing classes there. It was one thing for Cheever to sympathize with the difficulties of his suburban neighbors and quite another to declare his kinship with the murderers and swindlers, drug addicts, and three-time losers incarcerated at Falconer. *Newsweek* ran *its* cover story about "Cheever's Triumph" in 1977. Other media outlets took notice, and in a series of interviews, a heretofore reticent Cheever talked openly about his battles as a recovering alcoholic and even, at times, about the most intimate details of his private life. His celebrity

increased with the success of the collected *Stories* in 1978, a book that by bringing together the finest of his work made everyone alive and reading aware that Cheever was a master of the short story. By 1979 he had become a literary elder statesman, a brand name "like corn flakes, or shredded wheat" (*Journals*, p. ix).

In the decade after his death in 1982, biographical revelations tumbled out in a series of books: two memoirs by his daughter, Susan, a book of letters and a largely autobiographical novel by his son Benjamin, a book of interviews and a full-scale biography by Scott Donaldson, and a selection from the author's journals. Susan Cheever's moving *Home before Dark* (1984) opened the closet on her father's bisexuality and his troubled marriage. He had often addressed these issues in his fiction, but readers tended to ignore the hints. "Can't they see?" Cheever used to ask. Everyone did see, clearly enough, in *The Journals of John Cheever* (1991), a 399-page book edited by Robert Gottlieb and consisting of about one-twentieth of the three to four million words Cheever recorded in his journals. Looking back over these entries in 1968, Cheever was struck by their record of "two astonishing contests, one with alcohol and the other with my wife." The journals also revealed his ongoing struggle with homosexual yearnings. From time to time, he acknowledged, he suffered "a painful need for male tenderness," a need he could not satisfy without sacrificing a measure of self-esteem (Meanor, p. 181).

Another problem that frequently crops up in the *Journals*—one that besets many writers—was that of loneliness, loneliness so tangible that he could taste it. "Endeavoring to be a serious writer is quite a dangerous career," he remarked, for it had to be done alone. He was reminded of Hemingway in this connection, for "what we remember of his work is not so much the color of the sky as it is the absolute taste of loneliness" (p. x). Hemingway had been in his consciousness from the beginning. The second paragraph of "Fall River" (1931), published when Cheever was still a teenager, bears an unmistakable resemblance to the first paragraph of Hemingway's *A Farewell to Arms* (1929). "The house we lived in was on a steep hill and we could look down into the salt marshes and the high gray river moving into the sea," Cheever writes. And Hemingway: "In the late summer of that year we lived in a house in a village that looked across the river and the plain to the mountains." But all young writers learn from older ones (Hemingway was only thirteen years Cheever's senior), and if they are any good they eventually find their voice, as Cheever did in a lyrical limpidity distinctly his own.

Cheever's 1979 reference to Hemingway and the dangerous loneliness of their craft underlines their shared position among the great story writers of the twentieth century. Mary Hemingway, Ernest's last wife, supplied Cheever with one of the happiest memories of his life. Mary told him that Ernest awoke her from a sound sleep one night in November 1954. He had just read this marvelous story by John Cheever, he said, and then he insisted on reading the whole story to her, aloud. It was "The Country Husband" (*Thirteen Uncollected Stories*, pp. xv, xxii). Over the course of a fifty-year career, Cheever published four novels, a novella, and nearly 200 stories. Of the novels, *The Wapshot Chronicle* and *Falconer* seem likeliest to survive the test of time. A number of the stories will also undoubtedly survive.

## WORKS

*The Way Some People Live* (1943)
*The Enormous Radio and Other Stories* (1953)
*The Wapshot Chronicle* (1957)
*The Housebreaker of Shady Hill and Other Stories* (1958)
*Some People, Places, and Things That Will Not Appear in My Next Novel* (1961)
*The Wapshot Scandal* (1964)
*The Brigadier and the Golf Widow* (1964)
*Bullet Park* (1969)
*The World of Apples* (1973)
*Falconer* (1977)
*The Stories of John Cheever* (1978)
*Oh What a Paradise It Seems* (1982)
*The Letters of John Cheever* (1988)
*The Journals of John Cheever* (1991)
*Glad Tidings: A Friendship in Letters: The Correspondence of John Cheever and John D. Weaver, 1945–1982* (1993)
*Thirteen Uncollected Stories* (1994)

## FURTHER READING

Bosha, Francis J., ed. *The Critical Response to John Cheever*. Westport, Conn. 1995. Covers the critical reaction to all of Cheever's books, with a fine introductory essay by Bosha and incisive articles on *Falconer* by Glen M. Johnson and on the *Journals* by Robert A. Morace.

Cheever, Susan. *Home before Dark*. New York, 1984. Affecting memoir by the author's daughter.

Coale, Samuel. *John Cheever*. New York, 1977. First book devoted to Cheever's work and one of the most insightful.

Collins, R. G., ed. *Critical Essays on John Cheever*. Boston, 1982. The best collection of essays on Cheever's fiction.

Donaldson, Scott. *John Cheever: A Biography*. New York, 1988. The standard biography.

Donaldson, Scott, ed. *Conversations with John Cheever*. Jackson, Miss., 1987. Twenty-eight interviews, most of them from Cheever's later years.

Hunt, George W. *John Cheever: The Hobgoblin Company of Love*. Grand Rapids, Mich., 1983. Comprehensive study of Cheever's work, with emphasis on its religious roots.

Meanor, Patrick. *John Cheever Revisited*. New York, 1995. A much-needed updating of previous studies, dealing extensively with the posthumous publications.

O'Hara, James E. *John Cheever: A Study of the Short Fiction*. Boston, 1989. Analyzes about sixty of Cheever's stories, reprinting five important critical essays as well as Cheever's enlightening account of the composition of "Goodbye, My Brother."

Waldeland, Lynne. *John Cheever*. Boston, 1979. Discusses almost all of Cheever's writing and summarizes what others have had to say about it.

# CHARLES W. CHESNUTT

*by Robert M. Dowling*

America's first great black novelist, Charles W. Chesnutt, was a mixed-race, middle-class political moderate. He spent much of his life, both as a child and an adult, in northern cities and southern towns, particularly in Ohio and North Carolina. He was a product of the industrial Gilded Age and of agrarian Reconstruction, an author who fused tradition with new forms, realism with romance, ancient mythology with African-American folklore, and love stories with the law. "I am neither fish, flesh, nor fowl," Chesnutt confessed in 1881, "neither 'nigger,' white, nor 'buckrah.' Too 'stuck-up' for the colored folks, and, of course, not recognized by the whites." Chesnutt, who wrote during the period that in 1931 he called "Post-Bellum, Pre-Harlem," falls in between most American group identities. That station simultaneously equipped him as a realist, hobbled his ability to achieve an authentic social affiliation, and made him one of the most intriguing representatives of his period. As William Dean Howells wrote of Chesnutt's work in the context of the American race-writing tradition:

Charles W. Chesnutt. (*From McElrath, Joseph R., and Robert C. Leitz; "To Be an Author" Letters of Charles W. Chesnutt, 1889–1905. © 1997 by PUP. Reprinted by permission of Princeton University Press*)

> We had known the nethermost world of the grotesque and the comical negro and the terrible and tragic negro through the white observer on the outside, and black character in its lyrical moods we had known from such an inside witness as Mr. Paul Dunbar; but it had remained for Mr. Chesnutt to acquaint us with those regions where the paler shades dwell as hopelessly, with relation to ourselves, as the blackest negro. ("Mr. Charles W. Chesnutt's Stories," *Atlantic Monthly*, May 1900, p. 701)

## A STORY OF THE COLOR-LINE

Charles Waddell Chesnutt was born on 20 June 1858 in Cleveland, Ohio. His parents, Andrew Jackson Chesnutt and Anna Maria Sampson, were middle-class mulattos from Fayetteville, North Carolina, who had moved north in the mid-1850s to escape the increasingly virulent race laws caused by the growing threat of civil war. Andrew spent four years aiding the Union war effort as a teamster, after which he moved his family back to Fayetteville and opened a grocery store with financial help from Charles's white grandfather. Charles received a fine education at Fayetteville's Howard School, an institution for blacks established by the Freedmen's Bureau. But from the local patrons he gained an equally significant education working at his father's grocery, where he absorbed much of the southern black folk tradition. After a number of years, Andrew left the Chesnutt family and subsequently forced Charles, then fourteen years old, to teach at the Howard School, where he was both a student and now, a teacher. The responsibilities of an educational career at such a young age influenced his later work as a writer and activist; Chesnutt would consider it a lifelong duty to educate the American public. From 1873 to 1877 Chesnutt taught in schools across the Carolinas, solidifying his sense of duty to instruct. In 1877 he took up a position back in Fayetteville at the State Colored Normal School and in 1878 married Susan Perry, also a teacher. They had four children and remained together until his death in 1932.

Chesnutt's tendency to study exclusively canonical authors such as Ovid, Goethe, Molière, Thackeray, and Shakespeare left him at first with a snobbish attitude toward southern black culture. But through his parallel education in everyday life, he began to ascertain that the "universal truths" that were seemingly reserved for royal courts and ancient forums manifested themselves in the local groceries, street corners, and small farms of North Carolina as well. Knowing full well that a classical education was a privilege for a mulatto in the Reconstruction South and certainly not a right, Chesnutt realized that it was his duty to instruct not only the less privileged black population about white culture but also white people about black culture.

Nevertheless, he became disillusioned with the professional prospects of mixed-race professionals in the South during Reconstruction. At age twenty-two Chesnutt became principal of the normal school but abandoned his post after three years and traveled on his own to find work. His first stop was New York City, where he wrote articles for the Dow Jones and Company news agency and contributed a weekly column to the *New York Mail and Express*. In 1883 he returned to Cleveland, the city of his birth, where he settled with his family for good. Chesnutt found employment there as a clerk in the accounting and law offices of the Nickel Plate Railroad Company. In 1887 he took the Ohio bar exam and passed with the top score in his group. He worked for a time in Cleveland as a legal stenographer, but his passion for literature never subsided. In the 1880s, having found it difficult to make a living solely on stenography, Chesnutt resolved to become a full-time writer and began selling short stories to the S. S. McClure syndicate.

## LITERARY CAREER

Chesnutt's first short story, "Uncle Peter's House," appeared in the *Cleveland News and Herald* in December 1885. In August 1887 the *Atlantic Monthly* published his masterful dialect piece, "The Goophered Grapevine," the first story that magazine had ever published by a black author. Soon after, he befriended the famous storyteller of Creole life, George Washington Cable, who offered him a job as his personal secretary that Chesnutt graciously declined. Chesnutt's career as a professional writer was ratified in 1889 with the publication of several essays and short stories, including his treatise on race laws, "What Is a White Man?"; his story "The Conjurer's Revenge"; and another story, "Rena Walden," a novel manuscript that was accepted by Houghton Mifflin on 24 March 1900 with the stipulation that the title be changed to *The House Behind the Cedars* (1900).

Encouraged by positive reviews, Chesnutt set his mind to publishing a book. His editor at *Atlantic Monthly*, Walter Hines Page, was also an editor at the distinguished publishing house of Houghton Mifflin, and Chesnutt submitted many book proposals there with initially disappointing results: first Houghton Mifflin rejected a proposed collection of short stories in 1891; then a novel manuscript, "*Mandy Oxendine*," in 1897 (eventually published in 1997); and another novel manuscript, "A Business Career," in 1898. To ensure a popular audience, Page convinced Chesnutt to send him a collection of conjurer tales. Chesnutt responded in 1899 with *The Conjure Woman*, his debut collection. Another collection, *The Wife of His Youth and Other Stories of the Color Line*, appeared that same year. Meanwhile, he also convinced M. A. DeWolfe Howe, the editor of the Beacon Biographies of Eminent Americans series, to include a biography of Frederick Douglass, the most famous nineteenth-century African American. Thus, Chesnutt's landmark biography, *Frederick Douglass*, was published in 1899 as well. In September 1899 Chesnutt closed his stenography business and focused his energies solely on writing.

Chesnutt's first collection, *The Conjure Woman*, is widely considered his finest. Its opener, "The Goophered Grapevine," introduces the rural black "trickster" Julius McAdoo, who beguiles the narrator, John, into hiring him as a coachman. John is white, respectable, and kindly, although his ignorance in race matters demands some well-finessed instruction by "Uncle" Julius. In contrast to much of Chesnutt's later fiction, this artful narrative frame effectively opened his series of "conjure" tales to a broader, white audience while inventing the black vernacular (originally employed by white writers like Joel Chandler Harris and Thomas Nelson Page to revisit nostalgically the Old South) as a tool for African-American novelists in the decades to come. *The Wife of His Youth* is in many ways his most significant achievement, although it was not as well received as *The Conjure Woman*. In *The Wife of His Youth*, Chesnutt speaks to the same contradictions that make Chesnutt himself such an enigmatic public figure. He deals with blacks who pass as white in order to raise their status (although a self-professed "volunteer" black man who could have easily passed for white, he is understanding of those who choose to "pass" in white society); he sets half of the stories in northern Ohio and the other half in southern North Carolina; and many of his black characters, unlike the rural "bumpkin" Uncle Julius, are from the "respectable" black middle class.

Chesnutt's most anthologized story "The Wife of His Youth," which first appeared in the *Atlantic Monthly* (1899), explores the sociocultural complexities of ethnic and regional identity through dialect with a masterful blend of Northern realism and Southern sentimentality.

Chesnutt's mulatto protagonist, Mr. Ryder, is a self-educated social climber who circulates in the light-skinned black professional classes of the city of Groveland (Cleveland). One day a Southern woman arrives at his doorstep and requests assistance in finding her husband, for whom she has searched since the end of the Civil War. Ryder's moral dilemma, whether to acknowledge the dark-skinned wife of his youth or maintain his status among the light-skinned professional classes, is resolved by honoring his past marriage and thus his Southern black heritage.

The year 1900 saw the publication of numerous Chesnutt stories and essays in such journals as *The Critic, Atlantic Monthly, Southern Workman,* and *The Century,* along with the appearance of his first novel, *The House Behind the Cedars,* which explores the complexities of "passing" as white. Also in 1900, the "Dean of American letters," William Dean Howells—a kind individual, but one who could make or break an author's reputation—published a review praising Chesnutt's short stories as vital contributions to the realist movement. Comparing Chesnutt to other realists of the time, including Henry James and Sarah Orne Jewett, Howells wrote: "Any one accustomed to study methods in fiction, to distinguish between good and bad art, to feel the joy which the delicate skill possible only from a love of truth can give, must have known a high pleasure in the quiet self-restraint of ['The Wife of His Youth']" ("Mr. Charles W. Chesnutt's Stories," *Atlantic Monthly,* May 1900, p. 699). Howells thus ensured Chesnutt's legacy not just as a singular African-American voice, but as a significant figure in American literary history.

Chesnutt's unorthodox views of race and ethnicity also came to light in 1900 with his watershed essay, "The Future American." In this essay, which appeared in three installments from 18 August to 1 September in the *Boston Evening Transcript,* Chesnutt makes the controversial statement (even by early twenty-first-century standards) that for race to no longer exist as a destructive category, the black, white, and indigenous races must (and most likely will) merge into one American racial and ethnic amalgamation. A biological forerunner to Israel Zangwill's 1908 "Melting Pot" concept, Chesnutt's "The Future American" is separated into three sections provocatively titled "What the Race Is Likely to Become in the Process of Time," "A Stream of Dark Blood in the Veins of Southern Whites," and "A Complete Race-Amalgamation Likely to Occur." In the last of these, Chesnutt arrives at the conclusion that "there can manifestly be no such thing as a peaceful and progressive civilization in a nation divided by two warring races, and homogeneity of type, at least in externals, is a necessary condition of harmonious progress" (Chesnutt, *Chesnutt: Stories, Novels, and Essays,* edited by Werner Sollors. New York, 2002, p. 862).

### THE MORAL OF THE STORY

Chesnutt's didactic tone here, entirely appropriate for arousing public debate, harmfully carried over into his fiction. Rather than improving upon the subtleties of his conjure tales, ironically allowing a white narrator to demonstrate the misguided grotesqueries of racial prejudice, Chesnutt's novels, *The House Behind the Cedars* (1900), *The Marrow of Tradition* (1901), and *The Colonel's Dream* (1905), deal explicitly with the most controversial race issues of the day—miscegenation, segregation, "passing," and southern white supremacy movements—which, although historically imperative, was deemed unliterary by most critics. The moral statements in his fiction, the reviewers claimed, took priority over narrative balance and stylistic ingenuity. *The Marrow of Tradition,* for example, was a direct response to the race riots that had taken place in Wilmington, North Carolina, in 1898, in which white supremacists killed over twenty black citizens and overthrew the local government. *The Marrow of Tradition* was Chesnutt's most ambitious effort. Based on his thorough research of the region, the novel incorporated a multitude of narrative threads and character points of view. Although his publishers conducted a significant advertising campaign, sales were extremely low. Here is Howells again, this time on *The Marrow of Tradition*: "The book is, in fact, bitter, bitter ... it would be better if it was not so bitter" (Howells, "A Psychological Counter-Current in Recent Fiction," *The North American Review* 173.6 [1901]: 882). None of Chesnutt's last books made enough money to sustain him financially, and in 1902 he returned to stenography.

### FINAL YEARS: POLITICAL AND COMMUNITY ACTIVISM

After the last novel published in his lifetime, *The Colonel's Dream,* appeared, Chesnutt's literary career had all but ended. Instead, he turned his attention to family, the stenography business, and political activism. He was deeply involved in Cleveland politics and society and regularly addressed local and national audiences on the future of African Americans. Chesnutt was a friend to both Booker T. Washington and W. E. B. Du Bois, who often took opposing sides in the debate over how best to achieve racial equality. He was an active member of George Washington Cable's Open-Letter Club for aiding the South in the post-Reconstruction era, and he sat on the General Committee of the National Association for the Advancement of Colored People and Washington's Committee of Twelve for the Advancement of the Negro Race. Chesnutt retained his reputation as a prominent man of letters through his final years: he was honored with an invitation to Mark Twain's legendary seventieth birthday celebration at Delmonico's restaurant in New York City in 1905, and although for the most part he found the modernist literary productions emerging from Harlem in the 1920s unfit for respectable consumption, he was held in high regard by that movement's most prominent players. In 1928 he was awarded the NAACP's esteemed Spingarn Medal for his significant political and literary achievements. Chesnutt died of arteriosclerosis on 15 November 1932 at his Cleveland home. He left behind six unpublished and mostly unfinished novels at the time of his death. Three of these, *Mandy Oxendine* (1897), *Paul Marchand, F.M.C.* (1921), and *The Quarry* (ca. 1928), have been printed for the first time in recent years, thanks to a burgeoning revival of Chesnutt orchestrated by contemporary scholars such as Dean McWilliams, Charles Hackenberry, William L. Andrews, and Werner Sollors.

## SELECTED WORKS

*The Conjure Woman* (1899)
*Frederick Douglass* (1899)
*The Wife of His Youth and Other Stories of the Color Line* (1899)
*The House Behind the Cedars* (1900)
*The Marrow of Tradition* (1901)
*The Colonel's Dream* (1905)
*Paul Marchand, F.M.C.* (1921)
*The Short Fiction of Charles W. Chesnutt* (1974)
*The Collected Stories of Charles W. Chesnutt* (1992)
*The Journals of Charles W. Chesnutt* (1993)
*Mandy Oxendine: A Novel* (1997)
*The Quarry* (1999)
*Charles W. Chesnutt: Essays and Speeches* (1999)
*Chesnutt: Stories, Novels, and Essays* (2002)

## FURTHER READING

Andrews, William L. *The Literary Career of Charles W. Chesnutt*. Baton Rouge, La., 1980. A critical biography by the most prominent late-twentieth-century scholar of Chesnutt and of African-American literature in Chesnutt's time. Andrews has been integral in revising Chesnutt's reputation in the late twentieth century. Includes thorough analysis of Chesnutt's well-known work along with more obscure stories.

Chesnutt, Helen M. *Charles Waddell Chesnutt: Pioneer of the Color Line*. Chapel Hill, N.C., 1952. Sympathetic portrait of Chesnutt by his daughter. Extensive quotations from journals, letters, contemporary reviews, and Chesnutt's published material.

Crisler, Jesse S., Robert C. Leitz, and Joseph R. McElrath, eds. *An Exemplary Citizen: Letters of Charles W. Chesnutt, 1906–1932*. Stanford, Calif., 2002.

Dowling, Robert M. "Ethnic Realism." In *The Blackwell Companion to American Fiction, 1865–1914*, edited by Robert Paul Lamb and G. R. Thompson. Oxford, 2003. Dowling places Chesnutt in the context of ethnic authorship and the realist movement at the turn of the twentieth century.

Du Bois, W. E. B *Chesnutt*. 1933. In *Du Bois: Writings*, edited by Nathan Huggins, pp. 1234–1235. New York, 1986. Du Bois considers Chesnutt a white writer, but one who made important contributions to American race writing nonetheless.

Duncan, Charles. *The Absent Man: The Narrative Craft of Charles W. Chesnutt*. Athens, Ohio, 1998. Convincingly argues that critics who focus on Chesnutt's polemics in his fiction, something traditionally expected from black writers, will often come up empty-handed. His reputation, Duncan contends, would be better served if scholars viewed him as a more complex, less one-dimensional, thinker and author.

Ellison, Curtis W., and Eugene Metcalf Jr. *Charles W. Chesnutt: A Reference Guide*. Boston, 1977.

Fleischmann, Anne. "Neither Fish, Flesh, Nor Fowl: Race and Region in the Writings of Charles Chesnutt." In *Postcolonial Theory and the United States: Race, Ethnicity, and Literature*, edited by Amtitjit Singh and Peter Schmidt. Jackson, Miss., 2000. Fleischmann argues that prominent scholars tend to focus unwisely on Chesnutt's blackness, which makes them complicit with the *Plessy* v. *Ferguson* verdict, since "mulatto" was a category *Plessy* officially expunged.

Heerman, J. Noel. *Charles W. Chesnutt: America's First Great Black Novelist*. Hamden, Conn., 1974. Argues that Chesnutt should be regarded a highly gifted technical as well as social writer. Heerman attempts to undo, as the black novelist John Edgar Wideman did in the 1970s and 1980s, the critical consensus that Chesnutt's novels are artistically flawed.

Howells, William Dean. "Mr. Charles W. Chesnutt's Stories." *Atlantic Monthly*, May 1900: 699–701. Howells welcomes Chesnutt as an important new voice on the American literary scene, comparing him to the some of the finest realist writers of the period.

Howells, William Dean. "A Psychological Counter-Current in Recent Fiction." *The North American Review* 173.6 (1901): 872–888.

McElrath, Joseph R., and Robert C. Leitz, eds. *"To Be an Author": Letters of Charles W. Chesnutt, 1889–1905.* Princeton, N.J., 1997.

McWilliams, Dean. *Charles W. Chesnutt and the Fictions of Race.* Athens, Ga., 2002. McWilliams identifies and deconstructs oppositional binaries that inform Chesnutt's perspective on American racial inequity and regards Chesnutt's essays, journals, short stories, and novels as *texts* that can be integrated within his system. Chesnutt's trajectory from the 1870s to the 1920s, according to McWilliams, demonstrates the increasingly fragmented construction of racial identity as the American public progressed toward a more modern, and to some extent postmodern, historical condition.

Pickens, Ernestine Williams. *Charles Chesnutt and the Progressive Movement.* New York, 1994. Historical analysis of Chesnutt's political views in the context of turn-of-the-century Progressivism.

Render, Sylvia Lyons. *Charles W. Chesnutt.* Boston, 1980. A biography in which Render discusses Chesnutt's literary impact and its relation to social change. She discusses Chesnutt's literary techniques—characters, tone, point of view, themes—and how they subvert popular stereotypes.

Sollors, Werner. *Beyond Ethnicity: Consent and Descent in American Culture.* Oxford and New York, 1986. Discusses Chesnutt's work with many other ethnic texts as examples of the tension between ethnic heritage and new culture acquisition, a functional dichotomy he memorably stamped "descent" and "consent."

Sollors, Werner, ed. *Chesnutt: Stories, Novels, and Essays.* New York, 2002.

Sundquist, Eric J. *To Wake the Nations: Race in the Making of American Literature.* Cambridge, Mass., 1993. Places Chesnutt in the context of other African-American authors who employed African folk beliefs and other cultural influences from that continent to emphasize racial difference.

Wonham, Henry B. *Charles W. Chesnutt: A Study of the Short Fiction.* New York, 1998. A concise introduction to Chesnutt's short fiction. Includes major essays and often-quoted journal entries. Also includes critical statements from prominent Chesnutt scholars. Good place to begin.

# CHICAGO RENAISSANCE

*by Molly McQuade*

The "Chicago Renaissance," as it is called, can be regarded as a cheerfully inexact moniker for the simple reason that a city like nineteenth-century Chicago, with no literary past to speak of, would have had none to revive in a "renaissance" either. Yet Chicago did compel a surge of new and unprecedented literary activity from a varied corps of writers beginning in the 1890s and lasting through the 1920s. These writers wrote in Chicago, they wrote of Chicago, and whatever they wrote was shaped somehow by the city. In their turn, the poets and novelists of the Chicago Renaissance gradually worked a change on the local and national literary landscape. Their city, described in 1914 by Theodore Dreiser as "a maundering yokel with an epic in its mouth," led them all to scribble toward an epic that would fit their own sense of style, scale, and literary destiny. From Dreiser the monumental realist to Edgar Lee Masters the free-verse elegist, from L. Frank Baum the pop American allegorist to Harriet Monroe the poetry magnate, the protagonists of the "renaissance" relied on Chicago to twist their pens and turn their pages.

## REBUILDING EVERYTHING

Chicago began to draw new writers through its borders at about the same time as it began to attract new builders. In 1871 the calamitous Chicago Fire leveled the city's downtown, leaving 100,000 people without their homes and destroying $200 million in property. A disaster for the central city, the fire required extensive rebuilding, but it first required city planners and citizens to imagine the city as it could be, not as it had been. This they did by employing in the city's rebuilding vanguard techniques of iron and steel construction, allowing architects to design massive, looming skyscrapers—"expressions of primordial power in this city which honored power so highly," as the historian Carl Smith (1984) has noted. The rebuilding of Chicago enabled and inspired its rewriting by way of example. As one stage in the city's rebuilding, in 1893 Chicago hosted the World's Columbian Exposition, intended to mark the four-hundredth anniversary of Columbus's voyage to America. The installation at the exposition of a vast beaux arts–style "White City," impressively resembling the European classical tradition in palace and institutional architecture, was meant to awe the international audience of visitors numbering more than twelve million with American ingenuity. The spacious exhibition halls of the White City, the colossal Ferris wheel, and the circuslike midway area of raggle-taggle vaudeville and variety performers suggested to writers such as Baum and Dreiser a changing urban horizon and the opportunity of taking fresh views, fresh chances. Although each responded in his own distinct way—Baum with buoyant fantasy, Dreiser with anything but that—the exposition, like its host city, helped lead them forward.

## "THE ICONOCLAST IS A NECESSITY"

While Dreiser's novel *Sister Carrie* (1900) was the first major accomplishment of the Chicago movement, his fellow novelist Hamlin Garland had given significant cues to the Chicago writers well before then. Garland (1860–1940), a native midwesterner who sought an education in the East at Harvard only to return and set up shop in Chicago, gave voice early to Chicago's evolving literary conscience. In a group of essays published in periodicals from 1890 to 1893 and collected in *Crumbling Idols* (1894), Garland announced "a series of suggestions" to American writers and artists. Most generally, Garland advised them that "American art, to be enduring and worthy, must be original and creative, not imitative." More urgently, he stated that "The iconoclast is a necessity" and anointed the literary rebels as "a generation of veritists," meaning truth-loving realists. "We propose," he wrote, speaking for the veritists, "to use the speech of living men and women. We are to use actual speech as we hear it and to record its changes." Addressing the ghostly mythic figure of the literary traditionalist, his chosen adversary, Garland informed that revenant, "We propose to discard your nipping accent, your nice phrases, your balanced sentences, and your neat proprieties inherited from the eighteenth century. Our speech is to be as individual as our view of life."

Theodore Dreiser (1871–1945) wrote numerous voluminous novels—*Jennie Gerhardt* (1911), *The Titan* (1914), *The Genius* (1915), *An American Tragedy* (1925)—as if in fulfillment of such demands and injunctions. Born in Terre Haute, Indiana, Dreiser at age sixteen transplanted himself to Chicago, working first as a dishwasher and later as a journalist before trying his hand at fiction. His debut novel, *Sister Carrie* (1900), took the measure of his adopted city with a plainspoken, bulky vigor of style that routed any conceivable elegance left over from the eighteenth century. As the contemporary American writer and critic Cynthia Ozick observed in *Metaphor and Memory*, "Dreiser's driven prose uncovers the unmistakable idiom of a raw Chicago." And for that reason, according to Ozick, *Sister Carrie* should be considered "the first recognizably 'American' novel—urban American in the way we feel it now." *Sister Carrie* follows the eighteen-year-old Caroline, known as Carrie, as she takes a train from small-town Indiana to Chicago in 1889. Carrie seeks a life in the big city, a place entirely unknown to her. Yet as she learns only too quickly, Chicago and its huge, faceless institutions, from banks to factories to department stores, stand ready to crush her and any other lone questers. As Dreiser warns early in the novel, "There are large forces, which allure.... Half the undoing of the unsophisticated and natural mind is accomplished by forces wholly superhuman. A blare of sound, a vast array of human hives appeal to the astonished senses in equivocal terms. Without a counselor at hand to whisper cautious interpretations, what falsehoods may not these things breathe into the unguarded ear!" Even with the help of a needed "counselor," implies Dreiser, the unguarded ear may have a hard time navigating bad and good fortune. As the novel progresses, Carrie falls prey to other people's ruses, especially those devised by unscrupulous men; they nearly destroy her. By portraying urban American society as a lurid, frightening opponent to a well-meaning individualist like Carrie, Dreiser made the city itself a memorable American protagonist in fiction. His lifelike, unsentimental portrayal of women's sexual exploitation by men also provoked disgust and controversy.

L. Frank Baum. (*Courtesy of the Library of Congress*)

## THE WONDERFUL WIZARD OF CHICAGO

The year 1900 also saw another significant achievement of the Chicago Renaissance: publication of *The Wonderful Wizard of Oz* by L. Frank Baum (1856–1919). Although composed as a peculiarly American fairy tale and written mainly for an audience of children, the book swiftly transcended limits of genre and even of readership to become an American classic. Moreover, though set in a faraway mythical country, *The Wonderful Wizard of Oz* was born partly of Baum's deep affection for Chicago, his home at the time he wrote the tale. Chicago guided Baum toward Oz, if indirectly. Much like the band of sturdy pilgrims led by Dorothy through Oz, Baum had come to the land of Chicago in part thanks to bad luck: an epic string of failures in half a dozen professions, from theater actor and manager to axle-grease salesman to small-time Dakota shopkeeper, spurred his 1891 arrival in the city. Only in Chicago did chance seem eventually to favor him. Baum initially worked there as a salesman for a crockery company while writing stories and poems on the side.

His first children's book, *Mother Goose in Prose*, appeared in 1897, illustrated by Maxfield Parrish. His next two books, published in 1897, benefited from the extraordinary gifts of the illustrator W. W. Denslow, a Chicago artist with whom Baum had struck up an acquaintance. Denslow also transformed the warm yet wry allegory of *Oz* with his surreally swashbuckling full-page color illustrations, an innovation for the time. If in *Oz* Baum was chronicling with droll symbolism his own misadventures on a not-so-golden road, then the Emerald City may have found its genesis in the Columbian Exposition's White City—both places of marvels and would-be microcosms of cosmopolitan, humane harmony. Like the White City, Baum's green version foretold the development of the City Beautiful movement in American urban planning. Both the White City and the green one preceded by not so many years production of the comprehensive *Plan of Chicago* by the architect Daniel Burnham. In Burnham's ambitious, quixotic book-length proposal for redesigning the Chicago landscape, grown dear to Baum from 1891 onward, one can find American hope clothed in an opulence of pragmatism. Hopeful pragmatism guided Baum and

Dorothy equally. They were only trying, in the end, to find the right road to and through a city.

## FAME, BLAME, AND SPOON RIVER

Like other writers of the Chicago Renaissance, Edgar Lee Masters (1869–1950) ventured to the city from a distance—in his case, from the small adjacent towns of Petersburg and Lewistown, Illinois. Although he published eleven books before his legendary *Spoon River Anthology* (1915) and many more after it, Masters became so closely identified with the *Anthology* that its fame was eventually to irk him. This collection of brief free-verse epitaphs—each written in the voice and entitled with the name of the deceased—evokes an intimate community from beyond the grave with frank and mordant realism. Though written in Chicago, where Masters worked as an attorney, for the poet his work may have linked the freedoms of the city paradoxically with the social confinements of the country: for Masters, both were needed. Commented the later American poet May Swenson on the *Anthology*, "Few of the ingredients of human corruption and vulnerability are missing from the depositions of these underground witnesses" (*Spoon River Anthology*, p. 12). For example, the poem in *Spoon River Anthology* entitled "Rev. Abner Peet" reveals the sad fate of the reverend's sermons and how he felt about it:

> I had no objections at all
> To selling my household effects at auction
> On the village square.
> It gave my beloved flock the chance
> To get something which had belonged to me
> For a memorial. But that trunk which was struck off
> To Burchard, the grog-keeper!
> Did you know it contained the manuscripts
> Of a lifetime of sermons?
> And he burned them as waste paper.

Masters lightly mocks the transience of writing while also acknowledging anxiety about the life and death of fame. In another *Anthology* poem, "Petit, the Poet," the author comments slyly on the limitations of conventional metrical verse. Petit regrets his dedication to iambics and his blindness to the life around him:

> Seeds in a dry pod, tick, tick, tick,
> Tick, tick, tick, like mites in a quarrel—
> Faint iambics that the full breeze wakens—
> But the pine tree makes a symphony thereof.
> Triolets, villanelles, rondels, rondeaus,
> Ballades by the score with the same old thought:
> The snows and the roses of yesterday are vanished;

> And what is love but a rose that fades?
> Life all around me here in the village:
> Tragedy, comedy, valor and truth,
> Courage, constancy, heroism, failure—
> All in the loom, and oh what patterns!
> Woodlands, meadows, streams and rivers—
> Blind to all of it all my life long.
> Triolets, villanelles, rondels, rondeaus,
> Seeds in a dry pod, tick, tick, tick,
> Tick, tick, tick, what little iambics,
> While Homer and Whitman roared in the pines?

The poem suggests a motive for the rebellious poetic realism of Masters. His realism was to jump the fence of genre and leave tracks, also, on Chicago prose writers. As a senior member of the Chicago movement, Masters had already met other Chicago writers before the *Anthology* poems were published, bit by bit, pseudonymously in a St. Louis periodical, *Reedy's Mirror*. The poet tolerated wearily his long-lived literary anonymity while watching others gain public attention. Masters maintained a rivalry with Chicago writers, though seeming to appreciate their talents. In his autobiography, *Across Spoon River* (1936), he recalled of Dreiser: "I noticed his buck teeth, which were very white and well cared-for, and I studied his long fingers when he took off his gloves.... His mind was seething with ideas and plans, and I was astonished at its strength and fertility. In fact, I was not long in seeing that he was much greater than his books." Of the poet Vachel Lindsay (1879–1931), who like Masters hailed from a small Illinois town but found success in Chicago, Masters noted, "His mouth was large, with the upper lip overlapping. His nose was large and fleshy. His forehead ran back. The shape of his head was that of a zero tipped back." Lindsay' riotously rhythmic verse, which he declaimed theatrically in long-distance tramps from town to town, was the manic opposite of Masters's small-scale, ironic cameo portraiture.

## ANOTHER ICONOCLAST

And yet among the many books of Masters is none other than the biography *Vachel Lindsay: A Poet in America* (1935). Written at the invitation of Lindsay's widow, the book explores the life of the poet down to his youthful report cards. (The eleven-year-old Lindsay received good grades in drawing, writing, reading, and spelling but not-so-good ones in music. Later, during high school, he embarrassed himself in Latin and algebra.) In his biography, Masters was the first to reveal that Lindsay's death at age fifty-two was a suicide (he drank the cleanser Lysol). Also of interest is the biographer's account of

Lindsay's visit as a teenager to the Columbian Exposition in Chicago: "Evidently he was captivated with such things as the lions he saw, the strange people that crossed his vision, among them a Turk in a fez." Lindsay also "watched the production of a cartoon . . . whether his ambition to become a cartoonist began here or not, none can say." For one poet to undertake the biography of another, his peer, is rare in American letters, especially when the two might otherwise have seemed to be writing at cross-purposes.

Beginning in 1912, Lindsay was championed by Harriet Monroe, the editor of *Poetry* magazine, but he spent many years before and after wondering what he really should be doing—and getting lost in the meantime. Although publication of his poem "General William Booth Enters into Heaven" in *Poetry* made his name and led to book publications, Lindsay the itinerant idealist felt happiest while trudging country roads, offering recitals of his poetry in return for lodging and meals from strangers. While he wandered, he carried with him pamphlets for distribution to potential hosts and benefactors entitled *Rhymes to Be Traded for Bread*. The pamphlets laid down Lindsay's rules of the road: "Keep away from the cities." "Keep away from the railroads." "Have nothing to do with money. Carry no baggage." "Ask for dinner about quarter after eleven." "Ask for supper, lodging and breakfast about quarter of five." "Travel alone." "Be neat, truthful, civil and on the square." And "Preach the Gospel of Beauty." The gospel he preached, of course, was preached in his poetry.

## THE HAMMER OF THE CITY

Far away from Lindsay's bosky lanes and donated dinners, Carl Sandburg (1878–1967) introduced himself to Edgar Lee Masters in a court of law where Masters was representing a client and Sandburg had gone as a reporter to gather information for a news article. Like Lindsay and Masters, he was born in small-town Illinois (northwestern Galesburg), bravely shouldered the influence of Walt Whitman, and in his poetry revoked all possible claim to genteel verse. Also like Masters and Lindsay, Sandburg enjoyed a connection with *Poetry* magazine; publication there of his poem "Chicago" in 1914 gave the poet his first taste of notoriety for the poetry's harsh and unstinting recognition of the city.

More so than Lindsay or Masters, Sandburg evoked Chicago with sometimes brutal forthrightness in his writing. Perhaps Sandburg's unsparing depiction of Chicago in his poetry emerged partly from his experiences as a reporter for a series of newspapers and periodicals culminating in the *Chicago Daily News*. His main beat there

was labor unions and the struggle to gain legitimacy and respect for the rights of workers. One of his poems, "Onion Days," describes the livelihood of a Chicago laborer, Mrs. Pietro Giovannitti, who works twelve hours a day picking onions on a farm outside Chicago; she catches a streetcar to her job at 5:30 each morning. Instead of wringing a proletarian melodrama from her hardships, Sandburg holds the poem close to the earth it came from. And he chooses to begin by offering a brief portrait of her mother-in-law, the quietly stalwart Mrs. Gabrielle Giovannitti. The opening lines help to give the poem an undeniable dignity.

> Mrs. Gabrielle Giovannitti comes along Peoria Street every morning at nine o'clock
> With kindling wood piled on top of her head, her eyes looking straight ahead to find the way for her old feet.

Sandburg concludes by remarking that "there's no dramatist living can put old Mrs. Gabrielle Giovannitti into a play." The poet thus declares his allegiance to a poetry of the real—a poetry given to him by people like the Giovannittis. Sandburg wrote poems about ditchdiggers, skyscrapers, and Abraham Lincoln. (He also wrote a biography of Lincoln that received, as his poems did, a Pulitzer Prize.) He wrote exceptionally well of rank physical force in urban landscapes, rather as Dreiser had: the pounding of rivets, pickaxes, and hammers. He also exercised his lyric imagination by composing songs and children's books. And at times he wrote in homage to other Chicago writers. Sandburg's poem "Sherwood Anderson," for instance, includes the lines:

> he sleeps under bridges with lonely crazy men; he sits in county jails with iconoclasts and sab cats; he drinks beer with broken-down burlesque actresses; he has cried with a heart full of tears for Windy MacPherson's father; he draws pencil sketches of the wrists of lonely women whose flowers are ashes.

In the poem, Sandburg advises a reader to "Ask this guy. Get his number." Anderson, suggests the poet, knows something about life—that's why he can tell a good story.

## MILK BOTTLES

The stories told by Sherwood Anderson (1876–1941) in his short and long fiction came mostly from his restive love of place. Born in Camden, Ohio, he would later memorialize the thronging discontents of small-town existence in *Winesburg, Ohio* (1919), his collection of bitterly tender short stories. To Anderson, schooled in a hodgepodge and interrupted manner, Chicago may have given the best education possible. His several stints in the city, where he worked nominally as an advertising copywriter while struggling to compose fiction, taught him the difference between scribbling for a living and writing as a calling.

In "Milk Bottles" (collected in *Horses and Men*, 1923), one of his most personally revealing short stories, Anderson tells of a man, never named, who during a sultry August night in Chicago tries to write the true story—his own. But he is unable to, overwhelmed by the livid, somnolent summer city, "heavy with a sense of struggle," namely that of "two million people . . . fighting for the peace and quiet of sleep and not getting it." In the story, Anderson characterizes marvelously a writer's impasse. Yet he also charts an unsure course toward the writer's liberation, thanks to realism. For "Milk Bottles" follows, in addition, the similar attempt of the narrator's friend Ed, an advertising copywriter, to capture in his after-hours personal writing an accurate sense of the city. Ed first scrawls a few hasty pages, then discards them in disgust, and finally manages to produce the work he prefers, presenting Chicago as a "mythical town . . . [with] great streets flaming with color, ghost-like buildings flung up into night skies." To Anderson's narrator, Ed's mythic writing seems as "lifeless" as advertising copy. Instead the scrawled and abandoned pages, scorned by Ed for their wildly provisional quality, represent the beginning of truthful writing because they give a real picture of an impure city. "Milk Bottles" leads the reader through a writer's journey into realism. The story also gives literary credit where Anderson felt credit was due. In describing Ed's rough but true story, which is also the one that Anderson has written here, the author notes: "It was the kind of thing Mr. Sandburg or Mr. Masters might have [written] after an evening's walk on a hot night in, say, West Congress Street in Chicago." As a writer, Anderson was shaped not only by his life in the city but also by the writers who were, like him, writing of that city.

## THE EDITORS

Because they wrote from and of Chicago, poets and fiction writers of the Chicago Renaissance inscribed the city in their very signatures. Yet the editors of such writers also contributed significantly to the rise of the city in the writing. The newspaper editors who employed Dreiser, Sandburg, and others served as salutary early influences on the fledgling creative writers. More potently, Harriet Monroe and Margaret Anderson (no relation to Sherwood) helped to form them and their sentences. As the founding editor of *Poetry* magazine, Monroe,

a Chicago native, dedicated herself to discovering and rewarding poets whose public range would otherwise have been severely restricted in a era when very few magazines of note took poetry seriously. She established the monthly national magazine in 1912 and soon began to publish Lindsay and Sandburg as well as the glittering generation of international modernists—Wallace Stevens, Marianne Moore, T. S. Eliot, Ezra Pound, Hart Crane, and many others. Monroe also provided a social gathering place in *Poetry*'s offices for writers from far and near to gossip, nitpick, and debate. Her influence has previously been underrated.

Like Monroe, Margaret Anderson was a midwesterner, born in Indiana, who found Chicago a lively place to host a journal. The *Little Review*, which Anderson published beginning in 1914, took upon itself a broader mission than *Poetry*: Anderson included prose and artwork regularly in its pages. Anderson's more bohemian nature led to a different sort of social mingling than Monroe's did. As Anderson's friend Janet Flanner, the writer and *New Yorker* correspondent, would later say of her: "Lawless by nature, she always practiced a variety of polite anarchy as her basis of conduct" (in Molly McQuade, *Stealing Glimpses* 1999). The *Little Review* would eventually serialize James Joyce's novel *Ulysses* and embrace the Dadaists; the editor's taste was not to be trammeled, nor did she ultimately choose to remain in Chicago with the magazine. But, like Monroe and the others who gave the Chicago Renaissance its name, Anderson found herself in Chicago.

[*See also* Anderson, Sherwood, and his *Winesburg, Ohio*; Dreiser, Theodore; Lindsay, Vachel; Masters, Edgar Lee; *and* Sandburg, Carl.]

### FURTHER READING

Anderson, David, ed. *Sherwood Anderson: Dimensions of His Literary Art*. Lansing, Mich., 1976. Critical essays by Walter Rideout, Linda Wagner, and others.

Anderson, Margaret. *My Thirty Years' War*. New York, 1969. The first volume of the autobiography of Anderson, who edited the *Little Review* in Chicago before moving its headquarters to New York and, finally, Europe.

Burnham, Daniel, and Edward Bennett. *Plan of Chicago*. Edited by Charles Moore. New York, 1993. A visually pristine and impeccably designed reissue of the original 1909 plan for rebuilding Chicago.

Cahill, Daniel. *Harriet Monroe*. Boston, 1973. A brief yet thorough biographical and critical treatment.

Callahan, North. *Carl Sandburg*. University Park, Penn., 1987. A compact biography.

Cronon, William. *Nature's Metropolis: Chicago and the Great West.* New York, 1991. Offering a view of Chicago's pivotal role in the expansion of the American West, this book also reconsiders in detail the changing physical, commercial, and cultural structure of the city.

Crowder, Richard. *Carl Sandburg.* Boston, 1964. A concise biographical and critical treatment.

Crowley, John W., ed. *New Essays on* Winesburg, Ohio. New York, 1990. Critical essays on Anderson's best-known work of fiction.

Duffey, Bernard. *The Chicago Renaissance in American Letters.* Lansing, Mich., 1954. A helpful literary history.

Garland, Hamlin. *Crumbling Idols: Twelve Essays on Art.* Chicago, 1895. Garland's prescient critical essays, some with lasting bearing on the Chicago Renaissance.

Howe, Irving. *Sherwood Anderson.* New York, 1951. Full-length biography.

Lingeman, Richard. *Theodore Dreiser: At the Gates of the City.* New York, 1986. Copiously researched, up-to-date biography.

Lingeman, Richard. *Theodore Dreiser: An American Journey.* New York, 1990. Volume 2 of same.

Lydenberg, John, ed. *Dreiser: A Collection of Critical Essays.* Englewood Cliffs, N.J., 1971. Essays by Alfred Kazin, H. L. Mencken, and others.

Masters, Edgar Lee. *Across Spoon River: An Autobiography.* New York, 1936. Masters's account of his life.

Masters, Edgar Lee. *Vachel Lindsay.* New York, 1935. The authorized biography, written by Lindsay's peer and fellow poet.

Monroe, Harriet. *A Poet's Life.* New York, 1938. Although unfinished at her death, this autobiography gives direct access to Monroe's views of poetry, as well as her personal account of founding and editing *Poetry* magazine.

Monroe, Harriet, and Alice Corbin Henderson, eds. *The New Poetry: An Anthology of 20th-Century Verse in English.* New and enlarged edition. New York, 1923. As a representative anthology of poetry by the editors of *Poetry* magazine, this will suggest Monroe's editorial perspective on the poets of her time, including those of the Chicago Renaissance.

Niven, Penelope. *Carl Sandburg.* New York, 1991. An up-to-date and comprehensive biography.

Pizer, Donald, ed. *New Essays on* Sister Carrie. New York, 1991. Essays by Alan Trachtenberg and others.

Russell, Herbert. *Edgar Lee Masters.* Urbana, Ill., 2001. An up-to-date biography.

Smith, Carl. *Chicago and the American Literary Imagination, 1880–1920.* Chicago, 1984. An insightful assessment of the city's—and its writers'—role in American literature of the period.

Townsend, Kim. *Sherwood Anderson.* Boston, 1987. New and up-to-date biography.

Williams, Ellen. *Harriet Monroe and the Poetry Renaissance: The First Ten Years of Poetry, 1912–22.* Urbana, Ill., 1977. A detailed partial history.

Wrenn, John H., and Margaret M. Wrenn. *Edgar Lee Masters.* Boston, 1983. A compact biographical and critical treatment.

# CHILDREN'S LITERATURE

*by Sam Pickering*

"Language," Loren Eiseley wrote, "implies boundaries. A word spoken creates a dog, a rabbit, a man. It fixes their nature before our eyes." What does well for a rabbit or a man, however, is inadequate for literature. The phrase "children's book" resembles a tent, baggy and capacious, containing all kinds of writing and drawing. For some critics, any book a child reads or plays with is a children's book. A "Golden Touch and Feel" book, Dorothy Kunhardt's *Pat the Bunny*, is for preschoolers. The "reader" imitates the characters Judy and Tom as they touch things. While Judy pats an illustrated bunny, the child touches a piece of cotton. After Paul smells flowers in an illustration, the reader sniffs a scented page. For children slightly more advanced are "Board Books," small books whose pages are thick as cardboard to resist rough handling; Sandra Boynton's books are an example. At the other intellectual extreme are books read by precocious children. If a child reads John Steinbeck's *East of Eden* in the fifth grade, can the book be classified as a children's book? Or should it simply be labeled "extraordinary reading"?

Pedagogues have met this issue by creating lists of "developmentally appropriate" books. However, what is developmentally, or culturally, appropriate for one child may not be appropriate for another child of the same age. In the belief that to sell, one must divide, bookstores categorize their holdings: first chapter books, young reader picture books, beginning readers, young adult nonfiction, young adult fiction, and so on. Then, does Margaret Wise Brown's sweet, almost teary *Goodnight Moon* belong among illustrated books, first books, or poetry books? These subcategories are almost as baggy and inclusive as "children's books." A shelf devoted to nonfiction may hold *Pocket Scientist*, *Jokelopedia*, *The Kids 'n' Clay Ceramics Book*, and *Frank Lloyd Wright for Kids*.

Illustrated books also raise classification problems. Many of the most expensive are purchased by adults and are intended for bookshelves, not the hard wear of pillow and toy box. In contrast, Little Golden Books are cheap, suitable in price for the rough and tumble of early reading. (This is not to say that Little Golden Books do not entertain or educate; Gertrude Crampton's *Scuffy The Tugboat* [1946], for example, is a cautionary tale of wondrous charm.) Illustrated books vary greatly. Dav Pilkey's popular contemporary books blend cartoon and text. Pilkey's titles—for example, *The Adventures of Captain Underpants* and *Captain Underpants and the Perilous Plot of Professor Poopypants*—appeal to youthful delight in the untoward, the history of which in children's literature goes back to the seventeenth and eighteenth centuries and the first extant chapbooks. In *Tom Thumbe, His Life and Death* (1630), the hero's experience inside the Red Cow does not stop at mouth and cud; he makes a long journey through belly and intestine, eventually reappearing in a "Cowturd." At King Arthur's Court, Tom becomes a great favorite with the ladies, sleeping on their knees and in their pockets "with many such like private places" and tilting "against their bosomes with a bul-rush."

Among critics of children's books, particularly of fairy tales, literature-as-therapy has attracted an articulate following. Bruno Bettelheim has argued that fairy tales act as psychological dragon slayers. Not only do they awaken and expand children's imaginations, but they also help them master the problems of growing up. In fairy tales, the argument runs, children confront psychological problems in fictional form that they will eventually face in life. As the heroes and heroines of the tales resolve their problems, so children unconsciously learn that their difficulties are resolvable. Similarly, Judy Blume's novels, many of which explore the problems of adolescence, are often assigned reading in elementary school. The problem with the therapeutic approach to literature is that it is almost always restricted to the reading of children and young adults. If society really believed that reading influences behavior, pharmacists would dispense books instead of drugs. For the woman treating her aged parent cruelly, *King Lear* could be prescribed; *Othello* would be required reading for jealous husbands, while the uxorious would be urged to peruse *Macbeth*.

## SCHOOLBOOKS AND BOOKS PRINTED IN BRITAIN

In another category are books taught in schools to young adults, often in the hope of shaping tolerant, socially conscious adults. Initially, many of these books were published for adults, but time transforms, in the book world not turning readers gray but keeping them forever young. Some books enjoying widespread popularity in high schools are coming-of-age novels such as Kaye Gibbon's *Ellen Foster* and J. D. Salinger's *The Catcher in the Rye*. Other books commonly read awaken conscience, examine social issues, or make students aware of ethnic difference: *Black Elk Speaks* as told through John Neihardt, Harper Lee's *To Kill a Mockingbird*, Arthur Miller's *Death of a Salesman*, Anne Frank's *The Diary of a Young Girl*, Elie Wiesel's *Night*, George Orwell's *Animal Farm*, Sandra Cisneros's *The House on Mango Street*, and Erich Maria Remarque's *All Quiet on the Western Front* are a few examples.

Appearing on countless high school reading lists are the plays of Shakespeare, not so much for their potential social influence as for their literary value, particularly *Othello*, *Macbeth*, and *A Midsummer Night's Dream*. To stamp Shakespeare's plays as children's books at first appears absurd. Leaving aside adaptations of Shakespeare for young audiences, such as those crafted by Charles and Mary Lamb at the beginning of the nineteenth century, most readers of Shakespeare in the United States are adolescents tied to study. Generations of young Americans have read Shakespeare. His plays have long been published in the United States and are an integral part of school curricula.

In fact, many of the most popular and influential children's books in the United States first appeared in Britain. Despite describing imaginary doings particular to England, J. K. Rowling's Harry Potter novels have been wildly popular in the United States, selling millions of copies. The Muggles are everywhere, not just in England's suburbs, and any middle-class child knows them well.

Many books first published abroad, primarily in Britain, have been popular for three or more generations in the United States and have influenced other writings so much so that they seem, and in a sense are, American: Lewis Carroll's *Alice's Adventures in Wonderland* and *Through the Looking Glass*, *Tom Brown's Schooldays* by Thomas Hughes, Kenneth Grahame's *The Wind in the Willows*, Rudyard Kipling's *Kim*, A. A. Milne's *Winnie-the-Pooh* and *The House at Pooh Corner*, George MacDonald's *The Princess and the Goblin* and *The Princess and Curdie*, the Narnia books of C. S. Lewis, Beatrix Potter's animal stories, L. M. Montgomery's accounts of *Anne of Green Gables*, Robert Louis Stevenson's *Kidnapped* and *Treasure Island*, and, of course, the novels of Charles Dickens. None of these books was written by an American, but they have been appropriated by American readers, and to discuss American children's books and not mention them is to distort literary history. One title—*Tom Brown's Schooldays*, written for adults but now read mostly by children—exemplifies this influence. Hughes preached "muscular Christianity," a religion of action and good deeds, not contemplation or doctrine. Man was responsible for his fellows and was duty-bound to make forceful efforts to reform the world. In his book, fighting in war or in sport is emblematic of the constant fight of Christians to overcome sin. (This sort of moral earnestness is also evident in Victorian poetry appropriated by and for children, like Longfellow's "Excelsior" and "A Psalm of Life.") In *Schooldays*, Hughes explained:

> After all, what would life be without fighting, I should like to know? From the cradle to the grave, fighting, rightly understood, is the business, the real, highest, honestest business of every son of man. Every one who is worth his salt has his enemies, who must be beaten, be they evil thoughts and habits in himself, or spiritual wickedness in high places, or Russians, or Border-ruffians, or Bill, Tom, or Harry, who will not let him live his life in quiet till he has thrashed them.

During the Civil War, series novels for juvenile readers became popular in the United States. Among the better writers were Horatio Alger, Edward Ellis, Charles Fosdick, and William T. Adams, known as Oliver Optic. Hughes influenced Adams, who saw the war in muscular Christian terms: "The cannon balls that struck the walls of Sumter seemed at the same time to strike the souls of the whole population of the North, and never was there such a great awakening since the Pilgrim Fathers first planted their feet upon the rock of Plymouth," Adams wrote in *The Soldier Boy* (1864), the first in a series of six juvenile novels about the struggle. Adams's hero, Tom Somers, is cut from the same Christian cloth as Tom Brown. He carries his "Testament" to the front. Battling against not only the Confederate Army but also human weakness, Tom prays for courage and strength. The "high principle" learned from the Bible earns his comrades' respect. He endures almost inhuman temptation. When Tom is starving, a Confederate soldier gives him two ashcakes, bacon, and a bottle of whiskey. Although he is exhausted and knows the whiskey might invigorate him and save his life, Tom refuses to let bodily weakness become moral weakness and throws the bottle away, praying to the "Giver of all Good." Hughes also influenced the metaphors of sport stories, linking them to warfare. Describing a football match, he wrote naively, maybe perniciously, but nevertheless influentially for the language of athletics, "My dear sir, a battle would look much the same to you, except that the boys would be men, and the balls iron; but a battle would be worth your looking at for all that, and so is a football match." In later American sports stories, Christianity wanes into latitudinarianism, but metaphors of warfare and struggle remain vital.

## FAIRY TALES AND FOLKTALES

Despite the great influence exerted by British writers in the late nineteenth and early twentieth centuries, seining out American books of that period is easier than in the eighteenth and early nineteenth centuries. Fairy tales did not enter English and American literature until the eighteenth century, when many French tales were translated. In 1729, Robert Samber translated Charles Perrault's *Histoires ou Contes du temps passé*. The first American printing was in 1794, the second in 1795. Of the eight stories in the book, seven have become Mother Goose favorites: "Sleeping Beauty," "Little Red Riding Hood," "Bluebeard," "Puss in Boots," "Diamonds and Toads," "Cinderella," and "Hop o' My Thumb." In 1721–1722, a three-volume edition of the works of Madame d'Aulnoy appeared, containing such tales as "The White Cat" and "The Yellow Dwarf." In 1761, Madame de Beaumont's *Magasin des enfants* was translated as *The Young Misses Magazine*, introducing British readers to "The Three Wishes" and "Beauty and the Beast." The collections of the brothers Grimm appeared in the nineteenth century, as well the tales of Hans Christian Andersen. Educational critics initially treated the tales harshly, saying they presented false pictures of life. By appealing to the imagination, the tales led to "unnatural excitement" and "extravagant ideas." By the middle of the nineteenth century, however, the literary spirit had changed. Democracy had spread; the romantic poets celebrated the truth of feeling and impulse; and fairy tales suddenly appeared to be manifestations of the natural. Dickens thought fairy tales taught wisdom of the heart in contrast to wisdom of the head. Ever since, fairy tales and folktales have been popular, particularly ethnic tales from the Russian, Chinese, Irish, Arabic, Italian, and other traditions.

In part because most of the fairy tales dubbed "classics" were translated from other languages into English, writers have not hesitated to emend the tales. "Little Red Riding Hood" provided James Thurber with matter for a humorous sketch and Anne Sexton with material for a poem. During the Atlanta child murders in the late 1970s and early 1980s, copies of Perrault's version were distributed in the hope that the story would teach children to be wary of strangers. For contemporary writers, the form seems particularly appealing, and authors as diverse as Isaac Bashevis Singer, Philip K. Dick, Donald Barthelme, Ursula Le Guin, and Louise Erdrich have adapted the form and written fairy tales.

The popularity of the tales created a climate favorable to the reception of Joel Chandler Harris's volumes of African American–influenced folktales. Nine years after the appearance of *Uncle Remus: His Songs and His Sayings* in 1880, the American Folklore Society was founded. Some literary historians believe that American folklore as a discipline began with the Uncle Remus stories, which Harris collected from slaves and former slaves in Georgia. Today the stories evoke controversy, some critics damning Uncle Remus as an "Uncle Tom" (not realizing that in Harriet Beecher Stowe's *Uncle Tom's Cabin*, Tom is a heroic, virtuous embodiment of the Sermon on the Mount). Other critics, however, celebrate Uncle Remus as a man humanized by oppression and a warm, playful grandfather figure. Uncle Remus aside, however, these most American of folktales are not actually American in origin. More than two hundred seventy versions of the "tarbaby" story are known, the oldest appearing in a collection of Buddhist tales. The great source of the Uncle Remus stories is the Reynard the Fox cycle. Seven centuries ago, they constituted a recognizable animal epic. In 1481, Reynard made his appearance in English when Caxton printed his history. Other stories that Harris collected and shaped made their way from Africa on slave ships to the United States, where they became syncretized with European folktales. In many of the Reynard stories, the fox is the trickster and the bear the dupe; in America the rabbit is the trickster. A weak animal, the rabbit survives by using his brain—a natural hero for slaves, who to survive had to outwit their oppressors. He is also a natural hero for a child surrounded by adults looming like ogres. If stories are therapeutic, trickster tales teach underdogs that they can survive, and even nail the wolves' hides to the door. If the reader sympathizes with the fox, though, the stories are grim. No matter how well the fox or the dominant person plans, something small and weak—whether a rabbit or a disease—will eventually overcome him.

## GODLY BOOKS AND RELIGIOUS AND MORAL VERSE

At the beginning of the eighteenth century, few books were published specifically for children. Aside from chapbooks and Aesop's fables, the only other children's books were "Godly Books." In 1717, *The Holy Bible in Verse* was published in Boston. Bibles for young readers remain popular today, most prominently *The Children's Bible*, published by Golden Press. The earliest extant copy of the *New England Primer* dates from 1725, celebrated today for the rhyming alphabet that begins, "In Adam's fall / We sinned all." In 1798, Isaiah Thomas published the first American children's edition of John Bunyan's *The Pilgrim's Progress*, which enjoyed great popularity and influenced Louisa May Alcott's *Little Women* (1869). Instead of fleeing the City of Destruction, Alcott's pilgrims stay in Massachusetts, and while destruction rages in the country, turn home into a Celestial Country. Until the mid-nineteenth century, particularly in school stories, characters were flat, not rounded, resembling Bunyan's allegorical figures and having names like George Graceless, Ned Neverpray, Jacky Idle, and Timothy Thoughtless.

Aside from *The Pilgrim's Progress*, the most important early religious book was James Janeway's *A Token for Children. Being an Exact Account of the Conversion, Holy and Exemplary Lives and Joyful Deaths of Several Young Children.* Published in Boston in 1700, it was a reprint of a book that appeared in Britain in 1671. About twenty-nine editions had appeared in the United States by 1816. Janeway and other divines with Calvinist leanings preached right religion as the one thing necessary for life. The unsaved child was not merely the potential father of a demonic man; he was also "Satan's Brat" or "the degenerated Bough of the wild Olive tree" whose "grapes" were sure to ripen as "Sodom's pride and lust." At a time when many children died young, writers of godly books felt duty-bound to hurry young readers toward salvation. Nothing was more important than eternal life, and godly books urged children to concentrate their energies on attaining salvation. When she was only eight years old, Sarah Howley, Janeway recounted, heard a sermon that convinced her of "her Need of a Christ." Thenceforth she was "very much in Secret Prayer as," Janeway wrote, "might easily be perceived by those who listened at the Chamber-door, and was usually very importunate, full of Tears." Sarah spent her free time reading the Bible and

holy books until at fourteen she contracted tuberculosis. "Like a continued Sermon," Janeway wrote, she spent her last days, "full of Divine Sentences, in almost all her Discourse."

Scores of writers followed Janeway, joyously burying countless children. In George Hendley's *A Memorial for Children* (1806), nine-year-old William Quayle "never expressed the least desire for life" in his last sickness. Instead, he "wished to be removed to his heavenly Father's house," saying "I would rather die than live." When he becomes seriously ill, Robert Hill exclaims, "Oh, I am happy all over! I know I shall die." When offered medicine, he pleads, "Don't give it to me, for it will do me no good, for I shall die. Do let me die; for if I live, perhaps I shall sin against God." The day before Lucy Cole dies, she asks for a looking-glass. "It being brought," Rebekah Pinkham recounts in *A Narrative of the Life of Miss Lucy Cole* (1830), "she took it pleasantly, gazed upon her deathly countenance, and observed, 'Ah! Lovely appearance of death.'"

Godly books remained popular through the first years of the nineteenth century. From books for children, deathbed scenes migrated to books for adults, most influentially to Harriet Beecher Stowe's *Uncle Tom's Cabin*, in which Eva the "Little Evangelist" dies not just full of divine sentences but also pointing the way to the moral life, Uncle Tom at her side. After the 1860s, not only did more children survive childhood, but society also became more affluent and worldly, and deathbed scenes lost their stature, becoming an object of ridicule in Mark Twain's poem "Emmeline Grangerford's 'Ode to Stephen Dowling Bots, Dec'd'" and Eugene Field's poem "The Little Peach."

The most influential early book of poetry for children was Isaac Watts's *Divine Songs, Attempted in Easy Language for the Use of Children*, published in Britain in 1715. The first American edition appeared in Boston in 1730. By 1929, about three hundred forty-five editions had been published in the United States. Although Watts muted Janeway's Calvinism, "the Lake that burns with Brimstone and with Fire" steamed through the book. "Young Sinners" were taught that "One stroke of his Almighty Rod" could send them "quick to Hell." In addition, however, Watts composed moral songs teaching right conduct: "Against Lying," "Against Quarrelling and Fighting" (the well-known "Let Dogs delight to bark and bite"), "Love between Brothers and Sisters," "Against Idleness and Mischief" ("How doth the little busy Bee"), and "Against Pride in Clothes," and "The Sluggard"

("'Tis the Voice of the Sluggard. I heard him complain / You have wak'd me too soon, I must slumber again."). (In *Alice's Adventures*, Lewis Carroll turned "How doth the little busy Bee" into "How doth the little crocodile" and "'Tis the Voice of the Sluggard" into "'Tis the voice of the lobster.") In assessing the influence of the hymns, Wilbur Macy Stone said, "If *The New England Primer* was the 'little Bible' of New England, Dr. Watts' *Divine and Moral Songs* has a worth place beside it as the 'little Hymnbook,' not only of New England but of Old England as well." For many years, American verse for children was more moral than playful, though, of course, the two were often blended. Typical of early-nineteenth-century moral verse is "The Little Trout," published by J. Grout in Worcester in *The Child's Gem* around 1840:

"Dear mother," said a little fish,
"Pray, is not that a fly?
I'm very hungry, and I wish
You'd let me go and try."

"Sweet innocent," the mother cried,
And started from her nook,
"That horrid fly is put to hide
The sharpness of the hook!"

Now as I've heard, this little trout
Was young, and foolish too;
And so he thought he'd venture out
To see if were true.

And round about the hook he play'd
With many a longing look,
And "Dear me," to himself he said,
"I'm sure that's not a hook.

"I can give one little pluck,
Let's see, and so I will."
So on he went, and lo! it stuck
Quite through his little gill!

And as he faint and fainter grew,
With hollow voice he cried;
"Dear mother, if I'd minded you,
I need not now have died."

## NURSERY RHYMES AND POETRY

In contrast to didacticism of moral and religious verse, nursery rhymes seem anarchic. The earliest extant collection of nursery rhymes in English is *Tommy Thumb's Pretty Song Book* (1744). It contains many familiar rhymes: "Hickere Dickere Dock," "Mistress Mary Quite Contrary," "Little Tommy Tucker," "Sing a Song of Sixpence," and "This Is the House That Jack Built." The *Song Book* was not reprinted in the United States in the eighteenth century. More important in American publishing is *Mother Goose's Melody*, printed by John Newbery in 1780 or 1781, then reprinted in Worcester, Massachusetts, by Isaiah Thomas in 1786. The *Melody* also contains much familiar verse: "Jack and Gill," "Little Jack Horner," "Jack Sprat," and "Three Wise Men of Gotham." With some forcing, nursery rhymes can fitted into categories: riddles, games (especially hand and counting games), parodies, nonsense, and alphabet rhymes, among others. Some rhymes are remnants of popular song, others of advertising jingles. Some tell stories. Many rhymes undermine Loren Eiseley's contention that words form prisons. Nursery rhymes often disrupt the rational border between sense and nonsense. By playing with words and creating new words, by taking joy in words in and for themselves instead of for meanings, nursery rhymes can subvert verbal and indeed social culture. Isaac Watts thought the rhymes dangerous. Believing that they reduced words from the objective to the subjective and thus undercut truth, he called them "rubbish" and "lumber" and warned parents against them. Because many rhymes seemed mysterious or unfinished, they appealed to romantics who celebrated fancy and the shaping spirit of the imagination. In "Why Distant Objects Please" (1822), William Hazlitt wrote, "Whatever is placed beyond the reach of sense and knowledge, whatever is imperfectly discerned, the fancy pieces out at its leisure." Because many rhymes seemed open-ended and did not teach but instead entertained, they lent themselves to emendation and parody. Many of the parodies are bawdy, something that appeals to children raised on diets full of wholesome instruction. Typical of a mild parody is this version "Little Miss Muffet":

Little Miss Muffet
Sat on a tuffet,
Eating her curds and whey;
Along came a big spider,
Who sat down beside her and said,
"What's in the bowl, bitch?"

Not all changes in nursery rhymes, of course, are naughty. Because children enjoy nursery rhymes, religious groups have blended instruction with playfulness. In *My Jesus Pocketbook of Nursery Rhymes*, Humpty Dumpty becomes a vehicle of moral instruction:

Humpty Dumpty
sat on a wall,
Humpty Dumpty
had a great fall.
Don't be like Humpty

who fell and cracked-up.
Let Jesus be your King
as you grow up.

Familiar and malleable, nursery rhymes have also furnished the frame for many advertisements. Around 1890, "Baa-baa Black Sheep" helped sell thread:

Baa, baa black sheep
Have you any Wool?
Yes sir, yes sir,
Three bags full.

Two for little mother
And one for little Ted,
Who mends his little pants
With Clark's O.N.T. thread.

As much as they may have entertained children, nursery rhymes have often irritated writers of serious books for children. Samuel Griswold Goodrich's many books of instruction for children sold so well that some historians think he almost succeeded in banishing nursery rhymes and fairy tales from children's bookshelves in America in the first years of the nineteenth century. Goodrich detested nursery rhymes, the story goes, and said anyone could make them up. For his friend Hannah More, an English writer, he wrote:

Higglety, pigglety, pop!
The dog has eat the mop;
The pig's in a hurry,
The cat's in a flurry—
Higglety, pigglety—pop!

Ironically, Goodrich's rhyme became so popular that, in the 1980s, Maurice Sendak illustrated it. Goodrich wrote the Peter Parley books and became the most famous and successful American writer of educational nonfiction for children in his day. *The Tales of Peter Parley about America* appeared in 1827. By 1856, Goodrich had written or edited 170 books, 116 of them linked to Parley. Annual sales amounted to three hundred thousand, with total sales over seven million. As Peter Parley wandered over the globe and through the heavens, readers learned geography and astronomy, and always morality. The books became school and home reading. Goodrich also encouraged his brother Charles to write *A History of the United States*, which became a classroom staple for decades.

The effects of writing are complex, no matter the intentions of authors. Although volumes of early poetry were cautionary and warned children against the dangers of the imagination, they did so imaginatively. Their stanzas often roamed across landscapes that may have delighted readers more than nursery rhymes. Nevertheless, beginning in the nineteenth century, the poetry for children that sticks in anthology and mind is often more playful than instructive. Even when such poems tell stories, the tales delight more than they warn. Much poetry that American children read first appeared in Britain, including the poems of Ann and Jane Taylor, Christina Rossetti, Robert Louis Stevenson, Hilaire Belloc, A. A. Milne, and Eleanor Farjeon. Some American verse became the stuff of textbooks, notably Longfellow's "The Children's Hour," "Paul Revere's Ride," "The Village Blacksmith," and "The Wreck of the Hesperus." In the same classroom category are John Greenleaf Whittier's "The Barefoot Boy" and "Skipper Ireson's Ride," Oliver Wendell Holmes's "The Deacon's Masterpiece," and Edgar Allan Poe's "Annabel Lee," "The Bells," and "The Raven." Because her poems are good and short, most textbooks contain Emily Dickinson's poems, often "A Narrow fellow in the grass," "A bird came down the walk," "I like to see it lap the miles," and "I'm nobody, who are you?" Many nineteenth-century American writers are remembered for just one poem: Clement Clarke Moore, "A Visit from St. Nicholas" (1823); Anna Marie Wells, "The Cow-Boy's Song" (1830); Eliza Lee Follen, "The Three Little Kittens" (ca.1830); John Townsend Trowbridge, "Darius Greene and His Flying-Machine" (ca.1870); and Sarah Josepha Hale, "Mary's Lamb" (1830). Parody testifies to a poem's popularity, and "Mary Had a Little Lamb" has been parodied many times, one of the best of which continues the poem:

When Mary has been good,
Her daddy gives her lamb.
She puts it on her little plate
And covers it with mint jam.

But don't you worry little children,
For lambkin is not there.
The kindly butcher helped him climb
The golden heavenly stair.

And there he sits with angel wings
The happy woolly in the sky
Blissful in the shining though
Baby Jesus don't eat mutton pie.

Among American writers who produced a substantial body of memorable poems for children are Lucy Larcom (1824–1893), James Whitcomb Riley (1849–1916), Eugene Field (1850–1895), Laura E. Richards (1850–1943), John Kendrick Bangs (1862–1922), Gelett Burgess

(1866–1951), and more recently Elizabeth Coatsworth, David McCord, Ogden Nash, Theodore Geisel (Dr. Seuss), John Ciardi, Shel Silverstein, Nancy Willard, and Jack Prelutsky. Many of their varied poems are humorous; a few are sentimental, like Eugene Field's "Wynken, Blynken, and Nod" and "Little Boy Blue," whose "little toy dog is covered with dust" and "little toy soldier is red with rust." In contrast, humor snaps and then vanishes. Moreover, much children's humor is an oral tradition of grade school insult poems like "Fatty, fatty, two-by-four / Can't get through the bathroom door." The limerick is a form easily adapted to the rude, especially by adolescents. The first book of limericks was published by J. Harris and Son in London in 1820, *The History of Sixteen Wonderful Old Women*. Edward Lear's *A Book of Nonsense* (1846) contains a selection of respectable limericks, many of which became well known:

There was an Old Man with a beard,
Who said, "It is just as I feared!—
Two Owls and a Hen,
Four Larks and a Wren,
Have all built nests in my beard!"

Among children in America, the limerick has remained absurd. In oral, almost underground, culture, however, particularly that of adolescents, bawdy is stirred into the absurdity.

## NEWBERY, LOCKE, AND EARLY AMERICAN BOOKS

In 1744, John Newbery published *A Little Pretty Pocket-Book*. As a result, as F. J. Harvey Darton, a distinguished historian of early English children's books, put it, 1744 is "a date comparable to the 1066 of older histories." Until Newbery's success, children's books did not stand out as a branch of literature. Behind Newbery's success and the later success of trade in children's books lay many factors. Commercial prosperity had increased the size of the middle class and contributed to social mobility. As people climbed out of penury, they were able to afford books. Moreover, as the future seemed to promise more than laborious poverty, they demanded books that would serve as educational stepping-stones by which their children could climb even higher in society. Later, with the rapid growth of Sunday schools in the 1780s and 1790s, popular education began, and a new reading public of Sunday scholars was created almost overnight.

If commercial prosperity made the expansion of the book trade possible, the writings of John Locke provided publishers with a wealth of general and particular educational matter. Locke's importance to early English and American children's books cannot be overstated. Before the reign of Queen Anne, the *Guardian of Education* declared in 1802, there were "very few" books written for children. "The first period of Infantine and Juvenile Literature" began, the journal recounted, after Locke popularized "the idea of uniting amusement with instruction." In *Some Thoughts Concerning Education* and his closely related *Essay Concerning Human Understanding*, Locke not only popularized uniting amusement with instruction, but he also provided the eighteenth century with what seemed to be a scientific basis for the study of human development and an explanation of the crucial formative influence of education and thus of reading. According to Locke, the "great Thing to be minded in Education" was "what Habits" were settled. Since nine men out of ten were formed "Good or Evil, useful or not, by their Education," life for the orthodox Lockean became good habit rewarded, and the most important duty owed children was establishing them in sound habits of mind and body based on right principles. Locke said that a child's mind resembled a "white paper void of all characters." Experience on which knowledge was based, he argued, marked the paper. If one controlled the experiences, then one could shape a child, and thus making the child the father of the man could determine both moral and financial success. Locke convinced educators that youthful reading played a major role in a child's development. If impressions, as he wrote, made upon "tender Infancies" had "very important and lasting Consequences," then childhood reading was significant, and no right-minded parent, or society as a whole, could ignore what children read.

Newbery quoted Locke. In his books, he followed Locke's advice and blended amusement with instruction, capturing attention with humor and playfulness and then teaching both practicalities such as the alphabet and lessons for a good and proper life. Newbery's most famous book, *The History of Little Goody Two-Shoes* (1767), is an updated Cinderella story in which a poor girl rises from poverty to possess a coach and six horses, aided not by a fairy godmother but by education.

The most important American publisher of early children's books was Isaiah Thomas of Worcester, Massachusetts. In 1784, he wrote Thomas Evans in London, asking that he be sent a large shipment of children's books containing Newbery's best books and those published by his heirs and rivals like John Marshall. Thomas reprinted about forty-five of these books in Worcester editions. Most differences between the London and Worcester editions are small. Thus, while Master Friendly is "a Parliament-man" in Newbery's *Nurse Truelove's Christmas Box* (1750), he is a "Congress man" in Thomas's edition of 1789. While Newbery "humbly inscribed" *A Little Pretty Pocket-Book* "TO THE PARENTS, GUARDIANS, and NURSES in Great Britain and Ireland," Thomas inscribed his version to the same group in the "UNITED STATES of AMERICA."

## CAUTIONARY TALES AND BAD BOYS

Despite their playfulness, early American children's books are cautionary, teaching the perils of disobedience. In *The Holiday Present*, published by Thomas in 1787, Polly Ingrate's mother tells her to stay away from a pond in the garden. Polly does not listen, and one day while playing catch, she tumbles into the pond. On this occasion, she is fortunate to be rescued. Her mother also warns her to avoid "a little dirty yard" where pigs are kept. Polly pays no attention, and one day when she tries to pet a baby pig, a sow bites her fingers "so bad, that one of them was obliged very soon to be taken off." Polly's obstinacy brings only painful distress. Despite being forbidden to approach an open window, Polly leans out of a window in her mother's bedroom, falls out, and breaks her back. The fall cripples her, and "She is now a woman, and you cannot think how sadly she looks. She is never well: Her back sticks out worse than any thing you can imagine, and her shoulders are as high as her ears; and all this was the consequence of not minding what had been said to her."

Although most nineteenth-century children's books stressed obedience and duty, stories like that of Polly became less common. Sentimental primitivism thrived. In celebrating the natural, the romantic movement sentimentalized the earthy. The unschooled were seen as natural and wholesome repositories of innocence and decency. Experience in its multiplicity, writers like William Wordsworth implied, taught better than schoolmasters. In this attitude lay the seeds of more complex characters, no longer flat devices for instruction but rounded figures in whom both virtue and vice appear. Instead of celebrating the disciplined child, some writers made heroes of characters who violate convention and to the world's eyes appear naughty or even bad, but who are actually good—vagabonds who are dismal failures in school and in conventional society, and who seem to be drifting aimlessly but are actually developing an enormous capacity to cope with and succeed in life. Uneducated, they do not lose their natural, sometimes heavenly, innocence. As a result, they behave decently when it counts. In such books, the bad boy is really a good boy. The best of the "bad" characters are Rudyard Kipling's Kim and Mark Twain's Huckleberry Finn.

Late in the nineteenth century, mischievous boys often figure as the main characters of books like Thomas Bailey Aldrich's *The Story of a Bad Boy* (1869), George Peck's *Peck's Bad Boy* (1883), or Frances Boyd Calhoun's *Miss Minerva and William Green Hill* (1909), a book so popular with southern readers that it was reprinted more than fifty times. Not all bad boys were even human: Frances Trego Montgomery's hero *Billy Whiskers* (1902) is a goat. The best of such tales in the twentieth century are Booth Tarkington's gentle accounts of Penrod and his rag-tag gang of friends; in addition to serious adult novels such as *The Gentleman from Indiana* and *The Magnificent Ambersons*, this prolific novelist from Indiana wrote classics for children and adolescents, such as *Penrod* (1914) and *Seventeen* (1916).

## ILLUSTRATED BOOKS

Chapbooks became common in the seventeenth century. Printed unbound on rough rag paper, they cost from a penny to a shilling. Those with which children were most familiar in the mid-eighteenth century measured four by six inches and cost a penny or two apiece. They were written for both children and adults of the lower classes, and some credit for the spread of literacy in Britain in the eighteenth century can be attributed to their broad popularity. In the first years of the century, the chapbook was the most easily obtainable kind of children's book. The crude woodcuts that illustrate them have a primitive appeal today; Newbery's illustrations are crisper because he recut woodblocks and often used copperplate engravings. In the nineteenth century, John Harris began to market small booklets measuring five by four inches and containing sixteen leaves, with all the illustrations colored. The first was *The Comic Adventures of Old Mother Hubbard, and Her Dog* (1805). The book was a success and spawned imitators.

The first illustrated science book published in Britain was John Amos Comenius's *Orbis Pictus* (1659), starting a line of nonfiction illustration that runs to David Macaulay's *The Way Things Work* (1988). As technology exploded, so did the variety of illustration. Here again, defining an American book is difficult.

In the twentieth century, illustrations became so important a feature of children's books that in 1938 the American Library Association began awarding the Caldecott Medal to the most distinguished picture book published in America each year. Because technical innovation reduced printing costs and because the present is a visual age, the variety of illustration is now immense, and reading pictures has become a critical skill. The list of popular and successful twentieth-century illustrators is long, including among its notables N. C. Wyeth, Leo Lionni, Ezra Jack Keats, Robert McCloskey, William Steig, Gail Haley, Leo and Diane Dillon, Barbara Cooney, Chris Van Allsburg, Bill Peet, Garth Williams, Tomie de Paola, Maurice Sendak, James Marshall, Dr. Seuss, Arnold and Anita Lobel, and Shel Silverstein.

## MAJOR THEMES: ANIMALS

Many of the most memorable characters in American children's books are animals. Ian Falconer's Olivia the pig paints a Jackson Pollock on a wall in her house; Howard Garis's Uncle Wiggley Longears putters slowly along, nibbling on the turnip steering wheel of his car on the way to the Smiling Pool to see Thornton Burgess's Old Mr. Toad. In a nearby circus, Dr. Seuss's Horton sits on the egg of Mayzie the lazy bird, while in an orchard Eric Carle's very hungry caterpillar eats his way through three plums. If these characters had been written into early children's books, they would have found themselves in a less anthropomorphic world. Animals were simply devices to lead children away from cruelty to benevolence. Little Goody Two-Shoes gathers stray animals about her. One morning Jumper, a dog she has rescued from starvation, forces her and a student out of a schoolhouse, whereupon Goody orders all the children from the building; shortly thereafter, the roof collapses. As Goody's kindness to Jumper indirectly saves her life and the lives of her pupils, so compassion woven into the character of a child would, Lockeans thought, help shape the moral character of the future adult. Benedict Arnold betrayed the Revolution, a biography for children explained in the nineteenth century, because as a boy he tortured baby birds. For the first half of the nineteenth century, animals were generally flat vehicles for instruction. In 1877, however, appeared *Black Beauty*, written by Anna Sewell, a Quaker. Told from the point of view of a horse, the book is practically a tract, preaching kindness to animals not for the sake of shaping people but for the sake of animals themselves. Vast numbers of the book were bought and distributed, with its devotees estimating thirty million over one hundred years.

*Black Beauty*, however, reflected the past. Toward the end of the nineteenth century, animals behaved increasingly like people, often children, in the *Mother*

*West Wind Stories* of Thornton Burgess or Howard Garis's accounts of Uncle Wiggley, for example. In 1886, Ernest Thompson Seton published his first book. Seton continued to publish until 1940. Although born in Canada, he spent much time in the United States. Urbanization was partly responsible for the popularity of his animal books and those of Jack London, *The Call of the Wild* (1903) and *White Fang* (1906). Seton's animals appeared wild at a time when the frontier was disappearing, and Americans were far enough removed from adventure to hanker for it. Scouting became popular, and summer camps thrived. John Muir's *The Mountains of California* was published in 1894. At the *Atlantic Monthly*, Bliss Perry published Mary Austin's articles; "The Land of Little Rain" (1903) described the California desert in hopes of attracting eastern readers and boosting circulation. The emphasis on the wild was not long-lasting, however, at least in children's books. Albert Payson Terhune's *Lad: A Dog* appeared in 1919, and from then until the present, animals in children's literature were either domesticated or anthropomorphized—E. B. White's *Charlotte's Web*, for example, or Margaret Wise Brown's furry children. An old saw of children's tastes was that boys read books about dogs while girls read about horses. Black Beauty aside, the most famous horse in American children's books is Walter Farley's *The Black Stallion* (1941); Farley wrote twenty-one Black Stallion and Island Stallion novels, most of which remain in print.

After T. S. Eliot declared that the amount of good poetry in the world was small, C. S. Lewis responded, "The amount that can be read with pleasure and profit is enormous." Many best-selling books read by children are not good literature. Such books have, however, given great pleasure. Edgar Rice Burroughs's *Tarzan of the Apes* was first published as a book in 1914. By the early 1970s, it had been translated into at least thirty languages and had sold more than thirty-five million copies. For an orphan on the west coast of Africa, Tarzan has a distinguished literary ancestry in Kipling's stories of Mowgli and the *Leatherstocking Tales* of James Fenimore Cooper—also books very popular with children. To some extent *Tarzan* is a Robinsonnade, a distant offspring of *Robinson Crusoe*, of which there were scores of derivatives for children, the most famous being *The Swiss Family Robinson* by Johann Wyss. Isaiah Thomas printed two versions of Defoe's novel, one full-length and the other thirty-one pages long, for small children. (In the short version, Thomas warned children against copying Crusoe and wandering from home.) By the twentieth century, Robinsonnades, particularly *Tarzan*, were optimistic, shaped by expanding wealth and a confidence derived from Locke. With the right education, with effort, a person could shape success, moral and financial. The furnishings of his father's hut, like the materials Crusoe salvaged from the wreck, furnished Tarzan's mind and contributed to his ability to cope with a chaotic world. Burroughs wrote other books popular with the children, particularly the eleven books of the Mars series featuring John Carter, five books in the Venus series, and seven books in Pellucidar series, in which David Innes and Abner Perry invent an iron mole and journey to the center of the Earth. The Tarzan series alone amounted to twenty-five novels, which in turn led to more than forty movies and hundreds of comic books. To some degree Burroughs's novels lie behind the *Star Wars* films and much science fiction read by children, particularly Frank Herbert's six books of the *Dune* series and Anne McCaffrey's fourteen novels describing the planet Pern.

Many of the Tarzan books feature adventures in lost cities and among hidden tribes. In twentieth-century children's books, the lost city or world becomes a narrative cliché, drawn not only from Burroughs but also from Jules Verne. Many such books create a more adventuresome, often fantastic, less industrial other world, frequently set in the past: T. H. White's collection of three novels based on legends of King Arthur, *The Once and Future King* (1958), Lloyd Alexander's *Chronicles of Prydain*, the four books of Ursula Le Guin's Earthsea series, Terry Brooks's Shannara series, the Dark is Rising Sequence by Susan Cooper, and J. R. R. Tolkien's *The Hobbit* and *The Lord of the Rings*—books that in their popularity transcend the boundaries of nation-states. Some books that explore lost worlds are not chronicles of derring-do but hymns to times past, particularly the works of Laura Ingalls Wilder. Among the most imaginative explorations of imaginary worlds are those of Madeleine L'Engle, particularly *A Wrinkle in Time* (1962), and of L. Frank Baum. *The Wonderful Wizard of Oz* appeared in 1900. Forty *Oz* books were published; Baum wrote only fourteen of these, of higher quality than the other books in the series. Because of the Judy Garland movie, most children know only *The Wonderful Wizard*, a shame, because Baum was remarkably inventive and his other Oz books delight.

As Tarzan overcomes the dark jungle, so the heroes and heroines of sports books triumph over dark adversity. Leagues of writers composed sports books. Among the best known was John R. Tunis, whose most popular books were nine baseball novels published in the 1940s and 1950s. Eight describe a fictionalized Brooklyn Dodgers, a representative title being *The Kid Comes Back* (1946).

## BOOK SERIES

As America became industrialized, so did children's books. In 1896, in *Street and Smith's Tip Top Weekly*, Gilbert Patten published his first story starring Frank Merriwell, a Yale-educated athlete. Patten, writing as Burt L. Standish, produced about two hundred novels featuring Merriwell, making him the most famous athlete in America for thirty years. In 1889, Edward Stratemeyer, a clerk in a tobacco store, sold a magazine serial that was the genesis of the Rover Boys, Nancy Drew, the Hardy Boys, the Bobbsey Twins, Tom Swift, Ted Scott, Bomba the Jungle Boy, and about one hundred twenty other series. Stratemeyer founded a "Syndicate" in 1905 or 1906 to help him turn out novels for children, and since that time the Syndicate has published around 1,300 books, or 1,500 if dime novels, retitled reprints, and revised editions are counted. Each year, more than two million copies of the Syndicate's books are sold, and total sales by 1980 were estimated at two hundred million. Initially, Stratemeyer hired writers to expand his three-page outlines into two-hundred-page books. Among the first writers he hired was Howard Garis, who worked on many series, including most of the Tom Swift books. Lillian Garis, his wife, the Syndicate's first woman writer, worked on the Motor Girls and the Bobbsey Twins, among others. Stratemeyer's daughter, Harriet Adams, took over the Syndicate on his death in 1930 and, under the pseudonyms Carolyne Keene and Laura Lee Hope, wrote all the Nancy Drew and Dana Girl books. Stratemeyer and the Syndicate used more than a hundred pseudonyms, some of which—Victor Appleton, Franklin W. Dixon, Roy Rockwood, Arthur M. Winfield, Carolyne Keene, and Laura Lee Hope—are probably better known to their long-ago child readers than are the names William Faulkner and Robert Frost. The sales of the Syndicate's leading "authors" are astounding. The seventy-one volumes (as of 1981) of Franklin W. Dixon's Hardy Boys series and the seventy-six volumes of Laura Lee Hope's Bobbsey Twins have each climbed above fifty million copies.

Stratemeyer studied the pulse of his time, and the range of tales astonishes. When movies became popular, the Motion Picture Chums appeared in 1913. The Motion Picture Chums owned a theater and the Moving Picture Girls were actresses; the Moving Picture Boys and the Motion Picture Comrades were filmmakers. In 1906, the first three of an eventual twenty-two volumes of the Motor

Boys appeared. In 1910, the first two volumes of the Motor Girls were published. In 1912, the Baseball Joe series began. An "everyday country boy" who loves baseball, Joe progresses from a club team to a school team to Yale, and through the minor leagues to the Giants. By 1922, Joe is "the greatest pitcher and batter on record." In 1923, unlike the real-life "Shoeless" Joe Jackson, the Syndicate's star refuses temptation even though "throwing a game" would have brought him a fortune. After Lindbergh flew across the Atlantic in 1927, Franklin W. Dixon finished the first volume of the Ted Scott Flying series in two weeks. Two weeks later, *Over the Ocean to Paris* was in bookstores, and by the end of 1927, four Ted Scott novels had appeared.

The Syndicate produced books for children of all ages. From 1917 to 1922, seventeen volumes of Richard Barnum's Kneetime Animal Stories appeared. Written for children aged four to nine, the titles resemble names given stuffed animals: Flop Ear, the Funny Rabbit; Tum Tum, the Jolly Elephant; and Mappoi, the Merry Monkey. Perhaps the most famous series for young children were Laura Lee Hope's Bunny Brown and His Sister Sue (twenty volumes), and Helen Louise Thorndyke's Honey Bunch (thirty-four volumes), later continued as Honey Bunch and Norman (twelve volumes). Unlike numbers, influence cannot be quantified; suffice it to note that, by 1993, sales of the Nancy Drew novels had climbed above eighty million, and the books had been translated into fourteen languages.

## OPTIMISM

No puzzle has ever defeated Nancy Drew. In her Witch series, Phyllis Reynolds Naylor's heroines discover and thwart a witch, overcoming doubting adults. Optimism cascades through American children's books. In *The Little Engine That Could* (1930), Watty Piper's "Little Blue Engine" chugs over the mountain saying, "I think I can," words that could stand almost as an epigraph above libraries of books. Thus, the taurine hero of Munro Leaf's *The Story of Ferdinand* (1936) determines the course of his life and avoids the bull ring and the Spanish civil war to spend his days sitting under "his favorite cork tree" smelling flowers. Against the odds, Virginia Hamilton's *M. C. Higgins, The Great* (1975) saves his family home.

In the world of children's books, educators and writers learned from Locke that education and experience shape children. When these were the right sort, a child could achieve anything and rise to any level in society. Instead of being bound to position and place, the child was mobile. Life rewarded education and virtue, and many

books were almost unfailingly optimistic, such as Eleanor Porter's *Pollyanna* (1913) and *Hans Brinker; or, The Silver Skates* (1865) by Mary Mapes Dodge. From 1873 to 1905, Dodge edited *St. Nicholas*, the most outstanding children's periodical ever published in the United States. The ashes-to-happiness tale of Cinderella provided a narrative frame for optimistic novels. In books like Kate Douglas Wiggin's *Rebecca of Sunnybrook Farm* (1903), Frances Hodgson Burnett's *A Little Princess* (1905) and *The Secret Garden* (1911), Katherine Paterson's *The Great Gilly Hopkins* (1978), and Jean Webster's effervescent *Daddy-Long-Legs* (1912), the heroines are either orphans or children separated from family. *Daddy-Long-Legs* is a Lockean fairy tale. Education and a fairy godfather who sponsors the heroine's schooling enable an orphan to live successfully and beloved. In Burnett's *Little Lord Fauntleroy* (1885), innocence in the character of Cedric and the new world transform his ogrelike grandfather into a loving man of feeling.

Not all contemporary children's books are sunny: see Robert Cormier's *I Am the Cheese* (1977) and *The Chocolate War* (1974). Of special interest is Robert C. O'Brien's *Mrs. Frisby and the Rats of NIMH* (1971), an environmental novel that preaches against irresponsible consumption and foreshadows the dangers of genetic engineering. On the whole, however, contemporary children's books describe a green world in which happiness arcs over pages in rainbows, and endings show bright promise fulfilled.

[*See also* Alcott, Louisa May; Cooper, James Fenimore; Dickinson, Emily; Erdrich, Louise; Lee's *To Kill a Mockingbird*; London, Jack; Longfellow, Henry Wadsworth; Poe, Edgar Allen; Salinger, J. D., and his *The Catcher in the Rye*; Singer, Isaac Bashevis; Stowe, Harriet Beecher; Tarkington, Booth; Twain, Mark, and his *Adventures of Huckleberry Finn; and* White, E. B.]

### FURTHER READING

Avery, Gillian. *Behold the Child: American Children and Their books, 1621–1922*. Baltimore, 1994. A sensible summary of historical trends.

Baring-Gould, William S., and Cecil Baring-Gould. *The Annotated Mother Goose*. New York, 1962. Illustrated and entertaining.

Bettelheim, Bruno. *The Uses of Enchantment: The Meaning and Importance of Fairy Tales*. New York, 1976. Influential but quirky readings.

Bottigheimer, Ruth. *Grimms' Bad Girls and Bold Boys: The Social Vision of the Tales*. New Haven, Conn., 1987. A good reading of fairy tales.

Brant, Sandra, and Elissa Cullman. *Small Folk: A Celebration of Childhood in America.* New York, 1980. Informative and wonderfully illustrated.

Darton, F. J. Harvey. *Children's Books in England.* 3d ed., revised by Brian Alderson. Cambridge, 1982. An essential study.

Griswold, Jerry. *Audacious Kids: Coming of Age in America's Classic Children's Books.* New York, 1992. Intelligent readings.

Hall, Donald, ed. *The Oxford Book of Children's Verse in America.* New York, 1985. The selection of poetry is good, but the introduction is slapdash and unreliable.

Johnston, Clifton. *Old-Time Schools and School-books.* New York, 1963. A reprint with a new introduction of a book first published in 1904; contains much useful information.

Johnson, Deidre. *Stratemeyer Pseudonyms and Series Books: An Annotated Checklist of Stratemeyer and Stratemeyer Syndicate Publications.* Westport, Conn., 1982. A good introduction and a fine bibliography.

Kuznets, Lois. *When Toys Come Alive: Narratives of Animations, Metamorphosis and Development.* New Haven, Conn., 1994.

Lurie, Alison. *Boys and Girls Forever: Children's Classics from Cinderella to Harry Potter.* New York, 2003. Genial readings.

McClinton, Katharine Morrison. *Antiques of American Childhood.* New York, 1970. Almost four hundred pictures of the furnishings of childhood.

Nodelman, Perry. *About Pictures: The Narrative Art of Children's Picture Books.* Athens, Ga., 1988. Very good at reading pictures.

Opie, Iona, and Peter Opie. *The Lore and Language of Schoolchildren.* Oxford, 1959. A fine discussion of what children sing and play at school.

Opie, Iona, and Peter Opie. *The Classic Fairy Tales.* Oxford, 1974. Reprints and splendid historical introductions to famous tales.

Opie, Iona, and Peter Opie. *A Nursery Companion.* Oxford, 1980. A collection of colored booklets for children from the early nineteenth century.

Opie, Iona, and Peter Opie, eds. *The Oxford Dictionary of Nursery Rhymes.* Oxford, 1973. Essential for students and lovers of nursery rhymes.

Pickering, Samuel. *John Locke and Children's Books in Eighteenth-Century England.* Knoxville, Tenn., 1981.

Pickering, Samuel. *Moral Instruction and Fiction for Children, 1749–1820.* Athens, Ga., 1993.

Roscoe, Sydney. *John Newbery and His Successors, 1740–1814.* Wormley, U.K., 1973. A labor of love and a fine bibliography.

Russell, David L. *Literature for Children: A Short Introduction.* 4th ed. New York, 2001. Fine bibliographies and reading lists.

Sale, Roger. *Fairy Tales and After: From Snow White to E. B. White.* Cambridge, Mass., 1978. Appreciative readings.

Silvey, Anita, ed. *Children's Books and Their Creators.* Boston, 1995. A useful encyclopedia.

Tartar, Maria. *Off with Their Heads.* Princeton, N.J., 1992. On violence in fairy tales.

Thompson, Stith. *The Folktale.* Berkeley, Calif., 1977. Useful.

Welch, d'Alté. *A Bibliography of American Children's Books Printed Prior to 1821.* Barre, Vt., 1972. Essential for the historian and collector.

# KATE CHOPIN

*by Robin Kemp*

Katherine O'Flaherty Chopin is best remembered for her novel *The Awakening*, which was greeted by popular critics as scandalous when it appeared in 1899. The controversy centered around the main female character's dissatisfaction with married life and her romantic attraction to a younger man. Chopin, however, was never one to be bound by convention and had been raised and educated by a series of headstrong women. Her outlook granted her a freedom to write without an internalized social censor; however, society was not yet ready for her work.

## EARLY LIFE

Born on 8 February 1850 in St. Louis, Missouri, "Katie" was one of five children. Her father, Thomas O'Flaherty, was an Irish immigrant from County Galway, who escaped the Great Potato Famine and his father's real-estate business to seek his fortune supplying ships, soldiers, and explorers in the United States. He also was instrumental in bringing new technologies like the telegraph and railroad links to St. Louis. His wife Eliza Faris was twenty-three years his junior, and the marriage appeared to be more of a business arrangement than a romantic commitment. O'Flaherty provided well for his family: he owned four slaves, sent his son George to St. Louis University, and paid for Katie's early schooling at the prestigious Sacred Heart Academy.

When she was five, Katie lost her beloved father in the disastrous Gasconade train bridge collapse that killed thirty of St. Louis's leading citizens. Katie's mother, now a young widow with a decent estate, did not remarry. Madame Victoire Verdon Charleville, Katie's great-grandmother, took the child under her wing. She was an unusual woman for her generation, in that she was literate and largely self-educated. During the period

Kate Chopin, 1893.
*(Missouri Historical Society, St. Louis)*

of mourning, she took it upon herself to school her great-granddaughter in French, the piano, and the nuances of survival as an intelligent woman.

At age seven, Katie reenrolled at Sacred Heart, this time as a day scholar. There, she became best friends with Kitty Garesché, a neighbor child as daring as she was. The duo climbed trees, read novels, studied a rigorous, wide-ranging curriculum, and went on educational field trips together.

Just as some normalcy began to return to Katie's routine, the Civil War broke out. Neighbors became bitterly divided over slavery and secession, even though Missouri did not leave the Union. The O'Flahertys' sympathies were with the South. Katie's brother George joined the Confederate Army, later dying of typhoid. On more than one occasion, the Sisters of the Sacred Heart had to prepare their young charges to flee, but rumors that soldiers would capture the convent school's buildings and grounds never came to fruition. Shots were fired just blocks from Katie's home and school. The last straw came when a Union sympathizer hung an American flag—an act intended as an insult—on Katie's house. Incensed, she stormed over, ripped down the flag, and stashed it in the dirty laundry. Angry Union soldiers tried to arrest her, but a neighbor intervened. Thereafter Katie O'Flaherty was hailed as "The Littlest Rebel" of St. Louis. The O'Flahertys' slaves ran off as the war reached its climax, and news came that Katie's cousin, also a Confederate soldier, had been killed in combat. Crushed by this latest series of personal losses, the schoolgirl sought refuge in books and music.

Encouraged by a teacher, Mary O'Meara, Katie began keeping a journal. She filled it with character sketches, literary critiques, poetry, and copied passages about powerful women. In later years, Kate would deny she had any discipline as a writer, but this early training proved extensive. Katie also was a talented pianist with a gifted ear. She was known for hearing a piece one night and then performing it from memory the next day. She spent a year at a rival school, apparently only to study piano, and took up German.

In 1868, Kate O'Flaherty graduated with honors from Sacred Heart and made her social debut. Already, she was beginning to chafe at the role she was expected to play. On a trip to New Orleans, she took up smoking—taboo for women—and she complained in her journal about the duties of a debutante: "What a nuisance all this is—I wish it were over. I write in my book to day the first time for months; parties, operas, concerts, skating and amusements ad infinitum have so taken up all my time that my dear reading and writing that I love so well have suffered much neglect" (Toth, p. 87). The young writer finished her first serious short story during this time. "Emancipation: A Life Fable" (1869) is a very short piece about a caged animal—perhaps not unlike the young debutante who was eager to take up her pen—who finally, after several false tries, escapes through the cage's open door.

In 1870, Katie married the dashing Oscar Chopin, a cotton factor. After a honeymoon in Philadelphia, New York, and Europe, the couple settled in New Orleans. It was common practice at that time for wealthy Creoles (descendants of French and Spanish colonists) to live in town part of the year and to tend to the plantation at harvest time. In 1874, Oscar joined the First Louisiana Regiment, an arm of the Crescent City White League. The White League was a paramilitary group made up of Confederate veterans from New Orleans high society. No love was lost between Creole cotton factors, whose wealth depended upon slave labor, and the large free black population in New Orleans. On 14 September 1874, Chopin's regiment exchanged fire with the metropolitan police in the infamous Battle of Canal Street.

In 1879, Oscar's business failed, and he moved the family to Cloutierville (pronounced "KLOO-chee-vil"), a small town of about six hundred people on the banks of the Cane River in northeastern Louisiana. The Chopins took up residence in the house built by the town's founder, which is today preserved as a literary shrine to Kate Chopin, and Oscar opened a general store and ran the plantation.

Kate gave birth to six children, but Oscar soon contracted swamp fever (malaria) and died. The young widow continued to run the store and plantation; she was widely believed to have carried on an affair with a married man, Alfred Sampite. After a year, she moved with her children to St. Louis to be near her mother. Her mother died soon after; Kate was distraught. The family doctor urged her to supplement her small rental income by publishing her writing.

## WRITING CAREER

Writing for pay was a respectable occupation for well-to-do widows in the late nineteenth century. The feminist scholar Sandra M. Gilbert also says Chopin's motivation was "partly to supplement her income and partly to distract herself from her grief" (Gilbert, p. 10). However, the late scholar Nancy A. Walker challenges this assumption: "to suggest that writing was for her a compensatory activity . . . or that following the death of Oscar Chopin she was forced to find a socially sanctioned means of supporting herself and her children [is not] borne out by the facts of Chopin's life" (p. 2). After all, she was the beneficiary of both Oscar's and her mother's estates, so she was not writing to put bread on the table for her children. Walker points out that such a career choice would be highly unlikely for a woman at that time unless there was some preexisting ability and practice on the writer's part. Chopin had received a great deal of formal education and writing instruction as a girl. As an adult, she rarely revised her works, understood how to handle editorial criticism, knew how to sell a story, and learned quickly from her mistakes.

Chopin, like many nineteenth-century writers, first published poems and short stories in the popular magazines of the day. In 1889, Chopin's first published work, the love poem "If It Might Be," appeared in *America*. Later that same year, she began writing her first novel, *At Fault*, and her first published story, "A Point At Issue!," ran in the *St. Louis Post-Dispatch*. The following year, Chopin published one thousand copies of *At Fault*, ostensibly based on her rumored affair with Sampite, at her own expense. She finished the manuscript of a second novel, *Young Dr. Gosse and Théo*, in 1891. After several publishers rejected the manuscript, Chopin destroyed it. Her short stories began to appear steadily in *Vogue*, *Century*, *Short Stories*, *Harper's Young People*, and *The New Orleans Times-Democrat*, among other magazines and newspapers.

In 1894, Chopin published her first collection of short stories, titled *Bayou Folk*. This group included such local color pieces as "For Marse Chouchoute," her first Cloutierville-inspired piece; "Boulôt and Boulotte," a comic tale of childrens' values; "The Storm," a passionate tale of an adulterous encounter during a hurricane; "Desirée's Baby," which explores intersections of racism and sexism; "La Belle Zoraíde," the tale of a light-skinned black woman who wants a dark-skinned baby, but whose cruel mistress removes the baby and convinces her the child is dead; and "At the 'Cadian Ball," recounting a flirtation at a *fais-do-do* (Cajun dance).

A second short story collection, *A Night in Acadie*, continued in the local-color vein. "A Matter of Prejudice" depicts a French woman in New Orleans who refuses to cross Canal Street because the other side is occupied by "Americans." In "The Lilies," a child creates a match between a mother and a cranky bachelor. "A Little Free-Mulatto" is another effort to examine life through the eyes of African Americans: a man attempts to cheer his sad and isolated mulatto daughter by taking her to "L'Isle des Mulâtres," which was where the free *gens de coleur* lived in Natchitoches Parish. There, the child is transformed by the joy of being among others like herself. This story, like "Desirée's Baby" and "La Belle Zoraíde," offers a unique perspective from the "Littlest Rebel" who married a member of the White League.

### THE AWAKENING

One story that was too big for the confines of the short form, "At Chênière Caminada," later grew into the novel *The Awakening*. The book opens in 1899 on Grand Isle off coastal Louisiana, where wealthy Creoles (descendants of French settlers) spend their summers. Edna Pontellier, a young wife and mother, is there with her two young sons and her husband Léonce. However, Léonce's business frequently calls him back to New Orleans. Edna, an *Americaine* who has married into Creole society, spends most of her time with Madame Lebrun, the resort owner; Adèle Ratignolle, a model self-sacrificing Creole mother; Mademoiselle Reisz, a piano-playing spinster; and Madame Lebrun's son, Robert, a single man who is known for choosing a married woman to squire about each summer.

Edna experiences culture shock in this French Catholic milieu. Because Creole women are considered above reproach, they are ironically free to flirt and to speak frankly. Edna is shocked at first but grows accustomed to the openness that Adèle and the other women on Grand Isle display. Robert takes up their company, and the three often venture down to the beach and chat. He begins swanning Edna about in an exaggerated chivalry. Soon after, the parody becomes flirtatious, and the two find themselves more and more attracted to each other.

As the summer progresses, Edna learns to swim, takes up her forgotten paintbrushes, and spends more time with Robert. This is the beginning of her "awakening." Clearly, there is a spark between Edna and Robert, yet neither speaks of it.

Edna also is moved to tears by the piano playing of Mademoiselle Reisz, a spinster who lives a life of freedom, one to which Edna unconsciously aspires. Edna begins to dread spending time with Léonce when he is around; he in turn becomes more clingy and questioning. Robert feels himself on the edge of romance with Edna and leaves for Mexico so as not to interfere.

However, when the Pontelliers return to New Orleans, things have changed. Edna is obsessed with her painting; Léonce is troubled by her new self-assertiveness. He seeks counsel from the family doctor, who suspects an affair but tells Léonce to let this strange bout of noncompliance run its course.

While Léonce is away on business, Edna sends the boys to the country to stay with his mother. Free of family distractions, yet lacking any real role models, Edna dives into remaking herself. She rents a small cottage, nicknamed "the pigeon house," moves herself and her few possessions, and calls remodelers into the Pontellier home. In the pigeon house, Edna feels in control of her own destiny. However, the local rake, Alcée Arobin, has taken note of her isolation and "befriends" her. They begin going to the racetrack. Although Edna still has feelings for Robert, eventually she is seduced by Alcée. She enjoys the pure physicality of their sex, but refuses to turn over her soul—to him or to any man.

Mademoiselle Reisz lives nearby, and one day Edna seeks her out. Mademoiselle tries to counsel Edna on the demands of the artist's life. She also tells Edna that she regularly receives letters from Robert. Edna is consumed with a desire to read the letters. Mademoiselle, knowing of their mutual attraction, finally allows her to see Robert's letters.

Eventually, Robert can no longer deny his love for Edna, and returns to New Orleans. By chance, they meet at Mademoiselle Reisz's apartment. He confesses his feelings for her yet insists that she belongs to Léonce. Edna counters that she does not belong to anyone but herself. She tries to convince Robert to live with her in the pigeon house, but his Creole sensibilities prevent him from launching into an affair with another man's wife.

As the two embrace, a messenger interrupts with news that Adèle Ratignolle is in labor and calling for Edna's assistance. Edna begs Robert to wait for her return; when she leaves, he writes a goodbye note and slips away. Meanwhile, Adèle urges Edna to think of how an affair would affect her children. The weight of Adèle's admonition is especially great because she is in labor, and Edna becomes consumed with guilt.

On her return to the pigeon house, Edna finds Robert's note. Suddenly, she realizes she is truly alone in the world. She can only conceive of one way to escape. She goes back to Grand Isle, strips, and swims into the Gulf. The ending implies Edna's suicide—an unforgivable sin in Creole culture—without ever actually passing judgment on it.

*The Awakening* has all the zing and spice of a contemporary novel. Unfortunately for Chopin, many of her readers in the final throes of the nineteenth century could not conceive of a woman breaking the social code this way. The third-person narrator never condemns Edna's behavior; readers inferred that Chopin herself approved of Edna's nonconformist actions. Chopin herself was a nonconformist, but the analogy between the author and her character is false: Chopin did not commit suicide (she died of a brain hemorrhage), nor did she leave her husband (she was widowed). Chopin herself wrote, "I never dreamed of Mrs. Pontellier making such a mess of things and working out her own damnation as she did" (Toth, p. 344).

The spark of scandal no doubt was fanned by Chopin's gleefully unconventional behavior. Chopin rolled her own Cuban cigarettes when it was considered unladylike to smoke; sauntered unaccompanied through the streets of St. Louis, New Orleans, and Cloutierville; wore purple; played cards; took over her husband's business; and rode astride her horse. This was not at all the behavior expected of a former Sacred Heart debutante, now a mother and widow.

Chopin's critics also objected to the tone of the novel. While portraying Edna's second adolescence, Chopin's narrator never condemned Edna's missteps and selfish acts. Critics, interpreting this as tacit approval of Edna's behavior, savaged the book. *The Awakening* also presented a more serious side of Chopin the writer than did her local color sketches. Ironically, the artist herself suffered a fate similar to that of her main character. Just as Edna's paintings were more than socially acceptable decorations for others' pleasure, so did Chopin's writing present a threat once she began to explore issues that were important to her.

Chopin was deeply wounded by the way St. Louis turned against her. The following year, her publisher refused to print the third collection of short stories, ostensibly as a result of the scandal that *The Awakening* caused. On 20 August 1904, Kate Chopin suffered a cerebral hemorrhage after having spent the day at the World's Fair. She died two days later, at age 54.

Chopin's work lay largely ignored for almost thirty years, until Father Daniel Rankin, a Catholic priest and scholar, rescued it from slipping into even greater obscurity. In the late 1960s and early 1970s, a new generation of headstrong women rediscovered her work and praised its farsightedness. Today, both Chopin and her works are lively topics of scholarship, and *The Awakening* is required reading for many high school and college students.

## WORKS

*At Fault* (1890)
*Bayou Folk* (1894)
"Athénaise" (1896)
*A Night in Acadie* (1897)
*The Awakening* (1899)
*Complete Works of Kate Chopin* (1969)
*The Awakening and Selected Stories* (1986)

## FURTHER READING

Dyer, Joyce. *The Awakening: A Novel of Beginnings.* Twayne's Masterwork Studies, 130. New York, 1993.

Martin, Wendy. *New Essays on* The Awakening. Cambridge, 1988.

Rankin, Daniel S. *Kate Chopin and Her Creole Stories.* Philadelphia, 1932. First book of scholarship on Chopin and her work. Rankin, a Catholic priest, also researched and wrote about Joan of Arc.

Seyerstad, Per. *Kate Chopin: A Critical Biography.* Baton Rouge, La., 1969.

Toth, Emily. *Kate Chopin.* New York, 1990. Engaging, detailed survey of Chopin's life, work, and critical reception.

Toth, Emily. *Unveiling Kate Chopin: The Centennial Story.* Jackson, Miss., 1999. Toth, in characteristic wit, delves even further into Chopin's life.

Walker, Nancy A. *Kate Chopin: A Literary Life.* New York, 2001. The feminist scholar, late of Vanderbilt University, examines how social mores stifled Chopin's white-hot career.

# BILLY COLLINS

*by Mark Conway*

Billy Collins is the most popular poet in America, according to a 1999 article in the *New York Times*. Named Poet Laureate of the United States for 2001–2003, Collins appears often on public radio and his readings are packed with enthusiastic fans. Collins's work—funny, accessible, and wry—receives high marks from many corners of mainstream criticism, and he sells more books of poetry than anyone since Robert Frost. However, it is these very qualities that cause others to question Collins's achievement. Despite, or perhaps because of, the broad appeal of these poems, some think Collins's work is too clever or, because it is often funny, classify the work as light verse. Collins does not have much patience for the division that pits his poetry against "serious" work. "Poetry," he says, "isn't supposed to make you feel dumb, it's supposed to enhance your life."

Billy Collins, from *The Art of Drowning*, 1995. (*Reprinted by permission of the University of Pittsburgh Press*)

he has since come to ridicule. The breakthrough in this volume is the establishment of a character who can be the speaker of the poems. Collins says, "This character has a tone of voice, rather than a fictional life. He is a fairly attractive fellow, a greatly improved version of myself." The creation of this voice allowed Collins to achieve a balanced tone, equally serious and humorous, as a platform for his deadpan delivery.

Tone is perhaps the most important consideration for Collins. He calls it "the key signature for the poem. The basis of trust for a reader used to be meter and end-rhyme. Now it's tone that establishes the poet's authority." In *The Apple That Astonished Paris*, Collins creates a voice that provides the flexibility that Collins needs for the imaginative flights his work takes. For Collins, the beginning of a piece is important not only for setting the tone, but also for inviting the reader into the poem. "Another Reason Why I Don't Keep a Gun in the House" begins by setting the scene in straightforward, narrative exposition: "The neighbors' dog will not stop barking." This sets up the central imaginative leap that, as in most of Collins's poems, serves as the single controlling metaphor of the poem. After the speaker puts a Beethoven symphony on full blast to drown out the sound of the barking, he then can see the dog "sitting in the orchestra, / his head raised confidently as if Beethoven / had included a part for barking dog." It is as if the dog is "sitting there in the oboe section barking . . . while the other musicians listen in respectful/ silence to the famous barking dog solo." The barking continues after the recording has stopped, just as it seems to trail off at the end of the poem.

## EARLY CAREER

Collins was born in New York on 22 March 1941. He began his career in letters by earning a Ph.D. in Romantic literature from the University of California, Riverside, in 1971. His dissertation, noteworthy in relationship to his own long path to find a reading public, was entitled "Wordsworth and the Romantic Search for an Audience." Later in 1971, he started teaching at Lehman College (part of the City University of New York) in the Bronx.

Collins's first real success came after placing poems in a handful of the more prestigious literary journals. He then published *The Apple That Astonished Paris* with the University of Arkansas Press in 1988. The poems in this volume represent a break from his previous work. Collins says that up until this point he wrote in the obscure style

His second book, *Questions about Angels* (1991), was selected for the National Poetry Series and began attracting a larger audience to his work. In this book, Collins starts to perfect the character of the rueful, suburban man, a creature of habit who mainly wants to sit in his study thinking about poems or listening to jazz. Every once in a while, he (and it is always "he," a version of the "greatly improved" Collins) is forced to do chores or go shopping. The only way to deal with these disruptions is to let his imagination loose while it looks like he is simply standing in line or looking for a parking place. In the poem "American Sonnet," even the notion of a summer trip to Europe seems too ambitious. For Collins, the American version of the sonnet is the postcard where, instead of fourteen lines dictating the form, the length is whatever we can write "on the back of a waterfall or lake." This sonnet is not an occasion to express love or religious ecstasy; rather, "We express the wish that you were here / and hide the wish that we were where you are." Much of Collins's work is in celebration of the insignificant, the quotidian, and in this poem, the trip not taken.

In the wake of this award-winning book, Collins forged a relationship with the University of Pittsburgh Press. With *The Art of Drowning*, published in 1995, and *Picnic, Lightning*, published three years later, Collins settles into a sustained body of work, collections that show an increasing authority and a consistency of tone. He has mastered a jazzy, improvisational style, a tone that is often counter-balanced by setting the poems in a very domestic scene. While this might suggest that the work would become tamer and more predictable, in fact, the poems have a greater distance to travel between the poles of the actual suburban world and the wildly eccentric leaps that occur in the Collins cosmos.

The poems now settle into a familiar pattern. The syntax is similar to the syntax of prose: straightforward and direct, it is designed to communicate as plainly as possible rather than tickle the ear or dazzle the reader. Enjambment is rare, with most of the line-breaks occurring on a comma or natural pause. The poems typically create a sort of philosophical narrative. They begin by posing a central metaphor; the rest of the poem is a playful development of that single notion. The language is clear and American, in the slightly outdated diction of a wry, aging hipster who likes jazz slang. The flat delivery has a natural cadence and relies on colloquialisms for color. A poem will usually use only one or two figures of speech to complicate the texture of the poem, usually a well-turned image or small but apt metaphor. An example is "Osso Buco," a contrarian's poem that sings of the pleasures of a full stomach, "something you don't hear much about in poetry, / that sanctuary of hunger and deprivation." One

of the few images occurs when "the lion of contentment / has placed a warm, heavy paw on my chest." The poem ends with the speaker slipping into a deep, satisfied sleep where dreams carry him into the "broken bones of the earth itself, / into the marrow of the only place we know."

## RISE TO POPULARITY

After *Picnic, Lightning*, Collins became an overnight sensation—at the age of fifty-seven. He appeared on two nationally syndicated radio programs and sales of the book jumped sharply. At this point, Random House offered him a stunning six-figure advance for three books. This was a major event in the poetry world, not only because of the size of the advance but also because the offer sparked a major disagreement between the University of Pittsburgh Press and Random House. Random House wanted its first book to be a collection of new and selected poems, but the University of Pittsburgh Press was not ready to release the rights to its poems. The disagreement threw into high relief the role of small presses and the best way for a poet to reach an audience. Eventually, these differences were resolved and Random House published *Sailing Alone around the Room: New and Selected Poems* in 2001. The collection included representative work from the books discussed here along with twenty new poems, work very much in the same voice and tone as the previous two volumes.

Collins was named Poet Laureate of the United States for 2001–2002, and renamed to the post for 2002–2003. He was very quickly called upon to offer a poet's perspective in the wake of the terrorist attacks on 11 September 2001. He responded that poetry is not concerned with the transitory and so has little ability to make immediate sense of the moment. He said that it is the timeless aspect of poetry that unifies and that all poems, by speaking for life, speak against the tragedy of the day.

*Nine Horses: Poems* was published in 2002. No doubt Collins will continue to present his unique vision, that the world is more amusing than we acknowledge, more yielding to our careful attention, and more terrible. For all of its attractive qualities, Billy Collins's poetry does not sidestep the more difficult parts of life. Each new book brings new readers to poetry and sparks further controversy over this accessible and popular poet.

## WORKS

*Pokerface* (1977)
*Video Poems* (1980)
*The Apple That Astonished Paris: Poems* (1988)
*Questions about Angels: Poems* (1991)

*The Best Cigarette* (1993)
*The Art of Drowning* (1995)
*Picnic, Lightning* (1998)
*Sailing Alone around the Room: New and Selected Poems* (2001)
*Nine Horses: Poems* (2002)

## FURTHER READING

Gray, Jason. "*Picnic, Lightning.*" *Prairie Schooner* 75 (Spring 2001): 189.

Kirsch, Adam. "Over Easy (*Sailing Alone around the Room: New and Selected Poems*)." *New Republic* (29 October 2001): 38.

Merrin, Jeredith. "Art Over Easy." *Southern Review* 38 (Winter 2002): 202.

O'Driscoll, Denis. "*Sailing Alone around the Room: New and Selected Poems.*" *Poetry* 180 (April 2002): 32.

Plimpton, George. "The Art of Poetry LXXXIII." *Paris Review*, no. 159 (Fall 2001).

# COLONIAL WRITING IN AMERICA

*by John Gatta*

From the first, North America's natural grandeur offered European explorers and settlers ample ground to stir imaginative wonder. Virtually ignoring native settlements, they saw before them a limitless, unpeopled wilderness of woodland abounding in game, fish, watercourses, and timber. Thus, trader-adventurer Thomas Morton, in his *New English Canaan*, rhapsodized on the "faire endowments" of a country that looked to him like "Nature's Masterpiece" when he landed from England on a spot of paradise near present-day Quincy, Massachusetts, sometime after 1622. "If this land be not rich," he later declared, "then is the whole world poor." By 1690 the largest settlement in the colonies amounted to no more than seven thousand Bostonians huddled on the edge of a mostly unmapped continent. In proportion to the meager population of British North America, colonists produced a startling quantity of written material, much of which has been preserved. Why, then, have later readers sometimes ignored or discounted this early writing as something beneath genuine literature?

Part of the reason, surely, is that most colonial writing does not fit conventional modern expectations of what literature should look like. There is virtually no fiction or drama. Instead, we are confronted with a formidable array of sermons, treatises, chronicles, histories, letters, conversion narratives, political documents, travel reports, and promotional tracts. Poetry is the only traditional genre of literary expression well represented in this mass of published and unpublished material. But the verses that colonists, particularly New Englanders, penned so profusely can strike us at first as alien and unappealing. Frequently expounding religious doctrines, moral teachings, or aphorisms derived from folk culture, such writing forces us to recognize that colonial Americans, even those of English or other European extraction, understood the world very differently from most of us today.

To appreciate writing of the colonial period requires us, then, to expand our conception of literature as well as our sense of America and the world. This effort can be rewarding insofar as it reveals the imaginative intensity and range of inquiry that colonial writers brought to their engagement with a New World. An earlier generation of twentieth-century scholars, inspired by the brilliant work of Perry Miller at Harvard, has already highlighted the enduring force of Puritan thought and symbols within the history of ideas. Students of the period have also stressed the role that colonial writers played, for good and ill, in helping to shape a distinctive national mythology. Long-standing beliefs about "the American self" have been traced back to seventeenth-century discourse. Influenced by shifting cultural attitudes, analysts in the late twentieth century began to offer still more reasons for reevaluating colonial American writing. Instead of regarding it with condescension, as just a preliminary and primitive phase of American literary history, they are finding new motives for giving it serious attention in its own right.

## REASSESSMENTS OF COLONIAL LITERATURE
In our early-twenty-first-century culture, for example, renewed appreciation for the expressive value of nonfiction prose, and for writing that blurs the distinction between journalism and imaginative literature, opens the way to better understanding of colonial autobiographies, histories, and sermons. Attentiveness to irony and patterns of self-making enables us to read Benjamin Franklin's *Autobiography* (composed 1771–1790) not so much for its practical advice as for the way it dramatizes a prototypical American's capacity for endless adaptation and self-invention. It has become increasingly clear that Governor William Bradford did not record a straightforward factual narrative of the first Pilgrim settlement in his *Of Plymouth Plantation* (composed 1630–1650). Despite its supposedly "plain style" of exposition, this work reflects the tensions and ambiguities its author faced in trying to sustain a providential vision of history. Like Thomas Jefferson's fable of nationhood in the Declaration of Independence, Puritan divine Jonathan Edwards's idealized re-creation of his own life in his "Personal Narrative" (composed ca. 1740) and other prose pieces of the period, Bradford's narrative reflects genuine rhetorical artistry.

Instead of calling attention to itself, however, such artistry was expressly designed to serve some social purpose. The practice of art for art's sake did not exist during this period. Nor did writing as a full-time vocation or paid career.

Pursuing the rhetorical and cultural significance of writings that fall outside our usual notions of literature yields new understanding of early American experience—even with texts as unpromising as execution sermons, diaries, political pamphlets, and funeral elegies. Since the late twentieth century, interest in gender politics and cultural studies has led interpreters toward fresh scrutiny of texts such as Mary Rowlandson's gripping, personal *Narrative of the Captivity and Restoration of Mrs. Mary Rowlandson* (1682), Sarah Kemble Knight's *Private Journal of a Journey from Boston to New York* (composed 1704–1710), and Phillis Wheatley's poems bearing on her condition as a black house slave in Boston around the time of the Revolution. The emergence of ecocriticism, a green-inspired movement in literary criticism that redefines nature writing within the broader category of environmental literature, has likewise provoked new interest in colonial and early national writings such as Thomas Harriot's *A Brief and True Report of the New Found Land of Virginia* (1588), William Wood's *New England's Prospect* (1634), and William Bartram's *Travels through North and South Carolina, Georgia, East and West Florida* (1791).

Mounting awareness of the need to honor this land's ethnic and ideological pluralism has particularly influenced the canon of early American literature—that is, the roll call of texts most frequently judged to warrant inspection by readers and critics. Late-twentieth and early-twenty-first century anthology collections of early American writing typically begin with mediated transcriptions of the creation myths and other oral traditions of Native peoples who did not record their experiences directly in writing. Typically, too, these collections include writings in translation by explorers such as Christopher Columbus, Bartolomé de Las Casas, and Samuel de Champlain, none of whom settled permanently in the Western Hemisphere. Early America is thus understood to embrace New Spain and New France, encompassing geographies beyond current U.S. borders and languages other than English. Even within the narrower bounds of British colonization, the beliefs of early writers show considerable diversity. Some writers, settled mainly in Massachusetts and Connecticut, were Puritans. In the spirit of John Calvin, these rigorously devout dissenters from the established Church of England wanted to press

the Protestant Reformation further than Britain had thus far allowed. But other colonial writers were worldly adventurers, secular-minded Deists whose faith centered on human reason, Quakers, Anglicans, renegade Puritans such as Roger Williams in Rhode Island, or proponents of other ideologies.

Nonetheless, the literature of Puritan New England has retained a distinct prominence in early American studies. Some scholars regard this special attention as a form of regional favoritism that downplays the worth of writing produced throughout the southern and middle Atlantic colonies. Others voice skepticism about the much-discussed continuity between Puritan attitudes and those reflected by major American authors in later centuries. Still others complain that Puritan influences on the future of America have been pernicious, encouraging an ideology of conquest and false confidence in this nation's supposedly exceptional status within the world community.

Yet the Puritan imagination has in fact left an unmistakable imprint on American consciousness. The exemplary role of the Puritan community as "a city upon a hill," first invoked by Massachusetts Bay governor John Winthrop in a lay sermon delivered in 1630, still surfaces perennially in political speeches as an ideal figure of the United States. Not only the imagery and thought patterns, but also some modes of expression favored by colonial New Englanders, have shown an enduring presence in American letters. For example, rhetoric of the sermon figures significantly in imaginative writings by later authors as diverse as Henry Thoreau, Herman Melville, William Faulkner, and Harriet Beecher Stowe. Sermons by inspired, first-generation divines such as Thomas Hooker, John Cotton, and Thomas Shepard amply demonstrate the power of the word to melt souls. Stowe, despite her quarrel with Calvinist religion, respected the singular passion and urgency expressed by the Puritans of colonial New England. For "in no other country," she observed "were the soul and the spiritual life ever such intense realities"; and nowhere else has everything been so deliberately contemplated "in reference to eternity" (*The Minister's Wooing*, 1859). *The Nature of True Virtue* (1765) and other philosophic writings by Jonathan Edwards continue to provoke reflection on the largest questions of life and ethics.

Particularly if we extend the definition of colonial writing to include works published shortly after the Revolution by figures active before 1776, we can likewise speak without apology of the imaginative accomplishments represented in this era's secular writing. In the art of scripted political oratory, for example, no American—except, perhaps, for Abraham Lincoln—has ever surpassed the eloquence of Thomas Jefferson and Thomas Paine. Within the frame of an epistolary prose-poem, J. Hector St. John de Crèvecoeur's *Letters from an American Farmer* (1782) presents an enduring image of the New World Garden and of Americans as a "promiscuous breed" transplanted to this soil from diverse ethnocultural roots. No essay has ever captured the mood of popular American values, or expressed the American dream of achieving autonomous freedom through monetary success, more effectively than Ben Franklin's "Way to Wealth" (1758). Nor has any personal narrative touched the heart of American individualism more memorably than Franklin's *Autobiography*.

## LITERATURES OF COLONIAL HISTORY AND EARLY SETTLEMENT

Throughout the European colonies, settlers and visitors recognized the decisive importance of their encounter with America. Accordingly, they began from the first stages of contact to develop historical records of their experiences. Such regionally focused accounts include *The True History of the Conquest of New Spain* (1632), by Bernal Díaz del Castillo, a soldier who marched with Hernán Cortés into Mexico, and *The General History of Virginia, New England, and the Summer Isles* (1624), mostly attributed to English adventurer John Smith. Virginians Robert Beverley (in *The History and Present State of Virginia*, 1705) and William Byrd II (in *History of the Dividing Line*, composed 1728–1738) offered further perspectives on the unfolding of events in their region. Colonial histories were typically meant to justify, if not to glorify, conduct of the individuals or groups responsible for producing them. Their portrayal of Native Americans falling under European control through disease or force of arms must therefore be viewed with considerable skepticism. History is always someone's version of the story; and regrettably, no full-blown Indian chronicles could be written or preserved within the thirteen English colonies. Hints about how indigenous peoples in British America viewed colonial history must be gleaned from recorded samples of Indian eloquence, such as Chief Powhatan's "Speech to Captain John Smith" (1609)

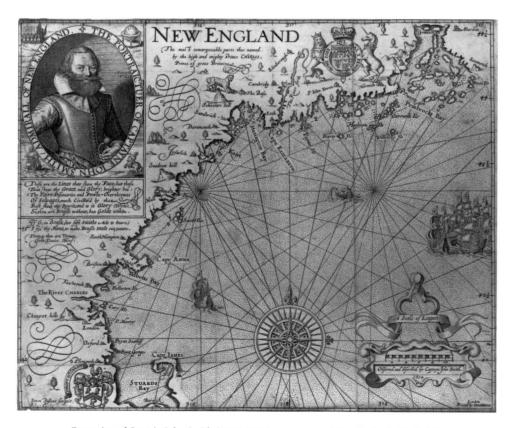

Engraving of Captain John Smith (1580–1631) over a map of New England. (© *Corbis*)

in Virginia or from remarks embedded in writings by sympathetic colonists, including Roger Williams's *A Key into the Language of America* (1643).

New England colonists began the venture of migration with a powerful sense of mission, a heightened desire to understand how their deeds fulfilled God's purposes within the drama of world history that began a new phase at the Protestant Reformation. Thus, they had scarcely stepped off the *Mayflower* and other ships of passage when they began to think about recording and interpreting the history of their enterprise. Just as Puritans scrutinized their souls individually for signs that they had been "elected" by God for eternal salvation, so also they sought evidence of divine favor or disfavor toward their covenanted community of "saints." For several generations, leading toward grand works such as Cotton Mather's *Magnalia Christi Americana* (1702) and Jonathan Edwards's *A History of the Work of Redemption* (1774), Puritan historians probed the meaning of New England's experiment and inquired how well this new chosen people was carrying out God's will.

William Bradford, for example, in telling the famous story of the Pilgrims who landed at Cape Cod in 1620, took pains to identify whatever instances of "special providence" emerged from his recollections of the community's history (*Of Plymouth Plantation, 1620–1647*). Particularly in earlier sections of his narrative, Bradford finds many encouraging instances of providential intervention on behalf of the holy fellowship. Surviving the perils of the first winter, meeting friendly Indians who happened to speak English, receiving rain just in time to water a rich harvest of corn—in such events Bradford saw visible evidence that Plymouth's struggle had been blessed by God.

Nowhere in the history does Bradford seem more confident that the Pilgrims were fulfilling a sacred destiny than in his account of the first landing at Provincetown. Writing ten years after the fact, he underscores the extreme vulnerability of this "poor people" who, having survived a perilous sea voyage, now faced the onset of winter in a bleak northern climate with no standing shelter or solace from friends. Yet Bradford pictures them falling on their knees with joy and gratitude upon reaching American soil. Cape Cod scarcely seemed then to offer Pilgrims the material abundance, the biblical milk and honey, of a new Promised Land. But if the ideal of Puritan faith was to live solely upon the divine Word, New Plymouth never came closer to realizing its vocation as a sanctified community than at this moment when

its people had nothing to rely upon or to "sustain them but the Spirit of God and His grace." Although these latter-day Pilgrims could not "go up to the top of [Mount] Pisgah to view from this wilderness a more goodly country to feed their hopes" as Moses had done in the Old Testament, Bradford shows them glimpsing their land of promise inwardly and imaginatively, at the very summit of their faith. His rhetoric magnifies both the occasion and his sense of audience. Writing in the third person, the aging author declares that as he looks back on these events, he stands "half amazed at this poor people's . . . condition." Bradford himself began the process of mythologizing these "Founding Fathers" as heroic models of faith and endurance.

Ironically, Bradford's confidence in the godly destiny of Plymouth began to fade as the community's material and economic condition gradually improved. With greater prosperity came greater interest in personal profit, the transformation of companionable Pilgrims into Yankee individualists, and the dispersal of Plymouth's godly fellowship into new settlements scattered throughout the region. *Of Plymouth Plantation* embodies the author's struggle to make sense of such developments and of social changes he associated with startling outbreaks of iniquity within the colony. Apparently unable to discern what providential meaning these events might bear, Bradford left his history incomplete. Before the work trails off, it shows the author dutifully recording a number of episodes that betray his final uncertainty and his elegiac sense of the community he once served as leader.

Contesting colonizers tell radically different versions of the same story. Beyond simply describing a given territory, colonial histories often set forth rival claims of possession. So it is fascinating to compare Bradford's sober history with the riotously exuberant, mock-epic interpretation of events supplied by Thomas Morton in his *New English Canaan* (1637). Both Morton and Bradford portray Massachusetts as a land of great promise for the future, although only Morton highlights its physical attractions. Both support the idea of colonization and reflect English cultural values. And although Morton displays much less piety than Bradford, both writers invoke biblical analogies that link New England to what Morton calls "the Israelites' Canaan."

But the two accounts clash in every other respect. As a free-spirited entrepreneur who was nominally Anglican but actually something of a neo-pagan hedonist, Morton aroused deep suspicion among Pilgrims and Puritans. Bradford portrays him as a dissolute troublemaker. *Of*

*Plymouth Plantation* deplores Morton's erection of a maypole, at his nearby settlement of Merry-mount, that becomes the focal point for orgiastic revelry. For Bradford, Morton epitomizes not only the resurgence of pagan licentiousness and idolatry, but also the lawless freedom of the woods. Such wild energy threatened to dissolve the godly order of Plymouth's community.

Morton, in turns, tells his story to defame the Pilgrims as bigoted fanatics who envy his success in the fur trade. According to *New English Canaan*, not Thomas Morton but these humorless "Separatists" and "cruel Schismaticks" are the real deviants whose behavior should trouble proponents of English colonization. In this account, the Pilgrim fathers come across as priggish busybodies. They take ludicrous measures to persecute Morton, Native Americans, and anyone else deemed unsettling to their repressive regime. Just as Bradford makes Morton an archvillain of his history, so also Morton enjoys developing a mischievous counternarrative in which the Separatists—including their un-Puritan military leader, Myles Standish, lampooned as Captain Shrimp—can be demolished through satire.

## COLONIAL POETRY

In several English colonies, but particularly in New England, writing or reading poetry was a popular pastime for settlers from all walks of life. Poetry was considered a suitable mass medium for instruction, edification, and entertainment. It may seem surprising to us that a long apocalyptic poem like Michael Wigglesworth's *The Day of Doom* (1662) not only attracted a phenomenal share of readers but was commonly committed to memory. Often set amid prose discourse in travel narratives, letters, histories, and other works, verse was likewise a familiar feature of almanacs and funeral broadsides. Plainly, most of this casual versifying does not qualify as literary art. Yet the era produced several accomplished poets whose work still draws attention today. New Englanders Anne Bradstreet and Edward Taylor are the leading examples. Widespread literacy, combined with the intensely verbal quality of the Puritan imagination, helped to encourage talents that were emerging in this region. Non-Puritan writers who continue to attract notice include Ebenezer Cooke, for his authorship of a humorous poem titled "The Sot-Weed Factor; or, a Voyage to Maryland, &c." (1708), about tobacco trading and plantation life; Richard Lewis, for his celebration of Maryland landscapes in "A Journey from Patapsco to Annapolis" (1730); and Phillis Wheatley, for poems such as "To the Right Honorable

William, Earl of Dartmouth" (1773) that subtly expose the contradiction between Anglo-America's love of egalitarian rhetoric and continued practice of chattel slavery.

For Edward Taylor, composing the 217 poems he eventually assembled in his *Preparatory Meditations* (composed 1682–1725) was an extension of his lifelong vocation as minister to the frontier community of Westfield, Massachusetts. Linked to sermons preached on the sacramental occasion of his celebrating the Lord's Supper, they reflect an interior process of meditation designed to relate scriptural texts to the state of one's soul. In seventeenth-century devotional life, meditation involved not only cogitation, but a disciplined effort to integrate intellect with the feelings and commitment of the heart. Taylor's poetic meditations, which remained unpublished until the modern era, display remarkable wit, exuberance, and artistry. Steeped in knowledge of sin but ultimately hopeful, they enact a representative soul's search for salvation. Taylor's sensuous metaphors and love of verbal play effectively belie stereotypes of Puritan gloom. So do accounts of finding his human nature raised to rapturous union with divinity, as exemplified by poems such as "The Experience" and "Meditation 8" within the first series of *Preparatory Meditations*.

Anne Bradstreet's acute awareness of her circumstance as a woman writer, demonstrated in her poetic "Prologue" to *The Tenth Muse Lately Sprung Up in America* (1650), is of particular interest to present-day readers. With *The Tenth Muse*, Bradstreet made history as the first colonist to publish a volume of poetry. For her long poem titled "Contemplations" (1678), Bradstreet also warrants recognition as the first poet to record a sustained, appreciative response to outdoor experience in British North America. Based on a solitary autumnal walk in the woods near her home in North Andover, Massachusetts, "Contemplations" expresses an untroubled fascination with the natural world that is rare in first-generation Puritan writing. As a spirited, passionate woman, Bradstreet also faced a continuing struggle to reconcile her love of people and things in this mortal world with her commitment to God's eternal realm of the spirit. This conflict, rendered more painful because of her deep affection for her husband and the eight children she eventually bore, is reflected in poems such as "Upon the Burning of Our House" (dated 1666) and "The Flesh and the Spirit" (1678). Despite the tensions and quarrel with God expressed in these poems, Bradstreet should not be misconstrued as a modern rebel against Puritan orthodoxy. Puritans of her day accepted such conflicted feeling as a recurring, inevitable part of the ongoing conversion process. Yet some of Bradstreet's poems do address secular subjects or reflect a more worldly orientation. Thus, "Before the Birth of One of Her Children" (1678) gives startling voice to an expectant mother's fear, envy, and unspiritual yearning to survive death in the earthly memory of others.

## WRITING NEW WORLD NATURE

At first, English settlers did not expect to find their cultural identity seriously changed by their encounter with North America's physical environment. They planned instead to refashion this land into a better England, remaining thoroughly English in the process. But as colonists pressed farther into the great woods and deepened their experience of the New World environment, the land itself began to reshape their group identity. Was this land a frightening "wilderness," as it first appeared to William Bradford while gazing on the shores of Cape Cod in November? Or was it a "garden" of superabundant promise tilled by freeholding farmers, as typically imaged in writings by St. John de Crèvecoeur and Thomas Jefferson? The body of colonial American writing reveals a broader urge to assimilate both perspectives into an original impression of nature. These polar images—of threatening but vital wilderness on the one hand, of cultivated prosperity yielding paradise on the other—suffuse the rhetoric of early American writing. They can even compete for dominance within the same text by a given author.

William Bartram's *Travels* is a case in point. As a bona fide though largely self-educated naturalist from Philadelphia with scientific expertise in botany, Bartram could not overlook the many troubling, threatening faces of untamed nature he encountered while wandering through the South from 1773 to 1777. His gripping tales of danger, especially the near calamity he faces while canoeing among a brood of attacking alligators in East Florida, should destroy anyone's fantasy of the South as a semitropical paradise. Yet Bartram does not dwell on the predatory horror of "primitive nature." Instead, his work highlights the awestruck gratitude he feels at discovering the ordered, prodigal diversity of creation. Absorbed with wonder at observing crystal fountains and remarkable plants like the Venus fly trap, he is drawn to contemplate the sublime benevolence of a world that seems to him "a glorious apartment of the boundless palace of the sovereign Creator . . . furnished with an infinite variety of animated scenes, inexpressibly beautiful and pleasing."

Consistent with his Quaker spirituality, Bartram also insists on respecting the animal life of "the brute creation."

Amazingly, he denounces the needless destruction even of hawks, rattlesnakes, and bears. Bartram traces his own education in this wider compassion to an episode that occurred while he was ascending Florida's south Musquito River in a canoe. After a hunter in his party thoughtlessly shoots a bear and then destroys the dam's cub as well, Bartram experiences a shock of distress—along with shame over his own complicity with the deed. This episode becomes a defining moment in the *Travels.* Comparable to the personal epiphanies featured in conversion narratives, it exposes for Bartram the heart of all ethical compassion. Typically, humans assume they enjoy an absolute sovereignty over nature. Bartram, however, offers intimations of that rarer outlook in which humans stand more nearly as kin beside nonhumans within the divine continuity of creation.

## VERSIONS OF PERSONAL NARRATIVE

Throughout the colonial period and beyond, Americans sought with peculiar urgency to locate and emulate those who might serve as models for their own lives. Fascination with the life stories of others became all the more pronounced in the New World as fresh avenues of social mobility and career choice emerged. But new opportunities for self-definition also produced new anxieties. How was a person to find his or her own way to success in a land without longstanding social institutions or traditions?

In his classic *Autobiography*, Ben Franklin shows how. The aim of this personal narrative is not self-expression or deep introspection, but the creation of a model that others could imitate on the way to shaping their own American lives. Addressed ostensibly to the author's son yet plainly responding to popular demand, this first-person testimony declares its rationale of utility at the outset. Franklin wants to tell others how he achieved celebrity, happiness, and affluence because they may find his experience "fit to be imitated." He artfully omits embarrassing details of his private life to portray the public self most relevant to needs of his eighteenth-century audience. Thus, without pretense of modesty, the author idealizes his own story so as to offer readers a secular counterpart of the saint's life and conversion narrative. Instead of passing from sin to salvation, however, Franklin describes his movement from poverty to wealth. He insists that the way to wealth is not an end in itself, but the means to building a self-reliant character empowered to perform public service. Yet the *Autobiography* shows that to achieve financial success in the first place, enterprising Americans must cultivate an appetite for self-serving individualism. Industry, frugality, ingenuity, and adaptability—all these traits paved Franklin's way to wealth. But the *Autobiography* suggests that some lucky breaks and shrewd business deals also smoothed the way.

For Puritan New Englanders, conversion narratives were the spiritual equivalent of Franklin's success story. From the standpoint of spiritual autobiography, though, success meant discovering in one's personal experience signs that divine grace had transformed the heart. Prominent clergymen wrote and sometimes published spiritual autobiographies as models of edification. But since personal testimony of conversion, or regeneration of the soul, was often required for full church membership, ordinary colonists—including many women—also recorded stylized narratives contrasting the older, depraved self with their newly "saved," authorial identity. Impelled by "a motion of love" to show how God's "tender mercies" operated in his life and throughout creation, New Jersey Quaker John Woolman offered another kind of spiritual autobiography in his *Journal of John Woolman* (1774). Other noteworthy personal narratives from the general period include *Some Account of the Fore-Part of the Life of Elizabeth Ashbridge* (1774), by an independent-minded woman who converted to Quakerism; *A Short Narrative of My Life* (dated 1768) by the Mohegan Indian, Samson Occom; and *The Interesting Narrative of the Life of Olaudah Equiano* (1789), by a former slave born in what would become Nigeria.

## POLITICAL WRITING ON THE VERGE OF REVOLUTION

Politically, the late colonial period was a time of heated controversy and high emotion. Yet in the spirit of that philosophic movement known first in Europe as the Enlightenment, it was also a time of surpassing confidence in the power of reason and in humankind's capacity to improve the existing social order. Both tendencies can be discerned in polemical pamphlets such as Thomas Paine's *Common Sense* (1776) and other incendiary writings by patriots, as well as in the many opposition pamphlets penned by Loyalists. Intense feeling also blends with reasoned argument in the era's most renowned work of political rhetoric, the Declaration of Independence. Youthful Virginian Thomas Jefferson, already known as a gifted rhetorician, became principal author of the draft presented to the Second Continental Congress. By virtue of his artistry, this document came not only to describe but also in some measure to create the governing ideology and political mythology of the United States.

The Declaration begins on a calmly majestic, authoritative note—even though the colonies at this stage possessed no legal authority in the world community. Nor did they possess anything like a centrally united government, despite the voice of unified assurance created by Jefferson's rhetoric. But instead of claiming authority through legal precedent or a legitimacy conferred by privilege from above, the Declaration appeals to the ground-up notion of a social contract formed among the nation's people. Thus influenced by philosophic theories derived from John Locke and others, Jefferson claims that governments derive "their just powers from the consent of the governed." This claim is founded, in turn, on the natural rights precept "that all men are created equal," at least for purposes of governance, an assertion supported by the "self evident" strength of human reason as evidenced directly in "the laws of nature and of nature's God." That the collective identity of a new nation could be based not on a common ethnic heritage or class grievances but on the dignity and liberty of individual citizens was indeed a revolutionary concept.

Despite the Declaration's reasoned respect for "the opinions of mankind," its argument is also driven by emotion. Jefferson's draft conveys poignant feelings of betrayal that Britain, by its abuse of America, had destroyed that vision of cross-oceanic harmony in which "we might have been a free and a great people together." The body of the Declaration also features a long, passionate denunciation of King George III. As though ritually exorcising the demon of liberty, Jefferson recites the litany of crimes committed by a British monarch he declines to name. Implausibly but significantly, he even tries to blame this mythologized source of all oppression for sponsoring and sustaining the American slave trade. By supporting that "execrable commerce" in which Africans are bought and sold, George stands guilty of waging "cruel war against human nature itself, violating its most sacred rights of life and liberty in the persons of a distant people who never offended him, captivating and carrying them into slavery in another hemisphere."

As Phillis Wheatley's poetry reminds us, colonial rhetoric of political protest often invoked the bondage metaphor, denouncing Britain's abuse of the colonies as a plot to "enslave" them. This myth of an America in chains appears not only in political tracts but also in sermons of the period. Yet pressing the metaphor to its logical conclusion would expose the disparity between egalitarian ideals championed by patriot leaders and their typical willingness to preserve chattel slavery. If the colonies succeeded in winning independence after issuing a declaration that carried a denunciation of the slave trade, they could no longer blame George if they subsequently failed to demand abolition—or, at least, major restrictions on slave commerce. No wonder Congress insisted on expunging Jefferson's slave rhetoric from the Declaration—a minor literary revision with momentous consequences for the nation's future. As a southern slaveholder who retains notoriety for his involvements with the "peculiar institution," Jefferson was fully enmeshed in these inconsistencies, despite his flashes of recognition that slavery was a tragic, unsupportable evil. Finally, however, the contradictory assertions written into the draft Declaration reveal something crucial not only about Jefferson's personal ambivalence, but also about ideological tensions in the national psyche that have yet to be resolved.

[*See also* Bradstreet, Anne; Crèvecoeur, J. Hector St. John de; Edwards, Jonathan; Mather, Cotton; Nature Writing: Poetry; Nature Writing: Prose; Poetess in American Literature, The; Puritanism: The Sense of an Unending; Taylor, Edward; *and* Wheatley, Phillis.]

## FURTHER READING

Andrews, William L., ed. *Journeys in New Worlds: Early American Women's Narratives.* Madison, Wis., 1990. Presents four revealing narratives, with pertinent introductions and annotations.

Bercovitch, Sacvan. *Puritan Origins of the American Self.* New Haven, Conn., 1975. Although this book has been challenged by recent attempts to minimize the standing of colonial New England within American Studies, it presents a seminal modern claim for the larger, enduring significance of Puritan thought and rhetorical expression.

Bercovitch, Sacvan, ed. *The Cambridge History of American Literature.* Vol. 1, 1590–1820. New York, 1994. Worth consulting for fuller treatment of topics such as "British-American Belles Lettres" (by David S. Shields) and "The American Enlightenment" (by Robert A. Ferguson).

Colacurcio, Michael J. *Doctrine and Difference: Essays in the Literature of New England.* New York, 1997. An intellectually challenging commentary whose opening chapters (together with an important statement in the Introduction) demonstrate the continuing vitality of studies focused on Puritan New England.

Daly, Robert. "William Bradford's Vision of History." *American Literature* 44 (January 1973): 557–569. A lucid account of ways in which *Of Plymouth Plantation,* through successive annals and narrative passages, reflects Bradford's attempt to interpret history.

Davis, Richard Beale. *Literature and Society in Early Virginia, 1608–1840.* Baton Rouge, La., 1973. Together with Davis's magisterial study *Intellectual Life in the Colonial South, 1585–1763* (Knoxville, Tenn., 1978), this authoritative work gives attention to England's southern or staple colonies, balancing regionally the numerous accounts of colonial New England.

Delbanco, Andrew. *The Puritan Ordeal.* Cambridge, Mass., 1989. A compelling reassessment of New England culture that focuses on the struggles and anxieties of first-generation Puritans as immigrants to America.

Elliott, Emory, ed. *Columbia Literary History of the United States.* New York, 1988. Within the limits of a single-volume collection of essays, Part One of this work provides a reliable summary of categories pertinent to understanding the literary history of the era.

Emerson, Everett, ed. *Major Writers of Early American Literature.* Madison, Wis., 1972. Remains an admirably clear and informative introduction to nine key figures, although its findings must now be supplemented with more recent commentary.

Franklin, Wayne. *Discoverers, Explorers, Settlers: The Diligent Writers of Early America.* Chicago, 1979. The leading treatment of travel and settlement narratives, especially those written in English.

Gittleman, Edwin. "Jefferson's 'Slave Narrative': The Declaration of Independence as a Literary Text." *Early American Literature* 8 (Winter 1974): 239–256. Highlights the significance of the slavery grievance in Jefferson's Declaration.

Greenblatt, Stephen, ed. *New World Encounters.* Berkeley, Calif., 1993. A collection of essays suggesting the variety of cross-cultural colonial encounters beyond British territories and throughout the Americas.

Gunn, Giles, ed. *Early American Writing.* New York, 1994. One of the more useful and compact period anthologies available, at least for its representation of relevant prose writings from diverse regions.

Gura, Philip F. *The Crossroads of American History and Literature.* University Park, Pa., 1996. The opening chapter, presenting one assessment of how literary and historical study of the colonial period changed in the late twentieth century, is particularly noteworthy.

Hammond, Jeffrey A. *The American Puritan Elegy: A Literary and Cultural Study.* New York, 2000. A commentary valuable not only for its appreciation of a specific, commonly scorned subgenre, but also for its clarification of cultural attitudes different from those that twentieth-century readers assume as normative.

Harris, Sharon M., ed. *American Women Writers to 1800*. New York, 1996. A topically arranged collection of primary sources.

Heimert, Alan, and Andrew Delbanco, eds. *The Puritans in America: A Narrative Anthology*. Cambridge, Mass., 1985. A topically organized collection of primary sources, with illuminating headnotes.

Lemay, J. A. Leo, ed. *Essays in Early Virginia Literature Honoring Richard Beale Davis*. New York, 1977. A collection useful for its treatments of figures such as John Smith, Robert Beverley, William Byrd, and Samuel Davies.

Levernier, James A., and Douglas R. Wilmes, eds. *American Writers before 1800: A Biographical and Critical Dictionary*. 3 vols. Westport, Conn., 1983. With entries covering 786 writers, this essential reference work includes familiar figures but also supplies rare information about lesser-known writers from the period.

Meserole, Harrison T. *American Poetry of the Seventeenth Century*. University Park, Pa., 1985. Admirably represents the abundance and range of colonial poetry. Particularly useful for extending awareness of writings produced by lesser-known figures.

Miller, Perry. *Errand into the Wilderness*. Cambridge, Mass., 1956. One of several classic volumes by Miller that remains in print, this work continues to offer a readable, stimulating account of the intellectual suppositions and aspirations that colonists brought to New England.

Mulford, Carla, ed. *Teaching the Literatures of Early America*. New York, 1999. With contributions from several teacher-scholars, presents a bibliographically supported overview of current topics, approaches, and debates pertaining to early American studies. Favors transatlantic comparative and revisionist approaches.

Mulford, Carla, and David S. Shields, eds. *Finding Colonial Americas: Essays Honoring J. A. Leo Lemay*. Newark, Del., 2001. Stressing comparative historical contexts, the assessments in this volume deal with Benjamin Franklin's world and a range of other topics related to British North America.

Shea, Daniel B. *Spiritual Autobiography in Early America*. Madison, Wis., 1988. First published in 1968. A readable, illuminating account of a significant mode of expression.

Wills, Gary. *Inventing America: Jefferson's Declaration of Independence*. New York, 1979. A readable, provocative account of the Declaration's character and intellectual context.

# CONFESSIONAL POETRY

*by Philip Hobsbaum*

Confessional poetry is verse in which the author describes parts of his or her life that would not ordinarily be in the public domain. The prime characteristic is the reduction of distance between the persona displayed in a poem and the author who writes it.

This genre of verse derives from the romantics, who put a high premium on the exploration of personal feeling. Poems such as "Nutting" by William Wordsworth, "Dejection" by Samuel Taylor Coleridge, and "Ode to the West Wind"—"I fall upon the thorns of life! I bleed"—by Percy Bysshe Shelley would seem to be precursors. More immediately, confessional poetry relates to "The Love Song of J. Alfred Prufrock" by T. S. Eliot and also "Hugh Selwyn Mauberley" and *The Pisan Cantos* by Ezra Pound, where intimate references to friends are worked into the verse:

> Lordly men are to earth o'ergiven
>   these the companions:
> Fordie that wrote of giants
> and William who dreamed of nobility
>   and Jim the comedian singing:
>     "Blarrney castle me darlin'
>     you're nothing now but a StOWne."
>
> (Canto LXXIV)

It would be an astute reader who could identify the figures to whom this refers as, respectively, Ford Madox Ford, W. B. Yeats, and James Joyce.

## ROBERT LOWELL

The term "confessional poetry" first appeared in a review by M. L. Rosenthal of *Life Studies* (1959) by Robert Lowell (1917–1977), a poet who is regarded as being central to any discussion of this school. Although he began with elaborately formal verse, Lowell in that book broke new boundaries. This critique by Rosenthal, recognizing the breakthrough, was published in *The Nation*, 19 September 1959, and has been frequently reprinted. The reviewer says, "Lowell's effort is the natural outgrowth of the modern emphasis on the 'I' as the crucial poetic symbol." Rosenthal points out that the speaker in Lowell's poems is unequivocally himself. When that speaker attacks his father for lacking manhood or refers to his breaking marriage, we are in no doubt that it is Lowell's own father who is under attack and Lowell's own marriage that is in reference: "you turn your back. / Sleepless you hold / your pillows to your hollows like a child" ("Man and Wife").

One advantage in this breaking down of distance is access to a mode of speech more specific and colloquial than was usual in earlier poetry. The showpiece of the whole school is perhaps "Skunk Hour," again by Lowell. This shows the poet in the unbecoming role of voyeur:

> One dark night,
> My Tudor Ford climbed the hill's skull,
> I watched for love cars. Lights turned down,
> they lay together, hull to hull,
> where the graveyard shelves on the town. . . .
> My mind's not right.

The ellipsis here is that of the poet. A frankness of statement is associated with a degree of precision—"my Tudor Ford"—that acts as a guarantee of authenticity. The admission that the speaker of the poem may in fact be deranged is especially striking. However, though authentic, the narration is slanted:

> A car radio bleats,
> "Love, O careless Love . . . " I hear
> my ill-spirit sob in each blood cell,
> as if my hand were at its throat. . . .
> I myself am hell,
> nobody's here—

Once more, the ellipses are those of the poet. "Love, O Careless Love" was a popular song of the time. "I myself am hell" is part of a speech spoken by Satan in *Paradise Lost* by John Milton. The poet is visualizing himself as a fallen angel, and the implication is that love has brought him to this pass. There is no attempt to disguise the fact that the speaker is Lowell, even though it is Lowell seen by himself in a theatrically gloomy guise. To that extent, the poem is spoken in character. Even so, the biographical facts are well known.

Lowell was a victim of cyclothymia, or manic-depressive illness. The symptoms include violent mood swings, hyperactivity, extreme verbosity, and pressure of speech. Lowell went through an annual cycle, rising to something of a climax in late summer, a season when he wrote most of his poems, going past that to a high peak involving grandiose behavior, followed by a descent into gloom and inactivity that took place in winter. What is remarkable is that Lowell regarded every aspect of his behavior as worth recording and, nearing the manic climax of the cycle, wrote like a poet inspired.

He was not an uncritical observer of his own conduct. This opened opportunities for various kinds of irony. Of his term of imprisonment—for refusing to serve in the armed forces during World War II—he wrote:

> These are the tranquillized Fifties,
> And I am forty. Ought I to regret my seedtime?
> I was a fire-breathing Catholic C.O.,
> and made my manic statement,
> telling off the state and president.
>
> ("Memories of West Street and Lepke")

"Seedtime" is an allusion to Wordsworth's great autobiographical poem *The Prelude*. The phrase "the tranquillized Fifties," describing the complacency of the United States a dozen or so years after the war, has passed into the language.

All this in fact happened. Lowell did indeed refuse the draft. He is not only dramatizing but mythologizing his own history because he thought it of importance. At the same time, he is looking back at his own youthful enthusiasm with a degree of adult disillusion, as though recognizing that his protest would have no effect upon the political outcome of the time.

The verse of *Life Studies* frequently rhymes and always has a firm rhythm that can be scanned. This is so even when superficially the author appears to be writing free verse:

> Father's death was abrupt and unprotesting.
> His vision was still twenty-twenty.
> After a morning of anxious, repetitive smiling,
> his last words to Mother were:
> "I feel awful."
>
> ("Terminal Days at Beverly Farms")

> In the grandiloquent lettering on Mother's coffin,
> Lowell had been misspelled LOVEL
> The corpse
> was wrapped like panetone in Italian tinfoil.
>
> ("Sailing Home from Rapallo")

"Panetone" is a dark and hard Italian bread. Some of the rhythmic authority is maintained by internal rhyming ("morning"/"awful") or by part-rhymes such as "Lovel"/"tinfoil." The meter is basically a three-stress beat capable of being pulled into a longer line, as with "After a morning of anxious, repetitive smiling," or compressed in such a way as to make the reader feel the meter is still proceeding beyond the bounds of the actual phrase vouchsafed—"The corpse . . . ," where ". . ." corresponds to the two light stresses and subsequent heavy stress of the anapestic foot in English meter.

### JOHN BERRYMAN

The skill and vision of Lowell put him at the head of the confessional school. However, he was not alone. A related impact was made by John Berryman (1914–1972). As had been the case with Lowell, Berryman first came before the public as a rhetorician, engaging in elaborate verse forms and distancing himself from his subject matter. He took on, for example, the persona of the earliest American woman poet, Anne Bradstreet. Admirers of his work were considerably surprised by *77 Dream Songs* (1964), a title deriving perhaps from a phrase in Eliot's poem "The Hollow Men." However, whereas Eliot took refuge in romantic reverie, Berryman's Dream Songs shove the actualities in our faces.

He does this by means of a persona, "Henry," who is patently the poet himself. This persona masquerades as a Negro minstrel; that is to say, a white man who has painted his face black for the purpose of entertaining the public. The persona is catechized through the Dream Songs—as used to happen in the singing troupe called the Kentucky Minstrels—by an interlocutor who in these poems represents death. This interlocutor addresses Henry as "Mr. Bones" but is himself sometimes so addressed. In his study of suicide, *The Savage God*, A. Alvarez said that the subject of the Dream Songs is mourning. Certainly a good many dead friends are evoked, and there is a central block of Dream Songs concerned with the alcoholic poet Delmore Schwartz. Berryman, himself an alcoholic, is additionally obsessed with his father, who committed suicide.

The following is extracted from a poem, "Henry's Confession," which may be found in the first batch of Dream Songs, those published in 1964:

> in a modesty of death I join my father
> who dared so long agone leave me.
> A bullet on a concrete stoop
> close by a smothering southern sea

spreadeagled on an island, by my knee.
—You is from hunger, Mr. Bones

(Dream Song 76)

It is a fact that Berryman's father, John Allyn Smith, shot himself dead at the back of the apartment building he inhabited with his family and was found by his wife, as John Haffenden, Berryman's biographer puts it, "lying in a spreadeagle fashion" (*The Life of John Berryman*, 1982). That is to say, he was sprawled out, not sitting down or in a sleeping posture. The name "Berryman" derives from a stepfather, and losing "Smith," the name the poet was born with, may have contributed to a wavering sense of his own personality.

The Dream Songs are a kind of modern equivalent to Shakespeare's sonnets. They are in three parts, rather than a sonnet's two, and are loosely related to the conceptual shape of the syllogism in logic. For example, in the Dream Song just cited, the first section states "Nothin very bad happen to me lately"; the second section—the one quoted—states "in a modesty of death I join my father"; and the third states "I saw nobody coming, so I went instead." The whole amounts to an exposition of stasis.

With some exceptions, each section of these poems consists of six lines. The third and sixth lines tend to be shorter than the others. Quite often the first line of a Dream Song has a feminine ending; that is to say the line ends on a heavy syllable followed by a light syllable, as in the word "lately."

As the Dream Songs proceed, Berryman engages in some astonishing feats of syntax. In an elegy for his friend, the much-feared critic Randall Jarrell, he writes:

Let Randall rest, whom your self-torturing
cannot restore one instant's good to, rest:
he's left us now.
The panic died and in the panic's dying
so did my old friend. I am headed west
also, also, somehow.

(Dream Song 90, op. posth., no. 13)

The apparent contortion of that initial sentence may be straightened out if we omit the second "rest," which is there by way of emphasis, and alter the word order to something like "Your self-torturing cannot restore one instant's good to Randall." However, in revising thus we are losing the intricate speech rhythm and indeed what may be styled as the characteristic tone of Berryman, which is something like a confidential signaling for attention—a huge presence in an intimately constricting room.

## SYLVIA PLATH

The confessional poets shared many points of subject matter and style—especially in the area of mourning—but there are variegations. Sylvia Plath (1932–1963) was a poetic generation younger than Lowell and Berryman, even though they lived on to lament her death. In her later work she learned from her elders, whom she greatly admired, and one thing she had learned was to place her personal predicament squarely in front of the reader. In fact, she projects her predicament with remarkable intensity.

The most famous of Plath's poems is an attack on her father called, with savage irony, "Daddy." He had apparently committed an unforgivable sin by dying when she was a child of eight. For this he is resurrected as a statue "in the freakish Atlantic," as an officer of the German air force with a "neat moustache," as a Nazi commandant "with a Meinkampf look," and as her errant husband, "the vampire who said he was you." This last is finally impaled by the villagers with a stake thrust into his "fat black heart," leaving his daughter exhausted and "through."

This would be a scream of hysteria were it not underpinned by an achieved technique, in part derived from a three-line stanza form, the triad or stepped verse, developed by William Carlos Williams and Elizabeth Bishop. In Plath's companion poem, "Lady Lazarus," the central figure dies every ten years and is resurrected. This is an allusion to Plath's childhood depression after her father's death, her suicide attempt at the age of twenty, and her final state of mind, which ended in suicide at the age of thirty:

I have done it again.
One year in every ten
I manage it—

A sort of walking miracle, my skin
Bright as a Nazi lampshade,
My right foot

A paperweight,
My face a featureless, fine
Jew linen.

Peel off the napkin
O my enemy.
Do I terrify?—

As with "Daddy," there is allusion here to Nazi death camps—where, in one notorious example, the skin of dead Jewish prisoners was made into lampshades. One may question whether the predicament of the author, who is so clearly her own persona, has earned the right to draw upon such sources. What has happened to her—her father's early death, her husband's adultery—is certainly serious. However, what happened to six million Jews at the hands of the Nazis is very much worse. A favorable critic could, however, reply that this is how life felt for the neurotic Sylvia Plath.

There can be little doubt that the last year of her life saw a state of clinical depression. In her very last poem, "Edge," Plath appears to be contemplating the murder of her two children. Everything appears to be at a slant. While she seems to be an authentic speaker, she is in fact highly biased. That does not alter the fact that her intensity captures the attention of the reader. She is iconic, gifted with a charismatic power of phrase. In "Tulips," which, perhaps, bears repeated frequentation more than those poems already quoted, the speaker is in a hospital, in bed. It, again, is a piece of biography.

After a violent quarrel with her husband, the poet Ted Hughes, Plath miscarried, had an inflamed appendix, and went to the hospital for an appendectomy. This afforded pabulum for a most remarkable poem. Here the author does not make use of the three-line stanza. As befits a calmer mood, the structure is that of seven-line stanzas, unrhymed, but with a steady five-stress beat that admits additional lightly stressed syllables. The poem, in form at least, is a sustained reproach to the world for bringing her tulips—red inducements drawing her out of a white world:

> The walls, also, seem to be warming themselves.
> The tulips should be behind bars like dangerous animals;
> They are opening like the mouth of some great African cat,
> And I am aware of my heart: it opens and closes
> Its bowl of red blooms out of sheer love of me.
> The water I taste is warm and salt, like the sea,
> And comes from a country far away as health.

That last line suggests the reason why Plath has to be taken seriously, as a major poet. She has the power to conflate unlike entities, to leap across conceptual boundaries, and to do all this within a formal structure that—while, in the more tempestuous poems, is bruised and shaken—never comes within any chance of collapse.

Plath is, however, not a good model. In order to write like her, it is not only necessary to feel but to have developed a considerable technique. This may be seen in the failure of several poems concerning her death composed, so to speak, in her wake:

> daddy you held me in the green rocker, read me the
> Sunday funnies, smoking your Chesterfields, blowing

> rings at the Dickeybird
> we fed him dandelions out of the yard in the
> summertime, dandelions still feel like Dickeybirds

*(Ellipsis*, November 1972)

## ANNE SEXTON

More literate, but also derivative, is "Sylvia's Death" by Anne Sexton (1928–1974). If Plath is the high priestess of the confessional school, Sexton is certainly its lady-in-waiting:

> O Sylvia, Sylvia
> with a dead box of stones and spoons,
>
> with two children, two meteors
> wandering loose in the tiny playroom,
>
> with your mouth into the sheet,
> into the roofbeam, into the dumb prayer,
>
> (Sylvia, Sylvia
> where did you go
> after you wrote me
> from Devonshire
> about raising potatoes
> and keeping bees?)

Sexton appeared before Plath did on the poetry scene. Their initial collections, *To Bedlam and Part Way Back* and *Colossus*, both came out in 1960, but Sexton was, well before that time, an object of Plath's envy (Plath, *Journals*, pp. 475, 483–484). Sexton's work had taken off in 1957, soon after she joined the creative writing class run by John Holmes at the Boston Center for Adult Education, and had been immediately published in *The New Yorker*, *Harper's* magazine, and other leading periodicals of the day. Yet, in Sexton's later poetry, the reliance on Plath's texts is obvious. Sexton has "two children, two meteors," but Plath has "You hand me two children, two roses" ("Kindness"). Sexton has "with a dead box of stones and spoons," but Plath has "this clean wood box / Square as a chair" ("The Arrival of the Bee-Box"). Sexton has "with your mouth into the sheet"; Plath has "They have propped my head between the pillow and the sheet-cuff" ("Tulips").

One may feel this particular mode was on the way, long before this lament. An early poem of Sexton is "Music Swims Back to Me," but we do not feel the control in this that may be sensed in its main influence, Robert Lowell:

> Wait Mister. Which way is home?
> They turned the light out
> and the dark is moving in the corner.
> There are no sign posts in this room,

four ladies, over eighty,
in diapers every one of them.
La la la, Oh music swims back to me
and I can feel the tune they played
the night they left me
in this private institution on a hill.

The last line is plain prose, the free verse is next door to unscannable, and there is a tone of self-pity alien to the ironic detachment of Lowell and the self-dramatization of Plath.

The New Zealand poet Fleur Adcock left Sexton out of her well nigh definitive *Faber Book of 20th Century Women's Poetry* because she found her "repellently self-indulgent." Looking even at Sexton's better poems, it is hard not to feel some justice in that severe comment: "I, who chose two times / to kill myself, had said your nickname / the mewling months when you first came" ("The Double Image"); "Father, this year's jinx rides us apart / where you followed our mother to her cold slumber; / a second shock boiling its stone to your heart" ("All My Pretty Ones"). The allusions to Shakespeare—"music swims back to me," "all my pretty ones"—seem not to have earned their position in her verse. Yet Sexton has her positive critics. Maxine Kumin, in an introduction to the *Collected Poems* (1981), tells us of what we had no doubt, that the stuff of the poet's life was in her poems. But she also claims that Sexton's work "evokes in the reader that sought-after shiver of recognition."

### MAXINE KUMIN

Maxine Kumin (1925– ) was a classmate of Sexton's in the Holmes creative writing seminar. There is a force in Sexton's poems that those of Kumin may seem to lack, but the advantage this latter poet has is a sense of humor. While omitting Sexton altogether, Fleur Adcock included in her anthology such likable poems of Kumin's as "In the Root Cellar" and, here, "The Retrieval System":

It begins with my dog, now dead, who
    all his long life
carried about in his head the brown
    eyes of my father,
keen, loving, accepting,
    sorrowful, whatever;
they were Daddy's all right, handed
    on, except

Maxine Kumin. (© *Bettmann/Corbis*)

for their phosphorescent gleam tunneling the night
which I have to concede was a separate gift.

Perhaps the final line lets down the stanza with rhythmic flatness where one might hope for an ictus, a lift. Nevertheless, the apparent nonchalance is prevented from falling into bathos by a pattern of internal rhymes and faintly heard pararhymes at the line endings.

Kumin is not, however, always so genial. The American father has had a hard time at the hands of Lowell, Berryman, and Plath, and at times Kumin is no exception:

Sundays my father
hairs sprouting out of
the v of his pajamas
took in the sitdowns
picket lines Pinkertons
Bundists lend-lease
under his moustache.

("The New York Times")

As is usual with confessional poetry, this has the virtues of specificity, and that specificity is not to the advantage of the poem's subject. It would not have been to Father's advantage, either, had he come down to breakfast in full evening dress. Perhaps the answer, sartorially and otherwise, would have been to adopt a happy medium. But this is the last attitude one is likely to find in a confessional poem:

these are the dream machines
the dream machines
they put black ants in your bed
silverfish in your ears
they raise your father's corpse
they stick his bones in your sleep
or his stem or all thirty-six
of his stainless steel teeth
they line them up
like the best orchestra seats.

("The Nightmare Factory")

Given Kumin's predilection in her poems elsewhere for areas of the body not hitherto usually alluded to in verse, it is fairly easy to infer what the "stem" stands for. Yet this very poem, like others of the confessional school that could be cited, is an emergence from verses of the late Victorian and indeed decadent 1890s period: "We are the music-makers, / And we are the dreamers of dreams" (A. W. E. O'Shaughnessy, "Ode"). So a good deal of such writing is not so much modern as harking back to a post-romantic pattern and adapting it to the pain and sorrow that are the pabulum of certain writers in more modern times: "These are the tranquillized Fifties...."

### DIANE WAKOSKI

The utterance of such major writers as Lowell and Plath made it easy for lesser poets to climb on the bandwagon. Such poets are "lesser" because they have imperfectly learned their craft. This results from education—missing, in the case of Sexton; incompletely absorbed, one may feel, in the case of Diane Wakoski (1937– ). On paper, she is formidable. Since 1962 she has published more than twenty collections of verse and more than forty books as a total. She is one of the few poets who has ever been able to support herself by public readings, in her prime giving between fifty and eighty a year.

This may afford a clue. There seems, at first sight, little in the way of art in such a poem as "The Father of My Country." It appears to be very much in the wake of the father poems voiced by Lowell and Plath, though nearer even than they to naked autobiography:

> My father;
> have you ever heard me speak of him? I seldom
> do. But I had a father,
> and he had military origins—or my origins from
> him
> are military,
> militant. That is, I remember him only in uniform. But of
> the navy,
> 30 years a chief petty officer,
> Always away from home.

So it is not a surprise to find, in various biographical accounts of Wakoski, that her father, a military man, deserted the family early on and visited only occasionally. The lines in verse above improve only marginally upon this flat prose account. In terms of meter, it is hard to find why some lines are longer than others. There seems to be no ascertainable rhythmic pattern.

What the layout most suggests is the lineation, be it prose or verse, likely to be adopted by an actor. The variegation of length in line will be readily understandable if we take it to be an actor's arrangement for a dramatic reading. Though in subject matter Wakoski finds herself a member of the confessional school, as regards her career she is a performance poet *en plein*. The art is not to elicit

meaning from a poem but, through histrionic use of voice and gesture, to drive it in:

> my father was not in the telephone book
> in my city;
> my father was not sleeping with my mother
> at home;
> my father did not care if I studied the
> piano;
> my father did not care what
> I did;
> and I thought my father was handsome and I loved him and
> I wondered
> why
> he left me alone so much,
> so many years
> in fact, but
> my father made me what I am
> a lonely woman.

From this point of view, Wakoski seems to be an exponent in a mixed genre.

### W. D. SNODGRASS

At the other extreme is W. D. Snodgrass (1926– ). He is formal, a master of variegated meters, a writer of considerable detachment—who nevertheless can employ distance as a device to evoke response from his reader. Here the voice emerges from the poetry. If the persona is ill, it is not with the almost punitive force with which Plath excoriates us. A kind of stoicism on the part of the poet prevents us from feeling guilty:

> From stainless steel basins of water
> They brought warm cloths and they washed me,
> From spun aluminium bowls, cold Zephiran
> sponges, fuming:
> Gripped in the dead yellow glove, a bright straight razor
> Inched on my stomach, down my groin,
> Paring the brown hair off. They left me
> White as a child, not frightened. I was not
> Ashamed. They clothed me, then,
> In the thin loose, light, white garments,
> The delicate sandals of poor Pierrot,
> A schoolgirl first offering her sacrament.

("The Operation")

This is witty; learned, even—it was at Zephyrum, a promontory of Cyprus, that Arsinoe, mother of Aesculapius, the god of medicine, made an offering of her hair to Venus, goddess of love. So, in one phrase, "Zephiran sponges," the author relates the shaving of the hair about his genital regions to love, medicine, and sacrifice, all in verse whose trisyllabic pattern of feet seems to associate it with the masters of classical Greek poetry.

Central to the work of Snodgrass is a sequence of poems concerned with a broken marriage. It is called "Heart's Needle," after a statement in an Irish legend: the loss of "an only daughter is the needle of the heart." This, again, is propounded with a degree of distance, in a series of what seem to be epistles addressed to a small daughter. It is separation seen from the father's point of view. The very control manifested by the verse, owing as much to Hardy as to Lowell, renders that pain of separation more and not less poignant than if it had been dealt with more directly:

> Now that it's turning Fall,
>  we go to take our walk
>   among municipal
> flowers, to steal one off its stalk,
>   to try and talk.
>
> We huff like windy giants
>  scattering with our breath
>   gray-headed dandelions;
> Spring is the cold wind's aftermath.
>  The poet saith.
>
> But the asters, too, are gray,
>  ghost-gray. Last night's cold
>   is sending on their way
> petunias and dwarf marigold,
>   hunched sick and old.

It is as though the poet needs this discipline of form—full rhyme, meter that is quasi-syllabic—to hold his emotion in communicable state. The sequence itself suggests that he is old to be a father. The season throughout is cold; if not winter, then certainly inhospitable autumn and delayed spring.

At one point he compares himself to a fox, captured but newly escaped, who has gnawed through his foot and left that part of his anatomy in a trap. The comparison is like and not like; we resemble and do not resemble the animals:

> Of all things, only we
> have power to choose that we should die;
> nothing else is free
> in this world to refuse it. Yet I,
> who say this, could not raise
> myself from bed how many days
> to the thieving world. Child, I have another wife,
>  another child. We try to choose our life.

Snodgrass is the poet of authoritative understatement. He shows the range that the term "confessional poetry"

can occupy. Thematically there is a reduction of distance between author and reader in this sense; we need have no doubt that what the author describes actually happened. Yet the mode of narration keeps the reader to some extent apart: there is a code in the formal meters, the patterned rhymes, the grave deliberation of tone.

## CONCLUSION

To that extent, the term "confessional poetry" may seem arbitrary. Fleur Adcock, also a divorcée, has a poem similar to this called "For a Five Year Old": "Your gentleness is moulded still by words / From me, who have trapped mice and shot wild birds, / From me, who drowned your kittens" (*Tigers*, 1967). Yet nobody has enrolled Adcock among the confessionals. Nearer home, Adrienne Rich may at the time have raised eyebrows with her nakedly frank "Twenty-One Love Poems" (1976) addressed to another woman. She, however, would not be identified with these others. To that extent, the term "confessional" may seem almost dispensable.

Yet the characteristics these poets maintain in common are quite apparent. There is a tendency toward the extreme in imagery, a following of the gradations of the speaking voice, a willingness to disclose that which had hitherto been kept private, a concern with breaking marriages, deviant parents, mental as well as physical sickness, death, mourning—inescapable mourning, as much for one's own deranged self as for those others one has lost. These points may be rammed home if the truth is told that, of the seven poets discussed in detail here, three—Berryman, Plath, and Sexton—committed suicide, Lowell underwent several mental breakdowns, and of the others, Wakoski and Snodgrass were divorced. Of course, such events as these have happened to others. It is part of the breakdown of family life in the twentieth century. The strange distinction of these poets, however, is to treat such matters as raw material for their art. At its worst, confessional poetry is a therapy that thrusts private experience upon an unwilling reader. At its best, as in Lowell's *Life Studies*, it is a way of creating character so as to inform the trauma of the past with understanding and, sometimes, compassion.

[*See also* Berryman, John; Lowell, Robert; Plath, Sylvia; *and* Sexton, Anne.]

## WORKS

John Berryman, *The Dream Songs* (1969)
Maxine Kumin, *The Nightmare Factory* (1970)
Robert Lowell, *Life Studies* (1959)

Sylvia Plath, *The Collected Poems*, edited by Ted Hughes (1981)

Anne Sexton, *The Complete Poems*, edited by Maxine Kumin (1981)

W. D. Snodgrass, *Selected Poems 1957–1987* (1987)

Diane Wakoski, *Inside the Blood Factory* (1968)

## FURTHER READING

### GENERAL

Alvarez, A. *The Savage God: A Study of Suicide.* London, 1971; New York, 1972. Personalized but readable account of suicide and literature (not suicide in literature) with especial relationship to Sylvia Plath.

Dodsworth, Martin, ed. *The Survival of Poetry: A Contemporary Survey.* London, 1970. Contains essays on Robert Lowell by Gabriel Pearson, on John Berryman by Martin Dodsworth, and on Sylvia Plath by Barbara Hardy.

Phillips, Robert S. *The Confessional Poets.* Carbondale, Ill., 1973. The standard study; puts these diverse writers in context.

Simpson, Eileen. *Poets in Their Youth: A Memoir.* New York and London, 1982. John Berryman's first wife writes about her late husband and about Robert Lowell, Delmore Schwartz, and others.

### JOHN BERRYMAN

Haffenden, John. *John Berryman: A Critical Commentary.* London and New York, 1980. A thorough and searching discussion, especially useful concerning the Dream Songs.

Haffenden, John. *The Life of John Berryman.* London and Boston, 1982. Sympathetic and detailed biography.

Mariani, Paul L. *Dream Song: The Life of John Berryman.* New York, 1990; repr. Amherst, Mass., 1996. Contains more recent information than above.

### ROBERT LOWELL

Doreski, William. *Robert Lowell's Shifting Colors: The Poetics of the Public and the Personal.* Athens, Ohio, 1999. Reconciles the public and private aspects of Lowell's work in terms of poetic entities.

Hamilton, Ian. *Robert Lowell: A Biography.* New York, 1982; London, 1983. Based on many interviews with those who knew the poet well, including Elizabeth Hardwick, Caroline Blackwood, Eileen Simpson, Mary Jarrell, Richard Eberhart, and Robert Giroux.

Hobsbaum, Philip. *A Reader's Guide to Robert Lowell.* London and New York, 1988. Poem-by-poem survey with *Life Studies* at the center but paying especial attention to "The Mills of the Kavanaghs" and *Imitations* as well.

London, Michael, and Robert Boyers, eds. *Robert Lowell: A Portrait of the Artist in His Time.* New York, 1970. Reprints M. L. Rosenthal, "Poetry as Confession," as well as essays by Randall Jarrell, Geoffrey H. Hartman, and Irvin Ehrenpreis, among others, and an interview with Lowell (1961) by Frederick Seidel.

### SYLVIA PLATH

Axelrod, Steven Gould. *Sylvia Plath: The Wound and the Cure of Words.* Baltimore, 1990. Penetrating account of Plath's poems together with many side glances at Lowell on whom this critic had already (1978) written a distinguished book.

Newman, Charles, ed. *The Art of Sylvia Plath: A Symposium.* London and Bloomington, Ind., 1970. Reprints an essay by M. L. Rosenthal concerning Plath in relation to confessional poetry, together with essays by A. Alvarez, Lois Ames, Annette Lavers, Ted Hughes, and A. R. Jones (on "Daddy"), among others.

Stevenson, Anne. *Bitter Fame: A Life of Sylvia Plath.* Boston and London, 1989. Perhaps too sympathetic toward Ted Hughes, but a clear-cut narrative detailing the events of this poet's complicated life.

### ANNE SEXTON

Colburn, Steven E., ed. *Anne Sexton: Telling the Tale.* Ann Arbor, Mich., 1988. Essay by Laurence J. Dressner on " 'The Abortion' and Confessional Poetry"; also essays by Kathleen F. McSpadden on "the religious quest" and Ruth E. Quebe on "the questing self."

Middlebrook, Diane Wood. *Anne Sexton: A Biography.* New York, 1991; London, 1992. Indispensable study of this self-reflexive poet.

Wagner-Martin, Linda, ed. *Critical Essays on Anne Sexton.* Boston, 1989. Essay by Steven E. Colburn, "Sexton as Storyteller"; also essays by Gwen L. Nagel on "death and time" and by Cheryl Vossekuil on the early poems.

### W. D. SNODGRASS

Gaston, Paul L. *W. D. Snodgrass.* Boston, 1978. A rare monograph on this most classical of the confessional poets.

# JAMES FENIMORE COOPER

*by Charles Robert Baker*

James Cooper (he legally added "Fenimore," his mother's maiden name, in 1826) was born on 15 September 1789, in Burlington, New Jersey, a little more than five months after George Washington took the oath of office as the first president of the United States. He was the twelfth of thirteen children born to William Cooper and Elizabeth Fenimore, one of only seven to survive childhood. William Cooper was the quintessential early American: a religious man, a shrewd land developer, and a willing public servant. By the time James was born, William had amassed great wealth; had founded the settlement of Cooperstown on the shores of Otsego Lake in central New York State, where he built the family estate; and had been selected to serve as the first judge of the court of common pleas for Otsego County. He served as the county's representative in the Fourth (1795) and Sixth (1799) U.S. Congresses and was a leading figure in the history of the state. A staunch Federalist, Judge Cooper agreed with Alexander Hamilton that men of property should govern the American masses. As his ambitions grew, so did the number of his enemies; he died after being attacked from behind by a political opponent in 1809.

Judge Cooper ruled his family as sternly as he ruled his community on the edge of the wilderness and insisted that his sons receive the best education possible. James attended lessons in Cooperstown and Burlington and was sent to board with an Episcopal priest, Thomas Ellison, who taught him Latin and gentlemanly behavior. There was, however, much of the untamed wilderness in Cooper when he entered Yale in February 1803. He was an indifferent student who enjoyed playing pranks on his professors and fellow students. After enduring his unruliness for three years, Yale sent Cooper home to his father. Judge Cooper determined that a career in the navy

James Fenimore Cooper.
*(Hulton Archive/Getty Images)*

would give his son the discipline he sorely needed, and to that end arranged for his training aboard a merchant ship. Cooper served as a sailor before the mast aboard the *Stirling* from October 1806 until September 1807.

On 1 January 1808 Cooper began his service in the U.S. Navy as a midshipman stationed at Fort Oswego on Lake Ontario. When his father died, Cooper was acting as a recruiter aboard the *Wasp*, anchored in New York City. He requested a year's furlough to put his father's affairs in order. But since his older brother was still living and would ordinarily handle family business, it would appear that the real reason for the request was to be free to court Susan Augusta De Lancey, the daughter of a prominent New York family. When the two were married in 1811, Cooper resigned his navy post, and with the help of an inheritance from his father of $50,000 plus a share of the interest earned from the family estate, established himself as a gentleman farmer. He built a home for his growing family close to Cooperstown and became active in the county agricultural society, the militia, and the Episcopal Church.

## FROM FARMER TO AUTHOR

There are two versions of how Cooper the agriculturalist became Cooper the author. One version, told by his daughter Susan in her introduction to his collected works, claims that Cooper—always an avid reader—became disgusted by the poor quality of a British novel he was reading and, hurling it across the room, declared that he could write a better one. His wife bluntly stated her doubts and challenged him to do so. The other version claims that he desperately needed money and had tried every other way he could think of to raise it. The War of 1812 had thrown the country into an economic depression, and Cooper tried to retrieve the family fortune by investing in various enterprises such as purchasing a whaling ship, *The Union*, in 1819. Lacking his father's shrewdness, however, he lost more money than he made. Whether provoked by his wife's taunt or driven by economic need, Cooper completed his first novel, *Precaution*, and in November 1820 paid a printer to publish it. Cooper fashioned his first work to the popular tastes of his day, using the novels of Jane Austen as his guide. Yielding to the prevailing sentiment in America that only imported cultural works had any artistic merit, Cooper had produced a work that was thoroughly British. *Precaution*, however, was a disappointment, not even selling enough copies for Cooper to regain his costs. Instead of looking for another source of income, Cooper decided to produce another novel, this time using the enormously popular historical romances of Sir Walter Scott as his model but making the work uniquely his own and uniquely American. Indeed, *The Spy; A Tale of the Neutral Ground* (1821) is considered the first American historical novel.

Cooper found the right combination of ingredients to make *The Spy* an immediate success: adventure, mystery, patriotism, romance, and a strong moral and ethical message. The novel's subtitle, *A Tale of the Neutral Ground*, refers not only to the lawless physical space that existed between American and British outposts during the American Revolution but also to the valueless wasteland in the hearts of those who would seek material gain during a time of social unrest. The system of values that Cooper believed must be embraced by Americans in order to overcome corruption is embodied in his title character—the spy, Harvey Birch. Assuming the disguise of a peddler, Birch travels between the camps of the contending armies gathering and dispensing information. Most Americans believe him to be a British spy and revile him, but in fact he is General Washington's most trusted and able double agent. A deeply religious man, Birch patiently suffers the indignities heaped upon him, content in the faith that he is advancing a greater cause. His virtues of self-sacrifice and self-discipline find full expression in the adventures of Leather-Stocking, a character Cooper introduces in his next novel, *The Pioneers; or, The Sources of the Susquehanna* (1823).

## A MAN OF LETTERS IN NEW YORK CITY

The success of *The Spy*, and an argument with his in-laws, prompted Cooper to move his family to New York City in 1822. For the next five years he enjoyed the life of a literary celebrity. He frequented the bookshop of his friend Charles Wiley and held court in a back room there that he dubbed The Den. He also established the Bread and Cheese, a luncheon club of notable New Yorkers who met weekly to discuss current affairs and American culture. Cooper's preeminence among the members is revealed by the fact that the Bread and Cheese soon became known as the Cooper Club. Feeling secure in his reputation, Cooper decided to write a novel, as he explains in its preface, solely to please himself. *The Pioneers* is an autobiographical novel of Cooper's childhood in Cooperstown. On the surface the story is a simple one: a stock dramatic tale of an inheritance illegally appropriated and the return of the rightful heir to claim it. But a closer reading reveals much about Cooper and his relationship with his father. The elder Cooper is portrayed as Judge Temple, founder of Templeton. Temple, although he has some regrets, is driven by an entrepreneurial desire to settle and civilize the wilderness no matter the irreparable damage to nature. Standing in opposition to this is Cooper's most famous creation, Natty Bumppo, nicknamed Leather-Stocking by the Templeton settlers. For the past forty of his seventy years, Natty has lived by his skills as a woodsman and hunter on the edge of the rapidly receding wilderness. With his friend, John Mohegan, a Delaware who has lost not only his land but also his Indian name, Chingachgook, and who represents all dispossessed American Indians, he despairs over the wanton destruction of natural resources caused by the judge and men like him. Natty prefers to keep his distance from civilized society, but when he and his particular skills are needed to rescue its members from danger, he does so willingly, returning to the forest when his work is done. Cooper makes it clear that Natty is fighting a losing battle and that it is up to the Judge Temples of the new country to find and enforce a balance between the needs of society and the wilderness that stands in its way.

*The Pioneers* was a commercial success; thirty-five hundred copies were sold before noon on 1 February, the first day of its publication. This, however, did little to alleviate the financial strain on Cooper. In 1823, at the age of thirty-four, he found himself responsible for the welfare of his growing family (four daughters and one son, his first daughter and first son having died in infancy); additionally, he had taken upon himself the care of his four deceased brothers' wives and children. In a flurry of creative energy Cooper published four books in the next three years: *Tales for Fifteen; or, Imagination and Heart* (1823); *The Pilot; A Tale of the Sea* (1824); *Lionel Lincoln; or, The Leaguer of Boston* (1825); and perhaps his best-known work, *The Last of the Mohicans; A Narrative of 1757* (1826). In the latter novel Cooper resurrected Natty

Bumppo, now known as Hawkeye, and Chingachgook and involved them in events that occurred some thirty-five years prior to those in *The Pioneers*. Against the backdrop of the French and Indian War, Cooper weaves a tale of high adventure, daring rescue, and treacherous murder and romance, with very little philosophizing about social and environmental concerns. Interestingly, however, Cooper—during a time of wholesale slaughter and displacement of Native Americans—strives in this novel to make a distinction between the tribes, contrasting the villainy of the evil Hurons and Iroquois with the nobility of the virtuous Mohicans.

## AN AMERICAN AUTHOR IN EUROPE

The hectic pace of his life and work in New York City took a heavy toll on Cooper's health. He took his family to Europe in 1826, seeking better health for himself and a better education for his children. For the next seven years they resided in Paris but traveled to England, Italy, Switzerland, Holland, and Belgium. In Paris he became close friends with a French hero of the American Revolution, the Marquis de Lafayette. The aged hero, sixty-nine years old when Cooper arrived in Paris, was passionately involved in political reform throughout Europe, but his attentions were primarily focused on his native France where, in 1830, at the age of seventy-three, he led a revolt that dethroned the Bourbon king and established a constitutional monarchy. The influence of Lafayette on Cooper was immediate and profound. No longer content to be a mere literary entertainer, Cooper hastily completed two manuscripts he had brought from New York—*The Prairie* (1827), wherein he kills off Natty Bumppo, and *The Red Rover* (1827)—and turned his talents to what he thought were more important matters.

Encouraged by Lafayette to educate Europeans and correct some misconceptions regarding his native land, Cooper wrote a stirring but often strident defense of American principles and ideals called *Notions of the Americans; Picked Up by a Travelling Bachelor* (1828). As Cooper became more involved in the politics of Europe, however, his readers in America became more puzzled by the direction their national author was taking. When Cooper wrote a pamphlet in support of Lafayette's position regarding France's finances in 1831, the American press soundly condemned him for his increasing involvement in European matters. He further distanced himself from his readers by writing three historical romances located in Europe: *The Bravo* (1831), set in Italy; *The Heidenmauer; or, the Benedictines*

(1832), set in Germany; and *The Headsman* (1833), set in Switzerland. Each is serious in tone and lacks the adventurous element that made his previous works so popular. Cooper was outraged by the attacks from the press and bewildered by the lack of interest shown in his new work. He briefly considered not returning to America, but changed his mind in 1833 and sailed for New York with his family.

## BACK TO HIS ORIGINS

Cooper spent a little time in New York City settling his affairs and avoiding old acquaintances. In 1834 he moved his family into his boyhood home in Cooperstown that he had purchased and restored and from whose grounds he rarely ventured for the rest of his life. In June 1834 he began *A Letter to His Countrymen*, in which he decried the lack of a truly American culture and declared that he would write no more. That resolve lasted less than one year. Over the following three years Cooper wrote a satire, *The Monikins* (1835); several nonfiction accounts of his impressions of Europe; and a sharply worded attack on American politics and provincialism, *The American Democrat* (1838).

A dispute with his neighbors in Cooperstown drove Cooper back to fiction. A dispute arose over the public use of a piece of land known as Three Mile Point. The Cooper family had long allowed picnickers and fishermen to enjoy this piece of their property on Otsego Lake. However, when Cooper noticed that some of his trees had suffered damage, he printed a notice in the local newspaper warning that anyone found on Three Mile Point would be prosecuted as a trespasser. The townspeople and the newspaper reacted strongly to this affront. Cooper defended his position in two novels, *Homeward Bound; or, The Chase* (1838) and *Home As Found* (1838). In both he asserts that the rights of the individual are in danger of being overtaken by a democracy that is out of control and calls upon his readers to return to the republican principles of the country's founders. The books were intensely disliked, and Cooper retreated even deeper into feelings of failure: not his own, but his country's failure to heed his warnings.

Perhaps to alleviate his pain, Cooper turned his imagination toward his earliest success. Natty and Chingachgook return in *The Pathfinder; or, The Inland Sea* (1840) and *The Deerslayer; or, The First Warpath* (1841). The two novels, set in 1759 and the 1740s, respectively, feature the coming of age of the two men of the wilderness. Interestingly, Cooper chose to add a new element to the suspense and adventure of the three previous Leather-Stocking novels: he allowed young Natty to experience the love of a young woman, the love, perhaps, that Cooper wanted again from his readers.

As much as he may have desired the love and admiration of the American public, he never passed up an opportunity to chastise and correct what he saw as its tendency toward mob rule. An event known as the Anti-Rent War (1844–1845) justified Cooper's pessimism. Large numbers of tenant farmers staged a rent strike in protest of the quasi-feudal system of land ownership in New York State. Violence broke out against the large landowners, and the state militia was called upon to quell the riotous behavior. Cooper addressed the issue in three novels known as the Littlepage Trilogy. The novels tell the story of the Littlepage family from their establishment of a settlement in colonial New York in *Satanstoe* (1845), through the American Revolution in *The Chainbearer* (1845), and culminating in the Anti-Rent War in *The Redskins; or, Indian and Injin* (1846). Cooper, in his growing conservatism, sided with the wealthy landowners and thereby brought down the condemnation of his readers and the press, who branded him as a would-be aristocrat.

Cooper found a harmless way to dispel the anger and disappointment he felt toward his countrymen in his next novel, *The Crater; or, Vulcan's Peak* (1847). One can imagine how pleasing it must have been for Cooper to write this tale of a man, Mark Woolston, who is shipwrecked on a deserted, volcanic island in the South Seas. His idyllic life is interrupted, however, when American settlers discover the island and transform Woolston's Eden into an unbearable hell. It must have given Cooper some measure of satisfaction to allow Woolston to escape from the island just before it and its inhabitants are destroyed in a volcanic explosion.

As he grew older and it became clearer to him that his countrymen would not heed his calls to reform, Cooper turned his thoughts to God and the hereafter. His final novels concern such end-of-life themes as conversion experiences, in *The Oak Openings; or, The Bee-Hunter* (1848), and travel to uncharted lands, in *The Sea Lions; or, The Last Sealers* (1849). Looking toward his own acceptance into eternity, Cooper was confirmed in the Episcopal Church in July 1851. Shortly thereafter his health, which had declined during the past several years, failed him and he died peacefully on 14 September 1851. He lies buried on the family estate in Cooperstown.

Cooper's reputation has waxed and waned over the years. Once the most popular author in America and Europe, he is rarely found on any school's recommended reading list in a time of cultural sensitivity and political correctness. He was held up to ridicule by Mark Twain in "Fenimore Cooper's Literary Offenses" (1895), but recognized as a major literary figure in D. H. Lawrence's *Studies in Classic American Literature* (1923). His innovative use of the sea as a setting greatly influenced Melville and Conrad, and his tales of a larger-than-life hero and his noble Indian companion find their imitators a century and a half later. Like his creation, Natty Bumppo, Cooper fought a losing battle to preserve and protect an America he cherished, and like Bumppo, he fought his battle courageously and skillfully.

[*See also* American Essay, The; *and* Nature Writing: Prose.]

## SELECTED WORKS

*Precaution* (1820)

*The Spy: A Tale of the Neutral Ground* (1821)

*The Pioneers; or, The Sources of the Susquehanna* (1823)

*Tales for Fifteen; or, Imagination and Heart* (1823)

*The Pilot; A Tale of the Sea* (1824)

*Lionel Lincoln; or, The Leaguer of Boston* (1825)

*The Last of the Mohicans; A Narrative of 1757* (1826)

*The Prairie* (1827)

*The Red Rover* (1827)

*Notions of the Americans: Picked Up by a Travelling Bachelor* (1828)

*The Borderers* (1829) (published in America as *The Wept of Wish-Ton-Wish* [1829])

*The Water-Witch; or, The Skimmer of the Seas* (1830)

*The Bravo* (1831)

*The Heidenmauer; or, The Benedictines* (1832)

*The Headsman* (1833)

*A Letter to His Countrymen* (1834)

*The Monikins* (1835)

*Sketches of Switzerland* (1836)

*A Residence in France; with an Excursion up the Rhine and a Second Visit to France* (1836)

*Recollections of Europe* (1837) (published in America as *Gleanings in Europe* [1837])

*England; with Sketches of Society in the Metropolis* (1837) (published in America as *Gleanings in Europe*)

*England* (1837)

*Excursions in Italy* (1838) (published in America as *Gleanings in Europe*)

*Italy* (1838)

*The American Democrat* (1838)

*Homeward Bound; or, The Chase* (1838)

*Home as Found* (1838)

*The Chronicles of Cooperstown* (1839)
*The History of the Navy of the United States of America* (1839)
*The Pathfinder; or, The Inland Sea* (1840)
*Mercedes of Castile* (1840)
*The Deerslayer; or, The First Warpath* (1841)
*The Two Admirals* (1842)
*The Jack O'Lantern* (1842) (published in America as *The Wing-and-Wing* [1842])
*Le Mouchoir: An Autobiographical Romance* (1843)
*The Battle of Lake Erie* (1843)
*Wyandotté; or, The Hutted Knoll* (1843)
*Ned Myers; or, A Life before the Mast* (1843)
*Afloat and Ashore; or, The Adventures of Miles Wallingford* (1844)
*Satanstoe; or, The Littlepage Manuscripts* (1845)
*The Chainbearer; or, The Littlepage Manuscripts* (1845)
*Lives of Distinguished American Naval Officers* (1846)
*Ravensnest; or, The Redskins* (1846) (published in America as *The Redskins; or, Indian and Injin* [1846])
*Mark's Reef; or, The Crater* (1847) (published in America as *The Crater; or, Vulcan's Peak* [1847])
*Captain Spike; or, The Islets of the Gulf* (1848) (published in America as *Jack Tier; or, The Florida Reef* [1848])
*The Bee-Hunter; or, The Oak Openings* (1848) (published in America as *The Oak Openings; or, The Bee-Hunter* [1848])
*The Sea Lions; or, The Last Sealers* (1849)
*The Ways of the Hour* (1850)

### FURTHER READING

Cooper, Susan Augusta Fenimore. *Pages and Pictures from the Writings of Fenimore Cooper*. New York, 1861; repr. Secaucus, N.J., 1980. A good source of biographical information from Cooper's devoted daughter and amanuensis.

Dekker, George. *James Fenimore Cooper: The Novelist*. London, 1967. A study of Cooper as American historian.

Grossman, James. *James Fenimore Cooper*. Stanford, Calif., 1949. The authoritative biography.

House, Kay S. *Cooper's Americans*. Columbus, Ohio, 1966. A good study of the social structure in Cooper's time.

Lawrence, D. H. *Studies in Classic American Literature*. New York, 1975. First published in 1923. "Fenimore Cooper's Leatherstocking Novels" and "Fenimore Cooper's White Novels" together offer an interesting appraisal of Cooper's America from the renowned British author.

Philbrick, Thomas. *James Fenimore Cooper and the Development of American Sea Fiction*. Cambridge, Mass., 1961. An exhaustive study of an often-neglected area of Cooper's works.

Spiller, Robert E., and Philip C. Blackburn. *A Descriptive Bibliography of the Writings of James Fenimore Cooper*. New York, 1934. Invaluable to any serious student of Cooper's work.

Twain, Mark. *How to Tell a Story and Other Essays*. New York, 1996. "Fenimore Cooper's Literary Offenses" is riotously funny but often inaccurate and unfair.

Walker, Warren S. *James Fenimore Cooper: An Introduction and Interpretation*. New York, 1962. A handy guide to the life and work of Cooper.

Winters, Yvor. *In Defense of Reason: Primitivism and Decadence, A Study of American Experimental Poetry*. Denver, Colo., 1943. "Fenimore Cooper, or The Ruins of Time" is one of the best early modern appraisals of Cooper's life and work, along with his place in American literature.

# HART CRANE

*by Cornelius Browne*

On 21 July 1899, Harold Hart Crane was born in Garrettsville, Ohio, the only child of Clarence A. Crane and Grace Hart Crane. Crane's short, troubling life in large measure parallels the tenor of the times in which he lived. His twenties in personal age correspond with the Jazz Age of the 1920s, with all its brilliance, excess, and celebration, and the end of his life in 1932 coincides with both the demise of his dreams for a poetic synthesis of American culture and history and the great crash of the American economy. His life is the arc of a great creative gift through ecstasy, dissipation, progressive alcoholism, and psychological deterioration to despair and suicide, when a few minutes before noon on 27 April 1932, Crane walked to the stern of SS *Orizaba*, removed his overcoat, folded it neatly over the rail, and dropped into the Caribbean Sea. In Crane's short life he created some of the most lasting, most vital poetry ever written by an American.

Hart Crane. (*Photograph by Walker Evans*)

## FAMILY MATTERS

His father, Clarence A. Crane, or C. A., was a wealthy confectioner and restauranteur. C. A.'s marriage to Grace Hart was disastrous from the beginning. All through Harold Crane's young life their quarrels were obvious, loud, and violent, as was the sex that often accompanied their resolution. Their arguments and reconciliations profoundly disturbed Harold, whose psychological turbulence often manifested itself physically in hives and fever. The Cranes settled at 1709 East 115th Street, Cleveland. A large Victorian structure, the house was dominated by two circular towers. Harold's room was in the northern tower, and it remained his until the house was sold in 1925. In this room, Harold Hart Crane began to write poetry and here he formed his first conception of his greatest work, *The Bridge* (1930), which he understood as a mystical "synthesis of America and its structural identity." It is difficult to underestimate the importance of this room and this house for Crane. His childhood, his midwestern roots, and even his impression of what America meant were bound up in the image and the reality of this place. In 1913 Harold Crane was enrolled in East High School, one of the most prestigious in the city. Unremarkable as a student, he attended irregularly, in part because Grace found solace from her marital squabbles in travel, and she often took Harold with her. On one trip she caused her sixteen-year-old son acute mortification when she insisted he share her berth in a sleeping car.

When home in Cleveland, Harold attended classes regularly, though he never graduated from high school. He immersed himself in Shelley, Coleridge, Byron, Poe, Hawthorne, A. C. Swinburne, and Wilde. In preparation for composing his own poems, he smoked cigars and sprinkled his mother's perfume about his room. All his writing life, Crane used music and later alcohol in preparation for writing, once claiming to have envisioned the ideal world under anesthetic in a dentist's chair. Outside stimulus aside, Crane believed that the poet could approach an ideal world, locating him in a long tradition of European and American romanticism.

## EARLY WORK

In 1916 Richard Laukhuff opened a bookstore in Cleveland devoted to works and periodicals at the cutting edge of contemporary literature. On its shelves Crane gained access to some of the little magazines so important to the dissemination of modernist literature: *Poetry, Soil, Seven Arts, The Pagan*, and *Bruno's Monthly*. After reading a series of essays in *Bruno's Weekly* in the winter of 1916 that sympathetically treated Oscar Wilde, Crane penned what would be his first published poem, *C33*, whose title is the number of Wilde's prison cell in Reading Gaol.

However, accompanying his public debut as a poet was the further deterioration of his parents' marriage. Divorce proceedings began in 1916 and Harold, who had already formed ideas of moving to New York City to be near the center of literary America, convinced his distracted parents to allow him to move there. Shortly after Christmas 1916, the seventeen-year-old Harold Crane boarded a train for New York City, the first step in many that led to a poetic reenvisioning of the United States which attempted to bridge the Midwest of his youth and urban America.

Jobs in New York City were difficult to find, and the impoverished poet steadily wrote his affluent father for money. C. A. was as much a believer in the American work ethic as his son was a staunch believer in the power of art and literature, and the growing tension between them abated only toward the end of both men's lives. Crane often shuttled between New York City and Ohio, working for his father when faced with destitution. The correspondence from this time between Harold and his family rehearses the marital battle in print, and most of the pain, intentionally or not, was visited on the child—the eighteen-year-old poet who, despite himself and them, deeply loved both his parents. Following one such letter from Grace in which she admonished him to acknowledge her side of the family, Harold—when *Echoes* was published in 1917—for the first time signed his name as Hart Crane, much to his father's irritation. Following the publication of *Echoes*, Crane published *In Shadow* in *The Little Review*, a primary vehicle for introducing the work of Ezra Pound, T. S. Eliot, W. B. Yeats, and other prominent modernists to an American reading public. The magazine was also the first to introduce James Joyce's *Ulysses* (1922) to the United States in serial form, resulting in the U.S. Postal Service burning several issues of *The Little Review* as obscene. He continued to publish poems—*North Labrador*, *Legend*, and *Interior* were published in *The Modernist*—and after enthusiastically reading several stories from *Winesburg, Ohio* (1919) in *The Little Review*, Crane reviewed Sherwood Anderson's work for *The Pagan*, instigating a short-lived friendship between the two Ohioans. Finally, broke again, Crane returned to Ohio to work for C. A. in one of his Akron stores. Along with him, he brought the idea of a poem, *My Grandmother's Love Letters*.

While many of the poems preceding *Love Letters* were imagistic in their conception, this poem represents an advance in Crane's early poetics. The poem more explicitly engages his personal milieu, but beyond that it engages memory, and this willingness to pry open personal memory in an era under the dominance of T. S. Eliot, who insisted upon the impersonality of poetry, represents an early glimpse of Crane's attempt to revise modernist aesthetics in order to create his own idiom within modernism. For most of his career Crane felt shadowed by Eliot, and although he greatly admired Eliot's technical virtuosity, he continued to write against what he saw as Eliot's destructive pessimism.

*My Grandmother's Love Letters* opens quietly with a night sky in which only stars of memory shine. The poet considers, "Yet how much room for memory there is / In the loose girdle of soft rain," attempting to walk a thin line between his respect and love for his grandmother (whose first name, Elizabeth, is given in the poem), and his desire to reach into her past, subtly eroticized by the evocation of a loosened girdle and the soft rain. Found bundled in an attic corner, her letters are "brown and soft, / And liable to melt as snow." The delicacy and whiteness of the snow are echoed by an old woman's white hair: "It is all hung by an invisible white hair. / It trembles as birch limbs webbing the air." Moving gently along, the poem is guided by subtle internal rhymes and assonance along with occasional end rhymes. The poet poses himself a question that ramifies into a query about the efficacy of poetry itself, though he never loses sight of the actual person who inspired the poem:

> "Are your fingers long enough to play
> Old keys that are but echoes:
> Is the silence strong enough
> To carry back the music to its source
> And back to you again
> As though to her?"

The question becomes one that wonders whether the music of poetry is able to retrieve a particular experience, and if so, can it provide a song that is as true to the poetry as it was to the poet's grandmother. It is the silence that must be powerful enough to enable the poetry; the silence provides a space for the poem. The query is of course unanswerable, but it provides the impetus to a poetry that evokes great love, intense sensuality, and a concern for how a poem can create a bridge between the past and the present, between a real life already lived and the poetic evocation of certain heightened moments in that life.

*Love Letters* becomes even more poignant when it is taken into consideration that Crane is coming to understand and embrace his homosexuality. In Akron,

Crane was befriended by Harry Candee, a member of an established gay community, and Crane began to feel more at ease with his sexuality. Crane, however, had also developed a taste for seeking out strangers for short and sometimes dangerous sexual liaisons. With Candee, also, his taste for Prohibition liquor increased. Late in the summer of 1920, Crane was sent as a sales representative to Washington, D.C., where he met another member of the gay community, Wilber Underwood, who enabled Crane to feel a part of a vibrant group of marginalized people. Crane experienced a strong attraction to the dangerous and potentially violent aspects of physical love, but though he often found it necessary to cloak his sexual adventures for practical reasons, especially from his family, he was not ashamed of them. Quite to the contrary, he seems to have enjoyed them greatly, and, difficult as it must have been to sustain, he exerts a stiff determination to see his sexuality as natural, not aberrant or diseased as his culture most often terms it. He created some of the most beautiful love lyrics in the English language, particularly the sequence *Voyages*, inspired by his love affair with the sailor Emil Opffer.

## POETIC ADVANCES

By the end of 1922, Crane's focus had matured and shifted to an attempt to incorporate American culture in all its bleakness, brutality, and beauty into poetry. This would demand the inclusion of jazz, bridges, subways, acetylene torches, airplanes, and elevators. Eliot's *The Waste Land* (1922) had appeared as one model, and though Crane admired it, he was unhappy with what he saw as its obsession with death. Eliot demanded a rejoinder, and in Crane's terms, that response must entail a "resurrection" of some kind. Already working on his most ambitious poem to date, *For the Marriage of Faustus and Helen*, Crane was gaining increased notice in widely circulated periodicals. In the 6 December 1922 issue of *The New Republic*, Crane's name joined those of E. E. Cummings, Edmund Wilson, Kenneth Burke, Malcolm Cowley, and John Dos Passos in an article by influential critic Louis Untermeyer called the New Patricians. Part of what distinguished these writers was a sense of strangeness in their work, and notably, a heightened complexity.

*For the Marriage of Faustus and Helen*, Crane's first foray into the long poem, is an attempt at the kind of poetic synthesis Crane will enact on a much larger scale in his masterwork, *The Bridge*. *Marriage* weds the hectic present of urban, commercial America to classical culture. Crane wrote to critic Waldo Frank that "the whole poem

is a kind of fusion of our own time with the past." The poet—the Faust figure—encounters Helen of Troy on a trolley car. Helen symbolizes beauty, and Crane explicitly states that Faust symbolizes not only a generalized poet but Crane himself. On a deeper level, the poem enacts "the transition of the imagination from quotidian details to the universal consideration of beauty." It attempts a resurrection. This sense that universals emerge from the everyday becomes thematic in most of his mature work. However, within this grand sense of beauty lodged in the quotidian resides a certain danger:

> There is the world dimensional for
> Those untwisted by the love of things
> Irreconcilable.

Clearly, for a poet like Crane—twisted by love of irreconcilable things—the dimensional world is a difficult place.

Crane, like millions of urban Americans, commuted by trolley to and from work in the world dimensional, and *Marriage* pivots on an evening trolley ride:

> And yet, suppose some evening I forgot
> The fare and transfer, yet got by that way
> Without recall,—lost yet poised in traffic.
> Then I might find your eyes across an aisle,
> Still flickering with those prefigurations—
> Prodigal, yet uncontested now,
> Half-riant before the jerky window frame.

The poet encounters Helen half smiling, framed in the streetcar window as the evening lights of the city flicker in her eyes. This first section of the poem evokes beauty, and the second section brings the poet and Helen to a rooftop party where

> Brazen hypnotics glitter here;
> Glee shifts from foot to foot,
> Magnetic to their tremulo.

The dance crescendos into a strange mixture of ecstasy and grotesquery, joined to a concise imaging of the American economic citizen, "Striated with nuances, nervosities / That we are heir to..." The closing lines of the poem then transcend the American urge to link bargains and prayer, the economic and the spiritual: "The imagination spans beyond despair, / Outpacing bargain, vocable and prayer."

While working on *Marriage*, Crane generated an idea for a poem that would use the Brooklyn Bridge as a central symbol. In a 1923 letter written to Gorham Munson from the tower room on East 115th Street, Crane makes the first written reference to *The Bridge* of which we know.

He confides, "I am ruminating on a new longish poem under the title of *The Bridge* which carries on further the tendencies manifest in 'F and H.' It will be exceedingly difficult to accomplish it as I see it now, so much time will be wasted in thinking about it." It was exceedingly difficult. Though many parts of *The Bridge* were published separately, the poem as a whole was not published until 1930, and its composition would shuttle Crane between ecstasy and despair through this entire range of years.

In 1923 Crane moved back to New York City, where he met the novelist Jean Toomer, the poet E. E. Cummings, the playwright Eugene O'Neill, the critic Kenneth Burke, and the writer William Slater Brown. Typically, Crane worked at advertising for a while and then resigned. He then moved to Woodstock, New York, to live with Slater Brown and Susan Jenkins. The following year he returned to the city, met poet Allen Tate, and worked with Malcolm Cowley at a catalogue service, finally moving to a room at 110 Columbia Heights in Brooklyn. This room is the second one that will exert a powerful influence on Crane. It had a view of the Manhattan towers across the East River, framed by the Brooklyn Bridge. Amazingly, the room was once inhabited by Washington Roebling, the architect who completed his father's work as chief engineer of the Brooklyn Bridge. Also living in the house in Columbia Heights was Emil Opffer, with whom Crane engaged in the most meaningful, though tempestuous, love affair of his life.

Throughout the winter of 1926 Crane lived in Patterson, New York, and worked on *The Bridge*, beginning with "Atlantis," which would eventually become the final poem of the book. Still desperate for the means to support himself while he worked on *The Bridge*, Crane asked for a $1,000 loan from New York financier and philanthropist Otto Kahn, who presented Crane with a gift outright of $2,000. Thus far, he had a rough outline of the ideas and dramatis personae of the poem. Some of the characters, such as John Brown, would fall away before the poem was completed, but the most important figures in the poem, Christopher Columbus, Pocahontas, Walt Whitman, the New York City subway, and the Brooklyn Bridge, were firmly in Crane's design. But although he was making progress on his poem, he bickered with his friends in Patterson, who eventually tired of late night tapping on the keyboard, loud music, and drunken rampages that sometimes sent typewriters sailing through second story windows.

## WHITE BUILDINGS

Crane needed someplace to write. A portion of the money from Kahn remained, so he appealed to his mother for the use of her family's house on Cuba's Isle of Pines—Villa Casas. Accompanied by Waldo Frank, Crane set sail on 1 May 1926 aboard the SS *Orizaba*. In an eerie twist, this was the same ship from which Crane would jump to his death in 1932. Frank shortly returned home, and Crane shared the house with the caretaker Sally Simpson, undergoing a splendid ten-week period of creativity, during which he completed much of *The Bridge*. Never again would he experience such productivity.

Good news arrived in July in the form of a contract with Liveright for *White Buildings* (1926), his first collection of poems, for which Allen Tate had agreed to write the introduction. *White Buildings* selects the finest poems Crane had written to date, and the collection concludes with the masterful cycle, *Voyages*, among the most accomplished love lyrics in the English language. Certainly, *Voyages* was written with Emil Opffer in mind, but the poem is also a powerful invocation of the sea. *Voyages* is more properly a cycle of six love lyrics; each stands alone, but together the poems sing. "Voyages I" opens with images of young boys playing on the beach, but quickly voices a warning about the transience of such happiness, "The bottom of the sea is cruel." "Voyages II" picks up where "I" left off:

> —And yet this great wink of eternity,
> Of rimless floods, unfettered leewardings,
> Samite sheeted and processioned where
> Her undinal vast belly moonward bends,
> Laughing the wrapt inflections of our love.

Although the sea floor may be cruel, the surface of the ocean arches toward the moon in a metaphor that links the natural phenomenon—the pull of the moon creating the tides—to the imagined act of the sea offering herself to the lovers, and laughing with them in a sensuous embrace. The waves become "scrolls of silver snowy sentences," and the Caribbean, "these poinsettia meadows of her tides,— / Adagios of islands." The sea becomes poetry and music, and Crane utters the power of poetry with the final lines of "Voyages VI":

> The imaged Word, it is, that holds
> Hushed willows anchored in its glow.
> It is the unbetrayable reply
> Whose accent no farewell can know.

But if the sea and the weather are excellent material for poetry, in the tropics they are also a violent threat. On 18 October 1926 a hurricane nearly flattened the Isle of Pines and heavily damaged Villa Casas. With the house in ruins, Crane returned to New York City and shortly thereafter *White Buildings* was published. Though the book received harsh reviews in *The Dial* and in the *New York Herald Tribune*, Ivor Winters, Allen Tate, and Waldo Frank publicly praised the book, ranking Crane among the country's most important poets. Ironically, Winters and Tate—who became powerful New Critics—were instrumental in the later dismissal of Crane's work.

In 1927 Crane worked sporadically on *The Bridge*. Through a friend he was introduced to Herbert Wise, a neurotic millionaire who had recently suffered a nervous breakdown and wanted a literary traveling companion to accompany him to southern California. Crane's only responsibility would be to keep Wise amused; also, Crane's mother, after the breakup of her second marriage, had moved to the Los Angeles area. Crane disliked the culture of southern California, and tension arose in his relationship with his employer. Crane left Wise's mansion and moved in with his mother and his sick grandmother, but his heavy drinking, cruising, and dockside brawls exacerbated his already pathological relationship with his mother. During an argument, Crane divulged his homosexuality to her, which resulted in a dramatic confrontation that ended with Crane sneaking out of the house on the night of 15 May 1928, leaving only a note. He never saw his mother again. The following autumn Crane learned that his grandmother had finally succumbed to her long illness. Elizabeth Hart left a behest of $5,000 to be paid upon her death to her grandson, but Grace used all her wiles to withhold the money until he returned to live with her in Los Angeles. Crane threatened suit, and upon receiving the money experienced a desperate need to put the greatest distance possible between his mother and him, finally sailing for Europe at the end of November.

## THE BRIDGE

Crane spent seven months in Europe, first London and then Paris, where he fell in with a fast-moving crowd dominated by Harry and Caresse Crosby, rich, flamboyant people who surrounded themselves with members of the cultural avant-garde. They also owned a small publishing company called the Black Sun Press. They were thrilled with the work Crane showed them—the drafts of *The Bridge*. The Crosbys agreed to publish *The Bridge* in a deluxe edition once Crane completed the poem; even so, Crane hardly worked on the poem while in Europe. His drinking spiraling beyond control, Crane spent the last week of his stay in a Paris prison for assaulting police officers following a row in a café.

Returning to New York City in July 1929, he worked strenuously on *The Bridge* to meet a 1 January deadline for the Black Sun edition. In the meantime, Harry Crosby and his mistress committed suicide on 10 December, further destabilizing Crane's already chaotic life. In January 1930 Caresse Crosby brought out the Black Sun Press edition of *The Bridge* in Paris, followed in April by the Boni and Liveright edition in the United States. Crane's masterpiece received mixed reviews; often, they were enthusiastic, but the book left many critics dismayed by either its complexity or its unfashionable Whitmanian echoes. Most devastating to Crane were the harsh reviews of his friends Allen Tate and Ivor Winters.

*The Bridge* consists of a proem and eight sections that themselves contain in total fourteen lyrics. The proem, "To Brooklyn Bridge," introduces the overarching metaphor of the entire work. The Brooklyn Bridge is transformed from a material object into a metaphorical structure that stands for the act of bridging and all its accompanying potentiality. "To Brooklyn Bridge" opens at dawn:

> How many dawns, chill from his rippling rest
> The seagull's wings shall dip and pivot him
> Shedding white rings of tumult, building high
> Over the chained waters Liberty—
>
> Then, with inviolate curve, forsake our eyes
> As apparitional as sails that cross
> Some page of figures to be filed away;
> —Till elevators drop us from our day.

The bird's wings dip and pivot like the cables of the bridge that chain the waters of New York Harbor and its famous statue. The gulls, like the bridge, trace an "inviolate curve." Then, abruptly, the lyrical musing shifts; we are dropped into the mundane "page of figures" and depart the lyrical mood via elevator.

Later, the poet—haunting the Brooklyn piers that may have moored Whitman's Brooklyn Ferry—awaits his inspiration in the night:

> Under thy shadow by the piers I waited,
> Only in darkness is thy shadow clear.
> The city's fiery parcels all undone,
> Already the snow submerges an iron year....
>
> O Sleepless as the river under thee,
> Vaulting the sea, the prairies' dreaming sod,
> Unto us lowliest sometime sweep, descend
> And of the curveship lend a myth to God.

In these last quatrains is a sense of foreboding, of the fleetingness of a lyrical vision in an iron year about to be smothered in snow. But the river and the bridge are sleepless, alive. And at this point, the lines are as much addressed to *The Bridge* as they are to the Brooklyn Bridge. *The Bridge* does indeed vault the oceans and the prairies in its attempt to create a myth of America from first contact to the physical and cultural landscape of Crane's United States, hovering on the brink of the Great Depression.

The poem travels time and space. The first section, "Ave Marie," takes the reader back in time to the deck of Columbus's ship on its return voyage to Spain. "Powhatan's Daughter," the second section, echoes Columbus's voyage with the contemporary "Far strum of fog horns," and trucks rumble past wharves. The bridge and ship are replaced by highways: "Macadam, gun grey as the tunny's belt, / Leaps from Far Rockaway to Golden Gate." All arteries of travel become intensely metaphorical.

In one of the finest lyrics in the poem, "The River," Crane hastens the lyrical pace, invoking familiar scenes from his Ohio years as seen from a railway car. In this way, the mythical landscape is merged with mundane, brand-name scenery. However, the mundane carries great power and energy, especially as the tempo of Crane's lines mimic the fast-moving rail car as it clips by a billboard world:

> Stick your patent name on a signboard
> brother—all over—going west—young man
> Tintex—Japalac—Certain-teed Overalls ads
> and lands sakes!

Here is a world inhabited by hobos and minstrels, and dominated by the incongruous trinity of "SCIENCE-COMMERCE and the HOLYGHOST." The poem then shifts to Crane's personal history with an invocation of "my Aunt Sally Simpson." The scene cuts to his father's cannery, behind which Crane recalls watching the hobos and recreates their conversation, "Jesus! Oh I remember watermelon days!"

The southbound train diesels alongside the Mississippi River, the central pulse of the nation, and the land becomes the body of Pocahontas, "Time like a Serpent down her shoulder, dark, / And space, an eaglet's wing, laid on her hair." This last figure returns to the surface a major concern in *The Bridge*. The poem bridges the gulf between time and space. Whitman is here, Columbus, Pocahontas, contemporary New York City and Ohio, the Great Plains of the pioneers, dockside drunks, Rip Van Winkle, Crane's adopted town of Patterson, a World War I dogfight, Yankee Clippers, the Wright Brothers, Edgar Allan Poe aboard a subway bound for Brooklyn—all these figures

yanked in and out of space and time in a warping poetic continuum.

And characters shift identities. The Indian princess is exchanged for a pioneer woman, and the roles are strangely juxtaposed, the pioneer woman heading east, and the Indian woman walking west. No longer a metaphor for the land, Pocahontas becomes a dispossessed person, "A homeless squaw." By the penultimate poem, "The Tunnel," the explorer from Genoa—Columbus—has morphed into a

> Wop washerwoman, with the bandaged hair[?]
> After the corridors are swept, the cuspidors—
> The gaunt sky-barracks cleanly now, and bare,
> O Genoese, do you bring mother eyes and hands
> Back home to children and to golden hair?

Columbus, who sailed to the Americas and, in Crane's vision at least, perceived the wondrous potential of the New World, has become a scrub woman riding the subway from Manhattan home to Brooklyn, traveling beneath the East River, not above it on the bridge.

The poem reaches its emotional depths on this bitter subway ride under the river, where love becomes "A burnt match skating in a urinal." However, the figure of Whitman—

> My hand
> in yours,
> Walt Whitman

—still presides over *The Bridge*, and his presence helps Crane emerge from the troglodytic despondency of the subway tunnel as he alights on the Brooklyn shore under the moon-shadow of the bridge. The Bridge began at dawn and now ends at midnight. The closing poem, "Atlantis," was the first section of *The Bridge* that Crane composed, and is in his own words "a sweeping Dithyramb in which the Bridge becomes the symbol of consciousness spanning time and space." Surfacing from the subway, Crane sees:

> Through the bound cable strands, the arching path
> Upward, veering with light, the flight of strings,—
> Taut miles of shuttling moonlight syncopate
> The whispered rush, telepathy of wires.
> Up the index of night, granite and steel—
> Transparent meshes—fleckless the gleaming staves—
> Sibylline voices flicker, waveringly stream
> As though a god were issue of the strings.

The bridge becomes a gargantuan Aeolian harp, not only the source of the imagination in the metaphor made famous by Coleridge, but also the symbol of the romantic imagination welded to immense industrial power and technical expertise. This is the vision Crane held for America—a culture that could fuse the power of the aesthetic imagination with the rawness of its industrial might. And this fusion entails not only the bridging of cultures past and present, but the synthesis of time and space, all accomplished through language:

> —O Choir, translating time
> Into that multitudinous Verb the suns
> And synergy of waters ever fuse, recast
> In myriad syllables,—

Finally, time and space, symbolized in this poem by the recurring images of, respectively, the serpent and the eagle, come to roost:

> —One song, one Bridge of Fire! Is it Cathay,
> Now pity steeps the grass and rainbows ring
> The serpent with the eagle in the leaves . . . ?
> Whispers antiphonal in azure swing.

One leaves the poem both exhilarated and with Crane's question mark lingering in the mind. How is such a vision sustained in America, then or now? Crane, though he believed that the poem is its own experience, suffered great difficulty sustaining whatever optimism he found in *The Bridge*, and exhausted after his massive effort, he feared for his creative gift. He had worked himself half to death and drank himself into near oblivion at the same time. He was physically and psychically spent.

To recuperate, in 1931 Crane visited his father, who had opened an inn near Chagrin Falls, Ohio. The two finally reconciled and each became tolerant of the other's worldview, though they must have chafed a bit. This was, perhaps, the calmest, happiest time in Crane's life. But he was never cut out for a sedate life away from books, art, and the company of creative people. He applied for a Guggenheim, which he was awarded in March, and he opted for travel to Mexico, with vague ideas toward a poem encompassing the conquest of Latin America. While living outside of Mexico City in Mixcoac, Crane associated with the writer Katherine Anne Porter, also a Guggenheim Fellow, and other members of the art community, including the Mexican artist David Sequeiros, who painted a portrait of Crane which, in a fit of drunken despair, Crane sliced to ribbons with a razor, beginning with the eyes.

While Crane was in Mexico City, Peggy—the estranged wife of his friend Malcolm Cowley—arrived in pursuit of a divorce. Both needed company, so Crane and Peggy were often together exploring the Mexican countryside, especially around Taxco, where Peggy was living. On Christmas night 1931, with the sound of cathedral bells ringing through the town, Crane and Peggy became lovers. Certainly, Peggy helped to kindle his last burst of creativity, but Crane's first and only heterosexual affair was anything but subdued. Crane's final poem, *The Broken Tower*, dates from this period, and in it Crane uttered what now can be seen as his famous parting words:

> And so it was I entered the broken world
> To trace the visionary company of love, its voice
> An instant in the wind (I know not whither hurled)
> But not for long to hold each desperate choice.

He was indeed desperate. He spent his Guggenheim year with only one poem to show, he drank suicidally, mourned the recent death of his father, made a spectacle of himself chasing Indian boys, had too many run-ins with the local police. He had to leave. Crane borrowed the money for passage home from his father's widow and cash for the train fare to the port of Vera Cruz from the Guggenheim Foundation. Crane and Peggy Cowley boarded the *Orizaba* on 24 April 1932, bound for Havana and New York City, and around noon on the 27th, Crane walked to the stern, folded his coat over the rail, and dropped into the sea.

Crane's poetry is among the most vital American work of the twentieth century. His *Collected Poems* was published posthumously in 1933, and though his reputation suffered during the reign of the New Critics, it has seen great renewed attention since the 1950s. Because the literary community has outgrown its reticence about homosexuality, solid critical attention has been paid to the relationships between Crane's sexuality and his art. We can now understand his alcohol abuse as an addiction, left tragically untreated. Robert Lowell, in *Words for Hart Crane*, put these lines in Crane's mouth:

> My profit was a pocket with a hole.
> Who asks for me, the Shelley of my age,
> Must lay his heart out for my bed and board.

Although Crane did not live to experience it, many hearts have laid themselves out reading his poems. Like Shelley, a great poet passed too soon from life into the sea.

[*See also* Fugitives, The (and Southern Agrarianism) *and* Long Poem, The.]

## SELECTED WORKS

*White Buildings* (1926)
*The Bridge* (1930)

*The Collected Poems of Hart Crane* (1933)
*The Letters of Hart Crane 1916–1932* (1965)
*Complete Poems and Selected Letters and Prose* (1966)
*Robber Rocks: Letters and Memories of Hart Crane, 1923–1932* (1968)
*Letters of Hart Crane and His Family* (1974)
*The Poems of Hart Crane* (1986)
*O My Land, My Friends: The Selected Letters of Hart Crane* (1997)

## FURTHER READING

Bloom Harold, ed. *Modern Critical Views: Hart Crane.* New York, 1986.

Butterfield, R. W. *The Broken Arc: A Study of Hart Crane.* Edinburgh, 1969.

Clark, David R. *Critical Essays on Hart Crane.* Boston, 1982.

Combs, Robert Long. *Vision of the Voyage: Hart Crane and the Psychology of Romanticism.* Memphis, Tenn., 1978. Sets Crane's work in the romantic tradition, drawing on Hegel's philosophy to examine Crane's poetry.

Fisher, Clive. *Hart Crane: A Life.* New Haven, Conn., 2002.

Guiguet, Jean. *The Poetic Universe of Hart Crane.* Orono, Maine., 1993.

Horton, Philip. *Hart Crane: The Life of an American Poet.* New York, 1937.

Lewis, R. W. B. *The Poetry of Hart Crane: A Critical Study.* Westport, Conn., 1978. Looks at Crane's life and poetry in one of the major texts in the critical rejuvenation of Crane's work.

Liebowitz, Herbert A. *Hart Crane, An Introduction to the Poetry.* New York, 1968.

Mariani, Paul. *The Broken Tower: The Life of Hart Crane.* Edinburgh, 1999.

Martin, Robert K. *The Homosexual Tradition in American Poetry.* Austin, Tex., 1979. A key text that examines poets from Walt Whitman to James Merrill and the centrality of the homosexual experience to their work. Crane is a pivotal figure in the study.

Paul, Sherman. *Hart's Bridge.* Urbana, Ill., 1972. Lucid, erudite biographical study of Crane's work.

Trachtenberg, Alan, ed. *Hart Crane: A Collection of Critical Essays.* Englewood Cliffs, N.J., 1982.

Unterecker, John. *Voyager: A Life of Hart Crane.* New York, 1969.

Uroff, Margaret Dickie. *Hart Crane: The Patterns of His Poetry.* Urbana, Ill., 1976. Examines the patterns of violence, flight, possession, images of stasis, and senses of mastery as they function to give form to Crane's poetry.

Weber, Brom. *Hart Crane: A Biographical and Critical Study.* New York, 1948. One of the earliest and most influential studies to claim Crane a major American poet.

Yingling, Thomas E. *Hart Crane and the Homosexual Text: New Thresholds, New Anatomies.* Chicago, 1990. Situates homosexuality as a central concern in contemporary literary studies and locates Hart Crane's work as the voicing of a new, modern homosexual subjectivity.

# STEPHEN CRANE

*by Mark Richardson*

Stephen Crane was born in Newark, New Jersey, on 1 November 1871, the fourteenth and last child of Rev. Jonathan Townley Crane (Methodist by denomination) and Mary Helen Peck Crane (an activist in the temperance movement). Eight of his brothers and sisters survived infancy. Crane's early years were spent in the cities of Newark, Bloomington, and Paterson, New Jersey, as his father moved from church to church in the way of Methodist ministers. In 1878 the Reverend Crane accepted a post at Drew Methodist Church in Port Jervis, New York, and there young Stephen lived for some five years, wandering about in the woods of neighboring counties and, from time to time, listening to veterans of the New York 124th Regiment, who often gathered in a park at the center of Port Jervis to swap stories about their service in the Civil War. (It was likely here that Crane's fascination with the war began in earnest, and he may have drawn on the Port Jervis veterans' recollections when writing *The Red Badge of Courage*.) Reverend Crane died in 1880, leaving Stephen and his siblings to be raised by their mother, whose devotion to the church her husband had served increased as the years rolled by; she died in 1891, after suffering a mental breakdown of uncertain duration and severity. Readers have been known to chuckle at the thought of so pious a father and mother giving birth to so irreverent a son as Stephen Crane. But the son seems less to have been in rebellion against his parents, whom he loved, than simply attuned to the knowing urbanity and cleverness that characterized the younger set in New York City, where he would make his start in the 1890s.

In 1883, Mrs. Crane moved with the younger children—the oldest remained in Port Jervis, where he practiced law—to Asbury Park, New Jersey, a resort town

Stephen Crane.
(*Courtesy of the Library of Congress*)

on the coast. Here Crane wrote his first short story. After several years at a Methodist school in nearby Pennington (where his father had once been headmaster), Crane transferred to a military boarding school in Claverack, New York, where he was instructed by (among others) General John Bullock Van Petten, a veteran of much hard combat in the Civil War. In the summer Crane returned to Asbury Park, where he began writing items for a news bureau run by an older brother. During 1890 and 1891, Crane matriculated in, and left, both Lafayette College and Syracuse University, as it became clear to him that writing (and not, say, engineering) would be his vocation. He drifted about from Lake View, New Jersey, where his brother Edmund lived, to New York City, where he stayed with friends and frequented the saloons, cheap boardinghouses, and theaters of the Bowery—the setting of his first novel, *Maggie: A Girl of the Streets* (1893), at which he was already at work.

By this time, Crane was regularly publishing (often irreverent) sketches in the *New York Tribune*, scandalizing, in a minor way, the genteel readers of that eminent Republican organ. But nothing could have prepared the readers of the 1890s for *Maggie*, the lurid tale of Bowery life that Crane published pseudonymously, and at his own expense, in 1893. When that short novel was well received by William Dean Howells, among others, Crane's career was launched. An abridged text of *The Red Badge of Courage* appeared in newspapers late in 1894, and Crane became, by the time the book edition appeared in 1895, a celebrity, dispatching sketches and stories for syndication from as far away as Mexico City.

In 1896, an agreement with the McClure syndicate to supply it with war stories sent Crane south to Florida, hoping to reach Cuba, where rebels had begun their struggle for independence from Spain; the steamer he took out of Jacksonville sank on 2 January 1897, incidentally yielding, among other things, Crane's masterpiece "The Open Boat." While in Jacksonville, Crane met the woman who was to become what biographical sketches sometimes call his "common law wife" (they never married). She was Cora Steward (a.k.a. Cora Taylor), the proprietress of what by some accounts was a brothel fittingly named the Hotel de Dream. She and Crane spent the rest of his short life together, in New York (briefly), in Greece (where they covered the Greco-Turkish War in 1897), and eventually in England (where the two settled into a shabby country house, and became friendly with Joseph Conrad, Henry James, H. G. Wells, and Harold Fredric). At the outset of hostilities between the United States and Spain in Cuba, Crane returned to New York, failed the physical examination that would have allowed him to enter the Navy, and signed on as war correspondent with Joseph Pulitzer's *New York World*. In that capacity Crane witnessed the fights at Guantanamo and San Juan Hill before retreating, exhausted and ill, to Virginia; his health—constitutionally weak—would never fully recover. As soon as he was able, Crane returned to the Caribbean to cover the Puerto Rican phase of the war, and when this didn't amount to much, he turned, pausing in Havana, to short stories, and began his novel of the Greek war, *Active Service*. Early in 1899 he returned to England and to Cora, and embarked on a remarkable period of literary productivity, even as his health declined alarmingly (he was suffering from tuberculosis and malaria). He died at a sanitarium in Badenweiler, Germany, on 5 June 1900, at the age of twenty-eight, having already written enough stories, sketches, articles, poetry, and novels to fill a typical library shelf.

## LITERARY NATURALISM

Crane is often associated with a phase of late nineteenth-century thought known to literary historians as "naturalism." A good way to understand the term is by opposing it to "*super*naturalism." The literary "naturalist" is skeptical, and often contemptuous, of religion; he tends to account for human origins, human conduct, and human destiny in terms rather more in harmony with Darwin and Nietzsche than with the New Testament. Also important in "naturalist" writing is a loss of belief in individual autonomy. True "individuality," and real freedom of will, are rare commodities in

thoroughgoing naturalist fiction. (Even Mark Twain's Huckleberry Finn, who learns to *act* as an individualist, never entirely learns to *think* like one.) The suspicion that "free will" and personal autonomy are illusions involves as well the corollary belief that we are subject to physical and social forces that simply dominate us. Ralph Waldo Emerson provides a good summary phrase, though he wrote a generation or two before the "naturalists" arrived, and is in other respects not in sympathy with them. In "Fate," Emerson speaks of "organization tyrannizing over character." That is pretty much what the world amounts to, according to the naturalist. For these reasons, among others, naturalism is incompatible with "humanism"—or, in any case, with the belief that humanity somehow stands at the center of the world, if not of the cosmos; or with the belief that we are somehow the chief concern, and ultimate product, of the universe. For the naturalist, "man" is not by any means the measure of all things. Naturalists, in fact, tend to regard *Homo sapiens* as a kind of epiphenomenon of the physical world. And here, the influence of Darwin, alluded to already, is paramount. The Darwinian–naturalist world is a world "governed" by physical laws and chance; it is in fact a world not "governed" at all in the sense in which we use that word in reference to social and political systems. Human experience comes to have a merely contingent, even an absurd, aspect. We see that any "meaning" experience holds for us is meaning we ourselves create. The world as such means absolutely nothing, and has nothing whatever to do with such human conceptions as "the just," "the good," "the moral."

The following passages, familiar to any reader of Crane, are characteristic of the "naturalist" habit of thought:

> When it occurs to a man that nature does not regard him as important, and that she feels she would not maim the universe by disposing of him, he at first wishes to throw bricks at the temple, and he hates deeply the fact that there are no bricks and no temples. Any visible expression of nature would surely be pelleted with his jeers. Then, if there be no tangible thing to hoot he feels, perhaps, the desire to confront a personification and indulge in pleas, bowed to one knee, and with hands supplicant, saying: 'Yes, but I love myself.' A high cold star on a winter's night is the word he feels that she says to him. Thereafter he knows the pathos of his situation.

> We picture the world as thick with conquering and elate humanity, but here, with the bugles of the tempest pealing, it was hard to imagine a peopled earth. One viewed the

existence of man then as a marvel, and conceded a glamour of wonder to these lice which were caused to cling to a whirling, fire-smote, ice-locked, disease-stricken, space-lost bulb. The conceit of man was explained by this storm to be the very engine of life. One was a coxcomb not to die in it.

The first of these passages appears in "The Open Boat," a story about, at least indirectly, a gun-running junket to Cuba that ends in disaster—perhaps (or so the rumors went) as a result of Spanish sabotage. The second is from "The Blue Hotel," a story about (among other things) the introduction into Nebraska of what a character, speaking the bumpkinish dialect Crane often resorts to, denominates "a line of ilictric street-cars." The cool, chastened temper of these two stories is quite characteristic of the 1890s—the great epoch of imperial capital in the United States, and the great era of dizzying, hyper-accelerated industrial development. And Crane's best-known stories and novels resign us not only to the vagaries of the "natural" environment, as in "The Open Boat," but also to those of the essentially "social" environments with which natural ones are so often confused in his fiction, as in *Maggie: A Girl of the Streets*, the novel of slum life about which Crane once said: "It tries to show that environment is a tremendous thing in the world and frequently shapes lives regardless." Against the forces of both natural and social environments, as also against the tides, resistance is simply absurd. Crane's great theme is futility: the experience of being inadequate to the project of really understanding, let alone managing, the forces that condition one's environment. Crane forever writes about the experience of not quite feeling at home in the world.

## CRANE'S PROSE STYLE

In Crane's case, this general frame of mind called for, or perhaps simply allowed for, the cultivation of a peculiar and unforgettable prose style—a style that is at once cool, whimsical, supremely self-possessed, and highly idiosyncratic; this style is his great legacy in American literature (its influence is felt in writers as diverse as H. L. Mencken, Ernest Hemingway, and James Cain). Often, for example, one encounters in Crane metaphors that startle and disorient the reader, at times to surreal effect. Here is a description of a house fire, as it begins, in *The Monster*, a short novel dating from Crane's later years: "A wisp of smoke came from one of the windows at the end of the house and drifted quietly into the branches of a cherry tree. Its companions followed it in slowly increasing numbers, and finally there was a current controlled by invisible banks which poured into the fruit-laden boughs of the cherry tree. It was no more to be noted than if a troop of dim and silent gray monkeys had been climbing a grapevine into the clouds."

Several things strike the reader. The first is the comparison of the smoke to water—a confusion of the elements that works by paradox: air, too, can be "poured," after all. But the truly odd feature of the passage is the suggestion in the last sentence that the progress of the smoke is "no more to be noted than if a troop of dim and silent gray monkeys had been climbing a grapevine into the clouds." *No more to be noted?* How are we to understand such a remark? Most observers would "take note" if they saw a troop of dim and silent gray monkeys climbing a grapevine into the clouds, even if they saw it in Crane's fictional town of Whilomville. To an extent, the metaphor works by visual analogy on the basis of color: a rising column of smoke is compared to a chain of *gray* monkeys—to a chain of something gray, anyway. But the monkeys and the grapevine are sheer extravagances, as is the disclaimer that there might be nothing at all unusual in the prospect they afford.

Any reader of Crane will be able to cite other such examples of disorienting metaphors. Consider the famous beginning of "The Open Boat."

> None of them knew the colour of the sky. Their eyes glanced level, and were fastened upon the waves that swept toward them. These waves were of the hue of slate, save for the tops, which were of foaming white, and all of the men knew the colours of the sea. The horizon narrowed and widened, and dipped and rose, and at all times its edge was jagged with waves that seemed thrust in points like rocks.
>
> Many a man ought to have a bathtub larger than the boat which here rode upon the sea. These waves were most wrongfully and barbarously abrupt and tall, and each froth-top was a problem in small-boat navigation.

"Colour" takes on a quietly figurative significance, as the subsidiary, and somewhat archaic, meaning of "aegis" comes into play (as in the phrase "under colour of law"): we are concerned with the "colours of the sea"—with its integrity, its agency, its antagonism, its character. To say that all of the men "knew" " this color is to understate the case, of course. They are sick with knowledge of it. The waves appear to the men like jagged points of rock, as if they, in the little boat, were negotiating a mountain pass and not a patch of ocean—again an arresting metaphor that paradoxically takes sea for land, water for rocks. Either way, the passage goes hard. A new element emerges in the second paragraph. The comparison of bathtub to boat is no doubt funny, pathetically so, because our relation to water in a bathtub differs so utterly from our relation to it in a storm-tossed boat: the one is recreational; the other, antagonistic. Also, bathtubs are meant to keep water in; boats, to keep it out. So it is not just the size of the boat that is the point here, not just the absurd proposition of fitting four men into a bathtub of such commodious size as most men "ought to have."

The waves are described as "most wrongfully and barbarously abrupt and tall." This language belongs to the parlor, or at least to polite society, where we sometimes meet with forces we call "barbarously abrupt." It is as if the waves had committed what an Englishman might regard as an unpardonable sin against good breeding—as if the waves were exhibiting genuinely uncivilized behavior, damn their eyes. One can well imagine this belief forming a part of the men's relation to the water. They feel not merely threatened; they feel insulted, indignant. But Crane turns us about yet again in the last sentence quoted above: "Each froth-top," he says, "was a problem in small-boat navigation." This understates the matter in a special way. *Problems in Small-Boat Navigation* might well be the title of a treatise or textbook, something we might study at the Coast Guard Academy, say. To use that language here puts the relation of men to water in an almost clinical light. With this idea, we are no longer in the game; we are watching a film of it in the locker room; we are being debriefed.

In the aggregate, as they accumulate page after page throughout Crane's fiction, these tricks and devices dislodge the reader from customary habits of attention to words; and that dislodging is what Crane's work is somehow always "about." Crane is much more interested in the texture of what he says than in the "weight" of it. He is all about levity, not gravity. The world he inhabits, on the evidence of the fiction he wrote, is absurd, silly, brutal, and, in the end, without point: "a high cold star" on a winter's night is "the word" it gives us, as we know from "The Open Boat." And what Crane proposes to equip his reader with is simply a *style*, a particular mode of stoicism that can accommodate us to our situation as "lice" clinging "to a whirling, fire-smitten, ice-locked, disease-stricken, space-lost bulb." That series of adjectives from "The Blue Hotel" begins ingenuously enough in its existentialism. But in its sheer extravagance, it moves toward parody of the view it would apparently advance—a drift utterly characteristic of Crane. (His fiction contemplates nothing like the program of action the existentialists would later

offer.) His work is never the work of protest, even when he writes about the slums of the Bowery, or about, as in *The Monster*, the fate of a persecuted African American in small-town America at the height of the lynching terror. He is neither activist nor exhorter, because, for him, activism and exhortation are discredited modes of literary art—relics, it may be, of an earlier and more innocently earnest phase of American intellectual life, when it was still possible to "believe" in things. His work is always about style.

## MAGGIE: A GIRL OF THE STREETS

Crane published his first novel, *Maggie: A Girl of the Streets*, at his own expense and under an assumed name. No commercial publisher was willing to attach its imprint to this sensational tale of a young girl's descent into prostitution in the Bowery (a district in lower Manhattan). The 1880s and 1890s produced a good deal of literature about the slum, much of it intended to stir the reader's compassion for the suffering of the poverty-stricken immigrants who lived in such neighborhoods as the Bowery. Crane's novel owes much to this body of writing, but he hardly writes as a reformer: *Maggie* isn't meant to move anyone to indignation.

Early in the novel we encounter the following description of the tenement in which Maggie and her family live:

> Eventually they [Maggie's brother and father] entered a dark region where, from a careening building, a dozen gruesome doorways gave up loads of babies to the street and the gutter. A wind of early autumn raised yellow dust from cobbles and swirled it against a hundred windows. Long streamers of garments fluttered from fire-escapes. In all unhandy places there were buckets, brooms, rags, and bottles. In the street infants played or fought with other infants or sat stupidly in the way of vehicles. Formidable women, with uncombed hair and disordered dress, gossiped while leaning on railings, or screamed in frantic quarrels. Withered persons, in curious postures of submission to something, sat smoking pipes in obscure corners. A thousand odors of cooking food came forth to the street. The building quivered and creaked from the weight of humanity stamping about in its bowels.

This sort of literarily squalid scene anticipates the urban environments of T. S. Eliot's "Preludes," as well as certain urban images in "The Love Song of J. Alfred Prufrock" and "Rhapsody on a Windy Night." The passage is an exercise in what we now call "slumming," as are Eliot's poems. But the mood evoked by Crane's writing differs notably from that evoked by Eliot's. A suggestion of the forbidden, and therefore of the alluring, usually hangs about Eliot's eroticized urban wildernesses; he has a Puritan's feeling for corruption, which always retained, for him, a glamour from which he needed to protect himself. Crane is hardly vulnerable in this sense. And his evocation of the slums approaches amused contempt. There are few intimations of pity. And as for the erotic implications of socially forbidden precincts, the striking metaphor that most generally controls the passage combines the ideas of parturition (doorways "giving up" babies to the street) and defecation (tenants inhabiting the "bowels" of a building). As William Butler Yeats's "Crazy Jane" says to the Bishop: "Love has pitched its mansion in the place of excrement." Crane writes in the language of disgust. There is nothing at all titillating in this tale of a woman's lost honor. Crane's Bowery is a sink of crime and dissolution, and his procreative metaphor, in the passage just examined, is seriously enough meant. In the slum, there is a shocking fertility; it teems with life, but teems as does a sewer with bacteria. It is sometimes difficult to tell, in reading *Maggie*, whether Crane asks us to conclude that the environment infects the people or that the people infect the environment.

*Maggie* is a comedy whose laughs to a great extent depend on our remarking the great chasm that separates the "real" situation it describes—the squalor, the brutality—from the "vain" ideas about the squalor that the slum dwellers themselves indulge. Crane allows them no quarter, not even the modest dignity of recourse to the illusion of "honor" (whether of a sexual or an ethical sort). If *Maggie* takes aim at anything—if it is at all to be understood as satire—it satirizes not an economic order that brutalizes men and women; it satirizes instead the pretensions of that supreme "coxcomb," man. The novel may be "topical"—ripped from the headlines, as we now say. But the emphasis is general and nonhistorical, as it is in "The Open Boat" and *The Red Badge of Courage*. Crane's cool remarks about the Bowery in an often-quoted letter are certainly to the point, uncharitable though they may sound: "I do not think much can be done with the Bowery as long as [the people there] are in their present state of conceit. A person who thinks himself superior to the rest of us because he has no pride and no clean clothes is as badly conceited as Lillian Russell. In a story of mine called 'An Experiment in Misery' I tried to make plain that the root of the Bowery life is a sort of cowardice. Perhaps I mean a lack of ambition or to willingly be knocked flat and accept the licking."

## THE RED BADGE OF COURAGE

*Maggie* was a commercial failure; hardly any copies were sold. But it was a critical success, and the warm reception accorded it by such luminaries as William Dean Howells encouraged Crane as he embarked on his next major project, a novel of the American Civil War. A number of scholars have traced the origins of the novel to conversations Crane had as a boy with veterans of the New York 124th Regiment in Port Jervis; to anecdotes he picked up from his teachers at Claverack Military Academy; to Civil War novels such as Wilbur F. Hinman's *Corporal Si Klegg and His "Pard"* (1887); to the great battlefield photographs of Matthew Brady; and, most important, to a multivolume work called *Battles and Leaders of the Civil War* (1888), which had originally appeared as a popular series of articles in *Century* magazine. But however that may be, *Red Badge* certainly bears witness to the history in which it took shape in the life of Crane's imagination. It is thoroughly a document of the 1890s, and of the post-Reconstruction era generally: there is not a trace in it of Radical Republicanism, nor, for better and for worse, one thread of what in those days was called the "Bloody Shirt," which politicians who spoke too triumphantly, and piously, about the Grand Army of the Republic, and the democratic cause for which it fought, were inevitably accused of "waving."

*Red Badge* is sometimes treated as a bildungsroman: the record of a young man's coming of age. Henry Fleming, we are told, confronts his own weaknesses and fears, overcomes them, and emerges from the fire of battle a man. However, such a reading hardly withstands a close examination of the novel, especially when we attend to its style, which is, as always with Crane, irreverent, mischievous, and often downright comical. Nowhere—and certainly no more at the conclusion than at the beginning—does Crane allow his hero to achieve the dignity and self-possession we properly associate with maturity. Consider the famous conclusion to the novel:

> It rained. The procession of weary soldiers became a bedraggled train, despondent and muttering, marching with churning effort in a trough of liquid brown mud under a low, wretched sky. Yet the youth smiled, for he saw that the world was a world for him, though many discovered it to be made of oaths and walking sticks. He had rid himself of the red sickness of battle. The sultry nightmare was in the past. He had been an animal blistered and sweating in the heat and pain of war. He turned now with a lover's thirst to images of tranquil skies, fresh meadows, cool brooks—an existence of soft and eternal peace.

> Over the river a golden ray of sun came through the hosts of leaden rain clouds.

We are told, here, that the world is now a world "for" Henry Fleming, "though many discovered it to be made of oaths and walking sticks." We are invited, in other words, to suppose that Henry is no longer "hobbled" by the world—that on the serene plateau to which he thinks he has ascended, no more vexations will elicit from him "oaths," nor any constitutional weakness send him reaching for his "walking stick." But the reader simply must conclude—Crane's arch tone leaves little choice—that for Henry the world will always be, as it is for every other character in Crane, made *precisely* of oaths and walking sticks; and that he is a coxcomb not to die in it. The mastery, the sheer *fluency*, that Henry supposes himself to have achieved is of course an illusion. And the picture-postcard pastoral of the scene here evoked—Henry is said to have emerged from "a place of blood and wrath" to "prospects of clover tranquility," "fresh meadows," and "cool brooks"—is but the emanation of Henry's still naively "youthful" state of mind. He has recovered what Crane dryly calls an ability "to see himself in a heroic light." He has acquired adequate breathing space, as Crane says after the first of the two climactic charges is done, "in which to appreciate himself"; and he does just that—with "much satisfaction." The successful charge against the enemy color guard only leaves him "preparing to resent some new monstrosity in the way of dins and smashes." And it would be hard to demonstrate that the following late passage is any less ironic in tone than those toward the beginning of the book, where, clearly, we are to regard Henry's self-knowledge as faulty in the extreme: "He found that he could look back upon the brass and bombast of his earlier gospels and see them truly. He was gleeful when he discovered that he now despised them. With this conviction came a store of assurance. He felt a quiet manhood, nonassertive but of sturdy and strong blood. He knew that he would no more quail before his guides wherever they should point. He had been to touch the great death, and found that, after all, it was but the great death. He was a man." These are Henry's assessments, not Crane's.

## "THE BRIDE COMES TO YELLOW SKY" AND "THE OPEN BOAT"

As we have seen, Crane is especially good at effects arrived at by "dislocating" the reader's point of view. A fine example occurs in "The Bride Comes to Yellow Sky," one of the most often reprinted (and often taught) stories

in English. "Bride" is a "western," or, more accurately, a kind of spoof of "westerns"—a literary genre well established when Crane began his career. A lawman, Sheriff Potter, has one last showdown with the local gunslinger, Scratchy Wilson, in the town's dusty streets. Potter has just that morning returned to Yellow Sky with his new bride, and his marriage, literary critics often tell us, somehow symbolizes the final "civilization," or taming, of the West, which by the 1890s had been fully assimilated into the rapidly industrializing nation. That is all well and good. But something more important to Crane than the taming of the West appears to be involved in this great story—something more closely associated with the writer's craft, and with Crane's general outlook on the world.

Notice what Crane accomplishes, for example, in the following description of Wilson as he sportively fires a few rounds at a dog in front of the Weary Gentleman Saloon:

> The dog . . . had not appreciated the advance of events. He yet lay dozing in front of his master's door. At sight of the dog, the man paused and raised his revolver humorously. At sight of the man, the dog sprang up and walked diagonally away, with a sullen head, and growling. The man yelled, and the dog broke into a gallop. As it was about to enter an alley, there was a loud noise, a whistling, and something spat the ground directly before it. The dog screamed, and, wheeling in terror, galloped headlong in a new direction. Again there was a noise, a whistling, and sand was kicked viciously before it. Fear-stricken, the dog turned and flurried like an animal in a pen. The man stood laughing, his weapons at his hips.

The gunshots are, of course, described from the dog's point of view. His way of making sense of the world simply doesn't include the equipment he needs in order to understand the connections linking the report of the gun, the whistling sound of the bullet in the air, and the burst of sand where the bullet strikes the ground. It is worth pointing out further that as the narrator, in what Crane allows him to know, becomes more "canine," the dog himself is subtly (and whimsically) humanized: he is said to "scream," to be unable adequately to "appreciate the advance of events," and so on. The comic personifications only point up the pathos of his real situation.

Now, the reader might take this analysis of the dog's situation a step or two further, the better to understand Crane's "naturalism." Let us imagine that Crane here shows us, by exaggeration, what he believes to be true about our own plight, not simply about the dog's. In his fiction, Crane everywhere wants to suggest that we lack the conceptual and intellectual equipment we need in order to make good sense of the social and natural worlds we inhabit. There are some things, and some connections between things, that simply do not "register" in our minds, and some things of which we remain aware in wrong or inappropriate ways. The difference between us and Crane's dog is that our limitations are culturally determined and can be changed, while his are natural or biological and cannot. You can't talk a dog into understanding banditry.

In "The Open Boat" and "The Blue Hotel," Crane places us in a world that makes no sense, that is indifferent to us, and in which, for the most part, we cut a fairly ridiculous figure (this, too, is the world as Henry Fleming experiences it). And Crane did not, it turns out, regard his late nineteenth-century compatriots as occupying a position very much superior to the dog's in "The Bride Comes to Yellow Sky." It is certainly true that, in this story, Jack Potter and his wife feel themselves, however dimly, to be the butt of some great joke at their expense, quite as if the new America in which they find themselves in the 1890s—and which is epitomized by the luxurious Pullman train that conveys them across Texas to their anticlimactic encounter with Scratchy Wilson—is so large and alienating as to beggar description. They flurry like animals in a pen. They hear the report of the Gun of History, hear an appalling Whistling Sound about their ears, and feel the Sand in Their Eyes. But they cannot put it all together. They can only achieve the vague feeling of having *somehow* been insulted: "Historically," the narrator tells us, "there was supposed to be something infinitely humorous in their situation." Theirs is a world turned upside down, whose social relations are unreadable, opaque; even the porter is able to "bully" them in ways that "do not make it exactly plain to them" that they are, in fact, being bullied. They are like Henry Fleming when he overhears the officer speaking of his fellow grunts as if they were "mule drivers," or as if they were merely some sort of regimental "broom" with which to sweep the woods clean of rebels: he is humiliated, as are Jack Potter and his homely bride ("It was quite apparent that she had cooked," we are told, "and that she expected to cook, dutifully").

Crane, then, certainly thinks of the world as an "alienating" place. And "The Open Boat," "The Bride Comes to Yellow Sky," and *Red Badge of Courage* reflect a specifically Gilded Age, American sense of what the existentialists would later call "nausea." What the men in the boat face—and what the grunts on the battlefield

ultimately face, if they have the wit to see it—is a world stripped of religious and sentimental illusions. We learn in "The Open Boat" that there are no bricks to throw at the temples; we learn, indeed, that there *are* no temples. Ours is a godless world, indifferent alike to our petty purposes and our unseemly suffering. Crane's response to the men's total situation in "The Open Boat"—and he seems to believe it is "representative" of our situation generally—is a cool irony and a fine stylistic rigor that operate at the level of the phrase and condition even his diction, which is as tightly managed and shrewdly austere as anything going in the 1890s, and for quite a while thereafter. Crane makes an ethic, a duty, out of being disillusioned. He wants to achieve and sustain a prose capable of expressing what the captain in "The Open Boat" expresses merely with a laugh: "Then the captain, in the bow, chuckled in a way that expressed humor, contempt, tragedy, all in one. 'Do you think we've got much of a show, now, boys?' said he." Crane's unsentimental detachment emerges as the only properly tough-minded and attractive posture to strike; it is simply all we have left in a world without temples—this standing delicately poised between faith and despair, between humor and contempt, between tragedy and farce. The captain's chuckle is what writers especially receptive to Crane, like H. L. Mencken, later appropriated and refined. And it is a chuckle Henry Fleming is never allowed to achieve—and never could achieve, as Crane imagines him.

### THE MONSTER

*The Monster*, which Crane completed toward the end of his life, tells the story of Henry Johnson, a black coachman who is horribly disfigured (and rendered an imbecile) by the house fire from which he rescues little Jimmie Trescott, the only son of the town's respected physician. The townspeople quickly turn from blaming Henry for having started the fire—a conclusion to which their native racism initially led them—to celebrating him as the self-sacrificing savior of Jimmie. But their generosity turns out to be as fickle as their bigotry: soon enough they shrink from Henry, who is no longer able to take care of himself, and ostracize Dr. Trescott for refusing to turn Henry out. Henry is a monster, they say, a thing too horrible to behold; and it would have been better all round if the good doctor had simply let him die, and dedicated a few fine words to his ashes. *The Monster* is a devastating satire of small-town pettiness. Some readers profess to see in it an attack, as well, on American racism, which was of course especially vicious in those years of epidemic lynching. But that view, however consoling, is hard to sustain: Crane, as in *Maggie*, seems only mildly committed to protest, and not at all to reform. His commitments in *The Monster* are what they always are: to the writing.

The following description of the fire illustrates the point. "At the entrance to the laboratory," Crane writes, Henry Johnson and the boy he carries meet "a strange spectacle. The room was like a garden in the region where might be burning flowers. Flames of violet, crimson, green, blue, orange, and purple were blooming everywhere. There was one blaze that was precisely the hue of a delicate coral. In another place was a mass that lay merely in phosphorescent inaction like a pile of emeralds. . . . There was an explosion at one side, and suddenly before [Henry] there reared a delicate, trembling sapphire shape like a fairy lady. With a quiet smile she blocked his path and doomed him and Jimmie." Henry is able, in his last exertion, to lay Jimmie down near a window. But he himself collapses onto the floor beneath a table on which sit beakers and jars of various chemicals, one of which seems "to hold a scintillant and writhing serpent. Suddenly the glass splintered, and a ruby-red snake-like thing poured its thick length out upon the top of the old desk. It coiled and hesitated, and then began to swim a languorous way down the mahogany slant. At the angle it waved its sizzling molten head to and fro over the closed eyes of the man beneath it. Then, in a moment, with a mystic impulse, it moved again, and the red snake flowed directly down into Johnson's upturned face. Afterward the trail of this creature seemed to reek, and amid flames and low explosions drops like red-hot jewels pattered softly down at leisurely intervals." What sort of mind could see this particular fire in this particular way? A mind utterly unaffected and unsentimental; a mind capable of seeing in the fire a show of light, color, and form. It is a mind provisionally indifferent—Olympian, even—to the exquisite suffering the fire causes the men and women immediately touched by it. After all, they are, such a mind must feel, a little selfish in seeing the fire only in terms of what it can do *to them*.

In other words, the fire that ruins Henry Johnson is described precisely as a fire might like to be described. The fire is done justice to. The fire is flattered. It has good reason to deploy its flames like "flags" "joyfully" waving in the wind, as Crane puts it. No wonder the townspeople look up with eyes that "shine" with "awe," as Crane says they do. For they, too, are pyrophiliac, and can appreciate a fire. To appreciate it—as theater, as a spectacle, as a thing of force and beauty—is in fact what

they "really" came to the Trescotts' burning house to do. (Their motives are not so sympathetic as they suppose.) They are, so far as their moral investment in the scene is concerned, rather like the narrator himself: indifferent, and, as the story soon permits them to show, for the most part incapable of kindness. They would as soon kill the disfigured Henry Johnson as look at him—at least if they could do so merely by taking thought. We are invited to condemn the townspeople for their callous detachment, and yet we never really judge the narrator. The reason is apparently that, under the circumstances, and unlike the narrator, the townspeople *ought* to be committed to seeing the fire in terms chiefly of what it can do to their friends and neighbors (that is, make them suffer). They *ought* to be self-centered in that very human sort of way, because that would be the beginning of empathy. But they are nothing of the sort. They are not, to be sure, narrators describing imaginary events, as is Crane; but they most certainly are characters in a story behaving like narrators describing imaginary events. And that is precisely the moral problem to which Crane's novella alerts us: at the end of the day, Henry Johnson is not, for the good white people of Whilomville, "real," which is why they are all quite willing to have him disappear. But no sooner do we reach this conclusion than we reach another one much more unsettling: for Stephen Crane himself, Henry Johnson is, in an important sense, unreal. As presented by the narrator, not by the characters in the story, Henry is compacted of the worst clichés of the blackface minstrel stage. He is a cartoon of a man—a caricature. He is "Zip Coon," the urban dandy counterpart, in minstrel theater, to the rural "Jim Crow."

Here is the scene describing the visit Henry makes to his girlfriend, Bella Farragut, at her home in what Crane calls "Watermelon Alley": "The duty of receiving Mr. Johnson fell upon Mrs. Farragut, because Bella, in another room, was scrambling wildly into her best gown. The fat old woman met him with a great ivory smile, sweeping back with the door, and bowing low. . . . After a great deal of kowtow," we are told, "they were planted in two chairs opposite each other in the living-room. Here they exchanged the most tremendous civilities, until Miss Bella swept into the room, when there was more kowtow on all sides, and a smiling show of teeth that was like an illumination. The cooking-stove was of course in this drawing room, and on the fire was some kind of a long-winded stew. Mrs. Farragut was obliged to arise and attend to it from time to time. Also young Sim came in and went to bed on his pallet in the corner.

But to all these domesticities the three maintained an absolute dumbness." Now, we might first suppose that Crane expects us to admire the studied dignity with which these three conduct themselves in their impoverished circumstances, as they politely ignore the fact that a single room serves for a parlor, bedroom, and kitchen (with its "long-winded stew"). But Crane expects nothing of the kind, no more than he expects us to be moved to sympathy by Maggie's embattled sense of "honor." He continues: "They bowed and smiled and ignored and imitated until a late hour, and if they had been the occupants of the most gorgeous salon in the world they could not have been more like three monkeys." Clearly, this is an example of what we might call "inappropriate affect" on the part of the narrator, though in this case we have to do with an impropriety of which Crane is not a conscious manipulator. Crane is himself talking like one of the more unsavory characters in his own story. He is a citizen of Whilomville in good standing (as he would perhaps acknowledge with a shrug). A continuity links the general mode of the comedy in this novella—what might be termed the narrator's strategically "inappropriate" affect—to the sort of racist stereotyping we find in this scene, with its Watermelon Alley, its unctuously toothy smiles, and its monkeyshines. These details, embarrassing to today's sensibilities, mark the story as very comfortably belonging in the 1890s.

That is why Crane's satire in *The Monster*, if satire is the right word for it, never rises into indignation. Crane isn't indignant at all. He isn't writing any jeremiads about the broken promises of Reconstruction and the Republican Party in the 1890s—the decade that in many ways marked the nadir of American thinking about race. As often as not, he is simply amusing himself. Crane's story about a persecuted black man is, for him, not a story about a man persecuted *because* he is black; it is about a much more generalized, historically nonspecific sort of intolerance—to the extent that it is *really* about intolerance at all. There is very little in *The Monster*, or anywhere else in Crane's fiction, to suggest that the suffering to which he bears witness ought to be, or can be very much, alleviated.

## CRANE IN A NATION OF DIMINISHED POSSIBILITY

What, then, is missing in Crane's world? "Truth with a big 'T,'" as the philosopher William James might say. There is nowhere any Truth for Crane; there are only ways of seeing. In certain respects, his thinking is what we would now call "antifoundational," or, in American contexts, "pragmatist." But his is the antifoundationalism, the suave "irony," that many writers on the left now complain about in certain strains of postmodern theory, on the grounds that it simply cannot support, let alone offer, a program of practical political reform. For example, we know that the battle described in *The Red Badge of Courage* was, "in real life," many things: an episode in a democratic struggle to abolish slavery; an episode in a national-Providential story about the Glory of the Coming of the Lord; an episode in the extension of politics by other means to settle a question about the nature of federal power, and to resolve for good and all the future of slave labor in the American West; an exercise in military strategy, in which warfare, particularly under Grant and Sherman, was decisively "modernized"; a "vast blue demonstration"; a theater for the staging of an adolescent crisis; or, as for interpreters like W. E. B. Du Bois, an episode in a centuries-old conflict over the right relations of whites to nonwhites everywhere in the world. The battle is undoubtedly all of these things at once. But not one of them, for Crane, is ever allowed "essentially" to characterize it. He lacks commitment. He had, in fact, perfected the art of "lacking commitment." For Crane, the Civil War is determined by nothing much at all. And the implication in *The Red Badge of Courage*, as in Crane's fiction generally, is that Henry Fleming's alienated situation is representative. It is pure egotism to think of yourself or of your nation as having a special claim to make on the sympathies of the onlooking world. The life of each one of us is, to each one of us, fraught with significance and interest. We love ourselves. But to others we may merely be an anecdote, a part of the scenery—what the Union officer whom Henry Fleming overhears contemptuously refers to as "mule drivers." We may be the butt of a grand joke somehow effected by George Pullman and the Pullman Palace Car Company, as Potter and his dishwashing belle dimly know themselves to be in "The Bride Comes to Yellow Sky." We may be culturally shipwrecked in some "Watermelon Alley" of the Jim Crow American 1890s, with Henry Johnson and Bella Farragut in *The Monster*. Like Billie the oiler in "The Open Boat," we may be dead on the beaches of Florida, having made it that far, and no further, from—as Crane's astute contemporary readers would have known—a sinking cache of weapons running a half-hearted Navy blockade. Or we may be, as the ravages of American history are in *The Red Badge of Courage*, simply invisible. To know these things as Crane did is to dwell in a nation of diminished possibility.

## WORKS

*Maggie: A Girl of the Streets* (1893)
*The Black Riders and Other Lines* (1895)
*The Red Badge of Courage* (1895)
*George's Mother* (1896) *The Third Violet* (1897)
*The Open Boat and Other Tales of Adventure* (1898)
*Active Service* (1899)
*The Monster and Other Stories* (1899)
*War Is Kind* (1899)

## FURTHER READING

Beer, Thomas. *Stephen Crane*. New York, 1941. Reprint of the 1923 edition. First book-length study of Crane, controversial and unreliable as to biographical detail, but highly suggestive and very well written.

Benfey, Christopher. *The Double Life of Stephen Crane.* New York, 1992. A biographical study.

Gullason, Thomas A., ed. *Stephen Crane's Career: Perspectives and Evaluations.* New York, 1972. A helpful collection of reviews, reminiscences, and criticism.

Kazin, Alfred. *An American Procession.* New York, 1985. The chapter on Crane is among the best short studies of the writer.

La France, Marston. *A Reading of Stephen Crane.* New York, 1971.

Mitchell, Lee Clark, ed. *New Essays on* The Red Badge of Courage. New York, 1986. An important collection of assessments of *Red Badge.*

Robertson, Michael. *Stephen Crane, Journalism, and the Making of Modern American Literature.* New York, 1997.

Solomon, Eric. *Stephen Crane: From Parody to Realism.* Cambridge, Mass., 1967.

Stallman, R. W. *Stephen Crane: A Biography.* New York, 1968. The most extensive biography published to date.

Wertheim, Stanley, and Paul Sorrentino. *The Crane Log: A Documentary Life of Stephen Crane.* New York, 1994.

See also the article on *The Red Badge of Courage*, immediately following.

# STEPHEN CRANE'S
# *THE RED BADGE OF COURAGE*

*by Mark Richardson*

Notwithstanding the often-repeated testimony of the credulous old veteran who read *The Red Badge of Courage* (1895)—"I was with Crane at Antietam"—Stephen Crane, of course, had never seen battle, at least off of the athletic field, when he wrote his great war novel. Much work has been undertaken to unearth his sources for *Red Badge*, which might have been based in part on the experiences of the New York 124th regiment, many of whose veterans he met in Port Jervis when he was a boy. And in 1893 Crane read *Battles and Leaders of the Civil War*, a series that had run in *Century* magazine in the middle 1880s; there he found, among other things, a detailed account of the battle of Chancellorsville, which seems to have provided the model for the battle described in *Red Badge*. Crane may also have had in mind the stories of a colorful teacher of his at Claverack Military Academy, General John Bullock Van Petten, who had fought, among his many engagements, at Antietam. For his part, Crane's first biographer, Thomas Beer, reports—perhaps apocryphally—that Crane undertook *Red Badge* on the dare, from a friend, that he could not best Emile Zola's account of warfare in *La Debacle*, which Crane appears to have read in 1893. But however things stand with regard to the sources of the novel, surely of more significance is the peculiar quality of Crane's prose therein, which is quite distinctive, for it became the instrument with which he gained a purchase on the American scene in the 1890s.

## "HEROISM" IN *THE RED BADGE OF COURAGE*

The most important and long-standing controversy surrounding *Red Badge* has to do with whether or not Henry Fleming, its protagonist, can rightly be called a "hero." Does Henry, or does he not, "mature" as the novel progresses? Does the conclusion of the novel mark a turn, an upward development, in his character? Or is he, all the way through to the bitter end, regarded with ironic condescension by the narrator (and by Crane)? Related to this is another important controversy: Do we encounter in Crane the acid sort of irony, the inexhaustible sort of impiety, of a writer like H. L. Mencken? Alfred Kazin

offers the best account of him in these terms, in *An American Procession* and elsewhere. Or, instead of a cynical ironist, do we encounter in Crane a writer genuinely in search of the providential sense of national and individual purpose that we Americans apparently lost in the Gilded Age? The best reading of Crane along these lines is Andrew Delbanco's in his essay "The American Stephen Crane." To be sure, the novel can be seen as a *bildungsroman*. As Delbanco points out, "It has long been an English teacher's favorite, because it has a conveniently interrogatory form: What, it obliges us to ask, does Henry Fleming learn?" (*Required Reading*, p. 104). This question has been variously answered by critics. Henry learns (we are sometimes told) to accept mortality as the inevitable fate of the body. Or he learns to become a soldier—to subordinate his merely private interests to the imperatives of the larger social body to which he belongs, the army. Or Henry learns how to be a "man": he faces his fears, disciplines and manages them, and in the end recognizes that honor (for example) is a higher principle than mere survival. Arguing along these lines, R. W. Stallman contends that "Henry progresses upward toward manhood and moral triumph" (*Omnibus*, p. 192). But perhaps none of these answers is quite compelling, chiefly because the question "What does Henry learn?" is really beside the point. Henry, in fact, learns nothing.

To some extent, the interpretive controversies to which I refer arise from a simple historical fact: the text of *The Red Badge of Courage* has been difficult to establish. The first text to appear was an abridged version, which ran in several newspapers late in 1894. The second was a much longer text published in book form in 1895 by D. Appleton and Company of New York. For decades readers assumed that this latter text was the most authoritative available, and it was upon the basis of it that the debate as to Henry Fleming's "heroism" arose. But beginning in the 1950s more documentary evidence came to light, and, as the textual scholar Herschel Parker demonstrated in a masterful 1986 essay, the Appleton text is not, in fact, reliable—or even, perhaps, quite coherent. Crane's editor at Appleton, Ripley Hitchcock, caused him, however indirectly, to delete a number of passages from the novel, and indeed an entire chapter (this would have been chapter twelve in the original, swelling the total to twenty-five chapters). The effect of the excisions—which total several thousand words—is to mute, somewhat, the severity of Crane's ironic treatment of Henry, with the result that it becomes possible to see, in the broad outline of the plot, a story of his redemption.

The extreme to which this reading of the novel may be taken is best illustrated by Stallman's influential interpretation of it as a Christian allegory of redemption: "The theme is that man's salvation lies in change, in spiritual growth.... Henry Fleming recognizes the necessity for change and development but wars against it. But man must lose his soul in order to save it. The youth develops into a veteran: 'So it came to pass ... his soul changed.' Significantly enough," suggests Stallman, "in stating what the book is about Crane intones Biblical phrasing" (*Omnibus*, p. 193). And in due course Stallman concludes that, as he witnesses Jim Conklin's death, Henry figuratively "partakes of the sacramental blood and body of Christ [Stallman makes much of the dead soldier's initials, "J. C."], and the process of his spiritual rebirth begins at the moment when the wafer-like sun appears in the sky. It is a symbol of salvation through death" (*Omnibus*, p. 200). This is a far cry from the usual reading of Crane as a wiseacre rebel against his parents' strict Methodism (his father was a pastor, and his mother an activist in the temperance movement). It is a reading that finds the father and the mother in the son, and, indeed, the Son of the Father Himself in that most famous "sun" in late nineteenth-century American literature, the one Crane "pastes" in the sky of *Red Badge* "like a wafer" (*Omnibus*, p. 137)—a Communion wafer, if Stallman is to be believed.

There is a sense in which this reading has integrity, a sense in which it holds together. And it has been an influential reading owing to the fact that Stallman's detailed biography of Crane, which recapitulates it, remains to this day a standard. But this "redemptive" sort of reading ought to make any reader wary, if only because its solemnity, its gravity, sorts so uncomfortably with Crane's playfully sardonic prose (and then there are always the textual problems any Christian/redemptive reading of the novel must overcome). The alert reader soon begins to suspect that the network of "ecclesiastical" metaphors with which Stallman is concerned—they are certainly there to be dealt with—is motivated less by any

aspiration of Crane's to probe matters eschatological than by a more or less opportunistic (and happy) tendency on his part to follow out, dutifully, the implications of the figurative language available to him. Thus, when, early on in *Red Badge*, we find a reference to the "cathedral light of the forest," we ought not think of it as anything other than an extension of what is, after all, a centuries-old figure (that is, the forest as "cathedral"). Nor should we be either surprised, or put on our guard for Christian allegory, when the youth stumbles into a grove "where the high, arching boughs made a chapel," which, as chapels tend to do, also has "portals" and "doors" (in this case, green) and a "carpet" (in this case, of pine needles). And what else would one expect to find in the "chapel" of a forest "cathedral" other than "religious half light"? And why would not the wind-swayed trees be said, there, to "sing a hymn of twilight" in "chorus," and the insects, their own song abating, be said to "bow their beaks" and make a "devotional pause"?

Crane's habit is to follow out even the most common-place of metaphors in careful, at times ludicrous, detail. His interest is precisely in what critics used to call the "vehicles" of his metaphors, more than in what we may suppose to be their "tenor," or cargo, which explains the characteristic fastidiousness with which he so often develops them. His prose everywhere has the effect of arresting our movement from "vehicle" to "tenor": the "vehicles" are, for Crane, simply too much fun to play with; they absorb him. In the passage before us here, for example, his mind is likely on the fact that "cathedrals" imply "chapels," and "chapels," "portals" and "carpets"; and on the fact that all of these things imply "hymns," "bowing," and "devotion." Nothing in a religious allegory would require him to lay it on so thick. In short, the famous "chapel" scene in chapter seven of the novel, whose verbal details we have been considering, is neither a particularly Christian inquiry into the fact of mortality—notwithstanding that a corpse is among the furnishings of this "chapel"—nor a seriously Christian crisis in the "spiritual growth" of Henry Fleming.

But *Red Badge* does have a plot, and that plot has an arc, which accounts for the illusion of "moral progress," on Henry's part, that the novel can both foster and sustain. We may speak of it as having, in fact, a three-part structure. In its first movement, we are introduced to the set of dispositions toward war, and beliefs about it, that Henry and his green comrades are equipped with at the outset. These involve sentimental ideas about heroism and battle, partly associated with boyish adolescence and partly arrived at from reading, in secondary school, too many accounts of "Greeklike struggles" (pp. 83, 86). Over against this, in a second movement, is set the experience of battle itself. The adolescent sense of integrity these young soldiers had felt is utterly shattered by battle; and it must be reorganized—reconsolidated around some new central ideal. This new ideal, which emerges in a third or final movement, goes in the novel by the name of manhood: the "youths" become "men" (pp. 193, 212). And here we might well ask: Does it very much matter that the battle effecting this transformation is "an episode of the *American* Civil War"? as Crane's subtitle reminds us. Would any other battle in any other war have done as well? It is a nice question because the Civil War, as many have suggested, marked America's "coming of age"—its loss of innocence (if it had any to lose) and its long-awaited maturation. The Civil War for the first time made America *real*—in promise, in maturity, in responsibility. And it is tempting to suggest, with Stallman, that Henry becomes "real" in precisely this serious sense. But if that realization is in fact what the war achieved, Henry and his comrades, as Crane portrays them toward the novel's end, can hardly be an index of it. Nothing about them is ever really dignified—not to Crane anyway. The "manhood," and the new integrity into which they emerge, are pretenses hardly tenable. No more tenable than the idea that America had, through the war, at last made good its promise of democracy: the reactionary 1890s made that idea preposterous—as Crane seems intuitively to have understood. In short, the state of affairs as *Red Badge* concludes is really not so different from the state of affairs with which it began: men, in Crane's assessment of them, are pretentious, naïve, fragile, and "infinitely humorous" in their "historical situation," to borrow a phrase from "The Bride Comes to Yellow Sky."

And what of the last sentence in the novel, the one so often quoted? "Over the river a golden ray of sun came through the hosts of leaden rain clouds." Readers who find in *Red Badge* an intricate pattern of contrasts—such as light/dark, haze/translucence, confusion/insight—regard this conclusion as the capstone to the whole symbolic edifice of the novel: Henry has at last emerged from the tempest of his youthful ordeal into something like a harbor. It is as if the weather of the novel exteriorizes Henry's state of mind. "That Crane plotted the entire novel by images and situations evoking contradictory moods of despair and hope is evidenced not only in this terminal image of the book," writes R. W. Stallman, "but in the opening image of chapter one," which describes

the breaking of dawn (*Omnibus*, p. 370n3). And yet this terminal image, so integral to the pattern of the book as Stallman understands it, is not present in the surviving manuscript of *Red Badge*, and there is some controversy as to whether it "belongs" in the book at all. As Herschel Parker sees it—and the evidence is strong—Crane's editor Ripley Hitchcock "prevailed upon him" to supply "a new and upbeat final paragraph," the better to send the reader home feeling suitably uplifted ("Getting Used to the 'Original Form,' " p. 40). And indeed, passages missing from the published text of the novel and present in the manuscript, or else present in the published text and missing from the manuscript, strongly suggest, when taken together, that the novel as Crane "really" wrote it is unremitting in its irony: Fleming is a youth who never comes into his majority; he remains perpetually a minor, in what Crane at one point calls "an ecstasy of self-satisfaction." Thus, I see no "education" worthy of the name as having taken place, nor any profound "development" in Henry's character. The elements of the bildungsroman are certainly there, but so are the elements of a Wild West tale "there" in "The Bride Comes to Yellow Sky": in both cases—and the point is hardly a new one, with respect to the latter story—the effect is essentially parody.

## "STYLE" IN *THE RED BADGE OF COURAGE*

But if Crane is not writing about the progress of a boy into manhood, or about the redemption of a boy from fear, or about "spiritual" growth, or about the sacramental blood of Christ, or even about the making of a veteran soldier, what is the "subject" of the novel? We can, I believe, best answer the question by attending to the prose. Crane's fiction is forever concerned with, forever captivated by, *writing*—by *style*. And here we are speaking of style in a fairly generally sense: style as a way of cutting a figure in the world; style as charisma; style as a mode of address; style as a thing cultivated not for the purpose of realizing any particular work of art, but for the purpose of creating, of making vividly real, a literary personality.

A good place to begin an inquiry along these lines is chapter one, which opens as follows:

The cold passed reluctantly from the earth, and the retiring fogs revealed an army stretched out on the hills, resting. As the landscape changed from brown to green, the army awakened, and began to tremble with eagerness at the noise of rumors. It cast its eyes upon the roads, which were growing from long troughs of liquid mud to proper thoroughfares. A river, amber-tinted in the shadow of its banks, purled at the army's feet; and at night, when the stream had become of a sorrowful blackness, one could see across it the red, eyelike gleam of hostile camp-fires set in the low brows of distant hills. (p. 81)

Informing these sentences is a simple equation: the army is like a single man; the army *is* in fact a man, which might, as men do, "stretch out on the hills, resting," and which might "awaken," and "cast its eyes upon the roads." Nothing seems out of the ordinary here, and the personification is, in certain respects, conventional—so conventional as not to be strongly felt "as a metaphor." But Crane is doing something new with this familiar metaphor, which, as he seems to remind us, is always implicit in military terminology anyway: an army is a "corps," a body. And as the novel unfolds, we see just how "literal" Crane takes this metaphor to be. If the army is a "body," a "corps," then the individual soldiers themselves must be its "cells" or "corpuscles"; and much later we find Crane developing precisely this idea: "A small procession of wounded men were going drearily toward the rear. It was a flow of blood from the torn body of the brigade" (p. 116). The corps is here in danger of becoming a corpse; and at one point on its march the great body divides to clear the way for exactly that, a "corpse," in which it no doubt sees itself mirrored (p. 102). The very metaphoricity of phrases like "a great body of troops" has been worn away through their sheer familiarity. Crane's achievement is to make them feel like metaphors again, as he does with another phrase in the following sentence: "At nightfall the column broke into regimental pieces, and the fragments went into the fields to camp" (p. 95). Crane takes what is usually not experienced as a metaphor—the column "broke"—and follows it out scrupulously as if it were one; he makes the metaphor live again.

More complex is Crane's handling of another conventional metaphor first introduced in chapter eighteen of *Red Badge*, in which Henry Fleming overhears two officers discussing tactics. This is the passage in which the officers dismissively call the infantrymen "mule drivers." It is a revelation to Henry: "New eyes were given to him. And the most startling thing was to learn suddenly that he was very insignificant. The officer spoke of the regiment as if he referred to a broom. Some part of the woods needed sweeping, perhaps, and he merely indicated a broom in a tone properly indifferent to its fate. It was war, no doubt, but it appeared strange" (p. 179). What startles Henry is the idea, forced upon him many times during the course of the novel, that he is merely an instrument in "a vast blue demonstration"—that he is not a "real" agent at all. He is

a broom, or, what is worse (and more accurate), a single straw in the homely regimental brush of a broom. The broom is first brought out of the closet by another soldier, and to another purpose, in a remark about the Confederate dead: "Lost a piler men, they did. If an' ol' woman swep' up the woods she'd git a dustpanful" (p. 176). He imagines his and Henry's regiment wreaking havoc and an old woman cleaning up after them; it is a satisfying thought, and "sweeping" or "mopping" up is commonplace military slang. But on hearing the officers confer, Henry reworks the regiment's relation to the "broom" along humiliating lines. He now feels that a broom is no sort of implement to carry into battle, let alone to *be* in battle; brooms are for women's work. It is a double indignity (Henry feels) for a soldier to think of himself as one; it unmans him. And soon after, a grunt along the line prophesies to Henry, as they contemplate the opposing Confederates: "We'll git swallowed" (p. 181).

The ideas of the broom and of the swallowing coalesce to absurd effect in chapter twenty: "As [Henry] noted the vicious, wolflike temper of his comrades he had a sweet thought that if the enemy was about to swallow the regimental broom as a large prisoner, it could at least have the consolation of going down with bristles forward" (p. 192). The thought is "sweet" not least because it redeems the figure of the regimental broom, here oddly imagined as a "prisoner" of war. If the soldiers are but a broom, in the eyes of haughty commanders, they may as well fight dirty. Thus, the "bristling" gunfire mentioned by the narrator a handful of sentences back, becomes the porcupine "bristles" of a "broom" reluctant to be "swallowed" by the enemy, as if in some terrible (and terribly undignified) kitchen brawl. It is not clear whether Henry himself appreciates the ludic quality of the metaphor as much, and in the same way, as does the narrator: Defeating a hostile and tenacious regiment is like swallowing a broom, bristles forward. True, in what is for him an impressive show of intellection, Henry himself draws together the broom and the swallowing; we are, here, given access to his thoughts. But I doubt whether Crane ascribes to him the full ironic purchase on his commander's disdain that this "sweet," "bristling" thought would allow. However that may be, the refreshing thing about the passage before us here is the way it recalls two distinct metaphors from two chapters back in the novel—the broom and the swallowing—and adds to them the lucky flourish of "bristles." The facility with which Crane performs the maneuver argues a spirited but leisurely sort of play carried on superfluously above the narrative and hard to associate with the business of war, let alone with the gravitas of much discourse about the Grand Army of the Republic. The effect is entirely characteristic of him. His writing is forever a commentary on the unexploited possibilities for play that exist in "ordinary" language.

## CRANE'S CIVIL WAR AND THE 1890s

All of this helps us understand why Crane should treat the Civil War as he does in *The Red Badge of Courage*—that is, with no sense at all of the ideological dimensions of the catastrophe. Crane simply cannot forget that he is *writing*, nor be persuaded that the writing isn't always the main thing. And Crane's general preoccupation with style, as against polemics or politics or ideological crises, is what, in my view, makes untenable Andrew Delbanco's suggestion—and he is otherwise a fine reader of Crane—that "if the character and destiny of American nationhood eluded him as the issues at stake in the Civil War, then, in the end, he felt their absence not as a means to taunt naive believers, but as the loss of an immensely valuable act of mind." But Crane, it seems reasonable to say, did not write *Red Badge* "out of" and "about" a "crisis of faith" in God and in "God's instrument, the American nation," as Delbanco goes on to say. He wrote it out of the more or less tacit assumption that "faith," whether in God, or in America as God's instrument, was probably the sort of thing about which only a certain sort of politician—Democrat *or* Republican: it would hardly have mattered in 1895—made "heartfelt" appeals to a certain sort of constituency. In any case, this is what the novel seems to "take for granted"; this is the assumption that grounds its peculiar comedy. Crane's is a book to disconcert Rotarian pieties, as Union General Alexander McClurg's oft-cited denunciation of it as impious and unpatriotic implies. In *Red Badge* there is always what Crane calls "a singular absence of heroic poses"—a singular "neglect" of "picturesque poses" (p. 114). And in that sense his novel is indeed "anti-heroic," and essentially satirical in its relation to the literature of war. Honor (it tells us) is a mere scutcheon.

But this sort of thing can be taken too far. After all, it was necessary in the 1890s to repudiate "romantic views" of the Rebellion if the Republican Party, and the businessmen it represented, were to consummate their rapprochement with a New South ready to draw Northern investments into its cheap labor markets. It was "ideologically" necessary (so to speak) to deflate anyone

breaking out in triumphant talk about the military (let alone the political) achievements of the Union Army. After 1877, the "Bloody Shirt" was no longer in good form at the North, not even among firm Republicans—as is clear from the decisive defeat in the Congress of the 1890 "Force Bill," which would have provided for supervision of federal elections in the South, with the constitutionally sound aim of enforcing the Fourteenth and Fifteenth amendments—the "war amendments." Crane's novel redescribes the Civil War—or at least a "representative" part of it—in such a way as to make impossible a "heroic" reading of it. *Red Badge*, we might say, is written expressly to make untenable all talk about the Glory of the Coming of the Lord. And it is well worth considering whether or not, in the 1890s, a general deflation of exalted views about the war *did* help facilitate a reconciliation, which, in due course, allowed—as historians of the period have long maintained—for a businesslike reinstitution of white supremacy in the southern states, and for the ascendancy of big business as the major player in American politics.

In any case, there can be little doubt that Crane's Civil War, as we find it represented in *The Red Badge of Courage*, is altogether a product of the 1890s. Of course, to say so is hardly a slander; quite the contrary, in fact. Crane's work registers the American scene in the 1890s like a mirror. And if we would know what America was making of itself as the nineteenth century drew to a close—if we would know what America had become as the twentieth century dawned—we can do much worse than to study Stephen Crane's peculiarly irreverent treatment of the Civil War.

## FURTHER READING

Beer, Thomas. *Stephen Crane.* New York, 1941. Reprint of the 1923 edition. First book-length study of Crane, controversial and unreliable as to biographical detail, but highly suggestive and very well written.

Crane, Stephen. *The Red Badge of Courage.* New York, 1895. This first book edition is considerably longer than the abridged serialized text published late in 1894.

Delbanco, Andrew. *Required Reading.* New York, 1997.

Delbanco, Andrew. "The American Stephen Crane." In *New Essays on The Red Badge of Courage,* edited by Lee Clark Mitchell. New York, 1986.

Gullason, Thomas A., ed. *Stephen Crane's Career: Perspectives and Evaluations.* New York, 1972. A helpful collection of reviews, reminiscences, and criticism.

Kazin, Alfred. *An American Procession*. New York, 1985. The chapter on Crane is among the best short studies of the writer.

Levenson, J. C., ed. *Prose and Poetry*. New York, 1984. This is the best single-volume edition of Crane's writings; all citations in the present article refer to it.

Mitchell, Lee Clark, ed. *New Essays on The Red Badge of Courage*. New York, 1986. An important collection of assessments of *Red Badge*.

Parker, Herschel. "Getting Used to the 'Original Form' of *The Red Badge of Courage*." In *New Essays on The Red Badge of Courage*, edited by Lee Clark Mitchell. New York, 1986. An indispensable study of textual problems in *Red Badge*.

Solomon, Eric. *Stephen Crane: From Parody to Realism*. Cambridge, Mass., 1967.

Stallman, Robert Wooster, ed. *Stephen Crane: An Omnibus*. New York, 1952. This text of *Red Badge* includes, within brackets, manuscript passages deleted from the 1895 first edition.

Stallman, Robert Wooster. *Stephen Crane: A Biography*. New York, 1968. The most extensive biography published to date.

---

See also the article on Stephen Crane, immediately preceding.

# ROBERT CREELEY

*by Lacy Schutz*

Robert Creeley arose from a generation of poets who came to consciousness during the Great Depression and World War II and for whom these events formed a vast awareness of loss. Creeley in particular felt loss on a national and a personal scale; before he was five, his father had died of pneumonia and one of his eyes was blinded in a freak automobile accident. His family was originally working class. Creeley's paternal grandfather was a wealthy farmer, but the wealth, forfeited in a family scandal, was not passed on to the next generation. That brief brush with fortune raised Creeley's father out of the working class long enough to pursue an M.D. By the time Creeley was born on 21 May 1926 in West Acton, Massachusetts, his father had his own clinic and the family maintained chauffeurs and maids; however, it all disappeared when his father died. The family income dropped precipitously, and his mother was left with only her public health nurse's salary to support Creeley and his older sister. Critics have made much of the effect of the loss of his eye at the age of four on later themes of loss and betrayal in his poetry. The accident, which occurred when he was two, involved an errant load of coal that drove a shard of glass into Creeley's left eye. The injury was increasingly problematic until, after his father's death, his mother had the eye removed under circumstances he later considered a betrayal of trust. On what seemed like a routine visit to the hospital where she worked, she checked him in and the eye was taken out.

Creeley has also examined in his poetry his father's loss of two grown sons, his half brothers, through a failed marriage. Creeley perceived his father as regarding himself and his sister as a second chance. He went on to emulate this pattern of family alienation not once, but twice—marrying three wives and raising a

Robert Creeley.
(© *Christopher Felver/Corbis*)

total of eight children. Creeley's poetry rages against an emotional impotence he seems to battle in his primary personal relationships. With the loss of his father, he was surrounded by women: his mother and sister, an aunt who wrote occasional poetry, and Theresa, a mentally challenged woman his father had brought into the family as a domestic and who remained there after his death. Creeley's poetry often seems entrenched in a kind of resentment and desperation, trying to find the set of instructions that will teach him how to be a man.

After attending Harvard briefly, Creeley dropped out to join the American Field Service, and served in India and Burma. After returning, he married his first wife, Ann McKinnon; failed to finish his degree at Harvard; and eventually moved to a subsistence farm in New Hampshire where he raised pigeons and chickens. Creeley's poetry draws heavily on lessons acquired at this time in his life, during which he claims to have learned much from the old men who bred pigeons, such as their utter attentiveness to the task at hand and the care they took with the smallest details. Creeley claims utter truth for his poetry. It is not fictive. His poetry represents his engagement with his own feelings via the possibility of words. This mode may lend itself to a psychoanalytic reading, but his work does not fall within the purview of the confessional poets, such as Robert Lowell and Sylvia Plath. These poets were committed to a narrative recitation of their individual inner lives and struggles, whereas Creeley brings forth the commonality of emotion through abstraction and engagement with form and composition. Creeley is identified with the Black Mountain poets and looks to Ezra Pound, William Carlos Williams, Fyodor Dostoyevsky, D. H. Lawrence, and Louis Zukovsky as his masters and ancestors.

Creeley grew interested in jazz when he went to Harvard in 1943. The intricate rhythmic structures captivated him, as did the notion that one could work outside prescribed forms. Charles Olson, whose essay "Projective Verse" was the opening salvo that announced and rallied those who became known as the Black Mountain Poets, was a close friend and mentor of Creeley's. One thing Creeley took from both Olson and jazz was an interest in the act of composition as integral to the outcome of the work. Olson advocated something he called "composition by field," which involved the idea that each perception must lead instantly to the next one; that a poem must be kinetic and constantly propelled forward by the energy of its own content. Creeley's poetry is intensely emotional and often abstract, using a plain language to describe his conflicts with, attachments to, and hopes for what he considers American, and more particularly the New England strain of Puritanism with its self-torment and constraint.

Creeley barely suppresses an anger in his poems, an anger and embarrassment at the difficulty of being human and specifically being a man, being in manhood. There is also a sense of hope and redemption in his poetry, and a forced quieting of the violence. Thus emerges the tautness, the tension and uneasiness, of his finest poems. Creeley's poetic voice is unique. Many imitators have attempted the kind of apparent simplicity and compression that are his trademarks, mistaking them for minimalism and failing to capture the emotional complexity his short lines and frugal language belie. He hangs his poems on a ligamental structure of enjambment, consonance, and off-rhyme, revealing an uncanny aptitude for and awareness of the broken music of actual human speech. A glance through the index of *The Collected Poems of Robert Creeley, 1945–1975* (1982) reveals no fewer than eleven poems titled "Song." Other themes and words appear and reappear almost as incantatory charms throughout his oeuvre: *here, there, place, echo, light, window, woman.* The work is often elliptical, turning back on itself, not only casting previous lines and stanzas in new light, but also revealing layered recognitions of his own past work. As the poem moves forward, it suggests that whatever notions a reader thought he or she held about a certain common word or idea (like *here* or *there*) are in fact continually mutable.

Creeley attempted but failed to start his own journal in New Hampshire, but in the process became acquainted with Cid Corman, whose magazine *Origin* provided a forum for many of the emerging new generation of writers: Olson, Denise Levertov, and Robert Duncan, among others. Creeley began his long and voluminous correspondence with Olson at this time. Creeley is considered an acolyte of Olson, but in their correspondence it is Creeley who often comes across as the voice of reason to Olson's blurting and hyperbole. Because they thought it would be easier financially, Creeley and his first wife moved in 1951 to France, where Levertov and her husband were their neighbors. They moved in 1952 to Mallorca, where Creeley started Divers Press, which printed his own work and that of Duncan and others. Creeley's first three books of poetry came out quickly from small presses during the years in Europe: *Le Fou* (1952), *The Kind of Act of* (1953), and *The Immoral Proposition* (1953). Olson invited Creeley to Black Mountain College in North Carolina in 1954, to be at the helm of the *Black Mountain Review* and later to teach. After his stint at Black Mountain College, Creeley settled in New Mexico, where in 1960 he took an M.A. from the University of New Mexico, though he had never finished the B.A. at Harvard. Then came a stint as a private tutor on a coffee plantation in Guatemala that his second wife, Bobbie Louise Hawkins, documented in her true-to-life novel, *The Sanguine Breast of Margaret* (1992), much as Creeley documented his life in Mallorca with his first wife in *The Island* (1963).

Creeley participated in both the Vancouver Poetry Festival (summer 1963) and the Berkeley Poetry Conference (summer 1965), which were seminal gatherings for many poets of the time, including Olson, Allen Ginsberg, Levertov, Duncan, Kenneth Rexroth, and Philip Whalen, helping to lay out and define their overarching goals and theories. *For Love: Poems, 1950–1960* (1962) brought Creeley his first national attention. Creeley's book of short stories, *The Gold Diggers*, was issued in America by Scribner's in 1965, after appearing from Divers Press ten years earlier.

Creeley began teaching at SUNY-Buffalo in the 1960s and remains there today. He has collaborated with many visual artists, including Robert Indiana, Marisol, Donald Sultan, and Francesco Clemente. Creeley has published more than seventy-five books of poetry, essays, and fiction, and served as editor for selections of Olson, Robert Burns, Walt Whitman, and others. Creeley's correspondence with Olson was published in a ten-volume set by Black Sparrow Press. Some of his most recent works include a collaboration with the artist Archie Rand, *Drawn and Quartered* (2001), and a collection of poems from 1984 to 1994, *Just in Time* (2001). He has been awarded almost every prize available to American poets, including the

Lannan Lifetime Achievement Award, the Bollingen Prize, the Frost Medal, and the Shelley Memorial Award. He was the New York State poet from 1989 to 1991.

[*See also* Black Mountain Poetry.]

## WORKS

*Le Fou* (1952)
*The Immoral Proposition* (1953)
*The Kind of Act of* (1953)
*The Gold Diggers* (1954, 1965)
*All That Is Lovely in Men* (1955)
*If You* (1956)
*The Whip* (1957)
*A Form of Women* (1959)
*For Love: Poems, 1950–1960* (1962)
*The Island* (1963)
*Words* (1965, 1967)
*Poems, 1950–1965* (1966)
*The Charm: Early and Uncollected Poems* (1967, 1971)
*Robert Creeley Reads* (1967)
*A Sight* (1967)
*Divisions and Other Early Poems* (1968)
*The Finger* (1968, 1970)
*5 Numbers* (1968)
*Numbers* (1968)
*Pieces* (1968)
*Mazatlan: Sea* (1969)
*In London* (1970)
*A Quick Graph: Collected Notes and Essays* (1970)
*1.2.3.4.5.6.7.8.9.0* (1971)
*St. Martin's* (1971)
*A Day Book* (1972)
*Listen* (1972)
*A Sense of Measure* (1972)
*The Class of '47* (1973)
*Contexts of Poetry: Interviews, 1961–1971* (1973)
*For My Mother: Genevieve Jules Creeley* (1973)
*His Idea* (1973)
*Thirty Things* (1974)
*Backwards* (1975)
*The Door: Selected Poems* (1975)
*Away* (1976)
*Hello* (1976)
*Mabel, a Story: And Other Prose* (1976)
*Presences: A Text for Marisol* (1976)
*Selected Poems* (1976)
*Myself* (1977)
*Thanks* (1977)
*Desultory Days* (1978)

*Hello: A Journal, February 29–May 3, 1976* (1978)
*Later: A Poem* (1978)
*Later* (1979, 1980)
*Corn Close* (1980)
*Mother's Voice* (1981)
*The Collected Poems of Robert Creeley, 1945–1975* (1982)
*Echoes* (1982)
*A Calendar, 1984* (1984)
*Mirrors* (1983)
*The Collected Prose of Robert Creeley* (1984, 1988)
*Memory Gardens* (1986)
*The Company* (1988)
*7 & 6* (1988)
*Window* (1988)
*The Collected Essays of Robert Creeley* (1989)
*Dreams* (1989)
*It* (1989)
*Robert Creeley: A Selection, 1945–1987* (1989)
*Autobiography* (1990)
*Have a Heart* (1990)
*Places* (1990)
*Windows* (1990)
*Gnomic Verses* (1991)
*The Old Days* (1991)
*Selected Poems* (1991)
*Life & Death* (1993)
*Echoes* (1994)
*Loops: Ten Poems* (1995)
*So There: Poems, 1976–1983* (1998)
*Daybook of a Virtual Poet* (1998)
*Life and Death* (2000)
*Collected Prose* (2001)
*Drawn & Quartered* (2001)
*Just in Time: Poems, 1984–1994* (2001)

## FURTHER READING

Butterick, George F., ed. *Charles Olson & Robert Creeley: The Complete Correspondence,* 10 vols. Santa Barbara, Calif., 1980– . Vols. 9 and 10 edited by Richard Blevins.

Clark, Tom. *Robert Creeley and the Genius of the American Common Place.* New York, 1993.

Creeley, Robert, ed. *Tales Out of School: Selected Interviews.* Ann Arbor, Mich., 1993.

Faas, Ekbert. *Robert Creeley: A Biography.* Hanover, N.H., 2001.

Fox, Willard. *Willard Fox, Robert Creeley, Edward Dorn, and Robert Duncan: A Reference Guide.* Boston, 1989.

# J. HECTOR ST. JOHN DE CRÈVECOEUR

*by Kathryn W. Kemp*

In *Letters from an American Farmer* (1782), a writer calling himself J. Hector St. John provides a firsthand view of the lives of ordinary Americans in the latter part of the eighteenth century. Because the author, a native of France named Michel-Guilliaume de Crèvecoeur, opposed the American Revolution, his work received scant attention until the twentieth century, when scholars recognized the value of its descriptions of the colonial world, including rural life, Indians, the frontier, the whaling communities of New England, slavery, and the flora and fauna of the Middle Colonies.

St. John de Crèvecoeur, after the portrait by Valliere, 1786. (*Courtesy of Picture History*)

Crèvecoeur lived a life of constant change. Born a minor aristocrat in Normandy, on 31 January, he later lived in England and America before returning to France. He was a soldier, surveyor, Indian trader, and farmer while in America. Upon his return to France he became a diplomat and man of letters, publishing in both English and French.

## EARLY LIFE

Educated by Jesuit teachers who urged students to write something every day, he spoke and wrote fluent English. His best-known work, *Letters from an American Farmer*, while not a true autobiography, draws on his experiences in revolutionary era New York. Crèvecoeur structured his book as a set of letters, ostensibly written to an English acquaintance, Mr. F. B., who wanted first-hand information about America. The author of the letters, however, is presented as "James," a simple English-American farmer, quite unlike the worldly Crèvecoeur.

His journey from Normandy to America was by way of England, where he lived in Salisbury with some elderly kinswomen. The reason for this first move is unclear, but may have involved a dispute with his father, Guillaume Jean de Crèvecoeur. He was nineteen, and the father and son disagreed frequently. After a romance ended with the untimely death of his English sweetheart, Crèvecoeur left England in 1755 for Canada, where he served in the French militia as a surveyor and cartographer during the French and Indian War. Wounded at Quebec, he became a British prisoner when the French were defeated there.

Here lies a mystery: the records of the arrangements for the repatriation of the French prisoners of war indicate that some cloud hung over his reputation. The officers of his regiment required him to resign in 1759 and the British transported him to New York. Historians speculate that Crèvecoeur's long-standing fondness for the British may have been the source of this difficulty. However, he kept total silence about the affair and nothing more is known about his troubles in the military. Whatever the facts, he remained in America and became a naturalized citizen of the colonies, using an anglicized variation of his birth name, J. Hector St. John.

He continued to work as a surveyor. This took him into the wilderness, where he learned the ways of the Indians with whom he traded. Throughout his writings, a generally respectful view of Indians prevails, although he views the European culture as superior. He said that in the 1750s he was adopted by the Oneida Indian tribe.

In 1769 he undertook the life of a farmer on rented land in New York's Hudson Valley. He married Mehitable Tippet, daughter of a prosperous Westchester family, and settled with her in a home known as Pine Hill on farmland he purchased in Orange County. The first chapters of the *Letters* reflect his experiences there.

## THE SCRIBBLING FARMER

Readers accustomed to the brisk pace of modern writing may find the first of these letters, devoted mostly to justifying the project, to be slow going,. Sharp criticisms from the farmer's wife, which reflect some of the prejudices of the time and place, underscore "James's" blushing disclaimers of his abilities as a writer. She frets that writing is impractical, will not pay the bills, and will undermine his reputation: travelers "would point out to our house, saying, here liveth the scribbling farmer." However, the warm encouragement of his clergyman friend moves him to write to Mr. F. B. But he warns the recipient of his letters: "for what reason I know not, you wish to correspond with a cultivator of the earth, with a simple citizen, you must receive my letters for better or worse."

Crèvecoeur then begins in earnest, describing the "Situation, Feelings, and Pleasures of an American Farmer" in Letter 2. In his America, honest and industrious farmers live free of the corrupting influences of the European world. Depicting James's (and presumably his own) life as a farmer, Crèvecoeur paints an image of cozy domesticity. Working the fields, he wrote, "I place my little boy on a chair which screws to the beam of the plough," and together they marvel at the natural world around them. Crèvecoeur continues elaborating on the virtues of American life in the next letter, called "What Is an American?" He repeatedly compares the people and customs of America to those of Europe, always finding the American to be superior—free of religious strife, social snobbery, and political rivalry. He attributes this to their opportunity to possess their own land and to the minimal government interference in their private affairs. As an example, Crèvecoeur recounts the success of Andrew, a penniless Scotsman who becomes a comfortable farmer because of "the happy effects which constantly flow, in the country, from sobriety and industry, when united with good land and freedom."

Five subsequent letters describe the whaling communities of Nantucket and Martha's Vineyard, including their hunting methods, the orderly customs of their society, and the general prevalence of thrift and kindness on both islands. Crèvecoeur ascribes this atmosphere to the influence of a large community of Quakers, a sect that receives repeated favorable comment throughout the *Letters*. So favorable are his representations of the Society of Friends that some have suspected that Crèvecoeur might have joined them, although no direct evidence of this is available. He later assisted in the founding of the first Catholic church in New York City, but his published comments on religion put him firmly in the camp of the skeptics.

## ON SLAVERY; ON NATURE

The mood of the *Letters* takes a sudden shift in Letter 9, a description of the slave-based culture of South Carolina, where Crèvecoeur no longer finds an America superior to all the world. Instead, he condemns the evil of slavery, both for its effects on the slaves and as undermining the character of slaveholders. In other letters he makes reference to slaves in different parts of the colonies, but asserts that in the North they are treated with humanity and respect and are not exploited. His condemnation centers on the large-scale plantation slavery of the South. In Letter 9 he also argues for the weakness of a slave-based economy by comparing the general prosperity of the northern and eastern colonies to the curtailed opportunities in the southern slave colonies. The letter ends with a horrific account of the slow execution, by exposure in a cage, of a rebellious slave. Blinded and tormented by birds and insects, he cries out, "the birds, the birds; aaah me!" Whether Crèvecoeur actually visited the Carolinas or witnessed such a scene is uncertain.

Two letters bring back something of the sunny mood of the earlier chapters. Letter 10, "Of Snakes; and on the Humming-bird," reports on the behavior of these animals, mixing keen observation with a number of folk beliefs. Letter 11, purportedly written by an aristocratic Russian traveler, describes a visit with a "celebrated Pennsylvania botanist...John Bertram [Bartram]." The "Russian" spent time with his Quaker host, whose benign treatment of his slaves contrasted keenly with the cold cruelty in South Carolina.

## THE FARMER AND THE REVOLUTION

The next and last of the letters, "Distress of a Frontier Man," reflects a change in the circumstances of the author. Loyal to the crown, Crèvecoeur was at odds with the revolutionary element among his neighbors. In the same manner, "James" finds his peaceable kingdom disrupted by revolutionary passions. He resolves to abandon his home and community to live among the Indians, who are "a mild, hospitable people, strangers to *our* political disputes and having none among themselves" In a remote, unnamed village, he hopes to find rest "from all fatigues, from all apprehensions, from our present terrors, and from our long watchings."

Crèvecoeur took a different route of escape. Leaving his wife and two younger children, Fanny and Louis, with friendly neighbors, he took the manuscript of the *Letters* and his eldest son Alexandre (Ally) in an attempt a return to France. His intention probably was to reestablish a connection with the rest of his family and to ensure Ally's possible inheritance. Getting to France proved difficult. Virtually destitute, Crèvecoeur aroused the suspicion of the British authorities in New York City, who held him in prison for three months while Ally was kept alive by the kindness of friends of his father. After a winter of illness and near starvation, the two set sail for Europe in 1780. How he financed their passage is unknown. The voyage ended in a shipwreck off the coast of Ireland, leaving the father and son little more than the clothes on their backs. However, the manuscript, or at least parts of it, survived, and he was able to sell it in London for thirty guineas to Davis and Davies, the publishers of the great Samuel Johnson.

## IN FRANCE

Reunited with his family in France, Crèvecoeur benefited from the patronage of Mme. d'Houdetot, a family acquaintance who was a close friend of Jean-Jacques Rousseau and other French intellectuals. She introduced the erstwhile farmer into her sophisticated social circle. As the author of the *Letters*, Crèvecoeur found his place in the salons of Paris and became recognized as an authority on America. He wrote short reports on American agricultural topics for the information of the royal government.

Appointed consul, he returned to New York City in 1783. Crèvecoeur sought to reunite his family but learned of the death of his wife and the destruction of Pine Hill by a fire. The two events are not necessarily linked and the cause of her death is not recorded. He discovered that a series of kindly persons had protected Fanny and Louis and that they now were in Boston. Bad weather prohibited his emotional reunion with the children until the following spring. Crèvecoeur and his children returned to France in 1790. Having once fled the American Revolution, he now was confronted by the French Revolution and the Napoleonic years. As an aristocrat with mildly monarchist sentiments, he had to tread carefully to avoid the destruction that befell many of his class. He managed to do so, at times living out of the country with his married children.

Crèvecoeur had begun his writing career in English, but upon his return to his homeland he rediscovered his native tongue and began to write in French. Reports on American agricultural topics for the government were followed by a published translation into French—with extensive revisions—of the *Letters* as well as other short articles. (In addition to the two authorized editions, other, pirated, editions of the English version appeared.) In 1801 he published his last major work, *Voyage dans la haute Pensylvanie et dans l'état de New-York (Journey into Northern Pennsylvania and the State of New York)*. He died in Sarcelles, France, on 12 November 1813.

Crèvecoeur had expressed the intention to publish another volume of the *Letters* but never carried out the plan. However, his papers were preserved by his family, and in 1925 Henri Bourdin, Ralph H. Gabriel, and Stanley T. Williams published a collection of his other English compositions. *Sketches of Eighteenth Century America: More "Letters from an American Farmer"* (1925) is similar in tone to *Letters* and broadens his view of the colonial era. Crèvecoeur's pro-British sentiments limited his readership in the United States for more than a century, but *Letters* was republished in 1904 and, along with *Sketches*, has remained available in various editions. Scholars consider Crèvecoeur's works to be valuable sources on life in late-eighteenth-century America and some rank *Letters of an American Farmer* with Benjamin Franklin's *Autobiography* (1868) and Thomas Jefferson's *Notes on the State of Virginia* (1785) as a valuable contribution to American literature.

[*See also* Colonial Writing in America.]

### SELECTED WORKS

*Letters from an American Farmer* (1782)
*Lettres d'un cultivateur americain* (1787)
*Sketches of Eighteenth Century America* (1935)
*Voyage dans la haute Pensylvanie et dans l'état de New-York (Journey into Northern Pennsylvania and the State of New York)* (1801)
*Journey into Northern Pennsylvania and the State of New York* (1964)

### FURTHER READING

Allen, Gay Wilson, and Robert Asselineau. *St. John de Crèvecoeur: The Life of an American Farmer.* New York, 1987. Thorough and readable account of Crèvecoeur's life.

Philbrick, Thomas. *St. John de Crèvecoeur.* New York, 1970. Succinct biography with a discussion of the literary significance of Crèvecoeur's works.

# E. E. CUMMINGS

*by Kate Cone*

Poet of satire, love, and lower-case letters, Edward Estlin Cummings was born on 14 October 1894 at his home at 104 Irving Street, Cambridge, Massachusetts, to the Reverend Edward Cummings and Rebecca Haswell Cummings. To distinguish between the two Edwards, the son was called by his middle name, becoming known as Estlin to family and friends. It was much later that he chose to be known professionally as E. E. Cummings, and although it was believed for many years that he had legally changed his name to reflect the use of lowercase letters that became his poetic signature (e. e. cummings), he did not.

The Cummings house on Irving Street was a big, comfortable, rambling one, added onto frequently by Edward, who was not only a well-respected Unitarian minister and social work activist but a talented carpenter. The household bustled with an extended family consisting at times of both maternal grandmothers, aunts, an uncle, servants, and a handyman, creating a thriving source of love and creativity for the young Estlin and his sister Elizabeth. Distinguished guests came and went, since Edward kept an office at home. Among them was the philosopher William James, who had introduced Edward and Rebecca to each other.

Encouraged to draw, sketch, keep a diary, and compose songs and poems, Cummings as a child displayed a curiosity about language and portraying his world in pictures that would shape his later work. Rebecca kept every piece of art and poetry the boy produced, and her insistence that he keep a daily journal became a habit the poet never abandoned. Always carrying a notebook and pencil, Cummings jotted down poetry and observations about the world and drew the people and places he encountered every day of his life. Rebecca's early practice

E. E. Cummings, reproduction of a self-portrait. (*Courtesy of the Library of Congress*)

and her son's diligence following it produced the most voluminous collection of papers, notes, and sketches left by any writer or artist of his time.

## HARVARD AESTHETE

Estlin graduated from the Cambridge Latin and High School and was admitted to Harvard in 1911 at age sixteen. Small for his age, he made up for his lack of size with brains, wit, and talent. He studied composition and continued the writing of poetry and essays he had done frequently and well at Cambridge Latin. By the time he graduated with a master's degree five years later, he was well published in the various Harvard magazines and journals. It was during his Greek studies at Harvard that Cummings, now called by his surname, became acquainted with the epigram, a form of short poem that ends with a witty twist. Cummings would use this form many times throughout his career, especially when he performed public readings, and it became one of his many signatures.

It was while at Harvard that Cummings began the process of separating from his protective world of 104 Irving Street. Estlin rebelled against his father, staying out late, coming home drunk and disheveled, and carousing with his friends at burlesque houses and strip joints in Boston's notorious Scollay Square. For a young man whose father had a high public profile as a minister and was one of the chief supporters of the Temperance movement, such behavior was the ultimate insult. This rebellion went far into Estlin's adulthood, yet for all the resistance Edward received, he remained Estlin's biggest supporter behind Rebecca, and he long indulged the artist's life his son demanded.

It was during this period also that Cummings began rebelling against the traditional compositional and poetic forms favored by his professors at Harvard, most notably Dean Briggs, a revered teacher of English composition. One can imagine the gentlemanly Dean, a Mr. Chips type who rode his bicycle to classes and chatted with students in Harvard Yard, with raised eyebrows and perhaps a deep blush in his cheeks while reading the poetry Cummings submitted for class work. His experimentation with form and especially content—the explicit mention of women's breasts and the lyrical depiction of a bawdy-house brawl Cummings had witnessed during one of his drinking forays into Boston—were not expected or approved. Here, though, was where Cummings was beginning to find his own technique. He had always imitated other poets, as writers do when learning the art of poetry, but he was stretching in these years, experimenting with free verse, imagism, cubism, and vorticism, placing his work among that of the modern artists he admired. The techniques he employed were becoming his own, allowing him to "make it new," the cry of the modernist movement.

### *i*, NOT *I*

Among his experiments was the arranging of words upon the page as if he had taken a paintbrush loaded with letters and, splattering let go—black on white. Another was his use of the pronoun *I* as a lowercase *i*. Critics and scholars have attributed this small *i* to several sources, one being Cummings's desire to turn the standard use of language on its head, mixing the use of capitals, omitting punctuation, and forcing the reader to adjust to his new technique. Another theory is that Cummings was imitating the unschooled handyman his parents employed in the off-season to take care of their summer home, Joy Farm, in northern New Hampshire. Sam Ward kept the family apprised of his progress on certain projects around Joy Farm with letters that reflected that he was literate, but barely. *I*'s were not capitalized and punctuation was used sparingly and inconsistently. But Estlin obviously loved Sam, and even penned a poem praising his steadfastness when the handyman passed on. Perhaps it was an emulation of Sam's simple, unpretentious way of expressing himself that prompted Estlin to imitate his small *i*. The use of a lowercase *i* could also be a part of the Zen-like spareness to his poetry—a spacing of letters and words that allowed much white space, negative space, to show on the page. This is supported by Cummings's study of Japanese poetry while at Harvard.

### THE EGOLESS *i*

There is a substantive Eastern influence to Cummings's poetry, however, that can be traced beyond a stylistic imitation of the Japanese or even the New England Transcendentalist writers who influenced him. Intuition—experiencing an inspiration rather than thinking of it—goes beyond the mind and body and brings one to another place where the sense of separateness disappears. One is no longer a capital *I* but, like every other molecule, a small *i* in the universe. The person becomes one with every other being—the sun, moon, and stars; the grass and flowers and trees. This oneness is the transcendence espoused by Emerson, Thoreau, and other transcendentalists, but while Westerners have traditionally considered intuition, the source of transcendental inspiration, as originating in the mind, Taoists, Buddhists, and other Eastern religions state that intuition comes from within the body. (What we now call a "gut feeling" is intuition.) So while readers and scholars labor to decipher Cummings's poetry by dissecting the syllables, pinning down references to determine the poems' meanings, and speculating on his moods and their origins, Cummings's poems are best experienced. One is unlikely to get all of the references or word breaks upon the first reading. But each subsequent reading will add layer on layer of meaning, a gradual "experiencing" of what Cummings meant when he wrote the poem. There is passion in every line of every poem, whether he misses his lover, observes the new moon, extols the beaten conscientious objector, derides the Cambridge ladies, or encourages us to be the opposite of *mostpeople*. A reading of a poem when one is seventeen changes when one is forty-seven, but only slightly. Where the innocence Cummings portrays has been betrayed by the time we are older and more experienced, a new reading of the same poem can carry us back to that time when our innocence made us beautiful. We can be beautiful and hopeful again, pain notwithstanding, because we have experienced the sentiment in the piece. It makes our heart throb a bit with each new reading. We close the book and put it down with a sigh, wishing we could live between its pages.

### THE TAO

One important piece of evidence surfaced recently that indicates that Cummings had explored Eastern philosophies on his own. Hundreds of his paintings that had been languishing in a New Hampshire barn were finally sold at auction by the girls' camp that had been given them by Cummings's daughter Nancy Andrews. There are two small watercolors depicting a small dirt path emerging from a New England wood. One of these has written on the back, in Cummings's hand, "The Tao." "Tao" means "the way" in Chinese and refers to the work of Lao Tzu, the *Tao Te Ching*. As the transcendentalists distilled their views from Western philosophers who had extracted them from the East, it is not evident that they were expressed in a form that Cummings would have picked up as a restatement of the Tao.

Cummings's poetry captures the true meaning of Taoism: that intuition is the purest form of knowledge, just *because* it does not emanate from the intellect but rather is felt or experienced. He spoke many times of being and becoming, is, alive and truth. The reader merely has to suspend the ramblings of the mind in order to savor the simple words of the poem to get the meaning. Splaying the syllables and meter upon a page and classifying them are beside the point. Transcendence of the intellect is reflected in Cummings's poetry over and over, whether he forces us to be the monkey on the end of the organ grinder's string, the cool sliver of new moon, the gatherer of buttercups, a willing lover in the throes of passion, or a grasshopper splattered across the page in different configurations. Cummings makes a point. But he makes it in the same way Zen monks did when they tossed their students out of a second-story window onto the cobblestones below. He startles us into enlightenment with each poem. In a twentieth-century world where creationism was being supplanted by evolution, where science was making a mess of nature, where big business was trying to sell us things we didn't need on credit, and where wars continued to kill our friends, Cummings relentlessly clung to the very core of existence, "is."

## MAJOR AND MINOR WORKS

Cummings had a hate-hate relationship with mainstream critics, who were so well known and depended upon by their sheeplike readership they became icons of literature themselves. So a categorization of his art as "major" or "minor" would have him turning in his grave. Cummings continues to fascinate and endear because of his stubborn resistance to going the way of the herd. If ever Henry David Thoreau had a protégé, it was Cummings, who marched to his own drummer and thumbed his nose at disbelievers. And even though many of Cummings' works were met with negative press, he always seemed to have critic friends and patrons who understood what he was trying to do and who persevered in defending and extolling his work. But in the interest of enlightening new readers and scholars, a list follows.

After his service in World War I as an ambulance driver, Cummings was detained at La Ferte Mace in France as a prisoner of war. His minister father raised

hell with the powers that be, including the incumbent President Wilson, and managed to get Estlin released, then encouraged his son to write about the experience as a prisoner of war. One theme that prevails throughout Cummings's writing career is his low tolerance for stupidity, especially the organized type of stupidity that takes the form of bureaucracy. *The Enormous Room* (1922) was Cummings's first published collection and endures today as a scathing indictment of the senselessness that held him for no better reason than that he was a fellow soldier and friend of William Slater Brown, a critic of the war.

*The Enormous Room* was well-received, perhaps because it was considered part of the war-novel genre that included *A Farewell to Arms* by Hemingway and John Dos Passos's *1919*. But critics panned later works such as *Eimi* (1933), Cummings's very negative account of his five-week trip to Russia to observe the socialist experiment; *Him* (1927), a play in the expressive tradition that Dos Passos and others were indulging in; *Tom* (1935), a ballet based on Harriet Beecher Stowe's book *Uncle Tom's Cabin*; and *Santa Clause* (1946), a morality play that mocked the world's blind acceptance of science. Nevertheless, Cummings refused to back down and pander to popular taste. He was dogged in his efforts to get his poetry published, and he remained unwilling to compromise. He battled editors and publishers who wanted to cut the sexual and profane from his work in order to avoid prosecution for producing obscene material. Being "banned in Boston" would sell books in later years, but being banned also meant not having your work available to the public when it could produce money to pay the bills. So as Cummings wrote and painted and worked to get his art in front of the public, he endured the barbs of critics. People who "got" it, got it, and eventually in his lifetime, he became acquainted with and adored by a new generation of college students who loved his poetry.

## POET AS READER

In the 1950s, when Cummings felt old and was burdened by chronic back pain, he began his career anew as a reader of his own work. Audiences loved his delivery, and Cummings loved their attentions. Playing to packed audiences, the poet managed to eke out a new source of income from reading to crowds, especially the college crowd. Despite his back pain, this renewed interest in his work felt good to a poet who had spent decades resisting the sirens' call to conform to the mainstream. Here he was, in the winter of his career, read and adored by a new batch of readers. It surely must have left a spring in his step. Among his most famous readings were excerpts from *i: six nonlectures* (1953), written during his Charles Eliot Norton professorship year at Harvard.

## WINTER, TWILIGHT, AND MOUNT CHOCURUA

Cummings mellowed in his old age. His poetry focused on nature rather than cityscapes, primarily because he was spending more time in the mountains near Joy Farm, and his paintings reflected his New Hampshire surroundings. He insisted that he was a painter and a poet, but because he declined to exhibit his paintings after the 1930s, with carefully chosen exceptions, his greatest reputation was as poet only. He drew or painted every day of his life. Early on he studied with noted artists and had exhibitions of his work in prestigious venues. He saw, however, that he was considered primarily a poet, and so he kept his painting to himself for the better part of his career. He died on 3 September 1962, after a day of splitting wood and making notes about a lingering delphinium that had defied all and blossomed long after its stem-mates had withered.

## A NEW CENTURY OF WORK

Upon his death in 1962, he left all of his art to his wife Marion Morehouse Cummings. Marion left it to Cummings's daughter Nancy, who gave it to a New Hampshire girls' camp. The camp tried to raise funds by showing the art but found it too expensive a venture. Stored in a barn for over two decades, the art went to an auction house and was bought by a rare-book and art dealer in Massachusetts. The artwork was cataloged and offered for sale, and it is expected to be available for research within a few years. As Ken Lopez notes in his catalog, this collection contains the finished works as well as the preliminary "thoughts" of the eventual finished products. False starts that other artists would have been thrown away were saved by the ever-retentive Cummings. There are sketches, portraits, still lifes, scribblings, nudes—all alive with his energy and experience.

Shortly before Cummings died, he said that he needed a hundred more years to complete his work. An artist like E. E. Cummings would never be sated with merely another century. But he left so many notes and so much artwork, there are easily that many years' worth of discoveries to enjoy. Over 180 boxes of his randomly collected papers are available at the Houghton Library at Harvard, as well as the hundreds upon hundreds of pieces of artwork that await scanning by scholars—so much more to discover about the artist and poet whose idea of discovery merely "is."

## WORKS

*Eight Harvard Poets* (1917)
*The Enormous Room* (1922)
*Tulips and Chimneys* (1923)
*&* (1925)
*XLI Poems* (1925)
*Is 5* (1926)
*Him* (1927)
[No Title] (1930)
*CIOPW* (1931)
*The Red Front* (1933)
*Eimi* (1933)
*No Thanks* (1935)
*Tom* (1935)
*Collected Poems* (1938)
*50 Poems* (1940)
*1 × 1* (1944)
*Santa Clause* (1946)
*Xaipe* (1950)
*i: six nonlectures* (1953)
*Poems, 1923–1954* (1954)
*A Miscellany* (1958)
*95 Poems* (1958)
*Adventures in Value* (1962)
*73 Poems* (1963)
*Fairy Tales* (1965)
*Complete Poems, 1913–1962* (1972)
*Poems, 1905–1962* (1973)

## FURTHER READING

Cohen, Milton A. *Poet and Painter: The Aesthetics of E. E. Cummings' Early Work*. Detroit, 1987. The only book-length treatment of Cummings's art.

Cowley, Malcolm. *Exile's Return*. New York, 1934. Excellent portrayal of the beginning, middle, and end of the Lost Generation of writers from someone who experienced it.

Dupee, F. W., and George Stade, eds. *Selected Letters of E. E. Cummings*. New York, 1969.

Friedman, Norman. *E. E. Cummings: The Art of His Poetry*. Baltimore, 1960. Coherent and comprehensive critical look at Cummings's poetry, his personas, and his meaning. Out of print, but indispensable for an understanding of the poet by a scholar and friend of Cummings.

Kennedy, Richard S. *Dreams in the Mirror: A Biography of E. E. Cummings*. New York, 1980. The definitive work on Cummings's life; the author had access to material previously unavailable because of stipulations of Cummings's widow.

Norman, Charles. *E. E. Cummings*. New York, 1967. Although Norman did not have access to the material Kennedy did, he had the advantage of being personally acquainted with Cummings, with full access to his subject.

# RICHARD HENRY DANA

*by Richard Everett*

On 14 August 1834, a nineteen-year-old Harvard student walked down a Boston wharf to board the brig *Pilgrim*. He was wearing the loose duck trousers and tarpaulin hat of a sailor, for which he had exchanged his usual silk cap, kid gloves, and tight dress coat. Richard Henry Dana was about to embark on the adventure of his life—a two-year working voyage to California and back. He had decided to sail "before the mast" as an ordinary seaman, living forward in the ship for over two years with men who could hardly be more different from him. This breech of the boundary surrounding educated society shocked his friends. It was an audacious decision.

Dana's written account of this experience, *Two Years before the Mast*, would mark a turning point in American and European maritime literature. Nearly all accounts of life at sea had been written by officers, captains, or passengers living in staterooms at the rear of the ship—behind the mast. To sail "before the mast" meant to serve as working crew and be quartered together in the dark, often wet "forecastle" below deck at the bow of the ship. Although his book would gain popular attention and influence scores of writers, including Herman Melville, *Two Years before the Mast* would remain the main literary achievement of Richard Henry Dana's life.

## EARLY LIFE

Dana was born into a prominent Boston family on 1 August 1815. His father had founded the influential literary magazine *North American Review* and was a well-known poet and essayist. His grandfather had served as chief justice of the Massachusetts Supreme Court. Although his mother died when he was six and family finances were ebbing, Dana excelled at some of the best

Richard Henry Dana.
(*Courtesy of the National Park Service, Longfellow National Historic Site*)

schools. He entered Harvard in July 1831, but near the end of his second year contracted the measles. It so affected his eyesight that he was unable to even look at a printed page. Feeling pitiful and confined after nine months in his father's house, he seized on the idea of a long voyage involving constant work. Reading would not be necessary and he might better restore his health. After rejecting more comfortable options, he located a berth on the *Pilgrim*, sailing to California by way of perilous Cape Horn. In California the ship would trade goods for cowhides from the Mexican ranches, and bring the hides back to Massachusetts shoe factories.

After leaving Boston Harbor, Dana immediately found himself hopelessly seasick and miserable. Writing about it, he introduces a sense of humor and naiveté that causes many readers to feel as though they too must pay close attention if they are to survive the rest of the voyage. After his wrenching initiation, he describes the meaning and pronunciation of shipboard commands, what it is like to grease the mast of a ship rolling heavily, and how to catch an albatross using a shingle. Yet such descriptions soon turn to more serious events. After observing the auction of a fellow crewman's clothes only hours after he had fallen into the sea and drowned, he writes, "a sailor's life is at best but a mixture of a little good with much evil, and a little pleasure with much pain. The beautiful is linked with the revolting, the sublime with the commonplace, and the solemn with the ludicrous." Later, when two men are tied to the rigging and flogged, a horrified Dana quotes the captain screaming, "If you want to know what I flog you for, I'll tell you. It's because I like to do it! Because I like to do it! It suits me! That's what I do it for!" That night, Dana considered "the prospect of obtaining justice and

347

satisfaction for these poor men; and vowed that if God should ever give me the means, I would do something to redress the grievances and relieve the sufferings of that poor class of beings, of whom I then was one."

Dana, however, could never be of that class, and despite his vow the incident was not the reason for his later choice of the legal profession. He wrote that he had "always considered it a settled thing that I must be a lawyer" and that despite his "dread of the profession" in which his ancestors had been distinguished, "it was an honorable one." On the voyage, one of his greatest fears was that he might "become a sailor in mind and habits, as well as in body." Finding that he in fact must spend another year with the ship, he feels condemned to "a fate, which would alter the whole of my future life." Only because of letters from influential friends at home is he released. Yet, Dana feels the sting of the crew's taunt, "Oh, yes! The captain has let you off, because you are a gentleman's son."

Upon his return to Boston, Dana entered Harvard's Dane Law School and immediately began to write his account, based on surviving notes and letters. (An original journal and sea chest had been entrusted to a relative and lost the day he arrived.) He gave his manuscript to a former teacher who brought it to the publisher Harper and Brothers in New York. Dana hoped the book would bring in business for the law office he was about to open, so he hastily, albeit reluctantly, accepted $250 for publication rights. He correctly believed it was worth much more.

Upon its publication in 1840, *Two Years before the Mast* became a popular and international sensation. As biographer Robert Lucid noted: "In an age dominated by fictional melodrama its tautly understated prose bit into the literary imagination." The public and critics alike were understandably thrilled with the novelty of "this voice from the forecastle." In England the poet Samuel Rogers wrote: "extracts from this book were chosen by the oculists of the United States for use in testing eyes on account of its clearness in style and freedom from long words." Dana included so much information regarding places visited, the hide-curing process, and the dress and customs of the Californians that the book would become a reliable and popular source of information for people traveling to California during the Gold Rush. It remains an important source of information for historians today.

Such notoriety earned Dana the respect of many writers, including Charles Dickens, Ralph Waldo Emerson, and Herman Melville, with whom Dana corresponded. In the midst of *Moby-Dick* Melville wrote to Dana about his need to "throw in a little fancy. . . . Yet I mean to give

the truth of the thing, spite of this." Dana must have understood the great influence his book had, because he frequently lectured on his experience, yet he never considered a career in writing.

## LIFE AFTER *TWO YEARS BEFORE THE MAST*

Within a year of his book's publication, Dana opened his law office; married Sarah Watson from Connecticut (with whom he would have six children); and published *The Seaman's Friend*, which he called "purely a business book." It contained useful nautical information and included laws pertaining to mariners. Driven by his desire to restore the former Dana family fortune and the need to provide for his aging father and large family, he threw himself into his work. He won nearly all his cases, and it was even said that his law office smelled of tar from the constant parade of seamen who came to seek redress.

Being an upper-class gentleman, lawyer, and famous writer suited Dana's upbringing and conservative politics. He even supported corporal punishment of sailors as a necessity, although his book had encouraged opposition to the practice. But now, debates in Boston on the issue of slavery were breaking the old social bonds and alliances that defined a person's politics. In 1848 Dana helped found the Free Soil Party, which stood against the proliferation of slavery. He represented, at no charge, the cases of fugitive slaves—and lost business and friends as a consequence.

As life went on, he often worked himself past the point of exhaustion, and the best remedy would be to go off on some long journey. Several years after traveling to England he took a small side trip to Havana, writing his little-known account *To Cuba and Back* (1859). The book contains excellent descriptions of the Chinese laborers and sugar cane harvesting, but also contains descriptions of his breakfast and the temperature of the seaside baths. Within a few months of returning, he left on another trip—this time around the world. When the copyright for *Two Years before the Mast* reverted to him in 1869, he added a chapter based on this trip, entitled "Twenty-Four Years After." It is a startling account of a California utterly transformed since he had last seen it. The poignancy and style of writing found here compares to anything in the original book.

Dana became a legal expert on admiralty and international law, testifying before the U.S. Supreme Court (1863) to establish the legality of a northern blockade of southern ports. During these war years he served as Abraham Lincoln's district attorney in Massachusetts. He was elected to the Massachusetts legislature for two terms, but became known as "The Duke of Cambridge" for his aristocratic demeanor. The reputation hurt him when he ran for the U.S. Congress in 1868 and received a mere 10 percent of the vote. In 1876 President Ulysses Grant nominated him to be ambassador to Great Britain, but a charge of plagiarism in a textbook he wrote derailed his confirmation. Although later exonerated, the experience deeply depressed him. At age sixty-three, he turned his law practice over to his son and retired to Europe, where he attempted to write one last major work on international law. He died in Rome four years later on 6 January 1882 and was buried by his wife in the same cemetery as John Keats and Percy Bysshe Shelley. Before leaving for Europe, he had written in a letter to his son: "My life has been a failure compared with what I might and ought to have done. My great success—my book—was a boy's work, done before I came to the Bar."

[*See also* Melville, Herman, *and Moby-Dick.*]

## WORKS

*Two Years before the Mast* (1840)
*The Seaman's Friend* (1841)
*To Cuba and Back* (1859)

## FURTHER READING

Adams, Charles Francis, Jr. *Richard Henry Dana.* New York, 1983. An early biography by a younger contemporary, with an introduction by Robert Lucid. First published in 1890.

Lucid, Robert F. *The Journal.* Cambridge, Mass., 1968. An excellent introduction along with photographs and extensive footnotes to the private journal Dana kept between 1840 and 1860 and which is in the collection of the Massachusetts Historical Society. Includes Dana's 1815–1841 *An Autobiographical Sketch.*

# DON DeLILLO

*by Joseph Dewey*

There is something coolly inaccessible about the fiction—and the person—of Don DeLillo. By any measure—productivity, longevity, influence, scope—a dominant novelist of his era, DeLillo nevertheless resists the expectations of celebrity: public appearances, promotional Web sites, prestigious university appointments, conference readings, talk-show blitzes; even his interviews can be dense and forbidding. In an era of tell-all glamour, what little DeLillo, born on 20 November 1936, has offered of his autobiography rarely figures in his fiction—his Italian immigrant family; his love of the street life of his native Bronx; his fascination with the ritual theater of his Catholicism; his indifference toward his own formal education (he "slept through" high school and "didn't study much of anything" while earning a 1958 communication arts degree from Fordham); his initial experience of serious literature—Faulkner and then gloriously Joyce—while, at age eighteen, killing time as a summer playground attendant; his five-year stint as copywriter for the Manhattan advertising firm of Ogilvie and Mather; his 1964 decision to quit, not to write (although he had published two stories) but rather to abandon work he found unfulfilling; his long struggle to write his first novel, which would not be published until his mid-thirties. Since then he has maintained a spectacularly low-key lifestyle. Since his marriage in 1975 to designer Barbara Bennett, DeLillo has lived in the suburbs of New York City and traveled some, but mostly he has written, a dozen novels as well as a scattering of essays, stories, and experimental plays.

The novels themselves, unapologetically difficult, resist the comforting intimacy of other narratives: no clear plot lines compelled by suspense and offering convenient symbols to interpret on the way to tidy closure and a handy

Don DeLillo.
*(Photograph by Joyce Ravid)*

theme, all staged within a recognizable geography peopled by recognizable characters who, in the familiar sound of colloquial chat, fret over love and death, family and work. DeLillo even resists a defining genre: novel to novel, he has experimented with and skewed Westerns, science fiction, murder mysteries, spy thrillers, the nonfiction novel, metafiction, disaster novels, the romance, sports stories, even ghost stories. Like Saul Bellow a generation earlier, DeLillo writes novels of ideas, less stories than episodic meditations, unsettling and provocative. Indeed, DeLillo disdains other sorts of fiction—"around-the-house-and-in-the-yard" realism, as he terms them—for their diminished scope. Not surprisingly, DeLillo has never produced a character embraced by the American imagination—no Huck or Holden or Gatsby. His characters are uncharismatic, aloof and unapproachable, witty and talky, and often distant from the action within their own narratives. His works have sustained critical dissection and have garnered accolades: the 1985 National Book Award for *White Noise*; the 2000 William Dean Howells Award, presented every five years for the most distinguished work in American fiction, for *Underworld*; the 1992 PEN/Faulkner Award for *Mao II*; the 1999 Jerusalem Prize for a body of work centered on the freedom of the individual—the first American to win it. But save for *Libra*, a best-seller largely because of its creative appropriation of the Kennedy assassination, his novels have generated only modest sales. Indeed, DeLillo is famously indifferent to the pressure of having an audience—he is a consummate stylist, engaged by his own admission in mastering the technology of language itself, experimenting with the sonic dimension of his sentences, testing their syllable beat for harmony. He even works on a manual typewriter, relishing the physical imposition of ink onto paper and the accumulating drift of drafts.

Finding pedestrian the anxieties of the heart, the hidden poetry of small lives, DeLillo binds his characters to their larger cultural moment. He tests nothing less than the viability, indeed the relevancy, of the self in late-twentieth-century America. What is the effect, DeLillo asks, of the unprecedented reach of electronic media? The problem, as he articulates it across four decades of fiction, is the loss of the authentic self after a half-century's assault of images from film, television, tabloids, and advertising that have produced a shallow culture too enamored of simulations, unable to respond to authentic emotional moments without recourse to media models, staring (like voyeurs) at a complex of screens, dislocated from history but enthralled by the news, and taught by an onslaught of commercials not to dream—that, after all, is a complex expression of the individual—but rather to want, part of the collective herd that mass media inevitably fashions. Whatever poignancy DeLillo's characters manage comes when they demand the privilege of a self to explore, fearing in their darker moments that it is simply not there. With such a provocative focus, DeLillo has emerged as a most articulate anatomist of fin-de-millennium America—but not a particularly comforting writer. As cultural anatomist, he confronts his age with an unblinking eye and an intimidating intelligence; he has tackled the difficult implications of popular culture, high and low. His topics have ranged from nuclear apocalypse to rock music, the Kennedy assassination to the porn industry, astrophysics to college football, terrorism to baseball memorabilia, environmental holocaust to garbage management. In conducting this wide-ranging cultural dissection, DeLillo has maintained two thermal settings simultaneously: the caustic cool of a satirist, full of insult and indictment; and the white-hot fury of a latter-day prophet, full of discontent and desperation. As authorial postures, both are necessarily aloof, unforgiving, and predisposed to seeing a culture in permanent crisis, thus resisting easy intimacy with a reader bound, unaware, within the same troubling cultural matrix.

## PROBLEMS/SOLUTIONS OF A CULTURAL ANATOMIST

If DeLillo's focus is on the heroic struggle to salvage the self in the late twentieth century, what has so threatened the individual? DeLillo centers on three specific cultural pressures: the intoxicating melodrama of the Cold War, the 1963 assassination of John Kennedy, and the irresistible pressure of electronic media.

For more than a generation, the Cold War provided the appeal of coherence, squaring a fractious world into manageable clarity by the ruthless imposition of order. Its embracing schema could account for every news event; there was no surprise, only the comforting certainty of paranoia, the easy spell of manageable intricacy, a perfect rendering of post-Hiroshima anxieties into plot. The eccentric logic of such tidiness is evident throughout DeLillo's canon: in terrorists and religious cultists; FBI agents and corporate wheeler-dealers; fascists and Catholics; spies and counterspies; mathematicians and football coaches. How greedily, DeLillo cautions, we accept the elegant simplicity of explanations that insulate us from anxiety over the freefall pitch into pure contingency. That freefall was perhaps best defined by the ambush of Kennedy in Dealey Plaza, which DeLillo has described as a generational trauma, the blunt intrusion of crude mortality that revealed not only the eggshell fragility of the human form but, absent a motive, left a culture forever suspended between explanation and mystery, between scripted terrorism and random madness. Despite a hillside of eyewitnesses and the unblinking testimony of twenty-two cameras, the Dallas shooting has never revealed itself. As such, DeLillo sees the assassination as the birth of the video age—of television news and the rush to pitch disaster into living rooms where stark images nevertheless frustrate revelation. Here, DeLillo sees, a culture began its addiction to spectacle violence, the itch for more graphic filmed sequences, that thrill inevitably deadening the ability to react with appropriate sensitivity to suddenly quaint notions of the sacramental dimension of life and the private privilege of death. From the Vietnam War fought on television to the trailing bone-white clouds of the space shuttle *Challenger*, from the street beating of Rodney King to the shootings of Pope John Paul II and Ronald Reagan, from the made-for-television Gulf War to that lone aircraft flying eerily, unerringly into the south tower of the World Trade Center, a culture has come to crave the image: faddish reality television programming, omnipresent surveillance cameras, the endless roll of amateur video cameras, news crews in a frenzy to entertain with catastrophe as violence and death have become as routine as mouthwash commercials.

DeLillo's dominant concern, perhaps from his brief career in advertising, is just this unprecedented reach of electronic media, not merely the news but advertising, films, television, the screech of tabloids, the faux intimacy of pornography, the enclosing artifice of the World Wide Web, the bang and sizzle of home entertainment technologies, even the wonderland labyrinths of theme parks. These relentless forces have created a virtual reality, an electronic mediascape of composed images and enhanced projections that did not exist fifty years ago. Such invasive technologies, DeLillo argues, create a narcotic addiction for the larger-than-life and thus anesthetize hapless consumers, film-fed and image-fat, to the apparently unspectacular life immediately about them. Indeed the real becomes distant, even terrifying, or simply irrelevant.

The solutions DeLillo offers are strikingly traditional but appear provocative largely because they are asserted in an era—and within narratives—where they can appear ironic. Relax, DeLillo counsels his era, into wonder, relish the thrust and drag of the immediate, accept its unpredictability and your vulnerability, step away from the protective bunker of depthless images and lifeless words and approach each moment for what it is, an imperfect respite from what the human creature alone understands is inevitable: closure. Those able to do so are rare in DeLillo's fictions. They come to embrace the horizontal plane: they accept the body as a living organism measured in time, subject to the persuasive itch of passion and inevitably succumbing to deterioration. They turn to the immediate world, often for DeLillo an urban geography, that once lovingly detailed is suddenly shot through with unsuspected radiance, the heft and press of an ordinary city block—its color, its jazzy welter of voices, its harshness, and its beauty—becoming jarringly real. DeLillo offers reconnection—joy, terror, and wonder—as remedy for the stifling ennui of the late century. But it is not enough to tap such immediacy. DeLillo has come to valorize the exertion of articulation that encodes such awareness into words, the act of writing itself that confers a kind of permanence to such moments and in the process creates the accidental community of reader and writer. He understands how the media age has threatened language itself, cheapened it into power clichés, advertising slogans, political spin-doctoring, techno-jargon, and the thick insulation of legalese. The writer, engaged in observation, reclaims language, constructs a massively subjective system of representation—called a novel—that (unlike photographs or music scores or films) contains, rather than freezes, the contradictory impulses of experience. In the act of recording, the transient becomes stable; the inconsequential, significant; the neglected, the examined.

Consider DeLillo's influences. Although he has recognized the tectonic impact of Faulkner and Joyce and of his contemporaries William Gaddis and Thomas Pynchon, DeLillo more often acknowledges three influences that in the 1950s shaped his evolving aesthetic sensibility: the driving hard bop of improv jazz, the avant-garde revolution in abstract expressionist painting, and the New Wave European filmmakers, particularly Jean-Luc Godard. Like DeLillo's novels, each challenges rather than invites. Much as DeLillo minimizes character and action as elements of narrative, each aesthetic expression discarded its traditional elements (bop dispensed with melody, abstract expressionism with representation, and Godard's films with story and character). Thus, like DeLillo's novels, each expression ultimately foregrounds its own medium and compels the participatory audience to acknowledge the artifact as just that, a marvelously engineered form. Indeed, as DeLillo will come to argue, the sole energy able to un-violate the self, to reanimate the self in the electronic age, is language itself within the precise engineering of prose—the writer as a culture's last hero.

## NARRATIVES OF RETREAT

DeLillo's four earliest works offer a quartet of shallow characters each trying to undergo a convincing spiritual crisis but just not entirely sure how. They elect flight, a problematic retreat from the implications of their cultural moment and seek in that doomed gesture to recover a self worth preserving.

Television executive David Bell (*Americana*, 1971) finds success a tedious round of office realpolitik and bored adulteries. More distressing, at age twenty-eight, he has lost any notion of an authentic self. He is a performance: a collage of film recollections (particularly Burt Lancaster and Kirk Douglas) and advertising promotions (his father, an advertising executive, had subjected him as a child to hours of test commercials in the basement). Determined to reclaim a self, he accepts an assignment to oversee a documentary on the Navajos out west. But he abandons that assignment in the Midwest to pursue a conceptual autobiographical film. To discover who he is, he scripts critical memories of his life into third-person monologues and films ordinary people from a small town reading the recollections, which center on a problematic relationship with his domineering father and confused attractions for his mother. The film project fails—the fragmentary ruminations cannot cohere. Determined then to dispense with the self entirely, David heads west alone to the desert wastes, traditional site of spiritual cleansing. What he finds rather is a Dante-esque inferno of debauchery in a commune and is nearly raped by a gay hitchhiker. In the end, David exiles himself to a nameless island where he watches the unfinished film of his own life, coolly sustained by its depthless images.

Like David Bell, Gary Harkness (*End Zone*, 1972), a talented halfback, struggles within a spiritual crisis. He has gone through four prestigious college programs, plagued by spiritual malaise and dealing with his part in a brutal tackle in which an opposing player died. Terrified by the vulnerability of the puny self amid blind chance, he retreats to tiny Logos College in the West Texas wastes. There he plays for an authoritarian coach, a control freak who motivates with power clichés, who defines every turn of a game within the iron logic of his playbook, and who will provide Harkness the protective system he so desperately seeks. But DeLillo sees the price for such retreat. He renders the big game between Logos and its cross-state rival in thirty pages of x's and o's, inaccessible playbook jargon, every moment drained of the emotional texture of spontaneity and passion. When an ROTC professor of military strategy argues the inevitability of nuclear holocaust, Harkness relishes the tidiness of self-inflicted apocalypse. Like football (and, as DeLillo suggests, like theology), nuclear war charms brutality into an uncomplicated exercise in control, a perfect closed system in which the individual exercises no responsibility and which, theoretically, resolves the death anxiety entirely. But Harkness finds no protective end zone from death or absurdity. The team is shaken by two deaths—a young coach commits suicide, a player dies in a car accident—and Harkness (like David Bell) takes to long excursions into the desert. When, during a meaningless late-season game, Harkness smokes a joint and actually walks off, he is surprised that not only is he not disciplined but he is made co-captain for the next season. Feeling the enclosing pressure of an absurd world, Harkness opts for a ruinous fast, yet another gesture of control and retreat that DeLillo rejects: the novel ends with the weakened Harkness being taken to the campus infirmary.

When burned-out rock star Bucky Wunderlick (*Great Jones Street*, 1973) abandons his celebrity lifestyle and retreats, like some latter-day Thoreau, to a spartan Manhattan apartment to find a self just by simplifying its context, DeLillo readers expect such a gesture to fail of its own irony. Distressed by the directionless violence his concerts excite and disillusioned by the inefficacy of his early protest songs, Bucky retreats to recover a self. But his exile is regularly violated by worried record executives,

eccentric neighbors, a drug-smuggling girlfriend, and ex-band members. In addition, he becomes entangled in a bizarre theft of a government test-drug. A bundled sample of the drug, which destroys language skills and was intended to (literally) silence political dissenters in the aftermath of the 1960s, is left at Bucky's apartment, where members of a sinister underground hippie cult, ironically named the Happy Valley Farm Commune, plot to secure it for their own testing. In another similarly bundled package is the sole copy of Bucky's latest recordings, impromptu songs about his spiritual agonies, which he taped while alone in the mountains. When the commune destroys the tapes, Bucky spirals into hopelessness. After commune thugs inject him with the experimental drug, he finds his ability to speak entirely short-circuited. Wordlessly he tours the Bowery neighborhoods and witnesses firsthand its brutal splendor. It is a cathartic moment of promising engagement. But Bucky closes the novel, the drug just wearing off, content to sustain the charade of muteness, thus accepting only private restoration, a disturbing variation on exile.

But engagement does not simply enthrall. *Ratner's Star* (1976), for all its eccentric allegorical plots and fantastic asides, its sheer encyclopedic command of arcane mathematics and its impenetrable vocabulary, its extravagant sci-fi speculations and its careful emulation of mathematical architectures, cautions that engaging the freewheeling ad lib of the immediate can terrify as well. Science, DeLillo argues, has provided twentieth-century culture with a smug certainty that the universe simply awaits mapping—it is, like the football games at Logos College, a closed exercise in predictability, cozily immune to the shell shock of surprise. The premise here is tantalizing: Are pulsations that are being picked up from deep space a message? Billy Twillig, a brilliant fourteen-year-old mathematician called in to help decode the message, is taken, Alicelike, into a think-tank wonderland where a gallery of self-absorbed oddball scientists, Swiftian cartoons, pursue without irony eccentric projects radically disconnected from any real-world application. Billy himself will be involved in an absurd project to create a language based on numbers, thus dispensing with the inelegant imprecision of words.

When Billy decodes the signal as a message actually sent from an ancient Earth civilization that correctly predicts an imminent unscheduled solar eclipse, the realization that science had somehow "missed" that otherwise predictable phenomenon shakes the think tank. Billy, however, resists panic—he is more adaptive (as children in DeLillo often are). Indeed, at the threshold of adolescence, Billy has started to register the first complex urges of his maturing body, confusions over sexuality and aging and death, and has intuited that science can do little but simplify such rich confusions. He is last seen madly pedaling a child's tricycle into the very shadow bands of the approaching eclipse, ringing the bike's tinny bell, a sound that signals as much joy as alarm. Like Bucky, he makes peace with nature's elaborate chaos. But, as a mathematician, Billy long ago dismissed words as unreliable and thus is shut off from the technology of language that could share such intuition with a needful community.

## NARRATIVES OF FAILED ENGAGEMENT

Finding retreat unworkable, DeLillo would explore in his next two novels the implications of Billy's impromptu gesture of engagement. But because characters in these works engage the stunning unpredictability and death-haunted chaos of the real world without the requisite awe that makes that gesture rewarding, they are left—emotionally or physically—dead.

When Wall Street stockbroker Lyle Wynant (*Players*, 1977) witnesses a terrorist shooting on the floor of the Exchange, he glimpses the unbearable slightness of his ordered life: the mercenary rituals of his professional success, the interminable evenings channel-surfing with the sound off, the bored friction that passes for lovemaking with his wife, a thin life DeLillo underscores with a stark minimalist prose line and by his refusal to provide any background or interior shadings to Lyle. Curious about adventure, Lyle pursues an attractive secretary and, in the course of a predictable affair (the sex is less than incendiary), becomes enmeshed in the underground world of urban terrorists bent on shaking the foundations of the capitalist system by bombing Wall Street itself. Fascinated by the intrigue but ultimately unable to commit to its fanatic agenda, Lyle plays double agent and feeds information to federal investigators. He cannot even sustain the raw heat of a heady fling with one of the terrorists and returns to the relative safety of his cliché affair with the secretary, its lack of authenticity underscored by her use of a strap-on dildo to spice up what has already staled into routine. Lyle closes the narrative in a Canadian hotel, waiting for a phone call from one side or the other, watching television and fantasizing about being a spy: suspended from authenticity, rootless, playacting.

In alternating chapters, DeLillo tracks Pammy, Lyle's wife, who, as a grief counselor entowered within the World Trade Center, professionally mollifies her clients'

authentic expression of emotion with colorful brochures and easy platitudes. Like Lyle, Pammy will also test passion—she will journey with two gay friends to the Maine backwoods to engage the tonic natural world. There she will share an unexpectedly passionate moment under the stars with one of the men who, she never cares to suspect, is painfully suspended between sexual identities and who, when they return to the city, immolates himself in a desperate gesture of suicide. After coolly studying the charred stump, Pammy retreats to her apartment and watches television to obliterate the possibility of awareness. Later, on a walk through her neighborhood, she studies a flophouse marquee that reads "TRANSIENTS"—a word that is terrifying to those who genuinely engage the reality of death but, to one so casually playing at life, is reduced to simple noise (Pammy actually sounds it out).

Glen Selvy (*Running Dog*, 1978) is also a player, serving on the staff of a prominent U.S. senator (his unofficial job is to secure pornography for the senator's private collection) and as a mole for a shadowy military-industrial conglomerate, Radial Matrix, which is eager to get dirt on the senator to head off congressional investigations into its covert paramilitary operations to "manage" domestic dissent. Unencumbered by authentic convictions (his code name, Running Dog, suggests an unflattering penchant for obedience), he maintains a spare rented apartment and indulges in only anonymous sexual encounters rather than risk love. Selvy becomes entangled in an international black market intrigue to secure the sole copy of a pornographic home movie supposedly made in the last hours in Hitler's Berlin bunker. When the shadowy Kurtzlike head of Radial Matrix suspects that Selvy may be less than committed to acquiring the film, he assigns a hit squad to eliminate Selvy. Unable to accept the complicated reality implied by his own side gunning for him even after its first attempt fails, Selvy heads for the West, a landscape, in cinematic lore, marked clearly by white hats and black hats. He travels to an abandoned government training facility in the wastes of Texas where he had been first indoctrinated into the simplified universe of recognizable good and identifiable evil. But DeLillo deliberately undercuts the possibility of Selvy's spiritual reclamation. Selvy's death is inglorious: he is indecorously decapitated by the hit squad (at the moment of death, Selvy longs only for a drink). A comrade wants to give the body a traditional Native American "air burial," elevating it and offering it to buzzards, thus achieving an ennobling transcendence. But the ritual is unworkable as it requires strands of hair, and Selvy's head is missing. Even the black market film proves a telling disappointment: in it, a playful Hitler cavorts, mimicking Charlie Chaplin in *The Great Dictator*, for the delight of a group of children, the twentieth century's darkest monster a sad little clown—an intolerable ambiguity for a character like Selvy, so needful of simplification.

## NARRATIVES OF RECOVERY

Intolerant of the ad-lib openness of the real world, destroyed by a brush with its passion, potent surprise, and knotty contradictions, the Wynants and Glen Selvy brought DeLillo, artistically, to something of an impasse. After all, withdrawal and engagement had both failed. Four years would pass before DeLillo would publish again. Not to tie DeLillo's evolution as a writer to autobiography, but there is a marked change in the novels after DeLillo spent three years in the late 1970s on a Guggenheim Fellowship in Greece and the Middle East, where, by his own account, he was reintroduced to the stunning power of language itself. Indeed, the two novels that followed his return are clearly touched by an expansive generosity absent in his earlier works: two alienated (and terrified) central characters (James Axton and Jack Gladney) move hesitatingly toward authenticity and community by embracing the complicated mystery of the late-century world.

James Axton (*The Names*, 1982) begins a familiar DeLillo character: an overseas-insurance risk analyst for corporations concerned over terrorist attacks, he is a tourist in his own life, aloof, mild-mannered, emotionless, shallow, overanalytical, insulated from both his own heart (his sole affair was a tepid interlude) and from the real; the data he gathers immure him from the bloody rage of the terrorists he studies. For the first time, however, DeLillo foregrounds language. Although the narrative teems with students of language, none taps its enriching power to connect to the immediate. Conversations are maddeningly indirect and disjointed. The archaeologist Owen Brademas forsakes a promising local dig to pore over stone inscriptions, language reduced to meaningless glyphs; Tap, James's precocious nine-year-old, lovingly writes a novel but in a made-up, private language; an ancient mountain cult kills according to the alphabet, selecting victims whose initials correspond to the initials of the murder site, an enslavement to language as a rigid (and entirely arbitrary) ordering system; a visiting filmmaker wants to shoot a documentary on the cult entirely without a script, dispensing with language entirely. It is Axton

alone who comes to reject such insulating strategies. At novel's end, when he discovers he has been an unwitting dupe for the CIA, he abandons insurance to return to freelance writing, language implicitly tied to audience. Before he departs Greece, he visits the Acropolis, a site he had long avoided as too imposing, and there communes with the tonic chaos of the noisy street crowd (he does not speak Greek) and feels a vibrant community animated by the intricate webbing of the brimming jazz of conversation. It is language alive and spontaneous, kinetic and connective. But language can do more than stir such epiphanies. The novel ends with a chapter from Tap's novel that recounts a midwestern boy's nightmarish experience of a prairie religious revival in which frenzied members of the congregation suddenly speak in tongues (an episode that counterpoints Axton's epiphany amid the babble at the Acropolis)—but even the terror of that experience is redeemed within the freewheeling music of Tap's audacious language.

In *White Noise* (1985), DeLillo directly confronts what had long haunted his late-century world: the fear of death. Professor Jack Gladney, at midlife, enjoys the trappings of middle-class success—a home, his health, a family, a career—and yet he cannot sleep at night; he is certain something nameless and terrifying lives in his basement. He clings to crowds—his lecture hall, the local malls, the grocery store—certain that they keep out death; he specializes in Hitler studies, mesmerized by a personage who trafficked in death with cool confidence and brutal efficiency. Unable to accept the vulnerability implicit in mortality, gratefully accepting the insulation of domesticity, Gladney is seduced by his sense of invincibility (he parades about campus in full academic regalia and dark glasses) and hides within a comfy bunker of middle-class plenty, mesmerized by the distracting noise of the television news and its nightly barrage of catastrophe that cheapens mortality by making it generic.

When a nearby train accident releases a massive toxic cloud, the Gladneys must evacuate their home. When they stop for gas, Gladney steps out of the car and confronts the approaching churning chemical cloud. He understands that here, at this bald moment, mortality has entered him. Terrified, he turns to an experimental drug advertised in a tabloid, Dylar, designed to short-circuit that part of the brain where death-anxiety lurks. His wife, he learns, had secured a test sample after sleeping with a drug company representative. When the drug fails, he implements a crude Hitleresque end run: master death by killing (suggested by a sinister colleague who convinces

Gladney that death necessarily cheapens every experience). He tracks down the drug company representative to shoot him. When that plan goes absurdly wrong and Gladney himself ends up with a gunshot wound in his wrist, he matures into acceptance: death cannot be graphed, understood, tamed, ignored, survived, or beaten (each a strategy undertaken by characters in the novel). Thermos in hand, he joins the crowds who gather each evening at a highway overpass to watch the ringing bronze of the evening sunset, made spectacular by lingering toxins, a luminous metaphor for accommodating the natural inevitability of the human sunset that is both ordinary and stunning, generic and magnificent. But DeLillo cautions against simple optimism: in the novel's two closing scenes, Gladney's youngest son pedals his tricycle furiously out into the highway, a terrifying image of vulnerability without awareness. And when the Gladneys visit the local market they are momentarily bewildered by the store's reorganized shelves, a reminder of a universe shot through with wonder but that nevertheless refuses stasis.

## NARRATIVES OF REDEMPTION

Axton at the Acropolis and Gladney at the overpass both undergo a quasi-religious awakening that comes from embracing community and accepting uncertainty in a universe that science and television, despite their smug efforts, cannot diminish into predictability. But DeLillo as artist understands that such moments cannot suffice. Passion is not in the experience of the immediate. Rather, passion is in the work of shaping that experience into language, sharing that experience with an unnamable but real audience using the aesthetic technologies of narrative: observation, pattern making, plot shaping, and invention. The spell must be spelled out or it is a pointless ecstasy, a momentary intensity cooling into private recollection. Thus, in the confident voice of his most accomplished novels, DeLillo focuses on narration itself, specifically the role of the writer in the electronic age who sets the brutal wonder of experience to the available music of language.

In any narrative that configures a plausible reading of the Kennedy assassination, the narrative center would appear to belong to Lee Harvey Oswald, the ur-loner, the alienated nobody fed on the tough-guy fantasies of television, spy novels, and war movies and determined to become an event, a domestic terrorist fueled not so much by fanaticism as by the hunger to be known. In *Libra* (1988), DeLillo meticulously re-creates a plausible Oswald, coaxing the paradox of Oswald's commitments to both the Left and Right, to the Soviet Union and the marines, to Marxism and the American Dream (Oswald's astrological sign, Libra, indicates this struggle for balance) into a compelling arc that leads to the Texas School Book Depository. In turn, Oswald is a perfect dupe, the credible lone gunman necessary for a complex intrigue fashioned by CIA renegades from the Bay of Pigs debacle who believe a near-miss of the American president blamed on Cuba would ignite a genuine effort to overthrow the dictator, a charade that, even as it is planned, evolves into the very real execution in Dealey Plaza.

Although the play between the conspirators and the unsuspecting Oswald is mesmerizing (indeed, initial critical response blasted DeLillo for irresponsibly confecting history), a plausible reading of the Kennedy shooting is clearly not DeLillo's aim. It is more about writing such a plausible reading. This is a novel that foregrounds its own presence. DeLillo invents a third narrative element, a retired CIA analyst named Nicholas Branch, hired by the Agency long after Dallas to write the definitive history of the shooting, who is entombed for fifteen years in a fireproof basement teeming with binders of testimony and boxes of physical evidence. As historian, Branch is eventually overwhelmed by its plotlessness. He concedes that shaping such material into coherence will always be preliminary and lamely concludes that the shooting succeeded because of luck: coincidental encounters among the principles, the arbitrary choice of a motorcade route, and even the Dallas weather. Yet even as the historian despairs (or fashions towering improbabilities such as the twenty-six volumes of the Warren Commission report), DeLillo, as novelist, subverts such inevitability like a terrorist in the works and provides the same events with the richness of plot and the reward of an ordering that accepts itself as provisional. Thus, narrative redeems history and at the same time refuses to accept its own patternings as final. Certain, yet flexible; clear, yet ambiguous, narrative stabilizes the difficult onrush of circumstances into a manageable line, content to recover a serviceable, rather than inviolable, truth.

From the failure of the historian who attempts to shape a narrative, DeLillo tracks the failure of the novelist who attempts to engage the brutal onrush of pure event. Bill Gray, the recluse-author in *Mao II* (1991), is restless with his elected life of radical withdrawal. In hiding from the reach of the world, endlessly revising a novel-in-progress that molders in scribbled drafts in stacked boxes, Bill Gray suggests the fragile integrity of the individual voice within the era of electronic herdspeak, a culture's addiction to conformity suggested here by the Sun Hyung Moon cult, the Chinese Communist crackdown at Tiananmen Square, the Iranian cult of Ayatollah Khomeini, hooded Middle Eastern terrorists, and, most disturbingly, by Andy Warhol's vision of the artist as pop commodity. When Gray reasons that withdrawal has, in fact, simply made him more of a celebrity, he decides to reengage the world. He first agrees to sit for a photo portrait and then, more dramatically, to assist in an international campaign to free a Swiss diplomat and poet taken hostage in Beirut. But when he participates in a public reading in London, he realizes the event will be used by his publishers to promote his long-awaited new work and, worse, will actually help the terrorists by according them media attention. Determined to engage events firsthand, he heads on his own to the Middle East to offer himself as a swap to the terrorists, only to be struck by a careening taxi in Athens and then to die days later from unsuspected internal injuries on a ferry to Beirut, ingloriously and anonymously—his ID documents are stolen even as he dies. Writers, DeLillo cautions, deal with ideas and design and exist within invention and expression; they execute formidable structures that are themselves guerrilla gestures of organization in a world that dismisses the very viability of order. But the writer cannot compete with the brutal force of violence and fanaticism, suggested here by the shadowy figure of the terrorist. Indeed, the novel closes with the photographer sent originally to take Gray's portrait abandoning writers as subjects and turning rather to photographing terrorists—the image displacing the word even as the terrorist displaces the writer.

What then is the writer to do? Can a writer, in fact, matter? In DeLillo's masterwork, *Underworld* (1997), he redeems the failures of both Nicholas Branch and Bill Gray. A nameless narrator, a felt rather than heard presence, boldly stage-manages a massive cultural history of America's Cold War era by ostensibly tracking the intricate (and entirely invented) movements of the home run ball Bobby Thomson launched on 3 October 1951 to give the New York Giants an improbable National League pennant. Juxtaposed against that trajectory is a portrait of Nick Shay, a successful executive in waste management who comes to own the ball and who, past midlife, has decided to make peace with his own history, specifically a difficult adolescence that included a runaway father, an incendiary affair with a teacher's wife, and the accidental shooting of a neighborhood heroin addict. What stuns first is the scope of the novel, comprising more than 800 pages and dozens of characters, historical and invented, with a mesh of crossing plot lines,

historical and invented. In the process, the narrator deftly shifts voice like a master ventriloquist: the prose line is at turns deadpan, jazzy, jargon-ridden, witty, spare, or deliciously detailed—the sheer delight of a sonic complex. The construction itself is unconventional. While sections on Nick Shay move backward from the 1990s, chapters on the baseball move forward from the 1950s—the intricate crossings of temporal lines maintained by the confident architecture of the controlling narrator. Along the way, careful rereaders discover a trove of suggestive patternings—striking coincidences (both actual and invented), a recurring system of numerology (centering on the number thirteen), recurring symbols, repeated names, the multiple changes on the idea of "waste"—that can sustain illimitable analyses as the reader can construct viable contradictory readings.

It is a stunning demonstration of what DeLillo has been arguing is the necessary role of the writer in the late twentieth century: the architect of imposing artifacts that resist the contemporary surrender to disorder and fragmentation and the presumption of chaos. The narrative is replete with artists struggling to fashion such artifices, determined to produce the something that does not hiss into chaos, does not diminish over time. The narrative is itself a heroic act of waste management, recycling bits of recollection, narrative, history, cultural flotsam, and striking imagery into a vast interlocking system that conjoins the writer and the reader in an accidental conspiracy, a cooperation of effort to vitalize this private, fluid textual space, a shared authority that celebrates the imaginative energies of both writer and reader.

Appropriately, DeLillo followed such a maximalist achievement that so confidently championed the muscle of the narrative art with a fragile parable of the artist abruptly dislocated from that shaping strength. In *The Body Artist* (2001), Lauren Hartke is a successful performance artist whose consummate confidence as artist is shaken by the suicide of her filmmaker husband. Stunned by the vulnerability that comes from any encounter with mortality, Lauren is suddenly compelled into time, the heavy horizontal plane of experience. In a familiar DeLillo-esque gesture of retreat (she has withdrawn to a rented ocean cottage), Lauren encounters a mysterious presence in the cottage's upper floors, a strange man of indeterminate age, who speaks in a fractured babble that appears to suggest more than it says, who appears able to predict approaching events, and who mimics the voices of her and her dead husband like some creepy tape recorder. He never identifies himself or justifies why he is in the house, and after a time simply disappears. Although Lauren considers explanations (an autistic former boarder, an alien, an angel, a muse, a schizophrenic drifter, a ghost, a grief hallucination), we learn only that Lauren has returned to her work—we read a glowing review of her latest performance piece in which she also channels others' voices in an extended artistic interpretation that seeks to slow down time itself, to master what has so terrorized her.

Mr. Tuttle (the stranger reminds her of a long-ago science teacher) thus can be seen as the artistic energy itself, temporarily dislocated: there is his protean physical form, his lack of identity, his ability to mimic voices, his disregard for the usual measures of time, and his evident love of language, his cryptic monologues. But without the tie to the flesh-and-blood experience of time, such a presence is disembodied and distant. Lauren struggles to adjust to the anxious reality that all artists must confront (even the narrator of the towering edifice of *Underworld*): language must exist within time, must coexist with experience, imperfect and bruising; the artist must inhabit an imperfect physical form. Lauren recovers her art only by recommitting to that physical form, suggested in DeLillo's graceful, near-poetic prose that infuses with nuance the simplest objects—garden butterflies, orange juice in a frosty glass, the slow music of the wind. In the closing, a recovered Lauren, at a window overlooking the ocean, relishes the tangy breeze, her artistic sensibility salvaged, at peace within the roiling flux of the immediate (suggested by the sea itself). This position of awareness, unlike similar reclamations achieved by Axton and Gladney, is done in the contemplative cool of isolation, the self repaired on its own, its healing shared with the intimate community of committed readers by the conjuring power of DeLillo's prose.

DeLillo then affirms the writer as the last, best vestige of voice and individuality in the electronic age, the instrument of engaged resistance to the cultural pull toward conformity and indifference. The narrative, he argues, is that rare aesthetic system that permits, indeed factors in, ambiguity and flux, and it embraces, much like the universe itself, both order and mystery, where coherence does not mean clarity and patterns do not imply meaning. It gives form to chance, design to chaos, and wonder to a world that can appear fearful. Thus DeLillo's fictions, despite their apparent inaccessibility, succeed only by provoking the deepest sort of intimacy: diligent writer and committed reader who meet, two lonely figures in separate rooms, and engage each other in the sustained imaginative act of reading itself, a heroic process necessarily flawed as it can be undertaken only by those aware of its fragility.

[*See also* Italian-American Literature.]

## WORKS

*Americana* (1971)
*End Zone* (1972)
*Great Jones Street* (1973)
*Ratner's Star* (1976)
*Players* (1977)
*Running Dog* (1978)
*Amazons: An Intimate Memoir by the First Woman to Play in the National Hockey League*. Credited to DeLillo; published under the name Cleo Birdwell (1980)
*The Names* (1982)
*White Noise* (1985)
*Libra* (1988)
*Mao II* (1991)
*Underworld* (1997)
*The Body Artist* (2001)

## FURTHER READING

Cowart, David. *Don DeLillo: The Physics of Language*. Athens, Ga., 2002. Articulate examination of DeLillo's evolving interest in language and the role of the novelist in the media age.

Keesey, Douglas. *Don DeLillo*. New York, 1993. Excellent, accessible introduction that focuses, book by book, on the theme of the impoverished individual in the media age.

LeClair, Tom. *In the Loop: Don DeLillo and the Systems Novel*. Urbana, Ill., 1987. Drawing on complex language and information theories, a dense but often penetrating look at DeLillo's novels as systems of information processing. An early proponent of DeLillo.

Lentricchia, Frank, ed. *Introducing Don DeLillo*. Durham, N.C., 1991. Valuable introductory collection of previously published essays along with an engrossing interview.

Osteen, Mark. *American Magic and Dread: Don DeLillo's Dialogue with Culture*. Philadelphia, 2000. Erudite, wide-ranging study that sees the prototypical DeLillo character as alienated within a stifling consumer culture and suspended between quasi-religious consolations and anxiety over their inaccessibility.

Ruppersburg, Hugh, and Tim Engles. *Critical Essays on Don DeLillo*. New York, 2000. Helpful gathering of initial reviews of DeLillo's novels as well as critical analyses of nine of his novels. The introduction is a particularly strong overview.

# DETECTIVE FICTION

*by Mary Hadley*

It is hard to imagine a time when Britain and France did not have a police force and detectives whose job it was to solve crimes. But until the growth of criminal investigation in the form of Scotland Yard in London, and the Sûreté in Paris, there was no formal detection. The Sûreté (the French crime bureau) was created in the 1820s, followed in Britain in 1842 by a detective branch that was part of the Metropolitan Police of London. Detectives as part of the police forces in New York and other American cities came later still. Therefore, it is not surprising that the detective novel did not arise until 1841 with *The Murders in the Rue Morgue* by Edgar Allan Poe (1809–1849). Since the United States lagged behind Europe in its policing, Poe set his three detective stories not in New York but in Paris, a city he admired. He based his detective, C. Auguste Dupin, on Francois-Eugene Vidocq, a criminal turned private detective, whose memoirs were published in 1832.

Considering that Poe wrote only three detective stories, *The Murders in the Rue Morgue* (1841), *The Mystery of Marie Roget* (1842), and *The Purloined Letter* (1844), it is amazing that they have had such a far-reaching effect. *The Murders in the Rue Morgue* introduced a type of detective and some plot characteristics that were imitated by other authors on both sides of the Atlantic for the next one hundred years. C. Auguste Dupin is the original omniscient godlike detective, with the narrator, who is never named, acting as an admiring sidekick. Here is the classical detective story as we knew it for years: the inefficient local police, the locked room, deduction, the surprising solution, and the final explanation of how the crime occurred by a rather condescending Dupin. There are numerous clues, which the reader is supposed to notice, and a puzzle formula, which appealed to all those people who enjoyed conundrums and would later enjoy crosswords. It is clear when one reads the Sherlock Holmes mysteries, which were published fifty years later, that Sir Arthur Conan Doyle was most familiar with Poe's three works.

When we are examining the beginning of detective fiction, we cannot fail to mention the "grandmother" or perhaps "great grandmother" of the genre, Anna Katherine Green (1846–1935). Born in Brooklyn, New York, the daughter of a criminal lawyer, Green wrote between thirty and forty mystery or detective fiction works. Her first novel was *The Leavenworth Case*, published in 1878, and she wrote at least one book a year until her death at age eighty-seven. Her better works feature Ebenezer Gryce, but she was also so ahead of her time as to feature a female detective, Violet Strange, in some works. Although many would denigrate her writing as melodramatic, Green nevertheless deserves an important place in the history of the genre as the first female writer.

Also important because she, too, advanced the detective genre is Mary Roberts Rinehart (1876–1958). Having begun her writing career as a short story writer who aimed to help her family in their financial troubles, Rinehart became one of the highest paid authors before World War I. *The Circular Staircase* (1908) and *The Man in Lower Ten* (1909) were her earliest works. Rinehart perhaps influenced later women writers of the cozy genre. Her protagonist is usually an official male detective, but the narrator is usually a woman, often a spinster, who helps solve the crime in an accidental fashion and protects the innocent from suspicion. Rinehart's blending of romance and detection has been criticized by purists, but can certainly be seen imitated in numerous mystery novels to this day.

## THE HARD-BOILED DETECTIVE—THE 1920s AND 1930s

A description of the American male hard-boiled genre has to include mention of the "Golden Age" in Britain, since the hard-boiled was a direct break from the perceived gentility of the Golden Age. The Golden Age writers—Agatha Christie, Dorothy L. Sayers, Margery Allingham, Josephine Tey, and Ngaio Marsh—wrote a type of detective story between the world wars that eschewed the violence and ugliness so much in evidence during World War I. These writers followed Poe's convoluted plot or puzzle formula, the omniscient detective, and the less than competent sidekick, and have little social criticism in their works. Many of their stories take place in small villages or towns where the criminal is shown as an aberrant personality whose capture will allow the setting to return to its former comfortable situation. These writers basically appealed to a conservative audience who wished to have its position ratified within the patriarchal society. When the readers solved the convoluted mysteries, they felt in control of their world.

Many Americans reading these British authors felt that their gentility had little or nothing to do with life in the big cities they knew so well, and it was not long before they rejected the Golden Age genre in favor of something particularly American. As George Grella reminds us: "Populated by real criminals and real policemen, reflecting some of the tensions of the time, endowed with considerable narrative urgency, and imbued with the disenchantment peculiar to post-war American writing, the hard-boiled stories were considered by their writers and readers honest, accurate portraits of American life" (p. 105). First introduced in the pulp magazines, such as *Black Mask*, of the 1920s and 1930s, the American male hard-boiled novels came out of the action adventure story. The hero is physically tough, a loner, skillful with a gun, at home in the city streets where he fights criminals. He prefers his own brand of rough justice to that of society, which is often shown as corrupt. Since his quest is more important than love, and since women are often shown as evil, he is forced to eschew a loving relationship.

(Samuel) Dashiell Hammett (1894–1961), one of the most important writers of the hard-boiled genre, left school at thirteen and had a series of jobs, including working for the Pinkerton private detective agency. His first novel, *Red Harvest* (1929), was followed by the hugely successful *The Maltese Falcon* (1930) and *The Thin Man* (1932), both of which were made into movies. Hammett's major claims to fame are his realistic dialogue, his violent, fast-paced action, and his ability to describe a character in sharp strokes. His protagonists, the Continental Op and Sam Spade, are not, like so many British detectives, from the upper classes; rather, they have the

Dashiell Hammett.
(*Courtesy of the Library of Congress*)

tough qualities that allow them to be successful in this hard world. The American private eye is also very different from the well-educated British detective in his speech patterns. His use of the vernacular and witty wisecracks allow him to show his disdain for institutions, expose villains, and, above all, demonstrate his masculinity. In addition, the private eye relies not on the deductive reasoning of the earlier detectives but on his hunches or male intuition.

Unlike the small, rather effete Belgian, Hercule Poirot, Agatha Christie's creation, who was always referring to his "leetle gray cells," twirling his magnificent mustache, and drinking a tisane, Sam Spade is particularly noteworthy for his fighting physique. It is important in Spade's world that he actually be able to subdue his adversaries, and it is the violent fight sequences that are memorable in many of the books.

American cities in the 1920s were often crime ridden, and it makes sense that Hammett should depict Personville, the city in *Red Harvest*, as an ugly place, and the violent acts that take place there not as aberrations but as normal. Hammett's urban settings reflect the corruption of their political leaders, and Hammett suggests that such cities cannot be redeemed while a few men in positions of authority pursue wealth to the exclusion of morality.

Raymond Chandler (1888–1959) created Philip Marlowe, a more refined version of Sam Spade, and his novels continued to make the hard-boiled genre respectable and popular throughout the 1930s and 1940s. *The Big Sleep* (1939) is interesting for its episodic structure and, like Hammett's works, its continued use of the West Coast landscape. Although Marlowe is stylish, he mocks the rich and elite in *Farewell, My Lovely* (1940), and his creator clearly despised the snobbery often shown in British detective fiction of the same period. For both Chandler and Hammett, the puzzle element of the plots of the Golden Age books is nowhere nearly as important as showing detailed characterizations, human beings with whom we can easily identify and who fascinate us, described as they are, in a wealth of adjectives. Chandler's own words in "The Simple Art of Murder" best describe the hard-boiled hero: "Down these mean streets a man must go who is not himself mean, who is neither tarnished nor afraid. The detective in this kind of story must be such a man. He is the hero; he is everything. He must be a complete man and a common man and yet an unusual man" (p. 53).

## THE 1940s AND 1950s

In the 1940s, the hard-boiled genre moved forward with the first work by Mickey Spillane, *I, the Jury* (1947). This masterful novel introduced readers to Mike Hammer, a P.I. (private investigator) in the tradition of Sam Spade but far more developed as a character. Spillane's first-person narration gives us a greater insight into the thoughts of Hammer than we received with Spade. In addition, Spillane's secondary characters are described in fascinating detail. Although Hammer admits that there is corruption in the police force, he enjoys a good relationship with his detective buddy, Pat Chambers, and the descriptions of an urban wilderness are not the focus of the novel. Hammer is seen as a man who enjoys the company of women and does not treat them badly. In *I, the Jury* his killing of the beautiful Charlotte Manning, to whom he had seriously contemplated becoming engaged, is an act of necessity and revenge both for the horrific way she killed his best friend and because she had murdered several others and was about to shoot him. In contrast, the punishment of the criminal was not mentioned in the earlier British mysteries. Once the criminal was caught, his fate was left up to the imagination of the reader. The hard-boiled detectives, on the other hand, often took vengeance into their own hands, and their treatment of the criminal, both male and female, could be savage. Spillane, of all the hard-boiled authors, describes some of Mike Hammer's executions in lurid, gut-wrenching details. Charlotte Manning is shot in the stomach, so her death is slow and tortured, while before shooting Doctor Soberin in the face in *Kiss Me, Deadly* (1952) Hammer deals with him in this way:

> I let him keep the gun in his hand so I could bend it back and hear his fingers break and when he tried to yell I bottled the sound up by smashing my elbow into his mouth. The shattered teeth tore my arm and his mouth became a great hole welling blood. His fingers were broken stubs sticking at odd angles. I shoved him away from me, slashed the butt end of the rod across the side of his head and watched him drop into his chair. (pp. 277–278)

Erle Stanley Gardner (1889–1970), in *The Case of the Velvet Claws* (1933), introduced readers to a different type of hard-boiled mystery. Gardner's protagonist was a criminal lawyer, Perry Mason, not a private investigator or cop. However, in the style of the hard-boiled genre, he introduces himself thus: "I'm different. I get my business because I fight for it, and because I fight for my clients" (p. 5). Willing to perform many actions that risk his disbarment or endanger his life, Mason never does dull probate work or draws up contracts. He works with a private detective, Paul Drake, and a personal secretary, Della Street, who is completely devoted to him and indeed half in love with him. A lawyer himself, Gardner gave Mason many of his own attitudes, and his legal details were always completely accurate. Writing three to four books a year, Gardner followed a formula that was enormously popular and successful. In most of the books, Mason is called upon to defend a client accused of murder. Although the client may appear guilty, Mason, by digging deep, manages to prove his or her innocence, often at the last minute, in an amazing courtroom scene.

In the 1940s there was a radio show based on the books, and in 1957 *Perry Mason* became a television show starring Raymond Burr; it ran for nine years, and the reruns can still be seen in many American cities and overseas. Interestingly, the television Mason is nowhere nearly as hard-boiled as the original book version. Although we rarely see Raymond Burr using a gun or getting into fistfights, he still keeps our interest throughout the convoluted plot.

## THE 1960s–1980s

For many readers, what makes Chester Himes's (1909–1984) books fascinating is that they show life in Harlem from the perspective of an author who was an African American and had spent seven years in the Ohio State Penitentiary. Thus, Himes intimately knew the dark side of the life he portrayed. In addition, he is unusual because he spent the majority of his later years not in the New York he describes but in Paris. Indeed, all his books were originally written in French and translated into English. His main characters are Grave Digger Jones and Coffin Ed Johnson, who is described thus: "Ever since the hoodlum had thrown acid into his face, Coffin Ed had had no tolerance for crooks. He was too quick to blow up and too dangerous for safety in his sudden rages" (*Cotton Comes to Harlem*, p. 31). For today's readers what continues to make Himes's books enjoyable is the humor articulated by the protagonists even while they comment on the violent Harlem world they inhabit.

Although Evan Hunter (b. 1926) may be known to many readers for his 1954 semiautobiographical novel

*The Blackboard Jungle*, it is his police procedurals about the 87th Precinct, written under the pseudonym of Ed McBain, that have brought him fame. Indeed, numerous police officers admit that they enjoy the series because the dialogue and events are such an accurate portrayal of their own lives. McBain's first book in the series, *Cop Hater*, was published in 1956; his fifty-first, *Money, Money, Money*, came out in 2001, and he continues writing. Although McBain calls his imaginary town Isola, it is clearly based on New York City and has all a big city's problems. By using a big city, McBain is able to interweave crimes that take place within the 87th Precinct with those which take place elsewhere, increasing the interest of the reader. To a great extent the city takes on a persona of its own, and as George Dove says, "She also has a leading role in the series, her moods and whims determining to a strong degree the actions and affections of the other characters" (p. 198). The female persona is deliberate because McBain refers to Isola as a woman. Unlike many police procedurals, which focus on only one or two main officers, the 87th Precinct is unusual in that it depicts the work and lives of several male and female police officers. Although the key detectives, Steve Carella, of Italian origin, and Arthur Brown, an African American, appear most often, we also meet several others, such as Lieutenant Peter Byrnes and Eileen Burke. The types of crimes that the officers face have differed enormously over the years, and it is clear that McBain is fully aware of the sexual harassment, racial, and drug-related issues that have plagued the police in recent years. However, probably one of the reasons why real-life police officers enjoy these books is because McBain is "[a] genius for making platitudes exciting . . . [and has a] skill in dramatizing the commonplace [that] becomes most obvious in those passages in almost every one of the novels in which McBain steps on stage and speaks directly as narrator to the reader" (Dove, p. 202). What also makes the books realistic is having the police concerned with several crimes concurrently. This may make our reading complicated, but it certainly adds to the fast-paced nature of the novels.

Robert B. Parker (b. 1932), a former professor of English at Northeastern University in Boston, is famous for his Spenser P.I. series. His first novel, *The Godwulf Manuscript*, was published in 1974, and Parker has written twenty-eight more novels in the series since then. Although Parker wrote his Ph.D. dissertation on Dashiell Hammett and Raymond Chandler, and was asked by Chandler's heirs to finish the manuscript Chandler was working on when he died, his own protagonist is very different from those early hard-boiled heroes. Spenser, whose first name we never learn, has a sensitive side that is evidenced in his ability to cook gourmet dishes, have a monogamous relationship with the psychologist Susan Silverman, and vomit in reaction to killing the bad guys who plague his work. Susan describes him thus in the 1975 book *Mortal Stakes*: "You are a classic case for the feminist movement. A captive of the male mystique, and all that. . . . I'd care for you less if killing . . . people didn't bother you."

To counteract the sensitive Spenser, Parker gave him a sidekick, Hawk, in book four of the series, *Promised Land*. Hawk is an African American who has no compunction about killing or any other illegal act. Despite respecting Hawk, Spenser describes him as "a hurter" and "a bad man" (*Promised Land*, p. 25), and in later books, it is Hawk who performs most of the tasks that call for really tough action.

Although Parker has continued to write the Spenser series, he has also begun two other detective series. Jesse Stone is the protagonist in *Night Passage* (1997) and other novels; and Sunny Randall is the new female private investigator in *Family Honor* (1999) and other books. Sunny, who has a mini bull terrier and a gay male sidekick, was invented because the actress Helen Hunt asked Parker to create a female investigator whom she could portray in a movie.

### THE 1980s: FEMALE HARD-BOILED FICTION

The 1980s proved to be a watershed in detective fiction, and because of the advent of female hard-boiled fiction, the genre would never be the same again. The early female hard-boiled novelists had enjoyed reading the earlier male writers but were faced with the major dilemma of reconciling traditional femininity with the conventional private detective. They solved it by altering their narratives to include subject matters that concern everyday life and, especially, relationships. The first writer was Marcia Muller (b. 1944) (*Edwin of the Iron Shoes*, 1977), who was followed by Sara Paretsky (b. 1947) (*Indemnity Only*, 1982) and Sue Grafton (b. 1940) (*A Is for Alibi*, 1982).

Muller's original aim was to use the classical puzzle formula but have a female private investigator with whom her readers could identify. Sharon McCone was not going to be too eccentric, but she was going to have some larger-than-life traits. Unlike the male hard-boiled detectives, McCone is not vengeful and cooperates well with the police. She is a feminist in her actions but does not voice feminist rhetoric.

Sara Paretsky's sleuth is the strongest and most overt feminist of the early female hard-boiled detectives.

V. I. Warshawski voices her feminist concerns, but manages not to be irritatingly radical, and it is more in her ability to cope both physically and emotionally with male criminals that we see her strength.

Sue Grafton's Kinsey Millhone is similar to McCone and Warshawski, especially in the way she is a fully rounded person. Unlike the early male hard-boiled detectives and those of the Golden Age whose private lives are never examined, the reader learns all the quirks and oddities of these female detectives. From the openings of the novels of these three women writers, we learn not only how their detectives got their jobs but also why, and what effect the work has on their families and friends.

These writers and others changed the detective genre forever because they pushed the mystery novel in new directions as a medium for discussion of serious themes, both feminist themes and wider themes of social justice to which a feminist slant contributes. The American, and indeed the British, female private investigators of the 1980s reflected the growing numbers of women in the workforce, women who chose to be single, were extremely efficient at their jobs, could defend themselves physically, were prepared to use a gun, and constantly questioned the patriarchal society in which they functioned.

Similar to the male hard-boiled fiction in its criticism of society, the female hard-boiled novels of Muller, Grafton, and especially Paretsky use the investigation of a crime to criticize patriarchal institutions. However, although the crime against the individual may be solved at the end of the novel, more usually the major cause of the crime—society or one of its institutions—is unresolved.

Whereas in the earlier traditional detective novels of Poe, Conan Doyle, and the Golden Age writers the world was a just place and the detective, the police force, or the judicial system would remove the criminal and reestablish the status quo, in the female hard-boiled novels, this restoration does not take place because the detectives question the worthiness of the justice system and the establishment in general. We are shown in several instances that villains do not get their just deserts: they escape, they do not serve a sentence, or they commit suicide rather than allow themselves to be captured. Of twenty murderers in Grafton's series, for instance, only two are prosecuted (Kaufman and Kay, p. 259).

Another significant difference from their early male hard-boiled counterparts is in their sexual relationships. Whereas the males may be tempted by villainous females but reject, arrest, or even kill them, the females often fall for men who take advantage of them and try to dominate them. Neither Kinsey Millhone, Grafton's protagonist, nor V. I. Warshawski, Paretsky's heroine, has a long-term committed relationship with an equal partner.

Another important trait of the female hard-boiled detective is her relationship with family and friends. In contrast to her male counterpart of the 1930s and 1940s who is essentially solitary, the female detective is often called upon by her relations to pursue a case concurrently with cases for high-paying clients. Also, V. I. and Kinsey often have family members questioning their motives for pursuing the truth after the authorities have told them to stop, and also questioning their authority to act, as in Paretsky's *Killing Orders* (1985). However, these new female detectives clearly see their role as righting wrongs. In *Dead Lock* (1984), Warshawski states that she became an investigator because she was incensed at the guilty going free because they were able to afford cunning lawyers. Muller, Paretsky, and Grafton continue writing interesting, topical, and provocative books, appealing to both feminists and nonfeminists.

## THE 1990s

The 1990s saw the advent of numerous minority writers: African American, Latino, Native American, gay, and lesbian. Although they began writing in the 1990s, all of these writers follow the traditions begun by the 1980s writers of using the novel as a medium to criticize social ills. Because of the proliferation of new detective fiction authors in the 1990s, space permits the mention of just a few here.

Following in the footsteps of Chester Himes, the African-American Walter Mosley (b. 1952) has written a series whose first novel was made into the successful movie *Devil in a Blue Dress* (1990). *Devil in a Blue Dress* is set in Los Angeles in 1948 and introduces us to Ezekiel "Easy" Rawlins and his volatile, amoral sidekick, Mouse. Easy is hired to find a young white woman, Daphne Monet, who is known to go to jazz clubs and hang out with African-American men. Finding Daphne is no real problem, but avoiding trouble is a whole lot harder for Easy, especially when it is discovered that Daphne is part black—an embarrassment to the important white man who loves her.

Although Mosley writes about the postwar era in his books, their content, in particular the way he analyzes race and gender issues, makes him very similar to the women hard-boiled writers of the 1980s. In his third novel, *White Butterfly* (1992), Easy is married, raising a baby as well as a boy, Jesus, whom he has adopted. Easy has numerous problems with his wife, Regina, because he doesn't want her to know that he is wealthy and a landlord of several properties. She, meanwhile, feels he doesn't trust her or confide in her, and finally leaves him. Easy muses: "I knew that a lot of tough-talking men would go home to their wives at night and cry about how hard their lives were. I never understood why a woman would stick it out with a man like that" (p. 181). Thus Mosley continues the hard-boiled tradition of the past, but with an added thoughtful, analytical twist that makes for fascinating reading.

Another African-American writer who adds to the hard-boiled genre, in this case the female one, is Valerie Wilson Wesley (b. 1947). Her P. I. Tamara Hayle has a teenage son, Jamal, from a former marriage, who at times impinges on the way she can do her work. It is unusual to have a female investigator who is a mother because of the inherent complications to her schedule and conflicts of interest in her investigations. Tamara gets around the problem by having her friend Annie look after Jamal when necessary. But the fact of being a mother affects Tamara because it makes her more cautious both in her private life and in her work. As she says, "I've always chosen my hard-won self-respect over a possibly delightful roll in the sheets, that was one thing I'd learned over the years. I come first. Me and my son, not the possibility of what could be" (*Where Evil Sleeps*, 1996, p. 49). Like the 1980s female writers, Tamara is called upon by her relatives; for example, in the first novel, *When Death Comes Stealing* (1994), her ex-husband asks her to investigate the deaths of two of his sons. This interaction between Tamara and her relatives and her own in-depth self-analysis give a flavor to Wilson Wesley's books resembling that of Mosley's.

Having written several young adult and mystery novels under the pseudonym Jack Early, the lesbian author Sandra Scoppettone (b. 1936) created Lauren Laurano in 1991. Laurano is a P.I. in New York City. She lives and works in Greenwich Village and has a female partner, Kip, who is a therapist and counselor. The series, which starts with *Everything You Have Is Mine* (1991), is very much in the social consciousness-raising mode of the female 1980s writers. Scoppettone, like Wilson Wesley, follows the tradition as described by Ian Ousby:

> In the female private-eye novels personal involvement is not just a convenience to get the story going but a signal that its theme will be the detective's own self-discovery and self-definition. She is not just there to solve a mystery but to learn about herself by understanding women from her family past better, or to see herself more clearly by comparing her life with the fate of women friends. (pp. 186–187)

Lauren, who had been savagely raped when she was eighteen, examines not only her past but also her relationship with her alcoholic mother and enabling father, her own rather judgmental character, and especially her intimate relationship with her lover and partner, Kip. In most of the books she is called upon to solve a murder of a friend or relative of a friend, which usually forces her to learn painful details about her friends. In addition, Scoppettone comments on many of the societal ills of New York, in particular the problems of the poor, the homeless, and the city's gays. Although Scoppettone is not the first lesbian writer to achieve success, she is one of the first to be published by a mainstream publisher. Earlier authors such as Katherine V. Forrest and Barbara Wilson, both of whom wrote in the 1980s, were published by small presses because the mainstream ones steered clear of them (Breen, p. 164).

From the opening chapter in her first book, *A Cold Day for Murder* (1992), Dana Stabenow's (b. 1952) unique qualities as a writer are apparent. She was born in Anchorage, Alaska, and grew up for a time on a seventy-five-foot fish tender in the Gulf of Alaska. Having had numerous jobs in different parts of Alaska, she is very qualified to describe not only that state's magnificent scenery but also the concerns of the Native Americans who live there. The setting of many of her books is the Alaskan bush, which she describes in such detail that it excites even the most seasoned of armchair travelers. Her characters are the independent Kate Shugak, formerly an investigator for the Anchorage D.A.'s office, now living twenty-five miles from the nearest village; the handsome Jack Morgan, her love interest, among other things; State Trooper Jim Chopin; Kate's assorted Aleut relatives and friends; and, most important, Mutt, part wolf, part husky, but wholly a main character in every book. All of these players are a far cry from the usual urban criminals and good guys found in many mysteries. Every book in the Shugak series is gripping, but *Breakup* (1997), *Hunter's Moon* (1999), and *Midnight Come Again* (2000) are unparalleled. Having written so successfully of a female protagonist, Stabenow created State Trooper Liam Campbell for her second series. *Fire and Ice* (1998), the first book, introduces us to Campbell, who has been demoted and disgraced because of his actions in Anchorage and sent to Newenham, a small fishing town on the shores of Bristol Bay. There he meets again the only woman he has ever loved, Wyanet Chouinard. This series, like the Shugak one, is filled with exciting action in a stunning setting and characters who fascinate us.

Cuban-born Carolina Garcia-Aguilera (b. 1949) has lived and worked for many years as a private investigator in Miami, Florida, which is probably why Lupe Solano, her P.I. protagonist, is so authentic. *Bloody Waters* (1996), the first book in the series, introduces Solano, her wealthy family, and the Cuban-American world of South Miami. Garcia-Aguilera depicts the Hispanic culture in fascinating detail, so that Cuba is as much a character as the characters themselves. In this first novel Solano is hired to find the birth mother of an illegally adopted baby girl who is dying of a rare disease curable only by a bone marrow transplant from her birth mother. When she discovers where the mother is living, Solano undertakes a dangerous journey by boat to Cuba to smuggle her into Miami. In all of her books, the author manages to combine a fast-paced mystery with some detailed analysis of how Cuban-Americans feel. For example, in *Havana Heat* she states, "Cubans in exile and Cubans on the island were separated by geography and politics, but I felt that our hearts beat as one" (p. 235).

It is clear from this description of American detective fiction that the genre has altered greatly from its earliest beginnings. The godlike male protagonist, who solved the puzzling crime with minimal violence and had little concern for the societal conditions of the time, became the tough, gun-wielding hard-boiled detective, who was actively commenting on the ills that surrounded him. Today, this same detective, now often female, solves crimes for friends and family and also addresses a wide variety of discriminatory practices. Detective fiction has moved from being a comforting diversion to telling us "something about the world we live in, and about the best way of living peacefully in it" (Symons, p. 23).

## FURTHER READING

Breen, Jon. "Gay Mysteries Introduction." In *The Fine Art of Murder*, edited by Ed Gorman et al. New York, 1993.

Chandler, Raymond. "The Simple Art of Murder." *Atlantic Monthly* (December 1944): 53–59.

Dove, George. *The Police Procedural.* Bowling Green, Ohio, 1982.

Grella, George. "The Hard-boiled Detective Novel." In *Detective Fiction*, edited by Robin W. Winks. Woodstock, Vt., 1980.

Hadley, Mary. *British Women Mystery Writers.* Jefferson, N.C., 2002.

Kaufman, Natalie Hevener, and Carol McGinnis Kay. *"G" Is for Grafton.* New York, 1997.

Ousby, Ian. *The Crime and Mystery Book.* London, 1997.

Symons, Julian. *Bloody Murder.* Harmondsworth, U.K., 1985.

# JAMES DICKEY

*by Henry Hart*

James Dickey liked to conceive of his life as a series of cyclical journeys in which he departed from the securities and prohibitions of home, struggled through trials in order to penetrate to a source of power, and then returned home to deliver the fruits of his quest to others. The main catalyst for this conception was his journey to the Philippines and Japan during World War II. He once observed: "I remember almost every day that I was in the war, and I think almost everything that I've done is influenced, at least to some degree, either directly or indirectly, most probably directly, by the fact that I was in the war" (Hart, p. 65). Before his

James Dickey.
(© *Philip Gould/Corbis*)

service in the Army Air Corps, Dickey had been a mediocre student whose main interests were dating southern girls, running the high hurdles on the track team, and playing football. The war shook him out of his intellectual torpor, dispelled many of the traditional values he had acquired from his affluent parents in Atlanta, and convinced him to pursue the vocation of a writer. When he returned to the United States from the Pacific, he transferred from Clemson Agriculture and Military College, where he had been an engineering cadet for a semester, and enrolled in Vanderbilt University, a center of the Southern Literary Renaissance, where he soon earned a reputation as the best poet and one of the best literature students on campus. The metamorphosis caused by the war became the seed narrative in most of Dickey's major works.

One book that Dickey studied at Vanderbilt—Joseph Campbell's *The Hero with a Thousand Faces*—helped him articulate this transformation more than any other. In a section titled "The Hero and the God," Campbell mapped out an archetypal pattern in mythical adventure tales for which Dickey felt an enduring affinity: "The standard path of the mythological adventure of the hero is a magnification of the formula represented in the rites of passage: *separation-initiation-return*: which might be named the nuclear unit of the monomyth. *A hero ventures forth from the world of common day into a region of supernatural wonder: fabulous forces are there encountered and a decisive victory is won: the hero comes back from this mysterious adventure with the power to bestow boons on his fellow man*" (p. 30). Dickey, who had enjoyed a pampered upbringing on a mansion-lined street in Buckhead, a suburb of Atlanta, had ventured forth into the war-torn islands of the Pacific; contributed to the decisive Allied victory over the Japanese; and returned to America a new man committed to the ideal of the writer as a "deliverer" who bestows boons—in the form of books—on his fellow men.

Many of Dickey's most successful poems and novels follow the archetypal pattern of separation-initiation-return that characterized what Campbell—borrowing a term first used by James Joyce—called the "monomyth." Dickey told the scholar David Arnett that his best-selling novel *Deliverance* (1970) grew directly from the mythic hero's "separation from the world . . . penetration to some source of power, and . . . life-enhancing return" (Hart, pp. 449–450). The four characters in *Deliverance*, who represent different facets of Dickey's personality, leave their comfortable homes in Atlanta, battle against violent antagonists in the north Georgia wilderness, and the three who survive the trip go back to Atlanta with a greater appreciation for civilization. Dickey's ambitious, 682-page novel *Alnilam* (1987) also tracks a cyclical journey, this time by a father (not unlike the older Dickey) who ventures forth from Atlanta to discover the circumstances of his son's fatal plane crash on an Army Air Corps base and returns to Atlanta with lessons learned. Dickey's last novel, *To the White Sea* (1993), dramatizes another heroic journey, this time by a World War II tail gunner who parachutes from his plane into Tokyo during a bombing raid and hikes to a snowy island in the northern Japanese archipelago that reminds him of his home in Alaska. Some of Dickey's most anthologized poems, such as "The Vegetable King" and "Cherrylog Road," follow the monomyth's archetypal pattern as well. "The Strength of Fields," the poem commissioned for President Jimmy Carter's inauguration, makes the pattern explicit in its epigraph and plot.

Like Ernest Hemingway, William Faulkner, Norman Mailer, and many other war veterans, Dickey chose to mythologize his military experiences for dramatic effect. It was at Vanderbilt, while stifled by his attempts to be too truthful in his poems, that he discovered the virtues of "the creative lie." In his book *Self-Interviews* (1970), he recounted: "I really began to develop as a poet . . . when I saw the creative possibilities of the lie. . . . Picasso once said something to the effect that art is a lie which makes us see the truth, or which makes truth better than it is. This is very much my feeling. . . . [Lying creatively] is what the poet wants to do; this should be his sovereign privilege, because the province of a poem is that poet's, and in it he is God" (p. 32). For Dickey, lying became a habit he refused to restrict to his literary fictions. Interviews, letters, and conversations all afforded him opportunities to exercise his imagination in self-aggrandizing ways. Before long, he had exaggerated, fabricated, or simply lied about almost every aspect of his life. And he had done it so convincingly that almost everyone—including close friends, family members, lovers, journalists, scholars, and ordinary fans—believed in a mythical James Dickey who bore little resemblance to the real man.

One example is enough to demonstrate Dickey's abilities as an inventive autobiographer. In an interview with the journalist Jean Lawler for the *Vanderbilt Alumnus*, Dickey flaunted the lessons about creative lying he had learned as a Vanderbilt student. Lawler rendered the "facts" she had garnered from her conversation with Dickey as follows:

> Born [in] 1924 in a suburb of Atlanta, Dickey grew up with the nickname "Crabapple Cannonball," prowling the dusty roads of north Georgia on a Harley motorcycle, trysting with farm girls in auto graveyards, and bootlegging liquor in a '34 Ford. At Clemson University, he was a prize football back but left after freshman year for the War, flying almost a hundred Pacific combat missions in a Black Widow night fighter. After the war, he transferred to Vanderbilt. When he was barred from football by a Conference rule designed to prevent coaches from stealing each other's returning service athletes,

he turned to track and became Tennessee state champion in the 120-yard high hurdles. He graduated magna cum laude in 1949 and got his master's degree the next year. (p. 16)

In fact, Dickey was not born in 1924 (he was born on 2 February 1923); his nickname was not "Crabapple Cannonball"; he did not drive around north Georgia on a Harley-Davidson, trysting with farm girls in junked cars (he adapted this story from a Vanderbilt roommate); he was not a pilot who flew one hundred combat missions in the Pacific (he was a radar observer on thirty-eight missions); he never bootlegged liquor; he was not one of the top football players at Clemson (he failed to make the starting lineup on the freshman team); he was not prevented from playing football at Vanderbilt because of eligibility rules (he quit the team during tryouts when he realized he wouldn't play); and he was not a Tennessee state champion hurdler.

Dickey regularly portrayed himself to the public as a rags-to-riches Renaissance man—a cross between Horatio Alger, Ernest Hemingway, and Lord Byron—who had excelled in all fields despite his inauspicious origins. He told many he had grown up in poverty in the north Georgia hills, and blamed foot ailments he had received in the Pacific during the war on the fact that his parents couldn't afford proper shoes for him during the Depression. Determined to do better than his impoverished parents, after piloting planes in two wars he wrote Coca-Cola ads as an award-winning executive (he nicknamed himself "Jingle Jim") for the McCann-Erickson advertising agency in Atlanta. He took up archery and bragged about winning tournaments and shooting wild boar in the Georgia swamps. In between white-water canoeing, playing the guitar in cafés, composing music (he regularly claimed he was responsible for the sound track of *Deliverance*), and signing multimillion-dollar contracts for screenplays, he maintained that he slept with at least two thousand women.

Dickey undoubtedly found one of the models for his shape-shifting and role-playing in Joseph Campbell's accounts of trickster myths in *The Hero with a Thousand Faces*. According to Campbell, the trickster was another avatar of the hero-savior-god who represented "the world's plenitude of both good and evil, ugliness and beauty, sin and virtue, pleasure and pain" (p. 44). By breaking down conventional notions of right and wrong, truth and falsehood, the trickster exemplified the fundamental amorality and multiplicity of existence. To illustrate the trickster's ability to illuminate others by first confusing them, Campbell told the story of Edshu, a West African divinity, who one day walked between two farmers' fields with a hat painted red on one side, white on the other, green in front, and black on the back (the hat was supposed to represent the four World Directions). After seeing Edshu, the farmers fell into a violent argument about his identity. One farmer contended that he was a white-hatted man; the other, that he was a red-hatted man. In their fury, they accused one another of blindness and drunkenness, fought with knives, and got dragged before a tribal leader for a judgment. At the council, Edshu revealed himself, acknowledged his prank, and admitted: "Spreading strife is my greatest joy" (p. 45). Edshu's goal, according to Campbell, was to teach the farmers that their confusion was merely an illusion, a mist obscuring the multiplicity of identity and profusion of reality. Edshu's hat was neither red nor white, green nor black; it was all of these. The mischievous Dickey, who loved to don different hats and masks, also spread strife while flouting his audiences' simpleminded views.

At Vanderbilt, Dickey was drawn to tricksters in other books besides Campbell's *Hero with a Thousand Faces*. He devoted part of his master's thesis to Herman Melville's protean hero in "The Confidence Man." According to Dickey, Melville's con artist, who dupes boat passengers on a journey down the Mississippi River from St. Louis to New Orleans, "shifts through a dazzling array of disguises and identities" ("Symbol and Image in the Shorter Poems of Herman Melville," p. 61). He resembles Christ and Satan and ultimately the multifaceted mask of all existence—the "many" that obscures the "one." Like Edshu and the Confidence Man, and like the many masked crime fighters in pulp magazines he read as a teenager, Dickey appeared to be many men to many different people. He did not have one identifiable self, but a plurality of selves. To use his own words, he was "the sum of all the roles he played" (Hart, p. xv). Reflecting on his love of posing and prevaricating, he told an interviewer in 1967: "Everybody has in himself a saint, a murderer, a pervert, a monster, a good husband, a scoutmaster, a provider, a businessman, a shrewd horse trader, a hopeless aesthete.... There are all kinds of contradictory selves. Essentially, the most exciting thing for a writer ... is to get as many of these energized as he can" (Hart, p. xvii). The world was his stage, and everyone he met was a potential audience for a new performance, a new role.

In his wide-ranging study, *Trickster Makes This World: Mischief, Myth, and Art*, Lewis Hyde makes distinctions that are helpful in understanding Dickey's histrionic character:

> Most of the travelers, liars, thieves, and shameless personalities of the twentieth century are not tricksters.... Their disruptions are not subtle enough, or pitched at a high enough level. Trickster isn't a run-of-the-mill liar and thief. When he lies and steals, it isn't so much to get away with something or get rich as to disturb the established categories of truth and property and, by so doing, open the road to possible new worlds. When Pablo Picasso says that 'art is a lie that tells the truth,' we are closer to the old trickster spirit. Picasso was out to reshape and revive the world he had been born into. He took this world seriously; then he disrupted it; then he gave it a new form..." (p. 13)

According to Hyde, tricksters operate in a sacred or artistic space; their goals are religious or aesthetic. They must use their wits, camouflaging themselves and tricking their opponents, because they continually cross boundaries between the sacred and profane, the civilized and barbaric. They resemble heroic questers in the way they depart from known territories, struggle to survive in dangerous zones "beyond the pale" of law-governed societies, and depend on their craftiness to cope with the exigencies of their home ground when they return.

Dickey, who felt compelled to outdo all his models, possessed more hidden motives and played more roles than the average trickster. An obsessive collector of real hats and real masks, he cavorted and confused not only to reveal neglected truths but also to compensate for his numerous failures and fit into the traditional society his parents had taught him to value. He was determined to make his life conform to the "thousand faces" of the all-American hero. Because he was a middling football player, he told a *Life* reporter that NFL scouts were interested in drafting him after he left Clemson. Because he washed out of flight training as an Air Corps cadet in Camden, South Carolina, he told everyone he was a decorated combat pilot who had shot down enemy planes over the Pacific and been shot down by them. Because he had little respect for the advertising business and performed so cavalierly at one firm that he was fired, he bragged about being an award-winning ad executive. Because he often suffered from impotence, he tried to convince his family and friends that he was a testosterone-crazed Don Juan.

The motives for Dickey's inventions were legion. He lied to advertise himself, to make his life seem glamorous, to sell his books, to put down his rivals. He lied because of a deep-seated insecurity about his sexuality; as his poems, novels, and close friends attest, he was attracted to sadoeroticism and homosexuality while maintaining the pose of a traditional family man. He lied because he was an alcoholic, adept at the art of denial, of blurring fact and fiction. He lied because, like the romantics and symbolists, he thought the imagination was a god and the poet a supreme maker who created—rather than mirrored—the truth. He lied because he prided himself on being part of a long line of southern storytellers, who, in his estimation, were the most creative liars in the world. He also lied because mundane facts bored and hurt him, because they spoiled his narcissistic self-image as a literary Hercules.

## THE MAN BEHIND THE MASK

Many of the facts of Dickey's life did not emerge until after his death. His claims to a rustic background notwithstanding, he actually enjoyed a privileged childhood in Buckhead, in a spacious house tended by half a dozen servants. His mother, Maibelle Swift, inherited a small fortune from her father's Atlanta-based tonic company, Swift's Southern Specific, that provided for the family's aristocratic lifestyle. His father, Eugene, was a lawyer who preferred cockfighting to legal work and, with the leisure made possible by his wife's money, pursued his hobby with a vengeance (he won several tournaments in Florida, where the sport was legal).

Dickey attended the prestigious North Fulton High School—not Crabapple High School, as he sometimes claimed—and in 1941 entered Clemson as a cadet. Having failed to distinguish himself during the football season, which was shortened to four games because of the war, he enlisted in the Army Air Corps. Although he desperately wanted to be a pilot, he nearly crashed his plane on his first solo flight and was reclassified as a radar observer. He joined the 418th Night Fighter Squadron in the Philippines early in 1945 and operated radar equipment in a P-61 Black Widow piloted by Earl Bradley. He worried about encountering enemy planes (he regularly told stories about parachuting into the ocean after his plane was hit and being rescued by a submarine), but in fact he was never involved in any dogfights.

During the war, Dickey devoted most of his free time to reading books and writing poetry. He was especially enamored of the Victorian aesthete Ernest Dawson, the poet who coined the phrase "gone with the wind." Dickey wrote a dedicatory sonnet to him in his pamphlet *Poetical Remains* (1945). Returning to the United States in 1946, Dickey startled his family and friends with his new

devotion to his studies, his lack of interest in football, and his determination to succeed as a writer. Having excelled at Vanderbilt, in September 1950 he moved with his wife, Maxine Syerson, whom he had married on 4 November 1948, to Rice Institute in Houston, Texas. While teaching in the English department, he filled notebooks with plans for novels, short stories, and poems. Because of the Korean War, the Air Force recalled him three months later and assigned him to bases in Alabama, Mississippi, and Texas, where he taught radar operation. He returned to Rice in 1952, but left for Europe to write on a *Sewanee Review* fellowship in 1954.

While Dickey was abroad, the southern writer Andrew Lytle, who had become his mentor, helped him secure a job at the University of Florida. After the freedom of travel, Dickey quickly grew disillusioned with the regimentation and tedium of his new job. As at Rice, he resented all the writing time he had to sacrifice to teaching and grading. His frustration erupted during a poetry reading to an elderly group of American Pen Women in Gainesville, during which he used profanity and read a provocative poem, "The Father's Body." Horrified by what they considered to be Dickey's extreme vulgarity, the women reported his conduct to the university president, who decided not to renew his contract. Furious, but also relieved, Dickey left Florida in the middle of the 1956 spring semester for Atlanta, where his sister-in-law helped him find an advertising job on the Coca-Cola account at McCann-Erickson. From 1956 until 1961, Dickey worked at three different Atlanta advertising firms. Behind closed office doors during the week and at home on weekends, he wrote passionate, superbly crafted poems about the way his wartime experiences had transformed his vision of life. Influenced by "the mythical method" of modernists like James Joyce, T. S. Eliot, and Ezra Pound, and also by the gorgeous, surreal rhetoric of the so-called New Apocalypse poets Dylan Thomas and George Barker, Dickey fashioned a highly original and powerful style that fused fantasy and fact. He repeatedly mythologized events in his life, recasting them as episodes on a heroic journey from despair to ecstasy, blindness to illumination, fear to love, death to renewal. Because of their universal concerns, narrative drive, and enchanting music, his poems quickly found a large and sympathetic audience.

On the strength of his first book, *Into the Stone and Other Poems*, which Charles Scribner's Sons published in 1960, Dickey received a Guggenheim Fellowship that allowed him to take his family, which had grown with the arrival of Chris in 1951 and Kevin in 1958, back to

Europe. Dickey's year of traveling in 1962 was one of his most productive. He published his second poetry book, *Drowning with Others*; began writing *Deliverance*; and completed many of the poems for his third collection, *Helmets*. With his poems appearing regularly in *The New Yorker* and his books being nominated for the Pulitzer Prize and National Book Award (his fourth book, *Buckdancer's Choice*, won the National Book Award in 1966), Dickey decided to test the academic market once again. He took writer-in-residence positions at Reed College in Oregon from 1963 to 1964, San Fernando Valley State College from 1964 to 1965, and the University of Wisconsin at Madison for a semester in 1966, then served as poetry consultant at the Library of Congress from 1966 to 1968, and finally accepted a tenured job as poet-in-residence and English professor at the University of South Carolina, where he remained until his death in 1997.

## DENOUEMENT

In his novels and poems, Dickey's heroes usually return to their home grounds with a new knowledge of reality and salvation, but they do so after suffering or witnessing terrible falls. As with the modernists, his heroes resemble vegetation gods and goddesses who embody the seasonal cycle of autumnal disaster, wintry death, and vernal resurrection. "The Vegetable King" is an early example of the way Dickey mythologizes his own life in terms of a hero-god who suffers a fatal wounding before he returns home. Sleeping beneath a suburban grove of pines on Easter Sunday, he dreams he is the crucified and resurrected Christ as well as the vegetation god, Osiris, whom Christ resembles. After his apocalyptic experience beneath "the unconsecrated grove," he returns as a messiah who blesses and damns with an energy he can't control, who imposes on his family "Magnificent pardon, and dread, impending crime." He pardons his wife and son, presumably because they are not poetically inspired; they have remained at home in their domestic routines while he was outside communing with the stars and gods. But he also condemns them for failing to live up to his sublime ideals. His yearning for transcendental experiences in nature and his potential criminality at home set in motion his expulsion to the unconsecrated pines for another round of crucifixion and renewal. Like the classic trickster, Dickey is one of civilization's discontents who continually vacillates between godly and human realms, making mischief—sometimes criminal mischief—in each.

Aware of the flaws that motivated his "dread, impending crime[s]," Dickey projected them onto the characters in his poems and novels, analyzed them, mapped their deleterious consequences, and, sadly, submitted to them or at least failed to resist them in his own life. His most dramatically successful self-diagnosis comes in *Deliverance*, where he shows how Lewis Medlock's "capricious and tenacious enthusiasms" (p. 9) ensnare his friends in a canoe trip that culminates in homosexual rape, suicide, and murder. Ed Gentry, the advertising man, who most resembles Dickey, is wiser by the end of the trip—he renounces his adolescent fantasies about the pretty Kitt'n Britches underwear model, develops a new respect for his caring wife, returns to his studio with renewed energy—but he, like Lewis, has agreed to abide by their lies, their stories that cover up their implication in the deaths on the river. Ed lies to save his skin, but he also realizes that he has become slightly schizophrenic in the process. He has a hard time distinguishing between fact and fiction: "I had made it [the lie] and tried it out against the world, and it had held. It had become so strong in my mind that I had trouble getting back through it to the truth" (pp. 227–228). By the time Dickey published *Deliverance* (1970), his own enthusiasms and the lies that bolstered them had become a kind of addiction. While his self-inventions had enhanced his career in the 1950s and 1960s, they were partly responsible for ruining his reputation in the decades that followed. Realizing how politically incorrect, passé, and boorish his macho fabrications were to his post–Vietnam War audience, in the 1980s he made halfhearted attempts to deconstruct them, but the "heroic" lies stuck to him like barnacles.

After the success of *Deliverance*, in tandem with his occasional attempts to demythologize himself, Dickey renounced the "mythical method" that had given his writing its narrative momentum and coherence. His poetry and fiction grew more fragmentary, more diffuse. Although the plots of novels like *Alnilam* (1987) and *To the White Sea* (1993), and poetry books like *The Zodiac* (1976) and *The Strength of Fields* (1979), tracked the journeys of mythical heroes, they lacked the emotional appeal of his earlier writing. His book-length poem *The Zodiac* was supposed to be the drunken ramblings of a visionary poet, an "unwell-made poem," as he once declared. His other writings—if not drunken rambles—also seemed to be detrimentally affected by his drinking and the general chaos of his life.

Having pursued his American dream of success with Gatsby-like cunning and passion, Dickey plunged into Dionysian excesses that carried him toward a tragic denouement. From the time *Deliverance* became a best-seller and John Boorman turned it into a blockbuster film starring Burt Reynolds and Jon Voight, Dickey frequently drank all day, every day. His associations with Hollywood (he was asked to write several screenplays) and his six-figure advances for future novels only abetted his delusions of grandeur. His family was one of the casualties of his erratic behavior. His sons virtually abandoned him. His wife, Maxine, died in the fall of 1976 from an alcohol-related ailment (the veins around her esophagus hemorrhaged). Two months later, Dickey married his student Deborah Dodson, an unstable but attractive woman who later became a heroin and cocaine addict. He started a second family; his daughter Bronwen was born in 1981. His sons grew more estranged, especially after learning of Deborah's drug escapades, the pimps and drug pushers who were her close friends, and her violent tantrums. (During one altercation, she stabbed Dickey near the heart with a razor-sharp hunting arrow; during another, she hit him so hard on the head that he needed surgery to remove a blood clot on his brain.) After a nearly fatal bout of hepatitis and cirrhosis in 1994, Dickey separated from Deborah and began divorce proceedings. With Deborah ensconced in a rehabilitation clinic for drug addicts in Statesboro, Georgia, Dickey spent his final days in Columbia, South Carolina, in relative peace, reading, working on a fourth novel, tinkering with poems, and advising screenwriters who were working on *To the White Sea*. Although his liver improved, he died of fibrosis on 19 January 1997, and was buried at Pawley's Island, South Carolina.

## WORKS

### POETRY

*Into the Stone, and Other Poems* (1960)
*Drowning with Others* (1962)
*Helmets* (1964)
*Buckdancer's Choice* (1965)
*Poems, 1957–1967* (1967)
*The Eye-Beaters, Blood, Victory, Madness, Buckhead, and Mercy* (1970)
*The Zodiac* (1976)
*Tucky the Hunter* (1978)
*The Strength of Fields* (1979)
*The Early Motion* (1981)
*Falling, May Day Sermon, and Other Poems* (1981)
*Puella* (1982)
*The Central Motion* (1983)
*Bronwen, the Traw, and the Shape Shifter* (1986)
*The Eagle's Mile* (1990)
*The Whole Motion: Collected Poems, 1945–1992* (1992)

### PROSE

"Symbol and Image in the Shorter Poems of Herman Melville" (1950)
*The Suspect in Poetry* (1964)
*Babel to Byzantium: Poets and Poetry Now* (1968)
*Deliverance* (1970)
*Self-Interviews* (1970)
*Sorties: Journals and New Essays* (1971)
*Jericho: The South Beheld* (1974)
*Night Hurdling: Poems, Essays, Conversations, Commencements, and Afterwords* (1983)
*Alnilam* (1987)
*Wayfarer: A Voice from the Southern Mountains* (1988)
*Southern Light* (1991)
*To the White Sea* (1993)

## FURTHER READING

Baughman, Ronald, ed. *The Voiced Connections of James Dickey.* Columbia, S.C., 1989. A sampling of interviews with Dickey that covers his career from 1965 to 1987.

Bloom, Harold, ed. *James Dickey.* New York, 1987. A representative collection of essays about Dickey's early and middle years.

Bowers, Neal. *James Dickey: The Poet as Pitchman.* Columbia, Mo., 1985. A sharply critical account of Dickey's deliberate self-promotion that is quite accurate.

Bruccoli, Matthew, and Judith Baughman, eds. *James Dickey, A Descriptive Bibliography.* Pittsburgh, 1990. An extremely useful record of publications by and about Dickey.

Bruccoli, Matthew, and Judith Baughman, eds. *Crux.* New York, 1999. A large and judicious collection of Dickey's letters.

Dickey, Christopher. *Summer of Deliverance: A Memoir of Father and Son.* New York, 1998. A candid and often intemperate memoir by Dickey's son about the difficulties of growing up with his alcoholic father.

Hart, Henry. *James Dickey: The World as a Lie.* New York, 2000. A lengthy biography that focuses on how and why Dickey mythologized his life.

Hyde, Lewis. *Trickster Makes This World: Mischief, Myth, and Art.* New York, 1999.

Kirschten, Robert. *James Dickey and the Gentle Ecstasy of Earth.* Baton Rouge, La., 1988. A good introduction to Dickey's poetry.

Kirschten, Robert. "*Struggling for Wings*": *The Art of James Dickey.* Columbia, S.C., 1997. A well-edited collection of reviews, essays, and interviews that spans Dickey's career.

Lawler, Jean. "The Poetry." *Vanderbilt Alumnus* 53 (September–October 1967): 16.

Suarez, Ernest. *James Dickey and the Politics of Canon.* Columbia, Mo., 1993. An astute assessment of the sociopolitical reasons for the rise and fall of Dickey's reputation.

Van Ness, Gordon. *Outbelieving Existence.* Columbia, S.C., 1992. A comprehensive description of the reviews of Dickey's books.

Van Ness, Gordon. *Striking In: The Early Notebooks of James Dickey.* Columbia, Mo., 1996. A well-edited collection of Dickey's early notebooks.

# EMILY DICKINSON

## by Molly McQuade

A clear sign of literary malady: The experienced reader begins to take Emily Dickinson for granted, failing to feel the insoluble, salutary shock of her poetry. And the cure for this malady: try paraphrasing any poem by Dickinson. If you do, you'll quickly learn that you will probably never be able to satisfactorily summarize—or maybe even fully understand—Dickinson's recondite, elated originality. The writing will faithfully resist any effort to possess it completely; her poetry belongs to Dickinson only. Marvelously, though, many readers have been able to borrow it, admire it, and glean wisdom from the lapidary brio of the author. Although writing in literary seclusion in western Massachusetts during the mid to late nineteenth century, Dickinson invented a poetry both unprecedented in form and long-lasting in impact. She wrote as if to bid farewell to the Victorians and to urge on the modernists.

Emily Dickinson. (*Hulton Archive/Getty Images*)

## A DAUGHTER AND HER PRECURSORS

Dickinson was born on 10 December 1830 in Amherst, Massachusetts, a part of the New England region that often witnessed "the blazing up of the lunatic fringe of the Puritan coal," as the contemporary American poet and essayist Adrienne Rich has commented (McQuade, p. 33). Emily Dickinson's father, Edward, was the eldest son of Samuel Fowler Dickinson, a "flaming zealot for education and religion" (Bianchi, pp. 76–77) who wished with outstanding ardor for "the conversion of the whole world" (Bianchi, pp. 76–77). In his dedication to higher learning and the Protestant faith, Samuel Dickinson, lawyer and businessman, reflected the preoccupations of his neighbors in Amherst, a Puritan stronghold subject to periodic evangelical revivals.

His granddaughter Emily, although she did not profess the faith with his unbounded zeal, often concerned herself in her poems with the spiritual life. The following example delicately considers a supplicant's potential claims and merits before a singular and all-sufficient judge. (All quotations in this article are taken from *The Complete Poems of Emily Dickinson*, edited by Thomas H. Johnson, 1951.)

> Few, yet enough,
> Enough is One—
> To that etherial throng
> Have not each one of us the right
> To stealthily belong?
>
> (No. 1596)

The uncanny unity of Dickinson's five lines embodies, with a selflessly ghostly reverence, both the divine unity of a god and the solitary, helpless unity of the lone congregant of one. In its absolute compression of form, the poem also supports its own claim of spiritual sufficiency.

Although Emily Dickinson's paternal grandfather served instrumentally in founding Amherst College, Samuel Fowler Dickinson did so at great cost to himself, neglecting his other affairs to his own financial injury and embarrassment: While still engaged in seeking funds for Amherst, he mortgaged all his property and then was unable to pay off the mortgages. As his firstborn son, Edward Dickinson was naturally compelled to make amends for his disgraced father, particularly after Samuel left Amherst in 1833 following foreclosure on his mortgages. The early burden of financial responsibility may have affected adversely the development of her father's character.

Edward Dickinson was for Emily, her older brother, Austin, and her younger sister, Lavinia, a distant though powerful figure whose law practice, various investments, political ambitions, and devotion to community service often combined to keep him from home during extended forays to Boston, Washington, D.C., and elsewhere.

Thanks to Edward's drive to succeed, the Dickinson home in Amherst was handsomely appointed, the children were well provided for, and their father's presence on Sundays could be counted on. Merely by reading aloud to his family regularly from the Bible, he may have helped to assure his elder daughter's fascination with richly aphoristic language in particular and with rhetoric in general—with the full, roving scope of it, from scrupling understatement to rumbling hyperbole.

## A TACIT MOTHER

Yet Edward's many absences also threw the younger Dickinsons into a greater dependency on their mother than might have been true otherwise. His growing distance from the family also isolated Emily Norcross Dickinson, his wife and their mother. Her steadfast resilience was demanded and perhaps not rewarded.

Regardless, Emily Norcross Dickinson would have been unlikely to provide perfect resilience under any circumstances, partly by dint of her innate temperament and partly due to her recurrent illnesses, which crimped her domestic role and abilities. Biographers have characterized Mrs. Dickinson as an uncommunicative, narrowly conventional farmer's daughter who did not receive from her husband the love or the support at home that a woman like herself would have needed.

If paternal absences and maternal silences, differently inflected, were facts of her home life from her earliest years, then perhaps Emily Dickinson learned the value, as well as the hardship, of tacit intimacy as a main bequest of the family. Tacit intimacy would rely on the listener's cultivated talent to interpret the unspoken—to "read" a silence, whether loving or troubled, intermittent or ongoing. The same interpretive talent also serves well a reader of Dickinson's spectrally concise poetry. The poetry's currency is silence as much as it is words:

> My Cocoon tightens—Colors teaze—
> I'm feeling for the Air—
> A dim capacity for Wings
> Demeans the Dress I wear—
>
> A power of Butterfly must be—
> The Aptitude to fly
> Meadows of Majesty concedes
> and easy Sweeps of Sky—
>
> So I must baffle at the Hint
> And cipher at the Sign
> And make much blunder, if at last
> I take the clue divine—

(No. 1099)

Physically and emotionally constrained by an unspecified distress, the narrator of the poem is unable to perceive or to speak. Even so, she feels compelled to "baffle" and to "cipher" at evidence of the divine—to interpret even when interpretation seems all but impossible.

## AN IMPROPER PURITAN

Apparently the infant Emily Dickinson was never baptized, although her mother underwent a conversion experience only seven months after her birth and although Edward's family prayed fervently for him to follow suit. (Their prayers were rewarded.) Her brother Austin was the last to convert, in 1855; Emily never did.

Still, beginning with her earliest schooling locally in Amherst at the age of five, Dickinson was surrounded by an intense and intimidating aura of Puritan devotion. She most likely learned by heart many of Isaac Watts's *Divine and Moral Songs for Children* (1788), for example. Watts's iambic rhyming quatrains embedded themselves in the poet's ear, as suggested in poem after poem by Dickinson, notably:

> No Rack can torture me—
> My Soul—at Liberty—
> Behind this mortal Bone
> There knits a bolder One—
>
> You Cannot prick with Saw—
> Nor pierce with Cimitar—
> Two Bodies—therefore be—
> Bind One—The Other fly—
>
> The Eagle of his Nest
> No easier divest—
> And gain the Sky
> Than mayest Thou—
>
> Except Thyself may be
> Thine Enemy—
> Captivity is Consciousness—
> So's Liberty.

(No. 384)

Describing the freeing of the soul, this poem paradoxically engulfs its very own words mainly in iambic rhythms, thus suggesting the serious limitations attached to any state of spiritual consciousness.

In 1840 Dickinson began attending Amherst Academy, only recently opened to girls, and continued there as a student for seven years. One of her teachers, Daniel T. Fiske, described Emily at twelve as "very bright, but rather delicate and frail looking." She impressed him as "an excellent scholar: of exemplary deportment," and yet "somewhat shy and nervous. Her compositions were strikingly original" (Habegger, p. 152).

Part of Dickinson's originality may have suggested itself early in her inability to experience conversion. The revival fevers regularly sweeping the region claimed many souls who were thus ready to regenerate their religious dedication. The discomfort felt by abstainers must have been considerable, and it was not merely social in temper: During an era when illness could easily cut life short, a public and official renewal of one's faith would ease the passage to eternal life. Failure to renew, especially over the long term, would therefore require a rare sort of self-reliance, however subject to doubt. Indeed, the ability both to invite and to withstand recurrent doubt during the decades of her youth and maturity may imply that Dickinson did affirm faith but of another kind and in another light. In her poetry she subtly broached her heterodox faith:

> We pray—to Heaven—
> We prate—of Heaven—
> Relate—when Neighbors die—
> At what o'clock to Heaven—they fled—
> Who saw them—Wherefore fly?
>
> Is Heaven a Place—a Sky—a Tree?
> Location's narrow way is for Ourselves—
> Unto the Dead
> There's no Geography—
>
> But State—Endowal—Focus—
> Where—Omnipresence—fly?

(No. 489)

Dickinson here expresses heretical doubt about the need of humans to specify, literalize, and "prate" about an afterlife, when all too evidently the dead have "no Geography." Her asperity serves, however, the purpose of an unconventional devotion perhaps too great for words.

When in 1847 Dickinson entered Mount Holyoke Female Seminary as a student who boarded at the school in South Hadley, not far from her Amherst home, she might have hoped for a surcease of religious peer pressure, but she didn't get it. Here the pressure to renew her faith increased—and was less easy to escape from. During the Christmas season of 1847, for instance, an audience of students was asked by Mary Lyon, headmistress of the school, to rise if they "wanted to be Christian" (Habegger, p. 201). According to an observer, Dickinson remained seated while everyone else stood. Moreover, her fellow students prepared written reports for inspection by

authorities conceding Dickinson's continuing failure to conform in the faith (Habegger, pp. 202–203).

## AFTER SCHOOL

When Dickinson left school for good in 1848, she returned to live at home—with only a handful of interruptions or substantial excursions—for the rest of her life. Although for a time she continued to pursue a sometimes social existence in public, she gradually and famously withdrew until few outside the immediate family circle of her brother (and eventually his wife), her sister, her parents, and their servants regularly caught sight of her. Even esteemed guests might be turned away at her doorstep if the moment were not right; neighborhood children were well known to receive surreptitious baskets of her gingerbread, lowered from a window by the virtually invisible "Miss Emily."

Although she was writing, at times furiously, from her twenties through her fifties—Dickinson died 15 May 1886 at age fifty-five—she chose voluntarily not to publish the poetry. Instead she circulated it selectively by inserting or weaving her poems into numerous informal notes and longer letters written and dispatched by mail or messenger to family and friends, whether distant or close at hand. (According to Victorian custom, she also bound her poems into stitched packets known as "fascicles" for the purposes of her own editing and revising.)

Any serious reader of Dickinson must thus contend, sooner or later, with the legend that surrounded and surrounds the writer as a self-anointed recluse without wings in the world. As her sister-in-law and confidant Susan Dickinson was to write in Dickinson's 1886 obituary, published in the Springfield *Daily Republican*: "Very few in the village, except among older inhabitants, knew Miss Emily personally, although the facts of her seclusion and her intellectual brilliancy were familiar Amherst traditions." Dickinson herself cultivated her legend, not only by withdrawing but by doing so with a cunning theatrical panache. Her studied effort at self-characterization, even after her secession, left potent word of her in her wake as the woman in white who tended flowers, baked bread, cosseted children, and fashioned words into unusual artifacts.

## HER "LONELY" WISDOM

Actually, Dickinson may have chosen wisely to secede from conventional life. Conventional life in western Massachusetts during the later nineteenth century would inevitably have meant marriage, the mortally dangerous matter of childbirth, and domestic subjection for decades to come, were the wife and mother to survive that long (many did not, despite all possible care). Thus, for a writer who happened to be female, the conventional life would have decreed the end of her writing. We would not have Emily Dickinson to read now if she had chosen to pursue the lot of an average woman of her place, time, and class.

Beyond those patent social constrictions, the poet also struggled against the apparently less insuperable bonds bestowed in any upstanding New England hamlet even when a respectable lady of the nineteenth century remained unmarried. One of those bonds must have been purely linguistic: the language of social custom and daily behavior. To conduct one's days and hours according to those linguistic conventions might impose an extreme or even cruel demand on someone such as Dickinson, whose genius was to speak and write as *she* knew how to and not as most did or were expected to. To obey such linguistic habits of diction, syntax, grammar, and rhythm on a regular basis would have annulled, transfixed, or strangled the language of her very genius—Dickinson would have seen her language taken from her. The acceptance of female subordination, in language as in most things, would only have intensified her need for liberty concerning words—a liberty always conditional and qualified yet undoubtedly more available within her family circle than outside of it. By minimizing in her own life social entanglements that would have corrupted her poetic language, Dickinson was seeking to preserve herself along with her writing.

Part of her uncanny intelligence was to work out a solution, according to her own necessary terms, with a boldness that disputes or negates her reputation, earned over time, for fearful retreats and sidling evasions. Rather than talk her life away on trivial social niceties, she conserved her singular verbal resources and decanted part of that stock into the famous handwritten missives, which sounded (and still sound) like no one else's. To her friend Elizabeth Holland, after Holland's visit, Dickinson dispatched the message:

The Parting I tried to smuggle resulted in quite a Mob at last!
The Fence is the only Sanctuary.
That no one invades because no one suspects it.

A contemporary reader cannot fail to notice the heightened aphoristic quality of this note, however quickly improvised it was.

To Adelaide Hills of Amherst, who never met Dickinson face to face, the poet wrote:

To be remembered is next to being loved, and to be loved is Heaven, and is this quite Earth?

Dickinson's rhetorical question provides an answer probably never foreseen or demanded by the recipient. She wrote to air her thoughts and secondarily to be heard.

To Sarah Tuckerman, another lady of Amherst never encountered in person, Dickinson mused at length:

I fear my congratulation, like repentance according to Calvin, is too late to be plausible, but might there not be an exception, were the delight or the penitence found to be durable?

Although the original context of the note is not known, Dickinson's words can be savored by any reader who appreciates extravagant and refined quibbling in a "routine" note of apology. By imposing on herself, and on others, the fastidious freedom to choose words, Dickinson surrounded herself with the art she most needed.

## ''A SUSAN OF MY OWN''

Even while successfully negotiating the terms of her survival, however, the very private Dickinson was nonetheless confronted, as anyone would have been, by the commonplace calamities: illness and death, the wish for love, the denial of love, and the loss of love. Perhaps more than most people, she relied on intense friendships to help sustain her imaginatively, and yet she found them unreliable.

Because she lived in seclusion by choice, and because her poetry also steadfastly reflects the author's coveting of privacy, to read the life in the poetry is perilous, if not impossible. Likewise, to search the life for the origins of her poetry would be treacherous. It is more feasible to regard each arena, the life and the writing, separately. A survey of the leading people and events in Dickinson's adult life would fairly include the following.

A signal element until Dickinson's death was her long-term friendship with Susan Dickinson, who married her brother, Austin, in 1856. She and Susan most likely met in Amherst during the late 1840s. The friendship was to mark her poetry decisively even when the two endured repeated fallings-out. Susan, an intelligent and sensitive woman close in age to Dickinson, shared with the poet a certain shrewdness and steeliness of temperament; she was also relatively tolerant of unconventional ideas and behavior. Susan was the intended audience and the frequent recipient of so many Dickinson letters and poems that even Susan must at times have felt overwhelmed or resentful. Also, as time passed and Susan bore several children, she found she had less time for the childless

Emily and her seductively winning demands. Quarrels and estrangements disturbed them in 1854 and more protractedly in 1861. Susan wrote Dickinson's obituary, however, and assisted with the posthumous editing and publication of her poetry.

To enjoy the full force of Dickinson's appeal to her friend, the evidence of the poet's letters and poems written for and to Susan is compelling. In the late 1870s, scholars estimate, Dickinson wrote this note to Susan in the form of a poem:

> I must wait
> a few Days
> before seeing
> you—You are
> too momentous.
> But remember
> it is idolatry,
> not indifference. Emily.
> (*Open Me Carefully*)

Dickinson charms by staging surprises meant to disarm and waylay the recipient.

On another occasion during the same era, she wrote to Susan:

> To the faithful
> Absence is
> condensed presence.
> To others, but
> there are no
> others—
> (*Open Me Carefully*)

Dickinson interrupted herself here in mid-sentence, precipitously dramatizing her deep regard for Susan.

And, with a renegade's childlike delight, Dickinson confessed:

> To own a
> Susan of
> my own
> Is of itself
> a Bliss—
> Whatever
> Realm I
> forfeit, Lord,
> continue
> me in this!
> (*Open Me Carefully*)

What was the real nature of Susan and Emily Dickinson's long-lived mutual affinity? Suggests Adrienne Rich, "Obviously, Dickinson was attracted by and interested in men whose minds had something to offer her; she was, it is by now clear, equally attracted to and interested in women whose minds had something to offer her" (McQuade, p. 37). Rich elaborates: "Women [in the nineteenth century] expressed their attachments to other women both physically and verbally; a marriage did not dilute the strength of a female friendship, in which two women often shared the same bed during long visits, and wrote letters articulate with both physical and emotional longing" (McQuade, p. 37).

In *The Passion of Emily Dickinson*, the Dickinson critic and scholar Judith Farr attributes ninety-four poems written by Dickinson as intended for Susan Dickinson, including numerous love poems. Like so much of Dickinson's private life, her relationship with Susan Dickinson remains enigmatic to us.

## LETTERS TO THE EDITOR

In general, the 1850s were socially, emotionally, spiritually, and intellectually momentous years for Dickinson, despite or perhaps partly because of her seclusion. In 1853 she met Josiah Holland, literary editor of the Springfield *Daily Republican*, then a well-regarded newspaper, along with his wife, Elizabeth. Their company was stimulating. In 1858 she first met Samuel Bowles, the editor in chief of the Springfield paper for which Holland worked. Bowles's liberal politics included feminist leanings, unlike Holland's, and as the redoubtably busy boss of the paper he was able to give Dickinson much-valued indirect access into the world of public affairs as well as an audience of one for her letters and poems. (Bowles was introduced to her, as were others, when he visited the home of Susan and Austin Dickinson.)

On the other hand, just as momentously, in 1855 Dickinson heard the inspiring Charles Wadsworth preach in Philadelphia. Wadsworth seems to have impressed her with a spiritual quality of tormented eloquence that touched her as a woman and as a writer. Some biographers feel that Dickinson was seriously smitten with him and may have written some of her most recklessly erotic love poetry with him in mind.

## MR. HIGGINSON

For the poet, 1862 was also a highly significant year, for it was then that Dickinson began to read the essays of Thomas Wentworth Higginson, an editor and a frequent contributor to the *Atlantic Monthly* magazine. Emboldened partly by her enthusiasm for his observations of nature, she initiated a correspondence with him by sending him four of her poems. Higginson helped to fill the gap left in her spiritual and literary life after Wadsworth's 1862 departure for San Francisco and following her apparent quarrel with Bowles in the same year. Higginson's hidebound and conventional taste prevented him from savoring as he might have done Dickinson's achievement in poetry. Still, as a representative from the world of professional letters, such as it was, he eased her isolation.

Her father's death in 1874 was followed a year later by her mother's major stroke. As she had also done before during less threatening maternal illness, Dickinson offered primary care to her bedridden mother, although she was sharing their house with her sister, Lavinia. This added responsibility may partly account for the diminution of her writing from the fiendishly productive 1860s.

With one exception, all of Dickinson's suspected romantic interests (Wadsworth, for instance) led her to no tangible success. But in the early 1870s she became a friend of the prominent Judge Otis Lord while he was a guest of Austin and Susan. In the years after the death of his wife Elizabeth in 1877, he began pursuing Dickinson and evidently sought to marry her. Although she shared his feelings, she decided against marriage.

She may have been wise to do so. The 1880s for the Dickinson family were parlous, for the long-married Austin Dickinson fell in love with Mabel Loomis Todd, the much younger wife, new in town, of a local professor. They carried on an active and long-lasting affair in his house and hers, to the grief of Susan and the supposed equanimity of the cuckolded husband. Although little known to Emily Dickinson, Mabel Loomis Todd and her daughter Millicent Todd Bingham later competed with Susan Dickinson and her daughter, Martha Dickinson Bianchi, in trying to bring Dickinson's poetry and her letters to publication after the writer's 1886 death from Bright's disease. Although she wrote poetry in secret and asked that her letters be destroyed on her demise, Dickinson left an immense cache of fascicles behind her, surprising everyone.

All in all, hardly a life empty of significant action. However, Dickinson's most significant life was given to and conducted through her poetry. While it is impossible to do justice to the body of her work, numbering 1,789 poems and three volumes of letters, many critics have tried and are still trying—among them Helen Vendler, Sharon Cameron, Judith Farr, Richard B. Sewall, R. W. Franklin, Thomas H. Johnson, Denis Donoghue, and others.

As Richard B. Sewall, a preeminent Dickinson critic and biographer, put it in 1963, "We still are not quite sure of her. We ask and ask." Perhaps it is better to keep asking, even now.

## DICKINSON'S DASH

One of the first questions a new reader of Emily Dickinson might justifiably ask is about the rate of speed pulsing through her generally very short poems. The staccato quickness of much Dickinson poetry is achieved partly by use of her iconoclastic punctuation, most notably by her multiple dashes. The dashes, introduced at the ends of lines or as a fleeting intersection at a line's midpoint, quicken some of the poems by bifurcating them, as if a gasp is being uttered as the poem goes on running.

Her dashes, while mandating fragmentation, also serve to unite a poem's various fragments—syntactic, rhythmic, metaphoric—into a composite fragment, a whole made up of undisguised parts. The dashes may also summon up for some readers the sensation of abridgment, curbing or cutting as they do the poem's approaches to a thought or thoughts. Dickinson's poems typically record the motion of her mind as she thinks in and through the words. Her dashes take fast steps forward that also exert a retractive pull, holding back when a poem seems impelled or poised to spill headlong out of itself.

## THE WICK AND THE FLAME

Many of Dickinson's poems show her interest in speed as a verbal mode. One poem that does so with finely adumbrated irony is No. 233.

> The Lamp burns sure—within—
> Tho' Serfs—supply the Oil—
> It matters not the busy Wick—
> At her phosphoric toil!
>
> The Slave—forgets—to fill—
> The Lamp—burns golden—on—
> Unconscious that the oil is out—
> As that the Slave—is gone.

The confident writer here contrives a richly simple scene that burgeons quietly into metaphor. The scene: A kerosene lamp, dependent upon oil as its fuel, continues to burn its wick (the source of the lamp's light) despite the gradual exhaustion of the oil, which the "slave" does not happen to refill.

As long as the oil exists in good supply, the wick "matters not," for the oil will enable the flame to burn. But once the oil has vastly diminished, the wick takes precedence, persevering despite the lack of both oil and attendant "slave" to aid the flame. What Dickinson does not say directly: Only the wick can burn in a kerosene lamp, and so without the wick a lamp cannot shed any light. As physically the smallest and visually the most recondite element, the wick—typically just a bit of densely knitted fabric or thread—is nonetheless the most significant constituent of lamp and light, selflessly and singularly enabling our sight by which to read.

Like the wick she cites, Dickinson's insight about the wick and its flame lies submerged in the body of the poem, which is itself like a lamp radiating intelligence as a deceptively modest essential ingredient—as, in other words, the poem's flame. Yet Dickinson employs her dashes here to qualify and cast doubt on the seeming stability of both the poem and the lamp it evokes.

The dashes undermine the lamp's security, which is as fleeting as the ever-consumed oil that dwindles in the vessel of the lamp. Dashes also dramatize the oncoming extinction of the flame igniting the ultimately oil-less wick. In a line such as "The Lamp—burns golden—on—" the dashes overtly dispute the lamp's observed action, eroding the announced continuity of light and instead imitating the unsure flickering of a guttering flame. But because Dickinson chooses not to visualize the flame's death, she leaves us with a paradoxical closing impression: of steadfastness in a state of conscious uncertainty.

That state is finally the poet's, since she is the author of the metaphorical lamp. In the poem, Dickinson ironically salutes her own indentured and overlooked strength. The self-effacing writer, like the wick, rests on her own unsteady bravado as creator while her sustenance and stamina recede.

Although the critic R. P. Blackmur has voiced a negative view of Dickinson's dashes, he also clarified her use of them for his own earlier critical era, claiming that her dashes acted as musical notation for her words, which he compared with musical notes. The notation of the dashes was, Blackmur argued, inadequate to guiding the reader through Dickinson's ambiguous "music." Even so, the very inadequacy of the notation encouraged successively different readings (or hearings) of any given Dickinson poem, thus highlighting and serving her propensity for lyric freedom.

## FAILING AT SEA

Similarly, in poem No. 226, Dickinson employs dashes.

> Should you but fail at—Sea—
> In sight of me—

> Or doomed lie—
> Next Sun—to die—
> Or rap—at Paradise—unheard—
> I'd *harass God*—
> Until He let you in!

Here the dashes insinuate an implicit undertone in the action of the poem and comment on it. This seven-line poem lacks the visual symmetry of the previous poem's twinned quatrains, and unlike No. 233, No. 226 also begins on an emphatically subjunctive note of unconfirmed future possibility. "Should you but fail at—Sea—" reads the first line, with seemingly gratuitous paired dashes fluttering up at its end. What could be the connotative meaning of those pronounced dashes?

At the very least, the dashes interject further doubt into the already unsure "sea" of the first line, where the identity of the "you," the locale of the "sea," and the full meaning of the anticipated "failure" all remain hazardously unknown. As the reader's eye travels down the lines of the poem, that eye is rocked by an unstable wake, thanks mainly to Dickinson's dashes.

She resolves No. 226 with a countervailing irony utterly unlike that imbuing poem No. 233. For after conjecturing the various possible future fates of the "you" addressed in No. 226, fates of doom and suspected expiration, the poem's narrator insists that she will save the day if need be: she'll "*harass God*" to forestall disaster and grant the "you" safe passage into heaven. While Dickinson may be mocking her own powers before God, she also asserts these powers merrily by crafting the poem in the first place, by summoning and then puckishly solving the poem's challenges. As an author she permits herself a godly kind of mischief.

## HYMNS AND ANTI-HYMNS

Emily Dickinson's mischief-making tendencies, whether construed from punctuation or by other means, were tempered almost always by her poetry's reliance on hymn meters, ranging from "common meter" (an eight-syllable line followed by a six-syllable line) to "short meter" (two six-syllable lines followed by a line of eight syllables followed by a line of six syllables) to "long meter" (lines of eight syllables only).

Hymn meter typically occurred in four-line stanzas and in Dickinson's work included mainly iambic or trochaic metrical patterns. The regularity of hymn meter gave Dickinson's poetry a steady base to work with and to deviate from, as well as a specifically liturgical point of origin for earthly and spiritual meditations alike. As the eminent Dickinson scholar Thomas H. Johnson has noted, Dickinson often mingled different hymn meters within a single poem and varied exact rhymes with imperfect and suspended rhymes. With the passing of time, she asserted with increasing frequency her right to expressive liberties.

As the contemporary Dickinson critic Timothy Morris has observed more recently, Dickinson's approach to rhyme developed comprehensively over her career. In her first poems, written during the first half of the 1850s, she preferred exact rhyme. Later in the same decade, she experimented consistently with what Morris calls "a much less conventional rhyming," meaning a less regular and a more sonically subtle kind.

As Morris has proved by surveying analytically her poems by year of composition, Dickinson also imposed another signature innovation upon hymn form: She typically enjambed her lines, whereas the lines of hymns are traditionally end-stopped. Enjambment—in which the end of one line continues, in its syntactical organization and in its sense, into the next line—confers on Dickinson's poetry a supple speed of impetus and delivery that would have been wholly exotic to hymn lyrics. Although Dickinson's early work contains end-stopped lines, Morris's quantitative analysis has demonstrated that over the years she increased the prevalence of enjambed lines in the poetry.

Clearly Dickinson was a poet who counted and measured even while she worked to subvert traditional forms. Why did she choose to subvert at all? Was the impulse a well-considered one?

### RULES OF SUBVERSION

Some of her poems, devoted to fathoming nullity or immensity as a spiritual quantity, may offer a partial answer to the question. For example, consider poem No. 546:

> To fill a Gap
> Insert the Thing that caused it—
> Block it up
> With Other—and 'twill yawn the more—
> You cannot solder an Abyss
> With Air.

The six lines of this poem, ranging dramatically in their length, seek, at least nominally, to provide a sort of prescription for the writing of a poem—at least, for a certain kind of poem as it might be written by a certain kind of poet.

"To fill a Gap," begins the poem in its prescription, "Insert the Thing that caused it." The counsel offered is so matter-of-factly pragmatic as to foretell the construction of this very poem. What is the Gap except the space between what may be left unsaid and what might instead be written?

If the poet fails to express herself, then the gap must remain as it is; she would thus prolong the gap. To "block it up" may serve to fill it but will also meanwhile press upon the edges of the gap, widening it. In other words, each poem presses on its own borders and presses against other poems, written or yet to be written. Although writing may fulfill the momentary beckoning of an unwritten poem, writing cannot conclude the greater work of poetry, which expands in its possibilities with each word written. Like a cubist ahead of her time, Dickinson seems to envision a poetry of shifting juxtapositions that will never fully occupy or settle the space of poetry or the mind that creates it.

If all poetry remains provisional and unfinished, forever shifting in place and extending in dimension, then the poet might do well to reflect such material facts of aesthetic life in the form of the poems she writes. The visual "yawning" of this poem does just that by carving gaps into itself and defying its own finishing. By closing her auspicious first line with the word "Gap" and by concluding her oracular last line with the word "Air," with both words capitalized like Platonic ideals or like reigning gods, Dickinson seems to salute the poem's ability to unmake itself, whatever the will of the poet.

Creation, especially for a maverick Puritan such as Dickinson, would needfully call to mind and into question the poet's heterodox and troubling position as a would-be rival of God. To concede truthfully the necessary originality of the poet in the effort of creating, she may have refused to mimic poetic tradition or to venerate theological orthodoxy. Creation by either God or man must, by definition, forgo mimicry and commit originality; formal rebellion may further poetic justice.

### BEYOND INGENUITY

Not even Dickinson's formal ingenuities should distract a reader for too long from what she writes about and how she feels—or how the poems feel. A fact of continual amazement in her poetry is the exacerbated emotion that infuses, with terrific selectivity, phrases and lines and single words that otherwise might mainly suggest by their spare singularity the poet's unusual restraint in writing.

Such emotion flourished with Dickinson's extreme verbal scruples and with her dictional precision. She relied on relatively few words to do the work and play of a poem, yet the combined effects of syntax, rhythm, diction, rhyme, and metaphor in her writing confer an uncanny power on the slimmest scaffolding. She was able to economize marvelously, seizing smallness and wringing it for feeling. Her style was grandly parsimonious.

Dickinson's poem No. 365, beginning with the line "Dare you see a Soul *at the White Heat*?," shows what may be asked by her poetry of reader and writer alike.

> Dare you see a Soul *at the White Heat?*
> Then crouch within the door—
> Red—is the Fire's common tint—
> But when the vivid Ore
> Has vanquished Flame's conditions,
> It quivers from the Forge
> Without a color, but the light
> Of unanointed Blaze.
> Least Village has its Blacksmith
> Whose Anvil's even ring
> Stands symbol for the finer Forge
> That soundless tugs—within—
> Refining these impatient Ores
> With Hammer, and with Blaze
> Until the Designated Light
> Repudiate the Forge—

To see the ore that "quivers from the Forge / Without a color" is to see the soul fully ignited and refined, a vision beyond the scope and ability of most eyes. To recognize the ore so vividly colorless demands a courageous, penetrating glance. So does Dickinson's poetry.

## NATURE IS WHAT WE KNOW

Visual perception was a mainstay of Dickinson's writing, nowhere more so than in her many poems observing nature. " 'Nature' is what We know" she declared, "But have no Art to say." Nature's art guided Dickinson's.

She conceived exquisitely stark and airborne metaphors of a bee's erotic conquests in poem No. 1224:

> Like Trains of Cars on Tracks of Plush
> I hear the level Bee—
> A Jar across the Flowers goes
> Their Velvet Masonry
>
> Withstands until the sweet Assault
> Their Chivalry consumes—
> While He, victorious tilts away
> To vanquish other Blooms.

The workaday bee, who nonetheless seeks sexual "Plush," finds it over and over again in the open (ajar) blossoms, whose "Velvet Masonry" excitingly evokes both a watertight floral construction and the possibility of entering it rapturously. Dickinson's unexpected merger in her metaphor of love with business eroticizes each, as though pollinating both. The poem marks a conquest of its subject, inspecting bee and flower as if conducting an "assignment" in love.

Another remarkable piece of more extended natural observation, poem No. 1575, describes the bat as a sort of anti-poet who is unable to sing anything. Yet Dickinson's eye lingers upon him with a covetous adoration.

> The Bat is dun, with wrinkled Wings—
> Like fallow Article—
> And not a song pervades his Lips—
> Or none perceptible.
>
> His small Umbrella quaintly halved
> Describing in the Air
> An Arc alike inscrutable
> Elate Philosopher.
>
> Deputed from what Firmament—
> Of what Astute Abode—
> Empowered with what Malignity
> Auspiciously withheld—
>
> To his adroit Creator
> Ascribe no less the praise—
> Beneficent, believe me,
> His eccentricities—

To visualize inscrutability in a creature is not far removed from conducting the devotional duty of a congregant, which may help to explain why the poem moves, in the last stanza, to consider the bat's creator. Immaculately imperfect—"dun, with wrinkled Wings"—the animal is as such doubly desirable and infinitely beloved. Dickinson's fine and sharp portrait leaves out so much that what persists is unforgettable, fiercely and religiously real.

## SOREST NEED

"There is a word / Which bears a sword / Can pierce an armed man—," wrote Dickinson in poem No. 42. Although that metaphor is for this poet relatively undistinguished, even mundane, her poetry aims to pierce in just such a way, and her narrators tend to welcome their share of piercing too.

"I like a look of Agony," reflects the speaker in poem No. 241, "Because I know it's true—." To be properly felt, truth must wound, as when, in poem No. 561, "I measure every Grief I meet / With narrow, probing, Eyes— / I wonder if It weighs like Mine— / Or has an Easier size." Poetic readiness was for Dickinson cued by pain, well received. "To comprehend a nectar," she wrote, "Requires sorest need."

Even so, her writing thrives on indirection as a technique, on the avoidance of explicit statements. When Dickinson's poetry is at its most cryptic and unfathomable, the writer seems to claim a stance of diabolical removal, deitylike, from which to preside, overlook, and administer. The stance recalls that of the lordly "He" in poem No. 315:

> He fumbles at your Soul
> As Players at the Keys
> Before they drop full Music on—
> He stuns you by degrees—
>
> Prepares your brittle Nature
> For the etherial Blow
> By fainter Hammers—further heard—
> Then nearer—Then so slow
>
> Your Breath has time to straighten—
> Your Brain—to bubble Cool—
> Deals—One—imperial—Thunderbolt—
> That scalps your naked Soul—
>
> When Winds hold Forests in their Paws—
> The Universe—is still—

The artful inevitability of death needs no announcing, all the more so as the mortal mind could not understand death anyhow.

## A DIMPLE IN THE TOMB

Dickinson's mind enjoyed danger and was wont to frisk with it. Her poem No. 1489 can be read as a mordantly earnest wisecrack.

> A Dimple in the Tomb
> Makes that ferocious Room
> A Home—

For the legendary secluded one, a sepulchral dimple was perhaps a redeeming joke.

When writing with the fewest possible words, as above, Dickinson seemed to compress and expose at once, to speak translucently in order to mete out a transporting justice. In the process, "she" vanished in the purity of her sight and insight. Although unmistakably hers, the poetry aspires to a wayward disappearing act:

> By homely gifts and hindered Words
> The human heart is told
> Of Nothing—

> "Nothing" is the force
> That renovates the World—

(No. 1563)

[*See also* Poetess in American Literature, The.]

## WORKS

*The Poems of Emily Dickinson* (1951; edited by Thomas H. Johnson)

*The Letters of Emily Dickinson* (1958; edited by Thomas H. Johnson and Theodora Ward)

*Selected Letters of Emily Dickinson* (*1971*; edited by Thomas H. Johnson)

*The Master Letters of Emily Dickinson* (*1986*; edited by R. W. Franklin)

*The Poems of Emily Dickinson* (*1998*; edited by R. W. Franklin)

*Open Me Carefully: Emily Dickinson's Intimate Letters to Susan Huntington Dickinson* (*1998*; edited by Ellen Louise Hart and Martha Nell Smith)

## FURTHER READING

Bianchi, Martha Dickinson. *Emily Dickinson Face to Face.* Hampden, Conn., 1932.

Cady, Edwin H., and Louis J. Budd, eds. *On Dickinson: The Best from American Literature.* Durham, N.C., 1990. An up-to-date anthology of criticism, originally published in the scholarly journal *American Literature*, on such topics as Dickinson's style, her links with the metaphysical poets, and "thirst and starvation" as a theme in her writing.

Cameron, Sharon. *Lyric Time: Dickinson and the Limits of Genre.* Baltimore, 1979. Analysis of Dickinson's use of time in her writing.

Cameron, Sharon. *Choosing Not Choosing: Dickinson's Fascicles.* Chicago, 1992. A leading contemporary Dickinson scholar's contribution to the field.

Farr, Judith. *The Passion of Emily Dickinson.* Cambridge, Mass., 1992. An incisive investigation of Dickinson's love poetry.

Farr, Judith. *I Never Came to You in White.* Boston, 1996. An epistolary novel, based on fact, about Dickinson's schooldays, written by the Dickinson scholar.

Ferlazzo, Paul J. *Emily Dickinson.* Boston, 1976. A compact biographical and critical study.

Gelpi, Albert. *The Tenth Muse: The Psyche of the American Poet.* New York, 1991. This collection of Gelpi's criticism includes the essay "The Self as Center," a highly regarded work of Dickinson criticism.

Gilbert, Sandra M., and Susan Gubar. *The Madwoman in the Attic: The Woman Writer and the*

*Nineteenth-Century Literary Imagination.* New Haven, Conn., 1979. Includes a chapter offering a substantial and significant feminist reading of Dickinson.

Habegger, Alfred. *My Wars Are Laid Away in Books: The Life of Emily Dickinson.* New York, 2001. A much-praised full-length biography of Dickinson.

Howe, Susan. *My Emily Dickinson.* Berkeley, Calif., 1985. The noted contemporary American poet's ruminations on Dickinson.

Johnson, Thomas H. *The Complete Poems of Emily Dickinson.* 3 vols. Cambridge, Mass., and London, 1951.

Johnson, Thomas H. *Emily Dickinson: An Interpretive Biography.* Cambridge, Mass., 1955. A significant contribution to Dickinsoniana.

Leyda, Jay. *The Years and Hours of Emily Dickinson.* 2 vols. New Haven, Conn., 1960. Essential reading.

McQuade, Molly, ed. *By Herself: Women Reclaim Poetry.* St. Paul, Minn., 2000.

Sewall, Richard B. *Emily Dickinson: A Collection of Critical Essays.* Englewood Cliffs, N.J., 1963. Essays by Thomas H. Johnson, R. P. Blackmur, Louise Bogan et al., that give a sense of how critical reactions to Dickinson have changed over time.

Sewall, Richard B. *The Life of Emily Dickinson.* 2 vols. New York, 1974. A milestone in the field of Dickinson studies.

Ward, Theodora Van Wagenen. *The Capsule of the Mind: Chapters in the Life of Emily Dickinson.* Cambridge, Mass., 1961. Useful early work on the poet.

# JOAN DIDION

*by Joy Arbor*

Joan Didion is an accomplished writer of essays, political journalism, and novels. A distinctive literary voice, she is known for her subjective yet unsentimental essays, her harrowing novels, and her astute political criticism.

Joan Didion was born in Sacramento, California, on 5 December 1934 to Frank Reese Didion and Eduene (Jerrett) Didion. A fifth-generation Californian, her sense of identity as the daughter of California's Central Valley is a core theme in her work. In her early work, her native California was a favorite subject; since the mid-1970s, she has broadened her concern about disappearing and imagined senses of place to locales all over the United States as well as in Central America and Southeast Asia.

Didion graduated from the University of California at Berkeley with a B.A. degree in English in 1956. She won *Vogue*'s Prix de Paris contest that year and moved to New York City, working at *Vogue* for eight years. While working her way up from promotional copywriter to associate feature editor, she was also writing for *National Review* and *Mademoiselle*. While at *Vogue* she met and married John Gregory Dunne and wrote her first novel, *Run River*, which was published in 1963.

A year later, Didion and Dunne decided to move to Los Angeles. In 1966 they adopted an infant daughter, Quintana Roo. Determined to make a living as a freelance reporter, Didion wrote for *National Review*, *Vogue*, and other magazines. But it was a series of magazine columns for the *Saturday Evening Post* that attracted widespread attention. These were collected and published in 1968 as *Slouching towards Bethlehem*. With the publication of the novels *Play It As It Lays* in 1970 and *A Book of Common Prayer* in 1977, she established herself as one of America's more talented contemporary novelists.

Joan Didion.
(© *Christopher Felver/Corbis*)

Over the years, Didion and Dunne have written screenplays together. They include *Panic in Needle Park* (1971) (based on the James Mill book), *Play It As It Lays* (1972) (based on Didion's novel), *True Confessions* (1981) (based on Dunne's novel), and *Up Close and Personal* (1996).

Continuing to write essays and novels, she extended her reporting skills to writing *Salvador* (1983), a book of nonfiction about El Salvador at the height of its civil war. In *Miami* (1987) she again discusses cultural, social, and political issues as she focuses on the immigration of Cuban exiles into that city. *After Henry* (1992) is a collection of essays organized loosely around the three geographical areas she has focused on during her entire writing career: Washington, D.C., California, and New York City. In 1988 the *New York Review of Books* asked Didion to look at and write some pieces about the political process. These essays have been collected in *Political Fictions* (2001).

## CLASSIC ESSAYS: *SLOUCHING TOWARDS BETHLEHEM* AND *THE WHITE ALBUM*

*Slouching towards Bethlehem*'s title comes from the Irish nationalist poet William Butler Yeats's "The Second Coming." In the poem, "the center cannot hold; / Mere anarchy is loosed upon the world." In Didion's preface, she states that she must attempt to come to terms with the far-reaching chaos of the 1960s. Her title essay, the crux of the collection, explores the drug-filled days of the naive and pathetic flower children Didion encountered in the Haight-Ashbury area of San Francisco. Other essays in this collection further dramatize the desperation of the 1960s, while some attempt to evoke a specific sense of place, usually California. A famous essay included here is "Goodbye to All That," an elegiac piece on choosing to move away from New York City. She explains that like many places, New York City exists primarily in the mind and is therefore only for the very young.

Didion's second collection of essays, *The White Album*, was published in 1979. In her title essay, she explains feeling cut adrift from narrative, seeing only flash pictures without meaning. In an essay that juxtaposes the Manson family, the Black Panthers, murderers, and mothers leaving their children on the center island of the interstate with the Doors and Janis Joplin, it is hardly surprising that her readers feel overwhelmed, as if the world has no meaning. Many of them comment that "The White Album" exactly captures the mood of the times. Other essays in the "Sojourns" section again attempt to capture a sense of place.

"The Women's Movement," an essay in this collection, alienated many feminists. In the essay Didion attacks feminists for being, as she calls it, obsessed with trivia. In Didion's view, feminists want to become children again, without responsibility, without the mess and loss of freedom childbearing demands. Didion also attacks feminist interpretations of literature, because explicitly political interpretations distort the very literature it purports to expose, fiction being generally hostile to ideology.

## FIVE NOVELS

The three novels *Run River*, *Play It As It Lays*, and *A Book of Common Prayer* seem to go together because they all center on unhappy married women trying unsuccessfully to find purpose in their lives. All three novels are also driven by sexual attachments.

*Run River* tells the story of the twenty-year marriage of Everett and Lily Knight McClellan. Both children of old Sacramento Valley families, they begin their life together by eloping to Reno. But shortly after the wedding and the birth of their two children, Everett joins the army during World War II.

Feeling betrayed and having difficulties adjusting to life at the McClellan ranch, Lily has an affair and gets pregnant. When Everett is discharged after the death of his father and returns home, he is unable to deal with Lily's confessions of infidelity; she slips away to San Francisco to have an abortion. They find themselves unable to communicate thereafter.

As the couple grows further apart, Everett's sister Martha has a relationship with a social climber, Ryder Channing. After five years with Martha, he abruptly marries someone else. Martha finds herself unable to

rebuild her life and drowns one stormy night. Over the years, Lily has affairs and finally takes up with Ryder. The story is framed around a single night when, getting ready to meet Ryder, Lily hears a gunshot in the distance. The novel then flashes back to the early period of her marriage. When we return to the present, Lily hears a second shot and realizes that Everett has killed himself. Lily has been unable to stop Everett, just as she had found herself unable to take control of her life and end her adulterous affairs.

In 1970 the best-selling *Play It As It Lays* appeared. While creating controversy because of its seeming nihilism, the novel received a National Book Award nomination. It is set in the middle of moviemaking Hollywood, where individuals suppress their real emotions so they can manipulate others to gain success, recognition, or sex.

Young B-actress Maria Wyeth drives the Los Angeles freeways in a Corvette, finding that negotiating a lane change is about all she can handle in her chaotic life. She is separated from her husband, Carter Lang, and her institutionalized, retarded daughter Kate, who is the only person she truly cares about. When Maria becomes pregnant (likely not by her husband), Carter strong-arms her into having an abortion by threatening that he will prevent her from seeing Kate. Like Lily McClellan, Maria also has affairs but seems attached to Carter, trying to work things out, albeit to no avail.

After slowly falling apart over the course of the novel, Maria unexpectedly finds herself assisting a suicide. Carter's producer, B.Z., explains that he just does not want to "play the game anymore," making suicide an act of defiance. He climbs into bed with Maria, takes pills, and dies in her arms. But Maria's family and upbringing taught her to "play it as it lays"; she does not believe in suicide. She ends up in a mental institution, still hoping to attain some kind of peaceful life that she can live with her daughter.

*A Book of Common Prayer* reflects Didion's increasing interest in politics and the ways in which politics infiltrate the lives of those, like protagonist Charlotte Douglas, who feel separate from politics. Charlotte is a twice-married San Franciscan whose life falls apart when her daughter Marin leaves home to join a group of terrorists. Pregnant, Charlotte leaves her second husband to travel with her dying first husband. When the baby dies, she goes to Boca Grande, a fictitious Central American country with its own domestic conflicts, often within the ruling family itself.

The narrator, Grace Strasser Mendana—an American expatriate and widow of a member of the ruling Boca Grande family—tells the story of Charlotte's life and death. Critics argue over the efficacy of this uninvolved narrator, who must speculate on things she would most likely not know. Because Grace claims to have been trained as an ethnographic anthropologist, she questions her own ability to report what she knows, making the story as much about Grace and the nature of her speculations as about Charlotte's life.

The novels *Democracy* and *The Last Thing He Wanted* extended Didion's international political concerns, already evidenced by *A Book of Common Prayer* (and also expressed by her political journalism in *Salvador* and *Miami*). *Democracy* was published in 1984. The novel centers on Inez Christian and her family. In the spring of 1975, just when the United States has completed its evacuation of Vietnam, Inez's father is arrested for a double murder with political and racist overtones. The Hawaiian family's tragedy allows Inez to break free of her marriage to a U.S. senator and escape to Malaysia with Jack Lovett, a freelance CIA agent and the man she has always loved. Though he dies abruptly, she holds onto her freedom, choosing to stay in Kuala Lumpur working among Vietnamese refugees.

Critics argue that one can sense a moral tension in the narrative. The narrative itself, they argue, struggles against doing what it must do: recognize that history is not a story of the personal will triumphing over reality, but a story of the ebbs and flows of power.

After a twelve-year hiatus, Didion returned to fiction with *The Last Thing He Wanted* (1996), set in 1984. It is the story of Elena McMahon, a political journalist who abruptly changes her life, leaving a presidential campaign she is covering to return to Florida and visit her widowed father. Since her father wants to sell guns to the contras, she flies to Costa Rica, getting caught in a web of gunrunners, CIA operatives, and a conspiracy that spans the John F. Kennedy assassination and the Iran-contra scandal.

## POLITICAL ESSAYS: *AFTER HENRY* AND *POLITICAL FICTIONS*

*After Henry* (1992) is a collection of twelve essays organized loosely around the three geographical areas that Didion has focused on throughout her career: California; Washington, D.C.; and New York City. In contrast with *Slouching towards Bethlehem*, here she often focuses on politics and media.

"Sentimental Journey," a three-part attack on New York City, explores the way in which the gang rape of a white investment banker was transformed by the media into what Didion calls a "false narrative." She points out that most rapes are not framed by so much media coverage, but pass by relatively unnoticed in the public eye.

*Political Fictions* (2001) collects together eight pieces on the political process that Didion wrote for *The New York Review of Books*. Here she says that in 1998 she began looking at the political process and found that it is not a mechanism which allowed the people to have a voice in their government. Instead she finds that a handful of people invent public life. This political class is further entrenched by nostalgia for an imagined America.

While Joan Didion is much admired in the literary and intellectual worlds, it is surprising how rarely she is mentioned in the academy as an important contemporary novelist. Perhaps this is because her essays have outshined her novels, or because history is just not done with her yet.

[*See also* New Journalism, The.]

### SELECTED WORKS

*Run River* (1963)
*Slouching towards Bethlehem* (1968)
*Play It As It Lays* (1970)
*A Book of Common Prayer* (1977)
*The White Album* (1979)
*Salvador* (1983)
*Democracy* (1984)
*Miami* (1987)
*After Henry* (1992)
*Political Fictions* (2001)

### FURTHER READING

Felton, Sharon, ed. *The Critical Response to Joan Didion.* Westport, Conn., 1994.

Friedman, Ellen G., ed. *Joan Didion: Essays and Conversations.* Princeton, N.J., 1984.

Henderson, Katherine. *Joan Didion.* New York, 1981.

Reaves, Gerri. *Mapping the Private Geography: Autobiography, Identity, and America.* Jefferson, N.C., 2001. An investigation of America and individual places as imagined in Didion's essays.

Winchell, Mark. *Joan Didion.* Boston, 1980. A thematic treatment of Didion's early work.

# ANNIE DILLARD

*by Ian Bickford*

Among the most distinctive forms of American writing is the meditative essay, as initiated by the nineteenth-century authors Ralph Waldo Emerson and Henry David Thoreau. Annie Dillard is a more recent practitioner of this tradition. Often relying on the natural world as a backdrop for her philosophical discourse, Dillard explodes the minutiae of science and environment into broad, spiritual speculation. Dillard was born on 30 April 1945, the eldest of three daughters in a well-off Pittsburgh family. By her own account, her parents were hilarious individualists, as engrossed with the details of life as Dillard would become. They taught her the value of a good joke and the importance of self-reliance. Her father introduced her to *On the Road* by Jack Kerouac, whose autobiographical style greatly informed Dillard's later methods of writing. Despite their maverick personalities, Dillard's parents were of an affluent, country-club set that disturbed Dillard in her teens. She began to rebel, at one point abandoning her Presbyterian roots and thus beginning a lifelong inquiry into the diversity and relevance of theology.

Dillard's maiden name was Doak. She changed it upon marrying Richard Dillard, her writing teacher at Hollins College in Virginia. There she studied English and theology, earning both her bachelor's and master's degrees and producing a thesis on Thoreau's *Walden* that dealt with the notion of concentrating on a single geographic location in order to bridge Earth and heaven. Some of this idea would prompt *Pilgrim at Tinker Creek* (1974), a series of linked essays exploring the landscape around the narrator's rural home. Dillard follows Thoreau's lead in describing a sort of self-imposed exile for the purpose of achieving a studied focus, a personal illumination through the contemplation of nature. The opening of the book is a dazed account of a tomcat that leaves bloody pawprints on the narrator's body as she sleeps. It is a wild image, an acknowledgment of an uncontrollable, animal world. Dillard spends the rest of the book veering between upholding and retracting this acknowledgment, applying neat theories to the workings of the world and

then insisting on her own absolute ignorance. This dance is designed to lead toward enlightenment. A building stock of factual knowledge and philosophical acumen creates tension with the idea that one cannot, in fact, know or understand the complex world: such a tension, for Dillard, compels a divine awe free of ego. Much of *Pilgrim at Tinker Creek* is about the art of seeing, or rather the practiced ability to see that which, most of the time, is invisible to most people. In one chapter, Dillard describes the process of learning to see the egg cases of praying mantises. Once she begins to find them, she finds them everywhere—she is suddenly in tune with her environment in a new, small way. Another chapter is given to the phenomenon of sight being restored to the blind, querying the meaning of physical forms when they are revealed to those who previously could not see them. Dillard works herself into a revelatory celebration of a kind of seeing that is perpetually fresh, unburdened of association or precedent. Together, the essays in *Pilgrim at Tinker Creek* are an investigation of human perspective, both spiritual and physical.

Dillard suffered a near-fatal case of pneumonia in 1971. It was after this brush with death that she decided she needed to engage life completely and moved to Tinker Creek, in Virginia. An obsessive keeper of journals, she composed *Pilgrim at Tinker Creek* largely in day-to-day deliberations over her surroundings. She legendarily became so fixated on her writing that she began spending fifteen hours or more daily on her journals, eschewing food and sleep to write. Although much of the book is decidedly secular, Dillard regards it as theologically based. Worried about the response an audience might have to a theological book written by a woman, she hesitated to publish the manuscript. However, *Pilgrim at Tinker Creek* was released to massive critical and popular acclaim, and Dillard received the Pulitzer Prize for it in 1975.

## THE WRITER AS READER

If *Pilgrim at Tinker Creek* is an appreciation of home and immediacy, the book of essays *Teaching a Stone to*

*Talk: Expeditions and Encounters* (1982) is a salute to travel. The title of the volume is in reference to the silent language of nature, the world's refusal to explain itself. Dillard finds this refusal in the Galapagos Islands, in the Arctic Circle, in a solar eclipse viewed from a hilltop in the state of Washington. She departs in *Teaching a Stone to Talk* from specificity and detail and begins to address the universality of places and ideas. In the long, fragmented centerpiece to the book, an essay entitled "An Expedition to the Pole," Dillard explains her perpetual spiritual exploration as analogous to Arctic expeditions. She argues that the impulse to reach beyond charted boundaries is vital to an understanding of one's self in the world. Her project is always to reveal the extraordinary within the ordinary, and she insists that to do so one must journey past everyday perspectives: rather than bending over mantis egg cases in a focused meditation, the idea now is to fling one's attention into the unknown distance.

Dillard has consistently presented herself foremost as a reader—literally of books as well as figuratively of environment. Her memoir of early life in Pittsburgh, *An American Childhood* (1987), can be taken as an account of the development of Dillard's reading, from her fascination with field guides as a child to the Bible to the French Symbolists. The sheer randomness of Dillard's personal reading list is characteristic of her approach to information and ideas. At times she seems to be cobbling together bunches of mismatched conjectures, but ultimately she manages to draw them together into a sensible, cumulative finish. The logic of the British Christian academic C. S. Lewis, the unruliness of the French poet Arthur Rimbaud, and the metaphysics of Emerson weave a diverse backdrop for Dillard's thinking, the common principle for all being a fanatical devotion to ideas—this, boiled down, is Dillard's concept of divinity. Dillard maintains that her aim in writing is to get people to recognize the mystical in a material universe. Her diagnosis of the problem of modern humanity, as stated in *Teaching a Stone to Talk*, is that science has erased faith in the mass population. Because we know so much about our natural environment, we are blind to the miracles of it. Dillard's curious approach to combating this problem is to incorporate science into faith, to scrutinize factual conditions in order to heighten the marvel of the thing. For Dillard, learning the intricacies of nature does not inescapably need to interrupt the mystery of it.

## CRITICISM, FICTION, AND POETRY

In 1982 Dillard had published a book of literary criticism called *Living by Fiction* in which she discusses the "contemporary modernists," a loosely organized group of writers including Argentinian Jorge Luis Borges, Italian Italo Calvino, and Americans John Barth, Donald Barthelme, and Thomas Pynchon—by and large the same group popularly termed the "postmodernists." In 1989 she turned from readerly concerns to writerly ones in *The Writing Life*, a chronicle of the habits and trials of a full-time writer. Because most of Dillard's writing is at least partly autobiographical, her own identity figures heavily into the direction of her discourse; Dillard's role as a writer is fundamental to her identity, and therefore a book about writing was an obvious next step for her. If her thematic preoccupations lean toward perspective and observation, they also involve the need to communicate those observations. However, Dillard is at her best in direct, Emersonian examination of the world rather than in secondhand examination as filtered through critique of other writers or of the act of writing itself, and neither *Living by Fiction* nor *The Writing Life* are among her strongest works.

*The Living* (1992) is Dillard's first foray into true fiction. An epic novel dealing with the multiracial population of the nineteenth-century Washington Territory, *The Living* treats history much as *Pilgrim at Tinker Creek* treats theology: as immediate, intricate, fascinating, and changing. Other books by Dillard include the small but popular volume, *Holy the Firm* (1977), about Dillard's time living on an island in Puget Sound, and two books of poetry, *Tickets for a Prayer Wheel* (1974) and *Mornings Like This: Found Poems* (1995). Dillard's more recent work, *For the Time Being* (1999), recounts her travels to China and Israel in the inclusive, essayistic style of her earlier compositions.

Dillard's marriage to Richard Dillard did not last, and she remarried several times. She teaches at Wesleyan University in Connecticut, where she is a writer-in-residence. Along with the Pulitzer Prize, Dillard has been the recipient of fellowships from the Guggenheim Foundation and the National Endowment for the Arts.

[See also American Essay, The; Nature Writing: Prose; and Kerouac's *On the Road*.]

## WORKS

*Tickets for a Prayer Wheel* (1974)
*Pilgrim at Tinker Creek* (1974)

*Holy the Firm* (1977)

*Teaching a Stone to Talk: Expeditions and Encounters* (1982)

*Living by Fiction* (1982)

*Encounters with Chinese Writers* (1984)

*An American Childhood* (1987)

*The Writing Life* (1989)

*The Living* (1992)

*Mornings Like This: Found Poems* (1995)

*For the Time Being* (1999)

## FURTHER READING

Johnson, Sandra Humble. *The Space Between: Literary Epiphany in the Work of Annie Dillard.* Kent, Ohio, 1992.

Parrish, Nancy C. *Lee Smith, Annie Dillard, and the Hollins Group: A Genesis of Writers.* Baton Rouge, La., 1998. Addresses both the development of private Southern Women's schools and the writing culture at Hollins College, from which Dillard emerged.

Smith, Linda L. *Annie Dillard.* New York, 1991.

# E. L. DOCTOROW

*by Patrick A. Smith*

E. L. Doctorow was born on 6 January 1931 in the Bronx, New York, the second child of David and Rose Doctorow. His parents, both second-generation Russian-Jewish immigrants, and his grandfather, who had settled in New York City from Russia, instilled in him a passion for books, intellectual curiosity, and an appreciation for history—no doubt punctuated by his having lived through the worst years of the Great Depression—that would influence him in his career as a writer.

Doctorow received the traditional education of the Jewish male, though it was the eclectic and diverse aspects of his grandfather's and father's personalities that would inculcate themselves most in the young boy's mind. He recalls that his grandfather, a printer by trade, was an intellectual, an atheist, a socialist, and a chess player. His father was more of a romantic and a dreamer (not unlike many of Doctorow's characters), a failed businessman who later became a salesman in order to support his family.

Doctorow graduated from the Bronx High School of Science in 1948 and subsequently attended Ohio's Kenyon College, renowned for its liberal arts programs, where he studied literature and philosophy with classmate and poet James Wright and under the noted scholar and Agrarian poet John Crowe Ransom. After obtaining a degree in philosophy in 1952, Doctorow returned to New York City to attend graduate school at Columbia University (he was forced to turn down an appointment at Yale with Robert Penn Warren, to whom Ransom had introduced the young aesthete, because of impending military service). After a year at Columbia, Doctorow joined the U.S. Army and spent time in Germany. In 1954, he married Helen Setzer, whom he had met at Columbia.

E. L. Doctorow.
(© *Bettmann/Corbis*)

## "I CAN LIE BETTER THAN THESE PEOPLE"

After completion of his tour of duty, Doctorow worked from 1956 to 1959 at various jobs in the entertainment and publishing industries, including one as a script reader for Columbia Pictures. During his fitfully satisfying stint evaluating other peoples' writing, Doctorow became convinced that "I can lie better than these people" (Trenner, p. 34), and he set out to pen a novel. Although he had never been west of Ohio, the result of his first foray into fiction was *Welcome to Hard Times* (1960), a Western that turned the genre on its ear.

For the next decade, Doctorow made a living as an editor and vice president with New American Library and Dial Press. While he was at Dial, Simon and Schuster published *Big as Life* (1966), a rarely mentioned science-fiction novel. He left the publishing world for a turn in academe, moving several times over the course of the next two years before finally settling at New York University, teaching creative writing since 1982.

While Doctorow's style has evolved into a distinctive mélange of historical fact, neatly drawn complementary fictive characters, narrative experimentation, and big ideas, he has managed to maintain a popular reading audience (a handful of novels have become feature films), at the same time becoming a respected literary writer. Most of Doctorow's published work has been in the form of novels, although he has also published short fiction in the collection *Lives of the Poets* (1984); a play, *Drinks before Dinner* (1979); and essays in *Jack London, Hemingway, and the Constitution: Selected Essays, 1977–1992* (1993).

*Welcome to Hard Times* received general critical acclaim, though the novel little predicts what would come later in the author's fiction. Still, as Doctorow points out, "You write to find out what you're writing. It was only after I had written those first two books, for example, that I developed a rationale for the approaches I had taken—that I liked the idea of using disreputable genre materials and doing something serious with them. I liked invention. I liked myth" (Trenner, p. 36). The author's first attempt at fiction details the massacre of a group of settlers in the Dakota Territory town of Hard Times and their response to the attack, perpetrated by the Bad Man from Bodie, Clay Turner, a character whose predilection for violence is nearly absurd. Set against Turner are the characters Molly Riordan and Jimmy Fee, two victims of the Bad Man's rampage.

The story is narrated by Blue, the town's titular mayor, who records the events and attempts to rebuild the town with Molly by his side; Blue's presence illustrates the ineffectuality with which the victims react to the unprovoked violence in their lives. The novel recalls the Westerns of Louis L'Amour and the naturalist fiction of Stephen Crane (the surname Blue, for instance, suggesting Crane's impressionism), though Doctorow managed to create a wholly original "anti-Western" myth in response to the genre's conventions.

*Big As Life*, which Doctorow has publicly decried as a failed attempt at science fiction, is a melodrama in the mold of H. G. Wells's (and Orson Welles's) *The War of the Worlds*, though the characters that Doctorow creates—a pair of unimaginably tall and slow aliens that have fallen into New York Harbor through a rip in space-time—do not lend themselves to the vitality of the genre. Rather, they set forth ideas on collective action and social responsibility that Doctorow treats with more suitable characters and contexts in his later fiction.

## REPEATING HISTORY

Doctorow's reputation as a literary writer begins with *The Book of Daniel* (1971), a narrative tour de force that combines an intimate association with history and its impact on the present with the author's politics of ideas. Unlike his previous two novels, *The Book of Daniel* eschews the traditional linear narrative and challenges the reader to piece together snapshot images and various voices in order to fully comprehend the novel's complex sociopolitical associations.

The plot has as its backdrop the execution for treason of Paul and Rochelle Isaacson, told primarily through the voice of the narrator, their son Daniel. The book is based on the highly publicized conviction and execution of spies Julius and Ethel Rosenberg in 1953. What is less transparent to the reader than the novel's

historical background is the number of angles from which Doctorow attacks the narrative, shifting from present time to the distant past (the political upheaval of the 1960s, for instance, interspersed with scenes from the Depression) and changing points of view, so that the novel's "meaning," finally, becomes an accretion of the different images conjured up by Isaacson and the author.

In addition to Daniel's voice, which casts him as several different characters with one identity, the narrative delves into the minds of his parents and contains digressions on such topics as American history, czarist Russia, and Disneyland. The climate of the times acts as a parallel to McCarthyism and the "Red Scare" of the 1950s. Of Doctorow's work, *The Book of Daniel* is his most overtly political.

Doctorow's preoccupation with history gained momentum in *Ragtime* (1975), his most popular novel and winner of the National Book Critics Circle Award. The narrative presents the historically based characters Harry Houdini, J. P. Morgan, Henry Ford, Emma Goldman, and a host of others involved in a fictive storyline that immerses itself in the American Dream, social identity, and America's discomfort with racial, immigration, and class issues in the opening decades of the twentieth century.

The successful family, whose members are unwittingly drawn into a scene that juxtaposes traditional values with the lure of materialism and the outward trappings of success, is comprised of quintessential American social climbers. Coalhouse Walker, an African-American musician, visits the family weekly to see his lover, who works for the family, and his child. When he is mistreated by a group of volunteer firefighters, Walker goes on a rampage, demanding retribution for their actions and, in an increasing circle of violence, threatening to destroy the Pierpont Morgan Library. Walker's dilemma is a stark reminder for the family of the inequities that exist in society.

*Loon Lake* (1980), which won the National Book Critics Circle Award, is a similar novel in its exploration of the American sensibility in a particular moment in time, and further examines the boundaries of narrative in a novel that requires the reader to construct reality from several versions of the same event. In the summer of 1936, a street tough named Joe leaves the comfortable world of Paterson, New Jersey, where he has made a name for himself as a petty criminal, and heads into the wilderness. After coming into contact with hobos and a carnival owner, whom Joe cuckolds, he has an epiphany when he sees a beautiful blonde woman standing naked in a train window. Lured by that image to the estate of F. W. Bennett, Joe discovers the reason that he has been compelled to travel to this place.

*World's Fair* (1985), which won the American Book Award, once again delves into the past to make sense, finally, of the present. The narrative, what Doctorow has deemed a "novel"—though the narrative's autobiographical component is at times apparent, and it takes the form of a memoir that concludes before the protagonist turns ten years old—is redolent with the sense of history and more than a touch of nostalgia. Edgar Altschuler is a middle-aged man who recalls the events of his life and focuses on the most important issues in Doctorow's fiction, namely family, the shifting nature of reality, and the privilege of the writing experience over any contrived "plot." Although he balks at the notion that any writer's work must be either autobiographical or wholly a product of the author's imagination, Doctorow concedes that there are facts in the book that coincide with the facts of his own life.

In much the same way, *Billy Bathgate* (1989), a tremendous critical and popular success (winner of the National Book Critics Circle Award and the PEN/Faulkner Award for Fiction), is similarly concerned with circumscribing a world that exists, if only for a time, in the minds of the author and the reader, the two connected by their common knowledge of the subject matter. In this case, the author leads a tour through the seedy historical underbelly of New York City in the 1930s, the heyday of organized crime, when the title character meets the infamous gangster Dutch Schultz and becomes privy to the inner workings of his gang. Drawing on his earlier career as a professional reader, Doctorow uses the generic conventions of film and the crime novel and translates those properties into a novel that neatly describes the period and the contradictory wonder and disillusionment that are part of the American experience.

## NOVELS OF IDEAS

Doctorow draws on the image of a drowned child in the city's reservoir from a short sketch, "The Waterworks," in his collection *Lives of the Poets* (1984) for the novel of the same name. *The Waterworks* (1994) also recalls Doctorow's early work, in this case his experimentation with science fiction in *Big as Life*, though here in the historical context of New York City in the 1870s, in which Tammany Hall, the corrupt sphere of influence of the infamous Boss Tweed, still holds sway—if only just—over the city's goings-on. The advance

of technology, embodied in the ethically questionable machinations of Dr. Sartorius, is seen as a suspicious endeavor even in a society obsessed with progress. The novel's narrator, an editor named McIlvaine, relates that one of his best freelancers, the passionate social reformer Martin Pemberton, has disappeared. Pemberton has insisted that he has seen his deceased father, the wealthy Augustus, riding in a carriage through the city.

The novel recalls the gothic horror of Edgar Allan Poe, although Doctorow maintains an ironic distance from his material that situates the focus of the narrative directly on the city-as-character and the culture of capitalism and greed that gains momentum during the Gilded Age. Pemberton's railing against the corruption of the Gilded Age provides a counterpoint to the work of Sartorius and the entitlement of wealth.

*City of God* (2000) is the culmination of Doctorow's quest for the quasi-fictional narrative and a book concerned with ideas and connections. As in *The Book of Daniel*, Doctorow keeps the reader off balance with different narrative strategies and points of view that, only in the abstract and only from a distance, coalesce into a narrative that resembles a "novel" (and this effort, less than any other, would be considered such in the traditional sense). The narrative's plot involves the case of a purloined cross, and the relationships between Pemberton, a priest, Joshua and Sarah, husband-and-wife rabbis, and Everett, a novelist given to philosophical meanderings. Fittingly, the novel combines the characters' memories of war and the Holocaust with commentaries on society (including appearances by Albert Einstein, Ludwig Wittgenstein, and Frank Sinatra) only loosely held together, it seems, by any recognizable context.

The work is significant in the body of Doctorow's fiction as a testament to the continuing evolution of his narrative technique and his thorough attention to—and an unflagging passion for—history cultivated over more than four decades. Doctorow has established himself as a dominant figure in American letters—and an influence on many writers of note, Steven Millhauser and Paul Auster among them—and his work recalls the greats of American fiction: Vladimir Nabokov, Philip Roth, John Barth, and Norman Mailer, as well as Poe, Melville, and Faulkner. Doctorow's legacy to American fiction is, in addition to his knack for attracting wide and diverse reading audiences, his ability to imaginatively examine events and characters under the lens of history. From those creations come narratives whose vitality and urgency give them significance in the present, as they examine the essential nature of identity, perception, myth, and injustice.

## WORKS

*Welcome to Hard Times* (1960)
*Big as Life* (1966)
*The Book of Daniel* (1971)
*Ragtime* (1975)
*Drinks before Dinner: A Play* (1979)
*Loon Lake* (1980)
*Lives of the Poets: Six Stories and a Novella* (1984)
*World's Fair* (1985)
*Billy Bathgate* (1989)
*Jack London, Hemingway, and the Constitution: Selected Essays, 1977–1992* (1993)
*The Waterworks* (1994)
*City of God* (2000)

## FURTHER READING

Bloom, Harold, ed. *E. L. Doctorow*. Philadelphia, 2002. Twelve essays that examine the theme of injustice in Doctorow's work. Includes a chronology and bibliography.

Fowler, Douglas. *Understanding E. L. Doctorow*. Columbia, S.C., 1992. A general critical overview and close reading of Doctorow's work up to *Billy Bathgate.*

Harter, Carol C., and James R. Thompson. *E. L. Doctorow.* Boston, 1990. Biographical/critical examination of Doctorow's work up to *World's Fair.*

Morris, Christopher D. *Models of Misrepresentation: On the Fiction of E. L. Doctorow.* Jackson, Miss., 1991. A collection of critical essays on Doctorow's fiction.

Morris, Christopher D., ed. *Conversations with E. L. Doctorow.* Jackson, Miss., 1999. A collection of interviews and features on the author that gives a comprehensive overview of Doctorow's life and work in his own words.

Siegel, Ben, ed. *Critical Essays on E. L. Doctorow.* New York, 2000. A collection of critical essays on Doctorow's fiction.

Trenner, Richard, ed. *E. L. Doctorow: Essays and Conversations.* Princeton, N.J., 1983. A collection of interviews and essays on Doctorow's early work. Provides access to articles that may be otherwise difficult to find.

Williams, John. *Fiction as False Document: The Reception of E. L. Doctorow in the Postmodern Age.* Columbia, S.C., 1996. A collection of essays that explores Doctorow's work in the context of postmodernism. A good introduction to critical work on Doctorow and a source for bibliographical material on both Doctorow and postmodernism generally.

# JOHN DOS PASSOS

*by Robert Dowling*

John Roderigo Dos Passos was a major twentieth-century American novelist and self-styled "chronicler" of the American scene. He is best known for his contributions to the literary avant-garde of the 1920s and 1930s, most notably *Three Soldiers* (1921), *Manhattan Transfer* (1925), and the *U.S.A.* trilogy—*The 42nd Parallel* (1930), *1919* (1932), and *The Big Money* (1936). The most influential American reviewers of the early to mid-twentieth century, Edmund Wilson, Malcolm Cowley, and Granville Hicks, all welcomed Dos Passos as a foremost contributor to the modern American tradition. Dos Passos combined the artistic practices of literary naturalism and modernism and, significantly, foresaw many of the literary agendas that dominated postmodern writing in the late twentieth century.

John Dos Passos.
*(Courtesy of the Library of Congress)*

War veteran and successful corporate lawyer of Portuguese stock. John senior, married to another woman at the time of John's birth, legitimized his relationship with Lucy only after his first wife died in 1910. In the meantime, John the younger spent his childhood moving from place to place with his unorthodox mother, an experience he later referred to as his "hotel childhood." The transient nature of his first fourteen years left him with a taste and tolerance for the traveling life that would serve his career well. Dos Passos enjoyed a privileged education, graduating from the Choate School in 1911 and Harvard University in 1916 (at which time his father publicly acknowledged him as his own son). While at Harvard, he befriended E. E. Cummings, who later became one of America's finest modern poets. He and Cummings were strongly influenced by the imagist poetry of Amy Lowell and Ezra Pound, and they both published early poems in a 1917 collection, *Eight Harvard Poets*. Dos Passos was also working on a novel manuscript in the 1910s concerning his time in Cambridge, which would later be published as *Streets of the Night* (1923). Both Dos Passos and Cummings volunteered as ambulance drivers during World War I. Dos Passos himself served for the Norton-Harjes Ambulance Group in France, the American Red Cross Ambulance Corps in Italy (which gave him a dishonorable discharge for writing critical letters about the war effort), and the Medical Corps in France. After a brief period studying at the Sorbonne in Paris, he finished a novel based on his experiences as a wartime ambulance driver, *One Man's Initiation—1917* (1920), which sold a disappointing sixty-three copies in its opening six months.

Just before the eruption of World War II, Dos Passos effected a notorious shift in his political views from radical to reactionary and subsequently alienated many friends and critics on the Left. By the 1950s—a period in which literary stature depended largely on the extent to which an author challenged, rather than affirmed, the conservative establishment—Dos Passos had fallen so low in the eyes of the literary elite that James T. Farrell ironically remarked, "Dos Passos's liberalism has so decayed that his lifetime of work is not as important as two short stories and a wooden novel by Lionel Trilling." Trilling's single novel, *The Middle of the Journey* (1947), is no longer widely read, and Dos Passos's work is—but definitely not his lifetime's worth.

## EARLY YEARS

John Dos Passos was born in a Chicago hotel on 14 January 1896 to Lucy Addison Sprigg Madison, a well-to-do southern lady, and John Randolph Dos Passos, a Civil

## ON THE LEFT

The sales and reviews of his second novel, *Three Soldiers* (1921), were far more encouraging. *Three Soldiers* is a stark representation of wartime France and faced some controversy for its unromantic portraits of fighting men; regardless, it was widely praised as the first great novel to emerge from the European front. Equating the inhumanity of war with the greed of industrial capitalism, Dos Passos became fascinated by the Soviet revolution in Russia and began supporting labor struggles back home.

The publication of *Three Soldiers*, along with more experimental novels to come, secured his reputation as a favorite in French intellectual circles (Jean-Paul Sartre hailed him as "the greatest writer of our time" in 1947); indeed, he may have had more impact on French letters than any American author save Edgar Allan Poe. He earned the respect of many American writers abroad as well, members of the so-called Lost Generation including Ernest Hemingway, F. Scott Fitzgerald, and Ford Maddox Ford, who took advantage of the free atmosphere in postwar Europe to perform "modern" experiments on language and behavior. In 1925, Dos Passos published *Manhattan Transfer*, a groundbreaking work that conferred a distinctly American flavor upon the modern novel. The narrative bounces along in a jolting, almost cartoonish pace, which powerfully echoes pedestrian life in New York City between the wars. This technique—allowing syntax and structure to reflect material realities—makes his contribution to American letters incalculable. Not only did he introduce this narrative device more effectively than any American author has done before or since, but he additionally introduced a distinctly journalistic, near-objective narrator, which endows his stories with an eerie sense of veracity.

In 1927, Dos Passos published *Facing the Chair: Story of the Americanization of Two Foreignborn Workmen*, a defense of two working-class Italian immigrants, Sacco and Vanzetti, who were arrested for murder and ultimately executed. The crime created a media sensation, as the evidence against them was inconclusive and the case became symbolic for the members of the American Left of the U.S. government's overtly anti-immigrant and anti-labor position. Thousands of American radicals and liberals from all walks of life protested the trial. *Facing the Chair*, written under the auspices of the Sacco and Vanzetti Defense Committee, was a failed attempt to clear the Italians' names, and their executions further substantiated Dos Passos's belief that the United States was ruled by inhumane conservatism. Along with his defense of Sacco and Vanzetti, he visited the Soviet Union in 1928, served as editor for a time for the radical journal *New Masses*, and joined Theodore Dreiser to investigate the life of Kentucky miners in 1931. All of this led the American and European radical Left to declare Dos Passos one of their own. Regardless of the ideological ambiguity of his early novels, there is ample evidence to substantiate their claim. In the final sequence of his 1936 novel *The Big Money*, he returns to the Sacco and Vanzetti case and makes the (perhaps overstated) case that left-wing politics had been fully routed by reactionary control:

> they have clubbed us off the streets they are stronger they are rich they hire and fire the politicians the newspapereditors the old judges the small men with reputations the collegepresidents the ward heelers . . . all right you have won you will kill the brave men our friends tonight . . . we stand defeated America.

### U.S.A.

In 1929, Dos Passos married the writer Katherine Smith, a good friend of Ernest Hemingway's, whom he met while visiting the Hemingways in Key West, Florida. He and his wife spent the next few years traveling about, making social connections, writing, and generally enjoying themselves. All through the 1920s and 1930s, he wrote plays, essays, and fiction, along with a number of travel books such as *Rosinante to the Road Again* (1922), *Orient Express* (1927), *In All Countries* (1934), *The Villagers Are the Heart of Spain* (1937), and *Journeys between the Wars* (1938). Travel was Dos Passos's favorite diversion, but it also importantly served to clarify the distinctiveness of his home country rather than lure him into permanent expatriate status.

In 1930, Dos Passos revisited the stylistic ingenuity of *Manhattan Transfer* with *The 42nd Parallel*, which he followed with *1919* and *The Big Money* to create his masterpiece trilogy *U.S.A.* This trilogy testifies to Dos Passos's genius for capturing the frenetic pace of modern American progress. Each of the three novels interweaves every conceivable literary genre—the novel, the essay, biography, autobiography, journalism, song lyrics, and poetry. To this day, these books have lost none of their freshness. The trilogy opens with a short preface that embodies the psyche of modern man and ironically critiques the process of fulfilling the American Dream:

> The young man walks by himself, fast but not fast enough, far but not far enough (faces slide out of sight, talk trails into tattered scraps, footsteps tap fainter in alleys); he must catch

the last subway, the streetcar, the bus, run up the gangplanks of all the steamboats, register at all the hotels, work in the cities, answer the wantads, learn the trades, take up the jobs, live in all the boarding houses, sleep in all the beds. One bed is not enough, one job is not enough, one life is not enough. At night, head swimming with wants, he walks by himself alone.

*(The 42nd Parallel)*

All of his characters are driven by an ambitious drive of untold provenance. They are unexceptional, unromantic, and believable. The character Janey, for example, is introduced as a "plain thinfaced sandyhaired girl, quiet and popular with the teachers." His tone calls to mind a small-town librarian sweetly reciting Poe's "The Raven" to a circle of seated toddlers, merging American innocence and experience into a morbid practical joke. Middle-class professional ambition and sexual desire combine in Dos Passos to create pathological and immoral citizens, like his rising entrepreneur J. Ward Moorehouse. Wishing to impress a snooty and promiscuous society girl by making his fortune, Moorehouse curses the "damn Frenchman" she is enamored with and would "clench his fists and stride around the porch muttering, 'By gum, I can do it.'"

The plot is relentlessly interrupted by chapters that on the surface seem irrelevant and are written in a stream-of-consciousness prose style; for this reason, Dos Passos is often compared to James Joyce, but his writing is not derivative. There are four dominant chapter types in *U.S.A.*: the prose narrative itself, "The Camera Eye," the "Newsreel," and what he termed the "minute biography." The "Newsreel" sections employ popular songs, advertisements, and actual headlines from the *New York Herald Tribune*, which together display the monumental backdrop of international events in ironic contrast to the comparatively minor historical functions each character plays. Yet there is no sense of condescension—we are all being thrust about, the author implies, by the unstoppable tides of the modern world. "The Camera Eye" is an autobiographical mode that enables Dos Passos to slip out of the newslike reportage of his narrator and confess, among other things, his general distaste for social convention. He writes this, for example, about his time at Harvard: "four years under the ethercone breathe deep gently now that's the way to be a good boy one two three four five six get A's in some courses but don't be a grind be interested in literature but remain a gentleman don't be seen with Jews or socialists . . . and all the pleasant contacts will be useful in Later Life say hello pleasantly to everybody crossing the

yard." In his series of masterful biographical portraits, Dos Passos jokes sardonically about the celebrity status of the period's most noted successes, such as Thomas Edison, whose career seems so fantastical in its consummation of the rags-to-riches American Dream that Dos Passos begins to relate Edison's career with the heading "*(This part is written by Horatio Alger.)*" Along with Edison, there are portraits of Eugene Debs, the socialist candidate for president; "Big" Bill Haywood, the WWI leader; Minor C. Keith, the founder of United Fruit; Frank Lloyd Wright and Isadora Duncan; Henry Ford and J. P. Morgan; John Reed, Thorstein Veblen, Randolph Bourne, and Emma Goldman; Woodrow Wilson, and William Randolph Hearst—twenty-seven in all, nine a novel. Each figure is distinctly American, most favoring success over happiness.

Historians from all disciplines have explained in concrete terms the transformation of the Western world from monolithic Victorianism to modern disillusionment. But in *U.S.A.*, Dos Passos guides us through the process step by step, delineating the psychological and historical motives for the transition. *The 42nd Parallel* presents twenty-somethings striving for success in the industrial era, *1919* sends them to war-torn Europe, and *The Big Money* brings them back to their homeland, wishing for the freedom they felt in Europe and bewildered by the commercial buzz surrounding modern America—cars, Hollywood, the stock market, and all the rest. His central thesis is best expressed by one of the popular songs of the era, which he quotes in a *1919* newsreel: "*How are you goin' to keep 'em down on the farm / After they've seen Paree.*" Writing from the point of view of the character Anne Elizabeth, a respectable midwestern girl who volunteers in Europe, Dos Passos poignantly explains her conversion to modernism in concert with the transformation he himself underwent with thousands of other Americans volunteering, working, and fighting abroad during the war. Anne Elizabeth gently blames the erotic European atmosphere for her loss of virginity: "there was something about the rainy landscape and the dark lasciviouseyed people and the old names of the towns and the garlic and oil in the food and the smiling voices and the smell of the tiny magenta wildflowers he said were called cyclamens *that made her not care anymore*" (italics added). Here is the conversion in shorthand. Up to that point his characters care too much, accept social conventions out of hand, and obsess over their career paths. The Great War, Dos Passos says, for better or worse, stopped people from caring,

caring about the consequences of their behavior either on themselves or on others.

Although many Marxist critics of the time praised Dos Passos's *U.S.A.* as a monumental socialist text, Dos Passos was not a Marxist. Henrik Ibsen once complained that his play *A Doll's House* was not, as so many believed, a feminist play but a "humanist" one. The same logic might be applied to Dos Passos's *U.S.A.* and his early social philosophy in general. His friend Hutchins Hapgood summed up Dos Passos's humanist views with a simple but telling anecdote:

> An incident . . . happened the other day when he was talking about a neighbor. This man is a lawyer and has no radical tendencies, but Dos likes him very much because he is, Dos said, "a good human being." This might not appear significant, except for the habit among our radicals to sneer at anyone who doesn't hold their views, and to have nothing to do with such a person. Dos, however, is not only a good man himself, but sees that the objective of all our social activities is to make a society of good men.
>
> (Hapgood, *A Victorian in the Modern World*, 1939)

## ON THE RIGHT

Before World War II, Dos Passos was a political pragmatist. Indeed, he remained allied to the Western Left only so long as he believed its practitioners defended human justice. But a reversal occurred in the spring of 1937 when Dos Passos and Hemingway accompanied Joris Ivens to Spain with the intent of making a documentary film about the Spanish civil war (1936–1939). The Spanish war acutely reflected the bipartisan political struggles back in the United States and throughout Europe; it was perceived as a confrontation between communists and anarchists loyal to the Republic on the left and insurgent fascist Nationalists on the Right. But American observers were naive to assume a clean divide: the Loyalists, as they were known, experienced often violent disunity. While Dos Passos was there, for example, a Republican friend of his, the physician José Robles, was executed by the communist secret police "with the butt end of a rifle," as he recounted it in his 1937 essay "Farewell to Europe." Robles's murder turned Dos Passos against both the Loyalist efforts in Spain and a number of his good friends who continued to support them, including his longtime companion Ernest Hemingway; it may have also been the straw that broke his tenuous trust of left-wing political movements.

"Farewell to Europe" was a public disavowal of the European Left in favor of American democracy. He described communism in the pre–Cold War era as a system that generated "giant bureaucratic machines for anti-human power." He remained consistent throughout his life in his defense of those "plodding among the snarling machineries of our world" ("The Communist Party")—his "snarling machine" had simply shifted from exploitative industrial capitalism to Soviet dictatorship.

Dos Passos's second trilogy, *District of Columbia*, includes *Adventures of a Young Man* (1939), a fictional reproduction of Dos Passos's disillusionment with leftist politics in the United States (it concludes with the execution of a misguided American idealist by Communists in the Spanish Civil War); *Number One* (1943), a novel based on the gubernatorial dictatorship of Huey P. Long in Louisiana; and *The Grand Design* (1949), a gloomy account of the Franklin D. Roosevelt years. These novels are generally regarded as major disappointments, and none has received much critical consideration. He continued to write at a furious pace over the next two decades, but none of his later work, aside from selections of his novel *Midcentury* (1961), matches the technical genius of *Manhattan Transfer* or *U.S.A.* Unlike the complex political ambiguities that single out those earlier novels, such as the socialist-humanist identity paradox, Dos Passos's later work relied heavily on the tenets of American conservatism—patriotic sentimentalism, emphasis on the evils of Stalin over Hitler, distaste for organized labor, and fury over younger generations' abandonment of traditional values. He even argued in interviews that Joseph McCarthy, the most rabid member of the House Un-American Activities Committee (HUAC), had been unjustly characterized in the years that followed. He complained to one journalist in 1959 that compared to past mistakes, "you can't take the 'McCarthy Terror' too seriously. Some people were inconvenienced, yes, but their shouts were out of all proportion to their injuries." In 1959 not even Richard Nixon, a former member of HUAC, would have made such a statement.

In 1947, Dos Passos lost his wife Katherine in a car accident. Two years later he married Elizabeth Holdridge. They had a daughter, Lucy, and remained happily married until Dos Passos's death at their Virginia home on 28 September 1970. Over the last two decades of his life Dos Passos turned to American history to bolster his views on American individualism, exploring the individualist ideologies, or lack thereof, of national heroes in massive volumes of subjective historical interpretation: *The Head and Heart of Thomas Jefferson* (1954), *The Men Who Made the Nation* (1957), *Mr. Wilson's* War (1962), and *The Shackles of Power: Three Jeffersonian*

*Decades* (1966). He published his autobiography, *The Best of Times: An Informal Memoir*, in 1966. His novel *Midcentury* (1961) is the only notable return to the stylistic mosaic that had made him a "great" American author—one who challenged and transformed the literary status quo. But though the prodigious novel brings in more recent historical figures—James Dean, Jimmy Hoffa—*Midcentury* recycles rather than reinvents his stylistic genius.

Dos Passos traveled the spectrum of American political thought over the course of his life. He started early in the radical Left, then adopted a more pragmatic liberal perspective, and finally moved swiftly from conservative to reactionary to radical libertarian. But the critical view of Dos Passos as a traitor to the literary Left has had tragic consequences on his legacy. "Thus the destiny," James T. Farrell wrote, "of any man who is guilty of the sin of disillusionment." A testimony to this author's genius is that John Dos Passos anticipated a number of major literary preoccupations that would follow his tenure as American "chronicler"—the stylistic inclusion of mass media, the blending together of disparate genres, the mordant portrayal of American materialism, the sense that monolithic ideologies are as blinding as they can be progressive. Further, he presented these concerns with more clarity, vision, and stylistic innovation than many of his more politically consistent contemporaries whose reputations have remained intact.

[*See also* Dreiser, Theodore; Fitzgerald, F. Scott; Hapgood, Hutchins; Hemingway, Ernest; *and* Wilson, Edmund.]

## WORKS

*One Man's Initiation—1917* (1920)
*Three Soldiers* (1921)
*Rosinante to the Road Again* (1922)
*A Pushcart at the Curb* (1922)
*Streets of the Night* (1923)
*Manhattan Transfer* (1925)
*The Garbage Man* (1926)
*Orient Express* (1927)
*Facing the Chair: Story of the Americanization of Two Foreignborn Workmen* (1927)
*Airways, Inc.* (1928)
*The 42nd Parallel* (1930)
*1919* (1932)
*Three Plays: The Garbage Man, Airways, Inc., Fortune Heights* (1934)
*In All Countries* (1934)
*The Big Money* (1936)
*The Villagers Are the Heart of* Spain (1937)
*Journeys between the Wars* (1938)

*U.S.A.* (in one volume) (1938)
*Adventures of a Young Man* (1939)
*The Ground We Stand On* (1941)
*Number One* (1943)
*State of the Nation* (1944)
*The Grand Design* (1949)
*The Prospect before Us* (1950)
*Chosen Country* (1951)
*The Head and Heart of Thomas Jefferson* (1954)
*Most Likely to Succeed* (1954)
*The Theme Is Freedom* (1956)
*The Men Who Made the Nation* (1957)
*The Great Days* (1958)
*Prospects of a Golden Age* (1959)
*Midcentury* (1961)
*Mr. Wilson's War* (1962)
*Brazil on the Move* (1963)
*Thomas Jefferson: The Making of a President* (1964)
*The Shackles of Power: Three Jeffersonian Decades* (1966)
*The Best of Times: An Informal Memoir* (1966)
*The Portugal Story: Three Centuries of Exploration and Discovery* (1969)
*Easter Island, Island of Enigmas* (posthumous) (1971)
*Century's Ebb: The Thirteenth Chronicle* (posthumous) (1975)

## FURTHER READING

Aaron, Daniel. *Writers on the Left: Episodes in American Literary Communism.* New York, 1992.

Becker, George J. *John Dos Passos.* New York, 1974. A critical biography of Dos Passos's writing rather than of his personal life.

Belkind, Allen, ed. *Dos Passos, the Critics, and the Writer's Intention.* Carbondale, Ill., 1971. Collection of Dos Passos criticism.

Carr, Virginia Spencer. *Dos Passos: A Life.* Garden City, N.Y., 1984. Contributes to our understanding (and Ludington's) of Dos Passos's personal life. Carr was assisted by many of Dos Passos's relations from his second marriage, including his widow, Elizabeth Dos Passos, his daughter, Lucy, and her husband.

Casey, Janet Galligani. *Dos Passos and the Ideology of the Feminine.* New York, 1998. Dos Passos supplied many women characters in his fiction. Casey's book studies these characters in the context of 1920s and 1930s feminism.

Doctorow, E. L. "Foreword." *U.S.A.* New York, 1991. Brief, artful biographical essay on Dos Passos by the contemporary American author most often compared to him.

Farrell, James T. "How Should We Rate Dos Passos?" In *Literary Essays*. Port Washington, N.Y., 1976, pp. 118–121. Farrell, a major American author, criticizes the literary Left's rejection of Dos Passos's work as a result of his political transition.

Feied, Frederick. *No Pie in the Sky: The Hobo As American Cultural Hero in the Works of Jack London, John Dos Passos, and Jack Kerouac*. New York, 2001. Treatment of Dos Passos's hobo characters as evidence of the failed efforts of the Left to curb the effects of industrial capitalism.

Hook, Andrew, ed. *John Dos Passos: A Collection of Critical Essays*. Englewood Cliffs, N.J., 1974. Major critics expound on Dos Passos's writing. Includes Jean-Paul Sartre's 1947 essay "John Dos Passos and '1919,'" in which he claims that Dos Passos is "the greatest writer of our time."

Landsberg, Melvin. *Dos Passos' Path to U.S.A.: A Political Biography 1912–1936*. Boulder, Colo., 1972.

Ludington, Townsend, ed. *The Fourteenth Chronicle: Letters and Diaries of John Dos Passos*. Boston, 1973. Biographical material by Dos Passos from 1910 to just before his death. Includes personal confessions, travel notes, and political analysis. Useful primer for Ludington's follow-up biography.

Ludington, Townsend. *John Dos Passos: A Twentieth Century Odyssey*. New York, 1980. A monumental, near-definitive biography. Employs every accessible scrap of biographical material. More than you would ever need to know about Dos Passos.

Maine, Barry. *Dos Passos: The Critical Heritage*. London and New York, 1988. Critical essays on Dos Passos from the 1920s to the 1980s.

Nanney, Lisa. *John Dos Passos Revisited*. Farmington Hills, Mich., 1998. Treats Dos Passos in light of his lesser-known writing, his friendships, and the visual arts. Synthesizes recent Dos Passos criticism with a concentration on aesthetics and artistic movements that contributed to Dos Passos's work.

Pizer, Donald. *John Dos Passos: The Major Nonfictional Prose*. Detroit, 1988. Reveals more than any other collection the discourse between Dos Passos and his critics from the Left. Fine biographical introduction by the editor.

Pizer, Donald. U.S.A.: *A Critical Study*. Charlottesville, Va., 1988. The finest explanation of Dos Passos's narrative strategies. Of particular importance is his explication of the four main generic modes Dos Passos employs—the prose narrative itself, "The Camera Eye," the "Newsreel," and the "minute biography."

Rohrkemper, John. *John Dos Passos: A Reference Guide*. Farmington Hills, Mich., 1980.

Rosen, Robert C. *John Dos Passos: Politics and the Writer*. Lincoln, Neb., 1981. A close study of Dos Passos's political transformation with a brief look at the critical reception of *U.S.A.* by the Left.

Sanders, David. *The Merrill Studies in* U.S.A. Columbus, Ohio, 1972. Collection of reviews and essays pertaining to Dos Passos's fiction. A good place to start.

Wagner, Linda W. *Dos Passos, Artist as American*. Austin, Tex., 1979. Close readings of the body of Dos Passos's work. Particularly useful for a critical understanding of his lesser-known writing.

Waldmeir, John C. *The American Trilogy, 1900–1937: Norris, Dreiser, Dos Passos, and the History of Mammon*. West Cornwall, Conn., 1995. Concentrates on the genre of trilogy and its relation to political culture.

Wrenn, John H. *John Dos Passos*. New York, 1961. Short biography from the Twayne series. Distinctive in its appraisal of Dos Passos as a thinker more than author.

# FREDERICK DOUGLASS

*by Mark Richardson*

Any writer attempting an overview of Frederick Douglass's life and work confronts an embarrassment of riches: Douglass himself undertook the task not once but three times—in *The Narrative of the Life of Frederick Douglass, an American Slave, Written by Himself* (1845), *My Bondage and My Freedom* (1855), and *The Life and Times of Frederick Douglass, Written by Himself* (1881), a volume itself reprinted with additional material in 1892. Each book is rewarding in its own right, each sums up a distinct phase in Douglass's long and astonishingly productive career, and together they give us an indispensable record of the nineteenth century: of the abolition

Frederick Douglass.
*(Courtesy of the Library of Congress)*

movement; the meteoric rise of the Republican Party; the Civil War, Reconstruction; and beginning in the mid-1870s, the bitter forfeiture of the great emancipating enterprise that the better angels of our nature (as Lincoln might have said) have always held in view.

The reader of Douglass's autobiographies will necessarily become acquainted with the details of his eventful life, so it will do here to give only the barest outline. Douglass was born a slave in February 1818 on Maryland's eastern shore, the son of a white man named Frederick Augustus Washington Bailey, whom he never knew, and Harriet Bailey, a slave. He labored for his white owner, or for members of that man's family, on a series of farms in Maryland, and also in the city of Baltimore, where he taught himself to read and first resolved, someday, to make himself free. In 1838, using documents he had forged to secure safe passage, Douglass escaped to Philadelphia and then to New York City, where he was joined by his fiancée—a free black native of Baltimore, Anna Murray—whom he then married. The couple settled in New Bedford, Massachusetts, and started a family. Douglass sought work as a caulker, a trade he

had learned in Baltimore, and soon found himself drawn into the abolition movement, of which William Lloyd Garrison was then the leading light. From 1841 to 1847 he worked with the Garrisonians, both in America and in the United Kingdom, before settling in Rochester, New York, where he inaugurated his own paper, *The North Star* (later *Frederick Douglass's Paper*). There, he joined in the work of the antislavery Liberty Party, which had been founded by a New York State landholder named Gerrit Smith. After the Civil War, he relocated to Washington, D.C., and became an important figure in the Republican Party, holding such appointments as U.S. marshall for the District of Columbia and recorder of deeds. He campaigned tirelessly in every major election from 1868 to 1892, and served as consul general to Haiti from 1889 to 1891. On 20 February 1895, Douglass died at his house in Washington, which he had named Cedar Hill and which is maintained by the National Park Service.

## THE ABOLITION MOVEMENT

We can distinguish several important schools of antislavery thought in the period extending from the American Revolution to the Civil War, in two of which Frederick Douglass was a major figure. Thomas Jefferson's generation had, of course, looked vaguely forward to the gradual abolition of slavery, if by no other means than by the work of Almighty God. Proslavery sentiment was not, then, the rule in the South, and opposition to the institution, on moral grounds, was spread fairly evenly throughout the new nation. Obviously, no coherent program of action follows from the hope that slavery shall, simply, evanesce. But in conjunction with the idea of gradual emancipation arose various colonization schemes that sought to repatriate slaves, and in some cases, free persons of color to Africa, or as was sometimes suggested, to Haiti or some other Caribbean nation. Colonization, although never practical, enjoyed a vogue in the early decades of the nineteenth century, and persisted even into the middle years of the Civil War; among its legacies is the West African nation of Liberia.

Against both colonization schemes and gradualism arose the Garrisonian school, named for its founder and animating force, William Lloyd Garrison. Garrison called for immediate and unconditional emancipation, a doctrine he propounded through *The Liberator*, the weekly antislavery paper he published in Boston beginning in 1831. Immediacy was not the only novel element in his abolitionism; he also demanded full citizenship rights for black Americans. And with Garrison's appearance, the character of the antislavery movement forever changed.

Garrison refined his doctrine over the course of the 1830s. In August 1831 Nat Turner led an insurrection among slaves in Southampton, Virginia. More than fifty whites died in the fighting, and more than a hundred blacks. Virginia authorities called on the federal government, under the terms of the Constitution, to assist it in suppressing the rebellion. For this reason, and because the Constitution obliged states where slavery did not exist to return fugitive slaves to their owners, Garrison concluded that the Constitution was, both in theory and in practice, a "proslavery" instrument. It took some years for the new thinking to settle out, but here was the beginning of Garrisonian "disunionism": the call for the dissolution of the union, and for nonparticipation in its electoral politics. By 1842 the masthead of each number of *The Liberator* bore this unequivocal banner: "THE UNITED STATES CONSTITUTION IS A COVENANT WITH DEATH AND AN AGREEMENT WITH HELL! NO UNION WITH SLAVEHOLDERS!" With that, Garrisonian doctrine had matured, and here it would remain until war came in April 1861.

Garrison and his adherents traveled from Maine to Illinois, and beyond. They held rallies; debated their opponents, both within and without the wider abolition movement; distributed pamphlets, books, newspapers; raised money; and, on occasion, ritually burned copies of the U.S. Constitution in town squares. This is the movement Frederick Douglass entered with such force in 1841, and within months he was its most popular orator. His first autobiography, *Narrative of the Life of Frederick Douglass, an American Slave, Written by Himself*, appeared in 1845 with a preface by Garrison; advertisements for it ran in the pages of *The Liberator*; it was published out

of the same office in Cornhill Street, Boston, that printed Garrison's weekly; and the closing paragraphs of the book take special pains to extol the newspaper. Douglass's debt to the Garrisonians is evident in the *Narrative* from beginning to end.

## NARRATIVE OF THE LIFE OF FREDERICK DOUGLASS, AN AMERICAN SLAVE

Douglass wrote his *Narrative*, despite the fact that it would expose him to danger, for reasons later set out in *My Bondage and My Freedom*: "People doubted if I had ever been a slave. They said I did not talk like a slave, look like a slave, nor act like a slave, and that they believed I had never been south of Mason and Dixon's line." Accordingly, Douglass "wrote out the leading facts" connected with his experience, and thus "put it in the power of any who doubted, to ascertain the truth or falsehood" of his story. In an address before the 12th Annual Convention of the American Anti-Slavery Society in New York City on 6 May 1845, Douglass for the first time publicly identified by name his master, overseer, and a number of other men and women who figure in the *Narrative*. The book was published within a few days and in August he set sail for England. While abroad, Douglass continued his energetic schedule of lectures, traveling throughout the United Kingdom. His fundraising efforts on behalf of abolitionist organizations were richly rewarded, and in addition, British supporters of Douglass raised $711.66 to purchase his freedom from his Maryland master and thereby put him out of danger of recapture on his return to the United States in 1847.

The prose of this first and briefest of Douglass's three autobiographies is brisk and relatively unadorned. Although it is chiefly narrative in character rather than argumentative, a withering analysis of slavery nonetheless emerges from its pages. Slavery, as Douglass represents it, degrades slave and slaveholder alike. It puts all men out of temper, so to speak—sets the passions over reason, and the body, with all its unruly appetites, over the soul. Quite literally, slavery forces men a few steps down what Garrison, in his preface, calls "the scale of humanity"—down toward the "beasts" and away from the "angels." Slavery brutalizes men. For that reason alone, if for no others, it is contrary to the whole tendency of enlightenment and progress. So poisonous is the institution in this regard that the only sure recourse left to those who would oppose it is the severance of all ties that bind together slaveholding and nonslaveholding sections of the union: if thy right hand offend thee, cut it off. Douglass's *Narrative* perfectly supports the exhilarating, but impractical, call to break apart the nation and purify New England of complicity with sin. He would—to borrow a phrase from Wendell Phillips's letter congratulating him on the publication of the book—"consecrate" anew the sacred "soil of the Pilgrims." The *Narrative*, in Garrisonian fashion, invites not so much the extension and perfection of the American political experiment as a redemptive negation of that experiment, which, for the Garrisonians, had in any event done nothing but compromise, in the most worldly and decadent ways, the original Puritan errand into the wilderness.

## MY BONDAGE AND MY FREEDOM

Douglass's first autobiography was in all respects a smashing success. By 1849 it had gone through two editions in the United States and three in Great Britain. Why, then, did Douglass publish a second autobiography in 1855? The question is the more intriguing because only seven percent of the new book, by word count, covers ground not traversed in the *Narrative*; therefore, *My Bondage and My Freedom* is hardly a supplement to the earlier book and is not by any means its mere continuation. It is instead a radical revision. Moreover, in *The Life and Times of Frederick Douglass* (1881), the portion of the book devoted to the period through 1855 remains materially unchanged from *My Bondage and My Freedom*. There can be little doubt that the latter is Douglass's definitive account of himself although, regrettably, it is the earlier, shorter, more Garrisonian, and less politically complex text that is generally taught.

Having examined the Garrisonian school with which Douglass's first book is so intimately associated, we should, before turning to *My Bondage and My Freedom*, take account of the competing school of political abolitionism. This movement got its start in New York State around the small but influential Liberty Party, whose central figure and financial backer was the philanthropist Gerrit Smith. Smith and the Liberty Party maintained, against the Garrisonians, that the Constitution was antislavery in spirit, notwithstanding the clauses therein that provide for the return of fugitives, for the qualified protection of the slave trade, and for the use of federal power in suppressing insurrection. This position was dubious as a reading of the Constitution. But when put into practice it allowed, as Garrisonian disunionism did not, for the vigorous pursuit, through electoral politics, of a policy of abolition; it held out the productive promise of perfecting the Constitution, a possibility in harmony with the general tendency of American political development. Douglass had begun his drift toward political abolition in the late 1840s. The move was complete in 1851, when he merged his paper, *The North Star*, with the *Liberty Party Paper* and accepted financial backing from Smith in the new enterprise. When *My Bondage and My Freedom* appeared four years later, published by a firm in western New York State, the stronghold of political abolition, it bore a dedication to "Honorable Gerrit Smith as a slight token of esteem for his character, admiration for his genius and benevolence," and in gratitude for his "ranking slavery with piracy and murder," and for "denying it either a legal or constitutional existence" (*Autobiographies*, p. 104). The break with Garrison was irrevocable, and Douglass was castigated in the Garrisonian press, often in tawdry ways, as an apostate who had allowed himself to be "bought out" by Gerrit Smith.

The reader of *My Bondage and My Freedom* soon discovers that Douglass's apprenticeship to the Garrisonians had not been entirely to his liking. In an account of his watershed inaugural appearance on the podium in 1841, there appears a telling remark. After Douglass spoke, we are told, Garrison "took [him] as his text." The metaphor is homiletic. Douglass is the text on which Garrison's sermon is based; he is the "matter," Garrison the expositor; he is the body, Garrison the mind; he is the storyteller, Garrison the interpreter; he deals in facts, Garrison in theory. This, anyway, is the idea, and in it we see intimated the more patronizing features of Garrison's patronage. John Collins, a confederate of Garrison, accompanied Douglass on his first lecture tour, and in introducing him, inevitably called him "a graduate from the peculiar institution" with "his diploma written on [his] back." Douglass's body was, for the Garrisonians, the originating site of his writing; his scars, and not his words and thoughts, authenticated him. "I was," Douglass reports, "generally introduced as a '*chattel*'—a '*thing*'—a piece of southern 'property'—the chairman assuring the audience that *it* could speak." "Let us have the facts," the people told Douglass. So also said George Foster, another Garrisonian, when he tried to "pin" Douglass down to a "simple narrative." Or again: "Give us the facts," John Collins would say, "we will take care of the philosophy." It was not necessarily gratifying to be "taken as a text" for the expounding of other men, or to be pinned down to mere storytelling. Douglass began to feel that he was being discouraged, at least implicitly, from thinking too much. His office, essentially, was to show himself, and to obey.

To be sure, Douglass was on display when he mounted the stage in a way that neither Collins nor Foster nor Garrison, nor any of the white abolitionists, ever was: his black body was the matter, not his mind. Collins enjoins Douglass to "be himself" and "tell his story," but this may really mean: put on blackface, be a white man's idea of what a black man truly is; otherwise (so goes the unstated argument), no white man will recognize you; to a white audience you will be, and in the most literal sense of the word, "incredible." The abolitionist lecture hall becomes a theater for the staging of a singularly highbrow sort of minstrel show, with the familiar—and deeply sympathetic, to white hearts and minds—"plantation darkey," the sort of black man with whom these white northerners could most be at ease. "It was said to me," writes Douglass, "better have a *little* of the plantation manner of speech than not; 'tis not best that you seem too learned."

Who, then, shall best represent the slave? The question has both political and literary implications, and it was to address both that Douglass wrote *My Bondage and My Freedom.* In it he would lay claim to the main and most productive tradition in American politics, thereby breaking out of the confinements of Garrisonian doctrine He would appear, in its pages, not chiefly as a black man, and certainly not as a sentimental plantation darkey in contemplation of whom white women might weep, but as, in the words of James McCune Smith's fine introduction to the first edition of the book, the "Representative American man"—as, in fact, the very "type" of his countrymen. This required that any trace of the deference he shows in the *Narrative* with respect to the Garrisonians be expunged, the better that he might emerge from behind the mask of white patronage. Instead of authenticating prefaces and letters from white eminences, there appears in *My Bondage* the introduction just quoted, written by a black, Edinburgh-trained physician, James McCune Smith. And he puts the matter unforgettably: "The same strong self-hood" that led Douglass "to measure strength with Mr. Covey," the "Negro-breaker" whom Douglass challenged and humiliated while still in his teens, led him to "wrench himself from the embrace of the Garrisonians."

## DOUGLASS'S "PHILOSOPHY" OF SLAVERY

But what of Douglass's philosophy? Douglass takes the view—authorized, if any authority is needed, by the Declaration of Independence—that the will to be free is in fact "an inborn dream" of "human nature," and thus a "constant menace to slavery" that "all the powers of slavery" are "unable to silence or extinguish." Slavery, then, can never relax; it is an institution most "unnatural," whose price is eternal vigilance. Elsewhere, Douglass likens it to a temperamental and delicate machine, which requires "conductors or safety valves"—for example, the "holiday" permitted slaves at the turn of the New Year—"to carry off explosive elements inseparable from the human mind, when reduced to the condition of slavery." Men and women have to be taught to be slaves and masters. Slavery requires "learned" habits of mind and bearing, of which children are born "naturally" free. "The equality of nature," Douglass says, "is strongly asserted in childhood." Young boys, he says, feel a hatred of slavery that "springs from nature, unseared and unperverted." Nature, in fact, does "almost nothing to prepare men and women to be either slaves or slaveholders." At such moments Douglass advances what might be termed a romantic, or Rousseauian, argument: social institutions—in this case, slavery—deform us, pervert our native inclination to charity, loving kindness, and fair play. Left in a state of nature, we would all be noble (and democratic) savages. To the hoary question, "Does 'civilization' distort or complement human 'nature'?" he appears to answer: "The former, not the latter." Dispense with slavery, then, and all will be well, or anyway well enough.

But the ignoble cruelty of slavery as it developed in North America seems to require a more worldly explanation of our inhumanity—a bleaker, less reassuring one; and this, too, emerges in Douglass's narrative. "Inborn" to us, as well as a love of freedom, is a will to power that has markedly cruel features. Douglass's master, we are told, could commit "outrages, deep, dark and nameless." These outrages, as we know from facts soon narrated, are at once erotic and violent; they are nothing less than sadistic. But lest we see in him a monster, Douglass assures us that Captain Anthony "was not by nature worse than other men," any one of whom, we are left to conclude, is therefore quite "naturally" capable of binding a beautiful young woman to a ceiling joist with her upraised hands, stripping her to the waist, and after "shocking preliminaries," and to the accompaniment of "tantalizing epithets," no doubt lewd in nature, lashing her almost to the point of death, all the while taking "delight" in the prospect. Such is inborn human "nature" when it is allowed an uninhibited self-expression, when it is allowed free reign to satisfy its darker appetites.

And with this notion we light upon a view of mankind rather more Calvinistic than Rousseauian. Men are by "nature" savage—even depraved. They need, desperately, the redemptive complement of "discipline," of some sort of curb against their "freedom" to act. This discipline may be, to adopt a secular vocabulary, "civilization," notwithstanding its inevitable discontents, which are simply the price we pay to become something more than "a nation of savages" (to borrow Douglass's phrase for it). As Douglass sees it—and the mild paradox with which he expresses the point is nicely Freudian—the great desiderata are "the just *restraints* of *free* society": reason and chastity. These effect a sublimation, into more socially useful channels, of the rapacious will to power that is, by all appearances, simply the birthright of men. To realize his humanity, to transcend his animality, man must be disciplined—but disciplined with the tempering "whip" of reason, not with the incendiary lash of passion. The problem with slavery is not so much that it entails too much discipline, but that it involves discipline of the wrong kind—discipline that is in fact an expression of license (and lust), rather than an instrument of control. The slave system everywhere "robs its victims," master and slave alike, of every "earthly incentive" to lead "a holy life." This fact should chasten us all, for as Douglass says, "Capt. Anthony might have been as humane a man, and every way as respectable, as many who now oppose the slave system; certainly as humane and respectable as are members of society generally."

The twofold idea, to sum it up, is this: slavery sets the passions free, when in fact they should be imprisoned, and men's passions are everywhere the same. There is in all this a challenge to the more transcendental foundations of New England abolitionism. And Douglass's "philosophy" of slavery, in its bleaker phases, may well explain his willingness to adopt the much more worldly, and much less absolutist, tactic of political abolitionism. It may explain also why he could not, at the end of the day, accept the Garrisonian proposal that New England purify itself of slavery by dissolving the union. Men being what they "naturally" are, we could purify neither them nor any nation they compose simply by cutting the slave states loose. Abolition of the most radical sort—the sort Douglass calls for—is the never-ending effort to conquer what Mr. Kurtz, in Conrad's *Heart of Darkness* (1902), calls the "horror." The "horror" is simply what slavery brings out into the open, and the events from 1861 to 1865 did not finish the job of dispatching that. Abolition of slavery to instinct, to passion, to intemperance, to the

gross sensualism that sees in a man or woman chiefly a body—this we can never take for granted as a thing achieved, or so Douglass implies. Why is this so? Because the plantation, as Douglass imagines it in *My Bondage and My Freedom*, is not so much a site in Maryland or Georgia as it is an uncharted region of the mind. The "dark continent" was in Kurtz the European, not he in it. Surely Douglass, like Conrad, points to something truly unspeakable in the makeup of men. The great optimism of *My Bondage and My Freedom* is not the somewhat mystical optimism of Emerson and his disciple Whitman—the sort that says there really is no death in the world, or that evil will bless and ice will burn. It is instead rationalist, secular, and progressive; in a word, it is the Enlightenment optimism of such early republican writers as Thomas Paine, Philip Freneau, and Joel Barlow. Notwithstanding its darker implications as to the nature of humanity—in fact, precisely because of them—*My Bondage and My Freedom* believes, and simply must believe, in the possibility of a genuinely New World empire of reason and "chastening" liberty, even if that possibility had never been made real. Douglass's worldly optimism quite naturally attended his break with the Garrisonians, and that break, in turn, opened up for his use the revolutionary tradition of the American Founders.

### THE COLUMBIAN ORATOR

This brings us to a schoolbook called *The Columbian Orator*. Had not Douglass immortalized it in his autobiographies, this volume, together with its author, Caleb Bingham, would have passed into oblivion and the Library of Congress. The book was published first in 1797, when opinion in America, even in the South, was generally antislavery. The speeches, poems, and extracts it collects, which were memorized by a generation or two of American schoolboys studying composition and public speaking, celebrate liberty and republican ideals, and incidentally include forthrightly antislavery material. The book figures prominently in *My Bondage and My Freedom*—having once obtained a copy, Douglass used it to learn to read and write—and its title and contents are altogether to the point. The book espouses Columbian ideals, imagining the New World, in the fashion of Bingham's contemporaries Freneau and Barlow, as the place where human liberty, along with redemption from the "feudal superstition" of caste, at last were to be effected. Over the course of his narrative, Douglass himself emerges as the essential Columbian orator. He is a self-emancipated man for a self-emancipated nation, and *My Bondage and*

*My Freedom* is his Columbiad—his New World epic. He is the real expositor of the American Revolution, the prophet of the New America. And as the instrument of *The Columbian Orator,* a primer in composition, would imply, his means of self-emancipation is literacy: he arrives at "self-possession" through mastery of the word—a fact intimated even in the nuanced style of the book itself.

In this connection, we should consider the figure of Sandy Jenkins, a slave to whom Douglass devotes a great deal of attention in *My Bondage and My Freedom.* Sandy finds Douglass in the woods, where he has retreated to hide from Edward Covey, a "Negro breaker" who had, the day before, beaten him into insensibility when he fell ill and could no longer work. Douglass introduces Sandy to us as "a genuine African" who had "inherited some of the so-called magical powers, said to be possessed by African and eastern nations" (*Autobiography*, p. 280). Sandy, a man locally renowned for his "good nature," takes Douglass in, feeds him, nurses his wounds, and then unfolds the secrets of a special "root": "he told me further, that if I would take that root and wear it on my right side, it would be impossible for Covey to strike me a blow; that with this root about my person, no white man could whip me" (p. 280). For proof, Sandy cites his own case: he had, he assures Douglass, "never received a blow since he carried it." Douglass takes the root, but remains skeptical.

The portrait of Sandy is complex. Sandy appears first as a savior of sorts, as "the good Samaritan." Doubtless we take as praise the affirmations of his "good nature" and "kind heart." The business of the root may be presented to us as "superstition"—as "very absurd and ridiculous if not positively sinful." But that alone is no real disgrace. No, our suspicion of Sandy is first aroused when we read this: "I had," Douglass says,

> a positive aversion to all pretenders to "*divination.*" It was beneath one of my intelligence to countenance such dealings with the devil, as this power implied. But, with all my learning—it was really precious little—Sandy was more than a match for me. "My book learning," he said, "had not kept Covey off me," (a powerful argument just then,) and he entreated me, with flashing eyes, to try this [root]. (p. 281)

This sets Sandy's "genuine Africanism," his conjuring, over against Douglass's New World "book learning"—the instruction he had imbibed from the pages of *The Columbian Orator* as he taught himself to read. The contrast is the more telling in light of certain facts of which we have already been apprised. Douglass tells us that he, "the only slave now in that region who could read

and write" (p. 280), is feared by whites and respected by slaves. Literacy is power; the only other slave who could read and write in those parts had just been sold South as a menace. So, when Sandy disparages "book learning," he reveals a great weakness. His African "superstitions," insofar as they discourage a slave to look toward "book learning" as a source of power, and encourage him to put his faith in his "roots," is an instrument quite useful to the slaveholder—which is precisely why slaveholders, as presented in *My Bondage and My Freedom,* indulge such customs as these, seeing in them no threat whatever.

Douglass quietly allows us to conclude that Sandy's celebrated "good nature" is not what it appears to be. It is, in fact, at least in certain of its aspects, perfectly unrespectable, a thing unbecoming a man: his meekness is what protects him from floggings, not his roots. Sandy, we later learn, is not free of what Douglass, speaking an anti-Catholic sort of language, calls the "priestcraft of slavery." He remains essentially feudal in outlook. Like too many Americans—to borrow a phrase from Joel Barlow's epic, *The Columbiad* (1807)—Sandy Jenkins "nurse[s] feudal feelings" on "the tented shore" of the New World. And this weakness, this distrust of "book learning," this effort to turn Douglass away from his *Columbian Orator,* all of this ultimately leads him to betray Douglass and the rest of the slaves once they determine to make their escape. This "genuine African" is an Old World survival, sadly complicit in his own oppression. In fact, through his actions Sandy had, Douglass intimates, "branded" himself a slave. "I did not forget to appeal to the pride of my comrades," Douglass tells us in the section recounting the conspiracy to run away.

> If after having solemnly promised to go, as they had done, they now failed to make the attempt, they would, in effect, brand themselves with cowardice, and might as well sit down, fold their arms, and acknowledge themselves as fit only to be *slaves.* This detestable character, all were unwilling to assume. Every man except Sandy (he, much to our regret, withdrew) stood firm. (p. 315)

Sandy Jenkins, it would appear, prefers to rely on his roots.

### THE LIFE AND TIMES OF FREDERICK DOUGLASS

Douglass's third and final autobiography incorporates the entirety of *My Bondage and My Freedom* and includes new chapters that take his story down from 1855 to 1881. Here, for the first time, Douglass narrates in detail his escape from bondage. (He had omitted an account of it from his

1845 and 1855 volumes for fear of alerting slaveholders to his methods.) Here the reader also finds accounts of Douglass's complex relationship to John Brown, of his several meetings with Lincoln, and of his work in the Republican Party during the Reconstruction years and after. Of particular interest, in connection with the latter, are two chapters appended to a second edition of the *Life and Times* published in 1892. These concern Douglass's tenure as consul general to Haiti in a period of great controversy, during which the United States sought a naval coaling station on the Caribbean island, and they reveal much about the American scene in the 1890s.

At the time of Douglass's appointment as consul general, Florvil Hyppolite was bringing his year-long rebellion against Haitian president François Légitime to a successful conclusion. With American backing, Hyppolite took power in August 1889, only weeks after Douglass had been named to his new position. Unbeknownst to Douglass when he was dispatched to Port-au-Prince by President Benjamin Harrison, the U.S. government expected Hyppolite, in return for military assistance rendered during the revolution, to grant it a lease at Môle St. Nicolas for a naval station. It, in turn, would be used to shore up U.S. military and commercial interests in the Caribbean. To effect acquisition of the station, Washington sent Admiral Bancroft Gherardi, together with a squadron of gunboats manned by two thousand sailors, into the harbor at Port-au-Prince. Douglass, angered that his authority had thus been undermined, nonetheless dutifully cooperated with Gherardi in the negotiations. Hyppolite ultimately refused to grant the lease. The restrictions it placed on Haitian sovereignty, he maintained, were unduly harsh. (The terms barred Haiti from leasing properties to any other foreign power.) At the time, Hyppolite was still consolidating his position. Guerrillas stood ready to exploit any hint of weakness on his part—indeed, a coup was attempted during Douglass's term in Port-au-Prince—and the new government could not afford to be seen as "repaying" the Americans for having brought it into power.

The New York City press blamed Douglass for the failure of the negotiations. His sympathies, they intimated, lay too much with the black republic: a white consul general would have succeeded where a black one did not. The charge was as unfounded as it was malicious, and Douglass responded, after his term as consul ended, in a pair of articles published in the prestigious *North American Review* and reprinted in the expanded 1892 edition of his *Life and Times*. There, he cites not only Admiral

Gherardi's arrogant gunboat diplomacy as the cause for the failure, but also the illicit actions of an unnamed agent of a large steamship firm based in New York City, William P. Clyde and Company. Early in his narration of the Haitian episode, Douglass notes without comment that important diplomatic papers had been dispatched from Washington to Port-au-Prince aboard a Clyde steamer. At the time, the Clyde company was attempting to persuade Hippolyte to invest $500,000 of his cash-poor national treasury in a new line of ships that would run between New York City and Port-au-Prince. Quite improperly, Clyde's agent sought to secure a promise from Douglass that the consul general's office would not merely lobby on behalf of the scheme, but in the future would refuse outright to negotiate on behalf of any competing shipping companies—a policy that would, if carried out, grant the Clyde company a government-backed monopoly. The proposition disgusted Douglass and he refused to be a party to the business. For this he was castigated in the New York City papers, which pretty clearly spoke for Clyde and its financial backers.

The Clyde affair, coming as it did in the midst of the Môle St. Nicolas negotiations, impaired Douglass and Gherardi's efforts to secure a naval station. And when Douglass lets us know, in a telling aside, that the agent working covertly for Clyde was a proud South Carolinian who made little effort to conceal his contempt for the very Haitians "whose good will it was his duty to seek," the implications are clear. The agent, we are told, accused Douglass of being "more a Haitian than an American," and in the richly evocative symbolism of American racial discourse, his meaning was unmistakable: Douglass was a "militant" black, not a docile and pliable one. After all, Haiti had, since it achieved its independence and overthrew slavery, always symbolized to South Carolinians, and to southerners generally, the terror of black autonomy. Douglass—or so the implication seemed to be—was what many in the South in the 1890s were already petulantly calling the New Negro: defiant, politically assertive, and determined to exercise his rights as a citizen. What the agent wanted was a deferential tool, and in Douglass he found instead "an unprofitable servant." The South Carolina agent epitomizes, in his actions, the ethic of the new regime in post-Reconstruction America: northern capital was to work with southern whites to effect the profitable exploitation of black labor—whether in the South or in Haiti—without regard for the dignity and independence of the laborers. The episode, as Douglass narrates it, is a sad but fitting allegory of the 1890s.

## THE AMERICAN ORDEAL OF "AUTOBIOGRAPHY"

We do not often speak of the plot of an autobiography. Lives (we tell ourselves) simply unfold, or happen; they are not thrown into shape by design. But there is something about peculiarly American lives that should give us pause, that should lead us to reconsider the relation between storytelling and living, and between the imagined and the real. For ours is a nation of "confidence men," of self-made men, of Walt Whitman, Mark Twain, Howard Hughes, Norman Mailer, and Jay Gatsby—of men who are also characters. Ours is a nation, for good and for ill, where autobiography actually can come first, and the life itself second; or perhaps more aptly, where a life can be "written out" even as it is lived.

As has been intimated, the book learning that Sandy Jenkins so easily dismisses ultimately secures Douglass his freedom. He writes in a chapter of *My Bondage and My Freedom* devoted to "The Runaway Plot":

> To [my friends], therefore, with a suitable degree of caution, I began to disclose my sentiments and plans; sounding them, the while, on the subject of running away, provided a good chance should offer.... That (to me) gem of a book, the Columbian Orator, with its eloquent orations and spicy dialogues, denouncing oppression and slavery—telling of what had been dared, done and suffered by men, to obtain the inestimable boon of liberty—was still fresh in my memory, and whirled into the ranks of my speech with the aptitude of well trained soldiers, going through the drill. (*Autobiography*, pp. 305–306)

That last metaphor neatly equates literacy with militancy, the pen with the sword (or, to be strict about it, words with well-trained soldiers). This equation is what Sandy the root man failed to understand, and that failure naturally issues in his treason. It is necessary, really, that Sandy Jenkins should betray the conspiracy, and for two reasons. First, Douglass has to force a choice upon the reader—a choice between New World "rationality" and Old World "folk" belief. (The two cannot coexist; the New World must be purged). Second, the manifest complicity of that folk culture with slavery must be demonstrated, even in the very arc of the plot. If Sandy Jenkins had not existed, Douglass would have had to invent him, at least if he were to make his argument genuinely narrative.

Of course, Douglass did not invent Sandy Jenkins, even if he did refashion him as a character. Douglass is not making these things up, no matter how well the details lend themselves to his narrative and thematic purposes. Nonetheless, the story he tells is peculiarly overdetermined, strikingly well-ordered, and in such a way as to suggest that he was writing it up, so to speak, even as he acted it out—back then, in the 1830s, as he wove his own actions into the text of *The Columbian Orator*. It is quite as if the "word" sets us free precisely because it organizes our lives in prospect, not merely in retrospect, when we pen an autobiography. It is impossible, Douglass intimates, to live outside of the stories we tell about ourselves; the living is the telling. That is why Sandy Jenkins died in bondage; really, the Old World story he was telling about his roots could end no other way. And the Enlightenment-republican story that Douglass learned how to tell so well, the story that organized his life toward freedom, the story of *The Columbian Orator*—this is the story he wants the nation never to stop telling itself. And that is why we have to read Frederick Douglass's great autobiographies. To be American is to fold stories like these into the accidents of your life; it is to live "as if" these stories were real, or might be made real. After all, that is precisely what Douglass did.

[*See also* Autobiography: Slave Narratives.]

### SELECTED WORKS

*Narrative of the Life of Frederick Douglass, an American Slave, Written by Himself* (1845)
*My Bondage and My Freedom* (1855)
*The Life and Times of Frederick Douglass, written by Himself* (1881)
*The Life and Writings of Frederick Douglass* (1950)
*Autobiographies* (1994)

### FURTHER READING

Frederickson, George M. *The Black Image in the White Mind: The Debate on Afro-American Character and Destiny, 1817–1914.* 2d ed. Middletown, Conn., 1987. Essential reading for any student of Douglass, or of American literature and culture generally.

McFeely, William S. *Frederick Douglass.* New York, 1991. The standard biography.

Preston, Dickson J. *Young Frederick Douglass: The Maryland Years.* Baltimore, 1980. Documents Douglass's early years.

Sundquist, Eric J. *Frederick Douglass: New Literary and Historical Essays.* New York, 1990.

Sundquist, Eric J. *To Wake the Nations: Race in the Making of American Literature.* Cambridge, Mass., 1993. A book of great breadth that includes extensive discussion of *My Bondage and My Freedom.*

# THEODORE DREISER

*by Jerome Loving*

By most accounts, Theodore Dreiser is considered a modern American writer, which is to say that philosophically and thematically his work belongs to the twentieth century instead of the nineteenth. As a result he is often compared to such writers as Ernest Hemingway and F. Scott Fitzgerald. Indeed, Fitzgerald's most famous work, *The Great Gatsby*, and Dreiser's most famous work, *An American Tragedy*, were both published in 1925. Both novels are set in the Roaring Twenties and concern the baneful influence of American materialism. Yet while the set for Fitzgerald's novel includes flappers and bootleg whiskey, Dreiser's work reaches back to the second half of the nineteenth century for some of its cultural artifacts, which he mixes freely with those of the 1920s. Whereas Fitzgerald and Hemingway, as part of the Lost Generation of Americans in Paris during the 1920s, responded to the heady materialism in America, Dreiser was equally concerned about the American malaise as it had existed in the 1880s and 1890s, during the era of the robber barons, whose American fortunes often relied on the exploitation of immigrants such as Dreiser's German-born father.

The moral question for this first major American writer of non-English stock was how badly the conspicuous rich were corrupting the poor and middle class. For Dreiser had not only grown up poor in Indiana, he had come to literary maturity during the first decade of the twentieth century, when John D. Rockefeller and his Standard Oil Company had fallen into serious disrepute for the corruption then being exposed in muckraker journalism. The so-called business novel of the 1880s, in which the protagonist is basically a good man who resists the temptation of corporate greed, gave way in the first decade of the twentieth century to the businessman as villain in many

Theodore Dreiser, 1933.
(*Photograph by Carl Van Vechten. Courtesy of the Library of Congress*)

novels, culminating with Dreiser's trilogy—*The Financier* (1912), *The Titan* (1914), and *The Stoic* (1947)—about traction king Frank Cowperwood.

Dreiser spent the first twenty-nine years of his life in the nineteenth century, where he grew up under the long shadow of the Civil War that was frequently the subject of his celebrated older brother's sentimental songs. The title of his first great novel, *Sister Carrie* (1900), may have derived from a Civil War song by the same name in which "Sister Carrie" (South Carolina) is chastised for leaving home (or the Union). Dreiser first came upon the literary scene at a time in which both the press and popular literature often presented a false picture of life, one that overlooked its harsher aspects. If the literature of the 1880s and early 1890s at all reflected Darwin's idea of the "survival of the fittest" (actually coined by the synthetic philosopher Herbert Spencer, one of Dreiser's early influences), it was couched in the terms of the Social Darwinists. They believed that the dog-eat-dog nature of life applied mainly to the lower classes, including minorities and immigrants. As a second-generation European immigrant, Dreiser counted as one of the "foreigners." It was during this era, as Reconstruction officially came to a close, that lynchings of blacks began and ran almost unpunished for fifty years, killing some 2,500 blacks in the South and Southwest. Dreiser's best short story is about a lynching he witnessed as a newspaper reporter in St. Louis ("Nigger Jeff" 1901). This period of Jim Crow and John D. Rockefeller was the cultural laboratory for the making of the Father of American Realism, so-called because Dreiser's novels challenged the puritanical standards of American literature and paved the way for the works of such writers as Sherwood Anderson, Sinclair

Lewis, Fitzgerald, Hemingway, William Faulkner, Richard Wright, and others.

## THE ROAD TO *SISTER CARRIE*

Dreiser was born on 27 August 1871 in Terre Haute, Indiana, the twelfth of thirteen children. The first three offspring, all boys, of John Paul Dreiser and Sarah Mary Schänäb died mysteriously before a fourth son was born around 1858. He was the other famous Dreiser—Paul Dresser, author of such pre-ragtime songs as "On the Banks of the Wabash" and "My Gal Sal." Dreiser's father had immigrated from Germany in 1844 to avoid the draft. He worked in New England and other eastern woolen mills before drifting westward. He married Dreiser's mother, the daughter of Mennonite farmers near Dayton, Ohio, in 1851. The couple soon settled in Indiana, where John Paul briefly prospered as the owner of a mill in Sullivan. It burned down in the late 1860s; Dreiser's father suffered severe financial losses and sustained an injury to the head during the attempt to rebuild the mill. The tragedy left John Paul Dreiser a defeated man who took odd jobs to support his family and otherwise devoted himself fanatically to the Catholic Church.

The Dreisers soon moved to Terre Haute, where their brood increased year after year. By 1879 the family had split up to make ends meet. Sarah took her three youngest children, including the eight-year-old Theodore, back to Sullivan. There she rented rooms and took in laundry. John Paul remained in Terre Haute, where several of the grown daughters held menial jobs. Paul Dresser, who had run away from a Catholic seminary and changed his name for the stage, now worked as a regular with a traveling minstrel show. The Dreiser daughters were headstrong and foolish, several eventually becoming pregnant out of wedlock. Two of them were the models for the heroines in *Sister Carrie* and *Jennie Gerhardt* (1911). In the first volume of his autobiography, *Dawn: A History of Myself* (1931), Dreiser records his early impressions of life in which the delights of nature merged with the harshness of his family's economic situation.

After living in Sullivan and Evansville, Sarah and her wing of the family moved to Warsaw, a lake district in the northeast corner of Indiana. Here she was joined by some of her wayward daughters in flight from the reality of their recklessness or by Rome, a ne'er-do-well son who every year or so would pay a visit and embarrass his younger siblings by becoming drunk and disorderly. Dreiser remembered in his autobiographies the shame these visits cast upon the youngest siblings under Sarah's

care, who were trying to develop social ties in school and the community. One visit the partial family always welcomed, however, was from Paul Dresser, who by this time had become financially well off as a songwriter. In the sketch "My Brother Paul" (1919) and elsewhere, Dreiser fondly recalled how Paul saved the day for his mother on more than one occasion. Dreiser quit school at age sixteen and (like Carrie in his novel) took a train to Chicago, soon to be followed by his mother and other siblings. There he worked at a lowly Italian restaurant and a poorly ventilated hardware store warehouse until one of his teachers from Warsaw gave him enough money to attend Indiana University for one year in 1889–1890. Dreiser was already a reader of literature, and the college experience extended his intellectual bounds into areas of social philosophy.

The following fall Sarah died in her mid-fifties, and the family members went off in various directions, leaving a mournful John Paul with only one or two adult children to support him. Dreiser eventually broke into the newspaper business as a reporter. After a brief stint on the *Chicago Globe* in 1892, he worked in St. Louis for the *Globe-Democrat* and the *Republic*. It was during his newspaper stint in Chicago that he wrote his first extant literary work, "The Return of Genius" (1892). Later he would write a novel titled *The "Genius"* (1915). The prevailing literary genre at this time was realism, which meant not what it might mean today—that is, stark reality—but a literary approach to life which was faithful in presenting adverse facts and circumstances, but romantic or idealistic in having its protagonist emerge from material loss or social disgrace with his or her dignity intact. In William Dean Howells's *The Rise of Silas Lapham* (1895), for example, the protagonist rises morally as he falls financially by refusing to cheat his competitors in order to save his business.

What Dreiser discovered, or said he discovered, as a journalist was that this idealistic image of the businessman did not in any way fit the Rockefellers, the Philip D. Armours, the Marshall Fields, or the Andrew Carnegies. Dreiser came to Pittsburgh in 1894 to work as a reporter for the *Dispatch*, not long after the notorious Homestead Strike in which Carnegie simply replaced the striking workers with other groups of immigrants. It was in the Steel City that the contrast between immense wealth and stark poverty in the United States was seared into the consciousness of the young Dreiser. He learned that the newspapers protected big business with bland stories about the good works of the rich and revolting reports about the decadent immigrant class of workers, who were dismissed as malcontents and socialists. As a reporter Dreiser was better, his colleagues said, at writing the news rather than finding it. He was frustrated, therefore, when his city editors forbade imaginative essays based on the news. He was not to write such "general stuff," his editors insisted. As one put it, "That's literature—not news stuff." Eventually, as a freelance magazine writer in New York City, he wrote essays such as "Curious Shifts of the Poor" (1899), which with slight adaptation went bodily into the text of *Sister Carrie*. His great empathy for the poor came from his own Indiana poverty.

Mainly, it was the result of his stint as a reporter in Pittsburgh that Dreiser became a full-fledged naturalist, one who believed that man's destiny is largely or even exclusively determined by heredity and environment. Its combination, the resulting personality or "chemism" of the individual, is buffeted by fate, usually to his or her detriment. While working as a police reporter in the Allegheny courthouse across the river from Pittsburgh, one day he wandered into Andrew Carnegie's very first public library and discovered the writings of Spencer, whose Social Darwinism suggested that the universe was becoming a friendlier place, but only for human beings who adapted themselves more along the lines of duty than desire. In the meantime, man was like a leaf in the wind—a metaphor that would dominate *Sister Carrie*. Dreiser also read the deterministic writings of Thomas Huxley and John Tyndall, which utterly destroyed any lasting remnants of his Catholic faith. At the same time he came upon his major literary influence, Honoré de Balzac, whose novels in the *La comédie humaine* series taught him to pile up minute and realistic details in his novels.

With the help of his brother Paul, Dreiser established himself in New York City in 1894. He founded and for two years edited *Ev'ry Month*, a house organ for Paul's sheet music company, and then became a freelance writer for leading magazines. Between 1897 and the publication of his first novel in 1900, Dreiser's bibliography swelled by almost one hundred items. In one magazine called *Success*, he wrote articles based on interviews (some faked) with such industrialists and persons of genius as varied as the steel king Andrew Carnegie and the "wizard" Thomas Edison.

During the summer of 1899, Dreiser and his wife joined Arthur and Maude Henry at their summer home in Maumee, Ohio. Henry, a former journalist whom Dreiser had first met in Toledo while working his way east, was living most of the year as a freelancer in New York City. Like Dreiser (who had originally hoped to become a playwright), he was an aspiring writer. That summer he repeatedly urged Dreiser to write. Dreiser wrote five or six short stories, including "Nigger Jeff" (1901), which were eventually placed in magazines. That fall he returned to New York City and began *Sister Carrie*, which he completed in the spring of 1900. After Harper's rejected the novel on the grounds that its realism was too uncompromising, the manuscript was accepted by Doubleday, where the senior reader was Frank Norris, then the celebrated author of the hard-hitting naturalism in *McTeague* (1899). Dreiser has often been compared to Norris, but he did not read his novel until after he had written *Sister Carrie*. Neither had he read any of the works of Émile Zola, the father of French naturalism who had deeply influenced Norris.

Generally, *Sister Carrie* was based on the life of Emma Dreiser, who ran off to New York City with L. A. Hopkins, a married man in Chicago. To pay his way, Hopkins stole from his employers. In the novel, Carrie does the same with George Hurstwood. The two first meet in Chicago through Charles Drouet, a traveling salesman who has been living with Carrie following their meeting on a train (where Dreiser met his first wife). Hurstwood is the manager and host of an upscale saloon catering to actors and prominent pugilists. When he is caught courting Carrie by his wife, who informs his employers, Hurstwood steals from the saloon's open safe and gets Carrie to board a midnight train to Montreal by telling her that Drouet has been seriously injured. Once in New York City, he tries to manage another saloon as part owner, but gradually loses it along with most of his money. In the meantime, he and Carrie move to less accommodating quarters in the city. She eventually gets on the stage and as her fortune there increases she leaves Hurstwood almost penniless.

In one of the most heart-rending sequences in American literature, Hurstwood slowly sinks into poverty and isolation on the mean streets of the Bowery in the winter of 1897. Once a proud manager of a popular saloon, he dies in the wretched cubicle of a hotel for indigents. Carrie, almost oblivious of Hurstwood, becomes rich and famous but remains somehow unhappy. Drouet, who risks nothing and gets nothing, remains the same. The emerging theme suggests that we are driven this way and that in life and have little or no say about where we go. It was not Hurstwood's fault that he failed, but his circumstance; it was not Carrie's industry, but her youth and good looks (which she did nothing to create); and Drouet's nontragedy is the result of the tragic nature of his inability to do anything other than follow his libidinous impulses.

With a first novel about to go to press, Dreiser had everything to live for in the spring of 1900, but storm clouds were about to gather. When Frank Doubleday, president of the publishing firm, returned from Europe and read the manuscript his editorial board had recently accepted on Norris's advice, he was appalled by its intimate revelations about such commonplace and immoral people as Carrie and Hurstwood. He urged Dreiser to give up the contract on the grounds that *Sister Carrie* would be a disastrous first novel for a young writer. Dreiser held his ground, however, and Doubleday reluctantly published the novel in November 1900, giving it no advertising and ultimately selling no more than five hundred or six hundred copies. Dreiser's total earnings for this American classic was a royalty check of $68.40. The relatively few reviews (because of the lack of advertising) were generally favorable as to the book's originality but doubtful as to its harsh realism. Dreiser never again fully trusted a publisher to keep his word and later turned the Doubleday affair into a legend in which the ultimate blame went to the publisher's wife. The commercial failure sent him into a three-year depression in which he made little money, was nearly homeless, and indeed looked much like the tragic Hurstwood he had so recently created.

## RETURN OF THE WRITER AND REALIST

Paul finally rescued his brother in 1903, sending him to a sanitarium in Westchester, New York. Afterward, Dreiser finished the cure himself through nearly a year of manual labor (recorded in the posthumous *An Amateur Laborer*, 1983) and eventually got back into the writing business as a magazine editor. Ultimately, he became editor-in-chief of a trio of women's magazines, including the *Delineator*, owned by the Butterick Corporation. Butterick was in the business of selling tissue-paper dress patterns to American women. Like *Ev'ry Month*, it also sold to dreams like Carrie's illusions of romance with images of beautiful, well-dressed women. As Dreiser prospered in this position, he found a small publishing house to reissue *Sister Carrie* in 1907 from plates he had purchased from Doubleday, and its second appearance eventually ensured its position as an American classic. At the same time he occasionally thought about finishing *Jennie Gerhardt*, which he had begun shortly after finishing *Sister Carrie*. Dreiser's reentry into full-time authorship finally came about in 1910. Because of a scandal in which the writer had an affair with the eighteen-year-old daughter of an employee, he was forced to give up his position at the Butterick Corporation. The incident led to the breakup of his first marriage and nearly another nervous collapse.

*Jennie Gerhardt*, largely based on the life of Dreiser's sister Mame, is about a young chambermaid who is seduced by a U.S. senator many years her senior. He intends to educate and marry her, but before he can do so he dies suddenly, leaving the girl an unwed mother. Jennie is of German ancestry. Her father, modeled closely on John Paul Dreiser, is a fanatical Lutheran who turns her out of the family home when it is learned that she is pregnant. Her mother and brother secretly help her. While working as a maid for a wealthy family, she is seduced again, this time by a man more her age—Lester Kane, one of two sons of a wealthy carriage maker. As was the case with Mame's husband, whose wealthy parents never accepted her because of her lowly social status, Lester cannot marry Jennie but instead lives with her in secret, not even knowing at first that she has a child. The same naturalistic forces are at play here as in *Sister Carrie*, but Jennie is much more lovable than the stolid Carrie. As a result many readers, especially students, prefer *Jennie Gerhardt* over *Sister Carrie* because of its sentimentality and formula-like plot of the lady in distress. One reason for the difference in the two novels (besides Dreiser's desire to write something that would get past the moralists and sell) was that Mame was probably a more caring person than Emma. Eventually, to save his inheritance Lester leaves Jennie, who afterward loses her daughter to typhoid. But she is forever loyal in her love of Lester and is secretly by his bedside at his death.

Dreiser took the plots for his first two published novels from the fragments of his sisters' lives. He also drew directly upon his own; while inventing upon reality to some extent, his novel *The "Genius"* was primarily autobiographical, long before he turned to that task officially in his autobiographies, *Dawn* and *A Book about Myself* (1922; called *A History of Myself: Newspaper Days* on its republication in 1931). The first draft of the novel was actually finished in 1911, only months before the publication of *Jennie Gerhardt*. It was not published until 1915, however, because he was already contracted to publish *The Financier*, a novel about an American business tycoon that would be the first volume of what became his "Trilogy of Desire." Furthermore, the Baltimore journalist and satirist H. L. Mencken, who had championed both *Sister Carrie* and *Jennie Gerhardt*, was doubtful about *The "Genius"* on the grounds that it would present a field day for Anthony Comstock and for John Sumner, his replacement as head of the New York Society for the Prevention of Vice. As it turned out, Mencken was right, but fortunately Dreiser delayed its publication so that it did not immediately derail his revived career the way *Sister Carrie* had undercut his debut as a novelist.

Armed with strong reviews and sales from *Jennie Gerhardt*, Dreiser brought out the first two volumes of his remarkable trilogy, *The Financier* and *The Titan*. The third volume, *The Stoic*, appeared posthumously in 1947. The long interlude between the second and third volumes was because sales for *The Titan* declined from those for *The Financier*. Furthermore, Dreiser was distracted by another project—*The Bulwark* (1946)—that took him as long to complete as *The Stoic*. It is with the trilogy of desire that Dreiser shifted his research away from family and autobiography to write what some even call a loose biography of Charles Tyson Yerkes, the streetcar tycoon whose name Dreiser had first heard as a teenager in Chicago. The idea of using Yerkes's notorious career as a basis for fiction came fully into Dreiser's consciousness in 1906, when the newspapers were full of stories about the collapse of the magnate's financial empire following his death the preceding year. In Dreiser's recycling of his flamboyant career, Yerkes became Frank Algernon Cowperwood (pronounced "Cooperwood"), who begins his ascent in Philadelphia. Here he is ultimately convicted of misuse of government funds and briefly imprisoned. He then moves to Chicago (in *The Titan*) and becomes rich and powerful all over again until defeated by competitors. Eventually he goes to London (in *The Stoic*), where he dominates that city's traction monopoly for a time before going down in defeat.

Frank Cowperwood is part Yerkes and part Dreiser. The biographer as author, of course, could not research Yerkes's personal life; he had no access to private letters, but it was well known that Yerkes was what Dreiser would call a "varietist" when it came to women. Here Dreiser merely substituted parts of his own promiscuous record of female conquests. Cowperwood's motto was "I satisfy myself" and Dreiser's was "I didn't make myself." He attributes the naturalistic stance to most of his protagonists, as he did indeed to himself in his private life, never publicly expressing regret for any of his actions, especially his "varietism." "For the second, third and fourth decades of my life," he readily confessed in his autobiography, "there appeared to be a toxic something in form itself—that of the female of the species where beautiful—that could effect veritable paroxysms of emotion and desire in me" (*Dawn*). Later he would find support for his determinism in the works of the behaviorist Jacques Loeb and Sigmund Freud. Generally, he believed that man was a tropism, much like a caterpillar drawn up a branch toward the sun. Men and women were drawn helplessly toward the object of their desires, as Hurstwood was fatalistically drawn toward Carrie in *Sister Carrie*.

With *The Financier* and *The Titan*, Dreiser brought to a culmination a series of American novels critical of the money moguls of the 1890s. Yet curiously, he also admired these men even though he himself had grown up in poverty largely because of their monopolies. This dual vision is suggested in the first chapter of *The Financier*, where young Cowperwood stands before the window of a fish market and watches a lobster devour a squid. "That's the way it has to be, I guess," the boy concludes about the organization of life. No Social Darwinist, Dreiser believed in the chance survival of the species. Whoever is accidentally strong will adapt and prevail. He believed this to be the way of nature; yet at the same time he held a deep-seated empathy for the weak that ultimately led him into a life of social activism in the 1930s. This was Dreiser's lifelong contradiction: he was both a determinist and a social reformer.

## CRIME AND PUNISHMENT

Dreiser published no novel during the ten years between *The "Genius"* and *An American Tragedy*. It was a difficult decade for the author, who had rebounded with *Jennie Gerhardt* and *The Financier* and who was now most famous as the author of *Sister Carrie*. Its turbulent publication history had become legend, and Dreiser was seen as a genius who may have already burnt himself out. Not only had *The "Genius"* become embroiled in a battle with the censors, but their condemnation also targeted Dreiser as being of German heritage during the period of anti-German prejudice stirred up by World War I. The book, Dreiser's biggest moneymaker before *An American Tragedy*, was withdrawn from sale by his publisher in 1916 in the face of threatened lawsuits by the vice societies. Naturally, this notoriety increased its value, and black market copies—to Dreiser's pecuniary frustration—were sold for many times the original price. The novel was not sold legally until 1923. By this time public support for puritanical standards in literature had faded and the vice societies soon went out of business.

Its healthy sale afterwards put much-needed money in Dreiser's pocket. Meanwhile, he had engaged in all sorts of literary enterprises. He fulfilled his original dream of becoming a dramatist by writing a dozen plays, symbolist and expressionist in anticipation of the work of his later friend, Eugene O'Neill, as well as Edward Albee. Most were one-act plays, modeled after ones he had seen performed by experimental theater groups such as the Washington Square Players and the Provincetown Players operating in Greenwich Village, where he lived during and after the war years. He was also inspired by Maurice Browne's Little Theatre in Chicago—as well as by an actress who became his lover for several years—while researching *The Titan* in the midwestern capital in 1913. One of the first one-acts to be produced was *The Girl in the Coffin* (1916), based on a silk workers' strike in Paterson, New Jersey, led by labor leader "Big" Bill Haywood. This was the most successful of the one-acts, as the others were highly symbolistic and some difficult to stage. His one four-act play is *The Hand of the Potter* (1918). Like *An American Tragedy* and other, shorter pieces that he published in the 1920s, it was based on a crime reported in the press.

It was also during this decade before the appearance of *An American Tragedy* that Dreiser published *Free and Other Stories* (1918). This collection combined pre–*Sister Carrie* stories with more recent attempts at the short story (a canvas generally too small for Dreiser's inclination toward the epic). The volume included "Nigger Jeff," whose title generally renders it too offensive to be included in high school and college anthologies at the turn of the twenty-first century. This is unfortunate because the story is both a sympathetic meditation on American racism and an early manifesto of the writer; he speaks through the cub reporter in the story, who after meeting with the dead man's dejected mother, says that he will report more than the spare facts of journalism. The following year Dreiser published *Twelve Men* (1919), which consisted of sketches about men who had made a deep impression on his life, ranging from his brother Paul to his father-in-law. Many of the stories had been written at the turn of the century. He also issued a collection of philosophical essays and two plays under the title of *Hey Rub-a-Dub-Dub* (1920).

It was around this time that Dreiser, almost fifty, met and fell in love with Helen Patges Richardson, a twenty-five-year-old divorcée who was the granddaughter of Dreiser's aunt. Like Edgar Allan Poe, whose work he had long admired and whose psychological strategies he used in *An American Tragedy*, he eventually married his second cousin. And while that did not happen until 1944, Helen became the main woman in his life. In 1919 he followed her out to Hollywood for three years as she tried to fulfill her dream of becoming a movie actress. A beautiful woman, she got bit parts and even a role in Rudolph Valentino's *The Four Horsemen of the Apocalypse* (1921). Dreiser was then under contract with his latest publisher to finish *The Bulwark* (1946), but instead turned to writing the first twenty chapters, later heavily revised, of *An American Tragedy*.

Ever since the publication of *Sister Carrie*, and indeed as far back as his reporter days in St. Louis in 1893, Dreiser had been fascinated by a particular kind of crime of passion. It was not the crime of killing for love or some other emotional impulse such as revenge, but instead involved sexual relations and the way they were connected to the American Dream of becoming rich. Having come from such dire poverty, Dreiser as a young man shared the fantasy at times of marrying a beautiful woman who was also rich, thereby ensuring the suitor of complete sexual satisfaction as well as a life of leisure and status. Too often, however, the young man fell in love and impregnated "Miss Poor" at about the same time he was about to get an opportunity to marry "Miss Rich," as Dreiser termed the choice in interviews following the success of *An American Tragedy*. Desperate to get ahead, the frustrated suitor murders the pregnant girl in order to marry the rich one.

This simple scenario seems worn out even for Dreiser's day until we consider its social ramifications at the turn of the century. First of all, at that time a young pregnant woman out of wedlock was the object of extreme shame, a consequence of an even stricter code around the Civil War, which demanded that irate parents eject their wayward daughters from their home. As Stephen Crane, one of the strongest literary influences on Dreiser at the turn of the century, showed in *Maggie: A Girl of the Streets* (1893), this attitude sent a good many young women into prostitution. The situation was further complicated as this strict morality weakened by the end of the century to the extent that more "good girls," or middle-class women, got pregnant outside marriage. Yet it was still a time in which abortion was illegal, as indeed was contraception. In the 1920s Dreiser was acquainted with Margaret Sanger and her campaigns for birth control. It was not simply a matter of sexual freedom, but one of social equality; for birth control devices and even abortion services were available to the rich. Though these services were still illegal, of course, physicians would simply look the other way in the cases of unwed mothers from affluent families. More generally, Dreiser saw this as a part of the larger pattern of social discrimination in which newspapers in the 1890s, before the muckraker era, protected the rich and powerful and criticized the poor.

After considering over the years several such crimes as the basis of his tragedy, Dreiser settled on the Gillette-Brown murder case of 1906 in the Adirondacks. Chester

Gillette came east to work in his uncle's skirt factory in Cortland, New York. He became intimately involved with Grace Brown, a worker in the factory. When this daughter of impoverished farmers became pregnant, she demanded that Chester marry her, apparently never considering abortion. Under the guise of running away to get married, Chester lured Grace up to Big Moose Lake. There on the lake she was knocked unconscious and left to drown. Gillette was quickly apprehended. His subsequent murder trial was a national sensation, mainly because it was trumped up in the press as a case of privilege over poverty, the murder of a poor pregnant woman by her affluent lover. Actually, Gillette had no money of his own and was convicted and executed solely on circumstantial evidence. But the issue of his innocence or likely guilt was drowned out by the public outrage the trial evoked, especially when the murder victim's pleading letters to the accused were read aloud in court and published in the newspapers.

Once Dreiser returned from the West Coast in 1922, he visited Cortland and the site of the murder. He became familiar with the case through newspaper clippings that reported the crime in minute detail. The plot of the novel is so much like the crime that some critics have denied it the name of art or literature. It is true that Dreiser followed the details of the murder and trial closely, but he invented the murderer's youth out of whole cloth, or from the facts of his own beginnings—at least insofar as the culprit had a fanatically religious father and an understanding mother. What he also invents is the psychological and economic environment that would likely produce such a murderer, for Clyde Griffiths is not simply a sex-driven killer (as Chester may have been) but an organism whose destiny is shaped beyond its control, even down to the trial, where state politics were involved in Clyde's conviction. Roberta Alden, Clyde's victim, is as much a victim of society and its inequities as Clyde because of her impoverished background and the duplicitous moral standards that keep her from an abortion and thus doom her to an early death.

Moreover, the trial and death house segments of the story—Book III of this eight-hundred-page novel—are invested with much more than the recorded facts of the Gillette-Brown case. Like Edgar Allan Poe, and Fyodor Dostoyevsky in *Crime and Punishment* (1866), which Dreiser may have reread before he wrote *An American Tragedy*, he equipped his novel with an interior monologue that depicts the conflicting thoughts of the killer. In this psychological intrigue, he was also influenced by his reading of Freud through the translations of Dreiser's friend, A. A. Brill. One other influence, born

from government suppression of civil liberties during and immediately after America's participation in World War I, was a developing sense of reform that favored socialism over capitalism and human rights over the right of the state. All this finally adds up in *An American Tragedy* to the Dreiserian contradiction in which the individual irrevocably caught up in a deterministic world might be helped through social reform.

Religion, a natural ally of the capitalistic status quo, is also part of the problem in *An American Tragedy*. Perhaps this represented Dreiser's lifelong reaction to the oppression he felt growing up as a Roman Catholic, but at any rate he saw religion as hypocritical and misleading in that it insisted on a morality that was contrary to human needs. The idea, for example, of one man for one woman that Dreiser himself could never abide was one of its commandments, one convention that Clyde cannot follow when it comes to both his economic survival and his insatiable desire for beauty. It must be said, however, that Dreiser does not present Clyde as personally admirable. He is no more loving of those other than himself than is Carrie Meeber. Like her—or any organism in Dreiser's view—he is primarily intent upon survival. Clyde's dilemma over the pregnant Roberta (whom he kills to be with the rich Sondra Finchley) is anticipated earlier in the novel with the out-of-wedlock pregnancy of his sister, a situation that Clyde does little to alleviate financially from his income as a bellboy. Later, Clyde rationalizes away again and again his obligations to the tearful Roberta. And the "victim" as well is not treated idealistically. Just as Clyde hopes to climb the social ladder of success with his uncle's connections and especially through Sondra, Roberta also values Clyde as a relative of the factory owner. While she loves him, she also loves the idea of how her marriage to Clyde will lead to her own social advancement.

It is in the matter of guilt where Dreiser is most intriguing. Gillette never confessed to murdering Grace Brown and, as already noted, went to the electric chair on circumstantial evidence. This is true of Clyde as well, for only the reader is an eyewitness to what really happened. In this regard, Dreiser drapes the whole matter in the same ambiguity he employed at the climax of *Sister Carrie*. When Hurstwood is threatened by his wife after she discovers his illicit connection to Carrie, he steals money from his employers and flees with her to New York City. But in the scene in which he commits the theft, Dreiser casts doubt on Hurstwood's guilt because the door of the safe accidentally closes while he holds out $10,000 of its contents. "Did he do it?" Dreiser asks rhetorically. The same question is asked of Clyde as he sits opposite the pregnant Roberta in a rowboat on Big Bittern Lake. Although he had brought her there to commit the murder, he falls into a catatonic trance at the moment of action and only inadvertently knocks her into the water, where she drowns. Although he was not legally required to risk his life in trying to save her from drowning, the fact that he allowed her to drown is used to convict him of premeditated murder. Yet it is only Clyde and the reader who know that this "first-degree murder" was committed accidentally.

## LITERARY FAME AND SOCIAL CRITICISM

*An American Tragedy* was a best-seller that earned Dreiser even more money when it was turned into a movie (the first of which, to Dreiser's outrage, turned Clyde into a sex-driven, cold-blooded murderer instead of the victim of a shabby childhood and heartless capitalism). The ten-year hiatus in his production of novels had ended, but he would never again complete another that was freshly conceived. Fame may have ruined him as an artist, but it is probably more accurate to say that the writing of *An American Tragedy* simply exhausted his talent as a major writer. He first turned to the book in the early 1920s and it took him until the fall of 1925 to complete it. He even worked on the story after it was set up in type, and wrote segments of it while earlier parts of the two-volume novel were being printed up in galley proofs. At its publication he was fifty-five and famous, having already enjoyed the fame without the royalties as the author of *Sister Carrie*. He went on a grand tour of the Scandinavian countries in 1926, securing contracts for the translation of his books and, on his way back home, even interviewing Winston Churchill in England for a magazine. The next year he was one of the world celebrities invited by the Soviet Union to see the results of its social experiment ten years after the Russian Revolution. Upon his return he bought himself a country estate in Westchester, New York, but also converted to communism. He issued *Dreiser Looks at Russia* (1928), a book partly cribbed from news reports and possibly from another book on Russia that year by journalist Dorothy Thompson, recently the bride of Sinclair Lewis.

In spite of his socialistic commitment, Dreiser tried to cash in on his recent fame. He reissued a shortened version of *The Financier* in 1927 and published *A Gallery of Women* two years later. The 1927 edition of *The Financier* eventually became the only one available in print, but it is not altogether clear that it is an improved version, since Dreiser depended so much on the amassing of detail to make his case. *A Gallery of Women* was much anticipated by the readers and reviewers of *Twelve Men*, but it proved to be disappointing. *Twelve Men* had dwelled on the compelling circumstances of the lives of men who had been meaningful to Dreiser, but in *A Gallery* the fifteen portraits were almost all of women Dreiser had known only casually, and were more psychological than circumstantial. They were also repetitive in their theme that women were their own worst enemies in trying to compete in the world (usually of art) with men. The book sold poorly, and to make matters (much) worse, Dreiser lost about half of his recently acquired fortune in the stock market crash of 1929.

Dreiser was a finalist for the Nobel Prize in literature in 1930, but the first such prize to an American writer went instead to Lewis, whose satires of America in *Main Street* (1920) and *Babbitt* (1922) may have been the deciding factor. Dreiser's brooding picture of American life, especially in *An American Tragedy*, attributed its tragedies to no particular person or country. Out of a sense of disappointment and with his interest in writing another novel waning, Dreiser turned in 1931 to fighting social injustice. Under the banner of the communist organization called the National Committee for the Defense of Political Prisoners, he was enlisted in the cause of the Scottsboro Boys, southern blacks unjustly accused of raping two white women. He also assisted the Communist Party of the United States in its investigations of the working conditions of miners in Pittsburgh and in Harlan County, Kentucky. He ended the year by issuing a biting denunciation of American capitalism in *Tragic America*, whose cobbled facts were often erroneous. Curiously, his social activism led him to begin a brief correspondence with President Franklin Delano Roosevelt, which culminated with a lunch on the presidential yacht in 1938. Evidently Roosevelt, who had read some of Dreiser's books and was being called a socialist himself for his New Deal approaches to the Great Depression, separated Dreiser the novelist from Dreiser the social radical.

As World War II loomed in the fall of 1938, Dreiser moved to southern California. In 1941 he issued another denunciation of American and world capitalism in *America Is Worth Saving*. His ancestry had made him initially sympathetic to Hitler's rebuilding of Germany until the harsh truths about the new leader became clear. He corresponded about the matter with Mencken, as he had during World War I. The two old friends were renewing their acquaintance after a ten-year estrangement following the publication of *An American Tragedy*. Mencken had given the book a battering review in his *American Mercury*, the culmination of his building unhappiness with the direction in which Dreiser's fiction had gone since the publication of *Sister Carrie* and *Jennie Gerhardt*. Dreiser had grown up almost dirt poor, while Mencken had been raised as the bourgeois son of a cigar maker in Baltimore. The one went to the left politically, while the other moved even more to the right, becoming a regular pundit at national presidential conventions. But they buried their differences out of respect for their initial years as friends and colleagues in the fight against the puritans and sentimentalists. Unfortunately, they never saw one another again after Dreiser moved to California, not even when Dreiser visited New York in 1944 to receive an Award of Merit from the Academy of Arts and Letters.

The award was for a lifetime of achievement, for Dreiser had done little in a literary way during the previous fifteen years to earn a specific prize. When not engaged in social protests, he had devoted himself to scientific investigations that were tinged with a religious or mystical nature. He sought to find spiritual solace at the end of his life as well as clues about the mystery of existence that he had come closer to discovering much earlier on in his greatest works. This quasi-religious quest also affected the development of his last two novels in the 1940s. With the help of several female editors, including Helen Patges Richardson—whom he had by then married—Dreiser completed *The Bulwark* and the third volume of the Cowperwood trilogy, *The Stoic* (1947). Neither book is worthy of the Dreiser power between *Sister Carrie* and *An American Tragedy*, but each tells us something about Dreiser's philosophical mood during the last three or four years of his life. He had begun as an "inoculated" (as he would have said) Catholic, thrived as a determinist or naturalist in literature, and died as a religious person, generally speaking. His full reconversion back to the idea of Providence shows in the revisions he made to the two novels that he had begun at the height of his naturalistic period. *The Bulwark*, which had begun as a novel critical of a religious man and a parent in the modern age of commerce and secular dominance, concludes as a monument to the patriarch's quiet faith in the face of the disasters that consumed his children's lives. In *The Stoic*, Cowperwood's second wife converts to Hinduism following his defeat and death. Shortly before his death on 28 December 1945, Dreiser became a formal member of the Communist Party, a move that biographers have viewed as part of his return to a religious or idealistic way of thought.

Theodore Dreiser is unique to American literature because he carried the torch of realism into the twentieth century. Along with Crane, Norris, and other literary naturalists of the 1890s, he challenged the surface realism of Howells, the dean of American literature at the turn of the century, with a realism—or naturalism—that was then considered devastating in its exposure of everyday life. What separates Dreiser from other post-Howellsian realists of his day is that he did not subscribe in any fashion whatever to Social Darwinism in its romantic embrace of the principles of evolution. His tragic figures are not necessarily Irish, like Crane's Maggie or Norris's McTeague, for instance. They are average Americans—the second generation of Walt Whitman's "divine average"—who wake up expecting the success of the American Dream and too often discover that it is instead an American Tragedy. George Hurstwood is the little guy who thinks too big and is ultimately crushed. His successor in American literature is Willy Loman in Arthur Miller's *Death of a Salesman* (1948). Clyde Griffiths can be found in Richard Wright's *Native Son* (1940) and elsewhere in the plots of novels based closely on case histories as well as the imagination. *Sister Carrie* and *An American Tragedy* rank among the literary masterpieces of the twentieth century. Their strength, however, is not necessarily in their form (as Dreiser was criticized throughout his career for his sometimes slapdash literary style) as in their substance. Few American writers in his time or out of it could tell a story as compelling as could Dreiser in his best work.

[*See also* Autobiography: General Essay; Fitzgerald, F. Scott; Hemingway, Ernest; Howells, William Dean; Lewis, Sinclair; Mencken, H. L.; Naturalism and Realism; *and* Norris, Frank.]

## SELECTED WORKS

*Sister Carrie* (1900)
*Jennie Gerhardt* (1911)
*The Financier* (1912)
*The Titan* (1914)
*The "Genius"* (1915)
*Free and Other Stories* (1918)
*Twelve Men* (1919)
*A Book about Myself* (1922)
*The Color of a Great City* (1923)
*An American Tragedy* (1925)
*Chains: Lesser Novels and Stories* (1927)
*Dawn* (1931)
*The Bulwark* (1946)

*The Stoic* (1947)
*Collected Plays of Theodore Dreiser* (2000)

## FURTHER READING

Dudley, Dorothy. *Forgotten Frontiers: Dreiser and the Land of the Free*. New York, 1932. Impressionable biography based in part on interviews with Dreiser.

Elias, Robert H. *Theodore Dreiser: Apostle of Nature*. New York, 1948; emended ed., Ithaca, N.Y., 1970. First critical biography.

Gerber, Philip L. *Theodore Dreiser Revisited*. New York, 1992. Perceptive, especially on the trilogy of desire.

Griffin, Joseph. *The Small Canvas: An Introduction to Dreiser's Short Stories*. Rutherford, N.J., 1985.

Lehan, Richard. *Theodore Dreiser: His World and His Novels*. Carbondale, Ill., 1969. Biography and criticism.

Lingeman, Richard. *Theodore Dreiser*. Vol. 1, At the Gates of the City, 1871–1907. Vol. 2, An American Journey, 1908–1945. New York, 1986, 1990. Cultural biography.

McAleer, John J. *Theodore Dreiser: An Introduction and Interpretation*. New York, 1968.

Moers, Ellen. *Two Dreisers*. New York, 1969. Valuable insights on Dreiser's two greatest novels.

Pizer, Donald. *The Novels of Theodore Dreiser: A Critical Study*. Minneapolis, 1976. Historically based criticism, exhaustively researched.

Pizer, Donald, Richard W. Dowell, and Frederic E. Rusch. *Theodore Dreiser: A Primary Bibliography and Reference Guide*. 2d ed. Boston, 1991.

Swanberg, W. A. *Dreiser*. New York, 1965. Distorted portrait in an otherwise thoroughly documented, readable biography.

# W. E. B. DU BOIS

*by Mark Richardson*

"Half-way between Maine and Florida, in the heart of the Alleghenies," wrote W. E. B. Du Bois in *John Brown* (1909), the year before he helped found the NAACP, "a mighty gateway lifts its head and discloses a scene which, a century and a quarter ago, Thomas Jefferson said was 'worthy a voyage across the Atlantic.'" Whereupon he continues citing Jefferson's words from *Notes on the State of Virginia (1785)*:

> You stand on a very high point of land; on your right comes up the Shenandoah, having ranged along the foot of the mountain a hundred miles to find a vent; on your left approaches the Potomac, in quest of a passage also. In the moment of their junction they rush together against the mountain, rend it asunder, and pass off to the sea.

The place is Harpers Ferry, Virginia (later West Virginia), where in 1859 John Brown, having shed blood in Kansas in an effort to make that territory free, struck his blow against slavery, and was hanged for it. In this passage from his biography of Brown, Du Bois sets up a genealogy of the real American "revolution," a genealogy whose lines converge at Harpers Ferry: there is Jefferson, as much as anyone the architect of the Revolution, and the man who taught us how to speak of liberty; then there is John Brown, who, by acting where others were content merely to speak of liberty, helped to start a civil war that would, at least in promise, perfect the American Revolution in what Lincoln called "a new birth of freedom"; and then there is Du Bois, who worked so hard to defend that infant liberty, born in 1863, when the reactionaries of the post-Reconstruction years set about to strangle it in its crib. In his astonishing career as writer and activist, Du Bois was all along simply trying to make America "worthy" of "a

W. E. B. Du Bois.
*(Courtesy of the Library of Congress)*

voyage across the Atlantic." He devoted his long life to the New World idea that men, if they but overcame divisions of class, caste, and color, could, at the moment of their junction, gather such uncontainable, liberating force as Jefferson thought he had found in those two rivers that rend a mountain asunder at Harpers Ferry and pass off to the sea.

## THE LIFE

William Edward Burghardt Du Bois was born to Albert Du Bois and Mary Silvina Burghardt in Great Barrington, Massachusetts, on 23 February 1868; he was of mixed French and African ancestry. Shortly after his birth, his father abandoned the family, never to see his young son again. Du Bois took his primary and secondary education in the local public schools, which were not segregated, and where he followed the college preparatory curriculum. In 1885, the year his mother died, Du Bois entered Fisk University, a black college in Nashville, Tennessee. Upon his graduation he gained admittance to Harvard University as a junior and completed an undergraduate degree there, studying with William James and George Santayana, among others. From Harvard he was awarded a bachelor's degree in 1890 and a master's degree in history in 1891. After a period of study abroad at the University of Berlin, and after having taken a teaching position at Wilberforce University in Ohio, he became, in 1895, the first African American to earn a Ph.D. from Harvard. (His dissertation was later published as *The Suppression of the African Slave Trade in the United States of America, 1638–1870* [1896], and is still consulted by historians over a century later.) In 1896 Du Bois married Nina Gomer and moved to Philadelphia, where he was attached to the University of Pennsylvania as a scholar. Out of his work there came a second book, *The Philadelphia Negro: A Social Study* (1899), a landmark in American sociology. Du Bois accepted a position at Atlanta University in 1897, and it would become the institution with which he was longest affiliated. There he directed an ambitious series of monographs in the sociology of African-American life and wrote the essays eventually collected in *The Souls of Black Folk* (1903), the first of his books to reach beyond the academy to a general readership. The turn of the new century found Du Bois more and more involved in political activism, and he soon emerged as the most powerful critic of Booker T. Washington's policies of accommodation; in 1905 he was a key founder of the Niagara Movement, dedicated to the pursuit of equal rights for blacks. When, in 1910, the National Association for the Advancement of Colored People was formed, Du Bois was appointed its director of publicity and research and relocated to New York City to take up duties as the editor of *The Crisis*. (Under his direction, circulation reached 30,000 within two years and peaked at 100,000 in 1919.)

In 1918, under threat of prosecution by the Department of Justice, Du Bois sailed for France to study the living conditions of black troops at first hand. (He was staunchly opposed to the army's policies of segregation.) The next year Du Bois organized the Pan-African Congress in Paris, which—at his urging—passed resolutions calling for the then-convened Paris Peace Conference to protect the rights of Africans still living under colonial rule. The year 1920 saw publication of a new volume of essays, *Darkwater: Voices from within the Veil*, which reprinted his searing indictment of empire, "The Souls of White Folks" (1910). In 1923 Du Bois visited Africa for the first time, touring Liberia, Sierra Leone, Guinea, and Senegal. In 1926, increasingly attracted to Marxism, he traveled to the Soviet Union (and subsequently published an article in *The Crisis* praising the achievements of the Bolsheviks). In 1928 he published his first novel, *Dark Princess: A Romance*, in which an international alliance of Africans, Asians, and American blacks is arrayed against the great colonial powers. Under pressure because of his espousal in the early 1930s of a nationalist program that deemphasized racial integration for the time being, Du Bois was forced in 1934 to resign his editorship of *The Crisis*, whereupon he took a position again at Atlanta University. Over the next few years he traveled widely in Europe, the USSR, China, and Japan. In 1940 came his autobiography *Dusk of Dawn: An Essay toward an Autobiography of a Race Concept*.

Retiring from Atlanta University, Du Bois moved back to New York City in 1944 to work once more for the NAACP, only to be dismissed a second time in 1948 when his public criticism of U.S. foreign policy in the early years of the Cold War raised an outcry. The Department of Justice indicted Du Bois in 1951 under the Foreign Agents Registration Act of 1938, citing his activities abroad and at home as a critic of U.S. policy, but he was acquitted of all charges. His difficulties did not end here, however. In 1952 the State Department denied him a passport with the explanation that the work he did abroad was not "in the national interest." He did not recover his passport until 1958, but once he did, Du Bois again undertook extensive travel overseas, in the United Kingdom, in Europe, in the USSR., and in the People's Republic of China. Along the way he met with Nikita Khrushchev, Mao Zedong, and Zhou Enlai. In 1960 he traveled to Ghana to celebrate its establishment as an independent republic, and the following year accepted an invitation from Prime Minister Kwame Nkrumah to immigrate to that country, of which in 1963 he became a citizen. In the same year, Du Bois died in Accra on 27 August, leaving behind him a body of writing all but unmatched by twentieth-century American writers in its breadth and variety, consisting of history, sociology, essays, novels, memoirs, poetry, biography, and more.

### THE SOULS OF BLACK FOLK

*The Souls of Black Folk* marks Du Bois's entry into the ranks of the radical civil rights movement; it might be said, as well, to mark the beginning of the civil rights movement as we came to know it in the twentieth century. Up to that point, Du Bois had lived in scholarly detachment, studying, teaching, working as a research fellow, and writing history and sociology. But events in the 1890s gradually made this sort of academic life impossible for Du Bois. He says in *Dusk of Dawn*: "One could not be a calm, cool, and detached scientist while Negroes were lynched, murdered, and starved" (*Writings*, p. 603).

*The Souls of Black Folk* is one result of his decision. It was written to put to rest for good and all—at least to those who could read, and would—the slanders against blacks that seemed to be issuing from every quarter of the country in 1903. David Levering Lewis rightly calls *Souls* an epoch-making book, the sort that divides history into a "before" and "after." Nine of the fourteen essays collected in *The Souls of Black Folk* had been published previously in periodicals, some of them professional journals of historical and sociological scholarship, but Du Bois reworked them all for the book. They range widely in character and subject. Two of them—"Of Our Spiritual Strivings" and "Of the Meaning of Progress"—combine memoir with a very literary blend of philosophy and polemic. Several are chiefly historical or sociological in bearing: "Of the Dawn of Freedom" (a revisionist account of the rise and fall of the Freedmen's Bureau); "Of the Quest of the Golden Fleece" (about cotton agriculture and black peonage in the postwar period); and "Of the Black Belt" (a study of the largely black counties of southern Georgia). One, "Of Alexander Crummell," is a portrait of a major figure in the history of American education. Another chapter, "Of the Coming of John," is a paradigmatic short story about the education of one young black man from Georgia. "Of the Passing of the First Born," an intensely personal elegy for Du Bois's first child, who died in infancy, approaches the intensity of a prose poem. There is an essay on religion in the South, "Of the Faith of the Fathers"; a polemical engagement in "Of Mr. Booker T. Washington and Others"; an essay on postwar education, "Of the Training of Black Men"; a suggestive, allegorical treatment of the ideal of a liberal education, titled "Of the Wings of Atalanta"; and a concluding chapter, "Of the Sorrow Songs," a pioneering inquiry into the meaning of the Negro spiritual, which had only lately begun to attract the attention of musicologists and historians.

*The Souls of Black Folk* was something of a sensation: twelve printings were exhausted by June of its first year in print, and by October two hundred copies per week were selling—remarkable figures for a book of such uncommon erudition. In 1905 *Souls* was brought out in England. Five years after it first appeared, more than 9,500 copies had been sold. Southern responses were intemperate and often savage, as might be expected. The *Nashville American* declared the book "dangerous for the Negro to read." A reviewer for the *Houston Chronicle*, in a fit of panic perhaps indicative of his own preoccupations, demanded that authorities arrest Du Bois for "inciting rape." Even the relatively moderate *New York Times* chose a white southerner to review the book, and, although he was not so severe as his compatriots from the South, he expressed grave reservations, and speculated that Du Bois, born and reared in Massachusetts, really did not know the South at all.

There is a deviously mortuary grace to the phrase with which Du Bois opens the book: "Herein lie buried many things," he says, "which if read with patience may show the strange meaning of being black here at the dawning of the Twentieth Century. This meaning is not without interest to you, Gentle Reader; for the problem of the Twentieth Century is the problem of the color line."

(*Writings*, p. 359). *Souls* will be an exhumation of sorts: after all, Du Bois, and his fellows "within the veil," know best where the American bodies are buried. And though it is arresting, Du Bois establishes at once that the "color line" of which he will speak separates not only whites and blacks generally in America, and throughout the world, but also separates him from his reader—a figure with whom, he intimates, his relations are perhaps to be difficult: "Need I add that I who speak here am bone of the bone and flesh of the flesh of them that live within the Veil?" he says, echoing Adam's words in Genesis 2:23.

We are made aware, here, of a fact of singular importance: almost always we simply take it for granted that the American reader is "white." When Du Bois startles us into the thought that the "American gaze" is, in the first instance, always a white gaze—even when situated (so to speak) in a black mind—he hints at an important idea: to read American literature or American history, both of which take for granted a necessarily unscrutinized "white" way of seeing, is—for black folk—to be given an education in self-distrust. For example, *Huckleberry Finn* (1884)—Twain's unimpeachable politics notwithstanding—somehow manages to admire a black man, Jim, chiefly by making an innocent, self-sacrificial child of him. And in 1903 our literature was, for better and for worse, constituted by books like these. Any black reader who would educate himself by reading them must undertake something of a struggle: he must "de-colonize" his mind, as the radicals used to say in the 1960s—and Du Bois was well ahead of them.

"After the Egyptian and Indian, the Greek and Roman, the Teuton and Mongolian," Du Bois writes in the first chapter of *Souls*,

> the Negro is a sort of seventh son, born with a veil, and gifted with second-sight in this American world,—a world which yields him no true self-consciousness, but only lets him see himself through the revelation of the other world. It is a peculiar sensation, this double-consciousness, this sense of always looking at one's self through the eyes of others, of measuring one's soul by the tape of a world that looks on in amused contempt and pity. One ever feels his twoness,—an American, a Negro; two souls, two thoughts, two unreconciled strivings; two warring ideals in one dark body, whose dogged strength alone keeps it from being torn asunder.
>
> (*Writings*, p. 364)

Double-consciousness is equivocally a gift and a curse. It is a gift insofar as it helps those who have it toward a purchase on the social world that those without the veil might never achieve: namely, the intuition (later, the conviction) that the social world we inhabit is not, in fact, of a "natural" kind, but of an "absurd" kind, as the existentialists say—that it is a contingent and historical world, a made world that can be remade in turn. But double-consciousness is at the same time a curse because, as Du Bois says, it first requires of a man that he "measure his soul" by "the tape" of a world that holds him in contempt, or regards him, simply, with pity: he can have no "true" self-consciousness; he cannot know himself as in himself he "really" is; the very language through which he "thinks" the world (and the self) is a white language, and in it he is Object, not Subject; Other, not Same; in it he is seen to act from passion more than from reason, to be more readily assimilated to nature than to culture, and more to the body than to the mind. The biological, literary, historiographical, and anthropological writing of the nineteenth century—especially of the period after 1840—is everywhere shaped by precisely these assumptions, such that it becomes difficult ever to think *entirely* beyond the reach of them. The literary language even of the most innovative African-American writers is, at times, inflected by imperfectly acknowledged "white" assumptions.

"Soul" and "spirit," then, are the ideals; for far too long black men and women had been thought of chiefly as "bodies." And over against the "souls" of black folk, Du Bois forever sets the prison house, the immanence, of the flesh. There is, in his thinking, an abiding idealist (or perhaps dualist) notion that self cannot be somehow identical with body, and this leads him to speak of the "unmanning" of men by the allure of the flesh, by which Du Bois means, in the farther reaches of his allegory, the allure of all things purely material. It must be admitted that there is a patriarchal drift to the language in which *Souls* is written, notwithstanding that Du Bois was a sincere feminist. The peculiar situation of African-American men probably made this inevitable: some reassertion of "masculinity" simply had to be made over against the predations of a culture that would assign the prerogatives of "manhood" to white men only—a culture that insisted, moreover, on articulating its power in more or less gendered (and sexualized) terms. So, the "aspiring self" Du Bois imagines in *Souls* is implicitly gendered "masculine"; the terms of the debate in which he was engaged—and these he certainly did not set—required it. (The character "Atalanta," who figures so largely in the book, is no exception; the allegorical meaning of her

ascetic self-discipline is what really concerns Du Bois, not her "femininity.")

For many in America, and for many in the West generally, "blackness" came to embody sexuality *as such*, the flesh *as such*: this is the idea Du Bois most wishes to chasten his "Gentle Readers" out of in speaking of the "souls" of black folk. To be sure, this "white" (and invidious) association of "color" with "sexuality" explains much about *Souls*: why it so often relies on metaphors of sensualist "decadence" to figure what had been done to the freedmen and their posterity (as in "Of the Wings of Atalanta"); why Booker T. Washington should so consistently be stigmatized in the book as a kind of "feminizing" force—as a seducer who would "unman" African Americans, giving them over entirely to the fate of the body, and to the abuse, as hewers of wood and drawers of water, of big capital; why Du Bois should everywhere be at pains to defend black Americans against the charge, urged constantly in those days, and often on so-called scientific grounds, of sexual immorality; and why Du Bois at times sounds rather monkish and otherworldly, rather, indeed, like an ascetic—as when he quotes with approval Goethe's injunction in *Faust*, "Deny yourself, you must deny yourself" (*Writings*, p. 420).

This brings us to the Wizard of Tuskegee, Booker T. Washington, and to Du Bois's great debate with him about the souls of black folk. In "Of Our Spiritual Strivings," Du Bois sketches out, in brief, the history of the postwar period for African Americans: there was emancipation itself; then the granting of citizenship and suffrage; then what Du Bois bitterly calls "The Revolution of 1876" (the election that put an end to Reconstruction); and with that, the freedmen and their sons and daughters were left to wander, like forsaken Israelites, in a desert somewhere between Pharaoh and a nation they could rightly call home. In this "wilderness" appeared before the freedmen, like the biblical pillar of fire, what Du Bois calls "the ideal of 'book learning'; the curiosity, born of compulsory ignorance, to know and test the power of the cabalistic letters of the white man, the longing to know. Here at last seemed to have been discovered the mountain path to Canaan" (p. 367). "Cabalistic" letters, says Du Bois—and the adjective is carefully chosen. The Cabala is the word of God handed down by Moses to the rabbis in the desert: the Talmud. Du Bois is setting up a rather exact allegory in *The Souls of Black Folk*: "ten thousand thousand" black Americans are adrift, and two men would be their Moses—Du Bois with his Cabala (all the "book learning" of the West), and Washington with his Tuskegee program of "industrial training." The one tends to the souls of black folk, the other to their bodies alone.

The chief underwriters of black educational institutions in the South in the post-Reconstruction period were organizations whose funds came for the most part from northern capitalists. The money was disbursed largely through two organizations: the Southern Education Board and the General Education Board. As David Levering Lewis points out, "a partial roster of the officers and trustees of the new SEB was a roll call of the arbiters of the Industrial North and the New South"—railroad money, money from the Wanamaker Department Store fortune, from Wall Street, from Standard Oil, and so on (*W. E. B. Du Bois: Biography of a Race, 1868–1919*, p. 266). The SEB, founded in 1901, and the GEB, created in 1902, disbursed some $177 million to white colleges and universities and some $22 million to black colleges and universities between 1902 and 1930. The directors of these organizations sought reconciliation between North and South and the development of southern labor and resources by northern capital, and these goals required that they defer to southern opinion on the "Negro Question." "The rich and dominating North," Du Bois explains in *Souls,* "was not only weary of the race problem, but was investing largely in Southern enterprises, and welcomed any method of peaceful cooperation" (*Writings*, p. 398). Booker T. Washington perfectly suited their purposes after his groundbreaking 1895 speech, familiarly known as the Atlanta Compromise. In it, he agreed to put off demands for real political and civil rights in favor of economic development. "As we have proved our loyalty to you in the past," Washington said to his white audience,

> nursing your children, watching by the sick-bed of your mothers and fathers, and often following them with tear-dimmed eyes to their graves, so in the future, in our humble way, we shall stand by you with a devotion that no foreigner can approach, ready to lay down our lives, if need be, in defence of yours, interlacing our industrial, commercial, civil, and religious life with yours in a way that shall make the interests of both races one. In all things that are purely social we can be as separate as the fingers, yet one as the hand in all things essential to mutual progress.
>
> (*Up from Slavery*, p. 156)

The studied "humility" of the address struck Du Bois as embarrassing; the concession to "social separation" struck him as reprehensible.

Washington reports in *Up from Slavery* (1901) that "one of the saddest things" he ever saw was a young black man "sitting down in a one-room cabin, with grease on his clothing, filth all around him, and weeds in the yard and garden, engaged in studying a French grammar" (p. 86). The youth, Washington implied, would be much better off, and much happier, if he practiced a trade instead of studying "big books" with "high-sounding subjects." To which Du Bois dryly retorts in *Souls*: "One wonders what Socrates and St. Francis of Assisi would say to this" (*Writings*, p. 393). Well, what northern capitalists had to say to it was plain enough: Washington on the merits of studying French grammar was music to their ears. He soon became a salaried field agent for the SEB, with the result (among other things) that Du Bois's Atlanta University was ignored by northern benefactors while Tuskegee flourished. Du Bois later remarked of the period in *Dusk of Dawn*: "The control [of the SEB and GEB] was to be drastic. The Negro intelligentsia was to be suppressed and hammered into conformity" (*Writings*, p. 608). All of which explains why Du Bois's attack on Washington in *The Souls of Black Folk* is so utterly devastating—although Du Bois manages, throughout, to sustain an essentially temperate, even cordial, tone: his iron fist is velvet gloved.

The heart of his argument against Washington is this:

> Mr. Washington represents in Negro thought the old attitude of adjustment and submission; but adjustment at such a peculiar time as to make his programme unique. This is an age of unusual economic development, and Mr. Washington's programme naturally takes an economic cast, becoming a gospel of Work and Money to such an extent as apparently almost completely to overshadow the higher aims of life. Moreover, this is an age when the more advanced races are coming in closer contact with the less developed races, and the race-feeling is therefore intensified; and Mr. Washington's programme practically accepts the alleged inferiority of the Negro races. Again, in our own land, the reaction from the sentiment of war time has given impetus to race-prejudice against Negroes, and Mr. Washington withdraws many of the high demands of Negroes as men and American citizens. In other periods of intensified prejudice all the Negro's tendency to self-assertion has been called forth; at this period a policy of submission is advocated. In the history of nearly all other races and peoples the doctrine preached at such crises has been that manly self-respect is worth more than lands and houses, and that a people who voluntarily surrender such respect, or cease striving for it, are not worth civilizing.
>
> (*Writings*, p. 398)

Washington becomes, in the story Du Bois tells, an instrument in the hands of white supremacy and of capital; and both institutions—the political and the economic—employ him for the purpose of "re-enslaving" the freedman, of "adjusting" him, more or less bloodlessly, to "submission" (the bloodier instruments of "adjustment" were wielded chiefly by rogue elements of the southern white working class under the protection of the local Democratic Party). In *Souls*, Du Bois associates Washington with what might be called the capitalist extremism of the Gilded Age, which, in its "astonishing commercial development," had grown "ashamed of having bestowed so much sentiment on Negroes," and which henceforth would be "concentrating its energies on Dollars" (p. 392). This "unusual economic development"—the word "unusual" carries the considerable force of Du Boisian understatement—had come to comprise as well the acquisition and administration of colonies in Hawaii, the West Indies, and the Philippines. The reassertion of white supremacy at home, in the post-Reconstruction period, was but a part of a larger project: the consolidation of white authority over peoples of color everywhere in the world—by the United States, England, France, Germany, Italy, and Belgium.

When set in this larger, global context, Washington emerges—under Du Bois's direction—as a veritable agent of colonial rule, as a figure who would sell out black "manhood," and who would, in fact, pander his race to a white ravisher. He had become, Du Bois pretty clearly implies, the Great Emasculator: he had "sapped the manhood" of the race, advocated a "policy of submission," withdrawn the demands of Negroes "as men," acquiesced in their relegation, again, to a "servile caste," yielded up their "manhood rights," and "overlooked certain elements of true manhood." It is exactly as Du Bois would have it in the epigraph he chose for this essay (and assay), "Of Mr. Booker T. Washington and Others": "From birth to death enslaved; in word, in deed, *unmanned*!" The line is from Byron's *Child Harold's Pilgrimage* (1813–1814) and it comes in a passage often cited in the literature of the more fiery abolitionists of old: "Hereditary bondsmen! Know ye not / Who would be free themselves must strike the blow?" It is no accident, as the saying goes, that when Du Bois convened a 1906 meeting of the Niagara Movement, he chose as the site Harpers Ferry, where John Brown—the "meteor of the war," as Melville put it—had staged his bloody insurrection in 1859.

### JOHN BROWN *AND* THE NEGRO

In November 1903 Ellis Paxson Oberholtzer invited Du Bois to write a book about the great abolitionist Frederick Douglass for the American Crisis Biographies series, of which Oberholtzer was the general editor. Du Bois agreed at once, only to have the invitation rescinded several months later. Booker T. Washington, it turned out, wanted the volume on Douglass for himself, and given Washington's fame, Oberholtzer gave the title to him, offering an irritated Du Bois the chance to choose another subject for his own contribution. Du Bois proposed a biography of Nat Turner, leader of a bloody slave insurrection in 1831, but when that was declined on the grounds that Turner was too incendiary a figure, Du Bois accepted Oberholtzer's suggestion that he write about John Brown instead. The reader should bear in mind the book's origins in these prickly negotiations because *John Brown* (1909) obliquely, but devastatingly, extends Du Bois's unforgiving critique of the accommodationist strategies he associated with Washington (though Washington is never mentioned by name). A kind of unspoken analogy lies behind the book: Du Bois is to Washington what John Brown was to the "moderate" abolitionists of his own day—a figure absolutely unwilling to compromise his principles, and whom time would fully vindicate. In identifying with Brown, as he surely does, Du Bois identifies with a prophet as misunderstood and feared in his own day as he would be held in awe by generations to come. At a time when even relatively liberal Americans spoke of Brown with a wary embarrassment—indeed, to many he was little better than what we now would call a terrorist—Du Bois made no bones about it: his book, he announces in a brief preface, is "a tribute to the man who of all Americans has perhaps come nearest to touching the real souls of black folk" (*John Brown*, p. xxv).

In telling Brown's story, Du Bois relies on what was then the best scholarship available, and he writes with his customary eloquence. But of most interest to contemporary readers is the last chapter of the book, "The Legacy of John Brown." There Du Bois points to a simple coincidence: 1859, the year of Brown's martyrdom, was the also the year of Charles Darwin's *The Origin of Species*. And "since that day," as Du Bois says, "tremendous scientific and economic advance has been accompanied by distinct signs of moral retrogression in social philosophy. Strong arguments have been made for the fostering of war, the utility of human degradation and disease, and the inevitable and known inferiority of certain classes and races of men" (p. 225). He refers, of course, to what came to be called Social Darwinism: the attempt to bend the new biology that Darwin had done so much to create to the purposes of empire, whereby one race or people is subjected to the will of another. The very complicated idea of natural selection had been travestied. To robber baron industrialists and unapologetic imperialists it seemed to explain, and also to justify, the global supremacy of Europeans and their descendants in North America; indeed, it seemed to consign to the dustbin of history the high end for which John Brown had died—what Du Bois calls his hope that "a more just and a more equal" distribution of property and power might be realized. Above all, the forces of reaction thought they had found in Darwin a thinker who could set their own privilege on a "natural" and therefore unchallengeable footing.

Du Bois could not abide that sort of thinking. And he devotes his closing chapter as much to the vindication of Darwin's legacy as to the defense of Brown's. "What the age of Darwin has done," he maintains, against the grain of current opinion, "is to add to the eighteenth-century idea of individual worth the complementary idea of physical immortality" (p. 227). By that last phrase he means the physical immortality of homo sapiens as a species, not, of course, that of any particular individuals. In other words, Darwin showed us that, contrary to what Christianity had always taught, the world has no end—no limit. Its ongoing development is potentially infinite and certainly unpredictable. "And this," adds Du Bois,

> far from annulling or contracting the idea of human freedom, rather emphasizes its necessity and eternal possibility—the boundlessness and endlessness of human achievement. Freedom has come to mean not individual caprice or aberration, but social self-realization in an endless chain of selves; and freedom for such development is not the denial but the central assertion of the evolutionary theory.
>
> (pp. 227–228)

Here, Du Bois anticipates the later insights of such politically progressive Darwinians as Stephen Jay Gould, which makes his book on John Brown a contribution not merely to history and biography but to the history of ideas.

With *The Negro*, published in 1915, Du Bois achieves three notable things: first, he offers a concise synthesis of the best scholarship available on the subject and writes for the general reader, who knew almost nothing of African history, rather than for specialists; second, he is uncompromising in his demonstration that "race" is neither an essential nor a scientifically valid means of distinguishing one people from another (that is, he demonstrates that "race" as we know it in the New World

is a product of historical and economic conditions, not of biological ones); and third, he shows how New World slavery was genuinely novel in the long history of human slavery, in that it arose alongside, and in the service of, the new industrial capitalist economies of America, England, and western Europe. Slavery, as developed in the colonies of the New World and in the United States, constituted an unprecedented means of production rooted in a racial caste system, and devoted to the mass production of a handful of commodities traded on a global market (chiefly rice, cotton, tobacco, and sugar). Du Bois's analysis in *The Negro*, coming as it did in 1915, alerts his reader to the fact that slavery, imperialism, and the European Scramble for Africa did much to bring on what Europeans were soon to be calling the Great War of 1914–1918. As any serious reader of Du Bois might expect, *The Negro* is at once exacting—Du Bois's training in historiography and sociology is much in evidence—and eloquent. Du Bois's estimation of the total cost of the slave trade is as shocking as it is moving. "It would be conservative," he writes, after having reckoned the total number of slaves expatriated from Africa, and the likely number that died along the trade routes and in the middle passage, "to say that the slave trade cost Negro Africa 100,000,000 souls. And yet people ask to-day the cause of the stagnation of culture in that land since 1600!" (p. 156). Furthermore, Europe in 1600 and after was hardly a decadent, barbaric realm, as Du Bois notes with caustic irony. The slave trade flourished not in the Dark Ages but in the epoch of the Renaissance and the Enlightenment. "Raphael painted, Luther preached, Corneille wrote, and Milton sung," Du Bois says bitterly,

> And through it all, for four hundred years, the dark captives wound to the sea amid the bleaching bones of the dead; for four hundred years the sharks followed the scurrying ships; for four hundred years America was strewn with the living and dying millions of a transplanted race; for four hundred years Ethiopia stretched her hands unto God.
>
> (p. 159)

*The Negro* is a book now too seldom read.

## THE LATER YEARS

It is difficult in so short a review of Du Bois's life to suggest the range and ambition of his writings, which, as already indicated, include works not merely of history, sociology, and essay but of fiction, poetry, and autobiography. He once said that of all his books he loved *Dark Princess: A Romance* the best. This novel, published first in 1928, never attracted a wide readership, and certainly Du Bois loses something of his usual elegance and guile as a writer when he turns to fiction. It will strike most readers as an awkward performance. But it is nonetheless fascinating.

The opening paragraphs of the novel tell the story of how Matthew Towns, the black protagonist, is compelled to leave the University of Manhattan in his junior year when he is refused admittance into the requisite course in obstetrics. The college dean (a new hire, and a southerner) dismisses him with the curt declaration that no white woman should be expected to permit a "nigger doctor" to deliver her baby. The attendance of a black obstetrician on the delivery of a white baby is, within the terms of white supremacy, unthinkable, and the reasons for this are worth going into. Simone de Beauvoir has suggested that, at the moment of parturition, the body of a woman is, at least as patriarchy would have us see her, somehow most essentially a body. ("Everywhere life is germinating inspires disgust," Beauvoir says in *The Second Sex* [1949]; hence the ancient taboos and proscriptions stigmatizing menstruation and childbirth, and requiring purification from them.) In speaking of the souls of black folk, of course, Du Bois had all along, and with devastating force, shown how white supremacy thinks of colored bodies as more purely physical and sensual, and less "intellectual" and spiritual, than white ones. The attendance of a "nigger doctor" on a white birth is intolerable because he would (so to speak) despiritualize the parturition all the more; he would desanctify it, animalize it, biologize it—he would put the white mind in an altogether unbearable relation to the prospect of its own reproduction (which it must, of necessity, view as not merely biological, not merely animal). The proscription is of course double because black fathering of white babies is also forbidden and hysterically feared (as if that route of insemination is radically unspiritual, radically biological; or as if that route of insemination does not "tie a subtle knot" between spirit and body but in fact reduces spirit to body). For white supremacy, blackness is everywhere a token of animality, of pure physicality. The racist assumptions of Social Darwinist thinking make this clear, as does also the behavior of white colonizers in Africa and Asia. "The horror, the horror!" say the latter with Joseph Conrad's Mr. Kurtz in *The Heart of Darkness* (1902). But the horror of which they speak is simply the horror of seeing in themselves a body. (Their unwillingness to think of themselves as animals perhaps explains why they could not assimilate Darwin without first distorting and refashioning his ideas.)

In any case, Matthew Towns, now banished from medical school, finds himself adrift. He goes abroad, to Europe, and there becomes acquainted with the "dark princess" of the novel's title: the daughter of a maharajah in British India. She is at the center of a loosely organized conspiracy of sorts: representatives of peoples in the colonized and "colored" parts of the world have come together to mount an organized struggle against empire and racism, a struggle that would unite American blacks with Chinese, Indians, Arabs, Africans, and Japanese. No doubt Du Bois has in mind, as a kind of model of how the thing might be done, the expatriate Bolshevik movement of the years leading up to the Russian Revolution. But to the Marxist analysis of the global situation in the early 1920s he adds, in *The Dark Princess*, an essential insight: it is not merely a question of capital exploiting labor on a global market; it is a question of white capital exploiting colored labor—as much in the American South as in the Belgian Congo.

The plot of *Dark Princess* is improbable, the characterization often puzzling. But it is a novel of ideas—a novel, in fact, of propaganda in the best sense. This is in keeping with Du Bois's argument in his seminal essay, "The Criteria of Negro Art" (1926). The artist, he maintains, must be not merely an "apostle of Beauty" but an "apostle of Truth and Right" as well:

> Free he is but freedom is ever bounded by Truth and Justice; and slavery only dogs him when he is denied the right to tell the Truth or recognize an ideal of Justice. Thus all Art is propaganda and ever must be, despite the wailing of the purists. I stand in utter shamelessness and say that whatever art I have for writing has been used always for propaganda for gaining the right of black folk to love and enjoy. I do not care a damn for any art that is not used for propaganda. But I do care when propaganda is confined to one side while the other is stripped and silent.

> (*Writings*, p. 1000)

The success of his undertaking in *Dark Princess* must be judged according to these criteria. And there can be no doubt that it is a major contribution to the field that we now know as postcolonial studies. Here, as in all his works, essay and fiction alike, Du Bois thinks through the problem of the "color line" in genuinely global terms.

When *Dark Princess* appeared in 1928, Du Bois was already sixty years old. But the next twelve years saw the publication of two of his most remarkable books: *Black Reconstruction: An Essay toward a History of the Part Which Black Folk Played in the Attempt to Reconstruct*

*Democracy in America, 1860–1880* (1935), and *Dusk of Dawn: An Essay toward an Autobiography of a Race Concept* (1940). The first is a monumental study of the United States in the post–Civil War period, whose Marxist interpretation of the collapse of Reconstruction remains to this day a major (if controversial) contribution to American historiography. The second is certainly one of the most unusual and provocative autobiographies ever produced in this country. Here the reader is, by stages, allowed to see emerge the real figure in the carpet of late-nineteenth- and early-twentieth-century European and American history: the color line, as it was etched across the whole of the globe by European colonizers and by American segregationists. In a series of withering chapters on "Science and Empire," "The Concept of Race," and "The White World," Du Bois tells the story of what was, in certain respects, the most astonishing invention of the Europeans: the idea of "race," which itself took on seeming life, and in a sense, became an "actor" on the world stage. The story of Du Bois's own life is necessarily tangled up in the story of that unreal but decisive "actor" (white folks had always already written the "biographies" of black folks—had always already determined the shape their lives might take). And so the reader finds in *Dusk of Dawn* not so much the story of an individual named W. E. B. Du Bois as "the autobiography of a concept of race," as Du Bois strikingly puts it in his preface to the volume.

Over the course of his career Du Bois published scores of articles and essays in *The Crisis*, which he edited, and in a number of other periodicals. These had a significant readership, as did such books as *The Suppression of the African Slave Trade*, *The Souls of Black Folk*, and *Dusk of Dawn*. And yet beyond them, the key to this extraordinary man's life and work might well lie in that much less widely known of his books, *John Brown*, the brief measure of which we have already taken. Like Shields Green, the black confederate of Brown who preceded him to the gallows, Du Bois chose, in his own way, to go with "the old man" (as Brown was sometimes called). And in this connection no reader of Du Bois can forget a scene described in *Dusk of Dawn*. The year is 1906 and Du Bois has called together, at Harpers Ferry, Virginia, a meeting of the Niagara Movement, the most radical civil rights organization then in existence. It was "in significance if not in numbers," Du Bois says, "one of the greatest meetings that American Negroes have ever held. We made pilgrimage at dawn bare-footed to the scene of Brown's martyrdom and we talked some of the plainest English that has been given voice by black

men in America" (*Writings*, pp. 618–619). The battle that these "pilgrims" waged, as they explain in a public statement, was not for themselves alone, but for "all true Americans." It was and still remains a battle "for ideals, lest this, our common fatherland, false to its founding, become in truth the land of the Thief and the home of the Slave—a by-word and a hissing among nations for its sounding pretensions and pitiful accomplishment" (p. 619). In America, Du Bois explains in *John Brown*, "we had built a wonderful industrial machine," and had done it on the backs of colored labor. It was a machine "quickly rather than carefully built, formed of forcing rather than of growth, involving sinful and unnecessary expense" (*John Brown*, p. 236). His admonition to his countrymen—and here Du Bois only follows Brown as he would have us understand that martyr's legacy—is still as crystalline in its simplicity as it is revolutionary in its implications for a world of global capital: "Better smaller production and more equitable distribution," he says; "better fewer miles of railway and more honor, truth, and liberty; better fewer millionaires and more contentment" (p. 236).

## SELECTED WORKS

*The Souls of Black Folk* (1903)

*John Brown* (1909)

*The Negro* (1915)

*Dark Princess: A Romance* (1928)

*Writings* (1986)

*Black Reconstruction in America* (1992). Reprint of *Black Reconstruction: An Essay toward a History of the Part Which Black Folk Played in the Attempt to Reconstruct Democracy in America, 1860–1880* (1935)

## FURTHER READING

Lewis, David Levering. *W. E. B. Du Bois: Biography of a Race, 1868–1919*. New York, 1993.

Lewis, David Levering. *W. E. B. Du Bois: The Fight For Equality and the American Century, 1919–1963*. New York, 2000. This and the preceding volume constitute the best biography of Du Bois, and in fact one of the best biographies of any American.

Rampersad, Arnold. *The Art and Imagination of W. E. B. Du Bois*. Cambridge, Mass., 1976.

Reed, Adolph, Jr. *W. E. B. Du Bois and American Political Thought: Fabianism and the Color Line*. New York, 1997.

Sundquist, Eric J. *To Wake the Nations: Race in the Making of American Literature*. Cambridge, Mass., 1993. A book of great breadth that includes an extensive, nuanced study of Du Bois.

# PAUL LAURENCE DUNBAR

*by David L. Dudley*

Paul Laurence Dunbar, a son of former slaves, was born on 27 June 1872 in Dayton, Ohio. His father, Joshua Dunbar, had escaped from slavery and fought for the Union Army. Dunbar's mother, Matilda Murphy, taught her son to read and inculcated in him a love of literature. Dunbar's parents separated before he was two and divorced in 1876. His father entered the Soldiers' Home, leaving his wife and son to fend for themselves. Dunbar excelled in high school, where he was elected class president and edited the school paper. More significant was his role as editor and publisher of several editions of the *Dayton Tattler*, a newspaper for and about the black community.

Dunbar had hoped to pursue a law degree after graduation but could not afford further study. Unable to find meaningful work, he ended up an elevator operator at four dollars per week. He read widely and wrote poetry, absorbing especially the work of the British romantics and the American poet James Whitcomb Riley.

### DISCOVERY AND EARLY CAREER

Paul Laurence Dunbar's break came in 1892, when he was invited to compose a poem for the Western Association of Writers meeting in Dayton. Impressed, some attendees invited him to join their association and wrote him letters of introduction. Thus, he came to the attention of his model and inspiration, James Whitcomb Riley, who sent him a letter of support.

Encouraged, Dunbar published *Oak and Ivy*, a book of verse, at his own expense. Appearing in 1893, it was printed in five hundred copies and sold well. That same year Charles A. Thatcher, a Toledo lawyer, befriended the young poet and arranged public readings for him. In June, Dunbar attended the World's Columbian Exposition in

Paul Laurence Dunbar. Frontispiece, *Lyrics of Sunshine and Shadow*, 1905. (*Courtesy of the Library of Congress*)

Chicago and landed a job working for Frederick Douglass, the famous civil rights champion.

In 1895, Dunbar's second book of poetry, *Majors and Minors*, was published. Consisting of ninety-three poems, it was privately printed in an edition of one thousand copies. The "Majors" were standard English poems that stood first in the volume; they were followed by the "Minors," which were dialect poems. This collection includes some of Dunbar's best and most famous poems, including "Ere Sleep Comes Down to Soothe the Weary Eyes," "We Wear the Mask," and "When Malindy Sings."

H. A. Tobey, a Toledo doctor who frequently gave Dunbar and his mother financial assistance, sent a copy of *Majors and Minors* to a friend, who passed it along to William Dean Howells, the novelist, editor, and encourager of young talent who was the most influential literary figure of the era. Howells praised Dunbar's dialect poems in a review published in *Harper's Weekly* (27 June 1896).

### "MAJORS" AND "MINORS"

Howells's *Harper's Weekly* review cut like a two-edged sword. It brought Dunbar recognition and helped him secure a contract for another book. In devaluing his standard English poems while praising the dialect poems, however, Howells seemed to be labeling Dunbar a dialect poet. He found nothing exceptional in many of the standard English poems, but asserted that in the dialect poems, Dunbar is

> the first man of his color to study his race objectively, to analyze it to himself, and then to represent it in art as he felt it and found it to be; to represent it humorously, yet tenderly, and above all faithfully.

Dunbar now faced a dilemma. America's most influential critic had dubbed him a dialect poet, uniquely gifted to represent his race to the white world. Dunbar knew himself to be his era's best writer of such poems and reportedly found pleasure and satisfaction in them. They were not, however, his "Majors"—works through which he hoped to establish a reputation. Yet critics, publishers, and the reading public, black and white alike, preferred them, and Dunbar would continue to write them to the end of his life.

Late in 1896 Dodd, Mead brought out *Lyrics of Lowly Life*. This volume of 105 poems, almost all of which had previously appeared in *Oak and Ivy* or *Majors and Minors*, was the turning point in Dunbar's life and is representative of the writer's achievement in poetry. Three other collections would follow: *Lyrics of the Hearthside* (1899), *Lyrics of Love and Laughter* (1903), and *Lyrics of Sunshine and Shadow* (1905). Since, however, Dunbar's talent as a poet did not grow dramatically and since he wrote excellent and representative verse from the beginning of his career, it is appropriate at this point to discuss the poetry as a whole, rather than to assess his collections individually.

## THE POETRY

A simple way to divide Dunbar's poetry is to separate it into two groups: the standard English poems and those in dialect. This division, however, oversimplifies matters. A more helpful division might be to speak of Dunbar's standard English poems on traditional subjects; poems of what one critic calls "racial fire"; poems with a strong autobiographical element; and dialect poems, consisting mostly of black dialect verse but including also poems in white midwestern dialect and even experiments with German English and Irish English.

Most of Dunbar's poems are in standard English and treat subjects and themes familiar in the British and American poetic traditions. Polished and masterful in their use of varied meters and forms, many of them are nevertheless of limited interest. Their themes are familiar—love, nature, life's disappointments, an examination of the speaker's moods and attitudes—and so are their tonal colors of irony, wistfulness, earnest appreciation of beauty, and sentimentality. Howells's opinion of them seems correct: many of these lyrics could have been written by other poets skilled in the forms and genteel language of late-nineteenth-century verse.

Of greater importance are standard English poems celebrating the achievements of black people, extolling their racial heritage, and deploring their unjust treatment at the hands of a racist society. These Dunbar wrote from the beginning of his career to almost its end. He placed his "Ode to Ethiopia" first in *Oak and Ivy*; in it, the poet pledges his loyalty to his "Mother Race," once crushed under slavery but now rising again in freedom, with black men and women working beside white people to build America anew. "Frederick Douglass," written shortly after Douglass's death, hails his fearless fight for freedom and declares that those who "have touched his hand" will continue his struggle until the coming day of triumph. "The Colored Soldiers" recalls the bravery of the black soldiers who fought and sacrificed valiantly for the Union in the Civil War, but wonders why they have not been afforded the rights of citizens since then.

"We Wear the Mask," one of Dunbar's most celebrated poems, first appeared in *Majors and Minors*. Its speakers are African Americans who feel compelled to show the world—presumably the white world—only the mask that grins and lies, while behind it human beings tortured by the effects of prejudice and injustice weep and cry out to God for help. Eight years later, in *Lyrics of Love and Laughter*, "The Haunted Oak" tells in ballad form the story of an innocent black man lynched by hooded white men, including a doctor, a judge, and a minister.

Also among the standard English poems are several that contain autobiographical elements, often expressing the frustration and disenchantment that some believe characterized Dunbar's life. "A Career," "The Crisis," "Unexpressed," and "Life's Tragedy" may all refer to the poet's troubles, but two other poems, among his best known, seem without question to express his pain. "Sympathy," which contains the famous line "I know why the caged bird sings," uses the caged bird as a symbol of the speaker's own sense of entrapment. Just as the bird sings when it is most unhappy and most desires freedom, so does the speaker use his song, or poetry, to express his desire for freedom to write the poetry he desires and escape the "cage" of publishers and public expectations. A short piece titled "The Poet" appears to be Dunbar's artistic epitaph. It speaks of one who sang of life and love—themes that did not receive popular approval. The poem ends, "But ah, the world, it turned to praise / A jingle in broken tongue." The "broken tongue" has been taken to mean the dialect poetry that caused Dunbar so much conflict.

It would be wrong to conclude that Dunbar disliked his dialect poems or that he did not want to write them—that he was somehow forced into it by the demands of publishers and readers. The problem for Dunbar was that these poems, of less value in his eyes than his other works, quickly came to be his most popular and seemed destined to become the basis of his lasting reputation. Some have criticized the dialect poems for presenting stereotypical portraits of black people as simple folk, easily contented with the simple pleasures of rural life, good natured, worthy to be regarded humorously or sentimentally. Two poems, "The Deserted Plantation" and "Chrismus on the Plantation," even present blacks who long for the old days of slavery. Another, "The Party," presents lively slaves decked out in their finery, dancing joyously and feasting on a bountiful spread that few real slaves ever enjoyed. Other poems, such as "A Banjo Song" and "When De Co'n Pone's Hot," describe black people finding pure pleasure in ordinary things such as music and food. But Dunbar never presents African Americans as debased or animalistic—images familiar in his time from the racist novels of writers like Thomas Dixon. Dunbar's blacks are loyal, generous, kind, and loving, and the poet regards them affectionately as part of a lost past rooted in communal life tied closely to the earth's seasonal rhythms. Famous dialect poems such as "When Malindy Sings" and "Lil' Brown Baby" exemplify how these poems celebrate African-American life and culture.

## NEW ENDEAVORS

In February 1897 Dunbar met Alice Ruth Moore, an accomplished writer with whom he had been corresponding for two years. They were married the following year and settled in Washington, D.C., where friends had secured Dunbar a job at the Library of Congress. In Washington he and his wife enjoyed the happiest and most productive years of his life. Meanwhile, between 1898 and 1902, Dunbar ventured into the field of the musical revue. In collaboration with Samuel Coleridge-Taylor, the racially mixed English composer, he produced *Dream Lovers* (1898), a romantic trifle in the style of Gilbert and Sullivan. With the American composer Will Marion Cook, he wrote the book and lyrics for *Clorindy, the Origin of the Cakewalk* (1898). With Paul Hogan, a popular black minstrel show comedian, Dunbar did *Uncle Eph's Christmas* (1899). He collaborated again with Cook on *In Dahomey* (1902), a large-scale work for which he wrote lyrics for three songs. The reviewer who dubbed Dunbar "prince of the coon song writers" may have intended to pay him a compliment, but the title must have galled. During these same years Dunbar saw the publication of several books of his dialect poetry illustrated with photographs taken by members of the Hampton Institute Camera Club. With titles like *Poems of Cabin and Field* (1899), *Candle Lightin' Time* (1901), and *When Malindy Sings* (1903), such books were obviously designed to capitalize on Dunbar's well-known themes and individual poems.

In 1898 Dunbar published *Folks from Dixie*, his first book of short stories. (Three more would follow.) Pointed social criticism appears in many of the stories. *Folks from Dixie* includes "Jimsella," which treats the theme of the harsh realities of life encountered by black refugees from the South in the large northern cities. "At Shaft 11" (1898), a story about the mining industry, treats corrupt labor practices and criticizes unions for not allowing black members, yet ends with whites and blacks working together in harmony for the common good. *The Strength of Gideon and Other Stories* (1900) shows Dunbar at his most outspoken. "The Ingrate," "The Tragedy at Three Forks," "One Man's Fortune," and "A Council at State" deal with such subjects as how blacks escaped slavery through the Underground Railroad, the horror of lynching, the detrimental effects of racism on intelligent and aspiring young black people, and the corruption of white and black politicians. But this collection also includes some that treat blacks as objects of sentiment and humor. Dunbar delivers much more of the same in his next collection, *In Old Plantation Days* (1903), all of whose stories are set on a southern plantation and feature a cast of stock black and white characters, including the faithful mammy; the comic preacher; the conjure woman; and the kindly, indulgent white master and his family.

Dunbar's true attitude toward the racial realities of his era are expressed not in his sentimental short stories or in his dialect poems. In July 1903, the same year that *In Old Plantation Days* appeared, Dunbar wrote an open letter to the *Chicago Tribune* deploring the fact that African Americans thoughtlessly celebrate Independence Day while they are being reduced to peonage through the sharecropping economy of the South, lynched in large numbers yearly, and denied the vote in the South and good jobs in the North. While some black Americans will sing "My Country, 'Tis of Thee," others more aware of the cruel ironies of the day will "kneel in their private closets and with hands upraised and bleeding hearts cry to God, if there still lives a God, 'How long, O God, How long?'" In his essays, moreover, he deplores the degradation of black life in New York City, the squalor and ignorance of black life in the South, and the stereotyping of African Americans as criminally inclined and unfit for higher education.

Of Dunbar's four novels, only one—his last—is of enduring significance. The first, *The Uncalled* (1898), has an all-white cast of characters and is of interest chiefly because some have seen in its protagonist, a young man urged into the Christian ministry against his own better judgment, an autobiographical reference to its author. Dunbar's mother had wanted him to enter the ministry, but he resisted. *The Love of Landry* (1900), inspired by Dunbar's sojourn in Colorado, where he sought a cure for his tuberculosis, is a western love story, again with white characters. *The Fanatics* (1901) is Dunbar's attempt at a large historical novel, featuring white families living in Ohio in the years before and during the Civil War, with sympathies among the characters divided between the two sides in the conflict. Despite respectable sales, none of these works received particular critical acclaim. His last novel, *The Sport of the Gods* (1902), is more significant because it deals with prejudices and legal injustices aimed at blacks in the South and the false promise of new lives in the North for those seeking social and economic freedom. Berry Hamilton, faithful black butler to an aristocratic white family, is accused of stealing a large sum of money. Despite the lack of evidence, he is found guilty and sentenced to a long prison term. His wife and children, forced to leave their home on their white employer's estate and shunned in their hometown, try to make a new life in New York City. But the son falls into dissipation and ultimately commits murder, while the daughter becomes a cabaret singer. Their mother takes up with an abusive husband. The city does not offer the family members the kind of haven they have sought, but proves itself to be a cold world, indifferent to the fates of the people it helps destroy. *The Sport of the Gods*, Dunbar's most successful novel, retains importance today for its strong social critique and for being the first work to dramatize black life in New York City.

## LATE CAREER AND EARLY DEATH

Paul Laurence Dunbar's life began to unravel in 1899. For one thing, his health failed. Never constitutionally strong, he contracted pneumonia in May and nearly died. Temporary recovery followed, but tuberculosis developed. The disease was exacerbated by alcohol, which Dunbar used in the mistaken hope that it would reduce the effects of tuberculosis and ease his physical and emotional pains. Additionally, Dunbar's marriage disintegrated. Paul and Alice separated briefly in 1900 and permanently in

1902. To the end of his life, he tried unsuccessfully for a reconciliation.

Dunbar continued to work relentlessly. Despite his illness, between 1900 and 1906 he wrote three novels, three collections of short stories, and three books of poetry. The end came on 9 February 1906. The poet was buried in Woodland Cemetery in Dayton. His grave marker is inscribed with the first stanza of his poem, "A Death Song." The last line reads, "Sleep, ma honey, tek yo' res' at las."

## DUNBAR'S ACHIEVEMENT

In his autobiography, *Along This Way* (1933), James Weldon Johnson asserts that his friend Paul Laurence Dunbar once said he had never gotten to the things he really wanted to do. Assuming that this is true, one might ask what it was that the writer wanted to accomplish. It has been suggested that Dunbar sought a new language with which to describe the lives of African Americans and with which to articulate—in poetry or prose—the challenges that faced them. Had he lived longer, perhaps Dunbar could have found a new voice, something between standard English and black dialect, with which to express all he wanted to say about African-American life. But what Dunbar did achieve is remarkable by any standard. A black man in a largely racist, white society, he found a biracial audience and became one of the most widely read and admired writers of his time. Since his death, Dunbar has been remembered primarily as a poet, but his short stories and last novel have been receiving the critical attention they deserve. His fear of being remembered only as a writer of dialect verse has proven unfounded, and Dunbar has taken his place as a black writer able to capture many of the complexities, problems, and strengths of African Americans during one of the most difficult periods of their history.

## SELECTED WORKS

*Oak and Ivy* (1893)
*Majors and Minors* (1895)
*Lyrics of Lowly Life* (1896)
*Clorindy, or the Origin of the Cakewalk* (1898)
*Dream Lovers: An Operatic Romance* (1898)
*Folks from Dixie* (1898)
*The Uncalled* (1898)
*Lyrics of the Hearthside* (1899)
*Poems of Cabin and Field* (1899)
*Jes Lak White Fo'ks: A One-Act Negro Operetto* (1900)
*The Love of Landry* (1900)
*The Strength of Gideon and Other Stories* (1900)
*Uncle Eph's Christmas* (1900)

*Candle-Lightin' Time* (1901)
*The Fanatics* (1901)
*In Dahomey* (1902)
*The Sport of the Gods* (1902)
*Lyrics of Love and Laughter* (1903)
*In Old Plantation Days* (1903)
*When Malindy Sings* (1903)
*The Heart of Happy Hollow* (1904)
*Li'l Gal* (1904)
*Howdy, Honey, Howdy* (1905)
*Lyrics of Sunshine and Shadow* (1905)
*Joggin' Erlong* (1906)

## FURTHER READING

Alexander, Eleanor. *Lyrics of Sunshine and Shadow: The Tragic Courtship and Marriage of Paul Laurence Dunbar and Alice Ruth Moore.* New York, 2001. Presents new information about the poet's marriage, including evidence that Dunbar physically abused his wife. Adds to our knowledge of the world of America's Talented Tenth—its black intellectual and artistic elite—at the turn of the twentieth century.

Best, Felton O. *Crossing the Color Line: A Biography of Paul Laurence Dunbar, 1872–1906.* Dubuque, Iowa, 1996.

Brawley, Benjamin G. *Paul Laurence Dunbar: Poet of His People.* Port Washington, N.Y., 1967. First published in 1936. The first full-length biography of Dunbar. Balanced but largely appreciative assessment of the poet's work.

Gayle, Addison. *Oak and Ivy: a Biography of Paul Laurence Dunbar.* Garden City, N.Y., 1971. Takes the view that Dunbar had to surrender his "poetical soul" in exchange for the fame that would come with writing the kinds of poetry the reading public demanded.

Martin, Herbert Woodward, and Ronald Primeau, eds. *In His Own Voice: The Dramatic and Other Uncollected Works of Paul Laurence Dunbar.* Athens, Ohio, 2002. Makes available some of Dunbar's works not readily accessible elsewhere.

Martin, Jay, ed. *A Singer in the Dawn: Reinterpretations of Paul Laurence Dunbar.* New York, 1975. Texts of papers delivered at a conference honoring the centenary of Dunbar's birth. An important collection that sparked the beginning of a reevaluation, largely positive, of Dunbar's work, the poetry in particular.

Martin, Jay, and Gossie H. Hudson, eds. *The Paul Laurence Dunbar Reader.* New York, 1975. An important one-volume source for the reader seeking representative works by Dunbar. It includes selections from his essays, short stories, poetry, and letters and most of *The Sport of the Gods.*

Metcalf, E. W., Jr. *Paul Laurence Dunbar: A Bibliography.* Metuchen, N.J., 1975. Exhaustive bibliography of published works by and about Dunbar. Dated, of course, but useful for studies of Dunbar publications up to the early 1970s.

Revell, Peter. *Paul Laurence Dunbar.* Boston, 1979. Features a biography and critical evaluation of Dunbar's work. A good introductory study for the general reader. Includes a bibliography.

Wiggins, Linda Keck. *The Life and Works of Paul Laurence Dunbar.* Nashville, Tenn., 1992. First published in 1907. The first biographical study of Dunbar.

# JONATHAN EDWARDS

*by Jane Beal*

Jonathan Edwards is perhaps best known for his sermon *Sinners in the Hands of an Angry God* (1741). The occasion for it was a Sunday service on 8 July 1741 in a church in Enfield, Connecticut. Edwards reportedly read his message in a level voice, as usual, without gesticulation or outburst. Yet his words had a very powerful effect on the congregation listening to him, members of which were brought to tears, and on a generation of New England readers who received the sermon in published form later that same year. Apparently, the power of his rhetoric was not solely in his delivery, whether spoken or written, but in the strength of his conviction.

In his sermon, Edwards combined rhetoric and conviction to move his audience. He selected Deuteronomy 32:35, "Their foot shall slide in due time," as his text for explication. The verse appears in a much longer passage called the Song of Moses. Deuteronomy depicts God giving the song to Moses and then instructing him to recite it to the Israelites because, as God informs Moses about his chosen people, "For when I shall have brought them into the land which I sware unto their fathers . . . then will they turn unto other gods, and serve them, and provoke me, and break my covenant. And it shall come to pass, when many evils and troubles are befallen them, that this song shall testify against them as a witness, for it shall not be forgotten out of the mouths of their seed" (Deuteronomy 31: 20–21). By his choice of text, Edwards set up a rhetorical situation in which he played the role of a new Moses, his congregants that of a wayward Israel. The sermon itself, like the song, serves both to remind and remonstrate.

*Sinners in the Hands of an Angry God* contains several allusions to the Song of Moses, including two to Deuteronomy 32: 41–42, Scripture verses that read, "If I whet my glittering sword, and mine hand take hold on

Jonathan Edwards. (© *Corbis*)

judgment, I will render vengeance to mine enemies, and will reward them that hate me. I will make mine arrows drunk with blood, and my sword shall devour flesh." Edwards reworks this passage into two images of God's fury at natural or unregenerate men: "The glittering sword is whet, and held over them, and the pit hath opened its mouth under them" and "the bow of God's wrath is bent, and the arrow made ready on the string, and justice bends the arrow at your heart, and strains the bow, and its is nothing but the mere pleasure of God, and that of an angry God, without any promise or obligation at all, that keeps the arrow one moment from being made drunk with your blood." These images reveal Edwards's characteristically vivid use of language to convey a theme. In this case, the preacher emphasizes the threat of hell, the justified wrath of God, and the fact that it is the absolute sovereignty of that same God, his "mere pleasure," that keeps his justice from being exacted from sinful men immediately.

It is at least partially from *Sinners in the Hands of an Angry God* that Edwards gets his reputation for being a "fire and brimstone" preacher. (Indeed, he uses the phrase in this sermon.) Yet even within a sermon ostensibly about God's anger, Edwards is careful to direct his listeners to God's grace and the "extraordinary opportunity," which they have on "a day wherein Christ has thrown the door of mercy wide open," to love God. The opportunity is extraordinary because after all, in Edwards's thought, it is God's mercy, not his wrath, that is arbitrary.

If *Sinners in the Hands of an Angry God* has become the canonical representative of Edwards's thought, it is because it is the message of his life. But it does not tell all. In fact, one gets a very narrow view of Edwards, the fullness of his spirit and his admiration for beauty, considering only his famous sermon. For a better understanding, it will be useful to consider his life, works, and influence on American culture.

## A NEW ENGLAND MAN: YOUTH, EDUCATION, FAMILY, AND EARLY WORKS

Jonathan Edwards lived an extraordinary life of self-discipline, service, and spiritual fervor. He was born in East Windsor, Connecticut, on 5 October 1703, the fifth child of eleven, the only son of the Reverend Timothy Edwards and his wife, Esther Stoddard, and the only brother to his ten sisters. His father was educated at Harvard, receiving the degrees of bachelor of arts and master of arts, and his mother, one of the Reverend Solomon Stoddard's ten children, finished her education in Boston. Their son would follow in their footsteps when he entered the Collegiate School at New Haven (later known as Yale) at age thirteen.

Before beginning his collegiate studies, Edwards studied at home. Here he learned the habit of writing well, endeavored to memorize Latin, and began his meditations on nature. His essays "On Insects" and "Of Being" indicate his scientific powers of observation as well as his ability to write with clarity and maturity. His parents obviously had some success with his childhood education, an education that was, it should be noted, thoroughly grounded in the study of Scripture. As a son and grandson of preachers, Edwards spent most of his time in Scripture-rich environments, either at home or in church, which encouraged his considerable knowledge and deep love of the Bible. Indeed, the Bible facilitated both his practical, intellectual development and his spiritual growth.

Edwards discusses his spiritual experiences as a child in his *Personal Narrative* (1739), a spiritual autobiography that has been compared to the *Confessions* of Augustine. In it, Edwards describes a "time of great awakening" in his father's church and his own response to it. He would pray privately as many as five times a day and talk about religion with other boys; he and his schoolmates "built a booth in a swamp, in a very secret and retired place, for a place of prayer. And besides, I had particular secret places of my own in the woods, where I used to retire by myself, and used to be from time to time much affected." Edwards would keep the habit of thinking and praying in nature for the rest of his life.

His interest in religion from childhood is also indicated in his earliest extant letter, dated 10 May 1716, which he wrote to his sister, Mary, about "a very remarkable stirring and pouring out of the Spirit of God" which occurred in his father's church. The letter discusses the new members

of the church, the deaths of five community members, and the illness and recovery of several sisters who had been sick with chicken pox. The concerns here are already pastoral, but also familial. Edwards expresses love and affection for his sister, and by his choice of subject, for his whole family. His family clearly shaped who he was and who he became; his continued education at the university level only built on this already-established foundation.

At the Collegiate School at New Haven, Edwards obtained his bachelor's degree in 1720 and his master's degree in 1723. He devoted himself to the study of theology and was licensed to preach in 1722. He held a position at a Presbyterian church in New York City from August 1722 to April 1723. He returned to his university to work as a tutor from 1724 to 1726. Among others, he read Calvin, Locke, and Newton, and he spent some time reworking their ideas into his own coherent system of thought. However, it was his Christian heritage and Puritan worldview that is most reflected in his personal writings from this period, writings that include his "Resolutions" and *Diary* (portions were published by Hopkins [1765] and Dwight [1830]).

During the final years of his graduate study and the beginning of his work as a minister, Edwards made several "Resolutions" for his life. The specific dates of his earliest resolutions are unknown, but he wrote the thirty-fifth one on 18 December 1722 and the last one on 17 August 1723. He recorded his progress in sustaining his resolutions in a diary.

The "Resolutions" of Jonathan Edwards have been compared to those of Benjamin Franklin, but they are in fact more numerous (seventy compared with thirteen) and more spiritual (rather than civic) in character. The first four relate to Edwards's desire to do everything for the "glory of God," a theme that recurs in the "Resolutions" and Edwards's later writings as well. The "Resolutions" set a high standard, one focused not so much on deeds Edwards could do in the world, but rather on the attitudes and thoughts of the heart that Edwards wanted to continually maintain. Not surprisingly, Edwards often found himself failing in his own spiritual ambitions, as his *Diary* testifies, leading him to conclude even fairly early on: "O how weak, how infirm, how unable to do anything of myself. What a poor, inconsistent being! What a miserable wretch, without the assistance of God's Spirit. While I stand, I am ready to think I stand by my own strength, and upon my own legs . . . when alas, I am but a poor infant, upheld by Jesus Christ." Yet the character of the life Edwards lived after making his resolutions suggests he was at least successful in keeping some of them, such as those "never to lose one moment of time, but improve it the most profitable way I can" and "to live with all my might, while I do live."

Like his "Resolutions," Edwards's *Diary* reveals the man's inner struggles, emerging maturity, and understanding of God. It contains several direct addresses to God, prayers in prose, which contain some of the loveliest writing in the *Diary*. For example, the day after leaving his pastorate in New York City, an occasion he termed "melancholy" and "difficult," Edwards penned this prayer:

> Lord, grant that I from hence may learn to withdraw my thoughts, affections, desires and expectations, entirely from the world, and may fix them upon the heavenly state, where there is fullness of joy, where reigns heavenly, sweet, calm and delightful love without alloy; where there are continually the dearest expressions of their love; where there is the enjoyment of the persons loved, without ever parting; where those persons, who appear to lovely in this world, will really be inexpressibly more lovely, and full of love to us. How sweetly will the mutual lovers join together to sing the praises of God and the Lamb! How full will it fill us with joy to think, this enjoyment, these sweet exercises, will never cease or come to an end, but will last to eternity.

Edwards's meditations on withdrawal from the world were not to be fulfilled permanently. He experienced a serious illness in 1725 and spent three months convalescing in the home of his friend Isaac Stiles, which gave him time for further spiritual reflection. He writes in his *Personal Narrative* that "in this sickness God was pleased to visit me again with the sweet influences of the Spirit. My mind was greatly engaged there, on divine and pleasant contemplations, and longings of soul." Edwards recovered, and not long thereafter he would engage with the world from the pulpit once again, and quite intensely, starting in 1727, when he began to assist his grandfather, Solomon Stoddard, at his church in Northampton, Connecticut.

Almost immediately after his ordination, also in 1727, Edwards married Sarah Pierrepont. He was twenty-three and she was seventeen. He had known her since 1719 and had written a now-famous tribute to her, if the date is correct, when she was just thirteen years old. It begins: "They say there is a young lady in New Haven who is beloved of that almighty Being, who made and rules the world, and that there are certain seasons in which this great Being, in some way or other invisible, comes to her

and fills her mind with exceedingly sweet delight." As this tribute suggests, from their earliest acquaintance Edwards admired Sarah's spiritual experience with God, and he maintained that admiration throughout their marriage. Indeed, he would describe it thoroughly, though without indicating her name or gender, in his work, *Some Thoughts Concerning the Present Revival of Religion in New England* (1743). He called Sarah his "dearest companion," and she was the mother of his ten children, Sarah, Jerusha, Esther, Mary, Lucy, Timothy, Susannah, Eunice, Jonathan, and Pierrepont. She stood with him through victory and defeat, steadfast in her faith in God, as her extant letters testify. She had need of that faith in her many experiences with her husband and family. In fact, one of the greatest spiritual experiences of the Edwardses' lives began only a few years after their marriage.

## A PASTOR AT NORTHAMPTON: THE GREAT AWAKENING

In 1729, after his grandfather's death, Edwards assumed full pastoral leadership and served Northampton for the next twenty years during a time of powerful religious revival that would be known to history as the Great Awakening. This spiritual movement had two distinct stages, occurring first in 1734 and 1735 and second from 1740 to 1744, though its effects were felt throughout this period and long after. Edwards both promoted this revival through his sermons and chronicled it in the histories he wrote in its defense: *A Faithful Narrative of the Surprising Works of God in the Conversion of Many Hundred Souls in Northampton and the Neighboring Towns* (1736), *Distinguishing Marks of a Work of the Spirit of God* (1741), and *Some Thoughts Concerning the Present Revival of Religion in New England* (1742). Edwards wrote an initial account of the Great Awakening in a letter to the Reverend Dr. Benjamin Colman (30 May 1735) which reveals his perceptions of events, their causes and effects, but withholds his beliefs about God's purpose in sending a visitation of the Holy Spirit to New England in the 1730s, leaving those to Colman's mind and his own later writings.

The letter sets out Edwards's understanding of a few initial causes of the revival: the death of a young man from pleurisy and the death of a young married woman who, during her illness, experienced full conversion and urged others to it as well. These events motivated the citizens of Northampton to give greater thought to the destiny of their souls. People became focused on "the great things of religion" and "their eternal salvation." The effects of these concerns were personal, influencing the doctrinal, physical, and emotional lives of individual Christians. They were also interpersonal, affecting the relationships between individuals, and ultimately social and evangelical, eventually affecting communities from Maine to Georgia.

On a personal level, individuals became convinced of their sinfulness, of their total dependence on God, and as Edwards wrote to Colman, of "a lively sense of the excellency of Jesus Christ and his sufficiency and willingness to save sinners, and to be much weaned in their affections from the world, and to have their hearts filled with love to God and Christ." At the same time, on a doctrinal level, they accepted the truth and authority of the Bible. Because of the intensity of their convictions and encounters with God, they responded emotionally and physically, sometimes weeping, fainting, or simply being filled with a sense of the glory of God. On an interpersonal level, such rapturous experiences had very practical applications. They led directly to the reformation of immoral behavior and the ending of old quarrels through "the confession of faults" and the "making up of differences." Ultimately, the personal and interpersonal effects had a profound social effect. The people of Northampton and the surrounding communities had an evangelical concern for "the salvation of any soul, of the meanest of mankind, of any Indian in the woods." In short, the first phase of the Great Awakening affected much of New England, either directly or indirectly, and news of it was reported and discussed quite widely.

The revival of the 1730s quieted down abruptly when, on Sunday, 1 June 1735, Joseph Hawley, a successful businessman and an uncle by marriage to Edwards, committed suicide by cutting his throat. Edwards perceived this event as a direct attack by Satan on the work of the Holy Spirit: "Satan seems to be in a great rage at this extraordinary breaking forth of the work of God. I hope it is because he knows he has but little time." Edwards appointed a day of fasting in response. During the next few years, Edwards comforted his community and continued to preach. After the arrival in New England in 1740 of George Whitefield, a persuasive evangelist from England, the latent spirit of the Great Awakening broke forth once again. In 1741 Edwards preached his sermon, *Sinners in the Hands of an Angry God*, but it was the cumulative effect of his prayerful passion and dedicated service that facilitated revival.

At the same time, Edwards was concerned about and careful to address the excesses of people's emotional responses to the spirit of revival. His book, *A Treatise*

*Concerning Religious Affections* (1746), considers two questions: "What are the distinguishing qualifications of those that are in favor with God and entitled to his eternal rewards?" and "What is the nature of true religion?" To answer these questions, Edwards first defined affections and their importance for religion, and then argued which signs (that is, evidences) demonstrate gracious (having the quality of the Holy Spirit's saving grace) and holy affections and which do not. Thus, for example, weeping, fainting, and other emotional excesses do not necessarily demonstrate gracious and holy affections, although they may accompany those affections. But "a love to divine things for the beauty and sweetness of their moral excellency," the ability to "rightly and spiritually understand divine things," and "a reasonable and spiritual conviction of the judgment of the reality and certainty of divine things," for example, do demonstrate holy affections.

Edwards's *Treatise* appeared between two important historical moments in his life: the Great Awakening and the conflict that arose between him and his church in Northampton. As such, it sheds light on the former and anticipates the latter. In his *Treatise*, Edwards took the position that Holy Communion should be closed except to those who have made a public profession of their faith in Christ and given evidence of their conversion. This position contradicted the one held by Edwards's grandfather, Solomon Stoddard; Edwards's own former practice; and thus the tradition of the church that he was leading. Edwards's position became the central theological conflict he had with his congregation and led to his eventual dismissal in 1750. However, it was not the only factor in the conflict.

First, in 1744 Edwards decided to denounce publicly, by name, several young people from prominent families for their involvement in reading books he deemed immoral. He requested salary increases that were not approved. There were struggles for power and control between the town and church leadership, and Edwards was in a dispute with his cousins, the Williams family. These disagreements were not resolved amicably. In 1748 Edwards required a profession of faith from an applicant for church membership, was denied, and consequently declared a "state of controversy" to exist between himself and church. Eventually, Edwards left his church of more than twenty years, ostensibly departing the pulpit with his *Farewell Sermon* (1750) but actually lingering in the town for several months, even preaching occasionally in his former sanctuary, before obtaining a new post.

During the height of this controversy, Edwards published *An Humble Inquiry into the Rules of the Word of God, Concerning the Qualifications Requisite to a Compleat Standing and Full Communion in the Visible Christian Church* (1749), a book that set forth the opinions that had already proved so unpopular with his Northampton congregation. He also wrote the *Life of David Brainerd* (1749), Edwards's most dedicated attempt at biography. It consists of portions of Brainerd's diary, variously edited or summarized, interspersed with Edwards's comments. Brainerd, a Yale man and missionary to Native Americans at Kaunaumeek, and later Crossweeksung and Susquehanna, came to stay with the Edwards family when he was dying of tuberculosis. Brainerd clearly had a close relationship to Edwards's daughter, Jerusha, who cared for him during his illness and died shortly thereafter of the same disease that had killed him. Jerusha was just eighteen at her death, and her family grieved over her loss. At her father's direction, she was buried beside David Brainerd in Northampton. Brainerd's impact on Edwards himself is evident not only from the *Life*, which is in some sense an extended eulogy, but also from Edwards's decision to become a missionary. It seems that Brainerd's example prepared and motivated Edwards for his own efforts to share the Christian gospel outside New England's comfortable borders. Brainerd's former mission at Kaunaumeek was just twenty miles from Stockbridge, the town in western Massachusetts where Edwards would live and work for the next seven years.

## A MISSIONARY AT STOCKBRIDGE: MATURITY AND MASTERPIECES

Edwards's new post at Stockbridge was an outpost, a missionary endeavor to the "people of the ever-flowing waters" (as they called themselves), or Houssatunnuck Indians (as Edwards called them). The town was located 160 miles west of Boston in undeveloped country. While there, Edwards ministered to white, Housatonic, and Mohawk congregations, as both a pastor and an educator. He preached simplified sermons and set up schools to teach English in order to overcome the language barrier between himself and his new community. In doing so, Edwards experienced several trials of faith and patience, including illness; conflicts with his Williams cousins over governance of the town; and an attack on his congregation by some Native American fighters incited by the French in Canada, after which the town had to be fortified against further attack. However, as some consolation Edwards was surrounded by his supportive family, and his congregants

appreciated them. Edwards wrote to his father that "the Indians seem much pleased with my family, especially my wife," and his son, Jonathan, became fluent in the Mohawk language, retaining it in memory and practice for the rest of his life.

While at Stockbridge, Edwards wrote extensively, bringing at least two theological masterpieces to press and working on additional books. In 1752 he published *Misrepresentations Corrected, and Truth Vindicated*, in which he again set forth his requirements for full church membership. It was a lengthy footnote to the communion controversy, a reply to the arguments of the Reverend Solomon Williams, but nevertheless an important antecedent for Edwards's two later and greater theological works. *A Careful and Strict Inquiry into the Modern Prevailing Notions of That Freedom of Will* (1754) and *The Great Christian Doctrine of Original Sin Defended* (1758) both reveal the intensity of his thought and engagement with contemporary theology.

In *Freedom of Will*, Edwards explored the nature of the will, attacked the Arminian conception of the liberty of the will, defended God's foreknowledge of the future volitions of moral agents, and asserted the consistency of the biblical command to obey with the moral inability to obey (because God's grace empowers human beings to overcome this inability), among other things. He directed his book toward other Christians who accepted the truth of biblical revelation and who exercised their own reason. His work is thus a philosophical expression of a Calvinistic theology. As part of his thesis, Edwards had cause to consider the role of original sin in the exercise of the human will, so it is not a surprise that he would go on to discuss the doctrine of original sin in his next treatise.

In *Original Sin*, Edwards answered Dr. John Taylor's book, *The Scripture-Doctrine of Original Sin Proposed to Free and Candid Examination* (ca. 1738–1740), specifically, and the Enlightenment attitude generally, which suggested that human beings are reasonable, rational creatures, not innately sinful, and that humanity only inherited the consequences of sin as a legal or contractual obligation, not an unavoidable condition. To sustain his argument, Edwards set out to establish the sinfulness of humanity as a part of fallen human nature and to show that man's free will, not God's, explains the presence of sin in the world. Edwards uses the Bible as evidence for his position, analyzing the fall of man depicted in Genesis 3, together with several other instances of scriptural support for the doctrine of original sin. He also answers several objections to the doctrine, concluding with a repudiation of Taylor's sincerity, which he took to be a rhetorical device "calculated to influence the minds and bias the judgments" of readers. Edwards objects to Taylor, ostensibly a Christian man, misrepresenting the Pauline epistles of the New Testament, and hence God and truth. Ultimately, Edwards said he left the matter up to the reader to decide, and asserted that "the success of the whole must now be left with God, who knows what is agreeable to his own mind, and is able to make his own truths prevail."

In addition to *Freedom of Will* and *Original Sin*, Edwards also composed while still at Stockbridge *The End for Which God Created the World* and *The Nature of True Virtue*, published together posthumously in 1765. Edwards begins the former by noting that reason alone could not deduce the end that Scripture reveals; he thus continues his debate with the rationalists, for whom reason could ascertain nearly everything, and insists on the priority of revelation. Yet Edwards does not repudiate reason entirely. Instead, he uses it in the first part of the dissertation to present his argument and then strengthens it in the second part with scriptural revelation. According to Edwards, God purposed the world to end and revealed this to human beings as one of many ways to communicate his goodness and demonstrate his glory. In a truly fascinating exposition of Scripture, Edwards posits that the glory of God and the name of God frequently "signify the same thing in scripture." Thus, in a sense, God's identity, insofar as that is connected to his name, is manifest in the future end of the world.

In *True Virtue*, Edwards defines virtue, discussing love, beauty, and conscience and distinguishing truly virtuous things from those things mistakenly identified as virtuous. He argues explicitly that "the general nature of virtue is love" and that its beauty consists in beings who have intelligence, perception, and will. Virtue is demonstrated by love to Being in general, and must be enacted by showing love to God, the Divine Being, and to other created beings. Virtue is particularly a matter of the heart, of its qualities and exercises, and the actions that result from them.

At this time Edwards also had in mind the composition of a universal chronicle called *A History of the Work of Redemption*. It was to have been based on a series of thirty sermons Edwards had preached between March and August of 1739 on Isaiah 51:8, "For the moth shall eat them up like a garment, and the worm shall eat them like wool: but my righteousness shall be for ever, and my salvation from generation to generation." The series followed two earlier ones, the first in fifteen parts about love derived

from 1 Corinthians 13 and the second in four parts about the fall based on Genesis 3:11. Edwards preached this third and longest series on redemption about a year and a half before the arrival of Whitefield in 1740 and the beginning of the second phase of the Great Awakening. A very small portion of his preparatory thought for this sermon cycle saw publication in an earlier work, *God Glorified in the Work of Redemption, by the Greatness of Man's Dependence upon Him, in the Whole of It* (1731), and the sermon cycle itself was published posthumously in 1774, but Edwards had to set aside the larger work of chronicling salvation history in a prose treatise or book because he was busy with other matters. He did intend to return to the project of turning the sermons into a book, however, as a letter to the trustees of Princeton College indicates.

This letter is a matter of interest not only because of its relation to the *History* but because of its relation to Edwards's life and its abrupt end. Following the death in 1757 of Aaron Burr, the president of Princeton College and Edwards's son-in-law, Princeton officials invited Edwards to become their new president. Edwards was hesitant to accept because he had many writing projects he still wanted to complete. In his letter Edwards detailed his concerns and wrote an outline of the *History*. After considerable negotiation Edwards did, after all, accept the position at Princeton. He arrived during an outbreak of smallpox, however, and in order to ward it off, he accepted an inoculation that was not, in his case, at all effective. He was seriously ill for a month and died on 22 March 1758, at the age of fifty-four. Although Edwards did not live to rewrite his work on redemption, he left enough material to permit publication of his edited sermons in London in 1774 and eventually New York City in 1786.

Edwards's *History* divides all of time into three periods: from the fall of man to Christ's incarnation; from the incarnation to Christ's resurrection; and from the resurrection to the end of the world (see the second sermon). It then subdivides these three periods according to the "seven ages" scheme established by Augustine for dividing salvation history, divisions that were repeated in universal histories and chronicles throughout the Middle Ages. The first twelve sermons elaborate the meaning of God's work of redemption, tracing its development from the fall to the Flood, the Flood to Abraham, Abraham to Moses, Moses to David, David to the Babylonian captivity, and the captivity to the coming of Christ.

The majority of the sermons that follow concern the seventh age between the Incarnation and the Last Judgment, that is, between the first and second comings of

Christ. Edwards is particularly concerned in these sermons with the preservation and triumph of the church of Christ over pagans and heretics, describing and rejecting purveyors of "corrupt opinions" in his twenty-second and twenty-fourth sermons. His list of these included Muslims, Anabaptists, Enthusiasts, Socinians, Arminians, Arianists, and Deists; against these, Edwards preached the success of the gospel. In the final sermons of the series, Edwards described the future end of the world and argued that the whole purpose of God's creation is to provide a spouse for his son and accomplish the work of redemption. Edwards regarded God's redemptive work in the world as the fulfillment of God's greatest purposes, and it is significant that Edwards meditated on this throughout his life, as entries in his *Miscellaneous Observations* (1793) attest, and particularly between the major upsurges of the Great Awakening and toward the end of his own life.

As the foregoing chronology of Edwards's life and works reveals, his life and thought were thoroughly intertwined, so much so that Perry Miller has concluded, and many subsequent critics have agreed, that the true life of Jonathan Edwards was the life of the mind. In fact, however, Edwards lived a life vigorously engaged with God and other people, a life perhaps as intensely physical as it was intellectual. He chopped wood daily, fathered ten children, and moved from the "civilized" environs of Northampton to the wilds of Stockbridge. Indeed, in terms of literary output, the most productive period of his life was at Stockbridge, which not coincidentally was also a period of rugged daily living in an American wilderness. While it is possible to extrapolate and summarize key aspects of Edwards's thought in order to examine them as a coherent system, it is important to keep in mind the realities, the lived experiences, that catalyzed and refined much of Edwards's thinking.

## AN AMERICAN INHERITANCE: EDWARDS'S THOUGHT AND ITS INFLUENCE

It is worth noting that Jonathan Edwards first and foremost communicated his ideas orally, to his primary audience of congregants, whether in New York City, Northampton, or Stockbridge. Edwards intended the most substantial part of his literary corpus, his sermons, for oral delivery. Writings not intended for oral delivery, such as the *Miscellaneous Observations* and studies of typology, provide observations from nature and examples from Scripture to be used in sermons, and many of Edwards's treatises, dissertations, and larger prose works were originally given as sermons in a series. In a sense, the whole of

Edwards's literary corpus may be viewed as either generically homiletic, supportive of the composition of homilies or derivative of homilies. As a pastor and missionary, Edwards viewed preaching as a primary vehicle for motivating others to love and fear God. All of Edwards's writing points to the fact that he intended to influence others, and to do so by articulating God's word in a rhetorically effective manner from the pulpit. Thus, in tracing the influence of his thought, readers should remember that it was accomplished by both the spoken and the written word.

It is somewhat more difficult to trace the influence of Edwards's oral performances than his literary masterworks, but there is nevertheless considerable evidence to substantiate and characterize it. Edwards's descriptions of individual conversions and consequent changes in hearts and lives in his histories of the Great Awakening provide one source. Other sources are letters and diaries written by members of Edwards's family and churches at Northampton and Stockbridge. The Reverend Stephen Williams, for example, wrote entries in his diary about the effects of Edwards's preaching at Enfield. By inspiring younger preachers and missionaries, such as David Brainerd and his own son Jonathan and grandson Timothy Dwight, Edwards extended the genealogy of both his oral and written influence, seeing it carried further into America and its native and immigrant peoples. Of course, Edwards himself would have viewed his own influence as negligible in comparison with that of the Holy Spirit.

While he was living, Edwards had not only a primary audience in churches but also a wide readership, consisting of both laypersons and pastors. Edwards communicated various aspects of his thought to his readership in letters and other published works. He was an influential minister, speaking and writing to many other ministers in New England, but his reach extended beyond America's borders to England and Scotland. In England, Samuel Johnson responded to Edwards's ideas about the human will, for instance, when he wrote, "All theory is against the freedom of the will, all experience for it," and Boswell, Johnson's biographer, only wanted to forget Edwards's book on the same subject. In Scotland, several ministers—including John Erskine, Thomas Gillespie, John McLaurin, William M'Culloch, James Robe, and John Willison—kept up regular correspondence with Edwards; they shared his view of religious affections, felt encouraged by his *Faithful Narrative*, and published *The History of the Work of Redemption* before anyone else.

After his death, Edwards's influence continued to be felt through his family and his writings in several different arenas, including various schools of theology and philosophy, literature and history, and American culture overall. As might be expected, Edwards exerted considerable influence on Puritan and Calvinistic thought in America on such major topics as revival, free will, original sin, true virtue, and God's sovereignty. Perhaps surprisingly, he also influenced Unitarians, especially in the 1830s, and Mary Baker Eddy, the founder of Christian Science, in her ideas about religious affections, the "spiritual sense," and the spiritual interpretation of the Bible. In the nineteenth century Edwards influenced various theologians, both as a model to imitate and a foil to contradict. Men like Lyman Hotchkiss Atwater, Edwards Amasa Park, John McLeod Campbell, and Thomas Chalmers accepted or appropriated him while men like Henry Philip Tappan and George A. Gorden rejected or dismissed him. In the twentieth century Edwards's theology continued to be reevaluated in light of new developments, perhaps especially as formulated by Karl Barthes, but many theologians believed that Edwards's ideas about the humanity's basic depravity were largely sustained by the horrors of world war, escalating violence, and the brutalities of human selfishness.

In literature Edwards directly influenced a surprising number of important poets and prose authors, including Harriet Beecher Stowe (*The Minister's Wooing*, 1859), Emily Dickinson (*My Life Had Stood—a Loaded Gun*), Edgar Allen Poe (*Eureka*), and Robert Lowell (*Mr. Edwards and the Spider, After the Surprising Conversions, Jonathan Edwards in Western Massachusetts*, and *The Worst Sinner, Jonathan Edwards' God*). Writings by these authors reveal not only the influence of Edwards's thought, but the power of his perceived presence. Edwards becomes a kind of cultural icon, a symbol, against which to read various kinds of spiritual and cultural experiences. Lesser-known writers have responded to Edwards as well. Thus, western poets like Ray Young Bear, Thomas Hornsby Ferril, and Clarice Short make typological use of the landscape, just as Edwards did, and Mary Ann Waters depicts Edwards coming home to Sarah in her poem, *Sermon for Jonathan Edwards*. Indeed, fictionalized renditions of the marriage of Edwards and Sarah constitute their own form of response to Edwards's life and legacy. Andrew Hudgin, to give just one more example, imagines Edwards just before his dismissal from Northampton in his poem, *Awaiting Winter Visitors: Jonathan Edwards, 1749*.

In addition, critics often compare Edwards to other great canonical authors of the American tradition, including Benjamin Franklin, because both men wrote resolutions and autobiographies, and Ralph Waldo Emerson and Henry David Thoreau, because all three shared experiences of the American wilderness. Edwards and Nathaniel Hawthorne clearly have a common Puritan heritage (cf. "The Minister's Black Veil" or *The Scarlet Letter*, 1850, with Edwards's person and beliefs) and William Faulkner seems to share Edwards's vision of order and the place of the elect depicted in Faulkner's narratives "That Evening Sun," "Delta Autumn," and "The Bear." These and other comparisons demonstrate that Edwards's thought can elucidate other literary endeavors quite profitably.

Edwards himself has been variously evaluated as a creative writer or American artist. He has been called a poet, although he never wrote verse. He confined himself to prose genres, exploring and exploiting these according to his own designs. Some critics, like David Laurence, cannot adequately account for his place in American letters and regard his influence as primarily negative. Indeed, Edwards's uncompromising faith, his belief in the absolute sovereignty of God and depravity of man, makes it very difficult to approach him with a lukewarm attitude, so his audience is frequently (and famously) divided between those who admire him and those who detest him. There can be little doubt, however, that Edwards was an accomplished prose stylist and that his use of allusion (particularly to Scripture), typology, and metaphor is masterful, powerful, and often very beautiful. His descriptions of nature are meaningful, and his thoughts on the intricacies of spiritual experience are unparalleled in American literature.

At the center of Edwards's life was his belief in a sovereign God who, out of love, redeemed sinful humanity through Jesus Christ. From a very young age Edwards purposed in his heart to think, speak, and act for the glory of that same God. The course of his life and the works that he wrote testify to both his failure and success in meeting his primary goal. His mistakes at certain junctures, perhaps particularly in alienating his congregation at Northampton, are clear. His values, however, sustained a spiritual victory in his own life such that he could say at the end of it, "Trust in God and ye need not fear." He would have been the first to admit his own personal depravity, but also among the first to offer hope of an "extraordinary opportunity" for salvation. From New York City to Northampton to Stockbridge, Edwards preached the same essential message of faith in Christ. He saw the beauty of holiness in both nature and Scripture. As he wrote in his *Personal Narrative*, holiness "appeared to me to be the highest beauty and amiableness, above all other beauties: that it was a divine beauty, far purer than anything here upon the earth, and that everything else was like mire, filth and defilement in comparison of it." For Edwards the defilement of sin opposed the beauty of holiness, and he had little toleration for it in any form, whether in himself or others. Thus, although Edwards has influenced theology and philosophy, history, and literature and culture in various ways, in fact his desire was to influence people's individual souls to love and serve God. To the extent he achieved that desire, he was successful as a pastor and a missionary, as well as a Christian theologian and author. In no small measure, the strength of his conviction explains why his life and work have become such an intricate part of our American inheritance.

[*See also* Colonial Writing in America *and* Puritanism: The Sense of an Unending.]

## SELECTED WORKS

*God Glorified in the Work of Redemption, by the Greatness of Man's Dependence upon Him, in the Whole of It. A Sermon Preached on the Publick Lecture in Boston, July 8, 1731* (1731)

*A Divine and Supernatural Light, Immediately Imparted to the Soul by the Spirit of God, Shown to Be Both a Scriptural, and a Rational Doctrine. In a Sermon Preach'd at Northampton* (1734)

*A Faithful Narrative of the Surprising Work of God in the Conversion of Many Hundred Souls in Northampton, and the Neighboring Towns and Villages of New-Hampshire in New-England. In a Letter to the Revd. Dr. Benjamin Colman of Boston. Written by the Revd. Mr. Edwards, Minister of Northampton, on Nov. 6, 1736* (1737)

*Discourses on Various Important Subjects, Nearly Concerning the Great Affair of the Soul's Eternal Salvation* (1738)

*The Distinguishing Marks of a Work of the Spirit of God. Applied to That Uncommon Operation That Has Lately Appeared on the Minds of Many of the People of This Land: With a Particular Consideration of the Extraordinary Circumstances with Which This Work Is Attended. A Discourse Delivered at New-Haven, September 10th 1741. Being the Day after Commencement* (1741)

*The Resort and Remedy of Those That Are Bereaved by the Death of an Eminent Minister. A Sermon Preached at Hatfield, Sept. 2, 1741. Being the Day of Interment of the Reverend Mr. William Williams, the Aged and Venerable Pastor of that Church* (1741)

*Sinners in the Hands of an Angry God. A Sermon Preached at Enfield, July 8th 1741. At a Time of Great Awakenings; and Attended with Remarkable Impressions on Many of the Hearers* (1741)

*The Great Concern of a Watchman for Souls, Appearing in the Duty He Has To Do, and the Account He Has to Give, Represented & Improved. In a Sermon Preach'd at the Ordination of the Reverend Jonathan Judd, to the Pastoral Office over the Church of Christ, in the New Precinct at Northampton, June 8, 1743* (1743)

*Some Thoughts Concerning the Present Revival of Religion in New-England, and the Way in Which It Ought to Be Acknowledged and Prompted, Humbly Offered to the Publick, in a Treatise on That Subject* (1743)

*The True Excellency of a Minister of the Gospel. A Sermon Preach'd at Pelham, Aug. 30, 1744. Being the Day of the Ordination of the Revd. Mr. Robert Abercrombie to the Work of the Gospel Ministry in That Place* (1744)

*The Church's Marriage to Her Sons, and to Her God: A Sermon Preached at the Instalment of the Rev. Mr. Samuel Buel as Pastor of the Church and Congregation at East-Hampton on Long Island, September 19, 1746* (1746)

*A Treatise Concerning Religious Affections, in Three Parts* (1746)

*An Humble Attempt To Promote Explicit Agreement and Visible Union of God's People in Extraordinary Prayer for the Revival of Religion and the Advancement of Christ's Kingdom on Earth, Pursuant to Scripture-Promises and Prophecies Concerning the Last Time* (1747)

*True Saints, When Absent from the Body, Are Present with the Lord. A Sermon Preached on the Day of the Funeral of the Rev. Mr. David Brainerd, Missionary to the Indians, from the Honourable Society in Scotland, for the Propagation of Christian Knowledge, and Pastor of a Church of Christian Indians in New-Jersey; Who Died at Northampton in New-England, Octob. 9th. 1747, in the 30th Year of His Age* (1747)

*A Strong Rod Broken and Withered. A Sermon Preach'd at Northampton, on the Lord's-Day, June 26, 1748. On the Death of the Honourable John Stoddard, Esq.* (1748)

*An Account of the Life of the late Reverend Mr. David Brainerd, Minister of the Gospel, Missionary to the Indians, from the Honourable Society in Scotland, for the Propagation of Christian Knowledge, and Pastor of a Church of Christian Indians of New-Jersey* (1749)

*An Humble Inquiry into the Rules of the Word of God Concerning the Qualifications Requisite to a Compleat Standing and Full Communion in the Visible Christian Church* (1749)

*Christ the Great Example of Gospel Ministers. A Sermon Preach'd at Portsmouth, at the Ordination of the Reverend Mr. Job Strong, to the Pastoral Office over the South Church in That Place, June 28, 1749* (1750)

*A Farewell-Sermon Preached at the First Precinct in Northampton, after the People's Publick Rejection of their Minister, and Renouncing Their Relation to Him as Pastor of the Church There, on June 22, 1750. Occasion'd by Difference of Sentiments, Concerning the Requisite Qualifications of Members of the Church, in Compleat Standing* (1751)

*Misrepresentations Corrected, and Truth Vindicated, in a Reply to the Rev. Mr. Solomon William's Book* (1752)

*True Grace, Distinguished from the Experience of Devils; in a Sermon, Preached before the Synod of New-York, Convened at New-Ark, in New-Jersey, on September 28. N.S. 1752* (1753)

*A Careful and Strict Enquiry into the Modern Prevailing Notions of That Freedom of Will, Which Is Supposed to Be Essential to Moral Agency, Virtue and Vice, Reward and Punishment, Praise and Blame* (1754)

*The Great Christian Doctrine of Original Sin Defended; Evidences of Its Truth Produced, and Arguments to the Contrary Answered. Containing, in Particular, a Reply to the Objections and Arguings of Dr. John Taylor* (1758)

"Personal Narrative." In *The Life and Character of the Late Reverend Mr. Jonathan Edwards, President of the College at New-Jersey*. By Samuel Hopkins (1765)

*Two Dissertations, I. Concerning the End for Which God Created the World. II. The Nature of True Virtue* (1765)

*A History of the Work of Redemption. Containing, the Outlines of a Body of Divinity, in a Method Entirely New* (1774)

*Sermons on the Following Subjects* (1780)

*Practical Sermons, Never Before Published* (1788)

*Miscellaneous Observations on Important Subjects, Original and Collected* (1793)

*Charity and Its Fruits; or, Christian Love As Manifested in the Heart and Life* (1852)

*An Unpublished Essay of Edwards on the Trinity with Remarks on Edwards and His Theology by George P. Fisher* (1903)

*Images or Shadows of Divine Things* (1948)

## FURTHER READING

Edwards, Jonathan. *The Works of Jonathan Edwards*. Vols. 1–19. Edited by John E. Smith. New Haven, Conn., 1957–.

Fiering, Norman. *Jonathan Edwards's Moral Thought and Its British Context*. Chapel Hill, N.C., 1981. Examines Edwards's moral thought in the context of such thinkers as Francis Hutcheson, David Hume, Nicolas Malebranche, and Gottfried von Leibniz and revises Perry Miller's estimation of the importance of John Locke for Edwards's thought.

Hatch, Nathan O., and Harry S. Stout, eds. *Jonathan Edwards and the American Experience*. Oxford, 1988. Essays by various authors examine Edwards regarding the American imagination, cultural context, and later reception.

Lesser, M. X. *Jonathan Edwards: An Annotated Bibliography, 1979–1993*. Westport, Conn., 1994. A comprehensive, chronological, annotated bibliography of Edwardsean criticism from 1979 to 1993 containing an author and title index but no subject index.

McClymond, Michael J. *Encounters with God: An Approach to the Theology of Jonathan Edwards*. Oxford, 1998. Evaluates apprehension, speculation, contemplation, valuation, narration, and persuasion in Edwards's works with special attention to *The Mind*, *Personal Narrative*, *Diary*, *End of Creation*, and *The History of the Work of Redemption*.

Miller, Perry. *Jonathan Edwards*. 1949; repr., 1981. An influential biography of Edwards. Readers may wish to supplement this with other biographies by Sereno Dwight (1829–1830), Samuel Hopkins (1869), Ola Winslow (1940), Iain Murray (1987), John E. Smith (1992), and Norma Jean Lutz (2001).

Miller, Perry. "Jonathan Edwards on the Sense of the Heart," *Harvard Theological Review* 41 (1948): 129–145. A seminal essay for Edwardsean criticism.

Scheick, William J., ed. *Critical Essays on Jonathan Edwards*. Boston, 1980. Reproduces several seminal essays in the history of Edwardsean criticism.

# T. S. ELIOT

*by Philip Hobsbaum*

Thomas Stearns Eliot was born on 26 September 1888 in St. Louis. The Eliots originally hailed from Somerset in England and settled in America in the late seventeenth century. They began as a Boston family, but Eliot's grandfather, William Greenleaf Eliot, settled in Missouri in 1834 to preach as a Unitarian minister, dying the year before Eliot was born. Eliot's father, Henry Ware Eliot, a prosperous manufacturer of bricks, was in his forties by the time his wife, Charlotte, gave birth to their last child, T. S. Eliot, who had four elder sisters and a brother.

T. S. Eliot had a congenital double hernia and had to wear a truss for most of his life. After attending a local school, he went at the age of ten to Smith Academy, where he ran his own little magazine, *The Fireside*, and contributed poems and stories to the *Smith Academy Record*. In June 1906 he passed the entrance examination for Harvard University. He read a great deal, especially French literature.

A literary acquaintance that ripened into friendship was with Conrad Aiken, a poet whose work often seems to bear a likeness to that of Eliot, although the influence was probably the other way around. One crucial book that Eliot discovered at the end of 1908 was *The Symbolist Movement in Literature* (1899) by Arthur Symons. Eliot had already read Charles Baudelaire; through this book he encountered Jules Laforgue. Nevertheless, he remained deeply and impressionably American. His very sense of rootlessness saw to that. He was a southerner in New England and a New Englander down South. To disguise his Missouri accent, he adopted something of a Harvard drawl. He enjoyed boating around Gloucester and, in one vacation, sailed along the coast of Massachusetts to the Canadian border. He was sociable rather than clubbable

T. S. Eliot. (*Courtesy of the Library of Congress*)

and retained a distance between himself and most of his contemporaries.

It was at that point, in 1908, that Eliot became a serious writer—not so much in quality of work as in concentration. Previously his verse had been derivatively sheepish stuff:

> While all the East was weaving red
>     with gray,
> The flowers at the windows turned
>     towards dawn,
> Petal on petal, waiting for the day,
> Fresh flowers, withered flowers, flowers
>     of dawn . . .

("Before Morning")

After, though still derivative, it acquired a sharp ironic bite:

> And Life, a little bald and gray,
> Languid, fastidious, and bland,
> Waits, hat and gloves in hand,
> Punctilious of tie and suit
> (Somewhat impatient of delay)
> On the doorstep of the Absolute.

("Spleen")

In June 1909 Eliot received his B.A., with grades that were adequate rather than distinguished. He went on, in this his fourth year, to study for a master's degree, finding two teachers of distinction in George Santayana and Irving Babbitt. From the latter he may have derived his idea of "tradition."

Eliot specialized in philosophy, for which he had no particular bent, and took time out to visit Europe. He sailed in October 1910 and for a time settled in Paris, attending at the Sorbonne the lectures of Henri Bergson and of the reactionary philosopher Charles Maurras. There he met and had a close friendship with Jean Verdenal, a medical student with literary interests. It was at this time that Eliot wrote the first two poems by which he deserves to be remembered.

## EARLY CAREER

"The Love Song of J. Alfred Prufrock" (1910–1911) was prefigured by his poem "Spleen." The name "Prufrock" has sometimes been said to be drawn from that of a Boston undertaker. It dramatizes the diffidence felt by Eliot, especially with regard to the opposite sex. Though the poem may be termed a dramatic monologue, it deals with the movements of the mind rather than with external action. The influence of Laforgue—self-deprecatory, ironic—is manifest throughout on the surface, but the form as a whole proceeds, like that of several American poets of the period, by qualitative progression. That is to say the narrative is suppressed in favor of a movement suggested by emotional affinities.

What is clear about Prufrock is that he has missed the opportunities of life. He is an antihero. This is brought out by his reference to John the Baptist.

> Though I have seen my head (grown slightly bald) brought
> in upon a platter,
> I am no prophet—and here's no great matter;
> I have seen the moment of my greatness flicker,
> And I have seen the eternal Footman hold my coat,
> and snicker,
> And in short I was afraid . . .

Only at the end do we find a token of experience that is positive, and that, too, comes from myth. This, however, is a secular myth, akin to childhood and fairy-tale—very apt for a persona who has never properly faced the responsibilities of adulthood:

> I have heard the mermaids singing, each to each.
> I do not think that they will sing to me.
> I have seen them riding seaward on the waves
> Combing the white hair of the waves blown back
> When the wind blows the water white and black . . .

This has the romantic beauty of much verse that Eliot wrote concerning the sea, for which, as a resolute boatman of the Massachusetts coast, he always had an intense feeling. It is as though he could emotionally engage with the tide and the shallows rather than with proximate human beings.

If "The Love Song of J. Alfred Prufrock" suggests a middle-aging man retreating from encounters with females, then "Portrait of a Lady" (1910) suggests an aging female confronting a prim young man. There is often in Eliot the sense of disgust at the physical aspects of womanhood. In "Prufrock" we see arms "downed with light brown hair." In "Portrait of a Lady" distaste is created largely by the cadences of the Lady's voice and the impressionistic description thereof:

> The voice returns like the insistent out-of-tune
> Of a broken violin on an August afternoon:
> "I am always sure that you understand
> My feelings, always sure that you feel,
> Sure that across the gulf you reach your hand . . . "

The accents of the voice are represented in the poem with what may be felt as astonishing authenticity: "Life, what cauchemar!"; "you do not know / What life is"; "these April sunsets, that somehow recall / My buried life." This character is said to be based upon a Boston hostess called Adelene Moffatt. The form of the poem is that of an interrupted monologue, with the Lady's plaints interspersed with the suppressed revulsion of the interlocutor, a version of "Prufrock" again: "My smile falls heavily among the bric-à-brac."

Eliot visited London, the city where he was to spend most of his life, in April 1911. Then he went on to Munich, where he completed "Prufrock." He returned to Harvard and, through the autumn term, continued his studies in philosophy, some of it Eastern in origin. However, when he decided to read for a doctorate under the aegis of Josiah Royce, it was the philosopher F. H. Bradley, whose *Appearance and Reality* he had bought in 1913, who became the center of his concern. At this point he met Bertrand Russell, who was deeply impressed by him and in due course secured his acceptance by that loose association of painters and writers in and about London known as the Bloomsbury Group.

Some confused poems—"The Love Song of St. Sebastian," "The Death of St. Narcissus"—date from this period. There is also the pornographic "King Bolo," which he continued for some years. These point to a degree of uncertainty in his life. He accepted the Sheldon Travelling Scholarship and decided to continue his studies back in Europe, at Merton College, Oxford, where he was to complete his doctoral thesis under the supervision of Harold Joachim, an expert on F. H. Bradley. After a brief prelude studying at the University of Marburg, Eliot went to London and, through the agency of his Harvard friend Conrad Aiken, made contact with his fellow American Ezra Pound, who already had a reputation as a modernist poet. For many years Pound was Eliot's most tireless advocate.

Through Pound's intervention the influential magazine *Poetry*, based in Chicago, published "Prufrock," followed in another issue by some satirical pieces: "Cousin Nancy," "Aunt Helen," and "The Boston Evening Transcript." Pound's friend Wyndham Lewis, in his magazine *Blast*, published some attractive poems such as "Preludes" and "Rhapsody on a Windy Night." Again through the agency of Pound, "Portrait of a Lady" appeared in a magazine called *Others*, edited by Alfred Kreymborg, who was at the center of a New York group of intellectuals.

Although by now Eliot was as often in London as in Oxford, it was in the latter city that he met Vivien Haigh-Wood. Her friend, an American called Lucy Thayer, had a brother, Scofield, a postgraduate student at Oxford whom Eliot had known at Harvard. Vivien was from an unthreateningly prosperous English family and much more experienced than the man she married on 26 June 1915, about two months after their first encounter.

Eliot left Oxford and took lodgings for them both. He always had an aversion to certain physical processes associated with females, and Vivien seems to have had excessive and prolonged periods of menstruation. It is debatable whether they had a full marital relationship. There was an unhappy honeymoon in Eastbourne, where they stayed for a time. However, Bertrand Russell, who had taken a predatory interest in the marriage from the beginning, offered them rooms in his flat in London, adjacent to Holborn and the Bloomsbury Group. It was necessary for Eliot to earn a living, and he tried teaching, first at High Wycombe Grammar School and then the Highgate Junior School, where he stayed until the end of 1916. He was building a reputation as a lecturer and, through the agency of Russell's friend the hostess Lady Ottoline Morrell, met a good many writers—Aldous Huxley, Lytton Strachey, Katherine Mansfield, and D. H. Lawrence among them. His completed thesis on F. H. Bradley had been sent to the examiners at Harvard.

By now Eliot and Vivien had settled in a flat near Baker Street. A friend of the Haigh-Wood family recommended Eliot for a job at Lloyd's Bank, which he joined in March 1917. His office was in Cornhill, central London. He had been taken on largely because of his presumed skill in foreign languages. Soon after this appointment his first book, *Prufrock and Other Observations*, was published. It appeared under the imprint of Harriet Shaw Weaver's Egoist Press, but the publication was financed—unknown to Eliot—by a subvention from Pound's wife, Dorothy. Few outside Ottoline Morrell's circle took much notice of the book. It was treated by the critics who reviewed it as a modernist curiosity. Eliot bridged what seemed to be an uncreative gap in his life by writing poems in

French, and in English as imitations of French poets, especially Théophile Gautier. The best of these is probably "The Hippopotamus," a deft piece of symbolism by which the hippo stands, sympathetically treated, as an ordinary sensual sinner, while the True Church is shown up as hypocritical. By this we can see how Eliot had left his family Unitarianism behind him.

Eliot has often been thought of as unproductive, but if we count literary journalism, the output is immense. He got into this because of an offer made to him by Harriet Weaver to become assistant editor on her magazine the *Egoist*, a post financed by the American book collector John Quinn. Not only did Eliot commission articles and correct proofs, he began to write a good deal of critical prose himself mainly for the *Athenaeum*. An attempt to join the American armed forces toward the end of the war came to nothing, on health grounds. In May 1918 he and Vivien rented a cottage in Buckinghamshire, and Eliot commuted to work in London. Vivien's physical condition was giving cause for alarm, with breathing difficulties, depressive episodes, and headaches. She was quite unable to find work and was regarded as a social liability by several of Eliot's friends.

Meanwhile a second book, containing "The Hippopotamus" and the French imitations, was published as *Poems* by his newfound friends Leonard and Virginia Woolf under the imprint of their Hogarth Press in 1919 and, nine months later, by Knopf in the United States. A third volume appeared in 1920, as *Poems* in New York and in London as *Ara vos prec* ("I pray you," after Dante, *Purgatorio* 26). It contained all the poems in the previous volume plus "Gerontion," which had been written between 1917 and 1919. This was Eliot's most important production so far.

It is a monologue spoken in the person of a little old man. That would seem an extraordinary work for a young man of thirty to write except that there is ample precedent in the monologues of Tennyson and Browning, the former of whom Eliot admired greatly and the latter of whom was admired by his influential friend Pound. The speaker of this monologue seems to be one for whom things have gone badly. He took no part in the wars, he has no settled home, and in fact we are mostly told where he wasn't and what he did not do.

What makes this a remarkable poem is the quality of the verse. It derives from Jacobean drama and is cast in the shape of a monologue whose structure relates to that drama as mediated by Browning and Pound. In vainly trying to explain a self that he, as a character, cannot rightly comprehend, Gerontion says, urgently,

> I that was near your heart was removed therefrom
> To lose beauty in terror, terror in inquisition.
> I have lost my passion: why should I need to keep it
> Since what is kept must be adulterated?
> I have lost my sight, smell, hearing, taste and touch:
> How should I use them for your closer contact?

These lines are based on a passage in Thomas Middleton in his play *The Changeling*, for which Eliot had considerable liking:

> I that am of your blood was taken from you
> For your better health; look no more upon't,
> But cast it to the ground regardlessly,
> Let the common sewer take it from distinction.

Eliot comments on his original: "in flashes and when the dramatic need comes . . . [Middleton] is a great master of versification" ("Thomas Middleton," in *Selected Essays*, London, 1932).

In the play, Beatrice-Joanna has hopelessly compromised herself and is explaining the nature of her disgrace to her father. In the poem, Gerontion is seeking to explain to the reader his hopeless lack of distinction. Yet the verse, fructified it would seem by the allusive nature of Eliot's art, is of remarkable power and, indeed, intelligence. Consider the line "To lose beauty in terror, terror in inquisition." This is a rendering of the degenerative process involved in what today is called "questioning." The victim is so brought down as to be incapable of feeling even quite palpable human emotions. The implication is that Gerontion has become a mere babbling head—whose utterances, nonetheless, are imbued with a random music.

There is perhaps no more sustained performance in verse among Eliot's poems than this monologue. Other works, though containing elements of great power or beauty, tend to be interrupted by ill-absorbed allusion, chunks of prose, or mannerism tending toward facetiousness. It is worth considering that at this period Eliot was writing with considerable haste book reviews commissioned by Bruce Richmond, the enterprising editor of the *Times Literary Supplement*, who was putting together a team of keen young critics that included Virginia Woolf and John Middleton Murry.

Several of Eliot's reviews were collected in *The Sacred Wood* (1920), one of the key texts in twentieth-century criticism. These essays relate the seventeenth century to contemporary poetry, and they are written with an edge that compels assent, as the following touchstones will show:

> Arnold—I think it will be conceded—was rather a propagandist for criticism than a critic. ("The Perfect Critic")

> after the Chinese Wall of Milton, blank verse has suffered not only arrest but retrogression. ("Notes on the Blank Verse of Christopher Marlowe")

> Hamlet (the man) is dominated by an emotion which is in excess of the facts as they appear. ("Hamlet and His Problems")

These essays, and several others that could be cited, brought something new into criticism, not least the sheer wit with which they were written. Like all good criticism, the aperçus echo well beyond their immediate subjects. What spoils the book, however, and prevents Eliot from assuming the place among major critics that he would seem to deserve, is the longest and most famous essay, "Tradition and the Individual Talent." This puts forward a theory that not only is false but can be shown to be false. It is adumbrated in several formulations, expressed with Eliot's characteristic youthful energy:

> the more perfect the artist, the more completely separate in him will be the man who suffers and the mind which creates.

> Poetry is not a turning loose of emotion, but an escape from emotion; it is not the expression of personality, but an escape from personality.

Here is the same apparent precision of utterance that is found in the lesser essays of *The Sacred Wood*, but it is not sufficiently attached to specific texts and demonstrates that, whatever his other virtues as a critic are, Eliot is no theorist. His doctrine of impersonality—the more separate is the man who suffers from the mind which creates—comes up against such works as *Samson Agonistes* (Milton), "The Castaway" (Cowper), *The Prelude* (Wordsworth), "Dejection" (Coleridge), "Ode to the West Wind" (Shelley), *In Memoriam* (Tennyson)—to take in only those works that Eliot knew at the time of writing. It is impossible to feel other than this: that, in his theory, Eliot was seeking to protect his own poems, past and most certainly future, against any biographical imputations that could be put upon them. "Tradition and the Individual Talent" is a magnificent piece of rhetoric, but it is not literary criticism in the same sense as other essays in the book, notably those on Marlowe, Massinger, and Jonson.

## 1920s: *THE WASTE LAND*

Eliot became famous both in the United States and Britain after the publication of the 1920 volume *Poems*. There was strong advocacy from progressive academics, especially I. A. Richards, F. R. Leavis, and William Empson in Cambridge. Eliot had, however, taken on tremendous commitments in poetry, journalism, and itinerant lecturing, in addition to his daily routine at Lloyd's Bank. This last was no sinecure but an executive post concerning, for example, foreign exchange, prewar debts, and fluctuations of currency. He eased his burden by occasional furloughs in France, but there were also occasional indispositions. His wife continued to be dangerously restive, and they moved once more, to an apartment block in Clarence Gate Gardens near Regent's Park. His friends noticed that he seemed ill and depressed. Eliot himself said that his depression was owing to world events. In 1921 they certainly seemed grim enough. There was worldwide financial collapse. In Britain alone there were two million unemployed. However, the poem that emerged from this misery is at least as much a personal statement as an account of a decaying civilization.

The poem in question, *The Waste Land* (1922), has often been censured for its obscurity, but it has remained popular with many readers. Though it may seem difficult to explicate as a whole, it has outbursts of imagery, together with Eliot's peculiarly attractive music, that can appeal before they are understood. In any case, appreciation is by no means the same as explication. Many of the clues as how to read the poem are found in the notes—added, it was said, to bulk out the original slim volume and make it appear more like a book. The principal clue comes right at the beginning of the notes. Eliot writes, "Not only the title, but the plan and a good deal of the incidental symbolism of the poem were suggested by Jessie L. Weston's book on the Grail legend, *From Ritual to Romance*."

This book discusses various medieval French romances, chiefly of the twelfth century. Most crucial from the point of view of *The Waste Land* are those concerned with the knight Sir Perceval. These legends relate the story of a country stricken with drought and a dying head of state, the Fisher King. To revive this monarch, and indeed this waste land, a hero must be found who will ride off and discover the Holy Grail. This was the vessel said to have contained some of the blood that poured out of the body of Jesus Christ when he was impaled on the cross. The Christian Church officially knows nothing of this story. It may well be that the legends are pagan, Celtic in origin, and form some part of a nature cult. Some of them,

however, may have been reworked by authors who were Christian. It would seem that the Grail is not found and the Fisher King dies.

Certainly in Eliot's recension there seems to be no hope. One must remember that the text we have was abridged by Ezra Pound from a much longer version. Pound's excisions were on aesthetic grounds. What he did was cut out weaker lines and passages in order to preserve the stronger ones. Thus the poem appears to be fragmentary. Eliot himself, early on, called it "a heap of broken images." One could say that he was representing the chaotic state of modern civilization by writing chaotically. But confusion cannot be represented through confusion. It would be more sensible to consider the poem as a collection of lyrics held together by suggestions of a suppressed plot; the plot of the search for the Grail.

This suppression of plot is characteristic of modernist poetry produced by Americans. It is a prime factor of the immense poem by Ezra Pound called *The Cantos*, which, as we have seen in Eliot's "Prufrock," moves not through narrative of external event but through qualitative progression, in which the separate passages in the poem are related not by logic but by emotion.

In the case of *The Waste Land*, one way of expounding it is to go to what may be felt as the dominant or core of the poem. If anywhere, we find it here:

> And I, Tiresias, have foresuffered all
> Enacted on this same divan or bed;
> I who have sat by Thebes below the wall
> And walked among the lowest of the dead . . .

Tiresias was a figure from Greek legend, said to be a prophet of Thebes who had changed sex on striking with his staff two serpents copulating and had changed back into a man some years later on repeating this action. He thus had experience of both sexes. He had been deprived of sight by Juno because he declared from experience that the pleasure in intercourse of a female was ten times as great as that felt by a man. In compensation, the gift of prophecy was bestowed upon him by Jupiter, who also permitted him to live seven times longer than is the lot of mankind. Eliot himself declares in a note that what Tiresias sees is the substance of his poem.

We are certainly conscious of a narrative linking the dramatic interludes, sometimes explicitly: "I will show you fear in a handful of dust," "But at my back in a cold blast I hear / The rattle of the bones," "When I count, there are only you and I together." More than this, there is the sense of a brooding presence observing the vagaries of the Waste Land, mostly sexual, with a regret bordering on despair.

One of the most beautiful passages, which could well stand on its own as an elegy, is section 4, "Death by Water":

Phlebas the Phoenician, a fortnight dead,
Forgot the cry of gulls, and the deep sea swell
And the profit and the loss.
A current under sea
Picked his bones in whispers. As he rose and fell
He passed the stages of his age and youth
Entering the whirlpool.
Gentile or Jew
O you who turn the wheel and look to windward,
Consider Philebas, who was once handsome and tall as you.

"Phlebas" is the title of a dialogue by Plato defining pleasure. The figure in the poem is reminiscent of a fertility cult, retailed by Jessie Weston, in which a papyrus head, representing the god Adonis, was thrown into the sea at Alexandria and borne by a current to Byblos, where it was received with rejoicing. This elegy was adapted by Eliot from the French of his own poem, "Dans le Restaurant": "Phlebas, le Phénicien, pendant quinze jours noyé, / Oubliait des cris des mouettes et la houle de Cornouaille . . ." ("Phlebas the Phoenician, a fortnight drowned, forgot the cry of the gulls and the swell of the Cornish seas"). One could in fact point to several other sources, including Homer, who tells of a drowned Phoenician trader; accounts of the Phoenicians in part 4 of *The Golden Bough* by Sir James Frazer; and of course Eliot's recollections of sailing along the coast of New England.

*The Waste Land* is three-quarters allusion, ranging from direct quotation to suggestive imitations, especially of Jacobean drama. Variegated though the versification seems, behind most of it is the beat of the freely modulated blank verse favored by the gloomy playwright John Webster and certain of his contemporaries. But Eliot, a fine critic characterized by his apposite quotations, knew where to look for his sources. He himself had written, "Immature poets imitate; mature poets steal" ("Philip Massinger"). And what he stole for *The Waste Land*, from a variety of sources, amounts to what Edmund Wilson called "a most distressingly moving account of Eliot's own agonized state of mind . . . almost the cry of a man on the verge of insanity" (letter to John Peale Bishop, September 1922, quoted in Southam).

No wonder Eliot had in some sort to shield himself behind his doctrine of impersonality. This, as Wilson said, was "a cry de profundis." Eliot was chained to the bank by the need of a steady income; he was matched with a neurotic wife whom he had ceased to love; he was overworked by the periodical journalism that had become his main contact with literature; and he had his own health problems with which to contend. He had finished *The Waste Land* in Switzerland during a period of nervous collapse. Vivien had resorted to a series of sanatoriums in France and England.

Despite all this, Eliot had promised to start a literary periodical, largely financed by Lady Rothermere. Vivien suggested its title: the *Criterion*. Eliot collected a nucleus of writers, some from the *Times Literary Supplement*, but he sought also to give the magazine a European dimension. The first issue was published in October 1922, and early contributors included Valéry Larbaud, Herman Hesse, and José Ortega y Gasset. *The Waste Land* appeared in the November issue that year and was published a month later in the American magazine the *Dial*. In volume form, it appeared in America from Boni and Liveright in December 1922 and in Britain from the Hogarth Press in September 1923. In these volumes the notes for the poem were published for the first time. They did not help. Many reviewers dismissed the poem as obscure. But the younger people took it up, especially at universities, apparently excited by the music of *The Waste Land*.

Some young writers produced verse straight out of the poem, imagining that they were writing under the spell of inspiration, when in fact all they had achieved was unconscious plagiarism:

I that am seed, root and kernel-stone
Buried in the present, I that exact fulfilment from every hour
Now tell you
Accept all things . . .

(Nancy Cunard, *Parallax*, 1925)

Still, such people constituted Eliot's true audience, and they looked to the future.

Although under strain, Eliot began to see his prospects in terms of drama and began a play called *Sweeney Agonistes*. There were many distractions, however, some of them strange ones. Eliot had taken an additional set of rooms in an apartment block on the Charing Cross Road where he received artistic friends, and others more anonymous, some of whom appeared to be young sailors. It may be that Eliot was seeking to re-create something of his happy time in Paris with Jean Verdenal, who had been killed by enemy action in May 1915. At this low point, at the end of 1923, he met a young American poet, William

Force Stead, resolute in his Christian faith. It was he who led Eliot, brought up as a Unitarian, toward the Church of England. *Sweeney Agonistes* was not taking shape, and Eliot produced what he called a suite of poems. This coalesced as "The Hollow Men" and was completed in the autumn of 1925. Here were jazzy rhythms similar to those in the unfinished play and also lyrics related to other poems:

> Eyes I dare not meet in dreams
> In death's dream kingdom...
>
> ("The Hollow Men")

> Eyes that last I saw in tears
> Through division
> Here in death's dream kingdom...
>
> ("Eyes that last I saw in tears," in *Collected Poems, 1909–1935*)

However, he could not get on with the play, and one reason for this was Vivien. It was plain by now that their marriage was a failure. They were by 1925 doing each other a considerable measure of harm. Even the prospect of release from the bank that Eliot had served for eight years was only a partial solution. Geoffrey Faber had gone into partnership with a firm of scientific publishers called Gwyer and wanted a presence with business experience on his board of directors. Eliot began work at Faber and Gwyer in the autumn of 1925, still with an office, still with a suit, but this time fully engaged on the literary side. He proved phenomenal as a talent-spotter, with the careers of W. H. Auden, Louis MacNeice, and George Barker—as well as those of older writers such as Ezra Pound and James Joyce—greatly to his credit.

In 1926 his new employers published *Poems, 1909–1925*, in which "The Hollow Men" appeared for the first time in volume form. In 1926 Eliot gave the Clark Lectures at Cambridge, entitled "The Metaphysical Poets of the Seventeenth Century." He had been reading theology, especially the work of Jacques Maritain. On 29 June 1927, through the agency of William Force Stead, who was now chaplain of Worcester College, Oxford, Eliot was baptized and received into the Church of England. This in due course led him to a new area of social intercourse—meeting people, for example, such as the bishop of Chichester, Dr. George Bell.

During an unproductive period Eliot had been translating from the French the poems of St. John Perse. But his conversion seemed to release his creative impulse, and he produced one of his most readily accessible poems, "Journey of the Magi":

> "A cold coming we had of it,
> Just the worst time of the year

> For a journey, and such a long journey:
> The ways deep and the weather sharp,
> The very dead of winter."

The words are those of a sermon from the seventeenth-century divine Lancelot Andrewes. But, as ever, Eliot knew where to look. The prose of the old sermonizer imparted something new to poetic meter; notably, the wintry shudder in these lines. This and poems following, such as "A Song for Simeon," "Animula," and the uniquely beautiful "Marina," were issued in the shape of Christmas pamphlets known as the Ariel Poems from the firm of Faber. Essentially they are the poems of a convert—a conversion sealed by Eliot's becoming a British citizen in November 1927.

These poems led on, under a load of journalism, to *Ash Wednesday*, finished in 1930 and published in London and New York soon after. The title refers to the first day of Lent, a period of forty days' penance and fasting. This work is best read as a sequence of lyric poems which, like the Ariel Poems that preceded them, are concerned with conversion. As in "The Journey of the Magi," we are told that the progress into religion is a difficult one. The first poem, originally entitled "Perch'io Non Spero" after a ballata by Guido Cavalcanti, enacts in its repetitions and pauses the torment of decision:

> Because I do not hope to turn again
> Because I do not hope
> Because I do not hope to turn
> Desiring this man's gift and that man's scope—
> I no longer strive to strive towards such things
> (Why should the agèd eagle stretch its wings)
> Why should I mourn
> The vanished power of the usual reign?

The second section, originally called "Salutation," introduces the figure of the Lady, suggesting that the new dispensation could be one of release and happiness or one, which may come to the same thing, of utter abnegation:

> Lady, three white leopards sat under a juniper tree
> In the cool of the day, having fed to satiety
> On my legs my heart my liver and that which had
>     been contained
> In the hollow round of my skull....

The leopards are agents of destruction, and what is being suggested is that conversion leading to the immolation of personality can be bad and bitter.

The temptations waiting upon conversion are demonstrated in the third poem, originally called "Som de l'Escalina" ("the topmost of the stair") after the same section of Dante's *Purgatorio* from which Eliot culled the title of his 1920 volume:

> At the first turning of the second stair
> I turned and saw below
> The same shape twisted on the banister
> Under the vapour in the fetid air
> Struggling with the devil of the stairs who wears
> The deceitful shape of hope and of despair. . . .

There is evocation of evil in that imagery. Note the strange felicity of "twisted" in "The same shape twisted on the banister." There is the effect of struggle in the obsessive rhyming, pararhyming, and internal rhyming: "stair," "air," "stairs," "wears," "despair." The stairs may have a significance, in that early manifestations of the Seven Deadly Sins, popular in medieval sermons, transpired in terms of demons lurking on each of seven ascending staircases designed to take the human spirit out of this world. The spirit is stripped of a fleshly attribute at each stair, and so the concept is one of suffering as well as purgation.

The fourth poem in the sequence was originally called "Vestita di Color di Fiamma" ("clad in the color of flame"). That again alludes to Dante's *Purgatorio*—this time cantos 30 and 33, which feature the figure of Beatrice, the poet's love on earth, now transfigured into divine beauty. In Eliot this marks the reappearance of the Lady, still in the garden but, as ever, ambiguous:

> The silent sister veiled in white and blue
> Between the yews, behind the garden god,
> Whose flute is breathless, bent her head and signed but
>     spoke no word. . . .

The fifth poem shares something of the vehemence of the third:

> If the lost word is lost, if the spent word is spent
> If the unheard, unspoken
> Word is unspoken, unheard . . .

We have to ask ourselves, what is a word when it is unspoken? How do we apprehend that which is unheard? The poem relates to one of Eliot's favorite quotations, "la sua volontade è nostra pace" ("his will is our peace") from Dante's *Paradiso*. The Lady appears toward the end of the poem which, like so many romantic lyrics, depends on a question:

> Will the veiled sister between the slender
> Yew trees pray for those who offend her
> And are terrified and cannot surrender?

The final section of the *Ash Wednesday* sequence shows the ambiguities of conversion. There is no perfect way. One lives in hope, but there is the possibility of despair. That, uniquely, is what we find at the end of the poem. It is a plea, not a statement, and a plea emanating from one who knows what it is to have been unhappy:

> And even among these rocks
> Sister, mother
> And spirit of the river, spirit of the sea,
> Suffer me not to be separated
> And let my cry come unto thee.

Although *Ash Wednesday* met with considerable appreciation, especially among Eliot's Christian friends, he was not able to write much in the way of verse for the next five years. The *Selected Essays* of 1932 had helped to make him a literary lion. They included most of *The Sacred Wood* plus articles on the metaphysical poets (especially Andrew Marvell) and John Dryden, and several essays about poetic drama that had a good deal to do with defining his later ambitions. In effect, this volume rewrote literary history and inspired the work of the rising generation of writers often termed the New Critics, William Empson, F. R. Leavis, and Cleanth Brooks among them.

However, public and personal life alike had become difficult because of Vivien's increasingly peculiar behavior. It is quite likely that at social gatherings she could not follow much that was going on. Be that as it may, Eliot in 1932 accepted the Charles Eliot Norton professorship at Harvard that gave rise to a volume of prose published the following year, *The Use of Poetry and the Use of Criticism*. As a book it lacked the sharpness of expression found in his earlier criticism. This would be his first visit to the United States in seventeen years and would keep him there for several months. He had many lecturing engagements other than those at Harvard, appearing in New York, Buffalo, Pasadena, Minneapolis, Princeton, and Los Angeles, and especially at the University of Virginia, where he delivered the Page-Barbour Lectures. These were published in 1934 as *After Strange Gods: A Primer of Modern Heresy*. That hastily contrived work showed less tact than other performances. Eliot has been castigated for anti-Semitism, an unfortunate remark about "free-thinking Jews" in these lectures being linked to the image of a squatting Jew in "Gerontion" and also a character in his would-be comic poem "Burbank with a Baedeker, Bleistein with a Cigar" (1918–1919). All one can say is that if Eliot was anti-Semitic, as with his background might be inferred, such an attitude does not manifest itself in the work that really matters: his major poems and key critical essays.

After all this activity, though Eliot would be going back to England he would no longer be living with Vivien. He stayed in Surrey near the farm of his publishing friend Frank Morley and paid visits to other friends, such as Leonard and Virginia Woolf. But he begged them not to disclose his whereabouts to his wife. In late 1933 he settled down in rooms at the presbytery belonging to St. Stephen's Church in South Kensington, the paying guest of Father Eric Cheetham, at whose church he had frequently worshipped. He stayed there for seven years.

When Eliot did not return to the flat at Clarence Gate Gardens but instead abstracted books and other belongings when Vivien was out, she became hysterical. Being presented by her solicitors with a deed of separation made her worse. She was convinced that Eliot would return to her and tried various stratagems to procure a meeting with him. But matters had gone too far. Her conduct became stranger and stranger, involving dressing up in Nazi uniform and shoving envelopes filled with excrement through the letter box of Faber and Faber. It was apparently her own doctor who, in the summer of 1938, arranged her committal to a mental home. This was not a state institution but a private hospital called Northumberland House, in Finsbury Park, North London. Eliot sacrificed a considerable part of his income to keep Vivien there until she died of an unexpected heart attack on 22 January 1947 at the age of fifty-eight. It is notable that Eliot never experienced any estrangement from her family, the Haigh-Woods—who may be presumed, therefore, to have exonerated him from undue blame.

## WORKS FOR THE STAGE

The mid-1930s was the period when Eliot made some decisive efforts at drama. *Sweeney Agonistes* had been abandoned and remains a tantalizing fragment of proletarian dialogue. However, he had been asked by E. Martin Browne, a theater director whom he had met through Bishop George Bell, to write the choruses for a pageant to raise money for London churches. He worked on this through much of 1933 and into 1934. It was produced at Sadler Wells Theater in May and June in the latter year.

*The Rock*, as the pageant was called, is a morality play showing a group of workmen building a church, their labors being interrupted by incursions from the past such as a monk turned king's jester, Israelites founding Jerusalem, a Danish invasion, and men and women from the time of Richard I. There are also interruptions by an Agitator raising a crowd against the church, and there are Communists caricatured as Redshirts and Fascists caricatured as Blackshirts. The basic script was by Martin Browne, revised by the Reverend Vincent Howson, but Eliot supplied the choruses, which are the only memorable part of this work.

Even so, the importance of this collaboration is that it led to more serious efforts. Bishop Bell liked the choruses sufficiently to suggest that Eliot write a play for the 1935 Canterbury Festival. *Murder in the Cathedral* told of the martyrdom of St. Thomas Becket (ca. 1118–1170). It was first performed in the Chapter House of Canterbury Cathedral on 19 June. The play itself was ingenious, making dramatic use of a chorus of Canterbury women, featuring magniloquent speeches from Thomas and involving interruptions by four Tempters, who in subsequent productions have often been doubled by actors portraying the four turbulent knights who commit the murder. The play ends in prose, with a dialogue among those same knights moralizing their deed in a mode influenced by Bernard Shaw. At last, it seemed, Eliot had fulfilled the desire voiced in his critical essays to revive the poetic drama. The production moved to the Mercury Theatre in London, went on tour, came back to London for a run at the Duchess Theatre, and then transferred to London's premier Shakespearean theater the Old Vic.

Encouraged by this, Eliot in early 1936 started on a new play. This was the first of several attempts to dramatize mythical plots in modern settings. The idea seems to have been to use contemporary West End comedy as a medium for deeper matters. The draft was revised many times, up to and including the rehearsals for the play, which was produced as *The Family Reunion* at the Westminster Theatre on 21 March 1939. It told of the fear felt by a man who may have been responsible for the death of his wife, a "restless shivering painted shadow." Since much of this play was written during the events that led to Vivien Eliot's detention in Northumberland House, some degree of autobiographical imputation seems inevitable. The comedy was not a success. It did better when revived at the Mercury Theatre in October 1946 and was performed, together with *Murder in the Cathedral*, at the first Edinburgh Festival in 1947.

Eliot had been thinking of a new play since the first production of *The Family Reunion*, and 1947 seemed a time propitious for its inception. He sent the draft of an early portion to Martin Browne, who tried to get rid of the philosophizing that had marred the earlier play.

*The Cocktail Party* was first performed at the Edinburgh Festival on 22 August 1949. Eliot said that the play was based on the *Alcestis* of Euripides, wherein the wife lays down her life for her husband and is in her turn brought back from hell by Hercules—Hercules, in this version, being Sir Henry Harcourt-Reilly, a psychiatrist. The play went first to New York in January 1950, was produced in London in May, and reached its largest audience when screened on television in 1952. Its success may be attributed to the actors it was able to attract. *The Cocktail Party* seems to pick up traits from such masters of popular entertainment as Noël Coward, Terence Rattigan, and Frederick Lonsdale: A loves B, B loves C, C loves D, while D is married to A. But its low-pressure verse does little to sharpen those relationships into wit.

By 1952, Eliot was working on *The Confidential Clerk*. It opened at the Lyceum Theatre, Edinburgh—again as part of the festival—on 25 August 1953. The play turned on father-and-son relationships. Its verse is less colorful even than that of its predecessor and abounds in verbal clichés. The response, however, was favorable, and the play went on to the Lyric Theatre in London. Though work went much more slowly, Eliot was drafting what was to prove his final play in 1957, and this was performed at the Edinburgh Festival in August the following year. *The Elder Statesman* centers on a dying public figure confronted with recollections of his past. Given this far-from-invigorating plot, though transferred to the Cambridge Theatre, London, it failed to run.

On the whole Eliot cannot be considered a major playwright. But a certain amount of spin-off has proved fruitful: we would not have had the early essays in dramatic criticism had not Eliot nurtured theatrical ambitions. And when Martin Browne excised some lines that held up the action of *Murder in the Cathedral*, these proved to start off one of the most intriguing of Eliot's later productions—albeit a production for the study rather than the stage.

## GENESIS OF *FOUR QUARTETS*

The lines excised by Browne impelled Eliot into a later stage of the meditative verse he had utilized in "Gerontion" and "Ash Wednesday":

Time present and time past
Are both perhaps present in time future,
And time future contained in time past . . .

It is hard to see what function these lines would have in a play, but they are put to good use in "Burnt Norton,"

where they are the initiating impulse. These are the tones of the lecture room, derived from F. H. Bradley's *Appearance and Reality* and, even more closely, his *Ethical Studies*. Insofar as the passage means anything, it is denying the existence of entities except as the product of direct experience. Were this denial valid, it would be impossible to imagine anything one had not seen. But that attitude is immediately contradicted by a lyrical change of tone:

Footfalls echo in the memory
Down the passage which we did not take. . . .

So it is possible to imagine that which did not happen, after all. To drive this home, Eliot produces a magic garden, with an insistent thrush, invisible watchers, unheard music, and, most movingly,

the leaves were full of children
Hidden excitedly, containing laughter. . . .

The imagery here and elsewhere is largely derived from a story by Rudyard Kipling called "They," about a blind woman who, whether in reality or in her imagination, evokes missing children. This initiating passage ends by stating what has already been shown, that it is possible to conjure up that which one has not experienced.

The poem falls into five sections, of which this is the first. The title "Burnt Norton" refers to the grounds of a country house burnt down in the 1740s by its crazy owner, a Warwickshire squire called Sir William Keyte. He had previously thrown out his wife and children. Eliot most probably visited this site with Emily Hale, an American friend who wrote to him constantly and most summers met with him in England. The references to the children—which he might have fathered had he married Emily Hale and not Vivien Haigh-Wood—are given with a peculiar intensity.

The second section of "Burnt Norton" is a lyric— "Garlic and sapphires in the mud / Clot the bedded axle-tree." "Garlic" would seem to represent the lower elements in life and "sapphires" the higher, both impeding the movement of the wheel, which represents experience out of time. This lyric is followed by a contrasting meditative passage which, despite its quasi-philosophical tones, reinforces the attitude voiced in answer to Bradley, that the mind can create experience: "only in time can the moment in the rose-garden . . . / Be remembered." "Rose" and "rose garden" in Eliot symbolize unearthly bliss.

In the third section time is represented as a one-way progress, like the metaled ways of an underground railroad. In the fourth, however, another lyric lightheartedly implies an alternative mode of progression. The fifth and final section indicates that words, with all their imprecision, create the world through which we move. The implication is that the greater the poet, the more he is able to create a universe in which he can be at ease.

"Burnt Norton" was written in the latter part of 1935, almost concurrently with the early stages of *The Family Reunion*. There is a certain amount in common linguistically between them—the dialogue between Harry and Agatha, for example: "I only looked through the little door / When the sun was shining on the rose garden /And heard in the distance tiny voices." At this juncture, Eliot did not know he was going to follow up "Burnt Norton" with a sequel, and the poem was incorporated into his *Collected Poems, 1909–1935*, published in 1936 and, as might have been expected, received with considerable acclaim, as was the prose book *Essays Ancient and Modern*, relating Christianity to literature and published two years later. However, by 1940 Eliot was drafting another poem related to a place-name, using "Burnt Norton" as a prototype on which to base this successor. "East Coker" was the village whence a distant ancestor, Andrew Eliot, emigrated in 1669. Eliot was there only once, in August 1937, when, however, he observed in the churchyard the indecipherable gravestones of those who might have been his ancestors.

The first section evokes an old England followed, as was the case in "Burnt Norton," by a romantic lyric, conjoined with its own commentary deprecating its own romanticism: "That was a way of putting it—not very satisfactory." As in the previous poem, the London Underground is described as simulacrum of a deterministic mode of existence. A further lyric suggests, after Baudelaire, that the world is one great hospital. However, the apparent contrarieties are partially reconciled. What was a celebration of art in the previous poem here is a celebration of tradition: "Home is where one starts from."

By now Eliot was aware that he was writing a sequence. The celebration of "home" in "East Coker" leads naturally to the concern with history that is at the heart of the final two poems. "The Dry Salvages" harks back to his youth in America. These are rocks off the coast of Gloucester, Massachusetts. Sea and river imagery preponderate throughout. However, the third section links the passengers on the subway with the fishermen setting forth on their difficult journey: "Fare forward, travellers."

As if to underwrite the would-be religious character of the sequence as a whole, the place-name of the fourth poem, "Little Gidding," refers to a place of retreat where Nicholas Ferrar in the 1620s founded a Christian community. The poem is full of references to the England of that period—when, as Eliot had written in his essay on Massinger, "the intellect was immediately at the tips of the senses." Nevertheless, the crux of the poem derives not from any English tradition but from Dante. The second section comprises a practiced imitation of the chosen meter of the *Inferno*, showing the Italian poet recognizing his former master, Brunetto Latini, in Hell. In Eliot this is a dialogue between the present author and a humanist who can give him no comfort at all. Instead, he reveals the gifts reserved for age as "the rending pain of re-enactment / Of all that you have done, and been." "Little Gidding" ends, in the teeth of this deprecation, "With the drawing of this Love and the voice of this calling." Only in Christ can the contrarieties be reconciled, and the whole ends with an invocation of some of the previous images of *Four Quartets*, as by now the entire cycle was called. The river, the children in the apple tree, the sea, the tongue of flame, the knot of fire are all called together to endorse Eliot's summation of the whole: "the fire and the rose are one."

From an external point of view, *Four Quartets* looks like an entity. The key element in "Burnt Norton" is air, that in "East Coker" is earth, in "The Dry Salvages" water, and in "Little Gidding" fire. If we take the seasons, that in "Burnt Norton" is autumn, in "East Coker" summer, in "The Dry Salvages" winter, in "Little Gidding" still winter but passing on to spring.

However, these are superficial aspects of the sequence, which is not a single entity but a cycle of poems. For one thing, the poetic level is uneven. There are passages in *Four Quartets* that read like self-parody and not of a very enlivening kind:

> I do not know much about gods; but I think that the river
> Is a strong brown god. . . .

There are, though, passages of remarkable poetry. "Burnt Norton" is the "quartet" that sustains the highest level, with its first section about the garden, the third section about the "place of disaffection," and the passage in the fifth section about language. "East Coker" has in its first section an intense description of an English summer afternoon and a third section of powerful disillusion concerning the impermanence of earthly existence. In "The Dry Salvages" there is a sestina about the fishermen sailing into the Northeast. "Little Gidding" is the most willed of the four and would be deemed almost expendable in poetic terms were it not for the dialogue with the stranger, which sits oddly in a poem having to do with the Ferrar community. Editing of Pound's sort would leave us with seven sustained lyrics of the kind termed canzone, but that would not be quite enough to form a book. Also Eliot apparently needed the place-names and their associations to bring about the *Quartets* after that first impulse of "Burnt Norton." One can, however, certainly say that this small volume contains poetry of considerable intensity.

*Four Quartets* was written under the shadow of World War II, impending and continued. Eliot shut down his magazine the *Criterion* in 1939, the year in which he published his book of light verse *Old Possum's Book of Practical Cats* and also *The Idea of a Christian Society*, based on lectures that presage the decline of Christianity and the vanishing of civilization along with it. Eliot's lodgings with Father Cheetham in Kensington proved uncomfortable now that the war had begun, so in 1940 he moved out to Shamley Green, a village in Surrey from which he could commute daily to his office, staying at intervals with friends in London. After the war, in 1946, he moved back to the metropolis, sharing a flat in Carlyle Mansions, Chelsea, with the editor and scholar John Hayward, already a close friend. Hayward had a progressive disease that confined him to a wheelchair but for all that was more extroverted than Eliot and introduced him to a wide variety of acquaintances.

## POSTWAR YEARS

Eliot's was the life of a sedulous editor and publisher, but he went a long distance out of his way to defend Ezra Pound. His old friend was accused of treason because of fascist broadcasts during the war and was confined to St. Elizabeth's, a lunatic asylum in Washington, D.C., as being unfit to plead at a trial. Eliot traveled to America in 1946 to act on behalf of Pound but also to see his family and his lady friend Emily Hale. He flew to America again in 1947, just before the death of his brother and, while settling Henry Ware's estate, had to give several lectures to pay for the expenses of his stay. His health had not been secure. When he returned to England he had to endure an operation on his hernia and also had most of his teeth extracted. On yet another journey to America in 1948, by ship this time, he once more gave lectures at several universities and, while at Princeton, heard he had won the Nobel Prize. This was in the wake of being awarded the O.M., the highest nonchivalric honor that the United Kingdom can bestow. He traveled to Sweden for the Nobel ceremony. In this same year, *Notes towards the Definition of Culture* was published, voicing a characteristically reactionary view of the class system by which a civilized society perpetuates itself.

There were other journeys to the United States and visits to other countries such as South Africa, Spain, and France, but there was no doubt that by 1952 he was quite a sick man. His perennial bronchitis was not helped by the fact that for many years he had been a heavy smoker. But on 10 January 1957 he married his secretary, Valerie Fletcher, and she seems to have made him happy in what were to be his final years.

This event was a surprise to his friends. He had departed from Carlyle Mansions abruptly, giving very little notice to John Hayward, with whom he had lived for ten years. The married couple moved into Kensington Court Gardens, off High Street, Kensington. At Faber and Faber he became more and more a part-time editor. His retrospective collection of essays, *On Poetry and Poets*, appeared in 1957. Bland in tone, it could do little by way of adding to his reputation as a critic, but it consolidated his fame in that area. In Italy, in America, in London, he was an acclaimed and smiling public man.

Although friends such as Father Cheetham and Geoffrey Faber were dying around him, Pound, largely as a result of Eliot's avocations, was released from St. Elizabeth's in 1958. There were holidays in the sun and perhaps too many public appearances in Britain and America. But on return from a visit to Nassau, Eliot succumbed to a stroke and died on 4 January 1965 at the age of seventy-six.

## ELIOT AS AN AMERICAN POET

One aspect of Eliot that has never been sufficiently raised is how American he was. He claimed never to have read Walt Whitman, but the parallels between his verse and that of his greatest American predecessor are manifest. The resemblances are in imagery:

> When lilacs last in the dooryard bloomed . . .
> (Whitman, "Memories of President Lincoln")

> The rank ailanthus of the April dooryard . . .
> (*Four Quartets*)

There are resemblances in syntax:

> What waves and soils exuding?
> What climes? what persons are here?
> (Whitman, "Salut au Monde")

> What seas what shores what grey rocks and what islands . . .
> ("Marina")

And there is a marked tendency toward cataloging, which is a representative trait of American writing, in prose as well as verse.

The structure of Eliot's poems aroused initial puzzlement in English critics, especially in reviews of *The Waste Land*. This too is an American trait: Eliot works through the association of images rather than the retailing of narrative. Thus, he will not seem unduly difficult if he is read without the expectations aroused by traditional English poetry. In Eliot's verse, as in that of Ezra Pound and Wallace Stevens, the plot is suppressed in favor of emotive vibrations arising from it. Matters are made easier still by the strange sad music, not itself precise in meaning but appropriate to the feelings of loss involved, that is curiously Eliot's own:

A woman drew her long black hair out tight
And fiddled whisper music on those strings . . .

*(The Waste Land)*

Eliot is likely to have a difficult time in the twenty-first century. A lobby in favor of political correctness is assembled to accuse him of anti-Semitism. Further, a feminist lobby, in the wake of Vivien Eliot, accuses him of misogyny. It would be better to concentrate on the texts. In "Gerontion," "Marina," "Ash Wednesday," and parts of *The Waste Land* and *Four Quartets*, Eliot composed some of the finest poetry in the English of his day.

[*See also* Auden, W.H.; New Critics, The; Pound, Ezra; Stevens, Wallace; *and* Whitman, Walt.]

## WORKS

*Prufrock and Other Observations* (1917)
*Poems* (1919)
*Ara Voc Prec* (1920)
*Poems* (1920)
*The Sacred Wood* (1920)
*The Waste Land* (1922)
*Poems, 1909–1925* (1925)
*Ash Wednesday* (1930)
*Selected Essays* (1932)
*Sweeney Agonistes* (1932)
*The Use of Poetry and the Use of Criticism* (1933)
*After Strange Gods: A Primer of Modern Heresy* (1934)
*The Rock* (1934)
*Murder in the Cathedral* (1935)
*Collected Poems, 1909–1935* (1936; includes "Burnt Norton" [1935])
*Essays Ancient and Modern* (1938)
*The Idea of a Christian Society* (1939)
*The Family Reunion* (1939)
*Old Possum's Book of Practical Cats* (1939)
*Four Quartets* (1943)
*Selected Poems* (1948)
*Notes towards the Definition of Culture* (1948)

*The Cocktail Party* (1950)
*The Complete Poems and Plays* (1952)
*The Confidential Clerk* (1954)
*On Poetry and Poets* (1957)
*The Elder Statesman* (1959)
*To Criticize the Critic, and Other Writings* (1965)
*Poems in Early Youth* (1967)
*The Complete Poems and Plays of T. S. Eliot* (1969)

## FURTHER READING

Ackroyd, Peter. *T. S. Eliot: A Life*. London, 1984. This useful biography, unauthorized, therefore produced without aid of quotations, perforce created a new mode of criticism.

Bodelsen, C. A. *T. S. Eliot's* Four Quartets: *A Commentary*. Copenhagen, 1958. The most sensitive analysis so far of Eliot's enigmatic work.

Gardner, Helen. *The Composition of* Four Quartets. Oxford and New York, 1978. Useful in showing how this extraordinary work was built up.

Harding, D. W. *Experience into Words*. London, 1963. Contains two essays on Eliot that constitute the most perceptive account of the poet's use of language so far and also an essay on Eliot's plays.

Hobsbaum, Philip. *Tradition and Experiment in English Poetry*. London, 1979. Puts Eliot into an American context.

Jones, D. E. *The Plays of T. S. Eliot*. Toronto, 1960.

Leavis, F. R. *New Bearings in English Poetry*. London, 1932. The pioneer work by one of England's greatest critics, setting Eliot in context among twentieth-century poets.

Matthiessen, F. O. *The Achievement of T. S. Eliot: An Essay on the Nature of Poetry*. London, 1935. Pioneer work by a contemporary of Eliot. Useful insights.

Menand, Louis. *Discovering Modernism: T. S. Eliot and His Context*. Oxford and New York, 2003. Up-to-date commentary; provides valuable context.

Moody, A. D., ed. *The Cambridge Companion to T. S. Eliot*. Cambridge, 1994. Selection of essays by various hands; helpful in providing insights into the works of Eliot.

Selby, Nick, ed. *T. S. Eliot: The Waste Land*. Columbia Critical Guides. New York, 1999. Selection of essays.

Southam, B. C. *A Student's Guide to the Selected Poems of T. S. Eliot*. London, 1968. Subsequent editions, each one larger than its predecessor, sixth edition 1994. Invaluable as an explicator of allusions in Eliot's major poems exclusive of the *Four Quartets*.

Traversi, Derek. *T. S. Eliot: The Longer Poems*. London, 1976. Good on the religious aspects; has benefited from work of previous critics.

Weston, Jessie L. *From Ritual to Romance.* Cambridge, 1920. The essential background book for *The Waste Land.*

Williamson, George. *A Reader's Guide to T. S. Eliot.* New York, 1953. Poem-by-poem commentary.

Zhang, Jian. *The Passage He Did Not Take: T. S. Eliot and the English Romantic Tradition.* Beijing, 1996. Good at showing Eliot's affinities with romantic poetry; analyzes in detail the nature of the influence upon Eliot of the West End stage.

See also the articles on *Four Quartets* and *The Waste Land*, immediately following.

# T. S. ELIOT'S
# *FOUR QUARTETS*

### *by Ronald Bush*

It is common to speak about T. S. Eliot's *Four Quartets* (1943) as a single poem, but it also misleading. Eliot wrote what was eventually collected as the first "Quartet" ("Burnt Norton," composed 1935, published 1936) without a sense that he would add a successor, and it was only when he was writing the second (or perhaps the third) poem that he decided on a sequence of four. Eliot's dislike of repeating himself played an important part in his composition, which both sets up the poems as responses to one another and helps account for the sequence's four-part structure.

"Burnt Norton" continues to engage with many of the concerns of Eliot's earlier poetry. He continues to ask himself, for example, why, although our lives seem to be justified only by moments of romantic intensity, we cannot be certain that these moments amount to anything more than ephemera. From the perspective of middle age, Eliot handles these themes with a new feeling for genre, style, tone, and structure. Compared with *The Waste Land*, "Burnt Norton" is meditative rather than dramatic. That is, it proceeds by thought rather than scenes or images, and for the most part it avoids strong ironies. It also displays a much clearer structural outline.

Eliot composed "Burnt Norton" in the period after he separated in 1933–1934 from his wife, Vivien, and started to seek out people and places from his youth. Most notably, Eliot made contact with his college sweetheart, Emily Hale. The two spent time together when she visited relatives in the English Cotswold villages near Oxford in 1934, and he agonized about what he should do with his life. One day they strolled in the garden of an abandoned mansion named Burnt Norton, and the poem that Eliot wrote after their visit struggles with the claims of life and religion (Eliot had converted to the Anglican church in 1927), past and present, dejection and hope.

Like the suite that would grow out of it, "Burnt Norton" is not simply a poem of personal reminiscence but, like Tennyson's "In Memoriam," a more generalized reflection on meaning in a world where experience and the self it gives rise to are in constant flux. The poem's opening lines (the ones that start "Time present and time past" and end "Into the rose garden") were adapted from a canceled draft of Eliot's religious drama *Murder in the Cathedral* (1935), where they comment on Thomas Becket's temptation to regret the way he has lived his life and recapitulate arguments St. Augustine made in the eleventh book of the *Confessions* about what happens when a Christian tries to reconcile the eternal promise of God's salvation with historical inevitabilities that seem to make salvation impossible. If the consequences of a choice made in the past are alive in the present, it is difficult to see how they can ever be undone.

Yet *Four Quartets*, as Helen Gardner (1949) points out, is not a poem of philosophic argument, though it contains philosophic argument. Or better: the poems imitate the way a sensibility absorbs philosophic argument. The result is that we are given the impression of getting inside the rhythms of a mind. We inhabit a meditation as it is happening. In an essay entitled "The Music of Poetry," published the same year (1942) as "Little Gidding," Eliot explains the way a poetry of ideas approximates music: "The use of recurrent themes is as natural to poetry as to music. There are possibilities for verse which bear some analogy to the development of a theme by different groups of instruments; there are possibilities of transitions in a poem comparable to the different movements of a symphony or a quartet; there are possibilities of contrapuntal subject matter." In this kind of poetry, we cease caring about the truth of propositions and start thinking of them as transitory tones of thought—attitudes to be taken up and counterpointed by other attitudes rendered in different tonalities. According to "The Music of Poetry," such effects are possible because the music of a word has as much to do with its significance as with its sound: "The music of a word is, so to speak, at a point of intersection: it arises from its relation first to the words immediately preceding and following it . . . and from another relation, that of its immediate meaning in that context to all the other meanings which it has had in other contexts."

## DISSONANCES AND CACOPHONIES

Take the opening movement of "Burnt Norton," which concerns itself with time—past, present, and future. As these words are repeated in different contexts, their possible meanings shift and expand. The word "present," for example, which at first only means "in the present," begins as we respond to the "music" of Eliot's repetitions to suggest both that sense and other senses: "apparent," "present to the imagination," "standing out." And once that happens, the poem's statements seem to question themselves and contradict their own initial pessimism. If the present is not just the here and now, but also continually alive for us, then time may indeed be redeemable. Similarly, if the future is not merely "contained" in the past in the sense of being located there, but also "contained" in the sense of being restrained there, then perhaps it might be liberated and the future changed—a shading and a mood that assert themselves when we read of children "containing laughter." So the words of the poem, like notes in music, alter their emotional coloring as the verse develops and sometimes change before our eyes. Which is what gives Eliot's heavy philosophical statements a curious lightness.

There are gains as well as losses in the *Quartets*, as one can see by comparing the moment in the rose garden in "Burnt Norton" with the "Hyacinth Girl" episode of *The Waste Land*. Because of its deliquescent language, "Burnt Norton" achieves a sense of enchantment, of a reality beyond our perception, of being in a world of potential marvels such as the one in *Alice in Wonderland* (one of Eliot's models). But nowhere in the rose garden passage do we find what had been Eliot's great achievement in *The Waste Land*, a way of dramatizing experience profoundly enough to make us feel another person's nerve endings. Structurally the trade-offs are also clear. Whereas *The Waste Land* floated from one luminous vignette to another, maintaining its intensity at the price of narrative obscurity, "Burnt Norton" concerns itself with patterns larger than instants of consciousness and possesses a musical structure that (like the late string quartets of Beethoven that Eliot so much admired) includes moments of slackness. In the words of "The Music of Poetry," "dissonance, even cacophony, has its place in music, just as, in a poem of any length, there must be transitions between passages of greater and less intensity... and the passages of less intensity will be, in relation to the level on which the total poem operates, prosaic."

The last of these remarks has an obvious relevance to "Burnt Norton." Section 1 intuitively explores the implications of the rose garden episode, and section 2 attempts to formulate those intuitions more rigorously, with only partial success. Section 2 is divided into two halves. The first, a lyric in the high style of George Chapman and the Jacobean dramatists, assumes a heavenly vantage point and frames the struggles of the world (the boarhound and the boar) within the perspective of eternity. But the lyric is arch and unsustainable, and the second half of the section takes up the task in a more prosaic way. Attempting to define the undefinable, it achieves some marvelously precise distinctions but finally falls back on the logic of negation and breaks down in an admission of failure: "I can only say, *there* we have been: but I cannot say where." The third section takes yet another tack. It introduces a specifically Christian vocabulary, counterpoints it with conversational and philosophic language, and then assumes a prophetic voice ("This is the one way") before it too acknowledges its own inadequacy. The fourth section, like the fourth section of *The Waste Land*, moves lyrically from despair to release and then to relief and momentary illumination, only to be followed in the fifth section by a lament that illumination cannot be prolonged. The fifth section explicitly acknowledges the inevitable inadequacy of language to represent reality ("Words strain...") but concludes with a renewed affirmation of order and peace, even though they remain outside our ability to comprehend them.

## "EAST COKER"

"Burnt Norton" was published as the last poem in a volume of collected *Poems* in 1936, and its strong and hopeful ending gave no indication that a sequel was to be expected. Three years later Eliot, like the rest of Britain, was caught up in World War II. "East Coker" was begun in January or February of 1940, finished within a month, and then published in March. By this time Eliot had some kind of larger sequence in mind, but it took another year before he got around to the third poem, "The Dry Salvages," which was also written in a matter of weeks and was published in 1941. The fourth poem, "Little Gidding," started just months after the third, took more than a year to complete.

The stress Eliot by then confessed is revealing. Not only was the last poem, he wrote his friend John Hayward, "to be written to complete a series, and not solely for itself," but Eliot once again began to wonder whether the whole project had become a barren exercise. The forced repetitions of the suite, so useful to explicators, to him seemed factitious. Starting with "East Coker" and incorporating wherever possible the existing idiosyncrasies of "Burnt Norton," Eliot sewed his poems together by utilizing groups of four—four seasons (spring, summer, fall, winter); four elements (air, earth, water, and fire); four spiritual presences (the unmoved mover, Christ the Redeemer, the Virgin, the Holy Ghost). And to the best of his ability he repeated the five-part skeleton of "Burnt Norton" (itself a variation on the five-part movement of *The Waste Land*). So every first section is organized around some special landscape, every second section begins with a highly wrought lyric and modulates into something looser, every fourth section attempts a religiously charged lyric, and every last section addresses first the problem of communication and then communication in a more spiritual sense.

What seems to have saved Eliot's faith in the poems was not the suite's consistency but its emotional texture. Consider Eliot's progression (in section one of each poem) through landscapes in which the poet's personal history makes contact with a more general past. "Burnt Norton" exalts a private moment of illumination, and the poem ends by reaffirming that moment despite its failure to translate it into something more logical.

> Quick now, here, now, always—
> Ridiculous the waste sad time
> Stretching before and after.

"East Coker" is set in the village of that name in Somerset, from which Eliot's ancestor, Andrew Eliot, left in 1669 for New England. In August 1937, Eliot made a pilgrimage to the village, visited the undecipherable stones in the churchyard, and perhaps decided that he too would one day be buried there (as he is now, in the church). "East Coker" reexamines the closing affirmations of "Burnt Norton," insisting that more than romantic intensity may be necessary to understand the pattern of divine love. That understanding now seems to require the experience of more than one life and includes deciphering the broken stones of history:

> As we grow older
> The world becomes stranger, the pattern more complicated
> Of dead and living. Not the intense moment
> Isolated, with no before and after,
> But a lifetime burning in every moment;
> And not the lifetime of one man only
> But of old stones that cannot be deciphered.

Readers who expected the new poem simply to support the affirmations of "Burnt Norton" with the aid of tradition, however, were surprised on two counts. First, the ends that "East Coker" discovers are terrifying.

Although Eliot's sense of beginnings may have been altered by his pilgrimage, his fear of what awaits him has not. As he approaches the village in section 1 of "East Coker," he notes with horror that nothing ever changes—that history, like the seasons of the year, represents simply "succession." Granted a vision of his ancestors, Eliot feels only the pastness of the past. And so the scene transforms itself into a horrified parody of the rose garden vision of "Burnt Norton."

A second shock in "East Coker" can be felt in the surprise and anger that join Eliot's sadness and disgust. Section 2 opens with a lyric about a summery spell in November. The weather stirs passion and hope that Eliot well knows will be crushed by the impending winter, and his receptivity to the deception startles him. But his annoyance only figures the deeper anger provoked by his willingness to believe something as silly as our traditional imagination of Elizabethan England. This rage drives the remainder of the lyric, as Eliot's images turn toward apocalypse and his language affects the seventeenth century in archaisms he cannot sustain. And so section 2 of "East Coker" shifts into another voice, the voice of a poet dissatisfied with his own poetry, and another expression of anger, in the form of simple prosaic statements. Eliot turns on his "quiet-voiced elders" and asks whether their traditional wisdom amounted to nothing more than "the knowledge of dead secrets / Useless in the darkness into which they peered." Out of this angry disillusionment comes the assertion in the last verse paragraph of "East Coker" that "Old men ought to be explorers."

## "THE DRY SALVAGES" AND "LITTLE GIDDING"

As "East Coker" works by creating expectations of entering a cozy tradition and then shatters them, the next poem, "The Dry Salvages" (named after a group of rocks near the northern point of Cape Ann, Massachusetts, where Eliot and a friend once were stormbound) does something comparable but more extreme. It begins by rehearsing the savage energies at the core of our lives, but does so in commonplace, almost comfortable language that the poem undermines with willful savagery. Eliot's draft plan for "The Dry Salvages" shows that he at first intended to write simply about the sea. The poem he wrote, however, pairs the rocky shore of Cape Ann he summered on with the Mississippi of his boyhood winters. In this pairing, the sea suggests rhythms outside man's boundaries or understanding—the rhythms of eternal pain. But the river announces a more intimate and perhaps a more piercing pain, the discovery that along with moments of private ecstasy, "moments of agony . . . are likewise permanent / With such permanence as time has." In a passage that recalls the wreckage of Eliot's marriage, he laments that—like the river's reappearing "cargo of dead Negroes, cows, and chicken coops," "the agony of others, nearly experienced, / involving ourselves"—this "agony abides."

After such an intense confrontation with life's pain, it is not surprising that the last section of "The Dry Salvages" reaches toward divine redemption ("the gift half understood, is Incarnation"), as does "Little Gidding." The latter carries the name of a short-lived Anglican community that flourished near Cambridge during the English civil war. Eliot had visited the site in 1936. Little Gidding, though, alone among Eliot's four landscapes, was not a place of private significance. Meant to conclude the sequence and to tie up the individual poems into a single work, "Little Gidding" also aims to lift the poems out of a personal perspective. So the opening section deliberately recalls the rose garden of "Burnt Norton," only to speak of a moment out of time and a season beyond the seasons. Here personal memory has lost its privilege. Christian revelation is available to anyone. In the fifth section we are told that the poem's individuals (including the contestants of the English civil war) "depart" only to return in "a pattern of timeless moments."

As we have seen, though, Eliot chafed against the deliberate abstraction of "Little Gidding." Even the one passage in the poem where he tried to fuse his experience with the voices of the dead caused him immense difficulty. Yet finally this passage in section 2 came to ground what might have become an arid tour de force. It presents Eliot on his rounds as an air-raid warden during the Blitz, prowling the streets of London. He encounters "a familiar compound ghost" made up of three masters of disillusionment: Dante Alighieri, Jonathan Swift, and most important, W. B. Yeats. Assuming "a double part," Eliot begins a dialogue on life's disappointments like the one in the fifteenth canto of the *Inferno* in which Dante defines his own poetic mission in relation to a distinguished but limited predecessor, Brunetto Latini. Eliot here might have used Yeats, whose fascination with spooks he had long ridiculed, to do something similar. Instead, he recalls some of Yeats's great poetry to speak the poem's most painful truths, and in the end pairs Yeats with Arnaut Daniel, whom Dante near the end of the *Purgatorio* exalts for an ultimate act of moral heroism, immersing himself in flames of purification hotter than molten glass.

FURTHER READING

Bergonzi, Bernard, ed. *T. S. Eliot* Four Quartets: *A Casebook*. London, 1969. A collection of important essays (some sharply critical) including pieces by Donald Davie and David Perkins.

Bush, Ronald. *T. S. Eliot: A Study in Character and Style*. New York, 1984. Biographical criticism, containing a full reading of *Four Quartets*.

Gardner, Helen. *The Art of T. S. Eliot*. 1949; repr., New York, 1959. The first major exposition of *Four Quartets*. Strong on the poem's significance to wartime England.

Gardner, Helen. *The Composition of "Four Quartets."* New York, 1978. An essential presentation of Eliot's drafts and of the evolution of *Four Quartets*.

Gordon, Lyndall. *T. S. Eliot: An Imperfect Life*. New York, 1999. First-rate critical biography, including a full reading of *Four Quartets*.

Kenner, Hugh. *The Invisible Poet: T. S. Eliot*. New York, 1959. Readings of Eliot's work by one of the finest critics of modernism.

Moody, A. D. *Thomas Stearns Eliot: Poet*. New York, 1979. A formal and historical analysis of Eliot's work, including an extensive reading of *Four Quartets*.

Ricks, Christopher. *T. S. Eliot and Prejudice*. Berkeley, Calif., 1988. An intense questioning of Eliot's work by one of England's finest contemporary readers.

See also the article on T. S. Eliot that precedes this article, and the article on *The Waste Land* that follows.

# T. S. ELIOT'S
# *THE WASTE LAND*

*by Ronald Bush*

T. S. Eliot's *The Waste Land* (1922), noted for its learned allusions to earlier poetry, also questions not only the verse it alludes to but literature's traditional claim to a status more profound than speech. This core paradox, which shapes the poem's style and conditions its fragmented narrative, helped define modern writing in English in the twentieth century.

As a graduate student in philosophy at Harvard in 1911–1914, Eliot became fascinated by border states of consciousness and skeptical of the way newly organized sciences like psychology "explained" such things. It is hardly surprising, therefore, that much of his early poetry concerned disconnectedness. In the first significant anticipation of what was to become *The Waste Land*, contained in letters to his friend and fellow poet Conrad Aiken in the fall of 1914, Eliot enclosed parts of a long fragmentary work ("the 'Descent from the Cross' or whatever I may call it") that explored both mysticism and madness. He wrote Aiken that there would "be an Insane Section" and "Then a mystical section, and a Fool-House section beginning 'Let us go to the masquerade and dance! / I am going as St. John among the Rocks / Attired in my underwear and socks. . . .'" But Eliot was "disappointed" in the verses. The stuff, he wrote Aiken in November 1914, seemed to him "strained and intellectual." "I know," he said, "the kind of verse I want, and I know that this isn't it, and I know why" (*Letters*, pp. 44–46).

"The Descent from the Cross" with its associated poems (some of which now appear in Eliot's published poetic notebook *The Inventions of the March Hare*, and some in Valerie Eliot's edition of *The Waste Land: A Facsimile and Draft*) undertook a quest for connection through an inner world of nightmare. But for Eliot, the irony, parody, and grotesquerie with which he treated this material was as important as the material itself. Producing camp juxtapositions between passages and mixing wildly different registers allowed Eliot to question the authority of any one way of voicing ultimate truths. In 1914, though, he lacked the ability to anchor such a poem in the

here and now or to orchestrate it without reducing its intensity.

By 1921 Eliot was living through his own brush with madness. Five years of a tortured marriage, the sudden death of his father, and a difficult, extended family visit in the summer of 1921 left him shattered. He suffered a nervous collapse and, on his physician's advice, took a three-month rest cure, first on the English seacoast at Margate and then at a sanitarium in Lausanne, Switzerland. Whether because of the breakdown or the long-needed rest it imposed, Eliot broke through the block that had prevented him from finding a form for the fragments he had been collecting and completed a poem of the kind he had envisioned in 1914. In the interim he had learned to draw on his own life and his immediate surroundings. Certainly *The Waste Land* renders Eliot's London with a journalist's eye. (One of Eliot's working titles for *The Waste Land* in 1921 was "He Do the Police in Different Voices," which is the way Sloppy's mother in Dickens's *Our Mutual Friend* describes what Sloppy does when he reads the newspapers out loud.) Eliot had also learned, though, to charge his fragments with the energy of a nightmare and to weave them into a rhythmic whole of great skill and daring. From the 1930s the poem would be forced into the mold of an academic set piece on the order of Milton's "Lycidas," but *The Waste Land* was at first correctly perceived as a work of jazzlike syncopation. In a contemporary review of the poem entitled "An Anatomy of Melancholy," his friend Conrad Aiken insisted that Eliot's "allusive matter" was important primarily for its private "emotional value" and described the whole as "a powerful, melancholy tone-poem"—a work like 1920s jazz that was essentially iconoclastic and provocative.

## "A POWERFUL, MELANCHOLY TONE-POEM"

Aiken's intuition may be confirmed by a close look at the opening of *The Waste Land*'s section 3 ("The Fire Sermon"). Here it is clear that for Eliot literary borrowings represent sites in which suppressed feeling struggles against the superficiality of the ordinary self.

The poem's attitude toward its borrowings, though, is anything but simple. Inspired by their emotional power, Eliot's composite narrator is also intensely aware of the artificiality, the literariness, of the works he recalls. One of his terrors, in fact, seems to be that he has forfeited life to books. And so, in a sequence like the opening of "The Fire Sermon," his descent into near-madness is complicated by a self-consciousness that shadows every attempt to escape into the shapely realms of poetry. In a passage like the following, allusions attempt to access genuine feeling and then suggest an awareness that poetry is only literature and that to quote poetry risks sinking deeper into solipsism:

> The river's tent is broken: the last fingers of leaf
> Clutch and sink into the wet bank. The wind
> Crosses the brown land, unheard. The nymphs are departed.
> Sweet Thames, run softly, till I end my song.
> The river bears no empty bottles, sandwich papers,
> Silk handkerchiefs, cardboard boxes, cigarette ends
> Or other testimony of summer nights. The nymphs
>     are departed.
> And their friends, the loitering heirs of city directors,
> Departed, have left no addresses.
> By the waters of Leman I sat down and wept . . .
> Sweet Thames, run softly till I end my song,
> Sweet Thames, run softly, for I speak not loud or long.
> But at my back in a cold blast I hear
> The rattle of the bones, and chuckle spread from ear to ear.
> A rat crept softly through the vegetation
> Dragging its slimy belly on the bank
> While I was fishing in the dull canal
> On a winter evening round behind the gashouse
> Musing upon the king my brother's wreck
> And on the king my father's death before him.
> White bodies naked on the low damp ground
> And bones cast in a little low dry garret,
> Rattled by the rat's foot only, year to year.
> But at my back from time to time I hear
> The sound of horns and motors, which shall bring
> Sweeney to Mrs. Porter in the spring.
> O the moon shone bright on Mrs. Porter
> And on her daughter
> They wash their feet in soda water
> *Et Ó ces voix d'enfants, chantant dans la coupole!*

The emotional logic of these lines grows out of subconscious anxiety that, as in a bad dream or a psychotic delusion, projects itself onto human and nonhuman objects. In synecdochic progression, a river, falling leaves, the brown land, bones, a rat, Ferdinand, his brother and his father, Mrs. Porter and her daughter, all become extensions of a whole (but not continuous) state of feeling. Eliot's narrator projects his isolation, sense of vanished protection, and loss first onto the river, whose tent of leaves is "broken" (the inappropriately violent adjective emphasizes the feeling of grief behind the loss), and then onto the falling leaves, which animistically have fingers that "clutch" for support as they sink into decomposition and oblivion. Then defenselessness becomes a shrinking from attack as the leaves fade into the brown land, "crossed" by the wind. (Ten lines later the crossing wind will become a "cold blast" rattling sensitive bones, and, metamorphosed, the insubstantial malevolence of a "chuckle spread from ear to ear.") Still later, after an interlude of deep-seated loss, isolation turns into self-disgust as the narrator projects himself onto a rat with a human belly creeping softly and loathsomely through the vegetation. (Both rat and vegetation are extensions of the decomposing leaves.) The rat's living body merges with a corpse's, and the narrator apprehends himself first as rotting and sodden flesh, "naked on the low damp ground" and then as dry bones, rattled by the rat's foot as before he was rattled by the cold wind.

But the opening of "The Fire Sermon" is not simply an English version of the kind of French poetry that uses symbols to express the ambivalence of the subconscious mind. In the way Eliot's poetry alternates elevated and colloquial language, it dramatizes a sensibility caught between two double binds: a yearning for the vitality of common life combined with a revulsion from its vulgarity; and an inclination toward poetry combined with a horror of literature. This drama begins as the literary word "nymphs" emerges from a series of more or less pure images. The phrase "the nymphs are departed" begins to suggest a desire to escape from the narrator's empty present into a world of pastoral poetry, and this desire is reinforced by appropriating Edmund Spenser's voice. ("Sweet Thames, run softly, till I end my song.") The not surprising consequence is a disgust with modern life, which in the following three lines can be heard in a series of jolting colloquialisms. But both Eliot's poetic nostalgia and his disgust with the quotidian soften in the ninth line. There is real sorrow in the speaker's statement that the girls and their vulgar friends have deserted him—a sorrow sounded in the quick repetition of "departed." By this point Eliot's speaker has begun to intuit that the great phrases of the past may be as unreal as they are beautiful. And when his reminiscence of Spenser's "Prothalamion" is compounded by an allusion to the Psalms and by yet a third quotation, this discomfort explodes in mid-flight. "But at my back," the speaker begins, and we expect to hear the rest of Andrew Marvell's immortal lines: "But at my back I always hear / Time's winged chariot hurrying near." Instead, the feeling of desolation that had called up the line swells out into bitterness. The cherished texts of the past cannot charm away the bleak realities of life. This realization causes Eliot's speaker to interrupt Marvell's lines with a sardonic assertion of the primacy of the here and now ("the rattle of the bones, and chuckle spread from ear to ear"). This tune, like Mrs. Porter's, is not Spenserian. Its leering swell can only mock.

## MYTH AND MEMORY

The opening of "The Fire Sermon" was not written until late 1921 and took its part in an organization that Eliot had improvised over a number of months in collaboration with Ezra Pound. Yet many readers of the poem, relying on the "Notes" that Eliot appended after the poem was first published, have trusted their assertion that Eliot took "the plan and a good deal of the incidental symbolism" of the poem from Jessie Weston's *From Ritual to Romance*, about the Grail legend. Such commentaries fix on the way Madame Sosostris's tarot card reading in the first section of the poem introduces elements of Christian symbolism such as baptism ("death by water") and point to the way the poem represents these symbols as powerful truths that have in the modern world degenerated into empty words. The poem's horrified presentation of the "unreality" of modern life, the commentaries imply, serves to turn us back to these truths. Parts 1, 2, and 3 intensify various aspects of that unreality and culminate in outcries from the Buddha and St. Augustine, which expose the passion of the world as the sinful "burning." Part 4 presents the death of the sinful self as a peaceful "death by water," and part 5 reenacts that death as a visionary quest, recapitulating the symbolism of *From Ritual to Romance* in twentieth-century terms and joining a realization that "we have existed" only through a selfless love for others to a symbolic descent of life-giving rain.

It is difficult, though, to believe that Eliot's "plan" for the poem was derived from the Grail legends, since his drafts show that he added much of the Grail material just before the notes and that they primarily concerned the fifth part of the poem (the last to be written). Also, Eliot later did his best to discredit such readings, though he was finally forced to acknowledge in a 1956 essay entitled "The Frontiers of Criticism" (in North, pp. 112–113) that he himself had been "not guiltless of having led critics into [the] temptation" of inventing a "puzzle for the pleasure of discovering the solution." He lamented in "The notes to *The Waste Land*":

I had at first intended only to put down all the references for my quotations, with a view to spiking the guns of critics of my earlier poems who had accused me of plagiarism. Then, when it came to print *The Waste Land* as a little book—for the poem on its first appearance in *The Dial* and *The Criterion* had no notes whatever—it was discovered that the poem was inconveniently short, so I set to work to expand the notes, in order to provide a few more pages of printed matter, with the result that they became the remarkable exposition of bogus scholarship that is still on view today.... [M]y notes stimulated the wrong kind of interest among the seekers of sources. It was just, no doubt, that I should pay my tribute to the work of Miss Jessie Weston; but I regret having sent so many enquirers off on a wild goose chase after Tarot Cards and the Holy Grail.

A better guide than the Grail legend to the five-part structure of *The Waste Land* lies in Eliot's canceled epigraph to the poem, from Joseph Conrad's "Heart of Darkness": "Did he live his life again in every detail of desire, temptation, and surrender during that supreme moment of complete knowledge? He cried in a whisper at some image, at some vision,—he cried out twice, a cry that was no more than a breath—'The horror! the horror.' " We discover in part 1 ("The Burial of the Dead," a title that suggests suppressed memory) that what forces the speaker to "live his life again" with nightmarish intensity is that the significance of the great moment of his life is still unresolved:

"You gave me hyacinths first a year ago;
They called me the hyacinth girl."
—Yet when we came back, late, from the Hyacinth garden,
Your arms full, and your hair wet, I could not
Speak, and my eyes failed, I was neither
Living nor dead, and I knew nothing,
Looking into the heart of light, the silence.

Could Eliot's speaker here not speak because speech had been transcended or because the limitations of speech prevented him from fulfilling the moment? Did his eyes fail because he experienced what was beyond vision or because sight prevented him from the vision that he sought? Did he know nothing because worldly knowledge had fallen away or because he had understood the nothing that is the ultimate truth? Generations of readers have tried to answer these questions, but it is clear from the poem's syntax, which puts the questions in the past tense and embeds them in the self-questioning drama of Eliot's speaker, that they are not ours to answer. They are his, and he can find no peace until he himself resolves their implications. Looking back at his moment in the garden, the speaker agonizes about what had seemed the transformative moment in his life and finds himself unable—or afraid—to say what it means. Is he "looking into the heart of light" or into "the silence?" Does love have a transcendent significance, or is the feeling an illusion, and is his life meaningless?

These still-unresolved questions hang over the first three sections of *The Waste Land*, along with the fears that make confronting them unbearable—that we are indeed alone, that what seems our most authentic emotional life is an illusion, and that reality itself is meaningless. In this sense the poem remains a half-serious, half-parodic "Descent from the Cross" in which the speaker repeatedly tries to reestablish the validity of a moment of transcendental ecstasy in his past. Until part 4, the poem returns continually to the same kinds of story, the same fears, like a nightmare that disperses and re-forms every time it becomes too intense. As with a criminal returning to the scene of his crime (a murdered girl, a buried life), all things lead back to that.

Rather than simply remaining within the terms of personal experience, though, the poem tries to validate experience by reference to historical, legendary, and religious narratives. In successive drafts Eliot progressively elaborated what had started as a confessional poem into a kind of anti-epic. Yet invoking history, myth, and religion does not answer either the speaker's or the poem's questions. On the contrary, along the way of this nightmarishly compulsive inquest, every instrument that the speaker uses to alleviate his doubt is itself questioned and found wanting.

Part 1 of *The Waste Land* surrounds the Hyacinth girl's agonized lover with contemporaries (Marie, Madame Sosostris's client, Stetson's friend) who are also by turns compelled and terrified to reexamine the buried significance of their past, and places them all in a hall of mirrors drawn from the Bible, Dante's *Inferno*, John Webster's drama, Baudelaire's poems, and Wagnerian opera. Part 2, a cat-and-mouse "Game of Chess," explores two extended contemporary London vignettes (one drawn from the "better," one from the lower classes) and depicts lovers trapped within failed relationships. The mood of the poem becomes darker still in part 3, where love's ecstasy has been reduced to an unfeeling grope in the dark between a typist and a house agent's clerk. Here invocations of wisdom from Homer, Ovid, Buddha, and St. Augustine become more prominent and frequent but amount to little more than anguished cries.

Part 4 is puzzling, but it announces a shift in mood. After the pure anguish of "burning," "Death by Water" suggests both relief and release. Still apparently enclosed within the process of "living his life again," the speaker in "Phlebas the Phoenecian" passes "the stages of his age and youth." But replacing the rats of parts 2 and 3, a peaceful ocean current picks at his bones, with the suggestion that, "entering the whirlpool," the fear and the defensiveness associated with the prospect of asking ultimate questions have diminished.

In the last section, the poem's anxieties return with a jolt. The first word ("after") of "What the Thunder Said" places the speaker in a place looking back to a moment of ecstasy conjured up out of the mixed language of romantic, political, and religious upheaval. He expresses heartfelt longing for the return of watery release but, provoked by the sound of thunder, is impelled once again to ask a series of more and more ominous questions. And although some readers conclude that the questions lead to a moment of genuine self-understanding ("By this, and this only, we have existed") and to an announcement of divine instruction (in the resonant "Datta," "Dayadhvam," "Damyata," or "Give, Sympathize, Control" of the *Upanishads*), others point out that each of these ancient precepts is presented as a human and fearful (and therefore equivocal) interpretation of the voice of inscrutable thunder, and that the poem ends with a fury of anguished fragments that conclude nothing.

Ringed round by Eliot's ironies, no authority goes unsuspected as *The Waste Land* interrogates the moment in the garden. Religion may be illusion, history may be lies, memory may be a fabrication, the rambling self may be but an artificial construct, sensation may be hallucination, literature may be rhetoric, even language may be nothing more than empty words.

## FURTHER READING

Bush, Ronald. *T. S. Eliot: A Study in Character and Style*. New York, 1984. Biographical criticism of Eliot, containing a full reading of *The Waste Land*.

Eliot, T. S. *Inventions of the March Hare: Poems, 1909–1917*. Edited by Christopher Ricks. New York, 1996. Includes some of the poems peripheral to *The Waste Land* in a splendid edition that also digests Eliot's most important comments on his work.

Eliot, T. S. *The Letters of T. S. Eliot, 1898–1922*. Edited by Valerie Eliot. New York, 1988. Some of the letters offer crucial commentary on Eliot's work in progress, and the extensive annotation adds invaluable detail.

Eliot, T. S. The Waste Land: *A Facsimile and Transcript of the Original Drafts Including the Annotations of Ezra Pound.* Edited and with an introduction by Valerie Eliot. New York, 1971. Eliot's raw materials for *The Waste Land*, with extensive notes provided by his second wife.

Eliot, T. S. The Waste Land: *Authoritative Text, Contexts, Criticism.* Edited by Michael North. New York, 2001. A Norton critical edition; fine collection of background material and commentaries. Excerpts Eliot's essays including "Ulysses: Order and Myth"(1923) and "The Frontiers of Criticism" (1956) as well as important critical articles such as Conrad Aiken's "An Anatomy of Melancholy" (1923) and Cleanth Brooks's "*The Waste Land*: An Analysis" (1937).

Gordon, Lyndall. *T. S. Eliot: An Imperfect Life.* New York, 1999. A first-rate critical biography that also contains an important essay on the composition of *The Waste Land*.

Litz, A. Walton. *Eliot in His Time.* Princeton, N.J., 1973. Includes excellent essays by Litz, Hugh Kenner, and others.

Mayer, John. *T. S. Eliot's Silent Voices.* New York, 1989. Concentrates on Eliot's poetry of consciousness and on the connection between *The Waste Land* and Eliot's earlier verse.

Smith, Grover. *The Waste Land.* Boston, 1983. A book-length treatment of many of the most important issues surrounding *The Waste Land*.

See also the articles on T. S. Eliot and *Four Quartets* that precede this article.

# STANLEY ELKIN

*by David Ryan*

The writer Stanley Elkin is perhaps known best for his prodigious ear for comedy, although his work is equally admired for its virtuosic prose: its legato phrasing and staccato rhythms, its unique mixture of high and low idioms, its mastery over extending metaphors, and its singular ability to push language to extremes rarely matched in American literature. Born to Phil Elkin and Zelda Feldman in Brooklyn, New York, on 11 May 1930, he spent most of his childhood in Chicago, Illinois, eventually studying English at the University of Illinois, where he earned his bachelor's degree in 1952, a master's degree in 1953, and a doctorate in 1961. In 1960 Elkin became an instructor in English at Washington University in St. Louis, Missouri, where he would remain for the rest of his life, becoming assistant professor in 1962, associate professor in 1966, and full professor in 1969. In 1983 Elkin was appointed Merle Kling Professor of Modern Letters at the university. Diagnosed in 1972 with multiple sclerosis, Elkin remained remarkably prolific despite his illness, writing ten novels, two collections of novellas, a collection of essays, and three scripts in his lifetime. He received numerous awards, including the Richard and Hinda Rosenthal Foundation Award in 1980 for his novel *The Living End* (1979). *The Dick Gibson Show* (1971), *Searches and Seizures* (1973), and *The MacGuffin* (1991) were nominated for the National Book Award in fiction. *Searches and Seizures* received the American Academy of Arts and Letters Award in 1974. The 1976 film *Alex and the Gypsy* was based on one of the novellas contained in *Searches and Seizures*. He was awarded two National Book Critics Circle Awards in fiction: the first came in 1982 for his novel *George Mills* (1982), about a one-thousand-year lineage of cursed losers all named George Mills, and the second in 1995, posthumously, for *Mrs. Ted Bliss* (1995), a novel published that year about a widow at an elderly retirement village who finds herself involved with a drug ring.

## A LITERATURE OF EXCESS

Elkin's first novel, *Boswell: A Modern Comedy*, was published in 1964, followed in 1966 with his story collection, *Criers and Kibitzers, Kibitzers and Criers*, mostly collected from stories published earlier (five of which were written in the 1950s, while Elkin was still in graduate school). Elkin would later note the dramatic difference in style between his early writing and the works that followed. The earlier prose—though full of Elkin's characteristic rhythms and energy—is stylistically more accessible than his later work, following realism's credo to let language remain subordinate to the foregrounding of a story's cause and effect. With certain exceptions ("A Poetics for Bullies," for instance), the earlier writing unfolds with the more conventional prose the writer would later strike from his trope and replace with long, loping sentences constructed using metaphor in a generative capacity—that is, with one image generating yet another, often creating a litany of associations, separated into extended clause constructions.

Possessing a remarkably muscular comic timing and insight, his work is equally remarkable for the tragedy hanging just beneath the humor of its subjects. Elkin claimed, in a 1990 preface to *Criers and Kibitzers, Kibitzers and Criers*, that one reason he felt his early work was more realist in its convention was that he had suffered little misfortune during the first decades of his life. This would soon change: His father died in 1958 and his mother grew ill and became incapacitated. Elkin himself suffered his first heart attack at the age of thirty-seven. As a result of the misfortunes, he argued, he sought a certain lashing out through his art: "a writer's revenge . . . the revenge, I mean, of style" (p. xv). Such revenge would become one of the more distinguishing characteristics of his writing style to follow, including 1967's *A Bad Man*, and in particular in the novellas collected in *Searches and Seizures* and in novels such as *The Franchiser* (1976), *George Mills*, and *The Magic Kingdom* (1985).

Placing the importance of the stylistic concerns, this extreme language—a kind of pyrotechnics of syntax, phrasing, metaphor, and language—over meaning, structure, and plot, Elkin would time and again suggest that the very existence of a beautifully rendered sentence justifies itself. He emphasized coherence not through the realistic chronological beginning-middle-end found in more traditional approaches to storytelling but by using parallel scene constructions and regenerating images, strung through his sentences like varying beads on a necklace.

This intentional foregrounding of language has prompted some critics to classify Elkin as a metafictionist along the lines of Donald Barthelme, Robert Coover, and Thomas Pynchon. Others would classify him alongside American-Jewish social realist writers of the 1950s and 1960s as typified in the writing of Saul Bellow, Philip Roth, and Bernard Malamud. Elkin claimed a debt to Bellow, in fact, especially where style was a consideration. One can actually see a similarity, particularly in the author's phrasing of dialogue and in his sentences' combinations of high and low rhetorical prose styles, mixing the erudite and intellectual with a gutter language comprising the commonplace and the crass, done with the rapid-fire delivery of a salesman. (Elkin's father sold costume jewelry.) His similarities to Bellow, Malamud, and Roth are most conspicuous in the short stories of *Criers and Kibitzers, Kibitzers and Criers*. However capable of approximating any of these "types," Elkin was uniquely capable of dodging, as well as reaching beyond, their combined breadth.

The enigma of Stanley Elkin is that he is neither realist nor antirealist and both at the same time. Although his fiction evolved over the years from that of the plotted social realism of his Jewish-American peers to the more absurdist, antirealist method of the metafictionists, the marriage of these influences to Elkin's own unique center of interest—language and style as an assertion of the self, the signature of a writer—created a sum quite different from its parts.

Another writer from whom Elkin drew influence was William Faulkner. In 1961 Elkin finished his Ph.D. dissertation, "Religious Themes and Symbols in the Novels of William Faulkner." Elkin's debt to Faulkner lies in the assertion that in language—that is, a distinctive prose style—one asserts identity as a writer. Elkin's style, as was his mentor's, is one of intentional excess. But where Faulkner wrote with a biblical complexity of background, history, and social reverberation, Elkin sought an excess of humor, metaphor, language, and absurd circumstance with often little in the way of Faulkner's dimension. Elkin's dominating language runs through the often surprisingly banal lives of his characters, and Faulkner's biblical proportions rarely enter Elkin's work, although Elkin deals with an equally grave fatalism. However, only occasionally—as in James Boswell, of Elkin's first novel,

*Boswell: A Modern Comedy*—do his characters exist in any other form than the mundane. Midlevel bureaucrats, elderly ladies, shopkeepers, traveling salesmen, franchise owners all attempt to find a pattern to their lives, as if in failing to do so their lives would fade, unjustified. Lacking substance of background, personal character, or goals in life, their heroism lies on the surface level of the language Elkin commits to their thoughts and voices. Suddenly finding themselves in circumstances beyond their control, they fashion their existence through verbs, nouns, adjectives.

## PARANOIA, ORDER, CHAOS, AND COMEDY

Elkin's novels also share a similarly motivated strain of paranoia common to those who feel they must arrange the randomness of things into some palatable focus. Elkin's underlying themes of illness, death, and circumstances too terrible to be excused as simple bad luck (absent any other explanation) launch Elkin's characters into suspicions that some conspiracy, some "enemy"—be it tangible, spiritual, or completely fantastical—lurks just out of the periphery of their grasp. The absence of control over one's fate forces a kind of internal, creative control in which the mind constructs whatever is needed to put a focus on chaos, to forge it into something graspable—even if the result is a kind of outwardly absurd inversion, a chaos of its own. Much of Elkin's comedy relies on this conflict between his characters' paranoia and the actual causality behind it. The spin created between the two creates one manifestation of his stories' essential energy.

In the first twenty years of Elkin's writing, his characters—such as James Boswell (*Boswell*), Dick Gibson (*The Dick Gibson Show*), Ben Flesh (*The Franchiser*), and many from his short stories—are solitary, intent on living among, although essentially outside, the typical American social web of interaction with others. Many of his characters, in asserting their awkward separateness from the world around them, come off as bullies. This is first seen in Push, the prototypical character from Elkin's early story "A Poetics for Bullies" (*Criers and Kibitzers, Kibitzers and Criers*), wherein asserting the self, even if it means ostracizing that self from others, is the most one can do with one's life. Readers find similar traits in subsequent, longer narratives.

These solitary heroes wander through various labyrinths intent on devising a structure for their lives, even if it is false, a hall of cards, and ultimately no less doomed than the world lurking behind their fears. The quest for structure where there clearly is none is, in a sense, an embodiment of metaphor—that is, the choice of one thing to help clarify another, an attempt to fashion the abstract "noise" of a thing into coherence. Elkin's characters' decisions and actions mimic the novelist's process in that they demonstrate why we need art: to convey something personally meaningful from the chaos of our world.

For example, in *The Magic Kingdom* Eddy Bale leads dying children through the comic nightmare of Disneyland in an attempt to re-create his own dead son. *The Franchiser*'s Ben Flesh travels a similar comic nightmare (or nirvana, depending on one's tastes) of America's strip malls and highways in an attempt to consolidate both his properties and the meaning they bring to his life. Dick Gibson, of *The Dick Gibson Show*, broadcasts his identity, in a sense, as a radio call-in host in an attempt to fashion the noise around him into some kind of coherent message. And in *The MacGuffin*—the title literally a term associated with Alfred Hitchcock's use of a device to generate plot where it is needed for a story—Bobbo Druff, entering his later years, creates a complex labyrinth of plots against him to redeem the relatively dull, bureaucratic existence he has made of his life. He fudges the math of his life so as to aggrandize its purpose.

Consequently, Elkin's characters often illustrate how mortality ultimately frustrates our attempt to create order from the chaos of the world. It is no small irony that his books have been criticized for being orderless—that is, plotless—and by suggestion for lacking a coherent verisimilitude to life. Elkin's response has always claimed the preeminence of language running through his characters—that this itself was sufficient justification for his books. His insistence on aesthetic beauty in language and style as a way of generating meaning forgoes all other considerations, even if his characters—into whatever extremes they land themselves—live in a kind of comical, plastic diorama of the "real world." Elkins intentionally trades realism's verisimilitude—an artifice unto itself, in which scenes, stories, and characters are carefully created and revised so as to *seem* real—for exuberant caricatures of the real, emphasizing how their chaos reflects an accurate assessment of the chaos in our lives. Indeed, his writing is so full of excesses and chaos, so heightened with the unreal, that we soon lose any sense of its hyperbole, so bombarded are we by so much at once. Everything about Elkin's work is pushed to excess, so that it no longer resembles the excess it represents. His caricatures compel one to read them as an inversion on reality. And yet his fiction captures the same basic truths of life and death and of the middle ground most of us tread between the two.

After a twenty-three-year struggle with multiple sclerosis, Stanley Elkin died on 31 May 1995.

[*See also* Faulkner, William; Jewish-American Fiction; *and* Metafiction.]

## SELECTED WORKS

*Boswell: A Modern Comedy* (1964)
*Criers and Kibitzers, Kibitzers and Criers* (1966)
*A Bad Man* (1967)
*Stories from the Sixties* (1971)
*The Dick Gibson Show* (1971)
*Searches and Seizures* (1973)
*The Franchiser* (1976)
*The Living End* (1979)
*Stanley Elkin's Greatest Hits* (1980)
*George Mills* (1982)
*The Magic Kingdom* (1985)
*Early Elkin* (1985)
*The Rabbi of Lud* (1987)
*The MacGuffin* (1991)
*Pieces of Soap* (1992)
*Van Gogh's Room at Arles* (1993)
*Mrs. Ted Bliss* (1995)

## FURTHER READING

Bailey, Peter J. *Reading Stanley Elkin*. Urbana, Ill., 1985. Good source of information on Elkin, dealing extensively with his use of language to convey individuality.

Pughe, Thomas. *Comic Sense: Reading Robert Coover, Stanley Elkin, Philip Roth*. Boston, 1994.

"Stanley Elkins, Alastair Day." *The Review of Contemporary Fiction* 15 (1995): 7–102. Great, if occasionally uneven, collection of essays on Elkins—some academic, others more conversational in tone, including one from Elkin himself on words and music.

# RALPH ELLISON

*by William R. Nash*

Although he published relatively little (several stories, two collections of essays, some prefaces, and one novel) in his lifetime, Ralph Ellison indisputably ranks among the most important writers of the twentieth century. His National Book Award–winning novel, *Invisible Man* (1952), is a masterpiece of form and content that set a standard by which all subsequent American philosophical novels have been judged. An African American who believed firmly in integration, Ellison created in *Invisible Man* a portrait of a black man who resolves his identity crisis by recognizing and embracing his link to American society, even as he acknowledges the injustice that white America has done him and all his fellow blacks. Because of his integrationist views, Ellison often appeared out of step with prevailing currents of the African-American literary canon, especially in the late 1960s and early 1970s, when the architects of the Black Aesthetic derided him as an irrelevant Uncle Tom. With the rise of multiculturalism and the reassessment of definitions of identity and race in the 1980s and 1990s, however, Ellison regained an unchallenged position of prominence in American letters. Regardless of whether his popularity was waxing or waning, Ellison never wavered from his intellectual course, always arguing that blacks were integral to any true sense of American identity and that one could not sever the ties that bind black and white culture in America. In many ways a prophet, he was among the clearest observers of life in twentieth-century America, where race was central to virtually all discussions of personal and national identity.

## ROOTS AND INFLUENCES

As Lawrence P. Jackson ably demonstrated in *Ralph Ellison: Emergence of Genius* (2002), Ellison's integrationist ethos was largely a result of his being brought up in Oklahoma City, Oklahoma. He was born in that city on 1 March 1914, when the state of Oklahoma was still very much the frontier; it had been a state for only seven years. As such, it did not perpetuate the limitations on

Ralph Ellison, 1964. (*National Portrait Gallery, Smithsonian Institution/Art Resource*)

468

personal expression and advancement that one found in other regions, such as the South. Furthermore, and of particular importance to blacks, the state had no legacy of slavery to shape interactions between the races. Ellison's parents, Lewis Ellison and Ida Millsap, were well aware of this, since they were children of former slaves who had grown up in, respectively, South Carolina and Georgia. They came to Oklahoma largely to save their children the anguish of racism and oppression that they had each known. The author and his brother, Herbert, spent their childhood years confident in the notion that opportunity would not elude them, that they could achieve whatever they desired.

That the boys internalized this attitude is all the more impressive given that Lewis Ellison died when Ralph was three. In addition to losing a valuable role model in their father, Ralph and Herbert Ellison also lost the presence of their mother to some degree, since she was forced to work a series of menial jobs to provide for her family. As a result, the author began to develop a sense of independence and self-reliance that he would retain throughout life. That early experience also gave him the strength to resist ideas and values that he did not respect; this would prove crucial to his artistic development and would sustain him when his intellectual integrity demanded that he take unpopular positions.

Ida Ellison's work as a stewardess at the Avery Chapel African Methodist Episcopal Church provided another kind of sustenance for Ellison. The Ellisons were allowed to live in the parsonage, which contained an extensive private library. Ellison read widely in the minister's collection, from genre fiction to classics of the Western tradition. His consumption of a great variety of books helped foster the eclectic intellectualism that would characterize him throughout his literary life. Even after circumstances dictated that the Ellison family leave the home and its library behind, Ellison kept up his avid reading.

Significantly, at this point Ellison harbored no literary ambition. Instead, after his experience in the music program at Frederick Douglass High School in Oklahoma City, he aspired to be a professional trumpeter. Because the family's financial situation was rather dire, his family could not afford to send him to college; fortunately, however, Ellison won a scholarship from the state of Oklahoma. (This was in some ways a mixed blessing, as the state used its minority scholarship program as a defense against the integration of Oklahoma colleges.) Seeking to further his musical career, Ellison chose to enroll in the music program at Tuskegee Institute in Alabama. He could not

go immediately because he had no money, so he worked for a year in Oklahoma City as an elevator operator and a musician, and in 1933 he rode the freight cars of several trains down to Tuskegee to matriculate.

## TUSKEGEE: THE MUSICIAN BECOMES A MAN OF LETTERS

More important to Ellison's literary development were his three years at Tuskegee, where he encountered attitudes and had experiences that profoundly shaped his literary work, including *Invisible Man*. On a broad level, Ellison's first sustained exposure to the South taught him about racial oppression and balanced his frontier optimism with an awareness of what some African Americans had to do to survive. In *Ralph Ellison* (1991), Mark Busby argues that Ellison's encounter with this legacy of oppression created a tension within him that became a pervasive theme of his fiction; certainly it is a key element of the narrator's character in *Invisible Man*.

His experiences at Tuskegee increased this tension, as his professors in the music program pushed students to embrace an elitist model of black identity. Jazz, for instance, was frowned upon as inappropriate, and music students were forbidden to perform it. This dictum rankled Ellison, who had already developed a passion for jazz that was to last his entire lifetime. Enthralled with the music, Ellison embraced it and other elements of what he called "the vernacular," or African-American folk and mass culture, as valuable expressions of black being. To be told that he must summarily reject these things was more than the young Oklahoman could bear. He asserted his independence by continuing to play and follow jazz and by increasingly devoting his energies to other areas of the Tuskegee curriculum, especially art and literature. Although this would ultimately compromise his position at Tuskegee, it proved essential to his becoming a writer.

Ellison did not begin writing fiction at Tuskegee; he did, however, continue to read avidly. Much as his years living in the Avery Chapel parsonage had formed him as a young reader, his job at the Tuskegee campus library gave Ellison access to another world of books. He was inspired by having read T. S. Eliot's *The Waste Land* (1922) and, with the assistance of Professor Morteza Drexel Sprague, having studied Eliot's notes and sources for the poem. Ellison began an intense program of reading that started with modernists like Sherwood Anderson, F. Scott Fitzgerald, Ernest Hemingway, James Joyce, and Gertrude Stein. From there, he worked backward, reading the works of nineteenth-century authors such as Herman

Melville and Mark Twain, both of whom had a profound influence on Ellison as he was writing *Invisible Man*. He also tempered his reading of literature with texts by such great thinkers as Karl Marx and Sigmund Freud.

Professors in the music department, in accordance with the wishes of the chair, William Dawson, tried to cleanse Ellison of his allegiance to the vernacular. However, his experience in the college library, guided by conversations with Professor Sprague, proved in many ways to be the ideal antidote to that attempt, as he found in his reading a way of engaging elite white Western culture on his own terms without sacrificing the vernacular. Freed from dicta about what he ought to value in the texts he encountered, Ellison read largely with an eye toward the transracial applicability of their themes. His ability to see literature in these terms would prove invaluable to him throughout his career as a writer; a careful reading of *Invisible Man* demonstrates his debt to a broad range of writers, black and white. Consistently in his corpus, Ellison fuses both traditions by filtering the larger human issues the writers raise (for example, humanity, community, and death) through the particulars of African-American experience.

Although the development of these attitudes toward literature empowered Ellison personally, they proved too liberal for Tuskegee, at least for the music school. As he increasingly resisted Dawson's imperious demands of full devotion to his study of classical trumpet, Ellison became somewhat estranged from the program that had brought him to Tuskegee and subsidized his education. In *Ralph Ellison* (2002), Jackson suggests that this strained relationship, exacerbated by student unrest in the music program at a point when Dawson was in crisis, is probably what led to the termination of Ellison's scholarship. Whatever the case, the sudden change in his funding precipitated Ellison's traveling to New York City in the summer of 1936, a journey he undertook with the hope of studying sculpture part-time while he earned his senior fees and tuition. He did not, however, return to Tuskegee in the fall; instead, he embarked on another educational journey, this time turning his hand to the task of becoming a writer.

## NEW YORK CITY AND THE EARLY YEARS OF A WRITING CAREER

Ellison did not come to New York City expressly to become an author; he was, however, deeply interested in literature and aware of the legacy of New York in the evolution of African-American literature. When Alain Locke had come to Tuskegee the previous year, Ellison engaged him in an impassioned discussion of both the Harlem Renaissance and the current state of black writing. As fate would have it, on his first morning in New York, Ellison encountered Locke again; the scholar remembered Ellison from Tuskegee, and he introduced him happily to his companion, the poet Langston Hughes. The latter found Ellison interesting and affable and offered to make introductions for him into Harlem's literary and artistic circles. Hughes and his friend Louise Thompson not only brought Ellison into contact with the elite artists of his day but also began his systematic education in leftist politics. The culmination of these processes was Hughes's arranging a meeting between Ellison and Richard Wright. It was Ellison's friendship with Wright that set him fully on the road to a literary career.

Wright's entry into leftist literary circles in New York City included his assuming the editorship of *New Challenge* magazine; in the summer of 1937, he persuaded Ellison to contribute a review of Waters Turpin's *These Low Grounds*, published that year. Impressed with the results, Wright then encouraged Ellison to write a story for the magazine. After some initial hesitation, Ellison agreed. Drawing on his experiences riding the trains to Tuskegee in 1933, he produced a story entitled "Hymie's Bull." Although the magazine ceased publication before the story could appear, writing the story proved a watershed moment for the young intellectual. From that point forward, he devoted himself to perfecting his literary craft with the same intensity and passion that he had initially brought to his study of the trumpet.

Over the next ten years, Ellison published over three dozen reviews and essays on literary and political topics. In his capacity as a member of the Federal Writers' Project staff in New York City, he wrote profiles of many Harlem residents. Ellison then resigned that job to take an editorial position at *Negro Quarterly*. During the decade, he also published nine short stories and began two novels, both of which he subsequently abandoned. He continued writing even after joining the merchant marine in 1943. In 1945, while on a transatlantic trip to France, Ellison developed a kidney ailment that sent him home to America and up to Vermont to recuperate at a friend's farm. While there, Ellison continued work on his second unsuccessful novel, abandoning the project finally on the day that he spontaneously typed what was to become one of the most famous first sentences in American fiction: "I am an invisible man."

## INVISIBLE MAN

The plot of *Invisible Man* is relatively simple: a naïve African-American male, whom the reader knows only as Invisible Man (IM), goes seeking greatness and finds, through a series of initiations into the hard realities of life in a racially charged America, self-knowledge instead. This basic description is misleading, however, as it masks the complexity of the novel's structure, of the web of allusions that undergirds it, and of the novel's ultimate message about racial unity in the United States. Only by understanding these elements can one grasp the full significance of Ellison's accomplishment. The structure bears the marks of Ellison's musical interests, especially his passion for jazz. Like a jazz piece, the first sections of the novel lay out all of the major thematic elements of the novel, which include issues of personal and racial identity, questions about the value of heritage in the identity formation process, and speculation about the individual's debt to society. Subsequent sections return to and riff on those themes, playing variations—which mark stages in IM's development—on the issues. As a result, like truly great jazz pieces, the novel has the textural complexity of a tapestry.

Ellison enriches the fabric of his text through his pattern of intertextual allusion, which draws equally on black and white antecedent texts. His opening sentence evokes the first words of another American classic: "Call me Ishmael." Like Melville's Ishmael in *Moby-Dick* (1851), IM is on a quest for enlightenment, a search for meaning and order in a world that has become profoundly unsettled for him. Unlike Ishmael, however, who focuses much of his attention on understanding what Moby Dick's whiteness means, IM goes seeking some awareness of what his own blackness means. In the prologue, IM describes a drug-induced dream in which he hears a homily called "The Blackness of Blackness." The situation suggests Ishmael's hearing of Father Mapple's sermon in *Moby-Dick*. Where Father Mapple translates his divine lesson into the vernacular of the sea, though, the minister of the prologue delivers his message in the rhythms of the black folk sermon.

With this detail, Ellison equates African- and European-American culture, an act that reflects his integrationist sensibility and that defines the major message of his text. He solidifies the point with an account of IM's listening to Louis Armstrong's recording of "What Did I Do to Be So Black and Blue?" (1929). The narrator's attempts to answer that question inspire his reflection on his past, which becomes the mechanism for the reader to learn what led up to this moment. In the course of exploring his past, IM comes to understand that blackness need not mark him for suffering and that he must, eventually, try to find a place for himself in American society.

When IM reflects on the origins of his quest, he remembers his first major initiation into the realities of racial oppression. Having been honored as the valedictorian of his class at Greenwood's segregated high school, IM receives an invitation from the leading citizens to deliver his commencement address once again, this time before a group of white businessmen. Unbeknownst to him, he will also be expected to participate in a battle royal, a humiliating affair in which ten adolescent black males are first forced to look at a naked white woman and then, blindfolded, put into a ring to fight one another. He is hoodwinked into fighting the last of the boys, Tatlock, and takes a humiliating beating. Finally, after he and the other boys are tortured on an electrified carpet, IM is called forward to deliver his speech.

That Ellison chooses Booker T. Washington's 1895 Atlanta Exposition accomodationist speech as his protagonist's text conveys his sense of IM's naïveté at this stage of his development. It also marks the beginning of Ellison's extended swipe in the novel at Tuskegee. Distracted by the catcalls of the audience, IM inadvertently substitutes the phrase "social equality" for Washington's charge of social responsibility. When the whites challenge him, IM quickly corrects his mistake and disavows any interest in equality. For his accomplishments, and implicitly for his obedience, IM receives a new calfskin briefcase and a scholarship to the State College for Negroes. This institution, which is clearly modeled on Tuskegee, is intended to be the next stop on IM's path toward the conformity and compliance that whites wish of him.

At first, IM seems fully prepared to follow the path laid out for him. He develops a real devotion to the ideals of the novel's Washington figure, who is referred to only as The Founder. By his junior year, IM has caught the attention of Dr. Hebert Bledsoe, the college's president; when the college trustees come to visit, he is instructed to chauffeur Mr. Norton, one of the powerful white members of the board. Through a combination of poor choices and bad luck, he inadvertently brings Norton to the home of Jim Trueblood, a poor black sharecropper who has gained notoriety in the community for impregnating both his wife and his daughter. Driven by his own unreconciled incestuous desires, Norton faints when he hears Trueblood's story. IM exacerbates the situation by taking Norton to the Golden Day, a local bar frequented by the inhabitants of an insane asylum, most of whom are World War I veterans. Norton's humiliation at the hands of the patients leads to an outraged complaint to Dr. Bledsoe; this, in turn, results in IM's expulsion from the State College.

This section of *Invisible Man* grounds one of the recurrent questions the text raises: Of what real use is the folk tradition to African Americans living in the modern age? One finds in Trueblood and Bledsoe two accomplished practitioners of black folk cultural forms. Trueblood is a skilled singer and an accomplished storyteller. This latter skill has proved especially valuable in the wake of his transgressive actions, as whites have rewarded him handsomely for recounting his exploits; Norton alone gives him one hundred dollars after his tale is done. He has less success commodifying his musical talents, but they save his life, or at least his sanity. It is his heartfelt singing of the blues that enables him to return and face his responsibilities despite his humiliation and grief.

Bledsoe has little interest in music or storytelling; his great skill as a member of the folk is his ability to use the appearance of weakness to manipulate people who perceive themselves as his superior. This practice, commonly referred to as tricksterism, affords Bledsoe a means of controlling the trustees and the college by maintaining a mask of servility. In his outrage at what IM has done, Bledsoe lets his mask slip, so that the narrator has a full view of the real man, if only briefly. What IM does not realize, however, is that Bledsoe can and will so easily turn against him, as he does when he crafts the letters of "introduction" that seal IM's fate. This section of the novel forces the reader to confront the folk tradition from an unromantic perspective and to see two men who have turned it to their own economic advantage. Faced with that cynicism, the reader becomes wary of unexamined celebration of the folk and wonders whether or not "pure," or at least positive, manifestations of this heritage might help IM defend himself. Ironically, he must leave the rural South to find anyone who can answer that question.

When IM comes to New York City, he is blissfully unaware of Bledsoe's machinations against him. Seeking a job that will enable him to earn his next year's fees and return to campus, he faithfully delivers Bledsoe's letters; he also reflects on what he must do to appear desirable to white employers. In his mind, this includes shedding every visible indicator of his southern heritage; he believes that changing what he eats, for instance, will mark him as one who belongs in New York instead of as the greenhorn that he is. Ironically, he holds fast to this notion even after he meets Peter Wheatstraw, a garbage cart man who reminds IM of his childhood and who demonstrates how he uses his folk knowledge to survive in the city. IM enjoys his talk with Wheatstraw but cannot relinquish his plan to "act white"; he comes out of this dream only after one

of his prospective employers shows him Bledsoe's letter, which requests that IM be kept unaware that he has been expelled and that he also be kept from finding a job.

Astonished at Bledsoe's betrayal, IM resolves to become a trickster himself; his first efforts yield him a job at Liberty Paints. Unfortunately, while he is working there, he finds himself overmatched in tricksterism by his new boss, Lucius Brockway. Injured in an explosion that Brockway engineered, IM awakens in the factory hospital to find that a team of doctors is attempting to erase his racial sense of self. This section of the novel answers the persistent query about folklore, as the process designed to destroy his racial identity sets him on the road to real self-awareness. As Robert G. O'Meally notes in *The Craft of Ralph Ellison* (1980), IM "thwarts" the official plan by calling the African-American folk tradition to mind. The narrator recalls one of his grandmother's songs, a scatological childhood rhyme, the identity of Buckeye the Rabbit and Brer Rabbit, and the mechanisms of the dozens, a ritualized exchange of insults designed to help players cultivate verbal skills; yet IM does not embrace this heritage uncritically. As the onslaught begins, IM thinks, "maybe I was just this blackness and bewilderment and pain, but that seemed less like a suitable answer than something I'd read somewhere." As essential as the African-American folk tradition is to him in this instance, he will not rest with a narrow view of himself as "just" one set of anything. Instead, he will make a concerted effort to know himself and to understand how he can use the tradition effectively against the machines of modern culture. This decision also leads him to a crucial realization: "When I discover who I am, I'll be free."

After tricksterism liberates him from the hospital, IM's quest for self-knowledge takes him back into Harlem. There, he literally stumbles into the arms of Mary Rambo, a maternal figure out of the folk tradition who becomes his mainstay in the next few months. Ultimately, however, his experience with Mary begins to wear on IM; although he appreciates her kindness, he resists her counsel that he must do something for the good of the race. He drifts along aimlessly until witnessing an eviction moves him to make a speech. The circumstances are telling, as the personal effects of the Provos, the old evicted couple, are in and of themselves a time capsule of African-American history. What IM does in the moment of moving to defend the old couple from the police who seek to evict them is try to put the feelings this folk couple inspires in him into language that will resonate with the modern Harlem community. Although he does not realize it, this marks a significant step toward IM's resolving his identity crisis, as he allows the past and the present to fuse into an expression of his authentic emotions and experiences. In a sense, the eviction speech is the first time in the novel that the reader sees IM speak the truth.

Unfortunately for him, members of a radical political movement known as the Brotherhood hear his speech and recruit him to be a spokesman for the movement in Harlem. Initially motivated by financial need to join the group, IM quickly embraces their promise that he can achieve prominence through the organization. Although he believes that he is doing good for the Harlem district by becoming a party member and a spokesman for the district, IM inadvertently falls into the Brotherhood's trap, as they first promote black and white unity and then abandon that stance when it proves politically inconvenient.

The betrayal results in a profound sense of outrage that is one of the causes of a massive riot in Harlem which will apparently solve the "Negro problem" for the Brotherhood. Another powerful source of unrest in Harlem is the murder of Tod Clifton, an alienated Brotherhood member who provokes a lethal altercation with a policeman. IM organizes a community funeral for him, only to be censured by the leadership of the Brotherhood for honoring the life of one who had betrayed their cause. Significantly, the speech that IM makes at Clifton's funeral is apolitical in the same way that his comments at the Provos' eviction are. This reaction of the Brotherhood to his honest efforts to fuse heart and mind awakens IM to the inadequacy of the that organization's approach and makes him determined to find his own way to help the community. His first choice is a familiar one—tricksterism—as he seeks to subvert the movement from within.

At first this seems to work; following the model of Bliss P. Rinehart, a Harlem resident who is all things to all people, IM apparently works his way back into the Brotherhood leaders' confidence. Unfortunately, because he does not yet know himself fully, IM is unprepared for the riot and its aftermath. Utterly alone and bereft, he flees a group of whites intent on harming him; when he accidentally falls into a hole, he elects to go into hibernation there. It is from this temporary home that he tells his story, struggling as he does to make sense of his experiences. In reflecting on his life, IM comes to see that the best way to overcome alienation, the hallmark of his quest for selfhood, is to embrace his position in the larger society, no matter how aggressively white members might try to drive him out. Armed with that insight, he prepares to emerge from his hole and rejoin the world. He also

challenges readers to set aside their preconceptions about race and identity and to understand and embrace the links joining blacks and whites, asking in the final sentence of the novel: "Who knows but on the lower frequencies I speak for you?"

## THE SECOND NOVEL AND THE LATER CAREER

The publication of *Invisible Man* and its winning of the National Book Award ensured Ellison's place in American literature. He did not, however, intend to rest on his laurels. By 1955, when he began a two-year term as a fellow of the American Academy in Rome, Ellison had conceived of a second novel. He began work on it in earnest in 1958, and in 1960 an excerpt from it was published in *Nobel Savage* under the title "And Hickman Arrives." In the course of his remaining lifetime, seven more sections of the second novel were published; the completed work never appeared, however. According to John F. Callahan, Ellison's literary executor, Ellison worked steadily on the manuscript; at his death, which occurred on 16 April 1994, there were reportedly more than two thousand pages of text extant.

In 1999 Callahan published *Juneteenth*, a coherent narrative constructed primarily from the second of three connected texts of which Ellison had written drafts. This text, which deals with the exploits of an old African-American minister named Alonzo Hickman and his relationship to Adam Sunraider, a racist senator from an unidentified New England state, suggests that Ellison's second book would have been even richer and more complex than *Invisible Man*. The excerpts Callahan published indicate that many of the same themes—especially questions of racial and personal identity and the value of a sense of heritage to contemporary Americans—resonate throughout the second work. The appearance of *Juneteenth* sparked controversy among African-American literature scholars, many of whom disagreed over the appropriateness of producing a posthumous work. Nevertheless, regardless of what objections some have raised about the work because it was edited, Callahan made clear that the prose itself is all Ellison's and that his editorial process preserves Ellison's design for the story. Given that, *Juneteenth* affords readers further insights into the craft and attitudes of Ralph Ellison.

One also gains much from reading Ellison's essays, published during his lifetime in two collections: *Shadow and Act* (1964) and *Going to the Territory* (1986). Here, as in his fiction, Ellison explored the complicated subject of

American identity and of the role blacks play in creating the national sense of self. In one of his later essays, "What America Would Be Like without Blacks" (1970), Ellison offered an example of both the concrete and the intangible contributions that blacks have made to the development of American culture. He also demonstrated how white culture has affected black Americans, thereby asserting the power of the links that bind blacks and whites in America. This essay, which appeared just one year before Addison Gayle's *The Black Aesthetic*, illustrates why Ellison was an anathema to many black writers of the late 1960s and early 1970s. As thought about race has largely moved away from essentialism, however, Ellison's vision of personal, racial, and national identity has gained new prominence.

The resurgence of interest in Ellison coincided with increased availability of his writings, which was largely the result of John Callahan's efforts. After being named Ellison's literary executor, Callahan edited and published Ellison's *Collected Essays* (1995); a collection of Ellison's early short fiction titled *Flying Home and Other Stories* (1996); *Juneteenth* (1999); and Ellison's correspondence with his friend and fellow author Albert Murray, entitled *Trading Twelves: The Selected Letters of Ralph Ellison and Albert Murray* (2000). Subsequently, Lawrence Jackson published the first book-length biography of Ellison, *Ralph Ellison: Emergence of Genius* (2002). The Ellison papers at the Library of Congress have also been partially opened to the public for research use. As students and scholars have increasingly gained access to Ellison's work, many questions have arisen as to what particulars they will find in studying his fiction, essays, and letters; the materials published as of 2002 offer interesting insights into the development of an author's craft. One thing is certain, however: readers can expect consistency in the richness of Ellison's prose and the complexity of his ideas. How fitting that the author who used the metaphor of invisibility to challenge notions about racial identity is himself so visible in the national literary consciousness.

[*See also* Black Arts Movement.]

## SELECTED WORKS

*Invisible Man* (1952)
*Shadow and Act: Essays* (1964)
*Going to the Territory* (1986)
*Collected Essays* (1995)
*Flying Home and Other Stories* (1996)
*Juneteenth: A Novel* (1999)

## FURTHER READING

Benston, Kimberly W., ed. *Speaking for You: The Vision of Ralph Ellison*. Washington, D.C., 1987. Among the best and most comprehensive collections of essays on Ellison's work.

Busby, Mark. *Ralph Ellison*. Boston, 1991.

Graham, Maryemma, and Amritjit Singh, eds. *Conversations with Ralph Ellison*. Jackson, Miss., 1995. A thorough collection of interviews with Ellison that spans his career. Especially effective for tracing the evolution of his thought and of his feelings about *Invisible Man*.

Jackson, Lawrence P. *Ralph Ellison: Emergence of Genius*. New York, 2002. The first extensive biography of Ellison, this work stops with his winning the National Book Award in 1953. An excellent study of Ellison's childhood and early career.

O'Meally, Robert G. *The Craft of Ralph Ellison*. Cambridge, Mass., 1980. An excellent study of Ellison's aesthetics, with a thorough treatment of *Invisible Man*.

Watts, Jerry Gafio. *Heroism and the Black Intellectual: Ralph Ellison, Politics, and Afro-American Intellectual Life*. Chapel Hill, N.C., 1994. An excellent reading of *Invisible Man* that situates Ellison in a tradition of black intellectualism.

# RALPH WALDO EMERSON

*by Sheldon W. Liebman*

By 1860, the United States had achieved what few Europeans and even fewer Americans of an earlier generation would have thought possible: a level of literary excellence so surprising that it took more than half a century to acknowledge it. By that year, half a dozen writers—Poe, Hawthorne, Emerson, Melville, Thoreau, and Whitman—had written such an astonishing number of important works that the preceding decade or so has come to be called the American Renaissance. However, at that point in the nineteenth century, Ralph Waldo Emerson (1803–1882) was the only one of these writers who had attained a degree of popularity commensurate with his later literary reputation. Even after the 1860s, his fame continued to grow, prompting a dozen or so memoirs, biographies, and studies between the time of his death and the revival of attention that was accorded the aforementioned writers shortly after World War I. He was also known widely in Europe, especially in England, where he was lauded by the most important members of the literary establishment: the essayist Thomas Carlyle, the poet-critic Matthew Arnold, and the novelist George Eliot.

Emerson gained his fame largely through his lectures and books. In all, he delivered 150 sermons (now collected in four volumes), gave more than 1,500 lectures over a span of forty years (now collected in six volumes), and wrote ten volumes of letters. He also published dozens of essays as well as two volumes of poetry. Encouraged by his aunt Mary Moody Emerson (his father's only sister and an important influence on his thinking before 1830) and by the example of his father, who had been a Unitarian minister at the First Church in Boston, Emerson decided to join the Unitarian ministry after he graduated from Harvard College in 1821 and taught at his brother William's school for girls. In 1825, he

Ralph Waldo Emerson.
*(Courtesy of the Library of Congress)*

returned to Harvard to attend the Divinity School, gave his last apprentice sermon in 1828, and became the junior minister of the Second Church in Boston the next year. Emerson's lecture career followed his resignation from this ministerial position. Though he continued to preach (often twice a week) until 1839, he wrote his last sermon in 1836. On the surface, Emerson resigned over the issue of the Lord's Supper, but the real cause of his departure was his growing dissatisfaction with traditional Christianity, particularly his doubts about the authority of the church as an institution, the efficacy of its rituals, and the veracity of at least two of its doctrines—namely, Adam's fall and Christ's redemption. As early as 1831, he had given a series of sermons on the gospels in which he argued that in the quest for spiritual fulfillment the individual needs no evidence for faith other than personal experience.

When Emerson attended Harvard as an undergraduate, the college, populated mostly by boys between the ages of fifteen and eighteen, was more an advanced high school than an institution of higher learning. Nevertheless, Harvard introduced him to the ideas of the Scottish Common Sense School (a halfway house between neoclassicism and romanticism), and he learned to read Latin and Greek, which provided a foundation for his later private study of French, German, and Italian. Perhaps most important, in 1820, he started to fill notebooks with passages from books and magazine articles, as well as his own ideas and poems. Before he published his first important essay in 1836, he had completed ten volumes of quotations and ruminations. A decade or so later, the number had climbed to more than two hundred fifty slim booklets (all of them now collected in sixteen substantial volumes), and Emerson had, in the meantime, compiled two four-hundred-page indexes to give himself easy access to everything he had ever written down. Although he ended this practice in 1859, he continued to spend two ten-hour days preparing a notebook for each of the dozens of lectures he gave annually. Emerson had been a mediocre student at Harvard, and he delivered the class poem at graduation only because several other seniors had turned down the opportunity. But it is clear that he acquired a passion for reading, became familiar with and deeply interested in the prevailing ideas of the day, and developed such extraordinary study habits that he was able to carve out the most successful literary career in nineteenth-century America.

## FRIENDSHIP

Emerson's success as a lecturer was due in part to his great personal charm. Both men and women adored him. Oliver Wendell Holmes, speaking for hundreds of younger men who heard Emerson lecture, called his Phi Beta Kappa address of 1837 "our intellectual Declaration of Independence." Meeting Emerson on his first European trip, in 1833, Jane Carlyle, wife of Thomas Carlyle, thought he was an angel. Mary Ann Evans, who would later write novels under the name of George Eliot, said Emerson was "the first *man*" she had ever met. And Margaret Fuller, author of *Woman in the Nineteenth Century*, fell in love with him. Emerson established lifelong friendships with many Unitarian ministers, such as Theodore Parker and William Henry Furness; numerous women writers, intellectuals, and reformers, including not only Fuller but also Elizabeth Peabody, Elizabeth Hoar, and the abolitionist Lucretia Mott; fellow Concord transcendentalists like Amos Bronson Alcott (father of Louisa May Alcott), Orestes Brownson (later the leading advocate of Catholicism in America), Ellery Channing (poet and nephew of the leader of the Unitarian church), George Ripley (the founder of Brook Farm), and Henry David Thoreau; and other kindred spirits like Henry James Sr. (father of Henry and William), William Lloyd Garrison (the leading abolitionist), and the sculptor Horatio Greenough.

By the time of his death, having traveled to Europe in 1833, 1847–1848, and 1872–1873, Emerson had also met (that is, had dined with, had visited, or had been visited by) almost all the important British poets, novelists, and intellectuals. He was enmeshed in a web of friendships, many of them quite close and enduring, including an intense personal relationship with his brothers Edward and Charles; a nearly half-century association with Carlyle, represented by a thick volume of correspondence; and a

connection with the English poet Arthur Hugh Clough, consisting of nightly dinner engagements in Paris in 1848, a volume of letters, and a visit to Concord by Clough many years later. Besides intimate (and sometimes difficult) relationships with Thoreau, Channing, and Alcott, almost daily companions for many years, Emerson remained friends with Abel Adams, who had been a member of his congregation at the Second Church, served as Emerson's financial advisor, and left Emerson and his children five thousand dollars at his death in 1867.

Some of the adulation and loyalty Emerson elicited came as a response to his apparently indefatigable willingness to help his friends and family, especially when they needed money or literary advice. Shortly after his twenty-fifth birthday, he became the financial supporter of his mother and brothers, an obligation that lasted for two or three decades and that included supporting his mentally retarded brother, Bulkeley. (This burden was later shared by his other surviving brother, William, a lawyer and later judge in New York.) Emerson was particularly helpful to fellow writers—urging them to lecture or publish, editing their poetry and prose, and even promoting their works. He spent countless hours encouraging Carlyle to lecture in the United States, planning editions of Carlyle's essays, and managing every aspect of their American publication. He collected and edited his aunt Mary's writings. He defended Alcott from attacks in the press on his experimental school in Boston, edited Alcott's writing, and paid for most of Alcott's trip to England in 1842. He edited works by his brother Charles, the poet and later Unitarian minister Jones Very, and Thoreau. He promoted the publication of *Walden* in England and edited Thoreau's unpublished letters and poems after Thoreau's death. He tried to help Fuller, James Elliott Cabot, and Ellery Channing find publishers for their work.

Emerson's most famous act of support was his enthusiastic response to Whitman's *Leaves of Grass*, a copy of which Emerson received shortly after its publication in 1855. While Whitman was roundly criticized in New England for the sexual explicitness of some of his poems, Emerson continued to defend him unflinchingly and, considering the outrage Whitman's poetry stirred, quite bravely. Emerson urged Whitman to tone down the passages in question, but mostly in the interest of making the book more widely acceptable. Emerson sought Whitman out in New York City, sent other writers to see him, wrote letters of support, and went out of his way to meet him several more times.

## ACTIVISM

The passion that prompted Emerson to maintain this vast array of friendships also manifested itself in his desire to create an intellectual community in Concord. His first effort in this pursuit was the Transcendental Club, which met regularly from 1836 to 1840. It was succeeded by *The Dial*, a quarterly magazine edited first by Fuller and later by Emerson himself, the contributors to which were mostly the former members of the club. He met with several like-minded friends to plan the establishment of a utopian community, which later became Brook Farm but which, ironically, Emerson decided not to join. In 1844, Emerson did become a member of Concord's Social Circle, a group of twenty-five citizens of various occupations who met to discuss the issues of the day. He also tried to start a group called the Town and Country Club in the late 1840s. And he was, at various times, an active member of numerous town committees responsible for schools, libraries, and other public institutions. He was one of the founders of the Concord Atheneum in 1842, and he participated in the establishment of the Free Religious Association in the mid-1860s. Emerson's most enduring connection was his membership in the Saturday Club, which he helped found and whose monthly meetings he attended from 1856 until his death. Meeting in Boston, the group attracted such celebrities as the novelist Richard Henry Dana, the historian William H. Prescott, the music critic John S. Dwight, and old friends like Holmes, Whittier, Lowell, and Hawthorne.

Emerson also made his home available to a large number of visiting artists and thinkers. In 1840, he and his wife, Lidian, considered merging households with the Alcotts. Fuller stayed for extended periods—once, in 1842, with the intention of determining whether she could live permanently with the Emersons. Thoreau had moved into the Emerson home in 1841 and returned for nearly a year at Lidian's behest (after his two-year stay at Walden) while Emerson toured Europe in 1847–1848. Various family members—aunts, Emerson's brother's wife, a cousin here and there—also visited, sometimes for weeks or months. Besides morning and afternoon hours set aside for reading and writing, Emerson's days were filled with walking through the nearby Concord woods with his good friends or his children, planting trees that yielded prize-winning pears on property that grew from two acres in the 1830s to more than fifty acres at Emerson's death, and apparently savoring the duties of husband and father for more than forty years.

These strong social connections are worth mentioning because they show that the individualism for which Emerson is famous did not exclude what seems to have been an almost daily immersion in the collective life of the community, both formally and informally. Indeed, his deep commitment to social, political, and economic reform is merely the large-scale public extension of his personal and private relationships. That is, whatever we call it—love, altruism, or a sense of duty—this impulse pervaded every aspect of his life. Furthermore, no doubt partly influenced by Lidian's abolitionist and feminist sympathies, as well as his brother Charles's opposition to the federal government's Indian policy and its attempt to annex Texas, Emerson was involved in all of the major reform movements of the pre–Civil War era. He invited an abolitionist to deliver an address from the Second Church pulpit in 1831. He gave his first antislavery speech in 1837 and spoke publicly the following year against war with Mexico and the removal of the Cherokees from east of the Mississippi River. In 1844, he lectured on the emancipation of slaves in the West Indies.

Emerson's house became a center not only for writers but also for reformers and activists. In the mid-1840s, both Emerson and Lidian became even more involved in the abolitionist cause, joining in the 1850s a group of Concord citizens who promised to aid escaping slaves. After the passage of the Fugitive Slave Law, he gave two important speeches on the subject (in 1851 and 1854) and encouraged his fellow Americans to break the law. At this time, the Emersons befriended the radical abolitionist John Brown, entertained him in their home, raised money for him, and defended him at every opportunity. During the Civil War, Emerson spoke in Boston and Washington, D.C., on emancipation and privately opposed the war as long as it was fought to preserve the Union but not to end slavery. At the end of the war, he wrote an elegy on Lincoln's death and composed a poem celebrating Colonel Robert Gould Shaw's African-American regiment. Emerson's involvement in the women's rights movement began in 1855, when he lectured before the second annual New England Women's Rights Convention in Boston. In the late 1860s, Emerson held leadership positions in the Massachusetts SPCA and the New England Suffrage Association.

## READING

Surrounded by friends and family, ever ready to help them in times of need, increasingly involved in the reform movements of the day, and always making his home available to artists and activists from all over the country, Emerson can be called the epicenter of nineteenth-century America. Indeed, he can also be considered the central figure of the age because of his vast reading and voluminous writing. That is, he seems to have imbibed every available idea that happened to be circulating in the English-speaking world during his lifetime. And as a result of copying the most interesting and important of them into his notebooks, using them in his lectures by either quoting them directly or assimilating them into his own way of thinking, and transforming the lectures into essays (through a long, often two-year, process), he seems to have disseminated his own ideas to every potential listener and reader and thereby created an army of nineteenth-century transcendentalists and fellow travelers (including Horace Mann, Emily Dickinson, and the elder Holmes) as well as a large number of twentieth-century poets and philosophers whose work bears the unmistakable stamp of Emerson's influence: Robert Frost, Wallace Stevens, Hart Crane, William Carlos Williams, William James, John Dewey, and even Frank Lloyd Wright and Charles Ives, to name the most prominent and most obvious. Friedrich Nietzsche read Emerson extensively, evidently with more delight than displeasure, and went on to develop his own ideas of nonconformity and self-reliance.

The influences on Emerson were amazingly diverse and abundant. While he was studying Scottish philosophy at Harvard, he read extensively in the poetry and prose of the seventeenth century, including the work of Milton, Ben Jonson, Francis Bacon, John Locke, George Herbert, Andrew Marvell, John Donne, and Shakespeare. He was particularly struck by the vivid and energetic writing styles of Bacon and Montaigne and by the neoplatonic ideas of the theologians. The most powerful and most enduring impact on his thinking came from the ancient Greeks whose works he read at college, especially Plato but also, later, Plato's disciples (especially Plotinus) and the Roman Stoics. Among the English romantics, he was first impressed by Walter Scott and Lord Byron, but Wordsworth's poetry and Coleridge's prose eventually had a more lasting effect on his ideas. The French novelist Madame de Staël introduced Emerson to Goethe and the German idealist philosophers (especially Herder and Kant), and he rounded out his education in this area by reading Richter, Schleiermacher, Schelling, Fichte, and Hegel, among others.

Emerson first encountered the religions of Asia by reading articles in contemporary American and British journals that were paying increasing attention to Hinduism, Zoroastrianism, Buddhism, and Confucianism. He developed a deep interest in Persian poetry, especially the thirteenth-century Sa'di and the fourteenth-century Hafez. (When he took over the editorship of *The Dial*, Emerson created a special section called "Ethical Scriptures," which consisted of excerpts from the sacred texts of Asia.) His contemporaries, like Joseph de Gerando and Victor Cousin, helped Emerson see Eastern religion in relation to the Western philosophical tradition and accord it as much authority as Christianity on spiritual matters. He began to believe that "true" Protestantism began not with Martin Luther but with the Quakers, whose works he read (especially those of George Fox) and whose contemporary leaders he met.

Emerson was drawn to these writers because he saw in the seventeenth-century religious writers, Plato, the German idealists, Eastern religions, Quakerism, the mysticism of Jakob Boehme and Emanuel Swedenborg, and even the writings of the Puritan minister Jonathan Edwards and the Unitarian minister William Ellery Channing the core of the philosophy he would, in 1836, call transcendentalism. Among these varied sources, he found a common thread that matched what he considered to be the essence of Christianity, whose truth he never doubted but whose exclusive hold on the truth he utterly denied. Like the humanists of the Renaissance—Erasmus, Pico, and More—Emerson found the truth everywhere, but unlike them he was so fully committed to defining the essence not only of Christianity but of religion itself that he was willing to elevate books like the Bhagavad Gita, poets like Sa'di, and religious leaders like Confucius and Buddha to the same status as the Holy Bible, the psalmist David, and Jesus himself.

## TRANSCENDENTALISM

What aided Emerson in this quest was his growing sense in the 1830s that the entire Western world was slowly beginning to make the same connections he had been making for a few years. Fellow Harvard student Sampson Reed introduced Swedenborg to Massachusetts in 1821. William Ellery Channing sermonized on revelation. Elizabeth Peabody translated Herder and Guillaume Oegger, a Swedenborgian. Carlyle wrote articles on German philosophy. New friends like Alcott, Frederic Henry Hedge, James Freeman Clarke, Thoreau, Parker, and Fuller seemed to be reading the same books, thinking the same thoughts, and encouraging him to consider the implications of his ideas for other fields, such as education and human rights. Emerson found eloquence in the words of a spokesman for the Cherokee cause, John Ridge, and in the sermons of a Methodist preacher, Father Edward Taylor, of the Seamen's Bethel in Boston.

However, what impressed Emerson most in this widespread and growing acceptance of the basic principles of transcendentalism was less its social and political ramifications than its religious and philosophical dimension. And despite his affection for and support of Parker, Alcott, and Ripley, for example, he was not entirely sympathetic with their analysis of contemporary problems. To these and other political activists, the social ills of the nineteenth century could, as structural and institutional problems, be solved by collective action directed against the churches, the schools, or the economic system. To Emerson, these problems were not unique to either his era or his country. Rather, they were universal and inevitable, and they were therefore not likely to be ameliorated or eradicated by even the most strenuous efforts of an inspired generation of reformers. As a result, Emerson's criticism of nineteenth-century America was not quite as urgent or as strident as some of his contemporaries wished. And his political activism—though often the product of genuine outrage and the expression of deeply felt principles—was sometimes less enthusiastic and certainly less optimistic than that of many of his friends.

To be sure, Emerson thought of the defenders of tradition and convention—particularly insofar as they supported injustice and oppression—as not merely wrongheaded and corrupt; he thought of them as purely and simply insane. Emerson's ruminations on the madness of society appear frequently in his works, early and late. In "The Protest," an early lecture, he says that every person is born sane but that every society brutalizes the senses, dulls the mind, and undermines the morality of its members. The reason is that conformity to any societal standard inhibits self-realization, and without a fully developed self, the individual is hopelessly mad. Emerson believed that although insanity was manifested in such contemporary fads as mesmerism, spiritualism, and phrenology—easy targets for anyone's diagnostic attack—it was, in any guise, caused by the pursuit of wealth and power. Therefore, he says in the essay "Power" that every age is dominated by imbecility, which is characteristic of almost everyone at all times.

Yet even those who are opposed to custom and conformity are likely to be insane as well. That is, Emerson regarded many, if not most, of the activists of the day as equally demented. Thus, he says in "Lecture on the Times" that many reformers are "narrow, self-pleasing, conceited men, [who] affect as the insane do. They bite us, and we run mad also." As a result, despite the strong commitment to social change, true reform never occurs. Every cause becomes a monomania because it becomes detached from its place in the larger scheme of things, to which the individual has access only through self-realization. Emerson explains in "The Method of Nature" that insane people are those whose embrace of one thought separates them from the course of nature. What is needed to change the world and to bring the universal St. Vitus's dance to an end is to awaken the heart and enlarge the vision. In light of his skepticism regarding cultural revolution, social regeneration, and political reform, Emerson counseled patience—not only in his later years, when he supposedly abandoned his original faith in large-scale change (that is, according to some of his critics), but also in his early lectures.

## REVELATION

Emerson approved of the activism of his contemporaries only to the extent that he could see it as a manifestation of their first step in the process of spiritual awakening. He says in "Doctrine of the Soul" that the alienation of the present generation from the ideals and values of the preceding generation is notable as a coming-to-consciousness. Specifically, he sees it as a "crisis" that is always natural and inevitable—a realization on the part of a young person that he or she has been shaped entirely by society and has yet to become a true individual. Self-realization comes as a result of a "fall" into disillusionment and an ascent to faith. It can be short-circuited if the individual retreats to the comfort of conformity. Positing nay-saying as a prelude to yea-saying, alienation from society as a first step in self-awareness, and nonconformity as a prerequisite for self-development, Emerson thus understood the crisis of youth to be a spiritual dilemma of extraordinary importance. Defining society as always and invariably insane, he believed that the "protest" was the only means by which the individual (and, by extension, society) could become sane.

This idea is at the center of Emerson's vision, for in all of his writings individual change is the basis for all human achievement, whether moral, political, intellectual, or aesthetic. Indeed, he says again and again that self-reformation is contingent on complete self-transformation, a revolution of mind and heart, a leap from one level of consciousness to another. He believed that there are basically two angles of vision, one social and one individual, and two kinds of knowledge, one derivative and one original. And the difference between them is a gigantic step, a total change, a metamorphosis. In this context, the universal crisis of youth is primarily a crisis of knowledge: a matter of not knowing the me and the not-me, self and other. Therefore, the crisis can be solved by self-recovery, by the reacquisition of the self or soul originally possessed but inevitably lost by every person in the course of growing up in society. At the same time, Emerson says in "Man the Reformer," the crisis of youth can be solved by the recovery of "primary relations" with the not-me, the world beyond the self. For the not-me, like the me, is the sacred source from which everything valuable derives. In short, the journey out and the journey in are two aspects of the same change.

To Emerson, the detachment from the personal self and the larger universal Self of which it is a part is the central dilemma of life and the single most important cause of every other problem, whether political, social, or economic. In the opening lines of *Nature* (1836), Emerson asks, "Why should we not enjoy an original relation to the universe?" But the reconnection to the source is not a matter of formal education, church ritual, or religious training. The problem of ignorance can be redressed only by the acquisition of knowledge—sacred knowledge—which comes from a kind of experience better understood in Emerson's day as "religious" experience and better understood today as "mystical" experience. Contrasting two kinds of poetry, one of "tradition" and one of "insight," and two kinds of religion, one of "history" and one of "revelation," Emerson defines revelation and insight as a beam of light or a bolt of lightning. Indeed, although these visitations make "holy days," Emerson more often calls them "moments," emphasizing the relative rarity of religious experiences in most people's lives. In "Montaigne," he says that people typically experience only a few "reasonable hours" in a lifetime.

These revelatory moments are, however, worth far more than their brevity and infrequency suggests. On the one hand, they are accompanied by unusually intense feelings. The experience is thrilling, joyful, inspiring. At its lowest level, it is a mild enthusiasm and at its highest an ecstasy or even a trance. On the other hand, the experience is also cognitive. That is, it is not only emotional but intellectual. Specifically, what he calls a beatitude in "Natural History of Intellect" is defined in "The Over-soul" as "the disclosure of the soul." And "soul" is simply one of a number of words Emerson uses as synonyms for a kind of universal essence. Thus,

revelation is the means by which the private mind comes into contact with the absolute mind.

In this respect, revelation is also a communication, which reveals something for which Soul and Mind and even God are metaphors. In the lecture "Being and Seeming," Emerson says that in moments of revelation one senses that "Something Is." There are two ways of understanding this point. First, the something-that-is, which is the thing revealed, is God, whose name, after all, is I Am. Second, as Emerson suggests in "Character," the word "God" is just a metaphor for an elemental, underlying, and universal reality that could be called by any number of names: "Devout men, in the endeavor to express their convictions, have used different images to suggest this latent force; as, the light, the seed, the Spirit, the Holy Ghost, the Comforter, the Daemon, the still small voice, etc.,—It is serenely above all mediation. In all ages, to all men, it saith, *I am*." Thus, revelation reveals the essential fact of life, the source from which all things come—Being itself. As both "something" and something that "is," this ultimate and irreducible reality is both a fact and an event, the source of things but also the continuing creation, being and becoming.

## SELF-DENIAL

To some critics, Emerson's theory of personal reform is founded on Stoicism. Although there can be little doubt that Emerson sometimes justified this interpretation of his moral vision, he did not believe that individuals achieve virtue merely by repressing their needs and controlling their appetites. Stoicism is rather a means to the end of opening the heart and mind to revelation. In other words, as Emerson says in "Self-Reliance," Stoicism releases human spirituality. It does so not simply as an exercise of continual effort and vigilance, which once relaxed results in backsliding and moral regression, but by making revelation possible. The soul, Emerson says in "The Divinity School Address," "wants nothing so much as a stern, high, stoical, Christian discipline, to make it know itself and the divinity that speaks through it." Distinguishing between Stoicism as an end and Stoicism as a means, Emerson attacked it as often as he defended it. He believed that in the experience of revelation, the appetite is neither eliminated nor controlled but transformed. And he regarded the denial of the flesh as a spiritual discipline preparatory to spiritual change.

This view of Stoicism shows why such a social person as Emerson—who had many friends, eagerly joined clubs and associations, and even maintained his membership in the Concord Unitarian church long after he had ceased to be a Unitarian—speaks at the same time so highly of solitude and nonconformity. Just as self-denial is a prelude to insight, so any practice that suspends the influence of conventional values can prepare the individual for revelation. Like Wordsworth rejecting a world that is "too much with us," Emerson says in "Education" that the path to knowledge and power is a retreat from too much involvement with ordinary affairs and material possessions. It is a path not through abundance but through denial and solitude. In this respect, "wood" and "waste" are not romantic abodes in which the fancy is permitted to run free and in which the individual is safely isolated from the demands of responsibility and the threat of criticism. On the contrary, solitude is a kind of spiritual desert to be visited briefly but also ritually and repeatedly—for the sake of spiritual riches.

To Emerson, solitude stands for a denial of self as well as a denial of society, which makes it in most respects indistinguishable from the *via negativa* of the Christian mystics. On this subject, Emerson emphasizes in his lecture on George Fox that although God is within us, his presence is accessible only in connection with a complete renunciation of the self. That is, as he says in "The Divinity School Address," only the person who gives up the self finds it. This denial or renunciation is not a repudiation of the whole self but a purgation of those aspects of the self that prevent it from becoming whole. It is a rejection of the individual will. It is also a rejection of the individual identity insofar as it is created entirely by external, institutional, social forces. What remains is the self in a state of humility or lowliness, in which condition the divine self emerges: "As the traveler who has lost his way, throws his reins on the horse's neck, and trusts to the instinct of the animal to find his road," Emerson says in "The Poet," "so must we do with the divine animal who carries us through the world."

This "abandonment to the nature of things" is not the exercise of whimsical impulse Emerson seems to enshrine in "Self-Reliance" but an apprenticeship, as a result of which the apprentice might be taken for a fool, especially if he writes "whim" on his doorpost and suffers from the inevitable misinterpretation of this sacred act. This letting go is the beginning of self-transcendence, not the end, as Emerson makes clear in *Nature*: "Standing on the bare ground,—my head bathed by the blithe air and uplifted into infinite space,—all mean egotism vanishes. I become a transparent eyeball; I am nothing; I see all; the currents of the Universal Being circulate through me; I am part or

parcel of God." In this passage, Emerson touches on all of the conditions for and consequences of revelation. The "bare ground" is a place of solitude. The loss of ego and the awareness of one's own nothingness are prerequisites for vision. The "transparent eyeball" is the now inoperative sense through which soul can perceive Soul. And the ascent into infinity, the feeling of omniscience, and the union with God are traditional features of the mystical experience that leave their beneficiary transformed.

METAMORPHOSIS

Emerson's favorite word for this ascent refers to the law by which it operates: metamorphosis. In "The Poet," Emerson explains that perception, or what he elsewhere calls revelation, reveals the metamorphosis that characterizes all of nature—the law that every creature has within it a force that impels it to ascend to a higher form. Revelation is, in fact, the moment at which the world, in the process of ascent, passes into the human soul, changes, and eventually reappears as a new and higher fact. Thus, metamorphosis is the recurring pattern of nature (and of human experience, at the deepest level) that once known gives knowledge of the infinite past as well as the infinite future. As someone who experienced several such heightened moments, Emerson believed that these insights, though rare, are indispensable because they transform hearts and minds and thereby provide the only sure foundation for morality and wisdom. Furthermore, just as metamorphosis is a law of nature, the insights that reveal this law are also natural—that is, are meant to be experienced by everyone: "I hold that ecstasy will be found normal," he says in "Inspiration," "or only an example on a higher plane of the same gentle gravitation by which stones and rivers run."

With a deep and enduring interest in science, Emerson saw no contradiction between the mysticism that led to this insight and the principles of scientific investigation. His experiences with revelation were, as far as he was concerned, *experiences*. One such experience occurred at the Jardin des Plantes in Paris (which at the time was also a school for teaching science and conducting laboratory experiments), while he was examining an exhibit of Cuvier's work and was moved, momentarily, beyond words. Always abreast of the latest scientific writing, Emerson was particularly impressed by J. F. W. Herschel's *Preliminary Discourse on the Study of Natural Philosophy*, which he read before his first trip to Europe in 1833; Emerson enthusiastically greeted new scientific ideas, such as Faraday's discovery of electromagnetism and Darwin's theory of evolution. It should come as no surprise, therefore, that he thought of metamorphosis as a natural law—invisible, like all laws, but accessible by means of a higher kind of perception than is adequate for more mundane observation and by which (Emerson believed) all laws of nature are apprehended.

To experience metamorphosis, Emerson says in the lecture "Society," is not merely to acquire knowledge; it is also to possess its power. In fact, so profound is the change wrought by revelation that Emerson often refers to it as an acquisition of life itself. As either conformists or egoists, men and women are not only insane; they are also dead. They are insane because of what they do not know, the *law* of metamorphosis; and they are dead because of what they do not have, the *gift* of metamorphosis—the gift of life. As Emerson says in "Lecture on the Times," "Only as much as the law enters us, we are living men." Revelation affects the mind because it provides a new way of looking at things, a new perspective. Everything is henceforth understood from the point of view of infinity; it is based on a fundamental grasp of the law that rules the universe. This intellectual revolution is accompanied by a moral revolution, for the light by which the mind is empowered to see all things anew also enters the heart. This is why all external change—reform in the political and economic spheres—must be preceded by internal change. For only our access to what is invisible but nevertheless true, the universal law, can guarantee that our actions will conform to truth. From this, Emerson says, comes every improvement in opinion, religion, and manners. As he explains in "The Sovereignty of Ethics," like the grub that becomes a butterfly,

> The man down in Nature occupies himself in guarding, in feeding, in warming and multiplying his body, and, as long as he knows no more, we justify him; but presently a mystic change is wrought, a new perception opens, and he is made a citizen of the world of souls: he feels what is called duty; he is aware that he owes a higher allegiance to do and live as a good member of the universe.

## MONISM AND DUALISM

The idea that nature is pervaded by a soul, that this soul is also manifested in human nature, and that the individual can, partly by an exercise of his will and partly as a result of God's grace, transcend his ordinary self, accede to a higher self, and actually not only participate in the actions of the universal soul but both understand it and draw power from it should sound familiar to anyone who has read Plato. And, indeed, Emerson sounds like Plato because he was strongly influenced by Plato's writings,

which he continued to read throughout his life and which were reinforced by his reading of Plotinus, Buddhism and Hinduism, George Fox, and the German romantic philosophers.

Yet, though Emerson valued the mystical experience as an indispensable introduction to the spiritual world, he was not a monist. For as much as he believed that knowledge of the spiritual—of the One—is necessary to a true understanding of things (that, in fact, awakening to this reality is the foundation of wisdom), he did not thereby dismiss the significance of the material world and its appearance to the senses as the Many. Emerson's universe, as he says repeatedly, is dual, containing as it does a number of bipolarities, which he listed whenever the occasion required: spirit and matter, man and woman, reason and understanding, motion and rest, change and permanence. Nature is thus composed of one essence (Soul, Mind, or God), but this unity has two aspects. Each thing in the universe is only a partial reality, he says in "Compensation," and requires another thing to make it complete.

Monism and dualism do not, however, constitute a contradiction in Emerson's worldview. For the two aspects or ends of each phenomenon are not merely opposites, not divisive and mutually destructive, but united and mutually creative: "The fact of two poles, of two forces, centripetal and centrifugal, is universal," he says in "Politics," "and each force by its own activity develops the other." The point is clearer in relation to the law of metamorphosis because, in this context, things are understood not statically but dynamically—that is, as existing in time. In this regard, the two manifestations of nature are not Manichean opponents, God and the devil, but parts of a process in which each thing turns into its opposite. Soul remains Soul, but in the course of time it is incarnated or expressed in a process of self-generation by which it dialectically saves itself by giving itself and, at its most severe, multiplies by dividing and grows by dying.

According to Emerson, the dualism that bisects nature also divides human nature. In "The Conservative," he traces the opposition between the Conservative party and the Innovative party to two contrasting psychological dispositions that are trivial expressions of a "primal antagonism"—in other words, the two opposing poles of nature. In "Fate," Emerson says that these opposites are manifested in individuals as "the double consciousness," which consists of opposing elements, like power and sympathy, that can exist peacefully together. This is not to say, however, that men and women cannot be self-divided, but self-division occurs when one tendency predominates too strongly over the other. It is thus the exaggeration of one or another aspect of the self that creates not only confusion but also insanity of the kind Emerson found everywhere in modern America: conflicts between thought and action, faith and habit, will and sense. The goal of every individual is therefore to become whole, in the sense that both sides of the self are reconciled. As Emerson explains in "Fate," the halves of the personality combine when the perception of truth is joined to the wish to make it prevail—that is, in the moment of revelation, the result of which is a restructuring of the self, a conversion or fusion of the personality.

Emerson frequently describes the creative act as nothing more than the individual's fulfillment of the metamorphic process, the means by which nature completes itself and reaches, through the individual's creation, its highest level of expression. Thus, Emerson often describes the experience of revelation as a passive event in which the potential poet or painter or sculptor (or, equally, nurse or friend or teacher) simply receives spiritual energy and imbibes spiritual knowledge and then equally effortlessly imparts that energy and knowledge to his or her audience. As Emerson says in "Spiritual Laws," "Place yourself in the middle of the stream of power and wisdom which flow through you as life, place yourself in the full center of that flood, then you are without effort impelled to truth, to right, and a perfect contentment." Elsewhere, however, he shows that, although reception may be passive, expression is a matter of labor rather than ease, an act of deliberation rather than spontaneity. Indeed, because it requires a primary encounter with things, beyond traditional concepts and ordinary language, it is an engagement not only with the center of Being but with its circumference. It requires, in this regard, a descent from genius to talent. In short, creation also involves a confrontation with the transitory material world and requires that the individual (whether artist or humanitarian), in obedience to the law of metamorphosis, transform these raw materials into something worthy of their spiritual source.

## THINKING

The experience of revelation is only half the story of what happens to the individual when he or she undergoes metamorphosis. For having experienced it, the individual necessarily becomes an artist, in the broadest sense of the word, who continues the process in his or her own labor. The sentiment or sensibility that is created in revelation does not rest in the heart, Emerson says in "Character," but must be enacted. It is not only insight but action, for it compels its recipient to express it to others. However, reception and rendering are not two separate events, calling forth two different aspects of the mind. They are parts of a single seamless process in which thinking passes through higher and higher levels of growth. As Emerson says of this ascent in "Poetry and Imagination," sensation mixed with memory becomes experience, and experience mixed with mind creates knowledge and eventually thought. And thought, like everything that precedes it, is a beginning as well as an end, a progenitor as well as a product. "In the healthy mind," Emerson says in "Natural History of Intellect," "the thought is not a barren thesis, but expands, varies, recruits itself with relations to all Nature, paints itself in wonderful symbols, appears in new men, in institutions, in social arrangements, in wood, in art, in stone, in books." The process unfolds, like any growing thing. It is not only continuous but inexorable. In this context, poetry (and all creative activities) is important not as a diversion or an entertainment, not as a kind of spiritual therapy or mental vacation, and not even as one form of communication among many but as an exemplary act that originates in the deepest of visions and eventuates in the profoundest of words.

Emerson never doubted the significance of creation in human life, particularly when he thought of it not as a process necessarily eventuating in a product but as the quintessentially human act of thinking, a subject he explores in his famous Phi Beta Kappa address of 1837, "The American Scholar." What Emerson means by thinking—at least, authentic thinking—can be understood by comparing it with a lower form of mental activity. Traditional scientific thinking, he says in the early lecture "Humanity of Science," is nothing more than classification. Once facts have been arranged into classes, the mind is able to understand new facts by fitting them into preestablished categories. The process is a matter of finding resemblances and abstracting certain elements and ignoring others. While this scientific method is advantageous (the similarities are real, and the universe is orderly), the most important disadvantages are that theories are always only partial and therefore transitory and that this kind of thinking proceeds not as a means of discovery and invention but as imitation: the scientist thinks in terms of already-existing categories—to Emerson, the bane of religion, literature, and thinking of all kinds.

The alternative, however, is not to refuse to systematize or generalize at all. Dispensing with classification as an intellectual crutch and rejecting mere description as an intellectual escape, the authentic thinker allows facts to become something other than either members of classes (and important only in terms of their common properties) or unclassified anomalies (and important only in terms of their uniqueness). In the absence of these pseudoscientific methods of perceiving, analyzing, and interpreting, the thinker is free to consider facts as symbols, which are not empty of meaning but are susceptible to an infinite variety of interpretations, primarily because meaning and value are functions of the encounter between subject and object, thinker and fact. In this reenactment of revelation, as Emerson says in "The School," the thinker, as soul, opens up, and the fact, as soul, takes its place in the scheme of things. In true seeing, the self perceives the thing-in-itself (which is the thing in relation to the rest of the universe) because the self abandons everything that interferes with its perception (propriety, preconceptions, and purpose) and allows the object to manifest itself in all of its splendor, fullness, and resonance. Both mind and matter come to life, the self out of the torpor and tyranny of rubricated thinking and the fact out of the anonymity imposed by oversight or classification.

## ANTAGONISM

Revelation, the prototype of all thinking in Emerson's worldview, is not as passive as Emerson suggests in much of his writing. On the one hand, once the self opens up, insight occurs automatically. On the other hand, getting to that point is not easy. In fact, Emerson often says that effort is required not only after revelation, when vision is turned into words, but also before. That is, this experience is contingent on grace, fortuitously given, and readiness, intentionally willed. Suspending the ego, after all, is not possible, as Plato knew, without discipline. Furthermore, the extension of thinking into creation is complicated by what Emerson thought of as the innate antagonism between all subjects and all objects—between self and world. That is, the marriage of opposites is always beset, at least initially, by their difference. Our higher achievements, Emerson says in "Man the Reformer," must be based on the work of our hands. Therefore, what we need is not a malleable universe made up of things that yield easily and effortlessly to our wishes. We need an antagonism in our efforts, or nothing will be created. Emerson explored this friction in nature periodically and regularly in his lectures, essays, and poems, most notably in "Tragedy," "Illusions," "Experience," "Fate," and "Brahma." As he says in the first of these works, "He has seen but half the universe who never has been shown the House of Pain." This dark (and sometimes demonic) element in experience is not something Emerson reluctantly acknowledged. It is a major and central aspect of his vision. For, he believed, there is no strength without antagonism, no knowledge without struggle.

As thinkers par excellence, artists are uniquely blessed with the problem of struggle and work. For one thing, they must begin with their materials—whether words or stone or sounds. In "The Poet," Emerson emphasizes the need for poets to confront "the conditions," by which he means the circumstances in which the sounds and sights available for poetic use can be heard and seen: the situations of ordinary life, extraordinarily apprehended. On the one hand, therefore, the poet must abandon the world; on the other hand, the poet's departure and return are, respectively, from and to the "conditions," which are difficult but not insurmountable. Because creation can occur only in the world of commonplace objects and events, Emerson encourages his readers in "Natural History of Intellect" to take for their subject no esoteric theme or remote problem but the ordinary circumstances of the present in order to transform the everyday occurrences of urban life into universal symbols.

This radically American theme, running from Edward Taylor to Whitman and Dickinson and then to Frost and William Carlos Williams, is at the heart of Emerson's vision and is fully manifested in his large embrace of the commonplace and ordinary in his lectures and essays. For contact with reality, Emerson says autobiographically in "Experience," "we would even pay the costly price of sons and lovers"—hardly an ad hoc response to his son Waldo's death, but a continuing theme from the beginning of his career to the end. Emerson gives three reasons for his insistence on the need to return to the ordinary world, particularly submitting to the necessity of work and confronting the sordid and painful facts of life. First, as he says in "Prudence," the soul must confront the external world because the soul is imperfect until it does so. Second, the world itself asks to be answered and completed, and this occurs only when the soul interprets it and thereby fulfills it. Third, the universe of things is as real as the universe of ideas, for ideas and things, causes and effects, centers and circumferences are dialectically related and mutually sustaining. They exist only by virtue of each other. Throughout his life, Emerson paid homage to what he calls in his great essay "Fate" the surliness of nature, the terror of life, and the tyranny of circumstance.

And invariably he advised, as he does in "Self-Reliance," "Let us advance on Chaos and the Dark."

## ACHIEVEMENT

Emerson had ample opportunity to transform darkness into light. His father died in 1811, two weeks before the boy's eighth birthday. He was one of only three children in his family, including Bulkeley, to reach middle age. Two sisters and a brother died in childhood, and his two surviving younger brothers, Charles and Edward, succumbed to tuberculosis before they reached thirty. His first wife, Ellen Tucker Emerson, died of the same disease in 1831, not quite halfway through their second year of marriage, at the age of nineteen. Emerson's firstborn child, Waldo, died at age five in 1842. Lidian lost her parents when she was sixteen, and she was one of only three of seven siblings to survive. Emerson understood the gravity of loss. He felt deeply the parade of deaths that haunted his otherwise rich, fulfilling life. And he met this always stunning reality directly in every collection of essays or poems he compiled, coupling love and death, grace and despair, freedom and fate.

By 1834, Emerson had developed a prose style that exploited three techniques: a sentence structure based on biblical and popular proverbs, a vocabulary drawn from everyday conversation, and a method of organization devoid of logical connections. Emerson's sentences are thus eminently quotable because they sound authoritative and definitive. His language makes his writing both accessible and unpretentious. And the loose (or nonexistent) structure of his essays, even when they are organized as a series of ascending and expanding concentric circles, makes them seem open-ended and exploratory. By these means, Emerson abandoned the eighteenth-century prose style that still dominated nineteenth-century America, and he created an idiom that perfectly expresses a worldview that is simultaneously rooted in certainty and yet open to infinite possibilities. It is as if he always knew where he was, but not necessarily where he was going.

Emerson's most famous essays and lectures bear repeated readings—from *Nature*, the clarion call to transcendentalists, to his controversial address at the Harvard Divinity School two years later; the essays "Self-Reliance," "The Poet," and "Spiritual Laws" (which express his ethics, aesthetics, and metaphysics); and "Experience," "Fate," and "Illusions," in which he explores darker themes. Emerson's poetry is far more traditional than his essays and generally less impressive. Despite his famous assertion that a poem is "a metre-making argument"—that is, the idea of a poem creates its own structure—Emerson usually used conventional poetic forms to express his transcendental ideas. Yet poems like "Days," "The Problem," and "Brahma" place him, among nineteenth-century poets, below only Whitman, Poe, and Dickinson. Everywhere in his poetry, Emerson is intelligent and thoughtful, and occasionally he is also inventive and experimental.

What sustains Emerson's reputation today is not so much an undiluted and universal appreciation of his ideas. His distinction lies rather in the fact that he managed to talk philosophy for forty years and, over that long stretch of time, establish for his peers a high standard of integrity and decency. He did so in an idiom unmatched before or after for energy, directness, and simplicity, mixed with an often oracular and sometimes rhapsodic tone that reflects the ecstasy he experienced and wished to communicate to his readers and listeners. He attracted large audiences to hear what he had to say, lived it in every dimension of his private and public life, and acquired an international reputation because he made his ideas accessible through a highly personal style that was evidently as inspiring to some as it was disturbing to others. In short, Emerson found his voice (a rare achievement in any age), used it, and thereby shared with thousands of people his wisdom and his humanity.

## WORKS

*Nature* (1836)
*The American Scholar* (1837)
"Divinity School Address" (1838)
*Essays, First Series* (1841)
*Essays, Second Series* (1844)
*Poems* (1847)
*Representative Men* (1850)
*English Traits* (1856)
*The Conduct of Life* (1860)
*May-Day and Other Pieces* (1867)
*Society and Solitude* (1870)
*The Letters of RWE* (6 vols., 1939)
*The Early Lectures of RWE, 1833–1842* (3 vols., 1959–1972)
*The Journals and Miscellaneous Notebooks of RWE* (16 vols., 1960–1982)
*The Collected Works of RWE* (5 vols., 1971–1987)
*The Complete Sermons of RWE* (4 vols., 1989–1992)
*Collected Poems and Translations of RWE* (1994)
*The Letters of RWE* (4 vols., 1990–1995)
*Emerson's Antislavery Writing* (1995)
*Emerson's Literary Criticism* (1995)
*The Late Lectures of RWE, 1843–1871* (3 vols., 2001)

## FURTHER READING

Allen, Gay Wilson. *Waldo Emerson.* New York, 1981. An updating of Rusk's biography of Emerson and now the best chronology of Emerson's life.

Baker, Carlos. *Emerson among the Eccentrics.* New York, 1996. A biography that looks at Emerson through the eyes of his contemporaries.

Buell, Lawrence. *Literary Transcendentalism.* Ithaca, N.Y., 1973. One of the earliest attempts to assess the literary accomplishments of Emerson and his circle.

Cavell, Stanley. *This New Yet Unapproachable America: Lectures after Emerson and Wittgenstein.* Albuquerque, N.Mex., 1989. This reading of "Experience" is one example of Cavell's influential studies of Emerson as an important philosopher.

Ellison, Julie. *Emerson's Romantic Style.* Princeton, N.J., 1984. Looking carefully at the religious and aesthetic influences on Emerson, this study concludes that, to Emerson, the interpretive act depends more on the reader than on the text.

Gougeon, Len. *Virtue's Hero: Emerson, Antislavery, and Reform.* Athens, Ga., 1990. A comprehensive study of Emerson's involvement in the antislavery movement, which sees Emerson's commitment as strong and lasting.

Hopkins, Vivian. *Spires of Form: A Study of Emerson's Aesthetic Theory.* New York, 1951. A still-interesting examination of Emerson's aesthetics. Thorough and well written.

Kateb, George. *Emerson and Self-Reliance.* Thousand Oaks, Calif., 1995. Argues that Emerson's self-reliance includes sympathy as well as independence. Emerson is a relevant thinker who has made a major contribution to democratic culture.

Lopez, Michael. *Emerson and Power: Creative Antagonism in the Nineteenth Century.* De Kalb, Ill., 1996. Presents a useful corrective to the idea that Emerson's ethics and aesthetics emphasize passivity. Emerson was part of a nineteenth-century movement that included Carlyle, Darwin, Nietzsche, and the German romantics.

McAleer, John. *Ralph Waldo Emerson: Days of Encounter.* New York, 1984. Made up of eighty vignettes, this biography focuses on the crises and people that affected Emerson's life and thought.

Mitchell, Charles E. *Individualism and Its Discontents: Appropriations of Emerson, 1880–1950.* Amherst, Mass., 1997. A study of the changes in the responses to Emerson's idea of individualism, emphasizing Emerson's impact on pragmatism.

Mott, Wesley T. *"The Strains of Eloquence": Emerson and His Sermons.* University Park, Pa., 1989. This first book-length study of the sermons stresses Emerson's Unitarian roots.

Neufeldt, Leonard. *The House of Emerson.* Lincoln, Nebr., 1982. Pieced together from previously written essays (and therefore uneven), this book looks at Emerson's philosophy. The key word therein is *metamorphosis.*

Patterson, Anita Haya. *From Emerson to King: Democracy, Race, and the Politics of Protest.* New York, 1997. On Emerson's stature as a social and political thinker, especially his influence on W. E. B. DuBois and Martin Luther King Jr.

Poirier, Richard. *Poetry and Pragmatism.* Cambridge, Mass., 1992. Emerson's importance in American thought, especially through his influence on William James as well as such modern poets as Eliot, Frost, and Stevens.

Porte, Joel. *Representative Man: Emerson in His Time.* New York, 1979. An earlier examination of Emerson's ideas, achievement, and place in nineteenth-century literary culture.

Richardson, Robert D., Jr. *Emerson: The Mind on Fire.* Berkeley, Calif., 1995. Now the definitive biography, with a firm grasp of Emerson's reading, friendships, political activism, and emotional life. Indispensable reading.

Roberson, Susan L. *Emerson in His Sermons: A Man-Made Self.* Columbia, Mo., 1995. Contends that the death of Emerson's first wife, Ellen, was the crisis that transformed Emerson into an idealist. Reads the sermons as a record of Emerson's inner life.

Robinson, David M. *Apostle of Culture: Emerson as Preacher and Lecturer.* Philadelphia, 1982. Emphasizing Emerson's Unitarian background, this book shows the origins of Emerson's transcendentalist ideas.

Robinson, David M. *Emerson and the Conduct of Life: Pragmatism and Ethical Purpose in the Later Work.* New York, 1993. Explores the changes in Emerson's ideas as he moved closer to pragmatism and shifted to political and ethical concerns.

Rusk, Ralph L. *The Life of Ralph Waldo Emerson.* New York, 1949. A gracefully written biography that provides the essential facts of Emerson's life.

Sealts, Merton, Jr. *Emerson on the Scholar.* Columbia, Mo., 1992. A successor to Henry Nash Smith's book on Emerson's vocational crisis, this work examines Emerson's changing concept of the scholar as an ethical category.

Van Cromphout, Gustaaf. *Emerson's Ethics.* Columbia, Mo., 1999. Shows how Emerson, influenced mainly by Kant and focusing on the conduct of life, fits into the development of philosophy from the eighteenth century to romanticism.

Van Leer, David. *Emerson's Epistemology: The Argument of the Essays.* New York, 1986. Argues persuasively that Emerson read and understood Kant's philosophy and became an important epistemologist in his own right.

Wider, Sarah Ann. *The Critical Reception of Emerson: Unsettling All Things.* Rochester, N.Y., 2000. Examines interpretations of Emerson's theory of individualism, his philosophical sophistication, and his overall achievement.

# LOUISE ERDRICH

*by Amanda J. Fields*

Louise Erdrich was born in Little Falls, Minnesota, in 1954, the eldest of seven children raised in Wahpeton, North Dakota, not far from the Turtle Mountain Reservation, where their mother was born. Her parents, of German-American and Ojibwe (Chippewa) descent, taught at the BIA (Bureau of Indian Affairs) school. Erdrich attended Dartmouth College, graduating in 1976, after which she earned her M.A. degree in creative writing at Johns Hopkins University. Since then she has written eight adult novels, one nonfiction book, three children's books, and two poetry collections. She received the National Book Critics Cir-

Louise Erdrich. (*Courtesy of the New York Public Library*)

cle Award for her first novel, *Love Medicine* (1984), and she was a finalist for the National Book Award for *The Last Report on the Miracles at Little No Horse* (2001). In addition, Erdrich's children's book *The Birchbark House* (1999), which she illustrated, was a finalist for the National Book Award for young people's literature. She also edited the 1993 edition of *The Best American Short Stories*.

## MULTIPLE PERSPECTIVES, FICTIVE WORLDS

Louise Erdrich has cited as influences Shakespeare, Toni Morrison, Philip Roth, J. E. Powers, and Flannery O'Connor. Indeed, parallels can be seen in critics' comparisons of Erdrich's and Morrison's work to that of William Faulkner. Like Faulkner, Erdrich has created a world through which her characters move, narrate, and live, and nearly every character the reader is introduced to in each successive novel is given a chance to speak within a construction of multilayered narrators and perspectives. The world encompasses a group of people in North Dakota, extended through various bloodlines, both German and Native-American. *The Beet Queen* (1986) and *Tales of Burning Love* (1996) take place in Argus, a town a few miles from the reservation setting where *Love*

*Medicine, Tracks* (1988), *The Bingo Palace* (1994), and *The Last Report on the Miracles at Little No Horse* take place. The only novel that strays from the fictive world of Argus and the reservation is *The Antelope Wife* (1998), which introduces a new set of characters and takes place in and around Minneapolis.

By concentrating upon one fictive world through a series of novels, readers can backtrack through time and events, reviewing them through the perspectives of others. In a sense, this rewriting of events might closely parallel the historical revisionism advocated by much feminist literature and criticism. The connective novels cover nearly a century, from around 1912 to the 1980s. Erdrich's shifting viewpoints affect readers' perceptions of memory and work within the characters' individual focuses. While this technique can be confusing, it creates and maintains a reality in which one story is never the only story. The reader does not see a single experience but instead is forced to see the individuals and the varying perspectives behind any sequence of events. In *The Antelope Wife*, Erdrich goes so far as to make one of the narrators a dog named Almost Soup. This narrative technique is reminiscent of the oral storytelling preserved by several American Indian cultures. Readers might compare Erdrich's presentation of multiple and ever-changing stories to, for instance, that of the writer Leslie Marmon Silko, who incorporates Laguna Pueblo storytelling into her work.

Another effect of multiple perspectives is the ability of the story to avoid the stagnancy of one "right" version or truth. Readers are not told which story (or which history) is the correct one; rather, they are given access to several layers. Perhaps one of the clearest indicators of Erdrich's devotion to multiple tellings is her introduction of a children's series about nineteenth-century Native-American life, set in the same period as Laura Ingalls

Wilder's Little House series. *The Birchbark House* is the first book in Erdrich's series about a little girl named Omakayas (Little Frog) who is adopted by an Ojibwe family on Madeline Island after her family dies from smallpox. *The Birchbark House* takes place in 1847, the year a historic outbreak of smallpox occurred. The Native-American viewpoint, in this case, is different than that of Wilder's pioneer family. Erdrich's series, then, indicates an awareness of the changes necessary in acclimating children to multiple perspectives.

Erdrich is also deeply passionate about preserving and learning the Ojibwe language and teaching it to her daughters; she wants the language to be present in a living, daily sense rather than merely memorized in an educational setting. In her nonfiction work *The Blue Jay's Dance: A Birth Year* (1995), Erdrich writes that the Ojibwe language "sounds like water hitting the bottom of a boat" as she listens to her maternal grandfather speak it fluently.

## IDENTITIES

Erdrich's intentions, however, are not merely rooted in exposing the white dominant culture and the treatment of American Indian cultures; her agenda, she has said, is connected to a search for overall identity and spirituality rather than a specific search for social or gender identity. Growing up under the influences of the Ojibwe tradition, missionary Catholicism, BIA schools, and a German, French, and Ojibwe ancestry, Erdrich has experienced the identity conflicts inherent in so many of her characters. For instance, her maternal grandfather integrated both Chippewa religion and Catholicism into his life.

In *Love Medicine*, Lipsha Morrissey, whose real blood origins have not been revealed to him, possesses a healing touch that he uses to help his grandparents regain love. When his grandfather dies, he believes it is a direct result of his own meddling with and mixing of different belief systems, especially since he doesn't have a real belief in any of these systems. In addition, characters in search of identity often spend much of their time running away, either literally or metaphorically. In *The Bingo Palace*, Lipsha returns from a stint away from home, still searching for a sense of self. In *Love Medicine*, Lulu Lamartine "runs away" by sleeping with many men after an initial betrayal by her first love; her reactions and descriptions of sexual bliss indicate the significance of intercourse in her attempts to avoid finding an identity rooted in herself.

*The Bingo Palace* is often seen as a sequel to *Love Medicine*, and a criticism of this sequel is that the stories

of these individuals whom the readers have followed through more than one book are not cohesive or do not reach resolution. Perhaps this desire for unity is a learned response, for it seems that Erdrich's novels do not aim for a clear, tidy interpretation with regard to most of these characters; readers are not given neat conclusions. In this way, the characters may be a reflection that the Ojibwe culture's wounds will never fully heal. While each may find a way of healing, he or she cannot escape change and identity conflict. Similarly, much of what has been thrust upon the Chippewa people and other Native-American cultures in a long history of subjugation cannot be ignored or forgotten. Despite Erdrich's clear intentions to simply portray human beings, political connections seem inescapable in a culture of heightened awareness.

Other critiques of Erdrich's work have pointed to her lavish use of sexual conquest and erotically charged language, which borders on the realm of the romance novel. In an era when popular and academic culture is skeptical of the sentimental or overly erotic, Erdrich has a unique ability to smoothly integrate vivid love scenes into the content of her novels. She keenly exposes the most intimate aspects of her characters' lives, no matter how beautiful or terrible. The passionate language that prevails in her work is also seen in her consistent dedications to her late husband, Michael Dorris, whose life and work had a profound effect on Erdrich.

## COLLABORATIVE EFFORTS AND PERSONAL INFLUENCES

Any discussion of Erdrich's life and work includes the influence of Michael Dorris. Erdrich met Dorris, of Modoc Indian ancestry, at Dartmouth, where he helped start the Native-American studies program. The two were a popular pair of married writers, both of whom had successful publications to their credit and wrote generous dedications to each other in their books. Erdrich married Michael Dorris in 1981, and they collaborated on several projects, including the novel *The Crown of Columbus* (1991). The novel received mixed reviews, but the intense interest of the public in these two writers as a unit certainly factored into its best-seller status.

Both, however, continued to be successful in their individual writing endeavors. Erdrich won the National Book Critics Circle Award for *Love Medicine*, and Dorris won the same award in 1989 for *The Broken Cord*, a nonfiction book about his adopted son Abel's fetal alcohol syndrome. Dorris and Erdrich also won a five thousand dollar Nelson Algren prize for a story called "The World's

Greatest Fisherman," a phrase that appears on a hat worn by a character in *Love Medicine*. In fact, many of the sections in *Love Medicine* were published as short stories, and the novel was revised, lengthened, and republished in 1993.

Erdrich and Dorris had three biological daughters (Persia, Pallas, and Aza), three adopted sons (Abel, Sava, and Jeffrey), and one adopted daughter (Madeline). The significance and impact of these children on both of them is obvious from their writing and interviews. Erdrich's nonfiction book *The Blue Jay's Dance* explores the deep intertwining of the birthing process with her writing and philosophy as she considers pregnancy, raising her children, writing, feminism, and the natural life around her in New Hampshire, a place where she admits feeling distant from the landscape in which she was born.

In 1991, Erdrich's son Abel died when he was hit by a car. In 1996 Erdrich and Dorris separated and began divorce proceedings. On 11 April 1997, Michael Dorris committed suicide at the age of fifty-two in a New Hampshire motel, after which it was publicly revealed that he was under investigation for child abuse. Eerily enough, in *The Antelope Wife*, which Erdrich completed before Dorris's death, a husband eventually commits suicide after being left by his wife. While Erdrich has refused to discuss specific details about the investigation or to defame her late husband's character, she has admitted that he suffered from chronic depression. In its simplest interpretation, Erdrich and Dorris's relationship might be examined as part of a history of intriguing relationships between writers, such as Sylvia Plath and Ted Hughes.

## CONTINUING CONTRIBUTION

Erdrich's work continues to draw a large readership and a healthy amount of academic debate. She has published new work nearly every other year since 1984, and her output shows little sign of slowing. A children's book (*The Range Eternal*) appeared in 2002, and a novel (*The Master Butchers Singing Club*) appeared in 2003.

Erdrich lives in Minneapolis, where she runs Birchbark Books, Herbs, and Native Arts with her sister, the poet Heid Erdrich, and her daughters. She gave birth to a fourth daughter, Azure, at the age of forty-six, with an Ojibwe father she has kept out of the media eye. Besides being named one of *People* magazine's "most beautiful people" and dealing with the remnant speculation about her late husband, Erdrich tries to stay out of the limelight.

Whether she desires it or not, Louise Erdrich has gained a rare status for a literary writer. She is respected by a popular readership, academics, and critics, who share a high interest in both her writing and her personal life. Her body of work can be examined in connection with the American Indian literary renaissance that began in the 1960s and 1970s, and she has provided an integral contribution to the growth of multicultural studies. Beyond issues of cultural identity, however, Louise Erdrich's work is an exquisite example of language taken to lyric and vivid depths, with characters who live complex and meaningful lives and perspectives that challenge readers to find joy and value in new visions of storytelling and literature.

[*See also* Faulkner, William; Morrison, Toni; Native American Literature; O'Connor, Flannery; *and* Roth, Philip.]

## WORKS

*Love Medicine* (1984)
*Jacklight* (1984)
*The Beet Queen* (1986)
*Tracks* (1988)
*Baptism of Desire* (1989)
*The Crown of Columbus* (with Michael Dorris) (1991)
*The Bingo Palace* (1994)
*The Blue Jay's Dance: A Birth Year* (1995)
*Grandmother's Pigeon* (1996)
*Tales of Burning Love* (1996)
*The Antelope Wife* (1998)
*The Birchbark House* (1999)
*The Last Report on the Miracles at Little No Horse* (2001)
*The Range Eternal* (2002)
*The Master Butchers Singing Club* (2003)

## FURTHER READING

Chavkin, Allan, ed. *The Chippewa Landscape of Louise Erdrich*. Tuscaloosa, Ala., 1999. Collection of critical essays, including a selected bibliography. Examples of essay topics: vision quests, spirituality, female power, and ethnicity in Erdrich's work.

Chavkin, Allan, and Nancy Feyl Chavkin, eds. *Conversations with Louise Erdrich and Michael Dorris*. Jackson, Miss., 1994. Interviews and discussions of two successful writers and their collaborative efforts.

Jacobs, Connie A. *The Novels of Louise Erdrich: Stories of Her People*. New York, 2001. A critical discussion of Erdrich's novels up to *The Antelope Wife*, emphasizing setting in relation to Erdrich's presentation of the Chippewa people and the German-American people amid the conflicts of change and culture.

Stookey, Lorena L. *Louise Erdrich: A Critical Companion*. Westport, Conn., 1999. Includes a biography, a discussion of the storytelling process in relation to a sense of place or community, criticism of six novels, and an extensive bibliography.

Wong, Hertha Dawn, ed. *Louise Erdrich's* Love Medicine: *A Casebook*. New York, 1999. Critical essays arranged within the following sections: "Contexts: History, Culture, and Storytelling," "Mixed Identities and Multiple Narratives," "Individual and Cultural Survival: Humor and Homecoming," and "Reading Self/Reading Others." Includes two essays by Erdrich and a selected bibliography.

# THE ESSAY IN AMERICA

*by Jenny Spinner*

Any discussion of the American essay must begin with the problem of definition, rooted in the bifurcate history of the essay and in the nature of the genre itself. Depending on the type of essay in discussion, one of two progenitors is named: the Frenchman Michel de Montaigne, father of the informal essay, or the Englishman Francis Bacon, father of the formal. In the years since 1580 and 1601, when, respectively, Montaigne and Bacon published their first volumes of essays, writers and critics have wrangled over the "true" characteristics of the essay in an attempt to nail down the form. But if anything has remained constant about the essay over the centuries, it is the essay's refusal to remain in one place, its chameleonic adaptability to the changing social, political, and literary climate. Thus, the essay may be labeled familiar, personal, autobiographical, literary, creative nonfiction, or academic; or it may be named for its chief subject: the nature essay, the science essay, the philosophical essay, the review essay. It may take the shape of a letter, a periodical serial, a political tract, a newspaper or magazine column. Whatever the prevailing label or shape, the American essay is as varied as its possibilities.

## EARLY COLONIAL ESSAYS

Essayistic writings existed prior to Montaigne, but the ninety-four chapters that make up his first two volumes of essays embody the characteristics most often attributed to the essay: a loose, meandering style; reflection rather than pronouncement; and personal observation and experience to illustrate a point. Most important, and indeed what made Montaigne's writing revolutionary, is the primary presence of Montaigne himself: his voice, his thoughts, his experiences. Although other seventeenth-century English writers developed their own versions of the essay or composed imitations of Montaigne—notably Bacon, Sir William Cornwallis, Abraham Cowley, and Margaret Cavendish—few American writers tried their hand at the form until the early eighteenth century. The hardships of early colonial life were not conducive to the leisurely art of essay writing as practiced by Montaigne.

Moreover, the dominating Puritan theology did not allow for such personal traipsing about seemingly trivial subjects like thumbs and odors and old age. Deceivingly, seventeenth-century American writers frequently labeled as essays straightforward nonfiction writings that ranged from sermons to scientific treatises. The Massachusetts colonist John Eliot, for example, subtitled his 1666 Indian grammar *An Essay to Bring the Indian Language into Rules*, but there is nothing remotely essayistic about the work.

The first American to produce a book of essays most true to Montaigne's form was the Puritan theologian Cotton Mather, who in 1710 published *Bonifacius. An Essay upon the Good, that is to be devised and designed, By Those who desire to answer the great end of life, and to do good while they live*. Distinct from other Puritan publications, and even from Mather's own writings, the *Essays to Do Good*, as they are commonly called, are short, self-contained reflections on how to live responsibly, with specific passages addressed to husbands, wives, parents, physicians, lawyers, teachers, and ministers. While certainly didactic and limited in subject matter, Mather's circuitous and suggestive essays exemplify a personal voice and simple diction rarely heard in early American nonfiction prose.

## THE EIGHTEENTH CENTURY AND THE PERIODICAL ESSAY

As in England, the prevailing essay form in eighteenth-century America was the periodical essay. By the 1750s, essay serials were standard fare in colonial newspapers and magazines. At least at first, American writers directly imitated popular English periodical essayists like Joseph Addison and Richard Steele, authors of *The Tatler* (1709) and *The Spectator* (1711), two of the most influential periodicals of the century in both England and America. Early American periodical essayists like Mather Byles and Benjamin Franklin openly acknowledged their admiration for Addison and Steele. In Part One of his *Autobiography* (1791), Franklin describes how he copied essays from *The Spectator* in order to improve his writing style:

By comparing my work afterward with the original, I discovered my faults and amended them; but I sometimes had the pleasure of fancying that, in certain particulars of small import, I had been lucky enough to improve the method or the language, and this encouraged me to think I might possibly in time come to be a tolerable English writer, of which I was extremely ambitious.

The periodical essayists were products of their age, focusing on society rather than on the individual, as had the English character essayists of the seventeenth century. No social phenomenon or human foible was safe from their witty, often biting, pens as they took on hoop skirts and masquerades, coquettes and French fops, in musings meant to instruct as much as to entertain. Rather than sign their names to their writings, the periodical essayists invented personae to serve as mouthpieces for their ideas and opinions. This signature feature of the periodical essay created a veil of objectivity for its writers, who need not stoop to the indecorous habit of familiarity, as it was then thought. In his farewell number of *The Spectator*, for example, Steele remarks, "It is much more difficult to converse with the World in a real than a personated Character. That might pass for Humour, in *The Spectator*, which would look like Arrogance in a Writer who sets his Name to his Work." A pseudonym also allowed a writer to hold a contrary position on a topic, for the sake of humor, as a rhetorical strategy, or to avoid charges of slander. Thus, Addison and Steele expressed their views on the morals and manners of English society from behind the characters of Isaac Bickerstaff (*The Tatler*) and Mr. Spectator (*The Spectator*). Likewise, in America, Benjamin Franklin wrote as Silence Dogood for the *New-England Courant*; Judith Sargent Murray as The Gleaner for *Massachusetts Magazine*; and Washington Irving as Jonathan Oldstyle for the *New York Morning Chronicle*.

## KEY PERIODICAL ESSAYISTS

In 1721, the *New-England Courant* (1721–1726) began publishing original essays, the first colonial newspaper to do so. Sixteen-year-old Benjamin Franklin was an early contributor to this paper, which had been established by his older brother James. Using the widow Silence Dogood as his persona, Franklin wrote fourteen essays for the newspaper. With the help of Mrs. Dogood's self-professed "natural Inclination to observe and reprove the Faults of others," Franklin covers in these essays such topics as love and courtship, drunkenness, religious hypocrisy, and free speech. While the persona of a single or widowed woman was also employed by English periodical writers (notably Mary Singleton, the persona of Frances Brooke in her publication *The Old Maid*), Franklin's widow is distinctly American, or at least distinctly Franklin. In her frugality and industriousness, not to mention her no-nonsense vernacular, she exhibits middle-class virtues that Franklin later espoused in his *Autobiography*. Franklin continued to write essays—under pseudonym and his own name—for the rest of his life. Of special note are "The Busy-Body" essay serial he wrote from 1728 to 1729 for the *American Weekly Mercury* (1719–1746) and the essays he contributed to the *Pennsylvania Gazette* (1729–1815). In style and voice, these essays are at once imitative of Addison and original to Franklin, whose clear and direct prose style combined with his down-to-earth diction—all atypical conventions at that time—make him one of the best and most readable of the early American essayists.

Franklin's contribution to the American essay tradition is significant, but other writers made their mark as well, notably Philip Freneau, John Trumbull, Judith Sargent Murray, William Wirt, and Joseph Dennie. An important and influential editor as well as a poet and essayist, Philip Freneau wrote four essay serials in the personae of The Pilgrim, Robert Slender, Tomo Cheeki, and Hezekiah Salem. "Tomo Cheeki," originally published between 1790 and 1795, is written in the voice of a Native American who criticizes the inconsistencies of European society and the colonial settlers. While Freneau's native character is in many ways problematic for modern scholars, what is significant is that Freneau chose to represent a minority voice that did not yet have access to the essay.

To speak frankly of oneself in the form of an essay required an authorial ethos, even if that ethos was a trope, that at the time belonged to very few writers other than educated white men. Another early periodical essayist, John Trumbull, wrote two essay serials while a graduate student at Yale University. "The Meddler" appeared in the *Boston Chronicle* (1767–1770) from 1769 to 1770; "The Correspondent," in the *Connecticut Journal* and *New Haven Post-Boy* (1767–1775) between 1770 and 1773. Many of Trumbull's satirical essays address conventional topics such as coquetry and religious pretense, but his patriotic essays, in their critique of English colonial rule, foreshadow the political essays that would dominate the years surrounding the Revolutionary War. Though inevitably tied to a political moment, these political essays transcend time, so well do they utilize the essay form. Key revolutionary war essayists include Samuel Seabury;

Samuel Adams; John Dickinson; John Adams; Thomas Paine, author of *Common Sense* (1776); and Alexander Hamilton, James Madison, and John Jay, authors of *The Federalist Papers* (1777–1788), a series of eighty-five essays published under the pseudonym "Publius" and written to persuade New Yorkers to ratify the Constitution. Marked by their clarity and grace, *The Federalist Papers* embody the simple yet effective prose style that defines the American political essay of the period.

The work of Judith Sargent Murray is significant not only because of its literary accomplishment and enormous popularity during Murray's lifetime but also because Murray is one of a handful of female periodical essay writers whose work is known to scholars. From 1792 to 1794, Murray contributed two columns to the *Massachusetts Magazine* (1789–1796), one of the most influential literary periodicals of its day. "The Repository," written under Murray's pen name Constantia, consists of twenty-seven *leçons morales* on such topics as dueling, death, and motherhood. For her column "The Gleaner," Murray created a male persona who offers his perspective on female equality, federalism, and friendship. In the concluding column of "The Gleaner," Murray reveals that Constantia is actually the column's author. Constantia explains to the reader that she posed as The Gleaner because of "the indifference, not to say contempt, with which female productions are regarded"—a revelation that highlights the difficulties for colonial women essayists, and women writers in general. (Even at that, Murray did not reveal her real name, only her pseudonym.) In 1798, Murray collected subscriptions (George Washington was among the subscribers) and reprinted "The Gleaner" columns in book form. By the late 1700s, it was common practice for essayists to gather their serials and publish them as books, but Murray has the distinction of being the first American woman to self-publish.

As in England, the heyday of the American periodical essay did not last more than a century. By the beginning of the nineteenth century, it had run its course. Although the form's demise was imminent, two Americans eked out successful essay serials at the turn of the century. William Wirt, a southern essayist, published in Virginia newspapers two serials, *The Letters of the British Spy* (1803) and *The Old Bachelor* (1810–1811), and contributed to a third, *The Rainbow* (1804–1805). Joseph Dennie was perhaps one of the last notable essayists of the century, not so much for his own writings—he produced two long-running essay serials, *The Farrago* (1792–1802) and *The Lay Preacher* (1795–1818)—but for his influence

on Washington Irving in the next century and for his creation of the *Port Folio* magazine (1801–1827), which would become an important repository for both male and female American essayists in the first half of the nineteenth century.

## THE NINETEENTH CENTURY

In both England and America, the nineteenth century ushered in a revival of the familiar essay and the development of new essay forms—particularly, in America, the nature essay. While the periodical essay lost favor on both continents, the periodical as a repository for essays did not. In America, essayists found reception for their work in the many new magazines and quarterlies founded in the wake of the Revolutionary War and peaking in the decades between 1830 and 1850. Literary critics favored the *North American Review* (1815–1940) and the *New York Mirror* (1823–1857), while both literary critics and personal essayists frequently contributed to the *Atlantic Monthly* (1857–), *Harper's Magazine* (1850–), the *Saturday Evening Post* (1821–1971), *The Nation* (1865–), and *Scribner's Monthly/Century Illustrated Magazine* (1870–1881).

Still, many of the early century's most prominent essayists began their careers writing periodical essay serials, as did Washington Irving, who is considered by many to be the first American essayist. Irving's *Letters of Jonathan Oldstyle, Gent.* (1824) originally appeared between 1802 and 1803 as an essay serial in the *New York Morning Chronicle* (1802–1807). Just four years later, Irving collaborated with his brother William and James Kirk Paulding to produce a popular parody of the periodical essay, *Salmagundi; or, the Whim-Whams and Opinions of Launcelot Langstaff, Esq., and Others* (1807–1808). By the time Irving published *The Sketch-Book of Geoffrey Crayon, Gent.* (1819–1820), a collection of short stories, literary essays, and travel sketches, he had abandoned the periodical essay tradition altogether.

HUMOR ESSAYISTS. Two periodical essay conventions—the use of an authorial persona and the blurring of fact and fiction—continued to characterize the essay well into the nineteenth century. More and more, however, such conventions were used for the purpose of humor rather than out of preference for objectivity and the need for an authorial veil. A popular persona in the social and political lampoons of the century was the backward Yankee oracle. Maine writer Seba Smith's "Jack Downing" character, though not the first loquacious Yankee bumpkin, paved the way for others, including Jonathan Slick, the creation of Ann Sophia Stephens, and Hosea Biglow, the character made famous by James Russell Lowell in *The Biglow Papers* (1848). Two other humor essayists who wrote popular satires of contemporary life and politics were David Ross Locke, the writer behind the bigoted Petroleum Vesuvius Nasby, and Charles Farrar Browne, whose Artemus Ward essays made him famous both in America and in England. One of the best humor essayists of the nineteenth century was Mark Twain. Nine days after Twain's death, an anonymous contributor to *The Dial* wrote of Twain: "If we are to group him at all, it must be with the essayists . . . there are humorists who make us laugh and have hardly any other influence over us, and humorists who are also creative artists, and critics of life in the deeper sense, and social philosophers whose judgments are of weight and import. If we are to classify Mark Twain at all, it must be with the latter distinguished company." Among Twain's essay collections are *How to Tell a Story and Other Essays* (1897), *The Man That Corrupted Hadleyburg and Other Stories and Essays* (1900), and *What Is Man?* (1906).

THE TRANSCENDENTALISTS AND NATURE WRITERS. Another important nineteenth-century essayist—many critics consider him to be the most important—is Ralph Waldo Emerson, the leader of the American transcendental movement and an avowed admirer of Montaigne. Emerson's influential *Essays, First Series* (1841) and *Essays, Second Series* (1844), based on popular lectures he delivered on the winter lecture circuit, were at once philosophical and personal, written in a stylistic voice that had no precedent. By 1850, Emerson was delivering more than eighty lectures each year, many of which he collected in *Representative Men* (1850) and, following a visit to England in 1847, *English Traits* (1856). Emerson also contributed essays to the transcendentalist magazine *The Dial* (1840–1844), first edited by Margaret Fuller and later by Emerson himself. Fuller was herself a prolific essayist. In 1843, she wrote for *The Dial* her famous essay on women's equality, "The Great Lawsuit: Man *versus* Men; Woman *versus* Women," which she later expanded into book form, *Woman in the Nineteenth Century* (1845). First as a regular columnist and then as a foreign correspondent for the *New-York Daily Tribune* (1841–1924), Fuller contributed more than two hundred critical essays, articles, and dispatches.

Often considered the father of American nature writing, Henry David Thoreau, a disciple of Emerson, shaped a tradition of essay writing that is distinctly American in its personal, philosophical, and scientific rendering of the natural landscape. Thoreau certainly was not the first American to write nonfiction prose dealing with the country's landscape, but his works were influential and wide-reaching, notably his famous political essay "Resistance to Civil Government" (1849) and such seminal collections as *A Week on the Concord and Merrimack Rivers* (1849), *Walden; or, Life in the Woods* (1854), *The Maine Woods* (1864), *Cape Cod* (1865), and *A Yankee in Canada* (1866). Written in simple language but rich in poetical detail, Thoreau's essays investigate the rhythms of the natural world and humanity's place in it. Other key nature essayists from the century include John James Audubon, John Burroughs, and John Muir. Women like Susan Fenimore Cooper and Caroline M. Kirkland also contributed to the development of the American nature essay, Cooper writing in *Rural Hours* (1850) about the seasonal cycles of natural life in Cooperstown, New York, and Kirkland contributing essays about life on the Western frontier to the *Union Magazine of Literature and Art/Sartain's Union Magazine* (1847–1852).

WOMEN AND THE ESSAY COLUMN. Indeed, the nineteenth century witnessed a remarkable growth in the number of women essayists, who often found their way into print as newspaper columnists. For many of these writers, though certainly not all, a pseudonym was not so much conventional as necessary both for expressing their thoughts and ideas in public forums and for maintaining nineteenth-century ideals of feminine decorum. Sara Payson Willis Parton, who for sixteen years wrote as Fanny Fern for the *New York Ledger* (1855–1898), was not only a popular essayist but also one of the most highly paid journalists of her time. Parton was a fervent advocate for social justice and especially sympathetic to women and children. Her columns deal with subjects ranging from motherhood to women doctors to venereal disease. In 1853, a collection of Parton's first essays was published as *Fern Leaves from Fanny's Port-Folio* and became an instant sensation. Fern published five additional collections of essays, including *Fern Leaves from Fanny's Port-Folio: Second Series* (1854), *Fresh Leaves* (1857), *Folly As It Flies* (1868), *Ginger-Snaps* (1870), and *Caper Sauce* (1872). Among other popular women essayists were Sara Jane Lippincott writing as Grace Greenwood, and Elizabeth Cochrane Seaman writing as Nellie Bly.

Another popular essay columnist was Lydia Maria Child, who served from 1841 to 1843 as editor of the abolitionist *National Anti-Slavery Standard* (1840–1871).

During that time, Child wrote a column called "Letters from New-York" that combined personal reflection with social protest of injustices toward Native Americans, slaves, and women. A book-length collection of Child's essays, bearing the name of the column, was published in 1843, followed by a second series in 1845. The topic of social justice did not belong solely to the women essayists; many men wrote on such issues as well, notably Thomas Wentworth Higginson, an abolitionist and campaigner for women's rights. In addition to his sociopolitical essays, Higginson composed nature and critical essays, publishing ten books of essays in all, including *Out-door Papers* (1863), *Common Sense about Women* (1882), and *Carlyle's Laugh, and Other Surprises* (1909).

In fact, many nineteenth-century essayists wrote political essays on two of the most relevant issues of the day: slavery and women's rights. Intended primarily to instruct, the majority of this substantial body of essays is formal by nature and often lacks the personal voice that gives lasting literary value to the works of such writers as Parton, Child, and Higginson. Ann Plato's (1820?–?) *Essays; Including Biographies and Miscellaneous Pieces, in Prose and Poetry* (1841) is significant for being the first essay collection published by an African American. Though an extraordinary achievement amid the obstacles facing early African-American writers, Plato's volume of sixteen devotional essays, with such titles as "Decision of Character" and "Obedience," is didactic and epigrammatic. Much more remarkable are the religious, sociopolitical, and critical essays of Catharine Esther Beecher, Harriet Beecher Stowe, Sarah Moore Grimke, Maria W. Miller Stewart, George Fitzhugh, Louisa S. McCord, Henry Ward Beecher, Frederick Douglass, Anna Julia Cooper, and W. E. B. Du Bois, to name a few.

LITERARY CRITICISM AND THE RISE OF THE GENTEEL ESSAY. One of the greatest advances of the nineteenth-century essay occurred in literary criticism. For the first time, American writers surveyed their own literature—and that of Europe—and pronounced judgment, regardless of the work's reception abroad. Many writers tried their hand at criticism at some point in their careers, but few withstand the test of time as does Edgar Allan Poe, author of the classic critical essays "Philosophy of Composition," "The Poetic Principle," and "The Rationale of Verse." Other notable writers include William Ellery Channing, Henry Wadsworth Longfellow, James Russell Lowell, William Dean Howells, and Edwin Percy

Whipple, the sole writer to devote his entire literary career to writing criticism.

While the nineteenth century delivered in England some of the finest familiar essayists of the age—Charles Lamb, Leigh Hunt, Robert Louis Stevenson, and Alexander Smith among them—America produced few purely familiar essayists, and even then, not until the last half of the century. Chief among these is the physician Oliver Wendell Holmes, who wrote medical essays as well as his popular "Breakfast-Table" essays for the *Atlantic Monthly*. Difficult to classify, these sometimes whimsical, sometimes philosophical essays are a potpourri of poetry and prose, held together by observation, reflection, and narrative. Holmes collected his columns in three volumes: *The Autocrat of the Breakfast-Table* (1859), *The Professor at the Breakfast-Table* (1860), and *The Poet at the Breakfast-Table* (1872). Another personal essayist, George William Curtis, achieved literary success with *The Potiphar Papers* (1853), a collection of essays that satirizes the New York aristocracy, and his "Easy Chair" column that ran for thirty-eight years in *Harper's Magazine* beginning in 1854. Donald Grant Mitchell, also known as Ik Marvel, was an early collaborator with Curtis on the "Easy Chair," but Mitchell is best known for his dreamy essays on the respectable middle-class life of the gentleman farmer and collections such as *Reveries of a Bachelor; or, A Book of the Heart* (1850).

THE TWENTIETH CENTURY

By the turn of the century, the genteel essay—proliferated by writers like Curtis, Mitchell, Samuel McChord Crothers, Logan Pearsall Smith, Elisabeth Woodbridge Morris, Katharine Fullerton Gerould, and Van Wyck Brooks—dominated the American essay scene. Socially conservative and often at odds with prevailing social concerns, the genteel essayists railed against what they saw as the excesses of contemporary society in favor of a softer, romanticized past that privileged respectability and good manners and that was European, rather than American, in flavor. One of the most popular and prolific of the genteel essayists was Agnes Repplier, who, like many of the country's most prominent essay writers, launched her writing career at the *Atlantic Monthly*. Between 1886 and 1940, Repplier contributed over forty essays to the magazine, collected in her more than ten books of personal and critical essays, including *Points of View* (1891), *Essays in Miniature* (1892), *In the Dozy Hours and Other Papers* (1894), *Compromises* (1904), *A Happy Half Century and Other Essays* (1908), *Americans and Others* (1912), *Points of Friction* (1920), and *In Pursuit of Laughter* (1936).

The genteel essay struggled for survival at the outbreak of World War I, when the concerns of the genteel essayist seemed outmoded and trivial amid the country's preoccupation with world affairs and its resulting crisis of identity. Even Repplier acknowledged, in a 1918 essay titled "The American Essay in Wartime," that "The personal essay, the little bit of sentiment or observation, the lightly offered commentary which aims to appear the artless thing it isn't . . . has withered in the blasts of war." Rather than hold themselves accountable for losing their grasp on the form, the genteel essayists often blamed the reading public as well as a new breed of writers—the "article writers"—who favored theses and exposition over the meanderings and musings perfected by the familiar essayists of the past, particularly Lamb. The genteel essayists filled the pages of periodicals with eulogies for the essay, certain that the form was dead, not understanding that it had gained new life in the hands of newspaper columnists.

NEWSPAPER ESSAY COLUMNS. Indeed, the 1920s and 1930s marked the heyday of the newspaper essay column, which specialized in social satire and featured voices that were anything but genteel. Prominent columnists included Franklin P. Adams, Don Marquis, Robert Benchley, and Christopher Morley. Perhaps the most abrasive of them all was the writer and editor H. L. Mencken. Mencken's tireless hammering at the sacred and the stupid, or what he called the "booboisie," made him one of the most influential voices of his time. His magazine and newspaper columns were reprinted in numerous book-length collections, including the six-volume collection of his essays and reviews titled *Prejudices*, published between 1919 and 1927.

The essay column also provided an outlet for the voices of women and minority writers who combined personal experience with political and social analysis in writings that addressed the concerns of Americans living at society's margins. Alice Ruth Moore Dunbar-Nelson wrote of the condition of African Americans and women for the *Pittsburgh Courier* (1907–1965); Edith Maude Eaton, writing as Sui Sin Far, described the plight of newly emigrated Chinese Americans in her essays for the *Los Angeles Express* (1901–1916) and the *New York Independent* (1848–1924); Gertrude Simmons Bonnin, or Zitkala-Sa, contributed essays on Native Americans to the *Atlantic Monthly* and *Harper's Magazine*. Perhaps the most widely read of such columns was Eleanor Roosevelt's "My Day," a syndicated column published from 1935 to

1962. The First Lady wrote of her public and private life in essays that covered subjects as diverse as Jim Crow laws, old-age pensions, the invasion of Poland, prohibition, and the work of housewives. These writers paved the way for essayists of later decades who used the essay to document their experiences as women, people of color, and gays and lesbians, notably James Baldwin, Adrienne Rich, Gloria Steinem, Nora Ephron, Alice Walker, Judith Ortiz Cofer, Gerald Early, Naomi Shihab Nye, and Gloria Watkins/bell hooks.

*THE NEW YORKER* AND THE PERSONAL ESSAY. One of the most significant events in the development of the American essay was the founding of *The New Yorker* magazine in 1925. *The New Yorker* provided an important outlet for the nation's new breed of essayists and attracted two of the best, James Thurber and E. B. White. Thurber landed a job on *The New Yorker* staff in 1927 with the help of White, and became a celebrity with his "Talk of the Town" essays, cartoons, and spot illustrations. It was White, however, who had the most significant impact on the development of the personal essay. The essays White wrote for *The New Yorker* while on its staff between 1929 and 1939, most of which appear in *Essays of E. B. White* (1977), and those he wrote for *Harper's Magazine* after he left *The New Yorker* and retired to his Maine farm, collected in *One Man's Meat* (1942), epitomize the defining characteristics of the contemporary personal essay. In simple prose style, White weaves personal experience and observation into a narrative that he uses to reflect on some larger life issue, almost always with gentle humor. In White's hands, the nineteenth-century familiar essay finally made peace with the modern literary world. Many writers—Edward Hoagland, Sam Pickering, Phillip Lopate, Nancy Mairs, Scott Russell Sanders, and Anne Fadiman, to name just a few—have followed in White's footsteps, choosing a form that lends itself to the paradoxes of human experience and the interplay of personal experience and sociopolitical critique, observation, and reflection, and discussion of historical and current issues.

To some extent, White legitimized the personal voice for contemporary writers and critics, making the informal essay as much of an intellectual endeavor as the formal essay and in fact blurring the line between the two. Thus, while the essays of mid-century writers and critics—Clifton Fadiman, Lionel Trilling, Irving Howe, Mary McCarthy, and Elizabeth Hardwick—are typically more reserved than those of their successors, a personal voice is still present. Indeed, one of the marks of the contemporary American essay is its hybrid nature, and many of the best essayists engage in a stylized yet personal cultural or literary criticism that lacks the pretense of objectivity found in the driest of informal essays. These writers include, among others, William H. Gass, Cynthia Ozick, Susan Sontag, Joan Didion, and Joyce Carol Oates. Didion's work in the field of New Journalism, along with Norman Mailer, Tom Wolfe, Gay Talese, and Hunter S. Thompson, opened up additional possibilities for the essay writer, adding to the essayist's craft techniques from both fiction and journalism.

CONTEMPORARY NATURE AND SCIENCE ESSAYS. American writers have continued to develop the form that is most their own, the nature essay. As were their nineteenth-century predecessors, contemporary nature essayists like Loren Eiseley, Aldo Starker Leopold, Edward Abbey, Annie Dillard, Barry Lopez, Linda Hogan, Gretel Ehrlich, Barbara Kingsolver, and Terry Tempest Williams are interested in human interactions, often their own, with the natural environment and the sometimes spiritual, sometimes political implications of those interactions. Moreover, they are concerned with the ways in which cultural values shape definitions of the myriad natural landscapes that make up the United States. An offshoot of the nature essay is the garden essay, distinctly American in its discussion of native fauna and proliferated in the United States by two centuries of writers, including Louise Beebe Wilder, Elizabeth Lawrence, Eleanor Perenyi, and Jamaica Kincaid, to name just a few. After her retirement in 1958 as an editor of *The New Yorker*, Katharine S. White contributed fourteen "Onward and Upward in the Garden" essays to the magazine for the next twelve years. In elegant and richly detailed prose, White turned gardening into a literary adventure with her reviews of garden literature and analyses of seed catalogs.

American science writers have also managed to make good use of the essay form in writings that navigate between specific knowledge and personal experience for an audience of lay readers. Key writers include Richard Selzer and Oliver Sacks writing about medicine; Lewis Thomas, Edward O. Wilson, Sue Hubbell, Stephen Jay Gould, and Natalie Angier about biology; Edwin E. Slosson and Roald Hoffmann about chemistry; and Carl Sagan about physics and astronomy. One of the most prolific of the science essayists, John McPhee, has published more than twenty-five books of natural history spanning three decades on subjects as diverse as the Alaska wilderness and the American shad, notably *Encounters with the*

*Archdruid* (1971), *Basin and Range* (1980), *In Suspect Terrain* (1983), *Rising from the Plains* (1986), and *The Founding Fish* (2002).

REVIVAL OF THE ESSAY. The last two decades of the twentieth century witnessed yet another revival of the American essay, particularly the personal essay. Testaments to this revival are the editor Robert Atwan's popular *The Best American Essays*, published annually since 1986; the publication of the *Encyclopedia of the Essay* (1997); and the birth of a number of literary magazines dedicated solely to the essay, chiefly *Creative Nonfiction* (1993–) and *Fourth Genre* (1999–). Atwan's annual series is reminiscent of popular essay annuals from the first part of the century that also attempted to promote the work of the country's most prominent essayists. Unlike the early annuals, however, *The Best American Essays* attempts to place each year's essays in some critical and historical context with the addition of a critical introduction by a guest editor/essayist. While the essay enjoys renewed status among American writers and readers, it continues to occupy bottom-shelf status in the hierarchy of literary criticism. Few critical and even fewer historical studies of the essay have been written. As early as 1914, Adaline May Conway, a doctoral candidate at New York University, lamented in her dissertation on the American essay that "the Essay has suffered an almost absolute neglect at the hands of scholars." That continues to be the case, with the exception of a handful of works. Despite critical neglect, however, the American essay no doubt will persevere in one shape or another as new writers find ways to adapt contemporary concerns and trends to a form that by its malleable, meandering nature seems well equipped for survival.

[*See also* Baldwin, James; Didion, Joan; Dillard, Annie; Douglass, Frederick; Du Bois, W. E. B.; Emerson, Ralph Waldo; Franklin, Benjamin; Freneau, Philip; Howells, William Dean; Irving, Washington; Kincaid, Jamaica; Longfellow, Henry Wadsworth; Mailer, Norman; Mather, Cotton; McCarthy, Mary; McPhee, John; Mencken, H. L.; Oates, Joyce Carol; Ozick, Cynthia; Poe, Edgar Allan; Rich, Adrienne; Stowe, Harriet Beecher; Thoreau, Henry David and his *Walden*; Thurber, James; Twain, Mark; Walker, Alice; White, E. B.; Williams, Terry Tempest; *and* Wilson, Edmund.]

## FURTHER READING

Atwan, Robert, ed. *The Best American Essays*. New York, 1986–.

Brodbeck, May, James Gray, and Walter Metzer. *American Non-fiction, 1900–1950*. Chicago, 1952. Chapter 2 provides a thorough survey of the last of the genteel essayists at the turn of the century and the satirical columnists who dethroned them.

Chevalier, Tracy, ed. *Encyclopedia of the Essay*. London, 1997. A mammoth volume of information on the essay, including entries dedicated to the history of the American essay and major American essayists.

Conway, Adaline May. *The Essay in American Literature*. New York University Series of Graduate School Studies, no. 3. New York, 1914. The only comprehensive book-length history of the American essay.

D'Agata, John, ed. *The Next American Essay*. St. Paul, Minn., 2003.

Granger, Bruce. *American Essay Serials from Franklin to Irving*. Knoxville, Tenn., 1978. A comprehensive treatment of writers of early American essay serials and periodicals.

Howard, Maureen, ed. *The Penguin Book of Contemporary American Essays*. New York, 1984.

Linkon, Sherry L., ed. *In Her Own Voice: Nineteenth-Century American Women Essayists*. Garland Reference Library of the Humanities, vol. 2043. New York, 1997. A rare critical work related to the study of women essayists, this book contains essays on Lydia Maria Child, Anna Julia Cooper, Fanny Fern, Margaret Fuller, Gail Hamilton, and Zitkala-Sa.

Matthews, Brander, ed. *The Oxford Book of American Essays*. New York, 1914.

Oates, Joyce Carol, and Robert Atwan, eds. *The Best American Essays of the Century*. Boston, 2000.

Pack, Robert, and Jay Parini, eds. *The Bread Loaf Anthology of Contemporary American Essays*. Hanover, N.H., 1989.

Starkweather, Chauncey C., ed. *Essays of American Essayists*. Rev. ed. New York, 1900.

Wann, Louis, ed. *Century Readings in the English Essay*. New York, 1939. A comprehensive anthology of essays, including early Greek and Roman influences through the first part of the twentieth century. Wann's excellent introduction offers an exhaustive historical and critical overview of the essay in each century.

# For Reference

**Not to be taken from this room**